AF605979

THE PAPERS OF

FREDERICK LAW OLMSTED

THE PAPERS OF

FREDERICK LAW OLMSTED

VOLUME VIII

THE EARLY BOSTON YEARS

1882–1890

ETHAN CARR

AMANDA GAGEL

MICHAEL SHAPIRO

Editors

THE JOHNS HOPKINS UNIVERSITY PRESS
Baltimore

Printed in the United States of America on acid-free paper
9 8 7 6 5 4 3 2 1

The Johns Hopkins University Press
2715 North Charles Street
Baltimore, Maryland 21218-4363
www.press.jhu.edu

Library of Congress Cataloging-in-Publication Data
(Revised for vol. 7)

Olmsted, Frederick Law, 1822–1903.
The papers of Frederick Law Olmsted.

Includes bibliographical references and indexes.
Contents: v. 1. The formative years, 1822–1852 — v. 2. Slavery and the South, 1852–1857 — v. 3. Creating Central Part, 1857–1861 — v. 4. Defending the Union, 1861–1863 — v. 5. The California frontier, 1863–1865 — v. 6. The years of Olmsted, Vaux & Company, 1865–1874 — v. 7. The Boston years, 1882–1890.
1. Olmsted, Frederick, 1822–1903. 2. Landscape architects—United States—Correspondence. 3. Landscape architects—United States—Biography. I. McLaughlin, Charles Capen. II. Beveridge, Charles E. III. Title.
SB470.05A2 1977 712 77-741
ISBN 0-8018-1798-6 (v. 1) ISBN 0-8018-4198-4 (v. 6)
ISBN 0-8018-2242-4 (v. 2) ISBN 0-8018-8336-9 (v. 7)
ISBN 0-8018-2751-5 (v. 3) ISBN 978-1-4214-0926-9 (v. 8)
ISBN 0-8018-3067-2 (v. 4) ISBN 1-4214-0926-7 (v. 8)
ISBN 0-8018-3885-1 (v. 5)

A catalog record for this book is available from the British Library.

The Johns Hopkins University Press uses environmentally friendly book materials, including recycled text paper that is composed of at least 30 percent post-consumer waste, whenever possible.

CONTENTS

ILLUSTRATIONS

ACKNOWLEDGMENTS

The editors wish to give special thanks to the National Endowment for the Humanities, the National Historical Publications and Records Commission, and the Andrew W. Mellon Foundation for their longtime support of the Frederick Law Olmsted Papers and the contributions they made for the preparation of this volume.

The project has also received substantial support from other foundations and individuals, including the Barkley Fund, the Friends of Fairsted, Furthermore: A Program of the J. M. Kaplan Fund, the Hubbard Educational Foundation, the National Endowment for the Arts, the National Trust for the Humanities, the Seattle Foundation, Susan L. Klaus, Caroline Loughlin, Jean McKee, Victoria Post Ranney, and George A. Ranney, Jr., as well as significant funding from individuals and foundations who prefer to remain anonymous.

We also would like to thank the National Association for Olmsted Parks (NAOP), the sponsoring institution of the Olmsted Papers project, for providing fiscal sponsorship and administration of the project and this volume in particular. The staff of NAOP, Executive Director Iris Gestram, and Hilary Dick, gave administrative and fundraising support and assisted in public outreach for the project.

The University of Virginia generously supplied office space and staff support for the volume editors and served as the sponsoring institution for its preparation. Dean of the School of Architecture Karen Van Lengen made it possible for Ethan Carr to edit this volume as part of his position as the Reuben M. Rainey Professor in the History of Landscape Architecture, and Professor Emeritus Rainey shared his wisdom and knowledge and gave much appreciated support to the editors. Also, many research assistants at the university contributed to finding the necessary sources for annotations and helping with proofing documents. Frances Macmillan, Deborah Galaski, Jennifer Chang, and Suzanne Morgan provided invaluable assistance with these tasks. Special thanks are due to Reuben Shank, who was with the project from the beginning and helped with many aspects of research and production, especially with building the sizable Index of Plant Materials. The University of Massachusetts, Amherst, provided Ethan Carr with time and space to initiate work on the volume. Jeffrey Blankenship provided excellent research assistance at that time.

The editors of this volume especially appreciate and acknowledge the extensive advice, help, and guidance given to us by the Olmsted Papers series editor, Charles E. Beveridge, who early in the process made the principal decisions regarding the documents selected for transcription and publication. Throughout the subsequent editing, annotating, and the adding and subtracting of documents to the table of contents, Dr. Beveridge generously gave his time and the benefit of his experience and thorough knowledge of the documents and their contexts. His unfailing goodwill and encouragement have been deeply appreciated by the volume editors, and his involvement made it possible to aspire to maintain the high editorial standards of the series.

Other assistance has been provided by a group of scholars and editors who willingly came forward when asked. Francis R. Kowsky was called on and generously shared his research on both the life of Calvert Vaux and the history of the Buffalo park system. Keith Morgan shared his insights on Olmsted, Charles Eliot, and the town of Brookline in the 1880s. Cynthia Zaitzevsky, through her published research, contributed to the editors' ability to contextualize the history of the Olmsted firm in Boston and in Brookline. Arleyn Levee was always ready to share her knowledge of the life of John Charles Olmsted and of the activities of the Olmsted firm, and David Schuyler, a longtime contributor to the series, assisted at various stages of the project. Peter Del Tredici of the Arnold Arboretum at Harvard University generously gave his time to edit the Index of Plant Materials, which could not have been completed without his assistance. Special thanks are due to Caroline Loughlin who provided numerous invaluable services, including proofreading the completed manuscript. Her skill prevented many errors and inconsistencies in this work. Also, Sue Perdue of Documents Compass gave us her help and expertise in the editing of the General Index and Index of Plant Materials.

We wish to acknowledge the assistance provided us by the staff members of numerous institutions, including staff at the Buffalo Olmsted Parks Conservancy, archivists and historians Bill Alexander and Jill Hawkins at the Biltmore Estate Archives, and archivists at the Stanford University Archives. Local historians at many smaller park and residential sites that Olmsted designed provided us with information that would normally have been difficult to find. Historians and archivists in North Easton, Massachusetts; in New London, Connecticut; at the Denver Public Library, Colorado; and at the Lawrenceville School, New Jersey, were especially helpful. Also, Alexander Yale

Goriansky, a descendant of landscape architect Charles Eliot, provided us with access to his private collection of Eliot papers, and Mary Daniels at the Frances Loeb Library at the Harvard Graduate School of Design greatly helped us with their collection of Eliot materials and with gathering of illustrations.

We have benefited from the assistance and goodwill of many persons for collecting the illustrations published in this volume. Most images came from the Frederick Law Olmsted National Historic Site in Brookline, Massachusetts. A significant number of images were also provided by the Architect of the Capitol archive in Washington, D.C., the Stanford University Archives, and the Biltmore Company Archives. Staff members of the New York State Archive, Easton (Massachusetts) Historical Society, Boston Public Library, Denver Public Library, Massachusetts Historical Society, New York Historical Society, and the Arnold Arboretum archives all generously helped us collect illustrations. Special thanks are due to Jeanne Gamble at Historic New England for her help with various visual materials related to the Olmsted parks and the Olmsted family.

Finally, our work would not be possible without access to the Frederick Law Olmsted National Historic Site, maintained by the National Park Service in Brookline, Massachusetts, the American University Archives, and the Library of Congress in Washington, D.C. To Myra Harrison, superintendent of the Olmsted site, we wish to express our appreciation for her dedication to preserving and making available the rich archive of materials in her charge. Site manager Lee Farrow Cook as well as Alan Banks and Mark Swartz have continued to share and interpret the significance of Fairsted with the editors of the Olmsted Papers, as well as the public at large. Archivists Michele Clark, Anthony Reed, Michael Dosch, and Supervisory Archivist Jill Trebbe gave us access to original materials and provided scans of documents. In light of ongoing restorations at Fairsted, the work they do is remarkable and invaluable. Susan McElrath, archivist at the American University Archives and Special Collections, aided us with accessing the Olmsted Papers research materials. Dr. Alice Lotvin Birney, literary and cultural historian in the Manuscript Division at the Library of Congress, and the staff in the LOC reading room assisted us throughout our research on the Olmsted Papers in their collection.

THE PAPERS OF

FREDERICK LAW OLMSTED

INTRODUCTION

When Frederick Law Olmsted published *The Spoils of the Park* in February 1882, he expressed his cumulative frustration with the politics and patronage that made public work in New York City as maddening as it could be rewarding.[1] Begun in the winter of 1881 and printed at his own expense, the tract was an emotional indictment of what he felt was the corrupt and inept mismanagement of Central Park that had occurred since he had been forced to leave his position three years earlier. The tone and content of the writing suggest he believed his future indeed lay elsewhere: "If I had been seeking office," he wrote in the preface, "it would have been a most foolish thing to write it." It was, as he wrote to his lifelong friend and correspondent, Charles Loring Brace, his "last blow" in the protracted political conflicts that plagued his public work in New York.[2]

A number of events had transpired in Olmsted's life that had changed his personal outlook and professional expectations by the early 1880s. In December 1878, the New York park board voted to abolish the Bureau of Design and Superintendence and with it Olmsted's salaried position as its landscape architect. The move, which resulted from changes in the composition and politics of the board, occurred while Olmsted was recovering from a breakdown in his health and was about to leave for a planned trip to Europe.[3] With his passage booked, he chose not to contest the action and instead sailed for Liverpool. The turn of events left him deeply embittered and culminated years of efforts by his detractors to restrict his influence in guiding the future development of the city. The innovative street and transit plan he and the engineer J. J. R. Croes had recently completed for the city's Twenty-third and Twenty-fourth wards, for example, had been officially adopted but after 1878 was never fully implemented. In the coming years, Olmsted sporadically was asked to consult or to comment on aspects of the designs for Central, Morningside, and Riverside parks, but he would never again be in a position to guide the expansion of New York and its park system, nor to implement an integrated plan for transportation, sanitary, and landscape improvements for that city.

Just months after Olmsted lost his position in New York, however, a competition was held in Boston for the design of the most important public landscape project to be implemented there for decades. In Boston, originally located on the narrow Shawmut Peninsula and surrounded by tidal estuaries and shallow bays, urban growth depended in large part on landfilling. The most significant of these projects in the mid-nineteenth century was the filling of what had been the city's Back Bay, an operation that took decades and in the late 1870s was approaching completion.[4] At the west end of the new Back Bay neighborhood, however, the confluence of the Stony Brook and the Muddy River formed a tidal estuary that had become severely polluted with sewage and other waste, creating a noisome health hazard subject to frequent flooding. Flood control and sanitary improvements in the area were needed for the Back Bay project to be completed. In 1877 the Boston City Council established what was described as a park on the problematic site. The city's park commissioners then organized the park design competition and, when Olmsted declined to submit an entry, negated the outcome of the contest and hired him anyway. His 1878 preliminary design of what later would be named the Back Bay Fens became the starting point for the design of a metropolitan corridor of parks and parkways, and from that year until he ceased active practice in 1895, Olmsted and his growing atelier of apprentices and partners would make metropolitan Boston, not New York, the subject of their most important public landscape designs and park planning innovations.

The work in Boston drew Olmsted to the area, and he gradually relocated his family as well as his business. Following his 1878 European trip, he and his family spent the summer living in Cambridge as the guests of his old friend and colleague from the *Nation*, E. L. Godkin. They continued to spend winters in their four-story row house on West 46th Street in New York, but during the summers, the Olmsteds returned to the Boston area, specifically to Brookline, an affluent and leafy suburb where his neighbors included friends and collaborators such as H. H. Richardson and Charles Sprague Sargent. In 1881, Olmsted rented out their New York home and leased a house on Walnut Street in Brookline, now with the intention of staying.

Fairsted, 1883–1890

Olmsted was fifty-nine and a grandfather when he relocated his family, which included his wife, Mary Perkins Olmsted, and the two surviving children they had had together since their marriage in 1859, twenty-year-old Marion, who was unmarried and living at home, and Frederick Law Olmsted, Jr. (known as Rick), who was eleven and remained in boarding school in New York for another two years. Of Mary's three other children by her earlier marriage to Olmsted's brother, John Hull Olmsted (who died in 1857), only one lived with them in Brookline, John Charles Olmsted, who had been Olmsted's assistant since 1875. Now twenty-nine and unmarried, he continued to be a key figure in his stepfather's practice. His sister, Charlotte Olmsted, had married John Bryant in 1878 and lived in Cohasset, Massachusetts, in a residence Richardson and Olmsted designed for them in 1880. The youngest of the three, Owen Olmsted, had been a promising young man who trained as a mining engineer and spent the previous two years working on a cattle ranch in Wyoming. In the fall of 1881, the news arrived that Owen was gravely ill with tuberculosis, the disease that had killed his father. John Charles immediately left Brookline to bring his brother home, but Owen died that November on the railroad journey back east. Further tragedy affected the family two years later when Charlotte, after the birth of her third child, was overcome by mental illness. She remained institutionalized for the rest of her life.[5]

In the spring of 1883, Olmsted finally purchased a house in Brookline, at 99 Warren Street, and began remodeling it to become the combined family home and professional office that he and Mary named Fairsted. The house and grounds became an important demonstration of Olmsted's principles of domestic landscape design. At the same time, working out of the north parlor of the old farmhouse, Olmsted and John Charles expanded their landscape architecture practice, which would remain the largest in the country for decades. During the period this volume covers, the circumstances and methods of Olmsted's design practice differed significantly from those of earlier periods in his life. Since the dissolution of his partnership with the architect Calvert Vaux in 1872, Olmsted had collaborated with a number of architects, landscape gardeners, and engineers, such as Thomas Wisedell on the U.S. Capitol grounds, Jacob Weidenmann on a number of projects, including the parks in Buffalo and Montreal, and George Radford, whom Olmsted considered the finest civil engineer in the country. Following the move to Brookline, Olmsted increasingly relied on his stepson and their own office staff to provide expertise in architectural construction and drafting, horticulture, and engineering that Olmsted felt he lacked. Olmsted now had the opportunity to develop his own atelier, with apprentices and others trained specifically to assist him. Projects of all types increased in number during the decade, including the planning of municipal park systems, the design of institutional and residential landscapes, and the laying out of subdivisions. By the mid-1880s, systems of job numbers, billing procedures, and correspondence copying and filing all became necessary as the number and variety of commissions and clients grew. Typewriters and stenographers were employed, beginning a commitment to technical innovation that would continue at the firm into the twentieth century. The firm's principals were often on the road in the 1880s, taking advantage of the mobility offered by an expanding national rail network. Olmsted traveled by train across the country three times during this period, for example, for work on the design of Stanford University and other projects. Fairsted was a family home, but by the mid-1880s, it also contained the first landscape architecture office of its kind, structured and run along lines recognizable to professionals today.[6]

John Charles Olmsted was essential to the organization, expansion, and success of the Fairsted office. He was born in 1852 in Switzerland, where his parents were traveling, and was five years old when his father, John Hull Olmsted, died. Two years later his mother remarried, making Frederick Law Olmsted stepfather to his dead brother's three children. The family relocated to Washington following the outbreak of the Civil War, and then to Bear Valley, California. When Olmsted resumed his working relationship with Calvert Vaux in 1865, the family moved again, to Brooklyn, briefly, then Staten Island, and later to Manhattan. As a teenager, John Charles returned west, where he was part of Clarence King's survey party in Nevada and Utah. By the time he entered the Yale Sheffield Scientific School, the decision that he should become a landscape architect apparently had already been made, since he began assisting his stepfather immediately upon his graduation in 1875, working out of the dining room office in the family's Manhattan row house. In 1877 he left for European travel to further his education in the field, returning the next year to resume work in the family business, in which his stepfather now gave him a financial interest. His technical education at Yale, his independent travel and reading, and the drawing and drafting skills he developed constituted John Charles's education in landscape architecture. He became vital to Olmsted's activities, providing not only some of the drafting and technical abilities the practice needed but also administrative organization for the expanding business.[7]

In the spring of 1883, as Olmsted was acquiring the new family residence in Brookline, Charles Eliot joined the firm as an apprentice.[8] Eliot was the son of Harvard University president Charles W. Eliot and the nephew of the architect Robert S. Peabody, another neighbor of Olmsted's in Brookline and an important architectural collaborator during this period. Charles Eliot had chosen his profession in the summer of 1882 in consultation with his father, and together they devised a course of study at Harvard's Bussey Institution, which offered technical courses in agriculture and the natural sciences. Eliot cut short his studies to begin his apprenticeship, however, and immediately began accompanying Olmsted on field trips, as well as working in the office drafting plans and other drawings, preparing grading calculations, and doing other tasks that would become typical for entry-level staff in a landscape architecture firm. Eliot's diary for the period provides an account of some of his training and experiences with Olmsted, and Olmsted's letters reveal his high regard for his protégé.[9] In 1885, Eliot left for Europe to advance his education in the field, making notes and sketches of the parks and gardens he visited. He wrote Olmsted with descriptions and opinions of landscapes they had clearly discussed before his departure. His travels, between the fall of 1885 and the end of 1886, were nothing short of a landscape design education, an itinerary for which he had the advice of his father, Olmsted, and others in preparing (and which was better documented than John Charles's travels of 1877–1878).[10] Olmsted's letters to him in 1886 encouraged and instructed Eliot. He also suggested that he pay particular attention to landscapes in Italy, Spain, and the South of France for design precedents that could prove useful for work in California. Olmsted had just secured the Stanford University commission and hoped that Eliot would return soon and accompany him there as a partner.[11] Eliot declined Olmsted's offer, however, and when he returned from his European travels at the end of the year, he opened his own office in Boston.[12]

In 1884, Olmsted had made John Charles a full partner in the firm, now named "F. L. and J. C. Olmsted." That summer, a second, equally promising apprentice joined the firm, Henry (Harry) Sargent Codman, the nephew of Charles Sprague Sargent. Codman graduated from MIT in 1884 and began working at Fairsted as an entry-level landscape architect in a similar capacity to Eliot. Codman stayed with the firm for the next three years and then departed for Europe. He remained in Paris for an extended period, where he worked with Édouard André, the landscape gardener of the Parisian system of parks and squares, whom Olmsted had known and admired since 1876.[13] Upon his return to the United States in 1889, Codman accepted Olmsted's offer to become a partner in the renamed firm F. L. Olmsted and Co. Olmsted wrote to his friend Charles Loring Brace in 1890 that with John Charles and Codman as partners, his office was "much better equipped and has more momentum than ever before."[14] By that time the amount of work in the office had increased, and at least two full-time draftsmen, Percy R. Jones and James G. Langdon, were employed. In 1888, Warren H. Manning, the son of a Reading, Massachusetts, nurseryman, also joined the office as a planting specialist and later became the firm's director of planting.[15] The number of draftsmen and clerks working at Fairsted varied, but in the early 1890s, as the office continued to grow, there were fifteen to twenty such employees, supervised mainly by John Charles.[16] During the 1880s, recorded business correspondence increased from 101 outgoing items and letters in 1884, the first year such correspondence was systematically copied and filed, to 2,032 items in 1890.[17]

Olmsted adapted the building and grounds of Fairsted for the use of both family and firm. During the initial remodeling of the farmhouse in 1883, carpenters added a two-story wing on the southwest corner of the house that included a bedroom above and a glazed "plant room" at ground level. New windows, chimneys, roofs, and utilities were part of the extensive alterations and modernizations of 1883. The Olmsteds also separated the domestic and business areas of the complex. A two-story courtyard space between what had been the farmhouse kitchen and the north parlor was enclosed to create a separate entrance area for the north parlor office. As the business grew, further construction accommodated additional staff. In 1887, Olmsted enlarged the north parlor, and in 1889, a new, one-story office wing provided needed clerical space. The office wing was separated from the north parlor office by a new business entrance and a reception area. The 1889 office wing established a pattern for keeping the main domestic spaces of the house relatively unchanged even as significant business additions were made to the northern part of the complex in the 1890s and later.[18]

Much of this work was done under the supervision of John Charles who, with his stepfather's advice and approval, also drew up plans for the improvement of the grounds of Fairsted. The landscape as it was developed in the 1880s featured a clearly defined entrance from Warren Street, a well-separated service area and office entrance on the north side, and a sunny, south lawn for the family. Flowing vines soon covered the old farmhouse. The Hollow, a picturesque, rocky area, occupied a natural depression on the northeast side of the house. Olmsted left little specific documentary evidence of his wishes for the Fairsted landscape, and no significant original plans survive. In an 1884 telegram to John Charles, however, he may have been referring to Fairsted when he wrote, "I don't object to the cutting away of certain bramble patches if other brambles are to take their place — or anything that will appear spontaneous & not need watering or care. More mowing or dug ground I object to. Less wildness and disorder I object to."[19] The grounds of Fairsted exemplified Olmsted's aversion to Victorian garden effects and plantings in residential landscapes. The elements of the design were suggested by the old farmhouse's existing setting, which the designers enhanced and adapted to its new uses through grading, selective thinning, and new planting. The wooded edges of the property were planted in hardy shrubs, trees, and ground covers, as were the entrance drive circle and other areas. Photographs taken by John Charles and others at the end of the decade show that the grounds of Fairsted resembled what Olmsted's colleague and admirer, the British gardener William Robinson, described as the "wild garden," with woody and hardy herbaceous plants thriving in naturalistic masses.[20] Annuals and other garden specimen plants were likely restricted to the indoor "plant room," the glazed room adjacent to the south lawn that integrated the principal indoor and outdoor domestic spaces of the residence.

In the north parlor of Fairsted, Olmsted developed a professional practice that would become the model for other design offices that followed, as well as the training ground for the individuals who went on to establish them. The work Olmsted undertook during this period included the design of Belle Isle in Detroit, the park systems of Boston and Rochester, a new series of parks for south Buffalo, the Niagara State Reservation, and Stanford University. The U.S. Capitol grounds were completed with the construction of the terraces Olmsted designed around the building. The residences Olmsted designed at this time included Shelburne Farms, Rough Point, and many others. At the end of the decade, Olmsted was sixty-nine and in charge of an office with two active young partners and a large staff of clerks and draftsmen handling major public park, institutional, and residential landscape projects all over the United States. Of the two most important projects the firm would undertake in the 1890s, Biltmore, George W. Vanderbilt's palatial estate in North Carolina, was already in preliminary design, and the World's Columbian Exposition, which Congress had determined would be in Chicago, was on the horizon. The early Boston years brought Olmsted a degree of personal and professional stability and satisfaction that had often eluded him in earlier periods of his sometimes peripatetic life. He was now well established with his family in a relatively serene community with supportive friends and colleagues living nearby. The Olmsted firm, taking advantage of national economic growth in the 1880s, grew to become a significant business success, and a legacy Olmsted could plan to pass on to a new generation of partners.

H. H. Richardson and Mariana Griswold Van Rensselaer

In Brookline, Olmsted was once again a neighbor of his friend Henry Hobson Richardson, one of the most influential American architects of the period and the design colleague with whom Olmsted developed perhaps his most significant collaborative relationship. Olmsted and Richardson met in New York sometime after 1865, the year Olmsted returned east from California and Richardson returned to the United States from Paris. Both men relocated their families to Staten Island in 1866. That year Richardson joined the Century Association, where Olmsted was already a member, and they may have met there. In any case, in 1867 Olmsted recommended the architect to design the Alexander Dallas Bache Monument, which was erected in the Congressional Cemetery in Washington, D.C. By 1869, they both lived in the Clifton neighborhood of Staten Island, where Olmsted rented a house and Richardson built his, still extant, at 45 McClean Avenue. In 1870, Olmsted asked that Richardson be appointed to join him on the newly created Staten Island Improvement Commission, and in 1871, Olmsted and Vaux collaborated with Richardson on the Buffalo State Asylum for the Insane. Richardson relocated to Brookline in 1874, drawn by the ongoing construction of the building that would make him famous, Trinity Church in Boston. His Brookline residence on Cottage Street also housed his professional office and his atelier of young apprentices, an arrangement that may have later influenced Olmsted's plans for the nearby house that became Fairsted. Beginning in 1876, the two men again worked closely together over a period of years when their mutual friend and client, New York State lieutenant governor William E. Dorsheimer, asked Olmsted to advise on the completion of the New York State Capitol in Albany. As a result, Olmsted, Richardson, and the architect Leopold Eidlitz assumed control of the project and formed a partnership for the purpose.[21]

In 1880, Olmsted asked Richardson to design two of the bridges required for his design of the Back Bay Fens, as well as a gatehouse for the floodgate between the Fens basin and the waters of the Stony Brook.[22] The

Boylston Street Bridge, in particular, which created a prominent portal in the Fens landscape while also carrying intersecting street traffic above, became an important example of how the two designers understood and influenced each other.[23] Built in irregular granite ashlar (Olmsted originally wanted more rugged, boulder masonry), the undulating, unornamented mass of the bridge suggested a geological, organic form consistent with Olmsted's landscape design, which also eschewed historical references. The Fens landscape evoked the estuarine wetland that the site had once been, albeit through extensive grading, landfilling, soil amendments, and planting. The new landscape bore no resemblance to the popular gardenesque style—evident, for example, in the nearby Boston Public Garden—which was characterized by visually striking horticultural displays, statues, ornaments, and structures that referenced historical garden types. Richardson produced an architectural analog to Olmsted's alternative to contemporary Victorian gardening, one that was inspired by the material and form of the landscape itself, as Olmsted had designed it. Olmsted and Richardson combined landscape and architecture in an original, distinctly modern expression that rejected historical and stylistic references and drew instead on the natural processes and forms—geology, hydrology, and vegetation—of an archetypical, regional landscape: the tidal estuary.

While Olmsted was looking for property to buy in Brookline in 1883, Richardson offered to design a house for his friend, on the same lot as his own, suggesting it be a "beautiful thing in shingles?"[24] Olmsted decided on the nearby farmhouse on Warren Street, instead, but during the early 1880s, the two designers worked on an important series of commissions together. In North Easton, Massachusetts, the Ames family commissioned Richardson to design the Oliver Ames Free Library in 1877. In 1879, he began work on the adjacent Oakes Ames Memorial Town Hall.[25] The Ames family asked Olmsted to design the landscape setting for the buildings, which he did in part by exposing and emphasizing the rock outcrops of the site. Directly opposite the memorial hall, he created a massive boulder terrace with a flagstaff to serve as the town's Civil War memorial. The joints of the boulder masonry of the terrace were filled with soil to support vines and other plants. An arched opening allowed passage through it, and steps were incorporated into its stones.[26] Nearby, at the F. L. Ames estate, Richardson created a memorable gatehouse that also employed boulder masonry, and the building itself served as an arched entryway into the estate. The two projects indicate a strong continuity between Olmsted's structured landscapes, and Richardson's landscape-inspired structures, during this period. In the case of the North Easton town hall and the adjacent Civil War memorial, Olmsted and Richardson suggested a complete vision of landscape and architecture together creating a new town center, joined to other public buildings and spaces nearby, and rooted in an enhanced geology of the site. The memorial cairn, which was intended to grow as children added stones during annual ceremonies honoring the town's war dead, made the community memorialization a continuing activity, analogous to the natural processes of the site, such as the growth of vegetation that would also act to change the landscape over time.

Before Richardson's death at age forty-eight in 1886, the two men collaborated on a number of projects, including a series of Boston & Albany Railroad stations, the Robert Treat Paine, Jr., residence in Waltham, Massachusetts, and others. In residences and institutional grounds, Olmsted complemented Richardson's use of boulder or rough-hewn masonry by exposing existing rock outcrops, creating landscape structures that resembled or were integrated into the site's geology, and planting naturalistic groups of trees and masses of shrubs. The collaboration Olmsted and Richardson initiated continued after the architect's death, in a sense, through Richardson's successor firm, Shepley, Rutan, and Coolidge, as well as through other Boston area architects, such as Peabody and Stearns who, like Richardson, understood Olmsted's goals in residential, institutional, and public landscape design. During this period, Olmsted was able to cultivate sustained and fruitful relationships with a group of sympathetic architects, many of whom Richardson had influenced. He also had a staff and partners at Fairsted who now could often provide structural details and minor architectural design as desired.

Richardson's illness and death were nevertheless both a personal and professional blow to Olmsted and foreshadowed the premature losses of both Codman and Eliot that he and his firm would suffer in the 1890s. The tragedy brought him closer, however, to one of his most important correspondents and intellectual collaborators of this period, the architecture and art critic Mariana Griswold Van Rensselaer. While Olmsted rarely communicated with his neighbor and family friend Richardson in writing (there are no letters to him in this volume), he corresponded with Van Rensselaer frequently. She first contacted Olmsted in 1883 regarding a series of articles she was writing for the *Century Illustrated Monthly Magazine*. Following Richardson's death, Olmsted and Charles Sprague Sargent urged her to write his biography, which became the first of an American architect when it was published two years later. In 1893, two years before he retired, Van Rensselaer also wrote the first biographical account of Olmsted, which was published as an article in the *Century*.[27] By that time, she and Olmsted had exchanged many letters and ideas on a variety of topics, and Van Rensselaer had contributed articles and editorials on landscape architecture to a number of journals but especially to *Garden and Forest*, the magazine established in 1888 and "conducted" by Sargent (with Olmsted as an advisor and early investor) and edited by another important colleague and correspondent of Olmsted's during this period, William A. Stiles. Van Rensselaer assembled her *Garden and Forest* essays, and others, in her 1893 volume *Art Out-of-Doors: Hints on Good Taste in Gardening*, which became the most important book on the theory of the new profession of landscape architecture, and one in which Olmsted's influence was significant.[28]

Boston Parks, 1878–1890

The development of a connected system of public parks and parkways in Boston and in Brookline during the 1880s gave Olmsted his greatest opportunity to realize an urban vision of integrated transportation, sanitation, and recreational infrastructure based in a response to regional landscape systems and the transformation of specific sites. This implementation of urban design ideas corresponded to the increasingly complex operations of the Fairsted office and in turn shaped the practice of landscape architecture that emerged there.

The Boston parks movement began before Olmsted's involvement, and several early iterations of park system plans had preceded his designs. In 1869, a number of prominent Bostonians attempted to secure Olmsted's endorsement for different park proposals, and in February 1870, he visited the city and, in a lecture to the American Social Science Association, gave one of his most comprehensive statements on urban design and the importance of public parks.[29] Boston finally passed a public park act in 1875 that empowered a board of commissioners to acquire and develop parks within the city, which at the time was expanding its boundaries through municipal annexations. The following spring Olmsted toured proposed park sites and advised the Boston park commissioners, who were about to publish their preliminary recommendations for a system of parks and parkways. This limited and tentative involvement in planning the Boston park system ended in 1878 when the park commissioners, led by board president Charles H. Dalton, rejected the results of their Back Bay competition and asked Olmsted to design the park instead.[30]

As with a number of his Boston park designs, Olmsted established a new type of public landscape for the Back Bay site, one that had no exact precedent. The design was intended to alleviate flooding, as required, but the necessary water retention basin fit into the regraded landform and followed its naturalistic contours. The landscape also functioned as a tidal estuary, allowing in brackish waters from the Charles River and establishing conditions suitable for the grasses, sedges, and bordering shrubs and trees found in such wetlands elsewhere on the coast. While a system of paths and drives would allow the public to experience the landscape, other features the public might associate with a municipal "park"—flowerbeds, music pavilions, lawns, conservatories—were notably absent. Olmsted became concerned about the nomenclature of the new public landscapes he was planning for Boston. The Back Bay "Fens," for example, was a name Olmsted preferred to the Back Bay "Park," because only the largest landscape in the Boston system, the West Roxbury (later Franklin) Park, would have the expansive, pastoral quality that for Olmsted specifically defined a "park" landscape.[31]

The 1876 Boston park system plan had also called for connecting the Back Bay to Jamaica Pond, a large, existing kettle pond that was to be acquired for park purposes, with a straight corridor of parkland going over Mission Hill. In 1880, Olmsted proposed that the connection should be relocated to the north, along the valley of the Muddy River. He suggested that the river valley could be restored, replanted, and in places relocated, creating a corridor that evoked another regional landscape type: a small river valley feeding into a coastal estuary. The proposed Muddy River Sanitary Improvement eventually would help restore water quality and control flooding. Bridges that carried intersecting traffic above it would also create uninterrupted bridle and pedestrian paths along the re-engineered river. Suggested by the existing topography and hydrology of the region, the creation of the landscape corridor nevertheless required extensive grading, soil amendment, planting, and construction. Although clearly an elaboration of his earlier parkway designs, the restored stream corridor again established a new precedent.[32] The design also required relocating the political boundary between the town of Brookline and the city of Boston — a factor that helped delay construction until the early 1890s — because the river that defined that boundary was moved.[33]

By the beginning of the period of this volume, Olmsted had delineated a plan for a connected series of varied and innovative landscape designs that decades later would be described as Boston's "Emerald Necklace" but which Olmsted suggested in 1887 be called simply "the Parkway."[34] The Back Bay Fens and the Muddy River Sanitary Improvement, along with the Arnold Arboretum, which Olmsted designed in collaboration with Charles Sprague Sargent beginning in 1878, were in various stages of design development or construction. The largest park of the circumferential Boston system, however, was still in the initial phases of its design. The West Roxbury Park, which after 1885 was known as Franklin Park, covered 500 acres of upland pastures and orchards. The area was considered a scenic remnant of the region's agricultural past and was identified in early proposals as appropriate for a large park with significant expanses of pastoral scenery. Olmsted agreed with this assessment in 1876 and recommended the acquisition of the farms that made up the site. In 1881, he submitted preliminary advice on the boundaries and character of the new park, and in 1883, the public began to use the area before improvements had begun.[35] But in 1884, as the topographic survey of the site was completed along with a preliminary design, Olmsted feared his plans for Franklin Park, and his work in Boston generally, were about to suffer from the kind of political turmoil he knew so well from his New York experiences.[36] That year Boston elected its first Irish Catholic mayor, Hugh O'Brien, a Democrat who soon replaced Dalton and the other Boston park commissioners with prominent members of his own political coalition. After a period of uncertainty, however, Olmsted found that the new administration supported his park system plans. Opposition arose, ironically, from Republican opponents in the Common Council, who refused to allow appropriations for further park construction under a Democratic administration. O'Brien defeated the tactic through state legislation authorizing the sale of bonds as the source of park funding. In 1886, O'Brien and his commissioners approved the final plan for Franklin Park, and construction proceeded.[37]

One of the first sections of Franklin Park to be completed was the Playstead, a pastoral landscape in the north corner of the park that accommodated a wide range of sports, gatherings, and other organized activities involving larger groups of people. At the edge of the Playstead, Olmsted designed a massive viewing terrace, known as the Overlook (or Playstead Terrace). Set on an existing rock outcrop, the 800-foot terrace was made up of puddingstone boulders moved from nearby in the park. Olmsted worked with mason John H. Watson, as he had at North Easton, Moraine Farm, and elsewhere during this period. Soil placed in the joints of the boulder masonry supported vines and other plants, as at the North Easton memorial cairn. Another longtime employee, horticulturist William L. Fischer, supervised planting at Franklin Park and other Boston parks beginning in 1884.[38] At one end of the Overlook, Olmsted designed the Overlook Shelter, a building with a refectory at the terrace level and locker rooms for ballplayers at the level of the playfields, below, which were entered through an arched opening in the terrace wall. The Overlook Shelter, completed in 1889, was covered with a massive, undulating shingle roof that appeared to rise organically out of the terrace's boulder foundation. As one of the most significant buildings Olmsted designed in his career, the Overlook Shelter was evidence of the influence of his collaborations with Richardson over the previous decade and perhaps his most complete built statement of the integration of landscape and architecture.[39] Many of the structures in Franklin Park (most of which, like the Overlook Shelter, have not survived) continued the naturalistic forms and irregular (or boulder) masonry that were also used in Richardson's Boylston Street Bridge. While the firm continued to work with consulting architects, in Franklin Park and elsewhere in the Boston park system, Olmsted was able to collaborate effectively to secure architectural designs he considered compatible with their settings (although exceptions and disagreements occurred). Many park structures were designed within the Fairsted office, which developed a distinctive and ultimately influential idiom of rustic architectural design during this period.

Most of the work on the Playstead, Country Park, and Wilderness sections of Franklin Park was completed in the 1880s. The addition of Scarborough Pond was made in a revised, 1891 plan by the Fairsted office. But the northeast side of the park, where a large, formal avenue called the Greeting was originally intended to provide a concert ground and create the principal gathering point for promenades and carriage drives, was never developed. In the twentieth century, the area became the site of the Franklin Park Zoo. Although it was not completed, Franklin Park was nevertheless one of the major artistic accomplishments of Olmsted's career. The meadows of the Country Park, in particular, powerfully demonstrated how a municipal park could offer city dwellers the kind of experience — a large expanse of pastoral scenery — that

Olmsted felt was necessary to physical and emotional health. Pedestrian walks and the carriage drive around the Country Park offered views into and across the landscape, and at selected high points on the rocky ledges of the site, distant vistas of regional scenery complemented the foreground of parkland. The picturesque Wilderness section of the park provided a wooded, rocky counterpoint to these bucolic scenes. The combination of these landscape experiences, the integration of the park circulation with the new parkway system, and the exploitation of the inherent character and potential of the site for what John Charles later called the "true purpose" of a large park made Franklin Park a tour de force, considered by John Charles (who, as a co-designer, was not a disinterested critic) to be his stepfather's finest work of the type.[40]

The Boston park system included smaller parks and playgrounds that served a variety of purposes, several of which had originally been proposed in the park commissioners' 1876 plan. Olmsted conceived of Pleasure Bay (later Marine Park) as the true termination of the "necklace" at Dorchester Point in South Boston. The beach and waterfront esplanade incorporated the federal property of Castle Island, a complicating factor that helped delay its completion until the twentieth century. Wood Island Park served East Boston and was also located on Boston Harbor. The park and its connecting parkway, Neptune Road, were constructed in the 1890s. In 1887, Olmsted produced a plan for Charlesbank, a small park on the embankment of the Charles River intended to serve another working-class neighborhood in Boston, the West End. Only ten acres, Charlesbank included play areas for children, a waterfront esplanade, and in the early 1890s, innovative outdoor gymnasium equipment, all accessible to residents of the nearby tenement neighborhoods.[41]

By the end of the period of this volume, Olmsted and his associates had completed most of the design and much of the construction of the most significant municipal park system the firm would ever create. The breadth of public landscape types and functions was remarkable: the unique Back Bay Fens and Muddy River Sanitary Improvement projects; one of Olmsted's finest large, pastoral parks; an arboretum that combined park purposes with the display of what would become the country's most significant collection of woody plants; glacial ponds incorporated into park landscapes largely unchanged; a variety of smaller parks and playgrounds; and a system of connecting parkways. The Boston park system was a comprehensive vision of how a response to regional landscape systems, combined with the design of specific public landscapes offering a range of experiences and functions, could structure American urbanization.

Boston Metropolitan Parks, 1879–1889

During this period, Olmsted helped extend the idea of landscape-based urbanism to the scale of regional planning. In the 1880s, several cities and towns around Boston already were acting to set aside scenic areas and watersheds that citizens and officials felt would prove vital to the continued health and prosperity of their communities. In 1881, citizens of Lynn established a public trust to accept gifts of land and later raised private funds, which were augmented by a municipal appropriation, for the acquisition of Lynn Woods as a "free public forest." Olmsted had visited Lynn Woods in 1879 and, with others, including local manufacturer Philip A. Chase, had advocated their preservation. The journalist Sylvester Baxter published an article that year in which he described (and named) Middlesex Fells, another scenic, wooded area in suburban Boston, and argued for its public acquisition. When asked for his advice on park improvements for Middlesex Fells, Olmsted advised Baxter to "take it as it stands, develop to the utmost its natural characteristics, and make a true retreat not only from town but from suburban conditions." Writing ten years later on the value of Lynn Woods, he again wrote to Baxter, "Its value as a roving ground not for Lynn and the northern suburbs only but for the people of Boston, in the future, cannot well be overestimated. . . . It shd be to Boston something like Fontainebleau to Paris and Richmond & Windsor to London." He warned Chase of the "hopelessness" of attempting to make Lynn Woods "park-like." Its special appeal rested in its wild and uncultivated condition. Any attempt to improve the wooded and rocky landscape along those lines would be futile and expensive, he insisted, as well as ill advised. "Being unparklike in other particulars," he explained, "the decorative features commonly seen in parks would appear fussy and impertinent, everywhere jarring upon the natural scenery."[42]

Perhaps Olmsted's most significant contribution to the metropolitan park movement around Boston was the training and inspiration he gave to Charles Eliot, who, with Baxter, went on to help establish both the Trustees of Reservations and the Metropolitan Park Commission in the early 1890s. These organizations helped realize a system of regional reservations planned to represent a range of regional landscape types, from river corridors and beaches, to upland areas and forests. Eliot called the new, larger public landscapes "reservations," not "parks," and he described in detail how any development in them should be sharply restricted to the provision of public access and the careful management of existing forests and other vegetation. Olmsted had already advised such practices for Lynn Woods and Middlesex Fells (which became two of the largest components of the new metropolitan park system). The new reservations were selected for their existing scenic and environmental values, making traditional municipal park amenities undesirable and large-scale engineered improvements unnecessary. The Boston municipal park system served as a precedent, nevertheless, for planning a park and parkway system based on a representational range of regional landscape types, now at a regional scale.[43] In 1893, the year Eliot finally joined the Fairsted office (renamed "Olmsted, Olmsted & Eliot"), Olmsted described the significance of the "Boston work" of the previous twenty years — referring to both "the Metropolitan quite equally with the city work" — to his office and his profession:

> Our reputation is still to be made in such dealings with pleasure roads outside of "parks", and in such "wild" public grounds, as those that we are now first to engage with about Boston. As much is to be made in this respect, as was to be made in Central Park. In your probable life-time, Muddy River, Blue Hills, the Fells, Waverly Oaks, Charles River the Beaches, will be points to date from in the history of American Landscape Architecture, as much as Central Park. They will be the opening of new Chapters of the Art. And there will be fashions starting from them, which will run across the Continent.[44]

Brookline, Massachusetts, 1886–1889

Some of Olmsted's most significant projects in the Boston area during this period were not park designs but plans for widening and extending streets and the layout of urban residential subdivisions. His 1884 design for extending Commonwealth Avenue from Beacon Street to Brookline Avenue (through the Beacon Street entrance of the Back Bay Fens) was one example.[45] His 1886 plan for widening Beacon Street through Brookline to the Chestnut Hill Reservoir was another. That plan included a second extension of Commonwealth Avenue from its western end south to the same reservoir and so described an entire circuit of improved streets that were not "parkways," because they were not legally parkland under the jurisdiction of a park commission and they were not restricted to noncommercial traffic. But they did extend the character and amenities of the Boston parkway system. Both extensions of Commonwealth Avenue, for example, were planned to be wide enough to accommodate separated lanes of traffic and to have pedestrian paths, trees, and grass along their length. Together with Boston's parkway system, the Chestnut Hill Reservoir circuit was part of a comprehensive transportation infrastructure for the Boston metropolitan region at the time.[46]

The town of Brookline, in particular, which was experiencing a period of intense urbanization, provided Olmsted with notable opportunities for both street and subdivision design. Unlike many of the towns around Boston, Brookline resisted annexation and retained its own government. Some influential and wealthy figures in Brookline, including town officials and land developers, were sympathetic to Olmsted's park and city planning ideas. One such developer was Henry M. Whitney, a wealthy businessman who had been investing in Brookline real estate for decades and who served (with Sargent) on the Brookline park commission. Whitney had acquired property along the Beacon Street corridor in Brookline for years before forming the West End Land Company in 1886 and then asking Olmsted to draw up plans for redesigning and widening the street. Beacon Street as Olmsted designed it in 1886 called for separated lanes to offer a more convenient express route for private traffic while accommodating local commercial traffic serving businesses along the street. The new street design also called for bicycle and bridle paths and street trees along its length.[47] The project had many of the design features of a parkway, and the same powerful effect on adjacent land values. Whitney later asked the Olmsted firm to design a subdivision of property he owned on Corey Hill, adjacent to Beacon Street, and Olmsted designed other subdivisions in Brookline during this period. Most (like Corey Hill) were not implemented completely as planned, but Brookline (Fisher) Hill was built according his design, as was the Aspinwall Hill subdivision, at least partially.[48]

The only large public landscape Olmsted designed for Brookline was the half of the Muddy River Sanitary Improvement (including what is today Olmsted Park, or Leverett Pond) that lay within the town's boundaries. Olmsted recommended that the town need not consider creating a large park. He felt the Muddy River landscape, which extended along almost the length of the town's eastern boundary, served that purpose adequately, and he suggested the town acquire school playgrounds and smaller parks, such as the summit of Corey Hill, instead.[49] Olmsted's move to Brookline in 1881 gave him the opportunity through a variety of landscape designs—the Muddy River project, the Beacon Street widening, and his completed subdivisions—to shape the growth of the town at a unique moment in its history, and to do so with a remarkable group of colleagues, including Richardson, Sargent, and other leading professionals, who were not only collaborators but also neighbors.

Calvert Vaux and New York Parks, 1885–1889

The early Boston years were a new beginning in Olmsted's life and in his career, but he never could completely leave New York, where he had many personal and professional ties and where the fate of his most significant single work, Central Park, remained always uncertain. Although his partnership with that park's co-designer, Calvert Vaux, officially ended in 1872, the two men continued to work together during the period of this volume and their professional lives and reputations remained at least partially linked. Several times during this period, New York park officials asked Olmsted to act as a consultant, and Olmsted consistently refused to do so unless it was with Vaux. Other New Yorkers, notably journalist William Stiles, kept Olmsted informed on park events and politics and occasionally enlisted him to defend Central Park from various threats and encroachments.

Following his departure from the city, Olmsted had little professional involvement there until 1885. That year, Ulysses S. Grant died, and his family elected to have his tomb placed in New York's Riverside Park. John D. Crimmins, a New York park commissioner, asked Olmsted to consult on how the site should be integrated with the park's design, which Olmsted and Vaux had completed in the early 1870s. Olmsted visited the site and gave general advice but asked Crimmins to have Vaux oversee the project.[50] The following year park commissioner Henry R. Beekman tried to retain Olmsted's advice on a more permanent basis. Olmsted entertained the possibility and asked that Vaux join him in something like their old roles. He and Vaux wrote a long letter to Beekman with observations on the condition and future of Central, Morningside, and Riverside parks and specifying the terms under which they would consult for the department in the future. Although the commissioners apparently thought they had appointed Olmsted "Landscape Architect Advisory" in 1887, politics and rivalries doomed his involvement before it began. Vaux was left with the impression that Olmsted had pursued the appointment without him, and Olmsted felt he had once again been misled by the New York Park Commission. Olmsted attempted to appease Vaux in letters explaining that he would not take a position in New York on his own and by writing an open letter in the *New York Tribune* explaining the situation. As late as 1889, Olmsted still had to insist to the park commissioners that he would not accept a position unless one was offered to Vaux as well.[51]

Olmsted and Vaux did work on one New York City park project together during this period, the revision of their 1873 design of Morningside Park, which had remained mostly unbuilt.[52] The Panic of 1873, followed by jurisdictional disputes over municipal responsibility for street and park construction, delayed the development of the park into the mid-1880s. In 1887, the New York park commissioners asked Olmsted and Vaux to revise their park plan, and the old partners agreed and visited the site together that summer. Their design was presented in August and responded to the new conditions on the site, including the partial construction of the massive retaining wall supporting Morningside Avenue (later Drive) and the construction of the nearby Ninth Avenue elevated train, which shifted assumptions about the points of arrival and number of park visitors. The new plan eliminated a small lake in the southeast corner as a result and no longer featured a large conservatory that had been proposed in 1873 as part of a scheme to relocate parts of the Central Park Menagerie.[53]

Olmsted also remained concerned during this period with policies he felt would harm Central Park. In 1887, he successfully opposed legislation that would have opened the park for military training and permitted the construction of a new zoo.[54] In 1889, he was drawn into a controversy over the thinning of trees in Central Park, a subject of particular concern to him at this point in his career. Because he had been responsible for planting thousands of trees in parks over the previous two decades, their proper maintenance — which included thinning plantations that had purposely been planted thickly in anticipation of such action — was now a timely consideration. Olmsted accepted a request from the West Side Association and the Torrey Botanical Club, two private organizations in New York, to report on the situation in Central Park, where recent tree thinning had attracted criticism.[55] Working with Jonathan B. Harrison, at that time the secretary of the American Forestry Association, Olmsted and his co-author did more than report on the conditions of the trees in one park. In their 1889 report, *Observations on the Treatment of Public Plantations, More Especially Relating to the Use of the Axe*, Olmsted and Harrison compiled many sources and elicited opinions from leading horticulturists of the day to support the contention that thinning, if done properly, was a necessary aspect of maintaining tree plantations.[56] Another controversy involving Central Park arose in 1889 as a group of New York citizens assembled proposals for making the city the site of the World's Columbian Exposition, scheduled for 1892. Olmsted supported Henry R. Towne in his proposal for establishing the principal fairgrounds on Bloomingdale Heights, the area between Morningside and Riverside parks. He also commented on various schemes to employ the north end of Central Park temporarily as an extension of the fairgrounds.[57] Congress awarded the fair to Chicago, however, obviating the need to defend the New York parks from encroachments, and putting into motion what would become, early in the next decade, one of Olmsted's final and greatest commissions, the design of the Chicago World's Fair grounds.

The U.S. Capitol Grounds, 1882–1889

The U.S. Capitol grounds, designed by Olmsted in 1874, had been largely completed by 1882 with one important exception: the proposed marble terraces that were to wrap around the north, south, and west sides of the building. These terraces — especially the large west terrace, which was to step down in two levels and feature monumental, symmetrical staircases — were fundamental to the overall Capitol grounds design. While the new Capitol dome and wings had been completed by 1866, relatively small earthen terraces still served as the only transition between the building and its site. The design of the marble terraces was intended to correct the situation and provide a visually proportional base for the Capitol, and to create a suitably monumental transition between the building and its enlarged and redesigned grounds.

Senator Justin S. Morrill and the Architect of the Capitol, Edward Clark, had given crucial support to Olmsted's work to complete the Capitol grounds project to that point, and they continued their alliance in the completion of this final and expensive phase of the project. In 1882, Olmsted produced an illustrated pamphlet for members of Congress describing the purposes, design, and benefits of the terraces and submitted the same arguments to Clark to include in his *Annual Report*.[58] Morrill succeeded in getting a small appropriation that year to build "approaches to the Capitol" on the north and south sides of the building, which in reality were the first phases of the larger project. This led to increased scrutiny from Congress on the total cost estimates for the project, which Olmsted provided.[59]

The efforts to fund the terraces succeeded, but not without struggle and some design revision. Olmsted's role in the project also changed. After Congress made a significant appropriation for terrace construction in December 1884, Olmsted wrote a letter of resignation, stating that the work on the Capitol grounds was nearly complete except for the terraces, work he said was better left to the supervision of the Architect of the Capitol. At the time, Clark's own position was threatened. Following the elections of 1884, Congress sought to reorganize the Architect of the Capitol's office in a manner that would have removed him from administrative control of Capitol construction projects. In part with Olmsted's help, however, Clark remained, and Olmsted, despite his "resignation," continued to serve as the advisory landscape architect for the Capitol grounds in charge of all planting and other improvements, although at a reduced annual rate. Both Olmsted and Clark oversaw the construction of the terrace project until its effective completion in 1891.[60]

Revisions to the design of the west terrace of the Capitol began in the mid-1880s, when construction crews were already laying its foundations. Olmsted designed the west terrace under the expectation that a new wing was going to be added on the west side of the Capitol to house the Library of Congress.[61] By the mid-1880s, plans called for an independent building to house the library, which changed the requirement that the terrace act in part as a supporting foundation for an extension that now would not be built. At that point, altering the terrace's design was suggested. Morrill, for example, recommended that a large fountain could be added between the staircases. The most significant suggested alteration to the west terrace occurred in 1886, when the Senate debated whether the entire base of the terrace should be pierced with windows to provide light and ventilation for the offices and committee rooms within. Olmsted opposed the idea and pointed out that the solidity of the lower terrace wall provided the visual foundation that the Capitol building then lacked. Olmsted enlisted architects to the cause, including Howard C. Walker and H. H. Richardson, but he also was willing to compromise, which he did in 1886. Between the flanking staircases on the lower level, Olmsted revised the design so that the terrace curved inward and featured apsidal niches and a fountain at the center (although not of the size or design suggested by Morrill). On the upper level, he added new committee rooms in the area between the staircases, rooms that had large windows facing out to the west. The compromise answered at least some of the demands of members of Congress, while retaining the visual solidity of the terrace. Congress funded continued construction based on the revised plan, and the west terrace was completed five years later.[62]

Buffalo Parks, 1885–1889

Olmsted began planning Buffalo parks in 1868 when he visited the city at the invitation of Buffalo lawyer, politician, and park advocate, William E. Dorsheimer. At that time, Olmsted suggested to an assembled group of interested citizens that, rather than choosing one site among several identified, the city should acquire three parks, each of a different type, and connect them with parkways. By 1876, Olmsted and the Buffalo park commissioners had created the country's first coordinated park and parkway system, including a large, pastoral park (later Delaware Park), a parade ground (later Martin Luther King,

Jr. Park), and a ceremonial point of arrival, called the Front, overlooking the Erie Canal and Lake Erie.[63]

In 1887, Olmsted and John Charles began the design for the South Park, which had been proposed to serve the growing working-class neighborhoods of the Thirteenth Ward, south of downtown. In March 1887, the park commissioners asked Olmsted to visit the site they had proposed along the shore of Lake Erie. Over the next year, Olmsted and John Charles developed a design for a 325-acre waterfront park, featuring a recreational waterway—a "water avenue" incorporating a promenade on a lakeside levee with a boating canal behind it—connecting to downtown Buffalo and the rest of the park system. The park included a variety of water-based and other types of recreation.[64] With meandering watercourses, islands, and opportunities for sheltered recreational boating, the South Park would have resembled the water parks Olmsted had proposed on the shore of Lake Michigan for Jackson Park in Chicago in 1871 or, to a more limited degree, the Back Bay Fens of Boston.[65] The awesome expanse of Lake Erie, which could be windy and forbidding, was incorporated as the background view in a more hospitable landscape of varied and accessible shorelines and enframing shrubs and trees. Olmsted knew the politics of park making in Buffalo, and he attempted once again to rally support for his plan by printing and distributing copies of his reports at his own expense and by corresponding with newspaper editors. He pointed out that years earlier he had encouraged the city to acquire a larger lakefront park, but the opportunities to do so had already been limited because of development. He wrote to Edwin Fleming, the editor of the *Buffalo Courier*, that the South Park project should "secure now, before it is too late, a place of popular diversion, healthful and enlivening, on the Lake Shore, the only place available for the purpose being of such a character that no ordinary type of a 'park' could, at any reasonable expense, be formed upon it."[66]

The park commissioners changed their minds about the waterfront site, however, ostensibly because of its expense and worries over the maintenance of an exposed site that could be prone to flooding. But clearly local interests concerned with property values and development opportunities also influenced the decision. Opponents of the South Park plan wanted the new park, or parks, to be sited farther inland, where they would perhaps more directly influence property values and be more accessible to the neighborhoods they would serve. By the end of 1888, the commissioners rejected the South Park site, and they later selected two smaller, less dramatic sites for park development, named South Park and Cazenovia Park, which Olmsted and John Charles designed in the early 1890s.[67]

Rochester Parks, 1888–1889

The city of Rochester, New York, established a park commission in 1888 and contacted Olmsted for advice on assembling a list of potential park design consultants. Olmsted responded by explaining the distinction between landscape gardeners, who were principally horticulturists, and landscape architects (of whom there were few), who had broader training in design and were better prepared to plan park systems. The commissioners decided to hire both Olmsted and Vaux, and Olmsted approached his former partner to ask if he would be interested. Vaux apparently declined, however, explaining that the arrangement would be unfair to his partner, Samuel Parsons, Jr., and that he could not take the time from his work in New York parks. The Rochester commissioners then hired Olmsted to begin planning the city's park system that October.[68]

His first recommendation was to acquire as much land along the corridor of the Genesee River Valley as possible. The scenic river, its falls, and the escarpments and meadows that lined its banks ran directly through the city and offered immediate potential for parks and park drives along its course. By the summer of 1889, the plans for Meadow (now Genesee Valley) Park were prepared and construction and planting were under way. Olmsted worked with an old colleague, the nurseryman Robert Douglas, to supply and plant trees. Between 1889 and his retirement, Olmsted also worked on the designs of Seneca Park and Highland Park, and the firm's work on Rochester's park system continued into the twentieth century.[69]

Belle Isle, Detroit, 1882–1885

Belle Isle, an approximately 900-acre wooded and poorly drained island in the Detroit River, was acquired for park purposes in 1879. The Detroit Common Council established the Belle Isle park commission in 1881, and that November the commissioners, with James McMillan (the future U.S. senator) acting as chairman, inquired whether Olmsted would design a portion of Belle Isle. Olmsted refused, insisting that a comprehensive design for the entire island would be required. That winter he came to Detroit to visit the site, and the following spring he was given a contract to design the entire park and superintend its construction over the next three years. Work was delayed while Olmsted waited for a topographical survey, always a prerequisite for his design process. Olmsted presented his preliminary ideas for the park in Detroit late in 1882. The preliminary proposal called for keeping and managing most of the forest intact while creating some meadows that could be maintained with grazing sheep. At one end of the island, where steamboats providing the only public access would dock, he suggested more intensive activities and programs could be accommodated. A system of canals, which Olmsted described as "rigolets," would help manage drainage on the island but also provide access for small craft on sheltered waterways through much of the forest.[70]

A change in park administration occurred in March 1883 when the state legislature replaced the Belle Isle park commission with a new Detroit Board of Park Commissioners. The same month, Olmsted traveled to Detroit to present his design for the park, which retained the intentions and organization he had described the year before. The final plan also called for building large piers for the steamboats to dock and an attached "1,600-foot-covered 'gallery'" that combined multiple park purposes. Curving along the shoreline and covered by a massive, undulating shingle roof, the gallery directly connected to the piers, and so organized and sheltered arriving and departing park visitors. The gallery also served as a waterfront promenade that on one side provided sheltered viewing of a beach that was to stretch along its length. On the other side, the gallery served as an observation terrace for the large, open parade ground and ball-field sheltered on the inland side of the two-story gallery structure. Ramps allowed people to move from one level to the other, and rooms and offices for various park activities and maintenance were all integrated into the building. The rest of Belle Isle's final design was just as unusual. A straight avenue proceeded from the parade ground down two-thirds of the length of the island and then split to form a curvilinear circuit around its eastern end. Throughout, a network of canals was suggested that would accommodate boating, and the majority of the island's existing forest was to be kept intact and managed. Olmsted returned to Detroit that spring and summer to explain and promote the plan for Belle Isle. In the spring of 1884, work had begun on the parade ground area and the foundations of the gallery building. At that point, however, opponents of the project pressed the City Council to withhold funding for what some felt was an overly expensive project. The pier and gallery structures, in particular, drew criticism apparently mostly because of their cost. The situation was exacerbated by the fact that the city park commission was directly dependent on the City Council for approval of park construction funds, which were raised through appropriations, not bond issues. Olmsted published his own justification for the project, "Belle Isle: After One Year," and continued to try to convince the city to develop the park as planned, and especially not to leave out the gallery, which he felt was the crucial element of the design.[71] As he put it, "The plan of Belle Isle Park grows out of the feature of the Pier and Gallery as out of a stem."[72] But the politics and finances of Detroit made funding park construction difficult.

The documents in this volume mostly relate to Olmsted's efforts to convince the Detroit commissioners not to give up on this feature of his plan. The pier and gallery building Olmsted designed for Belle Isle was the most significant landscape structure design of his career and the fruition of his collaborations with Richardson and his experiences with projects in North Easton, the Boston parks, and elsewhere. In the coming years, however, the Detroit commissioners kept only some aspects of the Belle Isle design, such as the axial avenue. They kept costs to a minimum and never built the proposed canals. Instead of the gallery, they erected a much smaller, one-story shelter meant to resemble the building Olmsted had designed. As of the spring of 1885, Olmsted had no further involvement in the project. In 1887, after a change in the makeup of the park commission, he was asked for a new plan for Belle Isle, but refused to be involved any further.[73]

School Campuses, 1883–1887

Olmsted's experience in campus design went back to his work in California in 1865 for the design of the College of California (later the University of California, Berkeley). From the beginning Olmsted thought of the campus as a specific type of community, one that therefore should be designed with housing and other aspects of community life foremost in mind. The plan for the College of California described a "Berkeley Neighborhood" as well as a campus in an integrated landscape design adapted to the climate and soils of the region. Olmsted felt that the character of student housing and the layout of the adjacent residential area were essential to the educational mission of the college. He rejected both large dormitories and off-campus boarding houses for students and advised instead building a number of smaller campus residences, with the appearance of "large domestic houses," in a setting that was neither rural and overly isolated, nor urban and lacking the seclusion necessary for academic study.[74] The Morrill Land Grant Act of 1862 (sponsored by Olmsted's future ally in the Capitol grounds project, Senator Justin S. Morrill) created opportunities for Olmsted in campus planning following the end of the Civil War. In his report for the Massachusetts Agricultural College in 1866, Olmsted again urged that campus design was not a matter of choosing sites for a group of large, institutional buildings, but of laying out a community that, in the case of agricultural colleges, should be a "model rural neighborhood" with strong relationships with surrounding towns or villages.[75] Olmsted emphasized that well-planned residences were key to the experience and education of students and would assist in inculcating the best values of rural life and society. He considered this instruction an essential part of the mission of the new institutions that were otherwise dedicated to teaching agricultural sciences and techniques.[76]

While opportunities to see his campus designs realized early in his career were limited,[77] during the period of this volume, Olmsted designed two of his most significant school campuses and saw them built. The directors of the Lawrenceville School in New Jersey contacted Olmsted in 1883 to design a new campus for their secondary boarding school, which recently had come under a new administration. James Cameron Mackenzie had become headmaster in 1882 and was in the process of instituting the "house system," based on English models, in which students lived in groups with instructors in a residential houses rather than large dormitories. Such objectives coincided with some of Olmsted's own ideas, and working with architects Peabody and Stearns and engineer J. J. R. Croes, he produced his most complete and fully realized campus plan. Olmsted insisted that the arrangement of houses create convenient patterns of daily life, with equal access to central facilities and classrooms. He also felt that all the houses should be oriented to give full sunlight to the students' rooms, for reasons of health, as well as views and shelter from prevailing winds. Wooded areas and adequate distances from main roads would provide a desirable sense of seclusion for the residential complex. After some struggle to produce a plan to meet these requirements (as described by then-apprentice Charles Eliot), Olmsted devised an oval arrangement of the residential houses, fitted to the topography, that accomplished his goals, and defined a central campus green. In 1886, he recommended planting the campus as an arboretum and produced an extensive planting plan that the school carried out in the coming years. The Fairsted firm remained involved in planning the campus as it grew and new buildings and facilities were planned.[78]

In California, however, Olmsted received his largest and most ambitious campus design commission, for Stanford University. Olmsted had not visited California since 1865. When he returned to meet with Leland Stanford in 1886, he traveled on the transcontinental railroad, not by way of the Isthmus of Panama, as on his last voyage there. He was accompanied by Henry Sargent Codman and by his sixteen-year-old son, Frederick Law Olmsted, Jr., on the first of three trips he would take to the state between 1886 and 1889.[79] The Stanford commission gave Olmsted his greatest opportunity not only to implement his design ideas for universities but also to demonstrate what he considered the best approach to landscape design in the semiarid climates of the American West. First, however, he would need to convince his powerful and opinionated client that a California university need not be an imitation of the grassy yards and quadrangles of prestigious New England institutions.

Leland Stanford, who was elected to the U.S. Senate in 1885 and had earlier served as the state's governor, had made a fortune through railroads and other businesses and investments in California. While they were traveling in Europe together in 1884, his only child died of typhoid fever, and Stanford founded the university the next year in his memory. He consulted with the president of MIT, Francis Amasa Walker, early in his planning for the institution. Walker recommended that Stanford also consult with Olmsted and the architectural firm Shepley, Rutan, and Coolidge. Even before accepting the commission, however, Olmsted expressed concern that Stanford wanted "English landscape gardening" for his campus, which Olmsted felt would never be desirable or even feasible in the climate. While in California in the 1860s, Olmsted had devised his own approach to landscape design appropriate for western conditions, where turf, for example, could only be established in most places with expensive irrigation.[80] The plants and design idioms of the Mediterranean (as he had suggested to the then traveling Eliot) offered landscape and architectural design precedents adapted to conditions similar to those found in California. Soon after Olmsted's arrival in the state, however, Stanford insisted on a high degree of participation and control over the design process. While Olmsted suggested that the campus be located on the slope of a hill, where views and breezes were available, Stanford insisted on building it on the valley floor. But Olmsted won the most important argument: the new campus plan would not attempt to recreate an eastern landscape. The design centered on three enclosed quadrangles, paved in stone and surrounded by continuous, open arcades. Planting was restricted to a series of circular plots consisting of palms and dense plantings of low trees and shrubs, which could be easily watered and maintained. The arcades offered shelter and shade, and the one-story, stone buildings featured Romanesque architectural details and red-tiled roofs. Small dormitories and faculty residences were intended to be directly adjacent to the central quadrangles of the campus in small neighborhoods, a feature of the plan Stanford rejected. Stanford made other significant revisions to the plan over the next two years, changes that are the subject of much of the relevant correspondence in this volume. Olmsted wrote to Van Rensselaer in 1887 that the Stanford project was going "not very well and not ruinously." Stanford later canceled plans for an extensive university arboretum, and by 1890, Olmsted had little further influence on changes to the campus plan.[81] But Stanford University remains the largest example of Olmsted's campus design, and his most significant built expression of landscape design adapted to the semiarid conditions of California.

Residential Subdivisions, 1882–1889

The subdivision of land for the purpose of residential development grew in importance for Olmsted's office during the 1880s, a period of urban and suburban growth, overall, in much of the nation. Olmsted's Brookline subdivisions, described above, were important examples not only of the firm's work but also of a national trend that changed the character of many towns and villages on the outskirts of American cities. In subdivision design, the Olmsted office continued to employ many of the basic techniques of landscape architecture perhaps best expressed in Olmsted's 1869 design for the community of Riverside, Illinois. Road alignments conformed to topography, for example, a priority that required a topographic survey at the outset of any project. The identification of locations for parks and smaller public spaces, particularly along water bodies or in areas with notable views, was a priority for Olmsted (if not always for his clients). Generous width and geometry of streets allowed for trees and grass, where appropriate, enhancing the suburban ideal as one that offered less dense patterns of construction and allowed for more vegetation, space, and fresh air.

During the 1880s, Olmsted designed several resort communities, a development type that perhaps allowed him to apply some of his principles of subdivision design more completely than he was sometimes able to do when working closer to cities. In 1883, the owners of Cushing's Island, a 250-acre island near Portland, Maine, asked Olmsted to create a subdivision plan for a summer community of "common lands and . . . Villa plots." Olmsted delineated forty such plots on 133 acres of the island and kept the rest open for common use, including the shoreline, overlooks, and footpaths.[82] In 1887, Alfred D. Chandler, a prominent neighbor in Brookline, asked Olmsted to design a small resort on Lake Sunapee in New Hampshire. Although Chandler never implemented the plans, Olmsted provided an insightful analysis of the character of the site and its potential for development, noting, "As the success of the undertaking will depend on the enjoyment of . . . that which is characteristic in the scenery, . . . it is important that all operations of improvement should centre upon a hotel planned and placed with sagacious regard to the object."[83]

Olmsted's trips to California to work on the Stanford University campus also allowed him and his partners to take commissions that could be visited on side trips along the transcontinental route. In December 1888, he traveled to Perry Park, Colorado, fifty miles south of Denver along the Front Range of the Rocky Mountains, where a group of investors led by Charles A. Roberts and Gen. Bela M. Hughes hoped to develop a summer community. Henry Sargent Codman, also on his way to California, visited the site in the summer of 1889. Olmsted and Codman developed a plan for a lakeside subdivision but warned the investors that without the provision of an adequate water supply and other infrastructure investment, the entire scheme would never be feasible (which proved to be the case). Although not built according to their plans, the subdivision was another significant example of a landscape design adapted to the semiarid conditions of the western United States. Noting that the lake was a major attraction and amenity in the dry landscape, the plan called for a narrow road set back from the lake, with a "nearly continuous belt of trees and bushes to grow with their roots in its moist edges." This road corridor would include a sewer and other utilities, and with the lakeshore vegetation would be maintained by the development company. On the other side of the road, one-story bungalows were to be built with their front porches and verandas facing the lake, each provided with a source of water to encourage further cultivation of the lots by the owners. The effect was to create a vegetated zone around the lake, with both the circuit road and the community contained within it. The compact village would leave the "park" around it (a term used to describe the naturally occurring grassland of the high, intermountain valleys of the Rockies) mostly unaltered, with the village appearing so that it would "not be a prominent feature in the general landscape but rather an episode."[84]

Residential Design, 1882–1890

As the Fairsted office grew, the design of residential landscapes increased in number and importance. While Olmsted had a limited number of residential commissions earlier in his career, during the 1880s, he and his associates developed a distinctive approach, exemplified by the design of the Fairsted grounds in 1883. Olmsted created what could be called residential landscapes, rather than gardens, in the sense that he eschewed the ornamental beds, horticultural specimens, statuary, and other features of many gardens of the era. Particularly on sites that possessed a strong existing character, such as a rocky coastline, he argued against lawns and flowers and urged clients to embrace the inherent interest of their property through subtle manipulations of topography and naturalistic plantings intended to enhance the site's appeal rather than create a competing attraction. Gardens often did have their place in Olmsted's residential landscapes, but as at Moraine Farm in Massachusetts (1880), that place was well defined by a garden wall or some other separation.[85]

During the period of this volume, Olmsted designed a number of significant residential landscapes and began the single largest of his career, Biltmore, in North Carolina, which he designed with the architect Richard Morris Hunt for George W. Vanderbilt beginning in 1888. Olmsted had known Vanderbilt's father, William H. Vanderbilt, when they both lived on Staten Island. His first project for the family (and his first collaboration with Hunt) was the design of the Vanderbilt mausoleum in New Dorp, Staten Island.[86] Olmsted went on to design the grounds of residences for five of William H. Vanderbilt's eight children, who inherited enormous fortunes after their father's death in 1885. That year Olmsted began work on Elm Court, in Lenox, Massachusetts, the summer home of Emily T. Vanderbilt and her husband William D. Sloane. Peabody and Stearns were the architects, and two old colleagues, the engineer George E. Waring and the horticulturist William L. Fischer, also worked on the project. In 1886, Eliza O. Vanderbilt and her husband William Seward Webb asked Olmsted to design Shelburne Farms, their estate on Lake Champlain, in Vermont. Olmsted divided the property, which eventually covered more than 3,000 acres, into zones dedicated primarily to either farming or forestry, in addition to an area developed as parkland around the principal residence. Olmsted laid out a network of roads, and the planting plan called for thousands of new trees, although the firm remained involved at Shelburne Farms only until 1889.[87]

In 1887, Olmsted also began plans for Frederick W. Vanderbilt for the grounds of the summerhouse Peabody and Stearns were designing for him in Newport, Rhode Island. Named Rough Point, the house was indeed located on a point of the rocky shore along Newport's Cliff Walk. Olmsted determined the location and orientation of the house with the architects and urged his clients not to create lawns and flowerbeds between the house and the sea but to retain and restore the rugged aspect of the rocky, windswept site. This would create the best setting for the architecture and an appropriate transition to the shore, which he described to Van Rensselaer as an "utter wildness of rocks, shingle and sand, sea wrack and storm-beaten things." In the same letter, he acknowledged that his clients were dubious, but he had been "trying to get the Vanderbilt owners to set their house well out near the rocks and then . . . make a clean division of the property, one part (being that opening from the Avenue and on the lee side of the house, walls &c.), having a {*fair*} normal lawn-like character; the other part, seen from the opposite side of the house, over the terrace walls &c. rocky, wild, sea beaten—all its elevated parts forming a foreground to the general distance of the ocean—with a middle ground of reefs, breakers and foam."[88] Frederick Vanderbilt apparently was not entirely convinced regarding the treatment of the grounds, and Olmsted explained further as work was ongoing that while "previous occupants had grubbed out the indigenous growth, had filled up natural depressions; reduced elevations, covered rocks, and done much to obtain a smooth garden and lawn-like character," his grading operations were "wholly directed to an approximate restoration of a natural surface."[89]

In 1888, Olmsted began consulting on the design of George W. Vanderbilt's summerhouse in Maine, Pointe D'Acadie. That fall Olmsted traveled to North Carolina to discuss with the same client his more monumental plans for what would become Biltmore, located in the Great Smoky Mountains near Asheville. Richard Morris Hunt was working with Vanderbilt on the original design of what had first been planned as a relatively modest countryseat, but which by 1889 had grown into a proposal for a chateau in the manner of the French Renaissance, which would eventually become the largest private residence in the country. Olmsted again worked with the architect to determine the location and orientation of the building, accounting for principal winds, views, and solar orientation. The Biltmore Estate eventually grew to about 120,000 acres, and during the seven years Olmsted was actively involved in the project, he was able to implement a range of management recommendations and landscape designs that made Biltmore his largest work for a private client. Perhaps most significantly, he convinced Vanderbilt at the outset that the mountainous topography and thin forest soils of the region would never make a park landscape, at least not in the specific sense of a pastoral landscape of greenswards and gentle terrain. The land Vanderbilt was acquiring—much of it cut over forests and submarginal farmland—would therefore be best served by applying the scientific principles of forestry to improve the health and value of the forests and prevent further soil erosion. In the immediate vicinity of the house, Olmsted designed a series of outdoor spaces that transitioned from the formal to the wild. The more arable bottomland along the French Broad River below was maintained in agricultural uses. Olmsted did design a relatively small "deer park" to serve as a foreground for the mountainous vistas to the west, the views that had first attracted Vanderbilt to the area, but this was a rougher, steeper version of a park landscape.[90]

Biltmore occupied much of Olmsted's attention during the last phase of his career and also became an important training ground for Frederick Law Olmsted, Jr., while he was in his early twenties. Vanderbilt's wealth made it possible to realize much of the vision described in the early project correspondence included in this volume. The estate became the first large-scale demonstration of scientific forestry in the United States (Vanderbilt hired Gifford Pinchot as forester in 1892 at Olmsted's suggestion), and the approach road, the esplanade, the ramble, the viewing terrace (bowling green), and the placement of the stables and other dependencies, were all carried out as Olmsted describes them here.[91] The approach road was a particularly intensive effort, and was one of the finest examples of roadway design, drainage features, and roadside planting that Olmsted ever completed. Despite the considerable engineering required to bring the road through the precipitous terrain and up to the house site, Olmsted was intent on making the road an intimate and subtly enriched experience of the diverse flora, flowering understories, and seasonal bloom sequence of the region. The forest edge along the corridor was thinned and planted with a variety of rhododendrons; low shrubs and groundcovers enhanced the feeling of richness and profusion of the place. The experience of the three-mile approach served as a prelude to the spectacular views that were experienced only after arriving at the house and gardens above.[92]

Five other significant residences designed during this period are also represented by correspondence in this volume. All were in Massachusetts, an indication of the growing importance of the professional connections and clientele in that state Olmsted established during the decade. In 1882, he designed the grounds of Elizabeth Henderson Guild's summerhouse on the shore in Nahant, giving advice similar to that he would later give to Frederick W. Vanderbilt for Rough Point.[93] Some of his correspondence reveals a straightforward, if not antagonistic, attitude toward clients who for some reason failed to appreciate his suggestions. Charles T. Hubbard, whose property in Weston Olmsted designed in 1883, was told, "I am a designer which I should not be if I did not know better than anyone else what is & what is not essential in my designing," and that while Hubbard was entitled to do what he liked with his property, he also might want to seek professional advice elsewhere.[94] Olmsted had known another client, Morris K. Jesup, since the 1850s, a fact that did not prevent constant disagreements when he designed the grounds of Jesup's Belvoir Terrace, in Lenox. After years of arguing over the basic location of the house and layout of the property, Olmsted finally gave up in 1889, and Jesup hired Ernest Bowditch.[95] Olmsted did sometimes succeed in convincing clients to alter preconceived ideas about the location and aspect of their residence, as he did William Caleb Loring, for his summer home in Pride's Crossing.[96] In 1883, Julia and Alice Appleton asked Olmsted to design the grounds of their summerhouse in Lenox, for which Charles Follen McKim was the architect. Olmsted had known McKim's father, James, an abolitionist who had been one of the backers of the *Nation* in 1865, but this was the first time he worked with his son, the architect. Julia Appleton and McKim were married in 1885 in the house McKim designed.[97]

Niagara, Yosemite, and Scenic Preservation, 1886–1890

While residential design became a significant category of work for the Fairsted office in the 1880s, Olmsted also designed one of the most important projects in the history of scenic preservation during this decade. He did so in collaboration, once again, with Calvert Vaux. Olmsted had advocated the preservation of Niagara Falls since at least the late 1860s, when he began his work in nearby Buffalo. Hotels and tourist attractions had grown up around the falls for decades, forcing tourists to pay to gain access to overlooks and creating what many considered an inappropriate setting for the awesome spectacle. In 1879, the New York legislature appointed Olmsted, with the director of the New York State Survey, James T. Gardner, to prepare a special report on conditions at the falls and to make recommendations on how to improve them.[98] Their report emphasized the need to preserve the surrounding landscape, especially Goat Island, which separated the American and Canadian falls, and the shoreline along the rapids above the falls, which was lined with buildings. The report also contained a petition, which Olmsted and his friend the Harvard art historian Charles Eliot Norton had drawn up and circulated. Signed by leading cultural and political figures in the United States, Canada, and Great Britain, the document urged the state to acquire the private property around the falls and to provide better public access. At this time, Olmsted worked with a number of colleagues, especially Norton, to orchestrate a campaign to influence public opinion. The two men hired journalists Henry Norman and Jonathan B. Harrison to write articles on conditions at Niagara and on the legislation proposed to remedy them. Their efforts received a boost following the 1882 election of a supporter, Grover Cleveland (then the mayor of Buffalo), as governor of New York State. Olmsted and Norton helped found the Niagara Falls Association early in 1883, a group that intensified the effort to persuade the state legislature to act. Later that year the legislature approved a bill to establish the Niagara Reservation, and Cleveland signed it. In 1885, the same body finally appropriated funds to establish the reservation, and it became the first park of its type to be created by a state government.[99]

The first president of the Niagara Reservation board of commissioners was Olmsted's client and supporter in several projects, including the Buffalo park system, William E. Dorsheimer, who at this time was lieutenant governor. But the board also included Olmsted's longtime nemesis from his Central Park days, Andrew H. Green, who had become New York City comptroller. While Dorsheimer urged that Olmsted be appointed to draw up the Niagara Reservation plan, Green predictably objected to the appointment and put forward Vaux as an alternative. In 1886, the commissioners finally reached a compromise and asked both men to prepare the plan. While Olmsted had been far more involved than Vaux in planning and advocacy for Niagara, he acknowledged that Vaux had an important role in creating a plan for the reservation, which they completed in early 1887. Their Niagara report demonstrated how landscape architecture could be used to preserve and to restore a scenic landscape by acquiring private property, removing previous development, and facilitating public access through the construction of park drives, paths, overlooks, and limited visitor amenities.[100] By developing the area as a park, destructive resort development was avoided, affording the public opportunities for meaningful experiences of a place that otherwise might have been dominated by commercial enterprises.

These ideas and intentions for preserving a scenic landscape as a public park had an important precedent: the Yosemite Valley report that Olmsted had prepared just a few years before he became involved in the campaign to preserve Niagara.[101] In 1864, Olmsted was living in Bear Valley, California, managing the Mariposa gold mines, when Congress passed the Yosemite Grant, which ceded the nearby Yosemite Valley and Mariposa Grove of giant sequoias to the state of California for public park purposes. Olmsted had no hand in the legislation, but the governor appointed him to head the commission charged with managing the new park. His first act was to send James T. Gardner, who was then a U.S. deputy surveyor in California, to survey Yosemite Valley.[102] (In the 1870s, Gardner was the director of the New York State Survey, and so worked with Olmsted on their 1879 report on Niagara, as well.) The Yosemite report Olmsted wrote in 1865 outlined a program of minimal, unobtrusive development, including paths, overlooks, carriage roads, and camping facilities, that would allow what he foresaw would eventually be millions of visitors to the valley to have a full experience of it while keeping the landscape as undeveloped and undisturbed as possible. He recommended that most of the park's budget should be spent to build a road between the park's entrance and the steamboat docks at Stockton. Such a road would have allowed easier visitor access and would have made it possible to bring in lumber, food, and other supplies to serve visitors without the need to plow up and fence the valley's meadows to feed both people and their stock.

Olmsted traveled to California three times from 1886 to 1890, but he never returned to Yosemite Valley. On the first trip in 1886, he did travel to the nearby Mariposa Grove and visited with Galen Clark, who had been a fellow member of the first Yosemite commission. Clark and Olmsted probably discussed conditions in the nearby valley where, since Olmsted's last visit in 1865, much of the development and damage that he had warned against had occurred. Without the road to Stockton, many of the valley's meadows were now cultivated or used for pastures. Large hotels were built, rather than the simple camping stations Olmsted had advised, and numerous other businesses were established through permits issued by the state commissioners. The valley was changing in other ways, as well. By the 1880s, some visitors complained that tree growth was cutting off views and changing the character of the landscape. Although it was not well understood at the time, for centuries Native Americans had used fire to control the growth of vegetation in the valley, a practice that ended after 1864. By the 1880s, vegetation was rapidly encroaching into the valley's meadows, and park concessioners and managers reacted by removing and pruning trees, a practice that soon incited a negative reaction among preservationists who felt such tree cutting was inimical to the park's purpose.[103] During his 1886 trip, Olmsted was under pressure to work on the Stanford commission and to complete other business in California. But he may have had other reasons for choosing not to enter the valley that he had described movingly in 1865 as "the greatest glory of nature."

Olmsted was later drawn into commenting on conditions at Yosemite, nonetheless. In 1889, Robert Underwood Johnson, the associate editor of *Century* magazine, spent two weeks camping in and around Yosemite Valley with John Muir, the writer and wilderness preservation advocate. Muir enlisted Johnson in the cause of creating a larger Yosemite National Park around Yosemite Valley itself, which remained a state park at this time. Muir and Johnson also sought to reform the state's management of Yosemite Valley and criticized many aspects of the Yosemite commission's policies. Johnson wrote Olmsted and described what he considered the destructive removal of trees and other vegetation and the generally poor condition of the valley landscape.[104] He wanted Olmsted to consider taking a consulting position with the state park commission, and he offered to intercede with Leland Stanford to make the appointment possible. At the very least, the editor wanted Olmsted to write on the subject for *Century Magazine*.[105] Olmsted, who had just completed his definitive statement on the "use of the axe" in park management—a long and thoroughly documented defense of tree thinning—replied to Johnson only after considerable reflection. He eventually declined to write the article or to become more actively involved in criticism of the Yosemite commissioners. Although he sympathized with his friend's position and knew the management of the valley needed improvement, he was unwilling to condemn the commissioners without better knowledge of what exactly had been done and why. "All I could say," he wrote that fall, "is that, having at an early day spent several months in the valley under peculiarly favorable circumstances for contemplating it, I know that the question is {*one of far greater*} importance and of far greater difficulty than can be generally realized; that it is most foolish to take it up in an occasional and desultory way as a question of details, or as a question the answer to which will be chiefly important to the people of the present century. It is preeminently a question of our duty to the future."[106]

Olmsted might have continued to remain silent on the subject of Yosemite Valley, but in the spring of 1890 the governor of California, Robert W. Waterman, made a ludicrous claim that Johnson was disparaging the Yosemite commission solely for the purpose of obtaining a professional appointment for his "uncle," Frederick Law Olmsted. Olmsted now felt compelled to address the situation, and did so with a pamphlet published at his own expense, *Governmental Preservation of Natural Scenery*.[107] He gave an account of his involvement with Yosemite Valley and the Mariposa Grove since 1864, and he declined once again to criticize the state commissioners since he had not made a thorough study of their policies and actions. He refused to condemn tree removal, per se, in the valley but clarified that done incorrectly (as Johnson and others had claimed it was) the effects would be disastrous. The Yosemite commissioners, who had other areas of expertise, should not be expected to know the difference; landscape architects, who were specifically trained to make such judgments, should. While Olmsted declined to give any further advice on the management of valley landscape specifically, he gave a long quotation from the 1887 Niagara report that he felt should serve the general purpose of guiding Yosemite policy, and in so doing made it clear how closely these two great experiments in landscape preservation were linked.

"Nothing of an artificial character should be allowed a place on the property," he and Vaux wrote in 1887, "no matter how valuable it might be under other circumstances, and no matter at how little cost it may be had, the presence of which can be avoided consistently with the provision of necessary conditions for making the enjoyment of the natural scenery available."

Other Projects, 1882–1889

Documents in this volume also concern a number of other projects in the Fairsted office, including several significant park plans. In Newport, Rhode Island, Olmsted designed improvements for Easton's Beach, a popular public beach in a city known more for its opulent "cottages" on the shore.[108] In 1883, Olmsted advised the newly formed park board of Wilmington, Delaware, on proposed locations for a new park, including along the Brandywine Glen. He urged them to "obtain public rights in the scenery of the Glen, to protect and rehabilitate this scenery, and provide suitably for the public use of it," before they lost the opportunity.[109] In New London, Connecticut, Olmsted designed a park on an unusual three-acre site that included both an old burying ground and a small quarry. The human remains were taken to another cemetery, and he designed a unique shelter for the collected grave markers.[110] In 1883, Olmsted responded to a request by the Chicago South Park commissioners for copies of the report he and Vaux had completed for that group in 1871. Much of their plan remained unimplemented, although by 1880, a large open green, pedestrian paths, and carriage drives were completed in the Western Division of South Park (later Washington Park). But Olmsted, who had toured the park site in 1880, noted that some of the work had not followed their design. "You have had two styles of park in view," he advised the commission, "either of which would be satisfactory if well carried out. But the result of pursuing either alternative at intervals of some years or of muddling them together . . . must eventually be offensive either because of the incongruities it presents or tame and insipid because of the neutralization of one element of beauty by another."[111]

In 1889, Olmsted also worked on another capitol grounds project, this one for the Alabama capitol in Montgomery. The project, which like the one in Washington, D.C., was located on a hillside, never reached the point of a developed design.[112] Finally, in one fragmented draft letter in this volume, Olmsted wrote to the painter Thomas Worthington Whittredge, who had written to Olmsted on behalf of the Ladies' Summit Village Improvement Society, to which his wife belonged.[113] The letter is significant as one of the few written statements Olmsted made on the phenomenon of "village improvement societies," which were being organized in many towns in the United States at the time.

Publications, 1882–1890

During the early Boston years, Olmsted's reputation, and perhaps the benefit of having partners in his firm, allowed him to write for popular publications more than in past decades. Olmsted had always been at some level a journalist and a public intellectual, and as a landscape architect, he continued to strive to reach the broadest audience possible. This effort is evident in park reports and brochures intended to support park advocacy and influence public opinion. This volume also contains articles Olmsted contributed to such periodicals as *Garden and Forest*, the *Century Illustrated Monthly Magazine*, the *Sanitarian*, *American Architect and Building News*, *American Garden*, *American Florist*, and the [New York] *Art Review*. Olmsted would never write a definitive treatise or textbook on landscape architecture, but during this period he published some of his most mature and powerful statements on his art.

Asked to write on the healthful benefits of trees in 1882, he responded in "Trees in Streets and in Parks" with a discussion of landscape design theory, describing the necessity of subordinating individual displays, such as specimen plants, to the larger effects of landscape scenery in order to promote "unconscious, or indirect recreation" that directly affected an individual's emotional and physical health, something no individual landscape element could do.[114] "On Points of View and Methods of Criticism of Public Works of Landscape Architecture" was his defense of the preliminary site work at Franklin Park in 1885. Here and in numerous other essays, Olmsted drew on eighteenth-century landscape theorists, including William Gilpin, Horace Walpole, and Humphry Repton, to begin to define a framework and vocabulary for the critical consideration of landscape design.[115] Writing for the *Art Review*, Olmsted asked, "Are works of gardening, then, to be considered works of Art?" He responds by analyzing at some length Francis Bacon's 1625 essay, "Of Gardens." He asked (and answered) the question, "What is there in common between the gardening had in view by Bacon and this which has since been added to the field of gardening? The answer in one word is — design."[116] To the editor of *American Florist*, he provided an involved definition and etymology of "landscape," in order to clarify "terms vital to the discussion." In this case, he sought to distinguish what he described as "landscape gardening" from "ornamental gardening" for the publication's readers, at least some of whom apparently expressed some doubt at the validity of such a distinction.[117]

One of his richest essays on the theory of landscape architecture and scenic preservation, "A Healthy Change in the Tone of the Human Heart," was published in 1886 in the *Century Illustrated Monthly Magazine*. Before he asked Olmsted to write on Yosemite Valley, Robert Underwood Johnson asked for a more general article on what Olmsted later described as the "danger to treasures of natural scenery . . . growing out of modern developments of commerce and modern habits of travel."[118] Olmsted rooted his response in John Ruskin's observations on the historical transition from medieval to modern sensibilities, which that art critic described as a "healthy change in the tone of the human heart." This change involved the appreciation of mountainous landscapes, and by extension the appreciation of other scenery beyond the garden or the pleasure ground. "But if we accept it," Olmsted asked the readers of the *Century*, "what are we to think of the neglect that is apparent at many of our centers of civilization to preserve, develop, and make richly available their chief local resources of this form of wealth?" He followed with a somewhat dismal account of the failure of most American cities to preserve readily apparent scenic places and to secure opportunities for people to experience them.[119]

Other articles Olmsted wrote during this period address basic aspects of his design practice, such as "Plan for a Small Homestead," and "Terrace and Veranda—Back and Front," and "Foreign Plants and American Scenery." This last article questioned the preference for, and even the definition of, native plants.[120] These essays were all published in *Garden and Forest* in 1888, the first year of its publication. Olmsted's involvement with creating that magazine, and his subsequent interest in writing for it, his encouragement of others to contribute, as well as advising its editor, William Stiles, recalled his professional roots as a reporter, editor, and publisher in the 1850s. That experience, as much as any, prepared him for his career as a landscape architect. Olmsted's literary production was as much part of the professional practice he established at Fairsted as were plans, drawings, and specifications.

Conclusion

During the early Boston years, Olmsted's personal and working environment gave him substantial opportunities for professional fulfillment. The parks in Boston and Brookline, the architectural collaborations with H. H. Richardson, Stanford University, the plan for the Niagara Reservation, and the initiation of the Biltmore Estate were all the outstanding projects of their respective types in his career. With the organization of his office, the growth of his business, and perhaps the personal satisfaction he gained from his successful projects, Olmsted reached a satisfying point in his life by the end of the decade. His son Rick, in whom he placed great hopes as a successor, turned twenty and was already at work assisting him. Recognition of the significance of his life's work increased, as indicated by Van Rensselaer's 1893 biographical tribute to him. The coming years would bring his final professional triumphs and profound personal losses. His stepson and son would reorganize and carry on the business, however, which would survive and further enshrine its founder's name.

Ethan Carr

1. Frederick Law Olmsted, *The Spoils of the Park*, 1882 (*Papers of FLO*, 7: 605–52).
2. FLO to Charles Loring Brace, March 7, 1882 (*Papers of FLO*, 7: 592–94).
3. *FLO, A Biography*, pp. 360–61.
4. Nancy S. Seasholes, *Gaining Ground: A History of Landmaking in Boston* (Cambridge, 2003), pp. 215–29.
5. *FLO, A Biography*, pp. 388–92.
6. See Susan L. Klaus, "All in the Family: The Olmsted Office and the Business of Landscape Architecture," *Landscape Journal* 16, vol. 1 (Spring 1997), pp. 80–95; Cynthia Zaitzevsky, *Frederick Law Olmsted and the Boston Park System* (Cambridge, Mass., 1982), pp. 127–35.
7. Arleyn Levee, "Olmsted, John Charles," in Robin Karson and Charles Birnbaum, eds., *Pioneers of American Landscape Design* (New York, 2000), pp. 282–85; James Sturgis Pray, "John Charles Olmsted," *Landscape Architecture*, 12, no. 3 (April, 1922), pp. 129–35.
8. Eliot probably began his apprenticeship while the Olmsteds were still living in a rented house on Dudley Street in Brookline. The exact chronology of the family's move into Fairsted is unclear, but it may not have occurred until early in 1884. See Cynthia Zaitzevsky, *Fairsted: A Cultural Landscape Report for the Frederick Law Olmsted National Historic Site* (Boston, 1997), p. 11.
9. Charles W. Eliot, *Charles Eliot, Landscape Architect* (Boston, 1898), pp. 32–44.
10. C. W. Eliot, *Charles Eliot*, pp. 50–200.
11. FLO to Charles Eliot, March 4, 1886, FLO to Charles Eliot, July 20, 1886, FLO to Charles Eliot, Oct. 28, 1886, all below; Keith N. Morgan, "Introduction" to the 1999 Edition, *Charles W. Eliot: Landscape Architect* (Amherst, Mass., 1999), pp. vii–xlix.
12. C. W. Eliot, *Charles Eliot*, p. 204.
13. FLO to Édouard André, June 6, 1879 (*Papers of FLO*, 7: 393–95).
14. FLO to Charles Loring Brace, Jan. 18, 1890, below.
15. Robin Karson, "Manning, Warren," in C. A. Birnbaum and R. Karson, eds., *Pioneers*, pp. 236–42.
16. Frederick Law Olmsted, Jr., and Theodora Kimball, eds., *Forty Years of Landscape Architecture, Frederick Law Olmsted*, vol. 1 (New York, 1922), p. 38.
17. The figures were provided by Anthony Reed, archivist at the Frederick Law Olmsted National Historic Site, and represent totals from the Letterpress Records (Series A) of the Papers of Frederick Law Olmsted at the Library of Congress.
18. Marie L. Carden and Andrea M. Gilmore, *Historic Structure Report: Frederick Law Olmsted National Historic Site*, vol. 1 (Lowell, Mass. 1998), pp. 46–66.
19. C. Zaitzevsky, *Fairsted: A Cultural Landscape Report*, pp. 16; FLO to JCO, Sept. 12, 1884, below.
20. For thorough documentation of the Fairsted grounds in the 1880s, see C. Zaitzevsky, *Fairsted: A Cultural Landscape Report*, 15–36.
21. FLO to William B. Duncan, Sept. 22, 1870 (*Papers of FLO*, 6: 389–91); Frederick Law Olmsted, "Preliminary Suggestions for the Grounds of the Buffalo State Hospital for the Insane," July 7, 1871 (*Papers of FLO*, 6: 452–55); Jeffrey Karl Ochsner, *H. H. Richardson: Complete Architectural Works* (Cambridge, Mass., 1982), pp. 46–49, 78–81, 157–67; *Papers of FLO*, 7: 7–8.
22. J. K. Ochsner, *H. H. Richardson*, pp. 221–25.
23. *Papers of FLO*, SS1: 42–43. For more on the mutual influence of Olmsted and Richardson in the 1880s, see James F. O'Gorman, *H. H. Richardson: Architectural Forms for an American Society* (Chicago, 1987); Charles E. Beveridge and Paul Rocheleau, *Frederick Law Olmsted: Designing the American Landscape* (New York, 1995), pp. 175–87.

24. C. Zaitzevsky, *The Boston Park System*, pp. 127–28.
25. J. K. Ochsner, *H. H. Richardson*, pp. 183, 204.
26. FLO to Oakes Angier Ames, April 1882, below.
27. Mariana Griswold Van Rensselaer, *Henry Hobson Richardson and His Works* (New York, 1888); Mariana Griswold Van Rensselaer, "Frederick Law Olmsted," the *Century Illustrated Monthly Magazine*, 45, no. 24 (Oct. 1893): 860–67.
28. Mariana Griswold Van Rensselaer, *Art Out-of-Doors: Hints on Good Taste in Gardening* (New York, 1893).
29. Frederick Law Olmsted, *Public Parks and the Enlargement of Towns* (*Papers of FLO*, SS1: 171–205); *Papers of FLO*, 7: 9–13.
30. C. Zaitzevsky, *The Boston Park System*, pp. 33–47; Carl Haglund, *Inventing the Charles* (Cambridge, 2003), pp. 80–99.
31. See FLO to Charles H. Dalton, Dec. 9, 1879 (*Papers of FLO*, 7: 428–31); FLO to Charles H. Dalton, Dec. 24, 1883, below; FLO to Charles H. Dalton, Jan. 18, 1884, below.
32. In the 1860s, Olmsted and Vaux had proposed using stream valleys as park corridors in both Newark, New Jersey, and Albany, New York, but neither city adopted the schemes. In Newark in 1867, they suggested connecting proposed park sites to the city's downtown via the Mill Brook Valley. In Albany, their 1868 plan would have used two stream valleys to create a horseshoe-shaped park corridor beginning and ending on the shores of the Hudson. See Frederick Law Olmsted and Calvert Vaux, "Architect's Report to the Board of Commissioners of the Newark Park," Oct. 5, 1867; Frederick Law Olmsted and Calvert Vaux, "Report on the Proposed City Park," Dec. 1, 1868 (*Papers of FLO*, 6: 210–20, 293–301).
33. Frederick Law Olmsted, "Suggestions for the Improvement of Muddy River," Dec. 1880 (*Papers of FLO*, 7: 517–22); C. Zaitzevsky, *The Boston Park System*, pp. 82–85.
34. FLO to Charles H. Dalton, Dec. 29, 1881 (*Papers of FLO*, 7: 567–73); *Thirteenth Annual Report of the Board of Commissioners for the Year 1887* (Boston, 1893), p. 22.
35. FLO to Charles H. Dalton, April 8, 1876 (*Papers of FLO*, 7: 192–99); FLO to Charles H. Dalton, "Mr. Olmsted's Report," May 17, 1881 (*Papers of FLO*, 7: 528–33).
36. FLO to William Macmillan, March 16, 1885, below.
37. See Frederick Law Olmsted, "Notes on the Plan of Franklin Park and Related Matters," 1886 (*Papers of FLO*, SS1: 460–534).
38. See FLO to JCO, [May 30], 1884, below; "Specifications for Playstead Terrace, Franklin Park," July 30, 1885, below; FLO to F. L. Temple, March 15, 1886, below; FLO to William L. Fischer, July 21, 1887, below; FLO to JCO, Oct. 5, 1887, below.
39. John Charles Olmsted reported that his father designed the Overlook Shelter, with assistance from the architect of record for the project, Arthur H. Vinal. See "Specifications for the Playstead Terrace, Franklin Park," July 30, 1885, below; C. Zaitzevsky, *The Boston Park System*, pp. 176–77.
40. John C. Olmsted, "The Boston Park System," *Transactions of the American Society of Landscape Architects* (Boston, 1908), p. 52; John C. Olmsted, "The True Purpose of a Large Public Park," *First Report of the [American] Park and Outdoor Art Association* (Louisville, 1897), pp. 11–17.
41. *Appendix, Report of the Landscape Architect Advisory*, Dec. 30, 1887, below; Frederick Law Olmsted, *Tenth Annual Report, Boston Park Commissioners, Reports on West Roxbury Park and Wood Island Park*, [December] 1884, below; Frederick Law Olmsted, *Twelfth Annual Report, Boston Park Commissioners, Report on Charles River Embankment*, [Dec. 1886], below; C. Zaitzevsky, *The Boston Park System*, pp. 91–102.
42. FLO to Sylvester Baxter, Nov. 9, 1880 (*Papers of FLO*, 7: 510–12); FLO to Sylvester Baxter, Aug. 20, 1889, below; see FLO to Philip A. Chase, Nov. 29, 1889, below.
43. See C. W. Eliot, *Charles Eliot*, pp. 380–81.

44. FLO to JCO and Charles Eliot ["Dear Partners"], Oct. 28, 1893.
45. See FLO to Charles H. Dalton, Sept. 6, 1884, below.
46. See C. Zaitzevsky, *The Boston Park System*, pp. 5, 110–14.
47. Frederick Law Olmsted, "The Beacon Street Plan," Dec. 4, 1886, below.
48. See Frederick Law Olmsted, "Talk to the Brookline Club, History of Streets," [Feb. 1889], below; Cynthia Zaitzevsky, "Frederick Law Olmsted in Brookline: A Preliminary Study of His Public Projects," *Proceedings of the Brookline Historical Society*, Fall 1977, pp. 42–65.
49. Frederick Law Olmsted, "Talk to the Brookline Club, History of Streets," [Feb. 1889], below.
50. FLO to John D. Crimmins, Aug. 6, 1885, below.
51. See FLO to Henry R. Beekman, [June 10, 1886], FLO to Calvert Vaux, June 30, 1887, FLO to John D. Crimmins, July 2, 1887, FLO to Calvert Vaux, July 9, 1887, FLO to Calvert Vaux, July 13, 1887, FLO to John D. Crimmins, July 15, 1887, FLO to Waldo M. Hutchins, June 8, 1889, all below.
52. FLO to Salem H. Wales, Oct. 11, 1873 (*Papers of FLO*, 6: 651–60).
53. Frederick Law Olmsted and Calvert Vaux, *General Plan for the Improvement of Morningside Park*, Oct. 1, 1887, below.
54. See FLO to Calvert Vaux, July 9, 1887, below.
55. See FLO to James H. Robb, March 30, 1889, below; FLO to Joseph S. Fay, April 10, 1889, below.
56. Frederick Law Olmsted and Jonathan B. Harrison, *Observations on the Treatment of Public Plantations, More Especially Relating to the Use of the Axe*, April 30, 1889, below.
57. FLO to Henry R. Towne, Oct. 2, 1889, below.
58. FLO to Edward H. Rollins [c. Jan.–Feb. 1882] (*Papers of FLO*, 7: 577–83).
59. See Frederick Law Olmsted, *Annual Report of the Architect of the United States Capitol*, July 1, 1883, below.
60. See FLO to JCO, Dec. 6, 1884, below; FLO to William Mahone, Dec. 9, 1884; Asa Rogers, Jr., to FLO, Jan. 12, 1885, AOC.
61. The library wing, for which Thomas U. Walter had produced a design, was shown in the view of the west terrace in the 1882 pamphlet prepared by Olmsted. See FLO to Edward Henry Rollins [c. Jan.–Feb. 1882] (*Papers of FLO*, 7: 578).
62. See FLO to Edward Clark, Feb. 15, 1886, below; FLO to William B. Allison, July 23, 1886, below.
63. Francis R. Kowsky, "Municipal Parks and City Planning: Frederick Law Olmsted's Buffalo Park and Parkway System," *Journal of the Society of Architectural Historians* 46 (March 1987), pp. 49–64; see FLO to MPO, Aug. 25, 1868, and FLO to Calvert Vaux, Aug. 29, 1868 (*Papers of FLO*, 6: 268–73); FLO to William E. Dorsheimer, July 21, 1886, below.
64. F. L. and J. C. Olmsted, "Plan for a Public Park on the Flats South of Buffalo," Oct. 1, 1888 (*Papers of FLO*, SS1: 576–96).
65. Olmsted, Vaux & Co. Landscape Architects, *Report Accompanying Plan for Laying Out the South Park*, March 1871 (*Papers of FLO*, SS1: 206–38).
66. FLO to Sherman S. Jewett, April 11, 1887, below; FLO to Edwin Fleming, Oct. 20, 1888, below.
67. FLO to the Buffalo Park Commissioners, Jan. 26, 1889, below.
68. FLO to Edward Mott Moore, Aug. 5, 1888, below.
69. FLO to Edward Mott Moore, Aug. 5, 1888, FLO to Edward Mott Moore, Jan. 26, 1889, FLO to Robert Douglas, April 18, 1889, all below.
70. Frederick Law Olmsted, *The Park for Detroit*, Nov. 1882, below.

71. Frederick Law Olmsted, "Belle Isle: After One Year," June 1884 (*Papers of FLO*, SS1: 419–36).
72. FLO to John Stirling, May 12, 1884, below.
73. *Papers of FLO*, SS1: 37–40.
74. Frederick Law Olmsted and Calvert Vaux, "Report upon a Projected Improvement of the Estate of the College of California, at Berkeley, Near Oakland," June 29, 1866 (*Papers of FLO*, 5: 546–73). University officials implemented only aspects of the plan as they built the college over the decades.
75. Frederick Law Olmsted and Calvert Vaux, "A Few Things to Be Thought Before Proceeding to Plan Buildings for the National Agricultural Colleges," [Dec. 1866] (*Papers of FLO*, 6: 130–50).
76. Olmsted's advice for the Massachusetts Agricultural College (later the University of Massachusetts, Amherst), and in general for agricultural colleges, was not acted upon. See *Papers of FLO*, 6: 10–16.
77. The Columbia Institution for the Deaf and Dumb (later Gallaudet University) in Washington, D.C., was Olmsted's most significant early campus design to be built according to his plans. See FLO to Edward M. Gallaudet, July 14, 1866 (*Papers of FLO*, 6: 95–99).
78. See FLO to James Cameron Mackenzie, May 21, 1883, below; FLO to James Cameron Mackenzie, Feb. 6, 1886, below. Olmsted and Croes also devised innovative systems of sewage treatment and heating for the school. Olmsted consulted on the design of another preparatory school, the Groton School in Massachusetts, beginning in 1884, the year the school was founded by Endicott Peabody. The center of the school, Groton Circle, was another oval road designed by Olmsted. See FLO to Endicott Peabody, April 19, 1886, below.
79. On the way across the country, Olmsted stopped in Minneapolis to visit H. W. S. Cleveland and tour the municipal park system Cleveland was planning. In California, Olmsted spent most of his time working on the design of the Stanford campus, but he also visited Golden Gate Park in San Francisco and the Mariposa Grove near Yosemite Valley. On his return trip, Olmsted separated from his companions in Salt Lake City and traveled north to the cattle ranch in Montana that his stepson Owen had owned and operated before his death in 1881. His two other trips to California were in the fall of 1887 and the fall and winter of 1888–1889 (*FLO, A Biography*, pp. 407–10; FLO to JCO, Oct. 9, 1886; FLO to JCO, Oct. 14, 1886).
80. See Charles E. Beveridge, "The California Origins of Olmsted's Landscape Design Principles for the Semiarid American West" (*Papers of FLO*, 5: 449–73). The relevant landscape designs, none of which were fully implemented, were the Mountain View Cemetery in Oakland, the Berkeley campus and neighborhood, and a system of "pleasure grounds" for San Francisco.
81. See FLO to Leland Stanford, Nov. 27, 1886, JCO to Charles A. Coolidge, May 22, 1887, FLO and JCO to Leland Stanford, July 14, 1889, FLO to Mariana Griswold Van Rensselaer, May 17, 1887, all below.
82. Frederick Law Olmsted, *Report of Fred'k Law Olmsted to the Trustees of Cushing's Island Co.*, May 10, 1883, below.
83. FLO to Alfred D. Chandler, Sept. 9, 1887, below.
84. FLO to Gen. Bela M. Hughes, [Jan. 15,] 1889, below.
85. C. E. Beveridge and P. Rocheleau, *Designing the American Landscape*, pp. 149–74.
86. See FLO to George W. Vanderbilt, Aug. 9, 1886, FLO to Richard Morris Hunt, May 5, 1887, FLO to J. J. R. Croes, May 30, 1888, all below.
87. FLO to William Seward Webb, July 12, 1887, below.
88. FLO to Mariana Griswold Van Rensselaer, June 29, 1888, below.

89. FLO to Frederick W. Vanderbilt, Oct. 11, 1889, below.
90. FLO to George W. Vanderbilt, July 12, 1889, below.
91. See C. E. Beveridge and P. Rocheleau, *Designing the American Landscape*, pp. 223–57.
92. See FLO to William A. Thompson, Nov. 11, 1889, below; FLO to James G. Gall, Jr., Feb. 8, 1890, below.
93. FLO to Elizabeth Henderson Guild, May 29, 1882, below.
94. FLO to Charles T. Hubbard, Feb. 2, 1884, below.
95. FLO to Morris K. Jesup, Oct. 20, 1888, Jan. 22, 1889, Jan. 31, 1889, Feb. 11, 1889, all below.
96. FLO to William C. Loring, April 2, 1888, below.
97. FLO to Charles Follen McKim, Dec. 24, 1883, below.
98. "Notes by Mr. Olmsted," in *Special Report of New York State Survey on the Preservation of the Scenery of Niagara Falls for the Year 1879* [c. March 22, 1880] (*Papers of FLO*, 7: 474–81).
99. See *Papers of FLO*, SS1: 46–53.
100. Frederick Law Olmsted and Calvert Vaux, "General Plan for the Improvement of the Niagara Reservation," 1887 (*Papers of FLO*, SS1: 535–75).
101. Frederick Law Olmsted, "Preliminary Report upon the Yosemite and Big Tree Grove," Aug. 1865 (*Papers of FLO*, 5: 488–516).
102. *Papers of FLO*, 5: 22.
103. Alfred Runte, *Yosemite: The Embattled Wilderness* (Lincoln, Nebr., 1990), pp. 38–39; 49–54.
104. See FLO to Richard Watson Gilder, July 10, 1889, below.
105. Robert Underwood Johnson to FLO, June 23, 1889.
106. FLO to Robert Underwood Johnson, Oct. 9, 1889, below.
107. Frederick Law Olmsted, *Governmental Preservation of Natural Scenery*, March 8, 1890, below.
108. Frederick Law Olmsted, *Improvement of Easton's Beach*, March 13, 1883, below.
109. Frederick Law Olmsted, *Report of Frederick Law Olmsted to the Park Commissioners of Wilmington, Del.*, Dec. 22, 1883, below.
110. FLO to Charles A. Williams, [Oct. 1884], May 9, 1885, both below.
111. FLO to the South Park Commission of Chicago, Feb. 28, 1883, below.
112. FLO to Thomas H. Clark, April 10, 1889, below; FLO to Thomas Seay, July 10, 1889, below.
113. FLO to T. Worthington Whittredge, 1882, below.
114. Frederick Law Olmsted, "Trees in Streets and in Parks," Sept. 1882, below.
115. Frederick Law Olmsted, "On Points of View and Methods of Criticism of Public Works of Landscape Architecture," June 20 and June 27, 1885, below.
116. Frederick Law Olmsted, "On Points of View and Methods of Criticism of Public Works of Landscape Architecture," June 20 and June 27, 1885, below.
117. Frederick Law Olmsted, "To the Editor of American Florist, 'Landscape,'" Jan. 15, 1890, below.
118. Frederick Law Olmsted, *Governmental Preservation of Natural Scenery*, March 8, 1890, below.
119. Frederick Law Olmsted, "A Healthy Change in the Tone of the Human Heart," Oct. 1886, below.
120. Frederick Law Olmsted, "Plan for a Small Homestead," May 2, 1888; Frederick Law Olmsted, "Terrace and Veranda — Back and Front," June 6, 1888; Frederick Law Olmsted, "Foreign Plants and American Scenery," Oct. 24, 1888, all below.

EDITORIAL POLICY

The purpose of the Frederick Law Olmsted Papers project is to publish, in annotated form, the most significant of Olmsted's letters, unpublished writings, professional reports, and articles for newspapers and periodicals. The letterpress edition will consist of twelve volumes: nine volumes arranged chronologically, one volume containing major documents on park design and city planning, and two large-format volumes of plans and views of landscape designs.

Document Selection Although the process is to some extent subjective, the editors require every document published to meet at least one of three criteria: that it provide insight into Olmsted's character, present valuable commentary on his times, or contain an important statement on landscape design.

Annotation The editors believe that it is their responsibility to make clear the context within which Olmsted wrote the documents selected and to explain the significance of certain statements that some readers might otherwise not adequately comprehend. They believe also that part of their function is to identify the persons, places, and events Olmsted mentions, and to explain his relation to them. The annotation in these volumes is fuller than it would be in a complete edition of Olmsted's papers, where the documents would more frequently annotate one another. To supply background information and provide continuity within each volume, the editors use volume introductions, biographical directories, and chapter headnotes, as well as chronologies, itineraries, genealogies, and other aids.

Treatment of Text The intent of the editors is to provide a text as close to the original as possible without causing undue difficulty for the reader. In some instances, we alter the original text in the interest of clarity: in such cases, we furnish guides to our alterations that permit recovery of the original text.

The complete existing text of each document is published. All of the words that Olmsted wrote and did not cross out are presented, with the exception of inadvertently repeated words. The treatment of illegible and missing words is as follows:

{. . .} indicates illegible words or words missing because of mutilation of the manuscript.
{*italic*} indicates the editor's reading of partially missing words.
{roman} indicates a word supplied by the editors.

Where needed, these braces are supplemented by an explanatory endnote.

In the occasional instance where a passage does not make sense without substitution of a word or words for those in the original version, the editors make the needed substitution and supply the original wording in an endnote. When the word that Olmsted wrote appears not to be the one he meant to write and the correct word cannot be discerned, the editors suggest, in an endnote, an alternative word or phrase that seems closer to Olmsted's meaning. Where the document is not in Olmsted's hand and what appears to be incorrect wording may be due to the error of a transcriber or typesetter, one of these two approaches is used as well.

The published texts include words and phrases deleted by Olmsted only when they add material that does not appear at some other point in the document. If they are integral to the document, such deleted words are presented in the text in italics and in braces. If the deleted words are less directly relevant to the theme of the document, they are given in an endnote.

The principles of transcription stated here are applied by the editors to all kinds of documents, including drafts of articles and lectures that exist in "fair copy" as well as to fragmentary drafts. When preparing a text from manuscript fragments that have no clear order, the editors construct a text, adding such indications as microfilm reel and frame numbers, extra spaces between lines of text, dividing lines, ellipses, and endnotes, to mark the transition from one segment of the original text to another. When a document exists in both printed and manuscript form, and Olmsted wrote the document for publication (as, for instance, with park reports), the most complete version is used as the basic text. If the other version or versions contain significant variations from that text, the differences are described and quoted in notes added at the appropriate places in the document. The first, unnumbered, endnote to the document explains the textual treatment in such cases.

For manuscripts that were published at a later date, the original version is used as the basic text. Differences between the two versions that appear to be printer's or transcriber's errors are noted in endnotes, as are changes apparently made by Olmsted for the published version; obvious typographical errors, such as incorrect, missing, or transposed letters, are silently corrected when a published version of a document is being used as the text.

At the end of this volume, the editors provide a list of textual alterations, giving the original form of texts or quoted material where a change has not been indicated in endnotes or by braces in the text. The list indicates the original form of contractions that have been expanded. It gives each deleted or altered punctuation mark with the word preceding and the word following it, and indicates added punctuation by giving the words preceding and following it. The list indicates the original form of misspelled words that have been corrected in the text, except as noted below.

Spelling Olmsted consistently misspelled words with double consonants (as "dissapoint" for "disappoint"). He frequently misspelled words with double vowels (consistently writing "lose" as "loose"), and he misspelled words with the diphthong "ie" (as "cheif" for "chief"). The editors silently correct these three kinds of Olmsted's misspellings. All other misspelled words are presented in the text as Olmsted wrote them. If the misspelling makes a word particularly difficult to interpret, however, it is corrected and its misspelled form is presented in the list of textual alterations. Terms such as "can not" and "no where" have been silently corrected to their modern-day forms "cannot" and "nowhere."

Paragraphing The editors follow Olmsted's indications of internal paragraphing. Where he indicated a paragraph by a long dash or a large space between sentences, we silently make a new paragraph. We do the same where he inserted a paragraph symbol or where a change in subject matter between two pages of manuscript indicates that he used the page change as a paragraph. Sections of conversations are silently rendered as paragraphs. Other paragraphing introduced by the editors is indicated in the list of textual alterations.

Contractions The editors present the original form of abbreviations and contractions. Superscripts are reproduced. Apostrophes are silently added if they are missing from the contraction "nt" (for "not"), from conjugations of the verb "to be," and from possessives. Particularly awkward or unclear contractions are expanded and the original form is indicated in the list of textual alterations.

Punctuation The editors do not regularize Olmsted's punctuation or make it consistently grammatical, but we do make changes in his punctuation when it would be difficult for the reader to work out the meaning of a passage in its original form. In long and convoluted sentences, or where the original text is likely to cause the reader to misread phrases, the editors alter punctuation. We occasionally delete punctuation where it unnecessarily complicates already difficult passages, and we add punctuation to clarify basic sentence structure. These changes are not indicated in the text by braces or other symbols, since that would introduce new distractions and complexity at the very place where they would be most troublesome. Instead, the changes are given in the list of textual alterations. We silently supply periods where the end of a line served for Olmsted as the end of a sentence.

Marginalia Material that Olmsted added in the margins is presented at the point where he indicated that it belongs. If such material has no clear place within the text, it is printed at the end of the document with an explanatory note. Notes or jottings on a document by other persons are not included in the text but if informative are given in an endnote. Olmsted's infrequent footnotes are presented at the bottom of the page.

Place and Date of Documents The place of writing and date of a document are given as they appear in the original, but when the date appears at the end it is given in the upper right-hand corner of the published document. If that information is partial, incorrect, or missing, the probable date or time period is supplied in brackets, with an explanatory endnote if needed. Printed letterheads that are misleading are not reproduced but are noted in the first, unnumbered, endnote of the letter.

Arrangement of Documents Documents are presented in chronological order except for occasional pieces such as autobiographical fragments or reminiscences written at a later time than the period covered in the volume. Such pieces are presented with the documents from the period they describe. Articles of Olmsted's published in periodicals are presented in the chronological listing according to the date of their publication. If he noted the date of composition of the article, it is given at the foot of the document.

Citation of Sources Full bibliographical information is provided in the first citation of a source in each chapter, except for sources that appear in a volume's list of "Short Titles Used in Citations." The latter are cited consistently by short title throughout the volume. A full listing of sources about an individual is given in the note accompanying the first mention of that person in the documents of a volume. In subsequent references, sources are given only for additional information supplied. Birth and death dates for persons mentioned in the text of the documents are given in the first note identifying them and, for selected persons, in the index.

If no repository is given for a manuscript, this means that it may be found in the Frederick Law Olmsted Papers, Manuscript Division, Library of Congress, Washington, D.C. For citation of manuscripts in other collections and repositories, documents with the same sender and recipient are cited in a series using "ibid." in place of the names of sender and recipient. The name of the collection is then given at the end of the series of citations so arranged.

SHORT TITLES USED IN CITATIONS

1. Correspondents' Names

BCCP	Board of Commissioners of the Central Park, New York City
BCDP	City of Boston, Board of Commissioners of the Department of Parks
DPP	Department of Public Parks, New York City
FLO	Frederick Law Olmsted
JCO	John Charles Olmsted
MPO	Mary Perkins Olmsted

2. Standard References

ANB	*American National Biography*
DAB	*Dictionary of American Biography*
DNB	*Dictionary of National Biography*
EB	*Encyclopaedia Britannica*
NCAB	*National Cyclopaedia of American Biography*
OED	*Oxford English Dictionary*

3. Published Works

Appleton's Cyc. Am. Biog. *Appleton's Cyclopedia of American Biography*, ed. James G. Wilson and John Fiske (New York, 1887–89).

BCCP, *Annual Report* [18–] New York City, Board of Commissioners of the Central Park, *Annual Report* (New York, 1858–70). Each annual report covers the calendar year preceding the year of publication.

BCCP —— *Minutes* New York City, Board of Commissioners of the Central Park, *Minutes of Proceedings of the Board of Commissioners of the Central Park* (New York, 1858–69).

BCDP —— City of Boston, [Massachusetts], Board of Commissioners of the Department of Parks.

BCPP —— *Annual Report* [18–] Board of Commissioners of Prospect Park, *Annual Report* (Brooklyn, 1866–68).

BPC, *Annual Reports, 1861–1873* Brooklyn, Park Commissioners, *Annual Reports of the Brooklyn Park Commissioners, 1861–1873* (Brooklyn, 1873).

BPC —— *Annual Report* [18–] Brooklyn Park Commission, *Annual Report* (Brooklyn, 1869–1886).

DPP —— *Annual Report* [18–] New York (City), Department of Public Parks, *Annual Report* (New York, 1871–72). Each annual report covers the calendar year preceding the year of publication.

DPP, *Minutes* New York (City), Department of Public Parks, *Minutes* (New York, 1870–74).

FLO, A Biography Laura Wood Roper, *FLO: A Biography of Frederick Law Olmsted* (Baltimore, Md., 1973).

Master List Lucy Lawliss, Caroline Loughlin, and Lauren Meier, eds., *The Master List of Design Projects of the Olmsted Firm 1857–1979* (NAOP and National Park Service, 2008).

FLO Papers/LC Microfilm edition of the Frederick Law Olmsted Papers, Manuscript Division, Library of Congress, Washington, D.C.

Papers of FLO *The Papers of Frederick Law Olmsted*, ed. Charles C. McLaughlin et al. (Baltimore, 1977–).

4. Unpublished Sources

AOC Office of the Curator, Architect of the Capitol Archives, Washington, D.C.

FLLHU Frances Loeb Library, Graduate School of Design, Harvard University.

OAR/LC Olmsted Associates Records, Library of Congress, Washington, D.C. Citations give box or volume number, followed by (respectively) folder or page number (i.e., A21: 624 for volume A21, page 624, or B74: #1032 for Box B74, folder number 1032). The folder number is the same as the job number assigned a given project by the Olmsted firm — in this case, project 1032 is Leland Stanford, Jr., University.

NPS/FLONHS National Park Service, Frederick Law Olmsted National Historic Site, Brookline, Mass.

SUA Stanford University Archives.

THE EARLY BOSTON YEARS
1882–1890

CHAPTER I

APRIL 1882–JULY 1883

The documents in this chapter indicate the range of projects Olmsted and his associates were engaged in during the early 1880s. Three letters relate to residential development: a letter to Elizabeth Henderson Guild concerning advice for a seaside residential landscape; a letter to Montgomery Schuyler in which Olmsted describes how he would design a residential development on the East Side of Manhattan; and a letter to the trustees of the Cushing's Island Company regarding the design of a summer community. Several letters concern significant public landscape projects. A letter to Oakes Angier Ames describes a memorial cairn that Olmsted proposed placing in front of the Oakes Ames Memorial Town Hall in North Easton, Massachusetts, a town where he and his friend and colleague H. H. Richardson collaborated on several commissions for the Ames family. Two reports by Olmsted that were published in the 1882 and 1883 annual reports of the Architect of the United States Capitol present a detailed list and description of the trees planted on the Capitol grounds and attempt to convince legislators to approve his plan for a large terrace on the west side of the building. *The Park for Detroit* is Olmsted's comprehensive description of his plan for a public park on Belle Isle, a design that included a large steamboat pier and gallery building and a series of canals for boating and drainage of the site. Olmsted's letter to James Cameron MacKenzie suggests how the buildings of the Lawrenceville School in New Jersey, one of a handful of campus designs Olmsted completed in his career, should be arranged.

During this period, Olmsted also provides advice on other projects, some not officially his commissions. In a draft report to the artist T. Worthington Whittredge, Olmsted presents his views on village improvement societies.

In *Improvement of Easton's Beach* he advises the mayor of Newport, Rhode Island, on how to create a seaside area for recreational use by the public. His letter to the commissioners of Chicago's South Park warns them against straying too far from plans he and Calvert Vaux had prepared for the park in 1871. In his article "Trees in Streets and in Parks," Olmsted provides a major statement on the psychological effect of his parks and landscape designs.

To Oakes Angier Ames[1]

[April 1882]

A triangular grass-plat is to be made in the fork of the roads opposite the Memorial Hall and a short cross road carried along the South side of it by which carriages coming from the East will be led directly to the South approach to the Hall. When this is done there will remain a bank and strip of higher ground between the new road and the old road in front of the school house. To support this bank a wall is to be built and on the terrace which will thus be formed a public walk is to be laid out with seats and shade trees.

The lowest point of this walk will be on a level with the highest point of the present side walk next the school house ground and it will be carried on to the eastward at about the same elevation. At the Eastern end there will be a circular space 30 feet in diameter, in the centre of which a flag- staff is to be planted to replace the old one which has to be taken down.[2]

The retaining wall is to be formed of rough field-stone laid up dry, with a considerable slope that its general aspect may be consistent with the rocky elevation of the Memorial Hall Grounds—numerous crannies, niches and pockets opening to soil behind will be formed in it with a view to the growth of rock plants and the face is to be everywhere decorated with foliage and flowers, that it may appear pleasingly from the walks about the lower grass plat and in the view from the Memorial Hall Terrace.

Having ultimately in view out-of-door concerts and meetings in front of the Memorial Hall, the terrace is designed to serve the purpose of a gallery for parts of the audiences.

The retaining wall will be carried up three feet higher than the floor of the terrace walk, forming a parapet in front of it. The top of the parapet opposite the flag-staff will be twenty five feet above the base of the wall and the road on the North of it, and as the line of the wall must here be curved in adaptation to the form of the circle it will appear like the base of a round tower or an old warlike bastion half obscured by drapery of peace in the form of evergreens, vines, shrubs and flowering rock-plants.

View of North Easton, Massachusetts, Memorial Ground, c. July 1882

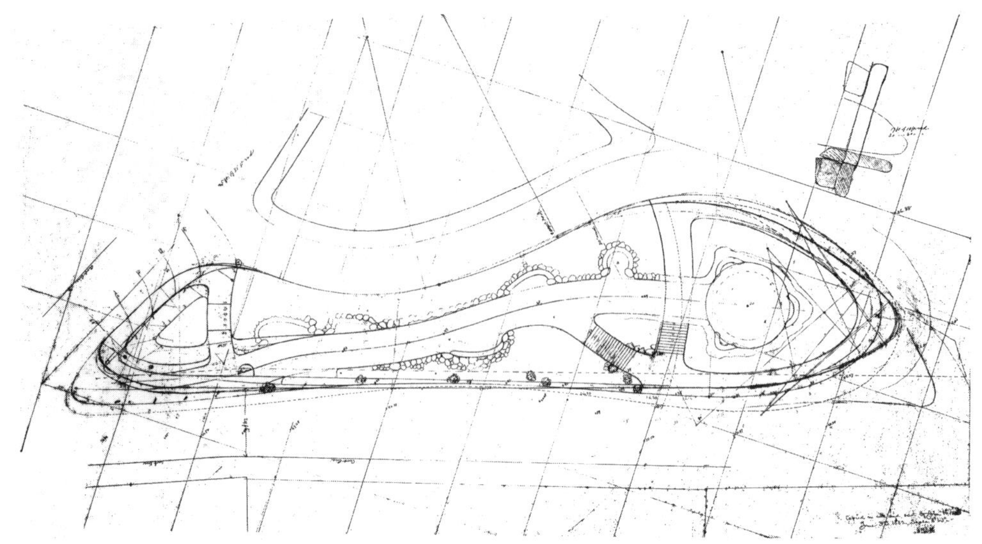

Plan for North Easton Memorial Cairn and adjoining grounds, June 3, 1882

In very old times it was customary to commemorate important events by a form of monument in the raising of which all the members of a community could have a direct part. This was done by their bringing together at a place agreed upon a great quantity of loose field stones and laying them up in a conical pile known as a cairn. The outside stones of a cairn are usually so heavy that they could only have been lifted to their place by machinery or with great labor of many men but the interior mass is more generally in part of smaller stones, some of which might have been brought by the hands of the youngest and feeblest of the community. The oldest and most enduring monuments in the world are of this class and some of them, because of the beautiful plants—that have become rooted in them and which spring out of their crevices or have grown over them from the soil at their base—are far more interesting and pleasant to see than the greater number of those since constructed of massive masonry and elaborately sculptured.

As the structure to be made at the East end of the proposed terrace-walk, above described, would otherwise have much the character of a cairn, being of the proper size, form, material and mode of construction, it is considered that it may be appropriately used to commemorate the anxious and heroic days of the great struggle through the results of which the American people are today a free and united Nation.

The better to carry out this idea, it is proposed that the names of all honorably discharged soldiers and Sailors going out from North Easton shall be deeply cut in the stones of the parapet; where they will always be conspicuous from the terrace walk and that the names of all who fell shall be inscribed upon a suitable stone at the foot of the flag staff. It is desired that the custody of the flag to be hoisted on this staff shall be with the veterans of the war living in North Easton

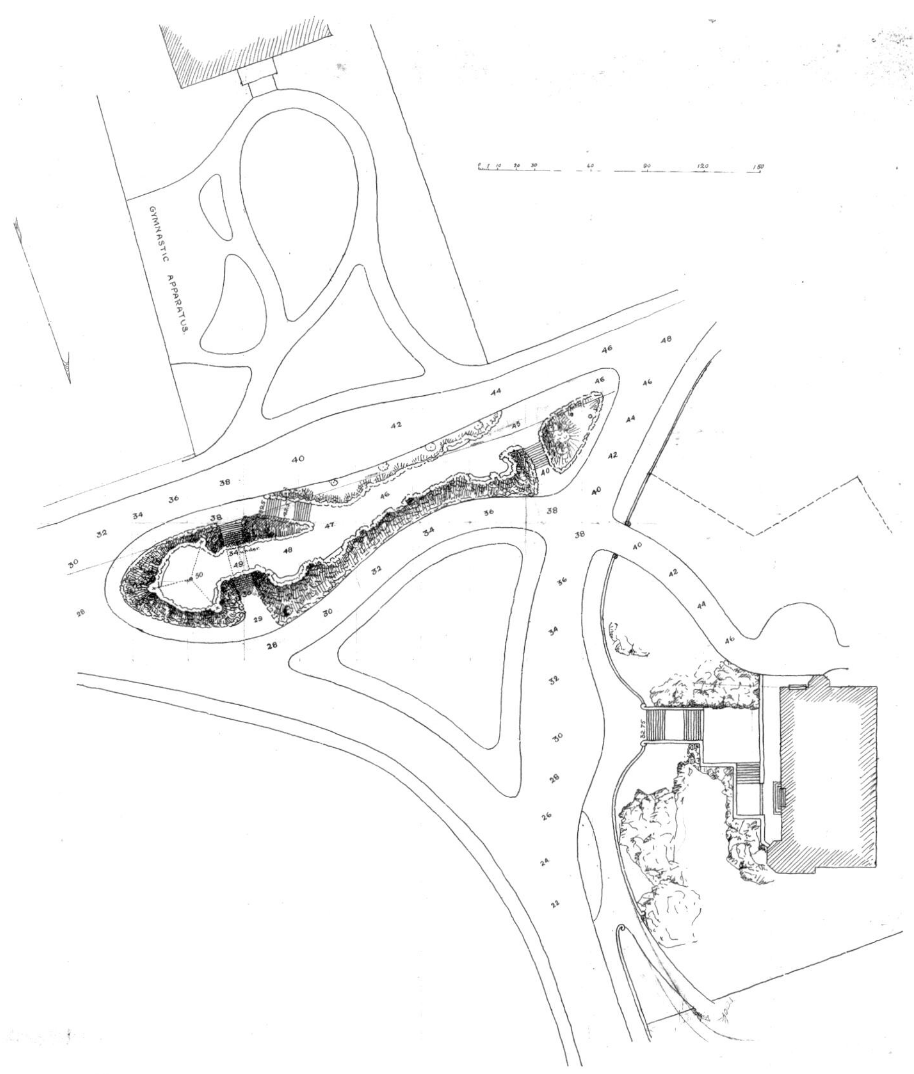

Plan for North Easton Memorial Cairn and adjoining grounds, n.d.

as long as any shall survive and that it shall be set by them on Decoration day and other suitable occasions.[3] It is further hoped that under their leadership, the school children of the village may be given conspicuous duties in all observances connected with the memorial; that in the first place for instance, they as well as all older persons, shall be asked to bring each a stone to be placed about the base of the flag staff; that their help shall be invited in the setting of plants and the sowing of flower seeds and that {*under the lead of the veterans of the war*}[4] a custom may be inaugurated of some simple annual ceremony suitable to be carried out by them and their successors, generation after generation, carrying down the lessons of the war and keeping green the memory of its heroes.

The text presented here is an unsigned draft in Olmsted's hand. The first section of the document appears to be missing, and a later annotation indicates the recipient and approximate date. The memorial cairn Olmsted describes is in front of the Oakes Ames Memorial Town Hall (1879–1881) in North Easton, Massachusetts, a building designed by H. H. Richardson for which Olmsted designed the landscape (1881–1883). Charles Eliot, Olmsted's apprentice at the time, wrote a detailed description of the cairn in May 1883:

> Before the Hall, at a meeting of three roads stands a great irregular pile of rocks — large boulders brought together from far and near — and forming a sort of Cairn which is to be the Soldiers Monument of *North Easton*. The mass of stones is of very irregular plan — is ascended by 2 or 3 flights of steps and is pierced by an archway. At the highest point, which is to be topt by a flagstaff, and whence a pleasant view of the village and the surrounding woods can be had, the stone-work structure is about 25' above the street level.
>
> Every chink is crammed with peaty soil, and about the foot of the higher rock walls runs a deep bed of rich earth . . .

(Jeffrey Karl Ochsner, *H. H. Richardson: Complete Architectural Works* [Cambridge, Mass., 1982], pp. 204–7; Charles Eliot Diary, May 6, 1883, pp. 1–2, FLLHU.)

1. Oakes Angier Ames (1829–1899) was the son of Oakes Ames (1804–1873). The elder Oakes Ames was an early industrialist and served in Congress from 1862 to 1873. With his brother Oliver Ames, Jr. (1807–1887), he built up the family's shovel and tool works in North Easton into a major industry by the 1860s. As a financier as well as a politician, Oakes Ames was instrumental in making the Union Pacific transcontinental railroad a reality. He was implicated in the 1872 Crédit Mobilier financial scandal, however, and died the next year. Oakes Angier Ames, with his cousin Frederick Lothrop Ames (1835–1893) and other family members, memorialized both Oakes and his brother Oliver in a series of architectural commissions. The Oliver Ames Free Library and the Oakes Ames Memorial Town Hall, both in North Easton, Massachusetts, and the Ames Monument in Sherman, Wyoming, were all designed by H. H. Richardson between 1877 and 1882. Olmsted designed the landscape of the Memorial Town Hall and later worked with Richardson on the town's Old Colony Railroad Station in 1883–84. In the early 1890s Olmsted laid out the grounds of four estates in North Easton for different members of the Ames family (*NCAB*; J. K. Ochsner, *H. H. Richardson*, pp. 183, 204, 212, 270; *Master List*, pp. 193, 269).
2. The firm provided detailed instructions and plans for the construction of the memorial cairn, including the flagstaff itself, which was to be seventy-five feet high, eighteen inches wide at its base, and made of well-seasoned white pine with brass fittings (JCO to Oakes Angier Ames, April 3, 1883, B63: #671, OAR/LC).
3. Decoration Day (later Memorial Day) began during the Civil War with informal commemorations honoring the war dead. These ceremonies often included decorating graves with flowers. In 1868 the U.S. Army officially designated May 30th as Decoration Day and encouraged local army posts and towns to devise their own ceremonies and services. Olmsted's landscape design for the memorial cairn and his proposal for placing stones as part of a commemorative ceremony make the North Easton site a unique Civil War memorial (George William Douglas, *The American Book of Days* [New York, 1937], pp. 293–94).
4. Sentence crossed out by Olmsted in manuscript.

To Elizabeth Henderson Guild[1]

Bkln 29th May. 1882

Mrs Sam[l] Guild.
Dear Madam,

In reply to your note of 27th I beg to say that the sketch to which you refer was not intended to be sent to you but to the contractor under the architects, and was not regarded as a final plan but as a memorandum to guard against further work being done under a mistaken impression of my views.[2] I wanted the whole affair to be left open until I could see you and explain on the ground what I should think best. Please try to sink any notions suggested to you by the sketch and let me begin at the beginning so that the minor features may be come to in their proper subordination to the general principles of design involved.

I should wish it to be manifest that you liked the place and pitched your summer tabernacle upon it because of a certain native and wild rudeness in its natural features fitting the margin of the ocean and making a consistent foreground for all to be seen off the gallery and out of the windows. I should like to have nothing beyond the rail of the gallery in the least out of character with this motive; therefore nothing in the least lawn like or garden-like; rather I would aim to sweep off anything suggestive of lawn or garden softness and fairness and avow more distinctly the fact of the dry rocky sea-breaking headland. But in such situations where soil lodges in pockets and is held by constructions there often occur special forms of vegetation fitted to cope with draughts and storms spreading beautifully over the rocks and some of these I would have you cultivate, seeking when you do so to secure density and naturalness, to decorate the cottage, cover the less interesting rock and heighten by contrast the interest of the craggy element.

As this part of the business has been left to well intentioned incompetent hands & they had proceeded either without or against instructions to do work which would have better been neglected, some slight departure from this policy has occurred, which to avoid expense I have not attempted to remedy. You can do so if you will, {*All that has been done under my advice is just.*}[3] and I shall advise you to at your convenience.

I don't think any other policy could have been carried out as inexpensively as this which I thus imperfectly suggest, nor will it cost as much in the long run to thoroughly pursue it as to compromise with and soften it, or adopt any of a mere common place character.

Such being the leading idea for treatment of the South, West and North sides of the cottage, there is only one satisfactory thing to do with the little front ground or balcony on the East. It is a formal artificial wholly constructional and architectural feature. It is an out of door projection of your hall, drawing room and gallery. Consequently the reverse of the rude natural policy applies to it. It constitutes all the garden and lawn elements of the place and demands the

TWO FEET OF GOOD SOIL TO BE LAID IN ALL THE YARD NOT COVERED BY TILE OR GRAVEL. THE GRAVEL-WALK TO BE ADJUSTED IN GRADE TO LEVEL OF STEP BEFORE THE PORCH AND TO THE LEVEL OF VERANDA, WITH A REGULAR INCLINATION BETWEEN.

SOIL TO BE GRADED EVEN WITH TOP OF RETAINING-WALL. PLANT-BEDS TO FALL FROM IT VERY SLIGHTLY, AND ADJUSTMENT OF GRADE BETWEEN TOP OF WALL AND LEVEL OF GRAVEL AND TILE TO BE MADE CHIEFLY BY SLOPE IN TURF.

Plan for Front Yard at Mrs. Guild's.

Scale, ¼ in. to 1 ft.

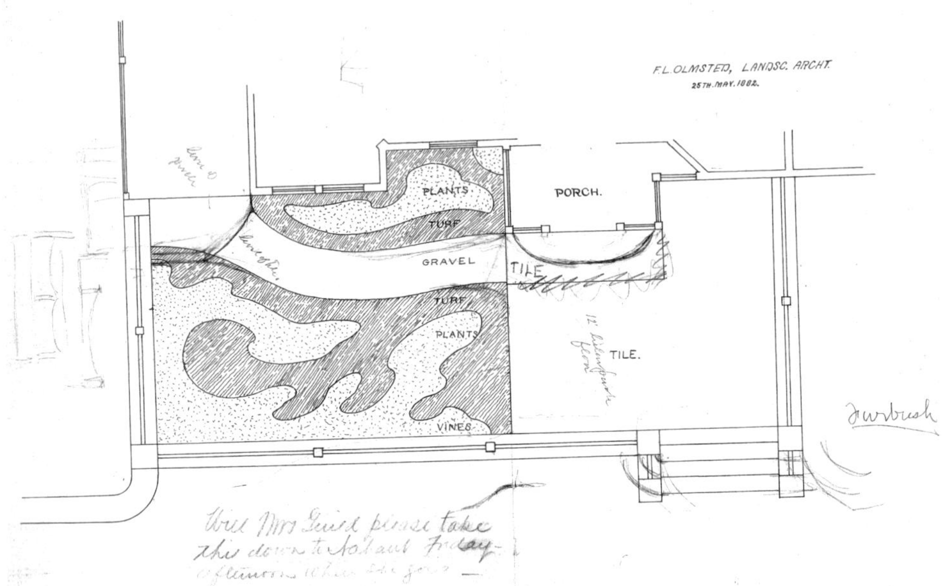

"PLAN FOR FRONT YARD AT MRS. GUILD'S," MAY 25, 1882, GIVING PLANTING SPECIFICATIONS. Note on bottom is not in Olmsted's handwriting. It reads: "Will Mrs Guild please take this down to Nahant Friday afternoon when she goes."

utmost refinement of lawn & garden treatment. It serves certain purposes of convenience. What is necessary to these purposes must be obviously suitable commodious and substantial. (tile gravel walk, fence & screening vegetation.) What is left of it after this should be choice and fine of its sort. It can if you prefer be all turf but it should be fine and nicely modeled turf. A dug border is desirable for the growth of the screening creepers on the outer trellis or fence work. If you are disposed to have any flowering plants they will be most cheaply as well as most suitably and effectively grown in association with these creepers and according to the amount you are disposed to have by a broadening of the dug ground for them. This is better & less, not more, costly than to grow them in circles apart as you suggest. But the extent of dug ground is no part of the design and is entirely adjustable at your pleasure. Only whatever you decide upon the intention should be to completely cover it. No dug ground should be apparent. It would be better in my judgment to confine the planting almost exclusively to such low perennials as require little care to be kept in the best condition. I should be satisfied with wood violets fretting a carpet of periwinkle. This if entirely neglected for an entire summer could be brought into good order in a week by a few hours of sweeping, dusting, washing, trimming and training.

The text presented here is an unsigned draft in Olmsted's hand. The advice Olmsted gives his client for the design of a seaside residential landscape bears similarities to his 1888 proposal for Frederick W. Vanderbilt's Newport residence, Rough Point. In both cases Olmsted urged his clients to limit the extent of lawns and flower gardens on rocky, coastal sites that already possessed a strong landscape character (see FLO to Frederick W. Vanderbilt, Aug. 2, 1888, below).

1. Elizabeth Henderson (Rice) Guild (1822–1894) was the wife of Samuel Eliot Guild, a Boston lawyer. Guild was also a first cousin to Charles W. Eliot, the president of Harvard University and father of landscape architect Charles Eliot, who began his apprenticeship with Olmsted in 1883. Mrs. Guild's summer home was designed by architects Peabody and Stearns and was being completed at this time on the island of Nahant, Massachusetts, near the entrance to Boston Harbor ("Death of Samuel E. Guild," *Boston Daily Advertiser*, July 19, 1862; *Boston Daily Advertiser*, June 25, 1894, p. 2; Walter Graeme Eliot, *A Sketch of the Eliot Family* [New York, 1887], pp. 26, 40–41, 50–51).
2. Mrs. Guild had written to Olmsted to say that she had received his "pretty & tasteful plans for my front yard at Nahant." She went on to say, however, "I do not think I would care for anything so elaborate as you propose—We should never have a gardener, & as we cannot make a long summer at Nahant we like to keep the place very simple & plain. I should be quite content with one or two circles for flowers & all the rest nicely turfed. I fear that so much space covered with tiles, would be too expensive." Olmsted responds to these specific concerns in this letter. The sketch referred to may have been the one completed at Fairsted on May 25th (Elizabeth Henderson Guild to FLO, May 27, 1882).
3. Sentence crossed out by Olmsted in manuscript.

To Montgomery Schuyler[1]

Dft

Brookline, 22d Aug. 1882.

Dear Mr Schuyler,

As I am to be away for a day I reply offhandedly to yours of yesterday, just recvd.[2]

The plan sketched w'd not be essentially affected whatever should be thought best upon the questions you raise. I made the suggestion of semi-

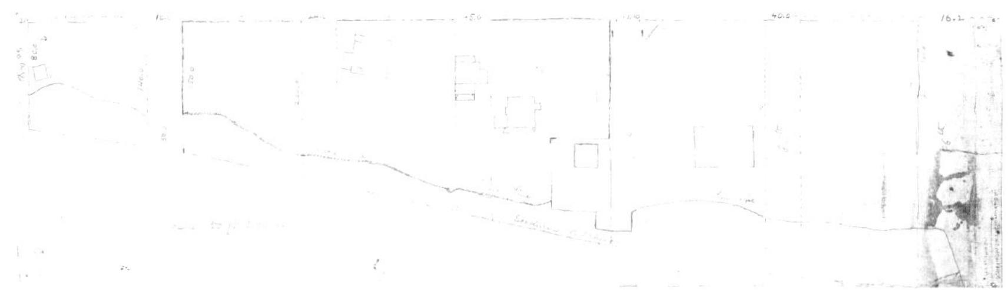

PLAN FOR COTTAGE RESIDENCES ON EAST RIVER, N. Y. C., AUGUST 1882, details land along East River between 80th and 86th Streets.

detached cottages only because you spoke of "cottages" and I thought semi- better than wholly detached. A continuous solid block wd be better if the owners will be prepared to build it. You might rule in intermediate lines giving 15 ft. lots. But in a revised drawing will not 16⅔ be better division — 6 to a hundred?

As to the question whether the lawn road should be private or public I am undecided. I am inclined to think the project can be better managed legislatively, municipally and between owners by making the fee private.[3] But in that case I should make a narrower road, gaining in depth of lots (15 or 20 ft.) and I should attempt as little as possible in the management of the common private property. I would accept the evil of a strolling and lounging rabble during the day under *ordinary* circumstances, simply locking the stairway[4] so it could not be a general thoroughfare to the beach. Having cottages with door yards in front I don't think it would be as serious a discomfort as the ordinary street traffic on the avenue side of the block. The administration would then begin and end with a night watchman, who during the night would sweep the road. Gates of course to be closed at nightfall. I don't think that locking would be necessary. If it should be found necessary the occupants would have pass-keys and there wd be a bell to call the watchman. At the most I would contemplate two watchmen to add say $50 to the rent of each cottage. Avoid a garden and gardener if possible. A little garden and a poor cheap gardener is a hard thing to manage and your tenants will be always grumbling & quarrelling over it. The vine covered bank, terrace & pergola, I propose, once well started could be well kept at an extra cost of $20 a year.

Your statement of the clothes yard difficulty takes the extreme case.[5] A slight retaining wall or an earthen bank sodded at the rear of the lot, would (at the worst) give a practicable yard. If not on account of ledge & expense the clothes yard could be worked in at the side of the kitchen L of the cottage.

These cottages should not be uniform: the lots not uniform, and of course the treatment of the ground not uniform. Economy of construction will, after actual survey, direct the curve of the lawn road, the depth of lots &c. I imagine.

Again, all this is to advance study on your part. Give me your conclusions

& send back the sketches & let me send you a "revise", then if you like to be an instrument to discussion with others.

Yours faithfully

Fred[k] Law Olmsted.

The text presented here is a signed draft in Olmsted's hand. In 1882 Montgomery Schuyler was proposing to build a residential development between East 81st Street and East 84th Street along the shore of the East River in New York. The property was just south of East River Park (now part of Carl Schurz Park), a park for which Olmsted had made preliminary design suggestions in the 1870s. Montgomery Schuyler and his family lived at the end of East 84th Street near the plot of land in question, which Schuyler did not own. Schuyler wanted to propose a development plan in any case because, as he wrote to Olmsted that summer, he felt the neighborhood was degenerating into a "tenement-house quarter." He hoped a "park-like" development of rental cottages on the waterfront would attract wealthy renters and forestall the trend. Since the property was divided among multiple owners, this scheme would have required assembling the site under single ownership as well as closing East 82nd and East 83rd streets between Avenue B (now East End Avenue) and the East River. Olmsted never succeeded in having this plan, or any other residential development in New York, realized. He had always wanted to implement a design that would offer amenity for domestic life, and at the same time withstand the encroachment of industry and commerce that had destroyed so many residential sections of the city. His concept for Washington Heights (1860) never reached the planning stage, and while the Riverdale section of the Bronx (1876) had the basic curvilinear street arrangement he had proposed for it, his concepts beyond this were not implemented. The only small subdivision in the region that he worked on more comprehensively was the Bryn Mawr subdivision in Yonkers (*Papers of FLO*, 7: 4; "Death Notice," Philip Livingston Schuyler, *New York Times*, July 1, 1880; Montgomery Schuyler to FLO, July 26, 1882; New York City Registry, Department of Finance Services, *General Statement of Early Title*, Section 5, Blocks 1589 and 1590; FLO to Henry H. Elliott, Aug. 27, 1860 [*Papers of FLO*, 3:259–69; FLO to John Olmsted, July 22, 1860 [*Papers of FLO*, 3: 256–57]; *Papers of FLO*, 3: 31–32; Frederick Law Olmsted and J. James R. Croes, *Preliminary Report of the Landscape Architect and the Civil and Topographical Engineer, Upon the Laying Out of the Twenty-third and Twenty-fourth Wards, Nov. 15, 1876*; Frederick Law Olmsted and J. James R. Croes, *Report of the Landscape Architect and the Civil and Topographical Engineer* . . . Nov. 21, 1876 [*Papers of FLO*, 7:242–66]; *Master List*, p. 91).

1. Montgomery Schuyler (1843–1914) was a journalist and author who wrote for the *New York World* and the *New York Times* and edited *Harper's Weekly* from 1885 to 1887. A founder of the *Architectural Review* in 1891, he wrote a number of books and articles on American architecture, including *American Architecture* (1892). A descendent of Arent Schuyler, who had emigrated from Holland in 1650, his branch of the family was one of the most prominent in New York. Schuyler had known Olmsted since the 1870s when he supported the position of Olmsted, H. H. Richardson, and Leopold Eidlitz in the controversy surrounding the completion of the New York State Capitol (*DAB*; Edward R. Smith, "Montgomery Schuyler and the History of American Architecture," *Architectural Record*, Sept. 1914, pp. 264–68; FLO to Edwin Lawrence Godkin, April 1876).
2. In his letter of August 21, Schuyler requested clarification on certain aspects of a plan

Olmsted had sent him. The scheme called for closing 82nd and 83rd streets east of Avenue B, so that two rows of building lots parallel to the avenue could be created on terraces stepping down the slope to the East River shoreline. The upper lots faced Avenue B, and a new private road along the lower edge of the property would allow access to the lower lots. A terrace extended below and along the new road, creating a private waterfront esplanade. Schuyler asked whether the road would be public or private, and whether the "park" (terrace and beach) would require "private policing." He also wondered whether "semi-detached cottages" would be a sufficiently desirable form of development for the site (Montgomery Schuyler to FLO, Aug. 21, 1882; plans 641-z19 and 641-14, NPS/FLONHS).

3. "Making the fee private," meaning retaining ownership and control of the road as private property.
4. The planned stairway would have allowed residents direct access to the "beach" along this part of the East River.
5. Schuyler was concerned with the "precipitous character of the backyards" on the sloping site, fearing they would be "unavailable for domestic uses" (Montgomery Schuyler to FLO, Aug. 21, 1882).

TREES IN STREETS AND IN PARKS.*

[September 1882]

I am looking upon a crooked, hill-side village street, lined with trees.[1] I was about to say beautiful trees. But this may be questionable, for I have a book on my table which says with distinguished authority that nature is not beautiful, the word being applicable, in the opinion of the author, only to matters of design,† and it occurs to me that what is of design in these trees cannot be called beautiful.[2] It is not symmetrical; it is not stately; it is not picturesque. A part of the trees crowd upon the gutter, a part upon the sidewalk so that two wayfarers can hardly pass between them and the fence. Soon a decision must be forced whether they shall be cut away, the street widened or the passage abandoned. The sidewalk is laid with tar-concrete on a base of stone; the gutter and wheel-way are laid a foot deep with road-metal.[3] Were moisture, air and mould of vegetation to be carefully kept from the roots, the arrangement could be little improved. The trees are, indeed, so poorly fed that others nearby of the same species and of the same age are nearly twice as large. Everyone bears great scars from wounds and mutilations, which a little

*From a letter written by request on the subject and read in abstract before the National Association for Sanitary and Rural Improvement, at Warwick Woodlands, N.J., July 10, 1882.

†ART IN ORNAMENT, by Charles Blanc, Member of the Institute of France, and formerly Director of Fine Arts.

care would have avoided. Several show dead wood. Having been challenged to find a perfectly thrifty and sound tree among hundreds, I pointed to one of extraordinary beauty. Upon examination I had to acknowledge that it was of spontaneous growth, taking by chance a position in which the line and grade of the street could be accommodated to it, and that it obtained its sustenance neither from tar-concrete nor broken stone, but through roots running under the sidewalk into a deep, rich alluvial soil.

I lament all that I have described of these my neighbor trees, and looking down upon it I say it is not beautiful. But looking up at the continuous green canopy which these maltreated trunks support, swaying in the light summer breeze against the serene blue beyond — swaying not only with the utmost grace of motion, but with the utmost stately majesty — I say that cheaply, inconsiderately as the planting work was done, if the result is not to be called beautiful, it is only because it has more of sublimity than beauty.[4] And, I ask, if man is not to live by bread alone, what is better worth doing well than the planting of trees?

Few who have not traveled with their attention specially given to the point can be aware how rarely trees are suitably selected, suitably placed, protected and cared for in our streets. There are not many towns that present a single example of a well-planted street, if even of a well-planted tree. I know of but one in which a well-considered planting system has been generally, or even extensively, carried out. I am glad to say that that one is our federal capital, in the streets of which more than fifty thousand trees now stand,[5] with but a single defect, and that not of intention but of incompleteness, to be repaired as soon as public opinion shall have been educated — educated, be it observed, not simply to admire and demand verdant vistas and canopies, but to admit and respect the elemental conditions of life and health in the trees of which they must be framed.*

But if public opinion is uneducated to sustain what it is educated to demand in the planting of trees, how much more in the planting of parks? Yet here the trouble lies, less in ignorance and the prevalence of inadequate and shiftless ideas, than in the cross-currents and want of co-ordination of right ideas.

Parks are now as much a part of the sanitary apparatus of a large town as aqueducts and sewers. Their management should be as much a matter of sanitary economy, and as rigidly subject to sanitary tests.

As it is, in applying such tests, two great errors prevail. As the second of these grows out of the first, I would like to trace the first up from what I believe to be its roots.

It is not long since the capital cities of the world were so ill-provided with means of cleanliness, that much of the waste now carried off by sewers

*There are some trees in the Washington planting of unsuitable species, and the beds of soil generally need enlargement.

was deposited in the streets. Not forty years ago hogs roved in the fashionable residence quarters of New York under protection of the law, and for the same reason that excuses the turkey-buzzards of Charleston and the dogs of Constantinople:—without them the odor from filthy garbage and putrid animal wastes would have been even more intolerable than it was.[6]

The custom of throwing offal and ordure into the streets had not gone out in large parts of Edinburgh and of Paris even thirty years ago, nor some time later in the principal cities of Italy. It had prevailed throughout London a few years earlier, and, there being no general water supply, it was a question of Heaven's pleasure how long the streets should remain uncleansed. No mere brooming over the rude pavements of that period being sufficient to fully remove the chief cause of offense, the air was nearly everywhere perceptibly foul, and this to a degree often provocative, in time of epidemics, of a panicky disposition to flee the town. Where there were parks, they gave the highest assurance of safety, as well as a grateful sense of peculiarly fresh and pure air. In London, besides the better known large parks, there were, early in this century, nearly a hundred small parks[7]—more than three times as many as we yet have in New York. The political economy of the day valued them almost exclusively because of their cleaner air, and few travelers' stories or other general accounts of London, until lately, failed to refer to them as "airing grounds," "breathing places," as "the lungs of London," and so on. It has been recognized by men of science and leaders of public opinion that they were pleasant and useful in other ways, but, until within a few years, these other ways have been considered as of incidental and relatively insignificant value.

The current of public opinion thus established is still so strong that scientific sanitarians are often carried off their feet by it. I have a pamphlet prepared by an eminent physician, not ten years ago, in which the project of a park, now being formed at great cost, is advocated solely with reference to the value of its air.[8]

Supposing the question to be taken up, as a problem of sanitary engineering, how to supply the people of a city with a certain amount of air, as the problem of supplying a certain amount of water or of gas-light often is, it may be considered certain that the solution would take nothing like the form which we find represented in our large parks.

An expedient is in general use, however, for reconciling the actual practice of park-making and management with an apparent adherence to the atmospheric theory of their value. It would be formalized briefly somewhat in this way: "It being desired that people should benefit by the sanitary advantage of breathing, even for one or two hours a week, the air of the parks, it is reasonable and economical to beguile them into doing so by making the parks *attractive*. Hence, besides building roads and walks and supplying shade, seats and opportunities of refreshment, large sums may be wisely expended in the planting of trees, and the introduction of other objects purely with *decorative* motives." (I say nothing of exercise, because it is an incident of taking the air, and is allowed for in any theory of value.)

But will the airing theory, as thus amended, account for the value which is generally recognized to be found in our parks?

Perhaps the shortest way to show that it will not, may be to state my own professional experience. Within four parks, there have been planted, under my supervision, more than half a million trees and shrubs,[9] in the selection, disposition, planting and care of which I am not conscious that the first thought has been given to their comparative air-purifying value or to their decorative effect. Beyond the number referred to, wind-breaks have been planted, and in small special districts — episodes of these parks, foreign to their main themes — a few trees, with a distinctly decorative motive. But much more than ninety-nine of every hundred have been planted and managed throughout, as far as under my direction, with a very different motive. Nor do I think that any flowers, fountains, monuments, statues, or other so-called decorative objects, have ever been placed in parks of my motion, with a decorative motive, except as just explained as to the few decorative trees.

Perhaps I have been disposed to resist overmuch those who could see nothing in a park but an airing apparatus, to be made attractive by decorations; perhaps, too little. I assume nothing in either respect, but only argue that I must have taken a very different view of the requirements of the public in a park, and that if this view had little to recommend it to the public and was perplexing and displeasing to common sense, the fact would have been much more clearly established than it has been. As it is, I have been pursuing a purpose of an entirely distinct character, and in so far as I have done so successfully, it would appear that the result is not unsatisfactory to the public. On the contrary, with every renewed attempt to set it aside, or to thwart it, on the theory that a park should be but a decorated airing ground, the more decorated at all points the better, and that nothing else is of consequence, the more plainly it appears that the public finds in the park something of value not to be thus explained.

I must not neglect to point out that the pursuit of this other purpose cannot in the least interfere with or lessen the value of a park as an airing ground; I claim that it does not make it less, but in the long run much more attractive than the exclusively decorative motive, while a consistent pursuit of it, if long sustained, would not be more, but much less the costlier. On the other hand, the pursuit of the decorative motive, in planting or otherwise, is in its tendency, destructive of the objects which I claim should be paramount.

Now to the question, what is this other motive? It is plainly not enough to answer that it is to move the mind recreatively, because that is equally the motive of Punch and Judy, of a flower-garden, of a cabinet of curiosities, of jewelry.

A skilled man may appraise a show-case of jewelry, considering, as to each piece in turn, the weight and fineness of its gold, the size and color of its stone, the refinement of its chasing, and the degree in which its design and workmanship are of the ruling fashion, and thus come in the end to a close estimate of the value of the whole. One may go through a park and take account of the decorative value of the trees and all other notable objects in much the same way. But when the inventory is complete, the estimate of the recreative value of the collection will hardly have been begun.

In attempting to distinguish the action in the mind, and through the mind upon the entire organization of men, that I suppose should constitute the special recreative and sanative value of large parks, I shall be obliged to grope my way in a branch of science in which I have no claim to be adept. My apology for doing so is my desire to interest in the search those better qualified for it.

If a convalescent, leaving a bed for the first time in months, tries to walk straight from door to door across a clear, smooth, level floor, he will be conscious that several distinct mental efforts are needed to the ordering of his every step. A month later it may happen that the same man shall walk through a forest, rough, stony and with tangled undergrowth, constantly adapting his movements to numerous and complicated obstacles, both near and distant, and this with so little mental effort that he is conscious of none. All the time he may be sustaining a conversation, whistling a tune, or keeping close watch of a bird or a dog. So far from the necessary exercise of judgment interrupting or disturbing consecutive thought, the most profound courses of thought known to man have been pursued under such circumstances and with such absorption of mind, that obstacles of considerable difficulty, ordinarily calling for watchfulness and skill, have been overcome so lightly that no recollection of having passed them has remained on the mind.

We all act much and often most wisely on opinions, or mental impulses which we use as opinions, that have come to us through no process of thought that we can recall. We say, while engaged in conversation, that we think thus and so, not having been aware of such thought until it was passing our lips. Much that we call tact, sense, genius, inspiration, instinct, is of this unconscious process.

Holding this experience in view, it will seem probable that the mind not only produces thoughts and gives direction to the body without conscious effort, or process to be recalled, but that it *receives* impressions, information, suggestions, the raw material of thought; that it stores and holds them for after use; that it is fed, refreshed, revived and restocked by what it thus receives, all unconscious of the process.

I write with no effort for verbal accuracy, being sure that everyone knows from experience that of which I wish these phrases to be a reminder, and with such experience in view, I am equally sure that the distinction will be intelligible that I propose to make between what I shall call conscious, or direct recreation, and *unconscious, or indirect recreation*.

The probability may also be recognized that objects and arrangements (a choice and disposition of trees for example), best adapted to supply or augment direct recreation, is not that which should be chosen with a view to indirect recreation. It may even appear that objects before which people are called to a halt, and to utter mental exclamations of surprise or admiration, are often adapted to interrupt and prevent, or interfere with processes of indirect or unconscious recreation.

I do not intend here to discuss how the motive of unconscious recreation would lead us to lay out or to plant a park; I do not assume to have defined with precision what this so-called unconscious recreation is. But after such light upon it as may have been given, if there be any to whom the idea is not familiar, I may be allowed to submit that the highest value of a park must be expected to lie in elements and qualities of scenery to which the mind of those benefiting by them, is liable, at the time the benefit is received, to give little conscious cogitation, and which, though not at all beyond study, are of too complex, subtle and spiritual a nature to be readily checked off, item by item, like a jeweler's or a florist's wares.

There is one thought more that comes to me in connection with this of unconscious recreation, that I may yet be excused for suggesting.

It will be felt, I think, that as between the beauty of a common wild flower seen at home, nearby others of its class, peeping through dead leaves or a bank of mossy turf, and that of a hybrid of the same genus, double, of a rare color, just brought from Japan, now first blooming in America, taken from under glass, and shown us in a bunch of twenty, set in an enameled vase against an artfully-managed back-ground, there is something of this difference: The latter is beyond comparison the more decorative, superb, attractive, only, perhaps, not quite as much so as it is rare, distinguished and—costly. But the former, while we have passed it by without stopping, and while it has not interrupted our conversation or called for remark, may possibly, with other objects of the same class, have touched us more, may have come home to us more, may have had a more soothing and refreshing sanitary influence.

There is an association between scenes and objects such as we are apt to call simple and natural, and such as touch us so quietly that we are hardly conscious of them.

Many of the latter class, while they have been the solace and inspiration of the most intelligent and cultivated men the world has known, have been enjoyed by cottagers in peasant villages, living all their lives in a meagre and stinted way. It is folly, therefore, to say of the art that would provide these forms of recreation, either that it is too high for some or too low for others.

But this is to be said and said sadly: As a result of the massing of population in cities; of the centering of communication in cities; of the increasing resort to cities for recreation; of the tendency of fashions to rise in and go out from the wealthy class in cities; of the prominence given by the press to the latest matters of interest to the rich and the fashion-setting classes, and of the natural assumption that people of great wealth get that for themselves that is most enjoyable — as a result of all this — the population of our country is being rapidly educated to look for the gratification of taste, to find beauty, and to respect art, in forms not of the simple and natural class; in forms not to be used by the mass domestically, but only as a holiday and costly luxury, and with deference to men standing as a class apart from the mass.

All this tends to our impoverishment through the obscuration, supercession and dissipation of tastes which, under our older national habits, and especially under our older village habits, were productive of a great deal of happiness, and a most important source of national wealth.

And I submit that, both in the planting of village streets and in the planting of town parks, this tendency is rather to be resisted by sanitarians than to be enthusiastically pursued.

Very truly yours,

FRED'K LAW OLMSTED.

The text presented here is from the *Sanitarian*, Sept. 1882, pages 513–18. This monthly magazine was published in New York (1873–1904) and covered a wide range of issues related to public health administration and reform. At this time, Olmsted was one of a number of influential individuals representing a range of professions who served as vice-presidents for the National Association for Sanitary and Rural Improvement, to whom he presented this paper before it was published.

While asked to discuss the importance of trees in streets and parks, Olmsted went much further and makes here one of his strongest statements of landscape design theory. Specifically he asserts the necessary subordination of individual elements in a landscape design in order to promote "*unconscious or indirect recreation*," a phrase that refers to the mental and physical benefits of experiencing large, pastoral landscapes, not just the individual specimen trees or floricultural displays that were common to many municipal parks. The latter displays might promote a "conscious, or direct recreation," but they only detracted from the needed therapeutic effects of more expansive landscape scenery.

1. Olmsted is presumably referring to Walnut Street in Brookline, Massachusetts, where he rented a residence and office beginning in the summer of 1881 (*FLO, A Biography*, p. 383).
2. Charles Blanc's *Art in Ornament and Dress* (London, 1877) is the English translation of *L'art dans la parure et dans le vêtement* (Paris, 1875). Blanc (1813–1882) was a French art critic and professor of aesthetics at the Collège de France as well as the author of a number of influential books on aesthetics. The argument Olmsted paraphrases here can be found on p. 1 in Blanc's introduction to *Art in Ornament*: "Nature, viewed in the grand spectacles, permanent or ephemeral, which she offers to our eyes, is not beautiful, but she is sublime. She is not beautiful, because she lacks the three conditions of beauty — order, proportion, and unity" ("Charles Blanc," *The New International Encyclopedia* [New York, 1914], 3, p. 374).
3. Road-metal is broken stone used in making roads (*OED*).
4. Olmsted uses the terms "sublime" and "beautiful" with specific meanings drawn from eighteenth-century British aesthetic theory, notably Edmund Burke's *A Philosophical*

Enquiry Into the Origins of Our Ideas of the Sublime and the Beautiful (1757). The aesthetic categories of sublime and beautiful corresponded to contrasting types of landscape experiences: an overwhelming response inspired by large mountains or otherwise awesome scenery, and a pleasing sensation created by the experience of pastoral, idyllic beauty.

5. See "Annual Report of the Architect of the United States Capitol," 1882, n. 11, below. Olmsted served on the Washington, D.C., Board of Public Works advisory committee when it created a "Parking Commission" in 1871. The Parking Commission oversaw the planting of over 60,000 street trees in the capital by 1887.
6. Turkey buzzards were a common sight around the markets of Charleston in the eighteenth and nineteenth centuries. "They are very industrious, and can be depended upon to clean the city, around the market, where they devour the offal. They are pronounced, by those who have tried them, to be the best scavengers in the world." The dogs of Constantinople were also famous scavengers remarked upon by nineteenth-century tourists (*North American and United States Gazette*, July 19, 1871, p.198; Edmondo de Amicis, *Constantinople*, translated from the seventh Italian edition by Caroline Tilton [New York, 1872], pp. 108–10).
7. Olmsted had seen and admired London's parks in 1850 during his first visit, with his brother, John, and friend Charles Loring Brace. In 1856 he lived there for several months while conducting business for the publishers Dix, Edwards & Company. He later wrote that during his residency in London "hardly a day passed" without a visit to the city's parks. He also visited London in 1859 and in 1878 (*Papers of FLO*, 1: 336, 394; 2: 23, 484; 3: 234–42, 346–48; 360, n. 2, 454; 7: 600–01; FLO to Mariana Griswold Van Rensselaer, June 11, 1893).
8. Olmsted is referencing Chicago Sanitary Superintendent John Henry Rauch's *Public Parks: Their Effects Upon the Moral, Physical and Sanitary Condition of the Inhabitants of Large Cities; With Special Reference to the City of Chicago* (1869). Olmsted and Vaux began working for the Chicago South Park Commission in 1869 and published the *Report Accompanying Plan for Laying Out the South Park* in 1871. Rauch knew Olmsted and admired his article "Chicago in Distress," written after Olmsted visited the city in the wake of the Great Fire of 1871 (Olmsted, Vaux, & Co. Landscape Architects, *Report Accompanying Plan for Laying Out the South Park*, 1871 [*Papers of FLO*, SS1: 206–38]; *Papers of FLO*, 6: 489, n. 12; Frederick Law Olmsted, "Chicago in Distress," Nov. 2, 1871 [*Papers of FLO*, 6: 479–91]; see FLO to Chicago South Park Commissioners, Feb. 28, 1883, below).
9. Olmsted's park projects that involved extensive tree planting included Central Park in Manhattan, Prospect Park in Brooklyn, Delaware Park in Buffalo, and the Chicago South Park, later known as Jackson and Washington parks (*Master List*, pp. 37–38, 47, 48, 70, 71).

THE PARK FOR DETROIT:

BEING
A PRELIMINARY CONSIDERATION OF CERTAIN PRIME
CONDITIONS OF ECONOMY FOR THE

BELLE ISLE SCHEME,

DESIGNED TO FURTHER DETERMINATIVE DISCUSSION OF THE
LASTING INTERESTS OF THE CITY IN THE MATTER,
WITH A VIEW TO

A SETTLED POLICY;

WITH
A SUGGESTION OF THE DISTINCTIVE CHARACTER OF A
PARK ADAPTED TO THE LOCAL CIRCUMSTANCES,
AND AN OUTLINE OF THE LEADING
FEATURES OF A SUITABLE

PERMANENT PLAN OF OPERATIONS.

"With this intent in view, I may, I think, hope to move you, I do not say to agree with all I urge upon you, yet, at least, to think the matter worth thinking about."—WILLIAM MORRIS.[1]

Printed For The Author.
November,
1882.

PREFACE.

As soon as I could, after receiving the survey of Belle Isle last summer, I came to Detroit to begin my study of a plan for laying it out.[2] The moment I arrived I was advised of some public impatience that operations of improvement were not in progress, and within a few hours received calls from several gentlemen wishing to know how soon my plan would be ready, and what it would be.

The Park Commission[3] had it in view before I left to obtain proposals for a thinning-out of the trees of the island during the coming winter, and, if the value of the wood to be removed should prove to more than compensate the expense of the operation, to ask the Common Council to confirm contracts for the purpose.[4]

As even this preliminary operation would imply some settled ideas of a plan, I saw that a statement of these ideas might reasonably be asked to be given to the public when the question should come before the Council. I saw, also, that any report that the Commission might wish from me for the purpose, which should fail to deal in a plain way with certain circumstances of the case, otherwise likely to be little considered, would be an evasion of the duty.

Those things in a park, which, when first seen, excite the most interest, soon fail, as a rule, to hold attention, and are often a disturbing element, rather than an enhancement, of the pleasure of its habitual frequenters. The number of those who make use of it, moreover, in the simpler ways of strolling, driving, riding, and boating, and through restful contemplation of its natural scenery, is ordinarily more than a hundred to one of those who use its less commonplace means of recreation.

Corresponding to this experience, within a few years after a community has begun to enjoy the use of a well-prepared park, it becomes evident, that, through that use, tastes are growing and habits of recreation developing in adaptation to its more permanently valuable conditions. This would be true, doubtless, as to any community; but it is a consideration of more consequence, the more unusual the character of the site to be improved.

It follows that a plan for a park adapted to the conditions of Belle Isle, and to the existing habits, demands, and expectations of the people of Detroit, or to so much of them as there is an obvious general willingness to be taxed to meet, is unlikely to fully accord with views that will later be taken of the matter.

To set to work with aims much beyond those that will be at once altogether pleasing, is to invite efforts directed to the frustration of the plan. On the other hand, to set to work upon a plan the aims of which will in a few years, as the tastes and habits of the public are educated through use of the park, come to be recognized as inadequate, and comparatively discreditable to the city, is as extravagant as building a house on insecure foundations.

In view of these considerations, if questions of plan or policy for the park are to be at this period opened at all to public discussion, it is best they should go to the root of the business.

With this conviction I had already written all of the first, and most of the second, part of the following paper, when I was advised that the Commission had concluded to bring the project of the winter's work before the Council without waiting for proposals, and that the Council had taken action on the subject.[5]

Since then, as I have been glad to learn from public prints, two propositions have been offered to discussion,—one to do away with the Park Commission; the other, to enlarge its responsibilities.[6] Each implies a disposition to abandon the arrangement first adopted but two years ago for carrying on the business of the park. It is probably of less consequence whether it shall be determined to sustain this arrangement, or to seek an improvement in either of the two directions proposed, than that divisions of opinion on the subject should lead to discussion tending in one way or another to more firmly fix some general policy. To this end, discussion should obviously range beyond the ordinary field of local city politics. It should have a distant future in view. It should refer somewhat to experiences with which few citizens of Detroit can be conversant.

This paper is, in part, a plea for such discussion, and it contains facts and suggestions that may be usefully referred to by those who shall lead in it.

Although, therefore, it is obsolete with reference to its original purpose, and I cannot, under the circumstances, ask the Park Commission to become its sponsors, I think it well to be prepared with a few copies of it, by which I may be permitted to meet such inquiries as have heretofore been addressed to me more fully than to an unready man is always practicable on the moment.

FREDERICK LAW OLMSTED.

CONTENTS.

Part First.

Part Second.

PART FIRST.

I.

The Occasion for Discussion, the Matter of Discussion, and its Importance.

If, upon the Commission's application, the Common Council consent to the preliminary operation advised for the improvement of the wood upon the island, nothing is to be gained through completing the general plan much before the next working-season. Something may be gained by deliberation and discussion.

A report of progress, for the information of the Council and the people, may, however, be desired of me. Such a report at this stage can but present the less popularly interesting parts of a plan,—the framework of principle, purpose, and method, upon which it is to be elaborated. Even this it can do neither very briefly nor prepossessingly. It can therefore serve a good purpose only as it may challenge a deliberate consideration of the lasting interests of the city in the matter.

Map-like drawings, however attractively they may present what it is practicable to exhibit by them of a plan, hardly give to most intelligent men a better idea of what a park to be formed upon them is to be, than a map of Michigan of the character of its people. The more attractive such drawings, the less are they apt, in fact, to hold general attention to the more important issues to be settled. It is possible, then, that, if patience to read a sufficiently full verbal explanation of some such issues in the present case can be commanded, it will better serve a sound public opinion than discussion of a finished drawing would do.

Taking this view, I shall steer clear, as far as I can in the present report, of the technical side of the subject,—shall address the common sense of the city, and shall urge nothing upon which immediate action is required. If my argument shall seem over-labored for the occasion, it will be because, after watching the growth and fluctuations of public opinion in twelve cities with whose park projects I have had more or less to do, I believe it unlikely that for many years to come there will be any matter of local public business brought before the people of Detroit, haphazard views of which will be more costly.

II.

The Prime Economical Difficulty of Park Undertakings in General, an Ill-defined and Unsteady Policy. Why so?

WHAT Detroit most wants in a park, as I am often advised, is economy. In every case within my knowledge, the most serious slips from economy in city park-making have been due to devious courses of management, such as would not have occurred had anything like a clear, common understanding been had, from the start, of the objects to be attained, and of what the purpose to attain them economically *excluded.*

The short history of this project of Belle Isle does not show that Detroit is starting upon a more secure footing. It was apparently the consideration, that, under private ownership, something was liable to be done with the island harmful to the interests of the city, that turned the scale of public opinion favorably to the project. Yet, when to the question "What can *the city* do with it?" the answer "Make it a park" was accepted, it must have been with varying and generally vague imaginings of what a park would be.

The more common central idea, undoubtedly, was that of a place away from houses, devoted to cheerful, rural recreation. Yet the first things afterwards proposed to be put upon the island were, I believe, two houses, each for a purpose as irrelevant to the purpose of cheerful, rural recreation, as any that could be thought of,—a mad-house and a pest-house.[7]

It is plain, that, wherever such buildings should intrude upon the park proper, the value receivable for every dollar invested with a view to its main purpose would be less than it would otherwise be,—as the value of the capital invested in a concert-hall would be lessened by the introduction of any noisy machinery in an adjoining building; of capital in a girls' school, by a lease of rooms under the same roof for a police court.

That nothing like this often happens when any other special form of public work is to be set about for the first time, even in a newly-formed community, is due to the fact that knowledge so much more prevails of what in a general way has been established by experience in hundreds of older communities. Although upwards of fifty millions of dollars are already represented by our American park properties, not one of them had even been planned six and twenty years ago:[8] hardly yet is the plan of one fully worked out. They so much differ in character, moreover, that numerous objects may be found prominent in the plan of some, that are not at all recognized in the scheme of others.

Hence, in so far as any understanding of what should be done with a piece of public property set apart for objects no better defined than they are by calling it a park depends on what is generally known of this brief, incomplete, and inconsistent experience, it is no wonder that it should prove an inaccurate understanding. It is no wonder that sensible men often imagine themselves at the end of a discussion upon it when they have only arrived at a beginning. Nor can it be held strange that men's judgment of what should be done with such a property, or with funds appropriated to its improvement, should vary from time to time with the interests that at any moment may happen to hold their attention.

It is not to be asked that the hurried people of an American city, sprung within the lifetime of men yet living from the condition of a frontier trading-post, shall stop to think much of what interest their children and their children's children may possibly have in the far-off results of any of their public works; but the sentiment that led to the building of the Detroit City Hall in a manner so much more substantial than any immediate profit could have been generally seen to warrant, may be appealed to against this common unsteadiness of public judgment in park business more pertinently than may be generally realized.[9]

In several of the town parks of Europe formed from one to three hundred years ago, no material modification of general design, or enlargement of scope, has, from the beginning of them, been made. The population using them has increased several fold: it has changed its forms of government, its forms of society, in some cases its forms of religion; it has changed its forms of building; it has widened, and lengthened, and sewered, and paved, and lighted, most of its streets; it has demolished its most solid constructions in walls and fortresses. In nothing else has so little change of general design occurred as in its parks; in nothing else so little been done, beyond the unnoticeable removal and repair of the results of decay, and wear and tear. While most other costly constructions have been losing in fitness and value for present use, the parks are recognized by all to have been, on the whole, gaining. In nothing else, then, that the people of one generation can leave behind them for others, is the economy of a steady pursuit of well-considered ends better established than it is by long experience in parks. I would not ask overmuch thought for this consideration. I would ask only that in a young and healthily-growing city,—rapidly enlarging in building-area, in population, in trade, in wealth,—the danger that the economy of what may be done in any single year upon a great park may be too much measured by the resulting, generally obvious, instantaneous dividends, shall not be overlooked.

III.

Aggravating Circumstances for Detroit.

It remains to be pointed out, that, however this difficulty in the way of sustained economy may be estimated as common to park undertakings in general, it is greater than usual in the case of Detroit, because of the unusual way in which she is taking hold of the business.

Having in view the fact that the value of parks under proper management increases with age, and that the immediate return for their first cost is comparatively small, nearly all large towns hitherto, both in Europe and America, when about to enter upon works of this class, have begun by obtaining a special fund for the purpose by some means not involving a very heavy immediate addition to their taxes; generally through loans secured by mortgages on the land to be improved. A part of the earlier outlays have been soon regained, also, by assessments on the adjoining lands benefited by the improvements. In some cases the same result has been accomplished by the purchase of such lands before making the improvements, and their later sale with profit. Again: these park works have in part supplied themselves with funds by the rapid advances to which they have led in the taxable value of neighboring property.

Not one of these expedients has been adopted in Detroit; and unless the tax-payers of the city are unusually confiding and considerate, not only must the work proceed slowly, but no appropriation will ever be proposed for the park without giving occasion for efforts to head off, in some particular, any well-considered policy of operations.

Yet again: it has been the custom, in undertaking a park, to provide for a less indirect, complex, and confused system of responsibility than would otherwise have obtained, by delegating with respect to it most of the duties commonly exercised by common councils in other city business to a board of citizens selected for their supposed special capacity and trustworthiness, serving gratuitously, from interest in the park enterprise.[10]

These boards have been authorized to employ forces; make contracts; start, press, restrict, or suspend parts of the work, according to their judgment of advantages offered by the season or the markets of the day; to enact ordinances, make regulations, and employ a special police,—all on their own unrestricted responsibility, rendering only annual account of their doings and outlays.

Generally, with these advantages, much work has been done rapidly at wholesale prices, so as to bring important features of the park soon to completion in a way adapted to impress the public with the true grounds of their value.*

By thus bringing considerable parts and features of a park rapidly into a condition of complete fitness for use, the public of all classes has been influenced to cheerfully accept at once whatever rules were necessary to the proper enjoyment of it, and thus to fall easily into customs, habits, and demands, harmonious with its design.

In Detroit it is arranged, I believe, that the outlay shall be limited from year to year by concurrent votes of both branches of the Council, to be taken in the midst of the park working-season; so that those in charge, when setting about work in the spring, will be uncertain of their means for carrying it on. It is further arranged that those in charge shall report, from month to month, of their doings, outlays, and intentions, and shall wait the concurrence of both branches of the city legislature, and of the mayor, before the determinations of their own judgment in the executive direction of the park-fund for the year can be made effective.[12] It has already occurred this summer that a vote on an important proposition from the Park Board has failed to come to a final vote after two months, and the object of the proposition has been lost through the delay.[13] More than once the decisions of the Park Board have, on review by the Council, been reversed.

There are doubtless compensations to be seen for the loss in efficiency that cannot fail to occur through such a division and attenuation of responsibility, and unfixedness of purpose; and no question is here raised of the wisdom of the arrangements on the whole. The difference between them and those employed in other cities is pointed out with two objects: first, that the importance, with reference to forming an economical park, of establishing as far as possible a fixed public understanding as to what shall, and as to what shall not, be attempted in it, may be better seen; second, that the necessity of a wide departure in this understanding, from what has been elsewhere generally attempted, may be more readily appreciated.

IV.

The Unusual Difficulties to be met. The Educative Function of a Park, and the Economy of it.

To fully realize how wide this departure may probably be, it must be considered that the ground to be operated upon is larger than that of most

*In New York a force of nearly four thousand men was at one time employed for this purpose within a space less than that of Belle Isle;[11] and the economy of the proceeding has never been questioned. The more extravagant operations, and the credible charges of corrupt practices, came later, when the original system was superseded, and the scale of operations had been reduced.

parks, and that, to respect at all the various classes of public demand, the annual outlay will necessarily be much scattered, and can at no point make a striking show, except through uneconomical meretricious work.

Under these circumstances, it will certainly appear to many, no matter how prudent the management shall really be, that their money is being frittered away to little purpose; and the usual difficulty of pursuing any well-considered plan of operations to large distant results, confidently, resolutely, and steadily, will not only thus again be greatly aggravated, but it will be especially difficult to secure such a use of the park site, during this long preparatory period, as shall lead on to customs fitting the ultimate design of the park.

Now, one of the more important elements of value in a park, never to be lost sight of in a study of its economies, lies in its power to divert men from unwholesome, vicious, and destructive methods and habits of seeking recreation, and inducing them to educate themselves in such as are, at the worst, less costly to the general interests of the community.

It is known, for example, that a large resort of young men to a park on Sunday means a falling-off in the back-door business of dram-shops, and resorts for petty gambling. Of what value this shall be, depends much on the pleasure such young men shall find in the park, consistently with a rigid exclusion of provocations to indulge in dishonest, destructive, blackguard, or law-outwitting smartness.

This consideration may be best brought home by again citing Detroit's own brief experience.

Something was spent last spring in preparing temporary accommodations for visitors upon the island.[14] Every dollar so used was a dollar the less available toward obtaining well-ordered permanent and substantial provisions for like purposes. But the numbers resorting to the island during the summer were, on occasions, much larger than the Commissioners had reckoned upon, and their over-frugal provisional arrangements proved, in consequence, unsuitable and insufficient; so much so, that there reasonably followed some public dissatisfaction, and the Common Council (holding the purse-strings, and taking sure back-sight where the Commissioners had acted on uncertain foresight) advised them of its disapproval. But the more important effect was not that, thus recognized, of the momentary public inconvenience that resulted: it was that some seed of rude and wasteful practices was thus scattered, the products of which must add to the cost, and lessen the value, of the park.

How so, will appear from the single fact, that, in that part of the island most favorable to efficient police control, not one of the benches for public use, set clear of the buildings, failed, in the course of the summer, to be torn from its fastenings, violently broken, bruised, shattered, befouled, or vulgarly cut and marked. These were not the only or the most significant incidents teaching the same lesson.

It must be a poor park that does not, through the impression of its fitness, and the adequacy and completeness of its provisions for public comfort, inspire enough respect to serve as a check upon the propensities thus evinced; and I have never seen one, moderately well equipped with reference to any tolerable standard of public service, in which the degrading tyranny that may be exercised, under circumstances favorable to it, by a few unfortunate scamps over a community of fortunate decent people, was as plainly exemplified.

In reckoning, therefore, the cost and difficulties to be overcome in acquiring a park, as is proposed in this case, by small annual instalments, with a complicated system of checks and rechecks, reviews and revisions, the necessity of putting up for years with cheap, temporary, inadequate arrangements in certain respects, and the drawbacks to public pleasure, and *consequently to public support*, of steady, economical, systematic courses, that will occur through the demoralizing effect of such makeshift arrangements, must not be left out of account.

V.

Necessity to Economy of Concentrating Early Outlays on a Few Popular Measures, to Success in which, at Moderate Cost, the Conditions of the Site are Specially Favorable.

IN determining the character and settling the primary plans for a park for Detroit, it is much less necessary to ask what the city can afford to pay as the first cost of the improvements proposed than what it can and will be willing to pay in the way of subsequent constant housekeeping expenses, and for annual repairs.

At the rate per acre of the cost of maintenance of the Buffalo park (independently of outlays for construction raised by loans), the annual tax for keeping up a park of the size of Belle Isle would be twenty thousand dollars a year; at the rate for the New-York park, two hundred and fifty thousand dollars a year; at the rate for the Common and Public Garden of Boston, five hundred thousand dollars.[15]

It is significant, that, where the expenditure is largest, there is plainly the least success in what is attempted. Great complaint has been made through the press of Boston, this last summer, of the dilapidated, shabby, ill-kept, and misused condition of the Common; and the superintendent has published long statements to show that the means allowed him are quite inadequate to supply what is called for. It has been much the same in New York. It is evident in both cases, as it is in many others, that a character of park is attempted to be assumed that the tax-payers will not allow to be creditably maintained. Economical management is constantly baffled between the cross currents of popular demand. The result is too much of shabby gentility.

If now, any still suppose that Detroit has but to follow a well-marked trail, only at a slower pace than has been customary with those who have gone before her, in order to obtain cheaply what they may have acquired extravagantly, in parks, the delusion will be dissipated upon more closely considering the unusual character of the site to be operated upon.

The area of the island is not materially less than that of the Central Park, and is greater than that of any single park of the more populous and richer cities of Brooklyn, Boston, Baltimore, Montreal, Buffalo, or Chicago. The average elevation of its surface above that of the surrounding navigable waters is little more than two feet. Large parts are covered with well-grown wood, with much close underwood, beneath which (the subsoil being a retentive clay), after every summer shower, there are puddles that gradually disappear more through evaporation than filtration. Other large parts are marshy; and in these there are constant pools, with rushy and bushy borders.

Conditions could not be chosen more favorable to the breeding and nursing of mosquitoes; and denser swarms of mosquitoes are nowhere to be encountered than in quarters of the island sheltered from the breeze. The pools, in September, I found discolored, and covered by bubbles and a green scum; and there was putrescent organic matter on their borders. They are thus available to the propagation of typhoid, malarial, and other zymotic poisons;[16] and it may be questioned whether the city is justified in allowing, not to say inviting, ignorant people and children to stray near them. Being in such relation to the city, even if the island had not been purchased, and was not desired for a park, common sanitary prudence would soon have suggested efforts to remove the danger they involve to the public health. Fortunately, as will be explained later, a complete remedy for all these evils would not be very costly; and the more serious may be at least greatly mitigated, if not fully removed, cheaply and speedily.

Looking all its disadvantages fairly in the face, it may not unreasonably be thought that they are outweighed, with reference to the more important common requirements of public parks, by the advantages offered in great numbers of promising trees of species the most valuable that could be selected, by openness to breezes, cooled and ozoned by passing over the adjoining flowing waters, and by the independence of many difficulties of management which will be secured by the isolation of the park from public streets and other affairs.

But what should be most firmly fixed in mind, as the more important result of a comparative review of the site, is the plain fact that Belle Isle has as little as possible in common with the little that is common among the sites of other American parks.

To bring this consideration to bear on the question of an economical plan of operations, it has only to be considered, that, if economy lies in a close adaptation of means to ends, it equally lies in a close adaptation of ends to means.

Suppose a limited sum to be available for your park,—no more than is necessary to attain, within a given period, certain results: then the attainment of these results will be hopeless, if within that period you apply any part of this sum to the attainment of other results. This is but another form of the first lesson in arithmetic for a child,—"You cannot have your cake, and eat it." But it is none the less certain, that, if the public opinion of Detroit can apply that lesson intelligently and steadfastly to the business of the park, a degree of economy will have been secured that cannot otherwise be approached by the most exacting comptrollership of accounts, the most intricate system of checks, and the most cunning and microscopic legislation of details.

But suppose it to be possible to start off next spring upon a plan adapted to this view: there will necessarily follow a critical period, during which the advantages to be attained by it will not be known by experience; when they will be wholly imaginary, and will be taxing imagination in fields far outside of the ordinary business experience of most Detroiters; when the taxation in behalf of the park will inevitably be large relatively, not only to the benefits immediately available, but even to those plainly recognized to be distantly coming due. During this period, consequently, there will be a pressure to turn the outlay that shall at any moment be available to results not essential to the plan, but temporarily pleasing,—a pressure such as it is hardly to be hoped can long continuously wholly fail to influence those in direct control of the business.

There comes, then, another condition to be met by the plan; namely, that to limit, as much as practicable, the liability to waste through unsteadiness, some of its designed permanent excellences shall be attainable in a degree popularly appreciable, in short time, and at moderate cost,—attainable, for instance, I will say, within three years, by a steady application to them of the larger part of such appropriations as may be hoped for.

VI.

Illustrations of the Economy of this Policy.

THE suggestion that a plan can be devised, promising, in important features of a park, excellences such as have not been attained by much larger outlays for the purpose in other parks, may be received with incredulity. As popular faith in this respect is essential to sustained economy, I think it best, before going further, to demonstrate the working of the principle I have last been advocating by reference to an experience as plainly open to the examination of citizens of Detroit as any not directly under their eyes could be.

It will stand in the form of a comparison between two of the parks that have been named, the most costly and the least so,—New York and (Detroit's nearest neighbor with a park) Buffalo.

In New York numerous objects have from time to time, and many intermittently, been had in view, upon a site unfavorable to a realization of them at moderate cost. Many of those first taken up are not yet fully attained; and work with reference to them is suspended in favor of others since taken up. Because of the position of this park in the midst of a great city, and because, also, of a certain yielding to a temporary epidemic of public taste,—of which in other things a spurious, so-called decorative aestheticism is the ridiculous outcome,—a general style of keeping is weakly attempted, approaching that suitable to lawns and gardens opening from drawing-rooms.

In Buffalo fewer objects have been had in view. They have been mostly pursued *exclusively*, and with a steady hand, upon ground fairly suitable to them, and with a simpler ideal of general effect. It is twenty-five years since work began in New York; fifteen since it began in Buffalo.

While I was last in Detroit, I heard the opinion of a gentleman, who would be selected by competitive examination as one of the half-dozen best qualified non-professional judges upon the subject in all the country, to this effect: that in respect to the more quiet, tranquillizing, and simply wholesome and refreshing forms of recreation,—in beauty of water, meadow, and woodland, which is the soul of a park,—Buffalo had already more of value than New York.

The Buffalo Park has some distinguishing defects: notably, in that the larger part of it lies upon a mass of flat rock covered with but a foot or two of soil, and is liable to become excessively dry; its ground available for picnic parties, is, because of a falsely economical curtailment of its original scheme, so contracted, that the numbers of those resorting to it cause great destruction, and make it so shabby that before many years there is danger that people of refined taste will keep away from it, and it will become a purely rowdy resort; it has no proper park police force, and practices are growing in the use of it destructive, demoralizing, and burdensome to its maintenance; lastly, its style of keeping is as yet a compromise between two ideals, and some of the results are consequently poor, relatively to their cost.

But, conceding all this, I cite the opinion above quoted, that I may not be thought unreasonable in saying, that, in the more important qualities of a park, that of Buffalo compares favorably with that of New York.

Look, then, at the following comparison as to costliness. For land, New York, $7,000 per acre; Buffalo, $400. For construction, New York, $15,000 per acre; Buffalo, $1,300. For maintenance, New York, $400 per acre; Buffalo, $30.*

The style of house in which men live, of the furniture they use, of the clothes they wear, of their streets, schools, jails, vehicles, even their creeds, morals, and manners, is mostly determined by currents of example and fashion. So is the degree of repair, and the method of use and keeping, of most of

*These figures are in round numbers, and partly approximate from recollection. About forty per cent of the construction cost of the Central Park has been in payments above the market-value, chiefly in wages to men recruited by "influence;" and much has been wasted through devious courses, compelled by political pressure, all which has been much better resisted in Buffalo. But reduce the New York expenditure one-half on these grounds, and the lesson will yet remain as above suggested.

these possessions. But, while the more the experience of other cities is studied, the higher the simpler elements of a park will be valued as a self-preserving institution of society, the plainer it will be, that to allow the style of park for Detroit, or the style in which it shall be kept, to be determined in the same drifting way, will be ruinous. It will be equally plain that the circumstances give opportunity for obtaining a park of distinctive style and merits with great economy.

VII.

The Necessity of Consistency of Style to Economy.

A PARK will have value mainly as the minds of those using it are acted upon by the different objects that come before their eyes; and the degree and method of this action will be more determined by the order, sequence, and relation one to another, of different objects, than by their intrinsic qualities. Different objects may be so used as to be counteractive, or to be co-operative; that is to say, to lessen or enlarge each other's value. The same principle of economy that leads to the keeping of parlor furniture and kitchen utensils in different divisions of a house, will lead to certain general, though less abrupt and definite, divisions in the planning of a park.

But the principle of economical consistency will carry us much further than this. When a woman of good taste, and thrifty, housekeeping qualities, sets out to furnish a room, the first article she buys for it, though but a single chair or table cover, settles much as to everything else. No curtains or wall-paper can be afterwards brought in, that are violently out of keeping with the table-cloth. No tawdry carpet can sustain a chair upholstered with light satin. Bring but one such chair, French polished and spindle-legged, into a room that has before been thoroughly respectable for its purpose, with cane-seated birch-timbered chairs, matted floor, window plants in red garden pots, and home-framed lithographs, and the room never appears satisfactorily afterward till it has a waxed and rug-strewn floor, Morris hangings, De Morgan vases, and, in short, an entirely new outfit.[17] And this is but the beginning. To keep it satisfactorily, ten times the former care will be required; and if this is at any time remitted, if dust comes in at the windows, if the chimney smokes or the roof leaks, it will soon be less satisfactory than before the improvements began. Such a difference accounts for the constant complaints of shabbiness, and the futile attempts to relieve it by additional finery, in certain parks.

There is a well-known public ground in Europe in which it is not quite true to say — as, in order to convey an idea of the precision of its style of keeping, it is often said — that the police are required to arrest every falling leaf before it strikes the ground.[18] There is one of our public parks in which, without approaching the same standard, men are now being paid at least twenty dollars a day to gather and hide the leaves that drift upon its surface; going over the same ground again and again in the duty, and this in parts where, for the thrift of the plantations, they would much better be allowed to lie.[19]

If one takes a walk in natural woods at this season, he finds beauty and pathos and poetry in the dying leaves. Why not in a park? It is a question of consistency. When you have been mowing and raking and watering and rolling a lawn all summer, have set out upon it exotics and bronzes, and other choice and elegant things, equally suitable to marble floors and frescoed walls, you cannot help regarding fallen leaves as so much dirty litter.

I am nearing one of those technical questions of which I meant to steer clear. But I will let a man you can better trust pilot you by it; and this man shall be one who, it is not unlikely, has done more to educate us all in the domestic enjoyment of the beautiful, and in increasing the value of what we buy in furniture, than all the royal academies and art associations in the world,—a poet, an artist, but also, if you please, a "practical man." It is a poor thing to say of him; but the prejudice is so common that a man of exquisite habits of thought is not likely to be practical, that, though not a chapter in the history of civilization fails to contradict it, before putting the helm in this man's hands, it may be well to recall the fact that he is a singularly successful manufacturer and trader, and that it is not in picture-frames alone that you see his art, nor between book-covers that you find his poetry: it is on sale in your shops by the yard; it is under foot and overhead (more or less adulterated) in your churches. It is a poor cottage that his pencil has not touched; and there is hardly a man in Detroit, there is hardly a civilized man in Colorado or Australia,—in the uttermost parts of the earth,—so favored by fortune that he can afford not to buy something that has come from him.

Bearing in mind, then, the analogy just now pointed out between park and household economy, apply to your park policy the spirit of the following advice:—

> "We must clear our houses of troublesome superfluities that are forever in our way,—conventional comforts that are no real comforts, and do but make work for servants and doctors. If you want a golden rule that will fit everybody, this is it,—
>
> "Have nothing in your houses that you do not know to be useful, or believe to be beautiful.
>
> "And, if we apply that rule strictly, we shall, in the first place, show the builders, and such like servants of the public, what we really want,—we shall create a demand for real art, as the phrase goes,—and, in the second place, we shall surely have more money to pay for decent houses.
>
> "Perhaps it will not try your patience too much, if I lay before you my idea of the fittings necessary to the sitting-room,—
>
> "First, a bookcase with a great many books in it; next, a table that will keep steady when you write or work at it; then several chairs that you can move, and a bench that you can sit or lie upon; next, a cupboard with drawers; next, unless either the bookcase or the cupboard be very beautiful with painting or carving, you

will want pictures or engravings (such as you can afford, only not stop-gaps, but real works of art) on the walls, or else the wall itself must be beautifully painted with some beautiful and restful pattern. We shall also want a vase or two to put flowers in, which latter you must have sometimes, especially if you live in town. Then there will be the fireplace, of course, which in our climate is bound to be the chief object in the room.

"That is all we shall want, especially if the floor be good. If it be not (as, by the way, in a modern house, it is pretty sure not to be), I admit that a small carpet which can be bundled out of the room in two minutes will be useful; and we must also take care that it is beautiful, or it will annoy us terribly.

"Now (unless we are musical, and need a piano), that is quite all we want; and we can add very little to these necessaries without troubling ourselves, and hindering our work, our thought, and our rest.

"All art starts from this simplicity; and the higher the art rises, the greater the simplicity.

"I have been speaking of the fittings of a dwelling-house,—a place in which we eat, and drink, and pass familiar hours; but, *when you come to places which people want to make more specially beautiful* because of the dignity of their uses, they will be simpler still, and have little in them save the bare walls made as beautiful as may be. St. Mark's at Venice has very little furniture in it, much less than most Roman-Catholic churches. Its lovely and stately mother, St. Sophia of Constantinople, had still less, even when it was a Christian church. But we need not go either to Venice or Stamboul to take note of that. Go into one of our own mighty Gothic naves, and note how the huge free space satisfies and elevates you even now, when window and wall are stripped of ornament; then think of the meaning of simplicity, and absence of encumbering gewgaws."[20]

I have quoted these sayings of William Morris, because the principle they urge is as applicable to a park as to a sitting-room or a cathedral; because they enforce with highest authority the one principle that must be held to steadily, year in and year out, if you are to succeed in obtaining a valuable park at moderate cost. You must have a few simple, distinct objects in view, and must provide for these in a liberal, strong, quiet, and thoroughly satisfying way, guarding with all possible care against inconsistencies and discords. Remember that the costliness of catchpenny, smart, "decorative" things, is not in what you first pay for them, or even in the labor of repairs and keeping that they bring upon you directly; but it is chiefly in the injury to everything else which comes with their introduction.

One word more of caution before we turn from principle to practice. A park is less fittingly compared to a dwelling than to a great public hall, attached to the main apartment of which there are several dependencies, vestibules, ante-room, cloak-room, refreshment-room, a counter for the sale of fans, lorgnettes, photographs, books of the music, and so on.

What is the great room that gives the whole this name of "park"? What is the difference between the entertainment to which it should invite us, and that of a concert-hall or an opera-house? It is a place in which to enjoy, instead of musical story-telling, dramatically or otherwise, the harmony and melody and poetry of actual nature; and it is just as important in the one case as the other to avoid bringing fussy, disturbing business into the main hall.

Every great park is valuable in proportion as it is the realization of an idyllic poem. As far as other objects are entertained upon the ground, economy requires that they shall be so pursued as to avoid disturbances, interruptions, and discords of the poetic theme.

PART SECOND.

I.

The Key to all Improvements of Belle Isle must be found in the Character of the Existing Wood.

THE leading object of all operations of improvement for the island being a consistent, harmonious, poetic entertainment, what shall be the general tone and character of this entertainment? Shall it, for example, be fine, delicate, and subtle, like most written poems, or shall it have more of the quality of Burns's verse, racy of the soil?[21] If we are truly seeking lasting economy, there can be but one answer,—it is determined by the condition of that element of the property, in which, with reference to a park, lies at present the larger part of its value.

To see this plainly, consider that the value of every large public park depends wholly upon the ultimate value of its sylvan elements. For example: take away the half-grown bodies of foliage which have already been formed in the New-York park, and it would be a ridiculous thing, wholly unfit for its purpose. The number of trees and bushes set out upon it exceeds three hundred thousand. Taking the preparation of soil with the cost of plants, planting, nursing, feeding, thinning, pruning, and guarding from injury, these plantations will have cost perhaps a million of dollars; but their actual value upon the above consideration is much greater (the value of what has cost fifteen million dollars, and is held to be well worth more than it has cost, being so largely dependent on them).

The area of wooded ground that you possess in Belle Isle is a little larger than that planted for the Central Park. So far as the woods upon it can be turned to good account, there is so much already paid for. Examining their present condition, comparatively few completely fine, and many distorted, decaying, and sickly trees, will be found. For convenience and safety in the park use of the ground, most of the latter must be taken out, and, by the removal of these and others, those of choicer qualities left to stand singly or in clusters, and further treated with a view to the development of pleasing forms, and compositions of healthful and luxuriant foliage. If this process is well managed, it is safe to say that you will have within ten years, in Belle Isle, elements of sylvan scenery of a far nobler type and character than in that time can have been attained from the original plantations on the New-York park at a cost of perhaps a million.

But the trees to be left for this purpose having gained their present size and form in a struggle from infancy with a crowd of older trees, while they can be gradually led to acquire much more graceful forms, and more fulness and luxuriance, have taken on characteristics that will always distinguish them from trees originally springing up apart, or in small groups in the open, and grown each with all the food and elbow-room and sunlight it could ask. There is nothing bad in these characteristics, but they are less expressive of lawn-like luxury, dressiness, and fine accomplishments, than the characteristics of most celebrated park trees; and the principle of economic consistency will consequently compel you to improve and furnish your park throughout with a more careful avoidance of a finical character than good taste might otherwise permit.

We have no terms that in their ordinary use convey a sound idea of the general character that should thus distinguish Belle Isle Park from others; but the only reason we have not, is that the terms "picturesque" and "rustic" have come, by misuse in respect to gardening matters, to suggest slight imitations suitable to go with the painted scenery of a theatre, rather than such elements of actual scenery as are substantially and permanently admissible.

As my present object, however, is to point out only the general direction in which departure should be made from the more common style of our American parks, if you would make a park of Belle Isle that the Detroit of today may be proud to give to her children, I will name an older and more beautiful park than any of them,—the Royal Park of Windsor.[22] I name it simply that I may say, that, if you can be satisfied with the general style of furnishing and housekeeping of which it is an illustration, the question "Can Detroit afford to maintain *so large* a park as that proposed on Belle Isle?" is answered. Large numbers of cows and sheep, as well as deer, are appropriately and profitably pastured in Windsor Park; and a reduction of the pastured area would lessen, not enlarge, the profits with which they are kept. Their presence does not prevent the royal family from walking through the park: it does not prevent the enjoyment of it by large picnic parties of working-people from London.

With an equal extent of roads and other structures to be maintained, the larger the area of a park upon which there can be good herbage closely cropped, the less, not the more, will the expense of keeping it be. It costs no more to build five miles of road within five hundred acres of park than within one hundred; no more to build two houses of given capacity, two miles apart, than one mile. The movements of a given number of people will cause less damage, and give occasion for less outlay for repairs, if they scatter over a large space, than if they concentrate on a space more limited.

Observe that the difference between the style of park thus suggested, and that more commonly seen in our city parks, corresponds to that between what is called the kept ground, and the outer ground, or park-proper, of those princely estates from which the idea of a park has indirectly come to us.

What is the reason for such a division? It is that the grazing animals, that keep the turf of the park-proper close and fine, and that form such a beautiful adjunct to its scenery, would be out of keeping with the distinctive beauty of a lawn opening from a drawing-room window, and would be destructive of such adjuncts of a drawing-room lawn as fine shrubbery and flowering plants. The animals are therefore fenced out, at least on one side, from the near vicinity of the palace, castle, or hall, which forms the central feature of the whole affair.

The principle is perfectly applicable to Belle Isle. You have no palace to build; but you may want a comparatively small area of the island nicely prepared, and kept for tennis, croquet, and other purposes in which ladies and children are more particularly interested. For this let there be such kept ground as may be desirable, and as can be afforded, but beyond it, the park-proper, which, once brought to a suitable condition, should be a source of income rather than of expense.

I know it will be thought that I am arguing the point at greater length than is necessary; but I know also, that, start with what strength of conviction you may, the chances are, that scrappy ideas of style and keeping, inconsistent with this, will, before many years, be pressed, or the means necessary to consistently realize this idea resisted, and that it cannot be too firmly planted.

Bear with me, then, while I point out again that the advantages of keeping park-surfaces by pasturage rather than by lawn-mowers or scythe, or, what is worst, not keeping them tidily at all, is recognized by the general practice of exhibiting a few cows and sheep in some parts of the larger city parks. This is done in Hyde Park, Central Park, Brooklyn Park, and Buffalo Park, for example. The reason the practice is not more generally and economically extended, is that where a park is entered from all sides directly from public streets, to be lined with stately buildings, and is designed to adequately accommodate within its limited space all who may at any time come to it, it must be much cut up with roads, and occupied by other artificial structures. In this case, convenience and congruity of aspect require in large parts of it a more garden-like quality; low-branched trees, underwood, and fine shrubbery ; and it is difficult to arrange fences and gates with a view to the pasturage of any part without making them ugly features, costly to keep in order. Even to the extent in which they are now used in the London parks, they are conspicuously ugly.

With an area to be dealt with so much larger, relatively to the population, than is generally the case; with no embarrassments from the occupation of the surrounding properties; from crossing streets, and numerous carriage entrances,—this difficulty of a pasturage style of keeping is likely to be little felt on Belle Isle. I need only add that an attempt to half carry out the idea will have bad results. The pastured ground must be well stocked, and the business should be large enough to profitably employ a good plant in all respects.

If a sufficient suggestion of the general character prescribed by the circumstances has thus been given, a few of the more important features of a plan may be outlined.

II.

The Question of Drainage.

THE site of the great park of The Hague[23] was a swamp, and presented, in an exaggerated form, every objection that lies against Belle Isle. The ground has been made dry; fitted for a royal residence, and for a general public health-resort, by a system of drains the discharge of which is effected by wind or steam pumps.

It would be a much simpler process to drain Belle Isle equally well. The advantage to be gained by it, and not otherwise to be gained, would be practically an addition of probably three months to the season in which the park would be an attractive and wholesome place of general resort; a more thrifty growth of trees; and a simplification and cheapening of various maintenance operations.

As park enterprises are ordinarily managed, the cost would not be formidable. It would not, for example, necessarily be a quarter the cost per acre that was incurred in the drainage of the Central Park.

It must be assumed in a plan that the park will finally be so drained. But this thorough system is not at once essential to a proper and wholesome use of the park; and it would be such a great and permanent misfortune to allow customs of using it in a bad way to be more firmly established through lack of suitable provisions for immediate public use, that I shall assume that all the money the Council will be willing to appropriate can for a few years be better used in other operations.

III.

Immediately Indispensable Surface-Drainage. Interior Waterways.

WITH reference principally to immediately indispensable superficial drainage, but also to other advantages, channels should be opened by means of which currents would flow through the several deeper pools in which water now stands permanently, stagnating in summer, and the bottoms of which are too low for drying by surface-drains. These channels, or rigolettes, should be so laid out as to serve as outlets for the minor surface-drains for which there would otherwise be insufficient fall.

Boating is likely to be a more generally popular means of recreation at Belle Isle Park than at any other nearer than the island park of Stockholm.[24]

Persons unaccustomed to boats, timid people, invalids, and children, would find boating upon these proposed shallow and sheltered park-waters very enjoyable. Forty licensed boats are found, at times, insufficient to meet the demand for a similar diversion on the still waters of Buffalo Park. Close alongside the open lake in Chicago there is a little sheltered park-pool, the boating of which yielded over eight thousand dollars of profit last summer; by so much diminishing the tax for park maintenance.[25] The proposed rigolettes of Belle Isle might, in a few years, be made incomparably more attractive. They would be highways of pleasure, in which boats would be used instead of carriages.

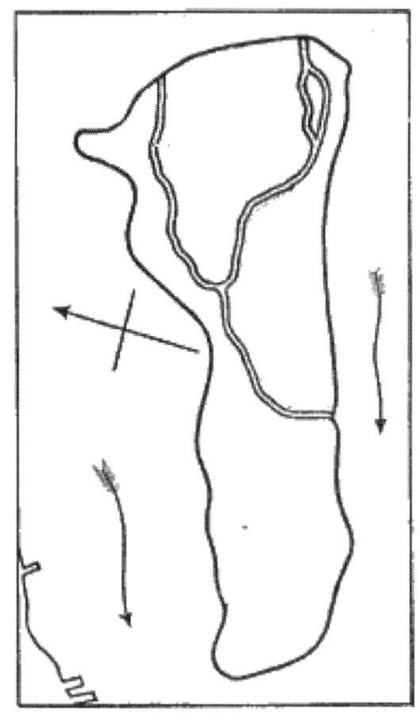

The cost of what appears barely necessary (*see cut*) to relieve the park, by this means, of conditions dangerous to health, and consequently imperative to be immediately set about, may be estimated at five thousand dollars; but as the work would be done by machinery, and by contract, there would be economy in connecting with it other desirable though less imminently necessary work; and this, with a proper disposition of material removed, and some piling at entrance-ways, would call for double that amount. This simply for wholesomeness. Later, ten thousand dollars more might be well spent in extending the system, giving it more interesting outlines, adding to the boating convenience, and to the attractiveness of the banks.

IV.

Opening the Woods.

With a view to driving off the mosquitoes; to the enjoyment on all parts of the island of the breeze from off the water, and to efficiency of police supervision,—all thickets should be removed, and all dense, low woods should be opened. The object generally to be sought in park plantations, of variety and picturesqueness through bodies of surface foliage, being thus excluded (as to be held or developed only at a cost greater than is warranted in this work), the following objects should be had in view as of immediate importance: (1) To give light and air to the ground with a view to more rapid drying of the surface, and establishing pasturage; (2) To remove dead, decaying, and badly-grown trunks, so as to allow of the development of a finer class of trees; (3) To gain a certain beauty of grouping and landscape composition throughout the woods,—all to be attained by a suitable thinning, and by grubbing and cleaning of the surface. The value of the timber and firewood should compensate for the labor needed to accomplish these results; and the sooner, the more economically they will be gained. The public should have considerable benefit from the work before next July.

V.

Access, Landings, Vestibule and Auxiliary Arrangements.

AMONG American parks, Belle Isle will be unique in its means and methods of access. In Stockholm only, where the most picturesque and the most locally popular public park in Europe is to be reached exclusively by boats, can anything corresponding be found. Even when Belle Isle shall be connected with the mainland by a bridge, the more favorite approach will be by boats; and to the mass of the population it will thus be more conveniently and pleasantly accessible than any other city park I know. A bridge is a matter for the future. When the park shall have been once well fitted for its purposes, and its value for those purposes generally realized, a bridge may be had with little direct outlay by the city.

The shorter the distance to the principal park-entrance from the centre of population of the city, the better. The shorter the boating distance, and the shorter the bridging distance, when the bridge comes, the better. This consideration would fix the main entrance, not, as at present, at the south-west, but at the north-west, point of the island. There is nothing in the way of placing it there at once but the expense of a new wharf. The necessary outlay, taking timber from the island, need be little more than a thousand dollars. But a great improvement will be gained by dredging a channel between this proposed wharf and that now used; so that boats may call at the first, and pass on without delay to the other, and up the river, to points on the south shore. A contract for this work can be made at this time for about seven thousand dollars: later, it will cost more.

Parties to be made up to go to any point of the island will be apt to gather first near the principal entrance. In uncertain weather, visitors will wait near the entrance to determine their plans, and to watch for friends arriving. When rain begins to threaten, visitors in all parts of the island will tend toward the entrance. Near the point of entrance above proposed is the highest and driest ground on the island. It is also the freest from mosquitoes, it is the breeziest, and it has the most animated and generally interesting outlook. For all these and other reasons, artificial shelter is here required; and nearby should be the principal promenade, or place of social gathering.

By "auxiliary arrangements" I mean those commonly to be met within parks, but to which trees, turf, rural beauty, and open air, are not essential. When such provisions are scattered through a park, they seriously injure its proper rural character. Of this class, are shows, exhibitions, arrangements for games and other entertainments requiring buildings or tents, of all which the germ is already established on the island under a rental or license system. The more all these can be kept together within reasonable limits, and the shorter the transportation between them and the town, the less they will cost; the more economical and efficient will be their police supervision; the less will be the discord between them and the more essential rural elements of the park; the less they will interfere with the proper quiet enjoyment and the distinctive economy of management of these elements; and the less will be the cost of their special water-supply, drainage, sewerage, roads, and walks. For all these reasons, ample space in the western part of the island should be reserved for provisions of this class. Such proposed reservation I will hereafter refer to as "The Fair Ground." (*See diagram*, A.)

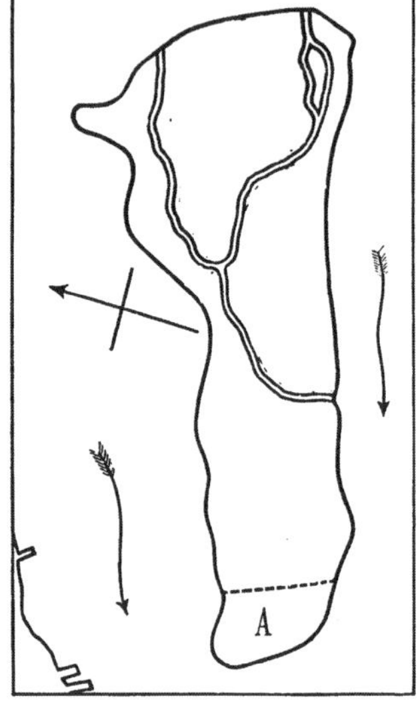

For the class of auxiliary arrangements thus brought in view, no immediate outlay need be made by the city. If nothing of the kind had been established, it might be better to contemplate nothing for a few years to come. For the present, temporary provisions, costing the city only about what they will return in rents and license-fees, need be considered. It may be hoped practicable, however, to obtain, later, a large investment of private capital upon this ground, for purposes and on terms advantageous to the general trade and repute of the city, and so used as to add largely to the value of the park-proper. The suggestion, which will be further developed, is made here, only that, in blocking out a general plan and policy, opportunity for such possible arrangements on a large scale may be held open. Provisions of the class in question– made from time to time, and often under the push of small speculators, or men of hobbies, with little reference to any comprehensive scheme for them — are sure, in the long-run, to become offensive, embarrassing, and demoralizing.

I have presented these considerations, in favor of making large reservations of ground in that part of the island nearest the city for auxiliary park constructions, with a view to the observation that the required provisions for shelter and promenade, near the main landing, should be laid out on a larger scale than would otherwise be necessary; that they should be well built, and suitable to stand before large concert, exhibition, and refreshment buildings, such as may hereafter be wanted. Whatever is to be built for the purpose for a few years to come should be either a section of such a fine, permanent construction, adapted to subsequent extension, or it should be of a plainly rough and temporary sort, evincing intention of its early removal and supersedure. A finished, cheap, showy affair, to answer immediate purposes, will be in every way uneconomical.

VI.

The Essence of the Park. The East Park.

THE essential element of a park is the enjoyment it offers of the beauty of natural sylvan scenery. Take everything else away that money may have procured in any park,—roads, walks, structures, play-grounds, menageries, circuses, race-courses, floral and other decorations,—and there will remain a park. Take this away, leaving all others, and there will be roads, walks, structures, a play-ground, a menagerie, a race-course, and a garden—but a park only in name; nor will any and everything else that may be added be as valuable to the people of a city as this single essence of a park.

To obtain this element in a high degree, it is, under ordinary circumstances, necessary to secure the foil and vantage for perspective of broad openings of unbroken greensward: to obtain a high degree of picturesque interest, it is necessary to have variety of surface, and desirable to have rocky prominences and declivities. The first is unnecessary in the instance of Belle Isle, because the purpose is served by the broad expanses of water with which its woodland scenery must be associated: the second is simply out of the question, since the result of any attempt, though at the cost of millions, would be but puerile, and serve only to call attention to what is naturally lacking. Such picturesqueness as is attainable must be attained with less obvious effect and affectation, in the disposition of the woods, the direct, truthful vigor of necessary constructions, and the refined fitness of details. But the essential merit of the park will lie in the extent, purity, congruity, and unsophisticated quality, of its main body of woodland; and the principal enjoyment of this will always be had in the depth of summer. The highest degree of it is to be obtained only after thorough drainage, by a gradual process of development of beauty in groups and masses and single outstanding trees, with glades giving light to them; but a good degree of it in summer is to be had soon and cheaply. The main thing to be insisted upon, both for the present and the future, is that a body of ground shall be managed *exclusively for this purpose*, sufficiently large to make a sustained consistent impression. This can rarely be afforded in a town park. There is not one in the country that has as large and adaptable a body of wood as that you possess on Belle Isle; and it needs only a trimming and growing process, with facilities for reaching it, and passing through it.

The broadest mass of this wood lies in the eastern part of the island, and it looks upon the broadest and least disturbed body of water. (Let the imagination add fifty years to the growth of the best of the trees, and then remember the last of the words quoted from Morris, p. 31.)[26]

The proposition to which all these considerations have been intended to lead up, is this: that in that part of the island farthest from the city, and nearest Lake St. Clair,[27] now occupied by one unbroken body of natural woodland, no object or motive of improvement shall at any time be entertained that will be unfavorable to that of unsophisticated sylvan scenery; such thinning out and trimming of the trees only being permitted as shall be aidful to a healthy, moderately open, and scattered but sturdy and umbrageous forest development, and such roads, walks, and other artificial constructions being introduced as are essential to the health, convenience, and comfort of visitors making the simplest use of it, and to economy of administration.

The space in question is less than a quarter of the whole space of the island. Its average elevation is not more than two feet above the river-level. The water off the shore on which it ends is the shallowest, and the locality is the least desirable for landings, of any on the island. For all these reasons there is no present temptation to encroachments upon it. But efforts to break in upon it with "improvements" inconsistent with the above proposition are as sure to come as there are sure to be found in the future of Detroit some men of immature tastes combined with pushing and persuasive ability.

VII.

Greensward Unpastured. Campus.

THERE is an area of land that has been in cultivation, lying in the southern half of the island, next west of the last woodland district. It has a suitable soil, and can be quickly and at little cost made into an unbroken green, or campus. It is low and moist and poachy in the spring, but, when covered with turf in summer, would, even without drainage, sustain a great deal of foot-wear uninjured, and would then be almost perfectly adapted to military parades or great field foot-sports. It would be faulty only in its crooked, northern outline, and narrowness relatively to length. Both objections can be removed by some clearing of the adjoining woods. The entire ground should be kept in tillage for one summer, after which one year should be allowed for the growth of grass. Supposing the clearing to be done this coming winter, by July of 1884 it might be in order for use,—the largest and best parade-ground by far possessed by any city in the country.

I have not now the necessary data for an estimate, but think that the cost of the operation would be within two thousand dollars.

The proposition is, that a plain of turf should be formed about eighty acres in extent, and large enough for the deployment of a brigade in line of battle. Its situation would be on the south side of the island, east of the second wharf. When not in use for parades or other large exhibitions, this ground would appear a simple meadow, with an umbrageous border on one side, and the river on the other. (*See diagram, D.*) It would be separated from the adjoining parts of the park by the rigolette, which would serve as a fence for it; and the excavated material from the rigolette thrown into an embankment would form a platform for spectators overlooking the parades. I shall advise that this eighty acres of grass be preserved from all intrusion from the opening of the spring till about a week before the local haying season usually begins; that the grass then be mowed before its seed has begun to harden, and made into hay for the support, during the winter, of the stock pastured on the park during the summer. Mowed at this stage, by the 4th of July the field would be in good order for reviews.

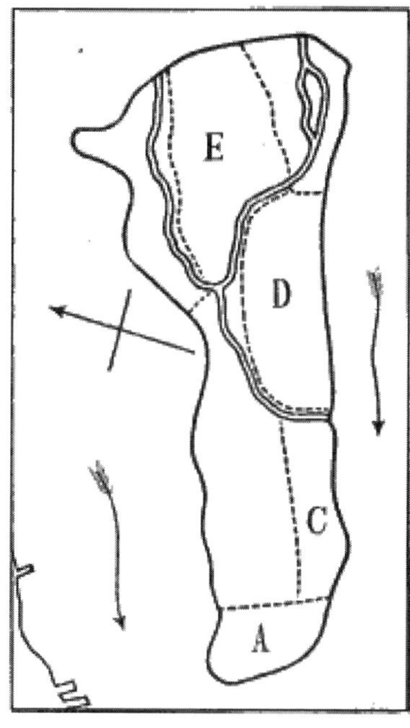

Between this ground, which I will here call the Prairie, and the Fair Ground along the south shore, there will be an intermediate district now cleared, and grassy or swampy, which will be most readily turned to account by a similar treatment to that of the Prairie. Not being held for hay, however, it would be available earlier in the summer. The western part of it would be useful for baseball and other athletic sports, being the nearest point of the island to the city, adapted to these purposes, breezy, and with convenient shade. (*See diagram*, C.)

VIII.

Opportunity for a Great City Fair.

THERE would be no definite division between the district last considered and that before proposed to be held as a Fair Ground. This term was used as slightly suggestive of a concentration of a class of provisions more or less found in most parks for some small trading and handicraft business in connection with means of amusement, as in old English fairs, our own agricultural fairs, the Dutch *kermis*, and French village *fêtes*.[28] An opportunity would thus be left for setting a large building beyond the limits of the original Fair Ground, should one ever be required, of the character of those used in national expositions, such as that last year held at Atlanta, this year at Denver, and next year proposed at Boston, Cincinnati, and The Hague.[29]

It will not be premature, perhaps, to refer to the fact that several large cities have been recently provided with such buildings,—not for national, but for local industrial exhibitions,—and that a tendency is apparent throughout the civilized world, as one of the results of the yet rapidly developing facilities of locomotion, to a return to a principle of commercial economy which has for some time been in a great degree left behind. I mean to that which in past centuries, as far back as authentic history goes, led to the drawing of an extraordinary amount of trade and of pleasuring together, to certain large towns at a particular period of each year; such gatherings being known to us as fairs. One of the more notable of them is held upon a green in the midst of the great suburban park of Copenhagen,—the Dyrhave.[30]

The increasing number and magnitude of trade conventions and expositions at points of general gathering, like Niagara and Saratoga, where there have been half a dozen this year, is one illustration of this tendency. Another is that of the wonderful confluences of people, brought together from distances hundreds of miles apart by steamboats and railroads, at such resorts as Nantasket, Martha's Vineyard, Newport, Narragansett Pier, Coney Island, Long Branch, Ashbury Park, Cape May, Round Lake, and Chatauqua Lake. A temporary local population larger than that of Detroit is sometimes thus gathered; and the trade so concentrated amounts annually to millions of dollars. Still another, in the multitudes of people drawn together by a class of festivals, of which the *Mardi Gras* of New Orleans and "The Oriole" of Baltimore are marked examples. (See *Studies in the South* in "The Atlantic Monthly" for December.)[31] The means for them are chiefly contributed by tradesmen, innkeepers, and transportation agencies, who find their profit in the trade they draw. The late Penn Celebration in Philadelphia was mainly of this order. Another is planned for this winter by the business men of Montreal.[32] We have not yet seen the full development of the tendency, and it will cost Detroit nothing to keep in view the possibilities she holds with reference to it on Belle Isle. I know of no other point on the lakes, possessing advantages of comparable value for the purpose.

IX.

The North Park and the Far Fields.

THE district between the Fair Ground and the park north and west of the Prairie (*B*, on *diagram*, p. 56) would be treated on the same general principles as the East Park, but for several reasons more openly, and with less of sylvan seclusion. The principal thoroughfares of the island giving access to, and communication between, all the other parts, would pass through it. Persons making short visits would be confined to it. By more thorough opening of the ground to light and air, and by better drainage, it would be available earlier and later in the season, and later in the evening, than any other part of the island. A main passage through it may be artificially lighted. On its northern side would be the regatta and bathing waters of the park, bathing-houses, boat-houses, and a grand stand, all branching from the Fair Ground, and in direct connection with the principal entrance: on its opposite side, the turf playing-grounds for ball, and other athletic sports; running and bicycling courses; and so on. These may suggest crude ideas of arrangements, requiring much study before they can be presented as distinct and coherent propositions of a plan.

There remain the two great swampy districts on the north and south respectively of the east park. After thorough drainage, these may eventually be given an ordinary park-like character, being treated and used like the main park in Buffalo, the north meadows in the Central Park, or the larger part of Phoenix Park, Dublin.[33] Pending that improvement, by the dredging of channels through them, as proposed under the head of "superficial drainage," and the distribution of some of the dredged material along their borders, it is believed that they can quickly, and at small expense, be sufficiently relieved of water to sustain a wholesome and nutritious herbage. They would then at once form the principal pasture-grounds of the park. They are now pestiferous: they would then be healthful. Speaking more definitely as to time and cost, I should think, that, with an outlay of from three to four thousand dollars, a tolerable result might be obtained after two years. (G and F on *diagram.*)

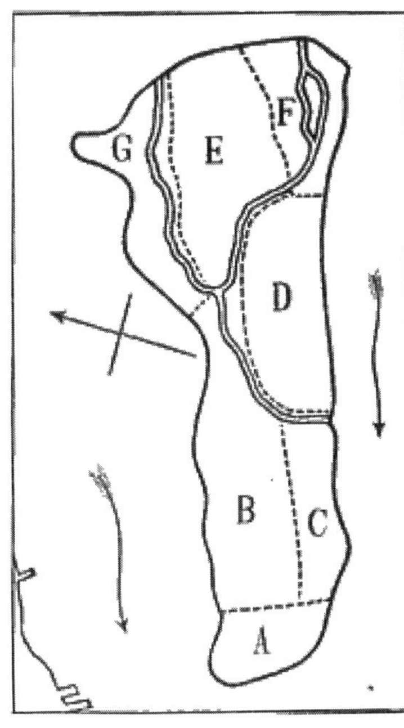

X.

Constructions.

Roads and walks will, of course, be proposed and located on the plan; but the study of them does not belong to this stage of it. They are no essential part of the park: they are but implements for making use of it, and are to be laid out and made only as other conditions direct, and when and so fast as necessary. Fortunately, there can at present be no large demand for wheel-ways; and great immediate expense for their construction may be avoided.

To provide means of rest, especially for invalids and children, shelters from showers, and well-managed retiring-rooms, a considerable amount of roofing will be required. It is economy to aggregate as much as practicable under one roof. It is economy, also, especially in respect to police arrangements, to avoid numerous points of gathering. Hence it will be desirable, first, as before suggested, as soon as possible to provide a shed stretching along the shore, south from the north-west landing, which will also serve as a vestibule

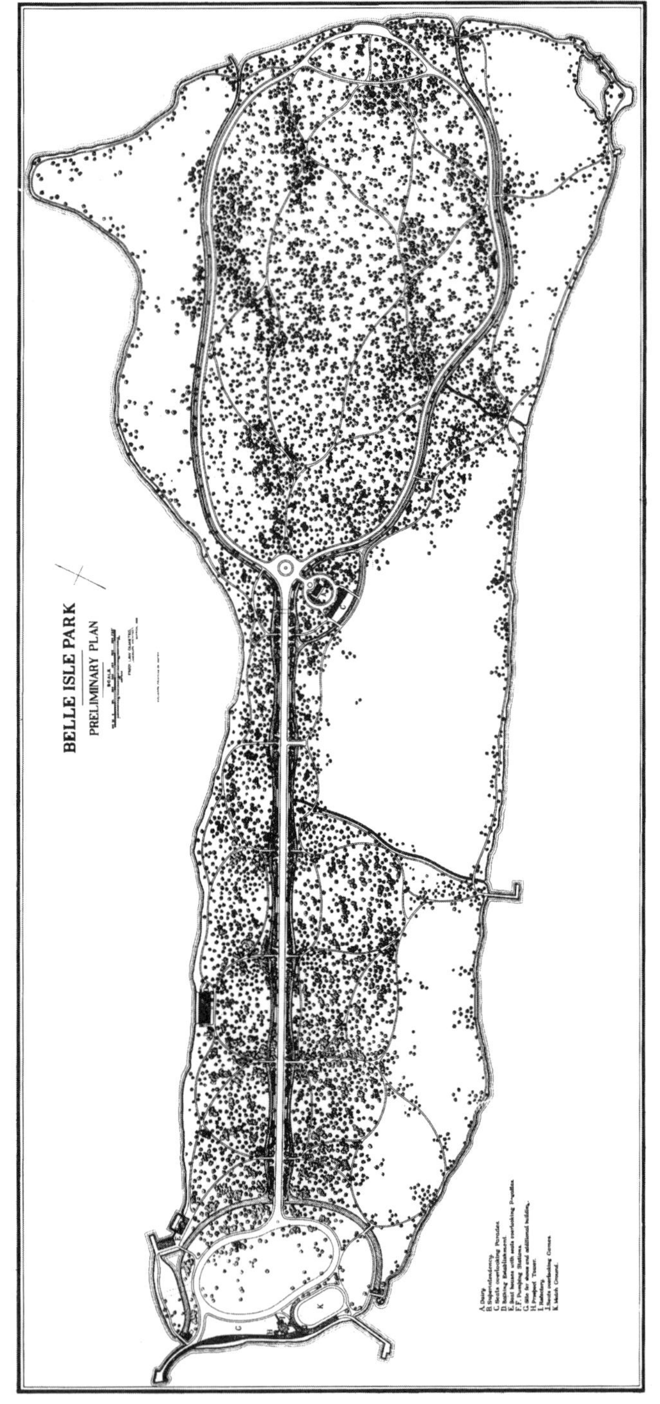

"Belle Isle Park, Preliminary Plan," March 1883

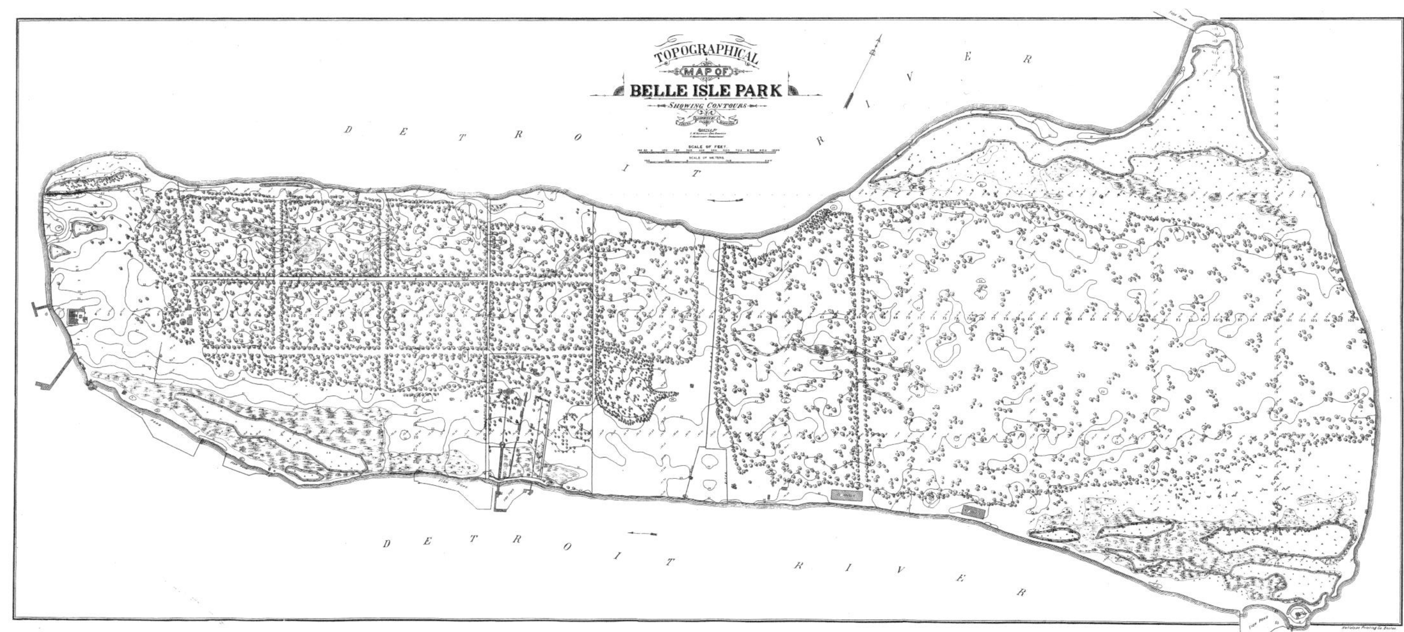

"Topographical Map of Belle Isle Park," c. 1882

and corridor to other buildings that may be later erected on the Fair Ground. For necessary *temporary* refreshment-rooms, and other public accommodations, I am disposed to largely advise canvas houses, or tents, because neater at their cost, and more easily repaired, than anything else, and because they would bear on their face the fact of the temporary use intended to be made of them, and throw no discredit on the permanent park.

The structures to be used in winter for the protection of the livestock could be made to serve, when necessary (in the emergencies of showers), for the shelter of large crowds. For this purpose they should be near the parade-ground, and on the east side of it, in the edge of the East Park, as best dividing the entire space of the island, with the shed at the north-west landing. The same vicinity will be best for all necessary farm-buildings, and for the superintendency. Here there should be also a house for a particular class of refreshments; namely, for the most part, milk and dairy products, to be sold at fixed low prices, it being desirable to encourage the use of them, as well as to make a cash home market for the products of the park stock. In connection with this establishment, there should be arrangements for gratuitously supplying boiling water and other requirements of picnic parties.

The text presented here was published, at Olmsted's expense, as *The Park for Detroit* (Boston, 1882). In August 1879 the city of Detroit purchased Belle Isle, an approximately 900-acre island in the Detroit River, for the purpose of creating a public park. An act of the Common Council established the four-man Board of Belle Isle Park Commissioners in August 1881, and the commission asked Olmsted that December to design a portion of Belle Isle. Olmsted responded by saying that a comprehensive design was needed, and in February the commissioners asked him to visit Belle Isle and begin preliminary designs. In April 1882 they awarded him a three-year contract to produce a comprehensive park plan and to supervise improvements to the island. That September the board reported that Olmsted's plans were delayed because the topographic survey of the island, always a prerequisite for Olmsted on such a project, had taken longer than expected. Olmsted presented his plan for Belle Isle to the park commissioners on March 23, 1883 (*Local Acts of the Legislature of the State of Michigan passed at the regular session of* 1879 [Lansing, 1879], pp. 215–16; "Chapter XVII: Belle Isle Park," *The Revised Ordinances of the City of Detroit, for the Year 1890* [Detroit, 1890], pp. 47–52; FLO to John Stirling, Dec. 30, 1881 [*Papers of FLO*, 7: 572–73]; *City of Detroit: Journal of the Common Council from January 10, 1882, to January* 9, *1883* [Detroit, 1883], pp. 145, 505; FLO to JCO, March 22, 1883; see also Frederick Law Olmsted, "Belle Isle: After One Year," June 1884 [*Papers of FLO*, SS1: 419–36]).

1. William Morris (1834–1896), the English designer and author, was a founder of the Arts & Crafts movement, along with John Ruskin and others. The quotation that Olmsted includes here is from William Morris, *Hopes and Fears for Art* (1882), p. 178. Olmsted also quotes Morris in his 1881 plan for Mount Royal in Montreal, as well as in other published articles (*DNB*; Frederick Law Olmsted, "Mount Royal. Montreal," 1881 [*Papers of FLO*, SS1: 350]).
2. Eugene Robinson made a survey of Belle Isle with the assistance of E. M. Veenfleet.

The work took longer than expected but was completed by early September, when Olmsted traveled to the site (*Journal of the Common Council from January 10, 1882 to January 9, 1883*, pp. 428–505; plan 614-15, NPS/FLONHS).

3. The members of the Board of Belle Isle Park Commissioners in November 1882 were August Marxhausen, William A. Moore, James McMillan, and William B. Moran (Silas Farmer, *History of Detroit and Wayne County and Early Michigan* [New York, 1890], p. 76; *Journal of the Common Council from January 10, 1882 to January 9, 1883*, pp. 116, 520).
4. According to the 1881 ordinance creating the Board of Belle Isle Park Commission, the board needed the approval of the Common Council "before accepting any bids, or entering into any contracts," including contracts for felling trees. No work, except for the possible erection of a public institution, was to commence on Belle Isle until "a thorough plan for the development and improvement" of the park had been submitted to and approved by the Common Council ("Chapter XVII: Belle Isle Park," *The Revised Ordinances of the City of Detroit, for the Year 1890* [Detroit, 1890], pp. 48–49).
5. The "winter's work" being the thinning of trees. On October 24, 1882, the Common Council approved a request by the park commissioners to "commence as early as practicable upon the work of felling certain timber and clearing underbrush" (*Journal of the Common Council from January 10, 1882 to January 9, 1883*, p. 572).
6. On October 28, 1882, the *Detroit Free Press* reported that city councilman Joseph T. Lowry said that the "Park Commission ought either to have more power or be abolished." The issue was not taken up in any official capacity by the City Council ("City Council," *Detroit Free Press*, Oct. 28, 1882; *Journal of the City Council from January 10, 1882 to January 9, 1883*, pp. 520, 116–17).
7. When the Common Council created the Board of Park Commissioners in August 1881, it stated that "any public institution for the care of the poor, insane and blind" would be welcome on the island. None were placed there. On July 19, 1881 Alderman Seymour Finney proposed locating a pest house, or hospital for people with communicable diseases, on Belle Isle, but the Common Council did not approve his proposal ("Chapter XVII: Belle Isle Park," *The Revised Ordinances of the City of Detroit, for the Year 1890* [Detroit, 1890], p. 48; City of Detroit, *Journal of the Common Council from January 10, 1881 to January 9, 1882, Inclusive* [Detroit, 1882), p. 363).
8. Olmsted draws attention to the year 1856, when New York's Common Council created the first park commission to oversee Central Park, the first public park of its kind (Frederick Law Olmsted, Jr., and Theodora Kimball, eds., *Forty Years of Landscape Architecture: Central Park, Frederick Law Olmsted, Sr.* [Cambridge, Mass., 1973], p. 31).
9. The Detroit City Hall was formally occupied on July 18, 1871, when the population of Detroit was still only 80,000 people. Designed by Alexander Chapoton, the building stood two hundred feet tall and cost $600,000 to build (S. Farmer, *History of Detroit and Wayne County*, pp. 475–77; Campbell Gibson, "Population of the 100 Largest Cities and Other Urban Places in the United States: 1790 to 1990," *U.S. Bureau of the Census* [June 1998]).
10. Olmsted was frustrated that the Board of Belle Isle Park Commissioners had to secure approval from the Common Council and the City Council for every expenditure made. He had expressed similar frustrations while working on the park at Mount Royal in Montreal, because the men in charge of the park were a committee of the Common Council and not an independent commission. Olmsted had better experiences with park commissions that submitted annual budgets and received annual appropriations, including those in New York City, Brooklyn, and Boston (Frederick Law Olmsted, "Mount Royal. Montreal," 1881 [*Papers of FLO*, SS1: 361]; Roy Rosenzweig and Elizabeth Blackmar, *The Park and the People* [Ithaca, N.Y., 1992], p. 263; Frederick Law

Olmsted, "Report to the Brooklyn Park Commission," Jan. 1, 1869 [*Papers of FLO*, 6: 321]; Cynthia Zaitzevsky, *Frederick Law Olmsted and The Boston Park System* [Cambridge, Mass., 1982], pp. 42–43).

11. Olmsted refers to Central Park. In 1859, 3,666 people were working there (New York City Board of Alderman, "Document No. 6, January 30, 1860," *Documents*, vol. 27 pt. 1 [New York, 1860], p. 21).
12. On the first of March of each year the park board was required to submit estimates of revenues and expenditures for the upcoming year and the Common Council then appropriated the "amount of said estimates as they deem proper and necessary." The park board was also required to submit monthly estimates of revenue and expenditures at the second session of the Common Council each month ("Chapter XVII: Belle Isle Park," *The Revised Ordinances of the City of Detroit, for the Year 1890* [Detroit, 1890], p. 51).
13. Olmsted refers to "An ordinance to license and regulate the running of vessels to and from Belle Isle," which was first proposed to the Common Council on June 20, 1882. The Council passed it on July 18, 1882, but on August 15, 1882, the City Council returned it to the Common Council with amendments. On September 12, 1882, the park commissioners declared that the inability of the city's government to pass the ordinance had led to a loss of money during that season. The Common Council and the City Council finally passed the ordinance in April 1883 (*Journal of the Common Council from January 10, 1882 to January 9, 1883*, pp. 341–42, 395, 440, 505; *Journal of the Common Council from January 9, 1883 to January 8, 1884*, pp. 137–38, 222–23).
14. Olmsted may be referring to the May 1882 purchase of a house then owned by Charles Rother, and the purchase of other structures on Belle Isle. Other houses on the island had been purchased in 1879 and most had been demolished. In June of 1882 the city built bath houses and sheds for visitors to the island (*Annual Report of the Controller of the City of Detroit* [Detroit, 1882], p. 94; City of Detroit, *Journal of the Common Council from January 14, 1879 to January 13, 1880* [Detroit, 1880], p. 495; Michael Rodriguez and Thomas Featherstone, *Detroit's Belle Isle: Island Park Gem* (Mount Pleasant, S.C., 2003), p. 20; *Journal of the Common Council from January 10, 1882 to January 9, 1883*, p. 314).
15. The "Buffalo park" was the large park of the Buffalo park system, at first called "the Park" and renamed Delaware Park in 1896. The 350-acre park consisted primarily of a large meadow with scattered groves of shade trees and a 46-acre lake. The "New-York park" referred to is Central Park (Francis R. Kowsky, "Municipal Parks and City Planning: Frederick Law Olmsted's Buffalo Park and Parkway System," *Journal of the Society of Architectural Historians*, March 1987, p. 52; *Twenty-Seventh Annual Report of the Buffalo Parks Commissioners* [Buffalo, 1897], p. 12).
16. Miasmas, or noxious vapors rising from stagnant water, poorly drained soil, or decomposing organic matter, were considered a source of infectious disease for much of the nineteenth century. The English sanitary reformer Edwin Chadwick and others supported the theory and therefore advocated environmental improvements, such as sewerage systems, improved drainage, and the creation of parks, all as means of eliminating miasmatic conditions. By the 1880s, the germ theory of disease was becoming more accepted, but here and elsewhere Olmsted refers to miasmatic disease theory to support the idea that parks would improve public health conditions (Edwin Chadwick and Benjamin Ward Richardson, *The Health of Nations, A Review of the Works of Edwin Chadwick* [London, 1887], pp. 18, 63–65, 206; Mervyn Susser and Zena Stein, *Eras in Epidemiology: The Evolution of Ideas* [Oxford, 2009], pp. 17, 75; see also Frederick Law Olmsted, "Improvement of Easton's Beach," March 13, 1883, below; Frederick Law Olmsted, "Report of the Landscape Architect," Dec. 24, 1883, below; Frederick

Law Olmsted, *Twelfth Annual Report, Boston Park Commissioners, Report on Charles River Embankment*, Dec., 1886, below).

17. A "Morris hanging" was a tapestry sold by William Morris's company. De Morgan vases were designed by William De Morgan (1839–1917), a leading producer of Arts & Crafts style ceramics and a former employee of Morris (Helen Dore, *William Morris* (London, 1996), pp. 98–101; *DNB*; Martin Greenwood, *The Designs of William De Morgan* [Somerset, UK, 1989]).
18. Olmsted is likely referring to the Jardin du Luxembourg in Paris. In Frederick Law Olmsted, Jr., and Theodora Kimball's *Forty Years of Landscape Architecture*, the same phrase is used to specifically describe park maintenance in Paris and in the Jardin du Luxembourg. The phrase is given in quotation marks, presumably quoting words of Olmsted's (F. L. Olmsted, Jr., and T. Kimball, eds., *Forty Years of Landscape Architecture*, p. 203; FLO to Andrew Jackson Downing, Nov. 23, 1850 [*Papers of FLO*, 1: 363]).
19. That is, New York's Central Park (Frederick Law Olmsted, *The Spoils of the Park* [*Papers of FLO*, 7: 633–35]).
20. William Morris, *Hopes and Fears for Art* (Boston, 1882), pp. 107–10.
21. Olmsted refers to Scottish poet Robert Burns (1759–1796) who was "racy of the soil" in the sense that he was strongly identified with his native landscape (*DNB*; *OED*).
22. Windsor Great Park is a large royal park near Windsor Castle in England. Originally a medieval hunting park, by the eighteenth century the park and its forest were a tourist destination and the subject of landscape paintings and poetry (Charles Lyte, *The Royal Gardens in Windsor Great Park* [Whinfield, UK, 1998], pp. 17–21).
23. Olmsted is likely referring to the *Bosch* (the woods), located in the western portion of The Hague. It encompassed over a thousand acres, was largely wooded, and contained several lakes and canals. The royal palace *Huisten Bosch* was located on the property. Olmsted may have visited the *Bosch* while in The Hague in 1878 (Russell Thayer, *The Public Parks and Gardens of Europe* (Philadelphia, 1880), pp. 63–64; Anonymous, *The Famous Parks and Gardens of the World* (London, 1880), pp. 193–94).
24. That is, Djurgård (or Djurgården) Park in Stockholm, which Olmsted wrote about in his article, "Park," for the *American Cyclopedia*. Djurgård Park was a two-mile-long wooded park in central Stockholm (Frederick Law Olmsted, "Park," *American Cyclopedia*, 1875 [*Papers of FLO*, SS1: 323]; Lars Nilsson, "Stockholm and Green Space, 1850–2000: An Introduction," in Peter Clark, ed., *The European City and Green Space* (London, 2006), p. 100; see also FLO to Sherman S. Jewett, April 11, 1887, below).
25. Olmsted is likely referring to Lincoln Park, on Chicago's North Shore, which by the 1880s had been turned from a cemetery into a popular destination for picnickers and boaters (Donald L. Miller, *City of the Century: The Epic of Chicago and the Making of America* [New York, 1996], pp. 134, 288–89, 290, 380).
26. Olmsted refers to the page number in his original published pamphlet. The quote from Morris' *Hopes and Fears for Art* given earlier, ending in ". . . and absence of encumbering gewgaws" appeared on p. 31 in the original pamphlet.
27. Lake St. Clair is located three miles northwest of Belle Isle between Lake Huron and Lake Erie.
28. The Dutch and French words for *fair*, or *festival* (*OED*).
29. The International Cotton Exposition took place in Atlanta from October through December 1881. The Denver Mining Exposition was held in the summer of 1882. In 1883, Boston hosted the American Exhibition of the Products, Arts, and Manufactures of Foreign Nations, and Cincinnati hosted the Eleventh Cincinnati Industrial Exposition. The event that Olmsted refers to taking place at The Hague in Amsterdam was likely the *Internationale Koloniale En Untvoerhandel Tentoonstellung* in 1883 (John E. Findling and Kimberly D. Pelle, eds., *Historical Dictionary of World's Fairs and Exposi-*

tions, 1851–1988 [New York, 1990], pp. 76–81; "The Denver Mining Exposition, *New York Times*, July 11, 1882, p. 5; "The Cincinnati Exposition," *New York Times*, Aug. 27, 1883, p. 1).

30. Each summer people gathered in the Dyrehave, or "Deer Park," north of Copenhagen Denmark to celebrate the feast of St. John the Baptist (E. C. Otté, *Denmark and Iceland* [London, 1881], p. 94).
31. "Studies in the South," *The Atlantic Monthly*, Dec.1882, pp. 751–52. In New Orleans, Mardi Gras is the celebration held on the day before the beginning of Lent. Carnival refers to the period beginning on Twelfth Night and ending with Mardi Gras. Similar celebrations, also called Carnivals, take place in many other countries. Citizens of New Orleans have celebrated Mardi Gras informally since the early nineteenth century, and the more modern Mardi Gras began in 1857. The Oriole Festival in Baltimore, begun in 1881, lasts for three days in autumn. The 1882 festival celebrated the battle of North Point, which was fought during the War of 1812 in Chesapeake Bay, and the founding of Maryland by Lord Baltimore. The festival ended with a masquerade ball and parade similar to those that took place during Mardi Gras (Steven Hoelscher "Mardi Gras," in Paul S. Boyer, ed., *The Oxford Companion to United States History* [New York, 2001]; Clayton Colman Hall, ed., *Baltimore: Its History and its People*, vol. 1 [New York, 1912], pp. 255–58; "Baltimore's Oriole Festival," *New York Times*, Aug. 9, 1882, p. 5; "Baltimore's Oriole Festival," ibid., Sept. 13, 1882, p. 2).
32. The Penn Celebration, which marked the bicentennial of William Penn's landing on the American continent, took place October 22–27, 1882. The first Montreal Winter Carnival, organized by the city of Montreal, took place January 23–27, 1883 (Gary B. Nash, *First City: Philadelphia and the Forging of Historical Memory* [Philadelphia, 2002], pp. 292–93; "The Penn Bi-Centennial," *New York Times*, Oct. 25, 1882, p. 1; William Henry Atherton, *Montreal, 1535–1914* [Montreal, 1914], p. 235; "Montreal's Winter Carnival," *New York Times*, Jan. 5, 1883, p. 4; "Good Promise for the Carnival," ibid., Jan. 24, 1883, p. 3; "Close of the Carnival," ibid., Jan. 28, 1883, p. 2).
33. Olmsted had visited Phoenix Park in Dublin on December 4, 1859, and wrote about it in an earlier draft of his article, "Park," for *The New American Cyclopedia*. The park was nearly eighteen hundred acres large and included the Zoological Society of Ireland (FLO to BCCP, Dec. 28, 1859 [*Papers of FLO*, 3: 234–42]; Frederick Law Olmsted, "'Park,' from *The New American Cyclopedia*, 1861 [*Papers of FLO*, 3: 347]).

ANNUAL REPORT

OF THE

ARCHITECT OF THE UNITED STATES CAPITOL.

[1882]

CAPITOL GROUNDS.

Relating to the Capitol grounds, Mr. Frederick Law Olmsted, landscape architect, furnishes the following report accompanied with an appendix, forming an index to trees about the Capitol, with advice to visitors interested in them. He says:

The principal construction works upon the Capitol Ground during the fiscal year ending July 1, 1882, have been the following:

PROGRESS OF CONSTRUCTION.

(1.) The southeast entrance-way, which is now completed, except in respect to lighting arrangements.

(2.) The entrance to the southern system of wheel-ways and walks from Maryland avenue, the stone work of which is complete.

(3.) The wall and coping on the east and south border by which the inclosure of the ground is completed.

(4.) The walls, coping, stairs, and drainage arrangements of the direct approach from Maryland avenue to the west entrance of the Capitol.

(5.) Foundation work of the parapet wall bounding the platform between the base of the Capitol and the central field of turf on the west.

(6.) Twenty-four thousand square feet of plain and 10,000 square feet of "mosaic" artificial stone flagging.

The ground adjoining the several new works of masonry, heretofore temporarily prepared, has been broken up, regraded, with improved modeling of the surface, and sodded or planted.

INCOMPLETE WORK.—THE TERRACE.

In reviewing the present aspect of the Capitol it should be borne in mind that the area within a distance of from 100 to 150 feet of the Capitol, including the slopes beyond the high earth works, remains as it was temporarily prepared twenty years ago pending the design of a general plan for the improvement of the ground. The more nearly the improvement beyond this space is brought to realize its local intention, the more unsuitable, shabby, and disorderly must the central and more conspicuous ground appear, so that the better the work done the less satisfactory is the result as a whole. The anomaly will be more and more marked until the terrace and western stairway shall have been completed and the adjoining ground graded and finished in adaptation to them.

The present Joint Committee on Public Buildings and Grounds have reviewed the plans for these structures adopted seven years ago by Congress, on the recommendation of their predecessors, and it is understood that all its members are convinced that they should be carried out without needless delay.[1] Until Congress adopts this conclusion the Capitol grounds must both be seen at disadvantage and produce impressions unjust to the general design incorporating them.

For the convenience of the committee a brief statement, with illustrative sketches of the plan of the terrace, was prepared last winter.

The construction of the terrace will involve no breaking up of ground or roads or walks already finished, and need cause no inconvenience to the ordinary business of the Capitol.

PROGRESS OF PLANTATIONS.

At the beginning of the year the effect of a summer of extraordinary heat and drought followed by a winter of unprecedented cold, was still marked in the condition of the plantations; with the exception of a few broad-leaved evergreens, they have since recovered and are now growing vigorously. The death of certain shrubs the present year has been traced to gas leaks, and it is to be hoped that the time is near when through the introduction of an improved economical method of electric lighting the danger attending the use of illuminating gas in planted grounds may be avoided.[2]

The four lines of plane trees on the west of the Capitol are growing very thriftily, but are checked and given lop-sided forms by the interference of what remains of the old avenue trees they are designed to supersede.

This will be obvious on comparing the crowded trees with others of their kind not so affected. The injury is not, as yet, so great that it may not be remedied, but the final removal of the remaining old trees, nearly all of which are plainly diseased or dilapidated, should not be delayed more than another year.

The temporary loss of shade will soon be amply compensated by the overarching of the new trees.

INDEX TO TREES.

There being trees on the ground unknown to many visitors from distant parts of the country, upon a suggestion kindly made by members of Congress, labels have been placed before a large number, giving their names, and a map, index, and references prepared for the use of strangers. To further foster, meet, and lead on to more useful fields any disposition of inquiry that might occur upon the ground in respect to sylviculture, especially with those having little knowledge of the subject, an explanatory account of the plantations has been added, with advice as to opportunities of fuller information. Copies of all are appended.[3]

APPENDIX.

INDEX TO TREES ABOUT THE CAPITOL, WITH ADVICE TO VISITORS INTERESTED IN THEM.

The interest shown by many visitors in the young growth about the Capitol and the character of the inquiries made by them is a gratifying evidence of the growing preparation of the public mind to give economic forestry its due national importance, and also of a rising disposition to study the choice of trees and methods of using them as aids to public health and comfort, and as means for the decoration of homes and the improvement of scenery.

As to citizens from all parts of the country and to visitors from abroad the Capitol is often the first and a more continuous attraction than any other in Washington, it is not surprising that its small plantations should receive more than their due share of attention relatively to other expositions of sylviculture nearby. It is for this reason desired not only that such information about them as is more commonly wanted may be made readily attainable and that misleading impressions of the purposes they are meant to serve may be guarded against, but that visitors may be advised of

The Advantages Otherwise Offered In Washington For The Study And The Enjoyment Of Trees.

The climate of Washington is subject to great extremes of heat and cold, dampness and dryness, but, for some not clearly established reasons, it seems to admit of an unusual range of vegetation, and allows of the growth in a more or less vigorous or depressed way of numerous woody plants not known far to the northward, and of some not common to the southward, except at considerable elevations. It is hospitable, also, to a larger number of foreign trees than the climate of most other parts of the country.

The Capitol ground is not planted with the least purpose to show what is possible in either respect; the aim in the larger part of it has been to avoid exciting interest through the exhibition of strange qualities in trees, especially of such as might be suggestive of unnatural or forced conditions, or of stratagems of horticulture, nor have the trees to be found in it been given position with a view to conspicuously presenting their individual qualities; rather, for reasons that will be later given, it has been designed to obscure these.

But, as visitors to the Capitol often find trees that happen to be new to them, and about which they wish to be better informed, labels have been placed before a large number, giving names under which inquiries can be made. With these as memoranda, and such other facilities as are supplied by the maps and tables herewith, it is hoped that the Capitol ground may serve to many as an introduction to such better opportunities as are offered in the city, there being few trees within it of which more instructive, because older, examples are not to be seen nearby and better exhibited because planted with the design of exhibition.

The several government plantations in which they may be looked for are unfortunately divided, fragmentary, and, each by itself, incomprehensive and incomplete, thus marking the result of sporadic and unsustained legislative efforts, and even of efforts in some cases a little at cross purposes one with another. Yet, taken together and with the natural growths accidentally available to supplement them, these plantations promise to be of no little value with respect to the long course of patient study upon which the infant science of

American forestry has yet to be brought up. Young as they are, nowhere else in the country can as wide a range of trees be found equally advanced, and this is of the more national value because of the close dependence of the science of forestry upon that of meteorology and the fact that nowhere else in the country are as full, accurate, precise, and scientifically collated local meteorological records accessible as in Washington.

Of the government plantations referred to, that of the National Botanic Garden adjoins the Capitol ground on the west. Its germ was a collection made by the Wilkes Exploring Expedition in 1842, of which but one hardy tree remains alive, an invalid Jujube (*Zizyphus*). The site was and is unsuitable and inadequate for the purpose, and the curator has had and still has to contend with obstacles of many kinds, the deadliest being a lack of intelligent public interest in the scientific objects of a botanic garden, and an excess of interest in its adventitious and recreative incidents.[4]

Among the exposed trees, visitors from the North may be glad to have their attention called to those named below.*

The Botanic Garden is managed directly by Congress through its Library Committees.†

Half a mile westward is another national collection, managed by the Agricultural Bureau of the Department of the Interior. It includes several hundred sorts of hardy trees and shrubs, most of which were planted between 1865 and 1870. The trees cannot yet, of course, begin to exhibit their mature character, but they are well grown for their age and generally of excellent promise, forming the most instructive collection in the country. As the first step toward a national forestry system it must be regretted that the bureau could not have been allowed more space and means. In twenty years, if thrifty, the trees will in many cases be crowding one another. An official list of the trees can be procured. The curator is Mr. William Saunders.[6]

The ground between the botanic and the agricultural collections, originally planned during the administration of the elder President Adams as a public promenade, under the name of "The Mall," but neglected, and its

*The Bull Bay, or great evergreen Magnolia of the South (*Magnolia grandiflora*); the Pecan (*Carya olivæformis*); the Whahoo (*Ulmus alata*); the Black Maple (*Acer saccharum nigrum*), a variety of the sugar maple growing better in the South than the common Northern kind; good sized specimens of the Colchican Maple (*Acer colchicum*), from Armenia; the Pride of China, the common avenue tree of the cotton States (*Melia azedarach*); the Asiatic nettle tree (*Celtis orientalis*); the Cedar of Lebanon (*Cedrus Lebani*); the Cedar of Mount Atlas (*C. Altantica*); the Cedar of the Sierras (*Libocedrus decurrens*); Christ's Thorn (*Zizyphus vulgaris*); European and Japanese Yews (*Taxus baccata stricta*); and *T. adpressa* and *Podocarpus taxifolia*; the Chinese Water Pine (*Glyptostrobus sinensis*); the Soapberry (*Sapindus marginata*); and *Sterculia platanifolia*.

†"A library filled with volumes written by nature, and which those who have learned the language of nature can read and enjoy with a satisfaction as much keener than anything that man-made books can give as it is nearer to the source of all truth,"—L.F. Ward, Bulletin of the National Museum, No. 22.[5]

design gradually lost sight of, is now provisionally divided into two widely different plantations. That nearest the Capitol was laid out and planted between 1872 and 1878 by Orville Babcock, colonel of military engineers.[7] It consists of small sections of mixed forestry, with borders of shrubbery framed within formal lines of standard trees, the different sections separated in one direction by straight streets retained from the earlier design, and in the other by roads of formal curvature with decorative planting near the junctions. The surface is generally low, the soil better than that of other grounds, the trees at present well cared for, and, except a few conifers, the removal of which will be a gain, of promising appearance. They are under the office of the Commissioner of Buildings, attached to the Executive Mansion, at present Colonel A.F. Rockwell, U.S.A.[8]

West of Colonel Babcock's work is what has been called the Smithsonian Park, but though originating in the impulse to which the founding of the Institution of that name gave rise, and contiguous to its building, it has unfortunately never been under the same enlightened management. It should have special and reverent attention, as representing the only essay, strictly speaking, yet made under our government in landscape gardening, for though the aim of the Capitol ground planting is more than decorative, it is necessarily too prim and niggling, and is too much controlled by engineering and architectural considerations to be entitled to that full rank. This of the Smithsonian was the last and the only important public work of Downing, who was not only a master of the art, but distinctly a man of genius, of whom his country should always be proud.[9] It was designed as a composition of natural scenery appropriate to be associated with a national seat of learning, and was regarded by him as the first step in a scheme of planting to be extended in one connected design to the White House and the Potomac. Upon Downing's untimely death, in 1852, the larger design was suspended, gradually lost sight of, and the ground has since been in considerable part laid out under successive acts of Congress by parcels, with a variety of local motives, none of which have as yet been fully realized. As to that actually planted under Downing's instructions, those to whom he gave them were soon dropped off; neglect and ill-usage followed; it is in parts stuffy and crowded, and in others run down and poverty-stricken, but in no other planted ground near Washington is there, or does there promise to be, any tree beauty to compare with what has been already attained in it.

Under its shades government has allowed a modest memorial of the artist to be placed by private subscription. Nowhere will a monument be found commemorating a riper fruit of the republic, more honorable aspirations, or devotion to a higher standard of patriotic duty.[10]

Near the Agricultural ground there is an interesting collection of hardy aquatic plants in the inclosure of the Government Fish Commission, and in adjoining buildings of the Smithsonian Institution and National Museum there are collections of woods and of tree products and of fossil woods and plants.

The public streets of Washington have been planted, mainly between 1870 and 1880, with upwards of fifty thousand (56,000) trees of twenty different sorts. A list showing where rows of each may be observed can be found in the report of the Parking Commission.[11] Though a considerable proportion are of quick-growing kinds, to which most experts object as too straggling in mature habit, too fragile, liable to accident, and short-lived, and though the amount and quality of soil provided is seldom adequate to a long-continued vigorous growth, the work on the whole is the best and most instructive example of town-planting to be seen on the continent. If well followed up in the care of the trees, the result will give Washington a distinction among the capital towns of the world — a distinction original, representative, and historic; natural, racy of the soil, congenial with the climate, in unquestionable good taste, indisputably excellent and admirable; little of which can be claimed of the results of most outlays that have been made by government for the improvement of the city.

The work thus far has been done with even over-strained economy, under the unbroken superintendence of three professional tree-masters, William R. Smith,[12] curator of the Botanic Garden, William Saunders, of the Agricultural Tree Collection, and John Saul,[13] who, under Downing, thirty years ago, planted the Smithsonian Park, of either of whom information may be obtained, and to whom thanks for a service to the nation, as yet too little appreciated, may well be given.

In the woods of natural growth about Washington, many sorts of trees may be found that are not indigenous in the extreme north. Among them there is the Liquid Ambar or Sweet Gum (*L. styraciflua*); the Willow Oak (*Quercus Phellos*); the Laurel Oak (*Quercus imbricaria*); the Persimmon (*Diospyros Virginiana*); the American Holly (*Ilex opaca*); the Black Walnut (*Juglans nigra*); the Swamp Magnolia (*M. glauca*); the Red Birch (*Betula nigra*), (a strikingly rustic beauty of extreme grace, as commonly observed on water banks hereabouts); and the Catalpa (*C. bignonioides*).

The first two may be found in low grounds, often in association with the Tupelo or Sour Gum (*Nyssa multiflora*); the White Ash (*Fraxinus Americana*); the Scarlet Maple (*Acer rubrum*); the Scarlet Oak (*Q. coccinea*); the Sassafras (*S. officinale*), which, rarely seen except as a shrub in the far North, is here a stout and lofty tree, richly furnished, very sportive in its forms of foliage, and often excelling all other deciduous trees in picturesqueness; and the Dogwood (*Cornus florida*), growing with a dense spreading head to a height of thirty feet. These, with other cornels, several of the shrubby sumacs (*Rhus*), the Climbing Sumac (R. toxicodendron), Bitter Sweet (*Celastrus scandens*), and Virginia Creeper (*Ampelopsis quinquefolia*), all being remarkable for their autumnal tints, and each in a different way, form combinations novel and delightful to the northern eye. In a favorable season, near the fall of the leaf, visitors from oversea will nowhere find a more gorgeous sylvan spectacle than is thus presented within a mile of the city, and this without a stroke of intentional aid from any human hand. The effect is often augmented by lower growths than any that have been named, as of huckleberries and brambles, by bright fruits and haws, and by golden and purple blooms of herbaceous plants.

Of trees to which Europeans may like to have their attention directed, in addition to those already named, there are growing wild, and of frequent occurrence, two American Elms; the Black Cherry (*Prunus serotina*), different examples of which vary much, but often a remarkably elegant and graceful tree, near Washington; the American Beech (*Fagus ferruginea*), a neater and more delicate tree than the European; the Tulip (*Liriodendron tulipifera*), growing to great height and in perfection; the Chestnut (*Castanea vesca Americana*), always, when well grown, a noble tree, but when early in June in bloom, the most glorious object of our woods; the Hickories (*Carya*); the Butternut (*Juglans cinerea*); and eighteen (indigenous) sorts of oaks, at the head of which the White Oak (*Q. alba*) is, under favorable conditions, fully as noble a monarch of the forest as its European brother, the Sacred Oak of the Druids (*Q. pedunculata*). Yet, perhaps, for broad landscape values others are of more consequence, and of these some, from their more feminine beauty, reward close observation also. The best scenery about Washington depends for its character chiefly on oaks. The Capitol ground has good examples of several (see list appended), of which the best were grown from acorns upon it or in the adjoining Botanic Garden. The largest, standing alone on the turf northeast of the Washington elm, was transplanted from a distance when eighteen inches in diameter.

A number of shrubs, known only as garden plants in the North, grow wild in profusion about Washington, the most striking and beautiful, both in leaf and flower, being the Virginia Fringe-tree (*Chionanthus Virginicus*). This, with the Silver Bell (*Halesia tetraptera*), and the Virgilia or Yellowwood (*Cladrastis tinctoria*), may often be seen in the form of small trees, the last two attaining a height occasionally of 30 feet or more, with graceful forms, and light and delicate spray and leafage. The Chinquapin or Dwarf Chestnut (*Castanea pumila*), also grows naturally about Washington.

Other small trees and bushes, all more or less planted now in Europe, but which foreigners may like to see in their native wild state, and which are common, are the Shad bush (*Amelanchier Canadensis*), a small tree of great refinement of aspect; the American Witch Hazel (*Hamamelis Canadensis*);[14] several Viburnums and Huckleberries and the Spice bush (*Lindera benzoin*). Wild grapes and Trumpet-creeper (*Bignonia radicans*) are also common, and both often lend a charm to situations that would otherwise be the reverse of attractive.

Such situations are unfortunately common near Washington, because mainly so much of the land has been ravaged of its natural fertility by a reckless agriculture, and because, when once cleared of its primeval vegetation, it does not, as it might further north, become naturally clothed by any form of turf or other close-knitting, surface-rooting growth, and is, in consequence, subject to be kept raw and gullied by the action of frost and rains.

Under these circumstances, whatever charm there might otherwise be in the landscapes is often wholly destroyed by foreground conditions of repulsive rawness and shabbiness. In most parts of Europe, not naturally turfy, such land would be systematically planted with trees. Here, with the relatively high market value of money for various other forms of commercial enterprise, such a use of it has not yet been proved profitable. It may be observed, also, that no plants are here indigenous like heather, gorse, or broom, such as in Europe often give a picturesque and at times exceedingly lovely aspect to sterile situations, otherwise of forbidding character. It is not certain that these plants might not be naturalized (a few plants of broom of several years happy growth may be seen in the Capitol ground). It is highly probable that the native American ally of the broom called Woadwaxen (*Genista tinctoria*), found in a few localities to the northward, if introduced, would serve their purpose. But at present woody vines of various sorts are chiefly of value in this respect, and of this value an admirable illustration may be observed in Mr. Saul's nursery, where a large extent of caving banks on the border of a small stream, occasionally becoming a torrent, have been made within a few years the most agreeable feature of the local scenery, the few plants of Japanese (sub-evergreen) honeysuckle (*Lonicera brachipoda*), originally set, having spread with the greatest profusion, so that in June there are acres of ground over which the air is loaded with the delicious perfume of their bloom. A characteristic exhibition of the same plant may be seen south of the summer-house on the Capitol ground, and near it a variety of plants adapted to dress rough ground unfit for turf. Among the best of these is the Saint John's wort (*Hypericum*), of which several species are native to the region.

The Red Cedar (*Juniperus Virginiana*), near Washington, generally assumes a form so different from that common in many parts of the north that it may pass unrecognized and an effect, distantly recalling one much beloved by Turner and seen in most of his landscapes of southern Europe, sometimes occurs (on the hills north of the reform school on the eastern road to Bladensburg Spa, for example),[15] the horizontal strata of the Italian Stone Pine being represented by the Yellow Pine (*Pinus mitis*), and the fastigiate Cypress by the form referred to of the Red Cedar.

Two short excursions may be recommended to the visitor wishing to cursorily observe the general character of the natural forest. One through the romantic woods of Rock Creek, best made on foot or in the saddle, taking by the way the government property of the Soldiers' Home, which contains many introduced coniferous trees of about thirty years' growth.[16] The other by rowing on the Potomac, above West Washington, where boats for the purpose can be had.[17] This offers a pleasing illustration of closely-wooded American river-side scenery, large in general outline and mass, with considerable picturesqueness of detail under the shadow of moderately well-grown forest trees. It is much resorted to and somewhat misused and damaged by boating and picnic parties. It is hard that in the interest of posterity these two sylvan treasures of the capital, the wooded declivities of the Upper Potomac and the wilds of Rock Creek,[18] cannot in some way be protected against the destructiveness which the hope of the smallest private pecuniary profit is liable at any moment to bring upon them. Samples may be already found of the hateful desert which may be thus quickly substituted.

The scope of the foregoing advice has been limited to trees and woody plants. Those who wish to have a more extended list of what may be looked for, as well as all interested, whether as botanists or as lovers of nature in local, annual, perennial plants, will find the best of aid in a government publication prepared by Mr. Lester F. Ward, of the Smithsonian Institution (Guide to the Flora of Washington—Bulletin No. 22, of the National Museum).[19]

Of the banks of the Potomac above referred to, Mr. Ward says: "The beauty of their natural flower-gardens in the months of April and May is unequaled in my experience." Elsewhere he states that fifty several sorts of plants may usually be found in flower before the 1st of April (p. 31), that is to say, before, in the latitude of Albany, the ground may be unlocked from ice.

Historical Notes Of The Capitol Ground.

The intelligent visitor, reflecting that it is nearly ninety years since the site of the Capitol was determined, and more than eighty since Congress first held its sessions upon it, will need some explanation of its present sylvan juvenility.

Since building work first began upon it several efforts for the improvement of the ground have been made before the present, but no plan for the purpose has long been adhered to, and little of the work done has been adapted to secure lastingly satisfactory results. There is, mainly in consequence of a wavering policy and make-shift temporizing operations, but one tree on the ground that yet approaches a condition of tree majesty, and beside it probably not one of fifty years' growth from the seed—not a dozen of ten years' healthy, thrifty, and unmutilated growth. It may be added that many hundred trees are known to have been planted in the streets of the city early in the century, of which not one remains alive, nor is it probable that one was ever allowed a full development of its proper beauty. Yet, to show what easily might have been, if due judgment and painstaking had been used, it is enough that one planted tree of even an earlier date may be pointed to, which is yet in the full vigor of its growth. (The "Washington elm" on the Capital ground, originally a street side tree.)

The following notes, chiefly upon the past misfortunes of the nation in its Capitol ground, have been largely based on conversations with the late venerable Dr. J. B. Blake, sometime Commissioner of Public Grounds.[20]

When government, near the close of the last century, took possession of the site of the Capitol, it was a sterile place, partly overgrown with "scrub oak." The soil was described (by Oliver Wolcott) as an "*exceedingly stiff* clay, becoming dust in dry and mortar in rainy weather."[21] For a number of years the ground about the Capitol was treated as a common, roads crossing it in all directions, and a map of the period indicates an intention to treat it permanently as an open public place. The year before his death, Washington built the brick house, still standing prominently, but injured by recent additions, a little to the north of the Capitol.[22] A picture showing this house, with a young plantation of trees (none now living) between it and the Capitol, together with an autograph letter about it from Washington to his business agent, may be seen in the Lower division[23] of the National Library. The first local improvement ordered by Congress, after occupying the rooms partially prepared for it in the incomplete Capitol, was a *walk* to be made between these and Georgetown (West Washington), where, there being yet no comfortable houses nearer, most of the members lodged.[24] The Capitol and the house of Washington had both been built upon the assumption that the future city, which Washington avoided calling by his own name, continuing to use the original designation of the "Federal City," would arise on the higher ground to the eastward. Both buildings were expected to stand as far as practicable in its outskirts, backing upon the turbid creek with swampy borders which then flowed along the base of Capitol Hill.[25] When this stream was in freshet it was not fordable, and members of Congress were often compelled to hitch their riding horses on the further side and cross it, first, on fallen trees, afterwards on a foot-bridge. There was an alder swamp where the Botanic Garden is now, which spread also far along the site of Pennsylvania avenue. Tall woods on its border shut off the views of the ground south and west of it. This wood, said to contain many noble trees, mostly oaks, was felled for fire-wood, by permission of Congress, as a measure of economy, sometime after the war of 1812.

These circumstances may give a little clue to the habit at the outset adopted, and of which Congress has since never been wholly disembarrassed, of regarding the ground immediately to the west of the Capitol as its "back yard," and all in connection with it as comparatively ignoble. With the city on the west, the transformation of the creek and swamp, and the opening of the magnificent view on that side, it is incomparably the nobler front.

It is a tradition, and is probable, that Washington, while building his brick house, planted some trees on the east side of the Capitol, of which the elm above referred to was one, and is the only one remaining.[26] Another of equal age, but rotting prematurely, probably from unskillful or neglected pruning, was blown down a few years ago, and a third was removed in consequence of the enlargement of the Capitol. The last was a tree of graceful habit, and Mr. Smith, of the Botanic Garden, has distributed, through members of Congress, many rooted cuttings of it to different parts of the country. The surviving tree, having a girth of but ten feet at four feet from the ground, has been of slow growth, and been badly wounded within twenty years, three cavities showing the removal of considerable limbs by barbarous excision. On the east side a strip of bark, the entire length of the trunk, has been torn off. The ground, at a little distance on three sides, having been trenched and enriched, and that nearer the trunk forked over and top-dressed, the tree has, within three years, gained greatly in health and vigor; its wounds are closing over, and it may yet outlive several generations of men.

Some years after the death of Washington a space of ground nearly half as large as the present ground was inclosed in connection with the Capitol, and a street laid out around it. The Washington elm stands near where this bounding street intersected another which formed the northern approach to the Capitol, and on the opposite side, to the north, an inn of some celebrity, long known as the "Yellow Tavern," was built.[27] This was the dining place for members still lodging at a distance.

Whatever improvement had been made upon the original ground before the burning of the Capitol in 1814 was probably then, or during the subsequent building operations, wholly laid waste, the three or four trees first planted alone escaping.

In 1825 another plan for laying out the grounds was devised, which was sustained in the main for nearly fifteen years, during most of which period John Foy had charge, and, as far as he was allowed, pursued the ends had in view in its adoption consistently.[28] It was that of an enlarged form of the ordinary village-door yards of the time, flat, rectangular "grass plats," bordered by rows of trees, flower- beds, and gravel walks, with a belt of close planting on the outside of all. So long as the trees were saplings and the turf and flowers could be kept nicely, it was pretty and becoming. But as the trees grew they robbed and dried out the flower-beds, leaving hardly anything to flourish in them but violets and periwinkle. Weeds came in, and the grass, becoming sparse and uneven, was much tracked across, and grew forlorn and untidy; appropriations were irregular and insufficient to restore it or supply proper nourishment. Foy was superseded for political reasons, and his successor had other gardening ambitions to gratify.

At this time, though even some years later, George Combe described the city as "a straggling village, reared in a drained swamp;"[29] it had become clear that it was not to grow up on the east front of the Capitol. John Quincy Adams, on retiring from the Presidency, had, like Washington, determined to build a town house for himself in Washington, and had chosen to do so far to the west.[30] Much other private building had followed, including one large and excellent hotel, and government had undertaken several important public buildings in the same quarter.

It was then determined to make an addition (about seven acres), and considerable improvement of the premises in the "rear" of the Capitol, and this improvement led on, without any special act of Congress, to a gradual change of motive in the management of the old ground on the east, under the management of James Maher,[31] who is described by his friends as a jovial and witty Irishman, owing his appointment to the personal friendship of General Jackson.*

The soil at the foot of the hill was much better than that of the east ground; but the trees planted by Maher were chiefly silver poplars and silver maples, brittle and short-lived. After doing more or less injury to the more valuable sorts, they have all now disappeared, but there remain of the planting of this period several fine occidental planes, scarlet maples, horse-chestnuts, a pecan, and a holly.

South of the "Washington elm," adjoining the east court of the Capitol, there are a dozen long-stemmed trees, relics of two circular plantations introduced in the midst of Foy's largest "grass plats," by Maher, for "barbecue groves," one probably intended for Democratic the other for Whig jollifications. These were also largely of quick-growing trees, closely planted, poorly fed, and never properly thinned or pruned. Forty years after their planting the larger number of those remaining alive were found feeble, top heavy, and ill grown.

Foy had planted in his outer belts some garden-like trees, very suitable to his purpose, magnolias, tree-boxes, hollies, and also some conifers, mostly thuyas, it is believed, but among them there was at least one Cedar of Lebanon. With them, however, or subsequently, more rapid growing deciduous trees unfortunately were also planted, and through neglect of thinning, the effect of drip and exhaustion of the soil the choicer sorts were nearly all smothered, starved, or sickened. A few crippled hollies (*Ilex opaca*) only remain. The violets and periwinkle (*Vinca*) now on the ground are largely of direct descent from those planted by Foy.

Most other trees within the limits of the Capitol inclosure before the enlargement of the Capitol in 1857 were removed to make way for the new building operations, or in consequence of the changes required in the grade of the ground to adapt it to the new work, or, later, to the grading done by the District government of the adjoining streets. It was found that the roots of most of the old trees, after having grown out of the small pits in which they were planted, had been unable to penetrate the clay around them, but had pushed upward and outward, spreading upon its surface and within a thin stratum of looser and darker material, consisting, it is believed, almost entirely of street sweepings which had at different times been laid on as a top-dressing. Though none were half-grown, nearly all had the characteristics of old age, many were rotten at the butt, and few were wholly sound. The more thrifty and manage-

*The following story is repeated from the best authority: The President once sent for Maher and said: "I am your friend, Jimmy, but I have often warned you, and this time I must turn you out." "Why, what's the matter now, General?" "I am told that you had a bad drunk again yesterday." "Why, now, General, if every bad story that's told against yourself was to be believed, would it be you that would be putting me in and putting me out?" He remained with another warning.

able of them were retransplanted in 1875, and under more favorable conditions, presently to be stated, the larger part of them now appear rejuvenated. When moved they were generally from 8 to 15 inches in diameter of trunk.

Except under the "barbecue trees" the entire ground east of the Capitol, and all that newly planted in the west, has been regraded. Near the eastern boundary the old surface was eight feet higher than at present; the Capitol standing at the foot of a long slope. The revised grade having been attained, the ground was thoroughly drained with collared, cylindrical tile, and trench-plowed and subsoiled to a depth of two feet or more from the present surface. (In the outer parts where evergreen thickets under scattered deciduous trees were to be attempted, fully three feet, and here the liming was omitted.) It was then ridged up and exposed to a winter's frost, dressed with oyster-shell lime, and with swamp muck previously treated with salt and lime, then plowed, harrowed, and rolled and plowed again. The old surface soil was laid upon this improved subsoil with a sufficient addition of the same poor soil drawn from without the ground to make the stratum one foot (loose) in depth. With this well pulverized, a compost of stable manure and prepared swamp muck was mixed. It is still found to have too much of the quality ascribed to the original by Wolcott, quickly drying very hard. It would seem, however, to be wholesome and sufficiently friable for the growth of the trees planted; the death of all the few that have failed being reasonably attributed to gas leaks, severe wounds, or to extraordinary cold, or to a severe attack of vermin before their recovery from the shock of removal. It is hoped that the more northern trees have been induced to root so deeply as to suffer less than they usually do in Washington during periods of extreme heat and drought, and that, in view of the thorough preparation and large outlay for the purpose, the methods of administration will hereafter be more continuously favorable than they had been for the longevity of the trees and their attaining the proper full stature of their families.

The Present Design.

Questions why, in the present scheme, certain trees and plants have been taken for the Capitol ground and others neglected, and why certain dispositions of trees have been made and others, offering obvious advantages in some respects, avoided, may be best answered in a general way by a relation of the leading motives of the design, some of which it is evident do not spontaneously occur to many inquirers.

The ground is in design part of the Capitol, but in all respects subsidiary to the central structure. The primary motives of its design are, therefore, that, first, of convenience of business of and with Congress and the Supreme Court, and, second, that of supporting and presenting to advantage a great national monument.

The problem of convenience to be met in the plan of the ground lay in the requirement to supply ready access to the different entrances to the building from the twenty-one streets by which the boundary of the ground was to be reached from the city. The number of foot and of carriage entrances is forty-six, and, as the entire space to be crossed between these and the open court and the terrace, upon which doors of the Capitol open, is but forty-six acres in extent, it had to be cut up so much as to put ordinary landscape gardening ideals of breadth and repose of surface, applicable to a park or private residence grounds, to a great degree out of the question. The difficulty was complicated by the hillside position of the building, compelling circuitous courses to be taken as a means of avoiding oversteep grades in the carriage approaches from the west.*

That the Capitol, in its several more admirable aspects, might be happily presented to view, it was necessary that the plantations should be so disposed as to leave numerous clear spaces between the central and the outer parts of the ground, and desirable that the openings or vistas should be disturbed as little as practicable by roads or other constructions. At the same time, the summer climate of Washington and the glaring whiteness of the great central mass made a general umbrageousness of character desirable in the ground, and a bare, bald, unfurnished quality to be, as much as possible, guarded against. It was then to be considered that customs are established that bring at intervals great processions and ceremonious assemblies into the ground, and that attending these, vast bodies of people, without order or discipline, surge through it in a manner that overrules all ordinary guardianship, and that, with increasing population and increasing means of communication, such throngs are likely to grow larger and more sweeping. This difficulty was increased by the long-established habit of regarding the Capitol ground as a common to be crossed or occupied in any part as suited individual convenience.

These considerations not only called for multiplied routes of passage, but for a degree of amplitude in pavements and flagging unfortunate with reference to the desired general effect of umbrageousness and verdancy. They also compelled a resort to many expedients for inoffensively restraining the movements of visitors in certain directions and leading them easily in others.

If these several more or less conflicting requirements are weighed, it will be seen that no attempt to reconcile them or compromise between them could be made that did not involve a disjointedness in the plantations unfavorable to the general aspect of dignity and composure desirable to be associated

*Some may ask whether, under these circumstances, a strictly architectural design would not have had advantages. It is enough to say that, for several reasons, no such plan, if understood, would have been acceptable to Congress or the public taste of the period. It would, therefore, have soon been ruined in the treatment of details. Public taste strangely admits topiary work to be mixed up with natural forms of vegetation, and applauds a profusion of artificial features in what passes for natural gardening. Nevertheless, it condemns, even in situations where they would be most pardonable, the grander and more essential aims of ancient gardening.

with so stately a building. Hence, where it remained permissible to plant trees at all, to have selected and arranged them with a view to exhibit marked individual qualities, would, as tending to increase such disjointedness, have been an unwise policy. The better motive was to select and place trees with a view to their growing together in groups in which their individual qualities would gradually merge harmoniously; to avoid a distinct definition of these groups, to aim to draw them into broader compositions, and to secure as much effect of depth and distance as possible by obscuring minor objects, especially in the outer part of the ground.

In the undergrowth, however, a degree of variety, cheerfulness, and vivacity, to be gained by moderate contrasts of form and color, might be studied. Hence not only the amount but the range of shrubbery used has been considerable, so much so that it must be admitted that at present it holds attention too much. As beyond a certain point the landscape effect of trees increases with age many times faster than that of bushes, the general effect will soon be much quieter. The chief reason for what would otherwise be an excessive proportion of shrubs and low growth is the necessity of mitigating the effect of the large extent of dead ground in the roads, walks, and adjoining streets, otherwise to be looked down upon from the Capitol and to be conspicuous in views across the ground.

Two minor motives influencing the choice and disposition of the undergrowth may be noted.

The summer climate of Washington being unfavorable to turf in situations where, owing to the number of trees growing in them, or for other reasons, the care of the turf would be difficult, the aim has been to cover the ground with foliage of creepers and of low perennials likely to retain greenness during droughts and requiring little labor to keep tidy. These low plantings also serve the purpose of connecting and merging the higher foliage with the verdure of the lawns and of increasing apparent perspective distance.

The shrubbery has been selected from regard to its fitness in foliage qualities, form, and size, when grown, to serve general purposes in the several localities in which it is placed. Its blooming qualities have been regarded as of subordinate consequence, but simple and natural bloom has been generally preferred to the more large, striking, and showy quality of flowers resulting from the art of the florist, the design being always not to make a lounging place or hold attention to details.

No spruces or other large-growing coniferous trees have been included in the recent planting, because if placed in the central parts they would obstruct views of the building; if placed on the outer parts they would disturb the general quiet and unobtrusive foliage effects desired, and lessen the apparent depth of the local sylvan scene. A few clusters of junipers, yews, and thuyas (*Chamœcyparis*), of established hardiness, will be found at points where they cannot interrupt views toward the Capitol, and where they will be obscured and overlooked in views from it.

The number of broad-leafed (laurel-like) evergreens that can be trusted to flourish in the climate of Washington is unfortunately limited. The fact that the ground is more visited in winter than in summer makes this the more regrettable. For this reason a considerable number of sorts have been introduced, the permanent success of which is not thought fully assured. All such are of low growth in this climate, and should they fail to meet expectations may be withdrawn without permanent injury to the designed summer landscape character. Should they flourish, it is hoped that others will be thinned out and the evergreens grow into moderate masses.*

The Capitol ground is declared by act of Congress to be formed "to serve the quiet and dignity of the Capitol and to prevent the occurrence near it of such disturbances as are incident to the ordinary use of public streets and places."[32] Incidentally to this purpose, however, it is much used as a public park, especially during the hot season or when Congress is not in session. The need to provide seats in which people could rest for a moment in passing up the Capitol hill from Pennsylvania avenue, which is the point of entrance for most, and the need of a place in which children could obtain water being apparent, and as the necessary extent of accommodation in these respects would otherwise cause an unseemly obstruction of the walks or become too conspicuous a feature of the scenery, a summer-house was designed, with a view to the following advantages: It is entered by a few steps from three different lines of walk; it contains separate seats for twenty-five people, protected under all circumstances from ordinary summer showers; it allows six children to take water from the fountain at once; it is very airy, the softest breeze passing freely through it. The seats are so disposed as, though shadowed, to be well lighted, and to be each under constant inspection of the passing watchmen and the public through an opposite archway. The house is closed at nightfall and in winter. These precautions have enabled ladies to use it in large numbers, free from the annoyances which often deter them from entering sheltered resting places in parks. Standing on sloping ground, the floor is kept at the lower level and the walls and roof of brick and tile as low as practicable, so that at a short distance the eye ranges over them. That they may be more inconspicuous, the walls are banked about with natural rock, and slopes of specially-prepared soils favorable to the growth of various creepers and rock plants, by which, except to one standing opposite to the entrance arches and turning to observe them, the entire structure will be wholly lost to view. From within the walls there opens on the up-hill side a

*The Evergreen Thorn (*Cratægus pyracanthas*), the Oregon Grape (*Berberis aquifolium*), the Coton-easter (*C. microphilla*), the Chinese evergreen Azalea (*A. amœna*), and an English hot-house shrub (*Abelia rupestris*), have each passed through without injury several severe summers and winters, and promise to be of the highest value for the landscape purposes for which they have been tentatively used. The three first are already to be seen in profusion and in vigorous health.

cool dark runnel of water, supplied from the overflow of the fountain at the west entrance to the Capitol. The spray of this rapid rivulet, with that from the waste water of the drinking-fountain, maintains a moisture of the air favorable to the growth of ferns and mosses upon the inner rock-work. What is chiefly hoped for, however, is that under the conditions provided, a growth of ivy may have been secured, gradually reproducing the characteristic exquisite beauty of this evergreen in its native haunts. Many good examples of it, though not of its best estate, may be seen about Washington. The visitor interested is particularly advised to see those in the cemetery at West Washington (Georgetown).[33]

The trees about the summer-house, though hardy and suited to the circumstances, will all have a somewhat quaint or exotic aspect. They include the Willow oak, the Cedrella, the Oleaster, two sorts of Aralias, and the Golden Catalpa.

The vistas or general lines of view to which all the planting and all the structures upon the ground have been fitted may be more fully stated.

Disregarding shrubbery, to be kept below the plane of sight toward the Capitol, openings are maintained, through which direct front views of the central portico and the dome will be had from the outer parts of the ground, upon opposite sides, and diagonal perspective views of the entire facades from four directions. In six other directions from the center of the structure only low-headed trees are planted, so that in each case the Capitol may be seen rising above banks of foliage from points several miles distant.

It is unnecessary to say that by the same disposition of the plantations, views outwardly from the Capitol are kept open, but attention may be called to the beauty and breadth, almost approaching grandeur, of the prospect up and down and across the valley of the Potomac, and to the design that when the present young plantations are full-grown this great advantage of the Capitol shall not be lost. The introduction of the proposed architectural terrace will indeed admit no trees to stand so near, or on ground so elevated, that they will ever obstruct the present distant view from the main or even the ground floor. The plantations in this direction, however, will in time obscure the nearer part of the city and form a continuous strong, consistent foreground to the further sylvan slopes.

From the terrace these plantations will in some degree limit the views to the northward and southward, but through the removal of the old central avenue and the broad gap left between the trees on the west an outlook is obtained between the northern and the southern divisions of the city in which a slope of unbroken turf, seen over a strongly-defined and darkly-shadowed architectural base, will be the foreground; a wooded plain, extending a mile beyond the foot of the slope, the middle distance, and the partly-overgrown, partly-cultivated hills beyond the depression of the Potomac, the background; the latter so far removed that in summer conditions of light and atmosphere it is often blue, misty, and etherial. Because, perhaps, of the influence of the cool waters of the river passing between the dry hills from north to south across this field of vision, sunset effects are often to be enjoyed from the west face of the Capitol of a rare loveliness.

LIST OF TREES AND SHRUBS IN THE UNITED STATES CAPITOL GROUNDS.

	Habitat
Abelia rupestris	China.
Acer campestre. English field maple	Europe.
Acer dasycarpum. Silver maple	Atlantic States.
Acer laetum	Caucasus.
Acer palmatum	Japan.
atropurpureum	Japan.
versicolor	Japan.
laciniata variegata	Japan.
rosea marginata	Japan.
reticulatum	Japan.
micranthum	Japan.
polycristata	Japan.
Æsculus glabra. Ohio Buckeye	Western States.
Æsculus hippocastanum. Horse-chestnut	Persia.
Aralia chinensis	Eastern Asia.
spinosa. Hercules' club	Atlantic States.
Amorpha fruticosa. False indigo	Atlantic States.
Aucuba Japonica	Japan.
Azalea amœna	China.
mollis	Japan
nudiflora	Atlantic States.
Benzoin odoriferum. Spicebush	Atlantic States.
Berberis aquifolium. Oregon grape	North Pacific States.
Fortunei	China
Japonica. Japan mahonia	Japan.
Thunbergii	Japan.
vulgaris. Barberry	Europe.
vulgaris atropurpurea. Purple barberry	Hort.
Betula alba. White birch	North Europe.
lenta. Black birch	Atlantic States.
Buxus Japonica	Japan.
sempervirens, var. Tree box	Europe.
Round-leaved box	Hort.

Golden variegated box. . . Hort.
Narrow-leaved box . . . . . . Hort.
Callicarpa Americana . . . . South Atlantic States.
Calycanthus floridus. Sweet-scented shrub . . . . South Atlantic States.
Caragana arborescens. Siberian pea . . . . Siberia.
Carpinus Caroliniana. Water beech . . . . Atlantic States.
Duinensis . . . . Caucasus.
Carya olivæformis. Pecan nut . . . . Western States.
Castanea pumila. Chinquapin . . . . Southern States.
vesca. Sweet chestnut . . . . Europe.
Catalpa bignonoides . . . . South Atlantic States.
Catalpa bignonoides aurea. Golden catalpa . . . . Hort.
Bungei, va. nana. Dwarf catalpa . . . . Hort.
Cedrella sinensis . . . . Northern China.
Celastrus scandens. Bittersweet . . . . Atlantic States.
Cercis Canadensis. Redbud . . . . Atlantic States.
chinensis . . . . Eastern Asia.
Chamæcyparis obtusa. (Retinospora) . . . . Japan.
nana. (Retinospora) . . . . Japan.
plumosa. (Retinospora) . . . . Japan.
squarrosa. (Retinospora) . . . . Japan.
pisifera. (Retinospora) . . . . Japan.
aurea. (Retinospora) . . . . Japan.
Chionanthus Virginica. Fringe tree. . . . . South Atlantic States.
Cladrastris tinctoria. Yellowwood . . . . Kentucky and Tennessee.
Clerodendron trichotomum . . . . Japan.
Clethra alnifolia. White alder . . . . Atlantic States.
Colutea arborescens. Bladder senna . . . . Europe.
Cornus florida. Flowering dogwood . . . . Atlantic States.
Mas. Cornel . . . . Europe.
variegata . . . . Hort.
paniculata . . . . North Atlantic States.
stolonifera. Red osier . . . . Atlantic States.
stricta. Stiff cornel . . . . Southern States.
Corylus Americanus. American hazel . . . . Atlantic States.
tupulosa atropurpurea. Purple hazel . . . . . . Europe.
Cotoneaster acuminata Simonsii . . . . Himalayas.
microphylla . . . . Siberia.
Cratægus Crus-galli, var. New Castle thorn . . . . Atlantic States.
oxyacantha. Hawthorn . . . . Europe.
var. Hawthorn . . . . Europe.
Daphne cneoreum . . . . Europe.
Deutzia gracilis . . . . Japan.
scabra . . . . Japan

flore pleno. . . . . .Hort.
purpurea . . . . .Hort.
Diervilla hortensis . . . . .Japan.
alba . . . . .Hort.
nivea . . . . .Hort.
grandiflora variegata . . . . .Hort.
rosea . . . . .China.
amabilis . . . . .Hort.
foliis variegata. . . . . .Hort.
grandiflora, var. Van Houttei . . . . .Hort.
Diospyros Virginiana. Persimmon. . . . . .Atlantic States.
Elaeagnus hortensis . . . . .Southern Europe.
Erica carnea. . . . . .Europe.
polifolia. . . . . .Europe.
Euonymus Americanus. Strawberry bush . . . . .Atlantic States.
atropurpureus. Burning bush. . . . . .Atlantic States.
Japonicus . . . . .Japan.
variegata . . . . .Hort.
radicans . . . . .Japan.
Fagus ferruginea. American beech . . . . .Atlantic States.
sylvatica. European beech . . . . .Europe.
purpurea. Purple beech . . . . .Europe.
incisa. Cut-leaved beech. . . . . .Europe.
Forsythia Fortunei . . . . .China.
suspensa . . . . .China.
viridissima. . . . . .China.
Fraxinus Americana. White ash. . . . . .Atlantic States.
excelsior. European ash . . . . .Europe.
Gymnocladus Canadensis. Kentucky coffee-tree . . .Western States.
Halesia tetraptera. Silver bell. . . . . .South Atlantic States.
Hedera Helix Hibernica. Irish ivy . . . . .Europe.
Hibiscus Syriacus. Althea. . . . . .Syria.
Hippophæ rhamnoides. Sea buckthorn. . . . . .Europe.
Hydrangea hortensea . . . . .Japan.
paniculata grandiflora . . . . .Japan.
Hypericum prolificum. St. John's wort . . . . .Atlantic States.
Idesia polycarpa . . . . .Japan.
Ilex aquifolium. English holly . . . . .Europe.
angustifolium . . . . .Hort.
ferox. Hedgehog holly . . . . .Hort.
argentea . . . . .Hort.
aurea . . . . .Hort.
opaca. American holly . . . . .Atlantic States.
Jasminum nudiflorum. Yellow jessamine . . . . .China.

Juniperus recurva squamata. . . . . .Nepal.
sabina. Juniper . . . . .Northern Hemisphere.
nana. Prostrate juniper . . . . .Northern States.
tamariscifolia . . . . .Europe.
Koelreuteria paniculata . . . . .China.
Laburnum vulgare. Golden chain. . . . . .Europe.
Lagerstræmia Indica rubra. Crape myrtle . . . . .India.
Ligustrum ovalifolium . . . . .Japan.
vulgare. Privet. . . . . .Europe.
Liquidambar styraciflua. Sweet gum . . . . .Atlantic States.
Liriodendron tulipifera. Tulip tree . . . . .Atlantic States.
Lonicera brachypoda. Honeysuckle . . . . .Japan.
aurea reticulata. . . . . .Japan.
fragrantissima. Bush honeysuckle . . . . .China.
Tartarica. Tartarian honeysuckle . . . . .Siberia.
Maclura aurantiaca. Osage-orange . . . . .Arkansas.
Magnolia acuminata. Cucumber tree. . . . . .Atlantic States.
conspicua. Yulan .China.
cordata. Yellow cucumber tree . . . . .South Atlantic States.
glauca. Sweet bay .Atlantic States.
grandiflora. Bull bay. . . . . .South Atlantic States.
tripelata. Umbrella tree . . . . .South Atlantic States.
purpurea. Purple magnolia . . . . .Japan.
Morus alba. White mulberry . . . . .Europe.
rubra. Red mulberry. . . . . .Atlantic States.
Neillia opulifolia . . . . .Atlantic States.
aurea . . . . .Hort.
Nyssa sylvatica. Sour gum . . . . .Atlantic States.
Ostrya Virginica. Hop-hornbeam . . . . .Atlantic States.
Paulownia imperialis . . . . .Japan.
Phellodendron Amurense .Manchuria.
Philadelphus coronarius. Mock-orange. . . . . .China.
grandiflora. Syringa . . . . .South Atlantic States.
inodorus . . . . .South Atlantic States.
Pirus coronaria. . . . . .South Atlantic States.
Japonica. Japan quince. . . . . .Japan.
Planera aquatica. Water elm . . . . .South Atlantic States.
Platanus occidentalis. Sycamore . . . . .Atlantic States.
orientalis. Oriental plane. . . . . .Western Europe.
Podocarpus taxifolia. Japan Yew . . . . .Japan.
Populus angustifolia. Willow-leaved poplar . . . . . . .Rocky Mountains.
Prunus Japonica. . . . . .Japan.
flore pleno. . . . . .Japan.
Sinensis. Sand pear . . . . .China.

Padus. Bird cherry .Europe.
serotina. Rum cherry . . . . .Atlantic States.
spinosa. Sloe. . . . . .Europe.
triloba . . . . .China.
Quercus alba. White oak . . . . .Atlantic States.
cerris. Turkey oak . . . . .Europe.
imbricaria. Shingle oak . . . . .Europe.
macrocarpa. Bur oak . . . . .Atlantic States.
palustris. Pin oak . . . . .Atlantic States.
phellos. Willow oak . . . . .South Atlantic States.
Prinus. Chestnut oak . . . . .Atlantic States.
prinoides. Chinquapin oak . . . . .Atlantic States.
Robur. English oak. . . . . .Europe.
concordia . . . . .Hort.
nigricans .Hort.
pedunculata . . . . .Europe.
Rhamnus Caroliniana . . . . .South Atlantic States.
catharticus. Buckthorn. . . . . .Europe.
Rhus Cotinus. Smokebush . . . . .Southern Europe.
glabra laciniata. Cut-leaved sumac . . . . . . .Pennsylvania.
Rubus leucodermis . . . . .Japan.
Rosa rubiginosa. Sweet brier . . . . .Europe.
rugosa . . . . .Japan.
Salisburia biloba. Gingko . . . . .China.
Sambucus Canadensis variegata. Variegated elder. . .Atlantic States.
Sassafras officinale . . . . .Atlantic States.
Shepherdia argentea. Buffaloberry . . . . .Western North America.
Sophora Japonica. . . . . .Japan.
Spirea Cantoniensis. . . . . .China.
chamædrifolia . . . . .Siberia.
Japonica alba . . . . .Japan.
rubra . . . . .Japan.
Lindleyana . . . . .Himalayas.
Douglassii var. . . . . .California.
prunifolia . . . . .Japan.
Thunbergii . . . . .Japan.
Staphylea trifolia. Bladder-nut. . . . . .Atlantic States.
Styrax Japonicum. . . . . .Japan.
officinale. . . . . .Europe.
Symphoricarpus racemosus. Snowberry . . . . .North America.
vulgaris. Indian current . . . . .Northern States.
Syringa Josikœa . . . . .Central Europe.
Persica. Persian lilac . . . . .Western Asia.

"GENERAL PLAN FOR THE IMPROVEMENT OF THE U. S. CAPITOL GROUNDS," DRAWN BY THOMAS WISEDELL DURING THE FALL OF 1874 AND PRESENTED TO CONGRESS IN EARLY 1875.

vulgaris. Lilac . . . . .Europe.
alba. White lilac . . . . .Europe.
Tamarix Africana. Tamarisk. . . . . .Southern Europe.
Taxus adpressa . . . . .Japan.
baccata. Yew . . . . .Europe.
aurea. Golden yew . . . . .Hort.
Tilia Americana. Basswood .Atlantic States.
Europæa. Linden . . . . .Europe.
heterophylla. White basswood . . . . .Atlantic States.
Ulmus Americana. American elm. . . . . .Atlantic States.
alata. Whahoo . . . . .Southern States.
campestris. English elm. . . . . .Europe.
fastigiata. Fastigiate elm . . . . .Hort.
microphylla. . . . . .Hort.
pendula. Weeping elm . . . . .Hort.
purpurea. Purple elm . . . . .Hort.
var. Huntingdon elm . . . . .Hort.
montana. Dutch elm . . . . .Europe.
Viburnum opulus. Guelder rose . . . . .Europe.
plicatum . . . . .Japan.
prunifolium . . . . .Atlantic States.
Zizyphus vulgaris. Christ's thorn . . . . .Southern Europe.

The text presented here is from the *Annual Report of the Architect of the United States Capitol for the Fiscal Year Ending June 30, 1882*, published in the fall of 1882. Edward Clark submitted the report and included this contribution from Olmsted.

In the spring of 1873 Olmsted was asked by Republican Vermont Senator Justin Smith Morrill (1810–1898) to consider improvements to the grounds around the Capitol in Washington, D.C. As a leading member of the Senate Committee on Public Buildings and Grounds between 1870 and 1898, Morrill was an advocate for public landscape improvements to the city. He introduced the 1872 legislation that expanded the Capitol grounds to their current dimensions and helped secure appropriations for the project. In 1873 the Architect of the Capitol, Edward Clark, recommended that Congress employ the services of a landscape architect to design the Capitol grounds. Clark and Morrill were Olmsted's closest allies in Washington and helped to assure that by the time Olmsted wrote this report, much of the landscape was complete as he had planned it. The proposed marble terraces and stairs conceived to replace the smaller earthen berms on the building's west side, however, had yet to be funded. In 1882 Olmsted drew up an illustrative pamphlet that described the proposed new terraces and distributed it to members of Congress. In September 1882 he submitted the text presented here to Clark (*Papers of FLO*, 7: 14–16; FLO to Justin Smith Morrill, Jan. 22, 1874 [*Papers of FLO*, 7: 36–43]; FLO to Edward Clark, Feb. 17, 1882; FLO to Edward Clark, Oct. 1, 1882, AOC; Glenn Brown, *History of the United States Capitol*, vol. 2 [Washington, D.C., 1900–1902], pp. 143–45; see also Frederick Law Olmsted, "Annual Report of the Architect of the United States Capitol," July 1883, below; FLO to Edward Clark, Feb. 15, 1886, below).

1. The Chairman of the Senate Committee on Public Buildings and Grounds in Congress in 1882 was Senator Edward H. Rollins from New Hampshire. The second ranking member, Justin S. Morrill, served as Chair of the Committee from 1870 to 1878, and later remained a strong supporter of legislation funding Capitol grounds improvements. The other Senate members were Angus Cameron of Wisconsin, Charles W. Jones of Florida, and George G. Vest of Missouri (David T. Canon, Garrison Nelson, and Charles Stewart III, *Committees in the U.S. Congress: 1789–1946* [Washington, D.C., 2002], pp. 266, 816).
2. In 1878 Congress appointed a committee to study the potential for switching from gas to electric lighting for the building and grounds of the Capitol. In 1882 the only lights that had been installed on the grounds were those on the piers at the Pennsylvania Avenue entrance. Over the next two decades electric lamps were installed throughout the grounds, and the last gas lamps were replaced in 1897 (G. Brown, *History of the United States Capitol*, 2, pp. 145, 159–60).
3. At this point in the published text, Clark inserts his reports on other federal construction projects under his supervision, followed by an account of his office's total expenditures for the fiscal year. Olmsted's text then resumes as an appendix to the report.
4. In 1820 Congress granted the Columbian Institute for the Promotion of Arts and Sciences five acres of land to establish a botanic garden. The site was adjacent to the Capitol grounds at the eastern end of the Mall. In 1837 the underfunded effort was abandoned, but in 1850 Congress appropriated funds for a second botanic garden at the same location to display the plant specimens collected from around the world by the 1838–1842 Wilkes Expedition. This larger garden, named the United States Botanic Garden in 1856, covered ten acres from First to Third streets between Pennsylvania and Maryland avenues (Karen D. Solit, *History of the United States Botanic Garden, 1816–1991* [Washington, D.C., 1993], pp. 5–6, 31–32).
5. Lester Frank Ward (1841–1913) was a scientist with expertise in several areas. He began working for the Geologic Survey in 1881 as Chief of the Division of Fossil Plants. The author of *Dynamic Sociology* (1883), Ward was also an important figure in the development of modern social science (*ANB*).
6. William Saunders (1822–1900) emigrated in 1848 from Scotland, where he had been trained in horticulture and landscape gardening. In the United States his professional practice included estate, park, and cemetery designs in New Haven, Baltimore, Philadelphia, and elsewhere. Many of these projects were completed in the 1850s during his partnership with horticulturalist Thomas Meehan. In 1862 he was appointed superintendent of the Department of Agriculture's new experimental gardens in Washington, D.C., and in 1863 he designed the Soldiers National Cemetery at the Gettysburg battlefield. In 1868 he established the Department of Agriculture's arboretum that Olmsted describes here. It was located on the Mall between 12th and 14th streets and existed until the early 1930s (*DAB*; Reuben M. Rainey, "William Saunders," in Charles Birnbaum and Robin Karson, eds., *Pioneers of American Landscape Design* [New York, 2000], pp. 327–32; Richard Rathbun, *The United States National Museum: An Account of the Buildings Occupied by the National Collections* [Washington, D.C., 1905], p. 189; Dana G. Dalrymple, "Agriculture, Architects, and the Mall, 1901–1905: The Plan is Tested," in *Designing the Nation's Capital: The 1901 Plan for Washington, D.C.* [Washington D.C., 2006]).
7. Orville E. Babcock (1835–1884) was a military engineer and Civil War general who served on Ulysses S. Grant's staff. When Grant became president in 1869 Babcock became an assistant personal secretary, and in 1871 he was appointed the Superintendent of Public Buildings and Grounds for the District of Columbia, a position he held until 1876. During those years he oversaw important improvements to the city's parks and squares. Babcock was also implicated in allegations of corruption during the Grant

administration, most seriously as part of the 1875 "Whiskey Ring" conspiracy (*ANB*; *Papers of FLO*, 7: 42, n. 7; Frederick A. Gutheim and Antoinette J. Lee, *Worthy of the Nation: Washington D.C. from L'Enfant to the National Capitol Planning Commission* [Baltimore, 2006], pp. 88–89).

8. Almon Ferdinand Rockwell was Superintendent of Public Buildings from April 1, 1881, to June 1, 1885 (Francis B. Heitman, *Historical Register and Dictionary of the United States Army* [Washington, D.C., 1903], p. 840).

9. Andrew Jackson Downing (1815–1852) was the foremost American landscape gardener of his day, made famous through his many publications, including *A Treatise on the Theory and Practice of Landscape Gardening* (1841). Calvert Vaux became his professional partner in 1850, the same year Downing was commissioned to design the landscape today known as the Washington Mall. Downing's plan for "The Public Grounds at Washington" consisted of a sequence of distinct public gardens and landscapes extending between the existing botanic garden at the foot of Capitol Hill, to the then incomplete Washington Monument, and then to the "President's Park" south of the White House.

   In the center of his plan Downing designed the "Smithsonian Pleasure Grounds" as an open park planted in a "natural style" around James Renwick's then incomplete Smithsonian Institution building. Following his death in a Hudson River steamboat disaster in 1852, Downing's designs for the Mall were never completely implemented (David Schuyler, *Apostle of Taste: Andrew Jackson Downing, 1815–1852* [Baltimore, 1996], pp. 192–202; Francis R. Kowsky, *Country, Park, & City: The Architecture and Life of Calvert Vaux* [New York, 1998], pp. 45–48; FLO to Justin Smith Morrill, Jan. 22, 1874 [*Papers of FLO*, 7: 36–43]; *Papers of FLO*, 3: 361–62, n. 13).

10. Following Downing's death in 1852, the American Pomological Society raised money for a memorial. Designed by Calvert Vaux and Robert E. Launitz, it took the form of a classical vase on an inscribed plinth. In 1856 it was dedicated in the partially completed landscape Downing had designed around the Smithsonian (D. Schuyler, *Apostle of Taste*, pp. 223–24).

11. In 1870 Congress passed legislation (introduced by Senator Justin S. Morrill) authorizing the city of Washington to "set apart portions of streets and avenues as parks for trees and walks." The next year President Grant signed legislation creating a Territorial Government for the District of Columbia, including a Board of Public Works concerned with drainage, sewers, pavements, and street improvements. The new board appointed an advisory committee that July that consisted of Olmsted, Orville E. Babcock, Quartermaster General Montgomery C. Meigs, Surgeon General James K. Barnes, and Chief of Engineers General A. D. Humphreys.

   As part of an ambitious program of improvements proposed in May 1871, the Board of Public Works called for a system of "parking" the capital's wide streets and avenues with lawn strips and trees, in part to reduce paving costs. Under the leadership of its dynamic vice president, Alexander "Boss" Shepherd, the board also established a "Parking Commission" whose members were William Saunders (at the time planting the Department of Agriculture's arboretum on the Mall), William R. Smith (superintendent of the United States Botanic Garden), and John Saul (an area nurseryman who had worked for Downing in Washington). The Parking Commission went on to plant over 60,000 trees in Washington between 1871 and 1887, making Washington famous for its street trees. As the landscape architect on the Board of Public Works advisory committee, Olmsted presumably influenced the board's "parking" policies, but there is no record of him attending its meetings (*Report of the Board of Public Works of the District of Columbia* [Washington, D.C., 1872], pp. 87–90; William Tindall, "The Origins of the Parking System of This City," *Records of the Columbia Historical Society* [Washington, D.C., 1901], pp. 78–81; William M. Maury, *Alexander "Boss"*

Shepherd and the Board of Public Works, GW Washington Studies, No. 3 [Washington, D.C., 1975], pp. 6, 9; *Evening Star* [Washington, D.C.], Sept. 6, 1871, p. 2; Peter Henderson, "Street Trees of Washington," *Harper's New Monthly Magazine*, July 1888, pp. 285–87).

12. William Robertson Smith (1828–1912) was born in Scotland and served as Superintendent of the United States Botanical Garden from 1853 to 1912. During his tenure he managed the plants from the Wilkes Expedition and oversaw the expansion of the gardens (Liberty Hyde Bailey, *The Standard Cyclopedia of Horticulture*, vol. 2. [New York, 1937], p. 1597; K. D. Solit, *History of the United States Botanic Garden*, pp. 32–36).
13. John Saul (1819–1897) was born in Ireland and emigrated to the United States in 1851, already an experienced horticulturist and nursery manager. He briefly joined his brother James, who was working at Andrew Jackson Downing's nursery in Newburgh, New York, before coming to Washington, D.C., to oversee planting for Downing's public grounds project. He held that position until 1853, but remained in the area and established his own successful nursery. He also laid out the grounds of W. W. Corcoran's residence, Harewood, in addition to his service on the Washington Parking Commission. Beginning in 1882 Olmsted made inquiries or requested plants from Saul for numerous projects in New England and elsewhere, including the residences of Joseph H. White and Col. R. H. Goddard, several Boston & Albany Railroad stations, the Boston parks, the Capitol grounds, and Biltmore (L. H. Bailey, *The Standard Cyclopedia of Horticulture*, 2, p. 1594; FLO to John Saul, May 12, 1882; FLO to John Saul, Oct. 23, 1884, A1: 82, OAR/LC; FLO to John Saul, March 30, 1888, A2: 316, OAR/LC; FLO to John Saul, Oct. 23, 1884, A1: 83, OAR/LC; FLO to John Saul, Jan. 12, 1885, A1: 137, OAR/LC; Bill Alexander, *The Biltmore Nursery: A Botanical Legacy* [Charleston, 2007], p. 85).
14. That is, *Hamamelis Virginiana*. The Latin name Olmsted gives is incorrect both in manuscript and the published report.
15. The Reform School of the District of Columbia stood on Lincoln's Hill near Bladensburg Road in northeast Washington, D.C., south of the Maryland border. Bladensburg, Maryland, was known for its mineral spring spa (De B. Randolph Keim, *Keim's Illustrated Hand-book of Washington and Its Environs: A Descriptive and Historical Hand-book to the Capital of the United States of America* [Washington, D.C., 1876], p. 228).
16. The United States Soldiers' Home was founded in 1851 on a site three miles north of the Capitol. In 1872 the home was expanded through the purchase of William W. Corcoran's adjacent property, Harewood. The grounds of the Soldiers Home were open to the public and offered views back to the city; and several presidents, including Buchanan, Lincoln, Hayes, and Arthur, used the Soldiers' Home as a summer retreat (Frank Flosser, *A Brief History of the U.S. Soldiers' Home, Washington, D.C.* [Washington, D.C., 1909], pp. 5, 8–9).
17. Georgetown was known for a period in 1880s as West Washington. A five-mile stretch of the upper Potomac, from Key Bridge in Georgetown to Little Falls, Maryland, was ideal for boating excursions then and now as it has high banks and was heavily wooded. Much of this section of the river has been preserved as parkland. The Chesapeake & Ohio Canal National and Historic Park and the George Washington Memorial Parkway, among others, are preservations that cover much of the land along the Potomac farther up-river to the Great Falls at the Maryland/Virginia border (De B. Randolph Keim, *Washington: What to See and How to See It: A Sightseer's Guide* [Washington, D.C., 1885], p. 11; F. A. Gutheim, A. J. Lee, *Worthy of the Nation*, pp. 147–51, 205–9).
18. Rock Creek extends northward from the Potomac at Georgetown through the northwest quadrant of the District of Columbia. Olmsted's interest in the wooded valley of Rock Creek dated back to his residence in the capital during the Civil War. Park

legislation was first introduced in 1867, but Congress did not authorize the creation of Rock Creek Park until 1890 (Timothy Davis, "Rock Creek and Potomac Parkway, Washington, DC: The Evolution of a Contested Urban Landscape," *Studies in the History of Gardens and Designed Landscapes*, Summer 1999, pp. 135–37; F. A. Gutheim, A. J. Lee, *Worthy of the Nation*, p. 85).

19. Lester Frank Ward, "No. 22 — Guide to the Flora of Washington and Vicinity," *Bulletin 26 of the United States National Museum, Department of the Interior, U.S. National Museum* (Washington, D.C., 1881).
20. John B. Blake (1800–1881) was a medical doctor and also a president of the National Metropolitan Bank. He was appointed to the Board of Commissioners of Public Buildings in 1851 and to the Board of Public Works in 1873 (Medical Society of the District of Columbia, *History of the Medical Society of the District of Columbia, 1817–1909* [Washington, D.C., 1909], p. 224; Charles Lanman, *Dictionary of the United States Congress and the General Government* [Hartford, 1868], p. 452; William Tindall, *Origin and Development of the District of Columbia* [Washington, D.C., 1909], p. 217).
21. Oliver Wolcott (1760–1833) was Secretary of the Treasury (1795–1800) under Presidents Washington and Adams and was governor of Connecticut (1817–1827). The quotation Olmsted cites comes from a letter Wolcott wrote to his wife dated July 4, 1800, in which he describes conditions in Washington. The letter had been published in an 1846 edition of Wolcott's papers (*ANB*; *DAB*; George Gibbs, ed., *Memoirs of the Administrations of Washington and John Adams, Edited from the Papers of Oliver Wolcott, Secretary of the Treasury*, vol. 2. [New York, 1846], pp. 376–78).
22. In 1798 George Washington purchased land on the west side of North Capitol Street between B and C Streets in order to build two houses that were designed by William Thornton. Washington died before construction was completed and the British burned the houses in 1814. The ruins were rebuilt in 1851, and two additional stories were added. The resulting structure was used as a hotel until its demolition in 1915 (Wilhelmus Bogart Bryan, *A History of the National Capital*, vol. 1. [New York, 1914–1916], pp. 311–12; John Clagett Proctor, "Houses Once Owned by Washington," *Sunday Star Magazine* [Washington, D.C.], Sept. 27, 1931, pp. 6–7).
23. The published version reads "Towner Division" and is corrected here to agree with the original manuscript.
24. Olmsted is referring to an act by Congress in 1800 to set up a "paving fund" to pay for the construction of sidewalks, or footways, "in suitable places." A surveyor was ordered "to stake out that part of Pennsylvania Avenue which lies between the President's Square and the Capitol for the purpose of paving a footway." A bridge over Tiber Creek was built where it intersected with the path at 2nd Street and the footway extended to Rock Creek where a new bridge was built connecting to Georgetown (W. B. Bryan, *A History of the National Capital*, 1, pp. 357–60).
25. That is, Tiber Creek, that flowed from the north to about present-day Constitution and 5th Street NW, where it turned to run to the west, becoming a tidal inlet of the Potomac River. In 1815 it became a part of the Washington Canal, which ran east-west along the line of Constitution Avenue, and then south along the base of Capitol Hill to the Anacostia River. The swampy areas around the Tiber Creek were filled in during the construction of the Washington Canal. The canal was enclosed during sewage and drainage work and the reclamation of the river flats in the 1870s and 1880s (Cornelius W. Heine, "The Washington Canal," *Records of the Columbia Historical Society*, 1953/1956, pp. 1–27; F.A. Gutheim, A. J. Lee, *Worthy of the Nation*, pp. 16–17, 22–23; 94–96).
26. The "Washington Elm" on the east side of the Capitol grounds was traditionally thought to have been planted by Washington. It was removed in 1948 due to disease

(Erle Kaufman, *Trees of Washington: The Man — The City* [Washington, D.C., 1932], pp. 39–40; *Washington Star*, May 13, 1948, p. B-1; *Papers of FLO*, 7: 98, n. 7).

27. Built in 1817 on what was the corner of Delaware Avenue and A Street, this building was a hotel that in the 1860s became known the Yellow Tavern. Square number 687, which included the tavern and several other buildings, was purchased and then cleared in 1872–1873 as part of the expansion of the Capitol grounds (G. Brown, *History of the United States Capitol*, 2, p. 144; John Clagett Proctor, "Congress Nearly Moved Out," *Sunday Washington Star*, Sept. 5, 1948, p. 2).

28. John Foy (1783?–1833) was born in Ireland and graduated from Trinity College, Dublin, as a civil engineer. He emigrated to America as a young man and became the first gardener of the Capitol grounds, overseeing their improvement after 1814. He also provided his services to the adjacent U.S. Botanical Garden.

    Foy's 1825 plan for the Capitol grounds that Olmsted refers to here was not found by the editors, but an 1830 survey depicts the grounds organized in three rectangular plats east of the Capitol, oriented with their longer dimension east-west like the surrounding blocks. West of the Capitol, the survey shows the grounds divided into four radial plats by extending the centerlines of Pennsylvania and Maryland avenues and adding a third path centered on the west elevation of the Capitol and its central staircase. Foy also described his vision for the grounds in an 1832 newspaper article, in which he proposed expanding the grounds and creating "meandering walks and clumps of trees" that would unify the Capitol grounds and the botanic garden to the west (*Annual Publication of the Historical Society of Southern California and Pioneer Register* [Los Angeles, 1900], p. 202; K. D. Solit, *History of the United States Botanic Garden*, pp. 11–12; G. Brown, *History of the United States Capitol*, 1, plates 87, 88; John Foy, "The Vegetable Kingdom," *Daily National Intelligencer*, Jan. 3, 1832).

29. Olmsted is quoting from George Combe's *Notes on the United States of North America During A Phrenological Visit in 1838–39–40* (Philadelphia, 1841), p. 264. George Combe (1788–1858), phrenologist and moral philosopher, was born in Edinburgh, Scotland. From 1838 to 1840 he traveled in the United States giving lectures (*NCAB*).

30. Following his presidency, John Quincy Adams (1767–1848) was elected to the House of Representatives and served from 1831 until his death. His family's home in Washington at the time was on F Street between 13th and 14th streets, east of the White House (Anne Hollingsworth Wharton, *Social Life in the Early Republic* [Philadelphia, 1902], p. 304; William Elliot, *The Washington Guide* [Washington, 1837], p. viii).

31. James Maher was placed in charge of the Capitol grounds by Andrew Jackson in 1833. He was later appointed public gardener for the city, a position he held until his death in 1859 (*The Constitution*, April 16, 1859, p. 2; W. B. Bryan, *A History of the National Capital*, 2, p. 327).

32. Olmsted is quoting from "An act to regulate the use of the Capitol Grounds" passed July 1, 1882. The act restricted the use of the grounds to "roads, walks, and places prepared for the purpose by flagging, paving, or otherwise" and prohibited commercial activity and political demonstrations ("An act to regulate the use of the Capitol Grounds," *U.S. Statutes at Large* 22 [1882], pp. 126–27).

33. Olmsted is likely referring to Oak Hill Cemetery, above Rock Creek in Georgetown. In 1848 William W. Corcoran purchased the land, already known as a scenic area, and paid for its development as a rural cemetery. Civil engineer George de la Roche designed the paths and drives and the first plots were made available in 1851 (Casimer Bohn, *Bohn's Hand-Book of Washington* [Washington, D.C., 1856], p. 109; Marisa Keller, "Oak Hill Cemetery Marks 150th Anniversary," *Washington History*, 1999, pp. 75–76).

To Thomas Worthington Whittredge[1]

[1882]

[24:652]
My Dear Whittredge.* A few months ago when your Village Improvement Society was getting under way and while it yet lacked the momentum of practical operations, I was asked in consultation with you to advise some of the ladies concerned about matters which they then had under consideration.[4] After such review as I was able to make of the local circumstances the advise which I had occasion to offer turned out to be almost entirely as to what should not be done. Otherwise, at least, it was simple and common-place, running in well beaten paths. In truth it has since weighed a little upon my mind that, stopping at the point where our conference adjourned, some might have been disposed to ask "Our local circumstances being what they are, what need for this new machinery of improvement?

The local circumstances to which I refer are in part these: that plans for [24:649] places of resort other than the streets were under commercial control and management and might best remain so; that the village had been improving with extraordinary rapidity, that it was in many respects in advance of villages which have acquired some reputation from their improvements and under existing arrangements had every prospect of continuing in a healthy and soundly economical course of improvement.

What under these circumstances, it might have been questioned, is the sense of asking two hundred ladies to band themselves together under the name of the Village Improvement Society—ladies most of whom have moved into the village within a few years, who have had little training in village affairs and whose habits [24:653–660] and tastes have been largely formed under conditions wholly impracticable for the village? Why should such funds as may be available for village improvement be drawn into new channels liable to cross, disturb or weaken those through which so much has been accomplished? Why should it be desired to supersede or overflow agencies which have not only been so far working well themselves but which correspond with those through which some of the most charming villages in the country have come to be what they are.

No confession of faith that may have been subscribed; no phraseology of agreement that may have been adopted will fully answer questions like these

*[An alternate beginning on 24:730]: My Dear Mr. Whittredge. The advice which the people of Summit chiefly want, in so far as it concerns the Village Improvement Association to obtain it, is mainly such as is wanted by the people of thousands of other villages and which can best be obtained through books prepared for the purpose, some as those of Col. Waring, Mr Mitchell and Mr Eggleston,[2] treating chiefly of matters of common concern to a community; and others applying to the imprvmt of private as well as public properties such as Kemp's How to Lay out a Garden; Scott's Suburban Home Grounds and Weidenmann's How to Beautify Country Homes.[3]

and if this leaves the smallest room for suspicion of insincerity, cant, or fustian attached to the Society it should be searched without mercy.

Taking this view of the case and asking what solid base does the Society stand upon, it has occurred to me that however local and spontaneous the forming of it may have appeared to be, it is to suggest that beneath all that is plainly visible there may be some deep roots of a growing public sentiment.

This being possible let us consider it under the name of the village sentiment.

What has it to do with improvement? This term has come to have with us a distinct commercial usage referring to a class of operations by which property in lands and buildings is supposed to improve in exchangeable value. Improvements, in this sense, are made by individual property owners, by societies of property owners and by communities through their political servants. None of these are moved by the village sentiment. To none are the village improvement societies allied: upon none are they dependent. They owe little to the suggestions or to the efforts of men active in business improvement. They have tended to overflow and disconcert village politics rather than otherwise. They have somewhat emphatically, as a rule, put commercial and political ideas of improvement out of view. They have been formed more by women than by men, their methods have been womanly methods and women of comparatively secluded domestic habits have been of more weight in their counsels than those accustomed to be forward in public activities. The leading members have in most cases been mothers of families and under their lead younger women, boys and girls have been drawn into active cooperation.

These considerations all favor the thought that the village sentiment is largely a social and domestic sentiment.

Not to compare it in importance but only as a further clue to its character, we may recall the fact that twice when forces acting malignly upon our national character, forces to which wealth, fashion, political customs, even ecclesiastical customs lent constant and most powerful aid; twice when these forces were apparently of more irresistible strength than ever before, a wide spread sentiment in resistance to them first began to make itself manifest through the springing up of local societies, mainly of unknown and modest people, largely in each case of women and much in the manner that village improvement societies are now forming.

In our rich, fashionable, respectable religious society there is nothing now sustained, fostered, encouraged as drunken conviviality once was; as the perpetuation and spread of slavery once was. There is no heat of sentiment apparent under the name of Village Improvement corresponding to that of the early temperance societies and the early anti-slavery societies. Nevertheless there may be moving in cooler and more moderate volume a sentiment of protest and a disposition to offer a united resistance to malign tendencies in our social and domestic national life which takes something of this historic form.

I should like to avoid trying to define what this tendency may be. The great forces and counter-forces of civilization are seldom clearly definable. I have an idea of it and I will call that idea the townward idea insignificant of what I vaguely have in my mind as the term may be. Not only insignificant, I reflect, but misleading; nevertheless as a rude instrument for want of a better let me tentatively use it. Only as, in a public discourse, as you may possibly recollect, more than twelve years ago I used the same word in a manner to include the village idea as opposed to that of rural domestic life[5] it must be understood that I mean such an intensification of townwardness as we have seen for example in the progress of the building {*out*} in respect to the shell of domestic life in New York. Let us consider what this has come to.

New York has gained under our observation more than a thousand fold in wealth-producing power of steam and electricity, and, while we know that this gain is as yet one of means and forces rather than of actual product in improved human life, we know that in certain respects the gain has been great—perhaps ten, perhaps a hundred fold in certain forms of real property, as of churches, preachers; schools, teachers; in libraries, collections of art and of Science; in funds of charity and in funds of elevated entertainment. But what has been gained for domestic life—in wealth of home—as far as can be told by buildings? I will not take the tenement-house, nor that later development of it specially adapted to the temporary shelving of young couples under the name of the apartment house but that form of house "in a good neighborhood" that would be first offered to the father of a family able to pay a rent equal to half the salary of a college professor or double the average salary of rural clergymen and not disposed to pay more: It is not to be described so that it may be compared with a proper village house; it is almost as much like a ship or a mine, being but 15 feet wide (some only 12½) sixty, deep; sixty, long; with flight above flight of stair case to the number of six or seven; with no openings for light or air except at the stem and stern. Passing vehicles are liable at any moment to fill it with the din of a nail-mill; its outward prospect is limited by a high sombre wall, twenty yards away and this seen over dirty pavements. Can cultivation in art, can the utmost esthetic refinement ruling the utmost lavishness in decoration make such a thing as this congenial with domestic tastes? Is it not rather the fact that much display of ornament under such circumstances is apt to strike a healthy and unsophisticated taste as a little barbaric?

But to the children going out from these houses which are fair illustrations of townwardness if not of fully and generally established town character everywhere, what does the town offer for the cultivation of good domestic tastes, instincts and habits? Can a boy go out to school without seeing and hearing by the way much more that his mother would wish could be avoided than of what she would choose to come to him? Can a father be quite satisfied to let his daughter walk through the streets unattended? Can children look out the window without becoming familiar with forms of extravagant luxury in such contrast with extreme destitution, degradation and brutality as seldom fails to harden the heart and bring into contempt that perfectly sensible, logical and respectable principle which was once well understood in America under the name of equality, though now seldom used but in extravagant caricature of that principle?

What then can village improvement be in distinction from the townward degradation of a village? It is the distinction of the idea of a village that we can associate with it, as we cannot with the idea of a town, the attribute of loveliness and homefulness. The terms lovely village, charming village do not come to us strangely.

***

[24:662–63][6]

Is there not in the townward tendency of our habits, customs and manners; in our townward building, townward gardening, townward ideas of scenery, of beauty, of decoration, sentiments & morals, a danger threatening the rising generation adequate to account for a deep underworking impulse kindred to those forces which have twice saved our nation from wreck?

We may be able to recall, as Colonel Waring invites us to, the general aspect and character of Old Hadley, Deerfield or Farmington.[7] If not we can hardly fail to have some picture in our minds of the villages of Mary Howitt, Miss Mitford, Mrs Gaskell {*or Dickens*}[8] or Miss Thackery[9] and if so we have ideas of a large class of graceful refining, wholesome, charming, humanizing, neighborly influences associated with the word village such as are wholly lost and wholly out of the question in towns as our towns are now being improved.

Let this distinctive quality be abstracted and add to the old village railroads, telegraphs, telephones, libraries, daily newspapers, public bakeries and laundries, macadamizing and concreting and all improved sanitary appliances; add what improvements you will like to the common, park, play and burying ground, and when it is done, the village will not be a whit more charming home like or neighborly. It will be less — Nay, you will have no village left. You will not even have a sub-urb, you will have only a small town. Add to and mix up with it all the contents of the finest garden and the largest conservatory in the world and you will only have got further & further away from the charming idea of a village.

***

[24:723–24]

An echo of Col. Waring's reflection is unavoidable: "The more we enjoy all that is excellent in the town the more we realize certain short-comings that would have been avoided under better social conditions."[10] What is called town imprvmt having come to this, what by distinction is village improvement?

Unquestionably there is much of old association with the word village that is far from pleasant — Narrow mindedness and bigotry, selfish insistence that all shall govern themselves by common theories of right and propriety; tyrannical social police; oriental submission to nuisances and habitual heathenish reference to Jupiter of the natural results of an indolent selfishness in public affairs. From all this the inconvenience and gloom of village life will sometimes have seemed intolerable. But village improvement can no more mean an intensification of this inconvenience and gloom. It cannot {more} mean than an effort to turn a village into a town. Narrower and more compact, darker and more inconvenient houses, or the covering of spaces between houses with paving and flagging. The more a village has of all this the less of a village it is and it must be confessed that more abhorrent than the unimproved town, more abhorrent than the old village at its worst, is the mingling of the two in what the slang of the day calls a "one horse town".

***

[24:664–68]

What sort of improvement then is village improvement seen apart from town improvement? How is it to be set about? how secured? Who are to do the work, who is to employ them and how are they to be paid?

Mainly the women are to do the work; they are to employ their children and their domestic servants; they are to be paid in the health and pleasure each obtains in her own share of the work and the most important part of the work is the carrying of the best spirit and method of ordinary house decoration and housekeeping a little outside the house door. How this is to be done I may partly show later but here I assert, knowing that every one well informed on the subject, will at once confirm my assertion that it has been precisely in this way that the greater part of the work has been done which has ever made villages attractive; which has ever made then an improvement on the least attractive of towns.

I urge the more distinctly & emphatically that this must be considered the central idea of village improvement, and that the impulse and purpose to realize this idea must be the cornerstone of the Village Improvement Society, because as I have shown in my review of the circumstances, there is not any such work pressing to be done in your village as it is reported has been first taken up and accomplished with a hurrah in some other villages. There is nothing there that should distract attention from it and we may be sure that in the long run it will in every village be the most important improvement work. It is modest, quiet, home-work as precisely congenial to every gentlewoman living under proper village conditions as any of those forms of decorative art that have lately come in vogue and which unfortunately have so far, also, become matters of fashion and fanaticism, of quackery and cant as to provoke the persecution of ridicule and buffoonery. Because this {*has been*} so it is best to keep in mind what lies at the bottom of it.

At the bottom of all good decorative art there is unquestionably a close, tender and loving appreciation of the beauty which in one form or another Nature is everywhere ready to offer us. Beauty such as poor women, even women who earn their living by hard manual labor have often seen to secure under a cottage window, directed by no purpose but their own enjoyment. Their own enjoyment directly in the beauty obtained and their own enjoyment in the pleasure given by this beauty to their households and their neighbors.

May it not possibly be of as much value to a boy or a girl to have been brought up in familiarity with such unambitious and frugal village decorations; to be familiar with them and with the simple processes by which they are attained, as to have lived in houses replete with forms of beauty selected by others, with however much art selected, idealized, combined and represented?

Let us have both in our village life if we can but let us not imagine that to have been richly educated in the beauty indoors of household art is a greatly more fortunate thing than to have had the beauty of outdoor household nature for our daily bread.

The nurture of proper village tastes and habits, in reasonable independence of modern town fashions, and the cultivation of original study and skill in out of door household art {is desirable}, first in its own membership and then through the influence and mainly the unconscious influence of its membership upon the entire community. Can you doubt that if a tenth as much study as is given to fashion plates, to the literature of indoor art, to choice and means in respect to furniture and dress could be drawn to the improvement of the little ground and the portion of the street lying before each woman's house there would in a few years be an improvement of the village to be honorably proud of?

The duty of my profession is that of reconciling landscape enjoyment with domestic and social enjoyment. The restrictions fixed by the compactness of building and the thronging of crowds in large towns are as uncongenial to it as the domestic and social hardships of the wilderness. It is habitually as much interested in men as in nature as much in nature as in men.

There is a touching testimony of the truth of this assertion which as it has other and more important bearings on the subject of village improvement, I should like to recall.

Humphry Repton,[11] the first man to bear the title of landscape gardener, was an English gentleman of good birth, parts and breeding whose scholarly accomplishments made him a welcome guest at all times in many noble and even in princely houses. He not only designed and directed more great works in his profession than any who have followed him in it but he remains to this day the most voluminous and the most scientific writer upon it in our language. The last words of his last book were dictated during temporary respites from the spasms of a very painful illness rapidly bringing his long and honored life to a close, and were, in part, as follows: "I will now conclude with the most interesting subject I have ever known; it is the view from the humble cottage to which for more than thirty years, I have anxiously retreated from the pomp of palaces, the elegancies of fashion or the allurements of dissipation: it stood originally within five yards of a broad part of the high road; xxxx.[12] I obtained leave to remove the paling twenty yards further from the windows and by this appropriation of twenty five yards of garden I have obtained a frame to my landscape; the frame is composed of flowering shrubs and evergreens [meaning broadleafed evergreen shrubs, not coniferous trees]; beyond which are seen the cheerful village, the high road, and that constant moving scene, which I would not exchange for any of the lonely parks that I have improved for others. Some of their proprietors, on viewing the scene I have described, have questioned my taste; but my answer has been that in improving places for others, I must consult their inclinations; at Hare Street, I follow my own."[13]

Revering the memory of this master and communing, in some degree with the spirit which prompted these last sacred words of his, I have been led to review those special local circumstances of your Society to which I have referred, with results some of which I wish to submit to you; to you rather than directly to the Society, because my knowledge of the circumstances is so meagre compared with yours and because I shall be led to briefly touch matters of art in which your judgment is much more to be valued than mine.

***

[24:672–75]

Apart from social advantages, not here to be weighed, the only meritorious distinctions that I have heard claimed for Summit as a village is that of healthfulness. {*Common experience is said*}[14] to testify that a greater and more invigorating change of air is recognizable in coming to it from New York than at any intermediate point. Residence in it is claimed to be a protection against and a remedy for the various forms of indisposition and depressed vitality attributed to malarial poisoning, so common and oppressive in New York and most of its suburbs. Finally it is alledged to be extraordinarily exempt from influences such as are found elsewhere to develop or aggravate weaknesses of the lungs and air passages.

If the most desert and dreary place to be found within a hundred miles of New York offered decided advantages over all others in the respects thus claimed for Summit it would be a sufficient reason for the settlement upon it of a much larger suburban colony than has yet been anywhere formed. This not because of its value alone to invalids but to all aiming to assure themselves of the highest use of their faculties and the most uninterrupted domestic happiness. Natural advantages in these respects would outweigh all others and yet when in addition to them wealth had done all that could be asked of it in the way of building, paving and sewering and in supplying water and gas, schools and churches, theatres and libraries, hotels and shops, fountains and gardens, the village would still be by comparison with hundreds of others have a dreary aspect. To find and supply a means of making it cheerful, attractive and charming as a village would then be a work of beneficence. And a successful result would be the more satisfactory because the difficulties existing in the natural desert conditions would have compelled the use of extraordinary methods giving the village an interesting distinctness of character, which being associated with its sanitary advantages would become a subject of pride and felicitation.

Summit is far from being a desert and dreary place and yet apart from evidence not yet to be accepted as of scientific fullness, the credibility of its claim of healthfulness over many other villages appears to rest mainly on the alledged fact that its soil and subsoil are unusually free, open, inadhesive and wholesomely aerated. But if this is true it is probably true also that the soil and climate is less favorable to many plants, (not by any means to all) than the soil and climate of many other villages thus brought to their disadvantage in comparison with Summit. It is to be presumed, for instance, and my observation tended to confirm the presumption, that the grasses which may, in these other places, be found to make the finest, cleanest and closest turf, are apt to grow more sparsely and spindlingly; to be more readily supplanted by weeds; to sooner "run out" and in general to appear less attractive. Especially is this to be presumed as to these grasses on all rough ground, hillocks and rapidly declining surfaces, such as are not infrequent in the natural topography of Summit. It is to be presumed also of certain trees that they will grow less luxuriantly, will have weaker constitutions, be more open to attacks of insects and diseases and appear less attractively

* * *

[24:677–89]

If, then, discrimination is needed in applying good general advice for the improvement of villages to the special case with which your association is concerned, it is probably on account of the conditions of soil & climate to which reference has thus been made. If Summit is to have a village beauty of its own it will probably come through the tact exercised by its people to make a merit of that which would be a misfortune if they were clumsily bent on following fashions set by others or on competing with others in courses which they can only enter heavily handicapped.

The question then is, what quality of village beauty is more particularly out of your natural line and what can you aim at with confidence of an easier success than can be generally looked for?

Before we ask for anything else in the general aspect of a village we require for our pleasure in it that it shall not have a dirty or untidy and slovenly aspect. If it has, no amount of fine building and flower gardening scattered through it, will make it attractive to us. Nothing tells against a village in this respect like patches of raw earth, nor is the case helped, rather it is made worse, if there is an appearance of a thin, spotty, dwindling, dying or dead vegetation upon them.

If then in Summit it is at all more than usually difficult to establish and maintain thick, close fine and fresh turf through the summer attempts to have it will be wisely limited to ground of favorable surface and to areas upon which more than usually through preparation to secure thrift and more than usual continuous care to maintain it can be afforded. The fashion of formal earth terraces dressed with turf will, for example, be particularly out of place in Summit, as will all short sharp slopes such as are elsewhere often made in the grading of roads or house sites.

It is as bad housewifery for a lady to present a slovenly slope of turf to the view of her visitors as ragged curtains, dirty windows or broken chairs. And if a clear, fresh and unimpaired aspect is ever requisite in turf about a house it is when the heat and drought of the summer are otherwise most oppressive.

Where in a public road a side walk is to be carried for the sake of economy at some little distance above or below the line of the wheel-way the same consideration will lead to the avoidance in Summit of an abrupt transition between the two levels. The slope should be never steeper than one in four: rarely if ever than one in six. It will be much better for the general rural effect of the village that turf gutters should be used wherever practicable and with the light grades of the roads and their open subsoil they will be nearly every where practicable but, wherever used, it is indispensable to a permanent tidy appearance that they should be broad and shallow and that the grass should not be allowed to grow long in them. Ditch like gutters and steep banks though but a few inches high cannot be long kept by turf from crumbling and getting clogged and littered with dust and rubbish. If smooth, broad and shallow they may be dressed with turf and the turf may be cheaply kept short. Kept short it may also be kept clean with a broom almost as easily as a carpet more easily than a door mat. Kept close and clean it will not appear untidy even if it loses greenness and positive beauty in a dry time.

Where banks, declivities or steep slopes of considerable extent cannot be avoided or have already been formed and cannot well be reformed to gentleness, tolerable turf may probably be maintained upon them by an annual reinvigoration of their roots by means of copious top-dressing by careful compression of the surface with rollers or otherwise, by thorough hand-weeding, by the repair every spring of all breaks and by close mowings at frequent intervals; as often perhaps as once a week, during the season of rapid growth. It will still be desirable to frequently drench the soil and wash the plants with water and if this is impossible to often sweep off the dust from the surface. With all care turf cannot probably be kept of satisfactory fineness, closeness and evenness in such situations under trees, because their roots will insist on the lion's share of what food and moisture comes within their reach. Except in the streets where nothing else is available, it will be better as a general rule not to attempt to dress such places with turf. Strips of it may be laid criss-cross upon them as a temporary precaution against washing sliding and crumbling but the aim should be to cover them by plants better adapted to the situation than the grasses.

Though these cautions may not be generally needed there are sure to be a good many places which will never be kept neat and green with turf and more upon which a fairly satisfactory effect can be obtained with much less cost and trouble if something else is aimed at than a door yard of the common type—a body of turf more or less cut up, dotted and decorated with walks, flower beds, and scattered trees & plants.

So accustomed are we to this type, however, that to many there will seem to be no alternative but a grove, wood or thicket such as will destroy all ground verdure, and leave no view open toward or from the house.

I will consider a case, then, as difficult as any likely to be found in Summit, asking what can be done to avoid the forlorn result pretty sure to follow the common practice, without interfering with any desirable prospect.

Suppose that before and adjoining a new cottage there is a space thirty feet or more across occupied by a ridge or knoll of gravel, cobble-stones and boulders, partly natural, partly resulting from the excavation of the cellar. Any little poor soil in it is covered, scattered and unavailable. To work it into an ordinary door-yard lawn the soil of the bordering ground must first be lifted and stored, the ridge must then be graded down till graceful slopes have been obtained over the entire surface of the intended improvement; the larger stones upon it must be buried, the stored soil returned and as much more brought from some outside source as will supply a depth of from one to two feet over all the space intended to be turfed or planted. (That will be 40 New York city dirt cart loads). A heavy dressing of manure must next be worked in; there must be the slow and risky process of growing turf from seed, sowing, raking, rolling, weeding and then always after is mowing eight or ten times a year and other, attentions. Nothing less than this will secure a tolerable result. After all the May Chafer[15] may any year come and make havoc with it.

Asking what else can be done it is to be considered that it is not an uncommon thing to see a plant of ivy thirty or forty feet long or an orange or oleander tree which nearly fills a window, the roots of which are confined within a tub holding much less than a wheel barrow load of soil and occupying less superficial space than can be covered with a handkerchief. The same amount of good soil filled into a hole in the gravel will sustain a Virginia creeper that may grow in five months to closely cover twenty square feet of the raw dirt of the door-yard. Using a series of holes or a continuous trench encircling the space in question and planting creepers two or three feet apart, the entire ground may be clothed with a beautiful living mantle within two years, probably in less than one. To hasten a satisfactory result temporarily, annual vines may be grown at points nearer the center from seed, little pockets of soil to sustain their roots being provided. Or they may have been brought forward during the spring in the house in pots, and the pots set in the gravel when the season is sufficiently advanced. There are half a dozen strong woody vines and creepers of other sorts that may be used instead of the Virginia, or that may be combined with it. The best in most cases is the commonest of the Japanese honeysuckles, (*Lonicera brachypoda*) as it has a delicious bloom, is perfectly hardy, stands drought heroically and holds its verdure with a good color even longer than grass in fact in sheltered places is essentially evergreen. There are however a great many more delicate perennial plants which by a like planting at intervals will just as effectually carpet the spaces as the Virginia creeper and honeysuckle; not with the smoothness neatness and smugness of fine, well kept closely mowed and rolled turf but, taking the summer through, a great deal more agreeably than turf of ordinary quality. Once well-started many plants available for this purpose will require much less care than turf: they may fare not at all badly if left wholly to themselves for a year or two at a time. If a considerable variety is used the worst to be apprehended is that some will smother or root out others a result not perhaps to be deplored because it will prove what plants are best suited with the soil and situation and afterwards to be depended on to at least keep the place neat and green. Among plants thus available may be mentioned the common periwinkle (*Vinca minor*) St John's Wort, Soap wort, Money wort and such violets as are probably running wild in Summit woods. All these grow, spread and propagate themselves in poor thin soils and hold green through severe droughts. They are beautiful both when in and when out of bloom and with very little trouble they may be made to nicely cover ground where good turf is out of question. Doubtless a little study in the neighborhood will discover others at least equally suitable for the purpose. A mere heap of pebbles can at the worst be made verdant by sprinkling a little poor sandy soil in the crevices and planting sedums, either of the coarser sorts, generally known in the country as House leeks or some of the numerous more delicate varieties now sold by the florists. These may cost too much to be freely used at first but if a few plants are once started and given a fair chance they will rapidly multiply and spread.

Another plant which may be used with capital effect to spread over poor dry ground in lieu of turf is the common prostrate Juniper. There are other evergreen (coniferous) plants of the same habit, the European Tamarisk-leafed juniper, for example, which would probably grow well with you but that which is best of all under favorable conditions, the Canadian yew or ground hemlock, though native of some parts of New Jersey, would need more moisture and shade. Each of the plants I have mentioned will grow much better in the shadow of trees and upon ground fringed by the roots of trees than turf or than most of the common lawn shrubs.

I have spoken of the common type of village door yard, meaning that which seems to have been of late generally admired and held in view in most of the advice given in the books. These, I think, aim to realize within narrow limits and under special restrictions of convenience, something of the beauty of the lawn and pleasure ground proper to a villa or country seat of many acres adapted to families of great wealth and a large retinue of servants. I don't mean to advise against this but I cannot neglect to point out that the chief value in landscape composition of a lawn or of an open glade of turf in a park or in park-like scenery is generally considered by those who have studied the subject scientifically, to lie in the relief to the eye which is found in the contrast of its simple expanse of smooth unbroken verdure with the adjoining masses of fluttering leafage and broken lights and shadows. It is therefore said to supply more particularly the quality of repose. But if the space of unbroken turf among trees and bushes is not of a certain breadth, it does not have this effect.

* * *

[24:691–94]
Rather by separating the foliage into distinct masses and parting them it becomes an element of disturbance. I doubt whether a small door yard in which everything centers on a lawn, even under favorable conditions of soil and exposure, is apt to be as pleasing as a door yard of the old fashioned kind which has been first shaped and graded so as to appear from the street as a simple table or pedestal for the house to stand upon, then crossed by one or two walks leading with directness though not necessarily in a perfectly straight course from point to point as would best serve purposes of convenience and in which at last decoration has been introduced as if an after-thought of all this, being made to fit and adorn the skeleton plan thus laid down, beds being formed for example in lines parallel with the walks, bordered with box edgings and set with flowering plants favorites of the women and children of the house, arranged and cultivated entirely by their willing hands with little thought if any of contrasts or harmonies of form or color. I find unstudied compositions under these circumstances seldom disagreeable and believe that plants suitable to be used at all under these circumstances are most unlikely to be very badly misarrayed except by a poor artist trying to go beyond her means. Along the fence, at the corners or other architecturally emphatic points of these yards there would generally be certain small trees as mountain ash and laburnum, refined and lady-like in aspect, and certain blooming and fragrant bushes as lilac and honeysuckle snow drop and rose of Sharon, which though originally set out formally had soon stretched out their shoots and branches freely, picturesquely and girl like. Patches of thin grass that were, probably, poor considered as turf but with such scattering undergrowths of lily of the valley, pansies, periwinkle, stone crop and daffodils all running wild, that its meagreness was not unpleasant. I must say that when I come upon an old door yard of this class, with a neat picket fence set upon a low, mossy retaining wall, especially if there is a stoop before the door half veiled by woodbine and prairie roses, tubs of oleander and pots of geraniums set out for the summer, I think it very inviting and respectable. If the later style of door yard is generally less so in spite of the vast advance made in horticultural materials again I question if it is not because more has been attempted than could be done with a sure hand.

I make these confessions not with a view to urging a recurrence to the old style but only that there may be less fear of a bad result if walks and plantings are so arranged as to leave less ground in turf than has of late become customary; the main precept I would urge being that there should be no more turf than is likely to obtain continuously for years {with} what would generally be thought lavish care. It should also be studiously so arranged as to be little crossed, broken or dotted by walks, single shrubs or trees, beds of flowers or other bits and spots of intended decorations. It will thus have more of the characteristic value of turf in the general composition of the place, and will be better, more effectually and more cheaply mown, rolled, and watered or swept. Small bits of turf, narrow points and gores, mounds and ramps should be studiously avoided, as likely to be weak, poor and expensive.

***

[24:706–7]
I do not think it has ever been very well defined in words, but without here attempting to define it, I may urge any to whom it shall happen to come as an inspiration not to shrink from following it because it has not been definitely recommended and is not the fashion. Fortunately it is no more a matter to be ordered or controlled by fashion than the writing or the painting of a poem. I believe that it is possible to give a poetic quality to a village door yard. I hold it conceivable that every door yard in a village shall be as a verse in a poem and that the village shall be that poem in full. I tried some years ago to illustrate what I mean by this saying and to show how such an idea is realizable in a paper on Landscape Gardening which was printed in Johnsons Cyclopedia.[16]

***

[24:696–701]
This policy prevailing as to lawns or turf, there are two dangers remaining in the outside housekeeping of the village. The accomplished inside housekeeper will understand them if I characterize one as that of a bare, stingy unfurnished aspect, as of a matted room with paper curtains, a centre and pier table and rows of straight backed chairs; the other as that of fussiness as of the same room after it has been over stocked with incongruous additions to its furniture and tricked out with a bushel or two of dollar-store brick a brac.

Both evils are likely to be escaped if it shall be aimed to form groups and masses of foliage in all those parts of house grounds near the street which are not likely to be well kept in turf and flowering plants, or, where open views are wanted to be carpeted by ground plants or creepers. (I will show what I mean by groups and masses of foliage and that it is nothing impracticable for the unlearned, a little later.) Having shown that a large part of a door yard, however poor its soil, may be made presentable with much less expense than would be necessary to obtain decent results in the prevalent fashion, I must say that whatever is to be done in the way of higher foliage than that I have been suggesting for the poor ground, should be done with more liberality of outlay than is common. First the soil to be planted in should be well-prepared as all the books will be found to advise. Less expense will be necessary for this purpose, however, than in hungry ground is necessary to secure first rate turf. Next it is advisable to get well-prepared trees and bushes from a nursery. Well prepared trees are such as have been at least twice transplanted since they sprang from the seed, and have had their heads trimmed back. This makes them compact in form and enables them to bear further transplanting (chiefly because of more fibrous roots) without a serious constitutional shock, or check or disinvigoration. They will be planted closer than is often recommended, vigor of growth should be afterwards sustained by annual top-dressings and a thin, scattered straggling and feeble habit of foliage guarded against by frequent pinching of the growing shoots or occasional shortening in of them with the knife or scissors.

It will probably be practicable in the next severe drought to make a list of trees and shrubs which have been little affected by it and which, being in all other respects found suitable, may be wisely suggested by the Association for general planting in the village.

To have much value however recommendations for this purpose should not be made without examination of the apparent vigor and promise of various sorts of trees when somewhat advanced in life. It will probably be found that most of the European and Californian pines and spruces, for example, show signs of feebleness and decrepitude when but from fifteen to twenty five years old while at the same age our own white spruce is still in the vigor of youth. The American White and Red Pines, the beauty of which is unsurpassed, will be as full of life, as healthy and in all respects as beautiful in Summit soils as in any. This will be true also I presume of any birches that can be found, of the Hop hornbeam, of the Staghorn Sumac as well as of the smaller sumacs, that called copalina looking as fresh and happy upon a dry ridge in August as most shrubs by a brookside in June.

Now let it be remembered first that it requires much less care and expense to avoid an appearance of poverty and thriftlessness with trees and shrubs than with grass. Second that it is much easier and less costly to provide what is necessary to secure health and continuous vigor in small trees than in large. Third, that it is unfavorable to the health of families as well as to village neatness to have large growing trees like the American elm or Sugar Maple tulip or Balsam poplar standing in front of any house which is within fifty feet of the street. Lastly let it be borne in mind, on the laying out and planting of door yards of moderate extent, that there are few plants — almost none of those commonly used for display — that flourish under the shade, in the drip or among the roots of trees, and that trees have to be planted as infants but with a view to ultimate great expansion of both root and branch.

For all these reasons the Association should aim to encourage in Summit door yard plantings of shrubs and small-growing trees rather than those which are more common and popular. There are a considerable number of trees to be had which in the soil and climate of Summit when of mature age will have grown to no greater height than ordinary apple-trees, or to less than a quarter that often attained by the more common shade trees. I will name several which by an unobjectionable use of the knife at least, will not in fifty years grow above the house tops. Most of them are of very delicate and refined character, particularly appropriate to the cottage door yard of gentlewomen. The distinction between a small tree and a shrub is that the one grows bushily from the ground, the other is lifted on a trunk. By pruning trees can be made shrubs; shrubs, trees. As there are many wooded plants classed as shrubs that grow naturally as tall as the trees referred to and others smaller down to the size of diminutive herbs it is simply a matter of selection and arrangement to obtain any form and mass of foliage before and about a house that within reasonable limits may be desired. For example, there are a number of closely-related shrubs to be found in your Summit Gardens known as Meadow Sweets of which some kinds, need grow not more than two and others not more than three feet high. They are abundant and beautiful bloomers and their foliage is light and elegant quality, appearing almost lace-like when they border standard bushes. There are other shrubs known to all which grow a little taller such as the flowering currants and {. . .}; again, others which push above these as the Persian lilac, others of yet higher growth as the Chinese or common lilacs, the tops of which are well above the lower branches of small trees like the mountain ash, Red bud, Shadblow and Dog wood. By planting members of these several grades one before the other at distances calculated with reference to the ordinary full growths of each a mass of foliage may be formed which the eye can {. . .} {*penetrate*} rising from the ground to a height of twenty feet or more. I have named but half a dozen well known species which can be used in this way. Varying their order masses of foliage may be obtained of many different forms and with parts in different relations as to colour and texture.

* * *

[24:708–13]

There are and, as the village grows out, there always must be spaces by the roadside not occupied by door yards and not to be improved by any such means as have been suggested. They are generally grassy but during much of the year have a dilapidated, ragged and dirty appearance because grass is thin weak, scattered starved and choked. The land being held on speculation for building sites the owners have little personal interest to improve it and cannot afford to expend much if anything upon it from regard to the general interest of the village. The association may, however, properly suggest and may aid in and cooperate toward some inexpensive improvements.

It will probably cost very little to obtain and set or plant enough cuttings, of small plants of poplar, willow, sumac or white birch growing in the neighborhood to make some improvement in the worst places of this class. A more effectual and yet inexpensive expedient will be to adapt the skeleton of an old fence or build a new one; fix a trellis upon it, form pockets of good soil at frequent intervals as before advised, plant vines and creepers, and take care to have them so grown, spread and trimmed as to make a complete screen or verdant curtain. Well done, the effect at a little distance hardly differs from that of a very nice hedge. I have never seen a more beautiful fence than one made in this way, and, as the constructed part of post, rails and trellis is to be wholly covered, serving only as a scaffolding or skeleton, it is of little consequence how rudely nor of what readily to be picked up materials it is made. The commonest farm fencing post and rails will answer, and two rails will be enough. Or short cedar stakes such as farmers use for bean or hop poles will serve, these being driven into the ground and lighter poles carried between them by a lashing of annealed wire for rails. For trellis work lathes may be used tacked to the rails with shingle nails at spaces somewhat wider than are usual in common back door screens. I suppose a piece of coarse strong twine seine[17] such as boys and girls can easily be taught to make would do very well, if thrown evenly over the top rail and pinned to the ground on each side. If the twine rots away after a year or two the desired effect will not be impaired for the vines will then be strong enough to run alone and hold one another in place. And so if a post or rail occasionally gives way it will not always need to be replaced. I have grown the Wisteria vine in the form of sturdy bushes as strong and self supporting as quince trees. Much the best form of trellis however will be one of wire. Machine made zinc-washed iron wire netting suitable for the purpose may be bought at from $2 to $3 the running rod. It is sold in rolls like cloth, for poultry yard fences.

Of course hedges will answer the purpose, if well made, even better but it will take longer to grow them and the extreme rarity of a well-made hedge testifies how hard it will be to obtain one. People are impatient of the slow and laborious processes advised in the books for hedge making but my experience testifies that the usual directions are less stringent than is desirable. So much is in print on the subject that I need only advise in respect to hedges that none should be attempted in Summit on a line upon which trees are remotely liable to encroach. A hedge must be well and evenly lighted on both sides, and must not be interfered with in its feeding to avoid growing ragged and shabby.

There will be a question of the necessary height of living fences whether trellis-grown or self-supporting, for screening off shabby roadsides? If a height otherwise thought to involve too much cost and delay is supposed to be necessary to the purpose, it may be well to consider that more can be accomplished by a low screen of fresh foliage than may at first thought be presupposed. The effect of a strongly marked foreground in weakening the impression upon the mental vision of objects seen over it at a little distance is very considerable, and a field of poor herbage which would affect us disagreeably if it came to our feet and its nearer parts were looked down upon and seen in distinctions of detail is not unpleasing at a distance when its detail merges in broader qualities of form and tint. When the detail consists of gravel, grass or stubble with slender weeds of a general tone less vivacious and effective than the nearer object beyond which they are seen no broad belt of actual obscuration is necessary to accomplish the desired purpose. A fence of unplaned boards four feet high if it can be kept in neat condition will allow a general impression of village neatness to be sustained when its absence or a dilapidated and defaced fence in its place will make a decided discord.

The editors assembled this document from undated draft pages of a letter in Olmsted's hand. The pages are in the Frederick Law Olmsted, Sr., Papers, Box 26, Subject File Series, Folder 12, and are recorded in the microfilm edition of the collection on reel 24, frames 644–741. The editors omitted draft passages that were repetitive or too fragmentary to integrate into the letter's narrative. The reel and frame numbers of the microfilm on which the text for each passage can be found is given in brackets preceding it, and if a passage occurs over multiple frames they are given inclusively. The symbol **** appears where there is a break in the narrative of the text. In all other respects the text is treated according to the Editorial Policy described in this volume.

Olmsted's comments on "village improvement" were written at a time when village improvement societies were being formed in rural and suburban towns in many parts of the country. Tree-planting organizations had begun to form in New England in the 1840s and 1850s, and one of the most well-known was the Laurel Hill Association in Stockbridge, Massachusetts, formed in 1853. It provided a model for those organizations dedicated to improving the physical environments of their communities. In 1883 Olmsted became a vice president of the National Association of Sanitary and Rural Improvement, an organization that reported on village improvement activities in many places, including Summit, New Jersey (Kirin J. Makker, "Building Main Street: Village Improvement and the American Small Town Ideal," [PhD diss., University of Massachusetts, 2010], pp. 1–26; D. Schuyler, *Apostle of Taste* [Baltimore, 1996], p. 118; "Summit, N.J. Association," *Indoors and Outdoors*, May 1, 1883, pp. 3, 5; William H. Wilson, *The City Beautiful Movement* [Baltimore, 1989], pp. 42–44).

1. Thomas Worthington Whittredge (1820–1910) was a landscape painter of the Hudson River School. He began his career in Cincinnati, Ohio, in the 1840s and spent a decade studying in Europe, beginning in 1849. He established a studio in New York on his return and was elected to the National Academy of Design in 1861, serving as president from 1874 to 1876. In 1867 he married Euphemia Foote from Geneva, New York, and settled with her in 1880 in Summit, New Jersey. Olmsted and Whittredge had probably known each other since the 1860s, as Whittredge had been an early member of the Union League Club and was involved in the founding of the Metropolitan Museum of Art (*DAB*; Worthington Whittredge to FLO, March 16, 1882; John I. H. Baur, ed., *The Autobiography of Worthington Whittredge: 1820–1910* [Brooklyn Museum Journal, 1942], p. 62; Anthony F. Janson, *Worthington Whittredge* [Cambridge, UK, 1989], pp. 92, 152, 168; *Papers of FLO*, 6: 493–94, n. 1; Worthington Whittredge (1820–1910), *A Retrospective Exhibition of an American Artist*, exhibit catalogue [New York, 1969]).
2. Col. George Edwin Waring, Jr. (1833–1898), sanitary engineer and author, was well-known for his work on urban sanitary reform. Waring and Olmsted had been friends since 1857 when Waring rented Olmsted's Staten Island farm. That year Olmsted also hired him to supervise the installation of the drainage system for Central Park, a position that set Waring on a new and successful career path. After the war, during which he earned the rank of colonel, Waring designed sewerage systems for a number of cities including Memphis, which had struggled for years with devastating yellow fever epidemics. From 1895 to 1898 he served as commissioner of street cleaning for New York, where the results of his work gained national recognition. Waring wrote a number of influential books on sanitation and urban and village reform, such as *Village Improvements and Farm Villages* (1877) and *The Sanitary Drainage of Houses and Towns* (1876), a volume Olmsted particularly admired.

   Donald Grant Mitchell, "Ike Marvel" (1822–1908), was an author known for his essays and novels on American life, beginning with *Reveries of a Bachelor* (1850). Later in his career he wrote mostly about the value of country life, farm management, rural architecture, and landscape design. He wrote *Rural Studies with Hints for Country Places* (1867) and was also editor of *Hearth and Home*.

Nathaniel Hillyer Egleston (1822–1912), minster and author, was born in Hartford, Connecticut, the same year as Olmsted, and graduated from the Yale Divinity School in 1844. In the 1870s and 1880s he advocated for the preservation of rural scenery and the creation of village improvement societies in books and lectures, one of his more famous publications being *Villages and Village Life* (1878). He was the minister of the Stockbridge, Massachusetts, Congregational Church between 1860 and 1869, and was vice president of the Laurel Hill Association in Stockbridge at that time. He also advocated for the conservation of the nation's forests and served on the Forestry Congress and as Chief of the Bureau of Forestry in Washington, D.C. (*Papers of FLO*, 3: 42, n. 34, 105, n. 5; Martin V. Melosi, *Garbage in the Cities: Refuse, Reform, and the Environment* [Pittsburgh, 2005], pp. 42–52; *DAB*; Brett Coker, "Donald Grant Mitchell," in Wesley T. Mott, ed., *The American Renaissance in New England: Fourth Series* [Detroit, 2001]; Waldo H. Dunn, *The Life of Donald G. Mitchell* [New York, 1922]; *NCAB*; "Rev. N.H. Egleston Dies," *New York Times*, Aug. 26, 1912; K. J. Makker "Building Main Street," pp. 105–8).

3. Edward Kemp, *How to Lay Out a Garden* [London, 1850]; Frank J. Scott, *Victorian Gardens, the Art of Beautifying Suburban Home Grounds* [New York, 1870]; Jacob Weidenmann, *Beautifying Country Homes* [New York, 1870]).
4. In March of 1882, Whittredge wrote to Olmsted on behalf of the Ladies' Summit Village Improvement Society, to which his wife Euphemia belonged and which was based "much on the Stockbridge plan." He asked Olmsted to visit and advise them on matters of village improvement. Olmsted went to Summit in early April and suggested that, before any attempts to "beautify" the community were begun, the grading and pavement of the village's streets be undertaken to keep them clean and well drained. He also suggested "macadamizing" (paving with crushed gravel to promote good drainage) the streets and area around the train depot. He then consulted with Whittredge on the landscape design of his residence. While apparently no plan was produced, Olmsted ordered plants for Whittredge and instructed him where to plant them (Worthington Whittredge to FLO, March 16, 1882; Euphemia Whittredge to FLO, April 3, 1882; FLO to JCO, April 11, 1882; "Summit, N.J. Association," *Indoors and Outdoors*, May 1, 1883, p. 5; Euphemia Whittredge to FLO, April 23, 1882; Euphemia Whittredge to FLO, May 8, 1882; Worthington Whittredge to FLO, May 9, 1882).
5. See Frederick Law Olmsted, *Public Parks and the Enlargement of Towns*, 1870:

   > Of the fact of the general townward movement of the civilized world, and its comprehensiveness, there can be no doubt . . . the strength of the movement at any point seems to correspond closely with the degree in which the habits of the people have been recently changed by the abolition of feudalism, slavery, and government by divine right; by the multiplication and cheapening of schools, newspapers, and books; and by the introduction of labor-saving arrangements, especially of that class which are only available at all where they can be used to the direct benefit of many, such as railroads and telegraphs (*Papers of FLO*, SS1: 174.)

6. The words "after farm & town &c" appear here in the top margin, an annotation of Olmsted's noting where in the sequence of his paper he wanted this section.
7. In Village *Improvements and Farm Villages* (1877), Waring comments on these villages in Massachusetts: "It so happens that the few farm villages to which we can refer — such as Farmington, Hadley, and Deerfield — have become so attractive by means of their full-grown beauty, or have been so encroached upon by the wealth that has come over the district to which they belong, that they are no longer to be taken as types of pure country villages" (pp. 151–52).
8. Crossed out by Olmsted in manuscript.
9. Mary Howitt (1799–1888) was an English author of poetry and stories of rural life and

natural history. Mary Russell Mitford (1887–1855) was an English novelist whose most famous work was the multi-volume *Our Village* (1824–1832) composed of scenes from small village life. Elizabeth Gaskell (1810–1865) was an English author who often wrote of the different strata of society in rural England. Anne Thackeray (1837–1919) was an English author whose stories were often set in rural villages (*DNB*).

10. Olmsted paraphrases from Waring's *Village Improvements and Farm Villages* (1877), in which the author observes what is lacking in village life in terms of culture and diverse pastimes:

> The main reason for preferring village life is principally because it is better for the women and children; but there are reasons, in the same direction, why better social conditions would give the farmer himself decided benefits. The life, too, would be more *attractive* for both boys and girls, and would be divested of that naked and dismal gloom and dryness which now drive so much of the best farmer blood of the whole country to work-benches and counters,—to any position, in fact, which promises relief from the stifling isolation of the country. . . . it is hardly necessary to disclaim the least want of appreciation of the sterling qualities which have been developed in the American farm household. But it may be safely insisted that these qualities have been developed, not because of the American mode of farm life, but in spite of it; and, as I think over the long list of admirable men and women whose acquaintance I have formed on distant and solitary farms, I am more and more impressed with certain shortcomings which would have been avoided under better social conditions (pp. 143, 150).

11. Humphry Repton (1752–1818) was the English landscape designer who coined the term "landscape gardening" to describe the profession he helped establish. In addition to hundreds of design commissions in Britain, Repton published three textbooks on "the theory and practice" of landscape gardening that remained fundamental and cogent sources of theory and technical advice for Olmsted and his contemporaries in the United States (*DNB*; John Nolen, ed., *The Art of Landscape Gardening by Humphry Repton, Esq.* [Boston, 1907]; see also FLO to Charles Eliot, Feb. 25, 1886, below).
12. Olmsted's placeholders for words he omitted from the quotation: "this area was often covered with droves of cattle, of pigs, or geese."
13. Humphry Repton, *Fragments on the Theory and Practice of Landscape Gardening* (1816). Repton concludes his final book with these observations on his own residential landscape in the village of Hare Street, in Hertfordshire. See FLO to Charles Eliot, Feb. 25, 1886, below.
14. This was crossed out in manuscript but no alternative beginning to the sentence was given.
15. The May chafer, or cockchafer, is a European beetle that feeds on plant roots as a larva and is destructive to foliage, flowers, and fruit as an adult (*EB*).
16. In his article, Olmsted outlined several suggestions for attractive landscape gardening around the dooryard of a village home:

> Let it be acknowledged that fitness and propriety require that there should be some place before the house of repose for the eye, and that nowhere in the little property, to all parts of which we may wish at times to lead our friends in fine attire, can we risk danger of a dusty or a muddy surface. Starting from the corner nearest the tree, and running broader and deeper after it has passed and before the house, there shall be a swale (a gentle water-way) of cleanly turf . . .

(Frederick Law Olmsted, "Landscape Gardening," from *Johnson's New Universal Cyclopaedia*, 1878 [*Papers of FLO*, 7: 353]).

17. "Seine" is a fishing net designed to hang vertically in the water, the ends being drawn

together to enclose the fish. Here Olmsted suggests one made of twine to serve as a trellis for vines (*OED*).

TO THE SOUTH PARK COMMISSIONERS

Brookline Mass
28th February 1883

Sirs;

I am glad to be able to supply at the request of your Secretary[1] four copies of the pamphlet twelve years ago issued by your Commission explanatory of the motives and intentions with which the work of improvement of the South Park was entered upon.[2]

The request for these gives me occasion to recall the concluding passage of that pamphlet (pp 53 & 54) in which as distinct a warning was given as was then proper for the designers of the park to offer, that whatever departures from particular local features of the plan might come to be thought expedient in the future it was of the "*utmost consequence*" that consistency of purpose in respect to general style quality and character should be steadily insisted on by the Commissioners.[3] The more obvious dangers of mal-administration extravagance and waste were believed by the writers to be much less than that which lay in the liability and temptation to pursue local & special ends in themselves attractive and commendable but antagonistic to others of a more general and comprehensive scope.

When I had the pleasure of driving through the park with some of your body two years ago[4] I could not but point out that this warning had been ineffective and that the work in detail had in fact been directed to results very different in quality style and character from those which had been had in view in determining the outlines and general features of the undertaking so much so that one hand was tearing down what the other was building up.[5]

You have had two styles of park in view either of which would be satisfactory if well carried out. But the result of pursuing either alternative at intervals of some years or of muddling them together though not unpleasing to an observer for the time being must eventually be offensive either because of the incongruities it presents or tame and insipid because of the neutralization of one element of beauty by another.

What is now needed is a studious review of the entire work not with a view to the recovery of what has been lost of the value of the original design but to bring about in connection with the necessary maintenance operations greater consistency between the larger and substantially fixed elements of the undertaking and the smaller and more accommodative elements. Could a revision of the design be now fixed upon and adhered to recovering as far as remains practicable without costly constructive operations to the style and character of work originally designed, the result would be much more valuable and less costly than can otherwise be hoped for.

Very respectfully yours

Fred[k] Law Olmsted

The text presented here is a letter written and signed in a clerk's hand. The Chicago South Park Commissioners hired Olmsted and Vaux to design the 1,000-acre South Park (now Washington and Jackson parks and the Midway Plaisance) the year after the commission was established in 1869. The plans Olmsted and Vaux completed in 1871 remained mostly unimplemented in 1883. Work had commenced but was halted after the great fire of 1871 destroyed most of the documents related to the project. The commissioners engaged H. W. S. Cleveland to be the project's landscape architect in 1872, and he implemented the plan by Olmsted and Vaux. By 1883 much of Washington Park had been constructed, but Jackson Park and the Midway Plaisance were not fully developed until they were chosen to be the site of the 1893 World's Fair (*Papers of FLO*, SS1: 19–23; A. T. Andreas, *History of Chicago*, vol. III [Chicago, 1886], pp. 171–72; Victoria Post Ranney, "Frederick Law Olmsted: Designing for Democracy in the Midwest," in *Midwestern Landscape Architecture* [Chicago, 2000], pp. 46–50).

1. The secretary of the South Park Commission at this time was H. W. Harmon. The commissioners were Paul Cornell, John. B. Sherman, John R. Walsh, Martin J. Russell, and Bernard Callaghan; M. W. White was the park's superintendent (H. W. Harmon to FLO, Feb. 23, 1883; A. T. Andreas, *History of Chicago*, vol. III, pp. 171–72).
2. The "pamphlet" was the March 1871 *Report Accompanying Plan for Laying Out the South Park*, by Olmsted, Vaux, & Co. Landscape Architects (*Papers of FLO*, SS1: 206–38).
3. "It is not to be expected that a plan will be made at the outset so complete, that no additions to it or modification of it in detail will be admissible, but it is of the utmost consequence that the essential ends should be clearly seen before the work is organized, and that from the moment it begins to the end, be that five or fifty years hence, and under whatever changes of administration and changes of fashion, these great ruling ends should be pursued with absolute consistency" (Olmsted, Vaux, & Co. Landscape Architects, *Report Accompanying Plan for Laying Out the South Park*, March 1871 [*Papers of FLO*, SS1: 234]).
4. Olmsted revisited the South Park site in 1880 on a tour with park commissioners Paul Cornell and Martin J. Russell and park superintendent W. M. Berry (FLO to Paul Cornell, April 12, 1881 [*Papers of FLO*, 7: 525–28]).
5. Some changes to South Park made in the 1870s included features Olmsted and Vaux had not suggested, such as greenhouses and elaborate floral displays. In 1872 the commission hired landscape architect H. W. S. Cleveland, a friend and former employee of Olmsted's, with the intention of implementing Olmsted and Vaux's plans. Cleveland's work for the commission became sporadic in the wake of the financial crisis of 1873, however, and in 1874 his salary was suspended. In 1875 he wrote to Olmsted that he was seeking steadier employment (Daniel Bluestone, *Constructing Chicago* [New Haven,

1991], p. 44; William H. Tishler, "Horace Cleveland: The Chicago Years" in William H. Tishler, ed., *Midwestern Landscape Architecture* [Urbana, IL, 2000], pp. 30–35; H. W. S. Cleveland to FLO, May 26, 1875).

IMPROVEMENT OF EASTON'S BEACH.

BROOKLINE, MASS., March 13, 1883.

THE HON. R. S. FRANKLIN, *Mayor of Newport.*[1]

Dear Sir,—Since you asked my opinion as to what could be wisely done for the improvement of Easton's Beach as a place of public resort, a large part of the ground has been so encumbered by ice and snow as to prevent more than a superficial examination of the circumstances; but, without further delay, I will advise you of the inclination of my judgment upon my present understanding of them.

The probable effect of proposed measures on the value of city property has not often to be considered where the highest utility of the property is of the character that it is in this case. It is desirable, therefore, to plainly draw the line which divides the question to be dealt with from such as are of more familiar occurrence.

To those who for the first time see from this property the ocean breaking upon a broad strand of slight and regular inclination, the sight is one of the most moving that nature anywhere offers; and it is one admiration of which never fails. This distinctive value—regarding the beach as a property to be dealt with on commercial principles—will advance as population and wealth and facilities for reaching the seaboard increase in the interior of the country. The city, therefore, should be on its guard against projects by which conditions on which it depends may be weakened, vulgarized, or made unnecessarily prosaic, artificial, and commonplace.

The broad, hard beach, and the waste of sand back of it, thrown up by the breakers, form the natural and the most appropriate setting, and the most telling foreground for the grandeur of the view toward the offing; and simply as a matter of taste, or of the value of the property as food for the eye and the imagination, nothing better can be done than to let it alone.

If, however, considerations of public convenience and comfort must in some degree overrule this of respect for nature, then whatever is to be provided may desirably be given one of two characters. It may be either simple, sturdy, and of storm-defying aspect, or it may be obviously slight and shiftable, like the dressing-rooms on wheels commonly provided for bathers on the English beaches.

But I am advised, that, if the city should be willing to adopt any such movable dressing arrangement for bathers, some fixed construction at which spectators can obtain shade, seats, and refreshments, will probably be thought necessary. If an affair for this purpose is required, it should be set as far from the surf as practicable; that is to say, well back upon the high sands, leaving the beach proper unbroken. The present structures on the beach are too shabby and incommodious to remain long; but, taking everything into consideration, it would, I feel sure, prove an injury to the city to replace them by such as have lately been set upon several beaches of public resort elsewhere. These are really of the same cheap and shabby class, but bigger, and made more obtrusive and incongruous by gingerbread work and paint; sometimes also by sorry attempts to put all the distinctive attractions of the local scenery out of countenance by displays of smug[2] turf and garish flower-gardening. I particularly advise against anything of this kind.

I have so far been writing of what, to my mind, is not desirable, rather than offering positive advice, because the question, what should be done upon the beach, appears to be secondary to another, any satisfactory determination of which would probably affect plans for dealing with the beach.

While the view seaward over the beach, when not artificially disturbed, is as fine as possible, the foreground of the landward view is discordant with the general character of all that is seen beyond, and most disagreeable.

It is formed chiefly by a quagmire, with large pools of shallow water and mud. As the summer advances, the water shrinks, and the muddy surface broadens. The mire, when stirred, has a fetid odor, and apparently contains a large amount of putrefying organic matter. These conditions have not as yet, it is said, been found harmful to the public health; but they are obviously menacing, and, by their resemblance to those of the most noisome and deadly miasmatic localities,[3] are a repulsive circumstance in the midst of a place otherwise of the highest distinction as a resort for health and cheering recreation.

The pleasure of a visit to the beach, and consequently the value of the beach as a property of the city, must be greatly marred by this circumstance; and if, by any means not excessively costly, it could be overcome, and the landward foreground made positively agreeable and harmonious with the general landward prospect, the value of all private property throughout the city would be favorably affected.

Because of the difficulty of obtaining accurate information of all the under-water conditions, and consequently of judging fairly the capabilities of the situation, I do not like to propose a definite plan for the object; but I will offer a tentative suggestion, which, if you please, may serve as a provocative to more practical discussion than has yet been had,—may at least draw out information of difficulties and objections not at present obvious to me.

The important facts to be considered appear to be as follows;—

The swampy district is about three-quarters of a mile long against the beach, and quarter of a mile broad. The surface of the muddy deposit is about half above and half below the surface of the water at its average height. The depth of

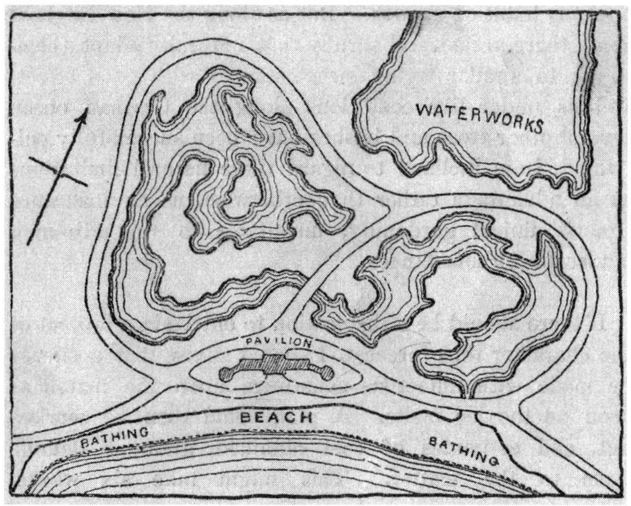

Plan for Easton's Beach and surrounding area, Newport, R.I. (1883)

the water in the deeper parts is from three to four feet; and a hard, sandy bottom is generally found at five or six feet.

The first object in any plan of improvement should be to obtain greater depth of water when water is to be permanent, and greater elevation, and consequently better drainage for the surface of all ground to be left above water.

This object can be gained at the least cost by the use of a steam-dredger, which (drawn over the beach by house-moving apparatus) would at once open a channel for itself by scooping the mud before it. The dredged material being swung out and deposited at its sides, the process could be so managed, that in the end the entire territory now occupied by quagmire would be divided between the dredger's channels, which would have a sandy bottom, at a minimum depth of perhaps four feet, and ridges between these channels, the surface of which ridges would have been raised by the deposits of the dredger to an elevation of three feet above the surface of the water,—more, if it should be found best, as it probably will be, to keep the ultimate level of the water considerably lower than at present.

But, to secure a pleasing aspect, means should be taken for spreading portions of the dredged material at a greater distance from the channels; and, with a view to a public promenade in connection with the beach, all along the outer part of the swamp the dredger should work below the mud, raising a sufficient amount of sand to form a continuous clean and solid embankment, with deep water adjoining it.

I give you here a rough sketch showing how the division of land and water might be arranged with a view to an economical use of the steam-dredging apparatus, and at the same time to picturesque effects.

On the outer embankment a pleasure drive, riding pad, and walk could be made within the outlines shown on the sketch. The circuit would be about two miles in length. Wherever required, ordinary streets would open into this circuit road.[4]

The circumstances are not favorable to the thrift of many sorts of trees or shrubs, though entirely so to turf and a great variety of perennials. The soil would be a little salty, subject to be harshly swept by the Atlantic gales converging between two headlands, and to be sometimes dashed with a little fine spray from the breakers. Unless, therefore, discrimination were used in the planting, trees and shrubs would be apt, if kept alive, to take an uncanny habit of growth. But as along the New England coast there are several shrubs that naturally adapt themselves to similar trying circumstances with good effect, and as under like conditions along the German ocean several other trees and bushes have been successfully cultivated. I am inclined to regard these natural limitations as an advantage rather than otherwise, as an insurance against finical gardening, unsuitable to the adjoining landscape circumstances.

If there should be a disposition to entertain a project of the character thus forecast, I should advise that a survey be made with numerous soundings upon the marsh as soon as the ice melts. A plan could then be worked out, and estimates of cost obtained, giving a definite form to the matter. This might take six weeks. The amount of material to be handled is large; but, by using steam in the manner suggested, it could be moved at less than half the cost of wheeling the same in the ordinary way on dry land. My impression is that the cost of the entire work would be within a hundred and fifty thousand dollars, and above a hundred thousand dollars.

If possible, the dredging should be begun early in the autumn, and completed before warm weather of the following summer. The mud, once frozen and thawed, would be harmless; but, if the operation were to be carried on during the summer, it might be difficult to prevent its becoming a nuisance. The work could be wholly completed, and the circuit roads opened to public use, the second year.

In conclusion, a trite remark may be excused on the ground that, because of its triteness, it needs on this occasion to be specially emphasized.

The degree in which the life of many of the summer residents of Newport is, to outward appearance, given to the pursuit of social enjoyments and ruled by fashion, tends to distract attention from the special root of the city's prosperity.

It was not fashion that first brought people of luxurious tastes, with means for indulging them, to Newport. It was a satisfaction found in its air and scenery by people of a rather reserved, unobtruding, contemplative, and healthily sentimental turn, little troubled by social ambitions. Social attractions came with them; and fashion, as is usual, followed social attractions. Little as it may be obvious on the surface, it is the same local advantage of air and scenery, and the same class of minds yielding to it, that yet retains for Newport so much larger a share of social advantages and of fashion than, with constantly increasing outlays and exertions, competing places of public resort are able to secure.

Whatever is to the disadvantage of the air or the natural scenery of Newport, to the sense of this inadvertent leadership of society and of fashion, is disadvantageous to the prosperity of the city. Whatever lessens any such disadvantage, and tends to strengthen the attractiveness of its air and scenery, even though it be by action on a listless imagination, as surely reduces its rate of taxation by enlarging the basis of assessment, and otherwise puts money in its pocket, as any other means by which capital might be attracted, and the profitable trade of the best customers of the country secured to a community.

Respectfully yours,

FREDERICK LAW OLMSTED

The text presented here was published as *City of Newport, Improvement of Easton's Beach, Preliminary Report of F. L. Olmsted* (Boston, 1883).

1. Robert Stillman Franklin (1836–1913) was born in Newport, Rhode Island, and served as mayor from 1882 to 1886. A local businessman and active in local politics, Franklin commissioned Olmsted to design improvements for Easton's Beach, also known as First Beach, which was popular with middle-class day trippers to Newport. In 1881 Easton's Beach had been the proposed site of a large hotel, but the project was thwarted by the summer "cottagers" who feared the new resort would not be exclusive enough (Albert Nelson Marquis, ed., *Who's Who in New England* [Chicago, 1909], p. 383; Annie Robinson, *Peabody & Stearns: Country Houses and Seaside Cottages* [New York, 2010], p. 58; "The Season at Newport," *New York Times*, July 10, 1881, p. 1; Richard M. Bayles, ed., *History of Newport County, Rhode Island* [New York, 1888], pp. 489–90; 494; 504–5).
2. Smug in the sense of smooth, clean, or neat (*OED*).
3. Olmsted refers here and elsewhere to miasmatic disease theory, which held that noxious vapors rising from poorly drained areas and swamps caused and spread disease (see Frederick Law Olmsted, *The Park for Detroit*, Nov. 1882, above).
4. The concept of an outer embankment serving as a pleasure drive suggests a later, more ambitious design Olmsted proposed for the Buffalo park system. His 1888 plan for South Park in Buffalo included a lakefront parkway connecting the park to the city's downtown to the north. The parkway featured a promenade built on a raised levee with a recreational canal behind it forming a "water-avenue" (F. L. & J. C. Olmsted, "Report on the South Parkway Question," in *Projected Park and Parkways on the South Side of Buffalo* [Buffalo, 1888], pp. 18–19 [*Papers of FLO*, SS1: 594, n. 10]; Charles E. Beveridge and Paul Rocheleau, *Frederick Law Olmsted: Designing the American Landscape* [New York, 1995], p. 94).

REPORT OF FRED'K LAW OLMSTED, LANDSCAPE ARCHITECT.

BROOKLINE, Mass., 10th May, 1883.

To the Trustees of the Cushing's Island Company:
GENTLEMEN:—I last week visited Cushing's Island with a view to giving you, as requested, my judgment of its fitness as a place of summer residence and as to measures desirable for its improvement.

The situation, dimensions, form and general character of the island as far as shown by maps, drawings and such written accounts of it as I have seen are probably known to all who may read this report, and such information as they present need not be repeated. I found that they had not impressed the more attractive qualities of its scenery upon me in several particulars. It is in parts much wilder and more rugged than I had been led to suppose, and has much more beauty of a delicate character, dependent on its minor vegetation, and the form, texture and color of its rocks. I will mention two incidents of its scenery which I found particularly enjoyable to which I had seen no reference. One is the rare picturesqueness of certain groups of vertically splintered rocks, close off the south shore against and among which the full swell of the ocean was surging at the time of my visit with a charm of motion and beauty of color quite indescribable; the other, the lovely tints, due I presume to lichens and mosses, in crannies and on the face of the beetling crags of White Head.

The Island is not a good place for a neighborhood of smart and fine suburban residences such as many prefer to pass their summers in. Streets suitable to such an occupancy of it would be difficult of construction, costly and a blemish upon its natural scenery. Villas and cottages of the class in question would appear out of place, tawdry and vulgar, upon it. Lawns and gardens appropriate to them are in large parts of the island out of the question. Notions of improving the island based on what has generally been attempted at many public favored places of summer resort should therefore be wholly abandoned. But to persons who wish to take as complete a vacation from urban conditions of life as is practicable without being obliged to dispense with good markets, shops and the occasional ready use of city conveniences; who have a taste for wildness of nature and who value favorable conditions for sea bathing, boating and fishing, the island offers attractions such as can be found, I believe, nowhere else on the Atlantic seaboard. To all such I recommend it unreservedly. The only danger of reasonable disappointment to such persons lies in the chance that others of incompatible tastes and ambitions will aim to make "improvements" of various sorts, and attempt a style of life incongruous with the natural circumstances and repugnant to tastes that the island is otherwise adapted to gratify.

If the island could in effect be owned by a club of families of congenial tastes united only for the purpose of preserving and developing its characteristic advantages and of providing convenience of habitation in a manner harmonious each with all, and all with nature, it would, under judicious management, soon acquire a value to each member such as could be obtained in a summer residence nowhere else nearly as economically.

It is with a view to a disposition of it essentially of this character that I shall suggest measures for its fittings and improvement.

From what has been said it will be obvious that the value of a summer residence upon Cushing's Island rather than in a thousand other localities along the coast, depends on scenery much of which can only be enjoyed either from points of view inaccessible to carriages and near which it will always be undesirable in the interests of those who will take the greatest pleasure in it, that carriages should be brought, or from elevated places in the interior. It is of the first importance to secure the free common use of these points of observation of both classes and to prevent their outlooks from being either obstructed or put out of countenance by structures for private convenience.

To this end certain elevated interior localities and a strip of land bordering the entire coast, should be made a constituent part of the property attached to each summer residence, these adjuncts being held in common. Certain other grounds should be disposed of for private use only in such large areas that houses to be built upon them will be scattered, leaving large spaces unencumbered by artificial objects. The deeds to be given for these large areas should provide against more than one residence within a distance of 500 feet, measured in a line parallel with the shore line, and with the condition that houses to be built upon them shall not be more than two stories in height: that at least their lower stories shall be of the local stone and that no fence or other structure shall be placed between them and the sea, except of rough local stone.

In the sketch plan herewith presented, about a hundred acres are proposed to be held as common property, this including all the outer parts of the island, its cliffs, crags, shingles and beaches, and sufficient space of the adjoining upland to allow continuous foot paths following the shore. At the more interesting points this upper space is enlarged. At each point of the island giving upon the ocean and the harbor's mouths considerable spaces are reserved and these are connected by a narrow common along the central heights which will command views both ways. Roads are projected with a view to a subdivision of the property and to a convenient connection between the interior building sites and the different parts of the shore. One main road, leading through the middle of the island from the present landing of the Portland ferry boat, is proposed to be seventy feet wide so as to admit of its being planted with trees. Other roads are generally forty feet wide and a few by-paths for short cuts between different points of interest are proposed.

Residence sites in that part of the island where houses will be overlooked from the heights, and where neither rocks nor declivities will make difficulties in building, are generally from half an acre to an acre in area, elsewhere they vary according to circumstances, from two to seven acres.

With a view to unity, harmony and congruity of general effect, it is advised that no house shall be allowed to stand within 30 feet of the road line on the smaller lots, nor within 60 feet on lots of over an acre in extent; that no house shall be more than two stories in height, or 30 feet to the top of the roof, or furnished in its upper or more exposed and conspicuous parts with jig-saw or other extrinsic and puerile ornaments.

All the northern part of the island is at present comparatively bare and bleak of aspect, but there is evidence enough in the existing foliage that trees, shrubs and perennial plants may be easily and satisfactorily grown. It is very desirable for the value of the property as a whole that trees should be planted and that the narrow roads should be lined with low hedges and thickets. For this reason, and with a view to suitably planting the roads, walks and common grounds, the Trustees are recommended to establish at once a small nursery from which a variety of plants, especially shrubs and low-headed trees, adapted to the local soil, topography and climate, shall be provided for private planting on the island, without charge or at cost. Also to encourage the building of stone houses and fences, the free use of the present farm walls and all loose stone is advised to be allowed and quarries are recommended to be opened from which building stone for use on the island may be taken without charge. The stone of the island may apparently be very cheaply quarried, and if the outside of all its buildings shall present to view only the local stone or shingles without paint or gingerbread work, or shall be draped with the foliage of vines natural to the locality, the general result will be most effective.

The abundance of stone is such that where railings, parapets or small structures for seats and outlooks are required in the common grounds, ordinary slight painted work should not be admitted, nor should any structure be made more conspicuous than its leading purpose requires, it being kept constantly in view that the value of the property in the long run and on the whole will be dependent on the art which conceals rather than displays itself, and which favors the large and most unsophisticated enjoyment of nature that can be reconciled with a fair measure of convenience.

To the same general end provision should at once be made for a gradual replacement of the present spruce and fir woods of the higher parts of the island. Such a removal and improvement of the old natural growth, if not delayed, can be secured at slight expense. A few years hence it is likely to be practicable only by an outlay many times as large. The present natural beauty of the island may, simply by the sowing of seeds at trifling cost, be greatly increased.

The topography of the island is favorable to drainage, and, as far as can

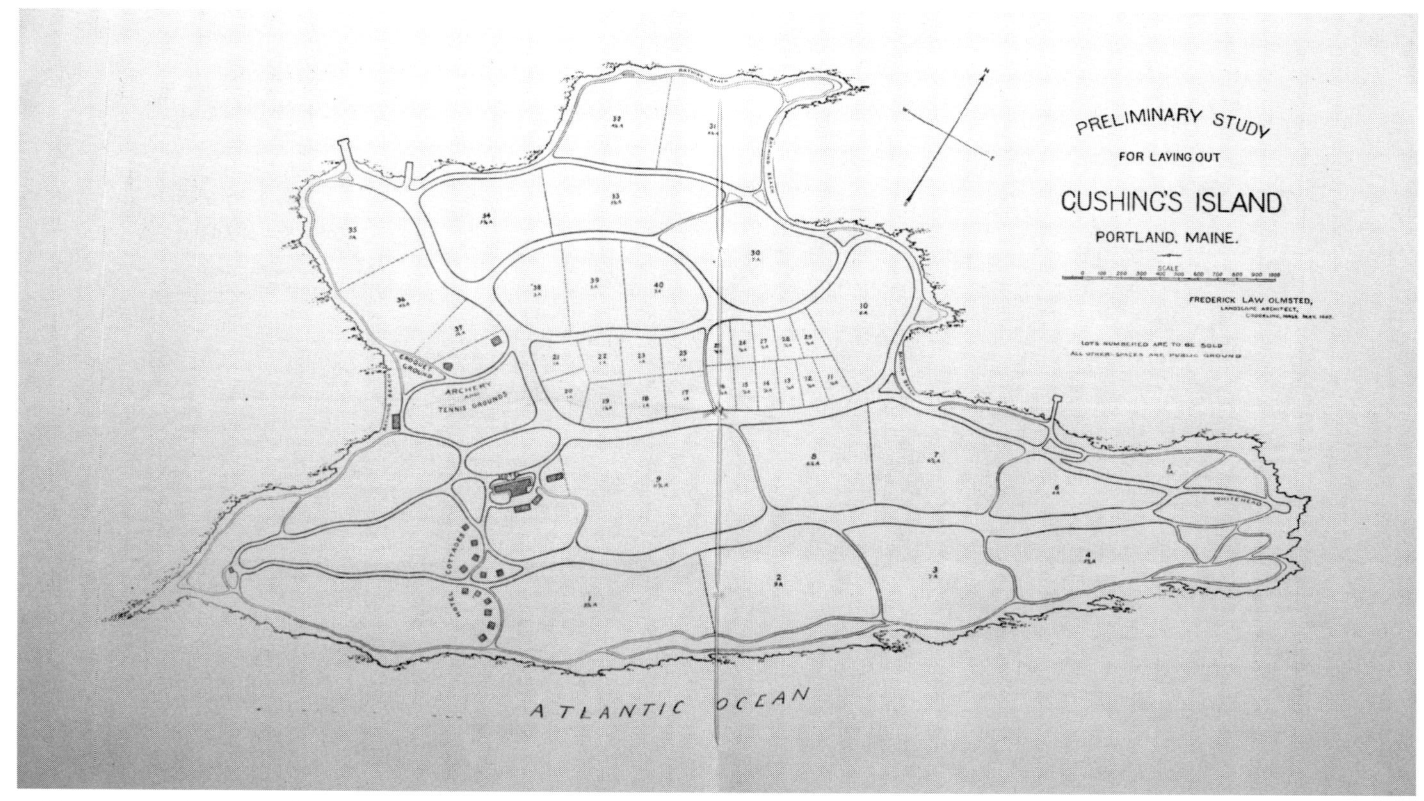

"Preliminary Study for Laying Out Cushing's Island, Portland, Maine," May 1883, from *Summer Homes, Cushing's Island* (1883); shows division of plots and land preserved along entire shoreline for walking paths

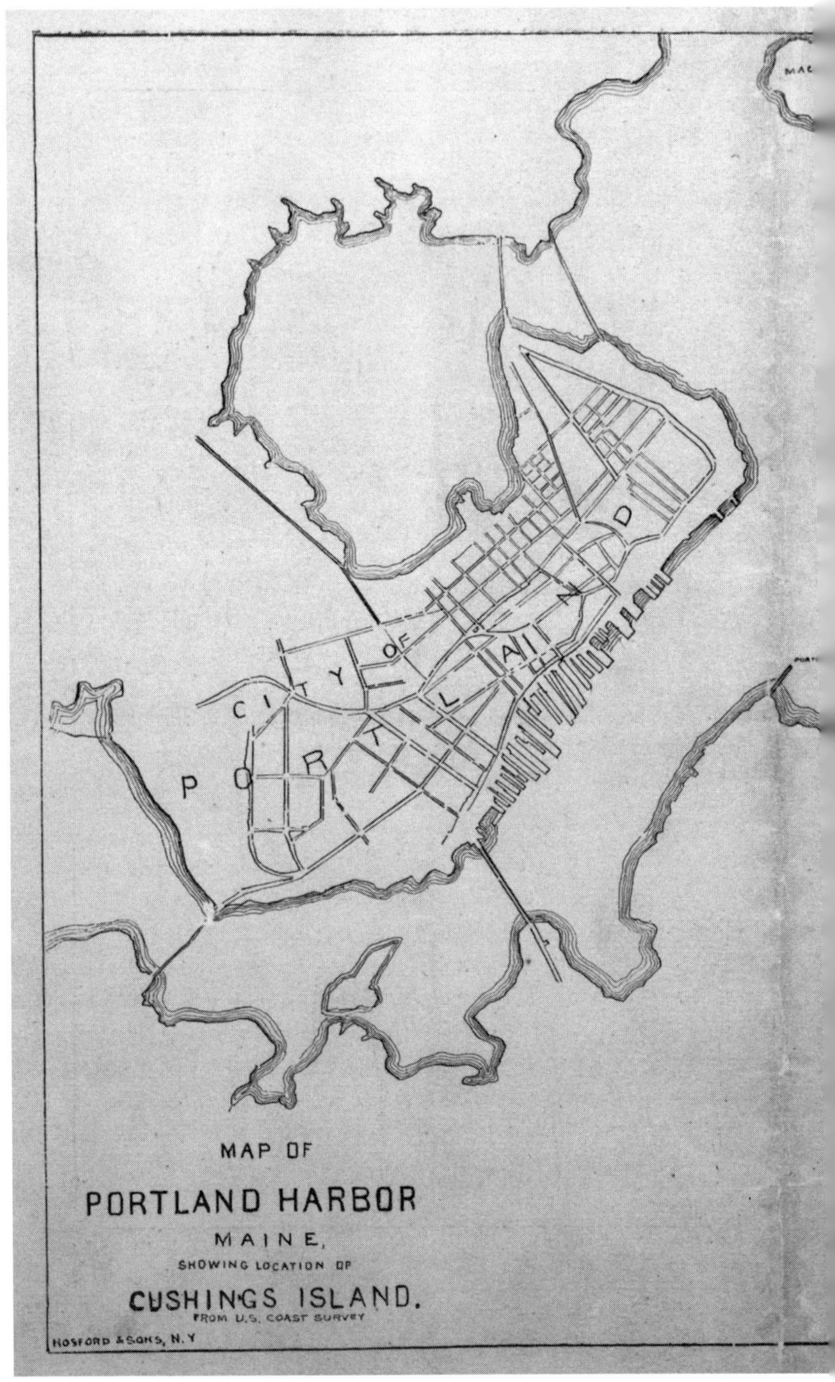

"MAP OF PORTLAND HARBOR, MAINE, SHOWING LOCATION OF CUSHING'S ISLAND,"

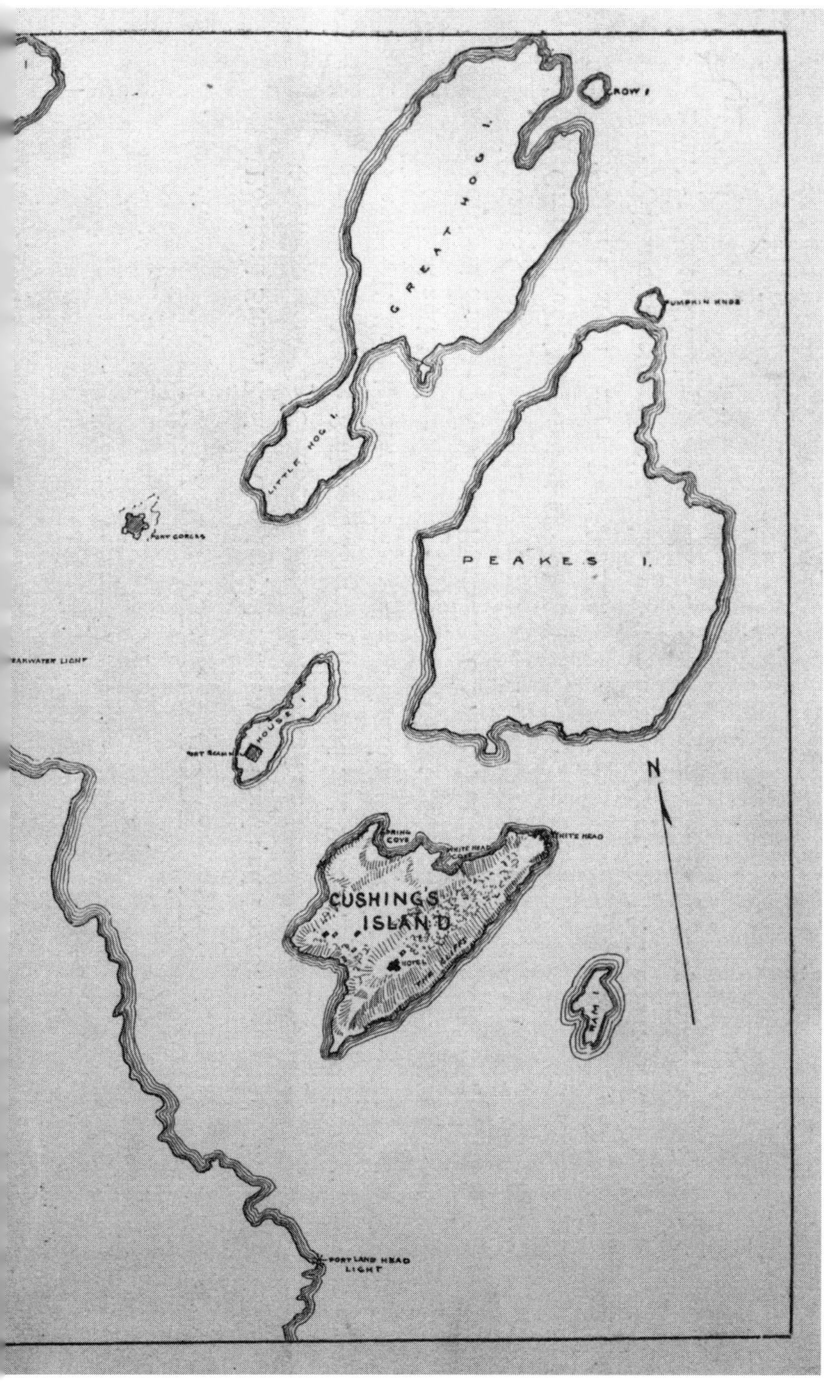

ROM THE U.S. COAST SURVEY, PRINTED IN *SUMMER HOMES, CUSHING'S ISLAND* (1883)

be judged in a cursory survey, there will be ready and moderately direct descent from all the lots shown on the accompanying plan, to the sea. Possibly in a few cases, to avoid rock cuts it may be desirable to carry outlets for short distances through adjoining properties, and the Trustees should retain the right to direct this when necessary.

Respectfully,

FRED'K LAW OLMSTED.

The text presented here was published in a real estate prospectus, *Summer Homes, Cushing's Island*, prepared by the trustees of the Cushing's Island Company (New York, 1883). Cushing's Island, which is about 250 acres, lies near the entrance to the harbor of Portland, Maine. Canadian businessman Lemuel Cushing bought the island in 1859 and left it to his sons, one of whom, Francis Cushing, incorporated the Cushing's Island Company in 1883. Francis planned to turn the island into a summer community centered around the Ottawa Hotel, which his father had built. The hotel burned in 1886, was rebuilt two years later, and then burned again in 1917. Cushing engaged Olmsted to design a subdivision of the island "laid out artistically in common lands and in Villa plots to be sold only to people who will build pretty cottages for Summer homes." Olmsted divided 133 acres of the island into forty plots with the remainder of the land held undeveloped by the company as common property. Olmsted devised the plan to assure that the shoreline remained open for public use, providing footpaths and overlooks (The Cushing's Island Company, *Summer Homes, Cushing's Island, Portland Harbor, Coast of Maine* [New York, 1883]; James A. Hudson to FLO, Nov. 22, 1882, B65: #675, OAR/LC; *Hull's Handbook of Portland, Old Orchard, Cape Elizabeth and Casco Bay* [Portland, 1888], pp. 207–8).

To James Cameron Mackenzie[1]

Brookline Mass.
(p.m.) 21st May 1883.

My Dear Doctor Mackenzie

You are at least bound to plant your institution on the firmest fully established ground of sanitary science. No authority on the subject for many years has failed to insist on the importance of so placing school rooms that they shall be open to the direct rays of the sun and so arranging dormatories that the sun shall, at some time of the day, shine upon every room.

If we plan and arrange the buildings without regard to these desiderata we shall assuredly be condemned.

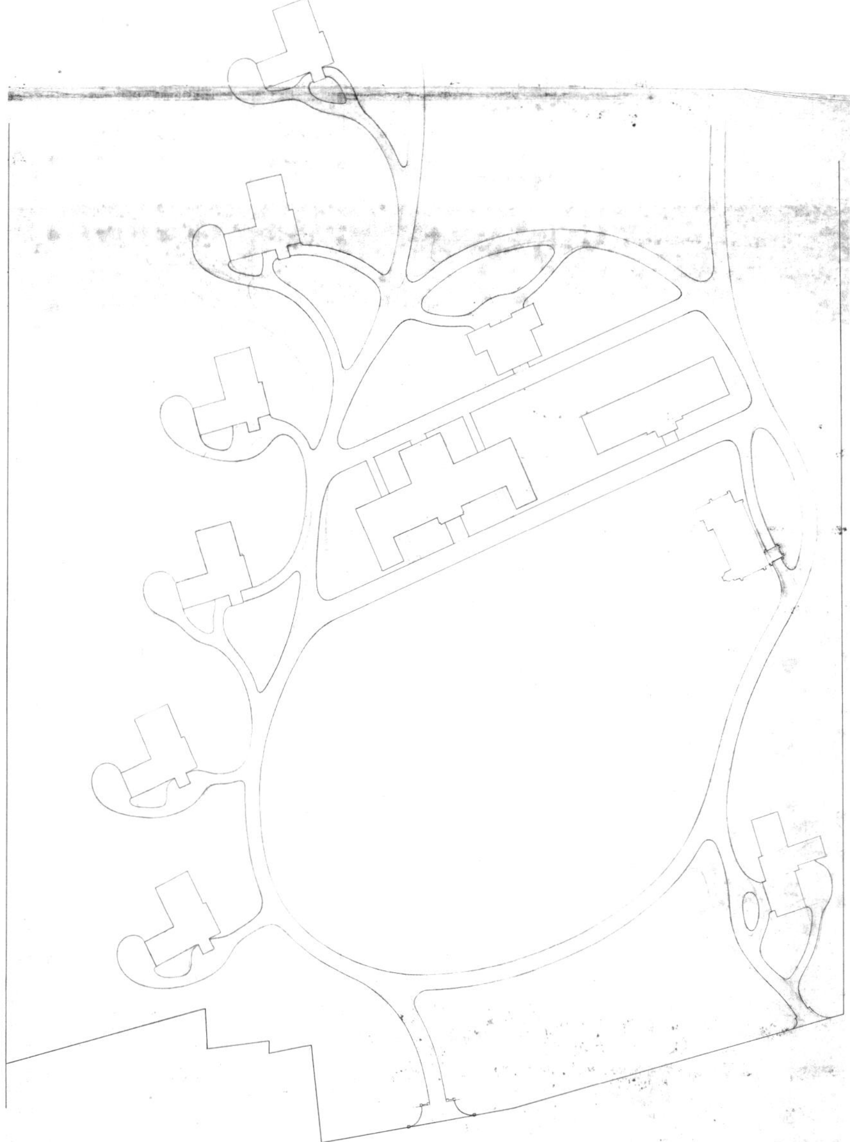

"PLAN FOR LAWRENCEVILLE SCHOOL, COPIED IN INK," APRIL 25, 1883, SHOWING THE FIRST PROPOSED LINEAR ARRANGEMENT OF BUILDINGS

Therefore the problem must be considered to include requirements to these ends before all others.

Secondary to them is that of placing the master's houses all within convenient distance of the Main School building and (less important) to the Chapel.

Again the buildings should not be crowded near the public street & the masters' houses shd not be more than 800 feet from it. (I did not see what determined this limit but we were so instructed.)

Lastly there should be some noteable spaciousness of verdant & umbrageous ground on the street side of the principal buildings, & room for enlargements on the West & for ample play grounds on the S.W. & {*sewage*} meadows on the S.E.[2] I have thus stated the main requirements of the problem. Of various arrangements that we have tried for solving it that of which I now give you a sketch best combines the required conditions.[3] It shirks none. It meets each fairly well.

E.G. It gives the morning sun on one set of Masters house bedrooms, the evening sun on another. It gives each family a fairly direct & short course to the main school building & the Chapel. It places the school rooms square to the South. It leaves room to place large dormitories so that each set of rooms on either side of a corridor would be facing the sun either forenoon or afternoon.

It meets all the other requirements as given to me but includes a sixth master's house which is beyond the 800 ft limit. It is practicable but not in my judgment advisable to squeeze all within 800 feet. It presents the principal building, Mr Peabody agrees, to the best advantage.

It leaves considerable additions to them practicable without much curtailing a general effect of spaciousness and seclusion of the buildings from the street.

I postpone the question of playgrounds & other matters till I receive the topog. map, & offer this as I promised this morning {. . .} for your private criticism.

Yours respy

F.L.O.

I have to leave home for a long professional tour next week & beg an early reply with return of the sketch, & I greatly regret the lack of the map.[4]

The text presented here is a signed draft in Olmsted's hand. In 1878 the family of John Cleve Green (1800–1875) acquired and endowed the Lawrenceville School and began a reorganization and expansion of it. In 1882 James Cameron Mackenzie became headmaster and established a "house" residential system in which instructors and students lived together in group houses in the manner of English public schools. Olmsted was hired in 1883 to create a campus plan that would accommodate the desired arrangement. Peabody and Stearns were the architects and J. J. R. Croes was the project engineer. In 1886 Olmsted proposed planting the school grounds as an arboretum consisting of all the species of trees that would be hardy in central New Jersey (Oscar Fay Adams, *Some Famous American Schools* [Boston, 1903], pp. 125–68; C. E. Beveridge and P. Rocheleau, *Designing the American Landscape*, pp. 127–38; FLO to James Cameron Mackenzie, Feb. 6, 1886, below).

1. James Cameron Mackenzie (1852–1931) was a prominent figure in American secondary school education. He was headmaster at the Lawrenceville School from 1882 to 1899 and a co-founder of the Headmasters Association of the United States in 1891. He later

established the Mackenzie School in Monroe, New York (*DAB*; "Dr. Mackenzie Dies; Noted Headmaster," *New York Times*, May 11, 1931, p.16).

2. Here Olmsted wrote and crossed out: "Leaving out for the present the question of the laboratory, gymnasium &c. Not intending at the moment to place the great dormitory or dormitories, the laboratory or gymnasium—only to see room for their subsequent placing." The "sewage meadows" Olmsted refers to were part of what he later described as the "complex, original, and ingenious" arrangements to address "difficult problems of water supply, drainage, sewerage, and of heating" that he and Croes devised for the school (FLO to George W. Vanderbilt, Aug. 1, 1891, A15: 405–11, OAR/LC).
3. The sketch mentioned here has not been found, but sketches dated April 23 and April 25, 1883, indicate a linear arrangement of the school houses. While working as an apprentice on the Lawrenceville plans, Charles Eliot wrote, "Difficult to arrange any way of giving the 5 Masters houses equally direct access to the school and chapel—without sacrificing all breadth and openness—and without resorting to a formal plan." Olmsted altered the draft proposal soon after it was criticized by the school's trustees in June. In his response to his clients, Olmsted pointed out that the topographic site survey, usually his first requirement upon beginning a commission, had not been available to him earlier. He also had not yet been able to meet the trustees or even visit the site. As a result, he suggested, the "theory" of the early sketch was adequate but the "detail of the arrangement" was not. Later that month the topographic survey was made available and a new plan, dated June 1883, showed the site topography with the cottages now shifted into an oval arrangement, maintaining both southern exposure for the student rooms and convenient access to the central classroom building (plans 52-14, 52-4-SH1, SH4, SH5; 52-21, NPS/FLONHS; Charles Eliot Diary, May 13, June 3, 1883, pp. 11, 17; FLLHU; FLO to Caleb S. Green, June 19, 1883).
4. This postscript is written in the left-hand margin, perpendicular to the main text. The "map" referred to would have been the still incomplete topographic survey.

ANNUAL REPORT OF THE ARCHITECT OF THE UNITED STATES CAPITOL

July 1, 1883

CAPITOL GROUNDS.

During the last year the north terrace approach has been built, and Congress at its last session ordered the corresponding work on the south of the Capitol. In the debate of the question apprehensions appeared that the plan of the larger work, of which these approaches are initial steps, had not been maturely considered, and that its ultimate cost could be but vaguely conjectured. Directions were consequently given that Congress should be supplied at the coming session with detailed information on the subject.[1]

The plan of the terrace was prepared under a commission which I had the honor to receive from Congress in 1874. It was submitted the following year in the form of large drawings of every part. A detailed estimate of the cost was at the same time presented, accompanied by offers from builders of the highest standing to contract for the work at the prices named.[2]

After prolonged consideration in joint committee, the proposition was adopted as a part of the general plan for the improvement of the Capitol grounds.

Since then the entire work of the terrace has been twice re-estimated in accordance with the market prices of the day. The last of these adjustments was made in 1882, and was based on the actual cost of the work then under contract upon the north terrace approach.[3] The rate thus established made the cost of the terrace entire about five per cent. less than the estimate originally given to Congress.[4]

Early in the last session this last estimate was laid before the Joint Committee on Public Buildings and Grounds, and at the time of the debate of the subject in the Senate was on file in your office. I do not know that it can yet be at all improved upon, and in order to meet the requirements of a detailed estimate to be presented at the opening of the next session, I will request, if you see no objection, that it may be printed precisely in its original form.

From the annual and occasional reports that I have prepared, and which have been printed for the information of Congress, in addition to the facts above stated, it will be apparent that[5] if I have failed to take the measures necessary to secure consideration for the plans and estimates of the terrace it can have been only from reluctance to exhibit a zeal in the premises which might be thought to carry me beyond the proper lines of my professional duty.

I hope that the small section of the terrace that has now been built, though at a point where the least advantage of the work can be realized, will be found to sustain, as far as it goes, the view of its value that I have at every suitable opportunity, in concurrence with you, sought to present.

The text presented here is Olmsted's report to Edward Clark, published in the *Annual Report of the Architect of the United States Capitol* (Washington, D.C., 1883). A draft of the report, dated July 26, 1883, is in FLO Papers/LC. In early June, while preparing this report, Olmsted visited the Capitol grounds with his apprentice, Charles Eliot (see Frederick Law Olmsted, *Annual Report of the Architect of the United States Capitol*, 1882, above; Charles Eliot Diary, June 10, 1883, pp. 20–25, FLLHU; FLO to Edward Clark, Feb. 15, 1886, below).

1. In 1882 Senator Justin S. Morrill secured a relatively small appropriation for the construction of "approaches to the Capitol" on the north and south sides of the building. These approaches were actually parts of the larger project that Olmsted had proposed in 1874 for marble terraces on the north, south, and west sides of the building. On March 1, 1883, Senator John J. Ingalls of Kansas and Senator James B. Beck of Kentucky who sat on the Committee on Appropriation questioned Senator Morrill on the estimated total expense for the construction of all the terraces. While $65,000 was appropriated

to continue the work, the following wording was also added to the appropriations bill: "Hereafter all changes and improvements in the grounds, including approaches to the Capitol, shall be estimated for in detail, showing what modifications are proposed and the estimated cost of the same" (Glenn Brown, *Documentary History of the Construction and Development of the United States Capitol Building and Grounds* [Washington, D.C., 1904], pp. 1217, 1221–28; William C. Allen, *History of the United States Capitol: A Chronicle of Design, Construction, and Politics* [Washington, D.C., 2001], p. 354).

2. Olmsted's first estimate for the cost of the terraces has not been found. A partial estimate, not including the "staircases leading to it," was $315,519 at that time (FLO to Committees on Public Buildings and Grounds, Jan. 5, 1875, B134: #2820, OAR/LC).
3. This estimate, prepared by engineer-in-charge of the Capitol grounds Frederick H. Cobb, was $657,402. In September 1883 Clark published another estimate submitted by Olmsted for $814,588.98, including work already done ("Estimate for new terrace," Jan. 11, 1882, B134: #2820, OAR/LC; G. Brown, *Documentary History of the United States Capitol*, pp. 1228–29).
4. When Olmsted estimated the cost of building the terraces in 1875, prices were falling in the wake of the Panic of 1873, and they continued to fall until 1879. By 1882, when Olmsted completed his more recent estimate, costs had almost risen to their 1875 levels (U.S. Department of Census, *Historical Statistics of the United States* (Washington D.C., 1975), p. 629).
5. The following sentence was deleted by Olmsted in the original draft: "I have from the first acted upon the conviction that the more thoroughly the full scope and intention of the terrace should be understood the higher would be the estimate of the fitness, convenience and dignity to be gained for the Capitol through its construction relatively to its necessary cost."

CHAPTER II

AUGUST 1883–SEPTEMBER 1884

One of Olmsted's most important commissions during this period was his design of the Boston park system. In a December 24, 1883, report for the Boston park board and a January 18, 1884, letter to park commissioner Charles H. Dalton, Olmsted attempts to convince them that the public landscape that he is designing in the Back Bay should not be called a "park," and why only Franklin Park among all the elements of the Boston park system qualified for that title. Three letters to nurseryman F. L. Temple provide instructions for planting the Beacon Street entrance of the Back Bay Fens. An additional letter to Charles H. Dalton describes how much time the Olmsted firm is spending on the plan for Franklin Park.

Regarding the grounds of private residences, Olmsted writes to architect Charles Follen McKim about the summer home of Julia Appleton in Lenox, Massachusetts, and to Charles T. Hubbard about his home in Weston, Massachusetts. This chapter also contains several letters to John C. Olmsted, now a partner in the firm, concerning the operation and organization of the Fairsted office. Other documents include a report to the park commissioners of Wilmington, Delaware, recommending sites for public parks in that city, a letter to John Stirling urging the importance of the pier and gallery building Olmsted had designed for Belle Isle, and a letter to Salem H. Wales about problems caused by political patronage in the New York parks department.

To Felker L. Temple[1]

Brookline, 21st Aug. 1883.

Mr. F. L. Temple;
Dear Sir;

You have said that you would like to undertake the planting of the Beacon Entrance district of the Back Bay upon a contract, payment dependent on success and have asked me for a statement of what is intended that you may present a proposition to that end.

The situation is bleak and arid; the plants largely on Southward slopes will suffer from reflected heat from walls in summer and in many parts will be raked by northerly winds passing over the Charles river which at this point are often extremely violent in winter. The lower part of the slopes will be soaked and occasionally sprayed on the surface with salt-water. There are numerous rocky buttresses along the shore. The entire area of ground to be planted may be reckoned as 2½ acres, of which a fifth part will be planted with trees and upright growing shrubs, leaving spaces to be otherwise treated aggregating two acres.[2]

As because of the broken surface of the ground and its contracted areas it would be too costly if not otherwise impracticable to keep these spaces nicely in turf, it is designed that they should be as soon as possible completely clothed with low growing foliage and that this foliage shall, through its variety of forms and tints acquire a more or less tufty, ruffled and mysteriously intricate surface. As the larger part of the ground cannot be efficiently protected or cultivated, plants of showy flowers such as would tempt pilfering and such as would require to be finely cared for are to be avoided.

To make sure of the leading results desired it is intended that the ground shall be closely planted with a selection of creepers and low growing shrubs mostly of sorts that are to be found growing naturally in exposed dry slopes along the seacoast.

The Commission has ready for this purpose the following plants of two years transplanted growth in nursery —[3]

7000 Myrica
7000 Comptonia
7000 Genista tinctoria
{*700 Junepirus prostrate*}[4]

It is intended that these shall be planted at from one to three feet apart and so as to average 11000 plants to the acre and so far mixed that if either one should generally fail to thrive the other two if successful would cover the ground but a perfectly regular and monotonous distribution is to be avoided.

To further insure a green surface under all contingencies and also to obtain more intricacy and variety of effect it is intended to set irregularly among the plants above named 5000 plants or rooted cuttings of hardy vines creepers and matting plants, such as sterile grapes, Cat briar (Smilax) Virginia creeper, Jap.

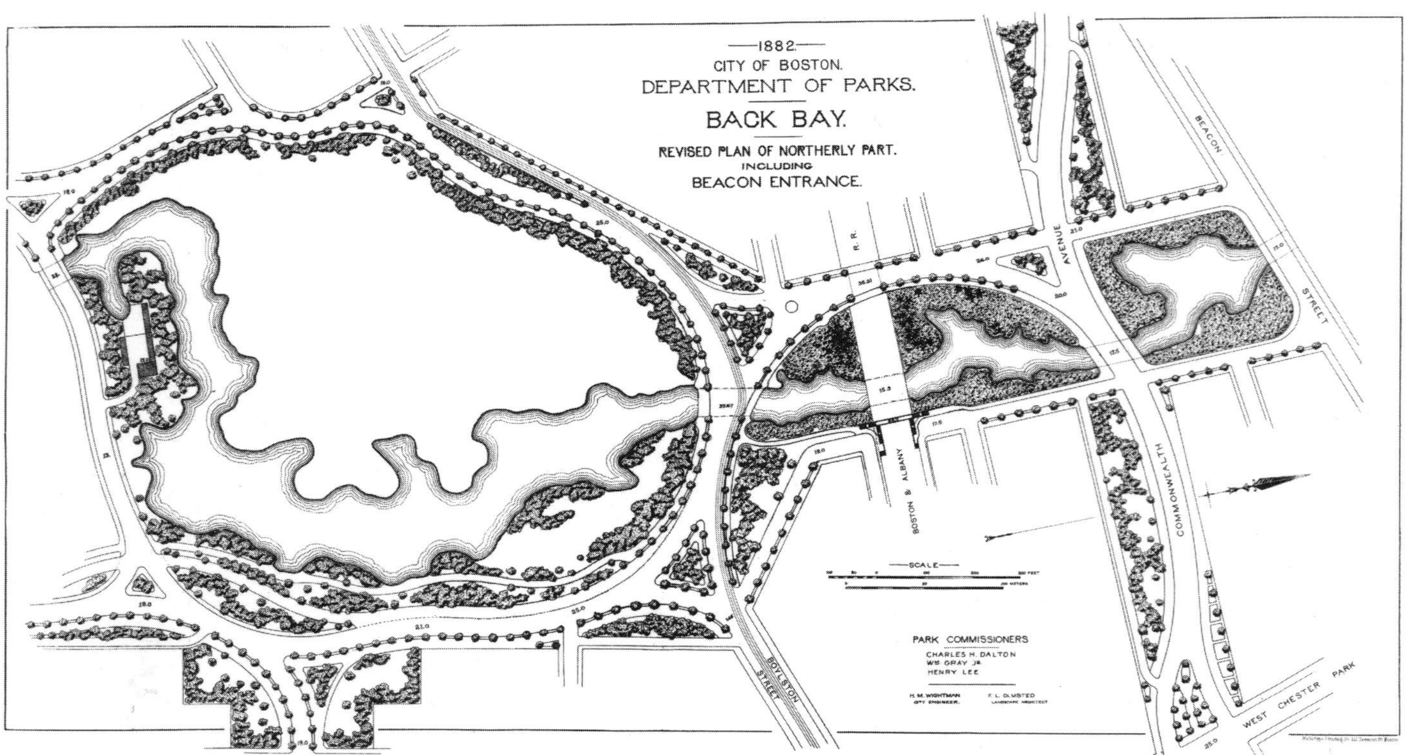

"Back Bay, Revised Plan of Northerly Part Including Beacon Entrance," 1882

honeysuckle, Periwinkle, Clematis, Rubus Canadensis and hispidus, bearberry, mountain cranberry, salix trista &c.

Upon the high ground not included in the above there are to be planted 200 White Pines, 200 red pines 100 white spruce 100 red cedar 700 prostrate juniper, 200 white birch, 200 dwarf birch.

On the knolls, and along the base of the walls 2000 shrubs mostly from the park nurseries. Along the shores above common flood of salt water but subject to occasional spray and at rare intervals to be washed with brackish water 5000 shrubs of beach plum, sea buckthorn, tamarisks and others natural to salty soils.

The margin of the water for a distance of 1600 feet to be set with plants and sods of sea lavender, golden rod, asters, beach peas and other plants obtained from like situations with an edging between ordinary high & low water of salt marsh sedge; the sedge to be supplied and delivered on the ground by the Commissioners.

The Commissioners will provide fresh water, hydrants and hose adequate to the watering of all parts of the plantations during the summer.

The present gravelly subsoil is to be covered with a coating of clayey silt from the bottom of the bay and upon this will be placed 2½ feet on an average of surface soil.

The coniferous plants will require to be protected during the first winter. The entire plantations will require to be thickly mulched during the summer.

I should be glad to receive from you a proposition to do all of the above planting and to provide all labor necessary to secure the thrift of the plants until the beginning of the winter of 1885; Payment to be made as follows:

One half the price that shall be agreed upon to be paid upon certificate that the planting has been completed to my satisfaction; one quarter in June 1885 upon certificate that all plants failing to live of the first planting have been satisfactorily replaced; the remaining quarter on certificate that the entire work required has been done and that the operation has been successful.

I shall be glad also to receive from you a proposition to furnish so much of the material called for as the Commissioners will not be prepared to supply, stating each sort and the price per plant, no packing or transportation to be charged for.

The Commissioners will supply 7000 myrica, 7000 comptonia 7000 Genistas, 1000 Berberis, 1000 clethra, 1000 Beach Plum, 700 Junepirus prostrata, 1000 Lonicera brachipoda, and such other plants as you have seen in good condition in their nursery.

The text presented here is an unsigned draft in Olmsted's hand. Olmsted and John C. Olmsted began working on the plan for the Back Bay Fens during the summer of 1878. The Beacon Street entrance, or Charlesgate, connected the Fens to Beacon Street and also created a transition between Commonwealth Avenue and the corridor of linked parks and parkways that came to be known as the "Emerald Necklace." By 1883 dredging and grading operations for the Beacon Street entrance were complete, as well as construction of many of the bridges in the Fens. Planting began in the Spring of 1884 (Cynthia Zaitzevsky, *Frederick Law Olmsted and the Boston Park System* [Cambridge, Mass., 1982], pp. 156–57, 187–90; *Eighth Annual Report of the Board of Commissioners of the Department of Parks for the City of Boston for the Year 1882* [Boston, 1883], pp. 7–10; Charles Eliot Diary, Dec. 2, 1883, pp. 82–86, FLLHU; Frederick Law Olmsted, "Report of the Landscape Architect," Dec. 24, 1883, below; FLO to Charles H. Dalton, Dec. 1884, below; see also Frederick Law Olmsted, "Paper on the {Back Bay} Problem and its Solution Read Before the Boston Society of Architects," April 2, 1886 [*Papers of FLO*, SS1: 437–59]).

1. Felker L. Temple (d. 1907) was the proprietor of Shady Hill Nurseries in Cambridge, Massachusetts. The Boston parks department made a contract with him in November of 1883 to carry out the planting of the Back Bay Fens. Olmsted made inquiries or acquired plants from Temple for a number of other projects in the 1880s, including Shelburne Farms in Vermont, the Vanderbilt Mausoleum on Staten Island, and Rough Point in Newport, Rhode Island (*Transactions of the Massachusetts Horticultural Society for the Year 1907* [Boston, 1907], p. 280; BCDP, City of Boston, *Minutes*, Sept. 4, 1883; *Papers of FLO*, SS1: 458–59, n. 36; FLO and JCO to F. L. Temple, April 26, 1887, A1: 757, OAR/LC; FLO to F. L. Temple, May 9, 1887, A1: 789, OAR/LC; FLO and JCO to F. L. Temple, April 24, 1888, A2: 382, OAR/LC; FLO to F. L. Temple, Nov. 22, 1883, below).
2. The Beacon Street entrance area, about 200 feet wide and 900 feet long, included a watercourse for the flow of the tide from the Fens basin to and from the Charles River. The entrance landscape and the watercourse were crossed by Boylston Street, the Boston and Albany Railroad, Commonwealth Avenue, and Beacon Street. Retaining walls and bridge abutments reflected heat in the summer and the tide brought in brackish and polluted water up the watercourse shorelines. While the "artificial salt meadows" Olmsted planned were successfully established in these conditions, trees, shrubs, and groundcovers planted on the slightly higher, adjacent ground did not thrive at first. Many of those planted in the Beacon Street entrance over the next two years did not survive. By the early 1890s, however, photographs show the intended vegetation well established.

   In the first half of the twentieth century, much of the Beacon Street entrance landscape was obliterated. In 1910 the Charles River was impounded, eliminating the tidal flow and salinity of the Fens basin, which could no longer function as an estuarine marsh. Later that decade Commonwealth Avenue was straightened where it crossed the Beacon Street entrance and two new bridges were built for it. In the early 1950s, Storrow Drive was built along the Charles River embankment cutting off the entire area from the river. Ten years later the Massachusetts Turnpike was extended into downtown Boston along the right-of-way of the Boston and Albany Railroad, crossing through the Beacon Street entrance to the Fens. In 1966 the Bowker Overpass was completed, covering the entire length of the Beacon Street entrance with highway ramps and four lanes of traffic (FLO to F. L. Temple, March 7, 1884, below; FLO to F. L. Temple, March 15, 1886, below; see also FLO to Charles Sprague Sargent, Jan. 27, 1879, and FLO to Charles Sprague Sargent, Jan. 29, 1879 [*Papers of FLO*, 7: 387–90]; *Eleventh Annual Report of the Board of Commissioners of the Department of Parks for the Year 1885* [Boston, 1886], pp. 27–28; John R. Freeman, "Concerning the Fens Basin and Its Pollution," in *Report of the Committee on Charles River Dam* [Boston, 1903], pp. 189–217; Karl Haglund, *Inventing the Charles River* [Cambridge, Mass., 2003], pp. 402–3).
3. No finished or formal planting list for the Beacon Street entrance survives but several partial lists, including this document and several descriptive diary entries by Charles Eliot, provided enough material for Cynthia Zaitzevsky to reconstruct a planting list for her book, *Frederick Law Olmsted and the Boston Park System* (1982). Further docu-

mentation is provided by a draft planting list included in this volume: see FLO to F. L. Temple, Nov. 22, 1883, below. In a contract dated December 1, 1883, Temple agreed to provide and plant "trees, shrubs, vines and plants" in the entrance area and "planting care" for two years. He also agreed to "assume all costs of losses for failure to grow" with an obligation to replace dead plants at 10% of cost. Olmsted also gave general instructions for planting the Back Bay Fens in his correspondence with Temple (Charles Eliot Diary, Sept. 9, Dec. 2, 1883, Jan. 6, 1884, pp. 71, 85–86, 101, FLLHU; C. Zaitzevsky, *The Boston Park System*, p. 188; BCDP, City of Boston, *Minutes*, Dec. 1, 1883; FLO to F. L. Temple, Nov. 22, 1883, below; FLO to F. L. Temple, March 7, 1884, below).

4. This line crossed out by Olmsted in the manuscript.

To Felker L. Temple

22[d] Nov. 1883.

To Mr. Temple
Dear Sir:

Please give a brief statement of your undertaking with the Park Comm.—It varies now from the last memo. I have from you. I have it that you are to supply plants as follows:

Class		
I	Mostly low wild bushes	15,500 a 5 = 775–
II	Brake & ferns	10,000 a 2 = 200–
III	Solidagos &c.	19000 a 3 = 570–
IV	Vinca	1000 a 2 = 20–
V	Woody vines	1000 a 4 = 40–
VI	Conifers	1666 a 40 = 666–
VII	{*Wild*} transplanted shrubs	4900 a 10 = 490–
VIII	Salt marsh & beach perennials	1500 a 3 = 45–
IX	Sedge &c.	25–
		54566 $2831–

The Comm. is to provide otherwise about 25000—perhaps more—and the entire amount to be due you for the two years work insurance, under my charge now authorized will be $3600.

Yrs Truly
FLO

Plat A—63000 sq. ft.
Low bushes & vines generally wild

We have engaged —	14,500		
Will buy Rubus odora. —	500		
Lonicera brach. —	1500[1]		
Berberis aquif. —	500		

—	17,100[2]		
Temple to supply bushes —	15,000	32,000	

Also Brake & ferns —	10,000		
″ Gold^{n} Rod asteroides —	19,000		
″ Periwinkle —	1000		
″ Woody vines —	1000	31,000	63,000

Plat B. 15000 sq. ft.
White and Red Pines & White Spruce & Junipers

---

1 to 9 sq. ft
1666 at 40^{c} = $666.40

Plat C. 24000 sq. ft.
High *Shrubs*. (*1 to 3 sq. ft.*)

We have	2000
Will obtain	
Ligustrum	1000 — (a 30/^{nt} + 15/ = 11.50)
Sweet briar	500 — (a 10/ + 5/ = 18.75)
Buxus	100 — (a 21 + 10/6 = 7.63)
Temple to supply	4400 — (a 10^{c}. = 440.00)

Plat D.

Shore line
We have 2000 B. Plums & S. Buckthorn[3]
Will buy 3500 Loni. brach.

Add			
Add	500 Tamarix	a	10 = 5000
	500 asparagus		3 = 3000
	500 Rosa lucida		5 = 5000
	500 Beach Pea		3 = 3000
	500 Sea Lavender		3 = 3000
	Sedge & Blk. Grass		2500
	8000		31500

(E)

For the border against the railing
(1800 ft.)
And to be scattered to cover ground under bushes & conifers—
Lonicera brachipoda
to be had of Saul — 3500 a \$2 pr m. 7—

In the class called low wild bushes there are to be not less than 1000 ea. of

Kalmia Angustifolia
Myrica cerifera
Bear berry
Mountain Cranberry
Salix tristis[4]
Running bramble
Linnea borealis
Cassandra caliculata
In the class of transplanted shrubs are to be included not less than 100 each of the fol.

Cornus stolonifera
Pyrus arbutifolia
Forsythia suspensa
Rhus copallina
" glabra
Ribes aureum
Azalea viscosa
Andromeda calyculata[5]
Amelanchier
Hamamelis
Symphoricarpus rasemosus (red)
Of Pines—
600=1 to 16 sq. ft. — 9000 sq. ft.

Recapitulation.

	Total	Temple	To be paid Temple
Plat A	63000	46000	1580
" B	1666	1666	666.40
" C	6000	4000	400
" D	8000	4300	215
	78666	55966	2861.40

Average plants to ac. 33050 Average price from Temple
About 1 to 15 sq. inches $5.11 pr 100

Plants to be set & cared for 78.666
Price ———————— 3600
Average pr plant about $4.60 pr 100

In the class III to be included
7000 solidagos
7000 asters
5000 tansy, yarrow, mints, cranberry, horseradish, hypericum, the smallest sunflowers, large buttercups, irises, asclepias, chicory, gentians, apios tuber.,[6] hops, columbine, lobelia, &c.
19000

Plants to be obtained thro' Temple.

Class I	(Low wild bushes, mostly)	15500 a 5	= 775 —
II	(Brake & ferns)	10000 a 2	= 200 —
III	(Solidagos &c.)	19000 a 3	= 570 —
IV	(Vinca ——)	1000 a 2	= 20 —
V	(Woody vines)	1000 a 4	= 40 —
VI	(Conifers)	1666 a 40	= 666 —
VII	(Trans. ptd. shrubs)	4900 a 10	= 490 —
VIII	(Shore perennials)	1500 a 3	= 45 —
IX	(Sedge &c. ——)		25 —
			2831

Plants to be obtained otherwise than thro' Temple

Rubus odorata — Woolson 500 a
Lonicera brachipoda, Saul, 5000 a 2 = 100
Rubus crataegefol. a
Berberis aquif., Waterer,[7] 500 a 15/[8] = 18.75
Buxus ———— " 100 a 31/6 = 7.63

Sweetbriar ——— " 500 a 15/ = 18.75
Privet ———— " 1000 a /30/ = 11.50

A list with total quantities from all sources
1 of low growing plants (such as genista comptonia, ferns, vines, &c., see memo. headed Plat A)
2 of Conifers – (Plat B)
3 of tall shrubs (suitable to Plat C)
(in this some from Poor Farm Nursery & the C. H. Reservoir)[9]
4 of stuff suitable for Plat D.

The text presented here is an unsigned draft of a letter in Olmsted's hand. Olmsted and Boston's park commission had corresponded with nurseryman F. L. Temple since the summer of 1883 regarding the planting of the Beacon Street entrance to the Back Bay Fens. This letter was written shortly before Temple was awarded a contract, dated December 1, 1883, to supervise the planting of the area. No final planting plan for the Beacon Street entrance has been found, but this list is consistent, with regard to the plants specified, with other letters to Temple by Olmsted, as well as with Charles Eliot's diary entries and the specifications of Temple's contract (C. Zaitzevsky, *The Boston Park System*, pp. 156–57, 187–90; Charles Eliot Diary, Sept. 9, Dec. 2, 1883, and Jan. 6, 1884, pp. 71, 85–86, 101, FLLHU; BCDP, City of Boston, *Minutes*, Dec. 1, 1883; see FLO to F. L. Temple, Aug. 21, 1883, above; FLO to F. L. Temple, March 7, 1884, below; FLO to F. L. Temple, March 15, 1886, below).

1. Below this, crossed out, "Rubus crataegefolia — 100."
2. That is, Rubus odoratus, Lonicera brachypoda, and Berberis aquifolium.
3. That is, Beach Plum and Sea Buckthorn.
4. Below this, crossed out, "Rosa lucida."
5. Below this, crossed out, "Mahonia aquifol."
6. That is, Apios tuberosa.
7. Throughout this list Olmsted refers to nurserymen he often worked with: Anthony Waterer (1822–1896), proprietor of Knap Hill nursery in Surrey, England; George C. Woolson (b. 1848) and George Thurber (1821–1890) of Woolson and Co. nursery in Passaic, New Jersey; and John Saul (1819–1897), proprietor of Maple Grove Farm nursery outside Washington D.C.
8. Olmsted uses the symbol (/) for "shilling," as Waterer's nursery was in England.
9. A "Poor Farm" was a generic name given to public institutions. Here Olmsted specifically refers to the Austin Farm nursery in Roxbury, Massachusetts, a home for poor women (*Hoffman's Catholic Directory and Clergy List Quarterly* [Milwaukee, 1886], p. 48; FLO to F. L. Temple, March 7, 1884, below).

REPORT

OF

FREDERICK LAW OLMSTED, ESQ.

TO THE

PARK COMMISSIONERS

OF

Wilmington, Del.

WILMINGTON, *Dec. 22d, 1883.*

TO THE PARK COMMISSIONERS OF WILMINGTON:
SIRS:—You have asked my professional judgment of the adaptation of certain lands to the furtherance of an object defined by the term park.[1] As the grounds called parks vary much in character, aspect, and method of usefulness, I will begin by stating what I regard as the most generally important object of a park, and the reasons of this importance.

It has been found by experience that when large numbers of people are living closely together, and especially if they are generally much confined by industrial pursuits or domestic duties, that it does them good to be brought occasionally under the influence of natural scenery. The reason it does them good is not that it brings them to breathe for the time better air, nor that it presents to their view things that gratify curiosity or taste. Equally good air, and things of certain kinds by which their curiosity or their taste would be equally gratified, such as flowers, birds, music, and fire-works, if found in a limited space in the midst of a town, might also do them good, but not in the same way, nor in as valuable a way. To understand the special value of natural scenery, we must first recognize that the artificial circumstances of a city, walls, windows, roofs, flags, pavements, plants in pots and gardens, all sorts of fabrics, and the constant evidence of work, intercourse, and traffic, gradually and insensibly have a wearing and depressing effect. Secondly, we must reflect that to enjoy natural scenery we must not only have escaped from all these artificial circumstances, and from the confinement of vision by walls and roofs, but that that which engages our admiration is the reverse of artificial. It is the result of nature working in a large, free, generous, and spontaneous way. Thus it supplies not simply relief, but a diversion or counteracting influence.

Whatever it may be called, a property adapted to give ready opportunities for such diversion is of great value to a city, and the most unquestionable duty of the bodies of public servants called Park Commissioners has been proved to be the devising and digesting and suitable presentation of sound schemes for securing such opportunities.

To a due performance of this duty the first necessity is a realizing sense of the fact that the benefits possible to be obtained in this way are not simply those of the luxury, but that they supplement necessary food, drink, and clothing, and that every man taxed to obtain them is better off for having a portion of his wages invested co-operatively for him in this form, precisely as he is when they are so invested skillfully in procuring a common supply of water, common means of protecting against fire, and other civilized requirements of a town community. If because of what a Park Commission shall do the people shall not be better able to carry on their various callings, and possess a larger measure of physical, intellectual, and moral vigor and ability for active industry during longer lives, its work had better have been left undone.

All this may be fully realized, and yet as we are accustomed to weigh and measure benefits that come to us in such intangible forms as those we derive from the influence of natural scenery less than those coming in the form of water, firm and clear roadways, security from fire, and other objects of city administration, it is found difficult to pursue this object in public grounds steadily and simply. The difficulty is aggravated by the circumstance that it is impossible to give any considerable town population the advantage of interesting natural scenery without providing extensive artificial arrangements for the accommodation of those seeking to make us of it, such as roads, walks, bridges and shelters. Very few can realize that these things are not an end in themselves, or that costing, as they needs must do, much more than the main elements of natural scenery, they should be designed with all possible art to be of subordinate interest. This difficulty is so great that natural beauty is often sacrificed to make a show of artificial beauty.

Taking the view that has been thus explained, of what a Park Commission should, if possible, aim to accomplish, and of the besetting difficulty oftenest found in the way, there is a question which should, in the case of Wilmington, have the most careful consideration at the very outset. It occurs in this way:—

The people of Wilmington, when the town was small, and no part of it very densely occupied and when it had much less of the stir, drive, and confining and nervously irritating toil of a manufacturing community than it has at present, enjoyed the use, by sufferance, of a passage of natural scenery which to a larger city would be of rare value,—so rare and desirable that in a number of cities several million dollars have been willingly spent to obtain results of which the best that can be said is that they somewhat distantly approach in character and expression such scenery as the people of Wilmington had provided for them without cost.

But, until recently, the need of the people of Wilmington to have their mental currents occasionally diverted into the poetic channels of natural scenery has been comparatively slight. As the need has increased, the means of freely supplying it has been lessened, and at the present moment, with a rapidly increasing population, it is so much restricted and interfered with, and it appears so likely to be wholly destroyed, that the public mind may be more ready to look elsewhere, and to wait upon the slow formation of a park by artificial means, than to give due consideration to the advantages still pertaining to the Brandywine Glen.[2]

Several sites are, no doubt, available for a park near Wilmington, comparing favorably with such as have been generally taken for parks by other cities. To one, more particularly, attention has been called, because of a generous proposal made by its present owners for conveying it to the city.[3] I believe that the city would find it profitable to accept this offer; but I cannot advise that it should do so if, by doing so, attention is likely to be for a moment withheld from the question whether it is yet possible to save and make suitably available any considerable measure of the scenery of its older, nearer, and more natural pleasure ground.

This question being asked me, I can now only answer that from such cursory examination as I have been able to make, there is at least abundant reason for a cautious, deliberate, and studious consideration of it. The first step in such study is a topographical survey, and the preparation of a topographical map. Upon this a plan could be formed, and upon this plan discussion could proceed in a definite and practical way. An intelligent understanding could thus be reached of the value of the advantages remaining available in the site, and of what the city could afford to pay to possess them and make them secure and available.

I want to speak well of the Salem Hill project, and with the highest respect for the views and motives that have led to it. For certain purposes of a park the Salem Hill ground can be made useful in a few years at moderate cost. But if it is to be considered as an alternative, and not as a supplement of a purpose to obtain public rights in the scenery of the Glen, to protect and rehabilitate this scenery, and provide suitably for the public use of it,—then I must advise that discussion of the Salem Hill project be suspended. With every advantage that a lavish outlay may buy, it cannot in fifty years be made nearly as valuable a ground for that form of public recreation that is most to be desired, with a view to the general health and education of the city, as that which is now in a fair way soon to be wholly lost.

A provision of a small airing ground nearer the centre of population of the city, and more readily accessible, is especially desirable with reference to the invigoration of very young children and women who cannot be gone long from home; but of this suggestion and all others to which my attention has been invited, I must say the same that I have of the Salem Hill project:—it is of secondary importance to that of recovering the Brandywine walk.

I am the more moved to limit my advice to this point, and to urge it upon you at this time strenuously, because of an oft-repeated experience elsewhere. In at least twelve cities where my counsel has been taken in park undertakings, situations have been pointed out to me more favorable for the purpose, and which could have been obtained a few years sooner at much less cost, than any remaining to be considered, and I have as often heard bitter expressions of condemnation of the seemingly insane shortsightedness that had allowed these opportunities to be lost. But in no one of these cases has there been as much to save at as moderate cost as there will have been at Wilmington.

Respectfully,

FREDERICK LAW OLMSTED,
Landscape Architect.

The text presented here is a published report. By 1883, the city of Wilmington, Delaware, had established a board of park commissioners to oversee the acquisition of land for one or more new parks. The interest in creating parks in Wilmington along the Brandywine River traces back to 1868, although no action was taken at that time. In 1882, a prominent Wilmington businessman, William P. Bancroft, offered forty-eight acres of his family's land on the west side of town for a park, and this prompted a renewal of interest in the initial Brandywine River location. A new park commission was formed that included Bancroft, U.S. Senator Thomas F. Bayard, and William M. Canby, who served as president. Olmsted's initial involvement in Wilmington was limited to this report, although in 1889 he and John C. Olmsted began the design of a parkway connecting the Brandywine Park (which by then had been acquired) and the newly established Rockford Park (located on the land that Bancroft originally offered in 1883). They prepared topographical maps and drawings for the proposed parkway between Rockport Lane and Scott Street along the river, but the plan was not implemented and their involvement ended by 1892 (J. Thomas Scharf, *History of Delaware, 1609–1888*, vol. 2 [Philadelphia, 1888], p. 671; *Laws of the State of Delaware Passed at a Session of the General Assembly, Jan. 2, 1883*, vol. XVII, part 1 [Dover, Del., 1883], pp. 404–8; William M. Canby to FLO, Nov. 15, 1883, B76: #1080, OAR/LC; FLO to William M. Canby, Nov. 21, 1883; William M. Field to FLO and Co., Jan. 14, 1890, B76: #1080, OAR/LC; FLO and Co. to William M. Canby, April 10, 1890, B76: #1080, OAR/LC; FLO and Co. to William M. Canby, Jan. 9, 1891, B76: #1080, OAR/LC; "Notes on conference with Wm. Canby," Dec. 16, 1892, B76: #1080, OAR/LC; Susan Mulchahey Chase, *Within the Reach of All: An Illustrated History of Brandywine Park* [Wilmington, 2005], pp. 15–19).

1. William Canby had written Olmsted in November of 1883 saying that their board of park commissioners had recently resolved to invite either or both Olmsted and Donald Grant Mitchell, the author and horticulturist, to come and "examine the land in the vicinity of Wilmington, with reference to its eligibility for Park purposes, and [determine] what expenses would attend such examination and a written report thereon." Canby preferred Olmsted's services and delayed contacting Mitchell until Olmsted replied. Olmsted accepted the invitation and visited Wilmington on December 22 (William M. Canby to FLO, Nov. 15, 1883, B76: #1080, OAR/LC; FLO to William M. Canby, Nov. 21, 1883; Brett Coker, "Donald Grant Mitchell," in Wesley T. Mott, ed., *The American Renaissance in New England: Fourth Series* [Detroit, 2001]; Wilmington Board of Park

Commissioners, manuscript *Minutes*, Nov. 13 and Dec. 28, 1883, Delaware Public Archives; S. M. Chase, *An Illustrated History of Brandywine Park*, p. 16).

2. The portion of shoreline under consideration was a one-mile stretch from the Market Street Bridge to the Augustine Bridge, terminating at what was then the Jessup and Moore Paper Company's Augustine Mill. The site featured hills, rocky outcrops, forests, and three stream falls in the river along the route. The city appropriated funds for the purchase of land in 1886, and when the park commission finished acquisitions in 1910 the park was 179 acres. The proposed Brandywine Park was roughly one and a half miles downstream from the land Bancroft was offering as a gift (S. M. Chase, *An Illustrated History of Brandywine Park*, pp. 17–25).
3. That is, Rockford Park, officially established in 1889 on land given to the city by William P. Bancroft (Wilmington Board of Park Commissioners, manuscript *Minutes*, April 26, 1883, Delaware Public Archives; S. M. Chase, *An Illustrated History of Brandywine Park*, p. 9).

Charles Follen McKim

To Charles Follen McKim[1]

Dft

Brookline, Mass.
24th Decr 1883.

My Dear Mr McKim:

I do not undertake to make plans providing for all contingencies and under which my occasional advice will be unnecessary to the attainment of the general result intended.

For small places my practice is to charge $100 for preliminary examination and advice. If what I advise is in a general way acceptable and it is desired

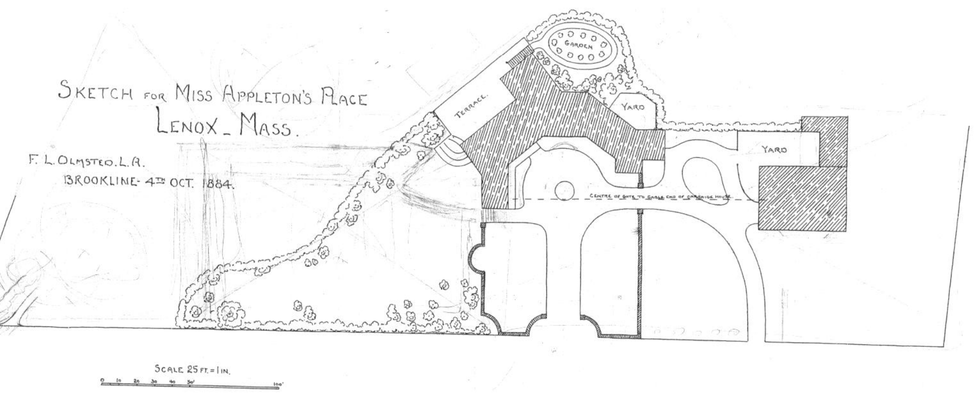

"SKETCH FOR MISS. APPLETON'S PLACE, LENOX, MASS," OCTOBER 4, 1884

that I should go further I undertake a general guidance of the work to be done. I furnish necessary drawings and make visits as I find necessary until the character of the place is sufficiently established. I select and buy trees & other materials if this is necessary. Commonly, half a dozen visits are necessary in the course of two or three years. Usually for such service my charge is somewhere from $200 to $400. In such a case as Miss Appletons[2] probably $200, plus travelling expenses; something depending on her local resources.

It is much harder to realize a simple, modest lady-like and convenient idea of a place than to carry out elaborate, showy and costly plans.

Yours Very Truly,

Fred[k] Law Olmsted

The text presented here is a signed draft in Olmsted's hand. In October 1883 the sisters Julia and Alice Appleton hired Charles Follen McKim to design their country house in Lenox, Massachusetts. They approached Olmsted at the same time to design the grounds, and Olmsted produced plans in the fall of 1884 (Charles Moore, *The Life and Times of Charles Follen McKim* [New York, 1970], pp. 50–52).

1. Charles Follen McKim (1847–1909) trained in architecture at the École des Beaux Arts in Paris between 1867 and 1870 and then worked at the New York office of Charles D. Gambrill and H. H. Richardson. He began working on independent commissions with architect William Rutherford Mead in the 1870s, and in 1879 they joined Stanford White and established the architectural firm of McKim, Mead, and White. Olmsted knew McKim's father, James Miller McKim, an abolitionist who helped raise the funds to establish the *Nation* magazine with Olmsted in 1865. That year the elder McKim also offered Olmsted the position of General Secretary of the American Freedman's Aid Union, which Olmsted declined. The younger McKim may have met Olmsted when McKim began working in Richardson's office in the 1870s. In any case, in 1881 he expressed a desire to work with Olmsted on the design of William D. Washburn's estate in Minneapolis and Olmsted responded with interest. That commission never materialized, however, and the Appleton residence in Lenox was the first project the

two men completed together. Olmsted later worked with McKim on Whitelaw Reid's *Ophir Farm* in White Plains, New York (1888–1892), the Vanderbilt/Twombly home, Florham, in Madison, New Jersey (1890–1900), and the Chicago World's Colombian Exposition fair buildings and grounds in 1891–1892 (*DAB*; C. Moore, *Charles Follen McKim*, pp. 14, 38–41, 50–52; FLO to James Miller McKim, Sept. 7, 1865 [*Papers of FLO*, 5: 439–40]; *Papers of FLO*, 6: 5–6, 567, n. 1; FLO to McKim, Mead, and White, June 4, 1881).

2. Julia Amory Appleton McKim (1859–1887) met McKim in May of 1883 when commissioning him to design the Lenox residence. She married him in 1885 in the newly completed home. Julia died in childbirth in 1887 and the house burned to the ground in 1905 (Richard S. Jackson, Jr., and Cornelia Brooke Gilder, *Houses of the Berkshires 1870–1930* [New York, 2006], pp. 77–81; Charles Follen McKim to FLO, n.d., B73: # 1022, OAR/LC; Charles Follen McKim to FLO, Dec. 6, 1883, B73: #1022, OAR/LC).

REPORT OF THE LANDSCAPE ARCHITECT.

CHARLES H. DALTON, ESQ., *CHAIRMAN OF THE PARK COMMISSION*:—[1]

Boston, December 24 1883.

SIR.—No results intelligible to the casual observer have been heretofore apparent from the tedious and costly city work on Back Bay, the operations having been scattered and mostly under ground or under water. North of Boylston street, however, the work has, within a few weeks, become coherent, and in part assumed a finished appearance, and south of Boylston street the leading features of the superficial design in land and water may be readily traced. In the course of next summer the slopes now formed will become in some degree verdant; streets will have been graded, bringing the whole under closer observation, and it is much to be hoped that the public will desire to be better informed about it.

The reason is this: The city has been for ten years preparing to enter upon a far-sighted and comprehensive scheme of public recreation-grounds which cannot be fully worked out in many years, but to an economical and successful pursuit of which an intelligent, steady, and patient public opinion is of the utmost importance. Looking to this object it is to be regretted that the first work of the department charged with the promotion of the scheme should be one in which recreation is but an incidental purpose, and in which, though the work is known under the name of a park, the principal circumstance that distinguishes a park from other pleasure-grounds will be wanting. With a view to a public opinion sustaining true economy and suitable design in park work proper, nothing could be more unfortunate than that the work in Back Bay should be regarded as park work, and, as such, should be found acceptable.[2]

A brief review of the history of the undertaking, and an explanation of its controlling ends, may therefore be desirably placed for reference in your next Annual Report.

The locality came to be known by the name of park,—"Back Bay Park,"—because ground was once bought upon it by the city, with a view to a public recreation ground. It was selected for the purpose because it could be obtained at a lower price than any other territory equally accessible. Its market value was low, because it was mainly occupied by a deep gullet,[3] through which the drainage and sewerage of a large area of Boston and its suburbs passed out to Charles river, and the cost of preparing it for building purposes was likely to be so great as to leave no prospect of profit in the operation.[4]

The project of a park, however, assumed that the body of water liable to flow through the territory could be as far as desirable, diverted and regulated consistently with the requirements of a park at reasonable cost.

With more exact knowledge of the circumstances, it not only became certain that this assumption was unwarranted, but that, before the adjoining region could be built upon, it would be necessary to provide a basin in which the waters of the two streams, here having a common outlet, could be allowed to accumulate, whenever the tide in Charles river rose so high as to prevent their outflow.

The quantity of water to be thus stored would be variable. In times of freshet the required amount would be many times larger than under ordinary circumstances.[5] The fluctuations thus occurring would cause the basin to be often noisome, a breeder of disease[6] and a very disagreeable object to the eye unless special means could be devised to avoid such a result.

The plan now being carried out was devised for this purpose.

It provides a basin with intercepting sewers, inlets and outlets, and a series of automatic gates so disposed that, under ordinary circumstances, the surface of the water within the basin will be at a level about midway between extreme high water and mean low water of Charles river, with a fluctuation not exceeding one foot, while that of the river may be sixteen feet. The water in the basin will then have the general aspect of a salt creek, passing with a meandering course, for the most part, through or along the border of a[7] sea-side meadow; but will not be subject to fall with the tide, so far as to exhibit the disagreeable aspect which in natural tide-basins, twice a day, appears in the form of slimy mud-banks. The water, when the work is complete, will ordinarily be clean and wholesome, and its immediate banks verdant.

When freshets of the streams flowing into the basin rise concurrently with extreme and prolonged high stages of the water in the river, preventing an outflow, the waters of the creek will rise rapidly until they overflow its banks, and then more slowly spread over the surface of adjoining salt meadows, until they wash the lower part of the meadow banks forming the margin of the basin, within which they will continue to rise until the falling tide reopens outlets into the river.

The public cannot be prudently admitted to any part of the basin except the slopes of its rim. Passage across it must be by causeways and bridges. Its boundaries, which will be over two miles in length, may, however, be followed by wheelways, bridle roads and walks; and these, together with any needed passages across the basin, will command views over it, and may be shaded by trees. This is what is intended. The exterior road will eventually be lined on one side by buildings, as the bounding streets of Boston Common are; on the other it will look into the basin, as Beacon street into the Common. It is thus of importance that the views over the basin should be made as pleasing as, at reasonable expense, and with a view to the highest efficiency of the drainage arrangements under all contingencies, they can be. To understand the design in this respect the following circumstances must be borne in mind:—

The water rising in the basin in times of flood will be less than usually salt; salt enough, nevertheless, to be destructive of turf or of ordinary park or garden plants. It follows that any beauty in the lower part of the banks must be obtained by a selection of plants specially adapted to the circumstances, and it will be evident to one reflecting upon the conditions as now to be observed on the ground that these plants, together with the plants of the meadows subject to be frequently soaked by strongly salt water, will be the leading constituents of the scenery of the entire territory. There will remain only a narrow border of generally steep slopes forming the sides and rim of the basin. They will be winding and irregular, will play insensibly into the meadows and water-sides at their base, and must be so treated as to maintain a certain consistency with them.

It will thus be apparent that the superficial verdant features of the locality must grow out of the constructive features of the drainage works, and that whatever beauty is to be looked for must be a very different beauty from that commonly looked for in parks and gardens. It does not follow that it will be less pleasing, in the long run, to good taste.

Two questions may be asked by visitors next summer which the above explanation does not answer:—

1st. Why should the water in the basin at ordinary stages be kept in a narrow and crooked channel?

The principal reason is that otherwise the difficulty of obtaining verdant shores and avoiding high, naked mud-banks at the foot of the slopes would be greatly increased, as, upon any extended surface of water, the wind would create an undermining surf. It will probably be found to do so to some extent with the designed arrangement, but it is hoped in such moderation that, where necessary at all, defences will suffice scarcely perceptible to the observer, and not at all destructive, when the foliage above them shall be developed, to the naturalness of the scenery.

2d. Why should the slopes on the outlet north of Boylston street, and in connection with the Beacon street and Commonwealth avenue bridges, be crowded with common wild bushes instead of being prepared in a lawn-like way, with detached groups of trees, shrubs, foliage-plants, and flowers, as other grounds bordering these streets have been?

CHARLES HENRY DALTON

There are several reasons: First, because were it otherwise practicable to obtain good results from this common mode of gardening it would be impossible to associate these results agreeably with what will be necessary upon the lower parts of the slopes, subject to the influence of salt water. Second, trees and delicate plants in this situation would suffer greatly from the unusual force of winds drawing through the pass. Third, trees would close out the fine view over Charles river from Boylston bridge. Fourth, the slopes being often steep, narrow, and twisting, it would be difficult and costly to keep turf finely, or otherwise maintain them in full dress.

For these reasons the aim will be to clothe these slopes with a dense, close, self-protecting hardy chaparral.[8] It is believed that in a few years this will be found to blend genially with the rough and weather-stained massive retaining wall of the road by which travel from Beacon street and Commonwealth avenue will be connected with the circuit road of the basin.[9] It will also play suitably into the salt shore plantations.

It was observed early in this report that the principal circumstance that distinguishes a park from other pleasure grounds will be wanting in the pleasure ground to be formed upon the basin of Back Bay. A park is a place for the enjoyment of rural scenery in a sense that a garden for instance is not. A town-park is a place of escape to such scenery from scenery of a town-like or artificial character. The circumstance that distinguishes a park, therefore, is that of sylvan seclusion. All parks properly so called are surrounded by screening plantations and it is a leading motive in their design to shut out of the view of those to be benefited by them whatever might be unfavorable to a continuous impression of consistent rural scenery. The site of the proposed park of West Roxbury is admirably adapted to this purpose; the requirements of the basin on Back Bay as distinctly exclude it. The Thames Embankment of London[10] which is also a great drainage work though embellished in a much more park-like manner than this on Back Bay can be is not called a park. Nor is the Ring of Vienna; the Chiaja of Naples, the Alameda of Seville or the Paseo of Havana.[11] Not being parks but public grounds of a distinctive character they are all much better named than if called parks. It is much to be desired that this designation for the basin on Back Bay may be abandoned.

Respectfully,

FRED'K LAW OLMSTED.
Landscape Architect Advisory.

The text presented here is from the *Ninth Annual Report of the Board of Commissioners of the Department of Parks for the City of Boston, for the Year 1883* (Boston, 1884). A draft of this report in Olmsted's hand is in FLO Papers/LC.

1. Charles Henry Dalton (1826–1908) was a Boston businessman and member of the Boston park commission from 1875 to 1885, serving as chairman for much of that time. In 1861 Dalton was named the Agent of the Commonwealth of Massachusetts for the U.S. Sanitary Commission, and so Olmsted, as the executive secretary of the organization, presumably became acquainted with him at that time. In 1873 Dalton wrote Olmsted on behalf of the Massachusetts General Hospital for advice on the relocation of the McLean Asylum. Two years later, as a new member of the Boston park commission, Dalton consulted Olmsted on the proposed sites for Boston parks, and that October Olmsted visited the Boston park commissioners. In the spring of 1876 he toured the proposed Boston park sites just before the park commission issued its first comprehensive park plan, in which Dalton acknowledged Olmsted's advice on "the general scheme." Dalton then helped organize the 1878 competition for the design of the Back Bay park. He later helped negate the results of that effort in order to hire Olmsted, who did not enter the competition, instead of the nominal winner. Until his departure from the Boston park commission in 1885, Dalton was a key ally and supported the implementation of Olmsted's Boston park designs (Roger Bigelow Merriman, "Memoir of Charles Henry Dalton," in *Proceedings of the Massachusetts Historical Society, October, 1908–June, 1909* [Boston, 1909], pp. 287–312; C. Zaitzevsky, *The Boston Park System*, pp. 43–47; *Second Report of the Board of Commissioners of the Department of Parks for the City of Boston, for the Year 1876* [Boston, 1877]; FLO to Charles H. Dalton, April 8, 1876 [*Papers of FLO*, 7: 192–99]; FLO to Charles H. Dalton, May 13, 1878 [*Papers of FLO*, 7: 363–65]).
2. Olmsted expresses his concern here and elsewhere that the public landscapes he created as part of the Boston system should be appreciated for their diverse, and sometimes unprecedented, purposes and appearances. Contemporary municipal parks in Boston, such as the Public Garden and the Common, were relatively limited in extent and featured flower gardens, fountains, monuments, and other activities and displays that the public had come to expect from a municipal "park." For Olmsted, only the West Roxbury (Franklin) Park possessed the expanse and pastoral character that defined it as a "park" landscape. The ponds, parkways, and river corridors that made up the rest of his Boston park system provided very different landscape experiences and func-

tions, and they were named accordingly. The Back Bay Fens, in particular, challenged contemporary assumptions about municipal parks. The landscape functioned as a salt marsh, in order to control flooding and improve sanitary conditions, and was designed as a hardy, evocative version of the tidal estuary that the site had once been (FLO to Charles H. Dalton, Dec. 9, 1879 [*Papers of FLO*, 7: 428–31]; FLO to Charles H. Dalton, Jan. 18, 1884, below; Frederick Law Olmsted, *Tenth Annual Report, Boston Park Commissioners, Report on Back Bay*, Dec. 1884, below; Henry Lee, *The Public Garden: Boston* [Boston, 1988], pp. 10–12; see also *Appendix, Report of the Landscape Architect Advisory*, Dec. 30, 1887, below; Frederick Law Olmsted, "Park" from the *American Cyclopedia*, 1875 [*Papers of FLO*, SS1: 308–30]).

3. Gullet, as in a narrow, deep channel through which a stream flows (*OED*).
4. In 1878 the Boston Common Council appropriated $450,000 for the acquisition of land for the Back Bay Fens, a meager amount considering that land was cheaper at this time due to the financial crash of 1873. The legislators also required that the park commissioners could buy not less than 100 acres with the authorized amount, further restricting the choice of land to less expensive parcels (FLO to the Board of Commissioners of the Department of Parks of the City of Boston, Jan. 26, 1880 [*Papers of FLO*, 7: 451–63]; "Paper on the {Back Bay} Problem and its Solution Read Before the Boston Society of Architects," April 2, 1886 [*Papers of FLO*, SS1: 440–41]).
5. In the draft manuscript, Olmsted states that the amount of water would be "several hundred times" larger.
6. Olmsted refers here and elsewhere to miasmatic disease theory, which held that noxious vapors rising from poorly drained areas and swamps caused and spread disease (see Frederick Law Olmsted, *The Park for Detroit*, Nov. 1882, n. 16, above).
7. In the draft manuscript the following words appear at this point but were crossed out: "sedgy meadow. These were the natural conditions of the locality before."
8. Chaparral, as in a dense tangled brushwood, composed of low thorny shrubs, brambles, and briars (*OED*).
9. The massive retaining wall described here was an extension of the abutment of H. H. Richardson's Boylston Street Bridge. The wall, about twenty-feet high at its highpoint near the bridge, carried the park drive in an arc over the Boston and Albany Railroad tracks and down to the extension of Commonwealth Avenue, defining the western edge of much of the Beacon Street entrance landscape. No detailed plans or views of the wall have been discovered, but one elevated view from the 1890s suggests its masonry was similar to the irregular ashlar of the Boylston Street Bridge. The retaining wall was destroyed in the twentieth century (see *Papers of FLO*, SS1: 449).
10. London's Metropolitan Board of Works built the Thames Embankment on the north bank of the Thames between 1864 and 1874. Designed by the engineer Joseph W. Bazalgette, the embankment channeled the flow of the river and improved sanitary conditions. The top of the embankment featured a roadway sixty-four feet wide and provided a pedestrian walk with shade trees, flower gardens, and benches (Karl Baedeker, *London and Its Environs* [London, 1894]; Dale H. Porter, *The Thames Embankment* [Akron, Ohio, 1998], pp. 31–38).
11. The Ringstrasse of Vienna was created in the 1850s after the defensive walls surrounding the city were razed. A wide boulevard, lined with cultural and government buildings and new residential districts, eventually replaced the ring of fortifications. Olmsted visited Vienna in 1856. The Riviera di Chiaja is a river promenade in Naples, which Olmsted also visited in 1856. He described it in 1875 as "divided into a ride, a drive, and a walk . . . nearly a mile in length, with a breadth of 200 ft. A part of it is separated from the shore of the bay of Naples by the villa Reale, planted in the garden style." The Alameda of Seville (Alameda de Hércules) was built in the sixteenth century along the Guadalquivir River in the center of the old city. The Paseo del Prado of Havana dates to the eighteenth

century and extends just over a mile from the Parque Central to the ocean (Donald J. Olsen, *The City as a Work of Art: London, Paris, Vienna* [New Haven, Conn., 1986], pp. 12–13; Frederick Law Olmsted, "Park," from the *American Cyclopedia*, 1875 [*Papers of FLO*, SS1: 324]; Karl Baedeker, *Italy, Handbook for Travelers* [London, 1883], p. 84; Elizabeth Nash, *Seville, Córdoba, and Granada: A Cultural History* [Oxford, 2005], pp. 12–13; Claudia Lightfoot, *Havana: A Cultural and Literary Companion* [Oxford, 2002], pp. 127–31).

To Charles Henry Dalton

Bkline 18th Jan. 1884.

Chas H. Dalton Eq.
Chairman of Park Commission:
My Dear Sir;

I am glad you propose to drop "*Park*" but though I have been advising it, there are considerations I would like to suggest before you officially adopt "Bay".

Back bay is a name topographically applicable to but a small part of your scheme as now developed. Looking ahead a few years you may find it desirable to use a more comprehensive designation than has yet been proposed for the whole affair between Commonwealth Avenue and Jamaica Pond.

The question is whether it would not be a good plan to take some short word if you could hit upon one that would be applicable to the entire district and use it in combinations that would designate sub-districts.

For example, take dale as such {a} common word (dale is a meandering shallow valley of a small stream in distinction from dell which is deeper and vale which is broader). Then the outlet on Charles River might be Charlesdale; the marshland, Sedgelydale or Lingerdale (the water being delayed there) or Marshdale, or Meadowdale or Opendale; the reach above, being narrow & to be overhung by foliage-Bowerdale, the next (Longwood) Dalewood; the next Brookdale; the next Waterdale or Dalemeer; the next Upperdale or Dalend. And the park-way throughout, the Daleway.

An address, for example, would then be: No. 307 Bowerdale. For streets facing the dale opposite the Daleway, terrace might be used as a terminal with a propriety wanting in the London use of the word. Thus: No. 10 Charlesdale Terrace East, or No. 30 Dalewood Terrace, &c.

By this system it would be evident 1st that the house so designated fronted on the landscape of the dale, 2d on which bank, right or left, 3d in which of several convenient divisions between Charles River & Jamaica Pond.

"Dale" is a word that lends itself rather nicely to such a system but if you don't like it others sufficiently euphonious might be thought of, as *Brook*, Brookway, Charles Brook, Sedgely brook Broadbrook &c. *Water*—Charles water, Sedgely water, Bower water, Waterwoodley &c.

Your scheme cannot develop much further without making a general name, & some local names a necessity of public convenience, and if you delay long to think out a good system, awkward descriptive terms will get into use and be hard to overcome. I saw in a newspaper lately a parkway that I laid out referred to as "the Sackett Street Avenue Parkway." This being a combination of the names by which people had begun to talk of it before the Commissioners gave it an official designation — I believe the lamps on it were labeled Eastern Parkway[1] ten years ago I believe — two years too late.

The text presented here is an unsigned draft of a letter in Olmsted's hand. These comments on the use of the word "park" to describe the landscape that would later be named the Back Bay Fens continued an ongoing discussion with Dalton and the Boston park commissioners about an appropriate name for the place (see Frederick Law Olmsted, "Report of the Landscape Architect," Dec. 24, 1883, above; *Appendix, Report of the Landscape Architect Advisory*, Dec. 30, 1887, below).

1. Olmsted and Vaux proposed what they called "parkways" for Brooklyn in 1868. The idea had precedents in the boulevards and avenues of European cities, but the neologism also implied that in the United States this new type of street would be planned and built by municipal park departments (and their consulting landscape architects) and placed under the jurisdiction of a park board. Although they did not adopt every aspect of the parkway plan Olmsted and Vaux described, the Brooklyn park commissioners created Eastern Parkway in the 1870s by widening what was then called Sackett Street to 210 feet between Prospect Park and the city line, a distance of about two miles. The parkway included separated carriage and pedestrian ways, rows of trees, benches, and grassy medians, as Olmsted and Vaux had suggested. The Brooklyn park commissioners hoped that the creation of Eastern Parkway would also help them secure the authority to lay out new streets in Kings County beyond the City of Brooklyn, but this did not occur ("Report to the Brooklyn Park Commission," Jan. 1, 1868 [*Papers of FLO*, SS1: 112–46]).

To Charles Townsend Hubbard[1]

Brookline Mass.
2d Feby 1884.

Ch. T. Hubbard Eq.
My Dear Sir,

I have yours of yesterday.

I did not doubt that you thought that you were as you say carrying out my ideas with only such immaterial variations as were judicious and required to make the result satisfactory to yourself but as to what my ideas were, what was essential of them, what immaterial & what judicious there is room for difference of opinion.[2] I did not mean to object to your going ahead on your own view but your doing so before consulting me in the points of difference relieved me of professional responsibility. The aid my son has given you since has been in carrying out your ideas of what was desirable. I do not expect you to take this view but you must not expect me to take yours. I am a designer which I should not be if I did not know better than anyone else what is & what is not essential in my designing.

If you will look again at my offer to serve you gratuitously, if you should desire in the matter of obtaining plants suitable to that part of the work in which you have been most led by my advice, you will find that I did not so much as suggest the desirability of your obtaining {*any outlandish*}[3] any tender or imperfectly hardy plants, I only said that if you wished any such I could get them for you. It is quite customary in such a place as yours, especially if it has a noble terrace to have some such plants & I thought you might wish some but I did not advise it. What I did advise was simply the cheap & ready way of accomplishing the local result that I had in view in advising the boulder foundation that you have made.[4] The larger part of the plants I had intended ordering if you wished are as hardy as the hardiest of your wild growth.

[5]And after declining the advice that I have thought it more important for you to act upon at this time in respect to planting you must allow me to decline aiding you to carry out the views in which you differ from me.[6]

The text presented here is an unsigned draft of a letter in Olmsted's hand. Charles T. Hubbard's home, Ridgehurst, was set on a ridge in Weston, Massachusetts, overlooking the Charles River valley and the New York Railroad line. Designed by Francis W. Chandler, the home was completed in 1883. Hubbard asked Olmsted to design the landscape of the residence that year. In addition to recommending how the site should be planted, Olmsted suggested a boulder retaining wall that would support a courtyard adjacent to the house and also help screen the view of the railroad tracks. The inventor Francis Blake had built his Keewaydin residence adjacent to Ridgehurst after marrying Hubbard's daughter in 1873. In 1883 Blake was renovating the house and had retained Ernest Bowditch to design formal gardens around it. Olmsted's involvement in the Ridgehurst project probably ceased by 1886. In 1911, Charles T. Hubbard's son, Charles W. Hubbard, hired the Olmsted Brothers to design a new garden for the residence (Pamela W. Fox, *Farm Town to Suburb: The History and Architecture of Weston, Massachusetts, 1830–1980* [Portsmouth, N.H., 2002], p. 506; Charles T. Hubbard to JCO, Aug. 10, 1883; Charles T. Hubbard to FLO, Feb. 1, 1884; Charles Eliot, Notebook Entry, May 13 and May 20, 1883, pp. 11, 13, FLLHU; *Master List*, p. 202; Pamela W. Fox, "The 'Eccentric Suburban' and the Quiet Idealist," *Wellesley Weston Magazine*, summer 2010).

1. Charles Townsend Hubbard (1817–1887) was a prominent Massachusetts businessman who made his fortune by founding the Boston Flax Mills in 1848 and the Ludlow Manufacturing Company in 1878. He lived in the Boston area and purchased land in Weston in 1867 for a summer home. He added more parcels of land over the years, giving his three oldest daughters land when they married. He died in 1887, and his son Charles W. Hubbard took over management of the estate (P. W. Fox, *Farm Town to Suburb*, pp. 501–7; Alfred Noon, *A History of Ludlow Massachusetts: With Biographical Sketches of Leading Citizens. . .* [Springfield, Mass., 1912], pp. 287–88).
2. In Hubbard's letter he writes that "I have endeavored to carry out your ideas in the spirit,

& almost to the letter, except the tunnel leading to the glen, if I may so call it. In the steep bank of bowldery, we tried to carry out your ideas exactly, & I think your son said it was just what you wanted." He also writes that he is in no hurry to plant flowers and shrubs, but when he does he prefers to use only the "most hardy" shrubs about the house, but is concerned about their survival. He reported that previously his neighbor and son-in-law Francis Blake had imported, through Ernest Bowditch, "a large quantity of so called hardy plants, & the most of them died that first winter." He concluded by requesting that Olmsted come out to direct where the trees and shrubs should eventually be planted (Charles T. Hubbard to FLO, Feb. 1, 1884; P. W. Fox, *Farm Town to Suburb*, p. 503).

3. Crossed out by Olmsted in manuscript.
4. In Hubbard's letter he describes the terrace to which Olmsted refers: "With the bank of large bowldery on one side, & the finished & capped wall on the other, it seems to me you will have what you planned for — an artificial court yard about the house, & all beyond that to be wild & wooded" (Charles T. Hubbard to FLO, Feb. 1, 1884).

    Charles Eliot, who assisted Olmsted on the project, also described Olmsted's plans for the site: "West of house a deep narrow wooded valley and on the slope of this Mr O. has planned a retaining wall of boulders built with great batter and with making crevices for planting — the whole carried on curve of roadway and ending close to house in a shed covered bastion giving a chance for wagons to stand at the kitchen door." Eliot also described Olmsted's statement of approach to the back part of the house: "Mr H. would rather have Mr O. fix things so that the 'back door' should not be made noticeable — he would rather pretend he had no 'back door' — but Mr O. is always firm on this point: — 'best to be perfectly frank about the kitchen region.'" (Charles Eliot, Notebook Entry, May 20, 1883, p. 13, FLLHU).
5. Crossed out here in manuscript is "That Mr Bowditch's advice did not result satisfactorily, may be a good reason [for] you to take that view of it but you must not expect me to take yours."
6. The rest of the manuscript is missing.

To Felker L. Temple

Detroit 7 Mch. 1884

To Mr. Temple.
Dear Sir;

At the earliest day practicable & before the ground is quite fit for planting please remove all available shrubs & vines from Chestnut Hill & the Austin Farm Nurseries and add them to the Back Bay stock.[1]

The following will be your general instructions for planting on Back Bay and you can proceed upon them at your discretion, except as more particular instructions shall be given later.

Class C Plats C You will best begin by planting most of the shrubs of Class C. because the space C will be earliest dry.

The larger growing sorts are to be planted never less than three of a kind together and mainly in patches of from twenty to two hundred of a kind, the average size of a patch (of berberis or ligustrum, for instance) being 40 sq. yards (4 yards wide by 10 long). The plants will stand on an average three to a square yard.

The smaller growing sorts of Class C are to be planted in a similar manner but enough of them to be so scattered along the outside of the plats C as to merge them in with the still smaller plants of Plats A.

For this purpose the plants must be more scattered—say 2 to a square yard, leaving room for the plants of Plat A to mingle with them.

The different patches of Plat C are also to dovetail together irregularly, and care must be taken that patches of the smaller growing sorts are not surrounded (so as to be hidden) by the larger.

Class A. Plat A. The shrubs of class A may then be planted in similar but generally smaller patches, the larger growing (as Mahonia, Myrica & Rubus) being more generally connected with the bushes of Class C, and also, set on the crown of the ridges. All the bushes of Class A are to stand four to a square yard, on an average. This will probably leave a few over to be crowded in here & there afterwards.

Classes D. E. & F: The plants of these classes are to be set on the corresponding plats (D. E. & F) and as directed in the accompanying lists, so as to be well distributed; generally in smaller and more mixed or dove tailed patches than those of Plats A & C.

The rocks will require special dispositions & care must be taken that each group of rocks has a somewhat different composition of plants from the others. Some for instance having a preponderance of Junipers; others few Junipers; others, none; so of Pines, &c. But in all cases the rocky points must be planted with the object of obscuring the rocks as soon as practicable and obtaining bold and salient bastions of dense foliage.

The bushes of Class D are to be in separated patches, each patch to contain clusters of several sorts and between these patches of bushes there are to be patches of herbaceous plants. There is to be a nearly continuous edging of sedge or black grass where the slopes meet the water; black grass, "samphire" & sea lavender where the slope is least abrupt; sedge along the steeper banks.

No large growing Pines or Spruces are to be planted north of Commonwealth Avenue.

The bushes and coniferous trees having been planted, the vines and herbaceous plants are to be inserted between them, evenly through all of Plats A and along the edges of the other plats. Golden rods especially among the bushes near the water.

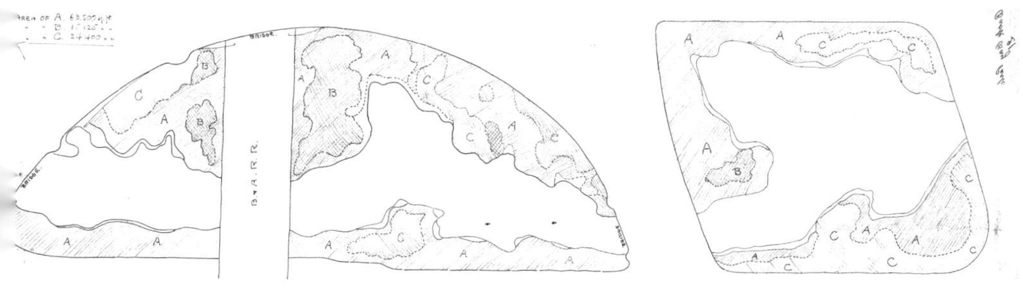

"Approximate Copy of Diagram Accompanying Planting Contract, Beacon Entrance, Back Bay," March 1884

Please make yourself and your assistant perfectly familiar with these instructions before the planting season opens; ask explanations of whatever is not quite clear, and be prepared to carry the work on at all points without hesitation or delay for lack of more particular instructions.

Please advise Mr Howe, the Engineer,[2] in good time, of any work needing to be done by his force before you can begin.

The text presented here is an unsigned draft in Olmsted's hand. Cambridge nurseryman F. L. Temple began planting the Beacon Street entrance to the Back Bay Fens in the spring of 1884. By the end of 1886 the sedges of the salt meadows had been successfully established, but many of the trees and shrubs described here had died (FLO to F. L. Temple, Aug. 21, 1883, above; Charles Eliot Diary, March 30, 1884, p. 120, FLLHU; FLO to F. L. Temple, Nov. 22, 1883, above; FLO to F.L. Temple, March 15, 1886, below; *Eleventh Annual Park Report, Boston Department of Parks,1885*, p. 27; BCDP, City of Boston, *Minutes*, March 21, 1884).

1. The planting lists that would have accompanied the final draft of this letter have not been found. In FLO to F. L. Temple, Nov. 22, 1883, above, and in the final contract dated December 1 of that year, Olmsted listed plants to be obtained from Temple's Cambridge nursery and elsewhere. In the November 22 letter, Olmsted lists them according to "plats" A, B, C, D, E, and organizes them into nine "classes" based on genus (FLO to F. L. Temple, Nov. 22, 1883, above; BCDP, City of Boston, *Minutes*, Dec. 1, 1883; Charles Eliot Diary, Sept. 9, Dec. 2, 1883, Jan. 6, 1884, pp. 71, 85–86, 101, FLLHU; see also FLO to F. L. Temple, Aug. 21, 1883, above).
2. Edward Willard Howe (1846–1931) was the assistant civil engineer for the city of Boston from 1874 until 1914. From 1883 to 1898 Howe was in charge of most of the engineering work for the park projects in Boston ("Edward Willard Howe," *Journal of the Boston Society of Civil Engineers*, June 1932, pp. 362–64).

To John Stirling[1]

Brookline, Mass.
12th. May. 1884

Mr. Jno. Stirling, Secy
B.I.P. Com.
Dear Sir;

Yours of 5th came duly but I have not since had a day at home.[2]

The plan of Belle Isle Park grows out of the feature of the Pier and Gallery as out of a stem.[3] If this feature is abandoned, the plan is permanently botched and will be very different from what it would have been had I been so instructed two years ago. If other parts of the park come into use long before this feature the public will accommodate itself to the arrangement which is a thoroughly bad one, the plan will be misunderstood, the park misused, your temporary arrangements be regarded as tolerably good and such opposition as has been met this year will be continuously increasing. To postpone the pier indefinitely and make other passable arrangements is therefore only an indirect way of abandoning your plan and fixing an extravagant & wasteful policy on the city. It was my conviction of this danger that led me to urge the large appropriation and the building of the gallery this year, the object being to fix the plan before the park came largely into use, and so make it possible to proceed steadily and systematically in carrying it out.

I would advise the new pier to be built this year if it took every dollar of

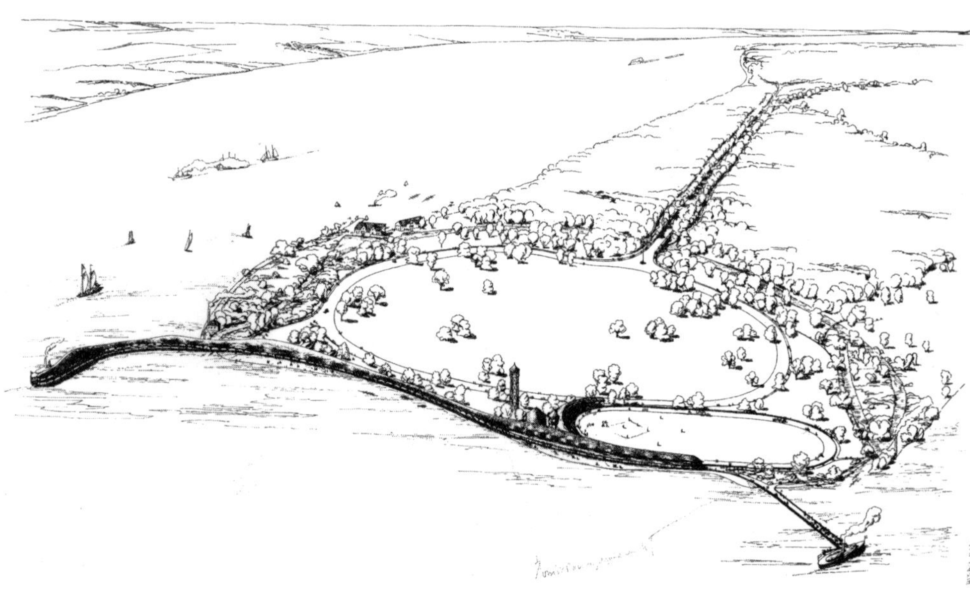

Rendering of Bird's-Eye View of Proposed Pier and Gallery Structure at Belle Isle, n.d.

MODEL OF PROPOSED PIER AND GALLERY STRUCTURE AT BELLE ISLE, N.D., DISPLAYING THE COVERED BI-LEVEL WALKWAYS

the appropriation not already in effect pledged to other work. To postpone it, in my judgment is to open the door to great continuous disorder and waste.

Yours respectfully

Fred[k] Law Olmsted
L.A.A.

The text presented here is a signed letter in Olmsted's hand. The Michigan State Legislature passed an act establishing the Detroit Board of Park Commissioners, which replaced the board of Belle Isle park commissioners, in March of 1883. The same month, Olmsted presented his plan for Belle Isle, first to the park commissioners and then to the Detroit Common Council. The park plan included a large parade ground, a central, axial avenue down the middle of the island, a network of canals, and a large pier attached to a 1,600-foot covered "gallery" along the water on the west shore. The commissioners balked at the cost of the gallery structure but Olmsted felt the innovative building, which was to serve multiple purposes relating to visitor circulation, recreational activities, and park maintenance, was essential to the success of the park. In the spring and summer of 1883 Olmsted made several trips to Detroit in order to explain the plan, and especially to justify the investment in the pier and gallery.

By March 1884 the site for the gallery was prepared and graded, but opponents of the project, those who felt that Belle Isle was an unsuitable site for the city's main park and those who simply objected to Olmsted's plan for it, pressured the Common Council to halt construction that spring. The *Detroit Evening News*, for example, ran several editorials disparaging the park's design and described the pier and the gallery, specifically, as a "colossal folly." These attacks prompted Olmsted to publish a report defending his plan, "Belle Isle: After One Year," a month after he wrote this letter (*Local Acts of the Legislature of the State of Michigan passed at the regular session of 1883* [Lansing, Mich.,1883], pp. 402–3; "Park Commissioners," *Detroit Evening News*, April 5, 1883, p. 2; John Stirling, "Belle Isle Park," *Thirteenth Annual Report of the Secretary of the State Horticultural Society of Michigan*, 1883 [Lansing, Mich., 1884], pp. 212–15; Charles Eliot Diary, May 27, July 8, 1883, and March 30, 1884, pp. 15, 41, 119, FLLHU; *Second Annual Report of the Board of Park Commissioners to the Common Council of the City of Detroit* [Detroit, 1884], pp. 3, 6, 24; *Third Annual Report of the Board of Park Commissioners* [Detroit, 1885], pp. 5, 30; Janet Anderson, *Island in the City: Belle Isle, Detroit's Beautiful Island* [Detroit, 2001], p. 32; *Detroit Evening News*, March 15, 1884; "Belle Isle Park," *Detroit Evening News*, May 30, 1884, p. 1; FLO to John Stirling, Feb. 13, 1884; FLO to John Stirling, Oct. 23, 1884, A1:84, OAR/LC; Frederick Law Olmsted, "Belle Isle: After One Year," June 1884 [*Papers of FLO*, SS1: 419–36]; see Frederick Law Olmsted, *The Park for Detroit*, Nov. 1882, above).

1. John Stirling was elected secretary of the first park board and served until his death in 1885, after which his son John R. Stirling was appointed secretary of the park board (Silas Farmer, City Historiographer, *The History of Detroit and Michigan or The Metropolis Illustrated, a Chronological Cyclopedia of the Past and the Present* [Detroit, 1884], p. 76; Paul Leake, *History of Detroit*, vol. 3 [Chicago, 1912], p. 1068; *Fourth Annual Report of the Board of Park Commissioners* [Detroit, 1886], p. 2).
2. The editors were unable to locate this letter, but apparently Olmsted was asked what the effect would be if the pier and gallery were removed from the park plan.
3. The pier and gallery were to be built on the west end of Belle Isle. The pier was necessary to accommodate steam ferries that would bring park visitors from the city. Adjacent to the pier, the long, curving gallery, with a massive, undulating roof, allowed passengers to get on and off the ferries efficiently, while also serving as a covered waiting area. The gallery was designed with two levels and inclined planes leading from one level to the next. On its west side, the gallery was to open onto the beach and provide a shaded area for viewing it. The east side of the gallery was to feature "tents or buildings" that Olmsted foresaw being used "for various purposes," creating what he called a "City Fair" for entertainments. The east side of the gallery also was to open onto large meadows intended for sports and other recreational activities, the gallery again providing a shelter for viewing the activity. Park paths issuing from the gallery were to connect to the central, tree-lined avenue down the center of the island. The gallery structure was to serve multiple purposes and was to be integrated fully into the circulation plan, activities, and landscape of the park.

   In July 1883, Charles Eliot wrote that the park commissioners had approved a modified plan of the pier and west end shore-walk developed by an assistant city engineer, Milo Davis. By August, however, Eliot was developing his own drawings for the pier. On October 7 he wrote, "Completed a set of *Belle Isle* drawings and Mr. O carried them off to Detroit. Scale of 1" = 50'—a sketch-plan of the whole shore—structure from pier to pier . . . Scale of 1" = 8'—a sketch-plan of the new pier with an elevation and sections of the same." Olmsted decided to turn over design of the pier to the architect Mortimer L. Smith in November (Frederick Law Olmsted, "Belle Isle: After One Year," June 1884 [*Papers of FLO*, SS1: 422–25]; FLO to John Stirling, July 25, 1884, A1: 21, OAR/LC; plan 661-z7, NPS/FLONHS; Charles Eliot Diary, July 8, Aug. 19, Sept. 29, Sept. 30, Oct. 7, Nov. 11, 1883, pp. 43, 61, 74–77, FLLHU; FLO to Mortimer L. Smith, Nov. 24, 1884, below).

To John Charles Olmsted[1]

[May 30], 1884

Decoration Day 1884. Detroit

Dear John, I was ill treated yesterday. The Ferry Company gave me their heaviest & deepest & most unwieldy boat and neither Captain Sullivan nor any of the pilots I know was allowed to go. It turned out that the pilot they sent never had been in our channel, did not know there was a channel there,[2] was very timorous and after we had started at 9 A.M. advised that we should put back and take a lighter boat. We had no lead line aboard and I made one of spun yarn and some scrap iron. There was a strong N. W. wind and the danger signal was flying. I felt so sure of my ground however that I insisted on going on and finally brought the boat alongside the buoy I had had Ludden[3] place the day before showing the end of our wharf. I found 3 fathom water within two feet of it and 6 fathom within 30 ft. So that the pilot said that no dredging at all would be required to land at a wharf so placed. Then I turned the boat round with some difficulty because of the high wind but she came and the Commissioners were fully satisfied that the project was perfectly feasible. Today we had a long session and I talked them an hour at a stretch, and at last President Moore[4] said laughing "I guess we shall have to build the pier, gentlemen, and the gallery also, but not this year." It ended in their instructing Ludden to submit working

John Charles Olmsted

plans for the pier & estimates, and authorizing more teams, plans, harrows, rollers, {*granite powder*} and men for the preparation of the Parade Grnd.

I expect to leave tomorrow at 3 for Washington via Pittsburg, Penna Central & Harrisburg & Baltimore.

I have two notes from you, the last written the 28th. Mr. Ellis's[5] wall has been built with openings at regular intervals for erecting the ramps (buttresses). I am not sure of the distances, Watson[6] knows. They may be 15ft. apart. It is necessary to know the exact number to obtain bids. There will be 20 to 30 and the price may be given by the piece.

Am not well and have been on my back ever since the meeting. I have not been able to digest anything since I came here—not even toast and milk—I try hardly anything else but asparagus. But I feel that this afternoon's rest has helped me & if I sleep tonight, I can travel tomorrow night. Affectly — FLO

The text presented here is a signed letter in Olmsted's hand (see FLO to John Stirling, May 12, 1884, above).

1. John Charles Olmsted (1852–1920) was the son of Olmsted's brother, John Hull Olmsted, and Mary Cleveland Bryant Olmsted (Perkins). He was born in Switzerland, where his parents were traveling in an attempt to improve John Hull Olmsted's health. The latter died of tuberculosis in 1857, and two years later Olmsted married John's widow, Mary, and so became stepfather as well as uncle to John Charles and his two younger siblings, Owen Frederick and Charlotte. John was groomed from an early age to become a landscape architect and his stepfather's assistant and partner. Following his graduation from Yale's Sheffield Scientific School in 1875, he began working full time with his stepfather in New York. In 1877 and 1878 he traveled in Europe, furthering his education. When Olmsted relocated to Brookline in the early 1880s, John moved as well and lived with the family at Fairsted. In 1884 he became a full partner in the firm, known from that point as F. L. & J. C. Olmsted, Landscape Architects. Working with his stepfather over the next decade John assisted in the design of park systems for Boston, Buffalo, Detroit, Rochester, Hartford, Louisville, Brooklyn, Chicago, and other cities, as well as numerous residential and institutional commissions. The deaths of Henry Sargent Codman in 1893 and Charles Eliot in 1897 left John as the only landscape architect in the firm with extensive and direct experience working with Olmsted, who himself retired in 1897 but had left active practice two years before. John's half-brother Frederick Law Olmsted, Jr.,

became a full partner in 1897, and the firm was again called F. L. & J. C. Olmsted. It was then renamed Olmsted Brothers in 1898.

In 1899 John married Sophia Buckland White and also that year was a founding member (with his half-brother and others) of the American Society of Landscape Architects. Over the next twenty years John continued the design of park systems begun with his stepfather and designed new parks or park systems for Portland (Maine), Portland (Oregon), Seattle, Spokane, Dayton, Charleston, Essex County (New Jersey), Chicago, and New Orleans, among other cities. He laid out the 1906 Lewis and Clark Exposition in Portland (Oregon) and the 1909 Alaska-Yukon-Pacific Exposition in Seattle. As the Olmsted Brothers firm grew, they designed many subdivisions, the grounds of residential institutions, university campuses, and hundreds of private homes all over the country (Arleyn Levee, "John Charles Olmsted," in Charles A. Birnbaum and Robin Karson, eds., *Pioneers of American Landscape Design* [New York, 2000], pp. 282–85; James Sturgis Pray, "John Charles Olmsted, A Minute on his Life and Service Prepared for the Board of Trustees of the American Society of Landscape Architects," *Landscape Architecture*, April 1922, pp. 129–35).

2. One objection to the pier and gallery structures Olmsted proposed for Belle Isle was that the approach to the pier would lack a sufficiently deep channel for large steam ferries. The park commissioners had expressed fears that ferries could run aground, and Olmsted wanted to prove the navigability of the area in question on the Detroit River (*Third Annual Report of the Park Commission* [Detroit, 1885], pp. 5, 30–31).
3. Henry D. Ludden (d. 1899) was the City Engineer of Detroit. He served from 1875 to 1878 and was reappointed in 1882 (S. Farmer, *The History of Detroit and Michigan*, p. 936; *City of Detroit: Journal of the Common Council from January 10, 1899 to January 9, 1900* [Detroit, 1899], p. 631).
4. William Austin Moore (1823–1906) was a prominent lawyer in Detroit, former Commissioner of the Police, and named President of the Board of Park Commissioners in 1884 (*The City of Detroit Michigan, 1701–1922*, vol. III [Detroit, 1922], pp. 262–66; *Third Annual Report of the Board of Park Commissioners* [Detroit, 1885], p. 2).
5. John W. Ellis (1817–1910) was a banker and railroad owner. His home, Stoneacre, was on Bellevue Avenue in Newport, Rhode Island. Designed by William A. Potter, it was completed in 1885. Olmsted at this time was working on preliminary plans for the design of the grounds (James L. Yarnall, *Newport Through Its Architecture* [Newport, R.I., 2005], pp. 96–97; "Recent Deaths: John W. Ellis," *Newport Mercury*, Dec. 31, 1910, p. 1; plans 1015-1 and 1015-10, NPS/FLONHS; *Master List*, p. 239).
6. John H. Watson was a stone mason Olmsted had worked with on several projects. His firm, Lawrence Watson and Son, was registered in Salem, Massachusetts. He built the stone grotto for the summer-house on the U.S. Capitol grounds in 1879 and built a stone wall and terrace for John C. Phillips's Moraine Farm in Beverly, Massachusetts, in 1880. In the 1880s he also worked on the memorial cairn in North Easton, Massachusetts, and on the Overlook (Playstead Terrace) in Franklin Park in Boston (John C. Phillips to FLO, Oct. 7, 1880; ibid., Oct. 21, 1880; ibid., Dec. 27, 1880; John H. Watson and Lawrence Watson to FLO, April 24, 1882; George Adams, *The Salem Directory 1886* [Salem, Mass., 1886], p. 97; *Papers of FLO*, 7, p. 554, n. 8).

To Salem Howe Wales[1]

Brookline, Mass.
5th July, 1884.

Dear Mr Wales:

My professional practice has taken a turn that keeps me personally much on the wing. I often fail to see New York papers and their reports about Central Park are so often sickening that I am apt to skip them. I have not followed the proceedings to which you refer and don't know the charges against the Commission.[2] I have before told you that I am confident that the Commission has been distinctly guilty of breaches of trust. I should be glad to contribute to a trial of that question before a Criminal Court.

But taking the most friendly view of your personal position and with every desire to strengthen it I don't see how I could help you to show that the park might not be maintained in better condition than it ever has been with a smaller sum than the smallest ever spent. I have not a doubt that it could be and never had. If you have found a report of mine that testifies otherwise it will be easily shown to be defective.[3]

Sometime before the date you {*mention*} I had found that to {*avoid*} professional disgrace I {*must*} insist on leaving the Commission's service (I had {*presented*} my resignation) or on being formally relieved of responsibility for the cost of the work and the worthlessness for their proper {*purpose*} of the police arrangements of the park. I had been so relieved and stood so relieved in 1878.[4]

I had had shortly before to make estimates for work on the Buffalo Park and had found it practicable to do so at about half the rates I was obliged to allow for like works on the Central Park. The reason was that they had a man for Superintendent who had not political influence enough to be employed in New York but whom they had employed at once upon my request in Buffalo.[5] He was a trained landscape gardener and was given entire charge of the work being the sole and absolute Executive officer of the Board. He was perfectly guarded from "influence." He had never employed or discharged a man or boy or sold an article or signed a certificate upon the "advice" of a Commissioner, much less of a legislator or alderman. In short, he was a bona fide superintendent, and remains so to this day to the entire satisfaction of the city.

I had stated this fact to the New York Commissioners & they knew my conviction that similarly treated I could get better results than they were getting at half the money they were spending.

I have supposed that in making estimates to go {before} the public I had always been careful to show that the rates at which the cost of labor were reckoned were those of the actual, not the honest, cost of like operations in previous years. This was certainly understood to be the case by the Commissioners and {if} it does not appear in the report I am unable to account for it.

Under the present organization of the Park service in New York it is quite impossible that there can be an approach to economy. The effort for it is child's play. Any man who thinks the management efficient either knows nothing about it or he takes for granted an enormous allowance for political necessities. Executive management by a Committee is never efficient management. Executive management of a technical work by an untechnical committee is silly nonsense. How would you like to sail in a steamship or invest in a Cotton Mill under such management?

You cannot successfully defend it. The only apology for it is custom and popular demand. And for you individually that you tried & failed to draw the Commission into a better way.[6]

Yours Sincerely

Fred^{k} Law Olmsted.

The text presented here is from a letterpress copy of a handwritten letter signed on the original in Olmsted's hand: A1: 2–7, OAR/LC. Olmsted had not worked for the New York City Department of Public Parks since he had been forced out in January of 1878 (DPP, *Minutes*, Jan. 23, 1878, pp. 556–57).

1. Salem Howe Wales (1825–1902) was the editor of *Scientific American* from 1848 to 1872, a longtime member of the Union League Club and the Century Association, and an active Republican in New York City politics. Mayor William F. Havenmeyer appointed Wales park commissioner in January 1873, and his fellow board members elected him president that August. While president of the New York park commission, he received Olmsted and Vaux's preliminary report on the improvement of Morningside Park. Wales resigned from the board in May 1874, after he lost the presidency to Henry Stebbins and also had disagreements with Andrew H. Green. After unsuccessfully running for mayor, Wales was reappointed a park commissioner in 1880. In 1881 he tried to convince the board to rehire Olmsted and Vaux as landscape architects to the commission, but allies of Green on the board refused to vote for Olmsted and ended up appointing Vaux alone as Superintending Landscape Architect. Despite the support Wales provided to him in this period, Olmsted felt Wales was too willing to allow the extensive clearing of vegetation that superintendent Aneurin Jones was carrying out in Central Park. Olmsted's curiously phrased reference to "worthy master Salem Wales" at the beginning of his pamphlet, *The Spoils of the Park* (1882), also displayed some ambiguity. He described Wales metaphorically as a sailing vessel, not a man-o'-war, but a "man-of-peace, across whose shapely bows my yet more peaceful shallop could never hold her course but with the falling topsail of deferential salutation" (*NCAB*; "Death of Salem Wales," *New York Times*, Dec. 3, 1902, p. 9; FLO and Calvert Vaux to Salem H. Wales, Oct. 11, 1873 [*Papers of FLO*, 6: 651–60]; "Resignation of Park Commissioner Wales," *New York Times*, May 29, 1874, p. 2; "Park Department Rows," ibid., Oct. 20, 1881, p. 7; "Park Department Affairs," ibid., Nov. 20, 1871, p. 13; "Park Commissioner Wales Resigns," ibid., April 5, 1885, p. 2; Salem Wales to FLO, July 10, 1884; Frederick Law Olmsted, *The Spoils of the Park*, Feb., 1882 [*Papers of FLO*, 7: 606]).
2. The Council of Political Reform, an organization of private citizens that was formed in

1870 to combat corruption in government, was arguing before a State Supreme Court judge that the park commissioners were not following the law when awarding contracts. The council focused their probe on a gravel contract that was not put out for competitive bids. Days before writing his letter to Olmsted, Wales had testified that the reason for this was that there was only one type of gravel suitable for New York City's parks ("Political Reform — Organization of the State Council," *New York Times*, May 17, 1870, p. 2; "Ways of the Park Road: The Judicial Investigation of the Department Begun," ibid., June 24, 1884, p. 8; "Commissioner Wales on Gravel," ibid., June 26, 1884, p. 3).

3. Wales wanted Olmsted to help him counter the testimony of William H. Grant (1815–1896), a reputable engineer who had worked with Olmsted on a number of New York City projects. Grant was the superintending engineer of Central Park during its construction, worked with Olmsted and J. J. R. Croes on their plans for the twenty-third and twenty-fourth wards of the city (the Bronx), and served as the constructing engineer of the Department of Public Parks until he formed a private practice in 1876. He testified that the sum appropriated for Central Park was sufficient to maintain it properly, yet it had fallen into disrepair ("Memoir of William Harrison Grant," *Proceedings of the American Society of Civil Engineers* 22 [New York, 1896], pp. 610–11; *Papers of FLO*, 7: 263–64, n. 2; "Central Park's Condition," *New York Times*, June 29, 1884, p. 7; "Expenses for Park Work," ibid., July 9, 1884, p. 8).
4. Olmsted presented his resignation to Wales on September 17, 1873, because the commissioners were threatening to reorganize the parks department in a way that would diminish Olmsted's control over Central Park's gardeners and police force. He offered to "go on with the duties of design." A week later the board "relieved" him of "all duties of superintendence until further order," but directed him to proceed with his plans for Riverside and Morningside parks. In March 1875, after the appointment of William R. Martin to the board, Olmsted regained control of the superintendence of Central Park, but not of the police force. In 1878 he was forced out by his opponents, who relieved him of all responsibilities related to the city's parks (FLO to Salem H. Wales, Sept. 17, 1873; *Papers of FLO*, 6: 43–46; Frederick Law Olmsted, *The Spoils of the Park* [*Papers of FLO*, 7: 619–20]; DPP, *Minutes*, Sept. 25, 1873, p. 297; ibid., March 19, 1875, pp. 594–95; ibid., Jan. 23, 1878, pp. 556–57; Frederick Law Olmsted, Jr., and Theodora Kimball, eds., *Forty Years of Landscape Architecture: Central Park, Frederick Law Olmsted, Sr.* [Cambridge, Mass., 1973], pp. 110–11).
5. That is, William McMillan (1831–1899), who was a superintendent of Buffalo's parks from 1870 to 1897 (see FLO to William McMillan, March 16, 1885, n. 1, below).
6. As a commissioner, Wales opposed many of the changes underway in the Department of Public Parks, and by 1882 regretted that he had taken the position since "the spirit of evil is upon the department." He repeatedly wrote of the corruption in the department and of his struggles with the other commissioners. He also made a series of unsuccessful attempts at restoring Olmsted as parks superintendent (Salem H. Wales to FLO, Jan. 21, 1882; Salem H. Wales to FLO, Jan. 28, 1882; Salem H. Wales to FLO, March 12, 1882; Salem H. Wales to FLO, March 6, 1882).

To Charles Henry Dalton

Brookline, Mass.
26th Aug. 1884.

My Dear Sir,

Thanks for your note of today.

Nothing could be further from my intentions than to intimate anything looking in the direction of what you suggest that I may have intended you to understand. I have no engagements that can stand in the way of your work. If I have said anything that seemed to you {to} imply that I had, & that for this reason, I was anxious to have the topographical map hastened, it certainly was not because I am not as able as I suppose any other man you can find will be to quickly prepare a strong drawing and say "here is your plan and my bill."

I want to bring your judgment and mine together. To do so may prove to require study upon study; essay upon essay. You may wish me to try again and again before you find your own judgment mature. How can I tell? How can you tell? As a rule, the longer the plan is incubating the better it is. And the incubating process should not begin until all the facts of a topographical plan are mastered. The question of a plan is not one of mechanical labor but of the pondering of possibilities.

I have had twenty assistants at work with me on plans, including the best in the country, and can have them again, when needed, I suppose, to hasten work that can be hastened with advantage. At present I have but two.[1]

Yours Truly

Fredk Law Olmsted.

The text presented here is from a letterpress copy of a handwritten letter signed on the original in Olmsted's hand: A1: 36–37, OAR/LC. Apparently Olmsted had requested the completion of a topographical map of the (West Roxbury) Franklin Park area from Dalton, Chairman of the Boston Park Commission. Olmsted often made a detailed topographical survey, paid for by the client, a prerequisite for a general plan (*Tenth Annual Report, Boston Department of Parks, 1884*, p. 17; FLO to JCO, Dec. 6, 1884, below).

1. The two assistants referred to by Olmsted were Charles Eliot, who had come to apprentice at the office in the spring of 1883, and Henry Sargent Codman, who had been hired the summer of 1884 after graduating from the Massachusetts Institute of Technology. After John C. Olmsted, who had become a partner in the firm that year, they were Olmsted's most important assistants at this time. Olmsted also hired draftsmen and other office employees as needed (*FLO, A Biography*, p. 393; Charles Eliot Diary, years 1883 and 1884, FLLHU; Charles Eliot to Grace Hopkinson Eliot, summer 1884, courtesy of Alexander Yale Goriansky).

To Charles Henry Dalton

Brookline, Mass.
6th Sept: 1884.

C. H. Dalton Esq. Chrm.
My Dear Sir,

I have looked at the "mounding" on Commonwealth Ave, as you requested. It is in accordance with my intentions and I am not afraid of it, but there would be nothing essential lost if the undulations were quieted and if you so instruct I will have the elevations reduced a foot or so.

In considering the question you will please bear in mind that a certain degree of undulation makes much less impression when uniformly covered with turf or in any way greened over than when of earth. Also that if there is to be shrubbery on these swells it will be effective sooner for the mounding, and that in any case, with shrubbery the views are to be obstructed.

The highest elevation, of the work done, is four feet above the grade of the main drive, three feet above the top of the rounded retaining curb on the right of the walk. The side road, (straight, before the houses) is lower than the main drive at this point, so that the top of the highest swell will be six feet above it. All these swells are planned to give lazy and graceful slopes toward the houses, the lower parts of which will thus have a certain seclusion and exclusiveness, which in my judgment will not ultimately injure their value. You will recall the swells & slopes between the main & side roads of the Avenue de l'Emperatrice (of late Uhrich).[1] The space is broader, the difference of elevation greater & the side roads are higher instead of lower than the main promenade. The swells as I remember them are larger, higher & the plantations more important, but what I am aiming at may be considered as an effect slightly of that character on a smaller scale. A decided difference of detailed treatment in the gardened spaces of Commonwealth Avenue, where its outlines change from a straight & formal motive to curves and irregularly broken views, is of course desirable. But it is a fair question whether I have not aimed at more than is necessary to accomplish what is desirable in this respect and I am perfectly willing to revise the plans if you think so. I hope that you will examine the entire grading plan before you decide. There is one point where a swell occurs, I think, a trifle higher than the one you have questioned.

Yours respy,

Fredk Law Olmsted.
L.A.A.

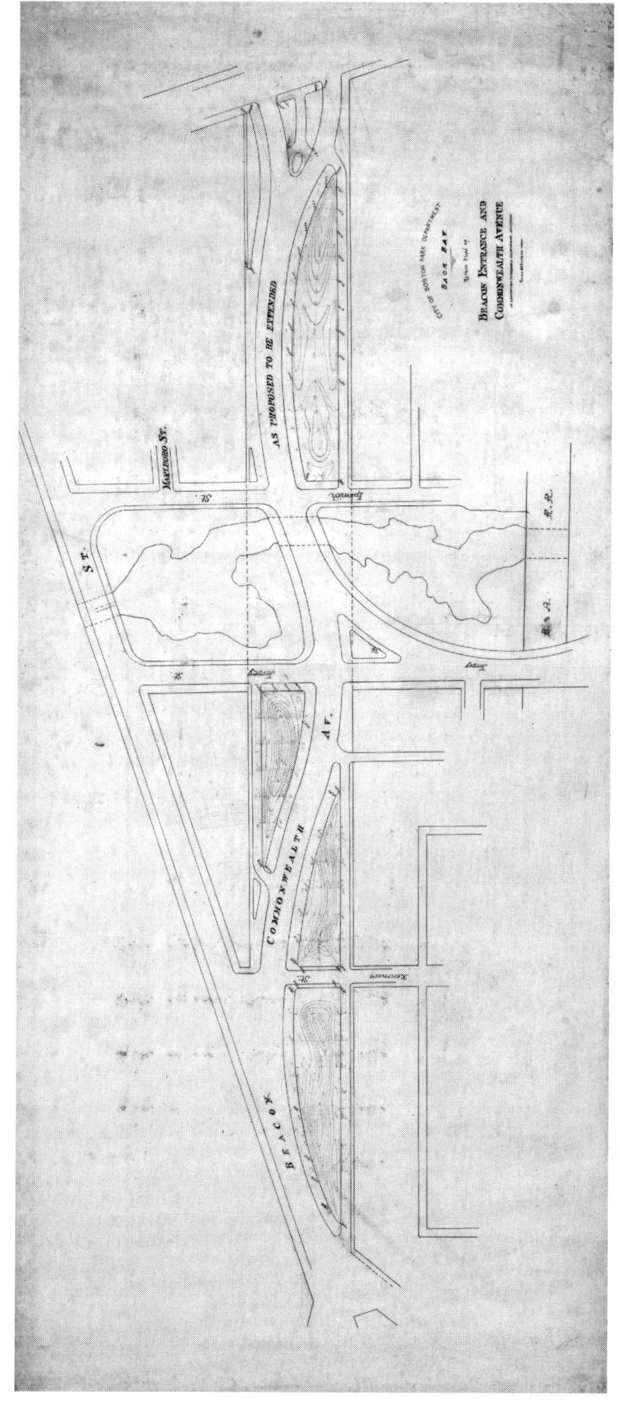

"Back Bay, Revised Plan of Beacon Street Entrance and Commonwealth Avenue," n.d.

The text presented here is from a letterpress copy of a handwritten letter signed on the original in Olmsted's hand: A1: 41–43, OAR/LC. When Olmsted began the design of the Back Bay Fens in 1878, Commonwealth Avenue terminated at the end of the Back Bay grid of streets. In 1879 the Boston Common Council authorized the extension of Commonwealth Avenue in a northerly direction to the intersection of Beacon Street and Brookline Avenue. The extension crossed the Beacon Street entrance (Charlesgate) of the Back Bay Fens at a right angle. Olmsted's preliminary plans in 1879 show the extended avenue with straight carriageways in each direction and parallel rows of trees. By the end of the year, however, Olmsted had designed a curvilinear avenue flanked by the "mounding" topography described here. As it moved through the Beacon Street entrance, the avenue divided, continuing on to Beacon Street in one direction and reversing back, over the Boylston Street Bridge, in the other. The latter roadway rose up to meet the elevation of the bridge and was supported by a large retaining wall. The portion of the avenue west of the Beacon Street entrance was probably redesigned in the late 1880s; in any case, this entire section of Commonwealth Avenue was reconfigured in the twentieth century (*Papers of FLO*, 7: 463, n. 21; see illustrations in *Papers of FLO*, 7: 429, 448, 452–53; C. Zaitzevsky, *The Boston Park System*, p. 239, n. 2; for more on the retaining wall see FLO to F. L. Temple, Aug. 21, 1883, n. 2, above; Frederick Law Olmsted, "Report of the Landscape Architect," Dec. 24, 1883, above).

1. The Avenue de L'Impératrice (Avenue Foch) was the widest and most park-like of the boulevards and avenues created in Paris under the prefecture of Georges-Eugène Haussmann in the 1850s and 1860s. About one mile long and 460 feet wide, it extended from the Place de L'Etoile to the Bois de Boulogne, and so it was the most important connection between central Paris (via the Champs Elysées) and the large park developed by Haussmann on the city's western periphery. The Avenue de L'Impératrice consisted of a central roadway flanked by pedestrian and bridle paths, all set in a generous corridor that featured undulating turf and extensive plantations of trees and shrubs. Olmsted saw the avenue in 1859 and met its designer, Jean-Charles-Adolphe Alphand. In 1868 he described it as a precedent for Eastern Parkway in Brooklyn. In the early 1870s the avenue was renamed for General Jean Jacques Alexis Uhrich, the French general in charge of the unsuccessful defense of Strasbourg during the Franco-Prussian War. It was later known as the Avenue du Bois de Boulogne, and in the twentieth century was renamed for Ferdinand Foch, the French World War I general and Marshal of France (*Atlas Historique de la France Contemporaine, 1800–1965* [Paris, 1966]; Jean-Charles-Adolphe Alphand, *Les Promenades de Paris* [Paris, 1867–1873, reprinted, Princeton, N.J., 1984]; FLO to the Board of Commissioners of the Central Park, Dec. 28, 1859 [*Papers of FLO*, 3: 234–42]; Olmsted, Vaux, and Co., "Report to the Brooklyn Park Commission," Jan. 1, 1868 [*Papers of FLO*, SS1: 134–35, 145, n. 33]).

CHAPTER III

SEPTEMBER 1884–DECEMBER 1885

In 1883, Olmsted purchased the farmhouse in Brookline, Massachusetts, which he and his wife, Mary Perkins Olmsted, named Fairsted. Renovations of the house that year adapted it to use as both family home and professional office, but few extant documents discuss this work. A telegram of September 12 to John C. Olmsted about plantings for the property is an exception. Another letter to his step-son, of December 6, provides insight into the operations of the firm during this period of growth.

Olmsted continues park planning for Boston and Detroit and submits a proposal to Mayor Charles A. Williams for converting an old burial ground in New London, Connecticut, to a park. His main challenge in Detroit, as he explains in a letter to the architect Mortimer L. Smith, is to make sure that the combined pier and gallery building that he designed for Belle Isle is built as he specifies, since it is essential to his concept for the park. For Boston, he writes two reports that appear in the *Tenth Annual Report* of the Boston park commissioners: one describes progress of work on the Back Bay Fens, while the other provides preliminary plans for West Roxbury Park (later named Franklin Park) and Wood Island Park. His work on Franklin Park is consuming much of his time, as is evident by a draft of notes that provides specifications for the terrace in the Playstead section of the park, and a two- part article for the *American Architect and Building News* that responds to a critic of his Franklin Park plan. Olmsted had cut his ties with the New York City park board, but they asked him to return to advise them on the location of the tomb of Ulysses S. Grant. Olmsted traveled to New York to see the proposed sites, and shares his views in a letter to John D. Crimmins.

Two personal letters in this chapter include a note to Charles Loring

Brace reminiscing about their lifelong friendship, and a letter of condolence to architect Stanford White after the death of his father, Richard Grant White, whom Olmsted had known for many years. Additional letters in this chapter include a note to Bronson C. Rumsey assessing whether property in Yonkers, New York, would be suitable for suburban development, one to Percival St. George recommending books on landscape architecture, and one to an unidentified woman about the desirability of separating suburban residences by fences.

To John Charles Olmsted

Washington, 12th Sept 1884. 6, P.M.

Have just recvd yours of 10th
I intend the Bridgeport[1] page with fair margin to take in map with one fold—i.e. to be half the depth of it, but it may be shorter, so that will fold over one half or more. It is only important that this should not be a very short fold. I propose 25 copies to be printed & then to stereotype. Printer understands I believe but if cannot you would do well to make sure by calling.

Brookline Heights or Hill hardly satisfactory for a station in a lyn[2] or gorge. Should prefer Lynwood or Playsted or Brooklyndale.[3] But mother will have a better one ready grown.

I don't object to the cutting away of certain bramble patches if other brambles are to take their place—or anything that will appear spontaneous & not need watering or care. More {*mowing*}[4] or dug ground I object to. Less wildness and disorder I object to.[5]

Have telegraphed Green[6] in reply to forwarded telegram that I am engaged tomorrow. Will come Monday, Wednesday or Thursday. If Monday shall return here.

F.L.O

The text presented here is a signed telegram text in Olmsted's hand.

1. Olmsted refers to his and John Charles Olmsted's report on Beardsley Park in Bridgeport, Connecticut (*Beardsley Park. Landscape Architects' Preliminary Report. September, 1884* [Boston, 1884]).
2. An obsolete form of linn, "a precipice, a ravine" (*OED*).
3. Refers to the naming of Brookline Hills train station. Olmsted designed a subdivision

Fairsted, 99 Warren St., Brookline, Mass., home and office of Frederick Law Olmsted, n.d.

named Brookline Hill for several landowners, including George A. Goddard. The station was built in 1892 and was designed by Shepley, Rutan, and Coolidge. In the end, Olmsted apparently did not design the station's landscape and the building was later demolished (JCO to George A. Goddard, Sept. 25, 1884, A1: 65–66, OAR/LC; Jeffrey Karl Ochsner, "Architecture for the Boston & Albany Railroad: 1881–1894," *Journal of the Society of Architectural Historians*, June 1988, p. 130).

4. Previous published transcriptions of this letter have read "moving" here, but the editors have determined this word to be "mowing."
5. Presumably refers to grounds at Fairsted.
6. Either Caleb or Charles Green, family members of John Cleve Green, whose legacy was used to acquire and expand the Lawrenceville School in Lawrenceville, New Jersey. At this time Olmsted was developing plans for that campus (Oscar Fay Adams, *Some Famous American Schools* [Boston, 1903], pp. 125–68; FLO to James Cameron Mackenzie, May 21, 1883, above).

To Charles Augustus Williams[1]

[October 1884]

C.A. Williams Esq.
Chairman of the Park Commission.
New London.

Dear Sir; In a large number of cases it is probable that the remains of the dead laid in the Grand Burial Ground of New London will have become so commingled with the earth in which they were deposited that, were it desirable, it would be impracticable to remove them to another locality. It is probable that the earth to which they have thus been fully returned will to some extent be disturbed in the adaptation of the ground to the purpose which your Board has been commissioned to serve. The removal of the grave stones will be a necessity. Under these circumstances the question must have arisen in many minds whether the project is not an ill-advised one?

In considering it, the following circumstances are to be weighed.

The ground was unsuitable to the purpose of a burial place as that purpose is now generally regarded. This is shown by the fact that a part of it has at different times been used as a quarry and large quantities of building stone taken out from and brought through it and the further fact that in digging graves rock has in numerous instances been found so near the surface that to secure a decent interment earth has been drawn from elsewhere and piled over the coffins. The position of graves has been determined with reference to no uniform system and their disposition as a whole is a desultory and disorderly one, in parts closely crowded, elsewhere scattered and straggling.

Provision has been {*evidently*} neglected for keeping the ground in a decorous or even in neat and tidy condition. The graves have for the most part not simply been neglected but have been tramped over without compunction. There are well defined foot paths through the ground leading over them and their ancient headstones have been often kicked and battered by irreverent wayfarers. So far as the general aspect of the ground expresses the sentiment of the community that sentiment is not one of honor or reverence for the dead but the reverse.

To fully understand how such treatment of a burial ground could have been established we have to recall the fact that in the old countries from which our ancestors came it was, as in many localities it still is unusual that the remains of the dead are left long in undisturbed graves. The gravedigger, as in Hamlet,[2] is constantly throwing them out by fragments and it is even customary in many grounds from time {to time} to collect skulls and the more lasting bones and heap them together indiscriminately in common charnel houses or ossuaries.[3]

To most of us at the present time this ancient custom in all incidents has become repugnant, and the thought is a natural one that where a burial ground still exists which appears in any marked degree dilapidated, neglected, & dishonored, it should be revised to some degree in accordance with the more modern sentiment.

But in this case the particular form of disorder depends too much upon the original topography of the ground to admit of anything like a complete or satisfactory remedy.

Under these circumstances, the ground lying in the midst of a city, it has been determined that the ground shall be appropriated to other purposes. No suitable plan for adapting it to these purposes can be devised that does not involve a general removal of grave stones from their original positions.

Under these circumstances the following proposition is submitted:

A portion of the original burial ground to be set apart as a place in which remains of the dead that your board may find it necessary to disturb may be reverently redeposited and in which all monumental records that may be collected from other parts of the ground may be decorously treasured. All monuments not in the form of slabs (head stones), to be reset entire and that part of all others in which the record is inscribed to be given the form of mural tablets in a uniform firm setting of masonry and so protected as to secure their lasting preservation. The means used for this purpose and all the accessories to be as little as possible discordant with the ancient, time-worn and historic aspect of the monumental stones. The part of the ground assigned to the purpose to be laid out, planted and kept as a distinctive general memorial of the body of people and of the portion of the history of the city of which the inscriptions on the stones would testify.

To carry out this suggestion it would be necessary as I roughly estimate to use little more than a tenth part of the entire space which the law places at your disposal.

Awaiting your instructions upon this point, before proceeding with the general design of the premises.[4] I am, dear Sir,

Respectfully Yours

The text presented here is an unsigned draft in Olmsted's hand. The draft was not dated, but a letter from Robert Coit to Olmsted dated October 22, 1884, referred to Olmsted's "report on the proposed park addressed to Mr. Williams," so this draft was likely written in October 1884.

Charles Augustus Williams offered to fund the creation of a park (later named Williams Memorial Park) on a three-acre plot of land in New London, Connecticut. The site was an old burial ground with an adjacent area that had been used as a quarry, located on the north side of New London at the corner of Broad and Hempstead streets. A park commission was formed with Williams as president, and commission member James A. Rumrill was the first to contact Olmsted requesting his assistance. Robert Coit, president of the New London Northern Railroad Company, served as secretary to the commission and corresponded with Olmsted on the progress of the project. During the summer of 1884, Olmsted visited New London and met with Williams, Coit, and civil engineer W. H. Richards (Robert Coit to FLO, Oct. 22, 1884, B73: #1001, OAR/LC; Benjamin Tinkham Marshall, ed., *A Modern History of New London, Connecticut*, vol. 1 [New York, 1922], p. 404; "Steps Toward Laying Out a Park," *New London Day*, June 9, 1884; J.A. Rumrill to FLO, June 18, 1884; see also FLO to C. A. Williams, May 9, 1885, below).

1. Charles Augustus Williams (1829–1900) was a New London businessman and, at this time, mayor of the city. As a young man he was in charge of Williams & Haven, which operated one of the largest whaling fleets in the United States, and his family owned the land of the park site as well as adjacent land ("Death of Charles Augustus Williams," *New York Times*, Jan. 1, 1900; B. T. Marshall, ed., *A Modern History of New London*, p. 404; *National Register of Historic Places, Nomination Form* [United States Department of the Interior, National Park Service, Oct. 1987]).
2. Olmsted references the dialogue between the gravediggers in Shakespeare's *Hamlet*, as they dig Ophelia's grave and Hamlet muses on the skulls they displace (Act V, Scene 1).
3. In Europe during the Middle Ages and later, graves in churchyards were often reused after a period. Bones recovered in the process were then stored in charnel houses, or ossuaries (James Stevens Curl, *A Celebration of Death: An Introduction to Some of the Buildings, Monuments, and Settings of Funerary Architecture in the Western European Tradition* [New York, 1980], pp. 72, 136).
4. The park commissioners were in favor of Olmsted's plans to remove the gravestones in any way he saw fit. Coit wrote him that "we defer to your judgment in the matter of disposing of the gravestones & monuments," and "I am quite sure that your way of preserving the stone records of the burial ground will be entirely acceptable to those who have an ancestral interest in them." He further suggested that they hold on to the report and publish it after the removal of stones had begun, so that it could act as a "sedative" to those angered by their removal. It is not known if it was ever published. The bodily remains themselves were removed to Cedar Grove Cemetery. The removal of the stones

commenced in the fall of 1884, and Olmsted made sketches and formal plans for the park that included an alcove in which to house them, as he describes here (FLO to C. A. Williams, May 9, 1885, below; Robert Coit to FLO, Oct. 22, 1884, B73: #1001, OAR/LC; W.H. Richards to FLO, Dec. 3, 1884, B73: #1001, OAR/LC; "Williams Park placed on historic register," *New London Day*, Nov. 10, 1987; *National Register of Historic Places, Nomination Form* [United States Department of the Interior, National Park Service, Oct. 1987).

To Bronson Case Rumsey [1]

Brookline Mass Nov 1884

B. C. Rumsey Esq
Dear Sir

Last week I made a cursory examination of the property shown on the map herewith returned and the country near it.[2]

The long steep slopes of a large part of the property are likely to be saleable only with reference to the larger class of suburban villas and the advantages offered for this disposition of it are considerably lessened by the circumstance that it is divided into five belts by a stream, an acqueduct a railroad and a carriage road, all slicing it from North to South and barring what would otherwise be the best system of roads for giving access to the hillside building sites. Some land may in consequence have to be sold either in undesirably small plots, or attached to larger plots without adding much to their value, or made public property. Still a division fairly satisfactory for villa sites a considerable part of which would be from four to six acres in extent is practicable.

Unfortunately there is little demand for villa property of this class near New York, less than almost any other city the environs of which are not specially inviting, and villas and villa grounds of the better sort rarely sell to advantage. Many can be bought at half their original cost. Thrifty men are consequently cautious of having much capital in them. The reason generally given is that so many of such properties have proved to be malarious or otherwise unhealthy. I have examined many with the result of a {*conviction*} that they could be in most cases made healthful at a cost that would not be inordinate but that the disposition of owners to sell and the indisposition of others to buy is only partially due to this cause. Remove it entirely and the fact would remain that villa life in the near vicinity of New York does not prove generally satisfactory and consequently that villa places and villa sites are comparatively poor property. Poor I mean comparatively with a similar class of property near other cities looking so far away even as London, Liverpool and Paris. The comparison that I am best able to make however is with Boston near which city I have been advised with as to several villa neighborhoods.[3] In each of these before land has been put in the market, good roads have been built, their borders made graceful and neat, drainage secured and the healthfulness of the locality secured. It follows that lots have been rapidly sold at prices fully meeting the calculations of the owners and that numerous villa houses have been built and grounds prepared of a much more attractive sort than any often seen near New York.

Among the people who have done this some are of abundant wealth and of the highest social standing and there is no doubt that they are following a strong bent of taste and a conviction that the health and well being of their families are better served by a suburban villa manner of life than by any other. Some of these suburban residents that I know have moved from New York. While there they did not think of taking out of town places. Here they do so at once and are glad of the opportunity.

The difference does not lie wholly or mainly in the more careful judicious and substantial way in which lands naturally well adapted to villas are prepared and put in the market near Boston. It is due in large measure to the greater assurance felt by purchasers that such lands will not only not be taken up for other and widely incongruous purposes but that in a large neighborhood there will be a constant advance and improvement in the direction of an unbroken community of people of not excessively uncongenial tastes purposes and modes of life; A community likely therefore to be measurably united and constant in its demands and its influence upon the management of local public affairs and in which there will be an active public opinion repressing roadside exhibitions of excessively bad taste shabbiness or slatternliness.

In 1875 when engaged in devising the street plan for that part of the City of New York adjoining your property on the South[4] I saw how little confidence a purchaser could have in a similar growth of a villa neighborhood within it. It contained not a few places in themselves attractive but always at no great distance from these were circumstances putting them out of countenance. Rough clearings in old wood land with blocks of gaunt trees left standing; patches of waste land and ill kept fields; raw banks by the side of the road, puddles and swamps; road side taverns and beer gardens; shanties; dilapidated stables or small groups of buildings such as are to be looked for in the most repulsive outskirts of cities with cinders and garbage strewn before them New York fashion. These things scattered at intervals neutralize the attractiveness of a suburban neighborhood no matter how nice its better parts may be. And being closely associated with most villa properties about New York they have come to be regarded as natural and necessary elements of suburban scenery, just as crowded cars and shabby and incommodious railroad stations are. There are a dozen stations about Boston finer and better kept than the best in the suburbs of New York.[5] So there are about Philadelphia.

After examining your property the other day I looked again through parts of this adjoining New Ward district and it seemed to me that in the progress from its original rural condition the recent drift had been rather more toward a squalid outskirt of the town than toward a permanently inviting suburb. I do not see how confidence can be had that any part of it will acquire a continuous fixed character such as seems easy to establish for neighborhoods about Boston.

There are many times more people in New York than in Boston of the tastes habits and inclinations that are represented in the more attractive Boston suburbs. If the same advantages could be secured in your property with the same confidence of a lasting attractive consistent character that are secured in many Boston suburbs I think that a corresponding demand might be reckoned upon.

There are two special difficulties in the way of giving these advantages and this public confidence for your property. The first is the topographical difficulty to which I have referred which can only be got the better of by devising arrangements of an unusual if not an entirely original character in respect to roads and drainage.

The second is the difficulty of overcoming the inert imagination of possible purchasers and of setting them to think out the problems of providing such a class of homes for themselves as they might obtain upon these hillsides. New Yorkers are not accustomed to build except on shelves or plateaux of land and know nothing that is good of hillside gardening.

They need some tangible illustrations of what can be well done in such a locality to put them in train[6] to a market demand.

I do not think that experience gives reason to suppose that any easy and moderate improvement such as has been characteristic of New York suburban real estate speculations will make your property saleable except at prices at which it can be again held for speculation by small investors or occupied scatteringly by people of small means such as those who are building on the outskirts of Brooklyn with a view to getting houses at less rent than they can be had for in the city. The ground is much less adapted to a method of subdivision suitable to such an occupation of it than it is to that which I have aimed to suggest.

The text presented here is an unsigned letter in a clerk's hand. Olmsted added a note attached to the letter: "Report to Rumsey & others, proposed villa neighborhood near Yonkers."

1. Bronson Case Rumsey (1823–1902), a Buffalo businessman involved in banking, railroads, and land development, was a Buffalo park commissioner from 1882 to 1898. Olmsted and Rumsey had known each other since at least 1869 when they both attended a meeting about establishing the Niagara Reservation. They also corresponded in 1870 regarding a subdivision in Tarrytown Heights, New York, that Olmsted and Vaux were designing. Olmsted did more work for Rumsey later in the 1880s on designs for the Parkside and Villa Park neighborhoods in Buffalo (*A History of the City of Buffalo: Its Men and Institutions* [Buffalo, 1908], p. 182; *Twelfth Annual Report of the Buffalo Park Commissioners* [Buffalo, 1882]; *Twenty-Eighth Annual Report of the Buffalo Park Com-*

missioners [Buffalo, 1898]; FLO to C. K. Remington, May 28, 1888, n. 8, below; B. C. Rumsey to FLO, June 7, 1870; FLO to B. C. Rumsey, Jan. 13, 1886, A1: 270A–270B, OAR/LC; FLO and JCO to J. B. Stafford, Aug. 10, 1886, A1: 395–96, OAR/LC; J. B. Stafford to FLO, Aug. 17, 1886, B74: #1035, OAR/LC; *Master List*, p. 107).

2. The property was located due south of the intersection of Midland Avenue and Yonkers Avenue in Yonkers, New York. A bill dated January 1, 1885, indicates that Olmsted examined and reported on the site for Rumsey at that time. Olmsted's involvement in this project does not appear to have progressed beyond the 1885 plans for surveys and excavations (*Minutes of the Board of Estimate and Apportionment of the City and County of New York, 1885* [New York, 1886], pp. 293–97; "Property Maps, New Croton Supply," Department of Public Works, City of New York; FLO to B. C. Rumsey, Jan. 1, 1885, A1: 154, OAR/LC).
3. Olmsted consulted on the Aspinwall Hill subdivision and the Brookline Hill (Fisher Hill) subdivision both in Brookline, Massachusetts (Cynthia Zaitzevsky, "Frederick Law Olmsted in Brookline: A Preliminary Study of His Public Projects," *Proceedings of the Brookline Historical Society*, Fall 1977, pp. 42–65; see Frederick Law Olmsted, "The Beacon Street Plan," *Brookline Chronicle*, Dec. 4, 1886, below; Frederick Law Olmsted, "Talk to the Brookline Club, History of Streets," Feb. 1889, below).
4. In 1876, Olmsted and his colleague, engineer J. J. R. Croes, proposed a street system and steam rapid transit plan for the recently annexed twenty-third and twenty-fourth wards of New York City, in what is now the Bronx. The rugged terrain and hillside between Broadway and the Hudson River, in particular, could not easily be subdivided in an orthogonal grid, and Olmsted and Croes designed curvilinear streets adapted to the topography. The plans for the twenty-third and twenty-fourth wards were officially adopted but not laid out accordingly by the engineers in charge. Such a neighborhood would have been suitable for the type of villa residences that Olmsted notes were lacking in the suburbs of New York (Frederick Law Olmsted and J. J. R. Croes, *Preliminary Report of the Landscape Architect and the Civil and Topographical Engineer, upon the Laying Out of the Twenty-third and Twenty-fourth Wards*, Nov. 15, 1876 [*Papers of FLO*, 7: 242–51]; Frederick Law Olmsted and J. J. R. Croes, *Report of the Landscape Architect and the Civil and Topographical Engineer, Accompanying a Plan for Laying Out that Part of the Twenty-Fourth Ward Lying West of the Riverdale Road*, Nov. 21, 1876 [*Papers of FLO*, 7: 251–66]).
5. Olmsted refers to the suburban Boston railroad stations of the Boston & Albany Railroad. James A. Rumrill, a friend of H. H. Richardson's, became vice president of the line in 1880, and Charles Sprague Sargent became a director of the railroad the same year. In 1881 the company commissioned Richardson (and later Shepley, Rutan, and Coolidge) and Olmsted to design a series of stations in suburban Boston and western Massachusetts. Olmsted designed site plans and planting plans for the Allston, Auburndale, Brighton, Brookline Hills, Brookline Reservoir, Chestnut Hill, Newton, Palmer, Wellesley, and Wellesley Hills stations, among others. He also designed the grounds of a number of existing stations for the railroad, which at the time were the largest in New England (Jeffrey Karl Ochsner, "Architecture for the Boston & Albany Railroad: 1881–1894," *Journal of the Society of Architectural Historians*, June 1988, pp. 109–31).
6. That is, in process.

To Charles Loring Brace[1]

Brookline, Mass.
1st Novr 1884

Dear Charles;

I rcvd yours of 19th on returning from Detroit. I had accidentally seen your paper on Kapp in the Times[2] and had judged that the initials at end had been intended for yours and am glad that the first knowledge of his death came to me in such sympathetic form. I was attached to Kapp & glad to get his daughter's note, which I return, as well as yours.

Social changes in our time have been so great that while I feel myself in the full fount of the life of today I feel that the life of our early days was almost another life and instead of being shocked by the death of old friends, I wonder that {they} could have lived till so lately—most of all that I am still living.

You decidedly have had the best & most worthily successful life of all whom I have known. The C.A.[3] is the most satisfactory of all the benevolent works of our time.

I have done a good deal of good work in my way too but it is constantly & everywhere arrested, wrenched, mangled and misused & it is not easy to get above intense disappointment & mortification. The politicians & the reporters & the editors don't torture me as they once did but still not a little and I am older and don't bear what comes as well—or without greater agitation—than I once did for I never bore it well. I think it comes harder to an old man to be grossly insulted.

I have felt the disgrace of the late Presidential campaign very much. Even the best newspapers with the best position to support have been most shamefully conducted. It was very saddening.[4]

The crisis of Civil Service Reform was to come upon a change of administration to the Spoils party.[5] I have not much confidence in the result but the best statesmanship could not have put us in a better position for meeting it. I think well of Cleveland but realize—no, I don't suppose any man can realize what assaults he will have to meet—they will be beyond anything that can be imagined—and have it strongly impressed upon me that he has had an extremely contracted & not a very elevating social experience; that he has been a solitary man of most industrious habits—industrious exclusively in his vocation of a small lawyer's practice that his range of knowledge of respectable & educated men has been very limited, & so on. With a good deal of confidence in his native sagacity and resoluteness, I expect to see him awfully imposed upon and led into humiliating positions.

Do you happen to remember him when he was a teacher under Colden Cooper?[6] I think you must have been present one night when Henry Barnes[7] made some of his experiments in phrenology. I should have forgotten him but he recalled it & then I remembered a hypothetical cousin of my wife, whose name you know is Cleveland. (Mary Cleveland Bryant Perkins)[8]

I keep working as close to my possibilities as ever, my possibilities, never large, growing perceptibly smaller with every year. John takes more & more off and I have two good young men as "pupils",[9] but the character of my business becomes smaller & brings a greater multitude of diverse concerns to me & I get very weary of turning so often from one thing to another and of so many long & short expeditions. Perhaps I all the more enjoy my house & place & the bits of quiet work I am able to do in it.

I rejoice with you in the condition & prospects of your children especially now, of course, Loring's[10] which seems to be as happy as possible.

With love & congratulations to Letitia.[11]

Ever Affectly Yours

Fred[k] Law Olmsted.

Who wrote the paper in the Nation on Kapp? Someone, surely, whom I have known well but can't make him out.[12]

The text presented here is a signed letter in Olmsted's hand.

1. Charles Loring Brace (1826–1890) was one of Olmsted's oldest friends. Brace met Olmsted and his brother, John Hull, Olmsted in Hartford sometime after the family relocated there in 1832. When Brace entered Yale College in 1842 he was John's roommate and, in the course of Olmsted's visits to his brother, he and Brace became friends. In the fall of 1845, while Olmsted audited courses on agriculture and botany at Yale, their friendship continued. Brace studied for the ministry after graduating from Yale in 1846, and in 1848 he began ministering to the poor and sick committed to Blackwell's Island in New York. In 1850, Brace joined Olmsted and his brother, John, on a six-month walking tour of Britain and Europe. As young men, Brace and Olmsted engaged in spirited discussions and correspondence on religious, literary, and other topics. Brace helped found the Children's Aid Society in New York in 1853 and served as the director of this charitable organization until his death. He introduced Olmsted to influential people in New York City and facilitated his being hired by Henry Raymond to travel in the South in 1852–1854 as a reporter for the *New York Times*. Brace wrote numerous books on theology and philanthropy as well as accounts of his European experiences. Brace and Olmsted shared many friends and acquaintances in Connecticut and New York, and they remained close friends and correspondents throughout their lives (*DAB*; *Papers of FLO*, 1: 67–70; Emma Brace, ed., *The Life of Charles Loring Brace* [New York, 1894]; see also FLO to Charles Loring Brace, March 15, 1887, below; FLO to Charles Loring Brace, Jan. 18, 1890, below).
2. Friedrich Kapp (1824–1884) was a German-American lawyer and newspaper editor who emigrated to New York in 1850 and became actively involved in charities and Republican politics there. Olmsted met Kapp in New York in 1854, after Olmsted's travels in Texas during which he visited German Free-Soil communities. In the mid-1850s, Kapp assisted Olmsted in his quest for land to purchase for free-soil settlers in Texas. Kapp became close friends with Olmsted and Charles Loring Brace, and he was a trustee of the German School of the Children's Aid Society. Brace's eulogy of Kapp, "Frederick Kapp," appeared in the *New York Times*, October 31, 1884, p. 3 (*DAB*; *Pa-*

pers of FLO, 2: 66–69; Frederick Law Olmsted, "A Tour in the Southwest, Number 12" *New-York Daily Times*, June 3, 1854 [*Papers of FLO*, 2: 299–306]; FLO to Secretaries of the Cotton Supply Associations of Manchester and Liverpool, July 6, 1857 [*Papers of FLO*, 2: 443–45]; FLO to Friedrich Kapp, April 6, 1864 [*Papers of FLO*, 5: 219–24]).

3. That is, the Children's Aid Society.
4. The 1884 presidential election pitted Democratic Grover Cleveland against Republican James Blaine, and much of the coverage in papers focused on scandals in the lives of both candidates. The press accused Blaine of various kinds of political corruption, causing a group of Republicans, nicknamed Mugwumps, to rebel and vote Democratic. The Republican press accused Cleveland of having a child out of wedlock ("Disgusted With Blaine," *New York Times*, June 9, 1884, p. 5; "Blain's Unclean Record," ibid., Oct. 6, 1884, p. 5; "Blaine and the Cleveland Scandal," the *Raleigh News and Observer*, Aug. 14, 1884; Mark Wahlgren Summers, *Rum, Romanism, & Rebellion: The Making of a President, 1884* [Chapel Hill, N.C., 2000], pp. 173, 179–96).
5. Civil Service Reform was a significant issue in the 1884 election. The assassination of President James Garfield in 1881 by a disgruntled man who was denied a federal appointment motivated Congress in 1883 to pass the Pendleton Civil Service Reform Act. When Cleveland was inaugurated in 1885, however, 110,000 out of 126,000 federal jobs were still subject to political appointment. The reform movement wanted to create a professional administrative service that was not corrupted by partisan and personal gain or by the "spoils" system. Olmsted had a long-standing interest in civil service reform, as documented by his pamphlet, *The Spoils of the Park* and the article "Influence," which he wrote for his friend George W. Curtis, president of the Civil-Service Reform Association (M. W. Summers, *Rum, Romanism, & Rebellion*, pp. 73–76; Allan Nevins, *Grover Cleveland, A Study in Courage* [New York, 1932], p. 199; Frederick Law Olmsted, *The Spoils of the Park*, Feb. 1882 [*Papers of FLO*, 7: 605–52]; Frederick Law Olmsted, "Influence," c. July 1881 [*Papers of FLO*, 7: 539–48]).
6. Thomas Colden Cooper (1821–1864) was superintendent for the New York Institute for the Blind when Grover Cleveland and his brother William taught there during the 1853–1854 school year (H. Paul Jeffers, *An Honest President: The Life and Presidencies of Grover Cleveland* [New York, 2000], p. 22–23; "Cleveland as a Teacher," *St. Louis Globe-Democrat*, July 19, 1884, p. 3; D. T. Valentine, *Manual of the Corporation of the City of New York* [New York, 1853], p. 236; W. J. Tenney, *The Military and Naval History of the Rebellion in the United States* [New York, 1865], p. 777).
7. Albert Henry Barnes (1826–1878), son of the influential Presbyterian clergyman Albert Barnes (1789–1870), was an old friend of Brace's and Olmsted's. He studied at the Princeton Theological Seminary and was ordained a minister in 1854. The three men visited each other in the 1850s in New York and Princeton, and they also went together to Brooklyn to hear Henry Ward Beecher preach at Plymouth Church, as did Grover and William Cleveland in 1853, while teaching at the Institute for the Blind. William Cleveland entered the Union Theological Seminary (where Brace had also studied) in New York in 1854. Given the men's similar vocations and interests, it is not unlikely that Olmsted, Brace, and Barnes came in contact with the Cleveland brothers in New York in 1853 or 1854 ("Obituary," *New York Times*, May 10, 1878, p. 4; *Yale Obit. Rec.*, 2d ser., no. 8 [June 1878], p. 302; Princeton Theological Seminary, *Necrological Report, April 29, 1879* [Philadelphia, 1879], p. 53; FLO to Charles Loring Brace, Jan. 11, 1851 [*Papers of FLO*, 1: 365–72]; *FLO, A Biography*, 77–78; A. Nevins, *Grover Cleveland*, p. 25).
8. Grover Cleveland and Mary Cleveland Bryant Perkins Olmsted, Olmsted's wife, were sixth cousins ("Cleveland Genealogy," *New York Times*, July 20, 1884; *FLO, A Biography*, p. 58; "Guide to Bryant-Mason-Smith Family Papers, 1767–1861," The Massa-

chusetts Historical Society; George Larson II, "An Extended Family," www.rootsweb .com).

9. The two "pupils" at this time were Charles Eliot, son of Charles W. Eliot, and Henry Sargent Codman, nephew of Charles Sprague Sargent (*FLO, A Biography*, p. 393; see FLO to Charles H. Dalton, Aug. 26, 1884, above; FLO to Charles Eliot, Feb. 25, 1886, below).
10. A reference to the impending wedding of Brace's son, which Olmsted was unable to attend. Charles Loring Brace, Jr., married Louise Warner on Jan. 15, 1885 ("Fashionable Wedding at Sing Sing," *New York Times*, Jan. 15, 1885, p. 1; Charles Loring Brace to FLO, Jan. 20, 1885).
11. Letitia Neill Brace (1822–1916) was Brace's wife, whom he had met at her parent's home in Belfast while traveling in Ireland with the Olmsted brothers in 1850. They were married in 1854 (*DAB*; E. Brace, ed., *Charles Loring Brace*, pp. 90, 197–98).
12. A tribute to Kapp appeared in the Nov. 6, 1884 issue of the *Nation*. The anonymous author described Kapp as a man who "seemed to fully understand every man the first time he met him, and we never knew him to err in the prompt judgment he passed on individuals and on measures." The article also touched on Kapp's friendships with Olmsted and Brace. "His earliest efforts socially in the free States were in company with his friend Frederick Law Olmsted, to obtain sympathy and pecuniary aid for his countrymen in Texas. . . . In like manner he and Brace and Norton and others promoted an important emigration of German vine-growers to Missouri." In Brace's reply to Olmsted's letter he does not answer Olmsted's question about who wrote the article ("Friedrich Kapp," *Nation*, Nov. 6, 1884, pp. 393–94; Charles Loring Brace to FLO, Jan. 20, 1885).

To Mortimer L. Smith[1]

Detroit, 24th Nov. 1884.

Dear Mr Smith;

The Park Commissioners wish to have a proposition laid before them for the Superstructure of the new pier as an affair complete in itself and that for this purpose you should prepare drawings and obtain estimates. The scheme would include so much of the entire gallery structure as would reach from the outer end of the pier well on to the high bank South of the inclined plane. No change of design is necessary but a few details or added features may require study.

First; as to arrangements for landing from upper deck of boats. The boats and the gallery must both be adapted to this purpose and you had better confer with Mr Schulenberg the Manager of the Windsor Ferry about it. A mere gang-plank arrangement will not answer. A fixed platform supported below extending from the upper deck of the pier nearly as far as the edge of the wharf will probably be necessary with a moveable bridge to fall from it to the deck of the boat. But of this you must judge.

2. Provision should be made for small boat landings[2] at about the middle of the stem of the pier, i.e. the lowest point of the lower deck. These might be floats with ladders, like the side ladders of a ship, the lower part on wheels, for passage between the floats and the deck.

Doubtless other matters will occur to you. Consider nothing settled in the plan that upon reflection you do not thoroughly approve. The scheme has to be acceptable to the Council or money will be refused. The chief objection will be the cost, which therefore it is desirable to make as low as possible without sacrifice of matters essential to the spirit of the design and to abundant strength. As I have said before I do not care for any paint or for any planeing except where hands falling there would be liability to splinter wounds,—I would prefer to see saw and axe marks if satisfactory to you.[3]

The text presented here is an unsigned draft in Olmsted's hand. By this time work was underway on the parade ground at Belle Isle, in Detroit, but work had not begun on the gallery and pier structures that Olmsted felt were essential to the park's design. By 1886 the park commissioners had not reached a decision on the gallery, but did build a modified version of the pier. Over the following several years Olmsted had little contact with the park commissioners as they implemented and altered his plan as they saw fit. In 1887 the commissioners asked Olmsted to produce a major revision of his design, creating lakes rather than canals on the island. Olmsted refused, ending his relationship with the park board and any further planning by him for Belle Isle.

By 1888 the Belle Isle park commissioners had built a simplified shelter adjacent to the pier, rather than the gallery Olmsted had designed. This covered platform maintained some aspects of Olmsted's design, such as an undulating roof, but it was one story instead of two and did not serve the multiple purposes Olmsted had envisioned. In their *Sixth Annual Report* the commissioners described the structure: "Realizing the necessity for the protection of visitors from heat and storms, nearer the landing of boats than the Casino afforded, the wharf at the northwest end of the island was provided with a shelter, extending from the land end of the dock to the water's edge, with a division of fence extending the whole length, allowing visitors to land and embark without accident or confusion. A platform dock was constructed at the south side of the wharf, running nearly the entire length of the same, for the accommodation of yachting and small boat parties designing to land" (*Second Annual Report of the Board of Park Commissioners* [Detroit, 1884], p. 22; *Third Annual Report of the Board of Park Commissioners* [Detroit, 1885], pp. 4–6; FLO to Elliott T. Slocum, March 15, 1886, A1: 675–78, OAR/LC; FLO to Elliott T. Slocum, April 15, 1887, A1: 709, OAR/LC; FLO to C. A. Roberts, July 1889; *Sixth Annual Report of the Board of Park Commissioners* [Detroit, 1888], p. 5; see also FLO to John Stirling, May 12, 1884, above, and FLO to JCO, [May 30], 1884, above).

1. Mortimer L. Smith (1840–1896) was an architect with a successful practice in Detroit. Working with his son, Fred. L. Smith, he received commissions for several prominent public structures in the city in the 1880s. He also designed the D. M. Ferry building in 1870 for Dexter M. Ferry, a successful seed merchant who later was a Detroit park commissioner (*Detroit-Illustrated, The Commercial Metropolis of Michigan* [Detroit, 1891], p. 170; *Fourth Annual Report of the Park Commissioners* [Detroit, 1886], p. 9; FLO to John Stirling, July 25, 1884, A1:21–23, OAR/LC).
2. Crossed out here by Olmsted is the word "embarcaderos."

3. This request for a rough, natural look to the woodwork of the pier is similar to instructions Olmsted gave for the construction of the stairs at Mount Royal Park in Montreal in 1881:

> Bear in mind that the stairs, like everything else on the park, should not be simply means of transit, but, . . . means by which a greater enjoyment of the beauty of nature will occur because of the art which they embody. They may be of wood with rough surface except on the seats and hand-rails, with many tool-marks of the axe and adze, yet should exhibit the talent of your best architects, for nothing is harder to get than good rude work fitted to nature.

Frederick Law Olmsted, *Mount Royal. Montreal,* New York, 1881 [*Papers of FLO,* SS1: 407].)

To John Charles Olmsted

Washington:
6th Decr. 1884.

Dear Jno,

I have yours of 4th on arriving here.

I did write E. C. Gardner.[1] Neither the New London plan nor the Arboretum[2] can be long delayed & the Choate & Ford plans[3] will soon be pressing, but in some way I must manage to absorb myself and be free in using assistance in getting the design of West Rox. It is far more important than everything else. Can't you manage to throw more upon Eliot & let him throw more on Codman, so as to put yourself strictly upon what you alone can do? I see all the New Year business close upon you.

I can see that Clark is in some trepidation as to his office.[4] Two bills have already been introduced intended to consolidate it with the Treasury Architects. None can pass this session but they presage trouble next year.

If you go out at all for exercise, try to get familiar with the rocks between Thomas St. & Glen road & to the S.W. so as to be able to judge, when we come to experiment with lines, where cuttings might go clear of solid ledges.[5]

Yours affctly

F.L.O.

The text presented here is a signed letter in Olmsted's hand.

1. Eugene Clarence Gardner (1836–1915) was an architect based in Springfield, Massachusetts, and author of works on homestead design such as *Homes and How to Make Them* (1874) and *The House that Jill Built after Jack's Had Proved a Failure* (1882). In

1884 he completed the West Brookfield, Massachusetts, Railroad Station for the Boston and Albany Railroad. No letters between Olmsted and Gardner are extant but Gardner may have written Olmsted regarding the station, since at this time Olmsted and H. H. Richardson were collaborating on other stations for the Boston and Albany Railroad (Eugene Clarence Gardner Papers, Manuscripts and Archives, Yale University Library, New Haven, Conn.; Jeffrey Karl Ochsner, "Architecture for the Boston and Albany Railroad: 1881–1894," *Journal of the Society of Architectural Historians*, June 1988, pp. 114, 120).

2. A reference to the ongoing work on the Arnold Arboretum, for which the firm delivered planting plans in 1884 and 1885, and also to Memorial Park in New London, Connecticut (plans 902-16 and 902-17, NPS/FLONHS; FLO to C. A. Williams, [Oct. 1884], above; FLO to C. A. Williams, May 9, 1885, below).
3. A reference to plans and surveys made for Joseph H. Choate's estate, Naumkeag, in Stockbridge, Massachusetts, and R. T. Ford's home in Staatsburgh, New York (Joseph H. Choate to FLO, Aug. 21, 1884; plan 1016-2, NPS/FLONHS; plan 1013-2, NPS/FLONHS; *Master List*, pp. 197, 225; Robin Karson, *A Genius for Place: American Landscapes of the Country Place Era* [Amherst, Mass., 2007], p. 327).
4. In 1884, following the Democratic victory in the presidential election, Architect of the Capitol Edward Clark, a valued ally of Olmsted's, was forced to defend his position. Three bills were introduced in Congress that December with the intended purpose of reorganizing the architect's position and replacing Clark. Representative Strother M. Stockslager (D) of Indiana, Chairman of the Committee on Public Buildings and Grounds, sponsored a bill (H.R. 7523) to create a position of Supervising Architect with a four-year appointment made by the President. The Supervising Architect would answer to the Secretary of the Treasury and "have charge of the construction, repair, and furnishing of all public buildings." Clark's job, as Architect of the Capitol, would fall within that of other architects working on commissions for the Supervising Architect, and he therefore would have lost administrative control of the Capitol grounds project. The bill failed to pass and Clark retained his position as Architect of the Capitol until he retired in 1898 (*Journal of the House of Representatives of the United States, Second Session of the 48th Congress* [Washington, D.C., 1884], pp. 38, 40; *Reports of Committees of the House of Representatives, Second Session of the 48th Congress* [Washington, D.C., 1885], pp. 23–26; Henry M. Congdon, "Proposed Law for the Erection of Public Buildings," *American Architect and Building News*, Oct. 24, 1885, p. 199; William C. Allen, *History of the United States Capitol, A Chronicle of Design, Construction, and Politics* [Washington, D.C., 2001], p. 369).
5. A reference to the ongoing work on Franklin Park, in Boston, where John C. Olmsted was apparently walking the site in order to finalize locations for roads and paths. Glen Road was an existing road through the park site, the general location of which was maintained and helped to create a natural division between the "Ante-Park" and the park's central, pastoral landscapes. Glen Road entered the site from the northwest, through an area of extensive ledges, or rock outcrops (see Frederick Law Olmsted, *Tenth Annual Report, Boston Park Commissioners, Reports on West Roxbury Park and Wood Island Park*, [Dec. 1884], below).

TENTH ANNUAL REPORT, BOSTON PARK COMMISSIONERS, REPORT ON BACK BAY.

[December 1884]

To the Park Commissioners:—

GENTLEMEN,—The principal work on the Back Bay continues to be that under the management of the City Engineer,[1] which advances steadily in pursuance of the plan originally adopted, with good results, economically acquired, but mostly under ground or under water and little open to public observation.

In the outlet section,[2] only, a near approach to finished condition has been attained, and, as this comes in view from much-used thoroughfares, increased attention is drawn to the work, and it may be desirable in your Annual Report to meet inquiries that the present appearance of it naturally suggests to those unfamiliar with the circumstances.

It should be understood by all to whom it may have recently come to be of interest that there had originally been a scheme for a public pleasure-ground in the locality, but that, upon representations of the City Engineer and the Superintendent of Sewers,[3] this was, after long deliberations, set aside, because of the necessity of occupying the space with basins in which salt and brackish waters could be temporarily stored, and with other arrangements for regulating the drainage and sewerage of the city.[4] The plan of the works now in progress is determined in its main features and controlled in its leading details by this necessity. It was anticipated that the elements of sanitary security would be so costly that at best it would be impossible to obtain appropriations for carrying on the work with the steadiness and rapidity demanded by the large interests at stake; and it was feared that any considerable modifications of them or additions to them possible to be made, with the object of obtaining results of architectural or gardening stateliness, would perilously overload the scheme.

When, in the midst of a city, much work is seen to have been done in the materials commonly employed in landscape gardening, as earth, soil, manure, trees, plants, rocks and water, it is difficult to suppose that the entire operation is not designed and directed for the gratification of taste. In this case the fact is quite otherwise. It is not from considerations chiefly of taste, for example, that the banks of the basin have been made in considerable part of somewhat monotonous steepness; that the central feature of the entire arrangement has been made with a soil of salt mud instead of a soil adapted to a turfy lawn; that a possibility has been accepted that the water in the basin could not at all times be kept of an agreeable approach to purity or its margin be kept perfectly nice.

There is a question whether, accepting difficulties such as are thus suggested, it will be possible to avoid an offensive incongruity of character between the basins and the structures presumably to be built in the neighborhood in extension of the Back Bay residence quarter of the city, and to be separated from the basins by a broad road and steep banks. The hope is that by means of formal lines of trees on the roadsides and an informal disposition of trees, copses, and thickets on the slopes falling away toward the basins from these lines, the two things will be so far separated by an intermediate element, agreeable in itself, and markedly inharmonious with neither, that the incongruity will be little felt.

However that may be, what is certain is this: that if a pleasing interest of character is to be obtained in views over the basins, it will be far from the interest of a park or a garden. It will necessarily be an interest dependent on conditions of unmitigated rusticity, not at all of the affectation of rusticity, sometimes playfully introduced in close association with polished and elegant conditions. It must depend on elements of scenery and largely on forms of vegetation that may be associated—as they often are by nature with most agreeable effect—with the margins of salt creeks and harsh, weather-beaten headlands. I have an increasing confidence that pleasing results may, in time, be thus obtained, and, probably, before the city will be built about the property; but if so, they will be wholly unconventional, and, it is to be hoped, will not plainly manifest their artificial origin.

In that part of the work now more nearly completed, being the outlet part, north of Boylston Bridge, there are special local features, some reasons for which may be stated.

The circumstances allow a contrast of character to be sought between the banks of this short narrow passage and the miles of banks to be found about the broad basins on the south side of the bridge and the parkway beyond them; and, to make the most of the opportunity, it is desirable here to aim at a degree of variety of form and slope that would otherwise be excessive.

The outflow channel is required by the plans of the Street Department to be carried between two straight lines of bridge abutments at five different points within a distance of less than 600 yards. The intermediate reaches of the channel are too short for expanded pools or a quiet character in the shores and what would otherwise be an excessively wriggling disposition of the banks has the advantage of avoiding a sewer or canal-like directness of channel. Much would have been gained if all the bridges had been of masonry; but the conditions would have made them excessively costly.

It is necessary to use a certain amount of stone at points in the facing of the banks to guard against drifting ice. This gives reason for a buttress-like

Bird's-Eye View of Back Bay Fens, n.d.

abruptness of bank at these points. Such abruptness being accepted, it is better to make a decided feature of it, and let it control the character of the scenery of the outlet in contrast with that of the basins above where there can be no headlands. Large field-stones, have, therefore, been procured from the waste of the city's gravel banks and piled together to obtain boldness of projection. At present the stones, somewhat unhappy in color, are offensively conspicuous, and the several points have too much repetition of character. They will not only, in time, lose their present rawness of color, but will all, in a great measure, soon disappear under leafage, while, through the difference in the forms of vegetation growing out from between the stones and upon their flanks, their similarity of aspect will be lost.[5]

The ground has been planted with a density which would be excessive were the conditions not extraordinarily bleak. It has been planted also with an excessive variety, and in parts not harmoniously, with the expectation of thinning out a part of the plants when they shall have served their purpose of nurses, and in the meantime of determining experimentally whether certain of them can be depended upon to grow satisfactorily under the extreme exposure of the situation.

Lombardy poplars have been planted on the side of the road by which Boylston Bridge is to be approached from Commonwealth Avenue. The situation is an exceedingly trying one, and, until buildings shall break the force of the wind from the north-west, hardly any trees can be expected to grow in it without acquiring stunted and distorted habits. It is hoped that the poplar, if frequently cut in, will by its vigorous, compact growth, for a time, serve a good purpose.

This row of poplars terminates on the north at a point where, if continued, it would interrupt the prospect from Boylston Bridge over Charles River. The entire scheme of planting is determined with regard to this view; to the reverse view from Commonwealth Avenue through the arch of Boylston Bridge, and to the subordination, as far as practicable, of the railroad and other rigid and uncongenial features of topography.

Respectfully,

FRED'K LAW OLMSTED,
Landscape Architect Advisory.

The text presented was published as part of the *Tenth Annual Report of the Board of Commissioners of the Department of Parks of the City of Boston for the Year 1884* (Boston, 1885).

1. The city engineer of Boston at this time was Henry M. Wightman, who succeeded Joseph P. Davis in 1880. The assistant city engineer in charge of much of the Boston park work between 1883 and 1898 was Edward Willard Howe (Cynthia Zaitzevsky, *Frederick Law Olmsted and The Boston Park System* [Cambridge, Mass., 1982], pp. 152–

53; "Henry M. Wightman Dead," *Boston Globe*, April 4, 1885, p. 4; "Edward Willard Howe," *Journal of the Boston Society of Civil Engineers*, June 1932, pp. 362–64).

2. That is, the Beacon Street entrance (Charlesgate) area, which had been planted earlier that year.
3. The Superintendent of Sewers between 1863 and 1883 was William Hammatt Bradley (b. 1835). The planning for the Back Bay Fens that Olmsted refers to would have been under his direction (*Papers of FLO*, 7: 483, n. 3; Charles Edwin Hurd, ed., *Representative Citizens of the Commonwealth of Massachusetts* [Boston, 1902], pp. 194, 196).
4. In 1876 a plan for a park in the Back Bay area suggested a long, narrow corridor, with a carriage drive along its length, winding between lagoons. In 1878, the Boston Park Commission held a design competition for the new park, but the results were discarded, ostensibly because none of the schemes adequately addressed the need for controlling the floodwaters of the Muddy River and Stony Brook. Olmsted was then hired and worked with the city engineers to create a design for a public landscape that would help control flooding, by storing flood waters and releasing them into the Charles River (FLO to the Board of Commissioners of the Department of Parks of the City of Boston, Jan. 26, 1880 [*Papers of FLO*, 7: 451–63]; *Papers of FLO*, 7: 365, n. 1; Frederick Law Olmsted, *Paper on the {Back Bay} Problem and its Solution Read Before the Boston Society of Architects*, Apr. 2, 1886, [*Papers of FLO*, SS1: 437–59]; see also Frederick Law Olmsted, "Report of the Landscape Architect," Dec. 24, 1883, above).
5. The boulder revetments Olmsted describes replaced the vertical walls first suggested by the city engineers for the waterways of the Beacon Street entrance area (FLO to the Board of Commissioners of the Department of Parks of the City of Boston, Jan. 26, 1880 [*Papers of FLO*, 7: 455]).

TENTH ANNUAL REPORT, BOSTON PARK COMMISSIONERS, REPORTS ON WEST ROXBURY PARK AND WOOD ISLAND PARK

December 22d, 1884

Report On West Roxbury Park.

To the Park Commissioners:—

GENTLEMEN,—I respectfully submit the following propositions in respect to the plan of West Roxbury Park.

1. The prime object will be to present favorably to public enjoyment a body of rural and sylvan scenery, large in scale, simple and tranquil in character; and, in contrast and as a foil to this, passages of a wild, rugged, picturesque and forest-like aspect.

2. It is desirable that the larger part of the park should be of such character that it can easily be kept in good order and sustain its design without

great expense, and that for this purpose it should have less of a garden-like and more of a distinctively park and forest-like character than is now generally attempted in American parks.

3. *If, apart from the main provisions above suggested, and without seriously interfering with them or excessively restricting their extent*, the following proposed arrangements can be included in the general design, it is desirable that they should be:—

A. A place of general congregation where carriages, horsemen, and foot visitors may be brought together without clashing and under conditions favorable to the enjoyment of a gay throng.

B. A ground suitable for public festivities, especially for parades of children such as are made on the Brooklyn Park; also for displays of fireworks, balloons, and other exhibitions. This would relieve the management of the park of a responsibility elsewhere found very embarrassing.

C. Provisions by which families will be encouraged to make basket-meals and picnics on the park, and by which, especially, mothers with young children, unable to go out of town during the summer, may be invited to make lengthened visits to it.

Lastly, if suitable ground can be found that may be reserved without crippling the park for its main object, it is desirable that the plan should admit of the city's holding in readiness a sufficient area to be leased to a proper organization for establishing, by private means, a public Zoölogical and Exotic Garden,[1] as has been done in connection with the public parks of the cities of London, Paris, Dublin, Antwerp, Amsterdam, Cologne, Philadelphia and others, and as has been repeatedly attempted in New York unsuccessfully because the primary plan of the park did not admit of it.[2]

Respectfully,

FRED'K LAW OLMSTED,
Landscape Architect.

Report On Wood Island Park.

To the Park Commissioners:—

GENTLEMEN,—I have the honor to submit to your consideration a plan for laying out the city property known as Wood Island Park, within which will be the continuation and terminus, toward the harbor, of Neptune Road, now under construction, which is designed to be the pleasure drive of East Boston. The site is a promontory, the stem of which is crossed, in a cutting, by the Revere

Beach Railroad, over which the Neptune Road must pass by an archway. On the north-east side is a bay, becoming a broad mud-flat as the tide falls. On the south-west there is marshy ground, with high land beyond. On both sides the bordering land is private property, and is liable to be embanked and built over. On the south-east only can a permanent outlook be depended upon. In this direction there is a fine view down the harbor. The attraction of the locality is found in this view, and in the sea-breezes by which it is swept in summer. The ground is now treeless, and, because of its severe exposure and dryness, only the hardiest class of trees are likely to be long-lived and flourishing in it. For this reason, and also because low masses of foliage would obscure the outlook and obstruct the sea-breezes, ordinary pleasure-ground treatment of this site is unadvisable. The principal planting should be of the different sorts of oak, hickory, maple, birch, elm, lime, and ash, that have been found most enduring in Eastern Massachusetts, and in standard rather than lawn-like form.

As proposed by the drawing herewith submitted, Neptune Road is to be divided on entering the grounds, forming a sweep, from all parts of which the harbor-view and the sea-breeze may be enjoyed. For this purpose the base of the drive must be in part an artificial shelf or terrace of earth for which material is to be obtained by spreading out the central ridge of the promontory. Upon the level to result from this reduction a field of turf is to be formed fitting to games of base-ball, cricket, lacrosse, tennis, and other sports. On its boundary a track is to be laid suitable to walking, running, and bicycle exercises, and between this and the roadway is to be a promenade for spectators. The play-ground is six hundred by three hundred feet, or about four and a half acres, in extent. The running track is a third of a mile in length; the driving course half a mile.

At the north end of the play-ground a structure is placed, the basement of which will contain lavatories, closets, and arrangements for the convenience of players; the upper part, entered from the level of the walk, a shelter for visitors in sudden showers, and a gallery for viewing the games; elsewhere, retired from general view, a police station, superintendency, and work yard, and on the shore at the south point, a boat-landing, with a shelter and arrangements for letting boats and fishing-gear and the safe keeping of boat-equipments.

A key-plan is presented on the same sheet, showing the manner in which the park is connected by Neptune Road with the existing street system of East Boston, and on the main plan a possible extension of the street system upon the ground adjoining the park is forecast. The need for a street railroad, to give access to the park is assumed, and a route laid down by which it will cross a corner of the ground and take up visitors at a siding, from a proper shelter within it. A park station for the Revere Beach Railroad is also shown, with a suitable station-house, and route therefrom to the play-ground.

The drive and adjoining walk of the park are to be considered as a necessary continuation of the Neptune Road as already laid out and begun. The small buildings proposed will be found indispensable to any consider-

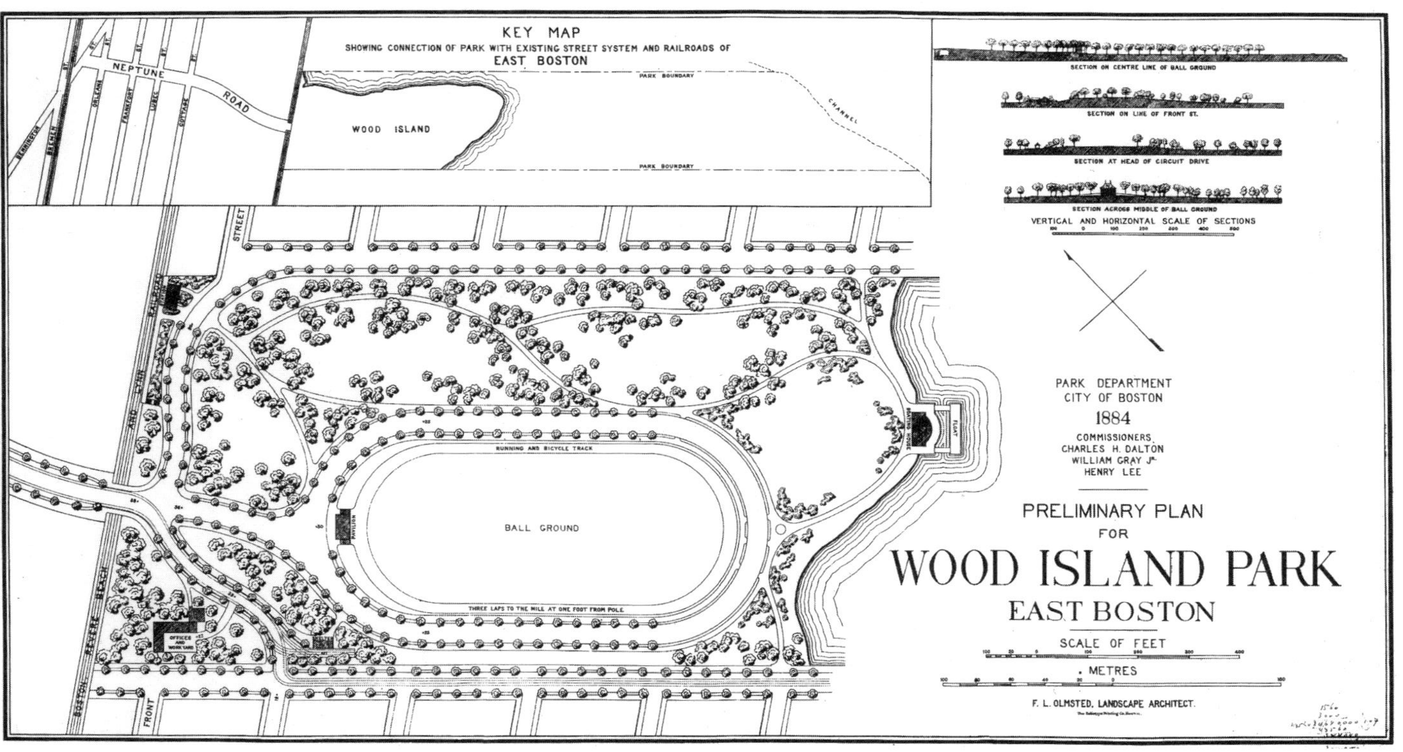

"Preliminary Plan for Wood Island Park, East Boston," 1884

able public use of the property. In other respects, though intended to provide every condition of a public ground desirable in the peculiar circumstances of this locality, making its distinctive advantages available, and controlling its disadvantages; the plan will, it is thought, be as little costly to carry out as any that could be devised.

Respectfully,

FRED'K LAW OLMSTED,
Landscape Architect.

The text presented here is part of Olmsted's contribution to the *Tenth Annual Report of the Board of Commissioners of the Department of Parks of the City of Boston for the Year 1884* (Boston, 1885). West Roxbury Park, proposed in the 1876 Boston park plan and renamed Franklin Park in 1885, was the large, pastoral park of the Boston system. In 1884, Olmsted wrote John C. Olmsted that its design was "far more important than anything else," and urged him to give it his attention. Wood Island Park was one of the smaller parks of the Boston system, intended to serve specific neighborhoods. Olmsted prepared a plan and report for the park in 1884, and when it was enlarged in 1891 Olmsted and John C. Olmsted provided a new design. Neptune Road, also designed by Olmsted, was the principal means of access to Wood Island Park. Both road and park were covered over by an expansion of Logan Airport in the 1960s (FLO to JCO, Dec. 6, 1884, above; *Papers of FLO*, SS1: 534, n. 70; C. Zaitzevsky, *The Boston Park System*, pp. 99–101; see also FLO to Alpheus Hyatt, March 24, 1889, below; FLO to Alpheus Hyatt, May 6, 1889, below; FLO to Matthias D. Ross, [Dec.] 1889, below).

1. The 1885 plan for Franklin Park included two areas labeled Deer Park, both between the Greeting (the formal promenade that extended from the Blue Hills Avenue park entrance) and the park's eastern edge. The adjacent Long Crouch Woods area, in the north corner of the park, was to be leased to a private organization to operate a zoological garden. The Greeting, the Deer Parks, and the proposed zoo were never realized as planned. Construction began in 1911 on the Franklin Park Zoo instead, which occupied the still unfinished eastern portions of Franklin Park (Frederick Law Olmsted, "Notes on the Plan of Franklin Park and Related Matters," 1886 [*Papers of FLO*, SS1: 488]; "Plans for Boston Zoo and Aquarium," *Boston Daily Globe*, Dec. 14, 1910, p. 9; also see FLO to Alpheus Hyatt, March 24, 1889, below, and FLO to Matthias D. Ross, [Dec.] 1889, below).
2. The Central Park Menagerie (later the Central Park Zoo) was not a feature of Olmsted and Vaux's 1858 plan for the park. As gifts of animals were made to the new park they began to be displayed in and around the pre-existing New York State Arsenal building, which was also used as a museum and an administration building during the park's early years. Numerous proposals for a permanent menagerie in the park were debated for decades, while the existing menagerie, in the meantime, became a permanent feature in its original location adjacent to the Arsenal (see FLO to Calvert Vaux, July 9, 1887, n. 4, below).

To "Madam"

Brookline, Mass.
16th Jan. 1885.

My Dear Madam,

I have received your note of yesterday asking me to aid you in securing a general removal of fences in Newton. I regret to say that the movement to dispense with fences in which many most intelligent and excellent people have for many years been engaged has never seemed to me a sound one. You will excuse me if I briefly suggest why, not at all with a view to your conversion to my way of thinking but as an apology for declining your invitation.

The value of a residence in a village or rural neighborhood over that in a compact town, should, it seems to me, lie largely in the advantage of adding something of out door life — the healthfulness, the comfort and the beauty to be had if suitable arrangements are made out of doors but in close connection with the interior of a dwelling — to a home. But it is essential to the idea of a home that the place so called should be exclusive, should have a certain retirement and separation from that which is public and everybody's. To express this idea — the idea that here is a home and here a street or a village of a strongly home like character — lines of demarkation between homes of separate families, and between all homes and the world at large out of doors, seem to me essential. The old custom of our civilization is to make such lines in the form of fences and I can't think it is an advance of civilization that prompts their removal.

As a rule our village & especially our suburban fences are so fashioned as to be very bad expressions of the idea and I would like to see them simpler, stronger, firmer; less ostentatious when built and less liable to become shiftless and shabby but as in so many other things I am inclined to think it would be better to urge patient and temperate improvement rather than radical revolution.

The text presented here is an unsigned letter in Olmsted's hand. The correspondent is unknown, and her letter prompting this response has not been found. For more of Olmsted's views on the subject dealt with in this letter, see Frederick Law Olmsted, "What is a 'Useless Fence,'" *American Garden*, Aug. 26, 1889, below.

To William McMillan[1]

Private. Please return.

Brookline, Mass.
16th March, 1885.

Dear Mr McMillan;

There has been a sudden upset of our park Commission. The leading new man is Patrick Maguire, editor of a small Irish paper, I am told & President of the Boston Association most nearly corresponding with Tammany in New York.[2] From all that is reported I shall probably be dropped at the end of my present official year if not sooner compelled to resign. Meantime I have to prepare my plan for the principal park of the city for which land has just been bought and with it to make a report.[3] The ground of change is, of course, economy and distrust. Boston is yet deeply in debt because of the great fire and taxes are so heavy as to drive many capitalists away. The conditions are tied with the class of men who chiefly rule in politics to a time-serving, penny wise, pound foolish policy. The general impression among intelligent citizens is that other cities have been led into the most reckless extravagance & to add enormously to their burdens of taxation by their park enterprises.[4] I mean as soon as practicable to record my protest against the course most likely to be pursued on the parks and to urge sound views. The most important and effective statement that can be made in this respect would be one of the history of the Buffalo Park. I propose to prepare a brief statement for this purpose, and I wish to consult you upon it. I will give you my idea of the statement and ask you to return what I write with corrections and comments. I am not perfectly sure of my ground but Mr Bowen[5] shortly before his death said: "We have very nearly completed all the work you first cut out for us at the meeting at Mr Jewett's[6] house and it is not going to cost us more than you said it would". Dorsheimer[7] told me last fall, that while it seemed to him that the plantations were going very slowly—more so than in the parks and not half as fast as those in Washington, and he thought much more should have been done for the improvement of the soil &c. he found that a great change in public feeling had occurred in relation to the park, the people were proud of it and it was generally thought a great success. I thought if you did not find occasion to materially alter the statement I will append, I would write it out more carefully & send it first to Dorsheimer; then ask you to obtain a few signatures to it of citizens holding positions of weight. My intention is to include the statement in a report to the Boston Park Commissioners, in connection with my plan.

Statement.

The principal park of Buffalo[8] was undertaken with a view to certain distinct ends. The site was selected as that best fitted to these ends of any within five miles of the center of the city. A plan was devised for improving {*it*} with reference to them, and this plan has been steadily pursued for fifteen years. There has been no change of the original purposes either by addition or deduction, though many have been proposed and urged. All details of the work have been worked out consistently with the plan as at first adopted. At the outset an executive staff was formed, drawn from the principal park of another city and familiar with its duties. It has since been changed only by promotions, or by deductions as the work has advanced to points where deductions could be afforded. The present Superintendent[9] has been employed without interruptions from the start. The work has been at times misrepresented and earnest efforts, largely inspired by misunderstandings have been made to break up the organization, without success. In the {*city*} reform movement led by Mayor Grover Cleveland[10] no reform in the park work was found necessary. No change of men or method was made. The result originally intended has been accomplished as far as time would permit and the park is meeting the public purposes had in view by its earliest promoters to their complete satisfaction. The opposition to it has gradually died out as its value has been developed and it is much used and very popular with all classes of the people; with none more than the small and frugal, house-owning tax-payers who constitute an unusual proportion of the population of Buffalo. The cost of the work has not exceeded expectations and is regarded as moderate relatively to the value of the results secured.

The above statement is certified to be true by the undersigned citizens of Buffalo.

Note. The signers represent both political parties; two? have been Mayors of the city — members of the City Councils; — members at different periods of the park Commission; — members of the state legislature; — Judges of — ; — members of Congress; &c.

F.L.O.

I should like to know, if you have the figures handy, what the park, exclusively, had cost up to the end of the last fiscal year — first, for land, second, for construction proper.[11]

I hope that you & your family are well and that you are not to fail of visiting us this summer.

Yours faithfully

Fred[k] Law Olmsted

The text presented here is a signed letter in Olmsted's hand. Olmsted included an expanded version of this testimonial in his 1886 Franklin Park report (Frederick Law Olmsted, "Notes on the Plan of Franklin Park and Related Matters," 1886 [*Papers of FLO*, SS1: 503–9]; see also FLO to Sherman S. Jewett, April 11, 1887, below; FLO to William McMillan, Jan. 2, 1888, below).

1. William McMillan (1831–1899), a Scottish immigrant, was general superintendent of Buffalo's parks from 1873 to 1897. McMillan operated Douglas Farm on Long Island in the late 1860s, providing plants to Olmsted for the Riverside residential development in Chicago and for Prospect Park in Brooklyn. He also worked as a gardener in Prospect Park for a brief period, and Olmsted held him in high regard. Olmsted recommended that the Buffalo park commissioners hire McMillan, and they appointed him superintendent of planting in 1870. In 1873, after engineer George Kent Radford retired, the commissioners appointed him general superintendent of parks. Olmsted continued to be impressed with McMillan's work, writing in 1888 that he had "unusual zeal, industry, and competency for his duty." The Buffalo park board fired McMillan in 1897, and for the final year of his life he served as superintendent of Essex County parks in New Jersey, another park system designed in part by the Olmsted firm (Stanton M. Broderick, "William McMillan" [unpublished paper]; The Western New York Horticultural Society, "William McMillan," *Proceedings of the Forty-Fifth Annual Meeting* [Rochester, 1900], p. 75; J. N. Larned, *A History of Buffalo* [New York, 1911], p. 178; William McMillan to Oliver C. Bullard, Sept. 15, 1869; William McMillan to FLO, Nov. 10, 1869; William McMillan to FLO, April 20, 1870; Oliver C. Bullard to FLO, April 21, 1870; *First Annual Report of the Buffalo Park Commissioners* [Buffalo, 1871]; *Fourth Annual Report of the Buffalo Park Commissioners* [Buffalo, 1874]; Frederick Law Olmsted, "Plan for a Public Park on the Flats South of Buffalo," Oct. 1, 1888 [*Papers of FLO*, SS1: 591]; "Wully Fired," *Buffalo Courier-Record*, Dec. 8, 1897, p. 6; *Meehan's Monthly, A Magazine of Horticulture, Botany and Kindred Subjects*, vol. IX [Germantown, Pa., 1899], p. 141; "William McMillan," *Buffalo Commercial*, Aug. 3, 1899, p. 6).
2. Patrick Maguire (1838–1896), a powerful Irish Democrat, was in the real estate business before he founded and became the editor of the *Republic* in 1882. In 1885 Hugh O'Brien, Boston's first Irish-Catholic mayor, appointed Maguire and two other Democrats to serve as park commissioners. Olmsted feared the new board would not be committed to implementing his Boston park plans, especially after the board rescinded his contract. The board reinstated Olmsted soon after, however, and over the following years worked productively with him ("Patrick Maguire Dead," *Boston Daily Globe*, Nov. 29, 1865, p. 85; C. Zaitzevsky, *The Boston Park System*, p. 67; FLO to Charles Eliot Norton, May 2, 1885; Charles Eliot Norton to FLO, March 5, 1885, Charles Eliot Norton Miscellaneous Papers, bMS AM 1088.2, box 5, Houghton Library, Harvard University; see also Frederick Law Olmsted, "On Points of View and Methods of Criti-

cism of Public Works of Landscape Architecture," *American Architect and Building News*, June 20 and 29, 1885, below; Frederick Law Olmsted, "Remarks about a Difficulty Peculiar to the Park Department of City Governments," Jan. 26, 1889, below).

3. That is, the West Roxbury Park, or Franklin Park. Olmsted developed the plans for Franklin Park in 1884 and 1885, and the published plan was publicly unveiled in January of 1886 (C. Zaitzevsky, *The Boston Park System*, pp. 68–69).
4. The Boston park commissioners had not yet fully determined how they were going to pay for Franklin Park. While funds from Benjamin Franklin's bequest to the city were anticipated (prompting the park's new name) and the city had begun land acquisition, the park board's actions were limited by the city's debt limit. Boston incurred large debts following the Great Fire of 1872 that burned over sixty-five acres of the business district. The city debt continued to increase during the depression that followed the financial panic of 1873. At Mayor O'Brien's request, however, in 1886 the state legislature passed a bill allowing Boston to increase its debt limit by $2.5 million. Funds made available under the legislation were used to pay for Franklin Park (C. Zaitzevsky, *The Boston Park System*, pp. 66–68; Charles Phillips Huse, *The Financial History of Boston from May 1, 1822 to January 31, 1909* [London, 1916], pp. 118–19, 169–70).
5. Dennis C. Bowen (1820–1877), a prominent Buffalo lawyer, was one of the organizers of the city's park movement. In 1869 he served on the first park commission as chairman of the committee on grounds, a position he held until his death (H. Perry Smith, ed., *A History of the City of Buffalo and Erie County*, vol. 2 [Syracuse, N.Y., 1884], pp. 480–81).
6. Sherman S. Jewett (1818–1897) was another organizer of the Buffalo park movement. He hosted a meeting of a group of prominent citizens at his house on August 25, 1868, at which Olmsted shared his ideas about the creation of new parks for the city. That summer, the same group of concerned citizens hired Olmsted and Vaux to prepare a report that their committee could use to make the case for establishing new municipal parks ("Letter from the Citizens' Committee," *Preliminary Report Respecting a Public Park in Buffalo and a Copy of the Act of Legislature Authorizing its Establishment* [Buffalo, 1869]; FLO to MPO, Aug. 25, 1868 [*Papers of FLO*, 6: 268–69]; see also FLO to Sherman S. Jewett, April 11, 1887, below).
7. William Edward Dorsheimer (1832–1888), lawyer and politician from Buffalo, was a friend and supporter throughout most of Olmsted's career. Dorsheimer had invited Olmsted to consult on the creation of Buffalo's municipal parks in 1868 and later helped to secure a number of important commissions for him (see FLO to William E. Dorsheimer, July 21, 1886, below).
8. That is, "The Park," as titled by Olmsted and Vaux in their original plans, and renamed Delaware Park in 1896. It was the largest of the initial three parks of the Buffalo system (*Twenty Seventh Annual Report of the Buffalo Park Commissioners* [Buffalo, 1897], p. 12).
9. That is, William McMillan (see, n. 1 above).
10. President Grover Cleveland (1837–1908) served as mayor of Buffalo for one year, 1882, before moving on to the governorship of New York. He was known as an honest Democrat who would not bend to political bosses or participate in the spoils system. His short mayoral term brought him national recognition for his reform efforts (A. Nevins, *A Study in Courage*, pp. 79–91).
11. According to Olmsted's final version of this statement, which appeared in "Notes on the Plan of Franklin Park and Related Matters," the Buffalo Park cost $1,400 per acre to construct. In 1885 the park consisted of about 350 acres (Frederick Law Olmsted, "Notes on the Plan of Franklin Park and Related Matters," 1886 [*Papers of FLO*, SS1: 503–9]; *Fifteenth Annual Report of the Buffalo Parks Commissioners* [Buffalo, 1885], p. 42).

To Stanford White[1]

Brookline Mass.
9th April, 1885.

My Dear Mr White;

I am much grieved to hear this morning of the death of your father.[2] Nearly forty years ago we were members together of a dining club and some years later some slight business relations ripened my personal regard for him. Though I have met him but rarely for a long time past I have always felt to him as to a friend and that he maintained a similar regard for me has been evident from repeated kindly references to me in his writings and otherwise.[3] You will perhaps remember that he took counsel with me as to your choice of a profession and the course of education you should adopt and that I introduced him to Mr Richardson.[4] I have enjoyed the satisfaction he must have had in the fulfillment of his faith in you and your remarkably successful career in the path that was then opening.

I assure you of my sympathy and am
Very Truly Yours

Fredk Law Olmsted.

The text presented here is a signed letter in Olmsted's hand. The original is in the Stanford White Papers, The New York Historical Society, New York City.

1. Stanford White (1853–1906) was one of the most important American architects of the nineteenth century. After serving as an apprentice in H. H. Richardson's firm, and studying art and architecture in Paris for almost two years, White joined Charles Follen McKim and William Rutherford Mead to form McKim, Mead, and White in 1879. The partnership went on to be one of the most prolific and successful architectural practices in the country. Olmsted and White worked together on Whitelaw Reid's Ophir Hall estate at Purchase, New York, in 1890, among other commissions that Olmsted collaborated on with the entire firm ("White, Stanford (1853–1906)," *Encyclopedia of World Biography* [Detroit, 1998]; Paul R. Baker, *Stanny: The Gilded Life of Stanford White* [New York, 1989], pp. 18, 40, 61, 99, 294).
2. Richard Grant White (1821–1885) was a literature, art, and drama critic who contributed to several journals, including *Putnam's Monthly Magazine, Morning Courier & New-York Enquirer*, and the *New York World*. White was the music and art critic at *Putnam's* when Olmsted became managing editor in 1855, and although Olmsted had White replaced at the magazine, they remained friends over the years, sometimes meeting at Fischer's (or the French ordinary) dining club on Barclay Street, where Olmsted often ate with George W. Curtis, Charles A. Dana, and other literary colleagues (*DAB*; FLO to John Olmsted, March 13, [1855] [*Papers of FLO*, 2: 347–49]; FLO to John Olmsted, April 27, 1855; *Papers of FLO*, 2: 53–54).
3. White wrote at least two editorials defending Olmsted and Vaux's Greensward plan, one being an unsigned editorial in the April 19 issue of *Courier & Enquirer* and another on

May 31, 1858. In 1866, White argued against Richard Morris Hunt's proposed monumental gateways for several entrances to the park, which Olmsted and Vaux opposed (FLO to Richard Grant White, April 16, [1858] [*Papers of FLO*, 3: 190–91]; FLO to Richard Grant White, June 3, 1858 [*Papers of FLO*, 3: 197–99]; *Morning Courier & New York Enquirer*, April 19, 1858, p. 2; ibid., May 31, 1858, p. 2; FLO to Richard Grant White, July 23, 1866 [*Papers of FLO*, 6: 101–4]; Richard G. White, "Gateways of the Central Park," *Galaxy* 1, Aug. 1866, pp. 650–56).

4. When Stanford was sixteen, Olmsted introduced his father to H. H. Richardson, and in 1870 Richardson hired Stanford to apprentice at his firm. White worked with Richardson on many projects, including the New York State Capitol, a project in which Olmsted was also deeply involved (P. R. Baker, *The Gilded Life of Stanford White*, pp. 18, 40, 61, 99, 294; H. H. Richardson to FLO, May 21, 1876).

To Charles Augustus Williams

Brookline, Mass.
9th May, 1885.

Dear Mr. Williams;

I have received your favor of 7th inst.

I do not think it practicable to make a very pleasing public ground of the site you have to deal with except in the introduction of some striking feature and by the adoption of some expedient by which the present conditions of the quarry region will be radically changed.[1]

The "natural conditions of the ground" have long ago been destroyed. When you have removed the grave yard element of interest, the existing conditions, except in the outlook toward the Sound, will be {*dreary*}. The outlook toward the Sound is not to be improved by {*producing*} superficially any suggestion of the natural or existing conditions (It would be very greatly improved by the purely artificial arrangements that have been suggested.) I can think of nothing better & nothing less costly to be done with the Quarry district than to handle it as I have proposed, making a defile by excavating a {*considerable*} amount of rock; building the terrace so as to increase the effect of depth and abruptness or declivity in this defile; establishing pockets & {*making*} deposits of soil from which to grow vines & rock plants by which to tie the rock in place to the rock {*artificially*} set up, and soften the asperity, {*hardness*} & coldness of the material, and by opening a convenient circuit of {*communication*} through the defile by which this otherwise intractable part of the property would be utilized and seem by contrast to give {*value*} to the other part in which there is a possibility of obtaining gracefulness of surface and more tranquility of character.

Now to proceed at all in this direction with any approach to economy

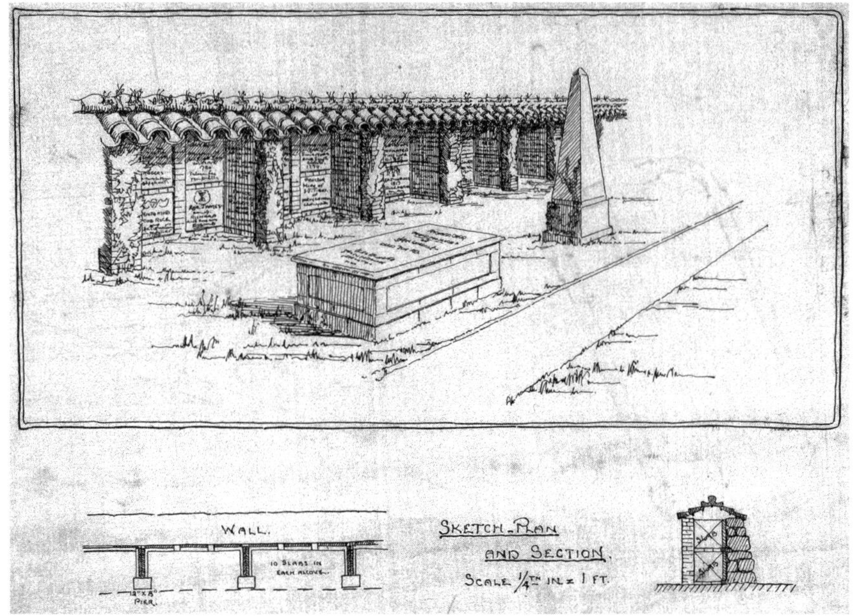

RENDERING OF PROPOSED CAMPO SANTO STRUCTURE AT NEW LONDON, CONN., MEMORIAL PARK, "SKETCH-PLAN AND SECTION," N.D.; DETAILS STORAGE SPACE FOR TOMBSTONES

you must begin by doing all the necessary quarrying that is to be done; you must thus have opened convenient passages and made everything ready so that when you begin grading in the earthy part of the property you can {*shovel*} soil for the pockets and slopes to be formed within the quarry region, easily, at one movement. I have been unable thus far with much pondering to devise any other plan the result of pursuing which would seem likely to be worth what it would cost. The mere slicking up and {*decoration*} of the existing conditions would give you a ground of no decided character and of no public consequence. It would be common place and incongruous.

Adopting the general motive of design I have above, as often before, sought to suggest, to try to carry it out in any other order of operations than we have thus far had in view would be wasteful and extravagant.

If you decide not to build the library, the same order should be followed, the quarried stone being disposed of elsewhere. If you are to build the library, you can build the terrace of stone, most of which would be of little value for the library & very cheaply. But in any case I would think the terrace a necessity. The place is the only place of interest on the ground (because of the outlook).[2] You must have a platform of some sort there to accommodate the numbers that will resort to it. Because of the undulating but wholly prosaic and dreary form of rock on the ridge this platform must be of an artificial character — must be *built*. Because of

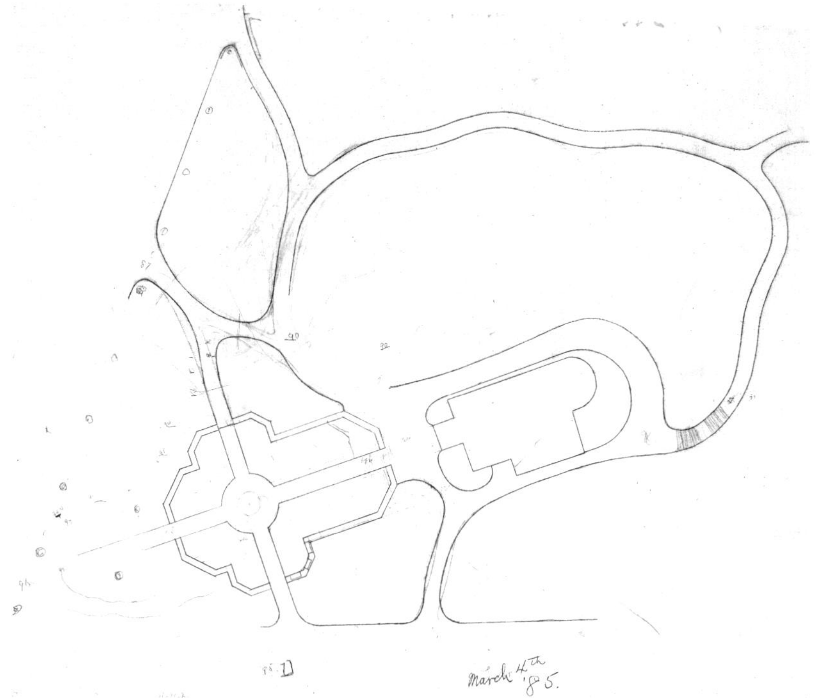

"STUDY OF MEMORIAL PARK, NEW LONDON," MARCH 4, 1885

the rock this, otherwise the most interesting spot in your ground, cannot be made very agreeable by suitable planting.

I am afraid I have not made the grounds of my convictions quite clear, but if I have put you on the track of them, you will, I am confident, with a little reflection, such as you would make if you were {*studying*} out a plan & scheme of operations for yourself, come to my conclusion. This is that, putting the grave stone matter wholly aside, and assuming that so much of the plan as had reference to the grave stones is to be revised, the scheme otherwise, as it has heretofore been considered, cannot be {*nicely*} changed. The first thing must be to get rid of the ugly, unnatural, useless, unsuitable and superficially unimproveable element of the quarries by carrying the quarrying to the point which will admit of a radical improvement.

I should come at once to you (I left home intending to do so once last week) but the extraordinary character of the planting {*season*} brings me pressing calls from all quarters all at once & unless you are urgent I shall delay doing so. Of course I could advise you much better on the ground.

But if you are decided to remove the graves, there is no reason you should not go right on with it.

Please consider that the last form in which I presented the "Campo

Santo"[3] idea here in view, by additional height of wall and by lengthening the line of wall while reducing the length on the ground of the whole affair, to leave a body of land clear at the corner, so that the view from the windows of the opposite dwelling house would be unobstructed. The structure would interrupt no view so much as any planting you are likely to substitute for it, and in connection with the library building, when covered with verdure, it would make the crown of the hill much more effective than it is otherwise likely to be. As to the view from the ground the less you have of it the better until you get to the best point of view. But I did not mean to argue the point. I think it entirely likely that all things considered your best way out of the difficulty is a complete removal of the grave yard. That is something people are used to hear of and can understand.[4]

Yours Very Truly

Fred[k] Law Olmsted.

The text presented here is from a letterpress copy of a handwritten letter signed on the original in Olmsted's hand: A1: 208–12, OAR/LC (see FLO to C. A. Williams, [Oct.] 1884, above).

1. The proposed park site in New London, Connecticut, was an old burial ground and part of the site had also served as a quarry. See FLO to C. A. Williams, [Oct.] 1884, above.
2. In addition to the alcove structure for the gravestones, Olmsted had indicated the location for a proposed library and terrace, on the high point of the site, with views out to the harbor. The proposal required further excavation of the quarry, using the stone for a retaining wall, and then filling and reclaiming the remains of the quarry. Robert Coit, a member of the park commission, criticized the idea in a letter to Olmsted: "I appreciate your suggestion that the building might be made the leading feature of the whole design, but if, in order to accomplish that, the finest part of the ground by nature must be covered up with it, perhaps it might be well to subordinate the building somewhat to the general design of a park of which it should be the chief embellishment." The library was never built in the park. Designed by Shepley, Rutan, and Coolidge in 1890, it was located a block away at State and Huntington Streets (Robert Coit to FLO, July 5, 1884).
3. Literally, a holy field or sacred ground. The *campo santo* style of cemetery, originating in Italy, consists of a cloistered or rectangular enclosed space housing remains and memorials. Olmsted is referring here to the stone structure he proposed to build for the displaced grave stones, one similar to the *campo santo* style. His 1884 sketches show that it would be built into an earthen declivity, within a retaining wall, enclosed and separated from the rest of the park. It would house close to 700 stones, being stacked on top of one another, three stones deep ("Preliminary Study for Memorial Park, New London," Oct. 7, 1884, plan 1001-5, "Sketches for New Memorial Park," n.d., plans 1001-z21 and 1001-7, NPS/FLONHS; James Stevens Curl, *A Celebration of Death: An introduction to some of the buildings, monuments, and settings of funerary architecture in the Western European tradition* [New York, 1980], pp. 150–51; "Notes for New London Memorial," B73: #1001, OAR/LC).
4. Olmsted's plans for the park through 1885 continued to incorporate the alcove structure and library, but sometime after this they must have been abandoned. No correspondence on the job after 1885 exists and the *campo santo* was not built.

ON POINTS OF VIEW AND METHODS OF CRITICISM OF PUBLIC WORKS OF LANDSCAPE ARCHITECTURE, — I.

June 20, 1885

In your issue of 18th of April (page 190) a gentleman tells of something that he has seen on one of the fields of work of the Boston Park Department, which, from his point of view, is a great wrong to the public, and an extreme illustration of professional morbid-mindedness. He asks how any other view of it is possible, implying that he is convinced that no other is possible. He adds that many persons are of his way of thinking. I think that I understand his point of view; that it is one from which I am every day taking much enjoyment of many things, and, looking at the occurrence exclusively from it, I respect and sympathize with the haste under which he has written. But I imagine myself, also, to have a moderately-clear idea of another point of view which may be taken with no less honesty and healthy simple-mindedness, and I am disposed to give some idea of it. I might have done so sooner, but since the letter appeared there has been an interregnum in the Department, and I have thought it more becoming to wait its termination.[1]

How is it possible? It is possible that a different understanding may be had of the purpose of the work. We can agree, I presume, that it is a purpose to provide means of recreation, and that the occurrence witnessed was the destruction of means of recreation. But there are different kinds of recreation, and the destruction of means for one may be the preparation of means of another. What, then, was the special character of recreation to be had in view in this case? There is no clear, full, official statement of it in existence. We must find the answer in the general drift of the proceedings that have led the work to be undertaken. The purchase of the ground to be operated upon — the raw material — has been lately determined after a discussion of the proposition in the City Council and otherwise, publicly, that had continued sixteen years.[2] The ground is five hundred acres in extent, and is situated at an extreme end of the city, seven miles distant from the dwellings of some of its people. Why should it have been thought better, after all this deliberation, to buy so much land in one place, and that so one-sided a place, rather than a dozen or more tracts equitably distributed, of the size, for example, of the Public Garden, all of which together would, perhaps, have cost less? There must have been some common-sense reason, or the obvious objection — an objection always having great weight, and which is generally recognized to have undue weight, in political bodies — would have made the result impossible.

The reason was, as is apparent from the course of debate, that something of a character that could not well be had on a site of the extent of the Public Garden, was, more or less clearly, felt to be wanted. Something different, also, from anything that could be seen in a long drive out of and around the city. Otherwise the argument against the scheme, that "we have a great park already, in all our beautiful suburbs,"[3] would have had more weight. Something different, also, from the best examples of landscape art in suburban villa grounds, and something yet again different from that which is enjoyed in passing through a rural neighborhood with scattered farmhouses, barns and other structures; with fields, diversified by a variety of crops and condition of tillage; with pastures, gardens, orchards and woodlands; but without striking natural features such as might be supplied by mountains.

What is this different thing? It must be something to which the topography of the site has been thought to specially lend itself, as well as something to the attainment of which a comparatively large extent of land was necessary. What, then, was to be found in the locality? First, and when the site was yet under debate, most conspicuously, there were upon it numerous homesteads, some of a villa character, some adapted to the wants of farmers and market-gardeners; with the proper following of barns, stables, ice-houses, glass-houses, poultry-yards, fences, lines of planted trees along the private boundaries, and so on. It was not because of these that the city wanted it. Imagine them out of the way; what then do we find? First, and most prominently, large woods and many small groves and separate shaws[4] of "natural growth" (wildlings, indigenous, spontaneous, strictly natural). These have not hitherto been cleared away, because the land where they stand is much broken and made intractable by ledges and huddles of boulders, so that it could not be brought under tillage or economically built upon. Then, within and between the outworks of these eminent, forest-like spaces we find glades often sloping from them and running out with more or less undulation, into meadow spaces through and over which, when the city acquired the property, it needed little more than the removal of the artificial features to open pleasing landscapes, extending in some directions to faintly blueish, dreamy distance. In these meadowy spaces there are also a few trees, seedlings, indigenous, native, natural, but so scattered chiefly on the upper parts of the slopes as not to materially disturb the generally simple, broad, quiet character of the scenery below the rugged woodlands.

There were four comparatively elevated points where the artificial features could be so far overlooked that the elements of this quality of scenery could be best realized, and on three of these sheltered seats had been placed in order that visitors might form a better idea of the more important capabilities of the site.

Plainly it was because of these special capabilities that a site of the character and extent of that purchased was selected. To what sort of recreation, then, does the history of the undertaking thus far point, as the special purpose that should be had in view in the further prosecution of it?

It will be convenient to give a name to it, and then consider what the name signifies. Let us name it the recreation of pastoral park scenery. I use the word pastoral to avoid any association of ideas with what is seen on the common, smaller class of parks, so-called, of our cities.*

What, then, is the distinctive characteristic of pastoral park scenery?

I answer, first, that if what is to be seen in gardens, villa grounds or rural neighborhoods is properly to be called scenery, it is by distinction scenery of a smaller scale. That is to say, the field of pastoral scenery is less occupied by incident and the details that go to make it up are less obtrusive; are broader, simpler, more combinative and composable. It offers more undisturbed perspectives. Perspectives, consequently, of more imperceptible gradation, softer, more ethereal, ineffable; leading toward "the sublimity of mystery."[6] Perspectives, consequently more persuasive to an unpurposed, drifting movement of the imagination. But, especially, pastoral park scenery, in contrast with what is to be enjoyed in gardens or in ordinary lowland villa or farmstead neighborhoods, illustrates what Hamerton in his new book calls "the curious truth that very much of the impressiveness [persuasiveness][7] of natural scenery depends on the degrees in which mass appears to predominate over details." ("*Landscape*," page 7.)[8] There being in such scenery less of incident calling for close attention, such as we find in a sparkling fountain, a bright, new, bronze statue, a freshly-painted pavilion, a blue spruce, a red Japanese maple or a rose of any tint, highly developed in form by the skill of the floral gardener, it the more works upon the organization of those coming into it out of a variegated, bright and bustling city, disposed to a tranquil musing in meditative and imaginative mood; a nerve-soothing mood. Such scenery, the result of purely natural processes, may be found in many parts of our country. I have seen it and experienced the influence of it in Kentucky, Texas, Colorado and California.[9] Such scenery, the result of art acting invitingly and suggestingly to nature (not masterfully), is often found in the old English parks; hence our term park-like.

The recreation to be obtained from such scenery is different from that to be obtained from many other types of scenery in which trees and turf and flowers are elements. Not as different as the pleasure we may take in perfumes from that we take in music, but so far different that means for obtaining it cannot be judged by the same standards of criticism without leading to misleading conclusions.

I have sufficiently indicated a possible point of view from which the occurrence witnessed by your correspondent might, I think, be seen in a different aspect from that in which he presents it. Having done so, I fear that you will think that I have used quite all the space that can be allowed me. I would like very much, however, if you would let me, to take up the subject proposed

*The beauty of park scenery," says Gilpin (1791) "is best displayed where hanging lawns screened with wood are connected with valleys, and where one part is continually playing in contrast with another." This is not the beauty that gives value to most of our city "parks."[5]

in my heading, and, without reproach to your correspondent, to examine his statements, simply as a means of exhibiting the method and manner of work that, as a critic, he has casually fallen into. Then, in another letter, I should like to show how greatly this method and manner of leading and educating the public prevails, and to point to some of its established consequences.

Besides what has been considered, there were on the property the remains of a number of small orchards. Your correspondent says they were of "native growth," but he cannot mean that they were so in the sense that the word native is commonly used with reference to trees. They were transplanted, nursery-grown trees. They had been distorted by grafting, and mutilated by trimming and heading-down. In one sense they were "natural," but no more so in the sense that that term is rightly applied to matters of scenery or garden art, than pig-tails or cramped feet or bouquets of "forced" flowers. They had been set, also, in rigid, straight lines, equidistantly and rectangularly, upon surfaces of naturally meandering contours, up hill and down, and often in positions that would have been chosen for them had it been considered an object to obscure the finest views of the neighborhood. Some, for example, had been so placed as to mar the outlooks from the commanding points chosen for the shelters before named. The most interesting and picturesque landscape on the site was thus divided and obscured. Many of the trees are very old, decaying, in parts dead, and limbs were often falling from them. They were in scattered squads standing in broken order, and from the point of view from which an artist regards pastoral park scenery, though not, perhaps, from that from which he would enjoy a garden, the outlook from a suburban villa or a pleasing prospect of an agricultural neighborhood, they were generally of an aspect that he would consider dissipating to the genius of the place.

Since the land came into the possession of the city, a few laborers have been employed when they could be spared from work elsewhere in progress, in removing obstructions to drainage, making gaps in walls, tearing down buildings not worth as much as it would cost to remove them, cutting out dead and dying trees, burning rubbish and so on. With the rest they have uprooted some of the remains of the old orchards. From the point of view that I have aimed to set forth, what has been done in this last respect would seem to be in as simple and direct pursuance of the purpose which led the city with so much deliberation to purchase this particular field of scenery, as the removal of old cottages, farm-houses and flower-gardens, the object in each case being the opening to public enjoyment of elements of scenery more truly natural to the locality; scenery of a rather broad scale, pastoral and park-like.

But your correspondent looking at it exclusively from the point of view, so far as appears from his letter, of admiration of things lovely in themselves, not as elements of composition, certainly not of scenery, sees in the removal of these particular trees, which for twenty days in the year might have been hoped for some years to come to exhibit a crop of flowers, an action similar in character to the setting on fire of the most valuable treasures of a public museum of art. Taking this view, he characterizes it in terms that could not be stronger if those responsible for it were detestable barbarians—"a vandalism; a wanton outrage." He describes the feelings to which the contemplation of it gives rise, as finding expression in "objurgations loud and deep." Under their influence he makes haste to give the public particulars of the atrocity. In his haste he says, first, that all of the fruit trees have been destroyed; afterwards all, he is "sure, with the exception of a few;" lastly, that apple blossoms have been "abolished forever over the whole stricken region." I attribute these expressions to haste and excited feeling because they are not of critical accuracy. Yesterday I had the pleasure of passing through the property with the commissioners recently appointed to superintend the undertaking, and while in movement, without interruption of conversation, I counted four hundred fruit trees, most of them apple trees, just breaking into bloom. I saw other blooming trees in the distance on both sides; saw boys, also at a distance, carrying branches in blossom. I know of many fruit trees that the party did not pass near—probably there are two or three hundred more trees of conspicuous blossoms yet standing on the ground.

But the letter not only thus exhibits the haste and hasty inaccuracy of observation and of statement that is characteristic of the class I wish to consider, it manifests another trait common to it. I mean the conviction that no other view of the subject of criticism than that of the writer is possible, except to a mind morbidly insensible to natural beauty, and that has become so as the result of professional training. The writer, in this case, accounts for the unnatural propensity to destroy apple trees to which he bears witness; for instance, as "a fine professional disesteem for so common and vulgar a poor relation as these natural growths"—meaning by natural growths apple orchards. He does not recognize the possibility of any other explanation.

The expression of the common notion that a professional life particularly unfits a man for professional duties, is addressed, in this case, to a professional journal and is pointed by an unnecessary reference, as to a marked example of a professionally disordered state of mind, to a gentleman, the most valuable part of whose professional capital was acquired in a series of rovings on foot, or in saddle or boat, and otherwise under conditions favorable to an absorbing, contemplative observation of scenery, and mainly of unsophisticated natural scenery. He was occupied in this training process several years, during which he traveled in the manner stated upwards of six thousand miles. There is no reason to doubt that he was moved to such a course by an unusual sensitiveness to the charms of natural scenery, and though he has had above sixty public grounds to deal with in a "practical" way since—most of them much too small to be illustrations of scenery of any kind—and this practice may have been a little demoralizing, on the whole, in his own judgment, the effect has been to strengthen the original impulse.

With reference to the frequent presumption of public instructors that no man of healthy mind can take a different view from their own of the occurrences which move them to write, another circumstance of this special case should be noted.

There were two well-known citizens of Boston who were exclusively answerable to the public for all work done upon this public property. The only person named by your correspondent had no formal official responsibility in the matter.[10] Your correspondent's impression to the contrary was a surmise, based on the fact that this person had been professionally employed by those in charge of the park work in question, with reference to other of the duties committed to them. Incidentally, it happens, to this other employment, they had conferred with him occasionally about the park work, and the squad of men engaged in the preliminary clearing of the ground having been drawn from his professional field, he had sometimes passed orders to it (of which orders he fully approved). But whatever he may have done in the premises was gratuitously done, was of unofficial character, was entirely known to and fully sanctioned by his principals, and there is no reason to suppose that if he had never seen the place one tree the less would have disappeared.

It follows that if your correspondent's theory were a sound one, these citizens must be afflicted with the same calamity of professional morbid-mindedness, distaste for nature and fine disdain for the "vulgar" view of a park with the person he names. The fact is, that both have had leading parts in other important movements for opening the higher enjoyments of taste to the great body of the people. Both have shown, otherwise than in public works, special interest in sylvan beauty. Both have country places, in which they have for many years been practising unprofessional landscape work and with distinguished success. One of them has been notably engaged in such work more than forty years.

Clearly, the point of view of these gentlemen is not that of your correspondent, nor is it a perverted professional point of view.

F.L.O.

Brookline, May 19, 1885

ON POINTS OF VIEW AND METHODS OF CRITICISM OF PUBLIC WORKS OF LANDSCAPE ARCHITECTURE.—II.

June 27, 1885

In a former communication (*American Architect* No. 495, page 295), I examined a letter which was only remarkable in that it had been addressed to a technical and professional journal of the highest standing. I did so because I found it a comparatively modest and moderate example of a class of criticisms of public works of Landscape Architecture, addressed to the public through the press and otherwise.

The leading traits of this class I indicated to be, first, that they were based on impressions of the subject of criticism which were the result of hasty, superficial and inexact observation of fragments of incomplete work; second, that they represented no adequate consideration of designed results to be reached by growth after a period of years through persuasion of nature in a choice of the ordinary ways of nature; third, that they confused one purpose or motive of design with another, or with several others; fourth, that they failed to recognize that the most important element of professional education of a landscape architect is that obtained through special familiarity with, and enjoyment of, the beauty of various aspects of nature, and assumed that the employment of professional education and experience in the conduct of the class of work they undertook to criticise could only lead into narrow, rigid, artificial channels of unnatural and depraved taste.

I wish now to narrate a few incidents in further illustration of the subject, and to add, perhaps, no more than a single example (since one of conspicuous character will fully answer the purpose) of the harmful results to public interests of such misled essays in criticism. I shall draw upon my own experience because of my familiarity with the facts of it. But let it not be supposed that the custom is of recent origin or that my experience is peculiar. Nearly forty years ago the venerated Downing,[11] acting under instructions received direct from the President, removed a few trees, which, in his judgment, were damaging a public ground in Washington. Upon this a gentleman asked in the Senate Chamber, "Who is this man Downing? Is it the famous Major Jack Downing?"[12] his object being to ridicule the idea that a man whose high standing in his profession was recognized by all who could speak with authority throughout the world was more competent, or to be safely entrusted with larger discretion than Tom, Dick or Harry. The logic of the position would lead to the conclusion that no tree on a public ground could be properly removed except by special act of Congress. Illustrations of the same frame of mind are constantly appearing. Since your correspondent's letter was printed, my name, for example, has been telegraphed through the land, not in the half-railing way of his use of it, but as might be that of a wretch, guilty of an atrocity so barbarous that its occurrence humiliates the nation. This for an act of professional duty as surely imperative as the amputation of a man's limb has ever been with a surgeon — an act contemplated and provided for ten years before; fully and specially sanctioned by those to whom I was officially responsible, and a temporary delay of which had led me to be remonstrated with by the highest authority in the country.[13] For like offenses against common-sense, I have been publicly denounced as a Vandal hundreds of times. It stands on the printed record that I have been given this title on the floors of Congress, after having been declared ignorant of the simplest duties of my calling,[14] and told that my most important work would disgrace the back-yard of a pioneer settler.

The first work in any ground, the surface of which requires modification, is that of taking off the soil and storing it in compact mounds until it can be returned to its place after a change of the substratum. It has more than once occurred that gentlemen, seeing these mounds half made, have rushed to a newspaper office to advise the public that the work was under no competent direction, for it was not at all in good modern gardening form to lay out such stiff, formal beds as they had seen making. Once the mayor of a city called the attention of the council to reports of this character. A committee of investigation was formed, it held several sessions, examined a number of witnesses, none of whom were connected with the work; finally, I suppose, came to the ground to look for itself, and let the matter drop — making no report.

Once a letter appeared ridiculing certain work in progress, upon grounds evincing a wrong-headed idea of its motive. Shortly afterwards I was advised by telegraph to see a legislator who, it was said, had the power and the intention to prevent any appropriation for the work until a change of plan was made in the particulars referred to. I hastened to the place, making a journey of a thousand miles for the purpose; found the gentleman in question and asked him to visit the ground with me. He said he could not, as he had to go at once to an office which he named. "You will pass through the ground in going there, and if I may go with you it will not detain you two minutes to have a matter set right in which I am told you have much interest." To this he consented, and when we reached the locality I began to show the necessity of the course adopted. Before I had half done so, in about sixty seconds, he interrupted me, saying: "Oh, I see you understand the business better than I do. I never thought there was so much in it. Go ahead and I'll support you."[15]

The marvel of such experiences, of which I could relate many, is that intelligent and educated men should be so unready, of their own motion, to reflect "that an artist *of whatever denomination*," as Charles Dickens once said, "may perhaps be trusted to know what he is about in his vocation, if they will concede him a little patience."[16]

But if this is marvelous, there is a thing more so. It is the want of root in the mind of the notions upon which the most sensational "criticisms" are uttered. Once a man wrote to a leading newspaper that he had seen in a place named an impossible object. He was known, was asked to look again at the place and the impossibility pointed out to him. "Obviously so," he said, coolly, "it must have been an optical delusion," but no correction of the report was ever made.

But of the shallow-rootedness of the sentiment, that appears so firmly established in many of the class of criticisms I am explaining, perhaps the best illustration appears in the fact that they have often been uttered by men who were at the time on familiar terms with me; to whom it would have been much easier to ascertain the facts and motive of the work criticised than to have written to a newspaper. It has happened that the authors of more than one of the reports to which I have referred in this letter have sought my professional advice for their private affairs, acted upon it in unquestioning faith, and expressed satisfaction with the results.

I do not know that my personal fortunes have ever been at all affected by this class of shallow, light-hearted but exciting criticisms. Those to whom I have been directly responsible, if they have not always fully sustained me and seen me through, have invariably expressed their confidence in me and their belief that I was right. But as to the effect on the interests of the public, I will refer to a case of which the essential facts must be generally known, so much have they, bit by bit, been publicly narrated.

In a daily paper of the largest circulation in New York, between 1850 and 1861 (more or less in others), a series of complaints were published upon the sparseness of the planting of the Central Park. For several years afterwards the entire work was extravagantly praised and all concerned in its design and management were set on a hazardously high eminence. Later, a systematic thinning of the plantations, much too long delayed, was entered upon; criticisms and protests then began to appear, and before long an excitement was worked up, which became violent when the vandalism was witnessed of taking out some of the larger trees — mostly cheap foreign trees, originally planted as nurses and for temporary effect, and in no way of permanent value, yet sure to be destructive to the designed sylvan effects if allowed to remain. This violence did not spend itself in the Press, it led on, in some cases, to proceedings of an almost riotous character, laborers being stopped at their work by gentlemen who left their carriages for the purpose. A man directed to fell a tree answered, "I beg your pardon, sir, but I hope you will excuse me. I really dare not do it."

The Commissioners professed to be satisfied that their professional advisers knew what they were about in their vocation, yet, after many cautions, were constrained by political considerations, or by respect for what they were made to regard as an irresistible public sentiment, first, to withhold the means necessary for proceeding with the work, and, at last, to forbid the removal of a single tree except the assent of a majority of their Board had been obtained and formally recorded.[17] This was practically a prohibition of all thinning of the plantations and was intended to be. What has followed? precisely what the Commissioners were over and over again warned would follow. For several years past I have seen no expression of dissent from the judgment expressed by many competent critics, that the value of this park, costly beyond parallel, has been cut disastrously short of what it was designed to be, and in its early stages fitted to be, by the course taken. It is too late to remedy the evil, and I have seen earnest appeals to those in charge to break into the plantations where breaks would only work to a more disastrous frustration of the design than has yet occurred.

The first step taken in the construction of the Brooklyn Park was the removal of one-third of the trees found growing upon the ground and the blazing of half the remainder as not to be reckoned to remain permanently. Later, some of the trees designed for permanence were subjected to such treatment as led to public denunciations of the ignorance and barbarity of those responsible for it, giving the Commissioners much concern and leading to earnest cautions. Three years afterwards the professional superintendents of the work invited a close examination of the results of disregarding the clamor of the Vandal-hunters and were thanked for their persistence. Let any competent critic examine the park now and ask whether a little more vigorous and sustained Vandalism would have been a misfortune to the city?

F.L.O.

Brookline, 1885.

The text presented here was published in two parts in *American Architect and Building News* on June 20, 1885, pp. 295–96, and on June 27, 1885, pp. 306–7, but composed a couple of months earlier. Olmsted wrote the article in reply to an anonymous letter to the editor written by a reader concerned about the "wholesale destruction" of fruit trees on the site of the future West Roxbury (Franklin) Park. "What attraction," the writer wanted to know, would "substitute for the glory of a New England apple orchard in May?" ("Vandalism, Excusable or Inexcusable?," *American Architect and Building News*, April 18, 1885, p. 190).

1. In December 1884 Hugh O'Brien, a Democrat and Irish by birth, was elected mayor of Boston, marking a historic shift in municipal politics. The new mayor replaced the original Boston park commissioners with three powerful Democrats: Patrick Maguire, John F. Andrew, and Benjamin Dean. When the new park commissioners took office in May 1885 Olmsted lost his powerful ally, Charles H. Dalton, the longtime chairman of the commission. Despite serious apprehensions expressed in correspondence with William McMillan and Charles Eliot Norton, Olmsted soon found the new administration and its park commission to be supportive of his park plans (C. Zaitzevsky, *The Boston Park System*, p. 67; FLO to William McMillan, March 16, 1885, above; FLO to Charles Eliot Norton, May 2, 1885; Charles Eliot Norton to FLO, March 5, 1885, Charles Eliot Norton Miscellaneous Papers, bMS AM 1088.2, Box 5, Houghton Library, Harvard University).
2. Preliminary discussions for a Boston park system had begun sixteen years earlier in 1869, when a group of Boston citizens and businesses petitioned the City Council to establish new public parks. In 1876 the commission published its first proposal for a park system, which was influenced by earlier proposals as well as some consultation with Olmsted. The plan included, in its earliest stages, the West Roxbury (Franklin) Park site, which Olmsted had endorsed. Appropriations for its acquisition followed in 1881, and a topographic survey was completed in 1884. Olmsted's plan and report for the park were published in 1885 while preliminary site work (discussed in this document) was already underway. Substantial appropriations followed the next year under the administration of Mayor Hugh O'Brien, and Olmsted published his "Notes on the Plan of Franklin Park and Related Matters" in 1886, in order to further explain how the park would have "greater lasting consequence to the city than those of any other of its

public works of the present time" (C. Zaitzevsky, *The Boston Park System*, pp. 34–44, 65–68; *Papers of FLO*, 7: 9–13; Frederick Law Olmsted, "Report of the Landscape Architect," Dec. 24, 1883, above; FLO to Charles H. Dalton, Aug. 26, 1884, above; Frederick Law Olmsted, *Tenth Annual Report, Boston Park Commissioners, Reports on West Roxbury Park and Wood Island Park*, [Dec.]1884, above; Frederick Law Olmsted, "Notes on the Plan of Franklin Park and Related Matters," 1886 [*Papers of FLO*, SS1: 460–534]).

3. Olmsted is paraphrasing the words of H. W. S. Cleveland in his chapter "What Boston May Do," from *The Public Grounds of Chicago: How to Give Them Character and Expression* (Chicago, 1869). Cleveland described the reaction of an imaginary visitor to Boston taken by the appeal of Boston's suburbs. The visitor asks rhetorically, "'What do you Bostonians want of a park, with such wealth of natural beauty all around you . . . tastefully improved by private hands?'" (p. 9). Taken in context, the observation is part of an argument for, not against, the development of a park system in Boston.
4. Shaw, as in "thicket, small wood, copse or grove" (*OED*).
5. Olmsted paraphrases William Gilpin: "The beauty, however, of park scenery is undoubtedly best displayed on a varied surface, where the ground swells and falls; where hanging lawns, screened with wood, are connected with valleys; and where one part is continually playing in contrast with another" (William Gilpin, *Remarks on Forest Scenery and Other Woodland Views* [Edinburgh, 1791], p. 295).
6. Olmsted presumably is quoting the English art critic John Ruskin. In *Notes on Some of the Principle Pictures Exhibited in the Rooms of the Royal Academy* (London, 1855), Ruskin wrote, "But as the years pass by, the artist concedes to himself, more and more, the privilege which none but the feeble should seek, of substituting the sublimity of mystery for that of absolute majesty of form" (pp. 8–9). See Frederick Law Olmsted, "A Healthy Change in the Tone of the Human Heart," *Century Illustrated Monthly Magazine*, Oct. 1886, below.
7. Olmsted inserted this word in brackets (as it is not in the original quotation) presumably to support his argument in the previous sentence about certain natural "perspectives" being more "persuasive."
8. Philip Gilbert Hamerton (1834–1894) was an English artist, art critic, and author who wrote many books on art and was a contributor to the *Fine Arts Quarterly Review*, *Cornhill*, *Macmillan's*, and other magazines in Britain and the United States. His treatise *Landscape* was published in London and Boston in 1885 (*DNB*).
9. Olmsted makes reference to American landscapes he had seen during his travels dating back to the 1850s. He visited Kentucky as a journalist and described "The Woodland Pastures of Kentucky" in *A Journey Through Texas* (New York, 1857): "Here spreads, for hundreds of miles before you, an immense natural park. . . . It is landscape gardening on the largest scale. The eye cannot satiate itself in a whole day's swift panorama, so charmingly varied is the surface, and so perfect each new point of view" (pp. 10–11).

   In the same volume, the "western prairies" of Texas were also seen as a naturally park-like landscape: "The live-oaks, standing alone or in picturesque groups near and far upon the clean sward, which rolled in long waves that took, on their various slopes, bright light or half shadows from the afternoon sun, contributed mainly to an effect which was very new and striking, though still natural, like a happy new melody" (pp. 129–30). He also described the natural, park-like beauty of this landscape in his "Address to {the} Prospect Park Scientific Association," May 1868 (*Papers of FLO*, SS1: 147–57).

   Olmsted journeyed through Colorado in the fall of 1880 while traveling with Charles Francis Adams, Jr., on one of his annual railroad trips for the Union Pacific Railroad. Olmsted was also on his way to Cheyenne, Wyoming, to visit his step-son

Owen, who would die the next year of tuberculosis. Unlike the other sites he mentions, Olmsted wrote no published description of the Colorado landscape (*FLO, A Biography*, p. 389).

Olmsted lived in Bear Valley, California, in 1864 and 1865 while managing the Mariposa Estate mine. He visited nearby Yosemite Valley among other locations in the state several times while there, and in 1865 he was named a commissioner of the state park board created to administer the valley as a public park, publishing that year his "Preliminary Report Upon the Yosemite and Big Tree Grove," Aug. 1865 (*Papers of FLO*, 5: 488–516).

10. The park commissioners serving in 1884 and the beginning of 1885 when most of the clearing of trees occurred were Charles H. Dalton, Henry Lee, and William Gray. The only two names attached to the *Tenth Annual Report* of 1884 that reported on the cuttings were Dalton's and Lee's, as Gray's confirmation to the board had been held up in January of 1885. All three men were replaced in May of 1885 when Mayor O'Brien's board took over. Olmsted's plan for the park had not been officially approved by the board until the spring of 1885, hence his statement here that he had had no official role in clearing the trees previous to that. Nevertheless, he is the only person the writer of the letter names in his article in *American Architect and Building News* (*Tenth Annual Report of the Board of Commissioners of the Department of Parks for the City of Boston for the Year 1884* [Boston, 1885], pp. 18, 25, 30; *Eleventh Annual Report of the Board of Commissioners of the Department of Parks for the City of Boston for the Year 1885* [Boston, 1886], pp. 19, 34–35; "No Quorum, and Hence, No Confirmation of William Gray, Jr.," *Boston Daily Globe*, Jan. 2, 1885, p. 2; C. Zaitzevsky, *The Boston Park System*, p. 43, 67; C. Zaitzevsky, "Frederick Law Olmsted in Brookline," pp. 42–65).
11. Andrew Jackson Downing was the foremost American landscape gardener of his day and author of *A Treatise on the Theory and Practice of Landscape Gardening* (1841). In 1850, Downing was commissioned to design "The Public Grounds at Washington" (the Washington Mall) (Frederick Law Olmsted, *Annual Report of the Architect of the United States Capitol*, 1882, n. 9, above; David Schuyler, *Apostle of Taste: Andrew Jackson Downing, 1815–1852* [Baltimore, 1996], pp. 192–202).
12. Major Jack Downing was a character created by popular American humorist Seba Smith. The Major's fictional letters first appeared in 1830 in the *Portland Courier*, and continued in the *National Intelligencer*. They were later collected in book form in *The Life & Writings of Major Jack Downing of Downingville* (1833). Major Jack was "a common man magnified as oracle, a Yankee full of horse sense and wise saws" (*EB*).
13. Olmsted began his work designing and supervising the improvement of the Capitol grounds in Washington, D.C., in 1874 and one of his first recommendations was the removal of about 400 trees, mostly in the eastern section of the grounds. Members of Congress and others objected on several occasions to the removal of trees and other aspects of the improvement and expansion of the Capitol grounds (Glenn Brown, *History of the United States Capitol*, 2 vols. [Washington, D.C., 1900, 1903], pp. 1154–55; FLO to Justin Smith Morrill, Jan. 22, 1874 [*Papers of FLO*, 7: 36–43]; *Papers of FLO*, 7: 67, n. 5; Frederick Law Olmsted, "The National Capitol," Dec. 5, 1874 [*Papers of FLO*, 7: 93–99]; W. C. Allen, *History of the United States Capitol*, p. 348).
14. On February 21, 1883, amendments were proposed on the House floor for H.R. 7595, a sundry civil appropriations bill, part of which requested appropriations for paying the salary of various men employed on the improvement of the Capitol grounds work, including Olmsted. Representative Benjamin Wilson from West Virginia, in protest to the slow progress of work on the grounds, proposed an amendment to the bill that effectively stripped away the request for payment for Olmsted and his workers. He said:

> Mr. Chairman, my object in offering this amendment it to stop this eternal work on the Capitol grounds. The despoiler has been here for ten years to my knowledge.

> The beauty and symmetry of these grounds have been in a great measure destroyed. Those who have carried on these so-called "improvements" have removed the most beautiful forest there was about the city of Washington — a forest containing shade-trees which cannot be replaced in less than a quarter of a century. In winter and in summers, in spring-time and in fall these grounds are being dug up, trees cut down, and changes everlastingly made. This damage to the public grounds around the Capitol has been going on for a series of years. I think any man of taste must fail to discover that any improvement has been made, though thousands of dollars have been expended.

Wilson's amendment was not agreed upon. According to an interview Olmsted later gave to the *Evening Star* in which he mentioned this statement of Wilson's, he said "I have since received a note from him acknowledging that he had been misinformed as to the facts and expressing regret that he should have made the statement" (*Sundry Civil Appropriations Bill*, HR 7595, 47th Cong., 2d. sess., *Congressional Record* 14 [Feb. 21, 1883], p. H3081; "The Capitol Building," *Evening Star*, Nov. 14, 1883, p. 1).

15. Olmsted refers to the construction and surrounding plantings of the summer-house on the northwest quarter of the Capitol grounds. In 1880 as the house was under construction, some Members of Congress questioned its aesthetic merits. Senator Eli Saulsbury from Delaware of the Committee of Public Buildings and Grounds threatened to introduce a resolution to have it removed. Olmsted traveled back and forth to D.C. and, along with Edward Clark and Senator Justin S. Morrill, convinced Saulsbury that the beauty of the structure would not be evident until the plantings were given time to grow (FLO to Edward Clark, c. Aug.–Sept. 1880 [*Papers of FLO*, 7: 507–10; W. C. Allen, *History of the United States Capitol*, pp. 356–58).
16. From Charles Dickens, *Our Mutual Friend* (London, 1865), from the "Postscript, In Lieu of a Preface" (p. 429).
17. The board of the Department of Public Parks of New York City passed an order banning the cutting of all trees without its approval on August 20, 1873. In *The Spoils of the Park, With a Few Leaves from the Deep-Laden Note-Books of "A Wholly Unpractical Man"* (1882), Olmsted describes a "standing order in force, forbidding me to have a single tree felled without a specific order, to be obtained by a majority vote of the Board. Before this order was passed, men seen cutting trees under my directions have been interrupted and indignantly rebuked by individual commissioners, and even by the 'friends' of commissioners, having no more right to do so than they would for like action on a man-of-war. I have had men beg me, from fear of dismissal, to excuse them from cutting trees, and, to relieve them, have taken the axe from them, and felled the trees myself." (DPP, *Minutes*, Aug. 20, 1873, pp. 217–18; *Papers of FLO*, 7: 621; see also Frederick Law Olmsted and J. B. Harrison, *Observations on the Treatment of Public Plantations, More Especially Relating to The Use of the Axe*, April 30, 1889, below).

SPECIFICATIONS FOR PLAYSTEAD TERRACE, FRANKLIN PARK

(30th July 1885)

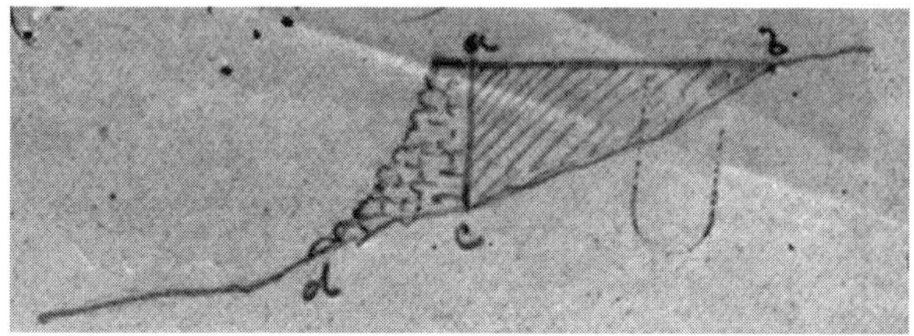

ab=deck.
acd=retaining pier.

a parapet is to {be}added at a.

Playsted Terrace. The outer line and grade of the deck of the proposed terrace having been given by stakes a series of piers are to be built along this line and to the height shown upon the stakes. The rear line of each pier is to be vertical and will correspond with the outer line of the deck (a). At the top the piers are to be 2 feet thick from front to rear and from 4 to 6 ft long.

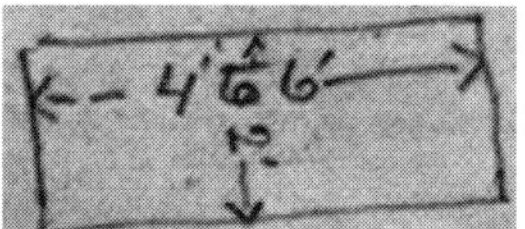

They are to have a batter on the front face sufficient to make their depth half way from top to bottom equal to half their height. (ab to equal b.c.)

The batter, or slope of the outer face, is not to be straight but slightly concave.

The piers as above described are to stand at a distance apart varying from three to five feet, average four, uniformity of distance not being desired. They are to be connected along the front by stones built in with the stones of the piers in such a manner as to form a continuous face but this intermediate structure is to be no deeper at any point than is necessary in order that it should stand and is to be laid in cob work; that is, so as to leave openings or fissures

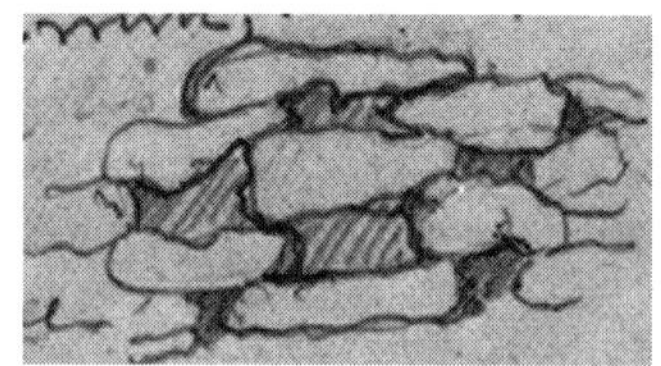

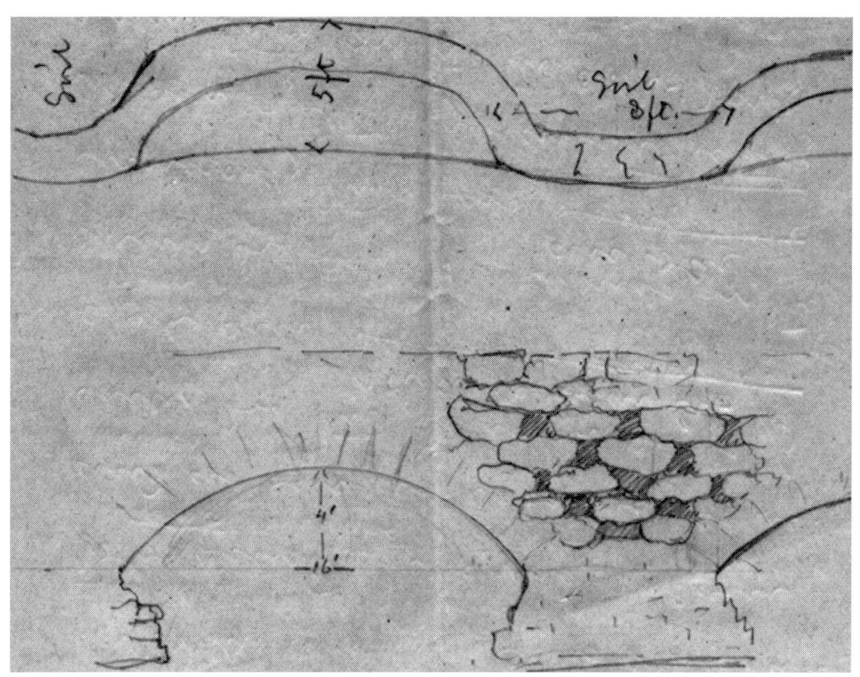
4'
16'

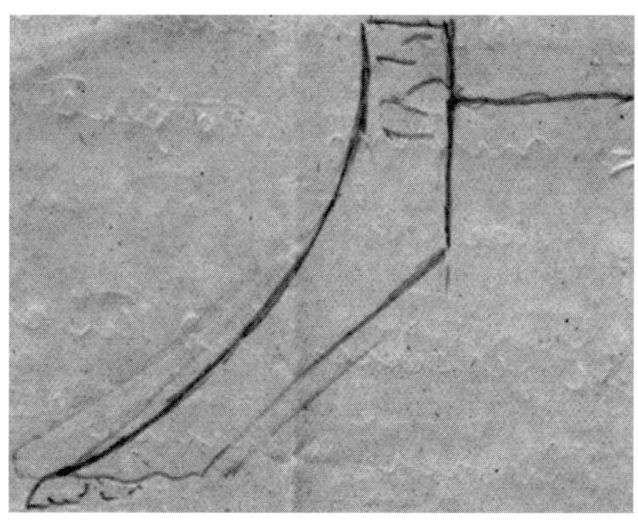

View Southwest Across Playstead, Showing Overlook Shelter, n.d.

between the stones and extending through the wall. These fissures to be at least large enough to let a man's arm pass through them, with some twice as large. The cob work stones are to be set pitching downward from front to rear rather than the reverse, (so that water falling on them may run inward). No fissures are to be left within two feet of the deck line.

The fissures, and the space between the piers behind the cob work to a depth of eighteen inches from the rear of the stones, is to be filled with soil rammed down, and the space in the rear of the soil with rip-rap and earth.

For the face of the piers stones are to be selected of good colour and as far as possible, especially for the central parts of each pier, such as {stones that} bear lichens or moss. Stones for the corners of the piers are to be chosen with reference to fitting connection with the cob-work. So far as the face of the piers can be so built without loss of strength small pockets are to be left between the stones, these being of such a form that they will hold each from half a pint to a quart of soil so that it will not be liable to wash out.

When the work is done no distinct up and down line should be noticeable between the piers and the cob-work, and the more nearly the whole appears an unbroken construction, (if there is, in fact, a sufficiency of fissures in the cob-work and sufficient solidity in the piers), the better. So far as the stones supplied will permit, with due attention to the above requirements, the entire wall is to have a smooth even face without marked protuberances. The stones near the base will in a few years be much covered by foliage those nearer the top less so, therefore stones of protuberant face will best be used if at all near the bottom and as the wall rises more and more pains should be taken to secure smooth work. For the upper courses to the depth of from one and a half to three feet from the deck, pudding stone[1] in blocks of nearly flat face and good color and that will lay with tolerably close joints without fissures or pockets are as far as practicable to be used. The upper stones will be a bed for a parapet to be added afterwards.

The text presented here is a draft of notes in Olmsted's hand. The Playstead section of Franklin Park is roughly thirty acres and occupies, with the Long Crouch Woods area, the north corner of the park. Designed to accommodate "athletic recreation" as well as "civic ceremonies" and other organized activities, the meadows of the Playstead connected with the northwest end of the proposed Greeting, a straight, tree-lined avenue that extended half a mile to the southeast, connecting to the Blue Hills Avenue entrance to the park. The Playstead and the Greeting were both part of what Olmsted called the Ante-Park, in which large events, organized games, and public gatherings could occur without encroaching on the quieter beauty of the somewhat separate, central areas of the park.

The Playstead Terrace, also called the Overlook, described here was an 800-foot long "elevated platform for spectators" built of earth and stone on the western edge of the Playstead. An existing "barren ledge" of rock served as part of its foundation, and the structure employed puddingstone boulders that were cleared from the Playstead meadow. In 1886 Olmsted wrote that the boulders of the terrace wall were to be "mainly overgrown with vegetation befitting the form and material of the structure, adapted to harmonize it with the natural scenery." The Overlook Shelter on the terrace was completed in 1889. According to John C. Olmsted, Olmsted himself designed the Shelter, which was integrated directly into the terrace structure (Frederick Law Olmsted, "Notes on the Plan of Franklin Park and Related Matters" [*Papers of FLO*, SS1: 487–88]; C. Zaitzevsky, *The Boston Park System*, pp. 68–70; 176–77; JCO to Sylvester Baxter, Jan. 17, 1898, A56:94–100, OAR/LC; see also FLO to JCO, Oct. 5, 1887, below).

1. Puddingstone is "a composite rock consisting of a mass of rounded pebbles cemented together by a siliceous matrix." It appeared in outcrops in the suburbs of Boston, and sometimes was used in construction (*OED*; *EB*).

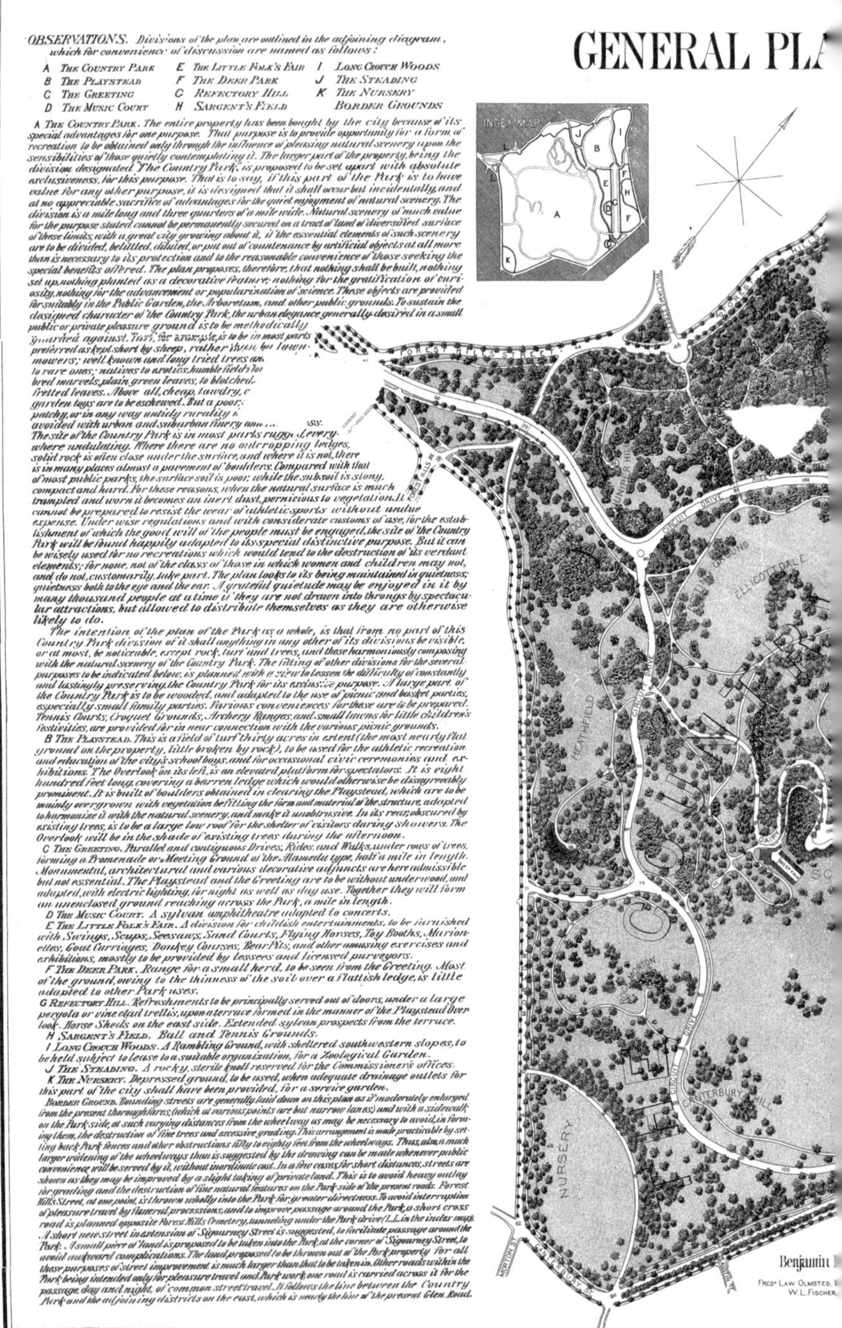

“General Plan of

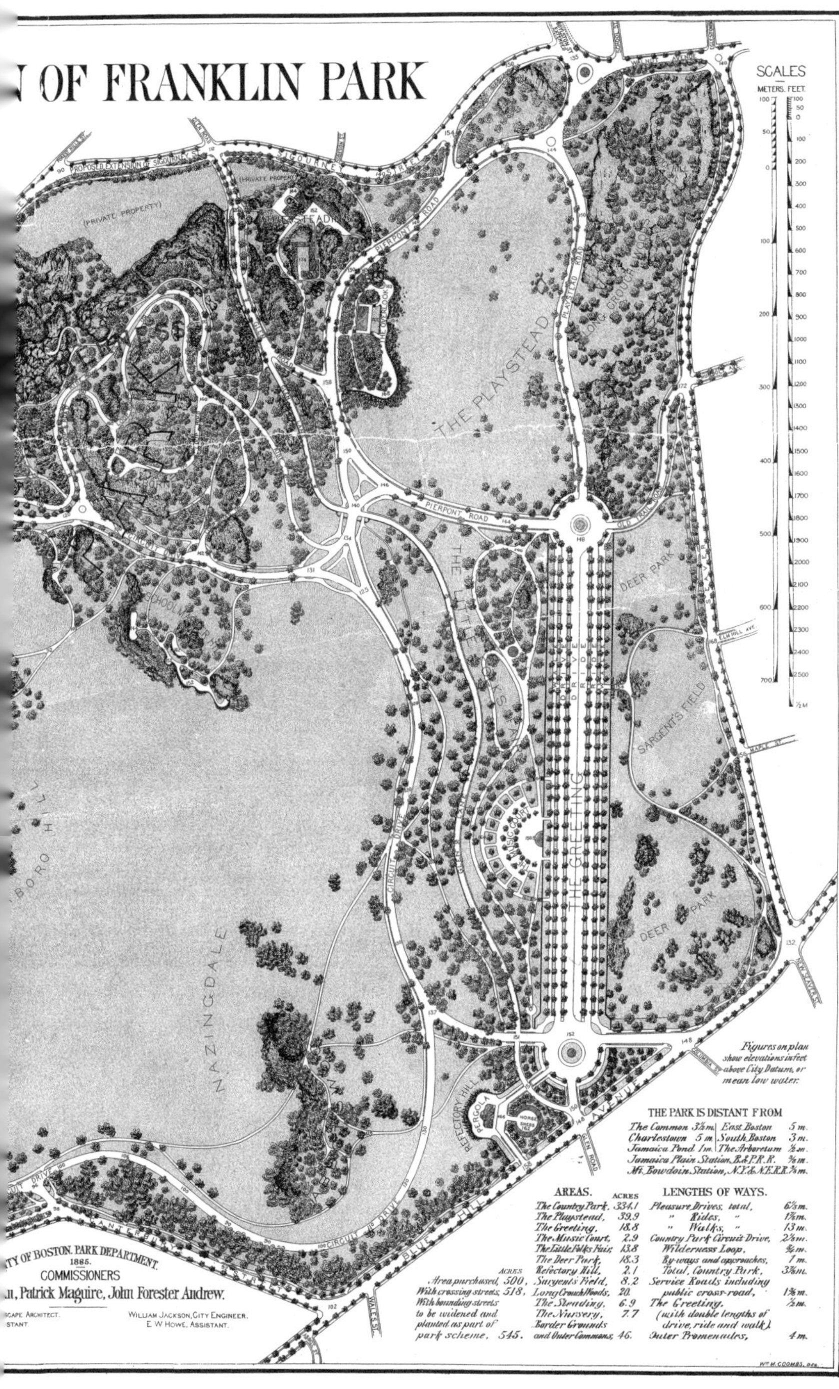

'RANKLIN PARK," 1885

To John Daniel Crimmins[1]

Brookline, Mass. 6th Aug. 1885.

Dear Sir;

You have asked me to communicate any suggestions for which I may see occasion in relation to the proposed tomb and monument at the end of the Riverside Terrace.[2]

Under the impulse to give expression to the ruling sentiment of the moment, the city is liable to be precipitated into courses that will afterwards be regretted. Many of the suggestions that have thus far been given seem to have been made with little recognition of certain conditions that I should regard as important to be kept in view.

The land to be dealt with has been bought by the city, has been some time held and considerable expenditures have been already made upon it, in consideration of its adaptability to a purpose very different from that now prominent in the public mind.[3] Should its value for this earlier purpose be hastily destroyed or seriously injured, the loss could not be repaired for a much larger sum than is likely to be expended on the proposed monument. It is therefore important in determining the position, the form and the immediately surrounding circumstances of the monument, that regard should be had to the preservation of this value.

There were originally two distinct properties, one called Riverside Avenue, the other Riverside Park, the latter being for the main part a steep often precipitous hillside, the former a strip of land one hundred feet wide adjoining the Park ground on the East and intended to be laid out as an ordinary street. In 1873 the city obtained authority from the legislature to annul this arrangement, in order to admit of the construction on the combined properties of a terrace over two miles in length upon which there might be formed broad, shaded passages, separate but closely adjoining, for driving, riding walking and resting, with suitable attendant decorative gardening.[4]

This project was devised because of the growing demand for provisions for recreation to which the Central Park had not been and, on account of its topography, could not, except at enormously greater cost, be adapted. The principal outlay upon Central Park—the entire outlay except for matters of superficial decoration—had been made with a purpose of favoring simple, tranquilizing, contemplative, rural recreation. The demand was growing for provisions more favorable to gay, social, festive, urban and {. . .} recreation. Such a demand appeared not only in the use of a crowded promenade of a certain stretch of the park road very ill adapted by courses, grades and otherwise for such use and in repeated impracticable suggestions for better adapting it to the purpose but also in the desire to have bits of garden finery upon ground of a natural character, in close association with rugged objects and under conditions unfavorable to suitable keeping. There was danger that this demand, if it could not eventually be met elsewhere, would lead to the destruction of the chief elements of value of the Central Park while substituting nothing of a different character of respectable quality. It was a demand that could not fail to increase with the growth of the city and that could not be suitably provided for in a few years.

The Riverside Terrace was devised as a means of forestalling attempts to meet the demand in a poor way at excessive cost.[5] The main work undertaken for this purpose is substantially done. What is principally lacking to its completion, except in horticultural matters, is a suitable terminal feature at its North end. Such a feature would principally be a place where having walked, driven or ridden several miles, there would be an invitation and opportunity not simply to turn around, but to halt and linger pleasantly before going back. Ground has been reserved for this purpose and some work has been done toward the fitting of it. The space available reaches from the end of the Terrace to the brow of a declivity from which a magnificent view is commanded up the valley of the Hudson. Properly used this view will eventually give a value to the entire promenade that could not be obtained by artificial means at a cost of millions. No other metropolis in the world has anything to compare with it. It will be one of the glories of New York and will go far to compensate for its lack of venerable architectural works. The loss of it would be an unending public calamity. Neglect of precautions to preserve it and hold its advantageous use would be criminal neglect.

The site proposed for the Grant sepulchre[6] is on a line, and about midway, between the end of the terrace already built and this point of view. It occupies the centre of the ground reserved for the terminal feature of the Promenade. It is a very fine site for a public monument. But it will be extremely unfortunate if, on the one hand, the remains of the dead are brought into close association with the gayety of the Promenade at this culminating point, or if, on the other, the city shall be forced to adopt plans for the terminal arrangements of the Promenade which will prevent its main character from being sustained, which will prove at all meagre and inconvenient, or which shall prevent the Promenade from having the great northern view as its terminus.

We cannot now entertain the idea that any monument to be here erected shall not be a lasting monument but no one would have believed even twenty years ago that in London the statue of Wellington could be taken down with the triumphal arch on which it stood and withdrawn entirely from the public eye, as it has been during the last year in order to make a better connection between Hyde and Green Parks and to improve the associated thoroughfares.[7] The warning should not be lost upon us.

The body of Grant should lie in a place specially adapted to its permanent undisturbed repose. It should be within a ground obviously set apart, if not consecrated to this special purpose. This ground should be separated in a distinct way from all adjoining ground. It should not be an incident of a festive promenade. It should have a distinctly solemn aspect.

It is not impossible that the two purposes — the festive and the funereal purpose may both be successfully carried out on Claremont[8] but the problem is one that calls for something more than native intelligence and horse sense.

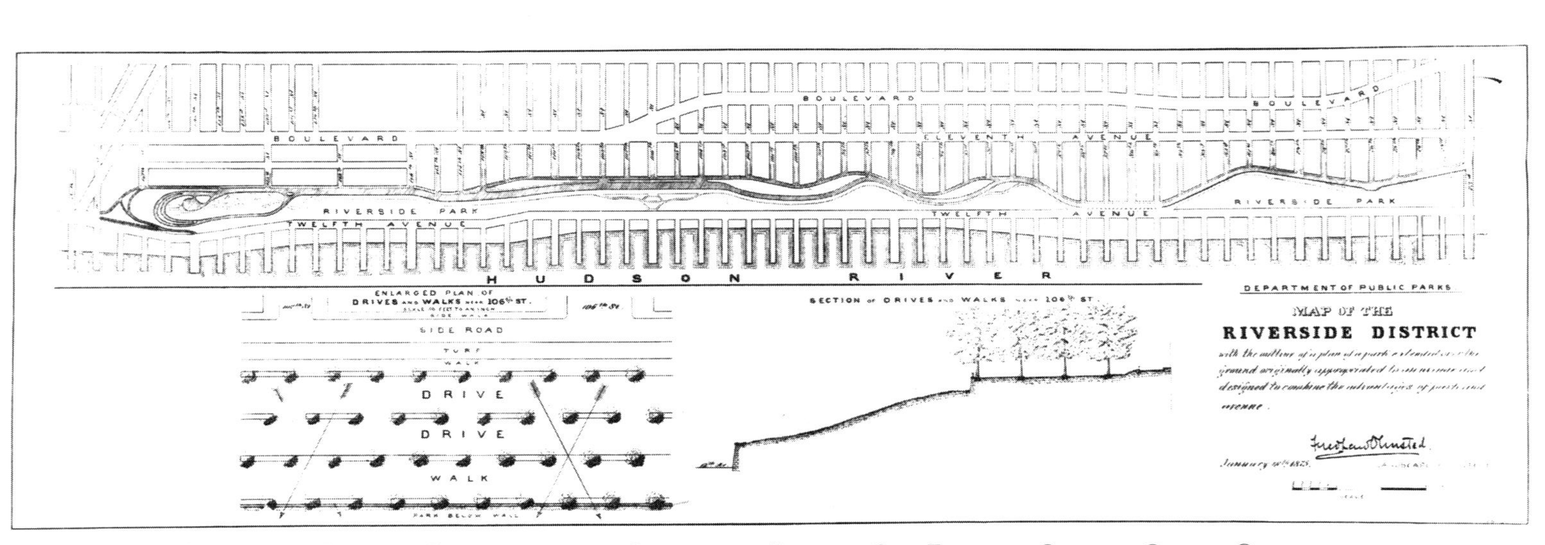

"Map of the Riverside District with the Outline of a Plan of a Park Extended Over the Ground Originally Appropriated to an Avenue and Designed to Combine the Advantages of Park and Avenue," January 18, 1875

To determine the extent of the monument ground, to so arrange its boundaries as to secure the necessary amplitude without over-much curtailing the space required for the adjoining Promenade; to devise its distinctive treatment is now a matter of primary importance. The position of the tomb and to some extent the dimensions and outlines of the monument should be secondary to it. It should, therefore, have immediate but deliberate and mature study.

Your board is at present employing Mr Vaux upon certain special problems of design.[9] No man is better qualified to advise the city upon such a question as that which has thus suddenly arisen and my counsel is that Mr Vaux be asked as soon as possible to give it careful consideration and furnish the board with a report of his conclusions.

Respectfully Yours

Fred[k] Law Olmsted.

The Hon J. D. Crimmins;
President of the Department of Public Parks.

The text presented here is from a letterpress copy of a transcription in a clerk's hand, signed in Olmsted's hand on the original: A1: 230–35, OAR/LC. After Ulysses S. Grant died on July 23, 1885, several cities were discussed as possible locations for his tomb. Mayor William Grace sent Grant's family a telegram on the afternoon of Grant's death offering to place his tomb in whichever city park they chose. Concerns were raised in New York regarding the potential effect of such a monument, and Olmsted received several letters from acquaintances who feared that Central Park would be chosen as the site. Grant's family did prefer Central Park at first, citing Grant's fondness for it; but after Grant's two sons, as well as Park Commissioner John D. Crimmins, Mayor Grace, and several others visited the potential sites on July 27, the family agreed that the north end of Riverside Park would be most appropriate.

The city began constructing a temporary vault, a cylindrical structure made of brick and bluestone, near the proposed site of the permanent tomb. Olmsted had developed the original plans for Riverside Park in 1873 with Vaux, and had worked on the project until 1878. At the request of Crimmins, Olmsted visited the temporary tomb on July 31. While at the site, Olmsted told a *New York Times* reporter, "In comparison with any other site that was available, I think the selection made is an admirable one. . . . My idea of a great monument, such as this will probably be, is that it should be altogether out of view of inharmonious objects surrounding it." Olmsted returned to Brookline and wrote the letter to Crimmins presented here, which Crimmins gave to the *New York Times* to publish (Joan Waugh, *U. S. Grant: American Hero, American Myth* [Chapel Hill, N.C., 2009], pp. 262, 271–74; Florence K. Howland to FLO, July 27, 1885; Howard A. Martin to FLO, July 27, 1885; "Riverside Park Chosen," *New York Times*, July 29, 1885, p. 1; DPP, *Minutes*, July 31, 1885, p. 240; "Good Progress on the Tomb," *New York Times*, Aug. 1, 1885, p. 1; DPP, *Minutes*, Aug. 7, 1885, p. 260; John D. Crimmins to FLO, Aug. 10, 1885; "Gen. Grant's Monument," *New York Times*, Aug. 8, 1885, p. 8).

1. John Daniel Crimmins (1844–1917) was a contractor and businessman in New York City and served as a park commissioner from 1883 to 1888. Most of his career was spent

working in the firm of his father, Thomas Crimmins, overseeing the construction of over 400 buildings, most of the elevated railway in the city, and much of the electrical wiring for the subway system. In addition to inviting Olmsted to consult on Grant's Tomb, Crimmins proposed that Olmsted be appointed Landscape Architect Advisory in 1887, and later that year he proposed that Olmsted be asked to prepare plans for Central, Morningside, Riverside, East River, and Mt. Morris parks. The park board voted against those proposals, but it did commission Olmsted and Vaux to revise their 1873 Morningside Park plans in August 1887. In the 1890s Crimmins commissioned the Olmsted firm to develop plans for his estate in Darien, Connecticut (*DAB*; DPP, *Minutes*, April 20, 1887, p. 515; ibid., June 22, 1887, p. 160; ibid., Aug. 24, 1887, p. 232; *Master List*, p. 155).

2. Olmsted conceived of what he describes here as the Riverside Terrace in 1873 in order to create a wide area along Riverside Avenue (also known as Riverside Drive) that would include paths and seating areas at the level of the carriage drive. Since Riverside Park sloped steeply down to the Hudson River in most locations, the terrace created more space to experience views and fresh air along the upper part of the park. Olmsted wrote in his 1873 plan, which was developed with Vaux, "The outer walk would generally follow a bold terrace, the slope below being planted with shrubs so arranged as to shut out of view the buildings and docks, and allow the eye to range over the expanse of the river beyond." In 1875 Olmsted added a riding-way between 104th and 120th streets. The site proposed for Grant's Tomb was a twenty-acre plateau located at what was then the northern terminus of the avenue and the park between 121st and 124th streets (*Report of the Landscape Architect on Riverside Park and Avenue*, March 29, 1873 [*Papers of FLO*, 6: 596–600]; FLO to Henry G. Stebbins, Jan. 15, 1875 [*Papers of FLO*, 7: 108–54]; "Plan for Riverside Avenue with Addition of Riding Way," March 15, 1875 [*Papers of FLO*, 7: 169]; FLO to Henry G. Stebbins, March 16, 1875; DPP, *Minutes*, March 17, 1875, pp. 571–72; Martha J. Lamb, "Riverside Park: The Fashionable Drive of the Future," *Manhattan*, July 1884, pp. 60–61; "Different Sites for the Tomb," *New York Times*, July 28, 1885, p. 1).

3. In 1865 William R. Martin proposed creating a park along the Hudson River above 59th Street, and in 1867 the state empowered the Central Park Board of Commissioners to acquire the necessary land for creating Riverside Park and Riverside Avenue (later Riverside Drive) above 72nd Street. The city acquired the land by 1872, and Olmsted and Vaux produced a plan for the park the following spring (William R. Martin, *The Growth of New York* [New York, 1865]; *Report of the Landscape Architect on Riverside Park and Avenue*, March 29, 1873 [*Papers of FLO*, 6: 596–600]).

4. The New York state legislature passed the act that Olmsted refers to on June 28, 1873. Since it involved the laying out of a park and the laying out of an avenue, it was not clear whether the Department of Public Parks or the Department of Public Works would be responsible for the project. Although Olmsted developed plans in 1873 for creating the terrace that would effectively merge Riverside Avenue and Riverside Park, little construction occurred over the next two years. In 1875 Olmsted presented a report to the Common Council describing what had been accomplished to that point and giving more details of the proposed Riverside Terrace. In June 1876, the Common Council gave the park department the authority to build the park and the avenue, and construction commenced. By 1880, while Riverside Park was still under construction, Riverside Avenue from 72nd to 127th streets had opened (*Report of the Landscape Architect on Riverside Park and Avenue*, March 29, 1873 [*Papers of FLO*, 6: 596–600]; FLO to Henry G. Stebbins, Jan. 15, 1875 [*Papers of FLO*, 7: 108–14]; FLO to Henry G. Stebbins, Dec. 3, 1875 [*Papers of FLO*, 7: 164–68]; "Riverside Improvement," *New York Times*, Dec. 28, 1878, p. 8; "Tearing Down Barricades," ibid., May 8, 1880, p. 8).

5. In 1875, the park commissioners were considering creating a promenade in the southern section of Central Park, where "drivers, riders, and walkers" could see and be seen. Olm-

sted suggested that the proposed terrace in Riverside Park would be a more appropriate space. He argued that the drives in Central Park had too many obstructions to allow for such a promenade, since carriages and other traffic would be crowded together in certain spots along the route. Olmsted was generally opposed to enlarging drives and walkways in Central Park because widening would require extensive grading of adjacent landscapes, affecting the character and purpose of the park. Olmsted preferred that Riverside Park act as the city's main promenade, and designed it as a landscape with enough width and length for different types of traffic and activity to be accommodated (FLO to Henry G. Stebbins, Dec. 3, 1875 [*Papers of FLO*, 7: 164–68]; see also FLO to Henry R. Beekman, June 10, 1886, below).

6. The proposed site of the monument, where it was later built, was between 121st and 124th streets in Riverside Park. The monument was designed by John H. Duncan and constructed over the following decade. The 150-foot tall rectangular structure was composed of granite and marble and opened on April 27, 1897 (J. Waugh, *U. S. Grant*, pp. 242–46, 283–99; M. A. Kellogg to FLO, July 7, 1885; "The Memorial Grounds," *New York Times*, Oct. 6, 1885, p. 5; "Mausoleum to Grant," ibid., March 14, 1897, p. 7; "Gen Grant's Body Removed," ibid., April 18, 1897).
7. A bronze statue of the Duke of Wellington on horseback was commissioned in 1840 and placed on the Triumphal Arch at Hyde Park Corner in 1846. In 1882, the Triumphal Arch was relocated a short distance to the top of Constitution Hill, the road that leads from Hyde Park to Buckingham Palace. At that time the Wellington statue was moved to Round Hill at Aldershot, a town forty miles southwest of London (Ben Weinreb and Christopher Hibbert, eds. *The London Encyclopedia* [New York, 1983], p. 822; Christopher Hibbert, *Wellington: A Personal History* [Reading, Mass., 1997], p. 377; F. Darrell Munsell, *The Victorian Controversy Surrounding the Wellington War Memorial: The Archduke of Hyde Park Corner* [Lewiston, N.Y., 1990], p. 104–6).
8. The Claremont section of Riverside Park was a plateau at about 122nd Street where the Claremont House had stood. In 1873 Olmsted had presented a version of his Riverside Park plan to the park commissioners at the Claremont House ("The Burial Place of General Grant," *Harper's Weekly*, Aug. 8, 1885, p. 519; DPP, *Minutes*, Oct. 30, 1873, p. 369).
9. In 1885 the park board had hired Vaux to work on individual commissions for the department. On August 17, a few days after this letter was written, the board asked Vaux and Samuel Parsons, Jr., to report on the "the proper boundaries of that portion of Riverside Park to be set apart for the Grant memorial grounds." They presented their report to the park board in October and the commissioners approved establishing the boundaries between 121st and 124th Streets (DPP, *Minutes*, June 19, 1885, p. 139; ibid., Aug. 17, 1885, p. 270; "The Memorial Grounds," *New York Times*, Oct. 6, 1885, p. 5).

To Percival Walter St. George[1]

8th Decr. 1885.

Percival W. St George Esqr
City Surveyor,
Montreal.
Dear Sir:

I have received your note of 5th inst. asking me as to works on Landscape Gardening showing designs in color for flower beds &c.

I am not accustomed to consider flower bedding of this kind that has been lately fashionable as a part of Landscape Gardening. On the contrary when such gardening comes in, as it may with great advantage in close association with buildings; in a small city square and other limited local conditions, Landscape Gardening goes out. It abolishes the fundamental purpose of landscape gardening. Landscape Gardening is a term first used by Repton[2] and in his voluminous works on the subject you will find this view everywhere sustained I believe.

It is equally so in the works of his opponent, Sir Uvedale Price.[3] This may {. . .} to you as it is to most intelligent students of the subject merely a verbal question, but the compression of the purpose of evocative and spectacular gardening with that of landscape gardening has been until recently so common in practice and has been, and yet generally is, so wasteful and unhappy in its results that you will excuse my {*reference*} to it, more especially as you have I believe, the charge of the grandest occasion for *exclusive* landscape gardening possessed by any city in the world. As to that, (flower gardening for the {. . .}), there are two capital books, of which I think that I left copies in your office, years ago. Robinson's Alpine Flowers & Robinson's Wild Garden, both published by Murrays in several successive editions.[4] Capital {. . .} for {. . .} of the proper function of flower gardening in landscape works.

As to flower gardening for formal, intramural public grounds, I am sorry to say I know of nothing giving what you ask for; nothing giving patterns of any value. Robinson's Gleanings from French Gardens & Robinson's Parks and Gardens of Paris are instructive inexpensive books.[5] Much more so, however, Andre's *L'Art des Jardins*, but it costs I think about $12 & would probably have to be ordered from Paris. Andre was the designer of the best garden grounds of Paris. (This book contains a grotesque blunder about Mt. Royal).[6] There is another book on the same subject, by Alphand,[7] which I believe does contain such patterns and particulars as you want, but its publication price was about $200, and it is now rare, and is really not nearly as instructive a book as Andre's.

I will make inquiries of Prof^r^ Sargent,[8] who has, I suppose the best private library of books relating to gardening in this country, and if I hear of anything that would serve you, will write again.

Yours Very Truly

Fred[k] Law Olmsted.

The text presented here is from a letterpress copy of a handwritten letter signed on the original in Olmsted's hand: A1: 256–58, OAR/LC.

1. Percival Walter St. George (1849–1923) was educated at the University of Edinburgh and came to Canada in 1866, where he first began working as a surveyor and assistant engineer for the Nova Scotia Railway and the Intercolonial Railway. He was appointed Montreal's deputy city surveyor in 1876 and served until 1882. St. George served as the Montreal city surveyor between 1883 and 1900, and was also a consulting engineer. Much of his work was devoted to instituting a flood protection plan for the city. Olmsted and St. George probably met in the late 1870s, when Olmsted was designing Mount Royal Park (Rev. J. Douglas Borthwick, LL.D., *History and Biographical Gazetteer of Montreal to the Year 1892* [Montreal, 1892], p. 224; Henry James Morgan, ed., *The Canadian Men and Woman of the Time* [Toronto, 1912], p. 989; Frederick Law Olmsted, *Mount Royal. Montreal*, 1881 [*Papers of FLO*, SS1: 350–418]).
2. Humphry Repton (1752–1818), English landscape designer who wrote textbooks on the theory and practice of landscape gardening, including *Sketches and Hints of Landscape Gardening* (1794), *Observations on the Theory and Practice of Landscape Gardening* (1803), and *Fragments on the Theory and Practice of Landscape Gardening* (1816) (*DNB*; see also FLO to Charles Eliot, Feb. 25, 1886, below).
3. Sir Uvedale Price (1747–1829), English landscape designer and landscape theorist. A friend of Humphry Repton, the two became antagonists during debates over landscape design theory in the 1790s. Price advocated the "Picturesque" over the smooth and "insipid" beauty of, for example, Lancelot (Capability) Brown's parks. Repton was a self-proclaimed successor to Brown, and became the subject of criticism by Price (*DNB*; Stephen Daniels, *Humphry Repton and the Geography of Georgian England* [New Haven, Conn., 1999], pp. 122–26; for Olmsted's views on this subject, see also Frederick Law Olmsted, "Trees in Streets and in Parks," Sept. 1882, above; *Papers of FLO*, 6: 478, n. 4 and n. 5).
4. William Robinson (1838–1935), the Irish horticulturalist and author. Olmsted particularly admired Robinson's *The Wild Garden* (1870) and *Alpine Flowers for English Gardens* (1870) (*DNB*).
5. William Robinson, *Gleanings from French Gardens: Comprising an Account of Such Features of French Horticulture as are Most Worthy of Adoption in British Gardens (London, 1868)*; and *The Parks and Gardens of Paris Considered in Relation to the Wants of Other Cities and of Public and Private Gardens; Being Notes on a Study of Paris Gardens* (London, 1869).
6. Édouard André (1840–1911) worked with Jean-Charles-Adolphe Alphand and Jean-Pierre Barillet-Deschamps, as Principal Gardener of the city of Paris, and over the years he and Olmsted had become friends. In his *L'Art des Jardins* (1879), a book that Olmsted greatly admired, André comments favorably on the parks Olmsted and Vaux designed. However, he mistakenly attributes the design of Mount Royal Park in Montreal to both Olmsted and Vaux, when in fact it was one of the first large commissions Olmsted took

on independently (Patrick Taylor, ed., *The Oxford Companion to the Garden* [London, 2006], p. 12; "Édouard André," the *Garden: An Illustrated Weekly*, July 6, 1895, pp. 5–6; Édouard André, *L'Art des Jardins* [Paris, 1879], pp. 384, 868; see also FLO to Charles Eliot, Feb. 25, 1886, below).

7. Jean-Charles-Adolphe Alphand (1817–1891), chief engineer in the Services des Promenades et Plantations between 1855 and 1870. He designed many of the parks, boulevards, and public spaces for the redevelopment of Paris. He published *Les Promenades de Paris* (Paris, 1867–73), which is a graphic record of that work, and wrote *L'Art des Jardins* (Paris, 1886) with Baron Ernouf (P. Taylor, ed., *The Oxford Companion to the Garden*, p. 8).
8. Charles Sprague Sargent (1841–1927), Olmsted's longtime colleague, was a noted horticulturist and author, and the director of the Arnold Arboretum for over fifty years. He designed the extensive grounds of his home in Brookline, Holm Lea, which was noted for its horticultural excellence. In 1878, he and Olmsted began collaborating on the design of the Arnold Arboretum in Boston, an important project of Olmsted's and a lifelong endeavor for Sargent. Olmsted and Sargent also collaborated in 1879 when Olmsted asked for advice on what plants would survive the conditions of the Back Bay Fens. As a Brookline park commissioner, Sargent influenced the plans for the Muddy River Improvement, particularly the planting on the Brookline side of the park. In the late 1880s, Sargent, Olmsted, and other interested parties together planned and financed a new periodical devoted to landscape architecture, forestry, and related endeavors, *Garden and Forest*. It was established in 1888 with Sargent serving as "conductor," or managing editor. Sargent also served as Professor of Arboriculture at Harvard from 1879 until his death, and he was a principal figure in forest research and conservation. He was the author of a number of important scientific studies and books, particularly the influential *Silva of North America* (1891–1902) (*DAB*; S. B. Sutton, *Charles Sprague Sargent and the Arnold Arboretum* [Cambridge, Mass., 1970], pp. 3–21; 53–55; 131–32; FLO to Charles Sprague Sargent, July 8, 1874 [*Papers of FLO*, 7: 68–69]; FLO to Charles Sprague Sargent, Jan. 29, 1879 [*Papers of FLO*, 7: 388–90]).

CHAPTER IV

FEBRUARY 1886–AUGUST 1886

This chapter contains some of Olmsted's most important personal correspondence from the 1880s. Three letters to Charles Eliot, who was then traveling in Europe, compare American and European landscape gardening, suggest places that Eliot should visit, and inform him on current commissions. Three letters to the art and architecture critic Mariana Griswold Van Rensselaer discuss the death of Olmsted's close friend H. H. Richardson and a biography of Richardson that she had recently begun to write.

Progress is being made on the U.S. Capitol building at this point, and Congress had recently approved appropriations for building the west terrace Olmsted designed for the building, but the details of the design were still being discussed. Olmsted's letter to Architect of the Capitol Edward Clark concerns a fountain proposed between the stairs of the terrace, and the letter to Senator William B. Allison requests that the Senate reconsider its recommendation to place windows in the outer walls of the terrace. Two letters that relate to school campus designs are to headmasters James Cameron MacKenzie of Lawrenceville and Endicott Peabody of Groton. Regarding Boston parks, Olmsted's letter to F. L. Temple deals with the failure of plantings at the Beacon Street entrance of the Back Bay Fens. His letter to sculptor Anne Whitney provides suggestions for placing her statue of Leif Ericsson on Commonwealth Avenue. The document addressed to park commissioner Henry R. Beekman contains a proposal for developing revised plans for several New York City parks in collaboration with Calvert Vaux. The letter to William E. Dorsheimer relates to Olmsted's desire to develop a plan for the recently-authorized Niagara Reservation. The letter to George W. Vanderbilt about the Vanderbilt Mausoleum marks the beginning of several commissions that Olmsted undertook for the Vanderbilt family.

To James Cameron Mackenzie

6th Feby, 1886.

My Dear Doctor,

We have been for some time studying a scheme for the planting of your school property with the idea that a purpose of instruction might be combined with that of making the place pleasant. We are now so far {*advanced*} with this study that I can say that it appears feasible to have upon the property a complete collection of all species of trees that it is known can be successfully cultivated in Central New Jersey. The idea we had is that aside from any value such a collection would have with reference to direct scholastic instruction, as to which it would serve as a cabinet library[1] and museum of Botany and Dendrology, if each tree shd be conspicuously labeled with common & scientific name, native country &c. &c. boys would gradually, during the stay with you, absorb, as from object lessons, a pool of information of a {*kind*} that is to be soon in rapidly growing demand.

To work out the project to its last details, find the trees and have them properly planted, catalogued, labeled &c. will be a good deal of trouble, and it will probably cost a little more than to plant the ground simply with reference to scenery.[2] I cannot speak very definitely about it at the present stage but before entering upon another, I should like to know how the idea strikes you — to know if you would think it likely to be acceptable to the Trustees, and — in short worth the trouble.

Very Truly Yours

Fred^k Law Olmsted.

Planting at Lawrenceville School.[3]

A clipped hedge to be planted along each terrace to give an effect similar to that of a parapet.

A clipped hedge to {*run*} from the street near the old dormitory along the new road in front of the masters' houses, to associate them together in appearance and to give them a somewhat retired domestic effect. Rhododendrons and other handsome shrubs to be planted near the houses to give a richly {*furnished*} effect.

A few large growing native or foreign but not strange looking trees to diversify the lawn and compose with the houses.

A few groves for the same purpose and a general mixed border of trees to form the background for the buildings and local scenery.

The whole to form an arboretum collection but all the strange or peculiar and the less desirable trees to be kept in the background.

Thin pass to be preserved from each house to every other as far as practicable.

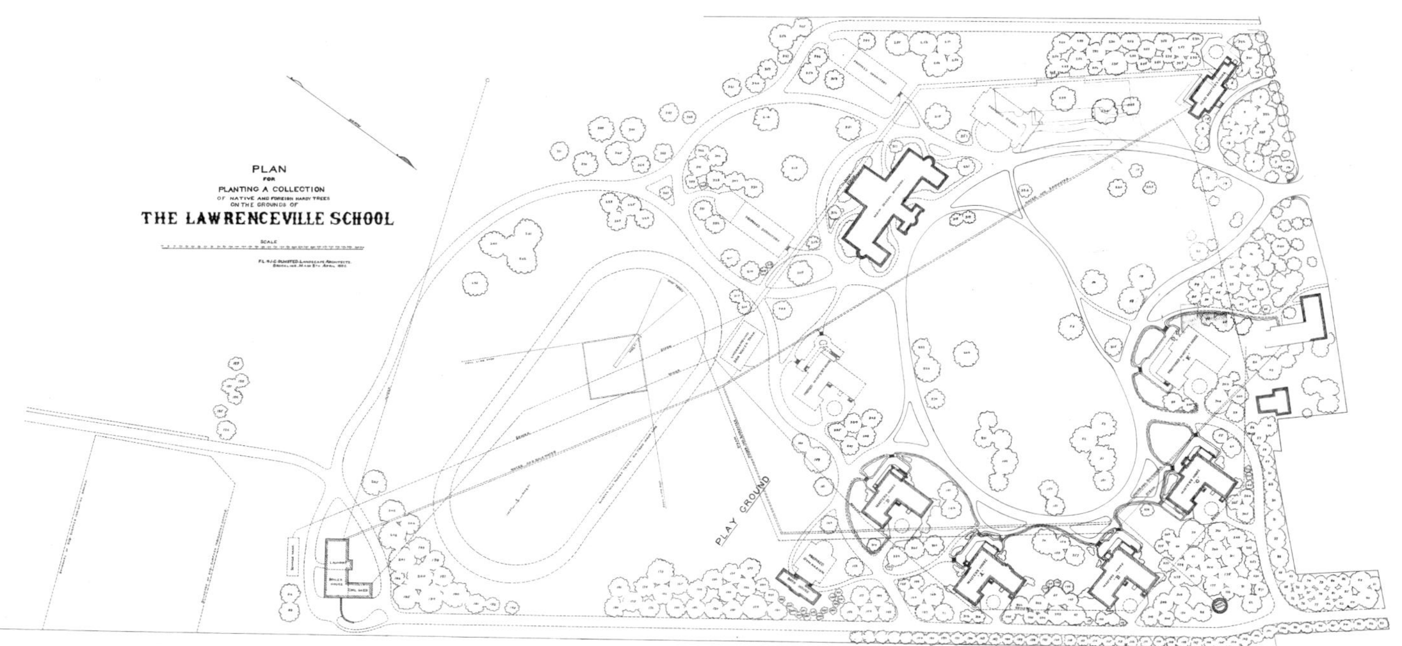

"Plan for Planting a Collection of Native and Foreign Hardy Trees on the Grounds of the Lawrenceville School," April 8, 1886

The text presented here is from a letterpress copy of a handwritten letter signed on the original in Olmsted's hand: A1: 278–79, OAR/LC. Olmsted had worked on the design of the Lawrenceville School campus since 1883. In 1884 the school had reopened with new central classroom buildings and the six "masters' houses" that Olmsted had arranged around a central oval lawn. Peabody and Stearns were the architects, and Olmsted and J. J. R. Croes designed innovative drainage, sewerage, and heating systems for the campus (Oscar Fay Adams, *Some Famous American Schools* [Boston, 1903], pp. 133–34; FLO to James Cameron Mackenzie, May 21, 1883, above).

1. Olmsted makes reference to the practice at the time of displaying items of scholarly merit in a cabinet space (i.e., a piece of furniture or small room) (*OED*).
2. Through the summer and fall of 1886 Olmsted produced plans for planting the Lawrenceville School grounds as an arboretum. According to Olmsted's original planting lists, in November, 371 trees were sent from the Arnold Arboretum to be planted at Lawrenceville. About thirty-five of the original trees from the 1886 arboretum plantation survive today on the school's grounds (FLO and JCO to Hugh H. Hamill, July 13, 1886, A1: 375, OAR/LC; FLO and JCO to Mr. Warren, July 19, 1886, A1: 377, OAR/LC; FLO and JCO to Charles E. Green, Nov. 16, 1886, A1: 545, OAR/LC; "List of Trees for Lawrenceville School," [Dec. 1, 1886], A1: 559–75, OAR/LC; Elaine Mills, *The Trees of Lawrenceville, The Lawrenceville School* (pamphlet) [Lawrenceville, N.J., 2009]; plan 52-30, NPS/FLOHS).
3. This text appears on a page attached to the original letter in FLO Papers/LC. It is uncertain whether it was sent with the letter to Mackenzie.

To Edward Clark

15th Feby 1886.

Dear Mr Clark;

Since our conversation last spring with Senator Morrill about the stair cases I have given much study to the matter and have made and discarded several drawings. I recognized the force of his objections to the place as it stood but have not been able to reconcile myself to his proposition of a cascade.[1] It seems to me that any attainable moderate stream of water seen in the midst of such great architectural masses would be trivial and wanting in scale and dignity. It is difficult to realize how little show a large stream of water makes when moving with a rapid descent.

On the other hand, if this objection could be removed by an adequate body of water, I am afraid that the result would be to lessen the impression of solidity and firm footing so desirable to be sustained at the base of so vast a pile. I have sent you a drawing showing a design which satisfies me better than anything before devised.

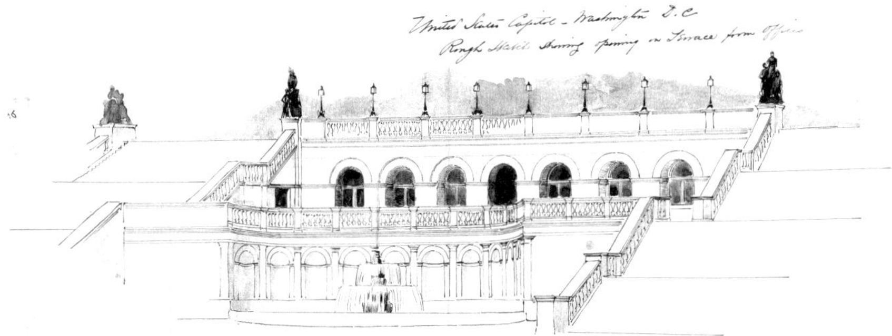

"UNITED STATES CAPITOL-WASHINGTON D. C., ROUGH SKETCH SHOWING OPENING ON TERRACE FROM OFFICES," N.D.

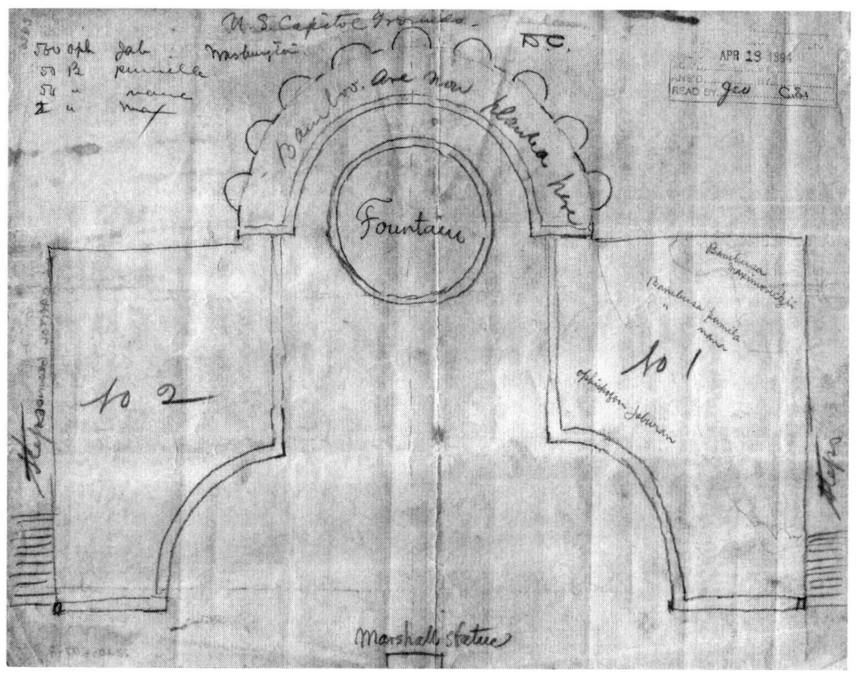

"U.S. CAPITOL GROUNDS, WASHINGTON D.C.," SKETCH OF TERRACE WITH FOUNTAIN, N.D.

The drawing does not show fairly what I consider the most important modification of the general design but with a little consideration you will realize it. I mean that there is more unity between the centre parts of the terrace and the flanks, and the centre is firmer and more self-supportive. The terrace is simpler, more massive, more classic, perhaps.

The greater strength given the main wall, justifies, I hope, the variation from the original idea of the fountains between the staircases, by which Senator Morrill's objection to the high and somewhat blank wall of the lower terrace is overcome and something gained of the sparkle of water that he desired.

The alcoves are designed to be of rough marble; their walls to be covered with evergreen creepers and plants in vases to be set in them.

As shown in the drawing some parts of this work would, it strikes me now, seem a little thin. Of course, this and probably other objections to be made to details may be remedied.

Please consult with Senator Morrill about it.

I will come on at short notice whenever you think it desirable.

Yours Very Truly

Fred[k] LawOlmsted.

The text presented here is from a letterpress copy of a handwritten letter signed on the original in Olmsted's hand: A1: 282–84, OAR/LC. Olmsted's involvement with the Capitol grounds project changed in the mid-1880s. In March 1883 several members of Congress questioned whether he was involved enough in the construction of the Capitol grounds to justify his salary, but no changes to his salary were made at the time. In December 1884, after Senator Morrill's Committee on Public Buildings and Grounds had helped persuade Congress to fund construction of the terraces, Olmsted wrote a letter of resignation to Senator William Mahone, stating that the work on the Capitol grounds was nearly complete except for the terraces and that the "direction of the terrace-work would lie more fittingly with the Architect of the Capitol." At the time, Edward Clark's position was also being challenged. In December 1884, three bills were introduced in Congress that were intended to reorganize the Architect of the Capitol's office and to replace Clark. The bills failed and he remained the Architect of the Capitol.

Despite his "resignation," after 1884 Olmsted continued to advise on the completion of the terraces as well the rest of the grounds, but at an annual fee that was reduced to five hundred dollars from his previous annual payment of two thousand dollars. At the time Olmsted wrote this letter, construction of the north and south terraces was well under way, and the foundation for the west terrace was being laid. Olmsted continued his involvement in the Capitol grounds project until its completion in 1891 (FLO to JCO, Dec. 6, 1884, above; FLO to William Mahone, Dec. 9, 1884; FLO to Edward Clark, Jan. 15, 1885; Edward Clark to FLO, Jan. 17, 1885; FLO to William Hammond Hall, March 28, 1874 [*Papers of FLO*, 7: 53–55]; William C. Allen, *History of the United States Capitol, A Chronicle of Design, Construction, and Politics* [Washington, D.C., 2001], p. 348, 354–55; Glenn Brown, *Documentary History of the Construction and Development of the United States Capitol Building and Grounds* [Washington, D.C., 1904], pp. 1156–59, 1219–20; 1237–38; *Annual Reports of the Architect of the United States Capitol* [Washington, D.C., 1875–1886]; see also Frederick Law Olmsted, *Annual Report of the Architect of the United States Capitol*, 1882, above; Frederick Law Olmsted, *Annual Report of the Architect of the United States Capitol*, July 1, 1883, above; FLO to Edward Clark, Feb. 11, 1889, below).

1. Senator Morrill had written to Olmsted on the need to redesign the space between the staircases of the west terrace. The original design for the upper west terrace had been for a quadrangular area with arched openings that led into a covered "crypt" that acted as a vestibule for adjacent offices. Just below, the lower west terrace had a high and featureless outer wall. The crypt had originally been designed with heavy piers to support a proposed library extension of the Capitol building above it, but with support growing to build a new Library of Congress at an independent site (which would be authorized by Congress on April 15, 1886), a revision of the terrace design was timely. Morrill suggested that the west terrace could now include a large fountain between the staircases. Olmsted characterized Morrill's idea for the fountain as "not a vertical jet, but a horizontal discharge (as in the Fountain of Trevi)" (W. C. Allen, *History of the United States Capitol*, p. 354–57; FLO to Edward Clark, May 30, 1885, AOC).

To Charles Eliot[1]

Brookline, Mass. 25th Feby. 1886.

My Dear Eliot,

Although I have been so long acoming to the point of saying so I enjoyed your letter from London exceedingly. I thought you had been both wise and fortunate in your proceedings and your comments on what you saw were most interesting.[2] I agreed with you at all points, though I should say with regard to Andre's work at Liverpool[3] I did no more than glance at it in a rainy day — not even leaving the cab that I remember — and it seemed to me that whatever the

Charles Eliot

HENRY SARGENT CODMAN

plan, it had been so perfunctorily carried out, as if by a commercial contractor, sticking closely to the letter of his specifications, and with such mean, mechanical and stinted detail that one could hardly judge what the designer had had in view.

I was particularly interested in what you said of the manner in which you found that large business in Landscape Gardening was conducted in London, or from London,[4] and I hope that during the summer you will be able to visit several of the works so managed, follow out details and judge how it works out from seeing also some finished results. The organization would seem to compare with Bowditch's[5] and I suppose that Andre has generally proceeded in the same way. I should think it difficult to avoid a good deal of crudity in the results, such as you see in some of Andre's public work even in Paris. I mean engineer's slopes and a prosaic quality in details which he accounted for by saying that his plans had been murdered by the engineers in superintendence.

We have had a call from a man who has been a curator of an English Botanic Garden and designer of a considerable public work. He had a slight reserved testimonial indicating that he had published something that did not displease Ruskin and altogether seemed to have been a man of some professional standing.[6] Assuming "a certain free masonry of our craft" he astonished us by the coolness and freedom with which he referred to alledged practices in it. No man, in his opinion, ever acquired a notable position or earned a decent living thro' Landscape Gardening except by taking advantage of the ignorance and credulity of his client. Nothing could be done directly by what we should regard as professional work. The making of plans was but the stepping stone to all sorts of underhanded commissions & profits through connivance or covert partnerships

PHOTOGRAPHS OF HUMPHRY REPTON'S COTTAGE AT HARE STREET, NEAR ROMFORD, ESSEX, TAKEN BY CHARLES ELIOT IN 1886 AND PUBLISHED IN *LANDSCAPE ARCHITECTURE, A QUARTERLY MAGAZINE*, VOL. 8, OCTOBER 1917–JULY 1918

with contractors, or by directly taking contracts to execute plans, being your own superintendent. He advised us with which of the large nurserymen profitable arrangements could best be made with and offered to make arrangements by which we could be sure of receiving a handsome percentage on all orders that we could influence. He was quite sure that all the leading men of the profession in

SKETCH OF VIEW FROM HUMPHRY REPTON'S COTTAGE FROM *FRAGMENTS ON THE THEORY AND PRACTICE OF LANDSCAPE GARDENING* BY HUMPHRY REPTON (1816)

England pursued his methods. All were tradesmen and contractors and brokers under the disguise of professional men. He could not believe that we were not. We thought he came out to get the Superintendence of the "Niagara Park" and that he meant to remain here at any rate.

My delay in writing you has happened mainly because when your letter came I was expecting to submit the Franklin (West Roxbury Park) and thought you would like to have the result. For various reasons it was thought best to postpone the delivery of it from week to week until the first of Feby. The Board and the Mayor then took a week or two to consider it and since its acceptance we have been waiting upon the lithographers. In a day or two we shall be able to send you a pamphlet about it.[7] The plan is accepted without a murmur but the fact is neither the Commissioners nor the public look at it or take any intelligent interest in it. We are in hopes that the legislature may be induced to authorize a fifty years loan for the parks. You will see that my paper is indirectly all an argument for its doing so. The Mayor and Commissioners have agreed to urge it. If they fail the outlook is not bright.[8]

I don't think that we have any new work in the office since you left. Harry Codman[9] is still with us and Coolidge[10] comes in twice a week. You will have heard of the great flood.[11] The Back Bay and Muddy River arrangements worked smoothly and with perfect success, the water never rising more than three feet and normal conditions returning without the slightest apparent damage.

I go to Washington tonight to try to persuade Congress not to order the terrace to be furnished with windows with a view to pleasant rooms for Committees looking out on the grounds — a fearful botching which Clark advises me they have determined on.[12]

If you are still to go to Venice, I hope you will have read Howell's Venetian Days. Somewhere in it he refers to old villas, still occupied by Venetians in summer, on the banks of the Po in a way that led me to think that they would be well worth visiting.[13]

When you are in England, again, if you can find the village of Hare Street and that it is not much out of the way, you might like to see the present condition of the cottage and its garden that Repton says, at the close of his book, has been the most interesting place in the world to him.[14] The house in which he died a few months later. If there happens to be a local photographer there I shall be glad if you can order a picture of it taken for me.

All the shop and the family send Greetings.

Yours Very Truly,

Fred[k] Law Olmsted.

The text presented here is signed letter in Olmsted's hand. Charles Eliot was an apprentice at Fairsted from 1883 to the fall of 1885. He then traveled in the United States and Europe for the purpose of furthering his education as a landscape architect. He visited major parks, gardens, and nurseries across Britain and Europe, and he described his experiences in letters to his family, to Olmsted, to John C. Olmsted, and to Henry Sargent Codman. Eliot returned in the winter of 1886 (Charles W. Eliot, *Charles Eliot, Landscape Architect* [Boston, 1902], pp. 50–203; see FLO to Charles Eliot, March 4, 1886, below; FLO to Charles Eliot, July 20, 1886, below; FLO to Charles Eliot, Oct. 28, 1886, below).

1. Charles Eliot (1859–1897), landscape architect, was the son of Charles W. Eliot, President of Harvard University from 1869 to 1909. He graduated from Harvard in 1882 and with his father devised a program of graduate education in landscape architecture. He began with courses at Harvard's Bussey Institution, which specialized in agricultural and horticultural studies. In the spring of 1883 his uncle, the architect Robert S. Peabody, introduced him to Olmsted, and Eliot began an apprenticeship at Fairsted soon thereafter. His first task was accompanying Olmsted to North Easton, Massachusetts. Over the next two years Eliot worked as a draftsman and traveled with Olmsted to many of the firm's project sites, including Easton's Beach in Rhode Island, Cushing's Island in Maine, the Lawrenceville School in New Jersey, and the Capitol grounds in Washington, D.C. He also worked on the Brookline subdivision plans, the Boston parks, plans for parks in Bridgeport and New London, Connecticut, and for Belle Isle in Detroit. Eliot took a particular interest in the firm's public park work.

   In 1885 Eliot traveled in the United States and Europe, where he visited cities, parks, and gardens through the end of 1886. When he returned home he declined to take a position at Fairsted and instead established his own practice as a landscape architect in Boston. Over the next ten years he designed a number of parks and residences. His greatest achievement during this period was his advocacy of The Trustees of Reservations, which was created in 1891, and for the Metropolitan Park Commission, established the following year. As the consulting landscape architect of the Metropolitan Park Commission, Eliot planned and designed an unprecedented regional system of landscape reservations around Boston in the 1890s. In 1893, following the death of Henry Sargent Codman, a partner in the Olmsted firm since 1889, Eliot accepted a second offer from the Olmsteds and became a partner that March. The firm was renamed Olmsted, Olmsted, and Eliot (the other partners were Olmsted and John C. Olmsted). Over the next four years Eliot worked on many of the office's projects, including the Metropolitan Park Commission work that he brought with him.

In March of 1897, Charles Eliot died of meningitis at the age of thirty-eight. Since Olmsted had ceased active practice with the firm in 1895, John C. Olmsted and Frederick Law Olmsted, Jr., then reorganized the firm, which by 1898 was known as Olmsted Brothers, the name it would keep until 1961 (C. W. Eliot, *Charles Eliot*, pp. 32–49; 316–57; *DAB*; Charles Eliot to Roland Thaxter, May 15, 1882, courtesy of Alexander Yale Goriansky; Charles Eliot Diary, May 6, 1883, p. 1, FLLHU; Charles Eliot to Grace Hopkinson Eliot, summer, 1884; Charles Eliot, Diary, 1885, courtesy of Alexander Yale Goriansky; Charles Eliot, Diary, 1884, FLLHU; FLO to Edward Mott Moore, Aug. 5, 1888, below; Karl Haglund, *Inventing the Charles River* [Cambridge, Mass., 2003], pp. 117–51; *Master List*, pp. 311–13).

2. In Eliot's letter, he described his travels through England late in 1885, shortly after beginning his European travels. Arriving at Liverpool, he saw and commented favorably on Birkenhead Park and Prince's Park, while he strongly criticized the design of Sefton Park. He also reported on his visits to Hampstead Heath, Richmond Park, Epping Forest, and Hampton Court, as well as his meeting with William Robinson and other landscape gardeners and architects (Charles Eliot to FLO, Dec. 19, 1885).
3. In 1867 Édouard André and architect Lewis Hornblower won first prize for their design of the 370-acre Sefton Park, which opened in Liverpool in 1872. Eliot did not admire the park: "André's *Sefton Park* fairly dumbfounded me. I liked neither the tiresome regularity of the road curves—(a continuity of radical curvature maintained in many cases regardless of topography), nor the foot paths that meander aimlessly in open greensward, nor the plantations invariably gathered close about the meetings or crossings of roads. Indeed I came across more monstrosities both in design and execution than I have ever yet seen in one place" (Hazel Conway, *People's Parks: The Design and Development of Victorian Parks in Britain* [New York, 1991], pp. 96–100; Charles Eliot to FLO, Dec. 19, 1885).
4. Eliot reported that he had visited landscape gardener Henry Ernest Milner and learned about "the methods of work and of charging in vogue here. *Surveyors* and also *Foremen*—beside draughtsmen—are regular members of the man's staff—he has works in progress in Belgium, France, & Sweden as well as in Gr. Britain—the trained foremen—he has 50 of these on his staff—are sent out with instructions and working plans and have sole command of carrying out the accepted design" (*DNB*; Charles Eliot to FLO, Dec. 19, 1885; see also FLO to Charles Eliot, March 4, 1886, below).
5. Ernest William Bowditch (1850–1918) was a civil engineer based in Brookline. He laid out paths and drives at Mount Auburn Cemetery in 1870 and opened his own office the next year. He worked for the Fairsted office on a number of projects as a draftsman and surveyor, and also consulted with prominent architects in the region, including H. H. Richardson and Peabody and Stearns (Kara Hamley O'Donnell, "Ernest W. Bowditch," in Charles A. Birnbaum and Robin Karson, eds., *Pioneers of American Landscape Design* [New York, 2000], pp. 32–35).

6. Olmsted is referring to Joseph Forsyth Johnson (1840?–1906), an English landscape gardener who had worked in England, Ireland, and Russia, and had worked as curator of the Royal Botanic Garden in Belfast. He came to America in 1886 and briefly served as superintendent of horticulture for Brooklyn's parks department. He had a successful career as a landscape gardener in the United States, designing Latta Park in Charlotte, North Carolina, and Inman and Piedmont Parks in Atlanta, Georgia. The publication Olmsted refers to is probably Johnson's *The Natural Principle of Landscape Gardening: Or the Adornment of Land for Perpetual Beauty* (1874) ("Obituary: Joseph Forsyth Johnson," *Gardening*, Aug. 1, 1906, p. 349; Ray Desmond and Christine Ellwood, eds., *Dictionary of British and Irish Botanists and Horticulturists* [London, 1994], p. 386; "Park Topics," *Brooklyn Eagle*, Feb. 2, 1887, p. 4; see also FLO to Calvert Vaux, July 9, 1887, below).
7. See Frederick Law Olmsted, "Notes on the Plan of Franklin Park and Related Matters," 1886 (*Papers of FLO*, SS1: 460–534).
8. On February 10, 1886, the Boston park commissioners officially adopted Olmsted's Franklin Park plan and asked him to prepare "Notes on the Plan of Franklin Park and Related Matters" for publication. The legislature passed a bill later in 1886 authorizing $2.5 million in bonds to pay for constructing Boston parks. Boston's Board of Aldermen blocked the funds until January 1887 (Cynthia Zaitzevsky, *Frederick Law Olmsted and the Boston Park System* (Cambridge, Mass., 1982), pp. 68–69; FLO to Edward P. Wilbur, April 29, 1886, below; see also FLO to Charles Eliot, July 20, 1886, n. 7, below).
9. Henry (Harry) Sargent Codman (1864–1893), the nephew of Charles Sprague Sargent, graduated from the Massachusetts Institute of Technology in 1884 and entered Olmsted's firm as an apprentice that year. He traveled with Olmsted, Francis Amasa Walker, and Frederick Law Olmsted, Jr., to California in August 1886 to meet with Leland Stanford and begin plans for the Stanford campus, a project for which Codman later took on a principal role. In 1887 he went abroad with his uncle Charles Sprague Sargent to study gardens and plant collections in Europe. He stayed in Paris for almost two years, working with Édouard André, and he then traveled along the African coast. After his return to the Olmsted firm in 1889, Codman was made a partner and the firm was renamed F. L. Olmsted and Company. Codman had a significant role in many of the office's most important projects, including Stanford University, Perry Park, and Biltmore. In Chicago, Codman was the firm's principal designer and representative for planning the grounds of the World's Columbian Exposition. In 1890, Olmsted noted that with John C. Olmsted and Codman working with him, his office "is much better equipped and has more momentum than ever before."

   Codman died unexpectedly in Chicago in January 1893 while recovering from an appendectomy. He was twenty-nine years old. Olmsted considered Codman a valuable partner and after Codman's death wrote, "I am one standing on a wreck and can hardly see when we shall get afloat again." When Charles Eliot rejoined the firm as a partner in March 1893, Olmsted wrote that, at least initially, Eliot had been unable to "fill Codman's place." Charles Sprague Sargent eulogized his nephew in *Garden and Forest* stating, "No man at his age had ever accomplished more in his profession." Codman was extremely well read and his collection of books on landscape architecture was one of the largest in the nation. He published an index of his works in *Garden and Forest*, and his parents donated his collection to the Boston Public Library in 1897 ("Henry Sargent Codman," *Garden and Forest*, Jan., 18, 1893, p. 36; Henry Sargent Codman, "Bibliography," ibid., March 12, 1890, pp. 131–35; "Books on Landscape Architecture," *Boston Daily Globe*, July 13, 1897, p. 12; FLO to Frederick Law Olmsted, Jr., Aug. 1, 1895; FLO to Leland Stanford, Aug. 17, 1889, A5: 154–56, OAR/LC; FLO to Charles McNamee, April 5, 1890, A7: 159, OAR/LC; FLO to Charles A. Roberts, Oct. 5, 1889, below; FLO to Charles Loring Brace, Jan. 18, 1890, below; "Henry Sargent Codman," *New-York Tribune*, Jan. 15, 1893, p. 3; FLO to Gifford Pinchot, Jan. 19, 1893; FLO to Frederick J. Kingsbury, Sept. 6, 1893; *FLO, A Biography*, pp. 393, 406, 407, 412, 425–30, 445).

10. David Hill Coolidge, Jr. (b. 1863), was employed full-time at the Olmsted firm beginning in 1888, after graduating from the Bussey Institute at Harvard University. He worked there until 1893, when he left and started his own firm, Coolidge and Titus. He was the brother of architect Charles Allerton Coolidge, of Shepley, Rutan, and Coolidge (*Harvard College Class of 1886* [New York, 1906], p. 43; *Fortieth Anniversary Report of the Secretary of the Class of 1881 of Harvard College* [Cambridge, Mass., 1921], p. 42; Charles Eliot Diary, Jan. 15, 1885, courtesy of Alexander Yale Goriansky; see also FLO to Charles A. Coolidge, May 22, 1887, below).
11. The Roxbury flood of February 1886 covered an area from Roxbury Street north to Camden Street, and west from Washington Street to the Fenway. The Back Bay Fens project was designed to allow waters from the Stony Brook, during flood events, to overflow into the Fens basin, where they collected and later flowed into the Charles River. During the February 1886 flood, the Fens basin successfully retained this increased level of water, as Olmsted observes here. Flooding in nearby neighborhoods occurred anyway, however, because the storm drains and conduits designed to divert the rest of the waters of the Stony Brook and the Muddy River directly into the Charles were overwhelmed ("Stubborn Waters," *Boston Daily Advertiser*, Feb. 15, 1886, p. 1; "Stony Brook has Cost Boston Much Over $1,300,000," ibid., Oct. 26, 1894, p. 2; *Congregationalist*, Feb. 18, 1886, p. 8; C. Zaitzevsky, *The Boston Park System*, pp. 154–55; FLO to the Board of Commissioners of the Department of Parks of the City of Boston, Jan. 26, 1880 [*Papers of FLO*, 7: 451–63]; E. W. Howe, "The Back Bay Park, Boston, Speech Read Before the Boston Society of Civil Engineers, March 16, 1881," *Proceedings of the American Society of Civil Engineers*, Jan.–Dec. 1881 [New York, 1881]; Charles Eliot Diary, Dec. 2, 1883, pp. 80–81, FLLHU; City of Boston Department of Parks, *Twelfth Annual Report of the Board of Commissioners for the Year 1886* [Boston, 1887], p. 29).
12. Olmsted had recently received a letter from the Chair of the Committee on Public Buildings and Grounds asking him to add windows to his plan for the outer wall of the lower portion of the U.S. Capitol's west terrace (Chairman, Committee on Public Buildings and Grounds to FLO, Feb. 15, 1886, AOC; see also FLO to William B. Allison, July 23, 1886, below).
13. William Dean Howells (1837–1920) was an American novelist and journalist who for a short time was employed at the *Nation*, which Olmsted had edited in the 1850s. Howells left the *Nation* after only a few months in order to edit the *Atlantic Monthly*. *Venetian Life* (1866) was one of Howells's travel books, which also included *Italian Journeys* (1874), which was another favorite of Olmsted's. In *Venetian Life*, Howells describes the patrician villas that were the scenes of their *villegiatura*. While he does not refer explicitly to villas on the Po River, he describes villas "on the banks of the Brenta," a tributary of the Po, from Fusina to Padua (*DAB*; Susan Goodman and Carl Dawson, *William Dean Howells: A Writer's Life* [Berkeley, 2005], pp. xxii, 325; M. A. DeWolfe Howe, ed., *Later Years of the Saturday Club, 1870–1920* [Boston, 1927], pp. 69–77, 183–87; William Dean Howells, *Venetian Life* [New York, 1887], p. 387; see also FLO to Charles Eliot, March 4, 1886, below).
14. The English landscape gardener Humphry Repton lived in, and worked from, a cottage in the village of Hare Street, Hertfordshire, throughout his thirty-year career. As at Fairsted, domestic and professional settings were combined in Repton's cottage. Repton also used his residential landscape as a demonstration of certain principles. At the end of his last book, *Fragments on the Theory and Practice of Landscape Gardening* (1816), Repton reflects on the growing significance of his domestic environment as old

age and infirmity limited the scope of his activities. He concludes with an observation on what he describes as

> the most interesting subject I have ever known; it is the view from the humble cottage to which, for more than thirty years, I have anxiously retreated from the pomp of palaces, the elegances of fashion, or the allurements of dissipation: it stood originally within five yards of a broad part of the high road: this area was often covered with droves of cattle, of pigs, or geese. I obtained leave to remove the paling twenty yards further from the windows; and, by this *appropriation* of twenty-five yards of garden, I have obtained a frame to my landscape; the frame is composed of flowering shrubs and evergreens; beyond which are seen, the cheerful village, the high road, and that constant moving scene, which I would not exchange for any of the lonely parks that I have improved for others.

Shortly before leaving England in October, Eliot went to Repton's cottage, as Olmsted requested, and photographed the site. The photographs were later published in *Landscape Architecture* magazine (Humphry Repton, *Fragments on the Theory and Practice of Landscape Gardening* [London, 1816], pp. 232–38; J. C. Loudon, *Landscape Gardening and Landscape Architecture of the Late Humphry Repton, Esq.* [London, 1840], pp. 603, 13–14n; C. W. Eliot, *Charles Eliot*, pp. 200–01; Percival Gallagher, "Repton's Cottage," *Landscape Architecture*, Oct. 1917 to July 1918, pp. 184–87; see also FLO to Percival Walter St. George, Dec. 8, 1885, above).

To Charles Eliot

4th March 1886.

My Dear Eliot;

Your letter of 13th ult°. to John & Harry has interested and delighted me greatly.[1] You have been most fortunate and in reading I said to myself constantly "that is just what I should think." I do hope that you will write something for the public on the present state of the art and the conditions of its practice in Europe.

As you refer to Milner as one to whom Johnson's statements cannot apply I will tell you that he particularly mentioned Milner. He said that Milner's father had made a fortune by taking contracts to carry out his own plans, had established a great business to which his son succeeded and which he was pursuing in the same way, i.e. a thoroughly speculative, brokerish, shopkeeperish, way. I did not believe him but I could not avoid your thought that there must be too much of trade & too little of art in his great business.[2] But it is a difficult question, and Morris's success in combining art & commercial profit in a large scale is to be reflected upon.[3] The important fact is that a master eye is needed in details of any gardening work for several years, as well as in the preparation of plans and specifications.

I wrote advising you to see the villas on the Po and to which Howells refers.[4] Talking with Walker[5] yesterday he spoke of villas that he had visited and enjoyed at or near "Laquercia" (?) a short morning's walk (perhaps 4 miles) N.E. of Viterbo, to which you go from Rome.[6] I think that you want to get hints for gardening in dry, hot regions of our country from Italy, Spain & South of France. You do not it seems to me get much of value from the show villas to which you go as a matter of course. But I remember moderate places which struck me as delightful, and one or two that I cannot now specify I made my way into and faintly recall always when I think of what should be done in California, Colorado, New Mexico, or, really in Georgia/Florida. I speak of a month in all Italy more than thirty years ago when I had no more thought of being a landscape architect than of being a Cardinal. Yet my experience has been of much value to me.[7]

Yours Very Truly

Fred[k] Law Olmsted.

The text presented here is a signed letter in Olmsted's hand (See FLO to Charles Eliot, Feb. 25, 1886, above; FLO to Charles Eliot, July 20, 1886, below; FLO to Charles Eliot, Oct. 28, 1886, below).

1. In a letter addressed to both John C. Olmsted and Henry Sargent Codman, Eliot described his experiences visiting parks and gardens in England and commented on the professional practice of landscape gardening there. He felt there was an over abundance of professionals in England and feared that those in need of work would come to the United States. He shared his impressions of several sites near London, including the estate of Ashtead Park, in Surrey, where landscape gardener Henry Ernest Milner was "working up" the property. He wrote of a sunset walk he took from Box Hill to Dorking, "by the valley that Gilpin speaks of as a perfect example of the combination of the moral and the beautiful," and of the gardens of the seventeenth-century English author and sylviculturist, John Evelyn. Following his visit to Oxford he wrote, "I never had a more interesting week" (Charles Eliot to JCO and Henry Sargent Codman, Feb. 13, 1886).
2. Henry Ernest Milner (1845–1906), landscape gardener, was the son of Edward Milner, also a successful landscape gardener. When his father became the principal of the Crystal Palace School of Gardening in 1881, Henry became a full partner in their business, and in 1890 he published *The Art and Practice of Landscape Gardening*. Eliot described him in his letter to John C. Olmsted and Henry S. Codman: "There is a certain wholesale quality about his practice that savors of trade rather than art. Milner's father was of the generation that . . . [is] said to have done good work and to have held the profession to a high standard in matters of practice." Eliot describes in detail a landscape Milner had created at Ashstead Park. Olmsted would meet Milner in 1892, describing him as "a nice fellow in every way." The statements of Joseph Forsyth Johnson that Olmsted refers to are those relayed in FLO to Charles Eliot, February 25, 1886, above (*DNB*; Charles Eliot to JCO and Henry Sargent Codman, Feb. 13, 1886; FLO to JCO, Aug. 6, 1892; see also FLO to Charles Eliot, Feb. 25, 1886, n. 4, above).
3. That is, William Morris (1834–1896), a founder of the Arts & Crafts movement, whom Olmsted admired (see Frederick Law Olmsted, *The Park for Detroit*, Nov. 1882, above).
4. In Olmsted's previous letter to Eliot, he suggested that Eliot visit a villa in Italy that

William Dean Howells refers to in *Venetian Life* (FLO to Charles Eliot, Feb. 25, 1886, above).

5. Francis Amasa Walker (1840–1897), president of the Massachusetts Institute of Technology, was a consultant to Leland Stanford on the creation of Stanford University while Olmsted was developing designs for the campus. Walker had traveled in Europe in 1878 when he served as Assistant Commissioner General for the Paris Exposition (*NCAB*; see also FLO to Leland Stanford, Nov. 27, 1886, below).
6. Viterbo is about sixty miles north of Rome. Olmsted refers to the villas near the Basilica Santa Maria della Quercia, which are within a mile or two of the Basilica.
7. A reference to a tour that Olmsted made of Italy in March and April of 1856 during his six-month stay in the British Isles and Europe, soliciting material for publication by his publishing firm, Dix & Edwards. Among the places in Italy that he visited were Genoa, Leghorn, Rome, Florence, and Venice, as well as a trip by carriage from Rome to Pompeii and Amalfi ("Memorandum by Bertha Olmsted," FLO Papers/LC; *Papers of FLO*, 2: 484).

TO FELKER L. TEMPLE

Brookline, 15th March 1886.

Mr. F. L. Temple;

Dear Sir; I have a recent brief note from you, without date, asking what plants will be needed from you this spring to replace such as have died, {*of*} earlier plantings at Beacon Entrance, Back Bay, and another, also without date, but received last Friday from Washington asking me {. . .} you can make an arrangement for taking care of the plantation during the coming summer.

I wish that you would try to realize the situation, or rather I wish that you would try to put yourself in my place and think how it appears to me.

When in 1883 the Commissioners wished Beacon Entrance to be planted, my official duty, as I explained it to you at the time, was simply that of an advisor, {*but it had been stipulated*} that in the conduct of the work professional service should be engaged satisfactory to me.

The situation and its purposes I had in view were such that I did not think that an ordinary extemporized gardening organization would be satisfactory. I was looking for someone especially expert in making plantations of such super hardy low native shrubbery as is not to be had in large quantities from nurseries and familiar with the difficulties of establishing it under bleak conditions, when you presented yourself and brought letters from two landscape gardeners *as a landscape gardener of precisely the special qualifications required*. You had just been studying the subject on the bleakest and coldest part of the New England sea coast: you had a nursery of your own and were interested, experienced and your business organized for undertaking just what was wanted. I had had no experience in this part of the country. You came as an authority upon the cultivation of the hardiest shrubbery in this part of the country and your confidence in what you could do under given {*conditions,*} based on your personal experience, overcame my doubts based upon my experience elsewhere, of the practicability of what I thought if practicable, desirable to be accomplished.

This was first, within three years to completely cover the ground in question, to within a few feet of the water, with low foliage in such a manner as to produce an {*enriching*} general resemblance to certain slopes along the sea coast that are covered by dense thickets chiefly of bay berry, sweet ferns and prostrate juniper but with some variety of other low vegetation and occasional clusters of higher bushes such as barberry, beach plum, wild roses, thorns and ground plants. Second, it was to so manage as to completely clothe the space likely to be influenced unfavorable to ordinary vegetation by salt water, with a large variety of plants to be specially sought for along the sea shore, that would flourish in the situation. The plans were devised, the list of plants made, the preparation of the site directed, the specifications of the arrangement drawn, in consultation with you, with the understanding that the Commission wished to spare nothing that would favor your success and to give you all possible discretion as to details by which you would be able to proceed in such a manner as in your own judgment would best enable you to accomplish *the few simple ends in view* such as have been stated. You were asked repeatedly, "Are you satisfied with this?" "Can you suggest any way in which the business can be put on a better footing for you?" and you have never made a request or offered a suggestion, or asked a modification of the terms of the contract in any detail that would not be an abandonment of the main comprehensive object in view, that you have not been accommodated. You could not have been used {*more*} liberally, and more, could not have {*been entrusted to your professional discretion, self-satisfaction and honor*} without dereliction of public duty. I have repeatedly pointed out to you that this was the footing on which I was dealing with you and you have always assented and accepted the obligations it implied.

I stated my own apprehensions fully to you and both in writing and verbally repeatedly warned you of the difficulties that your undertaking seemed to me to involve and my fears that you did not realize them or give them sufficient study.

Last spring I hesitated long as to certifying that the work had been done to my satisfaction and did so finally only after you had planted many thousand additional shrubs of more promising character and better planted than those set before. In June I found great numbers of plants in dying condition. The Commissioners saw the {*shriveling*} leaves in hundreds and the {*nearly*} dead stumps of many more. In July the condition of the plantation was still worse; I met your foreman on the ground and pointed out to him that not only nearly everything planted in the spring seemed to have failed but that nearly all the class of {*shrubs*} before planted that I was particularly interested in and with reference to which especially the engagement had been made with you, looked poorly, while thousands appeared to be dead or dying. He agreed with me; said that it was unaccountable; it looked as if the ground was being swept by a pestilence and everything was going to die. I asked him to report the state of the plantation to you and he said that he should do so. He showed such extreme disappointment and mortification that when I heard of his suicide[1] I suspected it to be due to the depression thus caused. I expected an immediate visit from you but you kept away and when, late in the fall, I at last saw you, I could not think you realized how great your failure had been. I told you so and though you said you had looked carefully over the ground and found a great deal of small stuff alive I was confirmed in my views by the terms upon which at last you proposed that your contract should be extended.

I then made a closer examination of the plantation and afterwards had Mr Fischer[2] with two men employed for a week in counting the plants one by one. The result satisfied me that the case was much worse than I had previously supposed. I did not tell you of the count as the winter had already set in, I did not think you would believe it accurate and I hoped that you would look more closely into the matter for yourself. I have a list of the numbers found by Mr Fischer to be alive last fall of every sort of plant on the ground.

I concluded as spring approached that you were unlikely to either count for yourself or to accept my count, therefore I obtained your consent to employ Mr Dawson[3] to go over the ground with your foreman and estimate what number of plants of {*all sorts*} there are now alive and in what proportion the dead stumps {*not removed*} in last summer's cultivation of the ground, are to the yet living plants.

He reports to me today that in his judgment there are in the vicinity of 35,000 living plants of all kinds, a large part of which are not woody plants but such as were to be supplied at the {*lowest*} price and are commonly ranked with weeds. This is a considerably larger number than Mr Fischer found by actual count last fall. I believe that it is an overestimate. You have been paid upon a basis of more than 100,000 plants.

Examining the plants on the ground left after the {*cultivating*} of last year, to determine the proportion of living to dead, Mr Dawson found as follows—

Christmas ferns 99 pr^ct^ dead
Salix tristis 95 " "
Smilax 95 " "
Rubus 80 " "
Genista 75 " "
Cassandra, Myrica, {*Comptonia*} (on the higher ground) 50 pr^ct^ dead.
Shore plantations of Beach plum, Hippophae, {*Rosa Lucida*}
and Tamarisk ——— all dead;
On higher ground 75 to 95 pr^ct^ dead.
The shore is bare of vegetation except a narrow strip of sedge here and there.

View of Beacon Street Entrance to the Back Bay Fens, Looking Toward Boylston Bridge, n.d.

Of Bearberry, Linnaea, Kalmia, Sea lavender, Beach pea, Asparagus, Euonymus {*radicans*} and others each of which your bills show that from 500 to 2000 have been planted, Mr Dawson saw, after searching several hours, hardly a score of anyone living, of most not a single specimen. Others largely planted in various parts he found only in one or two specially sheltered and moist localities.

The thriving plants are first the nursery grown, common commercial ornamental shrubs, mostly furnished by the Department, with some others not originally called for and not desired to remain, and Tansy, Asters and Solidagos, planted for temporary effect, which are rampant and spreading and which another summer will smother and kill nearly all that are left of the plants designed to permanently predominate as, Myricas, Comptonias, &c.

This mere loss of so many plants is the smallest part of the disaster. The whole design is a wreck. Of what remains of your planting that which should be most prominent and characteristic is least so, that which was desired to be an inconspicuous element merging in a mass of a certain quality, stands out exclusively; that which was to be subordinate, predominates. The ground and the rocks most strenuously to be covered are bare and the whole affair is recognized by the Commissioners to be exceedingly discreditable to all concerned.

I don't see how the plantation can be left longer under your management. I don't think that you should depend on me to think out your present duty in the premises. It is a question of professional obligation and character. But pray let me hear soon what, in view of the statement I have now made, you do think and intend about it. We must come speedily to some conclusion.[4]

Yours Truly,

Fred[k] Law Olmsted.

The text presented here is from a letterpress copy of a handwritten letter signed on the original in Olmsted's hand: A1: 304–11, OAR/LC. By this time, most of the plants that F. L. Temple had planted in the Beacon Street entrance to the Back Bay Fens had died. Temple wrote to Olmsted in November of 1884 inquiring about continuing the planting of the entrance the next season. Olmsted did not reply until February of 1885, and at that time explained that he had made a careful examination of the area and found that his count of the plants that had died differed from Temple's estimate. Temple was required by his contract to replace plants that died within the first two years of planting at 10% of cost. In 1886 Temple offered to replace the dead plants and asked Olmsted to state the number needed. Olmsted responded, "I am sorry to say that I cannot do so. I think that the number of plants alive is so much less than the contract calls for and than you believe" (FLO to F. L. Temple, Aug. 21, 1883, above; FLO to F. L. Temple, Nov. 22, 1883, above; FLO to F. L. Temple, Feb.10, 1885, A1: 281, OAR/LC; BPD, *Minutes*, Dec. 1, 1883; FLO to F. L. Temple, Feb. 22, 1886, A1: 296, OAR/LC).

1. The editors could not establish with certainty the identity of the foreman or the date or cause of his suicide.
2. William L. Fischer (1819–1899) was a gardener who worked at Central Park supervising planting from 1857 until 1870, and as superintending gardener from 1875 to 1878 and 1880 to 1884. In 1884 Olmsted brought Fischer to Boston to supervise the planting of the Fens, Franklin Park, and the Boston side of the Muddy River (*Papers of FLO*, 7: 133–34, n. 1; FLO to Boston Park Board, Oct. 7, 1884; C. Zaitzevsky, *The Boston Park System*, pp. 189–93; see FLO to William L. Fischer, July 21, 1887, below).
3. Jackson Thornton Dawson (1841–1916) was the Arnold Arboretum's first superintendent and plant propagator. He began in 1870 as head gardener for the Bussey Institute (FLO to F. L. Temple, Feb. 23, 1886, A1: 297, OAR/LC; Ida Hay, *Science in the Pleasure Ground: A History of the Arnold Arboretum* [Boston, 1995], p. 78; Charles Sprague Sargent and E. H. Wilson, *Jackson Dawson — in Memoriam* [Boston, 1916]).
4. Olmsted wrote to Temple in March and April describing the history of the failed plantings. He suggested that Temple did not understand his intentions for the Beacon Street entrance, making their continued collaboration undesirable. Olmsted wrote his final correspondence on this subject on October 19, 1886, and informed Temple that the park commissioners would no longer consider his offer to continue the plantings on the site. The replanting of the area presumably was done under William L. Fischer's direction. Photographs show that by the 1890s shrubs, ground covers, and trees were well established (FLO to F. L. Temple, March 19, 1886, A1: 312, OAR/LC; FLO to F. L. Temple, April 17, 1886, A1: 335–36, OAR/LC; FLO to F. L. Temple, Oct. 19, 1886, A1: 494, OAR/LC).

To Endicott Peabody[1]

19th April 1886.

My Dear Sir;

I want to be sure that you fully realize the considerations which had us after full discussion to place your buildings on the north side of the "campus". You never get a good thing except by sacrifices, and the question is one of compensations. Blessings heighten to the imagination as we contemplate them flying away.

The consideration which you are most likely not to have continued to give due weight to is this:—

Place your intended main school buildings on the north side, the north view may always be held from their north windows and from the flanks of the {*group*} of buildings; then on the south of them you may obtain a sheltered, comparatively sequestered assigning home-like ground without sacrifice of any important prospect. You rapidly move the institution out of its present somewhat bleak, bare, cold and hard aspect.

Place the buildings on the South Side and you have the view from a smaller number of windows and from the carriage front. There is no question of front and rear; buildings of the character contemplated should be conceived as of two fronts; the analogy being that of large villas, "halls" or palaces in which usually there is an entrance or court yard front used {. . .} fronts. (To bring carriages and general service roads between your best windows and your best view is to be avoided when practicable.)

But suppose you overrode this consideration. You have your buildings on the south side, and you have the view then to the north from their north windows—the smaller number of windows—that is your advantage. You cannot grow a higher tree without obscuring your view from some of your windows.

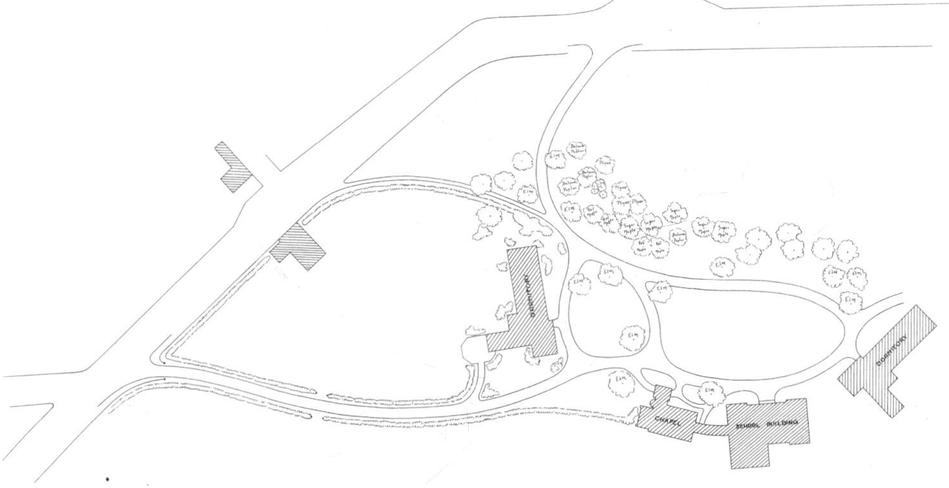

Plan for Groton School Grounds and Plantings, April 8, 1885

You can have no body of trees without destroying the advantage. For the sake of having the view from the smaller number of windows you accept the permanent disadvantage of a cold, bare bleak and hard aspect for the entire group of buildings as they will be seen by everyone intending to enter them or wishing to step out of them. Your approach roads and your campus will remain frozen two or three weeks later every spring. They will be damp and chilly longer. They will have an earlier winter and a shorter summer. Every man and every horse standing before a door will be raked by the north west wind.

You can think out the disadvantages on this line. I am strongly disposed to believe that if you do so fully—looking well ahead, giving the imagination its proper task and with due caution not to be imposed upon by purely temporary and transitional conditions and habits formed under different circumstances and with reference to different motives, you will come back to your original conclusion—that the balance of advantages lies with a plan which promises shelter, sunniness and geniality to the school centre.[2]

Yours Truly

Fred[k] Law Olmsted.

The Rev[d] S. E. Peabody.[3]

The text presented here is from a letterpress copy of a handwritten letter signed on the original in Olmsted's hand: A1: 336–39, OAR/LC. Olmsted began consulting on the design of the main campus of Groton School for boys in Groton, Massachusetts, in 1884. John C. Olmsted appears to have engaged in most of the correspondence for the project. In 1886, they were concerned with the placement of buildings, stables, and the gymnasium (See JCO to Endicott Peabody, April 17, 1885, A1: 189–91, OAR/LC; JCO to Endicott Peabody, July 22, 1886, A1: 382, OAR/LC; JCO to Endicott Peabody, April 24, 1889, A3: 562, OAR/LC; JCO to Endicott Peabody, June 13, 1889, A4: 869, OAR/LC; JCO to Endicott Peabody, July 9, 1889, A4: 942, OAR/LC; plan 31-z2, NPS/FLONHS).

1. Endicott Peabody (1857–1944) was an American educator and Episcopal priest. His father, Samuel Endicott Peabody, was a wealthy Boston merchant and banker and an associate of J. P. Morgan. Endicott moved to England with his family when he was thirteen years old and graduated from Trinity College, Cambridge, England, in 1878. He returned to the United States in 1880 and enrolled in the Episcopal Theological School in Cambridge, Massachusetts, the next year. He was ordained in 1884, and with backing from wealthy friends, including J. P. Morgan, he opened the Groton School for Boys that year. He served as its headmaster until 1940 (*DAB*).
2. The main campus of Groton consists of Groton Circle, an oval road designed by Olmsted with principal approach roads branching off from it. A sketch dated March 1884 placed three main school buildings on the north side of the Circle and a dormitory on the northeast side. An October 25, 1886, ink drawing shows only one main building on the north side of the Circle, with dormitories and classroom buildings on the west and east sides, and the gymnasium on the south. Apparently Peabody chose not to place the majority of buildings on the north side, leaving the north vista open. Due to additional

construction over the years, buildings were placed around the entire Circle leaving only the northwest corner open (plans 31-z2 and 31-3, NPS/FLONHS).

3. Olmsted mistakenly refers to Peabody as S. E. (Samuel Endicott) Peabody, which was Endicott Peabody's father's name.

To Edward Payson Wilbur[1]

29th April, 1886.

My Dear Sir;

Let me say a few words in explanation of my short reply to your inquiry in the State House this afternoon.

1. The purpose of the Back Bay work is already so far accomplished that there is no longer a nuisance there nor any danger to private property through freshets or tides. The property is already paying a good interest on its cost to the city; the policy and the plan are vindicated. They cannot be set aside to further any private or party interest. There is no danger that they will not be carried out. If the City Council compels the end to be reached two or three years later than it may be profitably, the result will neither be much less valuable nor much more costly.

2. But the result of such causes, as there is every reason to expect will be pursued without some such provision as is offered by the loan project,[2] in the case of the main park and the arboretum, are likely to be very different. For years to come the public will lose more than it will gain from these undertakings; the ultimate outlay upon them will be *much* greater, the value of the results *much* less. With the civil service law in operation[3] and such provisions as might be incorporated in a Bill limiting the purposes for which the money to be obtained by loan would be available and requiring the parts of the work not mainly horticultural to be done by contract, the objections that I believe to have the most weight against the proposition might, it seems to me, be overcome.

3. When all that is possible to be done under a loan limited to Back Bay, shall have been accomplished, the result, so long as it stands by itself will be disappointing and unsatisfactory. It will injure the prestige of the Back Bay district. As the opening feature of an obviously extended system of suburban recreation the Back Bay ground will be recognized as a good thing, it will escape the strictures and {. . .} that, regarded as a local "park", it will inevitably provoke and the locality will gain solid and enduring advantages from it.

Yours respectfully,

Fredk Law Olmsted.

The Hon {*E.*} P. Wilbur,

The text presented here is from a letterpress copy of a handwritten letter signed on the original in Olmsted's hand: A1: 344–45, OAR/LC.

1. Edward Payson Wilbur (1831–1901) was a businessman and Republican elected official in Boston. He served on the Common Council from 1872 to 1874 and in the State House of Representatives in 1884 and 1885. In 1886 and 1887 he was a state senator ("E. P. Wilbur of Boston Dead," *New York Times*, Jan. 7, 1901; *A Catalogue of the City Councils of Boston, Roxbury, and Charlestown* [Boston, 1909], p. 324; George F. Andrews, *Massachusetts Official Gazette, Biography of Members* [Boston, 1886 and 1890], p. 24).
2. Under the terms of the 1875 Park Act, funds for the acquisition of land for parks in Boston were obtained by issuing bonds under the provisions of the Public Park Loan. Separate legislation was needed, however, if the city's fixed debt limit were to be exceeded. At Mayor Hugh O'Brien's request, a bill to exceed the debt limit by $2,500,000 was introduced to the State Legislature, and passed in June 1886, two months after Olmsted wrote this letter. Republican members of Boston's Board of Aldermen, however, delayed approving the loan because they were concerned that the money would be misdirected by the Democratic administration. The Board of Aldermen finally approved bond issue in January 1887 (C. Zaitzevsky, *The Boston Park System*, pp. 68, 232–33 n. 14; *Twelfth Annual Report, Boston Department of Parks, 1886*, pp. 13–14; "Parks and Politics: Aldermen Wrangle over the Park Loan Order," *Boston Post*, July 20, 1886, p. 4; "The Park Loan: It is Laid Over by the Board of Aldermen," *Boston Daily Globe*, July 20, 1886, p. 6; FLO to Charles Eliot, Feb. 25, 1886, above; FLO to Charles Eliot, July 20, 1886, below).
3. In June 1884, Massachusetts became the second state to pass a civil service reform bill. The law required that applicants take civil service examinations and established a board of three commissioners who set rules for how state and municipal jobs should be filled. The commission instituted the first set of rules in December 1884, which had only been slightly modified when Olmsted wrote this letter ("On Beacon Hill. A New Civil Service Reform Bill Presented," *Boston Daily Globe*, May 15, 1884, p. 3; "On Beacon Hill. Closing of Year's Work of Legislation," ibid., June 3, 1884, p. 3; "Our New Civil Service," ibid., Dec. 18, 1884, p. 6).

To Mariana Griswold Van Rensselaer[1]

2[d] May, 1886.

Dear Mrs Van Renssalaer,

I do not know that any other of the friends of Richardson[2] who happen to have been near him of late will have thought of their duty to one who has been so good a friend to him as you have been.

He never had as much to do; never had such assurance of his leadership and the public a grateful acceptance of it, never had been as ripely strong and happy in his art as in his last days. My last interview with him was in Washington,[3] when having seemed at first extremely weak and downcast, hardly able to speak, some question of a building came into his mind and roused him, and for an hour

Bronze relief portrait of Mariana Griswold Van Rensselaer, by Augustus Saint-Gaudens, completed in 1888, this cast from 1890

he discoursed upon the works that he had in hand, upon his office, and upon his methods of work in the most animated, cheerful, sometimes even hilarious spirit, and so strongly and clearly that when I left I said to him "I shall have to report that I never saw you in better condition than you have been this evening", and he laughingly assented. He came home the next day, greatly worn down by the fatigue of the journey, and after that kept his bed mainly. I was told the last time that I called that the doctor said he would pull through, he had been down stairs, sitting on the veranda for a short time but the doctor advised that his friends should not see him. After that he slept a great deal but was busy when awake planning to go to Nantucket in order that he might pick up faster as a preparation for going to Europe. So he continued until the sleep came in which he passed away so quietly and softly that no one present knew when death occurred.

At his funeral in Trinity I saw every architect of Boston whom I know.[4] I think there were fifty of the profession present, three from New York besides

St Gaudens.[5] The Boston Society of Architects are to place a bust of him in Trinity—a bronze bust by St Gaudens.

His private affairs are left, I am sorry to say, in a condition showing his characteristic, unconquerable recklessness in personal matters. His professional income of late must have been very large—far larger than that of any other architect but he seems always to have been living ahead of it and his debts are thought to exceed his assets. It is hoped that Mr Shepley who is soon to marry Julu, the elder daughter, may be able with some assistance from Richardson's friends to retain and carry through the commissions now in the office.[6]

Mrs Richardson has a small independent income, $3000, I believe, and Mr Hooper[7] offers her the house, rent free, for five years, and something will probably be done privately for the education of the five children who are still of school age.

I have found Mrs Richardson composed and even cheerful, glad to converse and full of thankfulness that the death was so painless. I suppose that you have known her but little. She is an admirable woman of child-like simplicity, strong, brave, efficient. He could not have been happier in a wife. She is among the kindest of friends.

Sincerely Yours

Fred[k] Law Olmsted.

The text presented here is a signed letter in Olmsted's hand. H. H. Richardson, Olmsted's friend and collaborator, died on April 27, 1886, of Bright's disease. At the suggestion of Olmsted and Charles Sprague Sargent, Van Rensselaer would research and write *Henry Hobson Richardson and His Works*, the first biography of an American architect (Boston, 1888) (James F. O'Gorman, *Living Architecture, A Biography of H. H. Richardson* [New York, 1997], p. 13; FLO to Mariana Griswold Van Rensselaer, [May] 6, 1886, below; Mariana Griswold Van Rensselaer, *Henry Hobson Richardson and His Works* [Boston, 1888], reprint [New York, 1969], p. 36).

1. Mariana Griswold Van Rensselaer (1851–1934) was an author and architecture and art critic. From a privileged New York family, she was raised both there and in Europe. She married Schuyler Van Rensselaer in 1873. After her husband died in 1884 she concentrated on her career as a critic and author, contributing articles and some poetry to numerous journals, including the *Century*, *Garden and Forest*, and *American Architect and Building News*. Van Rensselaer and Olmsted began their correspondence in 1883 when she requested his advice on articles she was writing for the *Century*, and they continued to write to each other regularly throughout the next decade. She wrote extensively on landscape architecture in the 1880s and 1890s, and became one of the most important landscape critics and theorists of the era. In 1893 she wrote for the *Century* magazine the first biographical and critical assessment of Olmsted's life and work. That same year she published an influential collection of her essays on landscape design, *Art Out-of-Doors: Hints on Good Taste in Gardening* (1893). Some of her other books include *Henry Hobson Robinson and His Works* (1888), and *History of the City of New York in the Seventeenth Century* (2 vols., 1909) (*DAB*; Mariana Griswold Van

Rensselaer, *Accents As Well As Broad Effects: Writings on Architecture, Landscape, and the Environment, 1876–1925*, David Gebhard, ed. [Berkley, 1996], pp. 1–28; Mariana Griswold Van Rensselaer, "Frederick Law Olmsted," *Century Illustrated Monthly Magazine*, Oct., 1893, pp. 860–67; Mariana Griswold Van Rensselaer to FLO, Oct. 4, 1883; Mariana Griswold Van Rensselaer to FLO, Dec. 11, 1883).

2. Henry Hobson Richardson (1838–1886) was one of the most successful and influential architects of the nineteenth century. He knew Olmsted for many years and worked with him on a number of major projects in the 1870s and 1880s. The two men were close friends and neighbors as well professional collaborators. Born in Louisiana, Richardson attended Harvard and went to Paris to study architecture in 1859. The next year he was accepted at the École des Beaux-Arts and remained in France studying and working as an architect through the Civil War years. On his return to the United States he settled his family in a boarding house in Brooklyn, moving to Staten Island in 1866. He may have already known Olmsted at that point, since that spring Olmsted relocated his family from a boarding house in Brooklyn to Staten Island as well. The Olmsteds moved to Clifton, the neighborhood in which Richardson began building a new house for his family in 1868. Soon after, Olmsted recommended the young architect for the design of the memorial for Alexander Dallas Bache, an old friend from the U.S. Sanitary Commission. In 1870 Olmsted suggested that Richardson be asked to join him as an expert consultant to the newly created Staten Island Improvement Commission. The next year the consultants submitted their report, written primarily by Olmsted, that suggested new parks and other environmental improvements to the area. Olmsted and Richardson's professional association began in earnest that spring, when Olmsted, Vaux, and Richardson worked together on the design of the Buffalo State Hospital for the Insane. Olmsted and Richardson also collaborated on the design of Niagara Square in Buffalo.

   Richardson relocated to Brookline in 1874 after receiving the commission for Trinity Church in Boston. His house on Cottage Street became the home not only of his family, but also of the growing atelier of his successful practice. In 1876 Olmsted and Richardson, together with architect Leopold Eidlitz, were appointed to advise a New York State commission on the completion of the New York State Capitol in Albany. In 1881 Olmsted also relocated to Brookline. Richardson offered to design Olmsted a house next to his own on Cottage Street, but Olmsted decided instead to buy a farmhouse at 99 Warren Street, nearby. In 1883 Olmsted moved his family and office into the house, named Fairsted. Before Richardson's death the two men also worked together on Memorial Hall and other projects in North Easton, Massachusetts, a group of suburban train stations, and the Back Bay Fens, among numerous other public and private commissions (*DAB*; *FLO, A Biography*, pp. 299, 367–68, 390–91; Jeffrey Karl Ochsner, *H. H. Richardson: Complete Architectural Works* [Cambridge, Mass., 1982], pp. 46–49, 78–81, 157–67, 204–7, 217–25; J. F. O'Gorman, *Living Architecture*, pp. 81–82; *Papers of FLO*, 4: 81–83; *Papers of FLO*, 6: 34–35, 391, n. 4, 454–55; *Papers of FLO*, 7: 7–10).

3. Olmsted was in Washington for his work on the Capitol grounds, and Richardson could have also been there for one of several of his private commissions in the city (J. F. O'Gorman, pp. 183–84; J. K. Ochsner, *H. H. Richardson, Complete Architectural Works*, pp. 256, 345–46).

4. Richardson's funeral service was conducted on April 30 by Phillips Brooks at Trinity Church, Boston, which Richardson had designed nine years earlier (M. G. Van Rensselaer, *Henry Hobson Richardson*, p. 36).

5. Augustus Saint-Gaudens (1848–1907), the renowned American sculptor, was a friend of Richardson, Van Rensselaer, and Olmsted. Saint-Gaudens had a close professional relationship with Richardson and collaborated with him on a number of projects, including a mantelpiece portrait of Oliver Ames in the Ames Library, and decorative elements of F. L. Ames's Gate Lodge, both in 1881 in North Easton, Massachusetts. He also

completed granite portrait plaques on the Oliver and Oakes Ames Monument in Wyoming in 1882. In 1893 Saint-Gaudens worked with Olmsted, the architect Daniel Burnham, and others in the design of the World's Columbian Exposition fair in Chicago. In 1888 he created a bronze relief portrait of Van Rensselaer, and 1902 he completed the statue of Phillips Brooks that stands outside Trinity Church. But there is no record of Saint-Gaudens making a bust of Richardson, as Olmsted suggests here (*DAB*; John H. Dryfhout, *The Work of Augustus Saint-Gaudens* [Hanover, N.H., 1982], pp. 109, 122, 124, 171, 299–300).

6. George Foster Shepley (1860–1903) graduated from MIT in 1882 and joined Richardson's office shortly afterwards. In 1887, he married Richardson's daughter, Julia (Julu). Richardson wrote an informal will on the last day of his life in which he directed that his assistants, Shepley, Charles H. Rutan, and Charles A. Coolidge, continue his business. Between 1886 and 1915, the firm of Shepley, Rutan, and Coolidge went on to design Stanford University, the Harvard Medical School, the United States Building for the Paris Exposition of 1900, and the Art Institute of Chicago, among many other significant commissions (*NCAB*; J. F. O'Gorman, *Living Architecture*, p. 188; *Proceedings of the Thirty-Seventh Annual Convention of the American Institute of Architects* [Washington, D.C., 1904], p. 217).
7. Richardson's wife, with whom he had six children, was Julia Gorham Hayden. She was the sister of his Harvard classmate David Hyslop Hayden. When the couple settled in Brookline in 1874, they rented the Samuel Gardner Perkins House on Cottage Street in Brookline from Edward Hooper, another classmate of Richardson's and treasurer of Harvard College (1876–1898). The house was up the street from the house Olmsted moved to in 1883, and Richardson later expanded his house to include his professional studio, offices, and library (J. F. O'Gorman, *Living Architecture*, pp. 51, 78–80, 113).

To Mariana Griswold Van Rensselaer

6th [May], 1886.

My Dear Mrs Van Rensselaer:

I am glad to have your kind reply to my note. I feel all you say at all points. Mrs Olmsted and I had been remarking that Richardson's strong personality, breeding a habit with his friends of being always ready for something to occur concerning him not to be expected, seemed to have had the effect of making it particularly hard to become accustomed to think of him as gone.

And I have felt strongly with you of late that he was rapidly growing—gaining from experience and the testing of himself, and in the confidence and free-mindedness that success fosters.

As you speak of your responsibility, you will let me say how highly I esteem the value of the work that you are doing. I don't think that you can begin to realize its educational influence—of course you cannot. It is so widely scattered and "upon the waters."[1]

I shall be glad to call on you if I am ever in New York with the least leisure to do so. But I travel so much that I hardly ever leave home unless I am obliged to, and the obligations that take me through New York nearly always make me hasten through it.

One thing I have been hoping from you since I read your review of Hamerton's Paris. Some study of his big book entitled *Landscape*.[2] I fined myself $37 for my overeagerness to get it, and with reference to what I hoped for myself it was a great disappointment. There is much pleasant discourse in it upon the text of Landscape but with regard to what it seemed to promise, it is most unsatisfactory. Nor do I know of anything satisfactory on the subject.

Sincerely Yours

Fred[k] Law Olmsted.

The text presented here is a signed letter in Olmsted's hand. The original letter was incorrectly dated by Olmsted, "6th, April." The editors have determined through contextual evidence that the letter was most likely written on May 6th, not April 6th. After writing this letter, Olmsted wrote Van Rensselaer again on the same day suggesting she consider taking on an important memorialization of the architect: "I have been in conversation with Professor Sargent about Richardson and we agreed that a memorial book, giving some account of him and his works with illustrations should be prepared; that it should be set about at once, before his office is dismantled, his friends dispersed and while memories of him are fresh, and that you would be much the best person to undertake it" (FLO to Mariana Griswold Van Rensselaer, [May] 6, 1886).

1. Olmsted quotes from *Ecclesiastes* 11: 1, "Cast thy bread upon the waters: for thou shalt find it after many days."
2. That is, Philip Gilbert Hamerton's *Landscape* (1885). Van Rensselaer had recently given Hamerton's *Paris in Old and Present Times* (Boston, 1885) an unflattering review: "In short, the book reads like the work not only of a novice in architectural criticism, but of a novice in criticism of any kind, and indeed a novice in writing of any kind" (*DNB*; Mariana Griswold Van Renselaer, "Books and Papers," *American Architect and Building News*, Jan. 2, 1886, pp. 8–9).

To Henry Rutgers Beekman[1]

[June 10, 1886]

The Honorable Henry R. Beekman,
President of the Department of Parks, New York.
Dear Sir,

We have the honor to reply to your letter of 4th inst.[2]

1. Parts of each of three costly properties of the city, the Central, Riverside and Morningside parks are within six hundred yards of a common centre. If

the three had been brought together the value of the combined property would be considerably greater than that of the three separately. This consideration not having been regarded in determining their boundaries, the next best thing to do would appear to be that which your Board has in view, the adaptation of certain existing streets to the purpose of connecting pleasure roads and walks, bringing the three properties into one circuit.[3]

2. With regard to the proposition to enter at an early day upon the work necessary to make the Riverside and Morningside park properties available for use it is to be considered that the city can have no profit from these properties until operations are carried out that have not yet been begun; that their value will depend almost entirely on trees to be grown upon them that cannot be planted until these operations are ended, and that after they have been planted the profit of the entire property in each case will be increasing at a constantly advancing rate of increase. Unquestionably a general plan for their improvement should be settled upon as soon as this can be done with due forethought and deliberation, for the situation in each case presents difficulties to be overcome with economy only by ingenious expedients yet to be devised.

3. As to the Central Park the need for a comprehensive review of its plan and of various projects of alledged improvement to be made in it has for some time been obvious. The original plan has not yet been fully carried out. Features have been introduced in a manner making it impossible that it should ever be carried out in all respects. Important elements of the plan have been so marred in execution as not to serve the purpose originally had in view, and the public respect for the design and confidence in the pursuit of it has in various ways been much impaired.

But the reason commonly given for urging a revision of the plan is based mainly, in our judgment, on mistaken premises and as reference is made to it in your letter, much as we should like the opportunity of making such a review as you suggest, we should be sorry to have you engage us for the purpose without a clear understanding of the point of view from which we should proceed.

The reason in question may be stated in this form.

Since the Central Park was planned the city has gained greatly in population and wealth and the character, tastes and modes of life of its people have greatly changed. What was adequate for their wants at that time cannot be supposed to be so now. Therefore it is but reasonable to assume that a sweeping revision of the plan is now needed.

This reasoning would give occasion not only for upsetting such results as have been gradually gained at great cost during the last thirty years on this park but for radically revising the plan of all parks of growing cities at certain intervals.

That the facts of the case may be realized it is first to be considered that under the name of parks undertakings may be set about for innumerable purposes. Those to be provided for in one park may differ as widely from those of another as the purposes to be served in building a hotel from those to be served in building a church. Whether and in what way the plan of a park needs revision therefore, is wholly a question of the particular purposes designed to be met by that particular park. A park planned with reference to one set of purposes will be as bad as it possibly can be with reference to another.

Hence in planning a park to be found on any given body of land, the first thing to be done is to limit and fix the purposes to be had in view.

The purposes that were determined to be had in view in planning the Central Park were not to be fully well-served until in various parts of the site, (then mainly a body of rock without trees and without soil in which to grow trees), there should be great numbers of trees with a spread of branches and standing in relations one to another that could not be expected to be attained in less time than forty years, nor, except through processes to be patiently and steadily pursued during that time for the purpose. Accordingly the plan in all its parts was devised with reference not in the least to what the city then was or to the manifest wants of the day but to what the city might be expected to be and its probable wants after a period of forty years. As the degree of the forecast thus used is now merely[4] realized by those who discuss questions of revision we will recall a few illustrations of it.

One is to be found in the four streets carried through the park by subways as a means of avoiding the disturbance and vexation that would otherwise be caused in time by currents of all sorts of street travel crossing the lines of pleasure travel.[5] This element of the plan imposed cruel restrictions with respect to provisions for its main purposes and made the work of designing these in a satisfactory manner greatly more difficult. The sunken roads were very costly. They delayed the opening of the park to use and were a ground of antagonism to the plan with all who were indisposed to carefully consider what their value would be after many years. There was not the least immediate need for them. Even now not a tenth part of the advantages to be eventually expected from them is realized and yet it is plain that if they had not been provided {and} another plan of the park proper had not been accommodated to them the most important measure for the improvement of the property at this time would be one for their introduction, even though it involved a revision of the plan of the park of a much more radical, destructive and costly character than any one thinks of proposing.

Another illustration of the fact is to be found in the numerous archways by which the greater number of visitors moving through the park on foot are led to avoid crossing or following the driving and riding ways. Were it not for the precautions taken in this respect[6] at a time when the number of private pleasure carriages and riding horses used in the city was not a hundredth part as great as at present, the pleasure roads of the Park might have been double the width they are without accommodating the use now made of them nearly as well as they do.

One other fact of similar significance may be stated. Some of those who regard riding as a matter of supreme importance are disposed to think that the provisions they find in the park for the purpose were devised with reference to the demand of the period when the plan was made. The fact is that at that time not half a dozen citizens of New York kept riding horses and among the innumerable suggestions offered as to what should be provided for in the park there was not one from any quarter for a bridle road. Yet the space then proposed by the designers to be given to bridle roads was larger than that of all the bridle roads of all the parks of London and in three years after the plan had been settled upon more had been done in the Central Park for the encouragement of pleasure riding than had been done in ten times as many years in all the other cities of the world. Even with all that has since been done elsewhere for the purpose, there is not yet another city that has made as complete, as varied, as costly, or, all things considered, as good provisions for pleasure riding as had long ago been planned by us to be offered to the citizens of New York. And it must be remembered that New York is now acquiring lands[7] in which it is to be presumed that much larger and more perfect provision will be made for this form of recreation in which the interest of the great body of its taxpayers and voters is very slight indeed.

It is perfectly true that there are defects in the existing provisions. It is not true that they are defects of ignorance of what is desirable or of neglect of careful study to secure the best that it has been wise to aim at under all the circumstances. The bridle road is unfortunately winding. It is to be regretted that the course before a rider is as much concealed as it often is but there is not a curve in the road that was not compelled by overruling considerations of the safety of riders and the pleasure and convenience of the public generally in the park. It has always been recognized to be most desirable to have a Rotten Row[8] and a grand promenade in the Park. But conditions of topography and the requirements of general convenience have interposed obstacles that in the opinion of successive park commissioners could not be overcome except at a cost not to be justified. We should be glad to find your Board able to take a different view.

With the caution thus offered against mistaken assumptions we shall proceed to consider how it well may happen that a careful revision of the plan of the Central Park as it exists today may be pressingly desirable.

The profit of nearly all classes of public as well as of private works is dependent largely upon the degree in which defined ends are kept continuously in view. If before a certain point has been reached a work has been carried on with a view to the requirements of a church and later to those of a hotel, the result will be a structure built at excessive cost, to be kept at excessive cost, and not nearly as well adapted to any desirable purpose as it might have been.

The cost of forming the Central Park has been much more than it would have been, the maintenance of it excessively expensive, and in no particular do the citizens of New York obtain nearly the value from their outlay upon it that would otherwise have been due them, because of the pressure constantly brought to bear upon their agents to disregard the principle thus illustrated. The particulars in which the plan is lost sight of or deliberately put aside are seldom particulars of striking importance. There has perhaps been but one instance in which any considerable overruling of the plan has been plainly seen to be impending that public opinion has not been so strongly expressed against it as to force the purpose to be abandoned, but one little thing after another has been done, and a general spirit nursed, tending by the multiplication of departures in detail from the lines necessary to be followed in order that the ruling purposes of the plan may not fail to be realized, of which the outcome is in many respects disastrous to the original ends of the work.

To show how this comes about more than might be supposed, it may be observed that from the beginning there have been annual changes in the composition of the Park Commission. Of the thirty Commissioners who have come suddenly from pursuits in no way preparing them to deal with technical questions of park management to take active part in the management of the park, no two have entered upon their duties with the same ideas of the purposes to be served by it, and no one has retired from these duties after a few years experience without very different ideas of what purposes it is desirable and practicable to attempt to serve from those he originally had. The greater number of Commissioners have at first considered that the most important part of their duty was to make the park more agreeable not by providing for its uninterrupted growth and development upon plans already formed but by the addition of new features of special and immediate interest to serve particular divisions of the public—the riders, the drivers, the walkers, the skaters, the curlers, those who are fond of croquet, or archery or lawn tennis, or cricket or base ball; those who have a special interest in exotic plants, in flowers, in perennials, in specimen trees, in shows of bedding plants; those who think the park is too shady, those who think it is too sunny and so on. With every change in the composition of the Commission there has been more or less bending of the ruling purpose of the Department in respect to such features and it has happened repeatedly that a considerable amount of work has been done with a view to a particular result and before this result was reached regard for it has so changed that the plan for attaining it has been abandoned. In this manner hundreds of thousands of dollars have been thrown away. And this is not the worst of it.

As a general rule every new undertaking of the class indicated has given a certain degree of satisfaction to a small portion of the public but at a loss to the great body not generally recognized at the time. Because of the large aggregate outlay into which the city has been led for the accomplishment of results of this character to be quickly realized and applauded by those particularly interested in them and because of the attention diverted to these results, undertakings of which the results were to be more slowly realized, and which it was therefore desirable should be prosecuted as rapidly as possible—undertakings of far more general and lasting importance—have been neglected, delayed, advanced listlessly and intermittently, and conditions have been allowed to be established making it finally impossible to carry out the original plan with respect to them.

It is now, therefore, an exceedingly complicated and difficult question in what degree it is judicious to attempt to return to the original design, in what respects to abandon it, in what respects to add to it and in what respects to accept and make the best of the revisions that have, without comprehensive purpose or regard for the future interests of the city, been drifted into.

As to the scope of the revision desirable this is to be said.

In the further management of the Central Park one of these courses will be pursued.

First it will be managed with little continuous regard to any general design but in a time-serving, desultory, piecemeal way, largely by compromises between differing views of what at any time shall be thought desirable to be rapidly accomplished.

Second, it may be managed with a steady purpose to pursue the ends originally selected to be had in view and with reference to which the larger part of the outlay upon it has been expended, so far as the opportunity for doing so with economy has not been destroyed.

It is with a view to this course if any that we should expect to be of service to you.

But, thirdly, as the population and wealth of the city are multiplied and the park becomes less a central than a "down-town" park, it may be questioned whether the difficulty of maintaining it suitably to the ends had in view in the original plan will not so increase as to render that purpose impracticable.

In view of the constantly recurring demands that provision shall be made for the better accommodation of visitors in certain particulars not a tenth of which provisions can be made within the area of this park without destroying its value for its original purposes, the question thus presented should have the gravest consideration.

The prime object of the park as originally had in view was to provide for the mass of the population unable to go as much out of town as would be desirable, a retreat as completely rural in character as the circumstances would admit. The proportion of those who use the park in carriages relatively to those who use it on foot will be constantly lessening in the future, yet the number of carriage visitors will be constantly increasing. It may yet come to be double or quadruple the present number. What will happen then? Even today complaint is made that the drives are not wide enough and we understand that the Department is constantly pressed to enlarge them. Once already it has yielded to such pressure and widened a considerable stretch of road, destroying many of the finest trees in the ground in order to do so, and readjusting walks and other features to the injury of the rural character of the ground.[9]

Suppose, then, another enlargement of the drives having been made, the carriage using part of the public shall have continued to increase and to live nearer the park so as to use it more freely proportionately to its numbers and that demands again come for yet another enlargement, and so again and again, what is the final result to be? Plainly it is only a question of time when the park will no longer have any value as a rural retreat. Nay, it is but a question how far the process shall be carried to make that which will take the place of the Central Park, a series of broad, hot, glaring desert driving places, with strips of grass and trees between them as unrural as a conservatory or a flower garden.

We have wished simply to suggest toward what ends a large class of the demands tend that are addressed to your Department, for the most part privately, by persons who, having no public responsibility in the premises, naturally take narrow and short sighted views of the duty of the commissioners.

Before dropping the subject, we will refer to the fact that while London has been growing densely all about Hyde Park and Kensington Garden; while it has been doubling in population and while fashion has been crowding all about these grounds and the throng of carriages entering them has enormously increased, no material enlargement has been made of the park drives. They are yet generally narrower than those of the Central Park and, if filled with carriages would altogether contain not half as many as the Central Park drives as originally laid out would accommodate. The drives, rides and walks of the system of parks which you have in contemplation to form by connecting Riverside and Morningside with Central Park and which can be made ready for public use in two or three years, will not only comfortably accommodate several times as many people in carriages but several times as many in the saddle and several times as many on foot as the corresponding ways of Kensington Gardens, Hyde, Green and St James' Parks and there is no probability that there will ever be a quarter as many people living within three miles of this group of the pleasure grounds of New York as within the same distance of those named of London.

The fact is that the enjoyment of rural scenery, or of any approach to rural quiet and tranquility, cannot well be provided for in the midst of a city by arrangements that will also provide in a perfectly satisfactory way for the pleasure that people take in great throngs, in making displays of fine dresses, equipages, horses and horsemanship, and in watching such displays. Nor is the enjoyment of rural scenery as a counteractive to the irritating effect of confinement over long to urban scenery to be satisfactorily associated with such gorgeous floral displays as many urge that the Commissioners may with advantage make on the park, especially in a park formed in accommodation to such a rugged, wild and intractable topography as the Central Park has been. We cannot have our cake and eat it. Hitherto, the park has offered little of rural charm but now, three fourths of the forty years upon which the designers reckoned for the development of its foliage having been passed, it will be found that the artificial features, so generally supposed, with the greatest possible misconception of their purpose, to have been introduced as objects of decoration, are, except in two or three special cases, scarcely noticeable, not at all intrusive and wholly subordinate in interest to the broader rural elements of the work.

If the city is to throw away the advantage that has thus been gained; if a different sort of park, adapted to serve a widely different leading purpose from that had in view in the original laying out of the drives, rides and walks, the planting on their borders, the grading and outlining of the lawns and the massing of the woods, it will be far better that the work of providing it should be taken up deliberately, plans for it devised comprehensively with a fair counting of the cost than that it should proceed in the scattering, unpremeditated, stealthy way thus far pursued.

Having thus explained our view of the situation, if your Board should still desire to engage our services as proposed in your letter, we suggest that the best arrangement for the purpose would be one similar to that twice before made with us since we relinquished our first position of general superintendence of the Central Park and which the records will show to have worked satisfactorily to those making it and to the public.[10]

Under such an arrangement our duty would be to give the Department our best judgment on problems of general design of the Central, Morningside and Riverside Parks and the proposed connections between them and to such extent as we should think to be desirable upon methods necessary to the prosecution of the work consistently with the designs.

We propose that our salary should be the same that it was under the former engagements referred to, namely $5000 per annum, and that the engagement should be for three years. The Department to supply us with required data and information of all kinds as to the conditions to be dealt with in the form of surveys, maps and drawings and through verbal inquiry of others in its service. Travelling expenses and outlays necessary to the presentation of our advice in convenient form, as in drawings and otherwise, to be borne by the Department. The Department to take no action modifying the intended effect of works that have been advanced upon our designs until after opportunity has been given us to report upon propositions for such action.

{*If*} these terms should be satisfactory to your Board, {*we have*} only further to {*request*} that methods may be adopted for carrying out the arrangement in as prompt, simple and direct a manner as the laws permit.

The text presented here is an unsigned draft in Olmsted's hand. On May 10 Olmsted had declined an invitation to consult with New York City's park commissioners about modifications they were making to the northwest corner of Central Park. He explained that he would not "take occasional commissions with respect to detached features of the general design of the Central Park." His friend William A. Stiles, a journalist for the *Tribune*, wrote him several letters urging him to work with the commissioners in order to ensure that any modifications made to Central Park were done responsibly. According to Stiles, the commissioners had not solicited advice from Olmsted until the city's newspapers criticized them for failing to do so. Stiles wrote to Olmsted that Henry R. Beekman, the president of the park board, had suggested to Edwin L. Godkin, the editor of the *Post*, that he would seek Olmsted's advice if the *Post* stopped writing negative editorials about the commissioners. Beekman wrote to Olmsted on May 11, explaining that the "circumstances of the case about which your advice is sought are very exceptional," and asking him if he would change his mind about consulting. Olmsted agreed to meet with Beekman, and they decided that Olmsted would present the terms in writing under which he would consult with the commissioners. Olmsted submitted a preliminary proposal on May 20, where he wrote, "I respectfully suggest that it should be proposed to Mr. Vaux, who is equally responsible for the original design of the Central Park, to resume with me the position and duties that we formerly held." On June 4, Beekman asked Olmsted and Vaux to submit an official proposal, and the document presented here is their response. An annotation on the first page reads, "Sent to Vaux 10th June 1886." Although the *Tribune* reported on June 16 a "rumor" that Olmsted and Vaux were going to be hired again as advising landscape architects, the park commissioners never officially acted on this proposal (FLO to Board of Commissioners of the Department of Parks of New York, May 10, 1886, A1: 351 OAR/LC; William A. Stiles to FLO, May 7, 1886; William A. Stiles to FLO, [May 10, 1886]; "The Defacement of Central Park," April 30, 1886, *New-York Tribune*, p. 4; Henry R. Beekman to FLO, May 11, 1886; FLO to Henry R. Beekman, May 12, 1886, A1: 354, OAR/LC; FLO to Henry R. Beekman, May 20, 1886; Henry R. Beekman to FLO, May 24, 1886; FLO to Henry R. Beekman, May 28, 1886, A1: 362, OAR/LC; Henry R. Beekman to FLO, June 4, 1886; "Hope for the Parks," *New-York Tribune*, June 16, 1886, p. 4).

1. Henry Rutgers Beekman (1845–1900) was a New York lawyer with extensive real estate interests in the city. Mayor William Russell Grace appointed him a park commissioner in 1885 and again in 1886. Soon after this letter was written, Beekman was elected president of the Board of Aldermen and resigned his position on the park board ("The New Park Commissioner," *New York Times*, March 18, 1885; Marquis James, *Merchant Adventurer: The Story of W. R. Grace* [Wilmington, Del., 1993], pp. 198–208; "Justice Beekman Dead," *New York Times*, Dec. 8, 1900).
2. In his letter of June 4, Beekman asked Olmsted and Vaux to consult on Central, Morningside, and Riverside parks. For Central Park, Beekman specifically mentioned possible plans to "increase the area of the drives, footpaths and bridle paths." He also wrote that "suitable and appropriate plans" were needed for Riverside and Morningside parks and asked Olmsted and Vaux upon what terms they would undertake the work (Henry R. Beekman to FLO and Calvert Vaux, June 4, 1886).
3. In his letter, Beekman had told Olmsted and Vaux that the New York State Legislature had passed a law placing 72nd Street, from Central Park to Riverside Drive, 122nd Street, from Riverside Drive to Morningside Avenue, and 110th Street, from Morningside Avenue to Fifth Avenue under the control of the Department of Public Parks. He asked Olmsted and Vaux to design improvements for those streets, which connected Central, Riverside, and Morningside parks. Governor David B. Hill did not sign the bill that Beekman references, but signed similar legislation a year later. In the 1890s the parks department widened 110th Street (also known as Cathedral Parkway) based on a plan by Vaux and Engineer Montgomery Kellogg. The city did not widen the other roads until the twentieth century, and not based on plans by either Olmsted or Vaux (Henry R. Beekman to FLO and Calvert Vaux, June 4, 1886; "An Act in relation to the jurisdiction of the department of public parks in the city of New York over certain streets and avenues in said city," [April 19, 1887], New York State, *Laws of the State of New York, Passed at the One Hundred and Tenth Session of the Legislature*, [Albany, N.Y., 1887], chap. 179; "An Appeal for the Parks," *New York Times*, March 8, 1887, p. 8; "Cathedral Parkway Improvement," ibid., Feb. 16, 1893, p. 5; "Signed by the Governor," ibid., Feb. 23, 1894, p. 5).
4. That is, scarcely understood or realized.
5. That is, "sunken" transverse roads. Although the terms of the Central Park competition called for four or more crosstown transverse roads, only Olmsted and Vaux's Greensward plan called for the roads to be "sunk so far below the general surface, that the park drives may, at every necessary point of intersection, be carried entirely over it" (Frederick Law Olmsted and Calvert Vaux, "Description of a Plan for the Improvement of the Central Park, 'Greensward,' " March 31, 1858 [*Papers of FLO*, 3: 122]).
6. That is, the layout of carriage drives and walkways in the Greensward Plan that avoided having two kinds of traffic intersecting whenever possible. As Olmsted wrote in 1859, "A carriage coming directly upon the course of a pedestrian or of a man on horse-back is an annoyance, if not positively dangerous." Therefore, just as the "sunken and tun-

neled street-thoroughfares across the Park were planned to remove what would have otherwise been a ceaseless annoyance . . . several miles of broad graveled walks have been laid out, carried by arched passages under the drives when necessary, by means of which all parts of the lower Park may be traversed on foot without encountering a single carriage or horseman" (Frederick Law Olmsted, "Description of the Central Park," [Jan. 1859] [*Papers of FLO*, 3: 216]).

7. In April 1883 the New York State Legislature established a commission to acquire parkland north of the Harlem River in the 22nd and 23rd wards, and in December Salem Wales proposed that the park board hire Olmsted to suggest locations for parks. The board did not hire Olmsted, but by June 1884 it had made recommendations for park locations and the legislature passed an act establishing Van Cortland, Bronx, and Pelham Bay parks, as well as several smaller parks and connecting parkways (nearly 4,000 acres in total). Van Cortland and Bronx parks were located in the portion of the Bronx that had been annexed by New York City in 1874, while Pelham Bay Park was then in southern Westchester County. By the end of the century the New York Botanical Garden and the New York Zoological Garden (Bronx Zoo) covered much of Bronx Park, and a golf course had become a central feature of Van Cortland Park (DPP, *Minutes*, Dec. 19, 1883, pp. 447–48; "The New Parks of the City of New York," *Scribner's Magazine*, April, 1892, pp. 439–55; Evelyn Gonzalez, "From Suburb to City: The Development of the Bronx, 1890–1940," in *Building a Borough: Architecture and Planning in the Bronx, 1890–1940* [New York, 1986], pp. 9–13).
8. Olmsted refers to Rotten Row in Hyde Park, London. This straight, tree-lined avenue extended through the park from Apsley Gate to Kensington Gardens and was a popular promenade and carriage way. Rotten Row was famous for displays of horsemanship and equipages by London's elite. In 1881 Olmsted was quoted as having been in opposition to a proposed "Rotten Row" in Central Park, to which he wrote a letter to the editor of the *World* clarifying his position. He explained that he was not against riding in Central Park, but that as the park was then designed there was no straight stretch of park drive long enough to replicate Hyde Park's Rotten Row (Donald Edgar, *The Royal Parks* [London, 1986]; Frederick Law Olmsted, "A New York Rotten Row," *World*, April 10, 1881).
9. Under pressure to widen Central Park's drives in the early 1870s, the park commissioners decided to widen a relatively straight section of the East Drive between the reservoir and Fifth Avenue. Olmsted condemned the result: "[t]he Commissioners of 1871 thought to make an improvement simply by widening the wheelway, giving no consideration to any other public requirement of the locality, and accomplishing the little that was attempted with such narrow study of the circumstances that the relation of the widened drive to adjoining objects was left incomplete, unsymmetrical and offensive to the eye" (FLO to Henry G. Stebbins, Dec. 3, 1875 [*Papers of FLO*, 7: 167]).
10. Following their resignation in 1863 as landscape architects to the Board of Commissioners of Central Park, Olmsted and Vaux were twice reappointed together to oversee work on the park, once on July 19, 1865, and again on November 23, 1871. From 1865 until 1870 they were landscape architects to the Central Park board, but in May 1870 the New York State Legislature replaced the Central Park board with the new Department of Public Parks, and six months later the new park commissioners relieved them of their services. In 1871, after the fall of the Tweed Ring, Henry Stebbins became president of the Department of Public Parks board and reappointed Olmsted and Vaux as "Landscape Architects advisory." Vaux resigned on July 1873 to focus on building the American Museum of Natural History and the Metropolitan Museum of Art. The park board abolished Olmsted's position in January 1878. In 1881, park commissioner Salem Wales suggested engaging them both as consultants to the board, but his resolution did not pass. The board did hire Vaux in November 1881 with the title of Super-

intending Architect, a position he held until January 1883. In 1886 Vaux was working on projects for the park board, including drawings for greenhouses in Central Park, but had no official public appointment (Calvert Vaux to FLO, July 21, 1865 [*Papers of FLO*, 5: 405–6]; "The Central Park—Character of the Proposed Change—A Protest," Dec. 21, 1870 [*Papers of FLO*, 6: 392–95]; FLO to Charles Loring Brace, Nov. 24, 1871 [*Papers of FLO*, 6: 493–94]; DPP, *Minutes*, July 16, 1873, pp. 117–18; ibid., Jan. 23, 1878, pp. 556–57; ibid., Oct. 19, 1881, pp. 297–98; ibid., Nov. 19, 1881, pp. 386–89; ibid., Jan. 24, 1883, p. 467; ibid., June 19, 1885, p. 139; ibid, Aug. 9, 1886, p. 168).

To Charles Eliot

20th July 1886.

My Dear Eliot,

I did not much suppose that you would take a vacation from your European school for a visit to the Pacific but as you might feel an inclination before going further to see something of the larger range of American scenery and the time to be lost at sea is so little, I thought it best to propose it.[1] I don't doubt that you are right.

What you said in your note of 5th June about the charm of some of the old gardening work and the folly of some of the new English work in Italy pleased me very much.[2] I suppose that in at least half of our country the conditions are much less favorable to English gardening than in northern Italy yet nobody cares for any other. I find Governor Stanford bent on giving his University New England scenery,[3] New England trees and turf, to be obtained only by lavish use of water. The landscape of the region is said to be fine in its way but nobody thinks of anything in gardening that will not be thoroughly unnatural to it. What can be done I don't know but it will be an interesting subject of study.

I hear that you are going to Russia. I hope that you will find the Lothrops there.[4] They will be most agreeable friends. Please give my regards to them. I shall be much interested in your opinion of the very simple planting that André told me about—but three species of trees being used—in the park of the principal Imperial rural residence near St Petersburg.[5]

The terrace at Washington is in great peril and I am doing all I can to save it—the danger being that Congress will order the western retaining wall to be pierced with windows. The prime mover in the matter is not a frontiersman but Senator Dawes of Massachusetts.[6]

Work is still suspended on Franklin Park and on all the Boston Parks, the republicans being afraid to trust the Democratic Commissioners with funds for advancing it.[7] It looks just now as if nothing would be done this year, but I am inclined to think that before election a new light will be seen. They are not good politicians who take the responsibility of keeping laboring men out of employment.

We have an interesting private work in a great stock farm for Dr. Webb near Burlington V^{t} with a magnificent view over Champlain to the Adirondacks. I propose a perfectly simple park, or pasture field, a mile long in the lake half a mile deep, the house looking down upon and over it.[8]

I enjoy all your letters exceedingly. Pray let us hear as much from you as you can afford.

Yours Truly

Fred^{k} Law Olmsted.

The text presented here is a signed letter in Olmsted's hand (see FLO to Charles Eliot, Feb. 25, 1886, above; FLO to Charles Eliot, March 4, 1886, above; FLO to Charles Eliot, Oct. 28, 1886, below).

1. As part of his preparation to become a landscape architect, Charles Eliot toured European cities, parks, and gardens in 1885 and 1886. In July 1886, having traveled through England, France, and Italy, he was living near Kew Gardens and preparing to travel to Scandinavia and Russia. Olmsted had written to Eliot in June proposing that he interrupt his European travels to go with him to California to meet Leland Stanford and begin the design of the Stanford University campus. Olmsted felt Eliot's recent observations in Italy and the Mediterranean coast, in particular, would be relevant to their consideration of the California project, due the similarities in climate. Eliot wrote to Olmsted, however, declining the offer in order to continue his travels (C. W. Eliot, *Landscape Architect*, pp. 50–163; FLO to Charles W. Eliot, Sr., June 8, 1888; Charles Eliot to FLO, June 27, 1886).
2. In his letter Eliot recounted his trip to the Italian Riviera, describing the climate and plants. While there, he made observations on villa gardens and how they differed from English examples: "Many of these places have not a square foot of sod — and the plan of one of these placed beside that of an English park would seem a wild absurdity." His impressions of the "classic style" of gardens around Genoa were vivid: "striking verdure-framed views. . . . dark vistas broken in the distance by a burst of sunlight," and "in the depths of the wood a little stone-built open theater — and in another part a dancing floor — all cushioned with green moss." Around Lake Como he enjoyed "the intricate mingling of picturesque stonework with the luxuriant vegetation of the South" (Charles Eliot to FLO, June 5, 1886).
3. Olmsted had recently accepted the commission to design the campus of Stanford University in Palo Alto. Leland Stanford at first was determined to create a landscape that would evoke the settings of universities in New England. Olmsted argued that an approach to landscape design appropriate for the climate and soils of California was needed (see FLO to Leland Stanford, Nov. 27, 1886, below).
4. Olmsted is likely referring to George Van Ness Lothrop (1817–1897), a lawyer from Easton, Massachusetts, who served as a minister to Russia from 1885 to 1888 and was stationed in St. Petersburg (*DAB*).
5. A reference to the Imperial estate Tsarskoye Selo outside St. Petersburg, where a land-

scape had been created using only three species of trees — birch, larch, and fir. Olmsted's friend Édouard André had visited Russia and published an account of his travels in *Un Mois en Russie* (1870) (C. Piazzi Smyth, *Three Cities In Russia* [London, 1862], p. 175).

6. Henry Laurens Dawes (1816–1903) was a journalist, lawyer, and politician from Massachusetts. He was elected to the House of Representatives in 1857 and to the Senate in 1875, where he served until 1892. During the 1880s he was a member of the Committee on Public Buildings and Grounds and therefore involved in plans for the Capitol grounds. Olmsted had recently traveled to Washington to convince Senator Dawes and other members of the Committee on Public Buildings and Grounds to accept a compromise proposal to place windows in the west terrace wall between the two staircases. The committee ultimately accepted Olmsted's proposal (*DAB*; see also FLO to William B. Allison, July 23, 1886, below).
7. In June 1886 the Massachusetts State Legislature passed a bill to allow Boston to exceed its debt limit by $2,500,000 to help fund the construction of Franklin Park. On July 19 a majority of the members of Boston's Board of Aldermen voted to delay approving the loan ("The Park Loan: It is Laid Over by the Board of Aldermen," *Boston Globe*, July 20, 1886, p. 6; see also FLO to Edward P. Wilbur, April 29, 1886, n. 2, above).
8. William Seward Webb (1851–1926) was married to Eliza ("Lila") Osgood Vanderbilt, and they engaged Olmsted to design their estate and model farm, Shelburne Farms, near Burlington, Vermont, on Lake Champlain, which Olmsted first visited in June 1886. The house was not constructed as Olmsted describes here (Mitchell C. Harrison, *Prominent and Progressive Americans: An Encyclopedia of Contemporaneous Biography* [New York, 1902], pp. 367–69; "Dr. William Seward Webb's Great Park," *New York Times*, Jan. 31, 1895; FLO to William Seward Webb June 18, 1886, A1: 374, OAR/LC; see FLO to William Seward Webb, July 12, 1887, below).

To William Edward Dorsheimer[1]

Private

21st July, 1886.

My Dear Governor,

Mr Green's letter[2] is obviously written for a purpose other than any plainly appearing. It is "for record", to "{. . .}",[3] to be used by others. It is adapted to produce an impression with any who may read it without other knowledge of the fact that no one but Mr Vaux had hitherto been considered with a view to the duty in question. It would nearly imply to {. . .}[4] Mr Vaux had been the first man thought of, that his counsel had been mutually taken in the preliminary {*deliberations*} of the Commission, and that he had been the first to consider it desirable that the gorge of the river below the Falls should be controlled for the public. It is adapted finally, and as a whole to produce the impression that any delay in the adoption of a plan is due to your obstruction of the course that has thus been most plainly before the Commission. If the

WILLIAM E. DORSHEIMER

object of the letter had been to provoke you to impatience and draw from you a reply under the influence of that impatience it could not have been {. . .}[5] more skillfully. I have received as I presume that you have a cutting from the New York Times suggesting a claim upon the Commission based on Mr Vaux's suggestions about the {. . .}[6] and it has been referred to in correspondence.[7] I should be most cautious not to underrate the value of any action of Mr Vaux but you can hardly have forgotten that some sixteen years ago you heard me urge that the scenery of this entire gorge below the Falls and especially the Whirlpool part of it was of secondary importance to securing the Falls themselves only because it would be more difficult to destroy the value of the natural scenery anywhere else than just {*above*} the Falls. You will remember that with Richardson and others we drove first to the Suspension Bridge and the {. . .}[8] College Grounds, and afterwards followed the river bank as closely as we could all the way to Lewiston studying a scheme for securing action of the State favorable to the purpose.[9] You will remember that the first idea of the Survey Commission was to include the gorge to the Whirlpool, that the question was carefully considered by Mr Gardner and myself and reported upon;[10] that the desirability of including the Whirlpool was referred to by you in addressing the Ontario government and the reasons given for not proposing that on our side it should be for the time being included.

The word pupil does not I think carry a right impression of Mr Vaux's connection with Mr Downing. Mr Vaux was engaged by Mr Downing, in London, as an architect, and after a little experience in building on this side,

I believe, was associated with him as a partner in the business of planning country houses and grounds. He was never a pupil in the ordinary sense.[11]

The statement regarding Mr Vaux's connection with the Central and Brooklyn Parks is adapted to produce a wrong impression upon any reader not otherwise well acquainted with the facts.[12] I was employed on the Central Park before Mr Vaux, and several years after his employment, except in an occasional desultory way, ceased. Altogether, upwards of fourteen (14) years.[13] Our responsibility for the design of both parks is precisely equal. For the practical superintendence of the works mine is far the greater. Mr Green has repeatedly placed on record expressions indicative of the high value placed on my individual services.

Yours Truly

Fred^k Law Olmsted.

The text presented here is from a letterpress copy of a handwritten letter signed on the original in Olmsted's hand: A1: 378–80, OAR/LC. Since 1869 Olmsted and others had advocated the creation of a state reservation around Niagara Falls, and in 1879 the New York State Legislature asked Olmsted to write a report with James T. Gardner suggesting appropriate boundaries for the proposed park. Governor Grover Cleveland signed the law authorizing the (unfunded) reservation in 1883. Two years later, then governor David B. Hill signed the appropriations bill that established what became the first state park in the country.

Olmsted's old opponent in New York City, Andrew H. Green, and Olmsted's friend and supporter, William E. Dorsheimer, were both commissioners on the board of the Niagara Reservation, and they argued over who should be appointed as consulting landscape architect. Green preferred to hire Vaux alone, while Dorshemier supported Olmsted. The board voted to hire both Olmsted and Vaux to prepare landscape development plans, resulting in their "General Plan for the Improvement of the Niagara Reservation" (1887). Olmsted had predicted a rift between Green and Dorsheimer when he first learned that they had been appointed to the Niagara Commission in 1883. In a letter to Howard Potter, the President of the Niagara Falls Association, Olmsted wrote, "I hear that Mr. Green has been appointed on the Niagara Commission. This compels me to decline any responsibility I might otherwise have henceforth to you or others in the matter. . . . The only trouble I apprehend is with Dorsheimer who I am sorry to hear is on the Commission with Green. This makes divided councils inevitable" (FLO to C. K. Remington, May 28, 1888, below; FLO to Thomas V. Welch, Feb. 16, 1889, below; "Notes by Mr. Olmsted," in *Special Report of New York State Survey on the Preservation of the Scenery of Niagara Falls for the Year 1879* [c. March 22, 1880] [*Papers of FLO*, 7: 474–81]; Leighton Williams to FLO, Oct. 12, 1886; FLO to William E. Dorsheimer, Oct. 26, 1886; *Papers of FLO*, SS1: 46–53; Francis R. Kowsky, "In Defense of Niagara," in Buscaglia-Castellani Art Gallery of Niagara University, *The Distinctive Charms of Niagara Scenery: Frederick Law Olmsted and the Niagara Reservation* [Niagara Falls, N. Y., 1985], pp. 8–15; "General Plan for the Improvement of the Niagara Reservation," 1887 [*Papers of FLO*, SS1: 535–75]; FLO to Howard Potter, May 9, 1883).

1. William Edward Dorsheimer (1832–1888) was a lawyer, U.S. Attorney, and elected official from Buffalo, New York. Olmsted refers to him as "My Dear Governor" because

he was elected lieutenant governor of New York in 1874, on the ticket with Samuel Tilden, and reelected to that position in 1876. A longtime advocate of public parks, he was an important friend and supporter of Olmsted's for many years. In 1868 he invited Olmsted to consult with the citizens' committee in Buffalo that was formed to advocate for the creation of municipal parks for that city. Dorsheimer was on the board of the Buffalo State Asylum for the Insane in 1871 when Olmsted and H. H. Richardson were asked to design the building and grounds, and as lieutenant governor he created an advisory board consisting of Olmsted, Richardson, and Leopold Eidlitz to consult on the design of the New York State Capitol. As president of the board of commissioners of the Niagara State Reservation in 1887, Dorsheimer supported hiring Olmsted and Vaux to develop the general improvement plan for the park. He served in the U.S. Congress from 1882 to 1884, and then returned to New York to serve as a federal district attorney in 1885 (*DAB*; William E. Dorsheimer to FLO, Aug. 12, 1868; *Papers of FLO*, 6: 455; FLO to Samuel Bowles, May 13, 1872 [*Papers of FLO*, 6: 545–48]; Olmsted, Vaux, & Co. to William E. Dorsheimer, Oct. 1, 1868 [*Papers of FLO*, SS1: 158–70]; "New York State Capitol Testimony," [March 6, 1877] [*Papers of FLO*, 7: 288–304]; "General Plan for the Improvement of the Niagara Reservation," 1887 [*Papers of FLO*, SS1: 535–75]; see also FLO to Sherman S. Jewett, April 11, 1887, below; FLO to C. K. Remington, May 28, 1888, n. 6, below).

2. Andrew Haswell Green (1820–1903), in his role as Niagara Reservation commissioner, wrote to William E. Dorsheimer, president of the commission, to recommend appointing Calvert Vaux as the commission's landscape architect. Vaux had insisted in May 1886 that he wanted to work with Olmsted on the project, but Green insisted that Vaux alone should be appointed. In his letter to Dorsheimer, Green listed Vaux's qualifications, giving him credit for most of the design of Central and Prospect parks, as well as significant suggestions for Niagara's improvement.

   Olmsted had known Green since the late 1850s, when Green was comptroller of the Central Park board. At first a friend and supporter, Green soon attempted to curtail Olmsted's authority through close supervision of expenditures, and the two men became bitter antagonists as the park work progressed. Green served on the Central Park board throughout the 1860s. After the fall of the Tweed Ring in 1871 he was appointed city comptroller, a position he used to withhold Olmsted's salary and to abolish his position with the Department of Public Parks in 1878. Green briefly returned to the Department of Public Parks in 1880 and pushed to have Vaux appointed landscape architect, while resisting attempts to return Olmsted to that position. In 1883 Governor Cleveland appointed him a Niagara Park Commissioner, a position he held for almost twenty years (Andrew H. Green to William E. Dorsheimer, July 21, 1886; Calvert Vaux to FLO, May 21, 1886; FLO to Calvert Vaux, May 24, 1886; George K. Radford to FLO, May 26, 1886; *DAB*; *Papers of FLO*, 3: 55–59; *Papers of FLO*, 7: 4–5, 593–94, n. 4, 695–97; Leighton Williams to FLO, Oct. 12, 1886; *FLO, A Biography*, pp. 395–97).
3. Three words here are faded from the manuscript.
4. Four words here are faded from the manuscript.
5. Two words here are faded from the manuscript.
6. Two words here are faded from the manuscript.
7. The *New York Times* reported that in 1883 Vaux had encouraged the purchase and protection of land along the Niagara banks extending all the way to the whirlpool: "He proposed a driveway and walks along the river, forming a narrow strip of natural park, to a point below the whirlpool, at which it might be connected by means of a bridge with the Canadian shore." The article mentioned that Green agreed with Vaux's proposal, and made no mention of Olmsted ("The Niagara Reservation," *New York Times*, March 29, 1886, p. 4).
8. One word here is faded from the manuscript.

9. On August 7, 1869, at Olmsted's request, several men expressing interest in protecting the Niagara Reservation (including H. H. Richardson) met at William E. Dorsheimer's room at the Cataract House. The following day, according to a report in *Harper's New Monthly Magazine*, "the party drove to Lewiston, examining the banks to see if a public road could not be so laid out as to secure permanently for the public such views of the falls and the river as the land as yet unoccupied could furnish." The suspension bridge to which Olmsted refers was built in 1868 and was the first bridge to cross the Niagara River gorge just below the reservation. It would be replaced by the Falls View Bridge in 1898. The college grounds that Olmsted mentions were the grounds of De Veaux College (FLO to C. K. Remington, May 28, 1888, below; FLO to Thomas V. Welch, Feb. 16, 1889, below; "Editor's Easy Chair," *Harper's New Monthly Magazine*, Oct., 1885, pp. 801–2; Ralph Greenhill, *Spanning Niagara: The International Bridges 1848–1962* [Seattle, 1984], p. 32; George Washington Holley, *The Falls of Niagara and Other Famous Cataracts* [London, 1882], pp. 142–43).
10. James Terry Gardner (or Gardiner) (1842–1912), a surveyor and engineer, was appointed director of the New York State Survey in 1876. Olmsted had known Gardner since his years on the Mariposa Estate in California (1863–1865), when he had hired Gardner to survey Yosemite Valley for the newly appointed Yosemite Commission. In 1879 Olmsted and Gardner were asked by the commissioners to inspect Niagara Falls and prepare a report. They made their first official visit in May of 1879, and in September presented their report (*DAB*; *FLO, A Biography*, p. 380; FLO to James Terry Gardner, Oct. 2, 1879 [*Papers of FLO*, 7: 420–22]; FLO to James Terry Gardner, Oct. 3, 1879 [*Papers of FLO*, 7: 422–24]; "Notes by Mr. Olmsted," in *Special Report of New York State Survey on the Preservation of the Scenery of Niagara Fall for the Year 1879* [c. March 22, 1880][*Papers of FLO*, 7: 474–81]).
11. In his letter, Green wrote: "Mr. Vaux was the pupil of Mr. Downing and first in the field of landscape architects of this country" (Andrew H. Green to William E. Dorsheimer, July 21, 1886).
12. In the same letter Green wrote: ". . . he [Vaux] was the professional advisor in the improvement of the greater portion of the Central Park, New York; of Prospect Park of Brooklyn and of many other extensive enterprises. He is an educated architect, taking no second rank in his profession" (Andrew H. Green to William E. Dorsheimer, July 21, 1886).
13. The Central Park board appointed Olmsted "superintendent" of Central Park in 1857 and "architect-in-chief" in May 1858. From January 1859 to April 1862, Vaux held the title of "Consulting Architect." At the beginning of the Civil War, Olmsted left New York in order to direct the U.S. Sanitary Commission in Washington, D.C. In May 1863, Olmsted and Vaux resigned from the post of "Landscape Architects to the Board," which they had held jointly since April 1862. In July 1865, they were reappointed landscape architects and continued in that role until they were forced to resign from the newly-created Department of Public Parks in November 1870. They were reappointed in November of 1871. Vaux resigned a year later, and Olmsted remained as the head of the Office of Design and Superintendence until the abolition of that post in January 1878. Vaux went on to serve as architect for the park board from 1881 to 1883. Vaux rejoined the park department in December 1887, as Landscape Architect, serving with that title until his death in 1895 (Frederick Law Olmsted, Jr., and Theodora Kimball, eds., *Forty Years of Landscape Architecture: Central Park, Frederick Law Olmsted, Sr.* [Cambridge, Mass., 1973], pp. 533–37; Francis R. Kowsky, *Country, Park, & City: The Architecture and Life of Calvert Vaux* [New York, 1998], pp. 161, 299, 306, 316; DPP, *Minutes*, Dec. 22, 1887, p. 412).

To William Boyd Allison[1]

[July 23, 1886]

Hon. William B. Allison,
Chairman of Committee of Appropriations,
United States Senate:

Dear Sir: I respectfully ask that the attention of your committee may be invited to certain considerations affecting the question of opening windows in the outer wall of the terrace of the Capitol.

The essential purpose of the Capitol is provided for in a range of halls for legislative assemblies with connecting corridors, ante-rooms, and side rooms, and this range is manifested exteriorly by colonnades and other decorative features carried around the entire building. It is set well above ground, and is held up and made more conspicuous and notable by a very plain basement story.

Below this basement story there are foundation walls, and between these foundation walls a cellar. It is not customary in buildings of any importance to make a show of the foundation walls or of the cellar. It would detract from the dignity of such buildings to do so. That the cellar may be lighted and ventilated it is usual to make what in common city buildings is called an area, within which windows are opened through the foundation walls into the cellar in such a manner that they cannot be seen in a general view of the building from the outside.

This is essentially what has been done in building the Capitol, the area on the west side being a very large one. There are rooms of some importance in the cellar story, but these rooms are not designed to be presented to view, nor can they be presented to view with propriety any more than the coal vaults or any domestic offices in the cellar of ordinary fine large town houses.

The original design of the Capitol has thus been sufficiently explained. Now, as to the construction that is being added to it, called the terrace, it must not be supposed that this has been designed with the slightest idea of amending or re-organizing or overruling the original design of the building. It has not been intended to make a more important feature of the cellar part of the building, to bring it out of ground or to light it. Had there been any such purpose, had Congress asked for a plan for any such purpose, a very different plan would have been devised for it from that of the terrace. Nothing whatever of what has thus far been built of the terrace would have been proposed.

What, then was the object of the terrace? The answer may be given in this way:

Here is a great and costly building, the greater part of the cost of which has been directed to the purpose of producing a certain impression on the minds of those looking toward it, and an impression that should be associated with ideas of the strength and majesty of a great nation.

There is nothing more necessary to a successful realization of such a purpose in a building than that it should seem to stand firmly; that its base should seem to be immovable. There is a difficulty in making as strong an impression in this respect as is desirable when an extraordinarily massive structure is placed, as in the case of the Capitol, hanging upon the brow of a hill.

The object of the terrace was to more effectually overcome this difficulty. How was it to be accomplished?

It was proposed to be accomplished by setting a strong wall into the face of the hill in front of the foundations of the building; that is to say, in front of its cellar wall. Such an outer wall, it was calculated, would have the effect upon the eye of a dam holding back whatever on its upper side looked liable to settle toward the down-hill side. Every dollar thus far spent on the terrace, and on the grounds in connection with it, has been spent on the supposition that this calculation was soundly made. If it was soundly made, then it will appear that the opening of holes in this wall would leave the same effect as the opening of holes in a dam. It would make the building behind it look less secure in its foundations, less firmly based on the down-hill side.

Another way of stating the intended effect of the wall is that it would seem to overcome all tendency of the upper part of the hill to be squeezed out by the weight of the great mass of masonry above it.

Now, such a wall being seen a short distance in front of the cellar wall of the Capitol, it is of no consequence, with reference to the purpose stated, whether the space between the two is occupied by solid earth, or whether the earth is excavated, and in its place cross-walls built, by which any tendency of the cellar walls to slip out would be resisted. The result must be the same, a firmly reinforced base. In this case the arrangement of cross-walls have been adopted, and it has been thought that an advantage would be gained by making the spaces between these cross-walls available for storage vaults, and in those parts where, under the old arrangement,[2] a sunken area had been provided for the lighting of the cellar of the main building, that the spaces so gained should be prepared in a manner making them equally suitable with the best of the present cellar rooms in respect to the requirements of light and air. But the advantages to be gained in this way have always during the ten years in which the scheme has been under discussion been presented as incidental advantages simply, not as the main purpose.

With reference to this incidental purpose, and more especially to the requirement of additional committee-rooms, the Committee on Public Buildings and Grounds was asked to say how many additional well-lighted and ventilated rooms were desirable. The answer was that twenty would be enough. As the plan stands now, twenty-eight rooms are provided for. Their average area is 25 by 15 feet. Each has at least one window opening upon the area, and the smallest of these windows measures 8 by 11 feet. There is a large door opposite the window of each room opening from a spacious corridor, through which a thorough draught can be carried. The rooms would be large, lofty, airy, and well lighted.

Respectfully,

FRED'K LAW OLMSTED,
Landscape Architect.

The text presented here was published in the *Congressional Record of the Forty-Ninth Congress, First Session*, Vol. XVII (July 23, 1886), p. S7385. Olmsted sent this letter on July 15, 1886, to Senator William Boyd Allison, who read it into the record on July 23. Senator Allison was participating in a debate on the Senate floor over the question of including windows in the outer walls of the Capitol's west terrace, then under construction. The windows would have pierced the base of the terrace to provide light and ventilation for new offices and committee rooms within. Olmsted had first learned that members of the Committee on Public Buildings and Grounds wanted to add windows to the lower terrace when its chairman sent him a letter dated February 15, 1886, asking that he consent to this alteration. The committee needed his approval because the law provided that work on the terrace had to be done in accordance with Olmsted's plan. He was adamantly against the idea, writing several letters on the issue and traveling to Washington on February 25, 1886. He wrote a long letter to Edward Clark on March 21, 1886, that included many of the same arguments that he provides in this letter. Clark continued to pressure Olmsted through July to approve the changes, but Olmsted refused. In a July 20 letter to Clark, Olmsted wrote that the architects Charles Howard Walker and H. H. Richardson both "very strongly confirmed the view that I had taken of the prospect of the windows in the terrace." He proposed a redesign of the central space between the flanking staircases of the west terrace, a compromise that included some new windows. By the time the debate over the windows occurred on the Senate floor, Senator Allison and several members of the Committee of Public Buildings and Grounds had been convinced that Olmsted's proposal sufficed to address their concerns. An appropriation based on Olmsted's revised plan passed Congress on August 4, 1886 (FLO to Hon. William B. Allison, July 15, 1886, AOC; Chairman, Committee on Public Buildings and Grounds to FLO, Feb. 15, 1886, AOC; FLO to Edward Clark, March 21, 1886, A1: 316–21, OAR/LC; Edward Clark to FLO, March 29, 1886, AOC; Edward Clark to FLO, July 16, 1886; FLO to Edward Clark, July 18, 1886, AOC; FLO to Edward Clark, July 20, 1886; G. Brown, *Documentary History of the United States Capitol*, pp. 1238–60; W. C. Allen, *History of the United States Capitol*, pp. 349–57).

1. William Boyd Allison (1829–1908) was an Iowa Republican first elected to the Senate in 1873. He served as chairman of the Senate Appropriations Committee from 1881 to 1908 (*DAB*).
2. The "old arrangement" was Olmsted's original west terrace design that anticipated the construction of a library extension to the Capitol. In the revised design that Olmsted was suggesting in 1886, six new committee rooms were planned for the area between the staircases on the upper terrace. Windows provide light, air, and views to the west for the new commitee rooms. This area had been part of the vaulted "crypt" intended to support the weight of the library extension and serve as a vestibule for adjacent offices. On the lower terrace, Olmsted altered the outer terrace wall, curving it inward and lining it with a series of apsidal niches. The semi-circular wall was centered on a new, circular fountain with a modest jet. Olmsted hoped this compromise would preserve the integrity

of the terrace as a visual foundation for the building, while providing at least some new windows (FLO to Edward Clark, Feb. 15, 1886, above; W. C. Allen, *History of the United States Capitol*, pp. 349–57).

To Anne Whitney[1]

3d Aug. 1886,

My Dear Miss Whitney,

In your note to me of 1st July[2] you suggested that a conference between us would be desirable after your return to town in the Autumn. As I am likely to be away in September I think it better that I should write you on the matter of your inquiry. I presume that a letter to your town address will be forwarded.

The primary and essential purpose of the unpaved space A. B. C. of enclosed diagram is that of preserving as far as possible under the circumstances the continuity of the principal line of foot communication between the Public Garden and the Back Bay Promenade. There is a broad walk provided at each of the points D. E & F and there should be as direct a thoroughfare prepared for

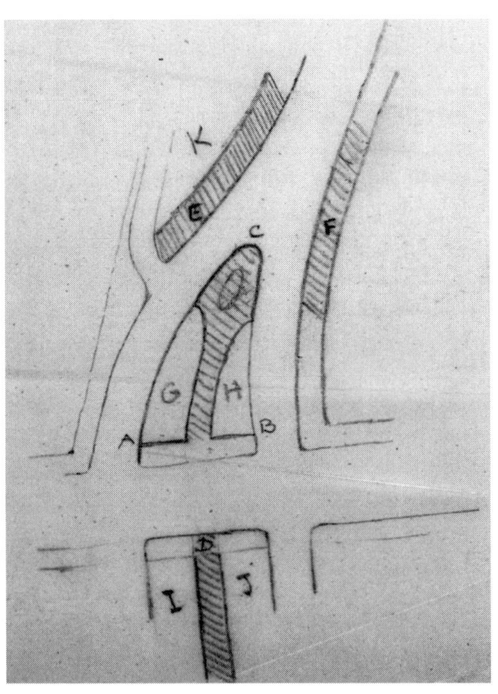

VIEW OF COMMONWEALTH AVE., BOSTON (POSTCARD), C. 1887, SHOWING PLACEMENT OF LEIF ERICSSON STATUE

footmen as is practicable between them. It is not necessary to occupy the spaces G and H for this purpose but as it would serve no good purpose to pave them I thought it best that they should be occupied in such a manner as would make a link of connection between the verdant spaces I-J and K.

Nor is all of the west end of the tongue necessarily to be prepared for the passage of footmen between D & E F. Consequently a fountain, statue or other monument can be given room at this point without interfering with the general design.

Perhaps, as you suggest, a simpler arrangement would be better but it could only be obtained by omitting the turf and letting the spaces G. & H be flagged or graveled. This would have the disadvantage of obliterating a certain expression of design in the lines bounding the walk which show the direction of movement.

You will see that from my point of view the place A. B. C. is not an island of turf divided for the sake of ornament by gravel but rather an island of gravel with these portions useless to footmen, lined off and left available for other occupations, as by turf, shrubs &c. But these are unessential.

The effect of what you suggest would be one of intentional and emphasized discontinuity of design — the reverse of that which from the first I have had in view.[3]

Submitting these reasons for not agreeing with you to your kind consideration, I am

Very Truly Yours

Fred[k] Law Olmsted.

The text presented here is from a letterpress copy of a handwritten letter signed on the original in Olmsted's hand: A1: 386–87, OAR/LC. It concerns the placement of Anne Whitney's statue of Leif Ericsson on Commonwealth Avenue at its intersection with West Chester Park (now named Charlesgate East). The statue's location was part of the Commonwealth Avenue extension through the Beacon Street entrance to the Back Bay Fens. Olmsted made the roadway curvilinear in order to provide an appropriate transition to the Fens landscape, as well as to allow traffic to run in a continuous curve to and over the Boylston Street Bridge (see FLO to Charles H. Dalton, Sept. 6, 1884, above; *Report of the Landscape Architect*, Dec. 24, 1883, above; plans 916-25, 916-24-SH1, 916-111, NPS/FLONHS).

1. Anne Whitney (1821–1915) was a sculptor and poet. In 1872 she established a studio on Mount Vernon Street in Boston, where she completed some of her most famous works, including the marble statue of Samuel Adams in the Capitol at Washington, D.C., and the bronze statue of Charles Sumner in Harvard Square. In 1886 she was working on her statue of explorer Leif Ericsson, which was finished and erected in the fall of 1887 on an eleven-foot pedestal (*DAB*; "Leif Erickson: The Statue of the Norse Explorer Erected at Back Bay Park," *Boston Daily Advertiser*, Oct. 24, 1887).
2. Whitney's July 1 letter to Olmsted has not been found. She wrote him again soon after, explaining that "the pedestal is ready to be set in its place." She asked if there was anything Olmsted needed from her while she was away for the summer and added, "My stone-cutter is fully possessed of all my plans models &c. & competent" (Anne Whitney to FLO, July 10, 1886; FLO to Anne Whitney, n.d. [fragment], Anne Whitney Papers, Wellesley College Archives).
3. Whitney and Olmsted continued to correspond in the fall of 1886 about her statue and the arrangement of the plants to be established around it. In December he responded humbly to her further requests for his advice, "You care a great deal too much for my judgment upon matters that lie beyond my professional field," he wrote, "If I differed with you on a point of your art you would certainly be wrong to be influenced in the slightest by my opinion" (FLO to Anne Whitney, Aug. 14, 1886; FLO to Anne Whitney, Dec. 4, 1886, Anne Whitney Papers, Wellesley College Archives).

To George Washington Vanderbilt[1]

Brookline 9th August, 1886.

George W. Vanderbilt Esq:
My Dear Sir;

When we came to study the plan of the Mausoleum Ground with the advantage of the topographical map, we found that the slope of the hill was much steeper than, in passing up through the trees, I had been led to suppose and the work required to realize the ideas I had formed for its treatment, more especially for the route of the approach road, much heavier. We found also in later visits that the distances being misty I had at first been deceived as to the direction of the outlook toward the ocean. This led us to try to form different plans but at the end we returned in the main to the views originally expressed to you. We did not however

GEORGE WASHINGTON VANDERBILT

feel inclined to elaborate our plan without being better satisfied on a few points nor without further conference with Mr Hunt. For that purpose I have been to New York and to Staten Island during the last week, have discussed the matter with Mr Hunt and also with Mr Ostrander, the Superintendent of the Cemetery, as well as with Captain Vanderbilt and your brother Cornelius,[2] whom I saw yesterday at Newport. I am very sorry that we cannot see you and that our present views can only be presented as imperfectly as they must be, even by a long letter.

I will first submit three propositions upon which the design must be formed:—

I. The approach should be at no point so steep as to make a strong impression upon the mind of those passing over it of being extraordinary in that respect. The line originally laid down and upon which a road has been begun would have a grade of one in seven which is far out of the question. The extreme grade that we think admissible would be one in fourteen (The grade of Fifth Avenue, 34th to 35th Streets is one in twenty five—of the steepest bye-road in the

Central Park, that by which "Vista Rock" is reached where the statue of Bolivar stands,[3] is one in seventeen).

II. A markedly zigzag course which would claim attention as a feat of engineering should not be taken to get up the hill. As far as possible in the end the road should seem to be following a course prepared by nature.

III. The Mausoleum is intended to resemble what are called hill-side tombs, these being caverns in the sides of hills with monumental entrances built up outside the natural entrances. This intention is not satisfactorily realized however, because the upper part of the masonry appears from all points to be above the highest part of the hill behind it. The effect would be much better if the ground behind were higher and on the flanks of the tomb more advanced, that is to say, if the masonry did not protrude from the hill side so much as it does — Mr Hunt entirely agrees with me in this opinion.

I will explain what we advise to be done by reference to the enclosed sheet labeled "Preliminary Plan".[4]

The present road of the Moravian Cemetery is to be followed to the point B, where a cutting has been made, as you will remember, with the intention of turning sharply to the left. Instead of this, the present proposition is to turn slightly to the left, strike into the hill, then with an easy curve turn to the right and approach the tomb with a single sweep, going as near the East boundary of the property as is practicable while leaving a screen of foliage to prevent an outside view in this direction.

The branch road is for the use of the custodian.

I proposed in conversation with you that the entire space of the terrace should be paved as a carriage court. The dullness and aridity of such an arrangement seems to be unnecessary. We now propose that the larger part should be a surface of flat turf flush with the carriage sweep shown. The carriage way is twenty feet wide. On the occasion of a funeral the procession would approach on the right of the tomb, the carriages stopping in succession at the steps before the entrance and then moving on without change of order until the rear of the procession was reached when they would turn and follow back, finally taking up their proper occupants at the steps and then move round the sweep and proceed down the hill out of the ground, keeping always to the right. This would be simple, orderly and in accordance with custom. If by any blunder or accident carriages were driven off on the turf it would occasion no disturbance or serious injury. The turf could be occupied by those on foot. It is intended to be kept flat and smooth as a tennis court.

The terrace is to appear of perfectly level surface bounded by a parapet three feet high of the same cut stone as the face of the tomb, to be designed in detail by Mr Hunt. This to be broken at intervals by piers and on those piers vases within which tubs of agaves or other suitable plants to be placed during the summer. The terrace to be sustained by a wall under the parapet. This wall to be built of field stone of the locality with considerable batter, to be much over-

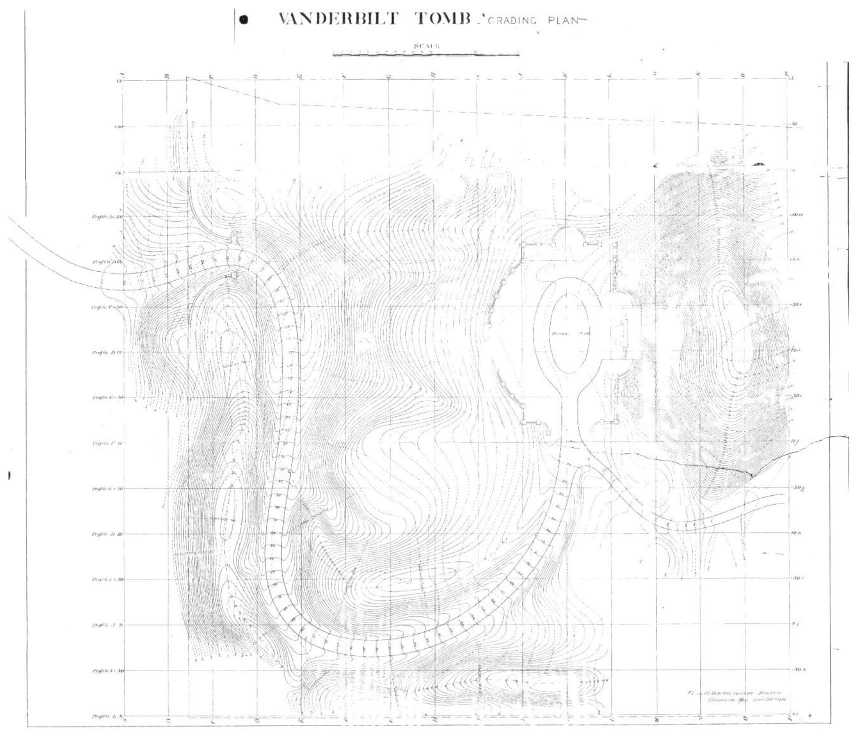

"Vanderbilt Tomb, Grading Plan," September 30, 1886

grown with creepers. If the outline of the terrace shown in the drawing should be retained, this wall would in its southern face be six feet high. But Mr Hunt would much prefer, and it may be practicable by changing the proportions of the terrace ground plan, to carry it farther out from the tomb and give it a greater elevation on the South.

In order to give the hill greater relative importance in looking toward the tomb, it is proposed to fill over it until a new surface is formed on all the space of about 150 feet back of the terrace, this new surface to be twenty five feet higher than the present surface and fifteen feet higher than the highest point of the roof. The proposition in this respect will be understood better by examining the *Section* on another sheet sent herewith. The embankment to spread to the right and left, its surface merging with the natural surface at points about a hundred feet from the lanthorns[5] i.e. from the middle of the tomb.

The objection to the entire proposition as thus presented, which has led us to be slow in advising its adoption is 1st the necessity it involves of removing a large number of trees both in the immediate vicinity of the tomb and on the hill side before it and, 2nd the heavy work of grading required. Neither of these objections can be overcome without (1) shutting the ocean out of view from

Vanderbilt Tomb with finished mounding, c. 1895

the terrace, (2) making the approach road longer and more tortuous in course, (3) leaving the face of the tomb to appear as it does now unfortunately large relatively to the hill side against which it stands.

The heavy work of grading referred to is that necessary to carry the road up the hill on the simple course laid down, with a rise of one foot in each fourteen of advance. To accomplish this the road must be in cutting nearly all the way, and at one point this cutting would be 30 feet deep. The material to be moved will be little short of 40,000 yards which is three times as much as could be used in grading up the hill back of the tomb and in forming the terrace. The excess we propose to throw out on the South side of the cut.

The result in time would be this:—

The road on leaving the general cemetery would enter through a gateway what would appear to be a natural winding defile, the slopes of which would be of varying undulation and for the most part closely wooded so that there would be arches of foliage over the road forming a deep shade. This would continue till the turn had been made by which the face of the tomb would be brought into view in a framing of foliage, when the road would come quickly out into the open table of the terrace.

The trees to be removed would have to be replaced by planting smaller ones but in a few years these smaller trees would be much finer than the existing trees can ever be, most of the latter having grown too closely and acquired a spindling habit.

The grading would probably supply all the stone needed for the retaining-wall of the terrace and for the bottoming of the roads.

The cost for grading would probably be from 25 to 35 cents per cubic yard, say $12000, the material being delivered where required. We have the addresses of three Staten Island contractors, recommended by Captain Vanderbilt and others, and, the specifications being very simple, we can, when desired, soon obtain bids from them.

I expect to leave for Oregon and California about the 20th inst. To be absent 5 or 6 weeks. If desired the work could be put under contract before that. We have an assistant engaged to set out the work and superintend it on the ground and my son[6] will inspect it as often as may be desirable.

Yours Truly

Fred[k] Law Olmsted.

The text presented here is a letter written in a clerk's hand and signed by Olmsted. There is also a draft of this letter, dated August 7, 1886, in FLO Papers/LC. The Vanderbilt family mausoleum in New Dorp, Staten Island, was Olmsted's first commission for the Vanderbilt family. Cornelius Vanderbilt (1794–1877) initially located a family mausoleum adjacent to the Moravian Cemetery on Staten Island in 1855. His son, William Henry Vanderbilt (1821–1885), once a neighbor of Olmsted's on Staten Island, commissioned Richard Morris Hunt to design a new mausoleum on the site late in 1884. After his death the next year, his son, George W. Vanderbilt, continued the project and hired Olmsted to design the landscape, which included an arched entrance to the grounds, a winding, uphill approach road, and terraces at the crest of the hill. Construction and initial landscape work were completed in 1889, but Olmsted and engineer J. J. R. Croes continued to consult on the project in the 1890s (Robert B. King, *The Vanderbilt Homes* [New York, 1989], pp. 176–81; Paul R. Baker, *Richard Morris Hunt* [Cambridge, Mass., 1980], pp. 290–91; FLO to JCO, April 10, 1886; FLO to Richard M. Hunt, July 22, 1886, A1:381, OAR/LC; FLO to Richard M. Hunt, Aug. 11, 1886, A1: 397–99, OAR/LC; FLO to J. J. R. Croes, Aug. 14, 1886, A1: 405–7, OAR/LC; JCO to Richard M. Hunt, Aug. 28, 1886, A1: 421, OAR/LC; JCO to J. J. R. Croes, Aug. 30, 1886, A1: 422–24, OAR/LC; JCO to Cornelius Vanderbilt, Sept. 1, 1886, A1: 425–27, OAR/LC; see also FLO to Richard M. Hunt, May 5, 1887, below; FLO to J. J. R. Croes, May 30, 1888, below).

1. George Washington Vanderbilt (1862–1914) was the son of William Henry Vanderbilt and so, with his siblings, was heir to one of the largest fortunes of the Gilded Age. Vanderbilt's privileged upbringing developed his interests in art, architecture, and collecting. His appreciation of the mountain scenery of western North Carolina resulted in his acquisition of thousands of acres of land, beginning in 1888, for what became his Biltmore estate. That year Olmsted began working on the project with Richard Morris Hunt (*DAB*).
2. Jacob Hand Vanderbilt (1807–1893) was the brother of the patriarch of the family, Cornelius Vanderbilt. He ran a ferry company that his brother had given him and was president of the Staten Island East Shore Railroad, built in 1864. Cornelius Vanderbilt II

(1843–1899) was George W. Vanderbilt's older brother, the eldest son of William Henry Vanderbilt ("Vanderbilt Dead," *New York Times*, March 20, 1893; *DAB*).

3. Olmsted errs and is describing here Summit Rock in Central Park, not Vista Rock. Vista Rock is the second highest point in the park at the top of the Ramble, on which Belvedere Castle is located. Summit Rock, the highest (although not the most prominent) point in the park, is at the western edge of the park near 83rd Street. An equestrian statue of Simon Bolivar was placed there in 1884 and later removed ("Sensitive About Poor Statues," *New York Times*, March 21, 1884, p. 3; "The Bolivar Statue Accepted," ibid., March 26, 1884, p. 8; "Unveiling the Bolivar Statue," ibid., June 17, 1884, p. 8).
4. A plan for the site dated August of 1886 has not been found, but other preliminary and topographical plans dating to the fall of 1886 do exist; such as plans 218-26, 218-19, and 218-9, NPS/FLONHS.
5. A nineteenth-century spelling for "lantern" (*OED*).
6. That is, John C. Olmsted, his stepson and nephew.

To Mariana Griswold Van Rensselaer

11th August, 1886.

Dear Mrs Van Renssalaer,

I have your very kind note of 6th inst. I was sorry to fail of seeing you again. It was {. . .} fault in miscalculating the time needing to reach the ferry.[1]

There are some things that cannot be done and there are standards that cannot be reached & which it is useless to set. Putting those out of the question, what have you to be afraid of? Who could more surely command the subject? It is exactly on the line that you have been following, and, the undertaking having taken the shape that it has, no one else is half as well fitted for it. It is not desirable that you should have been nearer to Mr Richardson than you have been. It would be better in order to take a thoroughly discriminating, candid historical view that you should stand further away. But on the whole if you can avoid the natural tendency to eulogy and partisanship no one could be better placed than you are to think out the true instructiveness of his life.

For my part I find it impossible to do so. But the conviction is rather growing upon me that there was a good deal of luck in Trinity and in all his best work until lately. Only toward the last was he constant to himself and able to proceed unexperimentally. His success was but partially that of an architect. It was very largely that of gaining the interest of common place men in matters that would otherwise have been of no concern to them, and in this way securing opportunities,—a freedom to work in his own spontaneous way—that no other architect could hope for. I do believe that it was in his ability to secure from clients a proper footing more than anything else that his success is due. Architects are so generally compelled to consider not what will be satisfactory to themselves but to their clients and the public. The public is so far behind good architects and finds it so hard to understand what they are driving at.

The book will be worth more to the public than to architects.

And this — the interpretation of artists to the public — is your public mission.

No, thank you ever so much, I can't think of taking any such refresh[t] as you offer at Southapton.[2] I expect to start in ten days for the Pacific and it is today decided that Harry Codman as well as my boy 'Rick[3] go with me. When we get back you will have got well over the bar of the book and going along with a clear sea before you.

Mrs Olmsted sends her kindest regards — Moll[4] is away on another drive. Sometime Mrs Sargent[5] will be away and we shall have the carpenters out of the house for a vacation, then we shall be looking for a visit from you.

Very Truly Yours

Fred[k] Law Olmsted.

The text presented here is a signed letter in Olmsted's hand. At this time Van Rensselaer was considering writing a biography of H. H. Richardson. In June, Olmsted wrote to her that "the best book would be the one most educative of the people — That means a book exactly in your accustomed current toward which you will naturally drift and in which you will move with the greatest ease and satisfaction" (FLO to Mariana Griswold Van Rensselaer, June 12, 1886).

1. Olmsted had just returned to Brookline from a trip to New York and to Newport, Rhode Island. Van Rensselaer vacationed in Newport and her permanent residence was in New York, and so Olmsted could have been referring to visiting her in either city (FLO to George W. Vanderbilt, Aug. 9, 1886, above; Cynthia D. Kinnard, "The Life and Works of Mariana Griswold Van Rensselaer, American Art Critic," [Ph.D. diss., Johns Hopkins University, 1977], p. 24).
2. That is, Southampton, Long Island, where Van Rensselaer also vacationed (C. D. Kinnard, "The Life and Works of Mariana Griswold Van Rensselaer," p. 24).
3. That is, Olmsted's son, Frederick Law Olmsted, Jr. (1870–1957).
4. That is, Olmsted's daughter Marion (1861–1948).
5. That is, Mary Allen Robeson Sargent (1853–1919), the wife of Charles Sprague Sargent. Van Rensselaer was a close friend of the Sargents and probably often stayed with them when in Boston (*DAB*).

CHAPTER V

OCTOBER 1886–JUNE 1887

This chapter contains several documents in which Olmsted reflects on issues of urbanization and landscape architecture, as well as specific jobs he has worked on. "A Healthy Change in the Tone of the Human Heart" for *Century* magazine is one of Olmsted's most comprehensive statements concerning the preservation of areas of natural scenic beauty in urban areas. The document addressed to Richard P. Hammond, Jr., regarding Golden Gate Park in San Francisco is one of several documents in this volume in which Olmsted emphasizes the appropriateness of thinning trees in public parks. The letter to Charles Eliot contains advice for starting his own landscape architecture firm, and a February 6, 1887, letter to Mariana Griswold Van Rensselaer discusses Olmsted's collaborations with H. H. Richardson. There are also two other letters written to her in May 1887, soon after Olmsted and Calvert Vaux published their "General Plan for the Improvement of the Niagara Reservation." The *Century* magazine commissioned Van Rensselaer to write a review of the plan, and Olmsted's letters to her offer a wide-ranging discussion of issues relating to it.

Two major commissions that Olmsted accepts during this period are for the design of the Stanford University campus and for South Park in Buffalo. The letter to Leland Stanford in this chapter argues that his California institution should not resemble a New England campus, and the letter to architect Charles A. Coolidge reflects Olmsted's frustration that Stanford is consistently trying to alter their campus design. Olmsted's letter to Buffalo park commissioner Sherman S. Jewett provides justifications for his plan for a park on Lake Erie in the southern section of Buffalo. Regarding the Boston work, Olmsted writes a description of the proposed Charles River Embankment and describes his plan for the extension of Beacon Street in Brookline. Other letters include a note to architect Richard Morris Hunt providing his concept for the design of the Vanderbilt Mausoleum landscape, and a letter to Oakes Angier Ames criticizing the selection and maintenance of plantings at the memorial cairn in North Easton.

"A Healthy Change in the Tone of the Human Heart."

(SUGGESTIONS TO CITIES.)

[October 1886]

This is the term used by a great writer[1] to describe what indolent people would be apt to call a difference of taste, the difference between the "taste" that led to the building of the Parthenon and that evinced in the building of cathedrals, and, again, between the public taste of the period of cathedral-building and the time of the building of—what shall be said?—our soldiers' monuments? our patent iron bridges?

In the fifteenth century, Mr. Ruskin tells us, the most cultivated of men found delight in scenes of which the chief characteristics were trimness, orderliness, framedness, surface fineness,—sources of gratification that could be so only through a conspicuous manifestation of human painstaking. The water in which they took pleasure was water flowing in a channel paved at the bottom, walled at the sides, rimmed at the surface, and bordered by parallel floral fringes, specimen trees, or hedges. The rocks they enjoyed were any but crannied, craggy, mossy, and weather-stained rocks. They liked best to look on forest trees when they had been trimmed, shorn, and disposed in rows by the side of a road. They disliked all that we mean by depth, intricacy, mystery, in scenery. They liked clear outlines, fences, walls, defining circumstances, scenes fretted with bits of bright color, turf patched with flower-beds, nature dressed on the principles of our drawing-room and garden decorative art.[2] They fairly hated the sight of the disorderly, unconfinable sea, with its fluctuating lights and shadows and fugitive hues. The civilization of our times, Mr. Ruskin thinks, finds a greater pleasure in rivers than in canals; it enjoys the sea, it enjoys the distinctive qualities of mountains, crags, rocks; it is pleasantly affected by all that in natural scenery which is indefinite, blending, evasive. It is less agreeably moved by trees when standing out with marked singularity of form or color than when the distinctive qualities of one are partly merged with those of others, in groups and masses, as in natural woodsides. It takes pleasure in breadth, sedateness, serenity of landscape. If modern art has any advantage over that of the middle ages, it is through its awakening to the value of these aspects of nature and its less respect for the more material wealth of man's manifest creation.

This doctrine is not Mr. Ruskin's alone. Scholars in general have substantially taken the same view from the time of Addison and Horace Walpole down.[3] Mr. Ruskin has but presented it more fully and accurately than others. But if we accept it, what are we to think of the neglect that is apparent at many of our centers of civilization to preserve, develop, and make richly available their chief local resources of this form of wealth? Let me refer to a few examples.

At our national capital, while we are every year adding to its outfit new decorations in marble and bronze, formal plantations, specimen trees, and floral and bushy millinery, we leave the charmingly wooded glen of Rock Creek in private hands, subject any day to be laid waste.[4] Once gone, the wealth of the nation could not buy for Washington half the value of landscape beauty that would thus have been lost.

Again, one of our Northern cities has always had lying at its feet a passage of scenery in which, with some protection and aid to nature, and a little provision of convenience, there might be more of grandeur, picturesqueness, and poetic charm than it is possible that this city shall ever otherwise be able to possess, though it should increase a hundred-fold in population and wealth, and command the talents of greater artists than any now living. No effort is made to hold the opportunity. No thought is given to it. The real estate in which it lies, as yet mainly if not wholly unproductive, is from year to year bought and sold as private property with regard alone to its possible future value for some industrial purpose to which thousands of acres nearby can easily be as well adapted. There is a river running through it, but its chief interest to "the human heart" does not lie in the water. The water is of no small value, yet it might be wholly drawn off to turn wheels and all that I have said remain true.

We have another fine city, a city of some repute for its poets, its architecture, sculpture, music, gardening, its galleries and its schools of art. Liberal, provident, thrifty, clean, it sits at the head of a harbor giving directly on the sea. The harbor has made the city. Various islands and headlands make the harbor.[5] The islands and headlands are thus the life of the city. Following Mr. Ruskin, one would suppose that whatever of beauty lies in them would long since have engaged all the art-sense of its people. But, in fact, hitherto, a stranger wishing to look down the harbor toward the sea could not find a foot of ground along the shore prepared for the purpose. Once the islands were bodies of foliage. Seen one against another and grouping with woody headlands, they formed scenery of grace and amenity, cheerful, genial, hospitable. But long ago they were despoiled for petty private gains, and the harbor made artificially bald, raw, bleak, prosaic, inhospitable. Each island now stands by itself, as sharply defined in all its outlines as the most mediæval mind could desire. Several of them are the property of the city and are in use for excellent purposes. It would not lessen but enhance their value for these purposes to dress them again with the graces of naturally disposed foliage; and under a well-prepared system, patiently followed, it would cost little more every year to do this than is spent for an hour's exhibition of fireworks. The harbor is often more crowded than any other on the coast with pleasure-seeking yachts and yachtlets; all that has been stated is perfectly plain; but the opportunity remains not only unused, but, so far as publicly appears, unconsidered,—a matter of no account.

One of the most impressive (and by its impressiveness the most recreative, and by its recreativeness most valuable) city grounds that I have known, I strayed into by accident, never having heard of it before. This was thirty years ago, and I have not heard of it since; but the impression it made was so strong that being asked for a note on this topic, it is instantly and vividly recalled.[6] The entire value of this city property lay in its situation. Otherwise it was barbarous—barbarous in its squirming gravel-walks, its dilapidated essays of puerile decoration, its shabby gentility; its hogs and its hoodlums. But far below flowed a great river, and one looked beyond the river downward upon the unbroken surface of an unlimited forest; looked upon it as one looks from a height upon the sea.

No matter what is beyond, an expanse of water, as you say, can never fail to have a refreshing counter interest to the inner parts of a city; it supplies a tonic change at times even from the finest churches, libraries, picture galleries, conservatories, gardens, soldiers' monuments, parks, and landward outskirts. What is easier than to provide a grateful convenience for such refreshment? Yet if one wants it at Troy, Albany, Newburgh, Springfield, Hartford, Middletown, New London, Trenton, Norfolk, Louisville, St. Louis, Memphis, Vicksburg, what is offered? What was lost for Brooklyn when the brow of its heights was wholly given up to paved streets and private occupation! What resources is Burlington wasting!

The wayfarer in Lynchburg may come to know by a chance glimpse at a street-corner that that city holds one of the greatest treasures of scenery at its command; but if he would see more of it, he must ask leave to climb a church-steeple, or, what is better, plod off by a dusty road to a point beyond the city's squalid outskirts, where the James river will give him undisturbed space for western contemplation. Many such illustrations of the general fact might be given.

But one who believes that Ruskin is describing tendencies of civilized movement rather than stages attained, as he looks over our land, is not left cheerless. Years ago a traveler arriving in Buffalo asked in vain where he could go to look out on the lake. "The lake?" he would be answered in the spirit of the middle ages; "nobody here wants to look at the lake; we hate the lake." And he might find that two large public squares had been laid out, furnished and planted, leaving a block between them and the edge of a bluff to be so built over as to shut off all view from the squares toward the lake and toward sunset. But lately land has been bought and prepared, and is much resorted to, expressly for the enjoyment of this view.[7] This new public property also commands a river effect such as can be seen, I believe, nowhere else,—a certain quivering of the surface and a rare tone of color, the result of the crowding upward of the lake waters as they enter the deep portal of the Niagara. Is the regard paid to these elements of natural scenery by the city less an evidence of growing civilization than is given in the granite statues on its court-house or in its soldiers' monument? San Francisco holds a grand outlook upon the Pacific; New Haven has acquired a noble eminence overlooking the Sound. Be it remembered, also, that at Chicago and at Detroit, at Halifax and at Bridgeport, sites have been secured at which the public interest in great, simple, undecorated waters may be worthily cared for.[8]

Between the two neighboring cities of St. Paul and Minneapolis the Mississippi flows majestically. Its banks are bold and nobly wooded, a virgin American forest. Mr. Horace Cleveland,[9] a veteran artist, a kinsman of the President's, is urging upon the people of these two cities that they secure the opportunity thus offered for a public ground common to both with which no other city recreation-ground could be brought in comparison. If Mr. Ruskin be right, it speaks well for the health of these two wonderfully growing communities that the suggestion has been gravely received and is earnestly debated.

A small space, it should not be forgotten, may serve to present a choice refreshment to a city, provided the circumstances are favorable for an extended outlook upon natural elements of scenery. This is seen in Durham Terrace at Montreal, the inward as well as the riverward characteristic scenes of which Mr. Howells has described in "Their Wedding Journey."[10] Another illustration of the fact may be found in a queer little half-public place, half-domestic back-yard, from which the river may be overlooked if anyone cares for it, at Hudson, New York. Yet another may be come upon at Providence, a public balcony, not more than a hundred feet square, thrown out from a hill-side street.[11] A trifling affair, but a trifle that expresses much of public civilization.

For low-lying towns upon the sea or lake coasts, promenade piers will generally offer the best means to the purpose. A simple promenade pier built with tree-trunks from neighboring woods, nicely hewn, nicely adzed, nicely notched, nicely pinned, without a bolt or strap of iron, with no paint or applied "gingerbread," built by a village bee, would be a work worthy to be celebrated in a woodcut poem of THE CENTURY.[12]

Frederick Law Olmsted.

The text presented here is an "open letter" published in the *Century Illustrated Monthly Magazine*, October 1886, pages 963–65.

1. Olmsted references John Ruskin (1819–1900), and specifically his *Modern Painters* (London, 1843–60). Olmsted read Ruskin throughout his adult life and was significantly influenced by him. He first read *Modern Painters* in 1849, shortly after it was published in the United States. Ruskin and Olmsted were contemporaries, but the two men never met and probably never corresponded directly. In 1879, however, Ruskin did provide a statement for the memorial Olmsted, James T. Gardner, and Charles Eliot Norton were preparing in support of the preservation of Niagara Falls. Norton

had a steady correspondence with Ruskin and was responsible for advancing his ideas and publications in the United States.

The title of this article is taken from *Modern Painters*, Volume III, Part IV, Chapter XIV, "Of Mediæval Landscape: First, the Fields," in which Ruskin describes the "great change" in the appreciation of landscapes that marked a transition from a classical to a medieval sensibility. Of three "vital points" in this change, first was a disdain for agricultural pursuits by the nobility and a related passion for gardens and ornamental horticulture. Second, was a "more sentimental enjoyment of external nature," epitomized by the medieval knight going "into his pleasance, to gather roses and hear the birds sing," a change Ruskin describes as "evidently a healthy, and a very interesting one." Third, was the realization that there was something to be gained from the landscape beyond this "hawking and apple-eating" and that "the mountains, as opposed to the pleasant garden-ground, are places where that other something may be best learned." This appreciation of mountainous landscapes was "evidently a piece of infinite and new respect for the mountains, and another healthy change in the tone of the human heart" (FLO to John Hull Olmsted, Feb. 10, 1849 [*Papers of FLO*, 1: 323–26]; FLO to James T. Gardner, Oct. 2, 1879 [*Papers of FLO*, 7: 420–22]; FLO to Charles Eliot Norton, Feb. 15, 1880 [*Papers of FLO*, 7: 471–73]; Roger B. Stein, *John Ruskin and Aesthetic Thought in America, 1840–1900* [Cambridge, Mass., 1967], pp. 47, 128, 240–53; John Ruskin, *Modern Painters, Volume III, Containing Part IV, Of Many Things* [London, 1843–60; reprint, New York, 1879], pp. 191–94).

2. In the chapter cited above from *Modern Painters*, Ruskin describes landscape illustrations in manuscripts of fifteenth-century "Romances," noting their depiction of paved waterways, and that "These central fifteenth-century landscapes are almost invariably composed of a grove or two of tall trees, a winding river, and a castle, or a garden: the peculiar feature of both these last being *trimness*; the artist always dwelling especially on the fences; wreathing the espaliers indeed prettily with sweet-briar, and putting pots of orange-trees on the tops of walls, but taking great care that there shall be no loose bricks in the one, nor broken stakes in the other" (J. Ruskin, *Modern Painters*, p. 201).
3. Joseph Addison (1672–1719), English writer and politician, contributed essays on literary criticism, politics, and landscape aesthetics, notably to the *Tatler* (1709–1711) and the *Spectator* (1711–12). In 1712 Addison wrote that "there is generally in Nature something more Grand and August, than what we meet with in the Curiosities of Art. When, therefore, we see this imitated in any measure, it gives us a nobler and more exalted kind of Pleasure than what we receive from the nicer and more accurate Productions of Art."

   Horace Walpole, (1717–1797), author, gardener, and patron of the arts, published his *History of the Modern Taste in Gardening* in 1771. This influential essay traced the development of the English landscape garden in the eighteenth century, emphasizing the work of William Kent and Lancelot (Capability) Brown. Walpole was a principal figure of the revival of interest in medieval architecture and history, and built his villa in Twickenham, Strawberry Hill, in the Gothic style (*DNB*, s.v. "Addison, Joseph" and "Walpole, Horace"; John Dixon Hunt and Peter Willis, eds., *The Genius of the Place: The English Landscape Garden, 1620–1820* [Cambridge, Mass., 1988], p. 142).
4. Despite Olmsted's concern for the preservation of the Rock Creek area of Washington, D.C., he never developed a park plan for it. Legislation for the creation of a park was not passed until 1890. Frederick Law Olmsted, Jr., was later a principal figure in the planning and design of the Rock Creek and Potomac Parkway (Timothy Davis, "Rock Creek and Potomac Parkway, Washington, DC: The Evolution of a Contested Urban Landscape," *Studies in the History of Gardens & Designed Landscapes* 19, no. 2, summer 1999, pp. 135–36, 167).

5. At this time Olmsted was advocating the reforestation of the Boston Harbor islands (See FLO to Robert Douglas, Dec. 5, 1887, below).
6. Thirty years earlier, in 1856, Olmsted traveled extensively in Europe on business for Dix, Edwards & Company, the publishing firm in which he had become a partner the year before. He may be referring here to any one of numerous cities he visited that year in Britain, France, Italy, Germany, Austria, and the Netherlands.
7. The land recently bought became The Front, a thirty-two-acre park designed by Olmsted and Vaux situated on a bluff overlooking the Niagara River where it flows out of Lake Erie. Olmsted initially visited the site in 1868, and the park was constructed in the early 1870s. The "two large public squares" in Buffalo he mentions are today known together as Prospect Park and are near The Front (FLO to MPO, Aug. 23, 1868 [*Papers of FLO*, 6: 266–68]; Olmsted, Vaux, and Co. to William E. Dorsheimer, Oct. 1, 1868 [*Papers of FLO*, SS1: 158–70]).
8. Olmsted refers to Golden Gate Park in San Francisco, California; East Rock Park in New Haven, Connecticut; South Park in Chicago, Illinois; Belle Isle in Detroit, Michigan; Seaside Park in Bridgeport, Connecticut; and Point Pleasant Park in Halifax, Nova Scotia.

   Olmsted had advised on the formation of a park system in San Francisco in the 1860s and he and Vaux later submitted a plan that was not adopted. Ultimately Golden Gate Park was designed by William Hammond Hall. Olmsted and Vaux designed plans for the Chicago South Park Commission in 1871. In Detroit, Olmsted began work on the design of the park on Belle Isle in 1881, but the plan was not fully implemented. Bridgeport's Seaside Park was designed with Vaux in the late 1860s. East Rock Park was designed by Donald Grant Mitchell in 1882 and Olmsted had no hand in it, though the later firm of the Olmsted Brothers designed improvements for it in the early twentieth century. Olmsted was not involved with Point Pleasant Park in Halifax, which overlooks the Atlantic, but he admired it (FLO to Richard P. Hammond, Jr., Oct. 5, 1886, below; Olmsted, Vaux, & Co. Landscape Architects, *Report Accompanying Plan for Laying Out the South Park*, March 1871 [*Papers of FLO*, SS1: 206–38]; FLO to John Stirling, Dec. 30, 1881 [*Papers of FLO*, 7: 572–73], [editor's note: our spelling of "Stirling" has been corrected from "Sterling," as it has been given in previous volumes]; FLO to John Stirling, May 12, 1884, above; *Papers of FLO*, 6: 28; *Master List*, p. 44; "East Rock Park, New Haven, CT," USDI/NPS, National Register of Historic Places Registration Form, 1997, pp. 10–11).
9. Horace William Shaler Cleveland (1814–1900) was a landscape architect and author, who, like Olmsted, came to his profession in part through his background as a scientific farmer. A native of Massachusetts, Cleveland was second cousin to President Grover Cleveland, and also a sixth cousin of Mary Cleveland Perkins Olmsted, Olmsted's wife. Cleveland began his professional practice as a landscape gardener in 1854 in a partnership with Robert Morris Copeland. In the 1850s the partners designed Sleepy Hollow Cemetery in Concord, Massachusetts, and made important initial suggestions for a Boston park system. Cleveland also entered the Central Park design competition, which may have been when Olmsted first encountered him.

   Cleveland and Copeland dissolved their partnership just before the Civil War, and in 1868 Cleveland worked for Olmsted and Vaux for one season supervising plantings in Prospect Park. He moved to Chicago in 1869 where he started his own practice and superintended the limited development of Olmsted and Vaux's plans for South Park. After relocating to Minneapolis, Cleveland published a plan in 1883 for an extensive municipal park system for that city, including parks along the bluffs of the Mississippi. He also developed plans for parks in St. Paul. Olmsted and Cleveland were long-time friends and colleagues and corresponded over many years (Theodora Kimball Hubbard, "H. W. S. Cleveland: An American Pioneer in Landscape Architecture and City Planning," *Landscape Architecture*, vol. 20, Oct. 1929–July 1930, pp. 92–111; William H. Tishler, "Horace Cleveland: The Chicago Years" in William H. Tishler, ed., *Midwestern Landscape Architecture* [Urbana, Ill., 2000], pp. 25–40; "Descendents of Henry Sewell of Coventry," www.sewellgeneology.com; George Larson II, "An Extended Family," www.rootsweb.com).

10. Durham Terrace, a public promenade, is in Quebec City, not Montreal. Howells describes it in his chapters "Quebec" and "Homeward Bound" in *Their Wedding Journey* (New York, 1871).
11. This is likely Prospect Terrace Park on Congdon Street in Providence, Rhode Island, which is at the top of College Hill and offers views of the downtown area.
12. That is, memorialized in an illustrated poem, such as the popular poems that appeared in magazines like the *Century* and were accompanied by ornamental woodcut illustrations.

To Richard Pindell Hammond, Jr.[1]

COMMUNICATION FROM HON. FRED. LAW OLMSTED.

Salt Lake,* October 5th, 1886.

R. P. Hammond, Jr.,
Chairman of Park Commission, San Francisco,

Dear Sir: I have the honor to reply to your note, received as I was about to leave San Francisco. You ask that I give you in a few words the result of my impression received from the examination which I have recently made of your Golden Gate Park, and especially my opinion as to the condition of its forest tree plantations, and the necessity of thinning out the trees composing them, etc.

The work of improvement of your park site, in common with that of others, naturally is divided into two classes, according to the purposes had in view — the one, the creation of a park, the other, providing for its occupation and use, and the amusement of people therein.

The more important is that of obtaining the apparently natural outlines and growths constituting a park fit for occupation by a city's crowds, and suitable for the distinctly rural recreation of people, as a relief and counterpoise to the urban conditions of their ordinary circumstances of life.

The attaining to this end must be largely the work of nature; but that the result may be altogether suitable, as well as pleasing and interesting, obstacles to

*This letter was written by Mr. Olmsted on his way East. His residence and business address is Brookline, Mass.

the necessities of use must be removed, the desired work of nature must be started and assisted, and the natural development of plantations be studied, guided, and encouraged in various ways. Beyond this, in the preparation of your park proper, nothing else is necessary but the provision of ways by which the results of nature's work may be enjoyed by the public without injuring and wearing them out.

In noticing, as you ask me to do, what has been accomplished on your grounds in this way, I am able to compare the site for the proposed Golden Gate Park, as I examined it last week, and as I saw it twenty years ago, when the question of its selection was being discussed.[2] And now I say that the result thus far obtained in the legitimate line of park creation, although as yet comparatively but little attractive to the public, or effective to the end in view, is an achievement far exceeding all that I have believed possible; and that it gives perfect assurance that if the work so well begun is as wisely carried on, no city in the world will have as good reason for taking pride in its park as San Francisco.

The Golden Gate Park, judiciously developed, is certain to have a unique and incomparable character; and this, not because of any striving after artificial originality, but because of the inauguration of its design and growth by a thoroughly studious, inventive, and scientific exercise of judgment in grasping such opportunities as nature afforded, and in the solving of an extraordinary problem presented in the circumstances of the locality.[3]

The creation of a park on this site in imitation of other great parks, is a result which could have been accomplished in a limited degree, by the expenditure of great sums of money, and its value would have been more than measured by its cost.[4] But the starting of growths which will successfully come to maturity, and be maintained at small cost on this site, having a park-like effect, unique and singular though it be, and the outlining of a plan admitting of its pleasurable occupation for rural enjoyment, is an achievement of value to San Francisco very far in excess of its cost. This, I think, has been effected. The foundation is laid and the possibilities demonstrated.

As to the other line of improvement which you are called on to carry out, it is that of providing grounds for public entertainment. This is done chiefly by a show of plants arranged and displayed in a manner the reverse of a natural or rural order.

What has been done for this purpose, chiefly in the garden of your Conservatory Valley, is a good piece of handicraft in the style that has for some time past been in fashion, but from which a reaction seems now setting in throughout communities older than your own.[5]

Your ornamented ground and flower garden being in no respect the product of local circumstance, or representative of distinctly local taste or study, and its full value being already realized, calls for no expression of judgment from me as to the possibilities of its future. I will only say that I am inclined to think that it was unfortunate that ground was taken for this purpose within the territory to which the term *park* has been applied, because it tends to confusion of public opinion between the wholly irreconcilable purposes of a rural park and those of an urban garden, and to favor neglect of the more substantial and more permanently important of the two.

In my view it is most desirable that the public, to whom you are responsible, should bear in mind that your fine garden ground, with its arrangements for crowds of people, its brilliancy, its bustle of carriages, and its brass band, is to gain nothing of importance through future growth, and that should it be swept away by a flood, or ruined by neglect or parsimony, a similar and as valuable a means of entertainment could be produced in a short time, at small expense, on the same site, or in any other part of the city.

It is no more an essential part of the rural park which you so much need, and in the future will absolutely require, for your people, than is a picture hung in a frame an essential part of the house which holds it. Two or three years from now it would be of little importance whether it is this year well managed or not. Lost ground in this class of improvement can quickly be recovered. Not so with the Park proper — the permanent and really valuable portion of your charge — the grounds at large, with their various growths of trees, and shrubs, and plants that produce, or are to produce, your rural effects. The degree of wisdom of its management today governs the value of results in years to come.

That which has been achieved points the way for future action. It is no longer an obscure problem. Observe and study well the results before you. Unless managed with disgraceful waste of the opportunities now offered, there is no reason why the park proper should not go on gaining in value through greater fitness for its purpose, year after year, indefinitely. It cannot fail, under decently conservative management and sustained study of the demands which nature makes apparent to be far more attractive and useful ten years hence than now, and a hundred years hence than ten.

As to the question you more particularly ask me to consider — the condition and management of the forest tree growths — I consider that Mr. Hall's views, embodied in the report you hand me, are unquestionably sound, and my examination of the place enables me to say that his statements sustaining them appear to me to be moderately made and accurately correct.[6]

The conditions of the case are in such degree unusual, and the results thus far attained so conclusive of the soundness of the course recommended, that it would be unjustifiable to turn aside from it, even if no evidence from the experience of others could be offered in support of it. His theory can stand on its own legs.

But, in fact, it is sustained by all experience the world over. No man with the slightest claim to speak with authority, can be found in the least at difference with him. I do not doubt that it was essential to the successful growth of the designed masses of foliage of the Golden Gate Park, that its trees should be planted as closely as they were. I do not doubt that it is equally essential to the growth in a healthy way of such masses that, as the trees advance in size, their number shall be greatly reduced. It is a common practice, as Mr. Hall states, after certain periods of growth, not to leave more than one out of five of trees originally planted. The best park plantations in the world (by which I mean the healthiest, sturdiest, longest lived, and most agreeable in natural aspect), have been obtained in this way.

The condition of the older plantations in Golden Gate Park has now become such, through neglect of the timely, continuous and gradual thinning originally intended, that very many comparatively large trees have to be cut out, and in many places the older groups cannot be judiciously treated without temporarily injuring their appearance. If to avoid such momentary apparent injury the neglect is allowed to continue, the trees will soon be ruined; that is to say, the majority will come to a miserable, lingering death, and those surviving, instead of presenting agreeable and effective masses of foliage, will be awkward, gawky, semi-detached trees. The purposes with which the plantations have been started, both as to effects of scenery and effects of bodily comfort for those visiting the park, will then be attainable only by cutting the old trees away altogether, and starting again with new plantations to be better managed.

In conclusion, let me counsel you, in general terms, to remember that your Park is not for today, but for all time — so long as you have a city. Its development is an interesting problem, no longer obscure, to be sure, but yet to be studied in a careful and sustained manner. You have your present population to satisfy and please. It is an intelligent population, beyond a doubt, and possessed of a high appreciation of good results. But it is to be expected that future populations will be more intelligent and more appreciative. The art of landscape architecture is a specialty which, in its exercise, peculiarly demands a forecast of the future. The materials of the work themselves grow and are progressive. To work with them demands sustained observation and intelligent making of deductions. I hope that Golden Gate Park may have these. It has been the ruination of many such grounds to have them pass rapidly under successive managements. The artistic direction of work on such grounds should, as far as possible, be continuous when once found fitting. It is not to be expected that the public will understand the necessity for and object of much that is done on such works. To do your duty, you will often have to sanction apparently reckless destruction of some present result. Such grounds are developed as to details, by stages of growth. When the time comes, one stage must give way to the next.

Yours respectfully,

FREDERICK LAW OLMSTED.

The text presented here was published in *The Development of Golden Gate Park and Particularly the Management and Thinning of Its Forest Tree Plantations* (San Francisco, 1886). William Hammond Hall (1846–1934) and John McLaren (1846–1943) also contributed to the report, which the San Francisco *Daily Evening Bulletin* reprinted on October 23, 1886. Hall designed Golden Gate Park and was its superintendent from 1871 to 1876. He was appointed California's first state engineer in 1879 and held that position for over a decade. In 1886 the park commissioners asked Hall to return as a consulting engineer (he had not been involved in the maintenance of the park since leaving in 1876) and to prepare a report on its current condition because of criticism concerning the cutting of trees in the park. He served as superintendent for the next three years. Hall asked McLaren, a landscape gardener, to contribute to the report, and a few months later the park commissioners hired McLaren as assistant superintendent. McLaren took over as superintendent after Hall resigned in 1889 and served in that position until his death in 1943. Olmsted visited the park and made his report on his way home in the fall of 1886 after visiting the Stanford University site in California ("Golden Gate Park," *San Francisco Daily Evening Bulletin*, Oct. 23, 1886, p. 4; Raymond H. Clary, *The Making of Golden Gate Park: The Early Years* [San Francisco, 1980], pp. 7–8, 69–71, 76; *DAB*; Terence Young, *Building San Francisco's Parks* [Baltimore, 2004]).

1. Richard Pindell Hammond, Jr. (1859–1900), William Hammond Hall's cousin, served on the San Francisco Park Commission from 1886 to 1894, at times as its president. Previously he was the U.S. surveyor-general of California. During his tenure on the commission he oversaw the development of several areas in the park, including the Golden Gate Park Zoo (R. H. Clary, *Golden Gate Park*, pp. 57, 89, 107; "Golden Gate Park, Annual Report by President Hammond," *San Francisco Evening Bulletin*, May 14, 1887, p. 4; T. Young, *San Francisco's Parks*, p. 141; "Death Notice," *San Francisco Call*, Sept. 22, 1900, p. 13).
2. Olmsted first advocated a series of "public pleasure grounds" in San Francisco in 1865, writing letters to San Francisco newspapers and the city's board of supervisors. The *San Francisco Bulletin* printed a letter from Olmsted on August 4, 1865, written under the pseudonym "Rusticus in Urbe," in which he described his vision for a system of public landscapes designed for the climate and conditions of the city. Olmsted and Vaux submitted their plan for a system of pleasure grounds in 1866, but it was never implemented (Frederick Law Olmsted, "The Project of a Great Park for San Francisco," Aug. 4, 1865 [*Papers of FLO*, 5: 425–32]; Olmsted, Vaux, and Co., "Preliminary Report in Regard to a Plan of Public Pleasure Grounds for the City of San Francisco," March 31, 1866 [*Papers of FLO*, 5: 518–46]).
3. Golden Gate Park was established in 1870 in an area of sand dunes and sandy soils west of what was then the boundary of San Francisco. William Hammond Hall drew up a plan to stabilize the soils, plant shrubs and shade trees, and establish turf, all of which required extensive irrigation. Despite the difficulties of the site, Hall successfully created a large park landscape inspired by eastern U.S. and European precedents. In 1866, Olmsted had suggested a very different approach for the city, proposing a system of smaller, sheltered public landscapes, none of which were described as a "park." The central space of Olmsted's proposed system was not a pastoral landscape, but a sunken promenade, running from the shore four miles inland, near the current Fillmore District. Planted with evergreen vines and shrubs, the promenade would be sheltered and would require less water, and was part of a system of public landscape designs adapted to semi-arid conditions. The San Francisco park commission decided instead, however, to be guided by more familiar precedents, even if they were less suited to the local climate and soils (R. H. Clary, *Golden Gate Park*, pp. 3–4, 14; T. Young, *San Francisco's Parks*, pp. 73, 78, 84–87; *Papers of FLO*, 5: 461–64).
4. When William Hammond Hall first undertook the design of Golden Gate Park, Olmsted warned him against relying on European and American design precedents and urged the necessity of developing approaches to landscape design that would be adapted to the semi-arid conditions of the west. "Experiences in Persia, Turkey, Smyrna, Spain and Portugal would afford more suggestions for what is practicable and desirable than any that could be derived from English authorities," he wrote. The situation called for "invention, not adaptation" (FLO to William Hammond Hall, Oct. 5, 1871 [*Papers of FLO*, 6: 468–70]).

5. Conservatory Valley, located within the park, was designed under the supervision of William Bond Pritchard, park superintendent from 1876 to 1881. At the heart of the Valley was a large glass hot house erected in 1879. The conservatory and its surrounding gardens were modeled after Kew Gardens in England in the fashionable, ornamental style to which Olmsted refers (R.H. Clary, *Golden Gate Park*, pp. 29, 35–36; T. Young, *San Francisco's Parks*, pp. 78, 116–17, 144–47).
6. In his report, Hall states, "I am prepared to show that this practice of planting thick, and afterwards thinning as the young trees commence to interfere with each other, in varied degrees, is a universal custom in the cultivation of forest growths, where systematically done, whether the object be that of business enterprise, of landscape improvement, or of growing belts or groups, to afford protection from winds" (*The Development of Golden Gate Park*, p. 11). For more on Olmsted's views on the necessity of thinning plantations of trees, see Frederick Law Olmsted and J. B. Harrison, *Observations on the Treatment of Public Plantations, More Especially Relating to the Use of the Axe*, April 30, 1889, below.

To Charles Eliot

28th Oct. 1886.

My Dear Eliot,

Welcome and use my name and welcome.

That which chiefly limits success in our profession is the fact that so few know that landscape architecture is a matter in which professional service is very desirable and payment for it is profitable. Many millions of dollars are misspent every year for want of good professional advice. It was nearly the same with architecture forty years ago. Forty years ago I employed an architect who had his office in the Merchants Exchange in New York to make me a design for a farm house.[1] He charged me $5 — for it. He was the only architect I then had knowledge of. Where there was one then, poorly paid, there are now a hundred much better paid. Why? Because people have learned through seeing the results of employing architects that it is profitable to employ them. So it will be with Landscape Architecture as Landscape Architecture comes to be recognized as a standard profession. The more work every good landscape architect is able to do, the more every other will have to do and the better he will be paid. The profession is a common wealth. I prefer that we should call ourselves L. Architects, following the French & Italian custom,[2] rather than l. gardeners following the English, (though Loudon uses "Garden Architect") because the former title better carries the professional idea. It makes more important also, the idea of design. "Gardener" includes service corresponding to that of carpenter and mason. Architect does not. Hence it is more discriminating, and prepares the minds of clients for dealing with on professional principles.

For a similar reason I think it best that we should never charge by the day or hour as most who call themselves landscape gardeners do. We should follow the custom of lawyers in good standing and charge measurably with reference to the importance of the trust undertaken. I believe that Cleveland, Weidenmann[3] & others have followed generally the plan of charging first adopted by O. & V. twenty years ago, shown in the memorandum enclosed.[4] I have never varied from it, except in reducing the preliminary charge for small places nearby to $50 — and abandoning the acre rate for very small places. Our custom now is to keep an eye on these for two or three years & charge for the whole, (collecting a due proportion each January), from $200 to $400 — This applies to such places as Storrow's[5] for instance. Only twice in twenty years have I received suggestions of abatement of charges & the exceptions were not significant, one being technical in which case I at once yielded the point, giving the benefit of doubt to the client. The other narrow mindedness, in which I insisted and carried my point. I have twice had to bring suit against city governments, & in one case had to appeal & appeal & finally been successful.[6]

I know that you will feel more than most men what you are to your profession — that is to "the cause." I mean beyond the zealous pursuit of it. In one way I wish to give you my opinion, derived from reading your letters, chiefly, that you are able to serve it better than any living English writing man. If you consider who and what they are who now write for the public on — or rather around — the subject, you will not think it flattering, if I say that you can easily give the public what the public most needs much better than any other man now writing. Perhaps the best, certainly the most honored & successful writers we now have are the two Parsons's, father & son;[7] I say so simply because they are in good company in the Century, for instance, & yet, how far they are from the root of the matter.

Everything that you have written of what you saw of scenery and gardening in Europe has been delightful to me. I can't say how refreshing by comparison with anything that even comes in the magazines, for instance. Really the subject is a very important one nationally. And is growing so rapidly. All the new fine houses in the Western cities are villas — there is a wonderful new crop of villas growing on the line of the Long Isd R.R. and good places for them have advanced several hundred prct in value, in five years. The fashion in suburban living is just setting in. (And such paltry work is done for it.)

I have seen no such justly critical notes as yours in Landscape Architectural matters from any traveler for a generation past.

You ought to make it a part of your scheme to write for the public, a little at a time, if you please, but methodically, systematically. It is a part of your professional duty to do so.[8]

I ought to have excepted Stiles,[9] but I suppose that I did not feel that regular hack newspaper work should count. Stiles does well but he has not half your advantages.

One thing more as to writing. Remember, that, duty, that I have talked of, aside, it will pay you, directly & indirectly. You write easily fluently, and in a critical way that is in demand. What you wrote off hand about the Italian Gardens—about the Baltic parks, (in this last letter),[10] and on various other matters you saw, would make a capital series of magazine articles, with a very little modification to the scale of a popular audience. I am sure that, greedy reader as I am, I have had nothing as good. And, perhaps a book. Anything of that sort (to speak of the indirect profits) will be worth much more to you than advertising in the Nation, for example.

As soon as you can find it convenient we shall hope for a visit from you. We shall always have a bed and want you at dinner.

Yours Truly

Fred[k] Law Olmsted

The text presented here is a signed letter in Olmsted's hand. Eliot had recently returned from his European travels and was in the process of establishing his own landscape architecture office in Boston. He solicited Olmsted's advice and asked if he could use his name as a reference in an advertisement he intended to place in the *Nation* (Charles Eliot to FLO, Oct. 10, 1886, courtesy of Alexander Yale Goriansky; Charles W. Eliot, *Charles Eliot, Landscape Architect* [Boston, 1902], pp. 204–5; see also FLO to Charles Eliot, Feb. 25, 1886, above; FLO to Charles Eliot, March 4, 1886, above; FLO to Charles Eliot, July 20, 1886, above).

1. Olmsted's first farm was on Sachem's Head on the Connecticut shore of Long Island Sound. He settled there in 1847 and consulted architect Alexander Jackson Davis, who maintained an office in the Merchant's Exchange from 1842 to 1862, about a design for a new farmhouse. Not happy with his prospects on Sachem's Head, Olmsted moved to a farm in Staten Island in March 1848 (*FLO, A Biography*, p. 54; Amelia Peck, ed., *Alexander Jackson Davis: American Architect 1803–1892* [New York, 1992], p. 19).
2. The French title that, for example, Édouard André used was *architecte-paysagiste*. The Italian title was *architetto paesaggista* (Édouard Ándre, *L'Art Des Jardins* [Paris, 1879]).
3. Landscape architects Horace William Shaler Cleveland and Jacob Weidenmann.
4. The editors have not found this memorandum or a table of charges for Olmsted, Vaux, & Co. from that period.
5. Likely the home of Charles Storrow in Brookline, Massachusetts, which was on a very small site. The firm worked on his estate from 1882 through 1886 (*Master List*, p. 177; plans 629-z1 and 629-1, NPS/FLONHS).
6. Olmsted brought suit against New York City in the fall of 1876 for salary owed him for the period from May to August 1876, totaling $1,637.14. The city's comptroller, Andrew Haswell Green, stated that he was withholding Olmsted's salary because Olmsted had accepted a position as commissioner on the newly-formed New York State Survey, asserting that a public employee could not hold two public offices. Green's action was part of a general effort by Green and several park commissioners to oust Olmsted from his position. Olmsted held appointment to the New York State Survey for only a short time, and he resigned as soon as the question arose as to whether the office conflicted with his position with the parks department. The suit was resolved in the summer of

1877 and was decided in Olmsted's favor. The court determined that Olmsted was an employee, not an office holder, at the parks department and therefore had never held two offices. The editors were unable to determine what other city government Olmsted may have sued (*Papers of FLO*, 7: 4–5; *FLO, A Biography*, pp. 350–53; "Superior Court of the City of New York, General Term," *Frederick Law Olmsted, Respondent, agst. The Mayor, Aldermen and Commonalty of the City of New York, Appellants* [May, 1877], court document; W. M. Prichard to FLO, Aug. 18, 1876; Smith E. Lane to FLO, Sept. 22, 1877).

7. Samuel Bowne Parsons, Sr. (1819–1906), was a nurseryman and horticulturalist from Flushing, New York. He was among the first to import and propagate popular species of rhododendron and Japanese maple, as well as many other ornamental shrubs and trees. He and Olmsted had known one another since Parsons supplied fruit trees for Olmsted's Staten Island farm in the 1850s. Olmsted also used the Parsons nursery for later landscape projects. Parsons lectured and wrote on horticulture, including his book *The Rose: Its History, Poetry, Culture, and Classification* (New York, 1860).

   Samuel Parsons, Jr. (1844–1923), landscape architect and author, worked in his father's nursery for five years until Calvert Vaux hired him as an associate in his office in 1879. Vaux made him a partner in 1887. When the New York park department hired Vaux to be its Superintending Architect in November 1881, Vaux asked that Parsons be hired as well. The board officially hired Parsons to be Superintendent of Planting over a year later, on January 24, 1883, the same day the board accepted Vaux's resignation as Superintending Architect. In May 1885 the board appointed Parsons the Superintendent of Parks. He served in that position until 1898, when the board appointed him to be the department's Landscape Architect. He served the city of New York until 1911, including periods as a park commissioner in 1905 and 1907. Throughout his career Parsons also worked on private commissions around the United States. He was a prolific writer who published books and articles in *Scribner's Magazine* (later the *Century*), *American Garden*, and *American Architect* among others (Byron D. Halsted, "Parsons, Samuel B.," in L. H. Bailey, ed., *Cyclopedia of American Agriculture*, vol. IV [New York, 1909], p. 602; *FLO, A Biography*, p. 65; DPP, *Minutes*, Nov. 19, 1881, pp. 386–89; ibid., Jan. 24, 1883, pp. 467–68; ibid., May 25, 1885, p. 75; Charles A. Birnbaum, "Parsons, Samuel, Jr.," in Charles A. Birnbaum and Robin Karson, eds., *Pioneers of American Landscape Design* [New York, 2000], pp. 287–91; Charles A. Birnbaum, *Samuel Parsons Jr., and the Art of Landscape Architecture*, monograph prepared in conjunction with an exhibition organized by the Catalog of Landscape Records in the United States [Wave Hill, Bronx, N. Y., 1994]; Mabel Parsons, ed., *Memories of Samuel Parsons* [New York, 1926]; "Samuel Parsons Dies at 78 Years," *New York Times*, Feb. 4, 1923, p. S5).

8. Eliot heeded this advice and began to publish articles in 1887. His first, "The Duty of the Garden," was published in the *Boston Transcript*, March 16, 1887 and re-published as "The Suburbs in March," in *Garden and Forest* in March 1888 (reprinted in C. W. Eliot, *Charles Eliot*, pp. 208–10). He continued over the years to write important articles and treatises on his profession for periodicals, most often featured in *Garden and Forest* (C.W. Eliot, *Charles Eliot*, pp. 204–5, 239–62).

9. William Augustus Stiles (1837–1897), editor and park advocate, began his career on the staff of the *New York Tribune*. He continued to write for the *Tribune* while also serving as managing editor of *Garden and Forest* from its beginning in 1888. Stiles was a friend of Olmsted and an advocate of many causes important to them both, including protecting Central Park from inappropriate development ("William A. Stiles," *Garden and Forest*, Oct. 13, 1897, pp. 399–400; M. B. Coulston, "William Augustus Stiles," in L. H. Bailey, ed., *Cyclopedia of American Horticulture*, vol. IV [New York, 1909], pp. 1724–25).

10. Eliot's letter to Olmsted, in which he asked Olmsted to be a reference for him on an advertisement about his new practice, also gave an account of his time in the nations around the Baltic Sea. He visited parks in Copenhagen, Stockholm, St. Petersburg, Potsdam, Dresden, and the parks at Schloss Wilhelmshöhe and at Muskau, in Germany. Of the last, he wrote, "[It] is probably the finest work of real landscape gardening on a large scale that this century has seen carried out in Europe. It is a work that has made me very proud of the profession — for here was a river valley in great part very barren, fringed by monotonous woods of P. sylvestris and in no way remarkable for beauty or interest. — but now one of the very loveliest vales of earth — and full to the brim, so to speak, of variety of pleasant change, of quieting and often touching beauty." Eliot's previous letters of 1886 to Olmsted and to John C. Olmsted and Henry Sargent Codman also gave critical descriptions of the scenery and gardens that he saw in England, Italy, France, and Russia. He also wrote home to his family during this period and kept a journal of his travels. Much of his journal and many of his letters home are excerpted or printed in full in C. W. Eliot, *Charles Eliot*, pp. 76–118; 164–203 (Charles Eliot to FLO, Oct. 10, 1886, courtesy of Alexander Yale Goriansky; see also FLO to Charles Eliot, Feb. 25, 1886, above; FLO to Charles Eliot, March 4, 1886, above; FLO to Charles Eliot, July 20, 1886, above; Charles Eliot to JCO, May 25, 1886; Charles Eliot to FLO, Dec. 19, 1885; Charles Eliot to JCO and Henry Sargent Codman, Feb. 13, 1886; Charles Eliot to FLO, June 5, 1886; "Charles Eliot's Diary," 1886, FLLHU).

To Amasa Leland Stanford[1]

Brookline Mass: 27th Nov: 1886.

The Honorable Leland Stanford,
My Dear Sir,

I presume that you will be arriving in Washington before long and may wish to hear from me. I have made no reportable progress, having been waiting for the topographical map, which (admirably drawn for my purpose) has just arrived. As, in any work to be done on the site that you have selected for the University, copies of this map will be of value to be used in the field, I have arranged to have it photo-lithographed.[2] General Walker has communicated to me the substance of the report that you will have received from him.[3] I am obliged to go next week to Niagara Falls on business of the State Reservation Commission which it is needful to get through before the ground near the Falls is much encumbered with ice.[4] As soon as I return I shall set about the drawing that you have wished of me, intending to embody in it the principles of General Walker's advice, as I shall find them adapted to the topography of the site. I cannot hope to complete this study before the latter part of December.

This is all I have to report at present but I should like to state my understanding of the object to be accomplished during the next month and something of the view with which I shall pursue it.

AMASA LELAND STANFORD FAMILY PORTRAIT, C. 1883

The immediate object is to present, in the form of a diagram, a coherent proposition, the critical discussion of which will aid you to formulate definite instructions as to the scope and as to many particulars, of a more mature study of the problem to follow. This problem I take to be the devising of a plan, that, spreading from a nucleus such as General Walker proposes, shall not only show how additions may from time to time be made to the primary building scheme that he defines, but how several series of buildings may be arranged, the buildings of each series radiating connectedly from the common centre of the primary buildings. (By several series of buildings, I mean, for example, the Academic series, the Collegiate Lodging series, the Work Shop series, the Outer Residence series and so on.)

It is not certain that such a problem can be solved except at a cost of convenience during the infant life of the University that will outweigh its advantages. But of this you will be able to much better judge with a drawing before you in the preparation of which the desired result has been tried for.

As I have been reflecting on what passed in our conferences at Palo Alto,[5] I have been led more and more to feel that a permanently suitable plan for a great University in California must be studied with constant watchfulness against certain mental tendencies from which neither you, nor General Walker, nor I, nor anyone likely to have influence in the matter, can reasonably be supposed to be free. The subtle persistency of the class of tendencies to which I allude is shown in the fact that the English in India, after an experience there of nearly two centuries, still order their lives in various particulars with absurd disregard of requirements of comfort and health, imposed by the climate, because they cannot dismiss from their minds standards of style, propriety and taste, which are the result of their fathers' training under different climatic conditions.

Because of less marked but not less positive differences of climate, with buildings and grounds arranged on the principles that have had control at Oxford and Cambridge, Harvard and Yale, Amherst and Williams, nothing like that which impresses a visitor as appropriate and pleasant in the general arrangement and environment of these colleges, can be had in California.[6] The same may be said with regard to other collections of buildings with semi-rural surroundings to which throngs of people are likely to resort. It would be impossible, for instance, in California, to maintain simply such degree of neatness as is seen in the Eastern or in English institutions of that description, at ten times their outlay for the purpose. Yet if to secure some tolerable degree of neatness all who have to do with them should be required to pass from one building to another only upon certain prepared passages, as we pass on ordered lines between the beds of an old-fashioned flower garden, the result in neatness would not pay for the trouble it would cost.

Neither turf nor any known substitute for covering unpaved surfaces between the buildings of a college can be used in California as turf is used in the East. Trees rooted in ground that is trampled as the ground is trampled about the college buildings of the East would be sickly, deformed and short-lived. Arrangements upon which, in the climate of the Atlantic States the beauty and comfort, not only of broad areas but even of streets and roads and yards depends, when reproduced as nearly as possible under the climate of California, will soon become unsuitable, dreary and forlorn. An example of what is to be apprehended in this respect already appears at Berkeley.[7]

It has often been observed that the character of the buildings and grounds, the scenery and atmosphere, of Oxford has greatly aided English veneration for learning and is to all Oxford students a highly important element of a liberal education. It is surely a sad misfortune that a young man seeking a liberal education, should be led, at the most impressible period of his life, to pass four years or more in an establishment the outward aspect of which is expressive of an illiterate and undisciplined mind, contemptuous of authority and that is essentially uncouth, ill-dressed and ill-mannered.

One of the largest of the college buildings at Amherst, of masonry construction, not old nor in bad repair, but graceless and gracelessly placed, has been lately taken down because as an offense to good taste, it had come through the advancing refinement of the times, to be no longer endurable.[8] The same experience will, probably, by and by occur at Berkeley on a larger scale. I may predict this with more propriety because before the Amherst Trustees had thought of getting rid of the building to which I refer and fifteen years before they screwed their courage up to doing so, I had advised them that it could be only a question of time when that conclusion would be reached.[9] What I have in mind at Berkeley is not alone that the buildings are in a "cheap and nasty" style but that the disposition of them and of all the grounds and offices about them betrays heedlessness of the requirements of convenience and comfort under the conditions of the situation and climate.

What I say, then, is that in the plan for a great University in California ideals must be given up that have been planted by all that we have found agreeable and have been led to regard as appropriate in the outward aspect of Eastern and English colleges. If we are to look for types of buildings and arrangements suitable to the climate of California it will rather be in those founded by the wiser men of Syria, Greece, Italy and Spain. You will remember in what a different way from the English methods, the spirit of which we have inherited, the open spaces about nearly all buildings that you have seen in the South of Europe to which throngs of people resort, have been treated. In the great "front yard" of St. Peter's, for example, not a tree nor a bush nor a particle of turf has been made use of.[10] This is not because Michael Angelo and his successors have been blind to the beauty of foliage and verdure in suitable places.

For reasons that I have thus, I fear not successfully, tried to indicate, as well as because opportunity must be left open for enlarging particular buildings in the manner advised by General Walker and for continuously extending special departments of buildings as suggested in the beginning of this letter, it appears to me that all spaces not thus specifically reserved for well-defined purposes of usefulness, should, as much as possible, be avoided and a degree of compactness of arrangement anticipated in public ways and places, especially near the centre of operations, that, having regard to Eastern and English standards would be regarded as illiberal and tasteless.[11]

If the principle buildings of the University could have been placed near the edge of an elevated table-land, commanding a fine characteristic California distance, an advantage might, with proper study, have been gained that would at once be felt to more than compensate for any shortcomings from standards of taste of the sort that I have indicated. Considerations, the wisdom of which I do not question, having determined such a situation to be inexpedient,[12] something is most desirable to be devised, appropriate to the circumstances, through which, when the University is born into the world, it may be saved from bearing on its face an expression of hard materialism and "Gradgrind" practicality.[13] This under General Walker's advice, cannot come from any stately beauty of the buildings, any picturesqueness in the manner of their disposition or any gardening or landscape appendages. It must be a matter

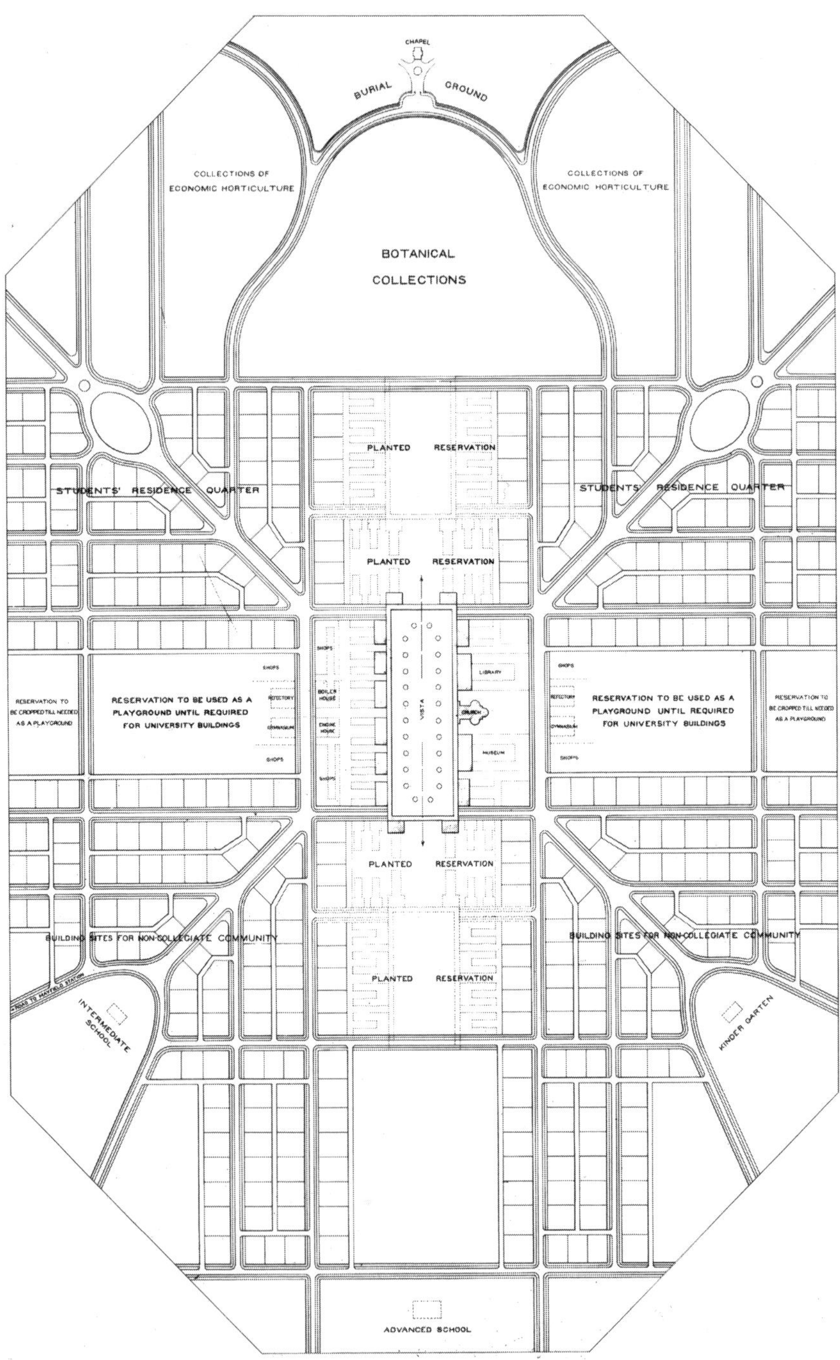

"Proposed Plan for Stanford University Grounds," December 28, 1886

of Art. It must have scholarly dignity. It must not be ostentatiously costly, and it must be unobtrusively incidental to a means of a manifestly useful purpose. Some element of this description I feel has yet to be designed.

With kind regards and my best service to Mrs. Stanford,[14]

I am, dear Sir,

Very Respectfully Yours,

The text presented here is a typed unsigned letter with edits in Olmsted's hand. Olmsted began working on the design of Stanford University in Palo Alto, California, in 1886. Stanford selected Shepley, Rutan, and Coolidge, the successors to H. H. Richardson's firm, as the architects. Olmsted traveled to California three times in the late 1880s to work on the project (see FLO to Charles A. Coolidge, May 22, 1887, below and FLO to Leland Stanford, July 14, 1889, below).

1. Amasa Leland Stanford (1824–1893) was a lawyer, businessman, Governor of California, United States Senator, and founder of Stanford University. Born and educated in New York, he moved to Wisconsin in 1848 and then to California in 1855. Elected Republican governor of California in 1862, he advanced the interests of the transcontinental railroad. From the time he left the governorship in 1863 until his death in 1893, he made a large fortune in the Central Pacific and Southern Pacific railroads and many other business interests. He served as a United States Senator from 1885 until 1893. While traveling in Europe in 1884, his only child, Leland Stanford, Jr., died of typhoid fever at the age of fifteen. Stanford founded Leland Stanford Junior University in 1885, one of the nation's first private, coeducational universities, in memory of his son. The university opened in 1891(*DAB*).
2. Olmsted had earlier asked John C. Olmsted to send "copies of our best photolithographical custom surveys" to Stanford at Menlo Park so that he could see examples of the type of topographic survey the firm required (FLO to JCO, Sept. 29, 1886).
3. Gen. Francis Amasa Walker (1840–1897), a Union general during the Civil War, was a well-known economist and president of the Massachusetts Institute of Technology from 1881 to 1897. Stanford met Walker while visiting northeastern universities in the summer of 1884 and offered him the presidency of Stanford University. Walker declined, but agreed to advise Stanford. Walker may have recommended Olmsted to be the landscape architect, since he had known Olmsted since at least the 1870s and they had both become members of Boston's Saturday Club in the early 1880s. In August 1886 Walker traveled with Olmsted, Henry Sargent Codman, and Frederick Law Olmsted, Jr., to Palo Alto to meet with Stanford. Upon returning to Massachusetts, Walker wrote a report to Stanford that outlined the uses of thirteen proposed buildings and suggested how they might be laid out within Olmsted's quadrangle design. He also expressed his approval of Olmsted's one-story arcade plan for the quadrangle (*DAB*; James Phinney Munroe, *A Life of Francis Amasa Walker* [New York, 1923], pp. 177–79; Orrin Leslie Elliott, *Stanford University: The First Twenty Five Years* (Palo Alto, 1937), pp. 1–38; Francis A. Walker to FLO, Jan. 10, 1876; M. A. DeWolfe Howe, ed., *Later Years of the Saturday Club, 1870-1920* (Boston, 1927), pp. 165–75, 183–87; Francis A. Walker to Leland Stanford, Nov. 30, 1886, B74: #1032, OAR/LC; FLO to Leland Stanford, Aug. 17, 1889, A5: 154–56, OAR/LC; see also FLO to Charles Eliot, March 4, 1886, n. 5, above).
4. In October 1886, the board of commissioners of the Niagara Reservation had appointed

Olmsted and Calvert Vaux landscape architects to the commission and asked them to prepare a plan for the reservation, which was presented in September 1887 (FLO to William E. Dorsheimer, July 21, 1886, above; FLO to Mariana Griswold Van Rensselaer, May 17, 1887, below; "General Plan for the Improvement of the Niagara Reservation," 1887 [*Papers of FLO*, SS1: 535–75).

5. Olmsted refers to his trip west earlier that fall when he went to Palo Alto to meet with both Walker and Leland Stanford.
6. Before Olmsted accepted the commission, he was concerned that Stanford had expressed a desire for his campus to resemble that of a New England college. He wrote in March 1886, before he met with Stanford for the first time, that he would not accept the commission if "it is English landscape gardening that is wanted." During his years in California in the 1860s and subsequently, Olmsted had developed an approach to semi-arid landscape design that was adapted to the climates and soils in the western United States. Important examples of this approach were his designs for the Mountain View Cemetery in Oakland, California; a municipal park system for San Francisco; and a summer community development, Perry Park, in Colorado (FLO to Charles W. Eliot, Sr., March 2, 1886; FLO to Charles Eliot, July 20, 1886, above; FLO to JCO, Oct. 31, 1887, Box H6, folder 1, OAR/LC; Frederick Law Olmsted and Calvert Vaux, "Preface to the Plan for Mountain View Cemetery, Oakland, California," May 1865 [*Papers of FLO*, 5: 473–88]; "Preliminary Report in Regard to a Plan of Public Pleasure Grounds for the City of San Francisco," March 31, 1866 [*Papers of FLO*, 5: 518–46]; FLO to Bela M. Hughes, [Jan. 15,] 1889, below; see also Charles E. Beveridge, "The California Origins of Olmsted's Landscape Design Principles for the Semiarid American West" [*Papers of FLO*, 5: 449–73]).
7. In 1865 Olmsted made initial studies for the private College of California, which was replaced in 1868 by the University of California at Berkeley when land grant college legislation made it feasible. He and Calvert Vaux submitted a completed plan for the campus and an associated residential development in 1866. The plan was not implemented, and in 1874 the Berkeley trustees hired landscape gardener William Hammond Hall to devise a new plan. As Olmsted implies here, the results of Hall's design were later criticized (Frederick Law Olmsted and Calvert Vaux, "Report Upon a Projected Improvement of the Estate of the College of California, at Berkley, Near Oakland," June 29, 1866 [*Papers of FLO*, 5: 546–73]; C. E. Beveridge, "The California Origins of Olmsted's Landscape Design Principles" [*Papers of FLO*, 5: 456–57]; *FLO, A Biography*, p. 409).
8. Olmsted refers to the East College dormitory building at Amherst College, Amherst, Massachusetts. Dedicated in 1858 and razed in 1883, the East College was an unpopular structure and, in the words of college president William A. Stearns, "destined some time or other to be removed." It was taken down in order to allow for the College Church to be built on the site (William Seymour Tyler, *History of Amherst College During Its First Half Century, 1821-1871* [Springfield, Mass., 1871], p. 405; "Amherst College: The New Buildings," *Boston Daily Advertiser*, Sept. 7, 1883, p. 5; Stanley King, *"The Consecrated Eminence," The Story of the Campus and Buildings of Amherst College* [Amherst, 1951], pp. 94–95).
9. Olmsted had consulted on the placement of new buildings at Amherst College in 1870, but he did not develop plans at that time. Although the editors discovered no record of an explicit recommendation by Olmsted to raze the East College dormitory, in an 1870 letter to President William A. Stearns about the selection of the site for the College Church, Olmsted discussed the inferiority of the design of some of the earlier college buildings. In 1883, the Amherst College trustees engaged Olmsted to develop a general scheme for the placement of new buildings, and he submitted several plans. The firm of Olmsted Brothers continued to develop plans for the college in the twentieth century

(FLO to William A. Stearns, April 5, 1870 [*Papers of FLO*, 6: 369–74]; Charles Eliot Diary, July 8 and Sept. 20, 1883, pp. 59, 75, FLLHU; *Master List*, p. 121).

10. The Basilica of St. Peter and Bernini's colonnade-enclosed Piazza di San Pietro in the Vatican made a powerful impression on Olmsted when he first encountered them in the spring of 1856. As he reported to his father, ". . . St. Peter's, poor as it seemed at a distance & mean as {*compared*} to my anticipations, still in some particularities, quite profounded me as I approached {*the*} front closely & through exceedingly different f{*rom*} all I had imagined, astonished and regularly {*awed*} me. Three or four times indeed I have been {*back &*} felt in a dream" (FLO to John Olmsted, [March] 27, 1856 [*Papers of FLO*, 2: 378]).
11. In an undated, unsigned draft of a letter in Olmsted's hand, he elaborates on what he considers to be "natural" in "the university site." The letter is addressed "Dear Sir," and was presumably intended as part of a letter to Leland Stanford. A portion reads:

> 'Natural' as thus does not mean simply that which results from the spontaneous and unassisted action of nature, as water plants growing in watery places and rock plants on rocks, but that which is natural as we say it is natural that a road passing through a hilly country or a forest should be winding and that a man passing from one point to another on an open plain should pursue a straight course. The natural style of gardening originated in England, a well wooded, well watered, naturally turfy country. Beauty of landscape in England lies mainly in the disposition of trees in relation to broad bodies of turf. Cactuses are not of natural growth in England, yet it is not in bad taste and it is not unnatural that close about a man's house, as a part of the house establishment there should be planted a few cactus plants. They are decorations of the home. But if a man should attempt to grow cactuses thickly over considerable spaces bringing them into association with masses of tree foliage as is customary with glades of turf it would not be natural. Any extensive use of turf in Cal[a] is equally far away from the principles of natural gardening. . . .
>
> So if, in a garden, exhibitions of ferns are made in close association with coarse wilted and dusty grass and weedy, knobly, dirty walks, they stamp the whole affair as in bad taste. Decorative objects should never appear in close association with things which are not themselves nice, complete and of their kind thoroughly good. (Papers of FLO/LC.)

12. Olmsted first suggested that the university be situated on sloping land southwest of what became the site of the campus. This suggestion recalled his proposed design for the residential grounds at Berkeley. Leland Stanford insisted that the University be situated on the level plain, and Olmsted acquiesced (FLO to JCO, Sept. 29, 1886; FLO to Leland Stanford, April 12, 1888, SUA; C. E. Beveridge, "The California Origins of Olmsted's Landscape Design Principles" [*Papers of FLO*, 5: 456–57]).
13. A reference to Thomas Gradgrind, a school headmaster in Charles Dickens' *Hard Times* (1854). He was "hard and cold," and his rote approach to public education was utilitarian—encouraging only practical, not intellectual, endeavors.
14. Jane Lathrop Stanford (1828–1905) was the wife of Leland Stanford and co-founder of Stanford University. Born and educated in New York, she traveled with Leland to Wisconsin and California where she became a leading philanthropist and social activist. After her husband's death in 1893, she became the University's sole trustee, overseeing its development through a series of legal and financial battles ("Jane Eliza Lathrop Stanford," *Encyclopedia of the American West* [New York, 1996], p. 1511; Robert W. P. Cutler, *The Mysterious Death of Jane Stanford* [Stanford, 2003], p. 5; Richard Joncas, David J. Neuman and Paul V. Turner, *Stanford University* [New York, 1999], pp. 5, 25–26).

TWELFTH ANNUAL REPORT, BOSTON PARK COMMISSIONERS, REPORT ON CHARLES RIVER EMBANKMENT.

[December] 1886

CHARLES RIVER EMBANKMENT.

The Board made applications to the Legislature for an extension of the time within which the Charles River Embankment must be completed, and for a change of line at the southerly end to provide for future extensions. These propositions were favorably entertained by the Board of Harbor and Land Commissioners, and resulted in chapters sixty-five and one hundred and thirty-four of the Acts of 1886.[1]

The contract for the construction of the embankment seawall was amended to conform to the new line, and the work proceeded without further interruption until the completion of the contract in October. Filling has since been going on by carts from the site of the new Court-House and various other sources without cost to the city.

A preliminary study of a plan for laying out these grounds is herewith presented, with the following explanation of the plan by the Landscape Architect:—

To the Park Commissioners:—

SIRS,—The preliminary plan which I have had the honor to submit for your consideration for the improvement of the lately embanked ground on Charles river, between Cambridge and Leverett streets, derives its special character from regard for the following circumstances:—

1. It is near a part of the city much occupied by extensive industrial establishments, and having a large tenement-house population.

2. It should be an important means of reducing the death-rate at midsummer of infants and young children.

3. To all others it is likely to be most useful at nightfall, when the finer beauty of gardens is lost, people coming to it then in great numbers who have been confined during the day in close and heated buildings, streets, and yards.

4. Its special sanitary value, both with respect to children and to the class of visitors last mentioned, will be in the broad expanse of tide-water upon

which it opens; partly because of the radical change of scene which it will offer from that of the compact town, and partly because of the radical change of air that it may provide.

5. It should offer some facilities for open-air exercises for people whose occupations are sedentary.

6. The site is one of extreme exposure for plants. Fine garden qualities could only be maintained at a greater cost than in the other public grounds of the city. It is well adapted to the growth of hardy trees.

7. The space is too small relatively to the number of people likely to resort to it for the introduction of plots of turf to be walked upon. It would be impossible to keep them in decent condition.

Governed by these considerations, the leading features of the plan are:—

First. A level promenade nearly half a mile in length, adjoining and overlooking deep water. This promenade is to have an unbroken width of twenty-five feet. It is to be bordered on the side opposite the river by a row of trees, back of which are to be shaded seats, the arrangements being spacious, simple, and convenient for keeping clean and in good order.

Second. On the side of the promenade toward the city the larger part of the ground is to be raised above the general level with slopes of a natural aspect, and is to be planted in the character of a natural grove, screening the air coming from that direction, shutting the buildings out of view, giving a certain degree of sylvan seclusion to the promenade, and smothering the roar of the streets to those upon it.

Third. A space 370 by 150 feet in extent is to be enclosed and prepared especially as an exercise-ground for women and children, no others being admitted. It is to be screened about with shrubbery, and is to be adapted only to simple forms of recreation in which many can be engaged at a time quietly, without compelling care-taking of excessive cost.

Fourth. A space 500 by 150 feet in extent is to be fitted with simple gymnastic apparatus,[2] and subject to use for more robust forms of exercise; but not games or feats likely to attract crowds in which it would be difficult to maintain order, and which would interfere with the comfort of women and children on the promenade.

Fifth. Two landings for boats are provided for, and it is intended that boats for hire should be offered at them.

Sixth. Two houses to contain water-closets, tool-rooms, and offices of administration are proposed, one at the entrance of the women's exercise-ground and near the southern boat-landing, the other near the gymnastic-ground and the northern landing.

Seventh. A row of lights at the edge of the embankment, and another

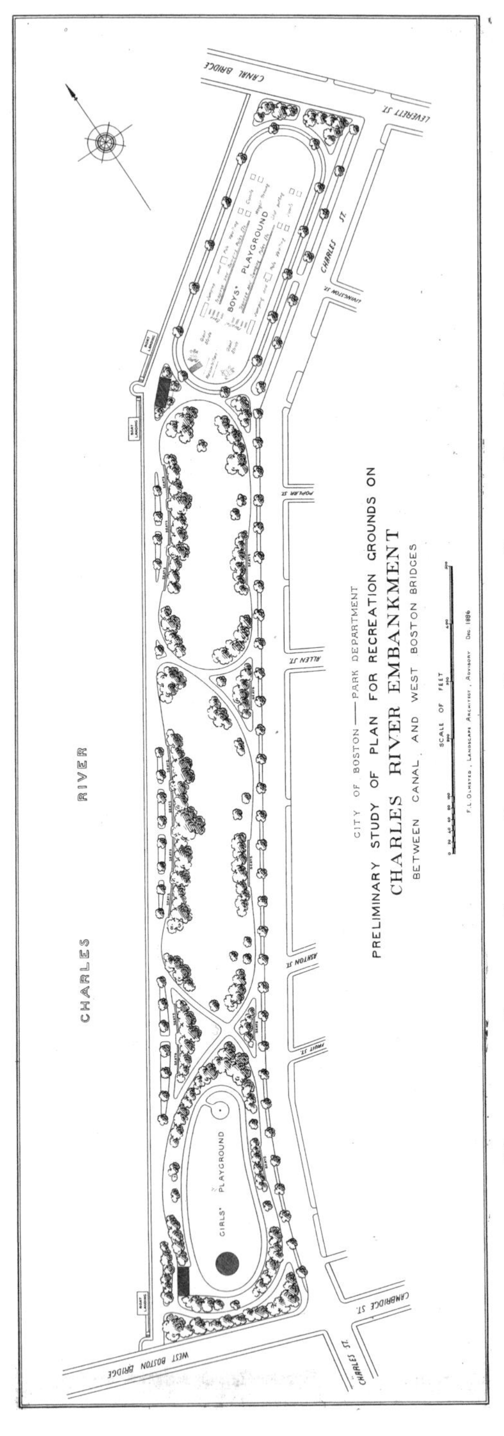

"Preliminary Study of Plan for Recreation Grounds on Charles River Embankment Between Canal and West Boston Bridges," December 1886

MEN'S OUTDOOR GYMNASIUM, CHARLESBANK, N.D.

along the street, will satisfactorily light the entire ground. No gas-pipes are to be laid in the planted parts.

Respectfully,

FREDK. LAW OLMSTED,
Landscape Architect.

The text presented here was printed in the *Twelfth Annual Report of the Board of Commissioners for the Year 1886* (Boston, 1887), pages 15–17. Plans for embanking and improving the shoreline of the Charles River had been part of Boston park proposals for years, most notably in the 1876 park system plan, which included a continuous waterfront embankment from Craigie's Bridge at Leverett Street to Cottage Farm (later Boston University) Bridge. In 1881, a reduced proposal for embanking and reclaiming the shoreline between Craigie's Bridge and the West Boston Bridge at Cambridge Street was approved. The park described here opened in 1889. Improvements and additions to the park are explained in the 1892 *Annual Report*, which included maps and descriptions of the popular gymnasia built there (FLO to Charles H. Dalton, April 8, 1876 [*Papers of FLO*, 7: 192–99]; "New Park Opened," *Boston Daily Advertiser*, July 30, 1889, p. 2; Cynthia Zaitzevsky, *Frederick Law Olmsted and the Boston Park System* [Cambridge, Mass., 1982], pp. 96–99; Karl Haglund, *Inventing the Charles River* [Cambridge, Mass., 2003], pp. 100–4; *Seventeenth Annual Report of the Board of Commissioners for the Year 1892* [Boston, 1893], pp. 47–62).

1. See [Chap. 65], *An Act Extending the Time for the Completion of the Public Park in the City of Boston, Known as the Charles River Embankment* and [Chap. 134], *An Act to Change a Portion of the Line of the Seawall of the Public Park in the City of Boston,*

Known as the Charles River Embankment, included in the *Twelfth Annual Report of the Board of Commissioners for the Year 1886* (Boston, 1887), pp. 33–34. These acts allowed work to continue on the creation of a sea-wall on the Boston side of the lower basin of the Charles River, between Craigie's Bridge and the West Boston Bridge.

2. The gymnasia that Olmsted designed were shown in more detail in his 1892 revised plan, and were, according to Sylvester Baxter, the first public, open-air gymnasia of their kind in the United States (*Seventeenth Annual Report of the Board of Commissioners for the Year 1892* [Boston, 1893], pp. 47–62; C. Zaitzevsky, *The Boston Park System*, pp. 96–99; Sylvester Baxter, *Boston Park Guide* [Boston, 1898], p. 35).

The Beacon Street Plan.

December 4, 1886

Messrs. F. L. and J. C. Olmsted, the Landscape Architects, make the following comments upon the preliminary plan for the widening of Beacon street, printed herewith:

This plan is designed to supply certain advantages, the lack of which is hindering a desirable, and inviting an unadvisable, occupation of the large and beautiful district lying on each side of Beacon street for three miles beyond Back Bay. It assumes that what is wanting to secure a natural, suitable, speedy and profitable outgrowth over this district from the Back Bay quarter, is, first, a spacious, direct trunk-line thoroughfare, specially adapted to pleasure driving, riding and walking; and, second, a means of direct communication between it and the city that shall be always ready for use, convenient, economical and expeditious.

As to the latter requirement, it is to be considered that an ordinary street railway laid in any one of the existing narrow streets would destroy any value it might otherwise have as a pleasure drive, and that the noise of cars passing so near would render property fronting on the street unsuitable for first-class suburban residences.

Under the plan here presented, a cable railway, with all the improvements that experience has proved to be desirable in the extensive cable systems of San Francisco and Chicago, is to be laid in the midst of an avenue of about three times the breadth of the broadest of the present streets of the district,[1] and is to be screened on each side by two rows of trees growing in well prepared borders. The usual objections to a residence upon a suburban street through which a house railway passes will thus be avoided.

It is to be further considered that the arrangement proposed will prevent ordinary road vehicles from being driven along the track of the railroad: that the track will be crossed only at infrequent intervals, and that at these, because of the breadth of the avenue, an approaching car will be seen well before the track is reached by any crossing vehicle, so that danger of collision may be readily avoided. For these reasons a much higher rate of speed can be maintained by the cars (and this with much less disturbance and noise) than is usual on street railways. With reference to travel otherwise than by railway, the designed arrangement of the cable road, and of the trees bordering upon it, involves the necessity of a drive on each side of the avenue, in order that houses facing upon it may be directly accessible by carriages. One of these two drives is planned to be wider than the other, in order that those using it may have greater enjoyment of the sociability of a promenade. A soft gravel course is provided for equestrians, and this, for the same reason, is placed adjoining the broader of the two carriage-ways.

The normal plan is modified where the line of the avenue crosses the steep slope of Corey Hill,[2] because, otherwise, the differences of elevation between the avenue and the adjoining properties would be inconvenient, and also because the cost of its construction would be excessive. It will accordingly be seen, by the lower of the two cross sections on the left of the plan, that the two drives are here designed to be at different elevations, one of the planting spaces at the side of the railway being widened and sloped to make such an arrangement feasible. The southern-most of the two drives is made the wider, because its grades will better adapt it in pleasure driving, and the bridle-way is carried with it.

The different means of locomotion, and the several lines of trees, provided in the plan, are expected to make the avenue attractive, not only because of the usual convenience secured, but also because of the sylvan beauty to be enjoyed in passing over it. As those to be drawn to use it on this account, will form in themselves, and by the elegance of their equipages and attire, a pleasing spectacle, as they pass by in daily procession, another feature will be gained, tending to make the adjoining building sites particularly attractive to many people.

Experience in the development of suburban districts elsewhere, both in the Old World and the New, justifies the conclusion that ready accessibility by cross-roads to an avenue having the advantages that have been thus explained, will also make a broad district on either side far more attractive as a place of residence than it is likely to become through any other means not greatly more costly. Many men of importance in the business of a city, and of abundant means, are found to prefer to live a little retired from the animation of such an avenue, who yet highly value it as a resort, and as a route of travel to and from their places of business.

"F. L. & J. C. Olmsted."

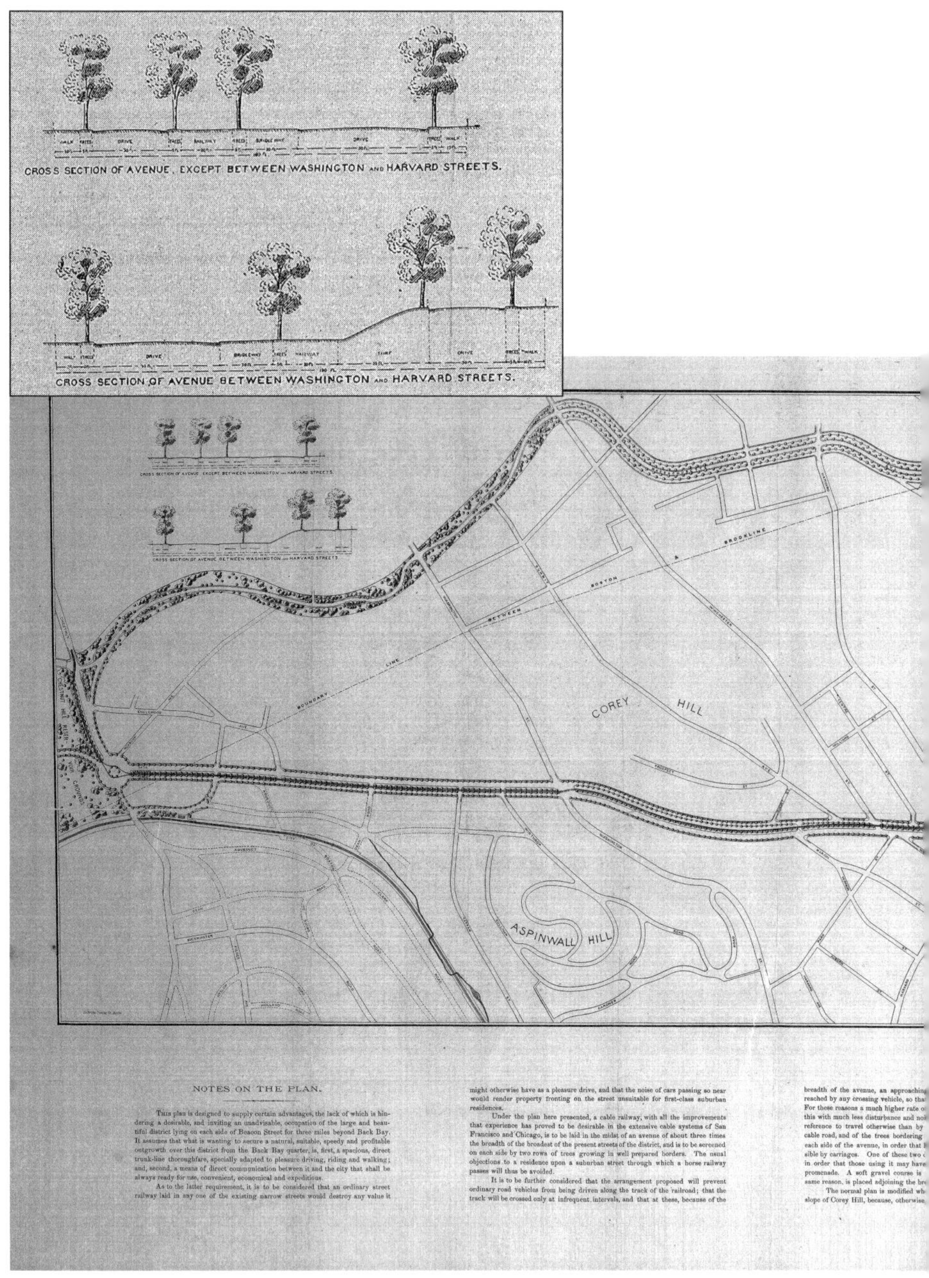

NOTES ON THE PLAN.

This plan is designed to supply certain advantages, the lack of which is hindering a desirable, and inviting an unadvisable, occupation of the large and beautiful district lying on each side of Beacon Street for three miles beyond Back Bay. It assumes that what is wanting to secure a natural, suitable, speedy and profitable outgrowth over this district from the Back Bay quarter, is, first, a spacious, direct trunk-line thoroughfare, specially adapted to pleasure driving, riding and walking; and, second, a means of direct communication between it and the city that shall be always ready for use, convenient, economical and expeditious.

As to the latter requirement, it is to be considered that an ordinary street railway laid in any one of the existing narrow streets would destroy any value it might otherwise have as a pleasure drive, and that the noise of cars passing so near would render property fronting on the street unsuitable for first-class suburban residences.

Under the plan here presented, a cable railway, with all the improvements that experience has proved to be desirable in the extensive cable systems of San Francisco and Chicago, is to be laid in the midst of an avenue of about three times the breadth of the broadest of the present streets of the district, and is to be screened on each side by two rows of trees growing in well prepared borders. The usual objections to a residence upon a suburban street through which a horse railway passes will thus be avoided.

It is to be further considered that the arrangement proposed will prevent ordinary road vehicles from being driven along the track of the railroad; that the track will be crossed only at infrequent intervals, and that at these, because of the breadth of the avenue, an approachin
reached by any crossing vehicle, so tha
For these reasons a much higher rate o
this with much less disturbance and no
reference to travel otherwise than by
cable road, and of the trees bordering
each side of the avenue, in order that
sible by carriages. One of these two
in order that those using it may have
promenade. A soft gravel course is
same reason, is placed adjoining the br

The normal plan is modified wh
slope of Corey Hill, because, otherwise

"Preliminary Plan for Widening Beacon Street from the Back Bay District o
Connections with Massachusett

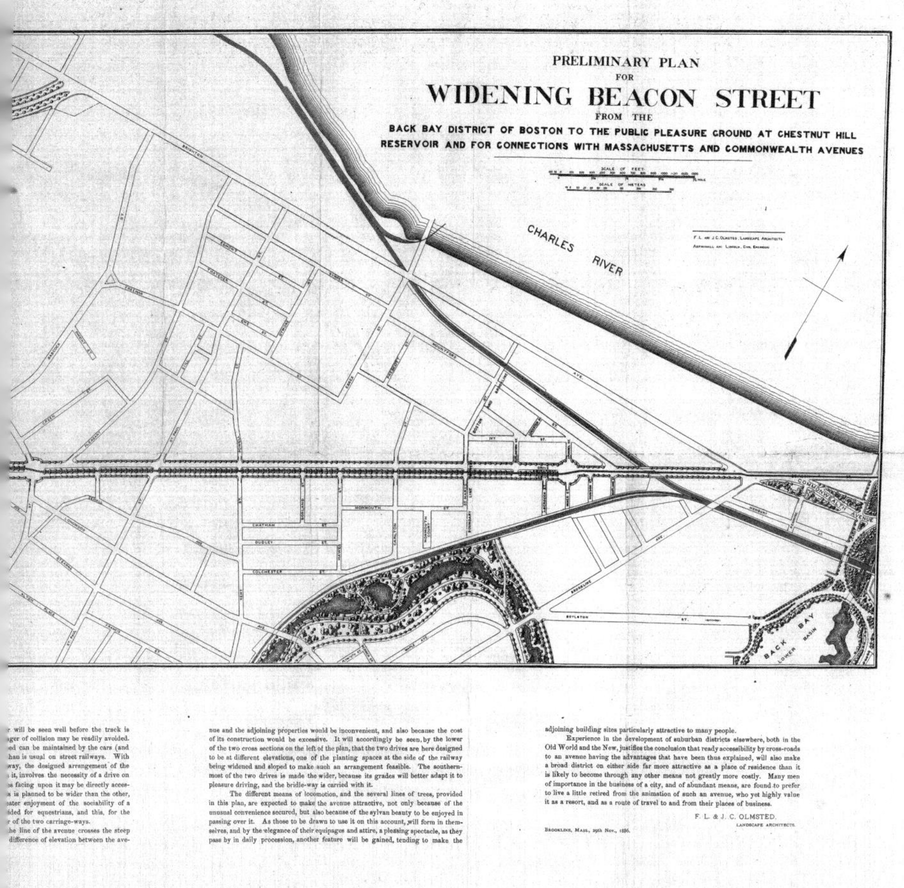

r will be seen well before the track is
ger of collision may be readily avoided.
ed can be maintained by the cars (and
han is usual on street railways. With
way, the designed arrangement of the
it, involves the necessity of a drive on
es facing upon it may be directly acces-
s is planned to be wider than the other,
eater enjoyment of the sociability of a
ided for equestrians, and this, for the
r of the two carriage-ways.
he line of the avenue crosses the steep
difference of elevation between the ave-

nue and the adjoining properties would be inconvenient, and also because the cost of its construction would be excessive. It will accordingly be seen, by the lower of the two cross sections on the left of the plan, that the two drives are here designed to be at different elevations, one of the planting spaces at the side of the railway being widened and sloped to make such an arrangement feasible. The southernmost of the two drives is made the wider, because its grades will better adapt it to pleasure driving, and the bridle-way is carried with it.

The different means of locomotion, and the several lines of trees, provided in this plan, are expected to make the avenue attractive, not only because of the unusual convenience secured, but also because of the sylvan beauty to be enjoyed in passing over it. As those to be drawn to use it on this account, will form in themselves, and by the elegance of their equipages and attire, a pleasing spectacle, as they pass by in daily procession, another feature will be gained, tending to make the adjoining building sites particularly attractive to many people.

Experience in the development of suburban districts elsewhere, both in the Old World and the New, justifies the conclusion that ready accessibility by cross-roads to an avenue having the advantages that have been thus explained, will also make a broad district on either side far more attractive as a place of residence than it is likely to become through any other means not greatly more costly. Many men of importance in the business of a city, and of abundant means, are found to prefer to live a little retired from the animation of such an avenue, who yet highly value it as a resort, and as a route of travel to and from their places of business.

F. L. & J. C. OLMSTED.
LANDSCAPE ARCHITECTS.

BROOKLINE, MASS., 29th Nov., 1886.

BOSTON TO THE PUBLIC PLEASURE GROUND AT CHESTNUT HILL RESERVOIR AND FOR
AND COMMONWEALTH AVENUES," NOVEMBER 29, 1886

The text presented here is from the *Brookline Chronicle*, Dec. 4, 1886. The same text appears on the lithograph of the "Preliminary Plan for the Widening of Beacon Street from the Back Bay District of Boston to the Public Pleasure Ground at Chestnut Hill Reservoir and for Connections with Massachusetts and Commonwealth Avenues" (Nov. 29, 1886). An earlier plan referred to the Beacon Street widening as the "Extension of Commonwealth Avenue along Beacon Street" but in the end Beacon Street kept its name.

The widening of Beacon Street greatly influenced the transformation of Brookline during this period. Twenty years earlier, Henry M. Whitney of the Metropolitan Steamship Company had recognized the development potential of the area and began buying property along the Beacon Street corridor. He later formed the West End Land Company and in 1886 employed Olmsted to devise plans for widening the avenue. That fall the Brookline Selectmen approved the Beacon Street project and asked Olmsted to draw up this final plan. Whitney also served on the Brookline Park Commission with Francis W. Lawrence and Charles Sprague Sargent. While work on Beacon Street and the development of adjacent property proceeded quickly, the proposed Massachusetts (Commonwealth) Avenue lagged and would only be completed, in a modified form, in the twentieth century (C. Zaitzevsky, *The Boston Park System*, pp. 110–14; "Beacon Street," *Brookline Chronicle*, Aug. 7, 1886; "Widening of Beacon Street," ibid., Aug. 21, 1886; "Beacon Street: Its Improvement in Brookline by Connection with Commonwealth Avenue, History of the Movement" [Brookline, 1887], pp. 1–8; "Report of the Brookline Park Commissioners," Feb. 15, 1886 [Brookline, 1886]; see also Frederick Law Olmsted, "Talk to the Brookline Club, History of Streets," Feb. 1889, below).

1. The new width of Beacon Street was reduced from 200 feet to 160 feet in the course of gaining approval from the city and developing the design. Beacon Street remained a public street and was not part of the Brookline park system. The original design described here, however, included a "cycle way," a "bridle way," and a wider roadway (fifty feet) on one side of the avenue (on the north side to the east of Coolidge Corner, and on the south side to the west), and a corresponding narrower roadway (twenty-four feet) on the opposite side. The wider roadway allowed for leisurely and recreational driving without interfering with business traffic and deliveries.

   The Beacon Street extension further realized Olmsted's concept of what he called in 1887 "the Parkway," which today is known as the Emerald Necklace, for the Boston metropolitan area. The separation of ways, the creation of a landscape corridor, and the connections between larger public landscapes all characterized Olmsted's Beacon Street plan, as they did the entire park corridor between the Public Garden and Marine Park (see *Appendix, Report of the Landscape Architect Advisory*, Dec. 30, 1887, below).
2. Beacon Street skirts the southern edge of Corey Hill between Washington Street and Harvard Street. The top of the hill offers views of Boston, and the area had been suggested as a park since at least 1869. Henry M. Whitney owned a portion of the hill when Beacon Street was being widened, and Olmsted began studies for the subdivision of the property in 1889. At that time Olmsted also suggested the summit of the hill become a park. Eventually the hill was terraced for residential development, although not according to Olmsted's plan. The summit became a park in the early twentieth century (Cynthia Zaitzevsky, "Frederick Law Olmsted in Brookline: A Preliminary Study of His Public Projects," *Proceedings of the Brookline Historical Society*, Fall 1977, pp. 42–65).

To Mariana Griswold Van Rensselaer

6th Feb, 1887.

Dear Mrs Van Renssalaer,

Thank you very much for writing me. My hurt is trifling and I keep my bed under the doctor's orders only because if I were knocking about I might get really hurt and also because I want to earn $15 from the Accident Insurance Compy.[1]

It had better be a secret between us three that he is too good a fellow to travel for if it should get abroad his occupation would be gone and there an end, for he gets his living by it.[2]

The book is growing well, I know, but I am glad to hear that you think so.[3] I have been to see the Ames Monument.[4] I heard from several sources and one that should have been authoritative that it was being spoiled by pebbles blown against it, and I obtained an order to have the Pacific train stopped long enough to let me go to it. I saw no evidence of injury. I never saw a monument so well befitting its situation, or, a situation so well befitting the special character of a particular monument. It is not often seen, apparently, except from a considerable distance, being on the peak of a great hill among great hills with a shanty village on the slope through which the train passes. A fellow passenger told me that he had several times passed it before and it had caught his eye from a distance but until he saw me looking at it he had supposed it to be a natural object. Within a few miles there are several conical horns of the same granite projecting above the smooth surface of the hills. It is a most tempestuous place and I have no doubt that at times the monument is under a hot fire of little missiles, but they will only improve it, I think. (I may be mistaken. I could only glance at it; there was some snow upon it and the wind and cold so horrible that my eyes were half drowned.)

Sincerely Yours

Fredk Law Olmsted.

The text presented here is a signed letter in Olmsted's hand.

1. Olmsted was injured in a train collision near Chicago, on January 31. He was on his way home from a trip to Salt Lake City to meet with members of the Union Pacific Railway about building a hotel in Garfield, Utah. In the accident Olmsted re-injured his lame leg, the result of an 1860 carriage accident (JCO to J. F. O'Shaughnessy, Esq., Jan. 21, 1887, A1: 609, OAR/LC; FLO to Chester M. Dawes, Feb. 9, 1887, A1: 630–31, OAR/LC; FLO to W. W. Riter, Feb. 14, 1887, A1: 635–38, OAR/LC; "Latest News Items," *San Francisco Daily Evening Bulletin*, Feb. 15, 1887; *FLO, A Biography*, p. 150, 433; see also FLO to Charles Loring Brace, March 15, 1887, below).

2. Olmsted may be referring to someone mentioned in Van Rensselaer's letter to him, but her letter has not been found.
3. Van Rensselaer was working on her biography of H. H. Richardson, about which she and Olmsted corresponded a number of times. In her 1888 book she quotes Olmsted's description of the Ames Monument from this letter (see FLO to Mariana Griswold Van Rensselaer, [May] 6, 1886, above; FLO to Mariana Griswold Van Rensselaer, May 2, 1886, above; FLO to Mariana Griswold Van Rensselaer, Aug. 11, 1886, above; FLO to Mariana Griswold Van Rensselaer, Dec. 21, 1887, below; FLO to Mariana Griswold Van Rensselaer, June 14, 1888, below; Mariana Griswold Van Rensselaer, *Henry Hobson Richardson and His Works* [Boston, 1888], reprint [New York, 1969], p. 72).
4. Presumably Olmsted saw the Oakes and Oliver Ames Monument, designed by H. H. Richardson (1882), in January 1887 on his way to or from Salt Lake City. Located in Sherman, Wyoming (between Laramie and Cheyenne), the massive granite, two-stepped pyramid was located three hundred feet from the Union Pacific portion of the transcontinental railroad at its highest point of elevation. Sixty feet square at its base and sixty feet high, the monument was faced in rough hewn granite. Augustus Saint-Gaudens created bronze portrait reliefs of the two brothers that were placed high on the east and west sides of the upper pyramid. Oakes Ames had been a central figure in financing the Union Pacific, and other family members remained important figures in that company. The Ames family were also the patrons of the North Easton, Massachusetts, projects on which Olmsted and Richardson collaborated in the early 1880s (Jeffrey K. Ochsner, *H. H. Richardson, Complete Architectural Works* [Cambridge, Mass., 1982], pp. 212–13; FLO to Oakes Angier Ames, Jan. 29, 1887, Ames Family Collection, Stonehill College; see FLO to Oakes Ames, April 1882, above; FLO to Oakes Ames, June 5, 1887, below).

To Charles Loring Brace

15th March. 1887.

My Dear Charles:

The more important change that age brings to me is a growing disposition to take no thought of tomorrow—none of today; to delay and postpone and be shiftless. In matters of business obligation I try to hold myself in reasonably good discipline but beyond that I indulge myself in going to sleep over the newspaper as my father did rather than pump up energy for pleasures of activity. And so, being overloaded with business all the time and held much more to the desk by it than is good for me, I have let your note of a month ago, which gave me great pleasure, lie unanswered.[1]

I was injured in my lame knee in a collision upon the C. B & Q returning from Salt Lake. I did not think it at all serious and when I heard that it was in the newspapers had the thought, where is the improvement of the Press going to stop, can't I stub my toe without its being telegraphed all over the country?[2] I kept my bed for a week under the doctor's orders and then thought I was well but in fact I do yet experience some inconvenience and am restricted in my movements by it and shall ask for some slight compensation of the Company. I cannot walk without a little pain. But I travel a good deal, using wheels for local movement as much as possible. We have all the professional work we can well manage to do justice to. I should like to feel free to undertake less. We are all as well as usual. Mary finds the winter tediously protracted; she was out yesterday looking at her plants in spots where the snow had melted off, but during the night there was another storm and they were buried again. She does not go out much in winter & is chiefly occupied in novel reading. Marion[3] is visiting in New Brunswick where it is still solid winter. There is no notable change in Charlotte's condition.[4] Her children are coming up very nicely under our excellent governess and housekeeper.

You ask what do I think of Major Walter.[5] I am ashamed to say, I don't remember any one of that name. Is it a friend of Field's[6] whom I saw in Liverpool. Yes, I think that was his name & I have seen him once since, in Chicago and have a book of his but I don't think I have any knowledge of him to be written. What brings him up?

Has Howard Potter[7] returned? I am sorry indeed not to have seen him. When is he to resettle here? I suppose Mrs. Brown Potter[8] must a little exercise him. I mean the newspapers' dealings with her. I have no other than the highest opinion of her. If she has the slightest talent for the Stage I should like to have it given to the public.

Tap, tap, tap. What a different world it is from that we used to know. I don't give much thought to it but every day it is driven in upon me. I have not forgotten the Sartor Resartus days.[9] I don't concern myself the least bit with speculations. I don't know and I don't care. I am occupied quite enough with "the duty that lies nearest to you."[10] The most horrible waste in the world seems to me the waste of mind in what is called theology and I repent of nothing more thoroughly than my own sin in superstitious meandering.[11] I take pleasure in observing how perfectly healthy our children are in this respect, how completely uninterested they are in all that used to be such a terrifically cruel burden upon me and how well they illustrate the fallacy in which we were steeped that the pondering of "eternal" things is favorable to good living. I think that living in a Greek family & community they would go to a sacrifice to Minerva, or if in Arabia to a Mosque in precisely the same spirit; with the same motives; the same sincerity and the same moral effect, that they go to church. I rather encourage them to go to church; to the Unitarian here; the English when with the bishop's children,[12] the Orthodox when in Litchfield,[13] the Roman Catholic when with the Perkins's[14] and I don't think that they feel separate from any of them which is a good thing. I should be sorry to have them feel that they were more enlightened or more "favored". I don't think so of myself. I only think it is queer that I could have ever thought myself to have such ideas as I did, and queer that anybody else can continue to have them. I talk so much as this to no one but you and it is a mark of the amazing progress of New England that nobody else ever invites me to. What a different, happier and better life I should have had, had it always been so. But I suppose in point of

JOHN CHARLES OLMSTED AND MARION OLMSTED, C. WINTER 1887/1888

fact that among the Presbyterian, Baptist & some other clubs, the same pharisaical habit with its delusions of inspired humility still prevails by which we were imposed upon. Yet there can be no question of the tremendous under current that is, everywhere, even among the niggers, sweeping it away. And in spite of the growth of a wretched leisure class and its consequence in the spread of anarchism I can't think than in any half century before the world has advanced nearly as far as in the last. In the old language I feel that we have been exceedingly blessed. Few men have more of the happy spirit of nunc dimittis.[15]

Yours affctly

Fred[k] Law Olmsted.

The text presented here is a signed letter in Olmsted's hand (see FLO to Charles Loring Brace, Nov. 1, 1884, above; FLO to Charles Loring Brace, Jan. 18, 1890, below).

1. In Brace's letter, dated February 13, he asked after Olmsted's health and reported good news about family and friends. He described that as he has aged "old memories come up," writing, "I often think gratefully of what you did for me in our Ruskin and Carlyle days, your influence on me was immense" (Charles Loring Brace to FLO, Feb. 13, 1887; see also *Papers of FLO*, 1: 225–37; FLO to John Hull Olmsted, Feb. 10, 1849 [*Papers of FLO*, 1: 323–26]).

2. For details on the accident see FLO to Mariana Griswold Van Rensselaer, Feb. 6, 1887, n. 1, above.
3. Marion Olmsted (1861–1948), Olmsted's daughter, was twenty-six at this time and still living at home. She never married and stayed at Fairsted, traveling with her father on trips in his old age and helping with secretarial work at the firm. She was later described by her mother as having a nervous temper. Olmsted described her in 1893 as delicate and suffering from rheumatic trouble, but "just the nicest girl—little old maid—possible; patient, happy, and indefatigable" (*FLO, A Biography*, pp. 391, 470–73; FLO to Frederick Kingsbury. Sept. 6, 1893).
4. Charlotte Olmsted Bryant (1855–1908), Olmsted's step-daughter. In her teenage years, Olmsted had described her as a "nice young woman, simple, straight-forward & self-possessed," but her health sometimes worried her parents. In the 1870s she was encouraged to pursue a vocation in the education of children, and worked for a time as a kindergarten teacher. Ending her career as a teacher in 1878, she married Dr. John Bryant, and they settled in Cohasset, Massachusetts, in a house and grounds that H. H. Richardson and Olmsted had designed for them (1880–81). By 1883, Charlotte had three children, the first of Olmsted's grandchildren. A month after the birth of her third child, Charlotte became severely mentally ill and never fully recovered. She was institutionalized in the winter of 1883 and died in a sanitarium in Norwood, Massachusetts, in 1908 (*FLO, A Biography*, pp. 338, 365, 391–92; FLO to John Olmsted, June 25, 1864; FLO to JCO, Oct. 7, 1877 [*Papers of FLO*, 7: 335]; J. K. Ochsner, *H. H. Richardson*, pp. 232–34; Calvert Vaux to FLO, Oct. 7, 1883; FLO to JCO, Oct. 7, 1877 [*Papers of FLO*, 7: 337, n. 31]).
5. Major James Walter (4th Lancashire Artillery Volunteer Corps) was an English writer and art collector who had recently published a book about the paintings of eighteenth-century English painter James Sharples, focusing on three portraits of he had done of George and Martha Washington (1796–97), which were part of a traveling exhibition in America in the early 1880s. The Century Club, of which Olmsted and Brace were members, housed the exhibit for a time. Walter wrote, "On the three pictures [of Washington and Martha] arriving in New York, the first to welcome them was the Century Club, to which they were formally introduced by Charles Loring Brace, one whose works of philanthropy are known throughout the world." Major Walter's book received mixed reviews, including a review in the *Nation* that claimed that the pictures were worth seeing but the book left much to be desired. Walter was already familiar with Brace and his career. In an earlier book about volunteerism in England, comparing it to the effort in America, Walter wrote, "such a man as Charles Loring Brace, of New York, who has devoted an energetic life to the rescue and sustenance of hundreds of thousands of waif and stray children of emigrants cast up on the streets of New York, and by his 'Children's Aid Society' gathered into God's fold" (James Walter, *Memorials of Washington and of Mary, his Mother, and Martha, his Wife, from Letters and Papers of Robert Cary and James Sharples* [New York, 1887], pp. 25–26; *Nation*, Nov. 4, 1886, p. 879; Kate Sanborn, "Coming to Washington: Some Rare and Valuable Portraits to be Offered to the Government," *Washington Post*, Nov. 15, 1886; James Walter, *Notes and Sketches During an Overland Trip from New York to San Francisco* [Liverpool, 1869]; James Walter, *England's Naval and Military Weakness. National Dangers. The Volunteer Force* [London, 1882], p. 38).
6. Alfred T. Field (1814–1884) was an English hardware manufacturer and merchant whose firm was based in Birmingham, England, and New York City. He had been a neighbor of Olmsted's on Staten Island and worked with him to promote the Richmond County Agricultural Society. He advised the Olmsted brothers and Brace on the itinerary for their 1850 walking trip in the British Isles. In 1854 Field moved back to England, but he and Olmsted remained friends and continued to correspond. His wife's sister, Harriet Errington, served as the Olmsted family's governess during their

time in California from 1863 to 1865, and ran a school on Staten Island that the Olmsted children attended in the 1870s (*New York Times*, May 28, 1884, p. 4; FLO to John Olmsted, March 14, 1850; *Papers of FLO*, 1: 342, n. 11; FLO to JCO, Oct. 7, 1877 [*Papers of FLO*, 7: 337, n. 31]).

7. Howard Potter (1826–1897) was a lawyer, banker, and philanthropist. He began his career as a lawyer in New York, then secretary and treasurer of the Novelty Iron Company, and then moved to England later in life to take over the merchant banking firm of Brown, Shipley and Co., the firm of his wife's family. Involved in civic and charity organizations, he was a co-founder of the Children's Aid Society and a long-time friend of both Brace and Olmsted. He assisted them in various ventures, including the founding of the *Nation* in 1863 and the campaign to protect Niagara in the 1870s. By 1887 he resided in both New York and London, and presumably Olmsted is asking here if Potter had recently returned from London. Potter eventually moved to London permanently (*Papers of FLO*, 4: 416, n. 3; *FLO, A Biography*, pp. 111, 235; "Howard Potter Dead," *New York Times*, March 25, 1897, p. 1).
8. Mrs. James Brown Potter (Cora Urquhart Potter) was Howard Potter's daughter-in-law, the wife of his oldest son, James Brown Potter. The couple married in 1877 and had one daughter. In 1886, Mrs. Potter began to pursue a professional acting career in spite of remonstrances from her husband and father-in-law. She signed a contract with a London theatre company in 1887 and moved to that city. She and her husband subsequently lived apart and divorced in 1900. As a society woman performing on the stage, Mrs. Potter received coverage in the press and gave interviews in which she spoke disparagingly of the Potter family, blaming them for attempting to stifle her artistic pursuits. The family tension and scandal resulted in Howard Potter disinheriting her in 1897 ("The Amateur Elocutionist," *New York Times*, May 2, 1886; "She Wants a Fortune," ibid., Dec. 31, 1886, p. 5; "Theatrical Gossip," ibid., March 5, 1887; "Society," ibid., May 9, 1897, p. 19; "Divorce for J.B. Potter," ibid., June 5, 1900, p. 1).
9. In 1846 Olmsted wrote to his brother, John Hull Olmsted, that he had just read Thomas Carlyle's *Sartor Resartus* (1831) and, ". . . if anybody wants to set me down for an insane cloud dwelling Transcendentalist, because I like Carlyle, I hope they'll gratify themselves. I do think Carlyle is the greatest genius in the world." As young men, Olmsted, John, and Brace enjoyed long discussions of philosophical, religious, and literary issues first at Yale, then at the Staten Island farm and during their walking tour of Britain, and in correspondence. Carlyle influenced Olmsted's personal convictions on matters of faith, salvation, and duty (FLO to John Olmsted, Aug. 12, 1846 [*Papers of FLO*, 1: 272]; *Papers of FLO*, 1: 225–27, 282–83).
10. In *Sartor Resartus*, Carlyle describes, through the words of the fictional Professor Teufelsdröckh, salvation that comes through dedication to good works:

    > Most true is it, as a wise man teaches us, that 'Doubt of any sort cannot be removed except by Action.' On which ground, too, let him who gropes painfully in darkness or uncertain light, and prays vehemently that the dawn may ripen into day, lay this other precept well to heart, which to me was of invaluable service: '*Do the Duty which lies nearest thee*,' which thou knowest to be a Duty! Thy second Duty will already have become clearer.

    (*Sartor Resartus* [London, 1831; reprint, Boston, 1836], p. 197).
11. As a young man in the 1840s, Olmsted was drawn into the religious revivals and doctrinal debates of the period. He later suggested he had been swept up by enthusiasm, but did not experience a true conversion and remained skeptical of religious dogma (*Papers of FLO*, 1: 225–81; *FLO, A Biography*, pp. 41–43).
12. William Woodruff Niles (1832–1914) was Episcopal Bishop of New Hampshire and the husband of Bertha Olmsted (1834–1926), Olmsted's half-sister. Of the six children

they had, four were living at this time: Edward Cullen, Mary, William Porter, and Bertha (Ezra S. Stearns, *Genealogical and Family History of the State of New Hampshire: A Record of the Achievements of her People in the Making of a Commonwealth and the Founding of a Nation* [New York, 1908], p. 520; "Bishop Wm. W. Niles Dead," *New York Times*, April 1, 1914, p. 13).

13. That is, members of the Congregational church who subscribed to strict Calvinist doctrine. A leader of the group was Lyman Beecher (1775–1863), who lived in Litchfield, Connecticut, and was the father of Henry Ward Beecher and Harriet Beecher Stowe. The Olmsted family had a number of friends and family in Litchfield, including the Beechers (*DAB*).
14. Presumably a reference to Catholic relatives of Olmsted's wife, Mary Cleveland Bryant Perkins.
15. A reference to the phrase in the Gospel of Luke (2:29–32): "Lord, now lettest thou thy servant depart in peace."

TO EDWARD WILLIAM BOK[1]

Brookline, Mass.
4th April, 1887.

E. W. Bok Esqr, Editor.
My Dear Sir,

Your circular and personal note of 24th ul^to were duly received.[2]

Through all his mature life Mr Beecher[3] was active in engaging the interest of the public in pleasure gardening and the results of pleasure gardening in all its forms but most beneficently so in those available for modest homes, for people of straitened means and living under conditions of horticultural difficulty. With these he was, I believe, more in sympathy than the world, of late, has been giving him credit for being, and I should be glad to give any help in my power to make him better understood in this respect.

I gratefully remember, also, the encouragement which at various times I received from Mr. Beecher[4] and have a warm sense of what he did in cultivation of an appreciative public opinion in respect to the class of works in which I have been engaged.

I have thus every disposition to comply with your request and have been slow to decline to do so. But the theme you give me — Mr Beecher's love of nature — can be justly treated only by one who has been in intimate communion with him in rural rambles, as I have not, and by one having some literary aptitude for the duty, as I have not.[5]

Yours Truly,

Frederick Law Olmsted.

The text presented here is from a letterpress copy of a handwritten letter signed on the original in Olmsted's hand: A1: 695–96, OAR/LC.

1. Edward William Bok (1863–1930), author, editor, and philanthropist, was collecting contributions for his *Beecher Memorial: Contemporaneous Tributes to the Memory of Henry Ward Beecher* (Brooklyn, 1887). Bok knew Beecher well and edited the *Philomathean Review* (which became *Brooklyn Magazine* in 1884), the official publication of Beecher's Plymouth Church. After selling the magazine in 1886, Bok began a newspaper syndicate, featuring a weekly column by Beecher, and, in 1889, he became editor of the *Ladies' Home Journal* (*DAB*).
2. Bok's letter stated that Beecher had been a great admirer of Olmsted. He wrote that Beecher had said that Olmsted "accomplished considerable towards ennobling, educating, and purifying the American people," and that "Olmsted, like the lamented, but never dying Andrew Jackson Downing, has beautified many a dreary spot, and made it a scene of perpetual beauty." Bok requested that Olmsted write an appreciation of Beecher, specifically speaking of the minister as a "lover of nature" (Edward W. Bok to FLO, March 24, 1884).
3. Henry Ward Beecher (1813–1887), Protestant minister and anti-slavery activist, was born in Litchfield, Connecticut, the son of Lyman Beecher and Roxana Foote, and the brother of Harriet Beecher Stowe. Olmsted had known Beecher since the 1850s, and in 1851 was briefly engaged to Beecher's niece, Emily Baldwin Perkins. Olmsted's close friend Charles Loring Brace also had a connection to the Beecher family, since his aunt, Harriet Porter, was Lyman Beecher's second wife and the two families had been neighbors in Litchfield. In 1847 Beecher became the minister of Plymouth Congregationalist Church in Brooklyn, where Olmsted heard his sermons on several occasions in 1853. A leading public figure of the day, Beecher, through public speaking tours, published sermons, and many articles in the *Independent* (which he edited during the Civil War years) reached a national audience. Beecher also had, as Olmsted notes, a serious interest in horticulture. In the 1840s he edited and wrote for the *Indiana Farmer and Gardener* and later published some of his articles as *Plain and Pleasant Talk About Fruits, Flowers and Farming* (1859) (*DAB*; *FLO, A Biography*, p. 77; *Papers of FLO*, 1: 68, 89).
4. For example, Beecher supported the campaign Olmsted and his brother, John Hull Olmsted, initiated in 1854 to raise funds to support their friend and fellow anti-slavery activist, Adolph Douai, in Texas. Douai needed funds so he could continue to publish his newspaper, the *San Antonio Zeitung*. Beecher, as well as Charles Loring Brace, were early supporters of the effort (Frederick Law Olmsted, "A Few Dollars Wanted to Help the Cause of Future Freedom in Texas," [c. Oct. 1854] [*Papers of FLO*, 2: 319–21).
5. Bok wrote to Olmsted again after receiving this letter, urging him to change his mind. He said that if Olmsted did not wish to speak to Beecher's love of nature he could instead write "a few lines speaking of him as a humanitarian, a friend of the slave and the down-trodden." He then went on to outline explicitly the things Olmsted should write about Beecher. Olmsted again declined to contribute, insisting that he was not a skilled enough writer for the job, claiming, "I always regret it when I travel out of the paths that nature and education have fixed for me" (Edward W. Bok to FLO, April 7, 1884; FLO to Edward W. Bok, April 18, 1887, A1: 720–23, OAR/LC; *FLO, A Biography*, pp. 400–01).

[APPENDIX.]

Proposed Extension Of The Park System.

Frederick Law Olmsted's Letter, Transmitted to the Common Council, April 11, 1887.

S. S. Jewett, Esq.,[1] President of the Board of Park Commissioners of the City of Buffalo:

Sir—The Common Council having asked your Board to take the necessary steps to realize the wishes of citizens of the Thirteenth Ward, petitioning for a park on the lake shore, and for a pleasure road connecting it with the existing park and parkway system of the city, and the Board having asked my counsel in the matter, on the 22d inst., in company with your Committee on Roads and Grounds, I made a tour of the Thirteenth Ward and of a part of the town of West Seneca, and the following day was present at a meeting of the Board at which a hearing was given to a number of gentlemen speaking for the petitioners. In a conversation that followed I was led to state something of the impressions that had been made upon my mind by what I had thus seen and heard and was asked by the commissioners to report the substance of my remarks in a written communication to you. Before doing so I should like to recall certain circumstances of the past, a consideration of which is necessary to an understanding of the present situation.

Nineteen years ago I was asked by a provisional committee of citizens to advise in the selection of a site for a rural park for Buffalo.[2] I said at once, that it should, if possible, be on the shore of the lake. This, more especially for two reasons: First, there is nothing so refreshing and grateful to a man escaping temporarily from the confinement of ordinary city life as an unlimited expanse of natural scenery such as would be provided without cost in any situation overlooking the lake. Every acre of park land, therefore, so situated, may be worth many acres elsewhere. Second, it is a great advantage to a city to have a park approachable by water. Boats are cheap and pleasant vehicles. Making the journey to a park in a boat, the refreshment of the visitor begins as soon as he takes water. It is a much better means of anti-urban recreation than that of moving in a wheeled vehicle through the midst of the city. The most beautiful place of resort in the world is said (in the *American Cyclopedia*) to be a public park in Stockholm.[3]

No other is more generally or better used by all classes of people. This park is on an island and is accessible *only* by boats. But when I said that I should think that the best place for a park near Buffalo must be somewhere on the shore of the lake, I was cautioned not to suppose that the people of the city had any sympathy with the sentiment by which, coming from the seaboard, it was presumed that I was moved. It was said that the lake brought to their minds, more prominently than anything else, harsh winds, wrecks and other disasters, dreary fields of ice and a tedious holding back of spring, and that, even in warm weather, boating was not popular, nor was there any custom prevalent corresponding to that which leads the people of cities near the ocean to flock to its shores. More than once it was said to me, "We hate the lake." I mention this because a directly contrary statement has been publicly made of late. If a change of popular sentiment in this respect has occurred it is probably because the habit of seeking recreation during the summer by excursions from the town has been growing rapidly and an education has been gained in sensibility to the refreshment of broad aspects of nature. What finally settled the question was the obvious fact that north of Buffalo creek[4] no large space could be found along the shore unoccupied by costly buildings or undivided by a railroad and, south of the creek, none which could be made pleasantly accessible except at immoderate cost. Giving up a large park on the lake, I nevertheless urged the importance of improving the Front, as has since been done, and that no time should be lost in securing the space of ground between the Front and the lake, which the city is now trying to obtain possession of at a cost many times greater than would have been necessary had my advice been immediately acted upon.[5] Making, next, a tour of the suburbs of the city at a distance from the lake, I found no ground offering valuable advantages for a rural park within the limits of the district to which the committee were willing to go. Looking (against their wishes and entirely of my own motion) beyond these limits, I found a situation in which the advantages for forming a park of an unusual and very desirable character, at moderate cost, seemed to be such as to more than compensate for its obvious disadvantages in remoteness from the people of the southern part of the city. I expressed this conviction and gave reasons for it and they were in time found sufficient to induce the city government, though not without strenuous opposition, to secure the greater part of the land advised. The little which it failed at the time to buy, it is now adding to the Park at a price, I believe, ten times greater than it would have had to pay.[6] I refer to these circumstances prefatorily to the following observation: If the population of Buffalo should increase at a rate not greatly below the average rate of its increase during the last twenty years, it will not be long before it is twice as large a city as it was when its present part was begun. It is improbable that it will wait even till that time before providing something in the way of a park at a point opposite that of the present park. It will, then, be improvident to let whatever tract of outlying land would be most suitable for the purpose become occupied with structures that will either prevent its purchase when wanted, or add greatly to its cost.

As to the choice of a site for a second park, the following propositions may be suggested. Whenever Buffalo wants another park, it will be best:

First, that it should be in a direction from the city opposite that of the present Park; second, that it should command a broad view over the lake; third, that it should be conveniently, safely and pleasantly accessible from distant parts of the town by boats; fourth, that it should be adapted to the production of natural features of rural scenery (other than in views over the lake) which will be pleasing and refreshing in a different way from those of the present Park, so that it cannot be said that one is better than the other; only that each is excellent of its distinctive kind. I find that the ground which the petitioners seem to have had more particularly in view, or ground near it, is satisfactory in each of these particulars. It is in the required direction from the center of the city; it is on the lake; when the breakwater shall have been extended, as I am told it is likely to be in a few years, there will be a still-water boating-way to it from the northern parts of the city; its topography is in strong contrast to that of the present Park.[7] Further than this, it is in part little better than waste land, and is in part farming land, at a distance from any improvements spreading out of the city, and will not be costly. Owing to numerous railroad embankments and bridges, interrupting the natural outflow of waters, a considerable quarter in the southern part of the city has been of late years increasingly subject to be flooded. To lessen this liability the city engineer has devised a scheme for turning the course of Cazenovia creek below a certain point, and giving it a direct outflow into the lake.[8] From evidences seen on the twenty-second, of the depth of a recent flood, covering all the roads and sweeping away bridges and fences on several square miles of land, I think the city will be compelled soon to provide some method of relief from this evil. Presuming that that proposed by the city engineer, which, at a glance, seems simple and effective, will be adopted, it is to be noted that the new outlet of the creek will come not far from the situation had in view for the park, and may easily be made to coincide with it.

Having been instructed to submit a preliminary design for the proposed park, I am disposed to consider whether advantage cannot be taken of the copious flow of water that the turned creek will supply, and of the movement of earth that will be necessary in forming its outlet, to establish the basis of a passage of natural scenery of an unusual type and of a park of unique character. If the park scheme and the drainage scheme are designed in certain respects co-operatively, economy will probably be gained for both. The precise situation of the land to be taken for the park should be determined with regard partly to the requirements of the drainage scheme, and partly to the price at which different properties that would answer the two purposes in view might be bought. In the meantime any plan for the park should be of a tentative character. In order that a better judgment may be formed of what is practicable and data obtained which would allow a preliminary estimate of the cost of the proposed work to be made, I shall wish to prepare such a tentative plan in consultation with the city engineer, and I advise that with a view to it a survey of the ground to be considered be made. This will best be done at once, before the leaves come out. As I have spoken of the advantages of water communication with a public park, it may be best at this time to mention that in laying out the present park north of the city the question of a water-way to it was considered, and it was concluded that it would be practicable at slight expense to make Scajaquada creek navigable for rowing craft and steam launches to the Park and a basin and landing for visitors arriving by that route was provided for in the plan. The arrangement is still available, and it will be feasible in the future to have a line of pleasure boats, moved, to avoid the heat of steam boilers, by electric motors (such as are now used by street cars), plying between the north and south parks and calling at various landings along the city front.

I shall now turn to another branch of the question upon which the Common Council has asked the commissioners to take action.

In connection with the plan of the main Park of Buffalo, a system of roads adapted to pleasure travel, by which the Park could be approached from different quarters of the city, was suggested by Mr. Vaux and myself in 1868. One branch of this system, which the Park Commissioners adopted and carried out, ran through the eastern outskirts of the city. From the southern end of this branch an avenue has since been extended, by order, I believe, of the Common Council, which is carried at grade over two railroads. Such a road is certainly not adapted to pleasure travel, but it seems to be classed as a part of the parkway system, and the present proposition is to further extend this road, under the name of a parkway, to the proposed new park on the lake. It differs in no respect from other ordinary tree-bordered avenues of the city.[9]

It was to be observed that the gentlemen who, on the twenty-second,[10] addressed your Board on behalf of the petitioners, scarcely mentioned the matter of the park, and did not at all discuss questions of its site, extent or character. But they were all warmly interested in the question of the route of the prospective parkway. Several routes for it were proposed and each was warmly advocated. All of them had the same point of departure, but while a direct route from this point to the point had in view for the park on the lake shore would be not more than three miles in length, the shortest of those advocated would be over four miles, the longest over six. Viaducts for getting over several railways were proposed in each case, but nothing was said of the grade crossings of railroads that would have to be passed before the initial point could be reached from the dwellings of a greater part of the people of the city, and even of the southern part of the city. That the park had been asked for not so much because the petitioners had felt the need of a park in the southern part of the city, as because they wanted what the city might be hoped to provide under the name of a parkway, would, I suppose, be denied by none of the gentlemen. The drift of the argument for each of the proposed routes for the parkway was such as to naturally suggest the comment made in a newspaper report of the proceedings the following morning, to the effect that each petitioner was of the opinion that the most suitable route for the parkway would be the one that would carry it nearer his front door.[11]

I indicate the impression which the debate was adapted to make as the leading motive of the petitioners with entire respect for them and with sympathy with that motive. It seems to me a wrong state of things which compels them to ask for cake when they are in dire need of bread. For, the matter which I understand to be at the bottom of their solicitude is, in my judgment, one of much greater moment than that of a park or of a pleasure road leading to a park ever can be. And, as I cannot advise any of the routes to be proposed to be adopted for its ostensible purpose, and am not prepared to recommend any other, it will be proper for me to say what chiefly lies in my way to do so.

In a paper that I prepared in connection with an exhibit made at the international exposition in Paris, it was said that the plan of no other city gave more evidence of shrewd forecasting study of the future interests of its citizens than that of Buffalo as originally devised, and as the limits of this plan were outgrown it was hoped that the same spirit might characterize the enlargement of it.[12] Since then Buffalo has begun to grow overground to the southward, presenting unusual difficulties in the way of a good plan, and the tendency to occupy this ground for certain purposes is probably irresistible. It is low, flat, liable to be flooded, difficult of drainage, and so cut by a broad, deep and exceedingly crooked water-way, that to extend a convenient street system through it under any circumstances would be a difficult undertaking; to construct streets over it, carrying sewers of suitable inclination and outflow, a costly work; to prevent a manner of building likely to invite pestilence and give the whole city a bad reputation as to health, an onerous piece of municipal administration.

But the difficulties natural to the situation in these respects are greatly increased by the fact that a number of railway corporations have been allowed to take possession of a great deal of the land immediately adjoining the well-built part of the city, and to obtain rights and establish structures, each with little regard to the interest of others, except, perhaps, a dog-in-the-manger interest. The rails of these companies are carried on low embankments, interrupting the natural surface-drainage, and extending in every direction through a belt, crossing the line in which the city is advancing, more than half a mile in breadth. Within this belt the railway lines cross and re-cross one another, and they are laid at an elevation which will be intermediate between the natural surface and the lowest level at which sanitary prudence will allow the surface of streets and the ground floors of dwellings to be placed. An idea of the number of these tracks, and the danger, difficulty and delay that they already establish for all who wish to pass in or out of the city on the south, except by rail, is given by a statement made at the meeting by one of the Park Commissioners, that in a single visit to a near suburb he had been compelled to cross twenty-four lines of railway, all on grade. It was stated by another commissioner that every few days someone is reported to have been killed in attempting the passage, and that in course of a year a more terrible loss of life occurs in consequence of the arrangement than that which has lately given rise to so much public feeling by the burning of the Richmond Hotel.[13] It is also said that as many as twenty loaded teams are already often to be seen at a

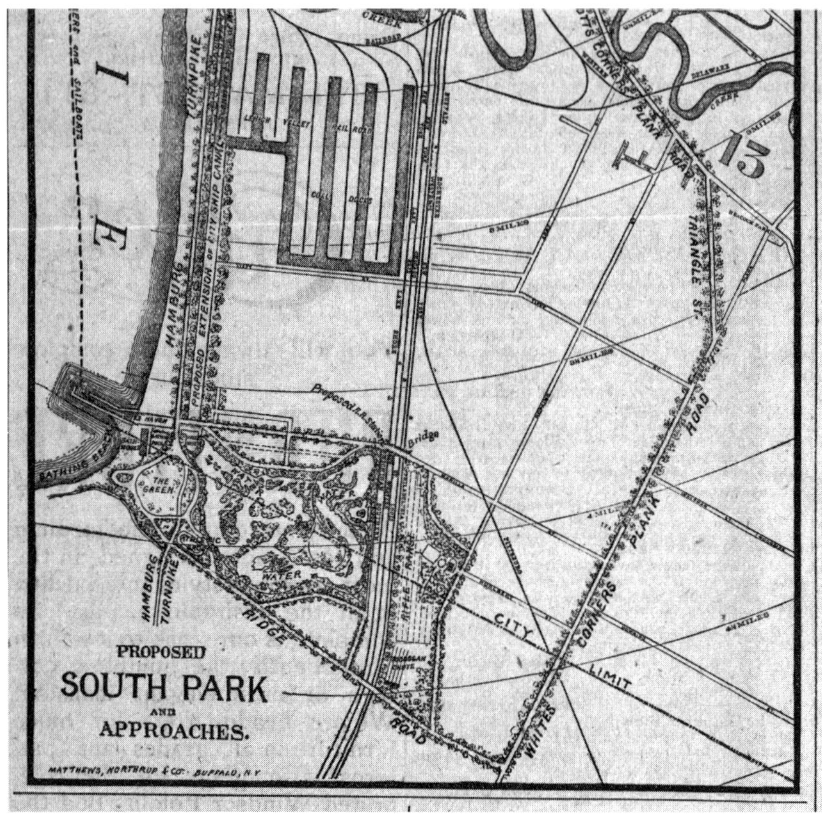

"Proposed South Park and Approaches," *Buffalo Express*, October 21, 1888

crossing, waiting for trains to pass, and that the delays and cost of transportation thus occurring are beginning to be felt as a heavy tax on certain branches of the business of the city.[14]

The difficulties in the way of establishing a judicious system for such enlargement of the city to the southward as is inevitable, presented in the circumstances that have been mentioned, are every year increased by new constructions planned without thought of the common and lasting interests of the city as a whole. Until the leading outlines, at least, of such a system shall be defined, no man, however forethoughtful and public spirited his intention, can be sure that any factory, warehouse, bridge, or road that he may build or urge the city to build, within or near this district, will not add to the complication of the problem.

There are currents of progress which, sooner or later, become irresistible in every growing city. From such knowledge of these as has come to me in a professional experience of thirty years in dealing with the corporations of numerous cities, I cannot doubt that Buffalo must before many years enter upon some broad, radical and far-seeing policy of improvement for this district and require that no

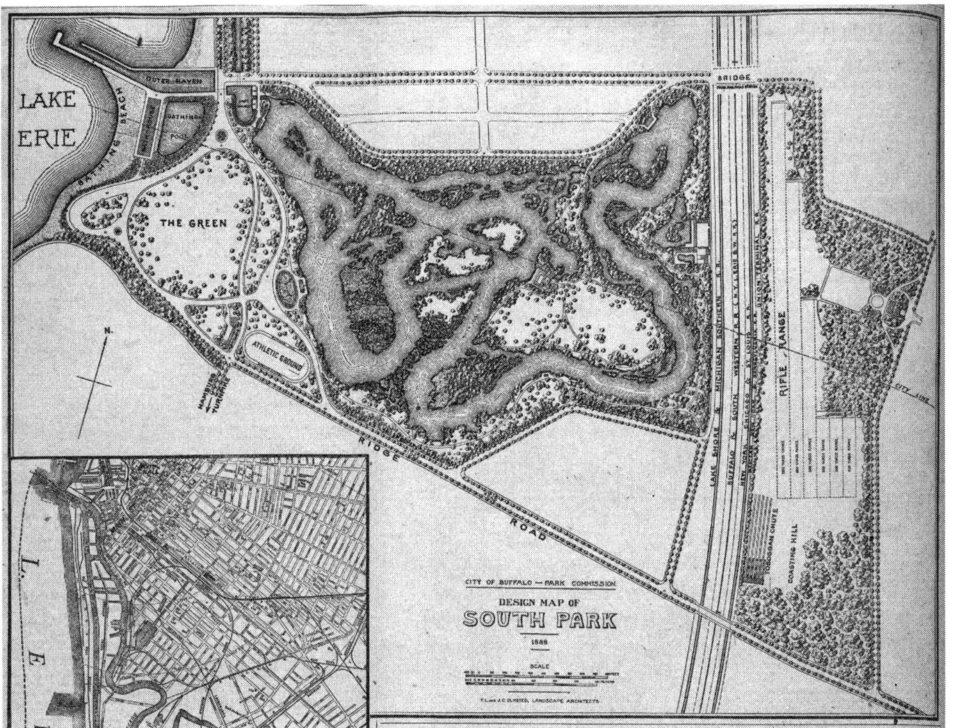

"Design Map of South Park, 1888," *Buffalo Express*, October 21, 1888

private or public work shall thereafter be prosecuted within it in a manner that will add materially to the cost of carrying out this policy.

I am told that the first step to such a policy has already been officially proposed; that it assumes that the several railroad corporations may be brought to work co-operatively one with another and with the city, to simplify the difficulty, by consolidating some of their lines, bringing others closer together, and then elevating all their tracks to a height that will allow street vehicles to pass under them.

If this scheme is ever realized and such a street system adopted as will thus be feasible and desirable, any parkway that may have been made in the meantime with regard only to the present system or no system, will be superseded and the city put to the expense of removing the materials that will have been used for getting over the railroads at their present level.

But it was said at the meeting that the opinion prevails among those likely to be well advised that the railroad companies would strenuously resist such a plan, and that in view of the means which they would be able to use for indefinitely prolonging a controversy with the city there will be no general disposition to adopt it.

Suppose it to have been decided, then, that the rails are not to come up, but that some consolidation of the different lines is practicable, that some lines may be abandoned and others relocated, so that the space of extreme difficulty will be narrowed and the problem made a little less complex.

Suppose that when this has been accomplished the duty and the interest of the city to provide for safe and convenient passage between its older parts and all of the different parts of the Thirteenth Ward has come to be recognized; the duty and interest of the city, also, to secure direct lines of common travel with all parts of the great tributary country beyond its borders on the south. In that case it is most likely that the first step toward a rationally comprehensive system of improvement for the southern part of the city would be to build a single viaduct carried in a straight line over all the railways. One end of it would be at a point where existing streets would be found conveniently diverging to all parts of the city. From the other end, lines would be laid down for broad avenues in several directions, so that, eventually, without excessive indirectness, branches from them would really come to every man's door, and all the country beyond be made conveniently accessible. One of these radiating avenues would certainly lead straight to any large park that had in the meantime been formed in that quarter. The viaduct would be broad enough to be divided into several ways, one suitable to heavy and slow traffic, one for pleasure carriages and light traffic, one for street cars, and one or more for footmen. The problem, in an administrative point of view, would be analogous to that which leads the City of New York to build bridges, causeways, and viaducts over the Harlem River and marshes, some of which pass over the railways also.

But suppose that before the necessary preliminaries to such a viaduct shall have been determined, devious roads have been made upon routes such as were advocated at the meeting of your Board, each having its own series of detached viaducts for getting over the railways, as the railways now stand. Suppose this, and it will be evident that when the time shall have arrived for planning a system of roads fitting the larger grand trunk viaduct, the difficulties now in the way of such a work will have been enormously increased.

And so, whatever comprehensive and broadly economical plan shall be finally adopted, until it is known what it is to be, nothing can be proposed with a purpose of mitigating present evils that will not be likely to have the effect of perpetuating and increasing them.

For these reasons, I submit that it is impracticable to determine at present upon what route a road adapted especially to pleasure and travel between the city as now built and the proposed Park site can be judiciously laid out.

If the Board should adopt this conclusion and so advise the Common Council, it may be within its province to represent also to that body the urgent occasion that exists for seeking radical, comprehensive and lasting economical expedients for meeting the wants that appear to have prompted the petition of the citizens of the Thirteenth Ward.

Respectfully,

FREDERICK LAW OLMSTED,
Landscape Architect.

The text presented here was published as in the appendix to the *Eighteenth Annual Report of the Buffalo Park Commissioners for the Year 1887* (Buffalo, 1888). Olmsted and Vaux began work on the Buffalo parks in 1868, planning a system of three new parks of different sizes and types connected with a system of parkways. In 1887 Olmsted began a second major period of work for the Buffalo park commission, which had been petitioned by citizens living in the Thirteenth Ward to expand the park system south of the city. In March 1887 the commissioners asked Olmsted to visit a potential lake-shore site for the new "South Park," and in April he submitted this report that brings attention to the need to address railroad track congestion on the south side of the city. In October 1888, Olmsted presented a plan for a 325-acre lakeside park: *The Projected Park and Parkways on the South Side of Buffalo* included two reports, "Plan for a Public Park on the Flats South of Buffalo" and "Report on the South Parkway Question." The Buffalo park commission never implemented the waterfront park plan, however, later acquiring two smaller sites farther inland, South and Cazenovia parks, which were designed by Olmsted in the early 1890s (Olmsted, Vaux, & Co. to William E. Dorsheimer, Oct. 1, 1868 [*Papers of FLO*, SS1: 158–70]; "The Park Extension," *Buffalo Morning Express*, March 24, 1887, p. 5; F. L. & J. C. Olmsted, "Plan for a Public Park on the Flats South of Buffalo," Oct. 1, 1888 [*Papers of FLO*, SS1: 576–96]; "Knocked Out, Mr. Olmsted's South-Side Park Decided Against," *Buffalo Courier*, Nov. 15, 1888, p. 6; Walter S. Dunn, ed., *History of Erie County 1870–1970* [Buffalo, 1972], pp. 102).

1. Sherman S. Jewett was a Buffalo businessman and longtime park commissioner. He served on the Executive Committee of the park commission until becoming president of the park board in 1879 (Perry Smith, ed., *A History of the City of Buffalo and Erie County with illustrations and biographical sketches of some of its prominent men and pioneers* [Syracuse, 1884], pp. 40–44; "Obituary," *Salt Lake Semi-Weekly Tribune*, March 2, 1897, p. 2; see also FLO to William McMillan, March 16, 1885, n. 6, above).
2. In 1868, on behalf of a committee of concerned citizens, William E. Dorsheimer invited Olmsted to Buffalo to advise on the development of the Buffalo park system. Olmsted visited proposed park sites in August, and his recommendations provided the design for what became three new parks, the Front, the Park (later Delaware Park), and the Parade, as well as connecting parkways (*Buffalo Commercial Advertiser*, Aug. 26, 1868, p. 3; William E. Dorsheimer to FLO, Aug. 12, 1868; FLO to MPO, Aug. 23, [1868] [*Papers of FLO*, 6: 266–68]; FLO to MPO, Aug. 25, 1868 [*Papers of FLO*, 6: 268–69]; FLO to Calvert Vaux, Aug. 29, 1868 [*Papers of FLO*, 6: 269–73]; Olmsted, Vaux, & Co. to William E. Dorsheimer, Oct. 1, 1868 [*Papers of FLO*, SS1: 158–70]; see also FLO to William McMillan, March 16, 1885, above).
3. That is, Djurgard Park in Stockholm. In his essay "Park" for *The American Cyclopedia* (1875) Olmsted wrote, "Stockholm has a great variety of delightful waterside rural walks; but the chief object of pride with its people is the Djurgard or deer park, which is a large tract of undulating ground about 3 m. in circumference, containing grand masses of rock and some fine old trees." Essays on parks in earlier and later editions of the *Cyclopedia* expressed similar reverence for the park ("'Park' from the *American Cyclopedia*," [1875] [*Papers of FLO*, SS1: 308–30]; "Stockholm," *American Cyclopedia* [New York, 1883], pp. 389–90).
4. Buffalo Creek (also called the Buffalo River) runs west to Lake Erie through the southern part of the city (Matthews, Northup & Co, "New Map of the City of Buffalo," *The City of Buffalo: Comprising Its Commercial and Financial Resources* [Buffalo, 1887]).
5. The Front was one of the first parks Olmsted designed with Calvert Vaux for Buffalo. Situated on a bluff above the point where the Niagara River flows out of Lake Erie, the Front overlooks a dramatic prospect. Olmsted had wanted to add a small stretch of industrial land along Lake Erie to the 35-acre park but the city did not acquire

it until 1886. As noted in the park commission's *Fourteenth Annual Report* (1884), had those acres been added to the Front when the park was established, "the cost of the land would have been a mere trifle compared with the benefits to our citizens. . . . [but] its value has largely increased." In 1891 Olmsted drew up a plan for the newly acquired land (Francis R. Kowsky, "Municipal Parks and City Planning: Frederick Law Olmsted's Buffalo Park and Parkway System," *Journal of the Society of Architectural Historians*, March 1887, p. 55; *Fourteenth Annual Report of the Buffalo Park Commissioners* [Buffalo, 1884], p. 19; *Seventeenth Annual Report, Buffalo Park Commissioners, 1887*, pp. 25–26; "Plan for Additions to the Front," plan 707-z2, NPS/FLONHS; see also Frederick Law Olmsted, "A Healthy Change in the Tone of the Human Heart," 1886, above).

6. Olmsted refers to "The Park," renamed Delaware Park in 1896, which was part of the original 1868 plan. Located in the northern portion of Buffalo, it was the city's largest park, composed mainly of a 230-acre meadow and a 46-acre lake. The park board purchased twelve additional acres for it in 1886, asking Olmsted to design a picnic grove in the space (F. R. Kowsky, "Frederick Law Olmsted's Buffalo Park and Parkway System, p. 52; *Seventeenth Annual Report, Buffalo Park Commissioners, 1887*, pp. 25–26).
7. That is, Delaware Park.
8. The Buffalo city engineer was George E. Mann. He was assistant city engineer and city engineer for eleven years and then was the engineer for the Grade Crossing Commission for eight years until his death in October 1897. While the park department did not end up rerouting Cazenovia Creek to build South Park, it later damned the creek to create a 20-acre lake in Cazenovia Park that has since been filled in (*Documents of the Senate of the State of New York* (Albany, 1897), p. 91; *Transactions of the Association of Civil Engineers of Cornell University*, vol. V (Ithaca, N.Y., 1897), p. 140; *A History of the City of Buffalo, Its Men and Institutions* (Buffalo, 1908), p. 204; F. L. Olmsted and J. C. Olmsted, "Plan for a Public Park on the Flats South of Buffalo [*Papers of FLO*, SS1: 576–96]).
9. The branch of the system that ran to the southeast from Delaware Park to the Parade was Humbolt Parkway. The road to which Olmsted refers is Fillmore Avenue, which extended to the south from the Parade and had recently been paved from Genesee and Seneca streets (*Seventeenth Annual Report of the Buffalo Park Commissioners*, pp. 5–7; Olmsted, Vaux, & Co. to William E. Dorsheimer, Oct. 1, 1868 [*Papers of FLO*, SS1: 158–70]; F. L. & J. C. Olmsted, "Report on the South Parkway Question," in *The Projected Park and Parkways on the South Side of Buffalo. Two Reports by the Landscape Architects. 1888* [Buffalo, N. Y., 1888], pp. 27–46).
10. The meeting took place on March 23rd, not the 22nd, and newspapers reported on it in their March 24th editions. The men Olmsted refers to were from the Thirteenth Ward ("The Park Extension," *Buffalo Morning Express*, March 24, 1887, p. 5).
11. About the meeting, the *Buffalo Morning Express* reported, "A number of interested parties . . . gave their opinions on the course of the proposed boulevard, someone remarking afterward that there was a peculiar coincidence in most instances between the course suggested and the location of the suggester's private property" ("The Park Extension," *Buffalo Morning Express*, March 24, 1887, p. 5).
12. Olmsted and Vaux integrated the city's parkway system with the 1804 radial grid street plan devised by Joseph Ellicott. Olmsted presented a drawing of the Buffalo park and parkway system at the Centennial Exhibition in Philadelphia in 1876, and in 1878 the Buffalo plan won an honorable mention at the Exposition Universelle in Paris (David Schuyler, "Cityscape and Parkscape," in Francis R. Kowsky, ed., *The Best Planned City: The Olmsted Legacy in Buffalo* (Buffalo, 1992), pp. 7–17; FLO to Dennis Bowen, [Sept. 10, 1876] [*Papers of FLO*, 7: 231–33]; Charles Beveridge, "Buffalo's Park and Parkway System" in *Buffalo Architectural Guidebook, Buffalo Architecture* [Buffalo, 1981], p. 19).
13. Fifteen people died in the fire that burned down the Richmond Hotel on March 18,

1887 (Cynthia Van Ness, *Victorian Buffalo: Images from the Buffalo and Erie County Public Library* [Buffalo, 1999], p. 97).

14. A public campaign was under way at this time to abolish as many railroad grade crossings as possible in the city, including in the Thirteenth Ward. As in other growing industrial cities in the United States, Buffalo experienced a dramatic increase in fatalities, accidents, and traffic congestion at rail crossings during the postwar decades. Olmsted's letter here to the Common Council was given just two days before the Council adopted a resolution to request the Board of Railway Commissioners of the State of New York to inspect the entire system of railroad approaches entering Buffalo. From April 1887 to January 1888, Common Council members, railroad engineers, and other New York politicians and railroad professionals met to discuss how to consolidate railways and to make the streets of Buffalo safer for pedestrians and drivers, ultimately deciding on a union station and elevated tracks. The project was completed in 1905. However, the single viaduct over the many railroad tracks separating the area south of Buffalo Creek from the city to the north, and connecting to a system of parkways running through the southside (which was the solution that Olmsted offers here) was not constructed (Robert B. Adam, "History of the Abolition of Railroad Grade Crossings in the City of Buffalo," in Frank H. Severance, ed., *Publications of the Buffalo Historical Society*, vol. 8, [Buffalo, 1905], pp. 153–64).

To Richard Morris Hunt[1]

5th May, 1887.

My Dear Mr Hunt;

Drawings are preparing and I hope may be sent tonight on which you will find all necessary data for planning the gateway, and indications of my notions of the substantial features of the design.[2] But, of course, the height and breadth of the central structure and the height and span and form of the arch are adjustable to a moderate extent. It is not necessary that there should be an arch. The thickness of the structure you can determine. So also the space above the arch. The planting trench overhead need not be as deep as shown (4 ft.). Two feet would serve my purpose or if you feel it to be desirable the planting trench can be dispensed with.

Back of the rough stone wall I have it in view to plant in a hedge like way shrubs that will mostly branch horizontally and some droopingly and pendantly, but mainly horizontal and close, so as to form a cornice and coping of foliage to the wall; then to plant at and near the base (among outcropping rocks) briars and brambles with acanthus-like plants and broom and small glistening leafed vines to grow up the face of the wall clinging like ivy. I should like more or less of this to be continued on your masonry walls. I mention it because it may effect your judgment about a coping for the curved part of the wall. I should prefer, for my purposes, an overhanging coping, which might be either of vitrified Akron tile, (as on the Tiffany & Villard houses)[3]. [illegible] The more project-

RICHARD MORRIS HUNT

ing i.e. shadow casting, the coping and, also, to any string course that you may use, the better for my purpose. The broader the joints also the better.

Of course, with my planting design, any coping will be in a few years mainly covered by foliage. But it would be seen here & there and foliage which has grown in adaptation to an overhanging coping becomes in time very picturesque. In broad joints with the mortar {*reamed*} out, I should here and there plant sedums — moss like plants — and, of course, the creepers would get better anchorage.

Yours Truly

Fred[k] Law Olmsted.

The text presented here is from a letterpress copy of a handwritten letter signed on the original in Olmsted's hand: A1: 779–81, OAR/LC. William Henry Vanderbilt commissioned Richard Morris Hunt to design a family mausoleum in New Dorp, Staten Island, in 1884. The next year his son George W. Vanderbilt continued the project and commissioned Olmsted to design the landscape, which included an arched entrance to the grounds, a winding, uphill approach road, and terraces at the crest of the hill (see FLO to George W. Vanderbilt, Aug. 9, 1886, above; FLO to J. J. R. Croes, May 30, 1888, below).

1. Richard Morris Hunt (1827–1895) was the first American architect to be educated at the École des Beaux-Arts in Paris, where he was admitted in 1846. He returned to the United States in 1855 where he worked with Thomas U. Walter on the Capitol in Washington,

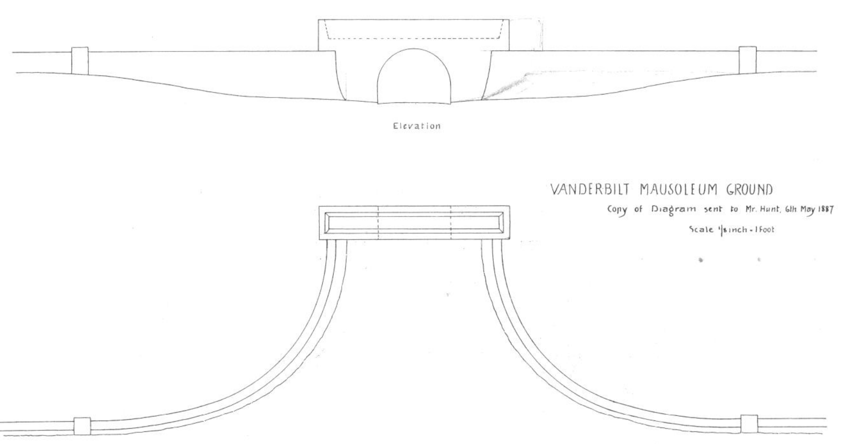

"Vanderbilt Mausoleum Ground, Copy of Diagram sent to Mr. Hunt," May 6, 1887

Arch at Entrance to Vanderbilt Mausoleum Ground, n.d.

D.C. He opened his own practice in New York in 1858 and went on to become one of the most successful architects of the era. After contentious interactions early in their careers, Olmsted and Hunt later collaborated well on projects for the Vanderbilt family and on other sites. The Vanderbilt family brought them together first for the family mausoleum in New Dorp, and later for the Biltmore estate in North Carolina. The two men also worked together on the 1893 Chicago World's Fair (*DAB*; David Schuyler, *The New Urban Landscape: The Redefinition of City Form in Nineteenth-Century America* [Baltimore, 1986], p. 96; Paul R. Baker, *Richard Morris Hunt* [Cambridge, Mass., 1980], pp. 146–61, 258–60, 290–91).

2. At the entrance to the mausoleum grounds, before the approach road to the tomb, Olmsted and Hunt designed a large stone archway, flanked on both sides by a high masonry wall that sloped and receded into the ground on either side. The arch was designed to contain soil across the top of the structure in order to plant vines and other plants that grew down over the gateway. A few feet in front of the high masonry wall was the lower "rough stone wall," described here by Olmsted. The space in between the two walls was to be planted with shrubs and other low-growing plants (photos 218-15, 218-17, Fairsted photo album, NPS/FLONHS; plans 218-28, 218-29, 218-33, 218-35, NPS/FLONHS).
3. Vitrified tiles are ceramic tiles fired at high temperatures to increase their strength and impermeability. One of the few factories in the United States that made vitrified roofing tiles at this time was in Akron, Ohio. The residence of Charles L. Tiffany, designed by McKim, Mead, and White, was built between 1882 and 1885 and was covered by a vitrified tile roof. The Villard houses, also designed by McKim, Mead, and White, were located on Madison Avenue between 50th and 51st Street and were also built between 1882 and 1885 (Heinrich Ries and Henry Leighton, *History of the Clay-Working Industry in the United States* [New York, 1909], p. 28; Samuel G. White and Elizabeth White, *McKim, Mead, and White: The Masterworks* [New York, 2003], pp. 10–11).

To Mariana Griswold Van Rensselaer

17th May, 1887.

Dear Mrs. Van Renssalaer;

You know men differ in degree as to endowment with the "literary faculty". If you put Shakespeare at 100, the average man at 50 you may set me down at 1. When I write it is as a man born without arms makes pictures. The subject about which the Niagara report[1] you refer to toils, probably interests me more than any other living man, but I can no more write what is in my mind about it than a crow can sing. I have a good many strokes of inspiration in my art (it was Horace Walpole who proclaimed it an art)[2] and if all the world did not seem to be conspired to spoil whatever good thing I set a going, I think that I should have been fairly successful in it, but successful in making people understand or even care to understand in advance what I design to have done and *why*, though I spend ten times the effort for it than I do upon design, plan, organization and superintendence, that, I never can be. Vaux and I have some differences but are fairly in accord. In the Niagara report he helped me and I helped him and at some points each of us crowded the other out a little. That you should have read it and got the impression from it that you say you did,[3] gives me more pleasure than you can imagine, and if you can translate the substance of it and boil it down to a palatable popular plateful you will take me off my feet.

Now let me try to say something which I can't say but which if it could be said and preached and made comprehensible might be worth many millions of dollars every year to this country through the saving and holding of wasted opportunities and the misapplication of effort.

There are two arts (the difficulty lies a good deal in this abused word) of design both of which are known by the name of gardening & are talked and written about with so little discrimination even by highly cultivated people as well as popularly that hardly any one keeps them mentally apart: no one fully so. (You can't, for you must think in words, and our mother Tongue is all muddled in the matter). Yet the principles of the two are as distinct as the principles of painting and sculpture. (Perhaps this is an exaggeration but it is only an exaggeration). Work-design- confusedly with reference to these principles and excellence is impossible. Apply to landscape painting the principle of mosaic art or of cameo work, what would you expect? But something very much like this is what everybody insists is right with reference to "*an art which has for its object the production (improvement & setting out?) of landscapes by combinations of the actual materials of nature, as landscape painting has for its object their imitation by combination of colors*" (pigments) (Loudon's Encyclopedia of Gardening.)[5] I have {not} been engaged in hardly any work of public interest upon which an entirely different *class* of art motives has not been engrafted or sought to be engrafted — overlaid would be the better term — and in several cases, enough has been accomplished to ruin it with reference to its original purpose. Even more has this been generally {*true, and even*} with private works. I design with a view to a passage of quietly composed, soft, subdued pensive character, shape the ground, screen out discordant elements and get suitable vegetation growing — come back in a year and find — destruction; why? "My wife is so fond of roses"; "I had a present of some large Norway spruces". "I have a weakness for white birch trees — there was one in my father's yard when I was a boy".

Why is it that I don't tell you what I want? Well, first, is it right to discriminate between the arts according to the classes of purpose or motives embodied in them, rather than according to the materials used, the tools and processes? Second, what, in popular usage, is the meaning of landscape? It is used by good writers with reference to flower gardens as artificial in purpose, design, character, sentiment, expression, as lace work or filigree of gold. And this is popular usage; at least when works of "gardening" of any kind are under consideration. And there are very few readers of the Century, or writers for it, who, having read the report of the landscape architects so called and accepted it, would not, if the work came under their control, direct work upon it with a purpose as radically different from that of the design as it lies in my mind, as the purpose of a sculptor is different from that of a painter.

The plan you ask about has been passed through the form of adoption by the Commissioners and they have asked the legislature to make an appropriation of a part of the sum estimated (in the report) to be required for carrying it out. I am advised that there is no probability that the legislature will make any appropriation for the purpose. I do not know that a word has been said about it in the legislature but it has been considered in committee. I think that the only way in which the plan is in the least likely to be carried out is by systematically stirring up, by personal preaching and newspaper cramming, a general popular agitation and thus operating on successive legislatures as we did before to secure the purchase of the real estate by the State. The Century's articles were of great value in the former agitation,[5] being much quoted by the newspapers & moving many men to thoughtfulness to whom the undertaking would otherwise have been far away.

By the way, speaking of the Century's influence, did you see — do you recall — a paper of mine that appeared in the Century last year — title, "A healthy change in the tone of the human heart". ("Open Letters").[6] In it I sought among other things to shame Boston for having made desolate its harbor and doing nothing and careing nothing for restoring its beauty. At the last meeting of the Park Commission a memorial[7] was received from prominent citizens asking attention to the subject and it was referred to me to report upon with the request that I would devise a scheme for carrying out the idea.[8]

There is a story to be told about the Stanford University which can be deferred until you come here, as I suppose you will in June or sooner. The matter is going not very well and not ruinously.

Yours respectfully,

Fred[k] Law Olmsted

The text presented here is a signed letter in Olmsted's hand.

1. "General Plan for the Improvement of the Niagara Reservation," 1887 (*Papers of FLO*, SS1: 535–75). Shortly after the publication of the Niagara Reservation plan in March, the *Century* magazine commissioned Van Rensselaer to write a review of it and of the work being done to preserve the falls (Mariana Griswold Van Rensselaer to FLO, May 16, 1887; "The Niagara Reservation," *Century Illustrated Monthly Magazine*, Aug. 1887, pp. 631–33; see also FLO to William E. Dorsheimer, July 21, 1886, above; FLO to Mariana Griswold Van Rensselaer, May 18, 1887, below; Mariana Griswold Van Rensselaer to FLO, May 21, 1887).
2. In his *History of the Modern Taste in Gardening* (London, 1771, 1780), Horace Walpole describes the development of British landscape gardening as a fine art, emphasizing the role of eighteenth-century landscape gardener William Kent in combining the sensibility of the painter with the techniques of a gardener.
3. In her letter to Olmsted, Van Rensselaer wrote that the Niagara report was a "remarkable & instructive & interesting essay, which has a general value, as explaining the true

'principles of things' outside of its special value as explanatory of this one case" (Mariana Griswold Van Rensselaer to FLO, May 16, 1887).

4. Olmsted quotes from J. C. Loudon: "Music, Poetry, and Painting are the principal imitative arts; to these has been lately added landscape-gardening, an art which has for its object the production of landscapes by combinations of the actual materials of nature, as landscape-painting has for its object their imitation by combinations of colors." (John Claudius Loudon, *An Encyclopedia of Gardening* [London, 1826], p. 998.)
5. *Scribner's Monthly* and the *Century* magazine published testimonials to the beauty and value of the Niagara Reservation that were generated by Olmsted and Norton's campaign to purchase the land. An open letter published in 1885 in the *Century*, for example, discusses the necessity of treating Niagara as a public trust, overseen by public funding:

   > The existing state [of private ownership] is one which no intelligent person can defend. The demoralization is natural and inevitable; competition between the owners of 'rival points of view' naturally develops a tendency to the employment of tawdry, sensational attractions . . . the only practicable remedy is ownership by the State, and permanent suitable guardianship over the lands. . . . No man in public life will hereafter be able to feel pride or satisfaction that he resisted the endeavour of the people of the State of New York to rescue the scenery of Niagara from destruction. (*CenturyIllustrated Monthly Magazine*, April 1885, pp. 954–55.)

6. Frederick Law Olmsted, "A Healthy Change in the Tone of the Human Heart," *Century Illustrated Monthly Magazine*, Oct. 1886, above.
7. A statement of facts forming the basis of a petition or remonstrance (*OED*).
8. The Boston Memorial Association, which was founded in 1880 and elected Olmsted a member in November 1887, was a group primarily concerned with the "future monumental decoration of the city" and with preserving Boston's history through the erection of memorials. The association responded to Olmsted's criticism of the management of Boston's Harbor Islands in the *Century* magazine by writing a letter to the Boston park commissioners asking for the islands to be reforested. Olmsted submitted his recommendations in a December report to the park commissioners suggesting that 400 acres of land in public ownership on the islands be planted with native and non-native trees. The plan was never implemented (*King's Handbook of Boston* [Boston, 1889], p. 268; Henry F. Jenks to FLO, Nov. 15, 1887; *Thirteenth Annual Report of the Board of Commissioners, Department of Parks* [Boston, 1887], pp. 44–45; *Appendix, Report of the Landscape Architect Advisory*, Dec. 30, 1887, below; C. Zaitzevsky, *The Boston Park System*, p. 108; see also FLO to Robert Douglas, Dec. 5, 1887, below).

To Mariana Griswold Van Rensselaer

18th May, 1887

Dear Mrs Van Rensselaer;

You may not know and may like to that the province of Ontario is making arrangements to set about this year what the bill for the purpose styles "The Queen Victoria Jubilee Park at Niagara", I believe.[1] It will not do to say so but I have reason to suppose that the Commissioners appointed and the public sentiment of the province favor a garden park character rather than a forest sceneric character. But there are a few people in Canada who are disposed to resist this tendency. The ruling idea is to make the affair pay its way by restaurants and play things and to draw business by attractions to picknickers. Of course the danger of a drift to another Prospect Park, to a Jones's Wood, Coney Island Big Elephant affair will be very great.[2] It is very desirable, therefore, to express and build up a public sentiment opposed to this tendency.

Yours Respy

Fred[k] Law Olmsted.

The text presented here is a signed letter in Olmsted's hand (see FLO to Mariana Griswold Van Rensselaer, May 17, 1887, above; FLO to Col. C. S. Gzowski, Aug. 15, 1887, below).

1. On April 23, 1887, the Legislative Assembly of the Province of Ontario passed the "Queen Victoria Niagara Falls Park Act," which established a reservation on the Canadian side of Niagara Falls. The reservation opened in May 1888. Olmsted had corresponded with Casimir Stanislaus Gzowski since 1885 about the Canadian reservation, and was asked to consult on the project in August of 1887. He visited the site and offered suggestions for a plan that would continue and extend the effect of the reservation he and Vaux designed for the New York side of the falls. Olmsted did not have further involvement in designing the Canadian reservation, however, and a unified design for both sides of Niagara Falls was not implemented ("The Park Act. An Act Respecting the Niagara Falls Park," *Queen Victoria Niagara Falls Park: Official Documents, 1880–1895* [Ontario, 1895], p. 23; FLO to Col. C. S. Gzowski, Aug. 15, 1887, below; "General Plan for the Improvement of the Niagara Reservation," 1887 [*Papers of FLO*, SS1: 537, 570 n. 5]).
2. Olmsted refers to several private landscapes open to the public on a commercial basis. Prospect Park was an amusement park established by the Prospect Park Company on the American side of Niagara Falls in 1872. As early as 1879 Olmsted suggested that the Niagara Reservation should include and replace Prospect Park, and in his 1887 plan for the reservation he placed the Upper and Lower Groves in its location. Jones Wood (also known as Jones's Wood) was a 150-acre plot between 66th and 75th Streets on the East River in New York and was initially favored by some as the site for a large park in the city. By 1853, however, the more central location of Central Park had been chosen instead. Jones Wood remained in private hands, available for picnics, festivals, and other activities and events. The Coney Island Elephant was a famous building in the shape of an elephant that housed a hotel. It was built in 1885 by James V. Lafferty at a time when carousels and other amusements were being built at Coney Island, in Brooklyn. The Elephant burned down in 1896 (FLO to James Terry Gardner, Oct. 3, 1879 [*Papers of FLO*, 7: 422–24]; "General Plan for the Improvement of the Niagara Reservation," 1887 [*Papers of FLO*, SS1: 540, 555]; Roy Rosenzweig and Elizabeth Blackmar, *The Park and the People: A History of Central Park* [Ithaca, N.Y., 1992], pp. 20–21, 233–36; Edwin G. Burrows and Mike Wallace, *Gotham: A History of New York City to 1898* [New York, 1999], pp. 791–92, 987, 994, 1133; Charles Denson, *Coney Island Lost and Found* [Berkeley, 2002], pp. 20–24).

To Charles Allerton Coolidge[1]

Brookline, 22[d] May 1887.

Dear Mr Coolidge,

We were taken aback by your letter of the 3[d] inst. and it has been difficult to get our minds on the new task.[2] The changes which you say Senator Stanford has required you to make seem to us not only to throw out important elements of the design which he had particularly expressed his pleasure in and fully adopted but to run counter to the spirit of his earliest instructions, upon which we have been proceeding for six months past.[3] There {*thus*} comes a danger of a mongrel sort of plan, with which when he comes to realize its character he will be dissatisfied. Therefore, as we have heard nothing from him and you do not make the reasons of his change of mind clear to us, we think that we had better drop the matter except as to what is essential for immediate operations, till after your return, which we suppose cannot be long deferred. As you may wish, however, to fix the position of the shops {*&c*}[4] before leaving we have proposed a plan and profile which will show what seems to us the best way of measuring the slope of the ground. With a little study of the drawings you will see what our purpose is and can explain it to the Senator.

If you have the surface of the street back of the church on the same level with the surface of the ground adjoining the church you must have either a higher and inconvenient retaining wall or a more inconvenient and permanently very ugly sharp slope or bank between the street and the surface where the shops are to be placed. You will also find the grading of the streets beyond the quadrangle's ends a costly and unsatisfactory work. Think out the plan in this respect for a {*second*} or two, take account of drainage requirements, and you will see — no doubt have seen. It seems to us that the street had better be kept, as shown in the drawings, nearly at the level of the natural surface; there should be a low retaining wall to carry it past the rear of the church, a few steps in this wall leading to a walk with a moderate slope to the church, and banks on each side with a shear like a ship's fore foot; these banks to be planted, so that from the front the church would seem to be backed by a cove of foliage and nothing be seen of the street, or of anything beyond except the sky. We have given the grade for the shop sites to correspond with this intention and have slightly changed the position in which they stood relatively to the street as given on the plan that you took with you.

Under the new arrangement the industrial buildings have been given a sort of {*back yard*} position, making them distinctly subordinate to the academic and the church {*has become*} the central and commanding feature. The colonnade, the quadrangle and the body of buildings of instruction lose dignity under this arrangement, the perspective effect upon which we so much counted is lost and we cannot think of any compensation for these disadvantages unless the Senator has reconsidered his decision in regard to the mausoleum and determined to place it in the apse of the church, letting the structure intended for the purpose be

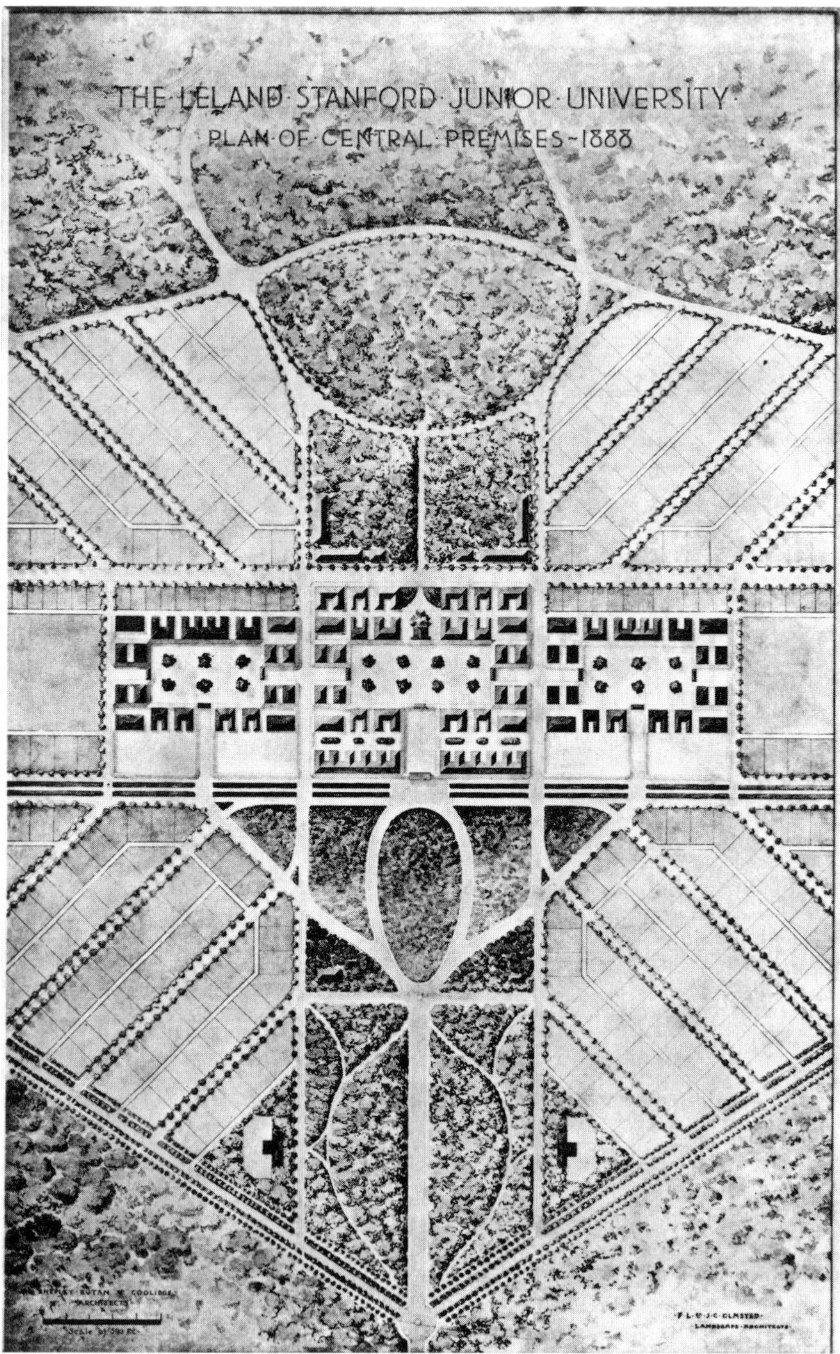

"THE LELAND STANFORD JUNIOR UNIVERSITY, PLAN OF CENTRAL PREMISES, 1888"

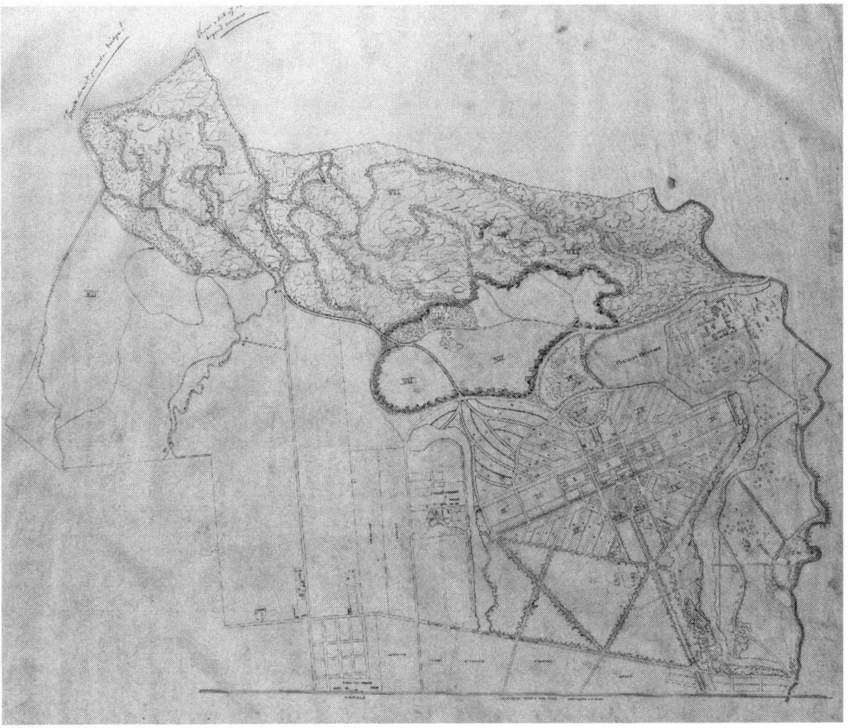

SKETCH OF GENERAL PLAN OF STANFORD CENTRAL PREMISES, APRIL 1888

built in the middle of the Cemetery & serve as a receiving tomb.[5] You say nothing of this but we hope that it will turn out so. This would in a measure justify the great injury to the quadrangle of the opening in its side. The introduction of this new element, the fracture of the quadrangle for the display of the church, will make necessary, as we think, a considerable revision of the plans north of the Quadrangle. The introduction of a great archway, disjointing and dwarfing the colonnade would be so unfortunate that we have no doubt that the Senator will come to see it.[6] We shall be able, certainly to devise an arrangement that will meet all his wants more satisfactorily but until we can confer together and with him personally it is only necessary that you should try to guard against anything being done on the ground opposite the church that would make further consideration of the whole plan in that direction more difficult.

Trusting that you have the summer's work well lined out and that we shall soon see you.

We are very truly yours

F. L. & J. C. Olmsted

The text presented here is from a letterpress copy of a handwritten letter signed on the original in Olmsted's hand: A1: 813–17, OAR/LC. Much of the text is taken from a penciled-in transcription (by a previous researcher) that has been inserted above the many faded and illegible words in the letterpress version (see FLO to Leland Stanford, Nov. 27, 1886, above; FLO to Leland Stanford, July 14, 1889, below).

1. Charles Allerton Coolidge (1858–1936) attended Harvard and MIT and began his career as an architect with the firm of William R. Ware and Henry Van Brunt. He entered H. H. Richardson's Brookline office in 1883. Upon Richardson's sudden death in 1886, Coolidge and colleagues George F. Shepley and Charles A. Rutan took over management of the firm, which became Shepley, Rutan, and Coolidge. Francis Amasa Walker recommended that Coolidge's new firm be given the commission, and Stanford officially hired Shepley, Rutan, and Coolidge in December, after spending Christmas as a guest of the Walkers in Boston. The Stanford University campus was the first large project for which Coolidge acted as the firm's lead designer, and he traveled to California frequently to oversee its progress. In addition to being a protégé of Olmsted's good friend Richardson, Coolidge was also a friend of Henry Sargent Codman, with whom he had attended MIT. He was also connected to the Olmsted firm through his brother David Hill Coolidge, Jr., a draftsman and landscape architect at the Olmsted firm between 1888 and 1893 (*DAB*; O. L. Elliott, *Stanford University*, pp. 1–38; Jefferson Elmore, "A New View of Some Stanford History," in *Stanford Illustrated Review*, Dec. 1921, pp. 135, 142, 152-53; Paul V. Turner, Marcia E. Vetrocq and Karen Weitze, *The Founders & the Architects: The Design of Stanford University* [Stanford, 1976], p. 22; FLO to Leland Stanford, Aug. 17, 1889, A5: 154–56; see FLO to Charles Eliot, Feb. 25, 1886, n. 10, above).
2. In his letter, Coolidge laid out some of the objections the Stanfords had to the design of the quadrangle, writing that they were "disappointed" in the model he presented. "They are very desirous of having the buildings look well at the start & therefore proposed instead of the seven buildings on the end to build all the buildings on the N.S. & W. sides," Coolidge wrote to Olmsted, "leaving E. side of Quad. open." When Coolidge explained to the Stanfords that this would make it look as if the main entrance should be on the east end, the couple replied that nevertheless they wanted the main drive (later Palm Drive) and vista, looking toward the southern hills, to be on the long side of the quadrangle, and also wanted a vista "up and down the valley thro' the side quadrangle." At this point, the family mausoleum was planned to be on the main axis, and the Stanfords' changes disrupted Olmsted's plans for an "open view" beyond the planned site of the family mausoleum. "We showed them how by this change they lossed [*sic*] the vista from the tomb to the back hills through the trees because the church [in its new position] would cut it off," Coolidge reported. But the Stanfords answered that now they preferred the church to be the termination of the vista and to be the dominant feature of the Inner Quad. Coolidge wrote that despite the important changes, "we did the best we could to preserve your plan as intact as possible" (Charles Coolidge to FLO, May 3, 1887; see also FLO to JCO, Oct. 31, 1887, Box H6, folder 1, OAR/LC; FLO to JCO, Nov. 4, 1887, Box H6, folder 1, OAR/LC).
3. Olmsted's design for the Stanford campus featured a main, or inner, quadrangle, from which outer quadrangles would "radiate" as the university expanded. In these earlier plans, the rectangle of the main quad was oriented from north to south, with its longest sides on the west and east ends. The church was on the long (west) side, and the main campus entrance came in from the short (north) side. After making the Stanfords' suggested revisions, Coolidge rotated the main axis of the inner quadrangle ninety degrees, making the long ends of the rectangle now on the north and south sides (Charles Coolidge to FLO, May 3, 1887; Shepley, Rutan, and Coolidge to FLO, April 9, 1887, B74: #1032, OAR/LC; Francis A. Walker to Leland Stanford, Nov. 30, 1886, B74: #1032,

OAR/LC; P. V. Turner, M. E. Vetrocq and K. Weitze, *The Design of Stanford University*, pp. 30–37; see also FLO to JCO, Oct. 31, 1887, Box H6, folder 1, OAR/LC; FLO to JCO, Nov. 4, 1887, Box H6, folder 1, OAR/LC; FLO to Leland Stanford, Nov. 27, 1886, above).

4. That is, the "work shops," or one of a series of instructional buildings that would radiate out from the original inner quad (FLO to Leland Stanford, Nov. 27, 1886, above).
5. In the early planning stages of the inner quadrangle in 1886 and 1887, the mausoleum was to be placed in an already existing cemetery outside the south end of the quadrangle, and was to be surrounded by plantings, including Olmsted's proposed botanical garden. With the suggestion to rotate the quadrangle ninety degrees, the Memorial Church became the visual terminus of the approach into the quad, with work shops behind it, and the family mausoleum was to be relocated to the apse of the church, as Olmsted says here. The planned location of the family mausoleum was later changed. The architects Caterson and Clark designed the final version, which was completed in 1889, on a four-acre site designed by Olmsted north of the campus. The old cemetery was moved in 1908 to make room for further development (plans 1032-100, 1032-108, 1032-120, and 1032-79-tp1, NPS/FLONHS; Shepley, Rutan, and Coolidge to FLO, April 9, 1887, B74: #1032, OAR/LC; FLO to John G. McMillan, May 29, 1888, A2; 542–43, OAR/LC; FLO to John G. McMillan, June 14, 1888, SUA; FLO to Thomas Douglas, Jan. 17, 1890, SUA; FLO to Leland Stanford, May 17, 1890, A8: 556, OAR/LC; Frederick Law Olmsted, "Memorandum of Instructions from Senator Stanford, May 20, 1888, as to position of tomb at Palo Alto," B74: #1032, OAR/LC).
6. "Both Mr & Mrs S. think the main entrance should be a large memorial arch with an enormously large approach & in fact the very quietness and reserve which we like so much in it is what they want to get rid of" (Charles Coolidge to FLO, May 3, 1887; for more on the Memorial Arch see FLO to Mariana Griswold Van Rensselaer, June 14, 1888, below).

To Oakes Angier Ames

Brookline, 5th June 1887.

Dear Mr. Ames:

There is a work at North Easton of which I am supposed to be the designer, which I have partly superintended and as to which you still encourage me to give you advice. I cannot if I would escape responsibility for it and it weighs on my conscience that I did not attempt to tell you the other day, when you took me to it, how far I am from taking your cheerful view of it.

The extremely rude and ungainly jumble of rocks first built is in itself an object of great ugliness and wholly unsuitable to the situation. Unless one had reason {*otherwise*} for thinking the man who planned it not a fool {*and*} could conjecture that it had been intended to be used as a foundation backing or core for some work to be done over it, it could be regarded only as a monstrosity and this view was expressed in the first name popularly given to it of "Jumbo".

To make it extremely ridiculous, it was only necessary that it should fall into the unfortunate courses that it since has which have provoked the name it now has of the "Rockery". [1] It is in fact, a cheap magnified caricature of a paltry garden rockery. But let its present promise be fulfilled in a few years it will get another name — "The Folly".

Now the structure was built for a purpose which if it could have been realized would have made the affair elegant, appropriate, becoming and with reference to its value not costly. It would have been an object fit to be associated with the noble structure, nobly placed, standing over against it. It would have graced the village and been as creditable to all concerned as that which now appears is discreditable.

There is no prospect in all that at present appears that it ever will be realized. There is less prospect of it now than there was last year or the year before. I do not know how to account for its present condition, for of all the plants that were arranged to be set out last year on the face of the jumble and along its base I did not see that a single one remained alive, while there were hundreds flourishing horribly that I had not advised.

It can never be a decent thing standing where it does until the Jumbo wall is covered with the originally designed close-fitting dress of fine, delicate foliage. The foliage of the plants now growing upward from the outer base work is and always will be worthless until the proper body dress is to be seen through it, or, as more particularly in the case of the glossy evergreens, blending with it. The Virginia Creeper will not supply this body dress. The great coarse sedums planted last year will not. The pallid anonymus[2] planted last year, (I am tempted to think as a practical joke by someone who knew how strongly I objected to them), will not. All these things only make the affair more nonsensical and the expenditure thus far made for it the more wasteful provided nothing more is accomplished.

I tell you this because you have allowed the planting season to go by without making another effort to secure the only means possible of turning the thing to any good account. I did not make a visit to it this spring because I thought that you perfectly understood what was wanted and if the arrangements of last year had failed you would know what to do and might think a repetition of my advice officious and intrusive. But apparently the bad luck of the thing has discouraged you. And now I must say that it would be shameful to let it stand as it is. If what the stone work was intended for cannot be realized the stone work ought to be torn down. In the prominent place it occupies, and in the presence of so much good work as has been done in the village, it is indecent and with its present planting will only grow more and more so.

Why should the attempt be abandoned and the design condemned and made a laughing stock? (as it is when you call it a rockery). The answer is that after three years, of hundreds of the plants principally depended on to supply the essential feature of the undertaking hardly any remain alive. (a part and an important part from the first reckoned upon, have never been planted). Three

"AMES MEMORIAL CAIRN, NORTH EASTON, MASS.," C. 1886

years in succession Robinson[3] has promised to supply them and to have them set by a competent planter and every time broken his promise.

Was I wrong in supposing that the plants in question were likely with proper care to live and flourish and accomplish the desired end? It would certainly appear so if you looked only at what has occurred at the Cairn. But I believe that a certain number of every one of these plants are growing on the Memorial Ground close by, and if not flourishing it is simply because the ground has been left too sterile for them. You will find one growing profusely upon the walls of the Lodge[4] up to the full height of the walls of the Cairn. You will find on the wall back of the Rosery[5] thousands of the house-leek and stonecrop that I have asked for that have been planted there since Robinson failed of his promise to supply them to the Cairn. All that are wanted to stock the Cairn could be taken from there and hardly be missed. As to the green Euonymus, I bought a lot for myself out of the same stock that I bought for you, and though I have lost some from mice I have hundreds of them flourishing, so that I have had in some cases to take a ladder to trim them. You have just enough of them growing yet along the base of the Cairn to show that there is nothing in the circumstances fatal to them. If the hundreds that have been planted and are not now to be seen have not

FREDERICK LOTHROP AMES GATE LODGE, NORTH EASTON, MASS., N.D.

been purposely destroyed or stolen (which I suggest because some of mine have been); if they have been rightly treated by your gardener, then the failure is to be considered due simply to an extraordinary run of bad luck such as a man must be prepared to encounter occasionally in any such undertaking, and there is no more reason to give up the original purpose than there was when it was started.

As I do not wish unnecessary risks to be taken in another trial I do not urge the replanting of the Euonymus this year. But I have had a hundred small plants that had been propagated on my own ground set in nursery rows which I shall ask you to let me set next spring, and I will send you a lot of runners in addition which your garden can grow. I will try to secure also a lot of good plants of Japan ivy, (unfortunately I don't know of any for sale in the country.) What can be done this year is to plant, in the upper part of the wall more particularly, a thousand or so of the various kinds of little delicate ferns that are growing in dryish rocky places all about you. A cart load of them could be gathered in an hour. I enclose examples of some of the best. Also, if Mr F. L. Ames was right in supposing that stonecrop and house-leeks are growing abundantly in the fields near you, a great lot of them should be used in all the upper parts of the work, inside and out, being stuffed into cracks, joints, crevices and crannies, where a teaspoonful of dirt can go with them. The next fortnight will be as good a time as any during the year for this business.

Take a charitable view of my importunities. If you can afford to have the undertaking fail I cannot. All that is likely to come of it unless the essential planting shall be made to succeed, would be regarded in a few years as disgraceful to me. For any further services that you will accept of me in the matter I shall make no charge.

Very Truly Yours

Fred[k] Law Olmsted.

The text presented here is a typed letter signed in Olmsted's hand. The memorial cairn he describes is in front of the Oakes Ames Memorial Town Hall in North Easton, Massachusetts, a building designed by H. H. Richardson and completed in 1881. That year Olmsted began work on the landscape, continuing through 1883. See FLO to Oakes Angier Ames, April 10, 1882, above (J. K. Ochsner, *H. H. Richardson*, pp. 204–7).

1. A "rockery" was a garden type popular in the nineteenth century. The term suggested a naturalistic pile of stones, planted with a collection of alpine and other plants that favored such conditions. In larger examples concrete was used to suggest naturally occurring rock formations. This kind of decorative garden feature differed from Olmsted's purpose and vision for the North Easton memorial cairn. The cairn nevertheless was popularly referred to as the "rockery" by 1885. An article that year in *Bay State Monthly* included a description of the North Easton landscape: "In the triangle near the centre of the village, formed by the converging of the principal streets, is a declivity, where art has so arranged the rough and irregular forms of New England boulders as to re-produce a unique scene from some Scotch or Swiss village. This 'rockery,' as it is called, is clothed in summer with verdure and flowers" (*OED*; Francis George Heath, *Garden Rockery: How to Make, Plant and Manage It* [London, 1908]; James W. Clark, "Oliver Ames" in *The Bay State Monthly: A Massachusetts Magazine of Literature, History, Biography and State Progress*, vol. 11 [Boston, 1885], p. 190).
2. *Euonymus* is a diverse genus of ornamental ground covers and shrubs. By using the word "anonymus," here, Olmsted derides the pale and inconspicuous appearance of the specific type of euonymus planted at the memorial cairn, against his wishes. He did not object altogether to the genus of *euonymus*, as he later explains in this letter. No contemporary planting list for the memorial cairn has been found, but the evergreen *euonymus radicans* was planted there sometime before 1902, when John C. Olmsted was developing plans for the rehabilitation of the site and wrote, "The evergreen creeper (*euonymus radicans*) is almost wholly satisfactory wherever it occurs. The general effect would be improved by having more of this creeper" (L. H. Bailey, *Cyclopedia of American Horticulture*, vol. 2 [New York, 1900], pp. 558–59; JCO to Winthrop Ames, Nov. 14, 1902, B63: #649, OAR/LC; J. F. Dawson, "Memorandum," Feb. 11, 1903, B63: #649, OAR/LC).
3. William Robinson (1851–1896), not to be confused with Irish gardener and author, William Robinson (1838–1935), was a horticulturist and head gardener at Frederick Lothrop Ames' Langwater estate in North Easton. Robinson was an expert in orchids and established one of the largest orchid collections in the world at that time at Langwater ("William Robinson," *Boston Daily Advertiser*, Sept. 19, 1896; L. H. Bailey, *The Standard Cyclopedia of Horticulture*, vol. 4, p. 3534; J. K. Ochsner, *H. H. Richardson*, pp. 183, 217–19).

4. Olmsted refers to the Gate Lodge at Langwater, the estate of Frederick Lothrop Ames (1835–1893), son of Oliver Ames II and first cousin to Oakes Angier Ames. F. L. Ames was a noted philanthropist with a particular interest in horticulture and was a longtime sponsor of the Massachusetts Horticultural Society and the Arnold Arboretum. While the main house at Langwater had been built in 1859 by Boston architects Snell and Gregerson, Olmsted and Richardson began consulting with F. L. Ames on the further development of his property in 1879. The Gate Lodge, designed by Richardson, was completed in 1881. The two-story structure served as an arched entry into the estate, as well as a residence. The boulder masonry construction supported vines and other plants. In addition to the landscape of the Gate Lodge, the Olmsted firm consulted on other areas of the estate into the 1890s (*DAB*; Massachusetts Historical Society, *Reconnaissance Survey Report*, Sept. 1981, p. 9; J. K. Ochsner, *H. H. Richardson*, pp. 183, 212–19; plans 1326-10 and 1326-27, NPS/FLONHS).
5. That is, a garden dedicated to the cultivation of different types of roses (*OED*).

CHAPTER VI

JUNE 1887–DECEMBER 1887

Throughout the summer of 1887, certain members of the New York City park commission urged Olmsted to accept a consulting position and to develop new plans for areas of Riverside, Morningside, and Central parks. In three letters to Calvert Vaux, Olmsted emphasizes that he does not intend to accept a commission from the park board unless the two of them are working together. He makes the same statement in a letter of July 2 to park commissioner John D. Crimmins. In the July 15 note to Crimmins and two letters to Dwight H. Olmstead he describes how revising plans for Morningside and Riverside parks would demand a thorough study of existing conditions and needs. The park board hired Olmsted and Vaux to develop a new plan for Morningside Park in August, which appears in this chapter as *General Plan for the Improvement of Morningside Park*.

Olmsted was working at this time on the design of Franklin Park in Boston, especially the Playstead area of the park. His letter to William L. Fischer describes how he envisions the plantings around the Overlook at the Playstead, and his letter to John C. Olmsted describes the parapet on the Overlook. Olmsted was also developing a program for reforestation of the Boston Harbor Islands, and his letter to nurseryman Robert Douglas discusses which species of trees would be appropriate for the purpose.

Other documents include a letter to William Seward Webb describing a general plan for his estate at Shelburne Farms in Vermont, while his letter to Col. Casimir Stanislaus Gzowski provides suggestions for treatment of areas of Queen Victoria Park on the Canadian side of Niagara Falls. The report to Alfred D. Chandler contains recommendations for building a resort hotel and cottages at Lake Sunapee in New Hampshire. Olmsted's essay "On Gardening," discusses the history of terminology associated with the aesthetics of gardening and landscape design.

CALVERT VAUX

TO CALVERT VAUX[1]

30th June, 1887

My Dear Vaux:

When I reached the Commissioner's office Tuesday P.M. I found that, owing, probably, to an error in the transmission of a telegram, I was misinformed as to the day of the meeting. I had previously agreed that if I got away from the office by 4'ck to go out with Cameron[2] on his yacht and did so, getting back next day just in time to keep deferred appointment with the Commissioners, and getting away from them just in time to catch the 4.30 train to Boston. Wherefore, I did not see you as I had intended to do.

At the meeting I was asked a number of questions, the more important relating to Central Park, to which, for some time, I was able to avoid giving definite answers. When at last it became unquestionable that I was expected to answer as one in the service of the Department and professionally responsible, I said as much and added that I did not accept the position[3] and concisely, as if for the information of Mr Hutchins, referred to an agreement of last year.[4] After some further cleaning up—all in few words,—and imperfect, with bare reference to the last correspondence with me, I was told that the Commissioners wished to make their arrangements exclusively with me. "Do you mean with reference to the Central Park as well as to Riverside & Morningside?" I asked. "Yes". "As I have told you before, repeatedly, I do not wish to make such an arrangement". Some little argument followed with me, and at this time Myer (?)[5] who had been absent came & I was introduced to him. Then it was said:—"It is evident that we can do nothing today. We had better adjourn". "When will you be in New York again, Mr Olmsted?" "Possibly in three or four weeks". "That won't do". "I will come whenever you wish". Then, (at last), I was asked to come next Thursday. Immediately upon the adjournment I stept to Mr Hutchins and in the hearing of Mr Crimmins[6] said, "I can understand why some of the Commissioners may object to direct dealings with Mr Vaux but you are not in their position and I should think that you would recognize that there can be neither justice, propriety nor policy in the intention to ignore him", & so on. I ended by saying, "two heads are better than one; discussion is always useful provided it does not lead to divided counsels in practical operations. You have no reason to suppose in this case that it will." "He answered:—"Yes I believe in discussion", (in an indifferent way) and I left.

Yours Truly

Fred[k] Law Olmsted.

The text presented here is a signed letter in Olmsted's hand. Since Olmsted's departure from New York's Department of Public Parks in 1878, certain park commissioners had proposed that both he and Vaux be reappointed, sometimes together and sometimes separately, as the department's landscape architects. In June 1886, Olmsted and Vaux together submitted a proposal describing the circumstances under which they would consult with the board on the design of Central, Riverside, and Morningside parks, but in the months following the board did not act on their proposal.

In the meantime, from November 1886 through March 1887, Olmsted and Vaux collaborated on the design of the Niagara Reservation. After they submitted that plan in March, for which they were not immediately paid, Vaux became increasingly agitated about his financial situation. He wrote to Olmsted on April 16 that he was "cramped on account of not being able to collect a bill," and Olmsted loaned him $300. The same month, the New York park commissioners again asked Olmsted to consult individually on the city's parks. In June the state legislature placed additional pressure on park commissioners to employ someone to develop plans for the parks when it passed an "Act to provide for the completion of the construction of certain public parks in the city of New York." Olmsted continued to insist that he would only work on the New York parks with Vaux. Vaux nevertheless wrote to Olmsted expressing his suspicion that Olmsted was trying to secure the New York park work on his own (DPP, *Minutes*, 1881–1887; FLO to Henry R. Beekman, [June 10, 1886,] above; Calvert Vaux to FLO, June 28, 1886; Calvert Vaux to FLO, July 8, 1887; "General Plan for the Improvement of the Niagara Reservation," 1887 [*Papers of FLO*, SS1: 535–75]; Calvert Vaux to FLO, April 16, 1887; FLO to Calvert Vaux, April 16, 1887, A1: 711, OAR/LC; Calvert Vaux to FLO, April 18, 1887; FLO to M. C. D. Borden & John D. Crimmins, April 23,

1887, A1: 777, OAR/LC; Calvert Vaux to FLO, May 6, 1887; New York [State]; *Laws of the State of New York, Passed at the One Hundred and Tenth Session of the Legislature*, [Albany, N.Y., 1887], chap. 575; FLO to Calvert Vaux, June 22, 1887, A1: 853, OAR/LC).

1. Calvert Vaux (1824–1895) worked for the Department of Public Parks in various capacities during the 1880s. In November 1881 the board appointed him Supervisory Architect (although several commissioners had nominated him to be Landscape Architect Advisory). He resigned as Supervisory Architect in January 1883 and for the next three years worked for the department on individual commissions, including the design of the grounds around Grant's tomb, with Samuel Parsons, Jr. The board hired Olmsted and Vaux to revise plans for Morningside Park in August 1887, and they appointed Vaux to be the department's Landscape Architect in December of that year, a position he held until his death (*DAB*; DPP, *Minutes*, Nov. 19, 1881, pp. 386–89; Calvert Vaux to FLO, Jan. 9, 1883; DPP, *Minutes*, Jan. 24, 1883, p. 467; ibid., June 19, 1885, pp. 447–48; ibid., Aug. 17, 1885, p. 270; ibid., Aug. 24, 1887, p. 231; ibid., Dec. 22, 1887, p. 412).
2. Roderick William Cameron (1823–1900) was a Canadian businessman who lived in the United States. In 1870 he founded a successful shipping line, R. W. Cameron and Co., in New York. From 1887 through 1889 Olmsted prepared plans for Cameron's Staten Island estate, Clifton Berley (*Dictionary of Canadian Biography*, vol. XII [Toronto, 1990], pp. 149–50; FLO to Sir Roderick Cameron, July 31, 1888, A2: 673–76, OAR/FLO; FLO to Sir Roderick Cameron, Jan. 19, 1889).
3. The park board had passed a resolution on April 20 appointing Olmsted to be the department's "Landscape Architect Advisory." He acknowledged receipt of the appointment, but never officially accepted it (DPP, *Minutes*, April 20, 1887, p. 515; Charles D. F. Burns to FLO, April 25, 1887; DPP, *Minutes*, May 12, 1887, p. 12).
4. Waldo M. Hutchins (1822–1891) was a New York City politician who served on the Central Park Board of Commissioners from 1857 to 1869 and on the Board of Commissioners of the New York Department of Public Parks from 1887 to 1891. Hutchins never supported Olmsted or the Greensward plan, and Olmsted doubted Hutchins's integrity and commitment, writing in 1861 that "Hutchins does not attend one meeting in fifty. Few people in New York know so little of the park." Their relationship remained antagonistic throughout Olmsted's involvement with the New York parks. The "agreement of last year" that Olmsted refers to here was likely the proposal that he and Vaux sent to Henry R. Beekman in June 1886 describing the terms under which they would consult together with the park board (Roy Rosenzweig and Elizabeth Blackmar, *The Park and the People* [Ithaca, N.Y., 1992], pp. 118–20; *Papers of FLO*, 6: 547–48, n. 7; FLO to John Bigelow, Feb. 9, 1861 [*Papers of FLO*, 3: 324]; FLO to Henry R. Beekman, [June 10, 1886,] above).
5. Theodore W. Myers (1844–1918) was a banker and broker who served as a park commissioner in 1887, leaving his post when he was elected New York City's Comptroller in 1888. He was unanimously elected by both Democrats and Republicans to a second term as comptroller (*Who's Who in New York City and State* [New York, 1904], p. 425; "Theodore W. Myers, Ex-Controller, Dies, *New York Times*, March 21, 1918).
6. John D. Crimmins served on the Board of the Department of Public Parks from 1883 to 1888 (see FLO to John D. Crimmins, Aug. 6, 1885, above; FLO to John D. Crimmins, July 2, 1887, below).

To John Daniel Crimmins

Brookline, Mass. 2^d July 1887.

The Hon. Jno. D. Crimmins;
Commissioner of Parks, New York.
My Dear Mr Crimmins; It was evident the other day that I had been asked to meet the Commissioners with expectations that I was unable to sustain. I may possibly have been to blame that they should have had these expectations and I am sorry for it. To guard as far as I can against further loss of time in a matter that must be growing urgent, through any possible doubt remaining in your mind, as to my position, I think it better to say that at no time since I left the service of the Department ten years ago have I been willing to take upon myself {*any*} obligations with regard to the Central Park unless they applied to the park as a whole, nor unless Mr Vaux was to be associated with me. I have repeatedly said this to Commissioners and others, successively inquiring, year after year, and had supposed that it was well known to you. The reasons for it are derived {*from experience*} {and} arguments you offer for a change of my {*mind*} do not apply to them.

With regard to the plans of Riverside and Morningside, Mr Vaux's responsibility and mine are not identical.[1] But there are problems to be solved in the revised plans for these works of much difficulty and no plans can be offered with regard to which there will not be heated differences of opinion. Mr Vaux's judgment upon them would be of great value & greater than that of any other man in the country, it would be more {. . .} for me to work at them and I should reach conclusions sooner, with confidence to present them, if proceeding in conference with him than if studying the subject independently. I have {*no doubt*} that you would obtain better plans, that they would stand fire better and be more likely to be carried out.

On the latter point it {*is to be considered that*} no plans can be had, if a {*hundred men*} were engaged to make them, which would not be thought by a selection of intelligent men of mighty importance to be {. . .} in essential particulars. The whole plan of the Central Park was shaped with regard to what the designers thought to be the necessity of sunken transverse roads. Take these out or essentially modify them and the plan in all its parts would be worthless. To the best of my information and judgment the necessity is today clearer and more obvious to the public than ever before, though its {*completest demonstration*} is yet to come. Yet you heard how differently Commissioner Hutchins looked upon the question the other day. He cannot yet see that the objections that he first put to them, theoretically, are ever to be compensated by the advantages to be secured by them.[2] Now, whatever arrangements {*you make*} you will never get a plan for Riverside Park to some important points of which there will not be a similar fixed, intelligent and respectable antagonism. Nor can you ever get one which some of the interested property-holders can be persuaded is the best that could be had, with reference to their particular interests, or which they will not be glad of a chance to upset or modify and weaken in points essential to its value. Thus, whatever your plan, it must stand fire and you should not subject it, unnecessarily, to mean, malicious and pettifogging attacks, appealing to ignorance, jealousy and the lower sort of political prejudices. On this ground you would find it unfortunate if your professional adviser, respect for whose trained judgment upon matters of his training, would be your strong hold with the community in general against such attacks, were a man who had not lived in New York for ten years and whose attention was divided between parks in New York and parks in Boston and other cities. You would find it much better that it should be recognized that you were employing the same Olmsted & Vaux under whose direction when, as designers and superintendents, the Central Park had been formed up to the time that it attained the highest and most undivided popularity, and one of whom had never ceased to be a citizen of New York, never lost his hold of New York life nor allowed his attention to be withdrawn for a moment from the park system of New York.

Considerations of this class are secondary, of course, but they are not unimportant, even considered with reference to the statesmanship of a large city in these days.

And, finally, if you are not to be influenced by them directly, yet think it desirable to secure my services, you should be influenced by the fact that they are important to me and to my doing satisfactorily what you want of me.

Yours Respectfully

Fred[k] Law Olmsted.

The text presented here is from a letterpress copy of a handwritten letter signed on the original in Olmsted's hand: A1: 867–72, OAR/LC).

1. Since the early 1870s Olmsted and Vaux had collaborated on the design of Morningside and Riverside parks, but they also had worked independently on them over the years. They developed plans for both parks in 1873, and Olmsted continued to refine his plans for Riverside Park until he was dismissed by the park board in January 1878. Vaux drew up additional plans for Riverside Park when he was employed as the Department's Supervisory Architect from 1881 to 1883, and he and Samuel Parsons, Jr., presented a report in 1885 providing the location and a general plan of grounds around Grant's Tomb (FLO to Salem H. Wales, Oct. 11, 1873 [*Papers of FLO*, 6: 651–60]; "Report of the Landscape Architect on Riverside Park and Avenue," March 29, 1873 [*Papers of FLO*, 6: 596–600]; FLO to Henry G. Stebbins, Jan. 15, 1875 [*Papers of FLO*, 7: 108–14]; "Plan for Riverside Avenue with Addition of Riding Way," March 15, 1875 [*Papers of FLO*, 7: 169]; FLO to Henry G. Stebbins, March 16, 1875; DPP, *Minutes*, March 17, 1875, pp. 571–72; plan 505-22, NPS/FLONHS; Francis R. Kowsky, *Country, Park, & City: The Architecture and Life of Calvert Vaux* [New York, 1998], p. 301).
2. Waldo M. Hutchins served on the Central Park Commission from 1857 to 1869, and Olmsted had a long and antagonistic relationship with him (FLO to Calvert Vaux, June 30, 1887, n. 4, above).

To Calvert Vaux

9th July, 1887

My Dear Vaux,
I had hoped to find a note at Cameron's[1] giving me some understanding to work upon of what you would like me to aim at & was disappointed. I had been asked to come to the park office at 11o'ck; had at the moment made a memorandum of it and verified it. Nevertheless, I was told when I arrived there that the Commission had met at ten and adjourned. It was said however, that if I would wait Commissioners would be sent for and a special meeting held. They were supposed to be about the City Hall. I waited and they came and went and came for some hours but no formal meeting was held.

I had before written Crimmins that to avoid further waste of time in discussion of impracticable propositions, such as presented to me the week before, he and they would do well to consider that no arrangement could be made with me which did not recognize you — essentially as in my discussion with them of last year.[2] Verbally with the Commissioners I held the same ground. But at last, when it was nearly time for me to go to catch a train for Boston, seeing no prospect of a move on that line, as they were plying me with questions about Riverside plan, having it in mind that the arrangement of last year was no longer satisfactory to you and that I had been unable to draw from you any indication of what you would like me to aim for, except that you had two or three times recalled to me that Riverside & Morningside plans were not the same to you that they were to me, I admitted that an arrangement might be practicable for revising the Riverside and Morningside plans which did not involve a partnership interest. Crimmins asked me to repeat this, and began taking a memorandum of it. I asked him not to as it had been said carelessly but then said "if you want a memorandum suggesting such an arrangement I will write one" and thereupon I did so. The President took the note and having read it said something to the effect that something like that might be feasible and he would like to talk it over with the then absent Commissioners and if I wanted to get the next train to Boston he would not detain me longer. We were not likely to come nearer to a point this time.

Since I began writing I have recvd your note of yesterday.[3] I must say that I do not see how you can put the construction you seem to upon my course or why it should please you to wish to. You write as you might if I had been coming to New York of my own notion with the purpose to obtain some employment of the Park Commissioners and that had moved for this purpose in such a manner as to crowd you — at least to take the "lead" out of your hands. You say that I have undertaken to lead but finding that I could not have been trying to ease myself of responsibility of leadership by teazing you for advice, or for information of your plans. I think that this is what anyone else reading your letter would suppose. I cannot suppose it because I know that you know that there is not the slightest word of truth in it. Yet even I cannot make anything else out of your letter and am obliged to think that you do not fully realize how far any such notion would be from the facts. If you don't, you ought.

For ten years past I have been sick of New York. Its infernal politics had wrought the most intense and ruinous disappointment with me. And occurrences made this, day after day, more and more mortifying and aggravating. After a time it did not appear that I had any duty to myself, my profession or to the public that should anchor me there. I came here for no business purpose. I had not a particle of business or prospect of business here when I came and I was further from such business as I had elsewhere when in Boston than when in New York and I left New York only because I was sick of it—its park commission and its infernal underground politics and after coming here I diligently cut myself away from New York and its associations. You must know that I have done so. I have not been to New York except for a business purpose, I have stayed no longer than was necessary and have rarely seen a New York friend in New York. I have done nothing that would help me to hold or extend influence there. I have meddled not at all with park affairs except in such organic public matters as the Menagerie and Parade[4] and when writing on these or other matters at special request have done so in a way to avoid connecting my name with the agitation. When Mr Crimmins wrote inviting me to come to him with a view to an arrangement for my employment, I had not seen him. I knew none of the Commissioners and wanted nothing to do with them; I declined the invitation. When it came again in an official form and as a business proceeding, I concluded after advising with several of our friends that it would not be right to refuse to give the Commissioners this counsel asked in their behalf by their President.[5] The first word I said to them was that you were the proper man for them to consult and that I wished to make no engagement with them. Since then in all that has passed nine parts out of ten of all that I have said to them has been with a plain purpose to strengthen you and Parsons[6] and to further your views as far as I could understand them. The first word I had with them and the last—addressed to the President as I was taking leave of him Thursday last was an earnest appeal to him to first of all put you on a proper professional footing. My last letter to Mr Crimmins was an effort to convince and persuade him that it was bad policy to keep you at arm's length and that it would be better to deal directly with you. I probably have never placed myself under bonds to have nothing to do with them until they had given you a proper position because I have never fully intended, if the obstacles to your appointment as resident Landscape Architect could not at last be overcome, to give them no alternative but to employ some one, as the Commissioners more than once had done before, not at all in sympathy with us, (as Mould or Jones or Johnson[7] who was with them last year with letters from Ruskin) but I have come as near to it as I could with truth and have gone far to create that impression.

Further, I have taken no step; have presented no suggestion to them which I did not believe to be in accordance with your wishes, or the least discordant with them that the circumstances allowed. It has never occurred to me that I was leading—much less that I was leading against your lead and I have no idea what you mean when you imply that. Certainly I have never desired to lead or to move in the matter at all except side by side with you. I have not thought of leading the Commissioners except in the view that I wanted nothing that, rightly informed, they would not want. I have had no concealed thoughts from them, have been plain and blunt. And so with you. If I have ever concealed anything from you that you ought to know or would wish to know, I am not aware of it. If I have in the least taken a lead that you did not wish me it has been your fault, not mine. It has been in some technical sense, not in spirit purpose or principle. I am not playing a game and am not ground[8] by technical rules.

—Here as I write comes in your second letter of yesterday, again, I have to say that I do not feel that I am on the ground of it. It would seem to bear the implication that I have been willing that, through the Tribune or otherwise, a wrongful impression, harmful, as it chances, to your interests and to Radford's,[9] should be spread, such an impression as you say Mr Duncan had received. I think that you would hardly be willing that I should understand just that from your letter. But what else can I understand? I see nothing else but an argument to that effect in all of these two pages. But I know that you have not the slightest ground for a suspicion that I have been willing that such a report should be propagated. But considering it a wrong report and one injurious to you, what could have been your reason for telling him that "*The Tribune was, of course right*" It was, *of course wrong*—(according to your statement, I have never seen the report). And you knew it to be wrong. I have not the remotest idea for what purpose you went out of your way to propagate the wrong.

I am apt to talk loosely when led on to do so in apparently friendly conversation and to overcome feebleness of expression by exaggerated rattle and I might easily have given some body with access to newspapers some wrong notion when asked what had occurred between me & the Commissioners. But in this I am sure that I have not. I have been twice interviewed with a view to a newspaper report but have at once said that nothing had occurred worth mentioning. I have referred to you as better able to talk about coming improvements, these in New York being matters of your business rather than mine, and have pleaded haste to get away. My aim has been to prevent newspaper reporting not lead it. And I suppose that I have succeeded.

My name has not been mentioned at any time since I left New York in connection with New York parks with my knowledge and consent. I have several times prevented it from being mentioned when it otherwise might have been.

I suppose that there is something lying back of what you say which you expect me to see and I cannot. Something "technical". If I were a prisoner before a criminal court and you the prosecuting attorney I should expect to be hanged by a technical rope. All the same I should know that I really was not guilty. I have been assuming that your letter meant what I say and have been contradicting it; but I don't quite think so—only if not that it is incomprehensible to me. That after all these years we should be no better able to understand one another is one of the strangest of life's experiences. I seem as near to you sometimes as to any old friend—I have not many left. Yet sometimes we have as little insight of each other's meaning and motives as if we were beings of two different planets.

I still hope that what is best on the cards for you and Parsons will come out of all this otherwise wasted time. Not that your interests are my primary object, of course. But I suppose that they lie right along with my primary object. I don't want to have to come back to New York but I am not sure that I shouldn't even do that rather than lose all chance of bringing the parks back to original principles so far as that is now possible. To that end, with you or without you, I shall always do what seems to me best. There is nothing else I care so much for.

Affectionately Yours

F. L. O.

The text presented here is from a letterpress copy of a handwritten letter signed on the original in Olmsted's hand: A1: 880–86, OAR/LC).

1. Roderick William Cameron was a successful businessman for whom Olmsted was developing plans for his Staten Island estate, Clifton Berley. In a July 5th letter to Vaux, Olmsted wrote that he would be stopping by Cameron's office when he next came to New York (FLO to Calvert Vaux, June 30, 1887, n. 2, above; FLO to Calvert Vaux, July 5, 1887, A1: 873–78, OAR/LC).
2. In Olmsted's July 2 note to Crimmins he wrote, "at no time since I left the service of the Department ten years ago have I been willing to take upon myself any obligations with regard to the Central Park unless they applied to the park as a whole, nor unless Mr. Vaux was to be associated with me" (FLO to John D. Crimmins, July 2, 1887, above; see also FLO to Henry R. Beekman, [June 10, 1886,] above).
3. Neither this note nor the letter that Olmsted references below have been found.
4. Olmsted is referring to his efforts to defeat two bills that were before the New York State Legislature in 1887 that called for placing a permanent menagerie in Central Park and allowing the National Guard to use the park as a parade ground. Alerted by William A. Stiles, the New York journalist and park advocate who in 1888 became the editor of *Garden and Forest*, Olmsted contributed fifty dollars to a fund organized to oppose the legislation and wrote letters to state legislators. The legislature passed a bill in May 1887, but Governor David B. Hill vetoed it.

   Since the establishment in the 1860s of an improvised Central Park menagerie adjacent to the Arsenal building at 64th Street and Fifth Avenue on the east side of the park, the commissioners had been discussing where to locate a permanent facility to keep and display their collection of animals. Olmsted was opposed to a menagerie in Central Park and, when asked to suggest a location in 1867, he and Vaux proposed Manhattan Square, on the opposite side of Eighth Avenue from the park between 77th and 81st Streets (later the site of the American Museum of Natural History). In 1870, the newly-constituted Department of Public Parks, under the control of Peter B. Sweeny, abandoned the Manhattan Square site and began building the menagerie in the North Meadow of Central Park. Olmsted and Vaux publicly protested, arguing that it would fundamentally alter important elements of their design. Construction was halted after the Tweed Ring lost its hold on municipal government. While working on their design of Morningside Park in 1873, Olmsted and Vaux suggested the menagerie be divided between several spots in Central Park and a new building in Morningside Park. In 1878 the park board had not yet made a decision on a permanent home for the menagerie, and the temporary structures around the Arsenal, holding about 700 animals, were falling into disrepair. Olmsted then suggested a menagerie be built in the park between 96th and 105th Streets on the west side. He continued to insist over the years that this would be the best spot. Finally, after the state chartered the New York Zoological Society in 1895 and gave the organization a large portion of the Bronx Park for a zoo in 1897, Central Park was relieved from having to accommodate the city's principal zoo, although the smaller Central Park Zoo remained (William A. Stiles to FLO, March 11, 1887; William A. Stiles to FLO, May 27, 1887; FLO to Calvert Vaux, July 5, 1887, A1: 873–78, OAR/LC; "News," *New York Times*, May 31, 1887; "News," ibid., June 28, 1887; To the President of the Board of Commissioners of the Central Park, 1867 [*Papers of FLO*, 6: 184-89]; "The Central Park—Character of the Proposed Change—A Protest," Dec. 21, 1870 [*Papers of FLO*, 6: 392–95]; FLO to Salem H. Wales, Oct. 11, 1873 [*Papers of FLO*, 6: 655]; "Document 51," DPP, *Minutes*, Oct. 11, 1873, pp. 1–5; To the Board of Commissioners of the Department of Public Parks, Jan. 2, 1878 [*Papers of FLO*, 7: 358–62]; FLO to Waldo M. Hutchins, March 18, 1890, A7: 34–46, OAR/LC; R. Rosenzweig and E. Blackmar, *The Park and the People*, pp. 340–49; William Bridges, *Gathering of Animals: An Unconventional History of the New York Zoological Society* [New York, 1974]).

5. See FLO to John D. Crimmins, July 2, 1887, above.
6. Samuel Parsons, Jr., was an associate of Calvert Vaux. The park board appointed him Superintendent of Planting, at Vaux's request, in January 1883, and Superintendent of Parks in 1885 (FLO to Charles Eliot, Oct. 28, 1886, n. 7, above).
7. Jacob Wrey Mould (1825–1886) was an English architect who came to New York in 1853. Working for the Central Park board, he collaborated with Vaux on the design of the Terrace, Belvedere Castle, and other projects. He was appointed architect-in-chief of the newly created Department of Public Parks in 1870 and served in that position until 1875, when he moved to Peru to serve as the architect-in-chief of Lima's public works. Upon his return to New York in 1880, the park board appointed him Architect of Morningside Park. He was suspended in December 1882, and rehired as assistant to the Architect in February 1883. He was fired that July, but in 1885 the park board rehired him as an Architectural Draughtsman, a position he held until his death.

   Aneurin Jones (1824–1904) was named Superintendent of Parks in August 1881. His decision to remove shrubs and understory trees from Central Park angered Olmsted, and was part of the reason he wrote *The Spoils of the Park* in 1881 and 1882. Commissioner Smith E. Lane tried to remove Jones from his position several times, claiming that he abused his power, finally succeeding when the board voted to replace him with Samuel Parsons, Jr., in 1885. Jones went on to serve in the 1890s as superintendent for the Brooklyn Park Department but was removed from that post as well. He ended his career as the chief engineer of boulevards and drives for Brooklyn and Queens.

   Joseph Forsyth Johnson (1840?–1906) was an English landscape architect who was appointed superintendent of horticulture and arboriculture by Brooklyn's Board of Park Commissioners on November 19, 1886 for a term of six months. Within the month of his appointment, the secretary of the civil service commission called his appointment illegal because he was not a naturalized citizen. Johnson also caused controversy by suggesting that a number of trees be removed from Prospect Park to give "the best trees plenty of space, light and air." By February 1887, the park board had removed him from his position (*NCAB*; R. Rosenzweig and E. Blackmar, *The Park and the People*, pp. 180–200; DPP, *Minutes*, Sept. 22, 1880, pp. 275–76; ibid., Dec. 6, 1882, pp. 380–81; ibid., Feb. 17, 1883, pp. 496–97; ibid., July 25, 1883, p. 200; ibid., July 20, 1885, p. 201; ibid., June 16, 1886, p. 84; ibid., Aug. 15, 1881, p. 190; ibid., Aug. 25, 1881, pp. 317–18; ibid., Aug. 16, 1882, pp. 174–75; ibid., May 25, 1885, p. 75; "Aneurin Jones Removed," *New York Times*, May 26, 1885, p. 2; "Aneurin Jones Dead," ibid., Sept. 7, 1904, p. 7;

"Scalps Taken By the Park Commissioners To-day," *Brooklyn Eagle*, Sept. 9, 1886, p. 4; "Park Affairs," ibid., Nov. 20, 1886, p. 4; "Municipal," ibid., Dec. 9, 1886, p. 4; "Prospect Park Trees," ibid., Dec. 14, 1886, p. 4; "Park Topics," ibid., Feb. 2, 1887; see also FLO to Charles Eliot, Feb. 25, 1886, above).

8. Olmsted may have meant "grounded in," that is, firmly fixed or established (*OED*).
9. George Kent Radford (d. 1908), an English civil engineer, collaborated with Olmsted on a number of projects from the 1870s through the 1890s. Radford also worked with Vaux on the American Museum of Natural History and the Metropolitan Museum of Art in Central Park (*Papers of FLO*, 6: 566, n. 11, 651, n. 3; FLO to Justin Smith Morrill, Aug. 16, 1874 [*Papers of FLO*, 7: 69–73]; F. R. Kowsky, *Country, Park, & City*, pp. 277–78, 347, n. 1).

To William Seward Webb[1]

Brookline, 12th July, 1887.

Dear Doctor Webb;

I understood from Mr Frederick Vanderbilt[2] that you had determined before going further with your plans to make a tour of England and thinking you would expect to pick up some notions there that might affect your plans I have supposed that you would hold everything in abeyance till your return. Perhaps I have been the more ready to pursue this theory because my son and Mr Codman who were with me when I was last at Shelburne Farms are both away on long vacations and, being pressed, I have tended to await their return before preparing drawings. In answer to your telegram, however, I will send you a sketch roughly embodying the leading ideas of the plan we had intended to submit to you before, going into further particulars or closer study.[3]

We have in view a general division of the estate inst.

1st Tillage and pasture lands in rotation;

2nd Parks or permanent pasture lands;

3d Forest: *Arboretum Vermontii*,

The last only requires immediate further consideration.

The first condition of forest husbandry is that cattle should be kept from running through the forest. Cattle also must be {*kept*} from the Arboretum and from frequenting the home grounds. Hence there must be fencing between the park and these {*grounds*}, parts of the estate. It is proposed to combine the Forest and the Arboretum in this way. Within the enclosure of the Forest there are to be roads. These roads (not shown on the sketch) are to be carried as far as convenient through parts of the enclosure which are not now wooded. Where they run through wooded ground, a {*border*} is to be made on each side of the roads by cutting away most of the wood for some distance back. The Arboretum is then to be planted on each side of the road; single specimen trees of each species in succession, generally, near the road; groups of the same species a little further back. Fine specimen trees of the old spontaneous growth are to be preserved and take their place in the Arboretum; even fine groups and masses are to be preserved close upon the road occasionally. Spaces between trees are to be occupied by undergrowth in a natural manner but this undergrowth when near the road is to be the shrubbery of the Arboretum.

I have satisfied myself by personal examination of the feasibility of such an arrangement and that a beautiful, interesting, instructive and publicly important Arboretum can be so attained, the present natural woods forming an appropriate and harmonious background for it and adding directly to its scientific value.

Assuming that this proposition is acceptable, we think it most desirable that approaches from the public roads on the borders of the estate to the house[4] should be so arranged that in passing through them it shall not be necessary to open gates, in other words that cattle shall be kept out of them and this without multiplying gate lodges. Hence the forest division of the estate is proposed to be extended to reach the public roads, or, roads fenced in, extending from the public roads to the borders of the forest. Thus you would get to and from the house without entering the park or the tillage or the pastured fields.

The sketch shows the general division of the estate into farm, forest and park lands. In the Northern part, the division is not perfectly defined because the bounds of the farm lands as separated from those of your brother-in-law and other friends do not seem to be unalterably fixed and much better arrangements are practicable by some variation from those provisionally fixed. We simply point out that gates on the leading lines of road in this quarter would be nuisances and that where the properties to be reached are in but few hands the existing public road has no justification. If possible the road suggested ("Road A") which would {*have*} better grades and the course of which is adapted with some grace to the natural landscape, should supersede the old straight and graceless public road. Whether it runs between two estates (by adjustment and exchanges of land to be made between you and your friends) or passes in the character of a party or neighborhood road along the border of your estate there should be no gate upon it. It should have the character of a luxuriously nice public road passing between two {. . .} of a fine farm.

The forest need not be divided by a fence from the home grounds. The home grounds must be divided from the park. The line of such division proposed is that marked b.b.b. on the sketch. At B and B' gates would be required to be opened when a carriage was to pass from the house into the park. There would be lodges at each gate, one at B for the family of a man employed in the adjoining garden, one at B' for the family of a man employed in the adjoining stable. But each of these gates is so situated that it could generally be left open, a dog being kept at the lodge trained to drive off cows coming toward it which training is a very

"Preliminary Study of Part of Plan for Laying Out the Shelburne Farms Estate of Dr. W. S. Webb," July 12, 1887

easy matter. But also these gates are so situated (being in inconspicuous positions) that self adjusting gates could be used during the pasturing season.

The fence b.b. is conceived to be a sunk fence (with possibly a low hedge or parapet on the upper side). Near the house it would merge into the retaining wall of the lower terrace. But the style of it and the degree in which the ground near it on the forest side shall be planted is to be further considered.

If you have an entrance in the manner you have assumed necessary on the approach from Shelburne it will be awkward, inconvenient and unbecoming. Therefore we venture to suggest a more radical and liberal arrangement than you may be prepared for. But as a decision of the question is not immediately necessary we will not now state its advantages. Mr Taylor[5] is, we think, aware of them. The School house[6] should sit in the triangle S.

We have intended at this time to indicate lines of road, only so far as your decision upon building sites might affect them or be affected by them.

We are decidedly of opinion with Mr Taylor that the South farm[7] would best be a complete establishment by itself, so that there would be little transportation necessary between it and the North farms.

Yours Respectfully,

F. L. & J. C. Olmsted.
F.L.O.

The text presented here is from a letterpress copy of a letter written and signed in a clerk's hand: A1: 887–91, OAR/LC. Shelburne Farms, located on Lake Champlain south of Burlington, Vermont, was the property of William Seward Webb and Eliza Osgood Vanderbilt Webb. The Webbs began assembling the property in 1886 and that year hired the New York architect Robert Henderson Robertson and Olmsted to design their model farm and estate, which eventually grew to about 3,800 acres. Olmsted visited the site that June and began work on a development plan that divided the estate into three complementary, functional areas: farm, forest, and parkland. Landscape plans included building a new system of roads, planting tens of thousands of trees, and creating a park landscape around the principal residence. Olmsted consulted on plans for the estate until 1889 (*National Historical Landmark Designation: Shelburne Farms*, U.S. Department of the Interior, National Park Service [2000], pp. 6–7; John Foreman and Robbe Pierce Stimson, *The Vanderbilts and the Gilded Age* [New York, 1991], pp. 73–101; FLO to William Seward Webb June 18, 1886, A1: 374, OAR/LC).

1. William Seward Webb (1851–1926) was a doctor, stockbroker, and president of the Wagner Palace Car Company. He was married to Eliza ("Lila") Osgood Vanderbilt, daughter of William H. Vanderbilt and sister to Frederick W. and George W. Vanderbilt. In addition to the creation of Shelburne Farms, Webb also built the St. Lawrence and Adirondack Railroad through the Adirondack Mountains in the 1890s. In 1893 he built Ne-Ha-Se-Ne, an Adirondack camp also designed by Robert Henderson Robertson (Mitchell Charles Harrison, *Prominent and Progressive Americans: An Encyclopædia of Contemporaneous Biography*, vol. 1 [New York, 1902], pp. 367–69; "Dr. William Seward Webb's Great Park" *New York Times*, Jan. 31, 1895).
2. Frederick William Vanderbilt (1856–1938), director of the New York Central Railroad, was the son of William H. Vanderbilt and brother to George W. Vanderbilt and Eliza Vanderbilt Webb. Olmsted designed the landscape of his estate, Rough Point, in Newport, Rhode Island (Wayne Andrews, *The Vanderbilt Legend: The Story of the Vanderbilt Family 1794–1940* [New York, 1941], pp. 325–26; see also FLO to Frederick W. Vanderbilt, Aug. 2, 1888, below; FLO to Frederick W. Vanderbilt, Oct. 11, 1889, below).
3. A sketch of a "preliminary plan" for the Shelburne Farms property dated July 12, 1887, is in the Frederick Law Olmsted National Historic Site archives (plan 1031-z19, NPS/FLONHS). The sketch references "A" and "B" road locations and shows the functional division of the land into farm, forest, and park.
4. Olmsted's 1887 plan was based on the Webbs' intention to build their principal residence on Lone Tree Hill, near the center of their property. They delayed construction of the main house, however, and Robertson designed a temporary dwelling, sited near the shore of Lake Champlain, in the fall of 1887. In 1893 the Webbs abandoned their plan to build on Lone Tree Hill and decided to enlarge their mansion on the lake instead (J. Foreman and R. P. Stimson, *The Vanderbilts*, pp. 83–85; plan 1031-z19,

NPS/FLONHS; *National Historical Landmark Designation: Shelburne Farms*, pp. 7, 12, 18, 35; FLO and JCO to Arthur Taylor, May 17, 1887, A1: 802–3, OAR/LC).

5. Arthur Taylor, a Scottish horticulturist and land-buying agent for Webb, was the first farm manager at Shelburne Farms and was responsible for implementing Olmsted's plans (*National Historical Landmark Designation: Shelburne Farms*, p. 6; J. Foreman and R. P. Stimson, *The Vanderbilts*, pp. 79, 81).
6. There is no evidence that this proposed school was ever built, but a location is suggested in the July 12, 1887, preliminary plan.
7. The South Farm did end up having its own entrance (South Gate) and gatehouse. The establishment included a breeding barn, a dairy barn, a sheep barn, a woodshop, a cemetery, and a variety of other small structures, most of which were designed by Robertson in the early 1890s. In 1913, the Webbs' son J. Watson Webb and his wife, Electra Havemeyer Webb, acquired and developed the area into their own estate residence, which they named Southern Acres (J. Foreman and R. P. Stimson, *The Vanderbilts*, p. 96; *National Historical Landmark Designation: Shelburne Farms*, pp. 26–32).

To Calvert Vaux

13th July, 1887.

My Dear Vaux.

I believe you are ahead of me now by six notes but then you don't write as long ones as I do.[1] The fact is, John being away, and Codman, I can't keep up with the calls on me and am so prostrated by the moist heat that I can't sit up more than half the day. The N. Yk crisis[2] being past I find it easier to put you off than anything else.

I return the Riverside study, which is all right, I think, thank you.

I don't think any such understanding between us, as you propose, seems necessary. I would not have you bound. I have told the Commissioners right along every time that I would make no arrangements as to Central Park that didn't comprehend you, and have suggested and entertained nothing with reference to any business in New York which did not include you. But I see nothing to be gained by pledging myself never to. But I am glad to know that you are not indisposed to cooperation.

The majority of the Commissioners did not behave honorably, to my notion, in their dealings with me. I believe that each man intended that I should be deceived. I cannot imagine for what reason. If there was an intention to draw me into some position or statement that could be quoted against me it signally failed. I did not shift my ground or at any time say anything that now I should be unwilling that any man should know. On the face of the entire record it would appear that they were willing to engage me without you, but I don't in the least believe that that was what they were after. I have no idea what it was. It is a great relief to get far from them.

Yours.

F. L. O.

The text presented here is from a letterpress copy of a handwritten letter signed on the original in Olmsted's hand: A1: 893, OAR/LC. The day after Olmsted wrote this letter he sent an open letter to his friend William A. Stiles, an editor at the *Tribune*, to distribute to the editors of other New York City newspapers. The letter provided a basic chronology of his communications with the park board. Stiles wrote to Olmsted on July 15 that he had read the letter to Vaux and that the architect was "delighted." The *Tribune*, *Times*, and *Sun* published the letter on July 16 (William A. Stiles to FLO, July 15, 1887; "Mr. Olmsted and the Park Board," *New-York Tribune*, July 16, 1887; William A. Stiles to FLO, July 16, 1887).

1. Much of the correspondence between Olmsted and Vaux written in 1886 and 1887 is extant, but the letters written by Vaux between May 7, 1887, and August 23, 1887, to which Olmsted refers, have not been found. During the same period, this letter and four others from Olmsted to Vaux exist (FLO to Calvert Vaux, June 22, 1887, A1: 853–54, OAR/LC; FLO to Calvert Vaux, June 30, 1887, above; FLO to Calvert Vaux, July 5, 1887, A1: 873–75, OAR/LC; FLO to Calvert Vaux, July 9, 1887, above).
2. The crisis to which Olmsted refers began on June 15, 1887, when, the New York State legislature passed an act to "provide for the completion of the construction" of the city's parks, including Central, Morningside, and Riverside parks. While Commissioner John D. Crimmins wanted to engage Olmsted as consulting Landscape Architect, the board could not reach the necessary consensus. They resolved the issue on July 11 by agreeing to ask Samuel Parsons, Jr., the Superintendent of Parks, and Montgomery Kellogg, the department's engineer, to study Olmsted and Vaux's 1873 Morningside Park plan and report to the board "what modifications, if any, are desirable" (New York [State]; *Laws of the State of New York, Passed at the One Hundred and Tenth Session of the Legislature* [Albany, N.Y., 1887], chap. 575; DPP, *Minutes*, July 11, 1887).

To John Daniel Crimmins

15th July, 1887.

The Hon.
John D. Crimmins
Dear Sir; I have received your note of 12th.

Your question about Morningside Park is not one to be answered without study. I can only say that it would be a very strange thing if after such development of the city and modifications of its customs and social spirit as have occurred in the last fourteen years, no new light should have come as to what is desirable in a park situated as Morningside is.

As to your other question you are much better acquainted with Mr Parsons than I am.[1] I have seen no original work of his except on the smallest scale and know nothing of his ability as a designer or an artist. Mr Kellog[2] is purely an engineer without the slightest profession of competency for the duty. I am mistaken if he would not prefer to decline the responsibility. It is in my judgment a much more delicate and difficult duty to make an extensive revision of a plan, aiming to preserve the main motives and spirit in which it was originally conceived but to extend it over additional ground of difficult topography [3] and to meet new requirements, (as in the case of Riverside) than to undertake an entirely fresh design upon a clear field and unhampered by anything settled. The so called park at Riverside must be a dependency of the great construction[4] already carried through the territory. It must be dominated by this. To preserve the proper subordination and to wisely solve the several special problems now presented, I regard as the most difficult professional duty I have ever contemplated. I have not the slightest desire to undertake it except as justice to my reputation concerned in the work that has been done and a certain fealty to the city of New York may require.

Yours Respectfully

Fred[k] Law Olmsted.

The text presented here is from a letterpress copy of a handwritten letter signed on the original in Olmsted's hand: A1: 895–96, OAR/LC. Crimmins' letter to Olmsted has not been found, but the day before he wrote it the park board had voted against his proposal that Olmsted and Vaux be hired to prepare new plans for Riverside and Morningside parks, instead voting to ask two park employees, Samuel Parsons, Jr., and Montgomery Kellogg, to review Olmsted and Vaux's 1873 plan for Morningside Park (DPP, *Minutes*, July 11, 1887, pp. 155–56; see also FLO to John D. Crimmins, July 2, 1887, above; FLO to Dwight H. Olmstead, Aug. 7, 1887, below).

1. Samuel Parsons, Jr., had been Superintendent of Parks since 1885 (see FLO to Charles Eliot, Oct. 28, 1886, n. 7, above).
2. Montgomery A. Kellogg (1830–1898) was a civil engineer who had been working on New York City parks since the construction of Central Park in the late 1850s. He served as engineer-in-chief for the Department of Public Parks between 1871 and his death, his most recent appointment occurring on June 6, 1883. He provided a preliminary design for Morningside Park in 1871 after the park board, then controlled by Peter B. Sweeny, let Olmsted and Vaux go. After the fall of the Tweed Ring, Olmsted and Vaux were rehired and developed the plans for Morningside Park that were ultimately adopted. Olmsted was not an admirer of Kellogg's abilities overall, as he comments in his letter to Dwight H. Olmstead, July 31, 1887, below, "If a stone desert, set on edge, were wanted, Mr Kellogg would be the man for it" ("Death List of a Day: Montgomery A. Kellogg," *New York Times*, April 20, 1898; FLO to Andrew H. Green, Dec. 28, 1860 [*Papers of FLO*, 3: 293–94]; DPP, *Minutes*, June 6, 1883, p. 93; FLO to Salem H. Wales, Oct. 11, 1873

[*Papers of FLO*, 6: 658–59, n. 2]; Frederick Law Olmsted and Calvert Vaux, *General Plan for the Improvement of Morningside Park*, Oct. 1, 1887, below).

3. The "additional ground" that Olmsted refers to is likely the area in the north end of Riverside Park between 121st and 124th streets that had been set aside in 1885 by the park board for the tomb of Ulysses S. Grant. The area around Grant's tomb was a plateau with steep cliffs that needed to be seamlessly merged with the rest of the park. By 1887, according to the *New York Times*, the area had "received a temporary treatment, owing to the uncertainty of what sort of monument will be erected there" (FLO to John D. Crimmins, Aug. 6, 1885, above; "The Memorial Grounds," *New York Times*, Oct. 6, 1885, p. 5; "Needs of the Park: Improvements Recommended by Superintendent Parsons," ibid., March 7, 1886, p. 3; "Park Improvements," ibid., Feb. 19, 1887, p. 8).
4. That is, Riverside Drive.

To William L. Fischer[1]

Brookline, Mass., 21st. July, 1887.

Mr Fischer:
My Dear Sir:

The piece of the parapet which has been set on the north curve of the "Overlook" wall may be taken as a sample of what is to be done all along the line. Although I gave no instructions that it should be set wholly from above I learn upon inquiry that it was so and that no man engaged went upon the face of the wall except the foreman (Watson)[2] who went below at times to see how the work appeared and direct the adjustment of the outlying boulders. With this demonstration of the possibility of doing the work wholly from above your objection to setting about the preparation of the ground below seems to be removed and I want you to take it up as soon as you well can. I shall hasten the building of the parapet as fast as I can but would not have you wait for it. Mr. Howe[3] promises to have water pipes laid as soon as you are ready to begin planting. If there is anything else to be done or obtained which will be of advantage to you or tend in any way to insure early and successful planting, please let me know. It may be better as I am writing on the subject to now set down distinctly a few points to be had in view in this planting.

The Overlook is an elevated platform upon which visitors can stand to witness the playing, parades and spectacles on the Playstead. There is a kind of natural platform here formed by ledges of rock. But as this is not high enough nor the surface of it regular enough for the purpose we construct an artificial platform. It is not intended to wholly disguise this artificial platform but it is intended that it shall be so much obscured that it will not be apparent how much is artificial and it is intended that to superficial observation the natural part shall seem to have been larger, more continuous and more favorable to the purpose of the platform than it actually was. It is also desired that the long line of the top of the wall, when seen from the opposite side of the Playstead shall not stand out very distinctly from the trees and bushes and vines that will be seen at a little distance behind it, the object being to avoid anything like a horizontal streak across the landscape and to subordinate the artificial elements as much as practicable to the natural.

But these landscape purposes must not be so pursued that the essential purpose of a convenient overlooking platform shall be lost. Hence the plants to be used in the upper part of the wall and which will grow from below up to the top of the wall should be plants of a *naturally snug, close, growth*, such as Euonymus radicans, Ampelopsis triloba, Rhus aromatica and dwarf small-leafed roses of compact and horizontal habit of growth.

Both along the upper part of the wall and along the base near the walk it is desirable that there should be prickly plants like roses and *dwarf* brambles growing thickly in order to deter trespassing and it is undesirable that there should be *any notable blooming* plants within reach of visitors. Near the lower walk there should, for the sake of variety and pictureseque effect, be some bushes that will grow to various heights and it will be desirable that a considerable proportion of these should also be thorny or prickly, like Berberis Thunbergii, Rosa multiflora and Rosa parvifolia and various thorns.

These considerations determining the top and bottom of the plantations, it is desirable that there should be no abrupt or rapid change of character in the intermediate space. Hence, along the base of the wall but out of hand reach there may be other roses, (Rosa rugosa being particularly good because of the fresh character of its foliage), in the recesses of the base of the wall; and Rosa rubiginosa because of the scent of its leaves, and both because self protective.

There then comes this consideration; First, it is very desirable to avoid the character of the ordinary artificial garden "rockery" and to have the whole affair appear old and "natural", that is to say, resembling places where, near ledges and ancient stone walls, there has been an interesting spontaneous growth of woody plants common in such places *near Boston* (especially to the Northward) there are barberry, cat briar, genista, Rhus copal., sweet fern and Myrica, and as these all would harmonize fairly well with the top and bottom planting, a good proportion of them should be used. Genista tinctoria I think it would be well to use very largely because it is likely to do well in spaces between the rocks and its habit is such that it will do a good deal to *obscure without quite hiding* the wall, and thus to disguise its artificiality.

Finally, it is desirable to green over the vertical part of the wall as soon as possible, and, especially, the cracks between the stones, for which sedums and sempervirens[4] will serve. These, also, should be used freely, for early effect, where spaces between the stones will be seen by people leaning over the parapet.

As this is the first planting to be done on the park,[5] as the work is a peculiar one, as it must attract a great deal of attention, and as its intention will be much misunderstood until the plants have attained some growth, every possible precaution should be taken to make them flourish. Be sure to call well in advance for everything that you will want and have a plan well laid out and a good understanding as to the men, teams and tools that will be useful.

Yours Truly,

Fred[k] Law Olmsted.
L.A.A.

The text presented here is from a letterpress copy of a typewritten letter signed on the original in Olmsted's hand: A1: 906–9, OAR/LC (see "Specifications for Playstead Terrace, Franklin Park," July 30, 1885, above; FLO to William L. Fischer, Aug. 6, 1889, below; FLO to William L. Fischer, Aug. 11, 1889, below; FLO to William L. Fischer, Sept. 30, 1889, below).

1. William L. Fischer (1819–1899) worked with Olmsted and Vaux in Central Park supervising plantings, and in 1884 Olmsted brought him to Boston to supervise the planting of the Fens, Franklin Park, and the Boston side of the Muddy River (see FLO to F. L. Temple, March 15, 1886, above).
2. John H. Watson, the mason in charge of building the Overlook (or Playstead Terrace), worked on a number of projects for Olmsted in the 1880s (see FLO to JCO, [May 30], 1884, above).
3. Edward W. Howe was a Boston city engineer who was the engineer in charge of Boston park construction at this time (*Thirteenth Annual Report of the Board of Commissioners for 1887* [Boston, 1888], p. 68; Cynthia Zaitzevsky, *Frederick Law Olmsted and the Boston Park System* [Cambridge, Mass., 1982], pp. 152–53).
4. Olmsted may have intended to refer to *sempervivums*, another genus of succulent plants, or perhaps *Euonymus sempervirens*.
5. The Playstead and the Overlook (or Playstead Terrace) were the first portions of Franklin Park to be planted and the only areas planted in 1887. Olmsted visited the site with Fischer in the spring of 1887 and this letter followed (C. Zaitzevsky, *The Boston Park System*, pp. 192–93; *Thirteenth Annual Report, Boston Department of Parks, 1887*, pp. 7, 18).

To Dwight Hinckley Olmstead[1]

31st July, 1887.

Dwight H. Olmstead Esq[r]
Dear Sir;
I have received your letter of 29th inst.

You tell me that the Park Commissioners are of the opinion that they can for a while longer put off taking {*competent*} landscape architects into counsel as to the requirements of their Central and Riverside works by directing all their expenditure to certain points at which, so far as they are able to see, they can get along safely without such advice. The calamity may thus be averted no doubt. But whenever for thirty years past their predecessors have undertaken to judge for themselves when and where and to what extent professional counsel should be taken in the management of any of their works, the results have not been gratifying I think. Are they more likely to be in the present case?

I will consider this question with reference to the first of the pieces of work that you mention. I conceived the design of this seventeen years ago and then, as no description of it was necessary, called it by the name you use.[2] But the term describes what I had in mind about as well as the term quadruped describes an alligator. It was an original device to meet a formidable difficulty upon a point of taste. I happen to have since had an opportunity of planning and carrying out essentially the same device elsewhere. Mr Vaux also has done something like it successfully. But there is no reason for supposing that Mr Kellogg[3] knows what it is and none for supposing that if he does he can {*satisfactorily*} carry it out. It is no more within his professional field than a case in Court or a case of malignant fever. If a stone desert, set on edge, were wanted, Mr Kellogg would be the man for it.

But suppose it had been my business at the time to draw out plans for this piece of work and frame specifications for it, so far as that were possible, (as it would have been about as {*possible that*} specifications could be framed for painting the eyes of a Madonna). Suppose this had been my duty and I had performed it and Mr Kellogg could be supposed competent to direct the work without advice from time to time as it advanced — there would remain a more important objection to what you think the Commissioners propose. In the course of seventeen years the conditions to which I was required to accommodate what I designed, calling it, for want of a readier and more suitable name, a retaining wall, have been wholly changed. Suppose I had made plans, not one measurement of those plans would now be applicable. Nothing, of all that the plans had been shaped with relation to, remains as it was. To proceed this year with any construction in the {*locality*} without a deliberate thorough and complete restudy of the problem would appear to me such an insensate proceeding that I cannot believe that it is intended. I suspect that it has been your turn to be bamboozled.

I must be excused from saying anything which going as it properly might from you to the Commissioners might yet go from them to the public in such a form as to convey the impression that I have been seeking business from them. There is no employment there that they could offer me that I should not accept at a sacrifice of my personal interests. I would never have listened to their overtures for a moment but for the hope that my reemployment by them would signify a disposition on their part of sincere respect for the designs, in the responsibility for which I share, that for years past have been so barbarously misused.

Yours Respectfully

Fred[k] Law Olmsted.

The text presented here is from a letterpress copy of a handwritten letter signed on the original in Olmsted's hand: A1: 921–24, OAR/LC. Olmsted had not worked on Riverside Park since his position with the New York Department of Public Parks ended in 1878 (see FLO to John D. Crimmins, July 2, 1887, above; FLO to Dwight H. Olmstead, Aug. 7, 1887, below).

1. Dwight Hinckley Olmstead (1826–1901) was a lawyer and landowner in Morningside Heights, New York City. He was a leading member of the West Side Association, founded in 1866 "for the purpose of promoting West Side improvements, and protecting the interests of property owners." The association advocated for the creation of Morningside and Riverside parks and remained interested in their design and development. Olmstead was also a member of the Morningside Park Association, appearing before the park board on several occasions on the association's behalf. In Olmstead's July 29 letter to Olmsted, to which this letter is a response, he wrote, "The Bill for the Morningside Park improvement was passed chiefly through the efforts of another gentleman & myself, & the park commissioners have at all times conferred freely with us about the work" (David M. Scobey, *Empire City: The Making and Meaning of the New York City Landscape* [Philadelphia, 2002], p. 197; DPP, *Minutes*, Aug. 15, 1881, pp. 180–82; ibid., Jan. 26, 1887, p. 389; ibid., Aug. 24, 1887, p. 232; Dwight H. Olmstead to FLO, July 29, 1887; Andrew S. Dolkart, *Morningside Heights* [New York, 1998], pp. 31–33, 285).
2. In his letter of July 29, Dwight Olmstead wrote that a large portion of the appropriated funds would be used to build the "Retaining wall at Claremont" in Riverside Park. This was a reference to a plateau located at what was then the north end of the park at the terminus of Riverside Avenue. The Claremont section of the park was receiving immediate attention because it had been designated as the site for Grant's Tomb in 1885. In Olmsted's 1875 plan for Riverside Park, he gave only preliminary indications for the design of the retaining walls necessary to his conception of the park:

   > What I have designated as the Riverside *territory* consists of two divisions: first, a strip uniformly 100 feet wide along its eastern side, named Riverside Avenue, and originally intended to be treated as other avenues of the city; second, a body of land of variable breadth named Riverside Park.
   >
   > Nearly all of the ground on both of these parts of the territory slopes with a rapid inclination to the west, so much so that the originally proposed avenue would require to be supported on the lower side by a strong retaining wall, generally not less than twenty feet in height.

   (Dwight H. Olmstead to FLO, July 29, 1887; FLO to Henry G. Stebbins, Jan. 15, 1875 [*Papers of FLO*, 7: 108]; see also FLO to John D. Crimmins, Aug. 6, 1885, above).
3. Montgomery A. Kellogg was the Engineer for the Department of Public Parks, working on New York City's parks for most of his professional life (see FLO to John D. Crimmins, July 15, 1887, n. 2, above).

To Dwight Hinckley Olmstead

7th Aug. 1887.

Dwight H. Olmstead Esqr
My Dear Sir:
Yours of 4th is received.[1]

You say that you "cannot see why plans for Morningside should wait the completion of plans for other parks," as if I had proposed that they should. I have not intended to say anything looking that way. It is my opinion that it is not desirable that any arrangement to be made for designing superintendence for Morningside Park should be of an exceptional character. If it is it will be of a makeshift temporizing and weak and inefficient character.

This is vacation season for my office force and I am personally much occupied with my regular business. But if it were otherwise I should not be disposed to give much time or thought to the affairs of the New York Department. I have no faith that anything satisfactory to me will come out of it. If I do not mistake the ruling purpose of the Commissioners even the arguments that the newspapers are addressing to them will have an effect the opposite of that intended and any apparent yielding to them will be deceptive.[2] I have been played with longer than is agreeable to me. I do not mean to be churlish but Vaux, Kellogg and Parsons are on the ground; they are more familiar than I am with the conditions to be considered and I think that you can get what you want from them better than you can from me.

You give a great deal too much importance to a piece of paper which you call a plan. It is but a {*mere*} imperfect memorandum of {*some particulars*} of what lies in a designer's mind. When you have got such a plan for Morningside there will remain any number of rocks under its lee[3] and so long as the Commissioners think it is their business with regard to any of their work to play the part of navigators and seamen as well as that of owners, directors, providers, comptrollers, auditors and paymasters, the danger that Morningside will be wrecked is about as great as if you had no plan. I have no wish to have anything to do with the New York Parks so long as the Commissioners can learn nothing from the experience of their predecessors for ten years past in this respect and their yielding a point exceptionally because of a pressure of private and local interests and newspaper urgency will not be reassuring.

Yours respectfully

Fredk Law Olmsted.

The text presented here is from a letterpress copy of a handwritten letter signed on the original in Olmsted's hand: 936–37, OAR/LC. The park board approved Olmsted and Vaux's plan for Morningside Park in 1873, and the sidewalks and entrances and a retaining wall on the west side of the park were built in the early 1880s. In 1887 the park commissioners were debating whether to proceed with Olmsted and Vaux's original 1873 plan or to hire them to revise it (FLO to Salem H. Wales, Oct.11, 1873 [*Papers of FLO*, 6: 651–60]; A. S. Dolkart, *Morningside Heights*, pp. 22–23; see also FLO to John D. Crimmins, July 15, 1887, above; FLO to Dwight H. Olmstead, July 31, 1887, above; Frederick Law Olmsted and Calvert Vaux, *General Plan for the Improvement of Morningside Park*, Oct. 1, 1887, below).

1. In his letter, Dwight H. Olmstead reported that he and his friends were trying to convince the Board of Estimate and Appropriations to adopt Olmsted and Vaux's original plan for Morningside Park and that the property owners preferred that the work be supervised by Olmsted. He pressured Olmsted for an answer as to how soon he could draw up more detailed plans, declaring that they wanted to begin work as soon as money was secured (Dwight H. Olmstead to FLO, Aug. 4, 1887).
2. In July 1887 the park board had approved of a resolution asking park employees Samuel Parsons, Jr., and Montgomery Kellogg to review Olmsted and Vaux's 1873 plans. On August 2, Parsons and Kellogg reported to the board that the old plan was satisfactory. Commissioner Crimmins disagreed, however, and presented a letter from Olmsted explaining why the plan should be revised. The following day the *New York Times* criticized the park commissioners for their unwillingness to pay Olmsted the $5,000 fee he requested for developing a revised plan. The editorial concluded that "the public will decline to believe that experts *ex officio* are experts at all. It will continue to hold that when the Park Commissioners are authorized to make a park they had better employ the best landscape architect they can get to plan it, and carry out his plan whether they happen to like it or not." On August 24, 1887, the park commissioners engaged Olmsted and Vaux to develop a revised plan of Morningside Park, which they presented later that year (DPP, *Minutes*, July 8, 1887, p. 161; ibid., Aug. 2, 1887, pp. 204–5; "A Vigorous Onslaught," *New York Times*, Aug. 3, 1887; FLO to John D. Crimmins, July 15, 1887, above; "Morningside Park," *New York Times*, Aug. 4, 1887; DPP, *Minutes*, Aug. 24, 1887, p. 232; Frederick Law Olmsted and Calvert Vaux, *General Plan for the Improvement of Morningside Park*, Oct., 1, 1887, below).
3. That is, any number of potential difficulties.

To Colonel Casimir Stanislaus Gzowski[1]

Clifton House, 15th August, 1887.[2]

My Dear Colonel,

If I had undertaken to give you professional opinions upon any of the questions which were approached in our conversation this afternoon I should do so only after much more careful study of the circumstances and after more deliberation than I can give them now, but I will trust that you will allow me to offer you some off-hand observations showing how I am inclined to {*think*} I should advise you if, after such study and deliberation, I found my present impressions confirmed.

There are local circumstances on your side of the river that from the {*same*} general principles might lead to a very different practice in some respects from that which Mr Vaux and I advised to be adopted by the New York Commission.

In the New York plan no refreshments are to be allowed to be sold to visitors on the Government property and none to be brought by visitors to be eaten upon it, except within an area of less than four acres which was bought especially with regard to the requirements in this respect of "excursionists," at a point which other visitors need have no occasion to occupy, and would not need to cross in order to enjoy all that is distinctive of Niagara scenery. In this area, called the Upper Grove,[3] permanent shelters and other conveniences are to be provided making it a gathering place for excursion visitors but nothing like what is ordinarily called a pic-nic ground is intended, the reason being that the space is too contracted to be so used.

Within your limits,[4] on the other hand there are two bodies of land, together nearly ten times as large as the Upper Grove on the New York side, equally removed with that from the river bank and out of the popular lines of transit. One of these is admirably adapted to the use of pic-nic parties, being nearly level, well carpeted with turf and a considerable part of it shaded by beautiful well grown and umbrageous trees scattered and grouped in a park-like manner. The other I am not as familiar with and could not examine closely today but I judge that it can be made equally suitable to the purpose at no great outlay. Both these areas could be used by large excursion parties and would accommodate several at a time without interfering with the movements of other visitors seeking to view the Falls and Rapids, or at all marring their enjoyment of the views. If desirable they might be in distinct enclosures.

There is, then, this further circumstance to be taken into account. Nearly all visitors to your ground will enter it, not as they enter the New York Reservation on its road side and with the necessity of crossing it in numerous streams, but at one end and on one line of march.

To pass from this end of your property to the other and return on foot by any route likely to be followed by those seeking to enjoy the river, will require a walk of not less than five miles, and with a moderate allowance of time to be spent on the way for the enjoyment of the scenery, visitors moving in a party with women and children will be likely to be three hours or more on the ground and much of this time at a distance of more than two miles from any existing place of refreshment outside the Grounds.

Under these circumstances it should be well considered whether it is not best to establish two pic-nic {*grounds*}, one some distance above and one some distance below Table Rock,[5] both as far back from the bank as practicable and secluded somewhat from the view of people passing along the bank. A shelter might be built in the back part of each of these grounds large enough in case of a shower to protect several hundred people. In these shelters rooms might also be provided in which rest and restoratives could be offered to any taken ill, and light refreshments to be sold for all needing them. The chief difficulty of such an arrangement would be that of resisting the tendency to enlarge it and make all the money out of it practicable. If it is adopted every cost should be taken to fix a limited scope to the refreshment part of the scheme and to prevent its coming unnecessarily into competition with proper commercial undertakings.

Whether the areas which have been referred as suitable for pic-nic grounds are to be used as such or not, it is, as I think, most desirable that they should be preserved in the character of park-like spaces; that is to say, glades of greensward broken only by a few scattered trees or groups of trees and measurably secluded by the other surrounding trees. No road or walk should be so laid out as to split them or in skirting them to unnecessarily encroach upon them.

Partly for this reason but partly also for others, I am disposed to question the policy of setting a carriage road so far from the bank as you are proposing to do. The route you have staked out would be suitable if the object were simply to provide for the conveyance of visitors from the Suspension Bridge to Table Rock and the Islands above the Falls and by taking it you would be relieved of some temporary complications. But there is this important objection to doing so.

The greater number of the visitors who are to come in carriages from the New York side, from whose fees you are looking for an important part of your revenue, will be moved to come, not in order to get a different near view of the Falls or the Rapids from that to be obtained on the New York side nor to visit the Islands but, to get a comprehensive front view of the Falls which is not to be had on the New York side nor from any place except the brink of the Chasm for a distance of half a mile from the lower end of your property. The road you have staked out passes so far from the brink (about {880} feet) that visitors wishing to get the view of which I speak would be compelled to leave their carriages for it.[6]

In nearly every carriage load of visitors there would be some who could not and others who would not willingly walk the half mile along the brink for this purpose and the knowledge that such a walk was necessary in order to obtain good front views of the Falls would deter many from crossing the river. {*Now*} as a matter of finance, in your case, it would be better to adopt an arrangement similar in principle to that adopted from other considerations by the New York Commission. This would lead two or three points to be fixed upon as the best for the enjoyment of a front view of the Falls in the furnishing there with seats perhaps with balconies and shelters, and to the providing near by of waiting places ("harbors") in which carriages would stand while those coming in them were enjoying the view.

If viewing places for visitors and waiting places for carriages are to be provided near the edge of the crags as thus suggested it would be undesirable that the route of the road connecting them should be very {*devious*}.[7] The only way to avoid making it so would be to lay {it} out by courses approximately parallel with and at no great distance from the edge of the crags.

If so laid out the further advantage would appear a broad quiet, simple unbroken park-like body of land between the road and the steep wooded slope on the border of your property. This would supply an agreeable contrast to the view on the other side of the road. It would be restful and grateful.

I am inclined to think further, that a walk on the land side of the road will eventually be desirable: first as a route for visitors returning, alternative to the often crowded walk along the edge; second, as a means of access to the pic-nic grounds.

Suppose such a walk to have been formed it will distinctly define the territory within which pic-nic meals are to be permitted and it will be much more practicable to enforce the regulation against them elsewhere.

I will add a few suggestions as to matters of detail.

The principal improvement to be made after the few works of construction that you have in view are completed is to be accomplished by planting. This, after a year or two, can be done cheaply if done gradually in the spring and autumn when your men will be little occupied by visitors, provided you shall have previously made arrangements for having ready suitable trees, bushes and vines in good condition for planting. To this end you should soon have a nursery started with small plants to be bought in quantities at low prices. If this is well ordered it will cost little to grow them to good planting size. You can buy at from five to ten cents trees which when grown to a size for final planting would cost you a dollar each. As you intend for other reasons to employ a gardener the business will be easily attended to.

There is no inexpensive way in which you can prevent much of your land above the Falls from being too wet and boggy on the surface for the healthy growth of most trees but at small cost it can in a few years be covered with beautiful masses of willow foliage.

The unsightly high, raw and sliding bank beneath the railroad,[8] if you cannot afford a more radical treatment, might in a few years be covered by foliage of vines and creepers to be started in beds and pockets of prepared soil made near the base and brink of the {*bank*}. Rooted cuttings of the wild grape vine and of Virginia creeper, which are growing profusely near by, can be prepared at trifling cost in any desirable quantity for the purpose by your gardener.

A thousand dollars spent within the next ten months for seedling nursery stock and means to such willow and vine planting as has been suggested would greatly set forward and make frugal a much to be desired improvement, one result of which would be a larger income through greater attractiveness of the road and walk on your bridges.

In making rustic railings as you propose for the bridges and paths of the Islands[9] I should think it better to attempt not the slightest "fancy work". Any variety of character in the railings will better grow out of a necessary adaptation in the form and arrangement of their parts to suit variations that may be found in the materials used and to special local suggestions and requirements. As a general rule that which as an engineer you would prescribe having regard simply to strength, endurance and utility, would give the best results from a high landscape gardening point of view. It is only in situations where there is no special natural interest to be considered that a decorative purpose should govern in the design of such constructions.

It appears to me that where you have further occasion to paint bridges and railings, a somewhat darker tint than that you are using may make them less conspicuous. It would be well to experiment a little upon the point. Regard must be had to the fading of the paint.

Very respectfully Yours,

Fred^{k} Law Olmsted.

Col. C. S. Gzowski.

The text presented here is from a letterpress copy of a handwritten letter signed on the original in Olmsted's hand: A1: 944–52, OAR/LC. In February 1887, two months before the Legislative Assembly of the Province of Ontario officially created Queen Victoria Niagara Falls Park, Gzowski invited Olmsted to Canada to advise the park commissioners. Olmsted, who was working with Vaux on the design of the Niagara Reservation, suggested that the Canadian and American plans should be "two complementary parts of one whole," and that he would be happy to consider the project as long as it was with Vaux. Olmsted visited the site in August of 1887, and this letter was the result. He also reported on his visit to the Commissioners of the New York State Reservation at Niagara, and the Canadian commissioners published that report in their annual report of 1888. There is no evidence, however, that Olmsted ever produced a design for Queen Victoria Park, with or without Vaux. The Olmsted Brothers firm advised the Canadian park commissioners from 1906 to 1926 (C. S. Gzowski to FLO, Feb. 21, 1887; FLO to C. S. Gzowski, Feb. 25, 1887; "The Park Act. An Act Respecting the Niagara Falls Park," *Queen Victoria Niagara Falls Park: Official Documents, 1880–1895* [Ontario, 1895], p. 23; Nancy D. Pollock-Ellwand, "The Olmsted Firm in Canada: A Correction of the Record," *Planning Perspectives* 21:3, July 2006, pp. 290, 305, n. 51; "Third Annual Report of the Commissioners for the Queen Victoria Niagara Falls Park, 1888," *Queen Victoria Niagara Falls Park: Official Documents, 1880–1895* [Ontario, 1895], pp. 54–55; see also FLO to Mariana Griswold Van Rensselaer, May 18, 1887, above; FLO to Thomas V. Welch, Feb. 16, 1889, below).

1. Col. Casimir Stanislaus Gzowski (1813–1898) was a Russian engineer of Polish descent who emigrated to the United States in 1834 and moved to London, Ontario, in 1842. After initially working as a public works engineer for the Canadian government, Gzowski began his own engineering and contracting business, and over several decades was responsible for major railroad, canal, and harbor improvement projects all over Canada. He was chairman of the first Board of Commissioners for Queen Victoria Niagara Falls Park from 1885 to 1893 and was president of the Canadian Society of Civil Engineers from 1889 to 1892 (H. V. Nelles, "Gzowski, Sir Casimir Stanislaus," in *Dictionary of Canadian Biography*, pp. 390–96).
2. Clifton House was a popular hotel on the Canadian side of the falls. It sat on the shoreline of the northern boundary of the Queen Victoria Park. The building was rebuilt after a fire in 1893 and today is the Oakes Garden Theater (Karl Baedeker, *The Dominion of Canada* [Leipsic, 1900], p. 183; Anne Marie Van Nest, *Niagara In Bloom: The Gardens of the Niagara Parks Commission* [Toronto, 2002], p. 9).

3. The Upper Grove occupied the site of the former Prospect Park (today known as Prospect Point) on the New York side of the falls (Frederick Law Olmsted and Calvert Vaux, "General Plan for the Improvement of the Niagara Reservation," 1887 [*Papers of FLO*, SS1: 555–56]).
4. In 1887, the Queen Victoria Park consisted of 154 acres from the Clifton House, across the river from Prospect Point on the American side, south to the Dufferin Islands (*Tenth Annual Report of the Commissioners for the Queen Victoria Niagara Falls Park* [Toronto, 1895], p. 10; E.A. Meredith, "Queen Victoria Niagara Falls Park," *Canadian Magazine of Politics, Science, Art and Literature*, vol. IX [Toronto, 1897], p. 229).
5. Table Rock projects out from the shoreline on the Canadian side at the top of the Horseshoe Falls (Irving H. Tesmer ed., *Colossal Cataract: The Geological History of Niagara Falls* [Albany, 1981], p. 188).
6. The carriage road referred to here was planned to replace a toll road acquired by the park commissioners in 1887. The new road, as built in 1887, was apparently closer to the edge of the gorge than the alignment originally staked out by Gzowski, roughly following the route of the current Niagara Parkway (George Siebel, *Ontario's Niagara Parks 100 Years: A History* [Ontario, 1985], p. 29).
7. That is, "off the main road, departing from the direct way; pursuing a winding or straying course" (*OED*).
8. A portion of the Michigan Central Railroad ran roughly from Chippewa (south of the Dufferin Islands) north to Niagara-on-the-Lake. The tracks came closest to the park at the shore at Falls View, close to Horse Shoe Falls (George A. Seibel, "Transportation: The Iron Horse," in *Niagara Falls, Canada, a History of the City and the World Famous Beauty Spot: An Anthology* [Niagara Falls, Ont., 1967], pp. 62–66; Christopher Andreae, *Lines of Country: An Atlas of Railway and Waterway History in Canada* [Ontario, 1997], pp. 128–29).
9. The Dufferin Islands (so named in 1887 in honor of Lord Dufferin's work to secure the park reservation) and Cedar Island (at the time a small crescent-shaped island along the shore near Horseshoe Falls) were the only Canadian islands that were a part of the reservation. The Olmsted Brothers' later work on Queen Victoria Park in the twentieth century included a revision of the shores along the Dufferin channel of the islands (*Tenth Annual Report of the Commissioners for the Queen Victoria Niagara Falls Park*; plan 6054-4-tp1, NPS/FLONHS).

To John Charles Olmsted

31 Aug '87
Hopedale.
Wednesday AM

Dear John,

Leaving the carriage at Mr Cutting's[1] door last night in the dark I stepped off the platform and fell badly for my knee, which snapped and was very painful. I felt sick and faint, was carried in and presently recovered but the knee remained in much pain and was a good deal more swollen than after the Chicago accident.[2] Have just been examined by surgeon who says I must lie still for a day or two as he cannot say what the injury is until inflammation {is} reduced. I don't think it is serious but will probably keep me anchored for a week or two. I shall expect to be moved home by sleeping car Friday, possibly Thursday night. Will write as to that after surgeon's next visit; tomorrow morning's mail. Will telegraph Morton House[3] if anything unexpected. May ask you to come here but think not.

What I want of you is to pick up my business with Vaux. It is important *you should master it and let no time or advantage be lost,* and I will tell you now what has been done and how it stands.[4]

Vaux and I have been twice on the ground together and had yesterday settled everything that could be settled before drawings, though there is one element of the project not very well-defined, and as to which there may be need of radical study. Except as to this (possibly) the primary drawing of the plan can go right on without more words. My intention had been to make a tracing with Vaux at his office today; tomorrow morning review on the ground, tomorrow pm. go to Bkline with tracing prepared to make complete revised tracing and start final drawing; sending revised tracing to Vaux for approval and then going on to furnish the final drawing being made at our office as in the case of Niagara.[5] My idea was that Jones would be back in time to do the rock and foliage.[6]

I want this programme carried out as fully as possible. Do all you can to prevent Vaux from disturbing it. Take it as a matter of course that the Niagara arrangement is to be repeated. Make it convenient to him & give him confidence in your ability.

The first thing is for you to take my place. Probably Vaux will today have got the preliminary tracing well advanced and will explain the plan to you so that you can go on & finish it tomorrow morning. Then go to the ground in the afternoon and get personal familiarity with the circumstances. Don't waste time in conversation more than is unavoidable. Make as short work as you can of Olmsted, Bixby, Elliot,[7] if you unhappily encounter them. They can't help you & they will cruelly detain you.

The only point that needs further consideration (at this time) and in which debate with Vaux may be necessary is the question of a revision of the old arrangements of entrances, carriage stand &c, where the outside street (Avenue) in our old plan is widened on the east side of park, south of 116th Street.[8] The occasion of such revision if any comes from the necessity of a line of through transit across the park from the grand stair case built by Mould on the west side of 116th Street to the elevator of the elevated R.R. on 116th Street east of the park.[9] As to this line of transit I consider that Vaux and I are essentially agreed and the new arrangement which he will explain to you supersedes an old and complicated arrangement for lines of cross transit to be kept open.[10] You will see by *close* study of our old plan (the original being in Vaux's hands) what this was. "Close", I say because the arrangement for a series of iron gates to close passage to the right and left will not otherwise be seen. And I want you to understand the principle of it because Vaux is not familiar with the arrangement and may be disposed to more revolutionary work at the point than is advisable. We are to do away entirely with the Zoological plateau & terrace — treating that place naturally.[11] The arrangement for the widening of Avenue at 116th Street on the east side, entrances that &c. had been designed with some reference to the now abandoned terrace. Perhaps now it should be wholly recast but I am inclined to think not. It is with reference to this question only that I think you will need to use any original study or not at once accept unquestioningly what Vaux may say. I am afraid that at that point he may not have fully taken in the problem or the conditions. Elsewhere don't waste time trying to understand or to improve on what he may tell you, as I am perfectly familiar with and can tell you better than he can.

Remember that *we have no time to spare*. We must get it and ready for delivery in three weeks at furthest, and there has been so much fuss about it and there are such interests against *us* (F.L. & J.C.O.) that the result must be as good as we can make it.[12]

The *drawing* should be strong and {on} course for newspaper reproduction & compare strikingly with Kellogg & Parsons's drawing.[13]

Prestige for further and better employment on N. York parks is to be gained through skilful adaptation of revision of old design to the new circumstances — mainly the rail road — but the grand stairs also. (Stairs grander than we had in view though the same in principle as ours). This leads to suppression — removal of interest from south end and magnification of 116th Street part.

On old plan there are two stretches of walks on the high rocks that I intend to omit but this you can do at Brookline. If you have time go rapidly over lines of walks. It {is} easy to get perfect command of topography looking down & looking up.

F. L. O.

After you have seen Vaux I should like to know that, so far, all is going as I expect.
Say "all right."

Telegraphic Address: —
Care W. Bayard Cutting Esq
Hopedale, Long Isd.

The text presented here is a signed letter in Olmsted's hand, Olmsted Family Papers, Box H6, folder 3, OAR/LC.

1. William Bayard Cutting (1850–1912) was a New York businessman, lawyer, and philanthropist. He increased his family's fortune through railroad ventures and devoted much of his energy to cultural institutions, including the New York Botanical Garden, the American Museum of Natural History, and the Metropolitan Museum of Art. Cutting first contacted Olmsted in 1886 to develop a landscape design for "Westbrook," his estate located in Great River (Oakdale) on the south shore of Long Island. Cutting had acquired the land in 1884 and commissioned Charles Coolidge Haight to design the house. In 1887 Olmsted was working on preliminary plans for the estate. In 1937, the Cutting family deeded two hundred acres of Westbrook to New York state to create the Cutting Arboretum ("W. B. Cutting Dies on Train," *New York Times*, March 2, 1912, p. 1; Robert B. Mackay, Anthony K. Baker, and Carol A. Traynor, eds., *Long Island Country Houses and Their Architects, 1860-1940* [New York, 1997], pp. 317–18; JCO to William B. Cutting, Sept. 28, 1886, A1: 468, OAR/LC).
2. On January 31, 1887 Olmsted was involved in a train collision outside of Chicago that aggravated an old leg injury. The accident he describes here delayed work on several projects, including plans Olmsted was preparing for Cutting's estate (FLO to Mariana Griswold Van Rensselaer, Feb. 6, 1887, above; FLO to J. R. Gapue, July 19, 1887, A1: 639, OAR/LC).
3. A hotel in New York City that was located on 14th Street between Broadway and Fourth Avenues, just off Union Square (Moses King, *King's Handbook of New York City* [Boston, 1892], p. 211).
4. On August 24, 1887 the New York City Department of Public Parks contracted with Olmsted and Vaux to revise their plans for Morningside Park, which they had originally developed in 1873 (DPP, *Minutes*, Aug. 24, 1887, p. 231; see also Frederick Law Olmsted and Calvert Vaux, *General Plan for the Improvement of Morningside Park*, Oct. 1, 1887, below).
5. In November 1886 the Commissioners of the Niagara Reservation commissioned Olmsted and Vaux to prepare plans for the recently established state reservation. They presented their "General Plan" to the commissioners a couple of months before Olmsted wrote this note ("General Plan for the Improvement of the Niagara Reservation," 1887 [*Papers of FLO*, SS1: 535–75]; see also FLO to William E. Dorsheimer, July 21, 1886, above; FLO to Mariana Griswold Van Rensselaer, May 17, 1887, above).
6. Percy R. Jones worked as a draftsman for the Olmsted firm beginning in the 1880s (C. Zaitzevsky, *The Boston Park System*, p. 134).
7. Dwight H. Olmstead and Francis M. Bixby (b. 1829) led the Morningside Park Association. Walter G. Eliot (1857–1931) was a member of the West Side Association with Olmstead and Bixby, and was also likely a member of the Morningside Park Association ("To Protect the Parks," *New York Times*, Jan. 17, 1888, p. 5; W. H. McElroy and Alex McBride, *Life Sketches of Government Officers and Members of the Legislature of the State of New York for 1876* [Albany, 1876]; Walter G. Eliot, *A Sketch of the Eliot Family* [New York, 1887], pp. 97–98; "Deaths," *New York Times*, May 6, 1931; see also FLO to Dwight H. Olmstead, Aug. 7, 1887, above).
8. Olmsted and Vaux's 1873 plan for Morningside Park called for the widening of Morningside Avenue between 114th and 116th streets on the east side of the park so "as to form a bay in which carriages may stand for the accommodation of visitors without interruption of general movement in the highway." They placed entrances to the park at 114th, 115th, and 116th streets (FLO to Salem H. Wales, Oct. 11, 1873 [*Papers of FLO*, 6: 651–60]).
9. The staircase to which Olmsted refers was initially designed by Jacob Wrey Mould,

appointed Architect of the Morningside Park in 1880. Julius Munckwitz, the Architect to the Department of Public Parks, supervised the work. The stone staircase led from Morningside Avenue West (Morningside Drive) into the park. Construction began in June 1885 and was mostly complete by August 1886. The elevated railroad station was located at 116th Street and Eighth Avenue, two blocks east of the park (DPP, *Minutes*, Sept. 22, 1880; ibid., Feb. 7, 1883; ibid., June 26, 1885; "Morningside Park, New York City," *Scientific American*, Aug. 7, 1886, p. 85; see also FLO to Calvert Vaux, July 9, 1887, above).

10. Olmsted wrote in a September 3 letter to Vaux, "In the original plan we had guarded crossings for the night at 116th and 120th, with which I should now be satisfied. Slight changes will be necessary because of the new plan of stairs introduced and because we want to emphasize the entrance to the park from the railway. Otherwise I don't think the original plan can be improved in respect to crossways" (FLO to Calvert Vaux, Sept. 3, 1887).
11. Olmsted and Vaux's 1873 plan included an "esplanade, the larger part of it occupied by a building" located in the western portion of the park between 113th and 115th streets. Originally the designers hoped to relocate at least part of the Central Park Menagerie to the location, but this never occurred (FLO to Salem H. Wales, Oct. 11, 1873 [*Papers of FLO*, 6: 651–60]; "Document No. 51," DPP, *Minutes*, Oct. 11, 1873, pp. 4–5; Calvert Vaux, "The World's Fair and Zoological Garden," *New York Times*, March, 7, 1881; see also FLO to Calvert Vaux, July 9, 1887, n. 3, above).
12. Olmsted may be referring to the three park commissioners who in July of 1887 voted against his and Vaux's appointment to revise their 1873 Morningside Park plan. Instead they voted to refer the plan to the Superintendent of Parks, Samuel B. Parsons, Jr., and the Engineer of Construction, Montgomery Kellogg, to determine what modifications would be necessary. It was only after Parsons and Kellogg submitted their report, which members of the Morningside Park Association and the park board deemed unsatisfactory, that the board voted to hire Olmsted and Vaux to revise their original plan (DPP, *Minutes*, July 11, 1887, pp. 165–66; ibid., Aug. 24, 1887, p. 231; see also FLO to Dwight H. Olmstead, Aug. 7, 1887, above).
13. Parsons and Kellogg submitted their report on the Morningside Park plan to the park board on August 2, 1887 (DPP, *Minutes*, Aug. 2, 1887, pp. 204–5).

ON GARDENING

Fall 1887

THE Art Review? on Gardening? Are works of gardening, then, to be considered works of Art?

Being permitted to raise the question, I solicit attention to certain recorded testimony upon it. The witness that I shall call may not be considered an expert in the technicality of art. I submit that it is not needed that he should be, the question being one in which studio wisdom is of less importance than knowledge of humanity and the manner in which certain forces delicately act upon it; and as an expert in this latter respect, no man can stand firmer and none speak with more scientific precision, or with more perfect freedom from cant and fustian. His name is Francis Bacon.[1]

It is the opinion of scholars, I believe, that more of what is sound in our present civilization is due to Bacon than to any other man. They say that the more important discoveries and inventions, the more critical advances of science of the last three hundred years, have been gained by holding to principles and pursuing methods that he was the first to clearly propound and systematically follow. They say, too, that he was a marvelously foreseeing man, and that it is unlikely that the best fruit of his study has yet ripened.

Like Darwin, and like Gladstone in later times, Bacon found relaxation from his profound studies and from social, political and judicial burdens, in what to most men would have been an exacting interest in matters of gardening.[2] Like Darwin, and like Gladstone too, he was disposed to turn his recreations to philosophic profit. After his death, a great body of manuscript—memoranda was found among his papers, in which he had recorded personal observations upon the growth of plants and other like matters. Their character is indicated by the fact that they were first published in the form of a French translation, in Paris, when the *Jardin des Plantes*[3] was there successfully cultivating a much more active, scientific interest in horticulture than existed in England.

But, while yet living, Bacon had given us in print a record of convictions to which he had been led, of much greater importance. To realize its significance, it is first to be considered that, wherever any other of the more sumptuous fine arts has been in high vein, it has been pursued contributively and subordinately to the art of Architecture; and that the greatest architects have been themselves masters of painting, sculpture and music. Architecture is the Art of Arts. Now, it was Bacon's conviction that it was only because of a one sided immaturity of civilization, that gardening had never come to be generally regarded as a branch of art more refined and of higher spiritual moment than Architecture.[4] He believed that it offered a larger and more productive field for the worthy exercise of specially-trained faculties, and that in no other class of works of art were men eventually to find such unmixed pleasure; in none, such vital relief from the depressing and repressing influence of over-much absorption in lay occupations.*

Suppose that this conviction had been reached by Bacon by no excessively un-Baconian process, what might be reasonably thought to follow? Might not this, for example: That the higher the social condition of a people, the greater will be the respect in which works of gardening are held; the more general and the more vitalizing the pleasure taken in gardening, the more critical the popular judgment of the management of such works, the more conser-

*See the first sentence of his essay on "The Royal Ordering of Gardens," this essay being one of a series said by Archbishop Whately to have been intended, not so much fully to express the author's views as, to set the readers of them a-thinking for themselves.[5]

vative the public dealings with them. And why not this again? That the lower the social condition of a people, the less will those ignorant of the higher fields of gardening be aware of their ignorance; the more supercilious will be their attitude to those who are less ignorant, and the less will they be held in restraint by public opinion from degrading and wasteful misdirection of gardening works.

It is not here and now asked whether all of Bacon's claim for gardening should be allowed. It is asked whether it is even reasonable that projects of gardening should be taken up and continuously pursued with the serious and reverent study that befits works of art? With reference to this question, it is now further to be submitted that the mature conviction of a man of Bacon's standing is entitled to much greater weight at this time than it might otherwise be, because of the limited resources of gardening and the restricted field that had been open for gardening works at the time when he wrote, compared with the present. The wealthiest man in England, let it be remembered, could not then command a single plant out of hundreds that are now common articles of the pleasure-gardening trade, so common that the poorest settlers in the remotest wilds of America or Australia may, for a few farthings, obtain nurslings of them through the mails.

As to the extent of the field of operations, to understand the difference between that open to Bacon's contemplation and that which is, at least theoretically, open to ours, we have first to think under what restraints of custom and conventional decorum his imagination was obliged to act. Compared with his contemporaries, he was a singularly free-minded man. He was, for example, able to wholly discard what was then "good form" in respect to what is now called color-decoration and bedding work; daring to say of it, "You may see as good sights many times in tarts."[6] How many people of refined tastes have had that thought lying back in their minds during the last twenty years, without strength to admit it to themselves, much less to live by it? Yet Bacon himself never thought, apparently, of carrying a work of gardening beyond a garden. And a garden to him was little more than a well-built and richly-endowed convent of plants; a convent in which nothing was so well expressed as the idea of the withdrawal of its inmates from the outer world and their subjection to methodism and discipline.

Wishing to picture a supreme work of the highest order of princely gardening, Bacon took for its site a field of thirty acres of flat ground[7] and, regardless of any distant beauty that might be had, first of all threw up an embankment all around it; and upon this set a lofty hedge, to be trained upon carpenter work and shorn into the fashion of a structure of masonry, with piers and alcoves, arches, battlements and turrets, but no windows. Beyond the limits thus established and so emphasized to the eye, he thought not that gardening was to be carried. And being thus compelled to have regard only to interior and confined effects, he went on to establish closer limitations by cross-lines of banks and hedges sub-dividing his space into apartments, each apartment having a style and expression of its own, like the successive apartments of a palace—stateliness being aimed at, for instance, in one; escape from stateliness in another (the latter called the heath, having the character of what is now called the wild garden). Respectable and excellent gardening of this order is still practiced, and there are situations and circumstances in which there can be no better. But in other situations and circumstances we may now have an order of gardening widely different, and calling for widely different talents, and to be judged, as to its excellence, with reference to widely different standards. Few think how very widely different, and I will try to make it apparent by presenting an extreme hypothetical case.

From the pains taken by some of our railroad corporations to advertise the pleasure to be had in looking from their cars and stopping-places, it would appear that means to this pleasure, and means of enhancing it, are already a commercial commodity.

If, in the laying out of these railroads and the arrangement of their stopping-places, there shall come a desire to some yet later generation to turn this commodity to account otherwise than as an advertisement, and if there shall come to be an inquiry for books educative of judgment in this respect, it will be found that the principles of economy applicable to the purpose have been carefully studied, with much of Bacon's faith and spirit, by men of erudition, industry and highly trained aptness for the work. In the few libraries and book-shops where the works of these instructors are stored, they are always ranged under the head of "Gardening." Of such writers in our own tongue, fountain heads of railroad gardening wisdom, as Stephenson was of railroad engineering wisdom, there are to be named—Whately, Gilpin, and Price.[8] It was a century ago that the first of these wrote, in his OBSERVATIONS ON MODERN GARDENING, that whatever was to be done to make nature (meaning scenery) more beautiful was a work of gardening;[9] and, though he did not in express terms add—whatever, also, is to be done to bring men to partake of scenery in such a way that it shall make a clean, unbroken coherent impression upon them, yet the context shows that this was his intention.[10] And many men of good general literary standing, Horace Walpole and Walter Scott among them, accepted this definition and it became good usage.[11]

Now let us think of a few operations that, under this view of the scope of gardening, are to be considered gardening-operations.

Clearing away trees, bushes or herbage, by which the more substantial and essential sturdy qualities of a headland had been obscured or softened. Felling a wood, in order that distant mountain-heights, or valley-depths, may be revealed. Demolishing obstructions, whether natural or artificial, in order to give a water course its old, natural, lively rippling way. Dredging a mud flat. Replacing painted and gilded structures of iron or wood with those of stone; and smooth, slick-faced granite with vigorous blocks raw from the quarry. Adjusting the site of a round-house, tank, coal-shed or signal station, with a motive to avoid unnecessary jar upon the foreground of a soothing prospect; or (leaving the railroad), fixing with a similar motive the position and outlines of a stable, gate or laundry-yard or of a bridge or landing pier, the course of a walk, the moorings of a yacht, or the height of a fence or of a hen-coop. These, I say, under modern usage, might all be operations of gardening. But as many confound horticulture with gardening, let it be noticed that not one of them is an operation of horticulture.

It may be questioned whether all that passes now, more than in Bacon's time, under the name of gardening, is wisely considered as simply a development of the old gardening. It might be that our ideas would be less confused, if what we call gardening outside of plant-convents had been classed as a different art and a different name had been given it. But it is only a question of expediency. Accepting the usage, we may consider how much more ground Bacon would have had for his opinions, how much greater the refreshment to be provided by gardening would have appeared to him, how much more a vital part of civilization, worthy of the highest thought of wisest men, he would have held gardening to be — could he have regarded it from a point of view that has thus been opened to us.

But it may be asked what is there in common between the gardening had in view by Bacon and this which has since been added to the field of gardening?

The answer in one word is — design.

The best dictionary-definition of design is that one of Dr. Johnson's, which says that it means "an idea to be expressed." If this does not go far, it is at least good as far as it goes.[12]

But design is one of those words to which a semi-technical signification may be attached by the circumstances under which it is used. We learn to use it discriminatingly only through familiarity with these semi-technical usages. Let us consider some of them.

We have an institution called the National Academy of Design.[13] It has for its object the fostering of what is called the Art of Design. Among them it includes Architecture, but not building; not engineering, not carpentry, nor plumbing. Among them it includes painting and sculpture, but not the manufacture of canvas, brushes, pigments or varnish; not quarrying, stone-cutting, or bronze casting.

When the Academy shall begin to take Bacon's view of gardening, it will not show it by inviting trees and bushes or samples of manures to be sent to its exhibitions. To foster improvement in these, is the business of horticultural academies. The Academy of Design will foster gardening as it fosters architecture (supposing that it does that a little).

But design is a word to be applied to works of gardening yet more discriminatingly.

When confectioners arrange various-colored sugary materials in a manner approaching that in which various colored yarns are arranged in a carpet, or as various colored stones in mosaics, their handiwork may be highly praised, but it is not praised with regard to the standard academically applied to "works of design."

Again, if a crop of flowers is raised with a view to a pleasure to be taken in them, similar to the pleasure that may be provided if they are cut and sent to a dinner-table or a sick-bed, or if they are laid upon an altar or heaped on a coffin, the work is not to be academically brought in comparison with "works of design."

Where does design in gardening begin?

William Morris, poet and unquestioned prince of certain provinces of design, gives this advice about a particular work of gardening:—

> "Don't have ferns. The hart's-tongue in the clefts of the rocks, the green things that grow within the reach of the spray of the waterfall, *these are right in their places*. Still more the brake of the woodside, whether in late autumn when its withered haulm helps out the well-remembered woodland scent, or in spring when it is thrusting its volutes through last year's waste. But all this is nothing to a garden and is not to be got out of it, and if you try it, you will take away from it all possible romance, the romance of a garden."* [14]

He is speaking of tiny gardens of the order of Lord Bacon's, though not lordly; tiny gardens of working-men, to be planned and carried out by them in the dingy outskirts of a crowded town; and of poetic ideas practicable to be expressed through gardening under such circumstances. He does not ask from the point of view of a milliner, are ferns pretty things? He does not ask from the point of view of a horticulturist whether, set in a peaty soil in a shady place and skillfully treated, their beauty can be secured in a town garden? He does not ask from the point of view of a decorative artist about the harmonies and contrasts of colors that may be obtained by the introduction of ferns. He asks: Would ferns be helpful to the expression of a general elevating and refreshing idea or sentiment, which it will be appropriate and, on the whole, practicable to lastingly secure in the place, and with the means and the technical skill at the command of the strong gardener and weak horticulturist in question?

This brings us round the corner; brings into view not high art, not great work, not costly or sumptuous work, not necessarily skillful work; brings us in view of very modest and not very beautiful work, but "work of design" in the academic sense, as appropriately to be so called as the most costly painting, the most imposing temple ever seen.

It is to be added, design is not a matter simply of expression, as Dr. Johnson's definition implies. It is also a matter of impression. If you say that gardening of design gives you, as a looker-on, no more pleasure than gardening not of design, remember that the same is said by many not only of works of building, of painting, of music, but of passages of natural scenery which to the better educated are singularly valuable. The word is not often used in this

*"Hopes and Fears for Art," p. 126.

way, but it is logically subject to such use, and the idea that would be thus represented is to be kept in mind—the idea that there is receptive, as well as constructive design, to be thought of in connection with gardening.

Frederick Law Olmsted

The text presented here is from *Art Review*, Fall 1887, pp. 31–34. The *Art Review* was a New York based monthly periodical edited by George F. Kelly from 1886 through 1889.

1. Francis Bacon (1561–1626), the English politician and philosopher, was known as a founder of modern scientific method. In the early seventeenth century Bacon oversaw the development of his grounds at Gorhambury House in Hertfordshire. His essay, "Of Gardens," was published in 1625 and describes an ideal, "prince-like" garden of about thirty acres (*DNB*; Richard Whately, ed., *Bacon's Essays with Annotations* [New York, 1857], pp. 415–22).
2. Charles Robert Darwin (1809–1882), the English naturalist who developed the theory of evolution, was an accomplished botanist and also took a great personal interest in gardening. He published many papers on botany and contributed articles to the *Gardeners' Chronicle*. William Ewart Gladstone (1809–1898) was Prime Minster of England from 1868 to 1874 and from 1880 to 1886. Gladstone's many interests included the design and management of his own gardens and grounds at Hawarden Park in Wales. Gladstone was known for a favorite form of exercise, "tree-felling," in which he engaged at Harwarden until late in his life (*DNB*; Wemyss Reid, *The Life of William Ewart Gladstone* [London, 1899], pp. 595–98).
3. Olmsted refers to the 1631 French translation by Pierre Amboise of Bacon's *Sylva sylvarum*, which included some of the author's observations on natural history. The work was originally published posthumously in English in 1626 with *New Atlantis*, though this combined volume may have had a limited distribution. The Jardin Royal des Plantes Médecinales, later the Jardin des Plantes, was founded in 1626. Louis XIII's physician, Guy de la Bross, urged the establishment of the garden in the belief that botanical science was essential to the practice of medicine. The garden was opened to the public as early as 1640 (*DNB*; Pierre Amboise, trans., *Histoire Naturelle de Mre Francois Bacon* [Paris, 1631]; *The Oxford Companion to the Garden* [New York, 2006], p. 364).
4. See Bacon's essay "Of Gardens," "God Almighty first planted a garden, and, indeed, it is the purest of human pleasures; it is the greatest refreshment to the spirits of man, without which buildings and palaces are but handyworks: and a man shall ever see, that when ages grow to civility and elegancy men come to build stately, sooner than to garden finely; as if gardening were the greater perfection" (R. Whately, ed., *Bacon's Essays*, p. 415).
5. Olmsted references Bacon's essay "Of Gardens," although he misquotes the title. The second sentence of the essay reads, "I do hold it, in the royal ordering of gardens, there ought to be gardens for all the months in the year, in which, severally, things of beauty may be then in season." Richard Whately (1787–1863) was an Anglican Archbishop of Dublin and the nephew of Thomas Whately, the author of *Observations on Modern Gardening* (London, 1770). Richard Whately edited an 1857 edition of Bacon's essays, and in the preface writes, "It ought to be remembered that an Essay, in the original and strict sense of the word,—an Essay such as Bacon's,—was designed to be suggestive of

further remarks and reflections, and, in short, to *set the reader a-thinking* on the subject" (R. Whately, ed., *Bacon's Essays*, p. iii; see also Frederick Law Olmsted, "Mr. Olmsted on Landscape Gardening," *The Garden*, Aug. 12, 1876 [*Papers of FLO*, 7: 223–28]).

6. Bacon writes in "Of Gardens," "As for the making of knots, or figures, with divers-coloured earths, that they may lie under the windows of the house on that side on which the garden stands, they be but toys: you may see as good sights many times in tarts" (R. Whately, ed., *Bacon's Essays*, p. 418).
7. Bacon describes his ideal garden, divided into three parts, "A green in the entrance; a heath or desert in the going forth; and the main garden in the midst; besides alleys on both sides" (R. Whately, ed., *Bacon's Essays*, p. 418).
8. Robert Stephenson (1803–1859) was the civil engineer who designed the Britannia Bridge spanning the Menai Straits between the island of Anglesey and Wales. Thomas Whately's (1726–1772) *Observations on Modern Gardening* (1770) was one of the most influential gardening texts of the eighteenth century, and Olmsted applied some of Whately's design principles to his own designs. William Gilpin (1724–1804) was an early enthusiast of "picturesque" landscape scenery who wrote a series of guide-books to scenic areas of Great Britain between 1782 and 1809. Olmsted was particularly influenced by Gilpin's *Remarks on Forest Scenery* (1791). Uvedale Price (1747–1829) was an influential picturesque landscape theorist who wrote *An Essay on the Picturesque, as Compared With the Sublime and the Beautiful* (1794), and other works (*DNB*).
9. "Whatever contributes to render the scenes of nature delightful, is amongst the subjects of gardening; and animate as well as inanimate objects, are circumstances of beauty or character. . . . The whole range of nature is open to him, from the parterre to the forest; and whatever is agreeable to the senses or the imagination, he may appropriate to the spot he is to improve: it is a part of his business to collect into one place, the delights which are generally dispersed through different species of country" (Thomas Whately, *Observations on Modern Gardening* [London, 1770], p. 256).
10. That is, Whately did not elaborate on his definition of gardening to include what specific tasks could be done on a landscape to provide a "coherent impression" on men's minds.
11. The novelist and essayist Horace Walpole (1717–1797) was a landscape theorist, novelist, and early proponent of the Gothic Revival. In "On Modern Gardening" (or, "The History of the Taste in Modern Gardening," published in 1771 but written earlier) he writes, "But it is not my business to lay down rules for gardens, but to give the history of them. A system of rules pushed to a great degree of refinement, and collected from the best examples and practice, has been lately given in a book intituled *Observations on Modern Gardening* (Thomas Whately, 1770). The work is very ingeniously and carefully executed, and in the point of utility rather exceeds than omits any necessary directions."

    In his critical essay "On Landscape Gardening," Sir Walter Scott (1771–1832) reviews the history of British landscape gardening and gives his own thoughts on garden design. He makes no specific reference to Whately but does single out Richard Payne Knight and Uvedale Price as the "champions" whose criticisms had caused "most landscape gardeners of the present day . . . to take a pride in preserving scenery, which their masters of the last age would have made conscience to destroy" (Horace Walpole, "On Modern Gardening," *Anecdotes of Painting in England*, vol. IV [London, 1771], p. 807; Sir Walter Scott, *The Miscellaneous Prose Works*, vol. XXI [London, 1848], p. 103; see also John Sutherland, *The Life of Walter Scott* [Oxford, 1995], p. 155).
12. Samuel Johnson defines "design" as "The idea which an artist endeavours to execute or express." This is the fourth and last definition he gives for the word (Samuel Johnson, *A Dictionary of the English Language* [London, 1775; reprinted, 1805]).
13. The National Academy of Design was incorporated in New York City in 1826 for the

purpose of "the cultivation and extension of the arts of design" (*Constitution and By-Laws of the National Academy of Design* [New York, 1839], pp. 7–9).

14. William Morris, *Hopes and Fears for Art: Five Lectures Delivered in Birmingham, London, and Nottingham, 1878–1881* (London, 1882), p. 126. See also Frederick Law Olmsted, *The Park for Detroit*, Nov. 1882, n. 1, above.

To Alfred Dupont Chandler

COPY

[A Summer Hotel & Cottages at Sunapee]

Report of F. L. and J. C. Olmsted

Brookline, 9th September, 1887.

Alfred D. Chandler, Esq.,[1]
Dear Sir:

It is proposed to organize a company for the improvement of certain property on Lake Sunapee. We have examined the premises and offer the following observations upon the local circumstances and the requirement of success in the enterprise. We presume those who are to read them to have a general knowledge of the geographical position of Lake Sunapee, but may briefly say that it is upon a spur range of the White Mountains of New Hampshire, between the Mt. Washington region and the Berkshire Hills of Massachusetts. It is nearer to Boston and to New York than the White Hills, and is reached by cars, leaving those cities in trains by which visitors to the White Hills usually travel.

1. In undertakings of the class of which this is now proposed, it is needful to any great success that the place of resort shall offer some combination of advantages not to be found elsewhere, being, in respect to them at least, superior to competition.

We believe that the claim can be sustained for Lake Sunapee that it offers an enjoyment of scenery of a refreshing, cheerful, genial and soothing character, at an elevation much above that not only of any other lake as conveniently accessible from large centres of population, but of any place in the Northern States at which scenery of the same character can be found. Its elevation is from two to ten times as great, for example, as that of the more popular inland places of resort, such as Saratoga, Trenton, Delaware Water-Gap, and those on Lake George and

Lake Champlain,[2] and the air has the invigorating quality of mountain air. As to the conditions of scenery, the shores of mountain lakes are apt to be either harsh, stern and gloomy, with spiky, rigid and stunted vegetation, or flat, monotonous, mirey and dilapidated. The shores of Lake Sunapee are comparatively steep, rocky and clean, the water laps them without losing its clearness, they abound with moderate projections and depressions and they are overhung by graceful and often luxuriant trees and bushes, backed by wooded hills rising into mountains with flowing sky-lines and sweeping indentations.

We have detected no local circumstances likely to be unfavorable to the health of visitors, nor any drawbacks to the special local advantages thus stated, except such, incidental to the wildness of the region and the sparseness of the population, as it would be the object of the proposed improvements to overcome.

2. As the success of the undertaking will depend on the enjoyment of those who shall resort to it of that which is characteristic in the scenery, and as the highest enjoyment of scenery, especially of the class of scenery here to be considered, comes when it is not specially sought for and incidentally to other occupations, it is important that all operations of improvement should centre upon a hotel planned and placed with sagacious regard to the object.

The property offers a suitable site for such a hotel. To take full advantage of it the house will be placed so that the windows of as many as possible of its guest chambers and of its principal rooms and the galleries before them will give to the southward as close upon the water as practicable, the galleries even overhanging it and the main floor being at an elevation of twenty-five to thirty feet above it. This will be found the most lastingly satisfying point of view. The main entrance and the offices will then be on the north or land side of the house and there will be a spacious basement to contain billiard, bar and reading rooms, and a water gate giving direct passage to arrangements for bathing and for pleasure boating.

As to parts of the house not facing directly upon the most attracting prospect, windows to the east will look across the main body of the lake, windows to the West upon a picturesque landlocked bay; windows of the entrance front upon a wooded slope and those of the upper stairs over a part of this slope with glimpses of the lake to the northward.

From the foot of an elevator in the basement there will be a covered way to the steamboat wharf. The basement story will be built of the rough, local stone as will the piers of the galleries. Such a house so placed, with the adjoining banks, rocks and trees, the dependencies that have been suggested and others growing naturally out of the circumstances, will have a character of its own by which even casual visitors will be impressed. It will be remembered, photographed, pictured, talked about and celebrated because of the unusually happy character of its situation.[3]

Among the advantages of the arrangement over others that might be suggested will be these:

The Lake, to the greater distance, and all the landscape elements grouping about it, will be seen in the most effective composition. The prevailing summer breeze will pass from over the water directly through the windows of the greatest practicable number of rooms. The larger part of the guests will seem to themselves to have been given rooms as fortunately placed as possible for the enjoyment of that which is the distinctive attraction of the locality. Guests will have access to the water for all aquatic amusements with the least possible personal exertion.

The nuisance of what is called a hotel lawn with all the incongruous and disturbing objects that are apt to be crowded upon it in the foreground of a fine prospect will be made impossible. The view from no window or gallery looking in the direction of the principal line of view can ever be shut out by any growth of trees.

3. Near the site, chiefly on rising ground to the northward, there are suitable positions for hotel cottages and in places less conspicuous and less well adapted to cottages, room for stables, a laundry, bowling alley and other conveniences.

4. There is also near by a body of pasture land rising with a moderate inclination into a low hill, wooded with groups and single trees and upon which are scattered numerous boulders, some of large size. Ground of this character near a rural place of resort is apt to acquire a forlorn aspect. After so much of the loose stone upon the ground in question as can be well used in the building of the hotel, wharf and other required structures, has been removed, and so much of it as may be desirable taken for cottages, the least costly way to turn this ground to good account for the enterprise will be to make a deer park of it. A little care to smooth over and make tidy some of the places from which stone will have been taken, will make it, when pastured by a few deer, interesting to visitors and a pleasing part in every respect of the establishment.

5. Along the main shore, on the islands,[4] on the mountain tops and in the mountain glens at various distances from the hotel, there are localities of special attractiveness, some to be reached by a short stroll, some by a long tramp, some only by boat, some suitable for picnic parties. We advise that these should be considered important elements of the enterprise and much more systematic care taken than is usual to stimulate guests to find enjoyment in visits to them. Some little preparation of them and of routes to them should be made, as, for instance, by direction boards, by the removal of poison ivy, by stiles at fences, by stepping-stones or logs thrown across wet places, by opening springs or otherwise arranging drinking places and making them accessible. Also by appointing times and giving notices of expeditions; assuming sometimes the management of them, sending servants with repasts, making adjustments if rain threatens; providing special conveniences for invalids and so on. It may probably be found best that the hotel should own some of the places at a distance likely to be attractive to picnic parties, that they may be held exclusively for the use of its guests. It is un-

derstood that the cost of them would be very little, as they are generally valueless for agriculture.

The necessary roads, walks, fences, seats, shelters and other artificial constructions required should be as simple, countrified and unpretentious as possible consistently with economy and efficiency. Similarity with constructions for like purposes in a city is to be avoided.

Somewhat more attractive boats, and boats of a more varied character, should be provided, than are often found at summer resorts, and there should be at least one capacious steam launch for the use of pleasure parties. As the regular steam packets on the lake are sometimes delayed at various landings and are sometimes crowded with excursion parties and freight, a boat to be run direct between the railroad station and the hotel for the special accommodation of its guests may be found desirable.

6. Access from the property to the nearest railway station and to the village of Sunapee is at present indirect and toilsome. For this reason, as well as to supply a convenient pleasure drive for guests, two or three miles of new road will be needed. It has so often occurred that in the beginning of similar enterprises to that now proposed, roads have been made without suitable comprehensive thought, that in laying out this new road regard should be had not only to convenience of passage over it and economy of construction, but to enjoyment of the scenery to be commanded from it; to the suitable division of adjoining land into attractive building sites and to the probable necessity, as a community shall grow up in the neighborhood, to the laying of sewer, water and gas pipes under the road.

These several requirements will be everywhere more or less conflicting. For example, the best building sites will be obtained by so laying out the road that houses can be built between it and the lake, but houses cannot be so placed without shutting the Lake out of view to those passing on the road. Looking only to the sewers and pipes other considerations will give way to the importance of steady grades and the avoidance of rock below the surface. The best course will be found only upon a discreet study of the balance of advantages.

7. Assuming a judicious management of the hotel and its dependencies, the scheme as it has thus been outlined, considered as a commercial undertaking, will yet be found deficient in one particular. While the value of the property would rest mainly on the attractiveness of the views to be obtained from it, there is a liability as it now stands that these views will be injured by operations on other properties. It often happens that views of similar character from given points are ruined by the felling or burning of woods, the opening of quarries or the erection of ice houses or other structures. To protect the property in this respect we think it important that the little island now owned by Mr. Craddock,[5] and the island lying between this and Great Island, should be possessed by the proposed company and that it is but little less important that it should also own Great Island and all the banks of the Lake between Colonel Dana's[6] and the point of the little cove.

The present cost of acquiring all this land would be small relatively to the cost of the improvement to be made and it is reasonable to expect that after having been made it can readily be disposed of for at least all that it will have cost, with restrictions embodied in the deeds of sale which will prevent such occupation of it as would be harmful to the enterprise.

The text presented here is an unsigned typed transcription of a report on proposed development on Lake Sunapee, in western New Hampshire. Olmsted and John C. Olmsted drew up this report at the request of Alfred D. Chandler, a prominent Brookline businessman who was interested in development opportunities there. Tourism at Lake Sunapee had increased after rail service reached the site in 1871. Olmsted's plans for Burkehaven, a small resort community along the west side of Lake Sunapee, were never adopted. It is unknown whether Chandler had any business partners in the venture, but he himself did not buy land in this area until 1890, and then only owned it for a year. He eventually did acquire land north of Burkehaven in Gardner's Cove (now Chandler's Cove) where he built a family cottage ("Sunapee" in *The Tourists' Guide-Book to the State of New Hampshire* [Concord, N.H., 1902], pp. 238–39; Theodora Kimball to Alfred D. Chandler, Dec. 7, 1920; Alfred D. Chandler to Theodora Kimball, Dec. 18, 1920; Alfred D. Chandler to Theodora Kimball, Jan. 5, 1921; *Sullivan County, New Hampshire, Registry of Deeds*, vol. 130, pp. 49, 621]).

1. Alfred Dupont Chandler (1847–1923) was a prominent lawyer, writer, and investor who lived in Brookline, Massachusetts. Chandler served on several Brookline government boards and committees and became acquainted with Olmsted by 1880 when Olmsted was working on the Muddy River improvement section in Brookline. They worked together throughout the decade on neighborhood planning in Brookline as Chandler was a prominent land owner there and served at various times as Chairman of the Brookline Board of Selectmen (*NCAB*; FLO to Alfred D. Chandler, Dec. 11, 1880; Alfred D. Chandler to FLO March 20, 1884; Alfred D. Chandler to FLO and JCO, Jan. 4, 1888; FLO to Alfred D. Chandler, Jan. 5, 1888).
2. Saratoga Springs, New York, was the largest resort town in the northeastern United States in the nineteenth century. By the 1880s, there were numerous hotels, a horse racetrack, and a casino. The gorge of the Delaware River between Pennsylvania and New Jersey, known as the Delaware Water-Gap, was a well-known scenic destination. Trenton Falls, in central New York, was another resort area known for its views. Lake George and Lake Champlain were the principal lakes of the Adirondack region of New York (Nathaniel Bartlett Sylvester, *History of Saratoga County, New York* [Philadelphia, 1878]; S. R. Stoddard, "Saratoga Springs" in *Lake George and Lake Champlain, A Book of To-Day* [New York, 1892]; Laura Obiso, *Delaware Water Gap National Recreation Area* [Charleston, S.C., 2008], p. 77; N. Parker Willis, ed. *Trenton Falls: Picturesque and Descriptive* [New York, 1851]).
3. This proposed hotel overlooking Lake Sunapee was never built. The Lake View House (later the Burkehaven Hotel), built in 1875, was the only resort hotel in Sunapee at this time, located just north of the area Olmsted discusses here. By the 1890s a number of other hotels were built, apparently none by Chandler (*Granite Monthly, A New Hampshire Magazine*, vol. XVII [Concord, N.H., 1894], pp. 112–14); *The Statistics and Gazetteer of New Hampshire* . . . (Concord, N.H., 1874], p. 348]).
4. Lake Sunapee covers approximately six and a half square miles. The islands in the harbor on the west side of the lake, where the town of Burkehaven was situated, are Burkehaven

Island (also known as Craddock Island or the Isle of Pines), Emerald Island, Star Island, Little Island, and Great Island (*Hancox's Indexed Map of Lake Sunapee, New Hampshire, 1897* [Boston, 1897]).

5. Ebenezer Craddock and his wife Sophia B. Woods owned Burkehaven Island (then named Craddock Island) from 1881 until 1902 (*Sullivan County, New Hampshire, Registry of Deeds*, vol.114, p. 120; vol. 156, p. 14).
6. George Hazen Dana (1837–1917) was a merchant who settled in Newport, New Hampshire, in 1871, and spent his summers on Lake Sunapee. His cousin was Olmsted's old friend from New York, newspaper editor Charles Anderson Dana. In 1882 Dana and his wife, Frances Matson Burke, inherited her father's property, which included the Lake View Hotel in Burkehaven. In the 1880s and 90s the couple acquired and developed real estate in Burkehaven (*Biographical Review Vol. XXII: Containing Life Sketches of Leading Citizens of Sullivan and Merrimack Counties, New Hampshire* [Boston, 1897], pp. 105–6; Elizabeth Ellery Dana, *The Dana Family in America* [Cambridge, Mass., 1956], pp. 546–47; "Summer Days on Sunapee," *New York Times*, Aug. 5, 1894; *Sullivan County, New Hampshire, Registry of Deeds*, vol. 125, p. 547).

GENERAL PLAN

For The

IMPROVEMENT

Of

MORNINGSIDE PARK.

NEW YORK, Oct. 1, 1887.

The Honorable M. C. D. BORDEN,[1]
President of the Board of Commissioners of the
Department of Public Parks of New York.
SIR:

The report which we have the honor to submit will be divided under several headings, the first being a statement of—

I.

THE QUESTION TO BE CONSIDERED; THE MANNER IN WHICH IT HAS ARISEN, AND CERTAIN CONDITIONS OF ITS FAIR DISCUSSION.

Had it been determined to carry streets through the property now called Morningside Park[2] at the usual intervals and by a continuance of the courses of those approaching it from east and west, the grades of those streets and the crossing avenues, and of all building lots opening from them for a long distance from the property on all sides, would have been so affected as to make (without any corresponding advantage) a difference of millions of dollars in the cost of preparing them in the usual manner for close permanent building.

The simplest way to avoid this was for the city to take possession of the ground, and the easiest legal way to take possession of the ground was to ordain, as a matter of form, that it should be called a park.

The city, having thus on its hands a piece of property which has come to it as an incident of an operation through which it has been saved a large profitless outlay, now asks how this property can be made useful.

To say that it can be made into a park is an insufficient answer.

Something may undoubtedly be made of it that will serve many of the purposes that are served by what are usually called parks, but it must be borne in mind at the outset that none of these have been made out of a piece of land of anything like the character of this of Morningside, consequently, that we must set aside, not only the commonly accepted notions of what is desirable, and the routine standards of excellence, but also the ideas of "value receivable" for a given expenditure that have been formed from observation of other pieces of ground called by the name of parks.

II.

THE OLD PLAN, AND WHY A REVISION OF IT IS UNDERTAKEN.

Fourteen years ago a general plan was prepared by us, hereinafter to be referred to as "the Old Plan,"[3] for turning the Morningside property to use. This was provisionally adopted by your Board, record being made that it would be subject to modification should circumstances arise making this desirable.* You have now asked us to consider whether such circumstances have occurred, and if so, to submit a revised plan.

*See Minutes of the Board, October 16, 1873.

We respectfully report that in our opinion occasion for revision has occurred, as follows:

FIRST.—When "the Old Plan" was proposed the elevated railroad had not been projected.[4] It has since been built, passing along the border of the property and having a station adjoining it. The tracks of the road are carried over, and their supports partly obstruct, the north side walk of One Hundred and Tenth street, which was otherwise likely to be the principal approach to the Park. Consequently, passing trains, moving slowly and with considerable noise upon winding tracks and at an extraordinary height will inevitably be a very disquieting circumstance of the southern part of any pleasure ground to be formed on the premises.

SECOND.—The elevated road, causing the locality to be much more accessible from all distant points of the city, makes it less of a local ground than it was formerly thought likely to be, and requires a larger estimate to be adopted of the number of visitors to be provided for in its walks and other accommodations.

The topographical limitations of the property remaining the same as before, this circumstance makes necessary a more careful avoidance of nooks and passages which, with crowds entering them, are likely to be glutted, and requires that precautions should be observed against dangers that increase with the pressure of throngs.

THIRD.—The elevated road makes an entrance to the Park at One Hundred and Sixteenth street of more importance than any other, and a commodious route of passage from One Hundred and Sixteenth street on the east to One Hundred and Sixteenth street on the west a prime necessity.

FOURTH.—The partial construction, since the plan was made, of the retaining wall of West Morningside avenue, and of outworks projecting from this wall into the Park property, on a somewhat different and more costly plan than that originally adopted, also makes adjustments necessary.[5]

FIFTH.—At the time the original plan was called for, the Park Department thought it might become desirable to place a large Exhibition Building on Morningside Park, and with reference to such a structure, a portion of the ground was proposed in the plan to be levelled at considerable expense and a system of approaches provided for, by which it would be accessible night and day.[6]

It is understood that it is no longer the wish of the Department that such a structure should be had in view. Hence the system of approaches designed for it is no longer required.

III.

SITUATION AND TOPOGRAPHY.

Having thus shown reasons for proposing a revised plan, we shall next briefly describe the leading topographical features to which a plan should be fitted.

The map shows the precise extent and shape of the property.

Roughly described, it is a strip of land of the length of that part of Broadway below the City Hall, and eighty to one hundred yards wide. As originally assigned to your Department, it was bounded by the adjoining thoroughfares, but (as we had presumed that at some time it would be when preparing the "Old Plan") the jurisdiction of your Department has been lately extended to take those in, so that improvements can be made upon them in connection with those of the ground they enclose.[7]

The leading circumstance of the topography of the entire property is a ledge of gneiss rock[8] running through it from end to end.

The western part of this ledge is about sixty feet higher than the eastern part (being the height of a four-story house).

Parts are precipitous and the face of most of it too steep to be passed across except by climbing. Below it there is a strip of flat land.

There are features of decided picturesqueness, almost of grandeur, in the ledge, but nowhere any trees or other vegetation of consequence, or any water. The general character of the ground is that of a rugged waste.

IV.

THE HEIGHTS.

We assume that any value the property can be made to have will be proportionate to the degree in which those resorting to it will find refreshing relief from the confined scenery of streets and buildings, and that the plan required must be adapted to furnish such relief and make it conveniently available with no costly disturbance of the natural features.

The best opportunity of furnishing it in large measure, without excessive outlay, does not lie within the territory originally taken for a park, but in the thoroughfare called Morningside Avenue West, to carry which a causeway supported by a retaining wall resting on the upper part of the ledge, has already been constructed. This wall is generally from twenty to thirty feet high, so that the surface of the avenue for a distance of more than half a mile is essentially a hanging terrace of the height of a six-storied house above the eastern side of the property.

When the city shall have been built up on the Harlem Plain,[9] there will be no outlook from any point within the park, but all along this high terrace walk a great expanse will be open to the eastward, the eye ranging over the ledge and over the roofs of houses to stand on the other side of the park.

Beyond the latter will be seen, first, the waters of the East River, with the shipping upon them, from Hell Gate[10] to the Sound; next, the suburban region of Long Island, and back of this, wooded hills, to a great distance. Provided it is seen under circumstances favorable to its enjoyment, it is not to be supposed that anything that can be provided by improvements within the park will be more refreshing than this broad prospect, reaching far out of town, and including much that is bright and rurally cheerful. All that is wanted for the full enjoyment of it is *first*, a safe and convenient shady place from which the visitor, while strolling easily, may take it in; *second*, a more congenial foreground.

The plan provides for the first in a Mall, to be shaded by two rows of trees, with a number of bays which will serve as resting places and invite contemplation at the best points of view. We shall hereafter refer to this arrangement as "The Heights."

It was the intention of the "Old Plan," that the wall supporting the walk on the Heights, the tourelles carrying the bays, the stairways leading from them, and the parapet required for the safety of visitors, should be built of stone in a rustic and inexpensive manner, dependence being placed on a garniture of vines and rock plants to make them beautiful.

A variation from this plan has since been adopted, following the same leading lines, but providing some additional bays and staircases, and requiring a much more massive, elegant, and obviously costly form of construction.

The greater part of this plan has been executed,[11] and as there is nothing in what has been done that mars the general design of the work as a whole, it is accepted and incorporated in the present plan.

The intention has been, however, in addition to what we have stated, to break the wall along the Heights into several level sections, to be connected by short stairways, the flanks of these stairways being decorated with piers, ramps, and vases of polished granite, and with flower beds.

However elegant, we think that such an arrangement would be seriously inconvenient, would lead to accidents, and would be difficult to maintain in good order. No part of it having been executed, we therefore advise a return to the original plan of an uninterrupted walk.

As to strengthening the effect of the distant prospect from the Heights by a more emphatic foreground, as much as possible is intended by the plan, to be accomplished by plantations on the park immediately below, care being taken that the choice and disposition of trees is such that those nearest shall in time form simple broad masses of foliage, pleasing to look down upon, and that, except at occasional points, none shall grow to a height at which they will hide the horizon.

The result of what shall be done in this way will be to put apparently further away, break up and make less strenuous upon the attention, the rows of buildings which will come into the view next beyond the park, and, by giving prominence, close at hand, to sylvan elements, secure unity between the nearer and distant parts of the landscape.

The value of the broad outlook from the high, breezy and conspicuous terrace walk that we have described will be so great that whatever may be offered in the park below it must be of minor importance. Consequently nothing should be aimed at which will at all detract from the value of what is to be provided on "the Heights."

This consideration rules out all artificial objects that would be so prominent as to engage particular attention when seen from above.

V.

THE LOWER GROUND.

What is next to be desired in this pleasure ground is a form of refreshment from the ordinary city scenery of streets and buildings which shall so differ from that to be obtained on the Heights that one shall be an agreeable contrast to the other, and each give a zest to the enjoyment of the other; the principle to be pursued corresponding to that which governs the order of courses in a refreshing repast. To this end the plan provides another broad walk of equal length with that on the Heights, but of a sheltered character, and carrying the visitor through sequestered rural scenery. The attention of those passing through this walk will be chiefly directed to features comparatively near at hand, and the pleasure to be had from resort to it will come in a greater degree from a sense of retirement and seclusion, and of immediately surrounding sylvan quietude.

The second walk thus proposed will be seen in the drawing between the foot of the ledge and the eastern boundary of the park, running near the base of the declivity in the middle part; and, in the northern and southern quarter, diverging so far from it as to allow spaces of turf to be introduced between it and the rocks which, in these quarters, are bolder than elsewhere, and will be seen in landscape composition with larger bodies of foliage.

The course of the walk, determined by regard for natural circumstances, is moderately winding and so ordered as to avoid steep grades or the necessity of stairs. An invalid will be able to move through it on a wheel chair.

Where it passes that part of the ledge, nearly a quarter of a mile in length, in which the rock, though less bold and salient, is most unbroken, and therefore affords the least opportunity for trees to grow upon it,[12] the walk is to follow near its base, at a grade below that of the original surface, and sloping banks are to rise on each side, which are to be planted with low spreading trees and underwood, so that the effect of a natural bowery passage will be had.

There are, however, to be frequent lateral depressions of the sloping banks, and openings of the foliage through these, looking upon grassy spaces, among trees on one side, and upon the rocky declivity and wall above it, on the other. Trees at a little distance on the east will everywhere obscure, not only the buildings but the rows of trees on the avenue, so that the latter will but give density to the general umbrage.

The present aspect of the declivity, as it may be looked to from the line of this walk, is comparatively hard, bleak, barren and gloomy; where it is most so, however, it is practicable to induce it to adopt a sufficient proportion of certain forms of vegetation to take on a cheerful and even gay character.

There would, for example, be that of various vines and creepers, especially of the smaller woody sorts; that of prostrate and low-headed conifers, dwarf brambles, myrica, comptonia, rock ferns, genistas, bearberry, the smaller sumachs and other bushes that flourish in dry ground, and that of certain yuccas, of Indian figs, sedums, semper vivum, of golden rods, asters and other low perennials.

Where seen through openings of the bowery walls of the walk at the base of the declivity, an interesting and refreshing effect will be produced by these modest forms of vegetation, their outer parts observed in perspective, as they will be in looking upward, fold upon fold of them mingling with projections of the gray ledge, and the undraped parts of the crowning wall with the spray of trees on the Mall hanging over it.

Between the southern part of this lower walk, and the base of the declivity we proposed in "the Old Plan" that there should be a body of water.[13] This will be a most desirable feature of the park, because its banks, being on all sides deep and sheltering, the water would generally have a still surface, reflecting masses of rock rising vertically from its western verge with foliage hanging over them, in entire consistency with the sequestered character which is to be aimed at in all these parts of the ground.

Nevertheless, we omit the feature from the drawing of the revised plan, not because we have come to think it undesirable or permanently impracticable, but because an adequate supply of water is not likely to be obtained for some years to come, unless your Board should conclude to make some special and, as yet, uncontemplated provision for it.

A space of turf will supply an element of scenery having a similar, though less attractive relation with that of the rocks and the Heights beyond them. Whenever water can be provided, as, sooner or later, in our opinion, it must be, in connection with the requirements of the Central Park, it can be made to take the place represented in the present drawing to be occupied by turf, by an excavation which will then cost but little more than it would now.

When this shall be done, the bodies of foliage designed to be planted on the borders of the turf will remain and will overhang the water.

VI.

THE SOUTHERN HILL SIDE.

Between the base of the western retaining wall and the brow of the rocks, which have just been under consideration in connection with the water question, there is a space less rocky and less steeply inclined than any other part of the declivity. For this reason, in "the Old Plan," it was taken as the site of the proposed Exhibition Building. In the present plan the main purpose to be accomplished on this ground is to present bodies of foliage, so disposed as to add to the freshness and beauty of the view downward from the Mall on the Heights, and of the view upward from the lower walk.

It is compatible with the purpose, however, to make a pleasant rambling ground upon it. The intention of which is indicated in the drawing by a walk making a circuit about a small glade among the trees and by a structure (The Rest-awhile) intended to serve the purpose of a general shelter in case of showers and also of a retiring cottage.

It is to be low-walled, and, when trees shall have been grown, is to be visible neither from above nor below. It is to be entered, in a manner to be explained later, from the Mall on the Heights.

VII.

THE CENTRAL HILL SIDE.

North of One Hundred and Sixteenth street, the face of the ledge, between the base of the retaining wall and the flat land is narrow and more inclined, its lower parts being generally precipitous, and much of its upper parts too steep for safe footing. From these upper parts there will be no outlook; on one side close at hand, will be the high retaining wall, as of a fortress, on the other, eighty yards away, blocks of buildings. There is so little soil and so little opportunity for forming artificial stores of soil upon it, that no continuous walk along the brow of the declivity would be well bordered either by trees or turf, nor could a convenient broad walk be constructed without violence to nature. No attempt, therefore is proposed to make this district, like the last, pleasant for rambling and rest. The designed treatment of it has been explained in describing the intended character of the view upward and westward from the long, lower walk; but, to facilitate the movements of laborers and police engaged in the care of the park, as well as to provide a passage for visitors between the foot of the stairs on the north, and the rambling ground last described, on the south, a path is shown, carried as near the base of the retaining wall as will leave planting space to be prepared for creepers to be grown upon the wall, and shrubbery to obscure what would otherwise be a harsh line at its base.

VIII.

THE NORTHERN HILL SIDE.

The northern part of the property is a mass of rock, and the walks carried through it, as shown in the drawing, are designed with reference to little else than convenience of passage across it to other parts, the purpose being to accomplish what is necessary to the result with no more blasting or building than is indispensable to the purpose. The heaviest part of the work has been already done.

The walls of a construction in this quarter, said to have been made as a part of a line of fortifications, and thus having a historical interest, are preserved and made accessible. It is intended that soil shall be banked up against the inside of these walls, being retained by a rough additional wall, the latter forming the backing of a seat, as shown, and that in the soil, vines shall be planted to droop over the rude masonry of the exterior.

IX.

THE OUTER PROMENADES AND THE CROSS-WAYS OF THE PARK.

One of the earliest determinations to be made, in forming a plan for a city park, is that of the question whether it shall be adapted to use at night. As a rule, a park for night use should be of a simple character; its foliage should be in the form of open groves with little underwood; its walks broad, of easy grade, and it should be free from stairs, which would be stumbling blocks, and from all conditions that would give ruffians special opportunities for sudden acts of violence and for escaping observation; it should be well lighted at all points and be free from dark shadowy places. To make it so it would be necessary to sacrifice much of the attractiveness which it might have, if fitted exclusively for use by daylight.

The topography of the Morningside property is all against an intention to adapt it to night use; to do this would add greatly to its original cost and compel a much more expensive system of maintenance. Out of the conclusion that it should not be prepared for night use grow two features of the plan that remain to be spoken of. The first is that of a continuous broad promenade all around the park, easily well lighted and in all respects suitable for night use, this to be separated from the interior park by a wall, not sufficient to prevent a determined man from making his way in, but sufficient to make it clear that no one who shall have made his way in has done so without intention to break the law.

SECOND.—It would be seriously inconvenient to the public not to be able to get across the park at night. Hence, two passages are proposed, one connecting the two parts of 116th street, the other, the two parts of 120th street. They are to be made as nearly direct as they can be without becoming unbroken flights of stairs, but so far indirect as to keep close to the natural surface, and to play smoothly in with the walks, the general direction of which is across their course. They are designed as shown on the drawing to be bordered with iron fences in which there will be gates where other walks lead out of them, these gates to be closed at night.

One Hundred and Sixteenth street being of greater width than 120th, and having the railroad station upon it, the crossing between its two points is likely to be much the more used of the two; it is therefore made of ampler dimensions and at a point between the two principal flights of stairs at the foot of the tourelle, a broad open landing is introduced giving opportunity for a resting place. This, together with the entire line of the passage, will be brightly illuminated by electric lights on the tourelles, and on the gateways upon the avenue.[14]

X.

SHELTERED CONVENIENCES.

As in the summer nights, great numbers of women and children must be expected to resort to the Heights for enjoyment of the brilliant spectacle which will there be presented, and of the breeze from the sea, it has been thought necessary that access should be allowed them to the cottage before spoken of, at which there would be a female attendant. This cottage (being situated so far below the level of the mall that the eye will range over it) is to be approached by a short flight of steps which in the daytime will also be an entrance to the park, while at night a fence and gates will restrict its use to those needing to enter the cottage, through which there will then be no passage. Another smaller shelter is proposed to be centrally situated in the northern section of the park, and the base of each of the tourelles is intended to be utilized, either as a shelter, or a place of retirement for the public, or as a tool-room, storage-room or sub-station for the Parkkeepers. Such use of them has not apparently been contemplated heretofore, and, that it may be had, doors and windows will have to be made in some of them.

XI.

APPROACH FROM CENTRAL PARK.

In "the old plan" it has been assumed that visitors approaching Morningside from Central Park would nearly all take the northern sidewalk of 110th street. The change made by the railroad destroys this approach. It has occurred too, since the old plan was prepared, that 110th street, from the Central Park to the corner diagonally opposite the south-east corner of the Morningside property, has been widened on the south side.[15] It seems advisable that this widening should be continued opposite Morningside Park, and if this can be done arrangement shown on the drawing will, we think, be the best that can be made for a foot approach from the Central to the Morningside Park, and for an entrance to the latter at the nearest point at which it can be reached.

XII.

NOTE ON THE ORDER OF OPERATIONS.

It is not our present duty to counsel you as to details of the general plan we submit, nor as to proceedings to follow should your Board see fit to adopt it. But we propose to offer one suggestion in this latter respect, because, if the course we indicate is not taken, it is probable that a very different result will follow from that which we have had in view in the preparation of the drawing now laid before you. We cannot, however, venture to make this suggestion without connecting it with some general observations more or less applicable to all considerable park undertakings.

The drawing submitted, and this report in which we aim to supplement the drawing, cannot possibly represent more than a dry and imperfect frame-work of what Morningside Park is designed to be. Endless drawings, and volumes of written explanations of matters of detail would not present the life and soul of the design, which can never be realized, except through a broad comprehension of, and sympathy with, its leadings motives in *the direction* of the required operations, and this not simply for two or three years, but constantly and permanently thereafter.

It is easily possible that something which might be called a park should be formed on this ground, in which every line on the drawing would be closely followed, and yet with a result egregiously different from that intended. It is easily possible that everything that is necessary to a realization of the design, shall be done, so far as this is practicable within a certain period, at the end of which period the construction of the park would be called complete, and yet, a few years afterward, that the park should have a character wholly different from that designed, and with a view to which all previous work had been planned. And the waste of such earlier work may occur with no definite intention but simply from ignorance, or irresponsible omission to do what is continuously necessary to the purpose.

Waste, through failure to follow up with due continuous operations the primary constructional work of a park, is apt to be (in a degree very difficult to realize) the result of self-seeking influences in its management, or of fallacious popular assumptions of what is necessary to produce desired results. Of such assumptions none are more common than those that relate to park plantations; and of these the most common, and influential on park management is the assumption that the planting of trees is in the nature of a final operation; that trees once well planted may shift for themselves.

In the examination upon which this report is based, we have come upon so striking an illustration of the manner in which this fallacy works wastefully that we wish to call your attention to it.

At some distance on all sides about the Morningside property, much building is in progress, population is moving in and land coming into use and tax-paying productiveness. Immediately about the property, there is no building. The chance that a park will be formed upon it, which will make it a particularly desirable place of residence prevents building about it for any other purpose than that of a superior class of residences; the ground is of a character so different from that upon which any satisfactory city park has ever been formed, that there is, unavoidably, a vague distrust of the possibility that anything satisfactory in the way of a park can be made of it. No one going upon the ground can avoid seeing that if residences of any description were to be built about it while it remains in its present condition, the so-called park would be an intolerable nuisance.

Under these circumstances, the city has been much urged to begin improvements, and has, during the last ten years, at different times, entered upon several pieces of work, which it has been led to believe would have the effect of improvements, in giving assurance that the present state of things at least, was not to last.

One of these pieces of work has been the planting of two rows, each nearly a mile long, of Oriental Plane trees on the north and east margin of the park property. These were well planted, large pits having been prepared for them with three feet in depth of mould, the trees were of suitable size, thrifty, well set, and each was duly provided with an iron hurdle as a protection.

It is common, all over the country, to assume that, by such an operation an improvement is accomplished, so far at least that nature may be left to complete it. The result in this case is that, so far from helping forward a park-like character, in the neighborhood, the operation has simply made the place look much more squalid than before, the chief result being a broken series of stumps standing among dusty weeds, and a lot of rusty and dilapidated iron guards, guarding nothing. More than ninety per cent. of the trees are dead. Of another series of trees planted a few years earlier on the south border of the property but five, we believe, remain. (We do not understand that your Department has been responsible for the wastefulness of either of these operations.)

The point to which these observations tend is this, that, in any well-conceived park design, the most important hostile influences to guard against are procrastination, incompleteness and inefficiency, in respect to matters of vegetation.

There is so much rock exposed and so much more close below the surface of the Morningside Park ground, that a desirably fresh, luxuriant and cheerful character can only be had in it by what would elsewhere be a more than liberal — a profuse — use of a variety of plants such as we have already mentioned; plants adapted to grow in dry shallow soils or to hang or creep over rocks from pockets of soil outside of them. If what we have advised in this respect shall be done, the result, in a few years, will be a park of a very distinguished character, and which in this special description of vegetation will have a unique interest.

The plants we speak of are nearly all American and natural to the circumstances — such as are not so are fully naturalized. With suitable arrangements they will be inexpensive to establish on this ground, and once established, will, better than most plants, take care of themselves.

The plants cannot be obtained in the necessary quantity ready grown from the commercial nurseries, and the demand for most of them, in ordinary gardening, is so little that, when grown, they are sold only at many times what their cost would be if a larger market for them could be calculated on. If, therefore, your Board should adopt the plan now submitted, and it is determined to do anything toward carrying it out during the next three years, we advise that large quantities of the desired plants be at once propagated in the nurseries of the Department, and that the business of furnishing the ground with suitable vegetation take precedence, as far as possible at all times hereafter, of other business. The outlay required for all that is to be desired in this respect will be a small item in the general cost of the park.

We have ventured to urge at length this special preparation of a suitable vegetation because it is the essence of our design that Morningside Park should, in a certain artistic sense, be considered a reservation for the illustration of a subtle and delicate though dormant landscape possibility, and not an opportunity for mere miscellaneous park treatment.

XIII.

THE QUESTION OF COST.

Much the larger part of the cost of executing this plan will be that of operations of preparing walks, stairs of rough stone, and other constructional work similar to what has been done on the rocky ground of the Central, East River and Mount Morris Parks.[16] We do not offer estimates of cost, understanding that it will be more satisfactory to the Board to receive such information as it may desire in this respect from its executive agents who have been engaged in the operations referred to.

We may point out, however, that (for reasons that have been given) certain costly items of the original plan are omitted from the revised plan; those, for instance, of the terrace for the Exhibition Building and the approaches to it,

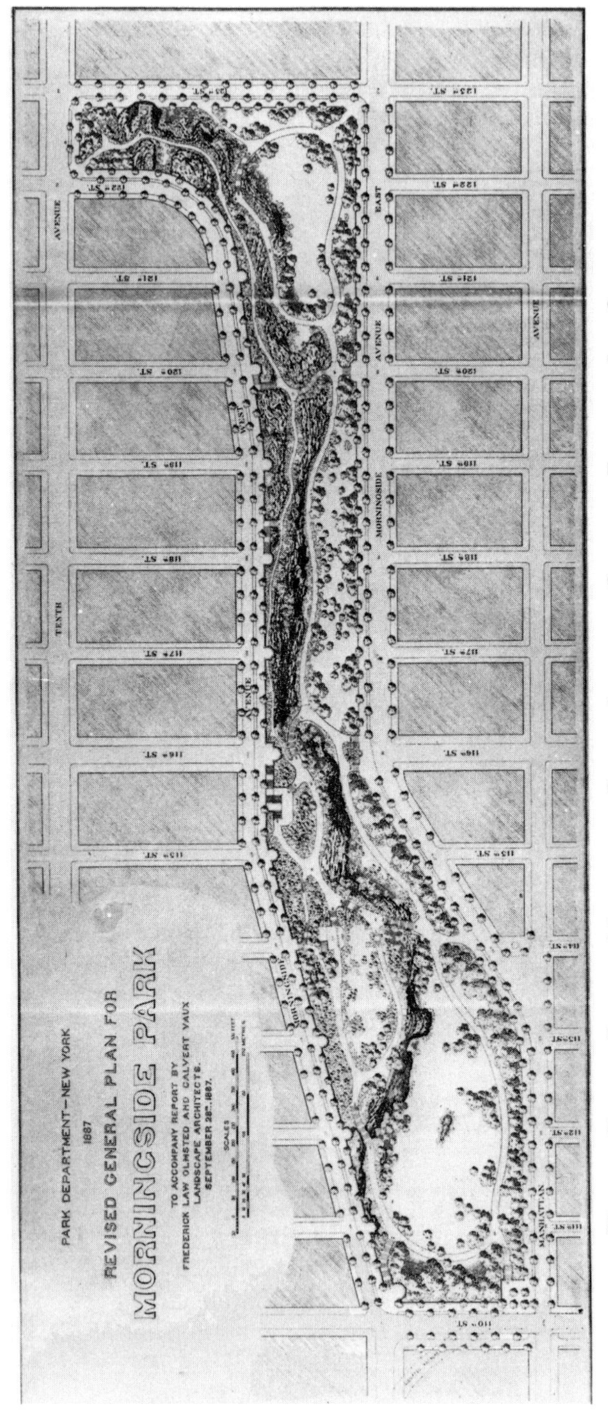

"Revised General Plan for Morningside Park to Accompany Report by Frederick Law Olmsted and Calvert Vaux, Landscape Architects," September 28, 1887

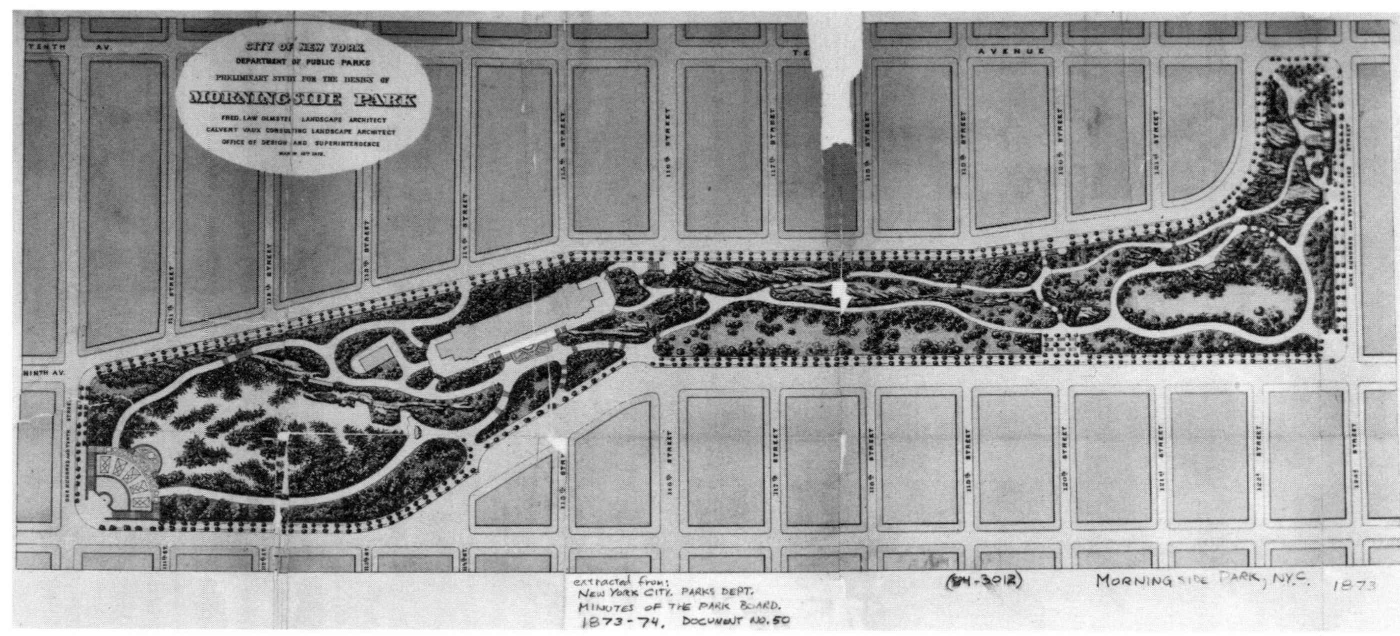

"Preliminary Study for the Design of Morningside Park, Fred. Law Olmsted Landscape Architect [and] Calvert Vaux Consulting Landscape Architect," March 10, 1873

and the extensive structure in connection with the south-west entrance. Also that much of the work required both by the original and the present plan has been executed.

Supposing that some part of the work must be delayed until further appropriations for it are authorized, we advise that no money shall be spent on any of the permanent outworks of the park, but that such inexpensive, temporary and provisional fences as are necessary to guard against accidents, shall be used in connection with the outer streets, until these shall be fully put in good order.

If this policy is adopted the fund that has been authorized to be appropriated would be available for the preparation of the ground to be dressed and planted, and for walks and other constructional work, which must be completed before the interior of the park will be in a condition to be conveniently, safely and enjoyably used by the public.

Careful calculation will, we think, show that the cost of accomplishing this would be within the amount authorized to be appropriated, provided the work is vigorously, steadily and systematically prosecuted.

Respectfully,

FREDERICK LAW OLMSTED,
CALVERT VAUX,
Landscape Architects.

The text presented here was published as the *General Plan for the Improvement of Morningside Park* (New York, 1887). Since Olmsted and Vaux had developed a plan for Morningside Park in 1873, the Department of Public Parks had begun and halted construction several times. The depression of 1873 stopped the project when work dredging a lake had only just begun. In the late 1870s, when the project was revived, disagreements between the Department of Public Parks, which controlled the parkland, and the Department of Public Works, which controlled Morningside Avenue, delayed construction. In 1880, Dwight H. Olmstead, a real estate investor and member of the Morningside Park Association, drew up a bill for the state legislature that assigned certain responsibilities to each department, and the law was passed on June 16, 1880. On September 22, 1880, the board appointed Jacob Wrey Mould Architect of the Morningside Park. In 1881 the board approved Mould's plans for the streets around and approaches to the park, and in 1882 it approved Mould's plans for sidewalks and entrances on the west side of the park, all of which were built. A year later the board asked Julius Munckwitz, Architect to the Department, to draw up plans and oversee construction of the retaining wall that was to support Morningside Avenue West. In 1887, when the park commissioners were prepared to proceed with the development of the park landscape, they first asked Samuel Parsons, Jr., and Montgomery Kellogg to review Olmsted and Vaux's 1873 plan and ascertain whether they could use it without revision. Parsons and Kellogg reported that the plan was satisfactory as it was; but pressure from citizens, especially members of the Morningside Park Association, caused the park commissioners to reconsider and invite Olmsted and Vaux to submit a new plan, which they did on August 24, 1887.

On August 30, after Olmsted and Vaux had visited the site twice and "settled everything that could be settled," Olmsted injured his knee and was bedridden for three weeks in Brookline. John C. Olmsted, under Olmsted's supervision, worked with Vaux to develop the revised plan. Olmsted felt compelled to address certain decisions, however, directly with Vaux. Since in the past Olmsted and Vaux had often worked out their collaborative designs through personal discussion, this circumstance led to a unique written correspondence between the two designers. They debated, for example, whether they should include paths on the steep hillside in the western portion of the park. Such paths existed in their 1873 plan, but Olmsted now wanted to remove them. Olmsted pressed for a simplified plan, creating a unified and more powerful landscape experience, and considered their earlier plan to be too complicated. Olmsted wrote to Vaux, "The great merit of all the works you and I have done is that in them the larger opportunities of the topography have not been wasted in aiming at ordinary suburban gardening, cottage gardening, effects. We 'have let it alone' more than most gardeners can. But never too much. Hardly enough." Olmsted's phrase "let it alone" was a reference to a statement reportedly made by Horace Greeley, who exclaimed after viewing Central Park for the first time, "Well, they have let it alone a good deal more than I thought they would!" The 1887 Morningside plan shows a path system that is nearly identical to that of the 1873 plan, suggesting that Olmsted deferred to Vaux's desires in this regard (FLO to Salem H. Wales, Oct. 11, 1873 [*Papers of FLO*, 6: 651–60]; A. S. Dolkart, *Morningside Heights*, pp. 22–23; Frederick Law Olmsted, "Patronage Journal" [*Papers of FLO*, 7: 654];"The Morningside Park," *Real Estate Record and Builders' Guide*, Aug. 20, 1881; New York [State], "An Act to Provide for the Improvement of Morningside Park [June 18, 1880]," *Laws of the State of New York Passed at the One Hundred and Third Session* [Albany, N.Y., 1880], chap. 565; DPP, *Minutes*, Sept. 22, 1880, pp. 275–76; ibid., Aug. 15, 1881, pp. 180–82; ibid., Oct. 18, 1882, p. 290; ibid., Feb. 7, 1883, pp. 496–97; ibid., July 7, 1883, pp. 148–49; ibid., July 8, 1887, p. 161; FLO to Dwight H. Olmstead, Aug. 7, 1887, above; Dwight H. Olmstead, "Resolution for Board of Commissioners of Department of Public Parks [draft]," Aug. 11, 1887; DPP, *Minutes*, Aug. 24, 1887, p. 231; Walter G. Elliot to FLO and JCO, Aug. 26, 1887; FLO to JCO, Aug. 31, 1887, above; FLO to Calvert Vaux, Sept. 3, 1887; Calvert Vaux to FLO, [Sept. 1887]; FLO to Calvert Vaux, Sept. 9, 1887; *Papers of FLO*, 3:18; see also FLO to John D. Crimmins, July 15, 1887, above; FLO to Dwight H. Olmstead, July 31, 1887, above; FLO to JCO, Aug. 31, 1887, Box H6, folder 1, OAR/LC; FLO to Waldo M. Hutchins, June 1889, below; The record of Horace Greeley's remark appears in Clarence Cook, *A Description of the New York Central Park* [New York, 1869], p. 110).

1. Matthew Chaloner Durfee Borden (1842–1912) was a merchant and manufacturer from Fall River, Massachusetts, who owned the American Print Company, the largest cloth printing company in the United States. He served as a New York City park commissioner from 1885 until 1890 and as president of the board in 1887 and 1889 ("Matthew C. D. Borden. John D. Crimmins Recalls His Services as Park Commissioner," *New York Times*, May 30, 1912; "Matthew Borden Goes into the Beyond," *Atlanta Journal Constitution*, May 28, 1912).
2. New York City purchased the site of what became Morningside Park between 1867 and 1870. Beginning near the northwest corner of Central Park, the three-quarter mile "strip of steep hillside" extended from 110th to 123rd streets, with Morningside Drive (then Morningside Avenue West) to its west, and Morningside Avenue (then Morningside Avenue East) to its east. The park site was less than one hundred yards wide in places and followed a steep, curving escarpment of bedrock that interrupted Manhattan's rectilinear grid of streets and avenues (FLO to Salem H. Wales, Oct. 11, 1873 [*Papers of FLO*, 6: 651–60]).
3. "The Old Plan" is Olmsted and Vaux's 1873 plan for Morningside Park (FLO to Salem H. Wales, Oct. 11, 1873 [*Papers of FLO*, 6: 651–60]).

4. In 1881, The Ninth Avenue Elevated Railroad reached 110th Street, just below the southwest corner of Morningside Park. There, the sixty-three foot high tracks curved east, running parallel to the southern edge of the park. From there the elevated tracks ran up Eighth Avenue to the Harlem River at 155th Street. The closest station to Morningside Park was located at 116th Street and Eighth Avenue, two blocks east of the park. The completion of the Ninth Avenue elevated train spurred development around Morningside Park and increased the number of people who were able to visit the park easily. When Olmsted and Vaux were developing their plan, Olmsted wrote to Vaux that "every change from the old plan might appear to have grown out of the Elevated Railroad" (Edwin G. Burrows and Mike Wallace, *Gotham* [New York, 1999], pp. 1053–58; A. S. Dolkart, *Morningside Heights*, pp. 30–31; James Blaine Walker, *Fifty Years of Rapid Transit, 1864–1917* [New York, 1970]; FLO to JCO, Aug. 31, 1887, above; FLO to Calvert Vaux, Sept. 3, 1887).
5. The retaining wall was built to support "the terrace road," later known as Morningside Drive. The 1880 legislation that empowered the Department of Public Parks and the Department of Public Works to improve Morningside Park directed the public works department to pave, grade, and regulate Morningside Drive and to build a retaining wall—while the parks department was to develop plans for approaches, steps, and railings. Julius Munckwitz, with the assistance of Jacob Wrey Mould, developed the working drawings for the retaining wall in 1883, after which construction began (FLO to Salem H. Wales, Oct. 11, 1873 [*Papers of FLO*, 6: 651–60]; "The Morningside Park," *Real Estate Record and Builders' Guide*, Aug. 20, 1881; New York [State], "An Act to Provide for the Improvement of Morningside Park [June 18, 1880]," *Laws of the State of New York Passed at the One Hundred and Third Session*, [Albany, N.Y., 1880], chap. 565; DPP, *Minutes*, Feb. 7, 1883, pp. 496–97; ibid., July 11, 1883, pp. 148–49).
6. In their 1873 plan, Olmsted and Vaux recommended placing a structure "of such moderate elevation, that it would present no obstruction to the view from the terrace road above" on an esplanade that would be "500 feet long and over 100 feet deep." It would have been located near the west side of the park between 113th and 116th streets (FLO to Salem H. Wales, Oct. 11, 1873 [*Papers of FLO*, 6: 654]).
7. In April 1887 all of the streets and avenues around Morningside Park came under the control of the Department of Public Parks (New York [State], *Laws of the State of New York passed at the One Hundred and Tenth Session of the Legislature* [Albany, N.Y., 1887], chap. 179; see also FLO to Henry R. Beekman, [June 10, 1886,] above).
8. The escarpment of Morningside Park that Olmsted refers to as gneiss is called mica schist by geologists today (Christopher J. Schuberth, *The Geology of New York City and Environs* [New York, 1968], pp. 74–75).
9. The Harlem Plain is a level area of upper Manhattan between the Harlem River and the higher ground of Morningside Heights and Hamilton Heights to the west. The bedrock escarpments that formed a natural topographic division between the Harlem Plain and the heights above were incorporated into Morningside and Saint Nicholas parks (C. J. Schuberth, *The Geology of New York City*, p. 75; Egbert Viele, "Sanitary & Topographical Map of the City and Island of New York," 1865).
10. Hell Gate is the channel between the East River and Long Island Sound (Gerard R. Wolfe, "Hell Gate," *The Encyclopedia of New York City* [New Haven, 1995], p. 538).
11. In addition to the retaining wall mentioned above, which included a large stairway, Mould prepared plans for the park's entrances and approaches. In September 1882 the commissioners adopted Mould's plans for the west side of the park, including a series of seven projecting "bays," or pedestrian terraces, overlooking the park along Morningside Park West (Morningside Drive). When the commissioners were ready to proceed with

construction in February 1883, they asked Julius Munckwitz to prepare final working drawings with Mould's assistance. In July the board commissioned contractor Charles Jones to build the retaining wall, and in June 1885 it commissioned Michael McGrath to build the stairway ("Document No. 89," DPP, *Minutes*, April 12, 1881; DPP, *Minutes*, Sept. 13, 1882; ibid., Dec. 6, 1882; ibid., Feb. 7, 1883; ibid., July 11, 1883; ibid., June 26, 1885; see also FLO to JCO, Aug. 31, 1887, above).

12. That is, the section of the walk between 116th and 120th streets.
13. In their 1873 design, Olmsted and Vaux suggested that a small lake, with several small islands and aquatic plants, be excavated in the southeast corner of Morningside Park. That section of park was later redesigned as an open field, and in the twentieth century it featured ball fields. In the 1980s the New York parks department constructed a new pond just north of where the lake had been proposed in 1873 (FLO to Salem H. Wales, Oct. 11, 1873 [*Papers of FLO*, 6: 656]; *Morningside Park: A Conceptual Master Plan*, prepared by Bond Ryder Wilson and Quennell Rothschild Associates [New York, 1985], pp. 24, 42).
14. In 1880 New York's Common Council began replacing gas lamps with electrical arc lamps along Broadway between Union and Madison squares, and in 1881 the park board approved the first electric lamp in Union Square. By 1886 fifteen hundred electric lamps were operating around the city, including in many of its parks (E. G. Burrows and M. Wallace, *Gotham*, pp. 1059–60; John A. Jackle, *City Lights: Illuminating the American Night* [Baltimore, 2001], p. 45; "Lights for Public Place, *New York Times*, May 5, 1881, p. 8).
15. In 1884 the park commissioners widened 110th Street between the northwest corner of Central Park and the southeast corner of Morningside Park to create a more significant connection between the two parks. In 1892 the park commissioners widened another section of 110th Street, between Seventh Avenue and Riverside Park, and also changed the name of the entire widened portion of 110th Street to Cathedral Parkway ("In and About the City," *New York Times*, May 22, 1884; "Laws of 1891," ibid., April 21, 1891; "For the Cathedral Parkway," ibid., Sept. 7, 1892; FLO to Henry R. Beekman, [June 10, 1886,] above).
16. The East River Park (later expanded and renamed Carl Schurz Park) was located along the East River between 84th and 86th streets. Mount Morris Park (now Marcus Garvey Park) is located between 120th and 124th streets, Madison Avenue, and Mt. Morris Park West ("Federal Writers Project," *New York City Guide* [New York, 1939], p. 250; James Riker, *Revised History of Harlem* [New York, 1904], p. 438).

TO JOHN CHARLES OLMSTED

Bal° 5th Oct 1887

Dear John

Over the Overlook arch the parapet should, I think be built of stone less deep (from front to rear) than elsewhere, there being no planting there and nothing to grow up over from below. You may consider

"[Franklin Park] Overlook Steps South from Pierpont Road Looking N. E.," n.d.

too whether they should not have a cut face on the Playstead side, and whether {or} not some approach to symmetry—at least balance, as thus.—

Again, it occurs to me that the best arrangement would be to have the cut stone parapet set as usual, the stone being a little less deep than average *and another line of stones set outside*, not tumbling against the parapet or elsewhere but built up flush with the ring stones, or a little overhanging, and laid in cement, so the face of the wall when pierced by the arch would be in effect uniform and solid.

As proper stones for the parapet will not be ready and Watson[1] will be going on and building part {of} the arch, you shd see to this as soon as practicable.

Until suitable stone in sufficient quantity have arrived for the parapet of the arch, he can leave a vacancy there and start anew on the South Side of the arch. As I had given him other instructions yesterday tell him that I have written this last, and also Mr Howe[2] that Howe may order such stone as you want for over the arch.

Talk the whole matter of the parapet beyond the double wall over with Watson and review the plan which I settled upon with him and with the engineer (Putnam)[3] for the southernmost steps, junction of walks, {*thinning*} out of parapet and disposition of curbs and ramps thereabouts.

Send me some Boston papers, copy Morningside Report & comments.[4]

Don't forget what I told you to say to Prof[r] Sargent. Attend meetings of Board.

F. L. O.

The text presented here is a signed letter in Olmsted's hand, Olmsted Family Papers, Box H6, folder 3, OAR/LC. The building of the Overlook (or Playstead Terrace) in Franklin Park was almost complete by the fall of 1887. The terrace, built of earth and boulders, was 800 feet long and provided a prospect for viewing sports and other events taking place in the Playstead section of Franklin Park. The details Olmsted describes here were for the arched entrance in the boulder terrace that provided access directly into the lower level of the Overlook shelter, which was built on top of the terrace and integrated into the structure. Athletes used the arched entrance to get directly from the Playstead fields to the lockers and other facilities that were housed in the lower level of the shelter building (see Frederick Law Olmsted, "Notes on the Plan of Franklin Park and Related Matters," 1886 [*Papers of FLO*, SS1: 487–88]; "Specifications for Playstead Terrace, Franklin Park," July 30, 1885, above; FLO to William L. Fischer, July 21, 1887, above; FLO to William L. Fischer, Aug. 6, 1889, below; FLO to William L. Fischer, Aug. 11, 1889, below).

1. John H. Watson was the stone mason for the Overlook (or Playstead Terrace). Olmsted also worked with him on the North Easton Memorial cairn and other projects. See FLO to JCO, [May 30], 1884, n. 6, above.
2. Edward W. Howe was the engineer in charge of Boston park work at this time (C. Zaitzevsky, *The Boston Park System*, pp. 152–53; see FLO to William L. Fischer, July 21, 1887, above).
3. C. E. Putnam, a Boston engineer, worked with Edward H. Howe at Franklin Park and continued to serve as a civil engineer for Boston and as engineer of the Boston parks department in the 1890s and into the twentieth century. He was also named Acting Superintendent of Parks in Boston in 1896 ("Proceedings of Boston Society of Civil Engineers," *Journal of the Association of Engineering Societies*, vol. VI [New York, 1887]; *Engineering and Contracting*, vol. XLIV, July–Dec. 1915 [Chicago, 1915], p. 22; *Twenty-Third Annual Report of the Board of Commissioners of the Department of Parks for the year 1898* [Boston, 1890]; "Superintendent of Parks," *Boston Daily Advertiser*, Sept. 11, 1896, p. 3).
4. See Frederick Law Olmsted and Calvert Vaux, *General Plan for the Improvement of Morningside Park*, Oct. 1, 1887, above.

ROBERT DOUGLAS

TO ROBERT DOUGLAS[1]

5th Decr. 1887.

Dear Mr Douglass;

I have your proposal for plantations at Palo Alto and as soon as I can think Senator Stanford prepared to give the matter suitable consideration will lay it before him.

With regard to Boston Harbor,[2] Profr Sargent observes that there are two trees, natural to the situation, more sure than any others to thrive in it and which are easy to propagate or be procured in large numbers at a year's notice—the Pitch Pine and the little white birch (*populi folia*). I think that he is right in advising that the bulk of plantations, at least on the more exposed ground, should be of these and that they should be planted closely. He says, for the Pine, four feet apart. With them he would mix a few other Pines, Spruces and birches. Elsewhere and dovetailing with them he would plant cherry, (*serotina*) which grows spontaneously, in thickets, on some of the outer islands; bass, which also thrives conspicuously on shores of the harbor, red cedar, oaks, willows, elm, aspen, hickory, ash, maples, of all of which there are good sized trees now growing on some of the islands or on the mainland close on its edge. I would add butternut and some of our low trees, thorns, dogwood and especially sumach (*typhina*). (Profr S thinks that in such plantations underwood, as R. glabra & copallina, Myrica, Bay berry, Brambles, Privet, Whortleberries &c. would spring up spontaneously.)

I should think that the average distance of plants might be six feet, that if Pitch Pine, birches and willows are more readily to be had than others and more sure to succeed they might be planted a little closer than the rest and constitute two thirds of the whole number of trees. I suppose that you have seen the Pitch Pine plantations on Cape Cod and have read Emerson's[3] story showing how tenacious of life the young plants are. He says also that they will bear drenching with salt water as will no other tree. In the sea coast plantations of England it is usual to plant thickets of the {. . .} willow on the outside. Mr Fay[4] has this tree growing with its roots in the beach sand, and offers me all the cuttings I may wish. On the coast at Quincy, C.F. Adams[5] told me that the little white birch was a nuisance, difficult to keep down.

I suppose that of these trees you would have to take one year for the growth of seedlings. Perhaps a few are to be had ready grown. Suppose that you have two years for the planting, that you have nursery ground provided on the islands; that you have free Transportation for trees by boat in the harbor, that one third payment is to be made on the planting of the trees and one third reserved until the required number of trees are satisfactorily established, (one third intermediate), the trees to be mainly if not wholly yearlings when planted. (Say 400 acres)

You see that I am trying to make the thing as easy, inexpensive and sure as practicable, without care for immediate effect.

I shall be glad if you can give me a proposition which can be given to the City Councils and the public in which the suggestions I have thus made would be regarded, with such variations as you may think judicious. My report on the subject is properly due before the New Year.

Yours Truly,

Fred[k] Law Olmsted.

The text presented here is from a letterpress copy of a handwritten letter signed on the original in Olmsted's hand: A2: 109–11, OAR/LC.

1. Robert Douglas (1813–1896) was a prominent nurseryman who started the first commercial production of evergreens in America. Born in England, he came to the United States in 1836 and in 1844 settled in Waukegan, Illinois, where he established R. Douglas & Sons. A founder and first president of the American Forestry Association, he was also active in the Illinois State Horticultural Society. He was a lecturer and writer and regular contributor to *Garden and Forest*, and worked with Charles Sprague Sargent when he was gathering data for the *Tenth Tree Census* (1880). The results were published in Volume IX of the *Tenth Census, Report on the Forests of North America* (1884). Douglas collaborated with Olmsted on several projects, including planning the tree nursery at Stanford University, and providing trees for the Biltmore Estate ("Robert Douglas," *National Nurseryman*, Jan., 1896, p. 157; "Who was Robert Douglas?" *Journal of Forest History*, Jan. 1975, pp. 22–23; see also *Appendix, Report of the Landscape Architect Advisory*, Dec. 30, 1887, below; FLO to Robert Douglas & Sons, [summer] 1889, below; FLO to Robert Douglas, April 18, 1889, below).
2. Olmsted wanted Robert Douglas to supervise the reforestation of the Boston Harbor Islands, and they corresponded about the types of trees that should be used. Douglas suggested a number of trees, including white pine, mountain pine, and white spruce. Olmsted wanted to keep costs low, and he suggested the trees listed here. Douglas agreed that Olmsted's suggestions would work, but argued that other trees, although more costly, "would make a better show in the future." Douglas offered to supply these other trees at

little profit because he believed it would be an honor to work on the project. To lessen his risk, however, he asked that two "dictators" be appointed (including Charles Sprague Sargent) to determine which trees should be planted and how they should be spaced. In March 1888, the park commissioners decided not to give Douglas the contract. Ultimately, the city council failed to pass an appropriation for the reforestation of the islands. Olmsted's protégé and later partner Charles Eliot was consulted by the Boston Park Commission concerning the planting of the islands in 1896, but the project was never undertaken (Robert Douglas to FLO, Sept. 5, 1887; Robert Douglas to FLO, Sept. 10, 1887; Robert Douglas to FLO, Dec. 1887; FLO to Robert Douglas, March 27, 1888, A2: 303, OAR/LC; C. Zaitzevsky, *The Boston Park System*, p. 108; Charles W. Eliot, *Charles Eliot* (Boston, 1902), pp. 699–700; see also Frederick Law Olmsted, "A Healthy Change in the Tone of the Human Heart," Oct. 1886, above; FLO to Mariana Griswold Van Rensselaer, May 17, 1887, above; *Appendix, Report of the Landscape Architect Advisory*, Dec. 30, 1887, below).

3. George Barrell Emerson (1797–1881) was an educator who participated in the formation of the Boston Society of Natural History and became its president in 1837. During his six-year tenure as president he was commissioned to make a zoological and botanical survey of Massachusetts. His study of the trees and shrubs of the state resulted in *A Report on the Trees and Shrubs Growing Naturally in the Forests of Massachusetts* (1846). Olmsted likely refers to the following passage from Emerson's report in which he describes the sturdiness of the pine: "The pitch pine has the great advantage of not being injuriously, at least not fatally, affected by salt water. Michaux observed it growing where the ground was overflowed by the spring-tides; and in many parts of this State it is found nearer to the sea than any other pine. It thus seems adapted to be planted on the extensive sands on Cape Cod, Nantucket, and in some other parts" (*DAB*; *A Report on the Trees and Shrubs Growing Naturally in the Forests of Massachusetts* [Boston, 1846], pp. 71–72).
4. Joseph Story Fay (1812–1897) planted one hundred acres on his estate at Woods Hole, Massachusetts, to see how different species could handle the weather conditions on Cape Cod. Douglas's tree recommendations for the Boston Harbor Islands were based on several trips he took to Fay's experimental forest (Joseph S. Fay to FLO, Sept. 25, 1887; "Fay, Joseph Story," *Appleton's Annual Cyclopedia and Register of Important Events of the Year 1897* [New York, 1898]; Robert Douglas to FLO, Sept. 5, 1887; Robert Douglas to FLO, Sept. 10, 1887; see also FLO to Joseph S. Fay, April 10, 1889, below).
5. Charles Francis Adams, Jr. (1835–1915), grandson of President John Quincy Adams, was a historian, educational reformer, and civic leader. In the early 1880s he oversaw the construction of the Thomas Crane Library in Quincy, designed by H. H. Richardson with grounds designed by Olmsted. In 1881 Adams invited Olmsted to Quincy to comment on a proposed "Water Park and Beach Drive" for the town, to be sited on Merrymount overlooking Quincy Bay. In 1892 Adams became a member of the Metropolitan Park Commission which, with Charles Eliot as landscape architect and Sylvester Baxter as secretary, planned the regional system of parks and parkways around Boston (*DAB*; *The Adams Papers: Diary of Charles Francis Adams* [Boston, 1986], p. xxi; FLO to Charles Francis Adams, Jr., Nov. 29, 1881 [*Papers of FLO*, 7: 566]).

CHAPTER VII

DECEMBER 1887–AUGUST 1888

This chapter contains a number of documents in which Olmsted reflects on past and current commissions, and writes about landscape architecture in theoretical terms. The first two letters to Mariana Griswold Van Rensselaer discuss the period in the 1870s when Olmsted, H. H. Richardson, and Leopold Eidlitz were commissioned to redesign the New York State Capitol building in Albany, and also consider the then current controversy about replacing the vaulted ceiling of the Assembly Chamber. The last three letters to Van Rensselaer discuss several of Olmsted's current commissions, including Stanford University and the Vanderbilt estate at Rough Point in Newport, Rhode Island. His letter to Cyrus K. Remington provides a reminiscence of the origin of the movement to create the Niagara Reservation. Two articles that Olmsted published in *Garden and Forest*, "Plan for a Small Homestead" and "Terrace and Veranda — Back and Front" are opportunities for him to recommend design principles for planning the grounds of modest residences.

The other documents in the chapter are written directly to clients. There is an 1887 report on a number of topics related to Boston parks, including suggestions for improving Boston as a summer resort, an analysis of the "Nomenclature of the Parkway System," and updates on the Beacon Street widening, the flooding of the Back Bay Fens, and tree cutting in Franklin Park. A letter to William McMillan discusses the plan Olmsted is developing for Buffalo's South Park. The letter to J. J. R. Croes is a detailed instruction on how to in-grade roads and roadsides. Two letters that relate to private residences are to William C. Loring and Frederick W. Vanderbilt, the first considering selection of a hillside site for a residence and the other recommending planting treatment for a site on the ocean. Meanwhile, Olmsted declines two commissions in New York City: in a letter to William R. Martin he refuses to advise on modifying the design of Riverside Park, while in a letter to John D. Crimmins he explains why he will not design the cemetery of St. Patrick's Cathedral.

To Mariana Griswold Van Rensselaer

21st Decr 1887.

My Dear Mrs Van Rensselaer;

I will take you at your word and, without loss of time, criticize frankly.

The general drift of the chapter strikes me as excellent.

It does not seem to me quite accurate to say that Richardson was brought by the Capitol "into conflict with public opinion".[1] A good many architects were wrought up by confidential circulars sent out by a few personal friends of Mr Fuller to hotly earnest contention in his behalf.[2] Very few other than architects. I now remember but one and he had been partly educated an architect and his criticisms and interferences have since forced McKim to resign a work in which he was greatly interested. The architects opposing us got first into the newspaper offices and carried away some editors and contributors by their "authority". But we were privately sustained by several architects of good standing and by others of authority, Profr Norton, for example, and the Profr of Architecture at Cornell.[3] We never felt that public opinion was against us. The Republican politicians at Albany made the most they could of the architects' attack upon us, as a means of harrying Tilden and Dorsheimer who were supposed to have backed us.

I should say that Richardson was brought into a professional contention *before* the public, rather than into a conflict *with* public opinion.

I am not sure that it might not be better that the statement about "pecuniary mismanagement" should be omitted. The important fact for the public, and for the vindication of Richardson from charges which did not cease to be made with his death seems to me to be this:—

From the day the foundations of the Capitol were laid to this, charges of reckless extravagance and scandalous waste in the management of the work have been incessantly made by politicians opposed to those for the time being in direction of it, and all holding any position of responsibility in connection with it have been roundly held up to public odium as faithless public servants.[4] As far as the Architects are concerned it should be better known than it appears to be that, in accordance with a custom fatal to architecture in public buildings, they were not employed to superintend the work but merely to give counsel on architectural questions and prepare plans for others to carry out. They had no responsibility for those parts of the undertaking in which, if anywhere, public money was likely to be wrongly used — in determination of the rates of wages and salaries and who should be selected to receive them, the length of a day's work, the organization and discipline of the great force employed, the purchase of materials, the making of contracts, the keeping of accounts &c. In repeated legislative investigations nothing calculated to throw a suspicion upon the integrity and faithfulness of the architects appearing to have been elicited. And that statement applies to Mr Fuller as well as to his successors.

Possibly it would be well to state that to bring the estimate of cost of completing the Capitol as low as $7000,000, in 1875. (p. 2 of MS.) it was necessary to assume that the great cornices all around the building and certain other decorative members should be made of sheet iron painted in imitation of granite.

Possibly, also, it would serve a good purpose to add after "Messrs. E. and R. proposed to complete it in a Romanesque style", (p. 5) that they did so chiefly for the reason that they were of the opinion that it would give a better opportunity for a true expression exteriorly of the internal structure, arrangements and special services of the building. (This was certainly the reason I gave my adherence to the proposition).[5]

Perhaps there is danger that the chapter will be overloaded or that the Capitol will have more than its proper share of the book but I shall feel a bitter regret if no reference is made to the Governor's room and the State Library. Richardson's drawings for the Library, are I believe, complete and a good beginning has been made in building upon them as well as upon his staircase plans.[6] A public sentiment favorable to proceeding with them is desirable to be cultivated.

I am in wondering and grateful admiration of all you have written that I have seen upon Landscape Gardening. I want to see more. I want especially to see the entire series of papers printed in the Independent. I have seen but one of them. I am sorry that you did not know that Vaux was equally with me the designer of the Central and Brooklyn Parks but it is one of these mistakes that one has always to be contending with hopelessly.[7] Sometime I must discuss the question of "Landscape Architecture" with you.

Very Cordially Yours

Fred^k Law Olmsted.

The text presented here is a signed letter in Olmsted's hand. Van Rensselaer had asked Olmsted to review a chapter about the New York State Capitol in Albany for her book, *Henry Hobson Richardson and His Works* (Boston, 1888) (Mariana Griswold Van Rensselaer to FLO, Dec. 20, [1887]; see also letters from FLO to Mariana Griswold Van Rensselaer in this volume: May 2, 1886; [May] 6, 1886; Aug. 11, 1886; April 6, 1888; April 9, 1888; June 14, 1888).

1. This phrase does not appear in the published book, which suggests that Van Rensselaer may have altered her text based on Olmsted's advice. In "Chapter XII: The Albany Capitol," she writes, "Richardson's Commission to work on the New York State Capitol at Albany placed him for the only time in his life publicly in opposition to other members of his profession" (M. G. Van Rensselaer, *Henry Hobson Richardson*, p. 73).
2. Olmsted refers to the protests of Thomas Fuller (1823–1898), the co-designer of the New York State Capitol and resident architect since 1868, after Leopold Eidlitz, H. H. Richardson, and Olmsted assumed responsibility for the design and supervision of the project in 1876. After Samuel Tilden was elected governor in 1874, he asked his lieutenant governor William E. Dorsheimer to form a commission to evaluate Fuller's plan. The project had proceeded slowly and was considerably over budget, and Tilden and Dorsheimer, who were reform Democrats, wanted to assume control of the project. The commission created an advisory board made up of Richardson, Eidlitz, and Olmsted, who sharply criticized Fuller's design for the building. The commission subsequently appointed Richardson, Eidlitz, and Olmsted to take responsibility for the building's redesign and for supervision of its construction. Fuller protested that he should have been allowed to revise his design before being replaced. Other architects, including members of the New York chapter of the American Institute of Architects, chaired by Richard Morris Hunt, protested Fuller's dismissal as well as many of Eidlitz, Richardson, and Olmsted's design decisions. In 1877, Republican legislators used the architects' protests to initiate a new round of hearings and ultimately passed legislation requiring that aspects of Fuller's design be incorporated into the final plans for the building (*DAB*; Frederick Law Olmsted, *New York State Capitol Testimony*, March 6, 1877 [*Papers of FLO*, 7: 288–304]; FLO to Charles Eliot Norton, April 2, 1876 [*Papers of FLO*, 7: 188–90]; *Papers of FLO*, 7: 7–8; Cecil R. Roseberry, *Capitol Story* [New York, 1964], pp. 21–41; Jeffrey Karl Ochsner, *H. H. Richardson: Complete Architectural Works* [Cambridge, Mass., 1982], pp. 157–60; Kathryn E. Holliday, *Leopold Eidlitz: Architecture and Idealism in the Gilded Age* [New York, 2008], pp. 112–20).
3. Olmsted refers to Charles Eliot Norton and Charles Babcock. Babcock (1829–1913) was an architect, educator, and Episcopal clergyman. He served as an apprentice with Richard Upjohn, was one of the founding members of the American Institute of Architects, and was the sole professor of architecture at Cornell University until 1880, where he designed buildings and taught from 1871 until 1896 (James Stevens Curl, "Babcock, Charles," in *A Dictionary of Architecture and Landscape Architecture* [Oxford, 1999], p. 54).
4. Van Rensselaer does not use the words "pecuniary mismanagement" in her final chapter, but begins her discussion of the history of the Capitol almost verbatim from Olmsted's letter, "From the day when the foundations of the Capitol were laid until this, charges of reckless extravagance and scandalous waste in the management of the work have been incessantly made by politicians opposed to those for the time being in power, and all persons holding any position of responsibility in connection with the building have been held up to public odium as faithless public servants" (M. G. Van Rensselaer, *Henry Hobson Richardson*, p. 73).
5. Van Rensselaer followed Olmsted's suggestion and later wrote that Eidlitz, Richardson, and Olmsted favored the Romanesque style because it offered "the best chance for a true expression in the exterior of the internal structure, arrangements, and special services of the different parts of the building" (M. G. Van Rensselaer, *Henry Hobson Richardson*, p. 76; for Olmsted's statement on this question at the time, see Frederick Law Olmsted, "To the Public," March 26, 1877 [*Papers of FLO*, 7: 315–17]).
6. Olmsted's concern for the Library and staircase stems from the fact they were not yet completed at the time of Richardson's death. Van Rensselaer does not spend much time on these features in her chapter on the Capitol, but she does address the Library and Governor's Room, concluding the chapter with a description of the great staircase:

"The design for the great staircase was perfected in Richardson's later years, and when complete will be one of the finest features of the building" (M. G. Van Rensselaer, *Henry Hobson Richardson*, p. 77).

7. Van Rensselaer's three-part series in *Independent: A Weekly Journal of Free Opinion ; Devoted to the Consideration of Politics, Social and Economic Tendencies, History, Literature, and the Arts* was chiefly on the negative aesthetic impact of the ornamental "bedding out" practice prevalent in some city gardens; see "A Word about Our Gardens I," *Independent*, Oct. 13, 1887, p. 6; "A Word about Our Gardens II," ibid., Oct. 20, 1887, p. 7; "A Word about Our Gardens III," ibid., Oct. 27, 1887, p. 7. The article, however, that Olmsted refers to here in which Van Rensselaer does not correctly attribute the design of Central and Prospect parks was in *American Architect and Building News*, "Of all our parks the Central Park is the most interesting and instructive. Others are more beautiful — Prospect Park in Brooklyn, for instance, which is also one of Mr. Olmsted's, and perhaps, in intrinsic charm of result, the best of all" ("Landscape Gardening — II," Dec. 3, 1887, p. 263). This was the second article in her three-part series on landscape gardening for *American Architect and Building News* (see also Mariana Griswold Van Rensselaer, "Landscape Gardening — I," *American Architect and Building News*, Oct. 1, 1887, p. 157 and "Landscape Gardening — III," ibid., Jan. 7, 1888, p. 3).

APPENDIX.

REPORT OF THE LANDSCAPE ARCHITECT ADVISORY.

Boston, 30th December, 1887.

The Honorable BENJAMIN DEAN, *Chairman of the Board of Commissioners of the Department of Parks:* —[1]

SIR, — In reviewing the operations of the Department during the last year, certain circumstances should be regarded that are not likely to recur. First, the City Councils had the previous year obliged all the works of the Department to be abruptly stopped, the forces employed to be disbanded, and the machinery to stand idle.[2] Second, work was not resumed until after an unprecedented demand had been established for all classes of service required by the Department; contractors were loaded with engagements; no contract for park work could be made except at greatly advanced prices, and those taking contracts found it impossible to meet their obligations because suitable workmen could not be hired. Third, the force employed by the day has been agitated at frequent intervals by projects for securing higher wages or for giving less work for given wages. Fourth, notwithstanding a large advance of wages, it has been evident that many men have entered the service of the Department with no care to remain in it, and so many have been falling out that to the end of the season the force has had to be constantly and largely recruited with raw hands.

Taking these adverse circumstances into account, it is thought that the amount and quality of the work accomplished at all points should be considered satisfactory. There has been no departure from the general plans set forth in the past annual reports of the Department; but in Franklin Park, where much obstructive rock has been found below the surface, making difficulties of construction, there has been a good deal of elaboration and adjustment of details of the design.

Reports, which it may be thought desirable to append to the annual report of the Department, will be presented below upon a number of matters of public concern.

I.

The Improvement Of Boston's Advantages As A Summer Resort.

Your Board has heretofore considered some aspects of this subject, and important operations are now in progress as the result of its deliberations, but the communication addressed to it last Arbor Day by the Boston Memorial Association, upon which a report has been asked, has obliged an inquiry to be made of broader scope than has hitherto been thought necessary.[3]

Between the wharves of Boston and the sea, outside of Boston Bay, there are seventy-five islands and islets, fifty notable projections of the main-land with bays between them, some of which are the mouths of streams, and a great many shoals and reefs which are exposed, or upon which the sea breaks, at low water. Between all these there are innumerable sub-channels more or less navigable, according to the stage of the tide and the depth of any object to be floated through them. The rise and fall of the tide varies from eight to sixteen feet, according to the age of the moon and the condition of the weather, and the tidal currents are liable to be strong and complicated. These circumstances not only make the harbor interesting because of what meets the eye of those passing through it or along its shores, but they give fleet, nimbly-turning boats a more marked advantage than they would otherwise have, and make close calculations and tact in trimming and steering them of more obvious importance than they are in harbors with fewer elements of picturesque character. Add to this the further consideration that from the time of the first settlers the people in Boston have been much engaged in fishing ventures, not only on the deep sea, but of a class to be pursued with boats of light burden, and the fact will be accounted for that there has always been an unusual interest among them in the modelling, building, rigging, and seamanship of small craft, both for commercial and for recreative use.

The city government has recognized this interest, and, in an exceptionally systematic way, wisely fostered it by the institution of an annual regatta with prizes to winners from the public purse. Latterly, at the suggestion of your Department, it has begun the building of a promenade pier, providing a fair outlook upon the harbor, and of a large basin especially as a mooring-place for pleasure-boats.[4] With a possible exception in Venice, it is believed that the people of no other city in the world make as much or as good use of their harbor, otherwise than commercially, as those of Boston have been long accustomed to do, and that none take as much or as justifiable pride in the character of their small craft, and their dexterity in handling them.

The success of the "Mayflower," the "Puritan," and the "Volunteer"[5] has called the attention of the world to the special talent thus gradually developed from the circumstances of Boston Harbor. It is, perhaps, more difficult for the people of Boston to realize the full value of their success than for others, taking a more distant view of it, to do so. A few incidents may be recalled to bring certain bearings of it better to mind.

This, for one:—To all appearances there had come, through inaction, to be scarce anything left of the old American regard for seafaring skill and prowess, when, one day last summer, through all the interior of the land, as well as in its seaports, hats everywhere went up with such enthusiasm over the result of a sailing-match of pleasure-boats, that no one could doubt that, in the heart of the nation, little provocation would be needed to stir all its old naval ardor into earnest action.

This, for another:—Certain men, of other parts of the country, send ten thousand dollars to a citizen of Boston as an expression of the gratification they have had in his work, adding, as an explanation, that, in their opinion, "nothing has, of late, redounded more to the credit of the country abroad" than the success of the "Volunteer," because of "the earnest concentration of ingenuity," of which it testifies, that Americans will be found capable whenever sufficient occasion comes to draw it out.[6]

This, for yet another:—That, because of the special talent, bred, as has been shown above, of Boston Harbor; which had been manifest in the successive triumphs of the "Mayflower," the "Puritan," and the "Volunteer," the master-workman of those pleasure-boats has been called to be a counselor of the Secretary of the Navy, in a matter of vital consequence to the country.[7]

And, lastly, this: that out of the recent history of Boston boats, and Boston pleasure-boating, measures of high statesmanship long culpably neglected, are plainly coming to receive a high degree of attention that can hardly fail to have great results for the country. The two bills now before Congress looking to a naval volunteer or militia system, being examples of the manner in which this new current of popular disposition appears.[8]

It is necessary to recall such facts as these, that too light a view may not be taken of that method of recreation in which Boston leads the world, and of those conditions of Boston Harbor out of which this leadership has grown.

Relatively to a large consideration of this subject attention is liable to be too much restricted to the more costly class of yachts. In Boston, boating is a thoroughly popular diversion; interest in it is wide-spread. More than one quarter of all the registered yachts of the entire Atlantic, Pacific, and Lake coasts have their home berths in the waters of the city and its suburbs. The whole number of masted pleasure-craft sailing the harbor is at least seven hundred. A large proportion of these are small and inexpensive boats, and, of the larger, some are owned by clubs of industrious men, individually, of moderate means. Many of the owners live in the interior, coming to Boston and using their boats only during a summer's vacation from business.

It is to be considered, also, that boating is an amusement much enjoyed by many who take no part in it except as lookers-on; and, with reference to the amusement the harbor affords to these, it must be remembered that, besides pleasure-boats proper, Boston has a large fleet of light fishing-craft, among which not a few are admirably fashioned and admirably sailed.

Owing to the enjoyment which the harbor offers many excursion trains are now run from a distance for the accommodation of those wishing to visit its shores. A number of large hotels, steamboats, and local railroads have also been built for them. Hundreds of families live, for a few weeks every year, in tents, pitched at points looking upon the harbor, and, of late, numerous light, wooden bungalows have been built in situations first occupied in this way. Many sojourners in these come from a distance.

It will be evident, from these facts, that as, throughout the country, the number of men increases who can choose their dwelling-places independently of

Rendering of Boston Harbor Islands

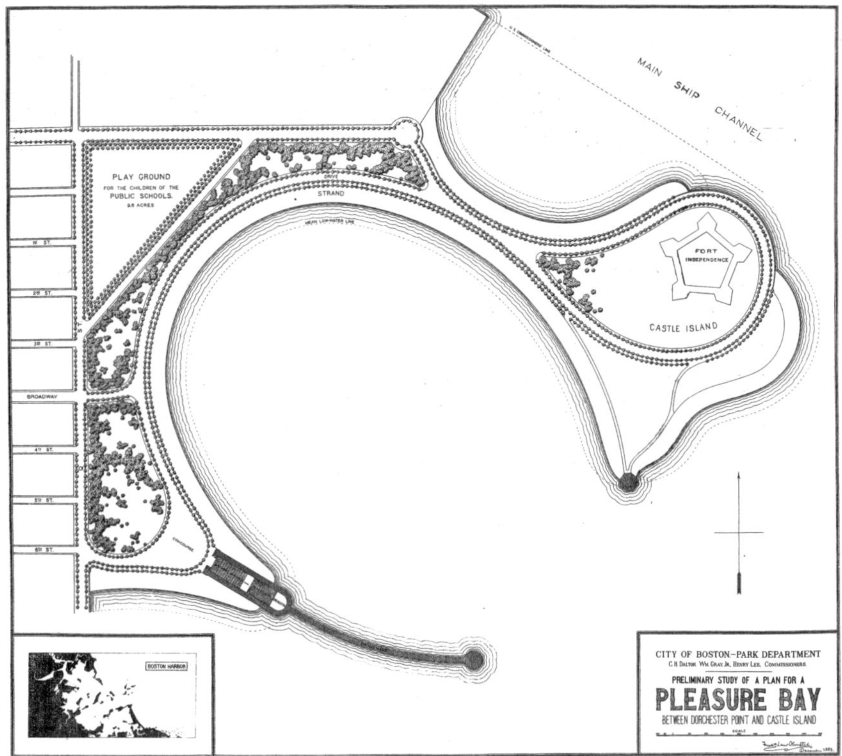

"PRELIMINARY STUDY OF A PLAN FOR A PLEASURE BAY BETWEEN DORCHESTER POINT AND CASTLE ISLAND," DECEMBER 1883

immediate money-earning considerations, and of men who are able and inclined to engage in pleasure-boating excursions, and that, as large numbers become interested in aquatic sports and seaboard scenery, the attractiveness of its harbor is to be reckoned no insignificant element of the trade and prosperity of the city. It will then be evident, further, that if its attractiveness, as a summer-resort, can be materially increased by a moderate outlay, it will be profitable to make such outlay.

In what, then, it is to be asked, other than in the play of its large and lively fleet of fishing and pleasure craft, does the special attractiveness of the harbor consist? The adjoining diagram shows the picturesque disposition of the principal headlands, bays, and islands (outlined, approximately, at half tide). The special attractiveness of the harbor lies partly in the contrast of the intricate passages and vistas among these, with the unbroken expanse of the ocean upon which it opens, and partly in the varied forms of the bluffs, crags, bars, beaches, and fens that form its shores.*

*A full description of the various natural features of the harbor will be found at p. 96 of the Appendix, compiled from the "Atlantic Coast Pilot."

What are the drawbacks to these attractive circumstances?

Chief among them must be recognized the generally hard-featured, bare, bleak, and inhospitable aspect of the headlands and islands. Let anyone, passing through the harbor, imagine them clothed with foliage of any kind, and it will be felt how much more agreeable its character would be if they were generally wooded.

Stumps, that still remain upon the most exposed, the rockiest, and bleakest of the islands show that they formerly were wooded. Once cleared, a second growth has been prevented by cropping and pasturing. The land being then much more open than before to frost and drying heat, rains, gales, and salt spray, it has ever since been losing soil and the soil remaining has been losing fertility. Hence the scenery of the harbor has been and is every year being despoiled more and more of its original beauty; its artificial features becoming more and more disagreeably conspicuous relatively to its natural features, and in these respects it is becoming less and less attractive.

The question whether the waste thus in progress can be arrested, and whether what has been lost can be recovered, is, happily, one to be answered by reference to the result of means used elsewhere for a similar purpose.

The difficulties to be overcome lie chiefly in the bleakness and dryness of much of the land most desirable to be planted; somewhat, also, at certain points, to its exposure to salt spray. They are such that trees of the sorts more commonly seen in the lawns, parks, cemeteries, and roadsides of the landward suburbs of the city could not be wisely planted. The suggestion offered by the Memorial Association is that the original forest may be restored.[9] Should this be attempted no results are to be expected that can be brought in comparison with those which are, unfortunately, associated in most minds with the term landscape-gardening. The beauty to be gained through such an operation is not the beauty of clusters, clumps, groups, or any artfully studied combination of trees; much less is it that of trees admirable for their beauty singly. It is the beauty of large compositions as these may be affected, to one looking in any direction across the harbor, by broad masses of foliage palpitating over the rigid structure of the islands and headlands; lifting their skylines; giving them some additional, but not excessive, variety of tint, greater play of light and shade, and completely overcoming the present hardness of outline of their loamy parts, without destroying the ruggedness of their rocky parts.

Having such an end in view, the trees to be planted will be of the same kinds with those formerly growing on the ground. That they may help one another to overcome the difficulties of the situation they will, when planted, be small, pliant and adaptable, offering little for the wind to tussle with; they will be low-branched, and will be set snugly together. A large proportion of all, intimately mingled with the others, will be of species the growth of which, like that of the little white birch of our rural roadsides, is rapid while young but not of long continuance. These, after a few years, will be overtopped and smothered by trees of slower and larger growth, greater constitutional vigor, and more lasting qualities. The former will have served as nurses to the latter while they are becoming established, and if timely thinning should be neglected, as it is so apt to be, they will gradually disappear by natural process before the permanent stock will be fatally injured by crowding.

Years must pass before the permanent growth can acquire a full-grown forest character, but almost at once the sapling plantations will give a pleasing softness and geniality to those elements of the scenery that are not contributive to its picturesque ruggedness. Three years after the planting is finished the harbor, as a whole, will have acquired a decidedly more good-natured, cheerful, and inviting character.

An impression is common that at most points of the harbor trees cannot be got to grow satisfactorily, and instances are referred to in which they have failed or, at the best, have grown very slowly and with distorted forms. So far as it has been practicable to ascertain, the trees, in these cases, have been ill-chosen and ill-planted, and the result has no bearing upon the proposition favored by the Memorial Association.

Reasons for confidence that, under a course of management judiciously adapted to the special difficulties of the situation, an undertaking of the kind that has been outlined would be successful, are found in the experiences of which those of Mr. Joseph Story Fay, at Wood's Holl,[10] supply an example.

The outer part of the sea-beaten promontory of Wood's Holl, had probably been devastated in the same manner as the islands of Boston Harbor. Thirty years ago it was even more bare of trees, bleak and cheerless than they are. As the result of operations which have been carried on within that period by Mr. Fay, about two hundred acres of it is now covered with dense woods of well-grown trees. Mr. Fay, visiting Boston Harbor islands last summer with the Commissioners, could see no reason to doubt that by similar operations upon them equally satisfactory results would be secured.

There is a large tract of barren land in a most exposed situation on the west coast of Lake Michigan which, a few years ago, was covered with drifting sand. Because it was supposed to be worthless, and that any attempt to improve it would be regarded as a "Folly," Mr. Robert Douglass chose to take it as a place to demonstrate the practicability of establishing forests under such special difficulties as the situation presented. He has been entirely successful, the sand is fixed and sheltered, leaf mould is beginning to accumulate upon it, and the ground is becoming comparatively moist and productive.[11]

The Kansas City, Fort Scott & Gulf Railroad Company, of which the head-quarters are in this city,[12] held in 1879 a body of bleak and arid land, of alkaline soil, naturally treeless. Some attempts to grow trees upon it had been unsuccessful, and it was generally believed to be incapable of bearing trees. In that year Mr. Douglass offered to take a contract to establish trees upon it, payment to be made him conditionally upon results. He was completely successful, and six hundred acres of the ground are now shaded by a thrifty and valuable wood. On this and other tracts, naturally treeless and supposed to present peculiar difficulties to the growth of trees, there are at this time three million flourishing trees that have been planted, under contracts with different landowners, from five to eleven years ago, by Mr. Douglass.

Mr. Douglass has had more experience in planting under trying circumstances, and has planted more extensively and successfully than any other man on the continent. It being known that he had a few years since critically examined the plantations of Mr. Fay and others within reach of the sea spray, and that he had some personal knowledge of Boston Harbor, it was thought best to ask his judgment of the scheme under consideration. After preliminary correspondence Mr. Douglass expressed his opinion of it by offering to enter into a contract to carry it out. The terms of his offer will here be stated as an indication of what a man of his experience considers practicable to be accomplished, and at what outlay.

Supposing that the aggregate areas to be planted would not be less than four hundred acres in extent, Mr. Douglass would engage to establish plantations such as have been suggested; to care for them until the trees should be well established, in thrifty condition, and so completely shading the ground that any further cultivation of it would be unnecessary. For this service he would agree to accept, as his compensation, payment at rates, which, with a reasonable allowance for incidental expenses of the Department in connection with and supplementary to the work, would be met by successive appropriations for five years of six thousand dollars a year. Payment of Mr. Douglass' part to be made in installments as the work satisfactorily advances, the last installment, amounting to 16% of the whole, to be due only when trees to the number of eight hundred thousand are certified by qualified agents appointed by the Department to have been found well-rooted and thriftily growing upon the ground.[13]

A compact statement is given on the adjoining sheet as to the position, area, ownership, and jurisdiction of thirty-seven islands; of the position and name of thirty-eight detached islets, ledges and beacons, and of the name, position, and some other particulars of fifty headlands, of Boston Bay.

The aggregate area of the islands is a little more than 1,300 acres. Of this the city owns 439 acres; the United States, 241 acres; and, of the remainder, 500 acres have but five owners.

So far as any part of this land has a productive value, it is chiefly because of the pasturage that is found upon it. On but few islands is this considered to be of more than trifling consequence. Where it is of any notable importance, it would, as a rule, be an advantage to have thickets planted along the shore borders of the high land, and clusters of trees at intervals through the pasture-ground, in the shade of which, when grown, cattle would rest.

On the islands owned by the city there are several public institutions, chiefly of a charitable character.[14] Much of the land of these is cultivated, pastured, or occupied by buildings and yards, and, of that which is available for woods, it would be better that much should be planted under the direction and by the forces of the departments in charge of them. It has been ascertained that the heads of these are well inclined to undertake this work, and especially so if supplied by the Park Department with nursery stock for the purpose. On each of them, however, it is believed that there are bodies of land, generally of small extent, which might be planted by the Park Department under an arrangement such as that suggested by Mr. Douglass, while, substantially, the whole of some of the smaller would be available. Conference with the War Department leads to a belief that it would not object to make arrangements with the Commissioners under which considerable portions of the government islands might be planted by the Department. It has been ascertained, also, that private owners of other islands important to be planted are well disposed to cooperate with the city in carrying out the scheme. It is to be hoped that the purpose of the city would likewise be aided by favorable action of towns bordering upon the harbor beyond the jurisdiction of Boston. A movement in this direction has already been made by the town of Quincy.[15] It is also reasonable to assume that when a demonstration shall have been made of the practicability of growing trees upon the more exposed points, there will be a great deal of planting about the harbor independently of any arrangement with the city, as there is in all its landward suburbs; an increased value of the land being sure to follow.

It is believed, as the general result of this review, that if the Park Department should be provided with the amount of $5,000 a year, for six years, to be used at its discretion for the purpose desired to be accomplished by the Memorial Association, it would, with such cooperation as it would be convenient for other departments of the city government to offer, be able to secure a substantial success. And it is believed that this success would have been gained with large profit to the city.

II.

The Outer Pleasure Circuit Of Back Bay.

An important addition to the means before had in view, for the open-air recreation of the people of Boston, has been well advanced during the last year, independently of your Department. It is that commonly called, but by no means described, as the widening of Beacon Street.[16] Its importance lies largely in the circumstance that it will form a short, direct, sylvan pleasure-way between the system of grounds preparing by the Department and the existing spacious but heretofore comparatively remote, inland, isolated, and little used public pleasure-ground at Chestnut Hill.

Before the plans of this work had been matured a suggestion of the undersigned was cheerfully accepted by the movers of it looking to a considerable improvement of the Back-Bay part of the general park scheme. The advantages to be gained were also apparent to the Park Commissioners. They are more intelligently presented in the accompanying map of the Back Bay Fens than they could be by any verbal description. It will be seen that the broad road, planned to lead from Audubon Circle on Beacon Street to the Audubon Road, as formerly planned, completes a circuit passage in the outer part of the Back-Bay district, a mile and three-quarters in length, all tree-lined, and in every respect adapted to pleasure-driving and walking.

III.

Nomenclature Of The Parkway System.

When the entire scheme has been carried out, towards the realization of which the works of your Department now in progress at Marine and Franklin Parks, the Arboretum, and Back Bay, are intended to promote parts, it will be plain that the complete system is of much greater value than the sum of the value of its different parts. But for some years to come those elements of its value which lie in the connecting parts of the scheme, will be but imaginary, and, as matters of imagination, but little taken thought of. Very few citizens have yet any clear idea of what is intended in this respect, or of the many advantages to be gained by carrying out the intention. Hence there is constant danger that other undertakings, public and private, will be devised and prosecuted in a manner that will make costly, if not disastrous, complications.

For this reason any expedient is to be welcomed that will tend to make the idea of federation and continuity, between the several principal works of the Department, familiar to the public.

The term *Parkway*, hitherto used to designate the continuous and connecting thread of the system, is probably as expressive of this idea as any that can be devised, and is as likely as any to come easily into familiar use with those having no special interest in the subject.

But, assuming a general public use of this term for the entire continuous way from South Boston to Back Bay, it has been thought that convenience would require distinctive names to be given to different parts of it. With this conviction the Commissioners, in 1885, directed the names *Rumford, Longview*, and *Riverdale*, to be used as the designation respectively of parts of the Parkway between Boylston Bridge and Brookline Avenue.[17] But these names are not as yet known to the general public, and it is now suggested for the consideration of the Board:—

First. That a uniform termination in all names to be applied to parts of the Parkway would, as it came into use, naturally aid in making the idea of continuity and unity familiar to the public, and, if such termination were short, simple and common, it would be in various ways a convenience.

Second. That the designatory parts of each local name might with advantage, as far as practicable without a harsh sacrifice of euphony, be derived from some topographical or historical local circumstance. For example, that part of the Parkway in which the course of the old Muddy River is followed might, under the proposed rule, instead of being called the Riverdale Road be called Riverway.

It is not particularly desirable that that part of the Back Bay improvement, which is intended to serve at times for the storage of flood waters, should be familiarly known to the public by its technical designation of *the basin*. This term is useful when it is desired to refer to its essential engineering function, but, regarding it as an accessory of a public pleasure resort, the more that function can be kept in the background the better. Looking for a name not open to this objection, it may be remembered that in the annual report of the Department for 1879, in which the scheme was first set forth, the designed landscape character of the basin was described as that of a clean, highly verdant, *fenny* meadow, set between steep banks, upon which banks plantations would be formed to eventually have more of a wildwood than of a park or garden aspect. Professional critics then and afterwards expressed the opinion that this proposition was chimerical, and the Commissioners were urged to abandon the scheme as likely to be wasteful. It was admitted by the Department that the purpose to artificially form a salt fen of the character proposed was to be regarded as in some degree experimental.[18] So long as the result of the experiment could be considered doubtful, it has not been best to give the place a name that would be appropriate only if it should prove successful. Its success is now so far established that next year, when the circuit road of the lower division of the basin shall be opened to the public, a sufficient approach to what was expected to be attained in the landscape character of its bottom will have been already accomplished to show that the result is not going to be unpleasing. It will, at least, be palpable, when the aspect of the finished part of the bottom is compared with what was to have been looked for as the result of any other method of treatment of it at any time suggested, that the course pursued by the Department should be regarded as a matter for congratulation.

In this view it is submitted that it will now be in better taste to call the bottom of the basin by a name significant of its landscape character, than either by one bringing to mind its primary utility, or by one provoking comparison with grounds prepared with exclusive regard to their use as pleasure-resorts. It is therefore suggested that instead of being called the Back Bay Basin, or the Back Bay Park, the place should be called the Back Bay Fens, or The Fens; that the sylvan bank of the basin should be called The Fenside, and that so much of the Parkway as is carried on the bank should be called The Fenway.[19]

IV.

Back Bay And Stony Brook.

Under an Act of the General Court of the present year, new plans for the drainage of the Stony Brook Valley have been adopted, which will have the effect, at times, of rapidly throwing a much larger quantity of water into the basin at Back Bay, than, when this basin was designed, the Department had been asked to provide storage for.

In the report of the Department presenting the plan of the basin to the Mayor and Councils (1880),[20] it was stated that according to the calculations of the City Engineer and the Superintendent of Sewers, a rise of water of one foot above the salt vegetation of the Fens would occur but rarely; a rise of as much as five feet, if ever, only at intervals of many years; a rise of more than five feet, never. It was assumed that, with the means used to check and break down heavy swells (described in the report), the planted banks of the basin would be little injured by a rise of from one to two feet, and that after the soil at a higher elevation, up to five feet, should be well interwoven with roots of woody vegetation, although some damage from the higher floods might rarely occur, it would not be of an irreparable character.*

But with the quantity of water which will be thrown into the basin under the new Stony-Brook drainage-plan more frequent and deeper floods are to be expected than had thus been provided for. The least of the unpleasant results to follow will be the occasional submergence of roads and walks that have been laid out above the highest previously assumed flood level. This will cause but temporary inconvenience and may be rightly regarded as of no great consequence. It is of much more importance that the higher the water in the basin, in any time of storm, the less effectual will be the precautions which have been taken to prevent a heavy swell from forming and spray from washing the higher parts of the bank, and the longer will the vegetation growing in the lower parts remain soaking in brackish water.

With the dash and undertow of a heavier swell the steeper the upper slopes of the Fenside must be expected to be fretted, undermined and washed away and trees to be loosened at their roots, blown down and thrown out. It may now be thought that this is a matter, also, of but little consequence; that the bank may be mended and new plantings made. But if the trees should have been allowed to grow to good size, all experience shows that such an occurrence would excite much popular indignation.

*The best account of the plan from the engineering point of view is to be found in a paper by E. W. Howe, Esq., C.E., printed by the Boston Society of Civil Engineers, 1881.[21] The expectations above stated as to the amount of water to be provided for in the basin under the arrangements assumed, have thus far been sustained. In the great flood of 1885[22] the water in the basin rose at no time more than three feet above the normal level.

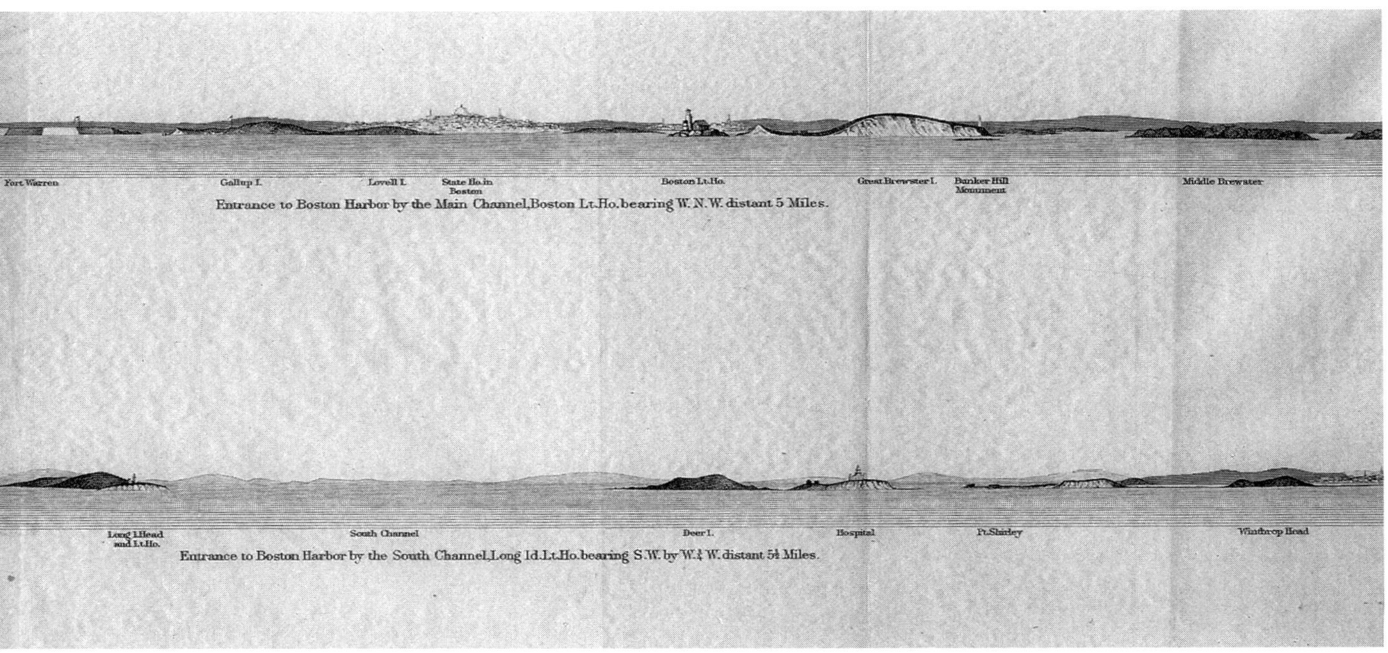

"View of the Entrance to Boston Harbor," from the *Atlantic Coast Pilot* (1879)

Had the requirements now to be made upon the basin been made when the plan was called for, provision would have been advised for them, either by an enlargement of the present basin; by flood basins to be formed higher up the stream, or by a conduit discharging directly into Charles River. But either of these expedients would now be so costly that the adoption of it is only to be expected under the immediate pressure of a public catastrophe.

Presuming that neither will be soon adopted and that the risk must be taken of an occasional soaking of the roots of the Fenside Woods in brackish water, it is probable that the worst injury to be apprehended under the present arrangement might be guarded against in a comparatively inexpensive way by reinforcing with rocks the face of parts of the bank which are from two to seven feet above the level of the Fens. Nothing like a complete paving of the surface would be necessary. Using chiefly rocks as large as could be conveniently handled without a derrick, and placing them with studied irregularity, and not with perfect continuity; training creepers over them and letting trees and underwood grow up between them, they would, after a few years, be inconspicuous. In the end they would give a more natural and agreeable aspect to the bank, while they would prevent land-slides, and any considerable undermining of the trees.

The public needs to be often asked to bear in mind that the cost of the basin in the Back-Bay district, preparing by the Park Department, is a necessary expedient for the economical drainage of another district of the city, parts of which are more than six miles away from the Back Bay.

Tree-Cutting On Franklin Park.

In the proper order of the work of Franklin Park many trees must be removed the coming season. To those who consider this operation without regard to the leading general purposes of the adopted plan of the park, the operation will appear a grievous one. During the last two years the Department has taken much pains to make the public familiar with these purposes. To this end a carefully prepared explanation of them was printed, with a map of the park, which has been circulated in different forms in large numbers.[23] It has been reproduced in the leading daily and weekly newspapers, and copies, on cardboard and in the form of roller-maps, have been hung on the walls of many offices and places of general resort. Several thousand have been distributed to individual addresses. Copies have been posted in the park, and, to aid those who might wish to trace out the plan on the ground, numerous guiding stakes have been set. Not a single remonstrance or objection to the general plan has been made, except where, along its boundaries, it has been supposed that individual interests might have been better promoted.

One feature of the plan, as thus fully made known in advance, is a series of roads and walks through existing woods. In planning these care has been taken that they shall involve the least possible injury to the natural features, and the least possible destruction of the finer and more promising trees. Necessarily many must be taken out to make way for the roads and walks, and more that slopes of natural character may be formed where the existing natural surface has to be broken. Not unfrequently, also, insignificant or decaying and unpromising trees are to be removed that others may be better developed, and that natural features of various kinds may be better brought into view. No trees will be removed at any point without careful consideration.

Respectfully,

FREDERICK LAW OLMSTED,
Landscape Architect Advisory.

The text presented here was published in the *Thirteenth Annual Report of the Board of Commissioners for the Year 1887* (Boston, 1888), pages 52–71.

1. Benjamin Dean (1824–1897), lawyer and Democratic politician, was appointed by Mayor Hugh O'Brien to the Boston park commission is 1885. He previously served in the Massachusetts State Senate from 1862 to 1863 and the U.S. House of Representatives from 1878 to 1879 ("At Break of Day Spirit of Benjamin Dean Passed from Earth," *Boston Daily Globe*, April 9, 1897, p. 8; Edwin M. Bacon, *Boston of To-day: A Glance at Its History and Characteristics* [Boston, 1892], p. 205; see also Frederick Law Olmsted, "On Points of View and Methods of Criticism of Public Works of Landscape Architecture," June 20 and 27, 1885, above).
2. The heavily Republican Board of Aldermen froze much of the park department's budget in 1886 apparently because they distrusted the newly-appointed Democratic park commissioners to allocate funds responsibly (see FLO to Charles Eliot, July 20, 1886, n. 7, above).
3. The Boston Memorial Association wrote a letter to the park commissioners, dated April 30, 1887, and included in the *Thirteenth Annual Report*, asking the commissioners to consider reforesting the Boston Harbor Islands (*Thirteenth Annual Report, Boston Department of Parks,1887*, pp. 44–45; see also FLO to Mariana Griswold Van Rensselaer, May 17, 1887, n. 8, above).
4. Olmsted refers to the pier that was part of Marine Park in Boston, which Olmsted originally referred to as Pleasure Bay. Designed by Olmsted with John C. Olmsted and Charles Eliot, Pleasure Bay included a long "strand" and a recreational pier. The protected "bay," suitable for swimming and boating, resulted from enlarging Dorchester Point in South Boston and linking it to Castle Island. Marine Park was not completed until the 1920s (Charles Eliot Diary, Feb. 3, 1884, p. 104, FLLHU; *Thirteenth Annual Report, Boston Department of Parks,1887*, pp. 16–17; Frederick Law Olmsted, "Cut of City Point and Castle Island," Dec. 1, 1883; Cynthia Zaitzevsky, *Frederick Law Olmsted and the Boston Park System* [Cambridge, Mass., 1982], p. 91).
5. The *Puritan, Mayflower* and *Volunteer* were yachts designed by the Boston naval architect Edward Burgess. They were successfully used to defend America's Cup in 1885, 1886, and 1887, respectively. The New York Yacht Club first won the America's Cup trophy from the Royal Fleet Squadron of Great Britain in 1851. Newspapers around the country covered the America's Cup races, and Burgess's successful yacht designs were a source of national pride ("Edward Burgess, Boston's Great Yacht Designer, is Dead,"

Boston Daily Advertiser, July 13, 1891; Howard I. Chapelle, *The History of American Sailing Ships* [New York, 1982], p. 341; Winfield M. Thompson and Thomas W. Lawson, *The Lawson History of the America's Cup* [Sheffield, U.K., 1986], pp. 44–45; Edward Burgess, *American and English Yachts* [New York, 1887]).

6. J. W. Hayward and F. W. J. Hurst sent a letter to Edward Burgess on December 23, 1887, with a check for $10,172.25, establishing the Burgess Testimonial Fund. The letter contained many praises for Burgess's yacht designs, noting that the national fund was created "in grateful recognition of your splendid genius and careful study, resulting in the modeling of the yachts Puritan, Mayflower and Volunteer, which so successfully, in turn, defended the America's Cup. . . . no event has in late years redounded more to the credit of this country abroad, reflecting as it did the earnest concentration of ingenuity of our people when occasion should require, and forcing the acknowledgment of the English press and people that they have met more than their match on the element upon which they held themselves pre-eminent" ("Modest Mr. Burgess," *New York Times*, Jan. 14, 1888, p. 3).
7. The Secretary of the Navy, William Collins Whitney, asked Burgess, among others, to sit on the United States Naval Board, a committee responsible for selecting "suitable designs for a 6,000-ton armored cruiser and an armored vessel of the same size" ("The 6000-Ton Cruiser," *Washington Post*, June 15, 1887, p. 2; "Edward Burgess, Boston's Great Yacht Designer, is Dead," *Boston Daily Advertiser*, July 13, 1891).
8. Republican Senator Eugene Hale of Maine introduced S. 1441 on January 16, 1888, and Democratic Representative Washington C. Whitthorne of Tennessee introduced H.R. 1847 on January 4, 1888. The bills proposed the creation of a naval reserve force, or militia. In 1887, Secretary Whitney had assembled a group of ex-naval officers, yachtsmen (possibly including Edward Burgess), and other interested parties to see if they would support the creation of a federal naval reserve force. Although the Naval Reserve would not be formally organized until 1916, states created naval reserve units as part of their militias before that date. Massachusetts became the first state to organize such a force in 1888 (S. 1441, 50th Congress, 1st Session, Jan. 16, 1888; H. R. 1847, 50th Congress, 1st Session, Jan. 4, 1888; "News," *New York Times*, Sept. 19, 1887, p. 4; Jack Sweetman, *American Naval History* [Annapolis, 2002], pp. 88, 121).
9. A portion of the Boston Memorial Association's letter to the park board read, "The Boston Memorial Association respectfully calls the attention of the Boston Parks Commissioners to the importance of restoring the islands in the harbor to their original beauty by the judicious formation of plantations of trees. . . . Would it not add very much to the beauty of the harbor if they could be properly planted; and is it not practicable for the City of Boston, or for private enterprise, or for both combined, to begin on some plan either permanent or experimental, with the above end in view?" (*Thirteenth Annual Report, Boston Department of Parks,1887*, pp. 44–45; see also FLO to Mariana Griswold Van Rensselaer, May 17, 1887, above).
10. Holl is an obsolete spelling of "hole," and Olmsted is referring to Woods Hole, Massachusetts (*OED*; see FLO to Robert Douglas, Dec. 5, 1887, above).
11. Robert Douglas (1813–1896) lived in Waukegan, Illinois. On the sandy flats two miles north of his home, he conducted an experiment planting "practically every variety of evergreen then in cultivation and several species of deciduous trees." These species included several varieties of pine and spruce trees, with the Australian and Scotch pines proving the most adaptable to those conditions (Emil Bolinger, "Pines That Grow Well in Lake Forest," *Billerica*, April, 1915, p. 11; see also FLO to Robert Douglas, Dec. 5, 1887, above).
12. The Kansas City, Fort Scott & Gulf Railroad Company had headquarters in Boston, as well as in Kansas City, Missouri, and Kansas City, Kansas. The company's president Horatio Hollis Hunnewell hired Robert Douglas in 1879 to plant a square mile of land on the Kansas prairie. The experiment was designed to see how well certain trees

could be established in those conditions (*First Annual Report of the Board of Railroad Commissioners, for the Year Ending December 31, 1883. State of Kansas* [Topeka, 1884], p. 143; *Transactions of the Massachusetts Horticultural Society, For the Year 1879* [Boston, 1879], p. 133; Sherry H. Olson, "Commerce and Conservation: The Railroad Experience," *Forest History*, Jan. 1966, p. 5; Roy V. Scott, "American Railroads and the Promotion of Forestry," *Journal of Forest History*, vol. 23, April 1979, p. 78).

13. Olmsted summarizes a proposed contract sent to him by Douglas earlier in December that offered to charge sixty dollars per acre for planting four hundred acres, guaranteeing at least two thousand trees per acre. The park commissions ultimately voted not to give Douglas the job (Robert Douglas to FLO, Dec. 1887; FLO to Robert Douglas, March 27, 1888, A2: 303–4, OAR/LC; see also FLO to Robert Douglas, Dec. 5, 1887, above).
14. The Boston Asylum for Indigent Boys and the Boston Farm School were located on Thompson's Island. A quarantine hospital was on Gallop's Island, and a city almshouse was on Rainsford Island. A penal institution was on Deer Island (M. F. Sweetser, *King's Handbook of Boston Harbor* [Boston, 1888], pp. 173, 191, 204, 221).
15. Olmsted refers to the establishment of Merrymount Park, overlooking the Quincy Bay portion of Boston Harbor. Charles Francis Adams donated the land for the park in 1885 (*First Annual Report of the Trustees of Public Reservations* 1891[Boston, 1892], p. 34; FLO to Charles Francis Adams, Jr., Nov. 29, 1881 [*Papers of FLO*, 7: 566]; see FLO to Robert Douglas, Dec. 5, 1887, above).
16. See Frederick Law Olmsted, "The Beacon Street Plan," [Dec. 4, 1886,] above.
17. The Boston park commissioners used "Riverdale" to refer to the park corridor between Brookline and Longwood Avenues, which was later known, with the section between Longwood and Huntington avenues, as the Riverway. There is no record in the published park reports of the names "Longview" or "Rumford" (*Eleventh Annual Report of the Board of Commissioners of the Department of Parks, For the Year 1885* [Boston, 1886], p. 15; Edwin Munroe Bacon, *The Book of Boston* [Boston, 1916], p. 151).
18. In 1880 an unsigned article in the *American Architect and Building News* objected to Olmsted's plans for the Back Bay, especially the proposed salt marsh. The Back Bay Fens landscape challenged contemporary assumptions of both municipal park design and flood control engineering ("The Back Bay Park in Boston," *American Architect and Building News*, March 20, 1880, pp. 117–18; Frederick Law Olmsted, "Improvement of the Back-Bay, Boston," April 3, 1880 [*Papers of FLO*, 7: 481–84]; see also FLO to Edward Mott Moore, Aug. 5, 1888, n. 6, below).
19. This appears to be the first time Olmsted suggests calling the Back Bay project the Back Bay Fens. He had been consistently arguing that the landscape should not be called a "park" because it would not resemble other public landscapes in Boston, such as the Common or the Public Garden, which the public associated with that word. Olmsted also wanted to reserve the use of the word "park" for larger, pastoral landscapes, such as Franklin Park in Boston. He offered several suggestions for naming the Back Bay landscape before settling on the "Back Bay Fens" (Frederick Law Olmsted, *Report of the Landscape Architect*, Dec. 24, 1883, above; FLO to Charles H. Dalton, Jan. 18, 1884, above).
20. See Frederick Law Olmsted, "Suggestions for the Improvement of Muddy River," Dec. 1880 (*Papers of FLO*, 7: 517–22).
21. E. W. Howe, "The Back Bay Park, Boston, Speech Read Before the Boston Society of Civil Engineers, March 16, 1881," *Proceedings of the American Society of Civil Engineers*, Jan.–Dec. 1881 (New York, 1881).
22. The flooding took place in February 1886, not 1885 (see FLO to Charles Eliot, Feb. 25, 1886, n. 11, above).

23. See Frederick Law Olmsted, "Notes on the Plan of Franklin Park and Related Matters," 1886 (*Papers of FLO*, SS1: 460–534).

To William McMillan

2[d] Jan. 1888.

Dear Mr McMillan;

I have yours of 31st, ult[o].

I should say the more thoroughly non-committal the Report as to the new park proposition, the better. Why not simply say that it is under careful consideration?

The intention of my last letter was, I said, simply to express a tendency of judgment with indecision. I shall be extremely reluctant to give up the original idea which I think would work into a park worth a great deal more, relatively to its cost, than anything else I can imagine.[1]

Shall we be perfectly sure, when we are obliged to come to a decision, that every expedient has been exhausted for providing an opening into the Lake? That anything of that kind is out of the question? It would be such an awful waste of opportunity to assume this that I don't think that I shall do it without coming again to the ground nor without the counsel of some expert of special qualifications whose judgment of the question we, and the public, ought to accept as conclusive — relieving us of responsibility. It is absolutely the most difficult of all branches of engineering and most engineers are prone to keep on the safe side by giving unfavorable opinions upon any new project. If Cap[tn] Eads[2] was alive I would think it well for the city to take his opinion at any necessary cost rather than abandon the idea. Neither you nor I want to take a professional responsibility on a question of that kind. All we could do would be to invent and, if our inventions looked to us promising, submit them to authorities.

I should say, off hand, that you were right in proposing to go just back of the rail roads.[3] (You say nothing of going further out on the Lake shore.) Yet I feel that it would never do to be as near even as that to a grand natural circumstance and make nothing of it. I should make a spacious outlet upon the Lake a feature of the plan.

Suppose a structure built upon the Lake of the general character of a New York ferry slip. Suppose a double line of piles, driven deeply on each side of the slip, braced and bolted together, and the interspace filled with stone. Reinforce the heads with close groups of piles. Built of rough timber and rough stone, boulders or quarried, the cost would not be appalling.

Suppose the two piers thus formed to extend out to where 3, (4 or 5) feet {of} water could be had at low stages of the Lake. Suppose them to be carried several hundred feet landward from the strand, well inside the dunes, then reaching a canal. This is the "slip". Suppose you excavate within the slip sufficiently to make a level floor, say three feet, below the ordinary low water level of the Lake. Make a timber and plank floor at this level, bolting to intermediate piles if required. Suppose a broad dyke, as strong as you can well make, enclosing your landward operations, the West arm of which would be about where the dune is. (I mean only the continuous hillock of sand) the "slip" running through it. Suppose the inner walls of the slip at this point to be ten or twenty feet apart—sufficient for a small boat to pass through it. Let there be here a very strongly constructed gate, so that, in {*summer*} when the Lake is at an extraordinary height it can be shut out. Suppose inside this gate a lock to provide for ordinary fluctuations–the whole arrangement making it practicable to keep the interior water within certain limits of fluctuation; the water within being commonly at the Lake level but controllable when the Lake is excessively high or low.

For the present let the stability of your dyke be assumed.

In certain storms the "slip", which we may now call the gullet, would sand up. But it would be easily cleared and so long as the deposit {. . .}[4] harm?

Everything would depend on the piles would it not? Let them be as strong and as deeply driven as practicable and loaded with stone. Could they be undermined? Could they be lifted by ice? Would sea and ice crush and break them {*destructively*}?

Consider this with regard to what has been done with piles at various points on the Atlantic. There are three pile piers at Coney Island two of iron piles, one of wood. They stand unharmed while every structure on lines parallel with the shore have been {*smashed*} to flinders.

A structure on the same principles, having in view a deep broad channel, for ships, would be very costly. But made to accommodate steam launches and row boats, and to serve as an inlet and outlet for a small and not violent stream of water, in fresh water, with no teredo[5] {*to bother*}, need it be excessively costly?

Yours Truly

Fred[k] Law Olmsted.

I would not have what I say to you while we are in the inquiry stage, go before anyone else.

The text presented here is from a letterpress copy of a handwritten letter signed on the original in Olmsted's hand: A2: 150–53, OAR/LC. After Olmsted submitted his preliminary recommendations for a park on the south side of Buffalo in April 1887, the park commissioners commissioned him to develop a "definite plan for the contemplated park" (FLO to Sherman S. Jewett, April 11, 1887, above; "Resolution of the Board of Commissioners to hire Frederick Law Olmsted," Nov. 29, 1887 [Copy sent to Olmsted], B47: #700, OAR/LC).

1. In Olmsted's letter of December 21, 1887, he explained to McMillan what would be needed to create an opening to Lake Erie at the proposed South Park site. He asked for a survey of the land to the west of the railroad along the shore in order to investigate whether it was feasible to make use of it for the park. Olmsted was concerned about flooding and storm damage that naturally occurred at lower elevations on the site. He later suggested in his October 1888 report that if naturally occurring banks of sediment did not prevent flooding, then a wall of boulders could be built for increased protection. A last resort would be a four and a half foot tall levee. For a detailed description of Olmsted's plan for the lakeside park see F. L. & J. C. Olmsted, *Plan for a Public Park on the Flats South of Buffalo*, Oct. 1, 1888 (*Papers of FLO*, SS1: 576–96) (FLO To William McMillan, Dec. 21, 1887, A2: 130–32, OAR/LC).
2. James Buchanan Eads (1820–1887) was a renowned American engineer and inventor. One of his projects was a system of jetties designed to keep the Mississippi River shipping channels open by controlling the locations of sedimentation. A portion of this system was completed near New Orleans in the 1870s (*DAB*).
3. That is, the three tracks of railroad located roughly a mile to the east of the shore (plan 718-15. F. L. & J. C. Olmsted, City of Buffalo, Park Commission, Design Map of South Park (1888), NPS/FLONHS).
4. A line of text here has almost completely faded from the manuscript.
5. A shipworm responsible for destroying submerged timbers in ships, piers, and sea-dikes (*OED*).

To William Caleb Loring[1]

2d April, 1888.

Dear Mr Loring;

John has gone to your place today taking the maps and I cannot reckon exactly what reducing the rock six feet would accomplish but I judge that six feet would not be enough to give you the advantage you imagine.

Before giving my reasons I may say in general that except for the consideration of expense I am convinced that the highest place that we have considered for your house, provided you had the outworks that we proposed, would have been much the most satisfactory to you, except only because the approaches and outworks would have cost too much. In this judgment I take fully into consideration Mrs Loring's liking to step quickly from the house into the service garden. I do not think that in practice there would be much to choose in that respect while in others there would be a good deal.

I consider that when you concluded to take the site last selected for your house you did so partly because of what you thought its greater convenience; partly because you thought that it would cost you less to build than that on the height; *accepting for these reasons the disadvantage of a comparatively confined situation and a narrow and one-sided outlook*. I have been inclined to think that you overestimated the comparative convenience of the lower site, not sufficiently

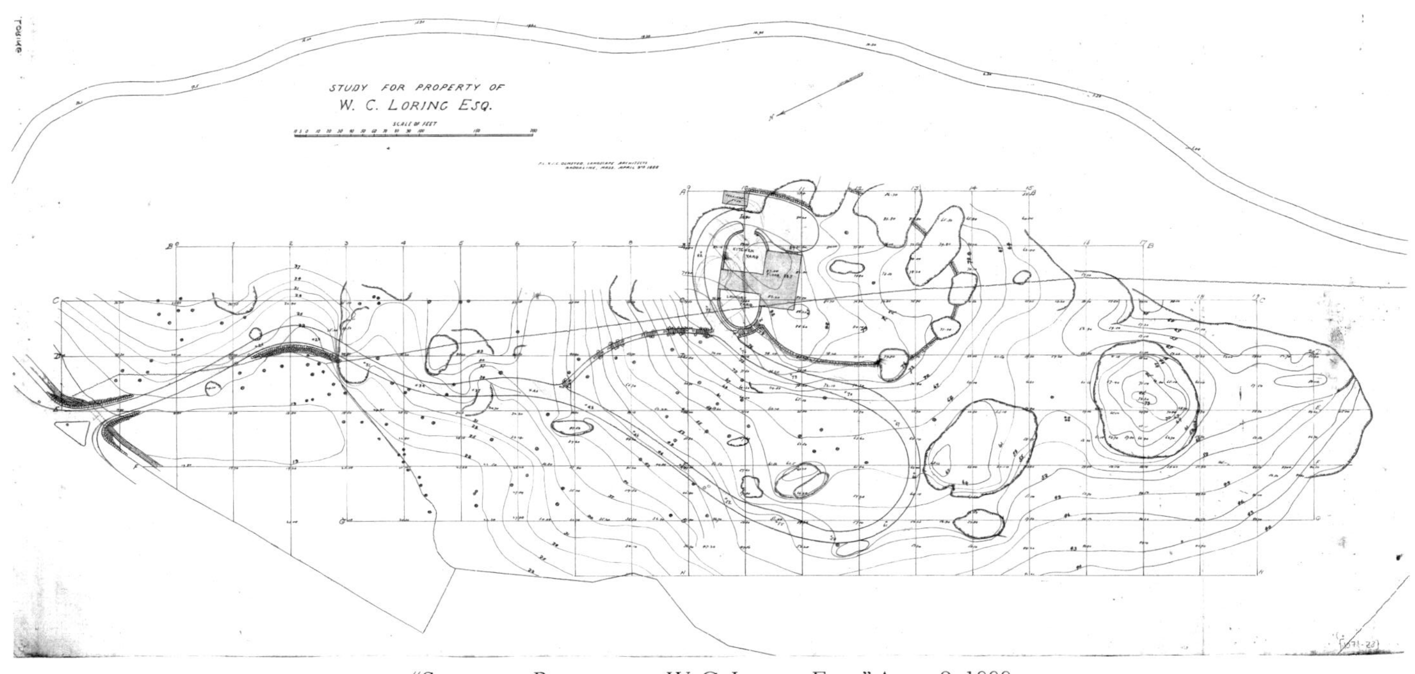

"Study for Property of W. C. Loring Esq.," April 9, 1888

Grounds of W. C. Loring Estate, c. 1916

realizing what would be gained by the snug arrangement of outworks that we had devised for the upper place. I have also been inclined to fear that you would never be quite satisfied with what you have had in view and that you would be tempted little by little to lessen your unsatisfied sense by after-improvements, the cost of which, being carried out in a desultory way and piece meal, would make the lower site the more expensive of the two. Something like this I have found to be a common course of prudent men in dealing with country places. But all depends on your personality. You might find that what you have had in view would exactly suit you. I might be satisfied with it, but I don't think that most men or most women would, and that you will note this suggestion of removing part of the rock immediately in your front makes me feel to be a little more probable.

Now, as to this question. If you are to have a body of low bushes to look upon and over in place of the rock they should have generally about three feet of loam and soil between them and the underlying ledge, otherwise just when you want them to be most surely fresh and cheering, (i.e. in very dry hot weather) they will be weak and sickly in appearance. Suppose that you confine your selection to shrubs not likely ever to grow above four feet high I should think that it would be a large amount of rock that would have to be taken out (in order that the tops of your bushes would not come too high), and that it would be years before the result would be quite congruous with the general natural aspect of your scenery. It rather seems to me, though I do not say so with perfect confidence, that it would

ENTRANCE AND PORTE COCHÈRE OF HOUSE, W. C. LORING ESTATE, C. 1916

be better to let your outlook be contracted in that direction, accept the rock as an important feature in your composition, lessen the apparent barrenness and aridity of the situation by a skirting of bushes and by leading vines, rooting at some distance from its shallow borders, over the less interesting parts of it, and then aiming at a character in what would stand for a lawn on its right that would not be inharmonious with its wildness.

I believe that this is the first time in forty years where a choice has had to be made between two neighboring sites for a dwelling, and my advice has been asked, that it has not been given in favor of the lower of the two. I ask myself how it comes to be otherwise in this case, for I have never had a doubt about it from the moment I approached the upper place of yours. The answer seems to be that an affair *first rate of its kind* can be had at a certain expense in this upper place; an affair of very distinct and complete and unquestionable advantages which no man, whatever his personal tastes, could help being much pleased with, while in the lower side-hill place, however nice and agreeable and convenient it may be, one will always have a sense of its not being perfect *of its kind* and a wish that the natural conditions had been a little different, so as to give a more direct, broader and more balanced outlook and either more or less show of rock, and, if more, a disposition of it with which the house would seem better compared.

If you ask why I said that I might be better satisfied with it than most men, I suppose that the answer is that I have a somewhat morbidly retiring and seclusive disposition, and, being an old man, my likings are better disciplined to my necessities than I expect other peoples to be.

You will not think that I am disposed to make you dissatisfied with your choice. As you have asked me *personally* to give you my opinion, I have tried to do so frankly and fully. I don't think your choice is a bad one but it involves the acceptance of certain drawbacks to which you must reconcile yourself. It is perfectly reasonable to do so.

Yours Truly

Fred[k] Law Olmsted

The text presented here is from a letterpress copy of a handwritten letter signed on the original in Olmsted's hand: A2: 325–29, OAR/LC. On January 4, 1887, William C. Loring asked Olmsted's advice as to the placement of a house he was planning to build at Prides Crossing, near Beverley, Massachusetts. Loring wanted to take an active role in the project, writing to Olmsted, "I want a simple place. In the general arrangement I should like your advice. But I want to make the place myself, after, with your aid, I have chosen the site for the house and the lay out of the avenue." Two sites near a knoll were considered, one on top and one just below. Loring wrote that he and his wife Susan preferred the higher location but felt the site work required would be expensive. The Lorings chose the upper site, however, as Olmsted advises here. The shingle style house designed by William Ralph Emerson was completed in 1893 (William C. Loring to FLO, Jan. 4, 1887; William C. Loring to FLO and JCO, Feb. 15, 1888; William C. Loring to FLO and JCO, Feb. 17, 1888; William C. Loring to JCO and FLO, [1888]; FLO and JCO to Charles F. Jackson, June 15, 1888, A2: 601, OAR/LC; William C. Loring to JCO, June 18, 1888; Susan M. Loring to FLO and JCO, Aug. 14, 1888; plans 1071-z12, 1071-z8, and 1071-z52, NPS/FLONHS; Cynthia Zaitzevsky, "Emerson, William Ralph" in *Macmillan Encyclopedia of Architects* [New York, 1982], pp. 24–25).

1. William Caleb Loring (1851–1930) was a lawyer in Boston and was appointed to the Massachusetts Supreme Court in 1899. He married Susan Mason in 1883, and the family spent their winters in Boston and summers in Prides Crossing, where Loring farmed and gardened and raised pedigreed cattle (Charles Henry Pope and Katharine Peabody Loring, *Loring Genealogy* [Cambridge, Mass., 1917], p. 336; "William C. Loring, Noted Jurist, Dies" *New York Times*, Sept. 9, 1930, p. 27).

To Mariana Griswold Van Rensselaer

Boston, 6th April 1888.

Dear Mrs Van Renssalaer,

I learn that Dana[1] intends to ask you to write a series of papers upon the text of the report of the expert Commission of this year upon the vault of the Assembly Chamber.[2]

I went to Albany some time ago and had a few words with these Commissioners. Bogart, (State Engineer), Clark, (railroad iron bridge builder), and Upjohn,[3] (who took an active part in the demonstration of architects versus Eidlitz, Richardson & Co *in re* change of style).[4] From all I saw and heard the impression came that no one of them was able to make a thorough study of the matter and that the result most to be feared would come through their desire to avoid committing themselves too positively on points beyond their reach.

Afterwards a report was made by Upjohn, speaking, as he represented, for his associates, one of whom was absent in Florida, which seemed to me shallow and rash. I was told yesterday by a close personal friend of Mr Bogart's that he repudiated Upjohn's report; that a final report would have to be agreed upon within a few days and that Bogart meant that this report should be confined if possible to the question:—Is the vault safe? Can it be made safe without being rebuilt? The answer being to the last, "it cannot". The question what shall be done, will, if Bogart can manage it, be avoided; though Upjohn means to have a flat ceiling ordered (perhaps an iron suspended ceiling as intended by Fuller, against which we protested). And my informant added, (no doubt representing Bogart's mind):— "The members of the Assembly almost without exception, *hate* a stone, vaulted ceiling and they hate Eidlitz, and they mean to have a flat ceiling more like what they are accustomed to and have been accustomed to admire in meeting houses and court houses".

You can hardly imagine how strongly the idea that a stone vault is suitable only to prisons and tombs and that lathe and plaster, or something indistinguishable from lathe plaster, though with their imitative decorative forms of ornament—forms imitative of stone construction—are the proper respectable and stylish materials for the ceilings of buildings of luxury is fixed in the mind of most of us practical, common sense Americans. There is a little bank in the Bowery, the Board room of which has a vaulted ceiling.[5] Eidlitz once, when we had come upon evidences of this feeling among the members of the legislature, told me that directors of the bank had consulted him about having a false ceiling of lathe plaster put under this vault, to relieve the gloom which oppressed them when they looked up and saw stones hanging over them, as if they were in a prison. Vaulted ceilings had affected me in such a way when I first came under them that it was not till after I had many evidences at Albany of what I am telling you that I could realize that men could be wholly insensible to their nobleness. But you had better have it in your mind that that is, and has been, the case and

View of the Assembly Chamber of the New York State Capitol in Albany, designed by Leopold Eidlitz, c. 1880

also consider that if the legislature had been all the time strongly under the influence of the sentiment I have tried to suggest (hating that which tends to awe), and wanted to bring about a state of things which would serve them as a sufficient apology with their constituents for tearing down the vault and putting a meeting house ceiling in place of it, they would have taken precisely the course that has been taken since 1881.

I suppose it to be true that in the construction of so large a vault as that in question, composed of such a large number of blocks and with so many joints and interstices to be filled with mortar, it is impossible to calculate in advance with *precision*, just what is necessary to keep the structure hanging well together and in perfect equilibrium. Consequently then it is to be expected that when otherwise complete, or nearly so, expedients shall be used for making good what was wanting in *precision* of the original calculations of design; that such has been the general course, and that many instances are known of strengthening and balancing operations used after the completion of a main structure by architects of high reputations and whose works have been regarded with respect and pride for many generations. I do not know accurately that such is the case but it seems to me that I have known it. And I suppose that we (E. I. & Co)[6] have proposed and advised and wished nothing that would put the question of what should have been done with the Assembly vault on a different footing. I don't believe that the report of the present Commission any more than that of 1882[7] will give any reason for thinking that *if the vault had been left under proper control of the architects*, there would be the slightest reason for taking it down, or that there can now, because of the refusal of the legislature to act on the advice of the architects, be any reason, if it is taken down, for not rebuilding it.

It would seem to me that it would be most disgraceful to the State of New York to proceed upon what I believe to be at present the ruling motive and spirit of the legislature in dealing with the question. At any rate that a hasty decision of the question at the close of a session would be a blot upon republican government.

We, the responsible representatives of architectural art, in the premises, cannot very well *urge* this view, but I think it is our duty in some way to see the legislature is not allowed to act without having it brought to their attention, and, if the report of the Commission is what I expect, we shall see that it is, as promptly as possible.

Yours Very Truly

Fred[k] Law Olmsted

The text presented here is a signed letter in Olmsted's hand. In September 1876 Olmsted and architects Leopold Eidlitz and H. H. Richardson replaced Thomas Fuller as architects for the New York State Capitol building in Albany. With Olmsted acting as advisor on the project, Richardson designed the exterior and the interior of the south side, and Eidlitz designed the interior of the north side, including the Assembly chamber (*Papers of FLO*, 7: 7–8; Mariana Griswold Van Rensselaer, *Henry Hobson Richardson*, pp. 73–77; see also Frederick Law Olmsted, *New York State Capitol Testimony*, March 6, 1877 [*Papers of FLO*, 7: 288–304]; FLO to Charles Eliot Norton, April 2, 1876 [*Papers of FLO*, 7: 188–90).

1. Charles Anderson Dana (1819–1897) was a newspaper editor, first of Horace Greeley's *New York Tribune*, and, as of 1868, of the *New York Sun*, which he owned and edited until his death. He and Olmsted had been friends since they edited *Putnam's Monthly Magazine* together in 1855. Dana commissioned articles on the debate over the Albany Capitol from Van Rensselaer, which were published that May (*DAB*; *Papers of FLO*, 5: 6; "The Ceiling of the Assembly Chamber," *New York Sun*, May 6, 1888, p. 16; "The Ceiling of the Assembly Chamber," ibid., May 13, 1888, p. 16).
2. Eidlitz designed for the Assembly chamber a ribbed groin vault ceiling that was fifty-six feet high and painted in patterns of gold, red, and blue. Completed in 1879, the ceiling began to crack in 1880 and eventually leaked. Reports and investigations were made in 1882 on how to fix the ceiling. Eidlitz suggested that the equilibrium of the vaults could be corrected, but nothing was done, and in 1888 chunks of stone began to fall from the ceiling and the room was declared unsafe. The legislature then invited outside architects to write a report with recommendations. At the time of this correspondence, Olmsted had not read the report, which was still being prepared. His information came from letters written by Eidlitz, who reported to him on the progress of the commission's investigation. The report was published a few weeks later as "Commission Concerning the Assembly Chamber of the New Capitol, Final Report" (Albany, April 26, 1888) and was reprinted as J. Bogart, T. C. Clarke, and R. M. Upjohn, "Report to the Governor on the Condition of the Assembly Chamber Vaulting at Albany," *American Architect and*

Building News, June 9, 1888, p. 270. The report recommended the vault be dismantled and replaced with a coffered wood ceiling, which was later done (K. E. Holliday, *Leopold Eidlitz*, pp. 120–29; C. R. Roseberry, *Capitol Story*, pp. 83–89; Leopold Eidlitz to FLO, Feb. 4, 1888; Leopold Eidlitz to FLO, March 24, 1888; Leopold Eidlitz to FLO, March 27, 1888; Leopold Eidlitz to FLO, March 29, 1888).

3. Civil Engineers John Bogart (1836–1920) and Thomas Curtis Clarke (1827–1901), and architect Richard Mitchell Upjohn (1828–1903) were asked by the New York State Legislature to ascertain the amount and type of work needed to repair or replace the vaulted ceiling. They later were the designers of the flat, coffered ceiling that replaced it (*DAB*; Joy Kestenbaum, "John Bogart," in Charles A. Birnbaum and Stephanie S. Foell, eds., *Shaping the American Landscape* [Charlottesville, Va., 2009], pp. 28-32; "Thomas Curtis Clarke Dead," *New York Times*, June 17, 1901; *Documents of the Assembly of the State of New York, 111th Session*, "Final Report of the Commission Concerning the Assembly Chamber of the New Capitol," April 26, 1888 [Albany, 1888]).
4. When Olmsted, Richardson, and Eidlitz replaced Thomas Fuller as architects for the Capitol in 1876, Fuller complained that he had been unfairly treated and should have been given the chance to make needed changes in the design himself. Many members of the New York chapter of the American Institute of Architects, including Upjohn, supported Fuller and urged his reinstatement. The "change in style" mentioned here refers to the new, Romanesque design by Richardson and Eidlitz, which transformed and replaced Fuller's original Renaissance style plans (J. K. Ochsner, *H. H. Richardson*, pp. 157–60; K. E. Holliday, *Leopold Eidlitz*, pp. 112–20; FLO to Mariana Griswold Van Rensselaer, Dec. 21, 1887, above).
5. That is, the Dry Dock Savings Bank, designed by Leopold Eidlitz and built in 1875. The bank was located at East Third Street and the Bowery and included a high vaulted ceiling supported by four piers, as did the Assembly chamber on a much larger scale (K. E. Holliday, *Leopold Eidlitz*, pp. 108, 124–25; "Bowery Building Conveyed by Bank," *New York Times*, Nov. 9, 1954, p. 46).
6. Olmsted refers informally to "Eidlitz, Richardson & Company," of which Olmsted was a part. This was a partnership formed specifically for the Albany Capitol advisory work in 1876. Olmsted referring to it here as "E. I. & Co." may represent a slip of an "I" for the "R;" or he meant to use the "I" as a pronoun, i.e., "Eidlitz, myself, & Co." (C. R. Roseberry, *Capitol Story* [New York, 1982], p. 33).
7. After the commissioners assigned to study the Assembly chamber in 1882 published their report, Eidlitz, Richardson, and Olmsted published a rebuttal. The commissioners argued that the foundation of the building had been settling unevenly, and therefore recentering the equilibrium of the vaults would only be a temporary solution, since future settling would cause the ceiling to become unstable again. They suggested instead that the vaulted ceiling be removed and replaced by a flat, wood ceiling. Eidlitz, Richardson, and Olmsted responded by stating that the survey was not conclusive. They argued that the fractured stone should be replaced and properly pointed, and "the equilibrium of the vaults should be reviewed and, if need be, corrected" (W. P. Trowbridge, Charles Babcock, and George B. Post, "Report of the Commissioners to Examine and Report on the New Capitol Building, Appointed by the Governor Pursuant to Section 9 of Chapter 295 of the Laws of 1882," [Albany, Sept. 26, 1882]; Leopold Eidlitz, H. H. Richardson, and Frederick L. Olmsted, "The New Capitol, An Examination of the Grounds on Which the Security of the Assembly Chamber is Held to be in Question," [Albany, Nov. 17, 1882]).

To Mariana Griswold Van Rensselaer

9th April, 1888.

Dear Mrs. Van Rensselaer,

I have yours of 7th, thank you.[1] I wrote you long and hastily with interruptions, while at a meeting of the Boston Park Board, thinking that if you were to take up the Capitol matter I might help you to get sooner on the track of what was passing. Something of what I said was hearsay & something came to me in confidence and I gave it to you only as suggestive of lines of inquiry.

The report of the Commission will not be favorable in the sense you hope but, compared with the report of the Commission of 1882 it will show that Eidlitz, Richardson & Co. at that time took the right view and that if their advice had been followed there would have been no occasion — no excuse — for taking down the vault.[2] It simply needed then slight repairs and adjustments such as it was no discredit to its architects that it should need. The advice then given has been annually repeated until this year, when notice was given by Eidlitz, Richardson & Co. that through continued neglect to take their advice, the legislature had allowed such progress in dilapidation to accrue that it must be warned that it was no longer safe to sit under the vault. I feel very sure that neither of these Commissions, either those of 1882 or those of 1888, has been able to examine

Portrait of H. H. Richardson, frontispiece of *Henry Hobson Richardson and His Works* by Mariana Griswold Van Rensselaer (New York, 1888)

PORTRAIT OF H. H. RICHARDSON BY HUBERT VON HERKOMER, 1886

the matter nearly as closely as to form as good an opinion upon it as the architects themselves. (On questions of construction Mr Richardson always deferred to Mr Eidlitz and he asked Mr Eidlitz to take upon himself the subconstruction of the Senate Chamber and he did so, though it has often been said that this subconstruction stood firm while Mr Eidlitz's is assumed to have failed. But before signing our joint report in 1882 on the condition of the vault of the Assembly Chamber,[3] Richardson looked into the question as searchingly as he could and was perfectly satisfied with the statements of that report, even enthusiastically so.)

There will be no occasion for you to give an opinion upon a question of construction, except perhaps to say whether the report of facts of the present Commission sustains or otherwise the theory of the facts presented by the architects in 1882.

If you write upon the subject you should certainly question Eidlitz. Do not hesitate to write to him asking him to come to your house, or anywhere else you please, to suit your convenience. (He is liable to be out of town.)

I was at the Sargent's last night and saw the portrait you are to have of Richardson.[4] I congratulate you. It is the man as he was rarely, at his best. It will add to the value of the book. It will add to the veneration in which Richardson's works will be held. I speak, of course, only of the expression of character. How

PORTRAIT OF H. H. RICHARDSON BY GEORGE COLLINS COX, N.D.

much better in this respect than Herkomer's.[5] How much better than that published by the *Architect*.[6]

As I told you that Mr. Frelinghuysen[7] declined to have communication with us, I must tell you that we have since heard from Miss Frelinghuysen and that John has been up to meet her at Lenox and we are to look after the planting of the place, as I knew that she wished.

Your Landscape Gardening no VI is very satisfying to me.[8] I suppose that I have spoiled quires of paper, laboring vainly to say what you say fully in half a page and as if it were as easy as falling off a log. And it seems to be that one has only to read it and accept it. Yet hardly anybody I have to deal with does accept it. How can you account for the rarity of a taste for organized beauty among people otherwise cultivated? You cannot know how great the rarity of it. But where were you, in respect to gardening art and its principles, a few years ago? I am strongly inclined to think that a taste for organized beauty in gardening affairs is much less common now than it was fifty years ago and Prof^r Sargent agrees with me. Cultivated people are much less open to be reasoned with, much more disinclined to give questions of gardening thorough consideration. I suppose that we must think that *fashion* (meaning a somewhat deeper current than we often have in mind when we speak of fashion) has been running another way. Perhaps interest in "decorative art" has crowded out interest in landscape art. "Decorative art" as a fad has about run its course, I suppose, with those who establish fashions. As it goes out landscape art may come in. It is not in yet. I really think that Garden & Forest,[9] though will, hereafter, be thought to have marked the dawn of a new day. And it gives me some satisfaction to think that though I seem to myself to have been all my life swimming against the tide I shall not sink before having seen it turn. By the way we have had five young men coming to us for "advice" about entering our profession, all referring to your articles.[10] All your bread thrown on the waters is not wasted, plainly.[11]

Most of them were very unpromising but the only one to whom we gave much direct encouragement or proposed to assist, was a man of near thirty who is studying at the Bussey[12] while supporting himself by woodcutting (not a la Gladstone[13] but engraving) in Boston.

Sincerely Yours

Fred^k Law Olmsted.

The text presented here is a signed letter in Olmsted's hand.

1. In her letter, Van Rensselaer wrote that Charles Dana had not yet asked her to write a series on the ceiling of the Assembly chamber of the New York State Capitol, as Olmsted had suggested to her (see FLO to Mariana Griswold Van Rensselaer, April 6, 1888, above). She added that if she were asked, however, she would use some of the information and arguments Olmsted had provided. She wrote: "I am glad to hear that the matter is not so bad as the papers have said and hope most sincerely that the right thing can be done with regard to it. It will indeed be a blow to the most vital interests of art in this country if such should not be the case. The pandering to unworthy feelings in the part of our legislators would not be so bad, even, as the slur on the architectural profession." Articles about the ceiling of the Assembly chamber did appear in the *New York Sun* on May 6 and May 13, and although there was no byline the content of the editorials suggest that they were written by Van Rensselaer (Mariana Griswold Van Rensselaer to FLO, April 7, 1888; Leopold Eidlitz to FLO, May 7, 1888; "The Ceiling of the Assembly Chamber," *New York Sun*, May 6, 1888, p. 16; "The Ceiling of the Assembly Chamber," ibid., May 13, 1888, p. 16).
2. At the time of this correspondence, Olmsted still had not read the actual report. His information came from letters written by Leopold Eidlitz, the architect of the Assembly

chamber. The final report, which Eidlitz sent to Olmsted on May 3, 1888, did not vindicate Eidlitz, Richardson, & Co. as clearly as Olmsted suggests here it might, but it did confirm their 1882 assertion that the building's foundation was settling evenly. It stated that the "ruin of the vaulted ceiling is due to the fact that the design and method of construction and loading of these arches and vaults have been such as to give pressures which have resulted in the disintegration of the structures," and not related to a "bad foundation." As long as the foundation was stable, Olmsted believed, the adjustment and repair of the vaulting could have been successful (Leopold Eidlitz, H. H. Richardson, and Frederick L. Olmsted, "The New Capitol, An Examination of the Grounds on Which the Security of the Assembly Chamber is Held to be in Question," Nov. 17, 1882, Papers of FLO/LC; Leopold Eidlitz to FLO, Feb. 4, 1888; Leopold Eidlitz sto FLO, March 24, 1888; Leopold Eidlitz to FLO, March 27, 1888; Leopold Eidlitz to FLO, March 29, 1888; Leopold Eidlitz to FLO, May 3, 1888; J. Bogart, T. C. Clarke, and R. M. Upjohn, "Report to the Governor on the Condition of the Assembly Chamber Vaulting at Albany," *American Architect and Building News*, June 9, 1888; W. P. Trowbridge, Charles Babcock, and George B. Post, "Report of the Commissioners to Examine and Report on the New Capitol Building, Appointed by the Governor Pursuant to Section 9 of Chapter 295 of the Laws of 1882," [Albany, Sept. 26, 1882]).

3. Leopold Eidlitz, H. H. Richardson, and Frederick L. Olmsted, "The New Capitol, An Examination of the Grounds on Which the Security of the Assembly Chamber is Held to be in Question," (Albany, Nov. 17, 1882).
4. This photographic portrait appears as the frontispiece of Van Rensselaer's *Henry Hobson Richardson and His Works* (Boston, 1888). The photographer is unknown. (See p. 505.)
5. Sir Hubert von Herkomer painted a portrait of Richardson in 1886 that shows him seated at his desk surrounded by his library and objects from his travels (James F. O'Gorman, *Living Architecture: A Biography of H.H. Richardson* [New York, 1997], p. 154; see p. 506).
6. The *American Architect and Building News* of March 24, 1888 advertised Ticknor & Co's *Monographs of American Architecture: Number Five*. The first subject was a portrait of H. H. Richardson in the robe of a medieval monk, from a series of photographic portraits by George Collins Cox (J. F. O'Gorman, *Living Architecture*, p. 153; see p. 507).
7. Frederick Frelinghuysen (1848–1924) was a lawyer and president of the Mutual Benefit Life Insurance Company of Newark for much of his career. He was the son of Frederick T. Frelinghuysen, the secretary of state under Chester A. Arthur. In 1887 and 1888, Olmsted worked on plans for his private estate in Lenox, Massachusetts ("Frederick Frelinghuysen," *New York Times*, Jan. 2, 1924; FLO and JCO to M. G. Frelinghuysen, April 19, 1888, A2: 361–63, OAR/LC; FLO and JCO to Frederick Frelinghuysen, April 25, 1888, A2: 392–95, OAR/LC; plan 1131-24, NPS/FLONHS).
8. Van Rensselaer wrote a series of articles for *Garden and Forest* that addressed the theory and practice of "landscape gardening," the term she preferred to "landscape architecture." In the article Olmsted cites, she notes that in the design of residential landscapes there is rarely "an appreciation of organized beauty—of the beauty of contrasting yet harmonious lines and colors and masses of light and shade, of intelligent design, of details subordinated to a coherent general effect" (Marianna Griswold Van Rensselaer, "Landscape Gardening VI," *Garden and Forest*, April 4, 1888, pp. 63–64).
9. *Garden and Forest: A Journal of Horticulture, Landscape Art, and Forestry* was published from 1888 through 1897.
10. Van Rensselaer's essays in *American Architect and Building News* in 1887 and in *Garden and Forest* in 1888 were early contributions to the establishment of landscape architecture in the United States as a profession with its own theory and artistic merits: "Landscape Gardening," Parts 1–3, *American Architect and Building News*, Oct. 1887–

Jan. 1888; "Landscape Gardening: A Definition," *Garden and Forest*, Feb. 29, 1888; "Landscape Gardening," Parts 1–6, ibid., March–April, 1888.

11. *Ecclesiastes* 11: 1, "Cast thy bread upon the waters: for thou shalt find it after many days." See FLO to Mariana Griswold Van Rensselaer, [May] 6, 1886, n. 1, above.
12. The Bussey Institute of Harvard University was established in 1871 on land that Benjamin Bussey had left to the University in 1835. It was planned and designed as a "scientific station" for the study of horticulture, botany, and agriculture for Harvard undergraduates. Charles Eliot was an early student at the Bussey Institute before entering into his apprenticeship with Olmsted. In 1872 Charles Sprague Sargent was named Professor of Horticulture at the Bussey, and the next year appointed director of the Botanic Garden of Harvard University as well as director of the Arnold Arboretum, which had been founded on land adjacent to the Bussey at this time. The five men who visited Olmsted, if all from the Bussey, were likely Theodore Lyman Bullard, Stephen Chase, Francis Sedgwick Child, Herbert Edward Everett, and Walter Gassett. The only other students enrolled at the Bussey in 1888 were Henry Sargent Codman and David Hill Coolidge, who were already apprentices at the Olmsted firm (*Bulletin of the Bussey Institution*, vol. 1, 1874–1876 [Cambridge, Mass., 1876], pp. 1–7; S. B. Sutton, *Charles Sprague Sargent and the Arnold Arboretum* [Cambridge, Mass., 1970], pp. 28–35; Ida Hay, *Science in the Pleasure Ground, a History of the Arnold Arboretum* [Boston, 1995], pp. 37, 81, 91-98; *The Harvard University Catalogue, 1887–1888* [Cambridge, Mass., 1887], p. 240).
13. William Ewart Gladstone (1809–1898), British politician, author, and Prime Minster. Gladstone was a self-described "tree-feller," which was a source of comfort and exercise to him, especially in his retirement years (*DNB*; Wemyss Reid, *The Life of William Ewart Gladstone* [London, 1899], pp. 595–98).

Plan for a Small Homestead.

May 2, 1888

Conditions and Requirements.—The site is upon the south face of a bluff, the surface of which is so steep that the rectangular street system of the city, to the east and south, had not been extended over it. The diagonal streets, *M* and *N*, have been lately introduced and building lots laid off on them, as shown in Figure 1. The triangular space between *L* and *M* Streets is a public property containing the graves of some of the first settlers of the region. Its northern and western parts are rocky and partly covered by a growth of native Thorns and Junipers, east of which there are Willows and other planted trees. At A there is a meeting-house and parsonage. Arabic figures show elevations above city datum.

The lot to be improved is that marked *IX*. The usual conveniences of a suburban cottage home are required, and it is desired that it should be made more than usually easy and convenient for members of the household, one of whom is a chronic invalid, to sit much and be cheerfully occupied in out-of-door air and sunlight. A small fruit and vegetable garden is wanted and a stable for a single horse and a cow, with carriage room and lodgings for a man. Water for the house, garden and stable is to be supplied by pipes. There is a sewer in *M* Street.

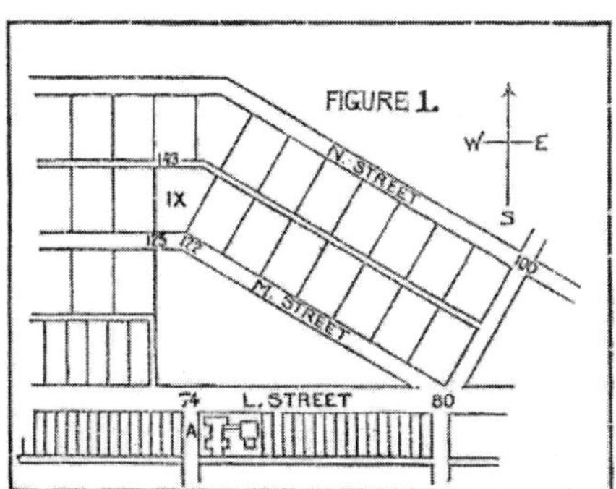

The problem is to meet the requirements thus stated so snugly that the labor of one man will be sufficient, under ordinary circumstances, to keep the place in good order and provide such gratification of taste as with good gardening management the circumstances will allow.

The north-west corner of the lot is 21 feet higher than the south-east corner, the slope being steeper in the upper and lower parts than in the middle. There is a small outcrop of a ledge of limestone about 30 feet from the south end, and the ground near it is rugged and somewhat gullied. *M* Street, which has a rapid descent to the eastward, opposite the lot, was brought to its grade by an excavation on the north side and by banking out on its south side, the bank being supported by a retaining wall. The excavation has left a raw bank two to five feet high on the street face of the lot.

Looking from the middle part of the lot over the roof of the parsonage a glimpse is had of a river, beyond which, in low bottom land, there is a body of timber, chiefly Cottonwood, over which, miles away, low, pastured hills appear in pleasing undulations.

The narrower frontage of lot *IX*, its irregular outlines, its steepness, its crumpled surface, the raw, caving bank of its street face and its apparent rockiness and barrenness, had made it slower of sale than any other on the hill streets, and it was, accordingly, bought at so low a price by its present owner that he is not unwilling to pay liberally for improvements that will give him such accommodations upon it as he calls for. From the adjoining lots and those higher up the hill to the north the view which has been referred to, over the roof of the parsonage, is liable to be curtained off by trees to grow, or houses to be built, on the south side of them. Either this liability has been overlooked or the view has been considered of little value by those who have bought them. "Most people," says the owner of lot *IX*, "find their love of Nature most gratified when they have a trim lawn and a display of flowers and delicacies of vegetation upon it in front of their houses. I find Nature touches me most when I see it in a large way; in a way that gives me a sense of its infinitude. I like to see a natural horizon against the sky, and I think that the advantage we shall have here in that respect will fully compensate us for the want of a fine lawn-like front, provided the place can be made reasonably convenient." Fortunately his wife is essentially like-minded. "I am a Western woman," she says, "and would not like to live in a place that I could not see out of without looking into the windows of my neighbors."

Controlling Landscape Considerations.—The only valuable landscape resource of the property lies in the distant view eastward from it. Looking at this from the house place, it can evidently be improved by placing in its foreground a body of vigorous, dark foliage, in contrast with which the light gray and yellowish greens of the woods of the river bottom will appear of a more delicate and tender quality, and the grassy hills beyond more mysteriously indistinct, far away, unsubstantial and dreamy. Such a foreground can be formed within the limits of lot *IX*, and, strictly speaking, the forming of it will be the only landscape improvement that can be made on the place. It is, however, to be considered, that when the middle of the lot is occupied by a house but small and detached spaces will remain to be furnished with verdure or foliage, and that anything to be put upon these spaces will come under direct and close scrutiny. Hence nothing should be planted in them that during a severe drought or an intense winter or in any other probable contingency is likely to become more than momentarily shabby. Further, it is to be considered, that when the eye is withdrawn from a scene the charm of which lies in its extent and the softness and indefiniteness, through distance, of its detail, the natural beauty in which the most pleasure is likely to be taken will be of a somewhat complementary or antithetical character. But to secure such beauty it is not necessary to provide a series of objects the interest of which will lie in features and details to be seen separately, and which would be most enjoyed if each was placed on a separate pedestal, with others near it of contrasting qualities of detail, each on its own separate pedestal. It may be accomplished by so bringing together materials of varied graceful forms and pleasing tints that they will intimately mingle, and this with such intricate play of light and shade, that, though the whole body of them is under close observation, the eye is not drawn to dwell upon, nor the mind to be occupied, with details. In a small place much cut up, as this must be, a comparative subordination, even to obscurity, of details, occurring as thus proposed, and not as an effect of distance, is much more conducive to a quiescent and cheerfully musing state of mind than the presentation of objects of specific admiration.

Anatomical Plan.—The important common rooms of the family and the best chambers are to be on the southern side of the house, in order that the view over the river, the southwestern breeze and the western twilight, may be enjoyed from their windows. (See figure 2.) It follows that the kitchen and the main entrance door to the house are to be on its north and east sides. Were it not for excessive steepness, the best approach to the house would be on a nearly straight course between its east side and the nearest point on *M* Street—*i.e.*, the south-east corner of the lot; this partly because it would be least costly and most convenient, and partly because it would make the smallest disturbance of the space immediately before the more important windows of the house. But to get an approach of the least practicable steepness the place will be entered at the highest point on *M* Street—*i.e.*, the south-west corner; then a quick turn will be taken to the right, in order to avoid the ledge, then, after passing the ledge, another to the left. On this course a grade of one in twelve and a half can be had. (The grade on the shortest course would be one in seven.) Opposite the entrance to the house there is to be a nearly level space where carriages can rest.

The caving bank made by the cut for grade of *M* Street requires a retaining wall four feet high along the front of the lot. This will allow a low ridge, nearly level along the top, to be formed between the wheelway and the street, making the wheelway safer and a less relatively important circumstance to the eye.

Even in the part of the lot chosen, as being the least steep, for the house, a suitable plateau for it to stand upon can only be obtained by an embankment on the south and an excavation on the north. The embankment is to be kept from sliding down hill by a wall ten feet in front of the wall of the house. This retaining wall is to be built of stained and crannied, refuse blocks of limestone which have been formerly thrown out from the surface in opening quarries on the back of the bluff. They are to be laid without mortar and with a spreading base and irregular batter. Where the ledge can be exposed they will rest upon it, and the undressed rock will form a part of the face of the wall. A railing two and a half feet high is to be carried on the top of the retaining wall, and the space (*b*) between this and the wall of the house will be an open terrace upon which will open half-glazed French windows on the south of the library, parlor and dining-room. At *c* (figure 2) there is to be a little room for plants in winter, the sashes of which are to be removed in summer, when the space is to be shaded by a sliding awning. At *d* a roof covers a space large enough for a tea table or work table, with a circle of chairs about it, out of the house proper, forming a garden room. This roof is to be sustained by slender columns and lattice-work, and lattice-work is to be carried over it and the whole to be overgrown with vines (Honeysuckle on one side, Wistaria on the other, the two mingling above). The space *ee* is reserved for a tiny pleasure garden, to be entered from the house and to be considered much as if, in summer, it were a part of it carpeted with turf and embellished with foliage and flowers. At *f* there is to be a retired seat for reading and intimate conversation, and east of this an entrance to the service gardens, to be described later. The laundry yard, *h*, and the kitchen yard, *i*, are to be screened by high lattices covered by Virginia Creeper. The court yard, *jj*, is to be smoothly paved with asphalt blocks or fire brick, which it will be easy to thoroughly hose and swab every day. In one corner of it is a brick ash house, *k*; in another a gangway to the cellar and a chute for coal, *l*; in another a dog house, *m*. The stable and carriage house are entered from the court yard, but hay will be taken into the loft from a wagon standing in the passage to the back lane. At *n* is the stable yard.

Landscape Gardening.—The soil to be stripped from the sites of the house, terrace, stable, road and walks, will be sufficient, when added to that on the ground elsewhere, to give full two feet of soil wherever needed for turf or planting.

Trenches, nowhere less than two feet deep, are to be made on each side of the approach road south of the terrace and to be filled with highly enriched soil, the surface of which is to slope upward with a slight concavity as it recedes from the approach. The base of the wall is to merge irregularly into this slope. The space between the terrace and the street is so divided by the approach, and, in the main, is so steep and dry, that no part of it can be well kept in turf, nor can trees be planted in it, because they would soon grow to obstruct the southward view from the house and terrace. The steep dry ground and the rock and rough wall of this space are to be veiled with vines rooting in the trenches. The best vine for the purpose is the common old clear green Japan Honeysuckle (*Lonicera Halliana*). In this sheltered situation it will be verdant most, if not all, of the winter, and blooming, not too flauntingly, all of the summer. It can be trained not only over the rough sloping wall of the terrace, but also over the railing above it, and here be kept closely trimmed, so as to appear almost hedgelike. Also it may be trained up the columns of the shelter and along its roof; the odor from its bloom will be pleasing on the terrace, and will be perceptible, not oppressively, at the windows of the second story. Other vegetation is to be introduced sparingly to mingle with it, the wild Rose and Clematis of the neighborhood; the Akebia vine, double flowering Brambles, and, in crevices of the wall, *Rhus aromatica*, dwarf Brambles, *Cotoneaster microphylla*, Indian Fig, Aster, and Golden Rod, but none of these in conspicuous bodies, for the space is not too large to be occupied predominatingly by a mass of foliage of a nearly uniform character. Near the southwest corner of the pleasure garden, *Forsythia suspensa* is to fall over the wall, and, also, as a drapery in the extreme corner (because the odor to those near the bloom of it is not pleasant), Matrimony vine (*Lycium vulgare*). Upon the walls of the house east of the terrace, Japanese Ivy (*Ampelopsis Veitchii*) is to be grown, and before it a bush of the fiery Thorn (*Cratægus Pyracantha*). For the ground on the street side of the approach, *pp*, smooth-leaved shrub evergreens would be chosen were they likely to thrive. But both the limestone soil and the situation is unfavorable to them. Next, a dark compact mass of round-headed Conifers would best serve the purpose of a foreground to the distant view, but there are none that can be depended on to thrive long in the situation that could be kept within the required bounds except by giving them a stubbed and clumsy form by the use of the knife. The best available material for a strong, low mass, with such deep shadows on the side toward the terrace as it is desirable to secure, and which is most sure to thrive permanently in the rather dry and hot situation, will be found in the more horizontally branching of the Thorn trees (*Cratægus*), which grow naturally in several varieties on other parts of the hill. Their heads may be easily kept low enough, especially in the case of the Cockspur (*C. Crus-galli*), to leave the view open from the terrace without taking lumpy forms. But as a thicket of these spreading thorn bushes, fifty feet long, so near the eye, might be a little stiff and monotonous, a few shrubs are to be blended with them, some of which will send straggling sprays above the mass and others give delicacy, grace and liveliness, both of color and texture, to its face. Common Privet, red-twigged Dogwood, common and purple Barberry, *Deutzia scabra*, Spice-bush and Snowberry may be used for the purpose. American Elms have already been planted on the lot adjoining on the east. The Wahoo Elm (*Ulmus alata*) and the Nettle tree (*Celtis occidentalis*) are to be planted in the space between the approach and the boundary. They will grow broodingly over the road, not too high, and mass homogeneously with the larger growing Elms beyond. Near the stable two Pecans (*Carya olivæformis*) are to be planted. The three trees last named all grow in the neighboring country and are particularly neat and free from insect pests. A loose hedge of common Privet having the effect of a natural thicket is to grow along the boundary. No other shrub grows as well here under trees.

As the pleasure garden is to be very small, to be closely associated with the best rooms, and to be not only looked at but used, it must be so prepared that no excessive labor will be needed (as in watering, mowing, sweeping and rolling), to keep it in superlatively neat, fresh and inviting condition. No large trees are to be grown upon or near it by which it would be overshadowed and its moisture and fertility drawn upon to the injury of the finer plantings. It must be easy of use by ladies when they are shod and dressed for the house and not for the street. Its surface is to be studiously modeled with undulations such as might be formed where a strong stream is turned aside abruptly into a deep and narrow passage with considerable descent. It will be hollowing near the house and the walk, and will curl and swell, like heavy canvas slightly lifted by the wind, in the outer parts. Wherever it is to be left in turf the undulations are to be so gentle that close mowing, rolling and sweeping will be easily practicable. The upper and outer parts are to be occupied by bushy foliage compassing about all the turf; high growing shrubs next the fences and walls; lower shrubs before them; trailers and low herbaceous plants before all. But there must be exceptions enough to this order to avoid formality, a few choice plants of each class standing out singly. The bushes are to be planted thickly, not simply to obtain a good early effect, but because they will grow better and with a more suitable character in tolerably close companionship. As the good sense of the lady who is to be mistress of this garden ranges more widely than is common beyond indoor matters of taste, it may be hoped that due thinnings will be made from year to year and that the usual mutilation of bushes under the name of pruning will be prevented.

The following little trees and bushes may be used for the higher range:

The common, trustworthy sorts of Lilac, Bush-honeysuckle, Mock-orange, Forsythia, Weigela, the Buffaloberry (*Shepardia*), common Barberry, the Cornelian Cherry and the red twigged Dogwood. In the second tier, Missouri Currant, Clethra, Calycanthus, Jersey Tea, Japanese Quince, Japanese Mahonia, Spiræas, and the Mezereon Daphne.

In the third tier, *Deutzia gracilis*, Oregon Grape, flowering Almond (white and red), *Spiræa Thunbergii* and *S. Japonica*, Waxberry, *Daphne Cneorum*, small-leaved Cotoneaster, and the Goatsbeard Spiræa. The Virginia Creeper is to be planted against the walls of the house, Chinese Wistarias near the garden room. Oleanders, Rhododendrons, Figs, Azaleas and Bamboos, grown in tubs, are to be set upon the terrace in summer. They are to be kept in a cold pit during the winter.

The service garden (*gg*, Fig. 2) will have a slope of one to five inclining to the south. It is intended only for such supplies to the house as cannot always be obtained in the public market in the fresh condition desirable, and is divided as follows:

g 1.Roses and other plants to provide cut flowers and foliage for interior house decoration;

g 2.Small fruits;

g 3.Radishes, salad plants, Asparagus, Peas, etc.;

g 4.Mint, Parsley, Sage, and other flavoring and garnishing plants for the kitchen,

g 5.Cold-frame, wintering-pit, hot-beds, compost-bin, manure-tank, garden-shed and tool-closet.

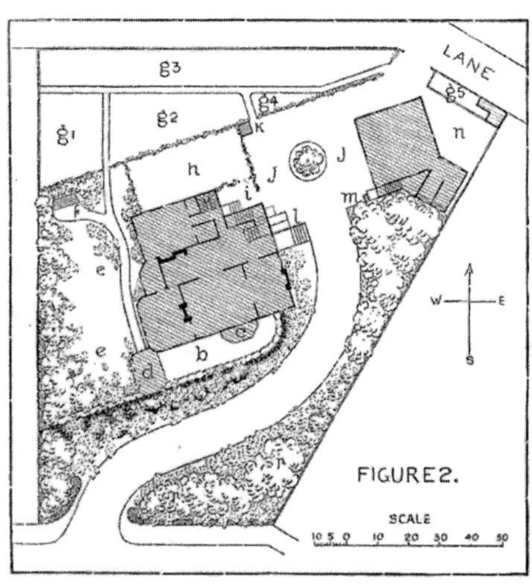

Fred'k Law Olmsted.

Brookline, Mass., 14th April, 1888.

This text presented here was published in *Garden and Forest: A Journal of Horticulture, Landscape Art, and Forestry*, May 2, 1888, pages 111-113, and it was composed on April 14. *Garden and Forest* was published from 1888 through 1897. It was established and "conducted" by Olmsted's sometime colleague, the founding director of the Arnold Arboretum, Charles Sprague Sargent. The periodical was the first of its kind and was highly influential in the formation of a number of professions at the time, above all landscape architecture. Olmsted was one of the early financial backers of the venture and also advised its managing editor William A. Stiles. Olmsted, Mariana Griswold Van Rensselaer, John C. Olmsted, Charles Eliot, Henry Sargent Codman, H. W. S. Cleveland, and other colleagues of Olmsted's published articles in it that ranged from discussions of the technical and theoretical aspects of landscape design, forestry, and horticulture, to advocacy for municipal, state, and national park creation (Stephen A. Spongberg, "*Garden and Forest*: The Botanical Basis of It All," *Arnoldia* 60, no. 2, 2000, pp. 7–9; Ethan Carr, "*Garden and Forest* and 'Landscape Art,'" *Arnoldia* 60, no. 3, 2000, pp. 5–8).

In the introduction to the issue in which Olmsted's article appeared, Sargent wrote that many readers had requested that the serial publish a plan for a small suburban lot. "When, therefore, we requested Mr. Olmsted to prepare a plan for an unpretentious homestead, we expected him to choose a lot with a character of its own and explain how he would adjust it to the wants and tastes of a particular household. . . . In a broader way it is useful as illustrating the class of problems that present themselves whenever thorough work of this kind is contemplated, and as illustrating, too, how these problems are solved by a trained and conscientious artist" (p. 110). The location of the project, which may have been a theoretical one, has not been identified.

To Cyrus Kingsbury Remington[1]

Brookline, Mass., 28th.May, 1888.

C.K. Remington, Esq.,
Dear Sir; I cheerfully reply as far as I can to the queries of your note of the 25th. inst.[2]

The conversation to which you refer was had at the Cataract House.[3] I had shortly before been engaged in establishing the State Reservation of California for the preservation and free Public use of the natural scenery of the Yosemite Valley and the Mariposa Grove and the question had been on my mind whether something could not be done with a similar purpose at Niagara. I had had some conversation as to the conditions of the property, the rights of the state and the dangers impending, with Mr. Whitney[4] of the Cataract House and I think also with Mr. Peter Porter and Mr. Townsend[5] but this may have been later. On the day of the meeting while rambling on Goat Island with Mr. Dorsheimer and Mr. Richardson[6] I brought the subject before them and, as there were, at the time, two or three other gentlemen at Niagara with whom we had been associated in the project of the Buffalo Park and the Buffalo State Lunatic Hospital Ground, they were asked to meet in the evening at Mr. Dorsheimer's room to consider the matter. The opinion prevailed that the State could not then be induced to entertain a proposition so unusual as that which was afterwards resolved upon; though possibly if certain threatened outrages should occur a public sentiment might be roused in the heat of which it might be, and it was agreed that should a propitious occasion arise those present should seek to promote such sentiment. It was then {*questioned*} whether land might not be taken for a public road to be so laid out from the Falls to Lewiston that from it a good free view could be secured to the public of the falls, the whirlpool and the entire gorge of the river. With reference more particularly to the latter project the gentlemen who had been at the meeting were taken next day in the private carriage of one of their number to various points on the river, going as far as Lewiston. The same gentlemen met afterwards, together with one or two others, at the Buffalo Club house and the matter was further discussed and at this time the project of a pleasure road connecting the Park at Buffalo with the suggested road at Niagara, (which has lately taken form in an Act of the Legislature),[7] was first bruited.

Except as to Mr. Dorsheimer and Mr. Richardson I cannot surely separate the gentlemen who first met at Niagara, from those afterwards taking part in the discussion of the subject at the Club house in Buffalo. Among them were, I think, Dennis Bowen, Joseph Warren, Doctor Carey, B.C. Rumsey and Henry Richmond.[8] I cannot fix the date but have an impression that it was September 1869. It can be determined by finding when Mr. Dorsheimer, Mr. Richardson and I were registered on the book of the Cataract House. My partner, Mr. Vaux, joined me, I believe, the day after the meeting and the entry of his name will further establish the date.[9]

I shall be glad to give you any further desired information that I can,
and am, dear sir,
Very Truly Yours,

Fred[k] Law Olmsted.

The text presented here is from a letterpress copy of a typewritten letter signed on the original in Olmsted's hand: A2: 531–33, OAR/LC A1 (see also FLO to Thomas V. Welch, Feb. 16, 1889, below).

1. Cyrus Kingsbury Remington (d.1899) was an historian of the New York region, and active in a number of historical societies in New York and Pennsylvania (*New Amsterdam Gazette*, Jan. 25, 1894, p. 13; *Year-book of the General Society of Colonial Wars (U.S.)* [New York, 1912], p. 138; "Editorial Notes," *Magazine of Western History*, vol. XIV, May–Oct. 1891).
2. Remington's letter has not been found, but Olmsted later recounted that Remington contacted him because he was preparing "some publication or report to an Association" on the history of the establishment of the Niagara Reservation (FLO to Thomas V. Welch, Feb. 16, 1889, below).

3. The Cataract House was a hotel on the bank of the rapids in the village of Niagara Falls, New York. The meeting Olmsted refers to took place on August 7, 1869 (William Pool, ed., *Landmarks of Niagara County* [New York, 1897], p. 407; Charles M. Dow, *The State Reservation at Niagara: A History* [Albany, 1914], pp. 11, 97–98).
4. Solon Miron Napoleon Whitney (1815–1907) was one of the proprietors of the Cataract House in 1869 (W. Pool, ed., *Landmarks of Niagara County*, pp. 408–9).
5. Peter Augustus Porter (1853–1925) was a prominent resident of Niagara Falls who served as the president of the village in 1878. He also served as secretary and treasurer of the Niagara Reservation from 1898 to 1903. Daniel Jackson Townsend (b. 1810) was related to the Porter family by marriage and was a partner in several ventures related to Niagara Falls, including the Niagara Water Works. Both the Townsend and Porter families had significant landholdings in the area, and the Porter family had owned and protected Goat Island for many years. The state acquired land from both families in order to establish the reservation (*Biographical Directory of the United States Congress* [Washington, D.C., 2005]; Edward T. Williams, *Niagara Country, New York: One of the Most Wonderful Regions in the World* [Niagara County, 1921], p. 427; Henry Porter Andrews, *The Descendents of John Porter of Windsor, Conn. 1635–9*, vol. 2 [Saratoga Springs, 1893], p. 619; New York [State], *Laws of the State of New York Passed at the Ninety-First Session of the Legislature* [Albany, N.Y., 1868], chap. 101; New York [State], *Documents of the Senate of the State of New York, One Hundred and Eighth Session* [Albany, N.Y., 1885], Doc. 35 and Appendix).
6. William Edward Dorsheimer was a leading advocate for the creation of the Niagara Reservation and served as president of the Niagara Commission from 1883 until his death. He supported hiring Olmsted and Vaux to develop the general improvement plan for the park, in opposition to the insistence by fellow commissioner Andrew H. Green to hire only Vaux. H. H. Richardson may have been in Niagara in 1869 because he was designing William E. Dorsheimer's house in Buffalo as well as the Buffalo State Hospital for the Insane, the latter in collaboration with Olmsted (C. M. Dow, *The State Reservation at Niagara*, p. 177; *FLO, A Biography*, pp. 396–97; FLO to William E. Dorsheimer, July 21, 1886, above; J. K. Ochsner, *H. H. Richardson*, pp. 54–55, 78–81; see also FLO to William McMillan, March 16, 1885, n. 7, above).
7. During the meeting in 1869, Olmsted and the other men present inspected the land along the gorge area for inclusion in the reservation and drove up to Lewiston to see if a connecting park road was possible. As explained in FLO to William E. Dorsheimer, July 21, 1886, above, Olmsted did not consider it to be of primary importance to include the gorge area in the reservation, and their ideas for a park road connecting the reservation to Lewiston from this route never fully materialized. However, Olmsted and Vaux proposed a riverway along the shore of the reservation from the Old French Landing site northwest to the Soldier's Monument at Prospect Point, in their 1887 report, "General Plan for the Improvement of the Niagara Reservation," 1887 (*Papers of FLO*, SS1: 535–75).

   Regarding a boulevard from Buffalo to Niagara, on May 23, 1888 a New York Senate bill entitled "An act providing for the location of a boulevard to extend form the city of Buffalo to the village of Niagara" was introduced. It proposed the creation of a boulevard 200 feet wide and 20 miles long. On April 2, it was read into the record and referred to the committee on cities. It was never printed or given a bill no., however, and by June 11 it was allowed to "expire without action" (FLO to William E. Dorsheimer, July 21, 1886, above; *Eleventh Annual Report of the Buffalo Park Commissioners for the Year 1880* [Buffalo, 1881], pp. 57–58; Charles E. Beveridge and Francis R. Kowsky, "The Distinctive Charms of Niagara Scenery: Frederick Law Olmsted and the Niagara Reservation," Buscaglia-Castellani Art Gallery of Niagara University [pamphlet][New York,

1985]; "Signed by the Governor," *New York Times*, May 24, 1888, p. 1; "Improvements at Niagara," ibid., May 27, 1888, p. 6; "Made Laws of the State," ibid., June12, 1888, p. 2; *Journal of the Senate of the State of New York at their 111th Session* [Albany, 1888], p. 492; *State of New York Public Papers of David B. Hill, Governor, 1888* [Albany, 1889], p. 169).

8. Dennis C. Bowen (1820–1877) was a lawyer in Buffalo who served on the first board of park commissioners. Joseph Warren (1829–1876), editor-in-chief of the *Buffalo Courier* from 1858 until his death, also served on the first board of park commissioners. In the late 1860s he was instrumental in establishing the Buffalo State Asylum for the Insane, the institution that H. H. Richardson and Olmsted designed in the early 1870s. Dr. Charles Cary, M.D. (1852–1931), was a professor of anatomy at the University of Buffalo and attending physician at Buffalo General Hospital. His father-in-law was Bronson Case Rumsey (1823–1902), a businessman and director of the Buffalo, New York & Philadelphia Railway Company, and he served as a park commissioner from 1882 to 1886. Henry Augustus Richmond (1840–1913) was vice-president of the Buffalo, New York & Philadelphia Railroad, a board member of the Buffalo Y. M. C. A., and one of the first Civil Service Commissioners of New York (*Papers of FLO*, 7: 718, n. 142; James Walsh, *History of Medicine in New York*, vol. V [New York, 1919], p. 293; FLO to Bronson C. Rumsey, Nov. 1884, above; Henry R. Rowland, "Henry A. Richmond: A Tribute," Paper Given for the Buffalo Historical Society, Buffalo, 1915; see also FLO to William McMillan, March 16, 1885, above).
9. The Cataract House and, presumably, its guest registry were destroyed by fire in 1945. Charles M. Dow consulted the registry for his history of the Niagara Reservation, however, and determined the date as August 7, 1869 ("Old Cataract House Destroyed by Fire," *New York Times*, Oct. 15, 1945, p. 15; C. M. Dow, *The State Reservation at Niagara*, p. 11).

To John James Robertson Croes[1]

30th May. 1888.

Dear Mr. Croes;

We send you line prints of contour plans sections and profiles upon which your assistant was instructed to proceed in directing the work at the mausoleum ground. We think it probable that the originals which he was supposed to have, had been lost, and we want you to carefully review the result and consider how far it {*varies*} from {*that*} intended and how far it would now be reasonable to attempt a revision of what is not as intended. You will observe that at a distance of fifty paces from the arched entrance the finished surface at a point fifteen feet away on one side and ten feet on the other was to be level with the crown of the road. I think that you will find that the surface rises directly from the side of the road. And almost everywhere the surface rises much more abruptly than it should. We repeatedly stated to your assistant and to Mr Madigan[2] that there was nothing as important in all the work as to secure all of the level or nearly level space on the sides of the road thus called for, and the last time that I was on the ground (before last week) I pointed that a large amount of excavation was still needed to accomplish the object.

The best approximation to what was originally designed should now be made both in this respect and in respect to the undulations of the surface shown by the contours and sections that is practicable without excessive expense. We must ask you to use your judgment and give directions accordingly. Not much can now be done in the upper two thirds of road except within three or four feet of the gutters. But below that and especially in the division from one to two hundred feet from the arch it is important that the surface should, after muck has been spread upon it, vary little from the requirements of the contour plan. You will see that a great deal of study was given to the preparing of this plan so that (with the sections) it would be but the simplest mechanical work for your assistant to give the contractor perfectly plain and precise instructions by stakes for the required grading. It seems to me that both of your assistants were greatly at fault in not having done this and the last greatly at fault in reporting to you that the requirements of the contract had been met. Nor can Madigan be held blameless for he knew perfectly well that I cared for nothing else in the matter so much as that the scooping out and undulations of slope required in the plan near the road should be fully realized. I said again and again that close exactness to the plan on the crest of the ridge and midway up the hill was not very important but that within twenty feet of the road precision was necessary.

Yours Truly

Fred[k] Law Olmsted.

The text presented here is from a letterpress copy of a handwritten letter signed on the original in Olmsted's hand: A2: 552–55, OAR/LC. Olmsted had begun the design of the Vanderbilt Mausoleum site in 1886 (see FLO to George W. Vanderbilt, Aug. 9, 1886, above; FLO to Richard Morris Hunt, May 5, 1887, above).

1. John James Robertson Croes (1834–1906), originally from Richmond, Virginia, was a civil engineer in New York City for more than fifteen years and collaborated with Olmsted on many projects. In 1860 he was employed by the Croton Aqueduct Department and worked on the large receiving reservoir in Central Park. He then moved to the Department of Public Parks in 1872, surveying the land north of 155th Street. He became chief engineer of the department in 1875 and collaborated with Olmsted on the street and rapid transit plans for the Twenty-third and Twenty-fourth wards of the city, which later became part of the Borough of the Bronx. Their Bronx plans were officially adopted but not faithfully implemented, and Croes left the department in 1879. In private practice, he continued to work with Olmsted on several projects, including the Vanderbilt mausoleum and the Lawrenceville School (*Transactions of the American Society of Civil Engineers* 58, June 1907, pp. 524–31; *Papers of FLO*, 7: 242–66; Frederick Law Olmsted and J. J. R. Croes to William R. Martin, Oct. 31, 1877 [*Papers of FLO*, 7: 340–50]; FLO to James Cameron Mackenzie, May 21, 1883, above).

2. Mr. Madigan was likely of Warner and Madigan, the construction company employed for the approach road to the mausoleum (FLO to Warner & Madigan, July 14, 1888; Charles Carroll Brown, ed., *Directory of American Cement Industries* [New York, 1901], p. 486).

Terrace and Veranda — Back and Front.

June 6, 1888

The following queries suggested by the "Plan for a Small Suburban Homestead," in the issue of GARDEN AND FOREST for May 2d, have been referred to me.[1]

"On the south side, where, in a typical American house, there would be a shady veranda, instead of it there is what is called a terrace — an uncovered platform — upon which the sun must fall and be reflected with burning heat and blinding light into the adjoining rooms. The house has no front door. To enter it from the street, visitors must go round by the back yard, close by the stable. What can be said for such arrangements except that they are striking from their originality or their foreign character? If a speaker chose to turn his back upon his audience he would offend a sense of propriety. Is there no question of propriety about the front and back of a house?"

I reply with pleasure to these inquiries.

A well-shaded apartment having been provided, outside the walls, at the south-west corner of the house, much better adapted for the seating of a family circle than an ordinary veranda, the platform called a terrace will serve desirable purposes that a veranda in the same situation would not. The family rooms giving upon it can be opened to sunshine, as it is best that all rooms should be occasionally, summer and winter. The sun can be excluded from them when it is better that it should be (leaving the air free course through the windows), by adjustable awnings. Interesting forms of decorative sub-tropical vegetation can be fittingly set upon such a terrace in immediate connection with the principal family rooms, as they could not be in the shade of a veranda. There are several months in the year when the terrace could be occupied for one or two hours of most days as a work-room for ladies or as an airing place for an infant or a convalescent, when it would be imprudent to sit in the shade out-of-doors, or to walk on damp turf.

As to a common sense of propriety and respectability in matters of the front and back of houses, let us consider how what may pass for such a sense has probably originated.

A feudal chief wishing to lodge a body of his vassals at a particular point, before unsettled, of his domain, would provide rows of huts set closely together on each side of a common passage or street. They would have the characteristics of such huts as are to be seen now by the score, for example, at Paso del Norte on our southern frontier;[2] a single room for a family, a door on the street side, a door on the other side, no windows, a little corral into which goats, swine and fowls are driven through the hut at nightfall.

As civilization advanced the manorial lords would find it to their profit to extend these villages, build larger dwellings, and, after a long interval, give them a little window on each side of the street door. Later, the roof would be pitched steeper and a sleeping-loft added. Then, on the street side, the walls would be built higher so that there could be upper rooms, also with windows, the roof still carried down to the first story on the opposite side.

At this stage of the evolution certain landlords might come to regard certain of their villages as a part of their lordly array; to conduct guests through their streets and to take pride in their cottages as they would be seen from the streets. It follows that new cottages would be built a little set off from the street and would be given a street door-yard; their street walls would be whitewashed and tenants would be encouraged to decorate the street yards with flowering plants and to line the ways from the street to the street doors with rows of boxes of shells or white stones. The other side of the house would still preserve the original hovel character; would have no windows, and the door would open upon a dunghill and rough shelters for the increasing personal wealth of the tenant in goats, pigs, donkeys, geese and fowls.

It can hardly be necessary to pursue the process of development nearer to "the typical American house."

Why is it that we so often see the family rooms of a house in the country on the least valuable part of the site of a homestead; the kitchen, wash room, drying yard and out-houses on the best part of it? Why is it that if one asks at a Seaside Hotel, where he can see the ocean, he is told to go out back of the stable? The answer is that it is because of a lingering superstition—a spurious semi-religious sentiment—which had its origin when one side of most houses—the side facing a public road—was the human side, the other the side of pigs and goats and geese, filth, darkness and concealment.

The front, *the* back, are terms no more applicable to a well designed house in America than anywhere else. Our Capitol and our White House have two fronts. Our beloved house at Mt. Vernon has two fronts. The old Hosack house at Hyde Park on the Hudson,[3] the finest country-seat in its natural elements in America, has four fronts, as have most palaces and many other monumental buildings, as those of our Interior and Post Office Departments.[4] (But this is a plan hardly ever to be recommended except where there is to be a spacious interior court, as in many French and Spanish country houses.)

Generally with us a country house, and often a suburban house, will best have three fronts. Except as regard for winter shelter or summer breeze may overrule, one of these will be on the side looking from which there is the most pleasing natural scenery, and here will be the more important family rooms (as at Mt. Vernon and at the White House). If the outlook from them has a fine distant background (as at Mt. Vernon and the White House),[5] then the nearer premises should be treated partly with a purpose to provide a place of common, quiet, domestic occupation, to be used in connection with the parlor or library, and partly with the aim of fitting the landscape with a foreground nicely conforming to, and helping the effect of, the middle distance and the background. It is desirable for neither of these purposes that there should be a sweep of gravel on that side of the house upon which horses may be driven or be kept standing, nor that there should be a public entrance to the house there. Usually a lawn, framed and sparingly furnished with masses of shrubbery that will not grow so high as to hide the distant view, will be best. But if the natural surface of the ground is rapidly declining from the house, especially if it is in the form of a broken and one-sided declivity, having a dislocating effect in connection with the distant view, then a level platform before the house, its further edge having a parapet, balustrade or hedge, will be desirable, both in order to give an effect of security and quiet to the immediate border of the house, and to make a strong foreground line by which the distance will be softened and refined.

Another side of the house will be its garden front, chosen because (of the three remaining sides) it offers the best conditions for a garden, properly so called. Another will be the entrance front, the treatment of which will be large in scale and less fine than either of the others. But here, if possible, there should be umbrageous trees. There will remain that part of the house containing the kitchen and laundry, from which will extend yards and sheds and spaces where wagons can stand and turn when bringing supplies or taking off wastes. Beyond them, perhaps, a carriage-house, stable and smaller out-houses. This should be the side on which the outlook is of the least value, and on which the natural circumstances favor convenient but not conspicuous lines of approach.

When such a complete arrangement, as has been thus suggested, is impracticable, the same general principles may be adopted as far as circumstances admit. It rarely occurs in any interesting place that the principal entrance can be best made on the more attractive side of a house. It often occurs, as in the finest places at Newport and Long Branch, that the best location for the stables, stable yard and laundry yard is on the street side of the house, and that the approach to its principal entrance passes near these, bringing them, exteriorly, under close view.

F. L. Olmsted

Brookline, May 18th, 1888.

The text presented here was published in *Garden and Forest: A Journal of Horticulture, Landscape Art, and Forestry*, June 6, 1888, pages 170–71, but composed in May.

1. "Plan for a Small Homestead," *Garden and Forest*, May 2, 1888, above.
2. El Paso del Norte refers to the pass of the north at the Rio Grande River that became the site of the border cities of El Paso, Texas, and Ciudad Juárez, Chihuahua. Olmsted visited El Paso in 1854 and wrote a brief description of it in *A Journey through Texas: Or A Saddle-Trip on the Southwestern Frontier* (New York, 1857), p. 451.
3. Olmsted refers to the Hudson River Estate near Hyde Park, New York, that the physician David Hosack (1769–1835) bought in 1828. In the 1840s, John Jacob Astor purchased the property for his daughter Dorothea and her husband, Walter Langdon, and the Langdons built a new residence. In 1888 the estate was owned by Walter Langdon, Jr., who had replaced his father's house with one designed by architects John H. Sturgis and Charles Brigham of Boston, which had porticoed entrances on four sides (*DAB*; Patricia M. O'Donnell, Charles A. Birnbaum, and Cynthia Zaitzevsky, *Cultural Landscape Report For Vanderbilt Mansion National Historic Site* [Boston, 1992], pp. 29–104; Charles Eliot, "Some Old American Country Seats, VI — Hyde Park," *Garden and Forest*, May 7, 1890, p. 222).
4. In 1888, the Department of the Interior was housed in the Patent Office Building in Washington, D.C., at F and 8th Streets. Based upon designs by Robert Mills and completed by Thomas U. Walter and Edward Clark, it was in the Greek Revival style with entrances on all four sides. At that time, the Post Office Department was next to the Patent Office Building, at E and 8th Streets. Designed by Mills and built under the supervision of Walter, it was a rectangular building in Italianate style, also with entrances on each side (David Edward Johnson, *Washington's Patent Office Building: How Its Design Evolved Over Time* [Charlottesville, Va., 1988]; John M. Bryan, *America's First Architect, Robert Mills* [New York, 2001], pp. 257–67, 274–81).
5. The west entrance to Mount Vernon faced a bowling green flanked by dependencies and gardens. The east, more public entrance featured a large piazza, or porch, and expansive views of the Potomac River and the opposite shore. The White House, since Thomas Jefferson's day, had a public entrance on the north, Pennsylvania Avenue side, and a more private entrance and grounds on the south side, with views toward the Potomac (Robert F. Dalzell, Jr., and Lee Baldwin Dalzell, *George Washington's Mount Vernon, At Home in Revolutionary America* [New York, 1998], pp. 90–93; William Ryan and Desmond Guinness, *The White House: An Architectural History* [New York, 1980]).

To William Runyon Martin[1]

9th June, 1888.

My Dear Sir,

I am much obliged to you and I should be glad if I could think it possible to take up the enterprise[2] again with any measurable prospect of affecting it favorably in a substantial way. I do not think there is or ever can be such a prospect. And I do not want to waste an additional hour of my time, further than courtesy imperatively requires, in discussing how, were New York not what it is and governed as it is, it could be made possible.

Such discussion has been going on with park commissioners themselves, as well as with many others, supposed to be interested with them and for them, and for the city in their affairs, at intervals for ten years past: never at my invitation, and never with anything but the reverse of satisfaction, self-respect or pecuniary profit to me.

Yours Truly,

Fred[k] Law Olmsted.

The Hon. W[m] R. Martin:

The text presented here is from a letterpress copy of a handwritten letter signed on the original in Olmsted's hand: A2: 583, OAR/LC. Olmsted had had little contact with the New York City park commissioners after he and Vaux submitted their revised plan for Morningside Park in October 1887. William R. Martin, representing the West Side Association, wrote Olmsted several letters in 1888 inquiring whether he would consider further consultation on the design of Riverside Park. Olmsted declined, however, writing on June 14, 1888, "I don't want to bother with New York politics & will not move a finger to secure any engagement with the Department nor have anyone else do so in my behalf" (*General Plan For The Improvement Of Morningside Park*, Oct. 1, 1887, above; FLO to William R. Martin, June 14, 1888, A1: 599 OAR/LC; see also William R. Martin to FLO, Feb. 29, 1888; William R. Martin to FLO, June 7, 1888; William R. Martin to FLO, June 11, 1888).

1. William Runyon Martin (1825–1897), a lawyer and real estate speculator, served as a New York park commissioner from 1875 to 1877, and was one of Olmsted's most important supporters. A longtime promoter of uptown development, Martin was the first person to call for the creation of Riverside Park, and as a member of the West Side Association urged that Olmsted be in charge of its development (*General Alumni Catalog of New York University, 1833–1905* [New York, 1906], p. 23; *Papers of FLO*, 7: 4–5; *Papers of FLO*, 7: 220, n. 1; William R. Martin, *The Growth of New York* [New York, 1865]).
2. In his letter of July 7, Martin informed Olmsted that the New York City park department was proceeding with work on the lower section of Riverside Park, from 72nd to 79th streets, and wondered whether there was "some way to get the benefit of your work or advice" (William R. Martin to FLO, June 7, 1888).

To Mariana Griswold Van Rensselaer

Brookline, 14th June, 1888.

My Dear Mrs Van Rensselaer;

Here and there I have heard some little criticisms of the illustrations and the back of the Richardson book[1] but nowhere anything but admiration and gratitude for all your part of the work. Sargent evidently feels triumphant.[2] I cordially congratulate you. I did not know that what I wrote at Clark's[3] request had come into your hands and am much pleased that you chose to make use of it.

My business with St. G. when I met you at his studio was to bring about a meeting between him, Coolidge and Senator & Mrs. Stanford. This was accomplished two days afterwards and resulted in a request from the Senator that St Gaudens should prepare a sketch to be submitted to him on his return from Europe in October for the frieze of the proposed Memorial Arch—entrance to the University. St Gaudens evidently thought it a great opportunity. But a few days afterwards, the Senator having sailed, I had the mortification to receive a note from him of which I will give you below a copy. I am glad that before it reached me, having observed that neither he nor Mrs Stanford appeared ever to have heard of St Gaudens, I had sent them a copy of your article and of the other published with it in the Century, upon his career and works.[4] I have a faint hope that it may do him good.

Yours Sincerely

Fred[k] Law Olmsted.

Copy. "Dear Sir, On reflection I think Mr De Gordon had better not attempt a model for the Arch, until we shall submit drawings of about what we think we would like to have. I shall try and bring home with me a design for our united consideration."[5]

The text presented here is a signed letter in Olmsted's hand. Van Rensselaer had just published *Henry Hobson Richardson and His Works* (Boston, 1888), and reviews of it had recently been published.

1. It is uncertain what reviews Olmsted read, but some mentioned that the book could have had more illustrations of Richardson's commissions. By "the back of the book," Olmsted may be referring to the Appendix, which lists the architect's commissions. The *Nation* offered this criticism of it, "The list of his works given by Mrs. Van Rensselaer, which she believes to be complete, counts only eighty buildings, distributed over twenty years of practice. A few of these were actually designed by Mr. Gambrill during their partnership, and nearly twenty were left for Richardson's successors to finish—some not fairly begun" ("H. H. Richardson's Life and Works," *Book Buyer; a monthly review of American and foreign literature*, July 1888, pp. 240–42; "The Architect Richardson," *Literary World; a Monthly Review of Current Literature*, June 9, 1888, pp. 9, 12; "Books and Papers," *American Architect and Building News*, July 7, 1888, pp. 10–11; "Henry H. Richardson," *Nation*, Aug. 2, 1888, p. 94).
2. Olmsted and Charles Sprague Sargent had been the first to suggest to Van Rensselaer that she write her biography of Richardson. Sargent apparently continued to be involved in the project, as Van Rensselaer reported to Olmsted in 1887, "I have taken infinite pains with every part of the book, and so has Mr. Sargent" (Mariana Griswold Van Rensselaer to FLO, Dec. 20, [1887]; see also FLO to Mariana Griswold Van Rensselaer, [May] 6, 1886, above).

3. Presumably Edward Clark, Architect of the Capitol. Olmsted is referring to an unattributed quotation in the Richardson biography offered, according to Van Rensselaer, by a "distinguished artist, though in another branch than Richardson's." The passage reads:

> I cannot express, or make those who did not know him even dimly understand, how much Richardson was in one's life, how much help and comfort he gave one in its work. It was not always that he could *do* much, but he would do what he could when other men would only have talked about it. And when he could not do anything he would yet take such an eager, unselfish, and really vital interest in one's aims and schemes, try so seriously to understand one's difficulties, and declare so imperiously that they must and should be overcome, be so intensely and intelligently sympathetic, give, in short, *so much of himself*, that he was the greatest comfort and the most potent stimulus that has ever come into my artistic life. (p. 40)

4. See Mariana Griswold Van Rensselaer, "Saint Gaudens's Lincoln," *Century Illustrated Monthly Magazine*, Nov. 1887, p. 37, and the article by painter Kenyon Cox, "Augustus Saint Gaudens," ibid., Nov. 1887, p. 28.
5. The Memorial Arch was built and stood over one hundred feet high, but was destroyed in the 1906 San Francisco earthquake. St. Gaudens designed the original frieze, titled the "Progress of American Civilization," near the top of the arch, and Charles A. Coolidge, the architect for the university with whom Olmsted was collaborating, designed the structure itself (Richard Joncas, David J. Neuman, and Paul V. Turner, *Stanford University* [New York, 1999], pp. 30–31).

To Mariana Griswold Van Rensselaer

29th June, 1888.

Dear Mrs Van Rensselaer,

I did happen to see the article on the Library that you were kind eno' to send me yesterday (and which I return) and I had sent it to Mr Clark, the Architect of the Capitol, and was intending to get another copy to send you. I suppose that Smithmeyer is very far from being the right man for the duty given him and I hope that he and his plan may have to go, but I doubt if the preparatory arrangements are as much in excess of what they should be as is represented.[1]

You know that it is the fashion at Newport to give a lawn-like finish to all the ground between the cottages and the very *base* of the "cliff"—so on one side you have what you might have in a forecourt of Fifth Avenue, on the other (of the "Cliff walk)",[2] utter wildness of rocks, shingle and sand, sea wrack and storm-beaten things. Rough Point[3] is a fascinating place to me, and from the first I have been trying to get the Vanderbilt owners to set their house well out near the rocks and then by means of the house, (long and narrow and not straight in plan),

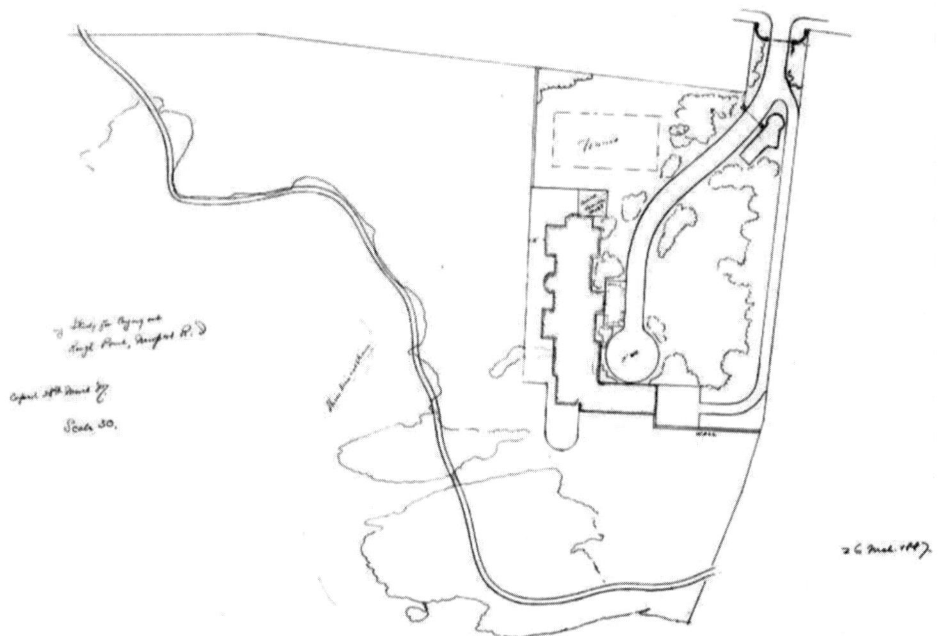

"Study for Laying out Rough Point, Newport, R. I.," March 26, 1887

terraces and yard-walls to make a clean division of the property, one part (being that opening from the Avenue and on the lee side of the house, walls &c.), having a {*fair*} normal lawn-like character; the other part, seen from the opposite side of the house, over the terrace walls &c. rocky, wild, sea beaten—all its elevated parts forming a foreground to the general distance of the ocean—with a middle ground of reefs, breakers and foam. Neither Mr nor Mrs (Fred) Vanderbilt take to the notion and tho' with various recessions from my original ground I have had a good deal done with reference to it, and if I was dealing with them alone I think that I should be able to hold to the essential principle, I don't believe that I can prevent them from finally trying to have a piece of decorated smooth flat turf between their sea-facing windows and the great rocks which will be from fifty to a hundred and fifty feet before them. And solely because of the *Vox populi*. As far as I know everyone they see tells them that what I want to do would be shocking. And I can't help asking am I possibly wrong? The former owners have drawn a great deal of soil from elsewhere in order to fill up the hollows and crevices among the rocks and make the surface as smooth and smug[4] as they could afford to do between the place where the house has been fixed and the line of bolder rocks that forms the cliff. I want to ream this out, expose the nearer side of the cliff rocks even more than nature had originally exposed it; step from the house upon natural rock, and let all seaward of it have a rugged moor-land character. I would either keep the grass down with sheep or I would have the ground between and above the rocks half overgrown with low wild bushes—the best substitutes I

Study and Rough Planting Plan for Rough Point, n.d.

VIEW OF CLIFF SIDE OF ROUGH POINT, C. 1895

could find for furze & broom & heath. But it really seems as if this would be an outrage upon public taste.

Very Sincerely Yours

Fred[k] Law Olmsted.

The text presented here is a signed letter in Olmsted's hand.

1. Van Rensselaer likely sent Olmsted one of many articles published on the controversy surrounding the building of the new Library of Congress. The architect John L. Smithmeyer (1832–1908) was born in Austria and practiced in Washington, D.C., after emigrating to the United States. He collaborated with Paul J. Pelz on a winning entry for the 1873 design competition for the new Library of Congress. Construction did not begin until 1886, and in 1887 Smithmeyer was implicated in a controversy that arose over the quality of concrete used for the foundation and possible improprieties in payments. The project was postponed while Congress investigated, and Smithmeyer was dismissed as the architect of the Library of Congress in 1888 (John Young Cole and Henry Hope Reed, eds., *Library of Congress: The Art and Architecture of the Thomas Jefferson Building* [New York, 1998], pp. 24, 42–43, 48–50, 301).
2. The Cliff Walk in Newport, Rhode Island, was a fashionable promenade from which

the public enjoyed views of the ocean as well as of some of the most prominent mansions that had been built along Newport's eastern shore. The walk followed the edge of the precipitous and rocky shoreline and so was a dividing line between what Olmsted considered the overly manicured grounds of residences on one side, and the surf and rocks of the shoreline on the other. The lawns of the residential grounds sloped down to the walk, and by the "base" of the "cliff," Olmsted apparently refers to the base of the Cliff Walk, which was below the grade of the private residences, although near the top of the cliffs themselves (James L. Yarnall, *Newport Through Its Architecture: A History of Styles from Postmedieval to Postmodern* [Newport, 2005], pp. 63–64).

3. Rough Point, a summer residence of Frederick W. Vanderbilt and his wife, Louise Holmes Anthony Torrance Vanderbilt, was built on a nine-acre, waterfront site near the end of Bellevue Avenue in Newport, Rhode Island. Olmsted began corresponding with Vanderbilt regarding the placement of the house and the design of the grounds in 1887, the year architects Peabody and Stearns were commissioned to design it. Olmsted urged Vanderbilt to retain the rugged, exposed character of the site, a rocky promontory with expansive views directly out to the Atlantic, and to limit the extent of the lawn on the ocean side of the house. The house and grounds were completed in 1891 (John Foreman and Robbe Pierce Stimson, *The Vanderbilts and the Gilded Age* [New York, 1991], pp. 261–64; Frederick W. Vanderbilt to FLO, June 17, 1888, B74: #1036, OAR/LC; Peabody and Stearns to FLO and JCO, May 17, 1888, B74: #1036, OAR/LC; FLO to William Seward Webb, July 12, 1887, n. 2, above).
4. "Smug" in the sense of smooth, clean, neat, trim, or tidy (*OED*).

To Frederick William Vanderbilt[1]

2d August, 1888.

Dear Mr Vanderbilt;

I think I ought to say to you that the more I reflect upon the matter the less I am near to reconciling myself to the conclusions reached in our last discussion.[2] As I said then, the place must be prepared with a view to your taste and your comfort and not at all to mine. But the question is for me to consider what plan when carried out, and, years hence, after mature results have been reached, you are likely to be permanently satisfied with. Taking fully into account your present predilections,[3] I do not believe that the arrangements to which you provisionally assented the other day would prove permanently satisfactory. In my opinion if you proceed upon them it will not be five years before you will abandon them and seek to make changes & variations. The result will be little less satisfactory, there being two classes of motives in conflict, producing a weak and imperfect compromise.

Therefore before anything is done in that direction, I must give you my advice distinctly against what I may have seemed the other day to have assented to.

The one thing that I hold to is that there should be no attempt at "lawn"

VIEW OF STREET SIDE OF ROUGH POINT, C. 1896, FROM "A CRITIQUE OF WORKS OF SHEPLEY, RUTAN, COOLIDGE, AND PEABODY AND STEARNS," *ARCHITECTURAL RECORD*, JULY 1896, PP. 82–3

treatment of the ground immediately in connection with the outcrop of ledge on the Rough side of the house. There should be an abrupt and clean separation between all dressy ground and these bold storm-beaten features of the place. Any attempt to have the dressed ground fade off into the wild ground will be a failure. As I said a thicket of shore growing shrubs, such as Myrica (candle-berry), lambskill, sweet fern and sweet briar, could possibly be interposed between the lawn and the rocks, but it would be years before it could be brought to satisfactory condition; it would be a failure with any ordinary gardening and the probability is that you would get tired of it and let your gardener seek to improve it by the introduction of elements that would destroy its character.

And the fact is that it would not accomplish your purpose. It would, if it succeeded, just as effectually separate visually your lawn from your wild ground as the terrace or a wall.

I am confident that you are mistaken in supposing that the effect of what I have advised would have the effect of belittling the place. I am sure it would have the contrary effect.

I am the freer to urge my opinion upon you (as to the division of the dressed ground from the "cliffs") because when first asked to take the matter up I gave my opinion in writing upon the point and if I did not clearly intimate in that note, I did distinctly state to Mr Peabody,[4] that if you should not be disposed to accept my opinion in this particular I should wish to decline the commission. So far as I advised you as to the form and position of the house it was with the object of making the house and its outworks constitute, as far as possible the desired separation, and while I have since urged the terrace on other grounds it is only as a means of completing this division that I think it, or some substitute in the same locality, essential to a good general design of the place.[5] I do not believe that you are as able as I am to forecast what will be permanently satisfactory to you in this respect.

I am bound to say, now that I am giving you a professional opinion on this point that I feel the design not to be quite satisfactory in one other. I have never liked the plat of turf that you have wanted between the two platforms on the rough side of the house and which you agreed the other day that you would discard. My reason for not liking it was that it was petty and insignificant and would make the two platforms which it separated petty also. It is much better to make one affair of the three things. But I think that the feeling which was at the bottom of your inclination to have a plat of turf (or of something) intermediate between the platforms, (and the house), and the undulating, broken and rocky ground before it was a sound one. A defined flat space of turf or of turf and gravel would be more convenient and would look more convenient and be in better taste at the foot of the steps than an abrupt passage from tiled floors and cut stone walk to rough ledges and undressed turf in slopes and declivities of various inclinations.

Yours Truly

Fred[k] Law Olmsted

The text presented here is a signed letter in Olmsted's hand. Olmsted was commissioned to design Vanderbilt's Newport, Rhode Island, estate, Rough Point, in 1887 (see FLO to Mariana Griswold Van Rensselaer, June 29, 1888, above; FLO to Frederick W. Vanderbilt, Oct. 11, 1889, below).

1. Frederick William Vanderbilt (1856–1938), director of the New York Central Railroad for many years, was the son of William H. Vanderbilt, and brother to George W. Vanderbilt, Eliza Vanderbilt Webb, and Emily Vanderbilt Sloane, all of whom commissioned Olmsted to design the grounds of residences for them. Besides his Rough Point property, Vanderbilt also built a mansion in Hyde Park, New York, completed by McKim, Mead, and White in 1899 (Wayne Andrews, *The Vanderbilt Legend: The Story of the Vanderbilt Family 1794–1940* [New York, 1941], p. 325–26).
2. Olmsted had been corresponding with Vanderbilt, Peabody and Stearns, and engineer Joseph P. Cotton on the subject of Rough Point throughout the spring and summer of 1888. The design of the ocean side of the house, the extent of lawn around the house, and the construction of a terrace were topics addressed (Peabody and Stearns to FLO and JCO, May 17, 1888, B74: #1036, OAR/LC; Frederick W. Vanderbilt to FLO, June 17, 1888, B74: #1036, OAR/LC; FLO and JCO to Joseph P. Cotton, June 19, 1888, A2: 604, OAR/LC; FLO and JCO to Frederick W. Vanderbilt, June 19, 1888, A2: 605–6, OAR/LC).
3. Vanderbilt expressed a preference for a smooth lawn between the house and the seaside cliffs, with a sloping terrace of earth creating the transition between the house and grounds. He wanted there to be no access from the public walk onto the grounds of the residence. He also asked that work near the Cliff Walk be stopped until he returned from a trip to the Adirondacks, and Olmsted complied (Frederick W. Vanderbilt to FLO, June 17, 1888, B74: #1036, OAR/LC; Peabody and Stearns to FLO and JCO,

May 17, 1888, B74: #1036, OAR/LC; see also FLO to Mariana Griswold Van Rensselaer, June 29, 1888, above).

4. Robert Swain Peabody (1845–1917) of Peabody and Stearns. Olmsted collaborated with Peabody and Stearns often, notably (in addition to Rough Point) at Moraine Farm, Elm Court, and the Guild Cottage in Massachusetts; and the Lawrenceville School in New Jersey (*DAB*; Annie Robinson, *Peabody & Stearns, Country Houses and Seaside Cottages* [New York, 2010], pp. 18–31).
5. Olmsted worked with Peabody and Stearns from the beginning of the project to determine the placement of the house, and he provided a plan for staking the location on the site. By February of 1888 he was working on a design for a stone terrace that would create the transition between the house and the grounds described here. Vanderbilt, however, wrote to the architects that he preferred a sloping earthen terrace, or perhaps no terrace at all. They reached a compromise by October of 1888 that comprised an earthen terrace along the bottom of a paved piazza built on the ocean side of the house (FLO to Peabody and Stearns, Aug. 2, 1887, A1: 925, OAR/LC; FLO and JCO to Peabody and Stearns, Feb. 11, 1888, A2: 192, OAR/LC; Peabody and Stearns to FLO and JCO, May 17, 1888, B74: #1036, OAR/LC; Joseph P. Cotton to FLO and JCO, Oct. 12, 1888, B74: #1036, OAR/LC; Frederick W. Vanderbilt to FLO, Oct. 13, 1888, B74: #1036).

To John Daniel Crimmins

2d August, 1888.

The Hon. Jno D. Crimmins:
My Dear Sir;

I am in receipt of your esteemed favor of 31st ulto. and thank you for thinking of me for the proposed service to the Trustees of the Cathedral and much regret that I must decline to accept it.[1]

I have never been able to reconcile myself to the principles upon which our great burial grounds and those of Northern Europe are designed; have never felt qualified to work under them and for more than twenty years have declined all engagements offered me to do so.[2] I have declined two within a few months.

The man in whom I shd have the most confidence for the duty is Mr J. Weidenman. He laid out the Cedar Grove Cemetery at Hartford, Conn., was afterwards connected with me in various private and public works; then went to Chicago to lay out a large Cemetery there, and lately wrote me that he was out of employment.[3]

Respectfully Yours

Fredk Law Olmsted.

The text presented here is a signed letter in Olmsted's hand.

1. Crimmins' letter to Olmsted is not extant, but was likely asking Olmsted to design a portion of the grounds of St. Patrick's Cathedral, located at 50th Street and Fifth Avenue in New York City. It had been completed in 1888. Crimmins served on the cathedral's Board of Trustees (Rev. Joseph F. Delany, Stephen Farrelly, and Thomas F. Meehan, eds., *United States Catholic Historical Society: Historical Records and Studies*, vol. XI [New York, 1917], p. 126; *DAB*).
2. Olmsted rarely designed cemeteries. The only exceptions were Hillside Cemetery in Middletown, New York, designed by Olmsted and Vaux in 1861, and Mountain View Cemetery in Oakland, California, designed by Olmsted in 1865. Olmsted wrote to William Robinson in 1875, "I do not think I could lay out a burial place without making conditions about the monuments such as I fear few but Quakers would be willing to accept" (FLO to William Robinson, c. March 20–30, 1875 [*Papers of FLO*, 7: 135–38]).
3. Jacob Weidenmann was a Swiss landscape gardener who emigrated to the United States in 1856, after which he designed parks in several American cities. In 1886 he had moved to Chicago to design the Mount Hope Cemetery, but lost the position shortly afterwards due to conflicts with the cemetery's directors. He had written to Olmsted in July 1887 asking for help securing new commissions (FLO to Jacob Weidenmann, March 16, 1889, n. 1, below; Jacob Weidenmann to FLO, July 11, 1888).

CHAPTER VIII

AUGUST 1888–FEBRUARY 1889

In 1888 Olmsted began consulting with the Rochester, New York, park board about planning a park system for that city. The August 5, 1888, letter to Edward Mott Moore advises him concerning the process of designing a park system and suggests several landscape architects whom Olmsted believes could handle the task. In the end, the Rochester park board commissioned Olmsted to develop plans for the city's parks. In his January 26, 1889, letter to Moore he explains the need to create a general plan based on a detailed topographical map and then creating a more detailed plan by a process he calls "involuntary and unconscious growth." Another major commission that Olmsted began in 1888 was a summer community in Perry Park, Colorado. His letter to Gen. Bela M. Hughes describes the potential of the site on which the developers want to build, points out the challenges of building a community in a semiarid landscape, and argues for the creation of a comprehensive plan and investment in infrastructure. In October 1888 Olmsted also presented his plan for Buffalo's South Park. His January 26, 1889, letter to the Buffalo Park commissioners reviews the history of the creation and reception of his plan.

During this time, Olmsted continues to design the grounds of private residences, but two commissions were not proceeding as he had hoped. His letter to William D. Sloane shows his dissatisfaction with the plants selected by the gardener for Sloane's estate Elm Court in Lenox, Massachusetts. Four letters to Morris K. Jesup describe the difficult course of Olmsted's planning for Jesup's estate Belvoir Terrace, also in Lenox, and indicate that they must come to a parting of ways after four years of desultory debate.

Three documents in this chapter discuss broader issues. "Foreign Plants and American Scenery" published in *Garden and Forest* argues that foreign plants need not be excluded in American landscape designs. "Remarks About a Difficulty Peculiar to the Park Department of City Governments" is an attempt to define the special purpose and responsibilities of park departments. "Talk to the Brookline Club, History of Streets" provides a history of city planning from ancient times through the nineteenth century.

To Edward Mott Moore[1]

Personal & Private
5th Aug, 1888.

Dear Doctor Moore:

You will not think that I would write you under the above heading with any purpose but to aid you to move to your own ends in your own way. I assume that your big and incoherent board cannot be brought to cordially unite in choosing us for its professional advisers. Cordial agreement on such a point at the outset is most important and you should be looking for someone else.

With reference to your undertaking there is less room for choice than may be supposed among the landscape gardeners or landscape architects of the country. (I have come to prefer the latter term, tho' I much objected to it when it was first given me. I prefer it because it helps to establish the important idea of the distinction of my profession from that of gardening, as that of architecture from building—the distinction of an art of *design*).

Of those who have given themselves the title of landscape gardeners not one of many more than a hundred have the smallest right to it. As a rule they are further from it than the average citizen of fair general education. This because the most of them have passed the best educational years of their lives in close and toilsome confinement to matters horticultural, botanical and in a small scale decorative. Pursuing a course in this and other respects in which faculties of close observation and handicraft skill are cultivated. A course, in fact, such as you might prescribe for a patient whom you wished to wean from too great susceptibility to and interest in grasses, bushes and trees as *components of natural scenery*. The gardening to which they apply the term landscape is just that, in its essence, which the term *landscape* gardening was first used as a means to rule out of view.

Hammerton in his treatise of Landscape says that "scape" in this word was from the same root and properly has the same significance with ship, e. g. in friendship[2]—meaning, that is to say, the comprehensive state, to the eye, of the land or region to which it is applied. (I should rather say the *character*, broadly considered of the scenery of a region.) Of late the training of gardeners has been not at all to landscape in this sense but to elements, incidents and features of the materials of landscape considered by themselves; to make them artists possibly in a certain way, as an ordinary, house furnisher may be trained to something of art in respect to articles of furniture, pictures, books and bric à brac, but not artists in respect to scenery, as scenery acts in the emotional nature of some of us. That a training that is innocently assumed to be a training in landscape gardening is a training in fact away from it, I have often seen evidence. For example a man came to me with a letter of introduction in which it was stated that he was a landscape gardener. As the best {*feast*} that I could offer a visitor of this description fresh from the old world, I dropped my business for a day to take him up the Hudson. It was soon apparent that he had less than ordinary interest in its natural scenery. When we came near to the best of it I had to urge him to move to a position on the boat where he could see it. Having done so, in a minute or two he left it, and, when near West Point, I found him below sitting at a table with a bottle of porter. Yet when I took him to the grounds of a friend's country seat he proved to be really an enthusiast in particular matters of gardening.

I have seen much of two of the most accomplished gardeners in the United States, but I never saw either of them look at anything a stone's throw away or show the slightest interest in our understanding of landscape. There is nothing to prevent them from presenting themselves in good faith as landscape gardeners. In conversing with one previously called a florist but who had offered himself and been appointed landscape gardener of an important public work, I found that he applied the term "harmony", with reference to the grouping of trees, on the supposition that it meant botanical kinship. In a gap between two masses of fine indigenous foliage he had planted some Chinese {*curios*} not only in complete discord with them but which, if they lived long, they would screen off his finest distant view.

Even of landscape gardeners rightly so called the practice of most has been at best upon small grounds or upon grounds in which the convenience and probable wants of but a single family and its selected guests were to be considered and a good design for which is a very different thing from good design for grounds in which the movements of many thousands are to be provided for and precautions taken not only against careless and erratic movements but against occasional malevolent torrents of a disorderly rabble.

Of the thirty four plans of so many assumed landscape gardeners offered to the Commissioners of the Central Park in 1857 but one made the slightest provision for requirements which every one now sees it was absolutely necessary should be provided for.[3] If either of the others had been adopted an almost complete reconstruction of the park would before this time have been necessary. Among the plans offered, that which, from the opportunities and well-earned reputation of the planner,[4] I had expected to be the best, aimed at nothing more than a connected and diversified *series* of effects appropriate to confined, private suburban pleasure grounds.

Of twenty two plans obtained ten years ago by the Boston Park Commissioners — several of which had cost the planners over a thousand dollars each and were most painstakingly studied, even that which they adjudged to be the best was after a few months entirely abandoned.[5] (They finally came to me for a plan which when published was bitterly denounced, declared publicly, by an alleged landscape gardener of large experience, wholly impracticable[6] and so held up to scorn that an association of citizens — large property holders — privately employed a civil engineer to professionally examine and report upon it. It has been carried out with no essential variation and all objections have fallen to the ground).

I have written all the foregoing to justify the opinion I now give you that in all Europe and America, among all the men who with no dishonest intention take the name of landscape gardeners (or architects) there are very few who have shown or are likely to possess any respectable power of dealing with problems of the class that properly come before the Park Commissioners of a large and growing city.

Of those among these likely to be available to you the man of highest proved ability is my old partner Calvert Vaux of New York.[7] There are respects of design in which he is probably the superior of any living man. He has had more experience of what is wanted by a city under the head of parks than any other whom you are likely to think of. There are in the country to my knowledge but two others (properly speaking landscape designers) who have had any experience that would specially qualify them to advise you.

One of them is H. W. S. Cleveland. He is a cultivated Boston-bred man, has been employed in responsible positions on the public parks of Brooklyn, Chicago and Minneapolis. He is the oldest landscape gardener in the country. He wrote me lately that he had almost for the first time in his life been under a physician's care and had been warned that he was too old to travel as much in hot weather and work as hard as he had been accustomed to but that he felt himself as active and energetic as ever. He is poor, has several dependent on him, is dissatisfied with his present position and I think wd gladly come to you for moderate compensation.[8]

The other is J. Weidenmann, the author of a book published by the Appleton's on Landscape Gardening; a Swiss by birth.[9] He laid out and superintended for years, the public park at Hartford, Conn. He was drawn to Chicago by speculators in a Cemetery enterprise, discharged by them two years ago, because he was faithful to his {*professional*} trust and has just {*received*} from them $14,500[10] by {. . .} at law. He wrote {*me*} that he had earned {*the*} last year less {*than*} {. . .} thousand dollars and {*has*} it in view to return to the east. (He may be addressed at Chicago — *Mr. Cleveland*, care of the Park Commission, Minneapolis.)

Of the men who are yet to win their spurs the most promising within my knowledge is Charles Eliot, son of President Charles Eliot of Harvard. He is a man of superior general education, has had special education at the Bussey

Institution and the Harvard Botanic Garden and in art under Prof[r] Norton, was two years as a pupil in our office, has traveled studiously in the best natural scenery of this country, and with uncommon advantages in Europe. He has been in practice by himself two years. He is laying out a small public park at Concord, N. H. and the Longfellow Memorial ground and some other small-public grounds at Cambridge.[11] If you could make it worth his while not only to prepare a general design for your work but to superintend it closely and actively for a few years, you would probably do exceedingly well. He is a real *landscape* gardener and is a well read, well-bred, cultivated man, enthusiastic but cautious and discreet—probably inheriting the remarkable business ability of his father. His address is no. 9 Park Street, Boston.

No doubt there are other promising men whom I don't know or think of—for the profession is not organized and every man fights on his own hook.

There are three or four men who tell fine stories of themselves as landscape gardeners, even in some cases showing what appear to be respectable testimonials, whom I should like to caution you against but I do not feel quite justified in mentioning them by name. One, an Englishman, I have good reason to believe a knave. Another, a clever Jeremy Diddler,[12] comes from the north of Europe originally, later from Paris. Another has published a pamphlet on Landscape Gardening in which he aims to appear a man of Science and shows himself a hopeless ignoramus. Another has publicly described himself a pupil of mine with less ground than my office boy would have. His private life is scandalous and he is in every way dangerous.

You have at Rochester opportunities of securing great results at comparatively small cost, one on the river (holding both sides) above the city, the other on the river below.[13] I don't know of another city in the country favored with {such an} opportunity. Your problem is to provide adequate accommodations for the movement and rest of the future population of the city without excessive encroachment upon the natural wealth of the localities. With respect to design the qualities to be most desired in your artist are modesty, reserve and patience.

Shall I say a few words about the direct work of the Commissioners themselves? If I venture to do so it is because I have been on confidential terms with a good many different park commissions, variously constituted and have closely followed their histories. I have been for a short time but at a critical juncture President and Treasurer of the leading Park Commission of the country and have attended its meetings and taken part in its debates under six different administrations.[14]

Park Commissioners, at first rarely begin to realize the importance or the difficulty of what is before them and are rarely willing to move at the outset as deliberately and cautiously as it is essential to a worthy success that they should. Everything afterwards depends on establishing sound lines of policy, adopting plans that will be good for all time and on determining the scope of discretion within which their executive agents are to work. Afterwards the principal duty of a Park Commission should be that of holding its agents to accountability. It should be exacting of reports, returns, accounts and records. It should not be stingy of clerks. And all reports should be reviewed and audited — not simply in a financial way but in the manner of an adjutant general, to see that instructions have been intelligently pursued. This chiefly in order that executive agents may themselves be obliged to think what they are about and have a clear mind as to their duties, and a due sense of accountability. It will be wise in much more nearly confining its activity to the class of duties thus indicated than Commissions often do, and in avoiding to the last practicable point every executive duty by which the sense of responsibility of its agents can be lessened. It is better that the Commissioners know as little as possible of their *subordinate* agents. It is a ruinous thing for instructions to be given by Commissioners individually; for reports or complaints or applications or suggestions to be received from subordinates by Commissioners individually. Orders should never go out except thro' the President or Secretary representing the Board or its executive Committee and thence through the head of the work or, if there is a divided responsibility on the work, through the head of a department.

All this may seem to you a matter of course. But in general it has not been so. And much as in the degree that Commissioners have directly concerned themselves with Executive details and taken upon themselves either individually or as a board the duty of bosses of their works the further have {*they been*} from economical management or creditable general results. The fewer offices a Commission has to fill by vote the better. The less it has to do with appointments and discharges the better. The more it proceeds by general and comprehensive orders the better.

I would not have written of this did it not appear to me that the larger the members of a Commission, the greater the difficulty must be of proceeding successfully on any other grounds than those suggested. And your Commission is the largest in numbers by much of all I know of.

Yours Very Truly

Fred[k] Law Olmsted.

The text presented here is from a letterpress copy of a handwritten letter signed on the original in Olmsted's hand: A2: 695–708, OAR/LC. The Rochester Board of Park Commissioners was formed in the spring of 1888, and that summer they invited Olmsted to come to Rochester and advise them on land acquisition. Apparently acting at least in part on the advice in this letter, the board later contacted other landscape architects to advise them: Calvert Vaux, Samuel Parsons, Jr., H. W. S. Cleveland, William S. Edgerton (superintendent of Albany, New York's parks), and William Webster (a local landscape gardener). By late September of 1888, all those contacted provided written comments to the board, except for Olmsted, who gave his in person. In October, the board decided to secure Olmsted's services for the Rochester park system. From then until he ceased active practice in 1895, Olmsted worked mainly on the design of Genesee Valley Park, Seneca Park, and Highland Park. The firm's work on Rochester's park system continued into the twentieth century (Edward Mott Moore to FLO, June 1, 1888, B77: #1100, OAR/LC; Edward Mott Moore to FLO, June 22, 1888, B77: #1100, OAR/LC; W. S. Kimball to FLO, June 26, 1888, B77: #1100, OAR/LC; FLO to W. S. Kimball, June 30, 1888, A2: 622–24, OAR/LC; FLO to Edward Mott Moore, July 27, 1888, A2: 667–68, OAR/LC; Edward Mott Moore to FLO, Sept. 23, 1888, B77: #1100, OAR/LC; Edward Mott Moore to FLO, Oct. 21, 1888, B77: #1100, OAR/LC; Alexander B. Lamberton, *The Public Parks of the City of Rochester New York, 1888-1904* [Rochester, 1904], pp. 15–16).

1. Edward Mott Moore (1814–1902) was the first president of the twenty-one-member Rochester Board of Park Commissioners, created by the New York State Legislature on April 27, 1888. Moore was also a practicing physician and surgeon and had settled in Rochester in 1882 to work as the chief of surgery at St. Mary's Hospital and to organize the Infants' Hospital. He was also a member of the Rochester Board of Health, the first president of the New York State Board of Health, and a member of the board of trustees of the University of Rochester (*DAB*; A.B. Lamberton, *The Public Parks of the City of Rochester*, pp. 13).
2. In the beginning of his book *Landscape* (London, 1885), Philip Gilbert Hamerton explains the etymology of the word "landscape" by tracing it to its Old English form, "landscipe." He writes, "It appears, too, that *scipe* or *skip* is the same as *ship* in 'friendship,' and means the state or condition of being, like the German termination *schaft* in *landschaft* and a multitude of other words" (p. 9).
3. A reference to the sunken transverse roads in Olmsted and Vaux's 1858 "Greensward" plan for Central Park, which avoided interruption of the visual continuity of the landscape, and the danger of collision of crosstown traffic with the carriages of park visitors. It also made possible safe passage across the park at night (Frederick Law Olmsted and Calvert Vaux, "Description of a Plan for the Improvement of the Central Park, 'Greensward,'" March 31, 1858 [*Papers of FLO*, 3: 117–87]).
4. Olmsted likely refers to the plan submitted by Howard Daniels, an architect and landscape gardener who had already designed a number of cemeteries and private grounds in the Midwest, in New York, and throughout New England (Roy Rosenzweig and Elizabeth Blackmar, *The Park and the People, A History of Central Park* [Ithaca, 1992], pp. 111–20; Sara Cedar Miller, *Central Park: An American Masterpiece* [New York, 2003], pp. 81–88; Christine B. Lozner, "Howard Daniels," in Charles Birnbaum and Robin Karson, eds., *Pioneers of American Landscape Design* [New York, 2000], pp. 73–76).
5. In March 1878 the Boston park board sponsored a competition for the design of a new park in the Back Bay area. Olmsted did not enter the competition. The park commissioners awarded the top prize to Hermann Grundel, a local florist. Soon after, however, the board effectively negated the results of the competition and hired Olmsted instead to design what became the Back Bay Fens (Cynthia Zaitzevsky, *Frederick Law Olmsted and the Boston Park System* [Cambridge, Mass., 1982], pp. 46–47).
6. Olmsted is likely referring to an unsigned article in the *American Architect and Building News* that objected to his plans for the Back Bay, especially the proposed salt marsh: "Mr. Olmsted has made the mistake — which would not surprise one in a beginner, but which is astonishing in a veteran landscapist — of undertaking to create in a small space, hemmed in narrowly by city streets, a great natural feature. . . . But a marsh is a feature of the natural landscape which needs, as much as any other, unlimited size. . . . to fill up thirty acres where the tide now flows, and cover it with mud to make such a marsh as this now proposed, would be nothing less than childish." Olmsted's reply to the article appeared in the April 3, 1880, issue of *American Architect and Building News* in which

he defended the purpose and design of the Back Bay Fens (*Papers of FLO*, 7: 481–84) ("The Back Bay Park in Boston," *American Architect and Building News*, March 20, 1880, pp. 117–18; see also Frederick Law Olmsted, "Paper on the {Back Bay} Problem and its Solution," April 2, 1886 [*Papers of FLO*, SS1: 437–59]).

7. Over a month after this letter was written, and before securing Olmsted as the sole designer of their park system, the Rochester park board inquired whether it would be possible for him to undertake the commission in collaboration with Calvert Vaux. Olmsted discussed the matter with Vaux in person and wrote to Edward Mott Moore on October 4 that Vaux felt his partnership with Parsons would not allow the arrangement: "I remained with Mr. Vaux till afternoon today and found his mind fixed in the conviction that his relations with Parsons precluded his entertainment of the suggestion of a joint responsibility with me in the matter." Olmsted went on to report that the only part of the park scheme that interested Vaux, in any case, was the "Southern Highlands," or the Highland Park site, and that Vaux also said that,

   > . . . they [Vaux and Parsons] made a proposition to you relating only to the laying out of that. If this is the case, (you will know), I am free to say that we (F. L. & J. C. Olmsted) would be much gratified to be engaged with reference to the river part of the scheme; the conservation and better opening of the river scenery, having been, as you are aware, for many years a matter of much interest to me. I believe that Mr Vaux would be pleased with such a division of duty between us and I do not doubt that we should assist each other with friendly counsel and that the result would be nearly the same, practically with that you were looking for in making the proposition for a partnership between us.

   Nothing appears to have come of Olmsted's suggestion, for by October 21 the board made an offer to Olmsted to take charge of the design of the "whole park system" (Edward Mott Moore to FLO, Sept. 23, 1888, B77: #1100, OAR/LC; FLO to Edward Mott Moore, Oct. 4, 1888, A2: 865, OAR/LC; Edward Mott Moore to FLO, Oct. 21, 1888, B77: #1100, OAR/LC).
8. H. W. S. Cleveland was a landscape architect and friend of Olmsted's who had been living in Minneapolis since the mid-1880s. He had recently written Olmsted describing his health problems: "The Dr. forbade my going any considerable distance from home in hot weather. I am as well, & for aught I can perceive as active as I was ten or twenty years ago, and cannot be thankful enough that I am so, for I have need of all the force I can muster, and dare not think of the time when I must stop work" (H. W. S. Cleveland to FLO, July 25, 1888; see Frederick Law Olmsted, "A Healthy Change in the Tone of the Human Heart," Oct. 1886, n. 9, above).
9. Orange Judd and Company, not Appleton's, published Jacob Weidenmann's book, *Beautifying Country Homes: A Handbook of Landscape Gardening* (New York, 1870) (see FLO to John D. Crimmins, Aug. 2, 1888, n. 3, above).
10. According to Weidenmann's letter to Olmsted, he was paid $14,700 as the outcome of his suit against the Mount Hope Cemetery directors in Chicago (Jacob Weidenman to FLO, July 11, 1888; see FLO to John D. Crimmins, Aug. 2, 1888, n. 3, above).
11. Charles Eliot returned from Europe in 1886 and established his own practice in Boston that December. Olmsted refers here to two of Eliot's early commissions, the design of White Park in Concord, New Hampshire, and the Longfellow Memorial Park in front of the home of Henry Wadsworth Longfellow in Cambridge, Massachusetts (Charles W. Eliot, *Charles Eliot, Landscape Architect* [Boston, 1902], pp. 2204–33; Keith N. Morgan, *Charles Eliot, Landscape Architect: A Research Guide* [Boston, 1999]).
12. That is, a swindler or cheat. The term originates from the character Jeremy Diddler in James Kenney's farce *Raising the Wind* (1803) (*OED*).

13. Olmsted refers to the Genesee River and the sites of Genesee Valley Park and Seneca Park.
14. Olmsted refers to his association with the New York City Department of Public Parks, created in 1870. Olmsted served as a commissioner on the park board from May 29 to October 23, 1872. During that time he acted as president and treasurer while Henry Stebbins was in Europe, surrendering those positions to Stebbins upon his return. The six administrations under which Olmsted had business with the Department of Public Parks were the two administrations of Abraham Oakey Hall (1869–1872), and one each of William F. Havenmeyer (1873), Samuel B. H. Vance (1874), William H. Wickham (1875), and Smith Ely, Jr. (1877–1878), (*Papers of FLO*, 7: 642–43, n. 15).

To William Douglas Sloane[1]

25th August, 1888.

Dear Mr Sloane;

I have just received your note of yesterday, thank you.

I shall be very glad if I can to make the visit you kindly propose. I think that I shall but speak with a certain doubt because I have to go to California before winter and have many engagements to meet before I can do so.

I was sorry not to find you at home when I called some time ago. Your place is very open to criticism because the gardener has been aiming too much to make it bright, gay and splendid, the consequence being a great lack of the quietness and repose of manner which should distinguish a gentleman's country place and a marked disseverance of the locality from the characteristic scenery of the neighboring region. This is what many people like but it is just what in the general plan, the location of the house and its immediate surroundings it was the purpose to avoid. Your note shows that you recognize that your shrubberies need thinning. They also need readjustments of the permanent plants, and the advice that I should give you surely would be to eliminate nearly all the shrubs that are *markedly* distinguished by peculiarities of form or colour from the general vegetation natural to the district, more particularly those which at a little distance have the effect of garish yellow blotches in the landscape.[2]

Yours Truly

Fredk Law Olmsted

The text presented here is from a letterpress copy of a handwritten letter signed on the original in Olmsted's hand: A2: 742–43, OAR/LC. Elm Court, in Lenox, Massachusetts, was the country home of William D. Sloane and his wife Emily Thorn Vanderbilt. The building was designed by Peabody and Stearns, and Olmsted began work on the grounds in 1885. At that time he recommended also hiring the engineer George E. Waring, a longtime associate, to oversee the installation of a drainage system and other site work. The horticulturist William L. Fischer, another longtime collaborator, who had worked at Central Park as well as the Boston parks and elsewhere, supplied and planted trees and shrubs. During the summer of 1886, Olmsted and John C. Olmsted sent Sloane and Fischer instructions for grading and planting, as well as their design for a stone wall that surrounded the grounds. The house was completed in 1887, but work continued for some time after on the grounds (FLO to William D. Sloane, Sept. 24, 1885, B75: #1027, OAR/LC; William D. Sloane to FLO, Sept. 25, 1885, B75: #1027, OAR/LC; William D. Sloane to FLO, n.d., B75: #1027, OAR/LC; FLO and JCO to Peabody and Stearns, June 8, 1886, A1: 367, OAR/LC; FLO to William D. Sloane, Aug. 11, 1886, A1: 400–02, OAR/LC; William D. Sloane to FLO, Aug. 26, 1888; FLO and JCO to William D. Sloane, Sept., 21, 1888, A2: 817, OAR/LC; John Foreman and Robbe Pierce Stimson, *The Vanderbilts and the Gilded Age* [New York, 1991], pp. 127–50).

1. William Douglas Sloane (1844–1915) was a director in the carpet-manufacturing firm W. & J. Sloane in New York and served on the boards of a number of corporations. In 1872 he married Emily Thorn Vanderbilt, sister of Frederick W. Vanderbilt, George W. Vanderbilt, and Eliza Vanderbilt Webb. Sloane was a benefactor of both Yale and Columbia Universities, and with his wife endowed the Sloane Hospital for Women in New York City in 1886. He was also active in preserving some of the landscape around Lenox, including Rattlesnake Mountain in the Berkshires (Jerry E. Patterson, *The Vanderbilts* [New York, 1989], p. 77; "William D. Sloane Dies in Aiken, S.C.," *New York Times*, March 20, 1915, p. 13).
2. In Sloane's reply to Olmsted's letter he writes, "We are anxious to have your advice and assistance in the beautifying of our grounds. As most of the shrubs are those of your selection, I am somewhat at a loss to understand what kind you refer to as having the effect at a distance of 'garish yellow blotches in the landscape,' for in looking them over today I fail to find such in any of the beds — So whatever there is that has produced so unfavorable an impression on your mind, please come and help me to eradicate them at the proper time" (William D. Sloane to FLO, Aug. 26, 1888).

To Edwin Fleming[1]

Private.
20th October. 1888.

My Dear Sir;

After my conversation with you I thought it better that the questions of the South Park should not be brought before the public any more than would be necessary until "after election",[2] and I am sorry to hear that the Express has had a mechanical reduction made of our lithographed plan and will bring it out tomorrow.[3] In my absence my son was asked to furnish electrotypes of the little cuts of our reports to be printed with it but could not do so.

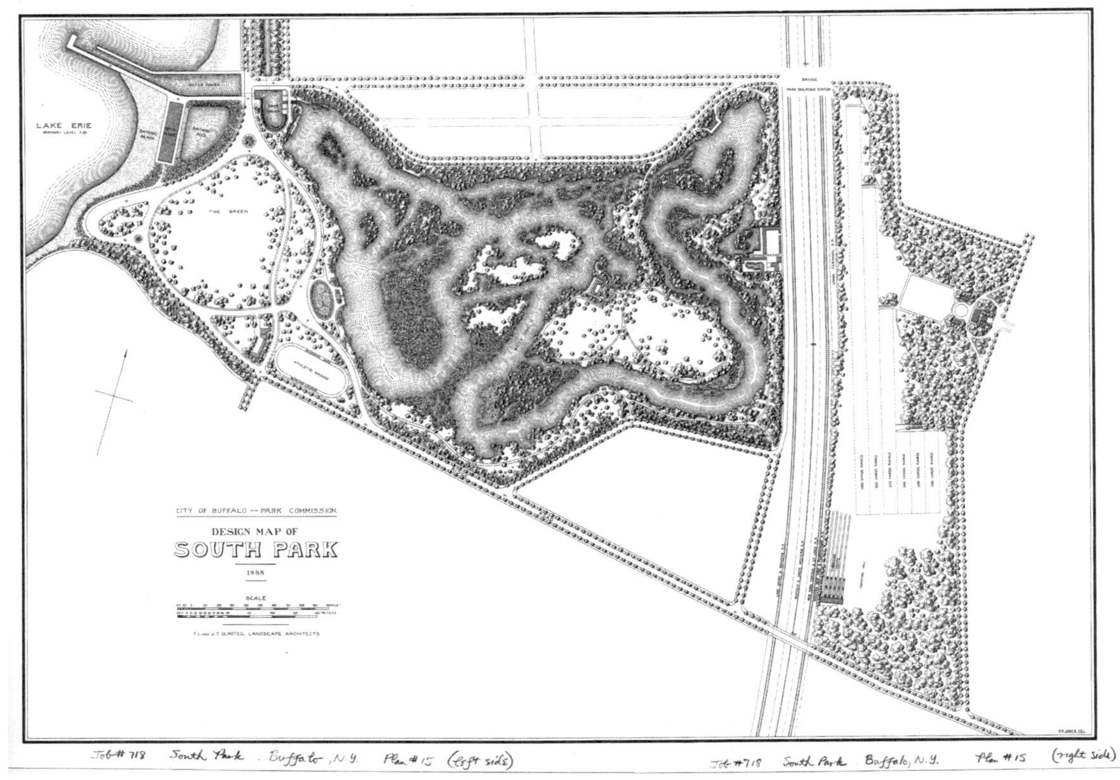

"Design Map of South Park," F. L. & J. C. Olmsted, Landscape Architects, 1888

But 100 copies of our reports have been printed. We are now having them consolidated and shall have a thousand printed with some addition of a statistical character; particulars of estimate, distances, areas &c. We have also been preparing with a view more particularly of your use of it, a new drawing of the plan, opening the lines, simplifying details, enlarging the lettering &c. of which we shall send you an electrotype suitable for rapid newspaper work. If there is anything else that we can do by which discussion of the subject will be aided we shall be glad if you will advise us.

What is wanted is not so much a favorable presentation of our plan as a rousing of the attention of the people of the city to the importance of the purpose of the scheme and to the problem, to the solution of which our plan is an essay. The problem has a number of branches but centrally it is, how to secure now, before it is too late, a place of popular diversion, healthful and enlivening, on the Lake Shore, the only place available for the purpose being of such a character that no ordinary type of a "park" could, at any reasonable expense, be formed upon it.

The Commissioners are little likely to take action, the Common Council much less, by which the opportunity can be saved, unless under conviction that there is some present public interest to have it saved. They will not do much against an apparent public apathy.[4]

Yours Truly

Fred[k] Law Olmsted

Mr Ed[d] Flemming.

The text presented here is from a letterpress copy of a handwritten letter signed on the original in Olmsted's hand: A2: 941–42, OAR/LC. On October 1, F. L. & J. C. Olmsted had completed two reports, *Plan for the Public Park on the Flats South of Buffalo*, and *Projected Park and Parkways on the South Side of Buffalo*, as well as a preliminary estimate for the construction of South Park. Olmsted presented the reports and the estimate to the park board on October 13. The commissioners agreed to consider the reports at a future meeting, and asked Olmsted to have one thousand copies printed and distributed. When this letter was written the Heliotype Printing Company was in the process of printing 1,225 copies under the title: *The Projected Park and Parkways on the South Side of Buffalo. Two Reports by the Landscape Architects, 1888*. As requested by Olmsted in this letter, Edwin Fleming, the editor of the *Buffalo Courier*, waited until December 9, 1888, to publish an explanation of Olmsted's plan with excerpts from the published reports ("How Do You Like It? Mr. Olmsted's Plan for a South Side Park," *Buffalo Express*, Oct. 14, 1888, p. 5; JCO to J. R. Marion & Son, Oct. 16, 1888; "The South Park. Mr. Olmsted's Novel and Elaborate Plan 'Illustrated,' *Buffalo Courier*, Dec. 9, 1888, p. 12; F. L. & J. C. Olmsted, "Plan for a Public Park on the Flats South of Buffalo," Oct. 1, 1888 [*Papers of FLO*, SS1: 576–96]).

1. Edwin Fleming (1847–1923) was a journalist who became the editor of the *Buffalo Courier* in 1885 ("Edwin Fleming Dead," *New York Times*, Aug. 14, 1923).
2. New York State held elections on November 6, 1888, for local, state, and federal offices.

3. Reproductions of the plan and excerpts from Olmsted's report appeared in the Oct. 21, 1888, issue of the *Buffalo Express*, p. 12.
4. When Olmsted presented his South Park plan at the park board meeting on October 13, some attendees objected to the proposed cost. In a letter to the *Buffalo Courier* published in November, an anonymous citizen articulated why many Buffalonians objected to the park: "That our citizens in the lower portions of the city are entitled to a park of modest dimensions which can be had at a reasonable cost is not denied. Such a park should be located in the interior of the Thirteenth ward, where the taxable valuation of the surrounding lands would be increased." As Olmsted predicts in this letter to Fleming, on November 13, the park board voted to reject his South Park plan. A movement to resurrect Olmsted's plan continued through early 1889, but the park board ultimately rejected it and chose to build smaller parks in the interior of the Thirteenth Ward ("How Do You Like It? Mr. Olmsted's Plan for a South Side Park," *Buffalo Express*, Oct. 14, 1888, p. 5; "The South Park Project," *Buffalo Courier*, Nov. 11, 1888, p. 6).

To Morris Ketchum Jesup[1]

20th Octr 1888.

Mr Morris K. Jessup:
My Dear Sir;

I was kept away longer than I expected to be when I last wrote you, arriving only yesterday. I am to leave again for a weeks journey Monday. All the engagements which thus keep me from meeting you at Lenox were made before your request was received.

I called immediately on my arrival yesterday on Mr Rotch[2] who told me that you had decided against the upper site suggested. This being understood you will excuse me for saying that I think that you overestimate the importance of another visit from me. The questions to be decided are not complicated, the local conditions not difficult for one accustomed to topographical studies to understand or to retain in memory. There have been already eight visits from my office, three from myself personally, three from my son and two from Mr Manning[3] and I had frequently looked at the grounds from the outside before. After learning your views on the ground I personally made a careful study of a plan over a sufficient topographical map and discussed it with my son, who after calculating grades and quantities and then again visiting the ground, made the drawing sent to you as expressive of our opinion. You have obviously an ideal in your mind and you are disappointed that we do not find that the local topography when studied with exactness, is well adapted to it. I should be glad if it were not so, but it is not a question of liking or disliking that you ask me. It is a question of facts.[4]

I am sorry that I cannot meet you again on the ground but as I cannot

MORRIS KETCHUM JESUP

without breaking engagements I must say that you miss very little in not getting me to do so.

That is to say, it is extremely improbable that another visit to the ground would give me a different understanding of the essential facts. Taking the facts as they are and using my best judgment in your behalf it is equally improbable that I should give you radically different advice as to the position of the house, the stable or the entrance and approach, from that I have already given you. It was not given without mature consideration and every desire to meet your predispositions, tastes and inclinations. I have not considered the question to be what I would like but what, in the long run, would prove most satisfactory to you.

Yours Truly

Fred[k] Law Olmsted

The text presented here is from a letterpress copy of a handwritten letter signed on the original in Olmsted's hand: A2: 935–38, OAR/LC. In 1885 Morris K. Jesup asked Olmsted to design a site plan for his property in Lenox, Massachusetts. The mansion, which he later built, was named Belvoir Terrace. Olmsted suggested that the house be placed in the upper part of the site but noted that if the house were to be placed any higher on the hill, where one might have even more expansive views in all directions, the slope would be too steep and the place would look "unfurnished and undomestic." When Jesup purchased adjoining lands in 1888, he again invited Olmsted to give advice. But when Olmsted sent a sketch of the property to him on June 26 of that year, Jesup responded on July 4 with his own sketch of the house in a different place. On July 17 Olmsted sent Jesup a description and plans for the grounds. Jesup continued to ask for changes, and in an October 7 letter asked Olmsted to return to the property to choose a final location for the house. Olmsted responded with this letter (FLO to Morris K. Jesup, Oct. 23, 1885, A1: 241–43, OAR/LC; FLO to Morris K. Jesup, July 17, 1888; FLO and JCO to Walter Watson, Aug. 4, 1888, A2: 710, OAR/LC; Morris K. Jesup to FLO, Sept. 13, 1888, B75: #1041, OAR/LC; see also FLO to Morris K. Jesup, Jan. 22, 1889, below; FLO to Morris K. Jesup, Jan. 31, 1889, below; FLO to Morris K. Jesup, Feb. 11, 1889, below).

1. Morris Ketchum Jesup (1830–1908) was born in Westport, Connecticut, and spent most of his life in New York. He made his fortune as a merchant selling railroad supplies and then as a banker. He was a longtime member of the Chamber of Commerce, becoming its President in 1899. Regarded as a philanthropist by his peers, he was a founder of the Young Men's Christian Association and supported the New York Mission and Tract Society, the American Museum of Natural History, and the Audubon Society. At the time of this correspondence he was funding construction of a boys' home in New York City, designed by Calvert Vaux, for Charles Loring Brace's Children's Aid Society. Jesup was also an amateur naturalist who advocated for legislation to protect the Adirondacks. In 1857 he had signed a petition supporting Olmsted's application to become superintendent of Central Park (*DAB*; "Morris K. Jesup," *New York Times*, May 28, 1899; *FLO, A Biography*, p. 128).
2. Arthur Rotch (1850–1894) was an architect trained at the Massachusetts Institute of Technology and the École des Beaux Arts. In 1880 he formed a partnership with George T. Tilden. Jesup hired Rotch and Tilden a month before this letter was written, at Olmsted's suggestion. Jesup wanted to lay out the grounds before hiring an architect, but agreed to retain Rotch when Olmsted wrote that he preferred "to work hand in hand with an architect" (*DAB*; FLO to Morris K. Jesup, July 9, 1888, A2: 635–36, OAR/LC; Morris K. Jesup to FLO, July 12, 1888; JCO to Walter Watson, Sept. 11, 1888, A2: 803, OAR/LC).
3. Warren Henry Manning (1860–1938), horticulturist and landscape architect, was born in Reading, Massachusetts, and from an early age worked in his father's nursery business. He joined Olmsted's firm in 1888 as a horticulturist, later becoming director of planting. He founded his own successful landscape architecture firm in 1896. Manning had advised Jesup on Belvoir Terrace as early as May 1888 (Robin Karson, "Manning, Warren," C. A. Birnbaum and R. Karson, eds., *Pioneers*, pp. 236–42; FLO to Morris K. Jesup, May 29, 1888, A2: 534, OAR/LC).
4. Jesup and Olmsted not only disagreed on where to locate the main residence on the property but also on the placement of the principal drive. Jesup wanted the main entrance on Pittsfield Road, but Olmsted insisted that would be impractical because the slope of the ground was too steep (Morris K. Jesup to FLO, May 22, 1888; Morris K. Jesup to FLO, June 6, 1888; FLO to Morris K. Jesup, June 26, 1888, A2: 616–17, OAR/LC; Morris K. Jesup to FLO, July 4, 1888; FLO to Morris K. Jesup, July 17, 1888, A2: 648–53, OAR/LC; Morris K. Jesup to FLO, Oct. 7, 1888, B75: #1041, OAR/LC).

Foreign Plants and American Scenery.

October 24, 1888

To the Editor of GARDEN AND FOREST:

Sir.—In GARDEN AND FOREST of August 1st, page 266,[1] the law seems to me to have been laid down that the introduction of foreign plants in our scenery is destructive of landscape repose and harmony. No exception was suggested, and the word harmony was used, if I am not mistaken, as it commonly is in criticism of landscape painting, not of matters of scientific interest; not as if the question were one of what, in matters of literary criticism, is called "the unities."[2]

That a fashion of planting far-fetched trees with little discrimination has led to deplorable results, no good observer can doubt. That these results are of such a character that we should, from horror of them, be led, as a rule, in our landscape planting, to taboo all trees coming from over sea, many of your readers will not, I am sure, be ready to admit, and if no one else has yet offered to say why, I will ask you to let me assume that duty.

Suppose anywhere in our Northern Atlantic States an abandoned clearing, such as in Virginia is called an "old-field;"[3]—suppose it to be bordered by the aboriginal forest, with such brushwood as is natural to its glades and skirts straggling out upon the open;—suppose that mixing with this there is a more recent, yet well advanced, growth of trees and bushes sprung from seed, of which a part has drifted from the forest, a part from a neighboring abandoned homestead, while a part has been brought by birds from distant gardens, so that along with the natives, there is a remarkable variety of trees and bushes of foreign ancestry;—suppose a road through more open parts of the old-field, and that on this road a man is passing who, having lately come from New Zealand (or the moon), knows nothing of the vegetation of Europe, Asia or North America, yet has a good eye and susceptibility to the influences of scenery.

Now suppose, lastly, that this man is asked to point out, one after another, so that a list can be made, trees and bushes in an order that will represent the degree in which they appear to him to have an aspect of distinctiveness; No. 1 being that which stands out from among the others as the most of all incongruous, unblending, unassimilating, inharmonious and apparently exotic; No. 2 the next so, and so on.

The question, as we understand it, is essentially this: Would all of the trees and bushes that had come of a foreign ancestry be noted before any of the old native stock?

Some of them surely would stand high on the list, and some of much popularity, such as Horse Chestnut and Ginkgo and numerous sorts of trees in themselves, at least, less objectionable on this score, as, for example, Weeping Beech and most of the more pronounced weepers; most of the Japanese Maples, also, and the dwarf, motley-hued and monstrous sorts of Conifers.

But, all? or, as a rule, with unimportant exceptions? So far from it, to our eyes, that we doubt whether, even of different species of the same genus, the visitor would not point out some of the native before some of the foreign—some of the American Magnolias, for example, before any of the Asiatic. We doubt if the European Red Bud, the Oriental Plane or the Chinese Wistaria (out of bloom) would be selected before their American cousins. It appears to us that *Rubus odoratus* would be noticed before *Rubus fruticosus*.[4] Passing from the nearer relatives, it seems to us likely, also, that many of the European and Asiatic Maples, Elms, Ashes, Limes and Beeches would be named *after* such common American forest trees as the Catalpas, Sassafras, Liquidambar, Tulip, Tupelo and Honey Locust; that the American Chionanthus, Angelica, Cercis, Ptelea, Sumachs, Flowering Dogwood, Pipevine and Rhododendrons would be placed before some of the foreign Barberries, Privets, Spireas, Loniceras, Forsythias, Diervillas or even Lilacs. We doubt if the stranger, seeing some of these latter bushes forming groups spontaneously with the natives, would suspect them to be of foreign origin, or that they would appear to him any more strange and discordant notes in the landscape than such common and generally distributed natives as have been named. We doubt if Barberry, Privet, Sweetbriar and Cherokee Rose, which, in parts of our country, are among the commonest wild shrubs, or the Fall Dandelion, Buttercups, Mints, Hemp Nettle and a dozen others, which, in parts, are among the commonest wild herbaceous plants, though it is believed all of foreign descent, would ever be thought, by such an observer, out of place in our scenery because of their disreposeful and inharmonious influence. Two hundred years hence are not Japanese Honeysuckle, "Japanese Ivy" and "Japanese Box" (*Euonymus radicans*) likely to be equally bone of our bone in scenery?

The forest scenery of northern Europe is distinguished from most of ours by greater landscape sedateness. It is to be doubted if many of the trees that come thence to us, judiciously introduced among our own, provided they are suited with our climate, will not often have more of a quieting than of a disturbing influence on our scenery.

We have much ground which it is difficult and costly, with any plants natural to it, to redeem from a dull, dreary, forlorn and tamely rude condition. There are parts of the world where, in ground otherwise of similar aspect, plants spread naturally, of such a character and in such a manner, that the scenery is made by them interesting, pleasing and stimulating to the imagination—picturesque, in short. Heather, Broom and Furze are such plants in the British Islands. It happens that neither of these has yet flourished long with us, though it is said that Broom appears to have got a foothold in some of our exhausted tobacco lands. But if we cannot have these, it does not follow that nowhere in the world are there plants that would serve the same purpose with us. If any such offer, should not every American give them welcome? The Woad-waxen[5] is a plant inferior to those above named as an element of landscape, but superior in cosmopolitan toughness. As a matter simply of scenery is such heroic settlement as it has effected (it is often winter-killed to the ground, but not to the root), upon the bleak, barren fells back of Salem, as lately described in GARDEN AND FOREST, a misfortune?[6] We believe that to most persons it adds (and otherwise than through its floral beauty) much to the landscape charm of these hills, while detracting nothing from their wildly natural character.

Again, may we not (as artists) think that there are places with us in which a landscape composition might be given a touch of grace, delicacy and fineness by the blending into a body of low, native tree foliage that of the Tamarisk or the Oleaster, that would not be supplied in a given situation by any of our native trees?

Is there a plant that more provokes poetic sentiment than the Ivy? Is there any country in which Ivy grows with happier effect or more thriftily than it does in company with the native Madrona, Yew and Douglas Spruce on our north-west coast? Yet it must have been introduced there not long since from the opposite side of the world. Would not the man be a public benefactor who would bring us from anywhere an evergreen vine of at all corresponding influence in landscape that would equally adapt itself to the climatic conditions of our north-eastern coast?

Imagining possibilities in this direction, let us suppose that, from remote wilds of Central Asia or Africa, we should be offered an herb, or a close-growing, dwarf, woody plant like the Leiophyllum,[7] as it occurs in the Carolina Mountains, that would form a sod with a leafage never rising more than three inches from the roots and never failing in greenness or elasticity during our August droughts. Would not the matting of many a large, quiet, open space among our trees, with such a plant, favor harmony of scenery much more than it is ever favored by the result of the best gardening skill, aided by special fertilizers, lawn mowers, rollers and automatic sprinklers, in dealing with any of our native grasses? Such an acquisition we may think too improbable to be considered. But is it really much more improbable than, 200 years ago, would have been a prediction of the present distribution in some parts of our country of Timothy Grass, Red Clover and Canada Thistle, or in other parts of Bermuda Grass, Alfalfa and Japan Clover?

Before agreeing that no addition can be made to our native forest, except to its injury, we should consider that trees for landscape improvement are not solely those that please simply from their fitness to merely fall quietly into harmony with such as are already established. Trees would be of no less value to us that, being adapted to our climate, would supply elements of vivacity, emphasis, accent, to points of our scenery, such as we see happily produced by the Upright Cypress and the horizontally branching Stone Pine when growing out of Ilex groves on the Mediterranean. And this is a reminder that some scholar has said that we can form little idea of what the scenery of Italy was in the time of Virgil from what we see there now. This because so many trees and plants, which were then common, have since become rare, and because so many, then unknown, have since become common. Is there reason for believing that the primitive scenery of Italy was, on this account, more pleasing than the present?

The large majority of foreign trees that have been introduced with us during the last fifty years, and which have promised well for a time, have been found unable to permanently endure the alternate extremes of our climate, but that there are many perfectly suited with it we have abundant evidence. Does the White Willow[8] flourish better or grow older or larger in any of the meadows of its native land than in ours? Was it not under this tree that the most American of our poets sung of the family of trees, "Surely there are times when they consent to own me of their kin, and condescend to me and call me cousin,"[9] forgetting that, if so, it was the case of "a certain condescension of foreigners"? How is it with the English Elm, the Norway Maple, the Horse Chestnut? The Ailanthus, the Paulownia, the Pride of China, all introduced from Asia within the memory of living men, are spreading as wild trees and elbowing places for themselves in the midst of our native forests. The Eucalypti, from Australia, have come, in thirty years, to be a marked (not generally an agreeable) feature in the scenery of California, and while the climate of our Atlantic coast does not quite agree with the Hawthorns, in Oregon, notwithstanding its greatly drier summer, they seem to be as much at home as in Kent or Surrey.

But on this point of the adaptability of many foreign trees to flourish in American climates, only think of Peaches, Pears and Apples.

Frederick Law Olmsted.

Brookline, September, 1888.

This text presented here was published in *Garden and Forest*, Oct. 24, 1888, pp. 418–19 and composed by Olmsted in September.

1. The anonymous author of the article to which Olmsted refers criticized the planting of garden shrubs that were not "native" to Prospect Park in Brooklyn, New York. He wrote, "They never seem out of place in a garden; but the moment they are placed in contact with our wild plants growing naturally as they do, fortunately, in the Brooklyn park, they look not only out of place, but are a positive injury to the scene" (*Garden and Forest*, Aug. 1, 1888, p. 266).
2. Aristotle first defined the three "unities" of time, place, and action in his *Poetics*, and they became fundamental theory for classical and neoclassical drama (J. A. Cuddon, *Penguin Dictionary of Literary Terms and Literary Theory* [London, 1999], p. 955).
3. An "old field" is land that has been exhausted through cultivation. The phrase also has been used to refer to land cultivated by North American Indians before the arrival of Europeans (*OED*).

4. *Rubus odoratus* (purple-flowering raspberry) is a perennial plant native to the eastern United States and eastern Canada. *Rubus fruticosus* (shrubby blackberry) is an invasive shrub native to northern Europe (L. H. Bailey, *Hortus Third: A Concise Dictionary of Plants Cultivated in the United States and Canada* [New York, 1976], p. 986; Fred J. Chittenden, ed., *Dictionary of Gardening: A Practical and Scientific Encyclopedia* [Oxford, 1951], p. 1835).
5. *Genista tinctoria* (Woadwaxen) is a robust European shrub with twigs that grow up to three feet high. It has spiny stems and bright green leaves, and in the early summer blooms clusters of bright yellow flowers. It is most often found in the midwestern and eastern United States (L. H. Bailey, *Hortus Third*, p. 500).
6. In the article to which Olmsted refers, the author explained that "Woad Wax" was introduced by John Endicott, one of the founders of Salem, Massachusetts. He wrote, "These hills, when the Woad Wax is in flower, seem to have been covered with a golden carpet, and present an appearance quite unlike anything which can be seen in any other part of the United States" ("Notes from the Arnold Arboretum," *Garden and Forest*, Aug. 1, 1888, p. 272).
7. *Leiophyllum buxifolium* (sandmyrtle) is an evergreen shrub, found commonly in coastal regions of the United States, especially in the southeastern states (L. H. Bailey, *Hortus Third*, p. 646).
8. *Salix alba* (white willow) is a willow native to Europe and western and central Asia. It is a medium-sized to large deciduous tree growing up to ten to thirty meters tall, with a trunk up to one meter in diameter (L. H. Bailey, *Hortus Third*, p. 995).
9. Quoted from James Russell Lowell, "Under the Willows," *Under the Willows and Other Poems* (Boston, 1869), p. 13.

To General Bela M. Hughes[1]

[January 15, 1889]

Gen'l B.M. Hughes,
President of the Redstone Company.[2]
Dear Sir:

I enclose a quotable professional opinion of the character of your property of Perry Park as a site for a summer resort.

In the present communication I propose to offer suggestions for the carrying out of your purpose to establish a small summer colony in the park at any early day.

The ultimate value of the whole property will depend much on the impression which this proposed early settlement will make upon possible future purchasers of land, even at considerable distance from it. The success of the early settlement, therefore, is to be measured but very partially by its immediate profit to you or by the satisfaction that shall be taken by those having part in it. The settlers you count upon will be, for some time, chiefly Denver people of a class disposed to make but very moderate outlays for buildings; not ambitious of display, yet unready to dispense with neatness and taste even while passing a vacation in a region mainly attractive to them because of its wildness and seclusion from the fashionable world. Among the people that you want to be prepared to impress favorably in the future there will be many of more luxurious tastes and who are readier to make liberal outlays to gratify them.

The point of policy to be considered is: How the pioneer settlement can be made, without excessive cost, to acquire and hold a character and reputation by which the value of the whole property will be favorably affected? Answering this question, there are, in my opinion, two reasons why you should stringently insist that the settlement shall not be made in a straggling, fragmentary or scattered way. They are:—

First, that spaces of bare ground which may have a not unpleasing aspect if in the midst of a region generally in a state of nature, when seen as waste places between neat houses and planted door-yards, are, in the climate of Colorado apt to appear forlorn, untidy and the reverse of attractive. If the houses are at all fine they will, by contrast with the vacancies, make the village as a whole appear a jumble of incongruities. If they are rude their association with the waste ground will give the village a raw and hopelessly mean character. A collection of even extremely rude cabins on the other hand, is apt to be pleasingly picturesque if they are seen to form parts of a group or composition the other parts of which are in good proportion pleasingly natural.

More or less this objection to scattered settlements is of general application but it often happens that in our eastern villages, what would otherwise be dreary waste places between houses are quite as agreeable elements of the local landscape as if they were under the highest garden cultivation because in the spontaneous course of nature they are clothed with rich turf and decorated with pretty bushes and perennials. The course of nature is very different on Colorado.

Second, the cost of providing common conveniences such as walks and roads and those of water supply and for the removal of waste, and of keeping them always efficient and neat, will be much less in a closely built than in a scattering settlement. And cost in this case does not mean money cost alone but house-keeping trouble. It is also to be considered that in a compact village a man would be ashamed to neglect the simplest requirements of good taste in the care of his place who, living in an isolated house, would allow its surroundings to fall into a condition likely to impress a passing stranger unpleasantly and injure the prestige of the property.

Assuming that the Company will not sell or lease land to people who are unwilling to live in a moderately compact village and to take obligations which will insure between each house and its neighbors a constant state of tidy verdure, what character in other particulars is it desirable than the village should acquire with respect to the lasting advantage of the park property as a whole?

It appears to me that the aim should be to give it some general excellence of its own, distinguishing it at least so far that no visitor will be liable to remember it only as one of numerous villages that he has seen. Even though to give it such a distinction there should be some elements to which many people would object it is better that it should provoke discussion on these points rather than fail to be distinguished. The great point is to make it complete in its own way and prevent the introduction of features confusing and out of character with that which is its notable excellence.

How could such a distinction be obtained without excessive expense?

Suppose that one who had been travelling for a few weeks in Colorado should come into a village in which there were no raw, dry, dusty and dirty places either in the streets or adjoining them: in which there were no houses so big and "stuck up" as to dwarf the greater numbers of all others; in which no house called for *particular notice* solely because of its evident newness or the freshness of its paint, none in which less seem to have been done for immediate display than for a kind of beauty that, nourished by nature would be increasing from year to year and would express unobtrusive domestic taste rather than fashion or smartness. Suppose that owing in part to local circumstances, in part to customs universally followed by its people, the houses of the village did not hold the eye of one passing among them more than the verdure growing before between and about them and that, notwithstanding the unassuming style of its constructions and the informal and apparently unarranged character of its natural elements, the village, *as a whole*, appeared strikingly pretty. Suppose a village so different as this must be from what is commonly brought about by the ambitions of those through whose efforts, moved more by a competitive than a cooperative spirit, villages are generally formed. Suppose this and you will see that situated in the midst of a naturally attractive region it could not fail to acquire celebrity in a degree greatly disproportionate to the necessary cost of securing it, a celebrity due, first, to its modesty and the apparent absence of effort with its people to make a display; second, to the evidence it presented of genuine refinement, good sense and good taste.

It is not to be supposed that such a distinction could be gained without cost both in the way of outlay for common improvements and by restrictions upon private enterprise that would prevent as rapid and early growth of the place as might otherwise be secured.

But it is my opinion that the cost would be well repaid in a few years and that much more would be gained by aiming steadily at such a distinction and keeping under control whatever would interfere with the pursuit of it than by taking a course more nearly parallel with that commonly followed in the building of summer resorts.

On one of the above points I will dwell a little more.

As a rule people will go to Perry Park rather than to some other place, under the lead of men who, in the first instance, will have taken land because its natural landscape was particularly pleasing to them. Now upon such a natural landscape a village — a settlement of summer visitors — never failed to jar unless its houses were not only subdued in color as houses only can be brought to be slowly, without paint, but unless they were comparatively unimportant features in the midst of a wealth of foliage growing on and about them.

But wealth of such foliage as would be desirable does not come of itself to a village, and when it is made to come in Colorado, it does not appear to belong to the natural landscape. Two precepts follow: First, you should choose a locality and devise a plan for your village favorable to a rapid growth of foliage in the midst of it. Second, you should seek to have the village so situated that it will not be a prominent feature in the general landscape but rather an episode.

The required conditions will be fully provided on the shores of the pond which you propose to form, surrounded as they will be at a short distance by hills that will frame in and give landscape seclusion to the locality.

Suppose that you have a road made along the natural margin of this pond, far enough from it to allow a nearly continuous belt of trees and bushes to grow with their roots in its moist edges, the road as narrow as convenience will permit in order to avoid all unnecessary exposure of dead earth and all unnecessary expense of keeping it smooth and tidy. Suppose that a little back from this road you let a series of "bungalows" be built, all low walled and roofed with only the face toward the pond presented distinctly to view and this face mostly shaded by verandas, galleries or awnings. Suppose that there is a little garden in front of each with a hydrant for watering it supplied by pipes from higher points of the brook which is to feed the pond,[3] and you will see that you have the leading elements of a very charming sort of village.

As a centre to such a village nothing could be so pleasing as a pond such as you expect to have embowered with such foliage as could be soon established on its banks. Given such an oasis with a road about it, and it would be natural and reasonable that a circle of cultivated people should cluster closely about it, and, having only summer quarters in view and an intention to live much out of doors, that they should build inexpensively just the class of rustic and unassuming but neat and cozy habitations that would be more desirable from the point of view of an artist. It would be equally natural and agreeable that, these houses being on a hill side, those living in them should terrace off little gardens before them from the road with rustic walls made of the loose stone abounding on the hill-side in their rear; that there should be seen a profusion of vines falling over these walls and climbing over the gate ways, trellises, porches and verandas of the cottages, and that they should be flanked and backed by such trees and bushes as with little effort could be grown for the purpose.

It is unnecessary at this point to carry the general suggestion thus presented into fuller particulars. If it strikes you favorably and you are disposed to have it elaborated in the form of a plan, the topographical map of the ground, for which we have already furnished instructions will be a necessary preliminary to our aiding you to obtain it.

It seems to me premature to undertake to plan the improvement of the park much further at present than has thus been proposed.

But to guard against others gaining to your disadvantage from such work as you may do, I advise that the Company get into its own direct possession enough additional land at a point that I indicated to you when on the ground to hold the control of all from which a good general view could be of the rock district and the two prairies, one stretching northwardly, the other southwardly, from near the old saw mill site.

Respectfully Yours

Frederick Law Olmsted
F. L. & J. C. Olmsted
Landscape Architects.

Brookline, Mass.
15th January, 1889.[4]

Having been asked to report on the availability of Perry Park as a summer resort, on the 26th and 27th of December, 1888, I made such examination of it as was at the time practicable.

The ground being frozen and lightly powdered with snow and an unusual drought prevailing, my observations were not such as would be needed for an assured judgment on questions of water-supply and cultural capabilities but I saw three streams flowing from as many ravines in the adjoining mountains, and evidences elsewhere of water beneath the surface. The form of the ravines seemed favorable for the storage of water at high elevations.

It was, however, as a place for the enjoyment of local scenery and for rural rides and rambles that I more particularly considered the park. In this respect it's more important features are to be found in several bodies of prairie land each bordered and separated from others by low and gently sloping, rounded hills. The comparatively small extent of the glade-like openings and the more continuous slight undulations of the surface, both of the openings and the wooded ground, make the term park a perfectly descriptive designation of the topography — much more so than it is as usually applied in Colorado to much broader and less varied surfaces, unbroken it may be for miles, by trees.

Although in Perry Park all trees of certain age had been taken out for timber some years since, enough remain of good size and so disposed, singly and in loose groups, as to give the landscape not only a well-furnished but in its distances an intricate and mysterious character. One can move in no direction that new and attractive passages do not open before him adapted to act subtly upon the imagination.

With the territory to which the above observations more particularly apply there is closely associated, first, the grandeur of an immense mountain range[5] with bold acclivities divided by darkly shadowed glens, and second, the interest of a remarkable body of rocks projecting in great variety of towering

"The Ideal Sketch of the Village of Lake Wauconda" from promotional pamphlet *Perry Park* (1890)

VIEW OF PERRY PARK, COLORADO

forms from the surface of the ground. Few of these are smaller than an ordinary dwelling, many are larger than the grandest of cathedrals. Most are so scattered and disposed, and associated with the other landscape elements as to form interesting and agreeable incidents of scenery. Looked at one by one, some are entertaining because of their extremely fantastic forms which bring to mind the quaint rocks often represented in Japanese pictures. Others might be taken from a distance for stately monuments. There are several extended ranges which present splintered, craggy and curiously crannied cliff-like faces. Often these are topped with lofty pinnacles and serrated crestings. Some have much beauty from the fretted texture of the stone of which they are composed and its varied soft tints.

Kept clear of such puerile and cockneyfied structures as are too generally allowed to put nature out of countenance in places of summer resort, as well as of such as would be offensive from their rudeness and shabbyness, I should think that Perry Park would soon be found very attractive, first, to tourists, led chiefly by curiosity, second, to persons seeking rest and refreshment under the influence of invigorating mountain air, of a landscape that will grow more pleasing as it becomes more familiar and of incitements to out of door contemplative occupations such as are to be found abundantly in the conditions that have been described.

I shall elsewhere offer a few suggestions as to the manner in which

VIEW OF PERRY PARK, COLORADO

provisions for sojourners in the park may be made with the least injury to its natural attractions.

F. L. & J. C. Olmsted,
Landscape Architects.

The text presented here is an undated, typed letter and report signed in Olmsted's hand. The editors have dated it according to information in Olmsted's Aug. 20, 1889, letter to Charles A. Roberts (below), in which he says that this letter to Hughes was written on January 15.

Olmsted had corresponded since June of 1888 with the owners of the Red Stone Town, Land, and Mining Company about developing a resort community at Perry Park, Colorado. (The term "park" here denotes a high plateau-like valley between mountain ranges.) Olmsted visited the site that December as part of his trip to California, and the firm developed plans over the next several years. In September 1889 the investors named the project the "Village at Lake Wauconda," after a lake they had created the previous year. The "summer colony" at Perry Park was one of a number of Olmsted's commissions in the western United States, including Stanford University and the University of California at Berkeley, for which he developed an approach to landscape design suited to semi-arid climates and conditions (FLO to Charles A. Roberts, Aug. 20, 1889, below; Charles A. Roberts to FLO, June 15, 1888, B76: #1091, OAR/LC; Charles A. Roberts to FLO and Henry Sargent Codman, Sept. 27, 1889, B76: #1091, OAR/LC; Ardis Webb, *The Perry Park Story*

[Denver, 1974], p. 30; JCO to William W. Dunnell, Dec. 27, 1888, A3: 86, OAR/LC; FLO to Leland Stanford, Nov. 27, 1886, above; Charles E. Beveridge, "The California Origins of Olmsted's Landscape Design Principles for the Semiarid American West" [*Papers of FLO*, 5: 449–73]; see also FLO to Charles A. Roberts, Oct. 5, 1889, below; FLO to Charles A. Roberts, Oct. 14, 1889, below).

1. Gen. Bela M. Hughes (1817–1902) earned the rank of brigadier-general during the Civil War. He settled in Denver, Colorado, in 1867 to practice law and became a major figure in the railroad and mining industries. As president and general counsel for the Denver Pacific Railroad, he was a colleague of John D. Perry, president of the eastern division of the Union Pacific Railway, with whom he later formed the Red Stone Town, Land, and Mining Company. Hughes also served as a member of the Territorial Council, helped organize Colorado as a state in 1876, and was elected a Democratic state senator. Hughes sold his shares in the Red Stone company in 1890 (William N. Byers, *Encyclopedia of Biography of Colorado: History of Colorado*, vol. I [Chicago, 1901], pp. 195–97; Thomas William Herringshaw, *Herringshaw's National Library of American Biography*, vol. III [Chicago, 1914], p. 251).
2. The Red Stone Town, Land, and Mining Company was formed in 1888 by John D. Perry, Gen. Bela M. Hughes, Charles A. Roberts, and other investors. They planned to construct a resort community on Perry Park, land that Perry had purchased in 1870 for ranching purposes. Perry Park is in Douglas County, Colorado, half-way between Denver and Colorado Springs. The stockholders in the company contacted Olmsted on June 15, 1888, to consult on the project (A. Webb, *The Perry Park Story*, p. 24; Charles A. Roberts to FLO, June 15, 1888, B76: #1091, OAR/LC; *OED*; FLO, "Memorandum," Nov. 12, 1888, B76: #1091, OAR/LC).
3. Olmsted was concerned from the beginning about an adequate water supply for the development, and he wrote to investor Charles A. Roberts on the necessity of investing in the needed infrastructure (FLO to Charles A. Roberts, Feb. 11, 1889, A3: 210–11, OAR/LC; FLO to Charles A. Roberts, July 27, 1889, A5: 76–80, OAR/LC; FLO to Charles A. Roberts, Aug. 20, 1889, below).
4. Olmsted wrote this "quotable" report for the Red Stone Town, Land, and Mining Company to include in its publicity materials. It was published under the title "Feasibility of Perry Park as a Resort" in the pamphlet *Perry Park* (Denver, 1890) (FLO to Charles A. Roberts, Jan. 16, 1889, A3: 107–10, OAR/LC).
5. Perry Park is at the base of the Rampart Mountain Range, part of the Front Range of the Rocky Mountains.

To Morris Ketchum Jesup

22^d^ Jan. 1889.

My Dear Mr Jessup:

I am satisfied that in what you want to do at Lenox[1] and in the manner through which you want to proceed to do it, I cannot help you. An attempt would lead to a frequent succession of misunderstandings for which neither of us would be at all blameably responsible but which would give us both a degree of anxiety and discomfort for which no desirable results to be obtained would compensate.

We regularly provide for such a contingency in our professional practice, always declining to take an engagement to plan and direct a work until opportunity has been had, through a stage of preliminary consultation to ascertain whether our views would be sufficiently in accord with those of our client to make it probable that such services as our office is {*fitted*} and organized to offer will prove to be such as he wants and expects of us. In spite of this precaution, which for thirty years I have been accustomed to take, it sometimes turns out that the result represents two notions of what was to be desired, both being partially, neither satisfactorily, realized.

Such a result is inevitably costly and disappointing to our client and mortifying to us.

It is more than mortifying to us. It is a lasting, and is liable to be a serious, professional and pecuniary injury to us. Should such a result occur through an engagement with you it would surely be so.

It is plain that you attach a much higher value to certain elements or possibilities of your property than we ever can and that we attach a higher value to others than you ever can.

This conviction brings us to a conclusion which I trust you have no need to be assured is reached most reluctantly.

Greatly regretting it, I am, with sincere respect.

Yours Very Truly,

Fred[k] Law Olmsted.

P.S. We send you the topog. map of the property. Will you please return the drawings made to aid the preliminary discussion.[2]

The text presented here is from a letterpress copy of a handwritten letter signed on the original in Olmsted's hand: A3: 125–26, OAR/LC.

1. Olmsted is referring to disagreements he and Jesup were having about the placement and design of Jesup's home, Belvoir Terrace (see FLO to Morris K. Jesup, Oct. 20, 1888, above).
2. Topographical maps and drawings from work on Belvoir Terrace in 1888 include plans 1041-6.tp2 and 1041-7, NPS/FLONHS.

REMARKS ABOUT A DIFFICULTY PECULIAR TO THE PARK DEPARTMENT OF CITY GOVERNMENTS, ADDRESSED, UPON INVITATION, TO THE NEW ENGLAND CLUB, 26TH JANUARY, 1889.

By Frederick Law Olmsted.

Note.—The Park Commissioners had been invited to address the Club,[1] and, at the request of its president, the following paper was prepared, with the object of presenting the affairs of the Department from another point of view from theirs. It is printed because the condensed reports of it which have been published, although correct as far as they go, do not present the leading purpose of the writer, which was to further the growth of a sound public opinion.

Having had better opportunities than the Commissioners who have addressed you for studying the history of the Park Departments of other cities, I propose to say how the affairs of the Boston Park Department look *from a comparative point of view*.

In all cities the business of a Park Department has to be carried on under a difficulty peculiar to itself. That I may suggest its nature I will first remind you that Park Departments are a new feature of city governments, and that before any of them were formed, nearly every city possessed public grounds, and an organization for taking care of them. In New York and many other places they were called parks, and the committees of the city council supervising them were called park committees. When the modern Park Departments were formed, they did not, as a rule, supersede these older arrangements. For example, here in Boston, before there was any Park Department you had the Common and the Public Garden, and a number of small grounds, some of which were designated parks; you had Commonwealth and West Chester Park avenues, with their strips of greensward and trees and beds. Moreover, you had Chestnut Hill, with its fine shade trees and its well-made pleasure roads and walks, passing between and around two broad artificial sheets of water, the whole more than 200 acres in extent. All these grounds remain and the business of taking care of them continues to be carried on as before. It may be questioned if any business of the city government is carried on more skillfully or more satisfactorily to the people.

Why, then, should another department, under the name of the Park Department, have been added to the already somewhat cumbersome machinery of the city government?

Carpers cannot say that it was to provide fat places for men to whom successful politicians had become indebted. The Park Commissioners get no salaries.

What then? There is but one way of avoiding the conclusion that all our cities have been doing a senseless thing in instituting these Park Departments. It is to assume that they are designed to supply a want not had in view under the old arrangements.

But, adopting this assumption, the question occurs, where is the distinctive duty in this respect of the Park Department defined? The Act establishing the Boston department states that its purpose shall be "to locate, lay out, improve, govern, and regulate one or more public parks." But this does not define a purpose distinct from that before provided for, nor is the distinctive business of the department anywhere, by any statute or ordinance, title or preamble, so defined that it can be clearly separated from the purpose of such institutions as the Public Garden and the Common, "Chester Park," "Union Park," and "Washington Park."

It is much the same elsewhere. In one of our great cities a site within a park was, some time ago, appropriated to a certain public purpose, and park funds voted to further advance that purpose. Commenting upon this action it was observed by a distinguished citizen, a lawyer and a law-maker, entirely in sympathy with the purpose, that if the action of the Commissioners in the matter did not go beyond their legal powers, then it must lie within their legal powers to set buildings, designed to promote any object which it appeared desirable to them should be furthered, at any point within the park. It would be competent for them to construct roads leading to these buildings. In fact they might occupy the entire ground with streets and buildings.

It is not necessary to my present purpose that I should undertake what the law-givers and courts have so far failed to undertake,—that is to say, to define the distinctive purpose of a Park Department; my aim is to show you where the difficulty lies, not to remove it.

The difficulty lies in the fact that the purpose to be served by a Park Department, not having been at all precisely defined, or by any form of long and well-known usage established, Park Commissioners cannot well be held—cannot well hold themselves—to a strict account for serving that purpose rather than serving numerous other purposes, such as even good citizens may think it right to urge upon them.

If a Sewer Department in any of our cities should set about building much-needed school-houses, or a Fire Department aim to supply the want of a Public Library, the work would not proceed far without a question being raised as to the authority for these operations. But when land has been taken, and money appropriated for a park, there is no clear popular working understanding, or active public opinion, as to the limits of purpose within which it is to be used. None, certainly, making an exact distinction between this purpose and that of the committees of the city council supervising what are classed as "the small parks."[2]

If the business of a Park Department is tolerably well directed, there comes, in time, a result, by familiarity with which public opinion becomes gradually educated to the point of rejoicing in work that really serves the specific purpose of the department, and of condemning its use, in any form, of public money or public property for purposes not peculiarly under its charge. In New York, for instance, after thirty years, it seems now to be approaching that point.

But, in the earlier stages of their works, the difficulty of strictly pursuing the distinctive objects for which Park Departments have been wanted, is apt to appear in many forms. I will refer particularly to two only:—

First, the results of any proper work of a Park Department are not apt to be fully reached for a long time after the work has been mainly done. Often the early results are decidedly unpleasing, as they have been, and in large parts, after many years, still are, in the work of your department, of the Back Bay Fens. The best intended results may not ripen during the lifetime of those to be chiefly credited with them. In most cases they never invite admiration as achievements. The best results of the best, most difficult, and most costly operations are likely to be accepted by the public as results of nature's work, almost exclusively. The aim of the department should be nearly everywhere, not to exhibit, but to conceal, the art it has used.

Under these circumstances, because of the vague understanding that is generally had of the purposes of the department, the value of the work it is doing is often, even generally, assumed to be found in results that are but provisional, temporary, and transitory. Even when this is not the case the public attitude toward it is apt to be an attitude of impatience, and it requires a more than usually stern sense of duty, and more than ordinary resolution and determination, both in the Commissioners and in those whom they employ in the immediate direction of operations, not to make large sacrifices to assuage this impatience.

Now, if I am asked to tell you from my comparative point of view how the business of the Park Department of Boston has fared with reference to this branch of the difficulty, I am glad that I can say that it has fared better than that of any other Park Department in the United States. I am moved to say so, more particularly in view of the patience of the public with respect to a costly work of an exceptionally tedious and unpromising character. I mean that of the Fens. In no other work of which I have knowledge has the purpose of a Park Department been so liable to be misunderstood, yet in hardly any other has the original controlling purpose been pursued so steadily, or with as little waste because of a desire to realize superficial and temporarily pleasing and immediately popular results.

Second, the worst thing that can happen to the business of a Park Department is that the lasting interest of the public in this particular division of its business shall be sacrificed, in order to further what may be assumed to be more important public objects. Objects, for example, that may be assumed to be of statesmanship: with reference to which parties are formed; with reference to which money must be raised, or the equivalent of money in various indirect and easily obfusticated forms of "patronage." You will see how the vague character of the charge given to the Park Department leaves an unusually wide door open for sacrifices of its proper purpose in this respect. You will see how such sacrifices can be made more easily in a Park Department than any other, for the reason that the motives of it can thus be better kept out of public view; can, for instance, be disguised under cover of an intention to remedy some assumed error of judgment or dishonest purpose on the part of predecessors of a different political camp. You will see that, there being occasion for such an operation, the public may be more easily misled, or, at least, brought to confusion of mind, in respect to the motives of it, than it can be in regard to the motives of any other department of city business. It may be more easily brought to applaud it because it is always easy in carrying out such an operation to gratify the public's constant impatience to have an early display of pleasing, even if meretricious, results.

How is your department getting on in respect to this branch of the difficulty?

It is a good time to answer this question, because three years ago a political revolution occurred in the Park Commission. Having been a republican it became a unanimously democratic board.[3]

The answer is, that neither under the former republican nor the present democratic administration has a man been dismissed, or a man been enlisted in any class of employment, with any motive (apparent to me), of serving a party, of rewarding party services, or of punishing failure of party services. I do not believe that a single purchase has been made, or a single contract manipulated in any manner, with any such motives.

And from my comparative point of view I may say that I do not think that there is another Park Department in the country, that at a corresponding period of its work has more successfully escaped the class of dangers that I have been trying to explain.

I do not think that with respect to any other a custom of conducting the work independently both of politics and of motives of temporary expediency has been so nearly established. I do not think that at so early a stage any other park work has come so nearly to be recognized and treated as a work of art.

Upon this conclusion I heartily congratulate your club and all good people of Boston.

The text presented here was published in the *Fourteenth Annual Report of the Board of Commissioners, Department of Parks, City of Boston for the Year 1888* (Boston, 1889), pages 48–53.

1. The New England Club, where members met weekly to hear speeches on economic and political topics, was founded in 1884. Its president in 1887 was Harvey Newton Shepard

(Edwin M. Bacon, *Bacon's Dictionary of Boston* [Boston, 1886], p. 311; Samuel Atkins Eliot, ed., *Biographical History of Massachusetts: Biographies and Autobiographies of Leading Men of the State* [Boston, 1911]).

2. In the late 1880s, many municipalities moved to create what were termed "small parks" in older, usually poorer and more densely populated neighborhoods. In 1887 New York State passed the "Small Park Act," which authorized the city to purchase land south of 155th Street in New York City for small parks in areas of the city meeting this description. In Boston, Olmsted designed the ten-acre Charlesbank in 1887. The waterfront park served the West End neighborhood and featured outdoor gymnasia, sitting areas, and play areas for children (New York [State], *Laws of the State of New York, Passed at the One Hundred and Tenth Session of the Legislature* [Albany, N.Y., 1887], chap. 320; Clarency E. Rainwater, *The Play Movement in the United States* [Chicago, 1922], p. 72; Frederick Law Olmsted, *Twelfth Annual Report, Boston Park Commissioners, Report on Charles River Embankment*, [Dec.] 1886, above).
3. In July 1875, Boston Mayor Samuel Cobb appointed Charles H. Dalton, William Gray, Jr., and T. Jefferson Coolidge as park commissioners. They served until the election of 1884, when Democrat Hugh O'Brien was elected mayor. O'Brien appointed a new board of park commissioners, all prominent and influential Democrats: Patrick Maguire, John F. Andrew, and Benjamin Dean. After initial apprehensions, Olmsted formed a productive working relationship with the new commissioners (C. Zaitzevsky, *The Boston Park System*, p. 67; see "On Points of View and Methods of Criticism of Public Works of Landscape Architecture," June 20 and 29, 1885, above).

To the Buffalo Park Commissioners

Office of F. L. & J. C. Olmsted;
Brookline, Mass,
26th Jany. 1889.

To the Park Commissioners:
Dear Sirs

The good opinion of the people of Buffalo being of value to me, in view of certain recent publications, I should like to have a true account of certain matters of my business with you set as follows, with your sanction, before them.

First; I have been employed by your Commission at frequent intervals, in small and large ways, for twenty years past. Bills for this service, unless at your request, have always been rendered in January. I have never been asked to explain or justify a single item of these bills. They have been promptly paid and I have had no reason to suppose that their justness has been at any time questioned by a single member of your large and yearly changing body. This fact is recalled because statements have appeared that might be thought to imply a different notion of my character from that which they suggest.[1]

Second: Nearly two years ago, I came to Buffalo upon the invitation of your park committee for a consultation in respect to a scheme that had been presented to your Board by the City Council in consequence of a petition of citizens representing the 13th Ward. The scheme looked to the formation of a park partly in Buffalo, partly in West Seneca, upon the Lake Shore. I was taken by your committee to this site and the question was asked:—What can be done with it? Upon this question I made a preliminary report which after discussion was accepted by your Board; laid before the Council and extensively published.[2] Under subsequent instructions the whole of the following year was occupied in a more thorough study of the question. Investigation gradually brought to light facts showing that the information upon which the preliminary report had been based was far from accurate or complete and that the problem of a plan was more complex and difficult than had been supposed. This led to the abandonment of one project of a plan after another, and at length, as was at the time reported to you and to the public, to a question whether it might not be better for you to advise the Council that a park on the Lake Shore could only be made at a cost which you would deem excessive. You were not recommended to do so because, upon a thorough examination of all the Southern part of the city, no other site was found upon which, even by a much larger outlay a park could be made that would distantly compare in value to the people of the city with one on the lake shore. The plan was then again recast and redrawn for the fifth time. It was finally presented to you in an unusually elaborate way and with an estimate of cost which had been prepared and submitted for review to respected citizens of Buffalo, qualified by long local experience to be considered trustworthy experts in matters as to which from lack of such local experience the judgment of the designers was liable to be faulty.[3]

The report of the plan was {*at once accepted*}[4] by your Board, as in full compliance with its instructions, and a note of thanks for it was, at the instance of his Honor the Mayor,[5] adopted with unanimity and apparent cordiality.

I wish these facts to be better known because I have seen no unofficial argument for an abandonment of the Lake Shore project that was not based on assumptions at variance with them. The term "Olmsted plan" has been applied much more to the proposition of a park on the Lake Shore, which neither originated with the designers of the plan nor with your Commission, than to the scheme and devices invented for making the proposition practicable for which the designers of the plan are responsible.[6]

Judging from the general drift of public opinion with reference to such matters, as I have had occasion to follow it in other cities, the project of a lake shore park will be from time to time revived until, from regard to the interests of the city as a whole, it is adopted. It is not desirable that when it again comes up a prejudice due to a misunderstanding of these facts should have been handed down to embarrass its fair discussion. Hence it is best that the above statement should go to the public with your verification. Your obedient servant

The text presented here is an unsigned draft of a letter in Olmsted's hand. Olmsted presented his designs for South Park to the park commissioners on October 13, 1888, and oversaw the printing of over one thousand copies for wide distribution. At the November meeting of the park board, however, the commissioners voted against the implementation of the South Park plans. John C. Olmsted described the opposition as "conservative short sighted taxpayers and . . . local speculators on the other side of the R. R. who want the improvement made in their district and of less cost." At the park board's December meeting, "interested property owners" from the Thirteenth Ward, where the park was to be located, submitted a petition asking that the board reconsider Olmsted's plan. William McMillan, the superintendent of parks, also presented a list of other possible sites in the Thirteenth Ward for smaller parks. The park commission ultimately acquired two smaller sites farther inland for what became South and Cazenovia parks, designed by Olmsted in the early 1890s (F. L. & J. C. Olmsted, *The Projected Park and Parkways on the South Side of Buffalo. Two Reports by the Landscape Architects: Plan for a Public Park on the Flats South of Buffalo* and *Report on the South Parkway Question* [Buffalo, N.Y., 1888]; "How Do You Like It? Mr. Olmsted's Plan for A South Side Park," *Buffalo Express*, Oct. 14, 1888, p. 5; "Knocked Out, Mr. Olmsted's South-Side Park Decided Against," *Buffalo Courier*, Nov. 15, 1888, p. 6; "The South Park," ibid., Dec. 9, 1888, p. 12; JCO to William McMillan, Nov. 16, 1888, A3: 25–30, OAR/LC; JCO to W. A. Stiles, Nov. 22, 1888, A3: 34, OAR/LC; *Master List*, p. 70).

1. On January 9, 1889 the *Buffalo Morning Express* reported that the park commissioners, when asked by Mayor Philip Becker to ask Olmsted to "present his bill for all services rendered," stated that "Mr. Olmsted's bill will amount to $10,000. Most if not all of his work has been in connection with the South-side Park." In Olmsted's records, there are two bills dated January 1; the first bill charging $808.79 for expenses incurred in 1888, and the other bill charging ten dollars per acre for his South Park and Southern Parkway proposals ($4,270). Olmsted claimed that this rate was based on the rate schedule agreed upon in 1868 ("Bills to Come: What Will Mr. Olmsted's South-Side Plans Cost?" *Buffalo Morning Express*, Jan. 9, 1889, p. 6; FLO to the City of Buffalo Park Commission, Jan. 1, 1889, B47: #700, OAR/LC; FLO to William McMillan, Jan. 26, 1889).
2. On April 11, 1887, Olmsted submitted his "Proposed Extension of the Park System," to the park board, which reprinted it in their annual report. It was also published in several Buffalo newspapers (FLO to Sherman S. Jewett, April 11, 1887, above).
3. Olmsted and John C. Olmsted had been corresponding with McMillan throughout 1888, continually refining their plans and estimates for South Park. On August 1, for example, Olmsted sent a plan to McMillan that was returned with notes and alterations. In his final report, *The Projected Park and Parkways on the South Side of Buffalo*, Olmsted included an appendix that contained a "Preliminary Estimate for Construction of Proposed South Park" (FLO to William McMillan, Jan. 1, 1888, below; plan 718-z28, NPS/FLONHS; F. L. & J. C. Olmsted to William McMillan, Sept 1, 1888, A2: 766–67, OAR/LC; F. L. & J. C. Olmsted to William McMillan, Sept. 3, 1888, A2: 775, OAR/LC; F. L. & J. C. Olmsted to William McMillan, Sept. 10, 1888, A2: 799, OAR/LC; F. L. & J. C. Olmsted, *The Projected Park and Parkways on the South Side of Buffalo. Two Reports by the Landscape Architects: Plan for a Public Park on the Flats South of Buffalo* and *Report on the South Parkway Question* [Buffalo, N.Y., 1888], pp. 47–48).
4. A phrase crossed out by Olmsted but not replaced with an alternate.
5. Philip Becker (1830–1898), Republican, was first elected mayor of Buffalo in 1875 and re-elected in 1885 and 1887 ("Death List of a Day: Philip Becker," *New York Times*, July 6, 1898, p. 7).
6. In a January 21, 1889, note to William McMillan Olmsted articulated his frustration more thoroughly:

> Looking over the newspaper account that we have, I am struck with the constant assumption implied that the proposition to have a park on the shore and lapping over the town line originated with the Olmsteds. This is spoken of as if it were the essence of our work. In fact the suggestion came to us, as we understood from the Common Council and to the Common Council from the 13th Warders. We were taken to the place by the Park Committee and the question asked of us, was, in effect, what can be done with such a place as this.

("That South Park: The Commissioners Again Consider the Question," *Buffalo Morning Express*, Dec. 5, 1888, p. 5; FLO to William McMillan, Jan. 21, 1889).

To Edward Mott Moore

26th Jan. 1889.

Dr E. M. Moore;
My Dear Doctor;

First, I must ask you to consider that all the advice that we have given you thus far is of a tentative character.[1] We rarely give final professional opinions upon such mere impressions of topographical conditions as can be obtained in advance of the thorough definite and exact knowledge that is supplied by a topographical survey and by conference with the surveyor as to details that he will have become familiar with but which cannot be represented graphically. One of the chief objects of the topl surveys is to enable questions of boundary; that is, of extent of land required to accomplish certain objects, and others which you ask me, to be definitely studied. In case of necessity we can give snap judgments but it is not desirable to take final action upon those if it can be avoided. What we have said thus far is, in effect, this:—"There is certain ground which you ought not to fail to get. There is certain ground (generally along the borders of the first) that probably would be wasted. With reference to an exact definition of boundaries, the topographical survey had better be carried to such and such points".

Second, the next step in your undertaking should be a comprehensive and broadly contemplative determination of *general design* with the advantage for that purpose of the entire topographical survey of the entire body of land previously proposed to be considered. Considerations of details should be strenuously avoided until all that is necessary for the characterizing broad features has been determined and secured. Then design can be pursued from larger to smaller, subordinately and supportively to the main purpose.

Third; good design means an operation of imagination. It is not altogether a process of inductive reasoning. It cannot be done upon the jump. It is a matter of *growth*: involuntary and unconscious growth. I cannot come to a designing conclusion just when I want to. I must muse upon the conditions to be dealt with, have them upon my mind, and, after a time, I {*furnish a conclusion*}. I do not make it. It has come to be in my mind without my knowing it. Of course, if necessary I can bring myself to a decision quickly, but such a necessity is unfortunate.

It does not require a moment for me to make up my mind that you should seize the banks of the river above and below the town. But I have never wanted to go a great way beyond this until I could study the survey, or rather the surveys, one for all the ground to be considered above, the other for all below.[2]

But your Committees {*wanted*} to get to work, and {*there was*} danger, especially up the river that delay in purchasing {*and*} acquiring rights would {. . .} harm. Therefore our first advice was, make sure of some space on the bank of the river above as soon as you well can, for in any case you should have a sylvan river drive. How much? To this our answer was, "let a space of at least 200 feet be surveyed. With this we can design such a drive (& walk); you can secure the land if it is critically important to have it secured quickly, and then, if it is also critically important that you make some demonstration next summer, that probably will be the place for it. It would be possible to do some planting along the bank next spring, and by May or June have 300 men at work grading and road making.

I did not suppose at the time that you could accomplish the purchase of the entire meadow adjoining the site of this proposed river road.

Now I must say that while the river road might be planned and work set about as stated, in an emergency, it would be much wiser that the river road sh[d] not be planned except as a part of a whole, which whole would be the entire meadow park from Elmwood Avenue up.[3] That is to say, until we have the complete survey of this and can ponder its possibilities comprehensively, with the advantage of exact knowledge of all parts of it, it would be much better not to deal independently with a small part of it. If another man should do so, and my advice were asked by a Commission he was serving I should feel compelled to say "your man does not know his business. Your Commission ought not to accept such a plan — a plan for a fragment of a great work — without knowing what the rest is to be to which this fragment is to be fitted".

Then, as to trees, our plan being done, it certainly wd be possible to plant trees along the land side of what, when I spoke of it, I had in view as the river road strip, but they would not at once produce any good effect and they would be in the way of grading operations and could not be protected from injury by the men and horses and teams employed. Much more so if on the river side, where probably it will be best to revise the brink and slope of the banks sometimes a little, sometimes considerably. Unless for reasons of expediency not evident to us, therefore, we should certainly not advise tree planting this spring. We probably shall advise, after a little study of the topographical map that a contract be made with {a} nurseryman to have ready for planting the revised river bank slopes next spring a large quantity of rooted cuttings of shrubs and vines perhaps twenty to thirty thousand. Possibly, if you think best to push this work — the grading of the river bank — we can get the cuttings in March, keep them in pits or quarries and be ready to see them in their final places in the early summer. They might be sufficiently well rooted to resist the next spring floods, with some special precaution for their protection at salient points.

We will come out if we can help you at this time but we would rather not begin any study of design until the whole of our topographical map shall be ready for use on the ground and everything else is ready for an {*intelligent*} final settlement of certain fundamental questions. It is always a bad thing to get ideas and motives of parts of such works as those lodged in a designer's mind in advance of a comprehensive study.

I doubt if you are quite right in thinking that I proposed an outlay of $10,000 for dredging the gulley.[4] I am far from having made up my mind what ought to be done with it. It is a difficulty of the situation. I have only got to the point of saying that it is not an {*insuperable*} difficulty, because if nothing better, a sort of bayou could be made of it by designing and Mr Laney[5] and I guessed that the dredging could be done for $10,000. We should want to think the problem over a good deal, with the topographical map {. . .}[6] and in {*consideration*} with some notion of the general plan before committing ourselves to the {*proposition*}.

You must not in the least imagine that we are not loyally and scrupulously under your lead in all the large questions of administrative expediency if we give expressions to *doubts* in a suggestive way. This I shall do in saying that it seems to us that you have been wisely bold and fortunate in securing such ground opportunities as you have. Adding what you must take with the Reservoir site, your undertaking is a prodigiously big one as it stands. No other city in the world of the population of Rochester has ever entered upon so large a one (in the "park" way).[7] I should be very cautious of increasing the load, at least until the plans of what you have are fully developed. I should also question whether as a matter of policy, it would not be better to avoid outlays anywhere else until a complete and comprehensive body of improvements had been made from the Lower Falls along the upper part of the bank[8] to the point where our last tour ended.

This is one reason for such a question:—It invariably occurs that as long as a park Commission is engaged solely on *work in progress* and not closely approaching completion, its operations are greatly carped and sneered at. They are unpopular, and the more extended they are the more unpopular. So the Commission loses esteem and confidence as its works advance, until some one big thing comes close to completion and its true intent begins to be realized with very little exercise of the imagination. Then there is apt to be a great reaction and the new-born faith applies to all that the Commission is intending to do later. We simply question, therefore, whether, with a given expenditure, you could not come to a striking result—a result that would give you prestige with your community—sooner and more surely on the line I speak of than anywhere else? We question whether you could make as great a popular success or stir the local pride of your citizens as much by anything you could do on the South Meadows. There is a grandeur in the scenery on the north that would take hold of people. And I believe that I am influenced a little in saying this by the suggestion that

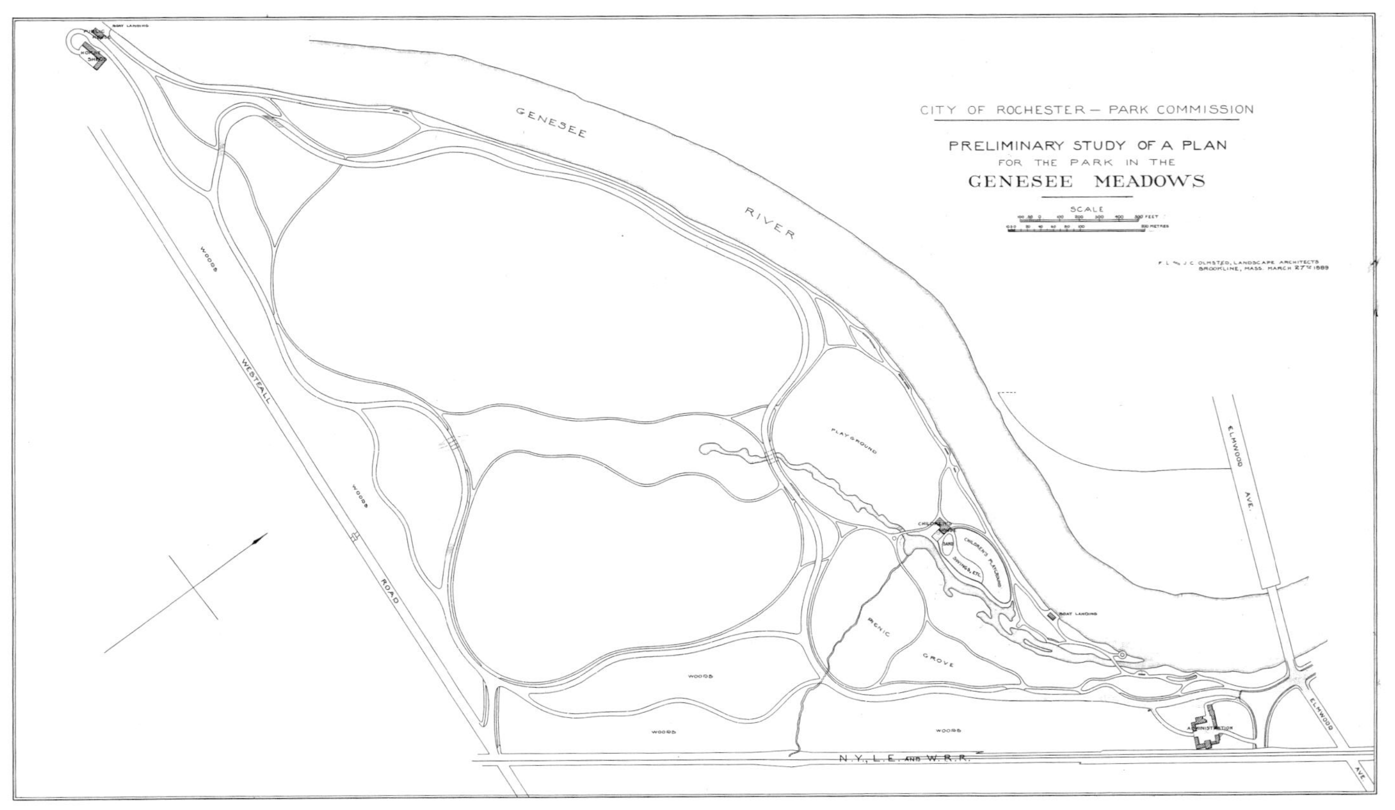

"Preliminary Study of a Plan for a Park in the Genesee Meadows," March 27, 1889

came to me in my last visit of possibilities of popular fine things in the situation that I could not define but that would grow with close study.

But all this, I repeat, is but a tentative and suggestive doubt—a reservation of opinion to be held until we get the topographical maps and can deal more exactly with the comprehensive problems.

It was our calculation that we should have the surveys, as Mr Laney supposed, by Christmas, and we had laid out to put in our time upon them during January. I am very sorry that this has proved impracticable, as toward spring we are more crowded. But it does not appear to me that it will take long to come to general conclusions as to the design of either of the works of which I have been writing. The Reservoir Park with its steep slopes, its narrowness, its irregular outlines, its springy ground, and its superb view to be kept open and presented to advantage will require much more pondering.

Yours Truly

Fred[k] Law Olmsted.

The text presented here is from a letterpress copy of a handwritten letter signed on the original in Olmsted's hand: A3: 148–57, OAR/LC. Olmsted had been working with the commissioners in an official capacity since October 1888, when they offered him a contract of $5,000 plus traveling expenses to "take charge of the whole park system." See FLO to Edward Mott Moore, Aug. 5, 1888, n. 7, above (Edward Mott Moore to FLO, Oct. 21, 1888, B77: #1100, OAR/LC; FLO to Robert Douglas, summer 1889, below; FLO to Calvin C. Laney, Aug. 9, 1889, below).

1. Olmsted began corresponding with Moore in June of 1888 about their park plans. In general, he had cautioned the board not to proceed too quickly with detailed park designs but to first address "considerations of policy and economy," and he also stressed the importance of securing as much parkland as possible along the river (FLO to Edward Mott Moore, Aug., 5, 1888, above; FLO to Edward Mott Moore, July 27, 1888, A2: 667–68, OAR/LC; *Report of the Board of Park Commissioners of the City of Rochester, N.Y., 1888–1898* [Rochester, 1898], pp. 19–20).
2. In February 1889 the Rochester park board reported spending $83,520 during the previous year to purchase the future sites of Genesee Valley Park and Seneca Park along the Genesee River. During the next months the topographical survey for Genesee Valley Park was completed and sent to Olmsted. Work on the park began that spring (A. B. Lamberton, *The Public Parks of the City of Rochester*, pp. 21–22; Edward Mott Moore to FLO, June 1, 1888, B77: #1100, OAR/LC).
3. That is, the entire area of what became Genesee Valley Park, with its large central meadow, extending southward from Elmwood Avenue for a mile and three-quarters along the right bank of the Genesee River (F. L. Olmsted & Company, "General Plan of Genesee Valley Park," 1890, NPS/FLONHS).
4. Olmsted refers to the excavation of Red Creek, an open ditch that ran through Genesee Valley Park. Olmsted eventually dredged and widened the mouth of the creek and redirected it for most of its length into an underground channel beneath a shallow swale (Edward Mott Moore to FLO, June 22, 1888, B77: #1100, OAR/LC).
5. Calvin Cooke Laney (1850–1941) was superintendent of the Rochester parks. His first

assignment was to survey the lands acquired for Genesee Valley Park (see FLO to Calvin C. Laney, Aug. 9, 1889, below).

6. Two to three words here are faded from the manuscript.
7. By January of 1889, the Rochester park board had acquired thirty-five acres along the river south of the city, part of what became Genesee Valley Park. In February 1889, additional land was secured in this area, and at the site of Seneca Park along the gorge of the Genesee River north of the city. The site of Highland Park, which Olmsted refers to here as Reservoir Park, was near a reservoir four miles east of the river. It was created from a donation of twenty acres from local nurserymen Ellwanger and Barry (given in May of 1888), and by transferring the reservoir itself to the jurisdiction of the park board. During 1889 the board continued to buy land along the river, and by February of 1890 parkland in the city totaled close to four hundred acres: 269 acres for Genesee Valley Park, 130 acres for Seneca Park and 20 acres for Highland Park, the latter growing to 60 acres by 1891 (*Report of the Board of Park Commissioners of the City of Rochester*, pp. 19–32; Edward Mott Moore to FLO, June 22, 1888, B77: #1100, OAR/LC).
8. The Lower Falls of the Genesee are north of downtown Rochester, at the south end of Seneca Park. Olmsted suggests here that the first concentrated improvements in the Rochester park system should be in the proposed Seneca Park, along the river gorge on the right bank of the river, for which he later designed a carriageway and path with several viewing concourses. He predicted that the development of this part of Seneca Park, which had dramatic views of the river gorge, would quickly create a welcome public amenity, while more extensive work on the meadow section of Genesee Valley Park was still underway (F. L. Olmsted & Company, "General Plan of Seneca Park, 1890," plan 1108-100, NPS/FLONHS).

To Morris Ketchum Jesup

Brookline, Mass.

31st Jany. 1889.

My Dear Mr Jesup.

I am very sorry that you take the view manifest in your note of 26th.[1] The question is not at all one of feeling. It is a question of business management. If what has passed between us since you first consulted me about the place in Lenox in 1885,[2] had passed between you and any man otherwise unknown to me—a man named {*Brown*}—and what had passed had become known to me, I should have said at once—"Mr Jesup; {*Brown*} is not the sort of man you want. What you want is not in his way of business." I might not be able to give you my reasons. One who has been for a long time following a particular channel of business, may, without arrogance or self conceit, come to conclusions about that business his reasons for which he is unable to state. His reasons may lie in a long course of experiences of which the larger number are no longer in his memory, though the *moral* of them remains. I have been on the track of my business more than forty years and no doubt I am more or less in that condition.

But it seems to me that if I may put you to the trouble of reading, I can give you sufficient reason for my conclusion.

My profession is that of a counselor in regard to a certain class of undertakings. Before I can give counsel I must have an understanding of what the undertaking is to be, its limits and conditions. What I need in this respect I must judge and I must therefore lead in the process of ascertaining it. I do not profess to be able to give any counsel which may be asked, at any time, offhand, on any branch or feature or detail of the undertaking. I must have a good general comprehension of the whole before I can deal to advantage with the parts. And in getting the needed understanding of the undertaking it is not my duty to be content with what my client is prompted to give me. Certainly I take his instructions, but not as a Secretary or an amanuensis takes instructions from a dictator. Rather as a lawyer takes instructions from one {who} wants his counsel. I do not limit my duty to giving such counsel as my clients may think they want. I give them what I find that they want.

Counsel, in my profession, is given largely in the form of drawings or "plans". It is not good practice to give such counsel in regard to particular members, elements or details of an undertaking before the main body of the scheme has been comprehensively studied and taken measurably definite shape, in a *general* plan—that is to say, until a plan has been prepared, discussed and approved, which, however vague and inaccurate in matters of detail, gives some idea of the principles of the undertaking, the relations of its parts to one another and to the whole, and of the character of the combination; in short, the design. That being done planning, (counsel) can go on in a deductive way, from comprehensive to incomprehensive, larger to smaller; from the more controlling to the less controlling features. Any other course leads to inconsistency, incongruities, blunders. It is putting the cart before the horse. It compels a sad waste of time and study. I say it is not good practice, not meaning that there is any professional etiquette or convention to that effect but that whether my reasoning is good or not, that is what experience has taught me. Accordingly, in your case, I had been from the first trying to proceed in that way. I don't think that to this time I have given you counsel on any point beyond what was directed to drawing from you such instructions as were required before a general plan could be begun. When you speak of plans that we have made, you refer to drawings of a perfectly tentative character—hardly that—simply drawings to serve a temporary purpose in *preliminary* discussion. Drawings to make clearer to you difficulties in the way of certain dispositions of yours which seemed to have come into your mind in advance of a realizing sense of the topographical conditions. You were in effect told "If you want such and such a house, with such an exposure and in such a place *then* some such arrangements as these will probably be necessary to convenience." Taking the difference of level between the different parts of the house; taking the necessary walls and cuttings; the courses and grades of approaches; the elevation of the domestic apartments above the natural surface; the disposition of yards in connection with the kitchen; *may you not think it better to modify your ideas of the house, its plan, exposure and situation*?

"You say you dislike a terrace; does not a house of the character you propose, placed in the proposed situation, almost make a terrace a necessity? At any rate, before undertaking to plan approach roads and entering upon their construction, (as you wished to do at once) would it not be better to consult an architect, and have your ideas more exactly defined?" To this last suggestion you finally and reluctantly agreed and your instructions that Mr Cook[3] must be set at work {on} roads making were countermanded. Wisely, as you must now, see. As to the approach from the Pittsfield road, your note implies an impression that you had obtained our counsel about it. You should not have so misunderstood us. Our position was that nothing ought to be planned—nothing could be safely planned—until the plan of the house had been more nearly defined, because until it was so, its place, its aspect, the elevation and grade of its various entrance ways could not be known, and until they were, the approaches to it could not be safely planned, unless in a very tentative and provisional way. You did tell us that you must have a road between the Pittsfield Road and your house. We advised you that it would be difficult—that is to say, that it would need very careful study and probably a heavy expense to get such a road and have it of a style and character consistent with that which you seemed to be having in view in the house and other points of the grounds. It would need very careful study to get such a road in without sacrifice of other elements that you valued in the property. But you urged us to study the problem, and (though we knew that we could not do so at all definitely until a nearer approach had been made to a settlement of some other matters), with reference to such a study we had the surveyor put in a line of stakes to indicate very approximately the course which you had seemed to have in view, in order that by measurements from them, we could study and define on the map a course laid out with regard to circumstances of the topography, the outlooks &c, which needed to be studied on the ground. To perfect the conception of an ideal for such a road along a steep, rocky and wooded hillside, determining what to abandon and what to secure and striking a judicious mean between respect for propriety of convenience and respect for nature would have been a most agreeable task but a task requiring a great deal of patient study of detail and a very cautious process of adjustment. The preliminary stakes had been set with regard to a suitable approach to a house to be set at a certain point, its entrance at a certain level. But after this, on the suggestion of your architects, you were considering the possibility that the house would better be placed in a widely different situation. Had all the other circumstances been favorable to a study of the road this fact showed that it would be premature. Hence, after once walking along the line of stakes and noting various points to be considered, we laid the question on the table. It had not had a day's study. Had we planned it we should have brought our plan to you for discussion. But we should have allowed you to defer a consideration of it, until it could be taken up in connection with other questions, after settling upon the place and plans of the house, and as part of a general preliminary plan.

This was the condition when you proposed last year a visit to Lenox and for the third time said that you wanted me and no one else to meet you there. Other engagements made it impracticable for me to do so at the time mentioned. Even if you had been willing to see my son, I could see no way in which the business could at the time be judiciously advanced. Everything was waiting the conclusion of your study with the architects. Until that point was reached a general plan could not be studied to advantage, and till a general plan had been at least provisionally settled upon, particular features could not be finally studied. Remember that I had already been four times on the ground and not the first step toward a real professional study had yet been made for want of a settlement of preliminary questions lying out of our field. I did not tell you that I did not wish to spend more time upon your work until such settlement had been made but finding that I could not come at the time you said that you would wait till next spring before asking for another conference with me. Later, however, you concluded to undertake the Pittsfield approach and without any information to our office, Cook was set about it. Of course on no plan for which we were in the slightest degree responsible. A line of stakes is no nearer to a plan than an alphabet is to a poem. But on somebody's plan it has been carried out so far that no other plan is now practicable. I don't want to criticize it. I don't know how I should have planned it differently. But I *do* know that I *should* have planned it differently if it had taken me a year to do it — either so or I should, after long time, have given it up and said it is beyond my power to make anything good of it. Perhaps what I should have planned would have suited you no better than what can be made of the essay in progress. Possibly as a plan on paper, you would not have liked it as well. If so, plainly I am not the counselor you wanted. But you say "You were away. I could not get you". There, again, the moral is, that I am not the man you wanted. I am not, because my business arrangements are such that a great deal of my business must be done by other men than myself. Everybody who has had to do with me knows this. I have not for years been responsible for any professional work, public or private, in which it has been my duty to do any particular thing — that could be named — personally. My business is of such a character that it would be very wrong for me to allow anything to be absolutely dependent on my abilities to be at particular points at particular days, and able to personally meet its requirements. It is quite necessary that I should make sure that what is to be provided — say, in the way of plans — drawings — shall be provided in a manner satisfactory to me and representative of my judgment, without the least work of my hands. You will see this necessity if you consider what the undertakings were with which we were charged last fall. Saying nothing of a dozen private works, we were dealing with eight important public (or semi public) works and were in correspondence as to others. There were six that I had appointments to visit, of which the nearest was five hundred miles away. From them we were constantly receiving reports and inquiries and to them we were sending plans and instructions. The outlays to be made upon them for the good direction and economy of which we had assumed a large responsibility were to be counted by millions. I could personally perform little of the work needed for a quittance of this responsibility. It was my duty to see that it was performed; that the performance of it went on from day to day, systematically, by competent men, in a manner that I could approve and accept as mine. Some of the men upon whom I had to depend were at all times a thousand miles or more away from me. I was liable to be called off from all of them any day. I was liable to be disabled in eyes or hand any day, and it was my duty to see that my business was so organized that no work would be blocked by such disability. I had to take care that all of the distant agents were in touch with the central office. I had to exercise such supervision and to personally do nothing else unless it was clear to me that I could do it better than any one else could be got to do it. Does this really imply any other methods of business than you would find exemplified in every large law office — counselor's office? That is the nature of my business, and I suppose that I may say that if tolerably successful results did not turn out from it you would not have asked my counsel. But it is plain, I think, that with such expectations as you had of me and for the manner in which you wish to have your business carried on, it is not suitable. I have never wished to conceal it. If you will refer to my letter to you of 20th Octr. last[4] you will recognize that I wished you to understand the fact, so far as it applied to you.

You may ask how can I be reasonably sure that plans prepared under these circumstances will represent what our clients may reasonably expect — my own judgment, my own counsel? To do so they must be made to suit me as well as if I did all the study upon them personally. Let us consider the case of your road and of my son — my son, rather than accept *my aid through whom* you preferred to do without it. (I am not blaming you for it.) My son has from early childhood been familiar with my works. He has lived with me on some of them. He has systematically taken lessons in our profession upon them. He has traveled thousands of miles with me while I have been inspecting and studying. He has been professionally educated under my direction, has studied abroad under my guidance. He has been at the head of my office ten years, has latterly taken an equal part with me in all my works, public and private. He is in the prime of life — a young middle aged man. More than one of our clients after experience have requested that I would allow him to lead in their affairs, finding him apter than they found me. Profr Sargent having to lay out a new approach upon broken ground among rocks and trees consulted him rather than me.[5] My experience leads me to believe that in such a case as yours, having walked over the ground and had some preliminary discussions with him, he would bring about a result more satisfactory to me than I could bring about in any way without him.

I don't in the least object to your saying: — "But that is not what I want". I can only reply — "I am truly sorry for it but I cannot supply you with what you want. It is not consistent with any business arrangements to do so. I can personally give only such degree of study to your undertaking as is necessary to the fulfillment of such professional responsibility as I am willing to assume about it. My personal work must be chiefly that of directing, reviewing and sometimes revising or amending the work of others."

You must take the frightful length of this letter to manifest my respect for your judgment, my regret that I could not and cannot answer your purpose and my desire to stand well with you.

I remain very sincerely yours,

Fred^{k} Law Olmsted.

The text presented here is from a letterpress copy of a handwritten letter signed on the original in Olmsted's hand: A3: 165–78, OAR/LC).

1. In his letter, Jesup explained that he had begun construction of an entrance drive for his property, connecting it to Pittsfield Road against Olmsted's advice. He apologized for his impulsiveness in implementing a plan contrary to Olmsted's, and said he would cease construction until Olmsted could consult with him on the ground. However, he said he still wanted to "convert" Olmsted to the idea of an entrance on Pittsfield Road (Morris K. Jesup to FLO, Jan. 26, 1888, B75: #1041, OAR/LC).
2. Olmsted had begun consulting with Jesup on the design of the grounds of his estate in 1885. See FLO to Morris K. Jesup, Oct. 20, 1888, above (see also FLO to Morris K. Jesup, Oct. 23, 1885, A1: 241–43, OAR/LC).
3. Presumably an engineer working on the project (FLO to Walter Watson, Aug. 7, 1888, A2: 711, OAR/LC).
4. FLO to Morris K. Jesup, Oct. 20, 1888, above.
5. Refers to work on Charles Sprague Sargent's estate, Holm Lea, in Brookline, which was close to Olmsted's home, Fairsted. John C. Olmsted had assisted on the design of the approach road during the summer and fall of 1888 (plans 1056-2, 1056-3, 1056-4-tp1, 1056-4-tp2, NPS/FLONHS; *Master List*, p. 176).

Talk to the Brookline Club Feb. 1889
History of Streets[1]

February 1889

I was invited to talk for an hour to a small circle of my neighbors upon some matter of local improvement with which I was having to do. As a servant of the town park commission[2] I could not discuss with entire frankness any such matters not yet fully settled. But I did not think that I had a right to decline such an invitation, and in casting about for a subject upon which I could feel more free to give my opinions, I remembered what it was that first attracted me to think of Brookline as a dwelling place. This led me to reflect that the undertaking of the parkway in the Muddy River Valley, the Beacon Street enterprise, the Aspinwall and Goddard Hill road system,[3] and several minor local affairs with which I have had something to do, were all alike illustrations of the working of a single common tendency of our civilization; that few communities are more interested than that of Brookline in forming an intelligent estimate of the true bearing and force of this tendency, and that the only way in which such an estimate can be formed is through a comprehensive study of the manner in which the tendency has been historically manifest.

Assuming, at some risk, that my vocation has given me occasion to reconnoitre the field of such a study a little more carefully than most of the other guests of the Club to-night, I have proposed to lead you in a glancing review of such of its leading features as I can conveniently point out in the time allowed.

We will start for this purpose, if you please, from the primitive town of the north of Europe.

This word town (from the same root with the German Zahn, a hedge or fence), did not originally mean either a place to live in or a trading place, but a place for the defence of life and property. The property often consisted chiefly of cattle and the paths formed mainly by movements of cattle were the nearest approach to streets to be found in the earlier towns.

As towns increased in population and wealth, their original slight defences were superceded by earth works or walls. The labor required for the construction of these and the advantage, in case of attack, of manning them closely with the force at command, made it important that they should not be unnecessarily extended. Consequently, as population further increased, lodging for it could only be had by gradually building houses closer and closer together within the walls. It followed that the spaces between the houses became narrower, and when second and third stories were added, they were, to get more room in the houses, often built jutting out over the paths.

Population still growing faster than accommodation could be found for it, herdsmen and other poor people were often driven to build huts and corrals outside the walls, again scatteringly, every man for himself, and again, foot paths and trails, afterwards to become streets, were formed accidentally, winding among them. After a time the protection of this outside population became important and then new and stronger walls were built enclosing it. And so, later, again and again, the town was enlarged; always in such a manner that the idea became inbred, as it were, in our race that the people of towns must live in a densely crowded way and that any degree of convenience for their private purposes to be found in streets must be a matter of luck rather than of *deliberate planning*. This, I suppose to be the origin of certain embarrassments to the exercise of good judgment that are operating here in Brookline and generally throughout our country, at this time.

If, in those days, any highways were laid out in towns, it was not with the slightest thought of what the effect would be upon the convenience and pleasure of the mass of the people in their ordinary industrial, social or domestic life; nor had the people anything to do with their laying out. They were planned and executed solely by military men, for warlike objects.

Paris, for example, had two straight roads, one crossing the other at right angles near the middle of the town. They were so laid out in order that re-inforcements could be hurried from the walls on one side by the shortest course to the walls on the opposite side. It was not till long afterwards that a road broad enough to admit a two-wheeled vehicle was carried through either of the four quarters into which Paris was thus divided.

We can hardly imagine the hardship to which, under these circumstances, even the more favored classes were subject; the filthy nuisances which they had to endure, the complete subjection that was required of all other aims in life to the one object of common defence. But you can see how naturally it fell out, that when, with the advance of society in other respects, it came to be tolerably safe for families to live otherwise than under the protection of walls and of large bodies of armed men, the excessive suppression of personal independence and individual inclinations which had before been required, caused a strong re-actionary ambition to possess each prosperous citizen to relieve himself as much as possible from dependence upon and duties to the general community. To secure greater independence and at the same time opportunity for the only forms of out-door recreation, in which the rich, after the days of jousts and tournaments, were accustomed to engage, all those who could command favor at Court, sought grants of land abounding in the larger game, and planted their houses in the midst of great enclosure of pasture land called parks, which not only kept neighbors at a distance, but served as nurseries for objects of the chase. With people of this class there was a sort of reaction toward the patriarchal form of society.

The habits of the wealthy, under these circumstances, though often gross and arrogant, and sometimes recklessly extravagant, were far from luxurious, according to modern notions, and as, in order to realize as fully as possible the dream of independence, every country gentleman had his private chaplain, surgeon, farrier, tailor, weaver and spinner; raised his own wool, malt, barley and breadstuffs; killed his own beef, mutton and venison, and brewed his own ale, he was able to despise commerce and to avoid towns. The finery his household coveted was brought to his door on pack-mules. The vocation of a merchant, in its large, modern sense, was hardly known, and the trade of even the most considerable towns was, in all respects, very restricted. Thus, for a long time, the old narrow, crooked streets of these towns served all necessary requirements tolerably well.

As the advance of general civilization continued, however, this indisposition to the exchange of services, of course, gave way; demands became more varied, and men of all classes were forced to take their place in the general organization of society. In process of time the enlargement of popular freedom, the spread of knowledge by books, the abatement of religious persecutions, the voyages of circumnavigators, and finally the opening of America,

India and the gold coast of Africa to European commerce, so fed the mercantile inclinations, that an essentially new class of towns, centres of manufacturing and of trade began to grow upon the site of the old ones.

Wagons, then, gradually took the place of pack-trains in the distribution of goods through the country, and, as one man could manage a heavy load, when it was once stowed, as well as a light one, wagons were made very large and strong, so as to carry cargoes like those of small sea-going merchant men.

The first considerable change in the streets of large towns that followed the invention of gunpowder was brought about by the necessity of widening some of them sufficiently to allow the passage of these great wagons. To a large extent this was accomplished by the removal of the wooden stalls and canvass booths that had before been built out in front of the walls proper of the shops and ware houses, as described by Scott in the first chapter of the Fortunes of Nigel.[4]

But with the new means of transport and the increase of trade and of population, the streets, as thus enlarged, soon proved inadequate for the uses required of them, and the consequences of their inadequacy, added to the results of ignorance and bad management in other respects, brought intolerable hardships upon all classes of towns people.

In Lanciani's Ancient Rome in the Light of Recent Discoveries,[5] a book published last year in Boston, which one does not need to be a scholar to find exceedingly interesting, there is one of those untwisting of old yarns by which we have of late years been so often surprised.

According to the author Rome, down to the time when Nero fiddled, had grown from a collection of herds-men's huts, into the greatest town in the world, never upon any pre-considered and comprehensive plan; its street arrangements being for the most part enlarged, from year to year, little by little, in a desultory, piece-meal way, with a view to local and personal, rather than general interests, much as those of Boston and Brookline are now. The slightest work of improvement was fiercely opposed by private owners of property and gave occasion, says Lanciani, to an endless amount of law suits and appraisals and fights among experts. The inconvenience and discomfort, the excessive cost of living, the sickness and misery that was due to this state of things had come to be appalling. The good Nero saw that no attempts at patch-work improvement would materially better matters. He saw that it would be an economical and in every way a beneficent operation to reduce the city to a heap of ruins, then clear the ground and begin building it over again upon a well-devised plan. And this he did, letting it appear, I believe, that the fires were accidental, yet providing with such noble, painstaking precaution for the safety of the people that not a life was lost either because of the fire, directly, or because of the destruction to which it led of shelter and clothing, and the interruption of the ordinary means of obtaining food and drink.

Even in our age of progress and material improvement, says Lanciani, we cannot help admiring the profound wisdom shown by the Architects Severus and Celer,[6] who were commissioned by Nero to design the new plan of the city. Large squares were opened where before had been filthy, thickly inhabited quarters. All new houses were to conform to new building laws designed to prevent the erection of ill-considered structures. These laws prescribed, among other things, that the height of no private house should exceed double the width of the street on which it fronted; that there should be porticoes covering the sidewalk in front of each for the protection of the public from rain and sun-stroke; Wooden ceilings were forbidden in the lower story of all buildings; It was forbidden also to build in blocks; Every new house was to have a clear space all around it; All building was to be under close official inspection.

The great fire of 1666[7] nearly secured for London the opportunity which Nero forced for Rome, and the greatest Architect of the time, Sir Christopher Wren, was alert to take advantage of it. He quickly sketched a greatly improved plan of streets, a plan that with all the advances that have since been made in the science of Municipal Administration, would still be considered a very good one. The immense advantages to be gained by it were undeniable. It was approved by the King and by everyone of liberal mind.

But it does not appear to have been even seriously considered by those with whom the decision was left, these being of the class whose motto is "I am a practical man," and London was re-built on much the same general plan, or the same no-plan, that it had been before.[8] Do you ask why?

I suppose mostly because of the unconscious subjection of the practical man to the tyrant custom. He could not be got out of the old ruts. And, however, the effect of a general almost monomaniacal dread of the opening of new channels of taxation which prevented any fair consideration of possible compensation for outlays for the general benefit.

Accordingly the city was re-built with little variation from the old lines. Then for another century it continued to become more and more crowded, more and more sickly, more and more inconvenient, debased and wicked. So gross, at last, became the evils resulting wholly, as we now know, from a senseless street plan, that they excited absolute consternation, and all the wise men of the kingdom were set to thinking how they could be contended with.

Did the wise men urge that the city should be deliberately burned over again in order that Wren's plan might be adopted? Did they even urge that a few buildings should be removed and the fronts of a few others set back, so that a few streets could be widened and straightened to serve as general thoroughfares? Did they advise that sidewalks should be provided and the big wagons confined between them? Did they suggest that Courts should be opened in which wagons could be loaded and discharged without obstructing the more important streets? Did they suggest better pavements?

They did nothing of the sort; first, because the immediate effect would have been a higher rate of taxation; second because all operations of the class would have made the city less disagreeable to live in, thus adding to the danger, always, as they supposed, attendant upon the gathering of great numbers of people. So great was the dread of these two evils that nothing could be thought of but projects for checking the increase of population, or, if possible, for declining it. A great many laws were passed for this purpose. Very queer they appear to us—as queer as some that we are passing will appear to our grand children, perhaps. In the end they seem all to have had the opposite effect of that intended. Among the less futile was one to prevent the building of any new houses in the borders of the city; one to prevent any additional accommodations from being provided for travelers within it; one requiring every man who had a house in the country to get out of the city in three weeks, and several for the transportation as bondsmen, of men and women found in the city without visible means of support, to Ireland, Virginia or Jamaica. And so on. But the business and the population, and the crowding and the filth and the discomfort and the disease and the vice of the town continued to increase frightfully. Within a hundred years after the real estate owners had rejected Wren's plan, the merchants were obstreperous in complaints that their profits were curtailed by the delays and miscarriages of all business caused by the constantly blockading of the streets. In time, nearly every house owner on many streets was ready to welcome increased taxation as the price of ever so moderate an improvement of his particular street. And little by little, by one movement after another, always of a limited local scope, time-serving and selfish, the street system of the old city of London was brought to be what it is,—and that is, even now, just as bad a system as the people can from year to year put up with.[9]

But I am getting on too fast. Let me get back to somewhere about the middle of the last century and see what the streets then were.

Their imperfect pavements never have been adequately revised since the days of hand-barrow and pack-horse transportation, were constantly being misplaced and the ground worn into deep ruts by the wheels of the great wagons. The slops and offal matters thrown out of the houses, combined with the dung of the horses and the mud to make a thick, deep, nasty mess through which the people on foot had to pick their way in constant apprehension of being run down or crushed against the wall. In the principal streets strong posts were planted at intervals behind which active men were accustomed to dodge for safety as the wagons came upon them. Coaches had been introduced, but though simple, strong and rudely hung vehicles, it was considered dangerous to use them in the streets. They were mostly employed for journeys out of town. Sedan chairs for all ordinary purposes were in common use by all except the poor upon every occasion of going into the streets. Even when George the Third went to open Parliament, streets had to be prepared for the safe passage of the state coach by laying faggots in the ruts. There was little or no sewerage or covered drainage, and heavy storms formed gullies of the ruts and often flooded the cellars destroying much merchandise.

Only by a good deal of scattered reading of books not very common, and by incidental and indirect evidence in these, can we now readily bring ourselves to believe what hardships women and children living in towns had, under these circumstances, to endure. Think of a housewife's daily shopping, think of little children going to school.

The condition of other European towns was in a few cases better than that of London, chiefly because the world had less business to do in them; the condition of most was worse because they had come more slowly out of the feudal military state. What the streets of Paris were in the latter part of the century we may imagine from the pictures that Dickens has given of them in the "Tale of Two Cities."

For us, the most instructive fact of the more recent history of cities is, that long after great improvements had been made in them, with the happiest results, and nearly to our day, custom still had such hold upon the minds of well-informed and intelligent men that they continued very generally to take for granted that the larger the business of a town should become, the greater would be the inconvenience and danger to which all its people would necessarily be subject; the more they would be exposed to epidemic diseases, the feebler, more sickly, and shorter their lives would be; the greater would be the danger of sweeping conflagrations; the larger the proportion of mendicants and criminals, and the more formidable, desperate and dangerous the mobs.

As a matter of fact, towns have gone on rapidly increasing, and in the largest the amount of disease is not now more than half what it formerly was; the chance of living to old age is much more than twice as great; epidemics are less frequent, less malignant and more controllable; sweeping fires are less common, less devastating and are much sooner got under; ruffians are much better held in check; mobs are less frequently formed, are less dangerous, and, when they arise, are suppressed more quickly and with less bloodshed; there is a smaller proportion of the population given over to vice and crime and a larger proportion of educated, orderly, industrious and well-to-do citizens. This is true of all prosperous, civilized historical cities.

Had our grandfathers been asked to look forward to such a state of things, they would have said that it could only come with the millennium, or by a series of miracles.

If we undertake to account for it less cheaply, we shall find it convenient to divide the agencies by which it has been more directly brought about under two heads. Under one would range such agencies as those of sewerage and water supply, compulsory vaccination, the isolation of people attacked by infectious diseases, provisions of bath and wash houses; police, fire and quarantine precautions, building laws, the widening of streets, reservations of open ground, provisions for recreation and so on, agencies which have been brought into use chiefly through town governments and by means to which the great body of the people have contributed but little except in the form of taxation, and in that form nearly always for the time reluctantly.

Under the other head we should range a variety of agencies that have been operating, as a rule, at least until very lately, without aid of government, without much public discussion, mainly by spontaneous action of the people, unorganized, and with leadership only of the kind which we have in mind when we speak of such and such a woman as being a leader of fashion.

The latter class of agencies have been of much more relative importance in the improvement of great towns than is apt to be recognized; therefore in continuing our historical study we need more particularly to look after such.

I have mentioned that in order to check the alarming growth of London building in the immediate outskirts of the city was for a time forbidden. With the widening of streets to admit the freer passages of wagons, the space covered by buildings within the city became less; as its business was at the same time rapidly increasing and with its business the number of people engaged in business, and as, beyond a certain point, closer stowage was impossible, we have the question, how was the increase provided for?

The answer is:—

First, within the city, dilapidated and burnt buildings were gradually replaced by new; the new were built much higher, and certain business formerly done on the lower floors was carried to upper floors.

Second, accommodations for increasing business and for the dwelling of those engaged in it, were found in the neighboring villages, and these villages were gradually much enlarged.

Third, the law to restrain building about the city became a dead letter and all the roads leading outward for long distances came to be lined with new buildings.

Lastly, and of most importance, a social movement began which was commonly regarded as a fashion, but which seen from this distance is no more reasonably to be described by this word than Christianity or Democracy or Irish Emigration.

It has been the custom for all, or nearly all, engaged in any business establishment, whether professional, mercantile, or mechanical, to form one household with the family of the proprietor. If it were a small household, the shopmen sat at table with the wife and children; if a large household, there might be a second table for the younger clerks and apprentices, and a third for the porters, laborers and domestics. Even the counting room and the vaults of a banker, as in the case of George Heriot,[10] were undivided from his dwelling house. Recalling the names of David Ramsey and Gabriel Varden,[11] you will be reminded how the custom worked with artisans and mechanics.

In the latter part of the last century business began to be done in many cases upon a larger scale than before, and certain merchants were coming to be very rich. With increase of wealth came more thoughtfulness for refined luxury and an enlarged social ambition. As business was forced into upper stories and families driven to higher apartments, and as, at the same time, need came to accommodate a larger business staff, it was occasionally impossible to fully maintain the old custom. For a time only those who stood at a considerable remove above the generality, perhaps only those who had become allied with the lower aristocracy, could break from it without subjecting themselves to much derision and giving rise to lamentations of the degeneracy of the age. But the number of those taking the step increased until the practice came to be regarded much as that of not going home to dinner in the middle of the day came to be about forty years ago in New York and Boston.

But more and more fell away, and at length a generation came to many of whom it was an inherited custom that business men should have homes apart from their places of business. A little later it became practicable to discriminate between different parts of a town under such heads as a fashionable, an unfashionable, and a low, residence quarter. Yet later, fashionable suburban residence quarters began to be heard of. And, as to this word suburban, I must point out that it has been gradually gaining a new significance. Originally a suburb meant a place where poor people overflowing from a dense city were forming a scattering hamlet of hovels outside its walls. Now it is coming to mean if it does {not} yet fully mean, a place in which a degree of the convenience of a town can be combined with a degree of the luxury of a rural home. In this sense not only are Brookline, and Brighton and Watertown and Waltham suburbs, but Beverley and Manchester, Lenox, Stockbridge and Newport.[12]

I have been giving you a few fragments of the history, for a thousand years, of London, bringing it down nearly to our own time, as a means of illustrating the method by which our present standard of propriety in respect to street arrangements has been developed from that of our pagan ancestors. Of the further development of the last half century I shall speak largely from personal observation.

Few American travelers, I apprehend, realize what a small part of London is that more compact part of it of which they see most, or, great as are the changes that have occurred through new streets and new buildings in that part, how much greater are those which have occurred in other parts.

I have made four visits to London, spending altogether something more than a year there. The first was forty years, the last ten years, ago.[13] I have had friends in different outskirts of the town, and from their homes have roved further outwardly in various directions. Through successive observations thus made the impression has been strongly fixed upon my mind that, outside of certain districts of comparatively small area, namely the commercial and the pauper districts, London is all the time growing more thinly settled. In other words, while London has been gaining greatly in business and in population (and population of a thrifty and fairly well-to-do character) it has been gaining more in area and the people engaged in its business are proportionately more widely distributed. It is, on the whole, a much quieter town; much cleaner; much healthier. Its people, without distinction of class, live in a more respectable way; are less crowded and enjoy a great deal more of that form of luxury that was formerly considered to be beyond the reach of townspeople. I mean domestic, suburban luxury.

In the village about London there had been from early times many pieces of waste land or of commons or bits of ground the titles to which were obscure and doubtful. A great deal of spirit has of late years been developed to make the rights of the public in all such places clear and definite; to extinguish adverse claims; to enlarge the spaces by the purchase of adjoining land, and then, partly by voluntary subscriptions, partly by funds from taxation, to make these places more commodious, beautiful and useful.

Add what has been gained in this way to the enlarged area of the more notable parks and such acquisitions as the Embankment[14] and those obtained by removing the grave stones of the old parish burial grounds and making shady public promenades through them and it will be found, I believe, that during the last fifty years the area of open and sylvan ground permanently secured for the use of the people of London has been more enlarged than the population.

But what has been gained in this way and in the opening of broader streets is, in my judgment, by no means the most important of the suburban gains of London.

You remember how Dickens, writing of a period in the history of London of about forty years ago, describes Mr. Jaggers as washing his clients off his hands before he left his office. "There were people slinking about who were evidently anxious to speak with him, but there was something so conclusive in the halo of scented soap that they gave it up for that day."[15]

Then he describes Wemmick as saying "My office sentiments must not be confounded with my Walworth sentiments," and he pictures Wemmick's moated castle, as being such a good thing for him.[16] What made it so? Certainly not the air. The air of the castle smelt of dry-rot and tasted like a bad nut, and Pip says the pig pen might have been a little further removed from his bed chamber with advantage. What then was the good of it? The good of it was the healthful effect upon the mind of a suburban home. That by which I have been most impressed in successive visits to the newer parts of London has been the apparent constantly increasing proportion since that time of houses that are set back from the street lines, and in the evidence that landlords and speculative builders are being forced, (generally with reluctance, and only by the overcoming of strongly indisposing habits), to adjust their plans to meet a growing popular satisfaction with homes in close connection with which there shall be some scrap of private lawn or garden or greenery of some sort.

I have no statistics of the progress made in this respect. When last in London, I called on one of the largest real estate agents of the city, hoping that he could put me on the track of them, but, though he confirmed my impression in a general way, he could offer me no definite statements about the movement, nor suggest how they could be obtained.

But one striking fact I can give you on the authority of Mr. Besant.[17] It is that the total average attendance upon the theatres of London is now actually less than it was fifty years ago, notwithstanding the enormous increase of population. This, Mr. Besant says, is due simply to the fact that the great body of what would otherwise be the play-going people of London, are now living at such a distance from the theatres that they prefer to find some local domestic, or social way of obtaining evening entertainment.

I have been citing the experience of London as the readiest way of illustrating a general tendency of civilization.

I do not think that there is any large thriving town in Europe in which the same tendency is not manifest.

Coming to our side of the ocean I will remind you, first, of a few of the forms in which it has been developing just hereabouts.

The Commonwealth of Massachusetts, wishing to sell a certain body of land on the border of the compactly built part of Boston, lays it out with streets broader than have been customary, and thus offers it to purchasers upon conditions designed to give them assurance that there will be no building upon it for mercantile or mechanical purposes, and that between every dwelling to be built upon it and the street line there will be a plot of turf at least 20 feet deep. In other words, the state guarantees purchasers that it shall be an unbroken residence quarter, with at least a slight element of verdure. Then, to give a little more of a suburban flavor to the district it provides, in Commonwealth Avenue, a continuous strip of turf and trees a mile and a half long to be formed through the middle of it.[18]

The immediate effect of these provisions is to make the land in question by far the most saleable of any in close connection with the compact town and to spread costly dwellings rapidly on it. Later, in the vicinity of this region, but further from the compact town, the city of Boston enters upon the difficult task of giving a pleasing sylvan character to the shores of a salt creek and a naturally repulsive drainage basin.

The owners of the adjoining land make provisions similar to those of the state, just described, to prevent building upon it for commercial purposes and to secure a strip of verdure between the streets and the house sites.[19] Then, at once, before the work is well begun and long before its success is secured, property doubles in market value.

Here in Brookline similar provisions to give assurance to purchasers that land in the neighborhood of that they are asked to buy shall be used only for dwellings, and that the front of no dwelling shall come within twenty or thirty feet of a street, are made by the Brookline, the Aspinwall, the West End and the Goddard Land Companies.[20] The Boston Park Department, when it buys a part of a man's land for the Parkway makes it a condition of its bargain that he shall be bound to sell no land fronting upon the parkway except with a restriction against building within 25 feet of it.[21] And land owners as a rule are found perfectly willing to agree to such an arrangement, recognizing that it tends to give a desirable character to the neighborhood. It all looks as if before long property fronting streets upon which building close up to the street line is permitted would be unsaleable except for commercial purposes, and for commercial purposes only where other special advantages are offered.

But let us look further from home. Let us consider how it is at our Capitol City.

Less than fifty years ago, visitors who wished to flatter our national vanity would make much of one or two small parts of Washington in which plain, solid, three and four story brick blocks had been lately built. "Washington is taking on quite an urban aspect" they would say. No one applies that term urban, in a complimentary way, to the present best residence quarter of the city. In this, most of the building of the last ten years has been done, not for occupants who would be tenants, but who would be owners of their dwellings. Nearly all the new buildings are set well back from the street, many are detached and have trees and foliage on all sides of them, like the best houses in our more attractive villages.[22] They have marked individual character and the streets they line have also more the aspect of broad village streets than of streets which not long ago must have been thought characteristic of the fashionable quarter of an important city. The greater number have lately been provided with bordering strips of soil to sustain trees; and in these strips, within the last twenty years, 60,000 trees have been planted and, under official inspection, have been *well* planted and furnished with guards.[23]

Illustrations of the same tendency are conspicuous in most of our cities, and the further we go from the seaboard, as a rule, the more conspicuous we find them. I cannot take time to review them, but there is one symptom that must not be slighted because it is more significant than all others, and is more marked in many of our new western cities than here or in Europe.

To realize the strength of the suburban tendency we must consider how it operates under difficulties; how it is affecting, if at all, that part of the people that is least able to follow its inclinations.

In most of our growing great western cities there are to be seen long lines, by the hundreds, of little homesteads. The streets on which they front are broad; often so much more so than seemliness, convenience, or economy would permit, that their breadth must be considered as due to an excessive revolt from the narrowness of streets in old towns. Their wheelways are often rutty, their gutters foul, their plank sidewalks dilapidated, the sapling trees on their borders badly selected, badly planted, badly treated in every way; not one in a hundred will ever make a tolerable mature tree. Generally the fences, gates, walks, the seedy turf and flower beds between the street and the houses are of the Cheap Jack and slop shop order of finery. Nevertheless, let the observant traveler reflect upon the obvious private history of the great body of the inmates of these dwellings; let him consider that not many years before, people of this class, (the class of Joseph and Mary) in all the large cities in the world, would have been living only in compact blocks upon narrow streets, lanes or courts, even as they yet live by thousands in Boston and New York and

Baltimore; let him consider out of what conditions the majority of those people must have come, and he will find that these shabby, dreary, dirty, straight, monotonous, broad streets of our western cities, lined for miles with front yarded, narrow dwellings of one story, or one story and a half, are about the most respectable things of our country. For what less do they tell us than this, that here are many thousands of laboring men, each of whom, under adverse circumstances has been stirred to make the attempt to provide his family with a separate home, (a separate dwelling house with a separate dwelling garden); and who has passed the necessary preliminary educational test of obtaining it, a test of self-control, self denial, temperance, frugality, thrift.

Give the utmost weight to the occasional childlike ignorance, the groping taste, the poor incongruities, of parts of the exhibition, yet it unquestionably evinces the first steps in a movement of humanity, the direction of which movement is just the best possible.

The Louvre, the British Museum, Harvard College, are not better tide-marks of the rising current of Christian civilization.

I have been showing you the pleasantest side of our new and coming great towns. You may naturally expect that at this point I shall tell you what degree of advantage the millions upon millions of people who are hereafter to live in these towns are to have, because those who are laying them out can apply to their work lessons taught by the history of older towns in the east and in Europe? I am sorry that I cannot give a satisfactory answer to this question.

Some few simple lessons, words of one syllable as it were, have been generally well learned. Streets are not laid out as they used to be in the walled towns of the barbarians. They are neither as short, nor as uselessly crooked as those of the older parts of London, Paris, Frankfort or Florence.

But let the question be:—what has been chiefly in the minds of those engaged in planning them, and I am obliged to answer that it can have been nothing nobler than a desire to get the job off their hands at the cheapest possible expense of thought.

Rarely can evidence be found in the plans of our young cities of the slightest ingenuity directed to the adjustment of the courses of streets to local circumstances, whether of topography or of trade.

As to the grading of streets, the Journal of the Association of American Engineering Societies represents that often (I believe it would be true to say, generally) in our younger western towns the grading of streets is controlled by regard for small private interests, or, at best, a compromise is made between immediate, small, private interests and lasting, great, public interests, in disregard of scientific principles and practical experience, creating irreparable incongruities, of which the result is financial loss and endless litigations.

With reference to the modern tendency of civilization toward a permanent division between business and domestic quarters, and toward the suburbanizing of the domestic quarters, in the original laying out of our western towns thus far, no thought is often given to it. Afterwards, attempts are sometimes made to modify plans with this motive. Generally the results are poor and excessively costly as compared with what might have been done by the application of judgment to the purpose before the primary plan had been adopted.

By chance, some of our recklessly prepared town plans answer tolerably well. Equally by chance, some as badly as the ingenuity of the devil could make them. If this seems a strong expression, it can be easily justified.

I do not think there is a city in the world which at the time it was first extensively laid out, was expected more confidently, by those responsible for the work, to come rapidly to be a great metropolis than the city of the Golden Gate.

There are streets in that city, the more nearly level parts of which you will now find crowded with traffic and lined with substantial buildings. In these buildings the most important business of the western half of the continent may be transacted. But move along quarter of a mile further on the same streets, and you may not see a single wheeled vehicle in an hour; you will meet few people on foot; you will notice many rickety wooden dwellings and not a few vacant lots. Go still further on the same streets and you will come to a good district of dwellings, factories and shops with every evidence of thrift and prosperity. How is the miserable condition of the intermediate district to be accounted for? Simply by the circumstance that it was less trouble to draw a straight line with a ruler on a piece of paper, than to find out by what courses a street could be taken over a hill, with grades less steep than the steepest possible. In some of the streets, crossing those to which I refer on the hill side, the surface is so canted laterally that the third story of houses on one side of them is on a level with the first story of the houses opposite.[24]

There is in the narrow crooked streets of Boston nothing to compare with the stupidity, the wastefulness, the hardship and the barbarous cruelty of the arrangement. Take my word that if anything like the amount of thought that a good architect usually gives to the plans of the simplest dwelling or stable, had been applied to the problem, the plan of San Francisco would have been bettered to a degree the value of which would be justly measured by millions upon millions of dollars. Even in saying this I do not suggest the worst aspect of the matter. Perhaps I can do so by adding that it has happened to me to see more striking examples of youthful brutality in just those quarters, within half an hour, than in many weeks in other parts of the city.

With no more study of the future convenience of its people than in San Francisco, the greater number of our cities have been laid out, and now every day there are ludicrously incompetent men, and men ludicrously unaware of their incompetency, determining the courses to be daily followed for centuries to come, in the aggregate by many myriads of men, with not nearly the degree of contrivance for their convenience that is often applied to the cabin arrangements of a fishing smack.

I hope that this strikes you as a very strange neglect of a most important duty. I am afraid it is hardly more strange than some facts with which you should be more familiar. For example, the fact that at this day additions to the street plan of Boston have been laid out without the smallest regard to the interests of those who shall be using them in years to come; without the smallest regard to the general public interests even of the moment; that the work has been under the direction of no public servant charged to regard the public weal in the matter; that it has been left to be done by private individuals acting privately, from a contracted individual point of view, and with regard to immediate private interests almost exclusively. I am afraid it is not more strange than that in the greater part of New England, the mending of common roads means merely slicking them over with vegetable mould thrown up from ditches into which the first heavy rain will wash it back again. How can we account for such things? I suppose that we can make one step toward an answer in saying that men who are thrifty in their private affairs are often thriftless in affairs of their community, and another in saying that none of us know in what degree our minds are fettered by custom. Our roads and streets are no more well ordered, no more convenient for our common purposes; no more economical, no more beautiful, than they are, because the current of our lives has its head in springs of barbarism. Even in the new world we but slowly get ourselves free from customs essentially uncivilized, and we do so much more slowly in matters political than in matters social and domestic.

In view of all the considerations that I have presented, it seems reasonable to conclude that there is a strong tendency in our civilization to build parts of towns with reference more and more strictly to business, and in such a manner that more and more business may be done within given limits of ground; and to built other parts of the same towns with reference more and more strictly to the enjoyment of life apart from business and in such a manner that more and more ground shall be appropriated to a given number of homes. It is reasonable to conclude also, that the sentiment that we attach to the word home will be less and less applicable, under the future working of this tendency, to dwellings which are wholly on the inside of the walls of a house. The word when applied to the dwelling of a family, in a large town, is growing more and more to call up ideas of verdure and foliage as well as of interior fire places, papered walls, pictures, books and house furniture. The effect of the tendency on the whole will be to spread out the domestic parts of a town and to include in the idea of a town a much larger proportion than at present of decidedly rus-urban elements.

The tendency in this direction is not only advancing; it is growing stronger and more sweeping as it advances. It first stimulates invention and business enterprise, and as inventions and new methods in business come into play the tendency is stimulated in turn. Street railways; electric and cable street railways; the special delivery of letters; the district messenger system, the telephone, and the extending custom of tradesmen's deliveries in the suburbs, are instances of what I mean. It is easier to keep house on an average four miles from the central parts of Boston now than it was two miles from it twenty years ago, and we cannot suppose that we yet see the end. I do not mean the end of the effect in this respect of what has already been invented, but we cannot suppose that the end of inventions stimulated by the tendency is yet near at hand.

We may reasonably conclude then, that, in choosing a dwelling place, people in the future will value nearness to the central parts of a town much less than they do now, and that they will care much more than they do now to have pleasant things about them the pleasantness of which is due to the operations of nature — the operations of nature as affecting the superficial texture and tone of rocks and of building materials and as evident in products of vegetable growth, and of *lasting* rather than evanescent, products of growth.

You may wish me to express an opinion as to the influence which this conclusion should have upon the conduct of the community affairs of this town.

It may be better to preface what little I can now say on this point by giving you a scrap of autobiography; my object in doing so being to make plain to you, first, my opinion of the present condition of Brookline, and the manner in which it may attract new comers.

When I was in Washington in 1861,[25] there was a man in my office that talked a good deal about Brookline, and always in a proud and affectionate way. He was the best man that I ever had so near to me as he was, and thus I came to acquire a good deal of regard for Brookline before I ever saw the place, and this regard grew the more at the time, I suppose, from the fact that no other people in all our country were as quick, as energetic, as discreet, as those of Brookline in sending to Washington, after each of the early disasters of the war, things of cheer — things not words. I had the pleasure once, of saying of a swift-footed messenger coming from them: — "This Mr. Lincoln, is Mr. Ginery Twitchell[26] of Brookline, Massachusetts; and he has brought us twenty tons of things for the soldiers — just the things that are wanted too — which the women made up in the meeting houses there last Sunday." I don't remember what day of the week it was but I know that we thought that Brookline had made the quickest time on record, and that circumstance added to my good opinion of the town.

In 1876 I was asked to prepare a plan for extending the street system of New York over a territory several miles in extent; a territory of extremely varied surface, with a resident population of many thousands, with numerous existing roads laid out when the region was wildly rural. I accepted the duty upon certain conditions, one being that I should have the assistance of Mr. J. J. R. Croes, an engineer who had made a topographical survey of the region and who knew it thoroughly. The first step in our work was to mark off several larger districts, being those the more undulating and rugged, and to determine that our plan for these should be of an unusual character. That we should not aim, for instance, to make them convenient for the purposes of commerce; or convenient for dwellings to be built in blocks smack on the streets, or in straight rows, or in rows parallel with the lines of the streets. That we should have in view a great variety of dwellings, large and small, modest and parade-full, the positions and frontages of which would often be adapted to the preservation of the natural topography of the locality, and to the enjoyment by their inmates of trees and bushes having a natural character and growing in a more or less natural way. We had in view in laying out each of these districts, that is to say, what had before never been had in view in laying out any part of the city of New York; a suburb and a suburb that should never be anything else than a suburb.[27]

We did not mean, of course, that these suburbs should be composed exclusively of dwellings. In our report made when we submitted our plan for the first of them, we said:—"an interrupted succession of private villas and cottages is not to be hoped for. Here and there a shop or a range of shops will be necessary, but being adapted only to local custom, they are not likely to be lofty or excessively obtrusive. Now and again buildings for other purposes would probably occur; as a school with its play grounds, a church set in a proper church yard; a higher institution of learning with its green quadrangle, academic grove or campus; a public hall, library or museum; a convent with its courts and gardens; a suburban inn or boarding house with its terrace commanding prospects. The nearest approach to urban building likely to be frequent, if once the general character proposed is obtained for the district, would be a range of dwellings set back from the public street and reached by a loop road, the crescent shaped intermediate space being either a quiet slope of turf, a play ground for children, or, if the topography favors, a picturesque rocky declivity. There will be, whatever the plan of roads, a great number of situations well adapted to such an arrangement, and which could be made suitable for no other except at much greater cost."[28]

We looked for a hot opposition to our plans and were not disappointed. Pamphlets were written and delegations of remonstrants were again and again heard, against them. But in the end they were adopted and to the extent of about a hundred miles of streets, turned over to the engineer to be carried out.[29] An engineer capable as such, and as a man, frank, sincere and of cultivated taste. But an engineer's first duty is to be safe. The path of safety is the well trodden path. Accordingly, it was on my mind that the engineer was probably prejudiced against the departures from custom of the plans, and if so it could not but affect his management of details unfavorably to a realization of the intentions of them. Some time after the work came into his hands I had the pleasure of a personal introduction to the streets of Brookline. So strongly were my old impressions of the town confirmed, that I immediately wrote to the engineer that I had seen realizations of nearly everything in our plans for new New York that, as they appeared on paper, had probably struck him as strange and odd and bizarre, beyond the point of propriety for permanent work, and that I should be greatly obliged if he would, under my guidance take a look at them. He was kind enough to accept my invitation and the result was what I anticipated it would be. As we drove back on the mill dam he said: "I confess that what we have seen has considerably changed my views and I shall proceed to carry out the policy you have advised with much more confidence that time will vindicate it than I could have had without seeing the demonstration you have shown me of its convenience, economy and pleasantness."[30]

For my part the predisposition to be pleased with Brookline that I before had was so nourished by what I saw of it that day that it brought me the next year to seek summer quarters in the place for my family. During that summer I came to like it, to respect it, and to feel at home in it, more and more. The summer following we took a furnished house on Walnut street and when the summer was passed the thought of going back to our urban home in New York was so unpleasant that week after week we kept putting off our departure. At length a fall of snow came. This was on a Saturday night. Riding out to enjoy the trees in their new dress the next morning, I was surprised to see squads of men with small snow plows, shovels and brooms, clearing the side walks under personal inspection of one of the selectmen on horse back. Before meeting-time women and children were comfortably walking to their places of worship from the outermost parts of the town.[31]

"Is it possible" I asked "that such a job can be so promptly, so cheaply and well done at the common expense of the community? If it is, taking the fact with everything else I have seen during the summer, I have not only found the advantages of town life better combined with rural and sylvan delights than I have in a long search found them anywhere else in the world but I have found a higher order of civilized people than I have found anywhere else."

I rode back to our furnished house on Walnut street and as I kicked the snow off my boots took care to cast it towards New York. The next day I ordered a supply of coal for the winter. We disposed of our house in New York as best we could and the first characteristic old Brookline homestead, well stocked with vines, bushes and rocks, that was afterwards offered for sale, was taken for our future home. My admiration for the place, my respect for its people, my willingness to pay my fair share of its honestly and intelligently spent taxes, and my conviction that I get a most satisfactory return for it, increases with every year of my dwelling here. I know of no reason why this individual experience may not be taken to indicate the line of policy by the pursuit of which the prosperity of the town will be best secured in the future.

Reporting to you, now, as a committee of one upon this question of the policy of the town. I should say, there is no reasonable prospect that old-fashioned, compact urban, block building will ever spread evenly over any considerable part of your territory. What you have to fear is that it will occur in bits and patches. The most forbidding part of a large town is apt to be an outskirt part in which big, pretentious, compact and block-like buildings are coming in sporadically, and the old and new mingle incongruously. From such quarters, while they acquire nothing of real urban grandeur, all suburban charm departs. The old houses become dilapidated, the rural elements become elements of squalor. Go North, East, South from Central Boston and you will easily find striking examples of what I mean. Be warned by them to guard the West.

There is no reasonable prospect that your territory will be wanted for *commercial* purposes. Commerce is apt to spread from navigable water, and prefers level ground and continuous straight streets such as the topography of Brookline resists. Nowhere near central Boston is commerce less likely to want land at all extensively than here in Brookline. No one can suppose that it is desirable to court commerce in a small way—success in doing so would mean the destruction of suburban attractiveness.

Suburban attractiveness, permanent, substantial, sterling, suburban attractiveness is the only important capital of the town. What are the chief elements of its suburban attractiveness that are possibly to be preserved and augmented? They are all of a picturesque and pretty order; nowhere continuously stately; nowhere grand or impressively beautiful. They have grown much out of the undulations, the ruggedness and the varied conditions of the topography of the town. These conditions, while it was inhabited by an essentially rural community, led to the laying out of many roads upon courses varying from directness little if any more than enough to give them gracefulness; impress the mind with a feeling that nature is leading the way, and to keep it interested in what is not fully revealed. The same conditions made it also convenient for land owners to spare many trees and bushes growing naturally along the borders of the roads and to plant others in such disposition that they now form before the wayfarer compositions essentially natural in effect. How to preserve this character; how to preserve it while making room for many times the number of houses that we have now, is probably the most critical question that lies before the town. If all individual owners could be led by moral suasion to do what every association of land owners is ready to do, led only by narrow personal interest, a fair and lasting solution of the problem would not be difficult. It would be reached by a contract that no land within a certain reasonable distance of a road should be built upon and that upon all land so reserved from building, trees and bushes where wanted should be planted and cared for in accordance with certain rules designated to secure their healthy growth at suitable but not quite regular distances.

But could such a voluntary arrangement be generally effected? I do not suppose that it could. I would then like to submit the question to those learned in the way of law-making whether legislation is out of the question under which the town could constrain citizens to come into an arrangement of the character suggested. If it is not—if it can be accomplished—I am entirely confident that the profit of it would be only greater for the whole town than that which the Boston Water Power Company, the Aspinwall Land Company, the Brookline Land Company, the West End Company and the Goddard Land Company are reckoning upon in making similar arrangements for their respective properties.

If such legislation is impracticable, then, I would ask whether by exempting from taxation all road side land so permanently reserved from building, and upon which there should be maintained certain prescribed foliage, the town might not profitably encourage the desired practice? I think that the town should be asked to consider whether, following a suggestion that has been recently made in Boston, it ought not to provisionally adopt a carefully studied general plan of streets by which all land owners could be guided in developing their individual properties, and whether it ought not to have a law preventing the erection of any building which would interfere with the ultimate carrying out of the plan. Authority might be left with some proper board for modifying the general plan when sufficient reasons could be given for doing so. Land thus rendered unavailable for building upon might be relieved from taxation as has been suggested for the borders of streets actually built—or it might be taxed on a valuation based upon its market value for garden or other purposes with which the restriction in question would not interfere.

Much advice of a more detailed character might be offered for furthering the same general object, which would not be in place at the end of such a paper as this. My purpose has been to indicate the *general direction* in which it seems to me it is for the lasting interest of the town that it should be moving.

The question has sometimes been asked if the town ought not to be acquiring land for a park? For a park properly so called, that is, a broad preserve of natural scenery, I think not. It would probably be a thrifty thing for the town to do, to acquire several small properties of flat ground here and there, chiefly where there is little building and land is not yet of high market value, to be used, as population increases, for play grounds for the children of the public schools. There are a few other small bits of land, also generally not very desirable as building sites, but on which there is some circumstance of natural interest, which I believe that it would be profitable for the town to get and hold possession of as a means of preserving and enhancing its attractiveness. There is a greater price of half an acre on Pond Avenue,[32] for example, which bears the finest oak tree, I believe, that we have. I think the town might buy and hold with profit half an acre of land, also, on the summit of Corey Hill for the prospect.[33] I question if the number and extent of such little planted triangles as those of which we have a number, like that near St Pauls church, might not be enlarged with advantage. You will observe that the aim of all these suggestions is to establish, preserve and augment the present character of the town without carrying it to largely increased outlays for the purpose.

The text presented here is a typed paper, unsigned, with annotations and edits in Olmsted's hand. The typescript, in FLO Papers/LC (microfilm 60: 393–418), is paginated 1 through 47 and the text given here follows that order. Olmsted presented the paper to the members of the Brookline Club and their wives on the evening of February 25, 1889.

Olmsted's observations here on the "history of streets" recall the report he and Vaux wrote for the Brooklyn park commissioners in 1868, in which they proposed the concept of the "park-way." At that time, Olmsted and Vaux presented a historical context for their idea by describing the "historical development of existing street arrangements" in four "stages," with the parkway being the fifth and most evolved stage. The first stage corresponded to the medieval walled city, which had essentially narrow "foot-way" streets. The next stage occurred as commerce increased and wheeled vehicles became more common, a change that made "the serviceable footways of the middle ages into the unserviceable wagon ways of the generation but one before the last." The third stage sought to remedy the situation through the introduction of sidewalks and curbs, improving drainage and traffic flow while reclaiming a place for the pedestrian. As in the paper presented here, Olmsted made a direct correlation between the physical evolution of the street and the technological, social, and economic trends shaping urbanization in Europe and the United States. Noting that cities had grown and prospered as never before in the nineteenth century, he observes that new conditions, such as the growth of suburban districts, required new "street arrangements." As an example of a "fourth stage" of street design, the authors cited the Avenue de L'Impératrice in Paris, and Berlin's Unter den Linden, both of which Olmsted had seen and admired. The parkways Olmsted and Vaux proposed for Brooklyn advanced "still another step" from such precedents by further elaborating the design in sections to create express carriageways, separate lanes for local traffic, and generous public walks lined by turf and trees. The result would be to generate a "parkway neighborhood" of "residences of more than usually open, elegant, and healthy character" along the length of the parkway.

Olmsted reiterates and elaborates the historical development of the street taken from the 1868 Brooklyn park report in the first half of these comments. He then turns to make general observations on the less dense, more "suburban" character of urban growth around many American cities over the last thirty years, and gives examples of his own efforts to shape the trend during that time. Brookline, in particular, exemplified the suburbanizing trend he describes, and Olmsted greatly influenced the pattern and character of Brookline's growth between 1880 and 1895 through the design of the Muddy River Improvement, the Beacon Street widening, and numerous other projects. He planned six subdivisions in Brookline during these years, two of which were executed as planned: Brookline Hill (Fisher Hill) and the Philbrick Estate (Pill Hill) (Olmsted, Vaux, & Co. Calvert Vaux, "Report to the Brooklyn Park Commissioners" Jan. 1, 1868 [*Papers of FLO*, SS1: 112–46]; "The Brookline Club, Members and Ladies Entertained with a Paper by Frederick Law Olmsted," *Brookline Chronicle*, March 2, 1889, p. 66; Ronald Dale Karr, "Brookline and the Making of an Elite Suburb," *Chicago History*, July 1984, pp. 36–47; Cynthia Zaitzevsky, "Frederick Law Olmsted in Brookline: A Preliminary Study of His Public Projects," *Proceedings of the Brookline Historical Society*, Fall 1977, pp. 42–65; see also Frederick Law Olmsted, "The Beacon Street Plan," Dec. 4, 1886, above).

1. The Brookline Club, composed of the "leading men of the richest town in the state" according to the *Boston Globe*, started meeting in the early 1880s. When Olmsted gave this talk to the Club at their clubhouse on Harvard Street, Dana Estes was president and the membership exceeded one hundred (*Boston Daily Globe*, Oct. 23, 1889, p. 5; "Government, By-Laws and Members of the Brookline Club, 1887–1888," pamphlet, [Brookline, 1887]; *Boston Globe*, April 26, 1885, p. 12).
2. The Brookline Park Commission was established in 1880 and Charles Sprague Sargent, Francis W. Lawrence, and Henry M. Whitney were the commissioners in 1889.

Since its formation, the commission had worked with Olmsted and the Boston park commission to plan the Muddy River Improvement, which followed the boundary between Brookline and Boston, with its western portion in Brookline. In 1889, the plan continued to be negotiated, and Olmsted produced a revised plan for the Muddy River Improvement in 1890 (C. Zaitzevsky, *The Boston Park System*, pp. 83–84).

3. Olmsted makes reference to several of his ongoing Brookline commissions of particular significance in shaping the town's rapid growth as a residential suburb of Boston: the Muddy River Improvement; the Riverway and Leverett Park (later Olmsted Park); the Beacon Street Widening; the Aspinwall Hill subdivision; and the Brookline Hill (Fisher Hill) subdivision. See note 20, below (C. Zaitzevsky, "Frederick Law Olmsted in Brookline," pp. 42–65; *Master List*, pp. 55, 102; see also Frederick Law Olmsted, "The Beacon Street Plan," [Dec. 4, 1886], above).
4. "The shop of a London tradesman at that time, as it may be supposed, was something very different from those we now see in the same locality. The goods were exposed to sale in cases, only defended from the weather by a covering of canvas, and the whole resembled the stalls and booths now erected for the temporary accommodation of dealers at a country fair, rather than the established emporium of a respectable citizen" (Sir Walter Scott, *The Fortunes of Nigel* [Edinburgh, 1822], p. 5).
5. Rodolfo Lanciani, *Ancient Rome in the Light of Recent Discoveries* (Boston, 1888).
6. The author describes how the imperial architects Severus and Celer rebuilt Rome after Nero burned the city and it was planned anew (R. Lanciani, *Ancient Rome*, pp. 122–24).
7. The 1666 Great Fire of London began on Sunday, September 2 and burned for nearly five days, destroying 13,000 buildings (*EB*).
8. Christopher Wren (1632–1723), mathematician and architect, proposed a new design for London in the aftermath of the Great Fire. His was the first plan submitted and initially favored, although other designs were soon put forward. Wren's plan included widened streets radiating from central points, such as St. Paul's Cathedral and the Tower of London. In the end, a group of commissioners appointed by the King and the Common Council organized a reconstruction effort that mostly followed the prior layout of the city. By 1676, much of the city was rebuilt with only slightly wider streets and strengthened building codes (*DNB*; Stephen Porter, *The Great Fire of London* [London, 1996], pp. 99–103; Adrian Tinniswood, *His Invention So Fertile: A Life of Christopher Wren* [New York, 2001], pp. 150–59).
9. Olmsted makes further observations on the rebuilding of London after the Great Fire in the 1868 Brooklyn park report referenced in the headnote (Olmsted, Vaux, & Co., "Report to the Brooklyn Park Commissioners" Jan. 1, 1868 [*Papers of FLO*, SS1: 121–23]).
10. George Heriot (1563–1624), who appears as a character in Scott's *The Fortunes of Nigel*, was an Edinburgh goldsmith, moneylender, and jeweler serving King James VI and Queen Anne of Scotland. Scott describes Heriot's counting room as being located on the main floor of his home (*DNB*; W. Scott, *The Fortunes of Nigel*, pp. 165–67, 170–72).
11. David Ramsay (1575–1660), who also appears as a character in Scott's *The Fortunes of Nigel*, was a Scottish shopkeeper and the chief clockmaker for James I and Charles I of England. Gabriel Varden, a character in Charles Dickens' novel *Barnaby Rudge*, was a locksmith (*DNB*; W. Scott, *The Fortunes of Nigel*, pp. 17–18, 148; Charles Dickens, *Barnaby Rudge* [London, 1841]).
12. Olmsted refers to communities that, while not close enough to Boston to be considered suburbs, had significant numbers of summer homes owned by residents of Boston or other relatively distant cities. In the 1880s, Olmsted had significant design commissions for summer estates in all the towns he mentions: J. C. Phillips's Moraine Farm in Beverly; G. N. Black's estate in Manchester; the Julia Appleton estate, the Frederick

Freylinghausen estate, the Morris K. Jesup estate, and the William D. Sloane estate in Lenox; J. H. Choate's Naumkeag estate in Stockbridge; and F. W. Vanderbilt's Rough Point, among other residences, in Newport (*Master List*, pp. 169, 186, 188, 197, 239).

13. Olmsted's first visit to London was in 1850, during his travels with his brother, John, and Charles Loring Brace. He resided in London during the spring and summer of 1856, during an extended business trip consigning books from English printing houses for the New York publisher Dix, Edwards & Company. His third trip to Britain and Europe, a tour intended to improve his health while he also studied municipal parks, was in the fall of 1859. In 1878 Olmsted returned to London as part of a three-month European trip (*Papers of FLO*, 1: 394; 2: 484; 3: 454; 7: 600–01; see also Frederick Law Olmsted, "Trees in Streets and in Parks," Sept. 1882, n. 7, above).
14. That is, the Thames Embankment, in London, built on the north bank of the Thames between 1864 and 1874. It channeled the flow of the river, improved sanitary conditions, and reclaimed land along the river that was used to create a roadway, a pedestrian esplanade, and public gardens (Dale H. Porter, *The Thames Embankment* [Akron, Ohio, 1998], pp. 31–38).
15. A reference to Mr. Jaggers, the attorney and guardian to Pip in the novel *Great Expectations*, by Charles Dickens. Pip describes the lawyer's habitual hand washing:

> I embrace this opportunity of remarking that he washed his clients off, as if he were a surgeon or a dentist. He had a closet in his room, fitted up for the purpose, which smelt of the scented soap like a perfumer's shop. It had an unusually large jack-towel on a roller inside the door, and he would wash his hands, and wipe them and dry them all over this towel, whenever he came in from a police-court or dismissed a client from his room. . . . There were some people slinking about as usual when we passed out into the street, who were evidently anxious to speak with him; but there was something so conclusive in the halo of scented soap which encircled his presence, that they gave it up for that day.

(Charles Dickens, *Great Expectations* [London, 1860], p. 199).

16. John Wemmick, Mr. Jaggers's clerk, befriends Pip and takes him to his home in Walworth, which was then a still a suburban village. Wemmick, influenced by the contemporary popularity of Gothic architecture, had created an imaginative retreat from the harsh realities of the city. Pip spends the night in Wemmick's "castle" and describes the remarkable residence: "Wemmick's house was a little wooden cottage in the midst of plots of garden, and the top of it was cut out and painted like a battery mounted with guns. . . the bridge [to it] was a plank, and it crossed a chasm about four feet wide and two deep." In addition to creating mock fortifications and a moat, Wemmick grows vegetables and fruit on his property and keeps a pig. He later remarks to Pip, "'Walworth is one place, and this office is another. . . . They must not be confounded together. My Walworth sentiments must be taken at Walworth; none but my official sentiments can be taken in this office'" (C. Dickens, *Great Expectations*, p. 273).
17. Walter Besant (1836–1901), author and historian, wrote a number of popular English histories in the late-nineteenth century. One of them, *Fifty Years Ago* (1888), describes the decrease of patronage to London theatres due, in part, to people moving to the suburbs (*DNB*; Walter Besant, *Fifty Years Ago* [London, 1888], pp. 125–27).
18. Olmsted refers to the 1857 gridded street plan for what became the Back Bay district of Boston, and specifically to Commonwealth Avenue, which was 200 feet wide and ran through the center of the grid. Since the land for development was created through land filling, the state had the opportunity to determine the overall design of the street pattern and also to require residential uses and twenty-foot building setbacks, through deed restrictions, on the plots of land it sold along the new avenue. The "mile and a half" strip of turf and trees Olmsted references was the 100-foot wide pedestrian mall

that ran down the center of Commonwealth Avenue plus the extension of it, which Olmsted had designed (Nancy S. Seasholes, *Gaining Ground: A History of Landmaking in Boston* [Cambridge, Mass., 2003], pp. 177–79; *Twelfth Annual Report of the Commissioners on Public Lands, Dec. 1863* [Boston, 1864], pp. 7–9).

19. In the early 1880s, as the filling of the Back Bay district neared completion, some new land that became available for development to the west, around Kenmore Square and the site of the Back Bay Fens, received building restrictions similar to those along Commonwealth Avenue. New buildings were to be residential, for example, set back twenty feet from the street, and constructed of brick, stone, or iron (N. S. Seasholes, *Gaining Ground*, p. 232; Bainbridge Bunting, *Houses of Boston's Back Bay, An Architectural History, 1840–1917* [Cambridge, Mass., 1967], pp. 250–55).

20. The Brookline Land Company was founded in 1860. Its holdings then were about eighty acres, covering land from Washington Street in Brookline Village to Jamaica Pond, and from the Muddy River valley to High Street. It later sold land to the city for the Brookline portion of the Muddy River Improvement and Leverett Park. Olmsted began work for the Aspinwall Land Company on the Aspinwall Hill subdivision in 1880. The development was completed only partially according to his plan. The West End Land Company was formed by Henry M. Whitney to advance the Beacon Street widening project and to develop property along that corridor. George A. Goddard of the Goddard Land Company was one of the Brookline (Fisher) Hill subdivision property owners, and Olmsted's plan for that development was completed (C. Zaitzevsky, "Frederick Law Olmsted in Brookline," pp. 42–65; Frederick Law Olmsted, "The Beacon Street Plan," [Dec. 4, 1886], above).

21. Olmsted's reference to "the Parkway" reflects the Boston park commissioners' vote on December 30, 1887, to refer to the entire park corridor "between Boylston Road and Marine Park, by the way of Jamaica Pond, the Arboretum, and Franklin Park, together with the adjoining strips of territory intended to be improved by the Department," as the Parkway, as Olmsted had suggested (*Thirteenth Annual Report of the Board of Park Commissioners for the Year 1887* [Boston, 1893], p. 22; see *Appendix, Report of the Landscape Architect Advisory*, Dec. 30, 1887, above).

22. Olmsted may be referencing neighborhoods north and west of Dupont Circle, along what later became Rock Creek Park, which were developed in the decades following the Civil War. Modest, free standing homes with yards were built near row houses and larger mansions, creating a diversity of housing types (Kathryn Schneider Smith, ed., *Washington at Home: An Illustrated History of Neighborhoods in the Nation's Capital* [Baltimore, 2010], pp. 175–95, 277–94).

23. For Olmsted's role in influencing the planting of trees in Washington, D.C., *Annual Report of the Architect of the United States Capitol*, 1882, n. 11, above.

24. In his "Preliminary Report in Regard to a Plan of Public Pleasure Grounds for the City of San Francisco," March 31, 1866, Olmsted suggested that, as San Francisco expanded westward, new streets be laid out on more gradual gradients, responding to the region's topography, and not according to a simple gridiron plan (*Papers of FLO*, 5: 542–43).

25. Olmsted was appointed executive secretary for the U.S. Sanitary Commission on June 20, 1861, and relocated to Washington to administer the organization. He remained in the position until the fall of 1863 (*Papers of FLO*, 4: 7, 59).

26. Ginery Twichell (1811–1883), Massachusetts businessman and railroad executive, organized the collection and shipment of donated hospital supplies from the Boston area to Washington, D.C., with remarkable expedition following the Second Battle of Bull Run. On September 5, 1862, just five days after the battle, President Lincoln wrote him a letter thanking him for the receipt of "a large amount of Hospital Stores, contributed for the use of wounded soldiers of the United States Army, by patriotic citizens of Brookline, Brighton, Newton, Watertown and Roxbury." From 1866 to 1873

Twichell served as a Representative in Congress (J. W. Denehy. *A History of Brookline, 1630–1906* [Allston, Mass., 1907], p. 136; Roy Prentice Basler, ed., *The Collected Works of Abraham Lincoln*, vol. 5 [New Brunswick, N.J., 1953–55], pp. 406, 407).

27. In 1874 New York City annexed a portion of Westchester County, creating the Twenty-third and Twenty-fourth wards of the city in what later became the Borough of the Bronx. The Department of Public Parks engaged Olmsted to lay out new streets for the area and to locate a steam rapid-transit system. Olmsted worked in partnership with chief engineer J. J. R. Croes, who since 1871 had done much of the surveying north of 155th Street for the city. They presented their plans in 1876 and 1877, first for the district overlooking the Hudson River north of Spuyten Duyvil, and then for the area just to the east, between Riverdale Avenue and Broadway. Certain portions of their plans rejected the conventional grid system of streets. Along the river and in most of the district west of Jerome Avenue (part of which is now occupied by the Jerome Park Reservoir), a suburban villa style plan was proposed with boulevards, tree-lined curvilinear streets, and little through traffic. In other areas, Olmsted and Croes did use a grid layout of streets, for example in neighborhoods where streets and buildings were already in place, such as near the former Van Cortlandt estate lands (now the southern border of Van Cortlandt Park) (Frederick Law Olmsted and J. J. R. Croes, "Preliminary Report of the Landscape Architect and the Civil and Topographical Engineer, Upon the Laying Out of the Twenty-third and Twenty-fourth Wards," Nov.15, 1876 [*Papers of FLO*, 7: 242–51]; Frederick Law Olmsted and J. J. R. Croes, "Report of the Landscape Architect and the Civil and Topographical Engineer, Accompanying a Plan for Laying Out that Part of the Twenty-Fourth Ward Lying West of the Riverdale Road," Nov. 21, 1876 [*Papers of FLO*, 7: 251–66]; FLO to William R. Martin, March 20, 1877 [*Papers of FLO*, 7: 306–13]; FLO to William R. Martin, Oct. 31, 1877 [*Papers of FLO*, 7: 340–50]; *Papers of FLO*, 7: 17).
28. For more on this plan, see Frederick Law Olmsted and J. J. R. Croes, "Report of the Landscape Architect and the Civil and Topographical Engineer, Accompanying a Plan for Laying Out that Part of the Twenty-Fourth Ward Lying West of the Riverdale Road," Nov. 21, 1876 (*Papers of FLO*, 7: 254–55).
29. Park Commissioner Henry G. Stebbins opposed Olmsted's plan, as did Comptroller Andrew H. Green, a long-time opponent of Olmsted's who had also previously submitted his own plan for the wards that proposed a grid layout of streets. The park board and a delegation of citizens nevertheless officially adopted both of Olmsted and Croes' plans in late February and early March of 1877, with only Stebbins dissenting. In 1878, William R. Martin, Olmsted's principal supporter on the park board, left after the expiration of his term, as did Stebbins. They were replaced by Tammany commissioners who opposed this and other of Olmsted's plans. Later that year when Olmsted left New York for a trip to Europe, his position with the New York parks was eliminated (*Papers of FLO*, 7: 4–5, 249 n. 1; for more on Olmsted's departure from the New York parks, see Frederick Law Olmsted, "Review of New York City Park Department Policies in 1878," Jan. 8, 1879 [*Papers of FLO*, 7: 373–87]; DPP, *Minutes*, Feb. 28, 1877, pp. 645–47; Frederick Law Olmsted, Jr., and Theodora Kimball, eds., *Forty Years of Landscape Architecture: Central Park, Frederick Law Olmsted* [Cambridge, Mass., 1973], pp. 104–16).
30. Edgar Beach Van Winkle (1842–1920) was chief engineer of New York City's Department of Public Parks from 1878 to 1884. It is not known when Van Winkle visited Brookline, but Olmsted did correspond with him in 1882 about the development of Brookline, sending him a copy of "Sanitary Improvement of Muddy River," (1880) along with his *Spoils of the Park* pamphlet (1882). In his reply letter, Van Winkle asked to meet with Olmsted to discuss park matters (George S. Greene, Jr., "Memoir of Edgar

Beach Van Winkle," *Transactions of the American Society of Civil Engineers* (New York, 1921), p. 933; Edgar B. Van Winkle to FLO, March 26, 1882).

31. The first home in Brookline that Olmsted took for his family was at the Allens' on Dudley Street in the summer of 1880. He took Mrs. Perrin's house on Walnut Street in the summer of 1881, staying through the fall and winter. His observation of snow removal probably occurred during the winter of 1881-82 (*Papers of FLO*, 7: 602–3; *FLO, A Biography*, p. 383).
32. Pond Avenue in Brookline runs along the edge of Leverett Pond in Leverett Park (later Olmsted Park).
33. Corey Hill is north of Beacon Street and south of Corey Road, between Winchester and Washington Streets, and just east of the Chestnut Hill Reservoir. The plan for the Beacon Street Widening curved the widened street around the hill, and Henry M. Whitney, the principal backer of the Beacon Street project, engaged Olmsted in 1889 to prepare a subdivision plan for the hill (a portion of which his West End Land Company owned). The plan was not implemented, but the top of Corey Hill was later made a park, as Olmsted suggests here (C, Zaitzevsky, "Frederick Law Olmsted in Brookline," pp. 42–65; see also "The Beacon Street Plan," [Dec. 4, 1886], above).

To Morris Ketchum Jesup

Brookline, 11th Feby, 1889.

Dear Mr. Jesup:

I have taken time for deliberation and conference before replying to your note of 4th inst. I cannot see that it places the matter in any new light. We do not complain, as you seem to assume, of what you have done.[1] Please dismiss that idea from your mind. The question may be considered to be how you can best get what you want? Upon that question we think that our familiarity with the required operations makes our judgment better than yours.

Practically your mind was long since made up as to certain particulars of your plan. We have told you that it was so in our opinion before you fully realized the facts of the topography. But having pointed these out to you your mind has remained the same. You may not have reflected that these particulars were controlling particulars of the plan as a whole but there can be no doubt that they were. It follows that what you have wanted is not counsel in framing a plan but help to find how the subordinate elements of a plan can be made to gear in satisfactorily with controlling elements that have been determined with no consideration of the problem thus afterwards to be dealt with. There are men whose common business it is to take up affairs of this class at just the point at which you want this taken up. But that has never been our business; we have always declined it and if we should depart from our rule in this case we are less likely to accomplish results that would be satisfactory to you than others would be who are less tied by habit than we are to guarded and methodical processes of design.

This being our opinion, the question is whether you cannot think it right that we should, in a perfectly respectful and friendly spirit, ask to be excused from taking up your work?[2]

Faithfully Yours,

Fred[k] Law Olmsted.

The text presented here is from a letterpress copy of a handwritten letter signed on the original in Olmsted's hand: A3: 207–8, OAR/LC (see FLO to Morris K. Jesup, Oct. 20, 1888, above; FLO to Morris K. Jesup, Jan. 22, 1889, above; FLO to Morris K. Jesup, Jan. 31, 1889, above).

1. Jesup's February 4th note is not extant, but it likely addressed continued disagreements the two men had about Jesup proceeding with the construction of an entrance drive at his estate in a location that Olmsted had advised against, due to the difficult topography. See FLO to Morris K. Jesup, Jan. 31, 1889, above.
2. Olmsted's involvement in Jesup's Belvoir Terrace project ended after this letter was written. Jesup then hired landscape gardener Ernest Bowditch to lay out the grounds, but it is uncertain if he finished the project. The architects Rotch & Tilden continued to oversee construction of Jesup's house, which was completed in 1891 (Richard S. Jackson Jr., and Cornelia Brooke Gilder, *The Houses of the Berkshires 1870–1930* [New York, 2006], pp. 121–22; William Adams Brown, *Morris Ketchum Jesup: A Character Sketch* [New York, 1910], p. 210).

CHAPTER IX

FEBRUARY 1889–APRIL 1889

In 1888, Olmsted first visited the site of George W. Vanderbilt's Biltmore estate near Asheville, North Carolina, which became his largest commission for a private client. His letter to architect Richard Morris Hunt discusses the planning and location of the mansion and outbuildings being designed by Hunt. The April 18, 1889, letter to Robert Douglas considers creating a commercial forest and major arboretum at Biltmore. Another project in the South at this time involved planning the grounds of the Alabama state capitol. Olmsted's letter to Thomas H. Clark considers possible ways of dealing with the steep hillside on the site. Other letters relate to ongoing commissions, including a letter to Edward Clark describing Olmsted's plan for placing a fountain between the stairs of the west terrace of the U.S. Capitol. The letter to Alpheus Hyatt begins a dialogue about placing zoological gardens and aquariums in several of Boston's parks. A letter to Thomas V. Welch discusses the origin of the movement to preserve the scenery of Niagara Falls.

An important topic dealt with in this chapter is the question of removal of trees and thinning of woods in parks and reservations. Members of the West End Association in New York asked Olmsted to write a report on thinning of the woods in Central Park. Written with Jonathan Baxter Harrison, *Observations on the Treatment of Public Plantations, More Especially Relating to the Use of the Axe*, argues that the thinning of tree plantations, performed by professionals and guided by the intent of the designers, is a necessary aspect of landscape maintenance.

To Edward Clark

11th Feby 1889.

Dear Mr Clark;

I send today plan, elevation and perspective, suggestion of revisions of plan for space between western stair ways of the Capitol. I am sorry that I could not send them sooner but it has not been a simple matter and one drawing fully made I have had to discard. The object of these drawings is to enable you and Mr. Morrill to discuss the subject more definitely and advise us of your judgment.

The fountain is designed to be used, as shown, with a moderate amount of water. It would be improved very much if better supplied, so that there would be a central broad jet and spray. But I do not think that the effect of it would be unsatisfactory with such supply as I suppose can be had soon.

The principal question submitted to you is that of the diameter of the lower basin. The plan expresses my judgment. The perspective, (included to present the fountain more particularly,) is not, I think, quite correctly drawn, the result being that the basin appears larger and the walk behind it narrower than they would be if of the dimensions shown in the plan and intended. My feeling is that a basin much smaller than that thus proposed would appear paltry under all the circumstances. Might it not be reduced slightly? Yes, I think that it might. I should not at all object, if you thought best, to give a foot of breadth on each side for the walk, or even two feet, but as it stands I do not feel as you do that the basin looks too large. Of course, I have always in mind the great portico and dome which do not appear in the drawing.

If the proposition, which I see has been offered, to have a passage from the level of the fountain to an elevator under the rotunda should be favored, I am

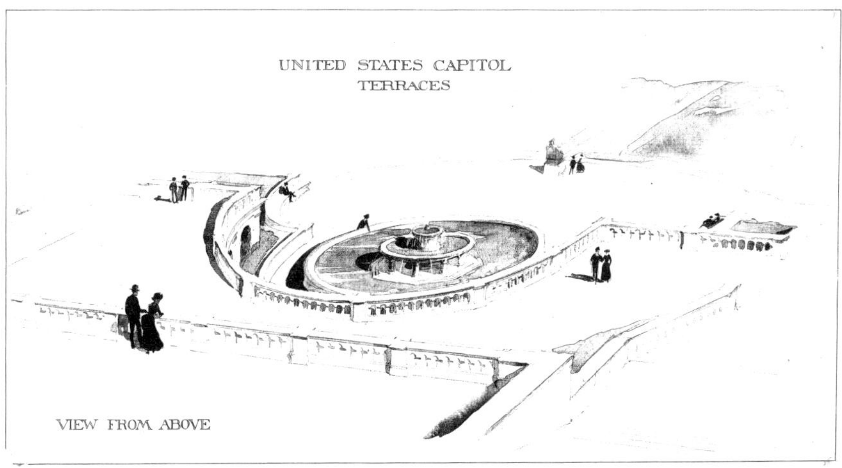

"United States Capitol Terraces, View from Above," n.d.

inclined to think that an opening at the central niche would answer for it, and the plan could stand without radical modification otherwise. Assuming that people could enter the elevator also from the next floor of the terrace, as in practice many would do I don't think that it would be an objectionable arrangement.

Yours Truly,

Fred[k] Law Olmsted.

The text presented here is from a letterpress copy of a handwritten letter signed on the original in Olmsted's hand: A3: 205–6, OAR/LC. The plans he describes here involve details of the redesign of a portion of the west terrace of the U.S. Capitol in Washington, D.C., specifically the fountain and apsidal niches on the lower level of the terrace. A month earlier Olmsted had written to Senator Justin S. Morrill regarding his concern that a fountain in this location, if too small, would be "weak, petty and trifling and . . . distracting from the grandeur of the whole." If too large, it would "often drench those passing around it" (FLO to Justin S. Morrill, Jan. 18, 1889, A3:114–15, OAR/LC; see FLO to Edward Clark, Feb. 15, 1886, above).

To Thomas Vincent Welch[1]

Private

16th Feby. 1889.

My Dear Mr Welch;

Many thanks for your note of 12th inst. I had seen a reference to the fall of rock and am glad to get particulars. I do not know the new Commissioner.[2]

I suppose that you invite my comments upon the memorandum enclosed in your note with regard more particularly to the statement that the gentlemen conferring at the Cataract House in 1869—

"Looked over the ground *in accordance with an idea that had been suggested* by Mr F. E. Church[3] xxxx who *had* intimated the preservation of the scenery to a friend xxxx who *had* intimated to Lord Dufferin[4] its importance."

I suppose that it has struck you that this is a somewhat overguarded and painstaking statement and that if you are to be responsible for the publication you would prefer to have it more circumstantial and precise.

In a notice by the New York World of the Report of the Survey Commission of 1880 it was observed that no credit had been given in it to Mr Church except in an obscure note by Mr Olmsted.[5] What I had said in this note was that my attention had been called by my friend Mr Church some ten years before to the deterioration of the scenery of the Falls. This was not an accurately true statement. Mr Vaux had said that before the meeting at the Cataract House in 1869, he had heard Mr Church talk at the Century Club[6] of the injury which was occurring to the scenery. I do not think that I had ever heard a word from Mr Church, or from any other source of what he had said on the subject. But as I was a member of the Century, (though not a frequenter of the Club House), and might have done so, I thought it right to assume that I had. Mr Dorsheimer told me afterwards that it had not been very uncommon for gentlemen visiting the Falls to bewail the condition of things there and to say that it was disgraceful and that something ought to be done about it. Mr Dorsheimer was also a member of the Century and though then residing in Buffalo was probably more at the Club House than I was. But he had not been aware of any talk on the subject there or anywhere by Mr Church. {*I do*} not in the least doubt that Mr Church had talked on the subject; I think it likely that he had before 1869 suggested that the state and transition Government[7] should take action in the premises but if he had it was wholly unknown to me, to Mr Dorsheimer or, as I believe, to any of the gentlemen meeting at Cataract House in 1869.

When I read the observation in the World it appeared to me that either the writer of it had a mistaken impression in some way of the facts or that I had, and, that I might know how it was, I wrote at once to the office and asked an explanation of Mr Hurlbert.[8] I then learned that the observation had not been written with any reference to Mr Church's interest in the subject before 1869, but solely to the fact that Lord Dufferin's note to Governor Robinson in 1878 had been written in consequence of a call upon him by Mr Hurlbert and Mr Church.[9] This circumstance was wholly unknown to me before; it had been unknown to Mr Dorsheimer and to Mr Gardiner,[10] (who edited the Report) and probably to Governor Robinson {*and all others of the commission.*} If it had not been {*well-known*}, and I have no reason to suppose that it had, Mr Hurlbert was wrong in suggesting that there had been a disposition to withhold due credit to Mr Church or himself.[11] But such an idea had been stated and Governor Dorsheimer afterwards had an impression that some pains had been taken to propagate it. {*He once*} said something publically in {*consideration*} of it and he told me not long before he died {that} he had partly written a statement of the facts which would in time be published.[12]

The implication of the memorandum above quoted that the conference of 1869 grew out of Mr Hurlbert's intimation to Lord Dufferin of Mr Church's intimation to him is entirely groundless. I think that you will find that Lord Dufferin did not come to Canada till long after the Cataract House conference.

I should be glad and should {*always*} have been glad to sustain and {*verify*} any claim of Mr Church's service in the matter. There is not the slightest ground for any supposition to the contrary. If there is any question about it, it is simply as to what proposition he advocated and when, where and how he advocated it, before September 1869? It seems to me a matter of trivial consequence but if you think it desirable to have it established why should you not ask Mr Church himself? You could do so simply in the interests of the truth of history. I think that it would be a desirable thing to put on record that Mr Church is a distinguished landscape painter—had not only been the main spring of the action of Lord Dufferin but that he had been among the earliest and most influential agents in propagating the public opinion that made possible the rescue of the scenery after Lord Dufferin acted. Whatever Mr Church could be got to say on the point would be conclusive.

Some time ago but within three years, I think, a gentleman whose name I do not now recall wrote to me from Niagara Falls, or possibly Buffalo, asking particulars of any meeting that had been held and in which I had part at the Cataract House in 1869.[13] He said that he was looking into the matter with a view to some publication or report to an Association. I replied as I conveniently could at the time and indicated in what way he could, if disposed, secure a more accurate account and correct or verify my statements. You are likely to know if there has been any publication on the subject and by calling on the author may learn something from my reply to his inquiries or something that he has ascertained by acting on my suggestions.*

Governor Robinson's recommendation to the Legislature of 1878 fell dead. Not the first move was made in the matter till the last day of the session. If you do not know and wish to how it was then brought to life and the course of action initiated that finally led to success, I could tell you.

Yours faithfully.

Fred[k] Law Olmsted.

The text presented here is from a letterpress copy of a handwritten letter signed on the original in Olmsted's hand: A3: 218–20, OAR/LC. Welch's letter to Olmsted and the memorandum mentioned below have not been found (see FLO to Col. C. S. Gzowski, Aug. 15, 1887, above; FLO to Cyrus K. Remington, May 28, 1888, above).

1. Thomas Vincent Welch (1850–1903) was a leader in the campaign to establish the Niagara reservation. A member of the New York State Assembly, Welch oversaw the bill establishing the reservation and then served as superintendent of the Niagara Reservation from 1885 until his death. In 1896, he wrote *How Niagara Was Made Free: The Passage of the Niagara Reservation Act in 1885* (Buffalo, 1896) ("Thomas Vincent Welch," *New York Times*, Oct. 21, 1903; Charles M. Dow, *The State Reservation at Niagara: A History* [Albany, N.Y., 1914], p. 180).
2. A severe storm in the Niagara region on January 9, 1889, caused extensive damage, including the destruction of a suspension bridge below the falls. The storm also resulted

*The books of the Cataract House will show when, in September, 1869, Dorsheimer and several Buffalo friends were at the Falls at the same time that Richardson and I were there. Among them (some perhaps at other hotels), may have been Bowen, Warren, Rumsey, Richmond & Dr Carey.[14]

in further erosion of rock formations at the crest of Horseshoe Falls. Descriptions of rocks breaking away at Horseshoe Falls were reported in newspapers through January and February, and Welch had likely provided Olmsted with his own description. The new commissioner Olmsted refers to was Daniel Batchelor, of Utica, New York, who joined the Commission of the State Reservation at Niagara on February 12, 1889, and served until his death in 1893 ("Niagara River Very High," *Milwaukee Daily Journal*, Jan. 10, 1889; "The Horseshoe Falls," *Morning Oregonian*, Jan. 18, 1889, p. 3; "A Second Rock Breaks at Niagara Falls," ibid., Jan. 24, 1889, p. 2; C. M. Dow, *The State Reservation at Niagara*, p. 181).

3. Frederic Edwin Church (1826–1900), an American painter of the Hudson River School, was one of the most prominent artists of the era. He was an early and important proponent of preserving Niagara Falls. (*DAB*).
4. Frederick Temple Blackwood (1826–1902), the first Marquess of Dufferin and Ava, was the governor-general of Canada from 1872 until 1878. He was one of the first politicians to call publicly for the creation of a Niagara reservation in Canada, and his communication with New York's governor Lucius Robinson was credited with advancing efforts in the United States to preserve the falls. He publicized the issue in Canada with an address given to the Society of Artists in Toronto in September 1878. A group of islands on the Canadian side of the falls was later named the Dufferin Islands in his honor (*DNB*; C. M. Dow, *The State Reservation at Niagara*, pp. 10–16).
5. The *New York World* published an editorial on James T. Gardner's *Special Report of New York State Survey of Niagara Falls for the year 1879*, which included "Notes" written by Olmsted. The article's criticism stated that "The only fault to be found with the report is that it fails to assign the credit of the project to the person to whom it is entirely due—to the distinguished American artist, Mr. Frederick E. Church, who besides doing this service has done more than any other person . . ." Olmsted's reference to Church in the report read, "I have myself been an occasional visitor at Niagara for forty-five years. My attention was first called to the rapidly approaching ruin of its characteristic scenery by Mr. F. E. Church, about ten years ago." Olmsted had also given credit to Church in a private letter to Charles Eliot Norton in 1880, writing that Church "was the first, as far as I know, to advance the proposition & I believed he brought it before Lord Dufferin" (*New York World*, April 7, 1880, p. 4; "Notes by Mr. Olmsted" in *Special Report of New York State Survey on the Preservation of the Scenery of Niagara Falls . . . for the Year 1879*, [c. March 22, 1880] [*Papers of FLO*, 7: 474]; FLO to Charles Eliot Norton, Feb. 15, 1880 [*Papers of FLO*, 7: 471–72]).
6. The Century Club in New York City. Olmsted and Vaux had both been members since 1859 (Edwin G. Burrows and Mike Wallace, *Gotham* [New York, 1999], p. 713; *FLO, A Biography*, p. 338; Francis R. Kowsky, *Country, Park & City: The Architecture and Life of Calvert Vaux* [New York, 1998], p. 137).
7. That is, the government of the Dominion of Canada, which had been created by the British North America Act of 1867. Under this act the provinces of Nova Scotia, New Brunswick, Quebec, and Ontario united to form the Dominion of Canada. The act served as Canada's Constitution, creating a bicameral parliament and delegating executive power to the British monarch, who continued to appoint a governor-general (Scott W. See, *The History of Canada* [Westport, Conn., 2001], pp. 77–88).
8. William Henry Hurlbert (1827–1895), journalist and author, was a friend of Olmsted's since they had worked together on *Putnam's Monthly* in 1855. He served as editor-in-chief of the *New York World* from 1876 to 1883 (*DAB*; "William Henry Hurlbert Dead," *New York Times*, Sept. 7, 1895, p. 5).
9. Lucius Robinson (1810–1891) was governor of New York from 1877 to 1880. According to a speech that he gave to the New York legislature in 1879 on the creation of the Niagara Reservation, Robinson said he had learned of the issue of preserving Niagara

in a meeting with Lord Dufferin in the summer of 1878, and not by a note, as Olmsted suggests in this letter ("Lucius Robinson's Death," *New York Times*, March 24, 1891, p. 4; "Message of Governor Lucius Robinson," Jan. 9, 1879, *Documents of the Assembly of the State of New York. One Hundred and Third Session, 1880* [Albany, 1880], pp. 41–42).

10. James Terry Gardner, director of the Niagara Reservation Commission, who compiled and edited the *Special Report of New York State Survey on the Preservation of the Scenery of Niagara Falls, and Fourth Annual Report on the Triangulation of the State, for the Year 1879* (Albany, N.Y., 1880) (see also FLO to William E. Dorsheimer, July 21, 1886, n. 10, above).
11. In other words, the authors of the 1879 Niagara report had not known the details of Church's and Hurlbert's early involvement in contacting Lord Dufferin, and Hurlbert had unfairly concluded that the report's authors had purposefully not given them credit.
12. William E. Dorsheimer died on March 26, 1888 (*DAB*).
13. Cyrus K. Remington wrote Olmsted in 1888 inquiring about the 1869 meeting at the Cataract House (FLO to Cyrus K. Remington, May 28, 1888, above).
14. See FLO to Cyrus K. Remington, May 28, 1888, above.

To Richard Morris Hunt

2[d] March, 1889.

Dear Mr Hunt:

Mr Vanderbilt had written that he should be in New York till the first of March but afterwards changed his plan so I missed seeing him and you, to my regret.

I very much like your new plan[1] and your suggestion as to position &c, satisfy me. Upon more exact study slight modifications may be found desirable. I should think that it might be better possibly, to set the house a little higher (not further to the Eastward) a little further north and to swing it a trifle nearer, north and south[2]—the object being a nicer fit to the natural situation.

There are two or three considerations which would have great weight with me in planning the dependencies to which I think that you and Mr Vanderbilt may not have attached as much importance as I do. I want to mention them and indicate vaguely to what they would lead in order that if they are outweighed by other considerations more prominent in your mind, you may guard me against what you would consider a false start.

The value of the site is in its outlook; the local scenery is not attractive. The soil is extremely poor and intractable. There is not a single circumstance that can be turned to account in gaining any desirable local character, picturesqueness, for instance, or geniality. Whatever we aim at must be made "out of the whole cloth".

What Mr Vanderbilt wants, as I understand, is a place in which to spend the winter and the harsh spring. But it is an exceedingly bleak place. When the wind chops round from south to north the effect is often terrible. In all the neighboring region fruit buds are oftener killed than they are here or in Washington. Being so much more open to the north west, the climate will *at times* be more severe than that of Asheville. Now and then the force of a gale sweeping from the {*snowy peaks*} in the north will be frightful. The compensating circumstances are that the greater part of the time the winter and spring air is of temperature pleasant to anyone exercising even moderately, and is of a {*bracing*} quality. Various facts of vegetation indicate that even though the mercury falls at rare intervals for a short time, {*lower*} than at Washington — or even I believe at New York — the climate is much less trying on the whole. Plants, and probably men, of such hardy constitution, are happier in it.

That is one compensating circumstance. The other is the advantage offered for making it pleasant for people to be out of doors; that is to say, first, for a short stroll or a promenade which shall be as it were a part of the house — from which *while walking* the great view {*westward*} — the valley and the distance with its far away snow-capped hills can be enjoyed. (This would suggest more terrace walk, closely associated with the house than your plan yet provides).

But no promenade south of the house with a western outlook would be available for use with an icy northwester sweeping across the valley doubled in force as it would by the current deflected and concentrated by the walls of the house. Hence a place out of doors is wanted, which attractive at all times in a different way from the terrace, will be available for a ramble even during a northwester and in the depth of winter. This would be a glen-like place with narrow winding paths between steepish slopes with evergreen shrubbery, in the lee of the house on the Southeast. Look at the map and you will see that the topography favors the suggestion. You will see also that a terrace thrown out southwardly from the house, a little but not much lower than the floor of the house, would still further fend off the cold winds from such a place and make it more secluded and genial.

One thing more. East of the entire length of the house you have in view, I presume, a broad plateau; the hill top being raked down so as to open a view to the eastward from the lower story.[3] A carriage approaching the house will be facing {to} the northward and if nothing is done to prevent it will catch the northwest wind sweeping around the north end of the house and the plateau will have a very bleak character, far from welcoming to guests coming from the north with anticipations of a milder climate and Southern hospitality.

On this point much would be gained if there was a substantial wind break stretching eastward from the north end of the house, such as would be supplied by a range of offices and stables. Let there be walled courts in front of these, some warmth of color in the material, green ivy spreading over them, a columbarium with doves hovering about, and I think the establishment would be much less bleak-looking. As neither you nor Mr Vanderbilt have said anything about stables near the house I suppose that there may be objections in your minds

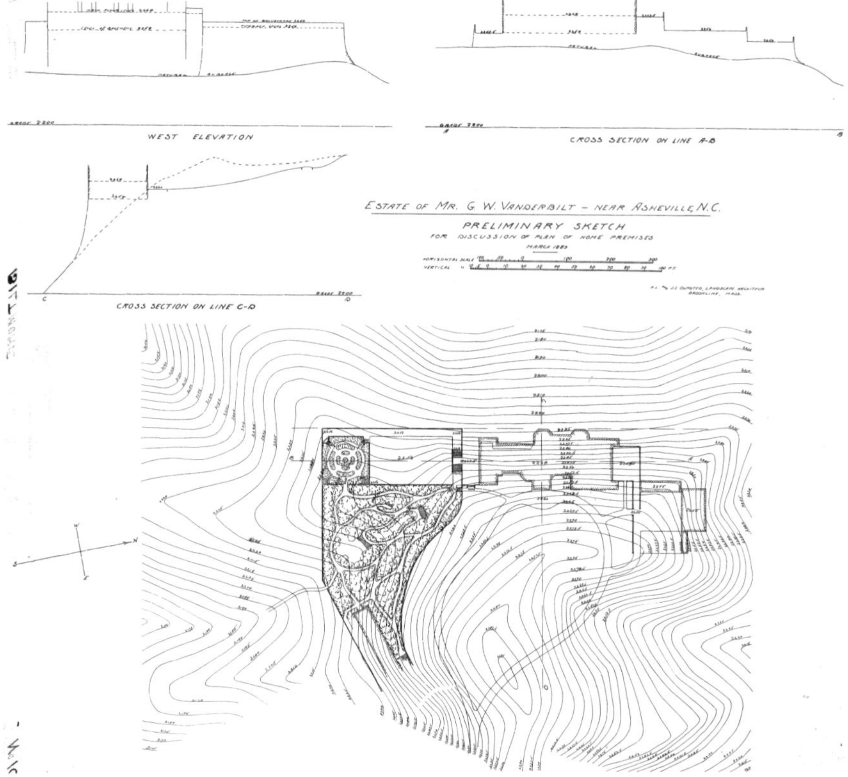

"Estate of Mr. G. W. Vanderbilt—Near Asheville, N. C., Preliminary Sketch for Discussion of Plan of Home Premises," March 1889, displays placement of structures in reference to existing topography

that I don't take sufficiently into account. If so I want you to advise me as I find something of the kind is rather a starting point in all my imaginings of what can be made of the place.

In a fine summer's day it would be pleasanter to look past the house into a fine body of wood as one drove up. Take the year through I don't think it would. In considering the suggestion you must remember that the wood is not fine. It is very poor wood and yet to have wood there on the north of the hill is so desirable that we should never think of wholly removing it. Therefore, if the stables are not to be there, there can be no fine view to a distance in that direction. But a range of low stables there and, poor as the wood is for a foreground, nothing could be better for a background, seen over roofs and walls.

I think that a good place for glass can be made east of my winter garden at an elevation about 30' below that of the plateau, the nearest point of it being about 350 ft southeast of the library window, the roof ridge being well below the

VIEW OF CONSTRUCTION OF BILTMORE, C. 1892

line of the eye of those passing along the approach road and easily planted wholly out of view from the house and the entire entrance plateau, if that is desirable.[4]

This is a long letter but I hope that you can answer it very shortly. All I want is to know before going into more exact study that such outlines as I have suggested would not cross your views. I think it desirable to make some preliminary graphic study as soon as possible because there is the possibility that out of it would grow some suggestion by which details of your design would be affected, as, for example, outside steps, (stairs) place of coal hole, base of terrace walls, entrance to kitchen court &c.

Yours Truly

Fred[k] Law Olmsted.

The text presented here is from a letterpress copy of a handwritten letter signed on the original in Olmsted's hand: A3: 252–58, OAR/LC. Since the fall of 1888, Olmsted had been corresponding with George W. Vanderbilt, Richard Morris Hunt, and others involved in preliminary plans for Vanderbilt's estate, Biltmore, outside Asheville, North Carolina. Olmsted was already consulting with Vanderbilt on his summer residence, Pointe d'Acadie, near Bar Harbor, Maine. Vanderbilt was also overseeing work on the family mausoleum in New Dorp, Staten Island, another project on which Olmsted and Hunt collaborated. Vanderbilt asked Olmsted to design the grounds of Biltmore in 1888, and the two men visited the site shortly after the initial two thousand acres were acquired.

Over the next seven years Vanderbilt's wealth made it possible for Olmsted to carry out much of what he envisioned for Biltmore. Following the initial advice Olmsted gave in 1888, Vanderbilt made his estate (eventually growing to 125,000 acres) the first comprehensive demonstration of the application of the principles of scientific forestry in the United States. Many of the basic design features described in this letter—including the approach road, the terrace, the Ramble, and the placement of stables and other dependencies—would be carried out according to Olmsted's plans (Charles E. Beveridge, "The Olmsteds at Biltmore," *National Association for Olmsted Parks Workbook Series, Vol. 5, Biography* [Bethesda, Md., 1995], pp. 1–10; John M. Bryan, *Biltmore Estate, The Most Distinguished Private Place* [New York, 1994], pp. 29–38; FLO to J. G. Aston, Oct. 29, 1888, A2: 950–51, OAR/LC; FLO and JCO to George W. Vanderbilt, Feb. 20, 1889, A3: 228, OAR/LC; FLO to George W. Vanderbilt, March 2, 1889, A3: 248–49, OAR/LC; Frederick Law Olmsted, Jr., to Laura Wood Roper, Nov. 21, 1952, Laura Wood Roper Files, LOC; see also FLO to George W. Vanderbilt, Aug. 9, 1886, above; FLO to Richard Morris Hunt, May 5, 1887, above; FLO to George W. Vanderbilt, July 12, 1889, below).

1. Vanderbilt's original ideas for the house, suggested in Hunt's first designs in 1888 and early 1889, were for a relatively modest country seat. An early scheme suggested a two-story brick colonial revival house. By the spring of 1889, however, Hunt, with Vanderbilt's approval, moved toward a larger French Renaissance inspired design. This inspiration was further elaborated after Vanderbilt and Hunt toured Europe together in the summer of 1889. Hunt still had not visited the Biltmore site, however, when Olmsted made the suggestions in this letter regarding the location of the house and dependencies (Paul R. Baker, *Richard Morris Hunt* [Cambridge, Mass., 1980], pp. 412–15; Frederick Law Olmsted, Jr., to Laura Wood Roper, Nov. 21, 1952, Laura Wood Roper Files, LOC; J. M. Bryan, *Biltmore Estate*, pp. 38–41).
2. Olmsted suggests, in other words, raising the elevation of the house, adjusting its location on the sloping site, and rotating it closer to a north to south axis in order to better fit it into the existing topography.
3. That is, cutting into the hill east of the house in order to create a level, rectangular esplanade at the principal entrance. To the east, the view down the esplanade was later terminated by a *rampe douce*, with a statue of Diana placed on the remaining hilltop above.
4. In Olmsted's March 1889 plans, a glass conservatory was placed, as explained here, east of the proposed "winter garden." This garden, which Olmsted describes earlier in this letter as "a glen-like place with narrow winding paths," was on a hillside protected from the north wind, with southern exposure. Olmsted later renamed it the Ramble, and it was later referred to as the Shrub Garden. The conservatory, however, was later moved south and downhill from the location described here, and adjacent to a four-acre walled garden.

To Jacob Weidenmann[1]

16th March 1889.

My Dear Mr Weidenmann;

I have received your favor of 14th inst. and am glad to hear of your welfare; particularly glad to hear that such a scheme as that of the Brooklyn University Ground has been committed you.[2] I wish that I could think that you were much more likely to see satisfactory results from any labor you may give the problem than I am for what I have done in Brooklyn.

The present course of the Brooklyn Park Commissioners is sadder than anything else I know of in American public affairs.[3] Until it is frankly reversed no man whose judgment should be allowed the slightest weight in the more important matters before them can, it seems to me, have part in any consultation even as to such operations within the park as those which your duty outside of it obliges you to speculate upon. During the last ten years I have repeatedly declined to be employed upon any particular question of the Central Park under a form of employment that did not involve an obligation on the part of the Commissioners to receive, (not necessarily to follow) advice from the original designers of the park, upon any and all questions affecting that design. I have declined to give such advice in any form, directly or indirectly, to any commissioner. I have advised Commissioners of the Brooklyn Parks that I should take the same view of any duty in regard to Prospect Park. I cannot waste my time in trying to help a body of men who have so little idea of their duty as the Brooklyn Park Commissioners. I cannot put myself in the least between them and the public condemnation which they are diligently earning. I must most reluctantly decline your request. But I thank you for making it and remain faithfully yours

Fredk Law Olmsted.

The text presented here is from a letterpress copy of a handwritten letter signed on the original in Olmsted's hand: A3: 352–53, OAR/LC.

1. Jacob Weidenmann (1829–1893) was a Swiss landscape gardener who emigrated to the United States in 1856. He designed City Park (later Bushnell Park) in Hartford, Connecticut, and went on to design other parks in that city. In 1870 he published *Beautifying Country Homes*, a catalog of his residential design work that both Olmsted and Mariana Griswold Van Rensselaer praised. Weidenmann worked at Prospect Park beginning in 1871 and, after the termination in 1874 of Olmsted's partnership with Calvert Vaux, he assisted Olmsted over the next decade on a number of commissions, including the Buffalo parks, Mount Royal in Montreal, and the U.S. Capitol grounds. They also collaborated on the Schuylkill Arsenal in Philadelphia and Congress Park in Saratoga Springs, New York. In the 1880s Weidenmann worked on his own and moved to Chicago in 1886 to design Mount Hope Cemetery. After being fired by the

cemetery's directors in 1887, he successfully sued them and returned to New York. In 1888 he published *Modern Cemeteries*, a guide to cemetery planning and management (David Schuyler, "Weidenman, Jacob," in Charles A. Birnbaum and Robin Karson, eds., *Pioneers of American Landscape Design* [New York, 2000], pp. 439–42; FLO to William Hammond Hall, Sept. 13, 1875 [*Papers of FLO*, 7: 149–51]; FLO to Rev. J. H. Miller, Feb. 28, 1876 [*Papers of FLO*, 7: 179–82, n. 1]; Rudy J. Favretti, *Jacob Weidenmann: Pioneer Landscape Architect* [Hartford, Conn., 2007]).

2. Weidenmann had moved back to New York from Chicago in 1888, at which time Brooklyn College commissioned him to advise them on a campus plan (R. J. Favretti, *Jacob Wiedenmann*, p. 142).
3. The Brooklyn Park Commissioners first appointed Olmsted, Vaux, and Co. landscape architects in 1865, and approved their plan for Prospect Park the following year. Olmsted oversaw construction of the park and continued to report to the Brooklyn park board until 1874. During that period, Olmsted and Vaux prepared plans for Washington (Fort Greene) Park, Carroll Park, and Tompkins Square, as well as Eastern and Ocean parkways. Olmsted's opinion of the Brooklyn Commissioners declined in the 1880s, especially after James S. T. Stranahan, the powerful and supportive president of the Brooklyn park commission since its earliest days, was not reappointed by Mayor Seth Low in 1882. In 1886 Olmsted wrote, "At several points in Prospect and in Fort Greene parks important intentions of the original design have been completely frustrated through the omission of a few simple and inexpensive operations needed to make available the results of large outlays."

   The leading editorial of *Garden and Forest* on July 4, 1888, likely written by William A. Stiles, stated that "the ideas held by the Board of Park Commissioners with regard to the responsibilities of their office, are not calculated to inspire confidence in the future." The park commissioners, he argued, had not been gradually thinning out the trees in Prospect Park and now a new board was "determined to make up for the neglect of their predecessors . . . [without] any understanding of the original motives of the plantations." Additionally, the park commissioners had chosen to erect a music stand in a portion of the park not meant for such an accommodation and were threatening to turn the plaza in front of one of the principal entrances of the park into a garden.

   The "present course" that Olmsted refers to may have been the Brooklyn Corporate Council's interpretation of a law passed by the New York State legislature in 1888, as part of a broad consolidation of the city's laws. The Council determined that the Brooklyn park board had to secure approval from the Common Council for individual expenditures. The effect of this interpretation was controversial, causing one Brooklyn park commissioner, who resigned in April 1889, to describe the situation in an open letter to the *New York Times*: "The board has no real authority to use its own funds. It is at liberty to propose plans for their approval, but is not at liberty to approve them . . . it is painful to me to see the parks already suffering and destined to suffer more and more for want of work which the board has no power to order to be done." The New York State legislature remedied the situation by passing a law in June 1889 clarifying that the Department of Parks had control over its own contracts (*Papers of FLO*, 6: 20–27; *FLO: A Biography*, p. 403; "The Park Commission," *Brooklyn Eagle*, June 16, 1882; p. 2; FLO to Andrew A. Smith, Oct. 18, 1886; John Y. Culyer to FLO, Dec. 18, 1886; "Prospect Park," *Garden and Forest*, July 4, 1888, pp. 217–18; New York [State], *Laws of the State of New York, Passed at the One Hundred and Eleventh Session of the Legislature* [Albany, N.Y., 1888], chap. 583; "Dr. Storrs' Resignation," *Brooklyn Eagle*, April 23, 1889, p. 2; "Bricks Without Straw," *New York Times*, April 21, 1889; New York [State], *Laws of the State of New York, Passed at the One Hundred and Twelfth Session of the Legislature* [Albany, N.Y., 1889], chap. 562).

To Alpheus Hyatt[1]

24th March, 1889.

Mr A. Hyatt:
My Dear Sir,

I write at once to say that I am very glad to receive your note of 22d which has but just reached me and that I am in cordial accord with all it suggests. The three localities are still open to your Society and the only change in the plans or forethoughts of the Department is in the direction of improved facilities for the purposes that you have in view.[2]

We have the topogl map of the Long Crouch district on a larger scale

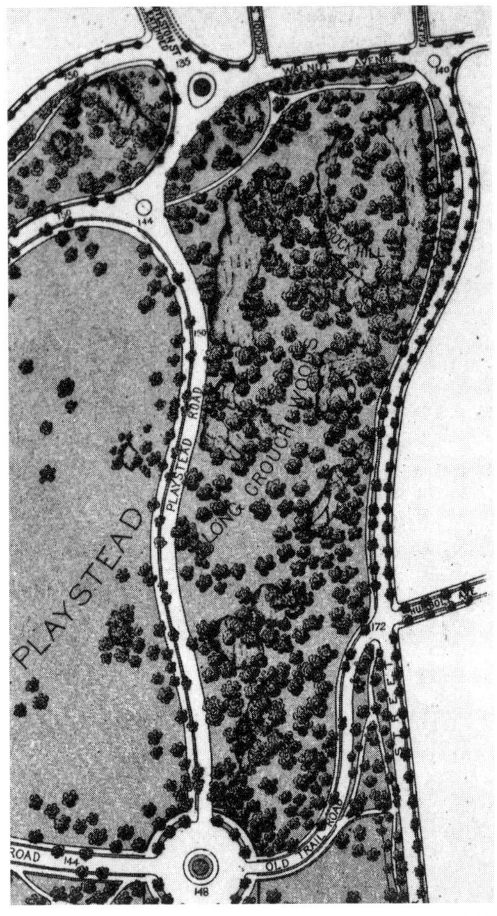

Detail from "General Plan of Franklin Park," December 1891, showing the location of Long Crouch Woods in relation to the Playstead in Franklin Park

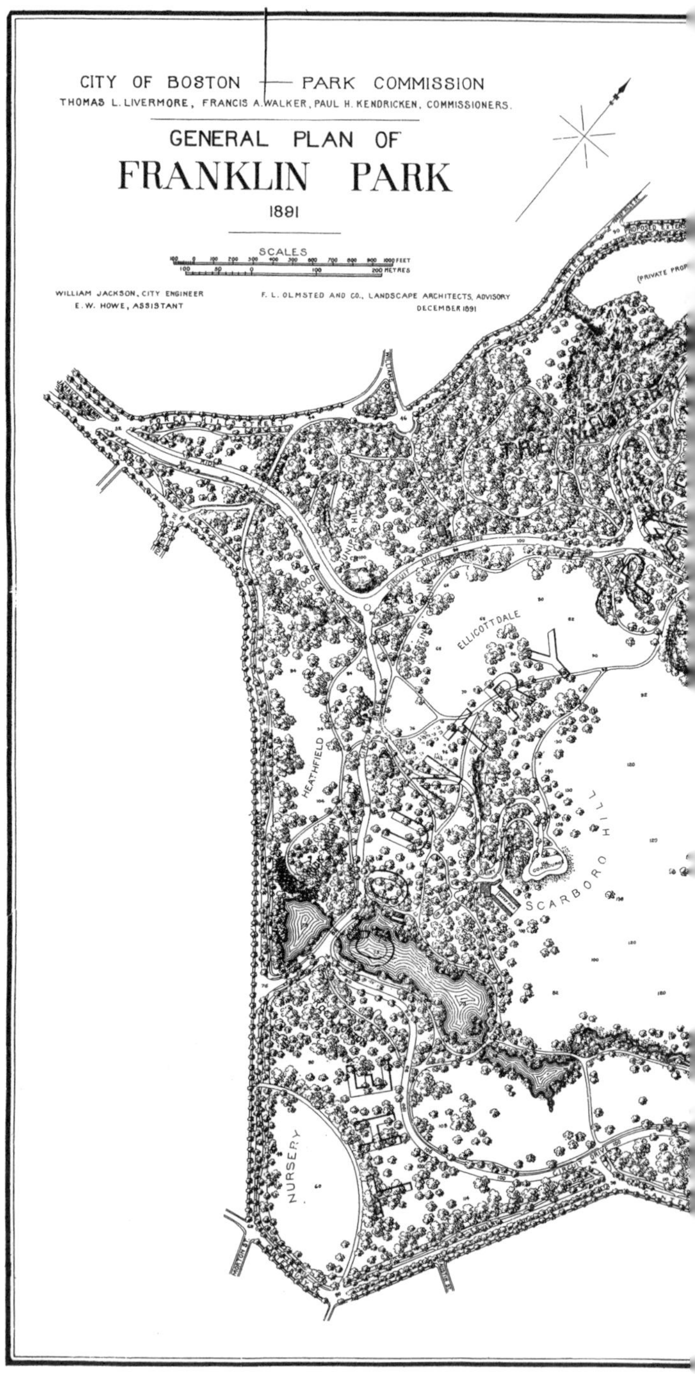

General Plan of Franklin

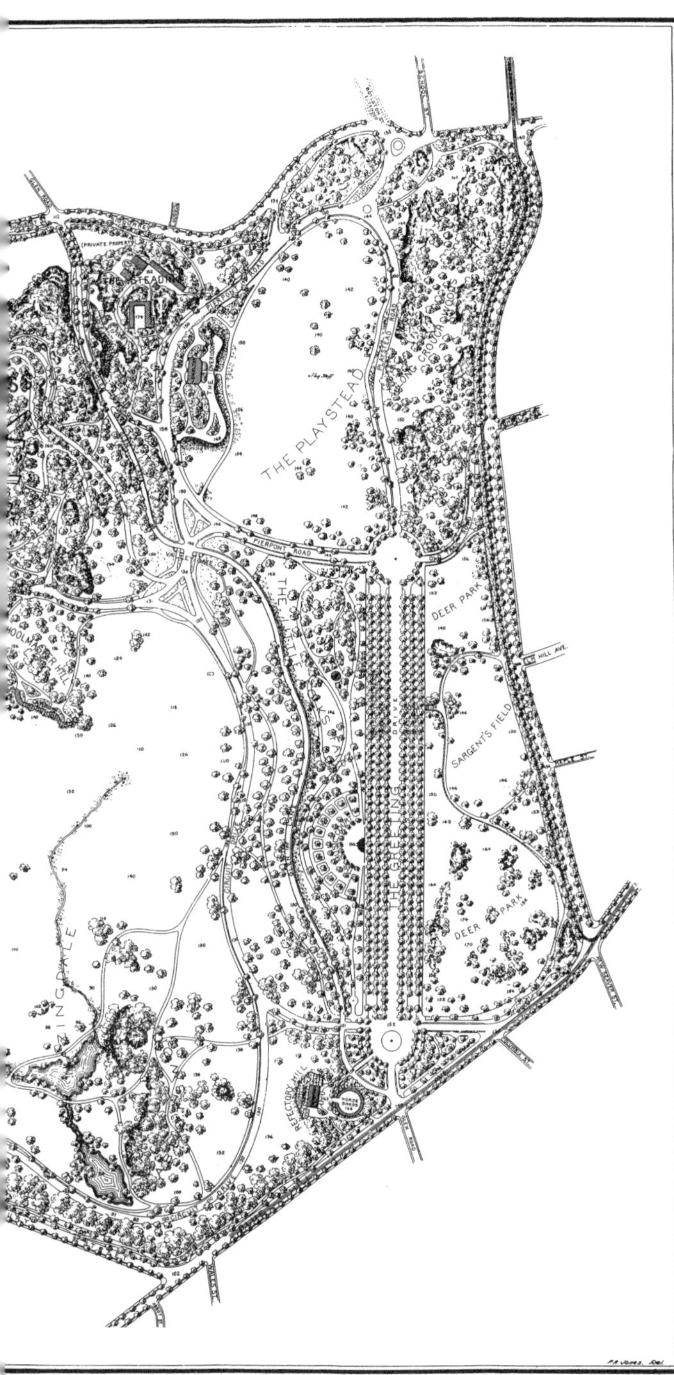

Park, December 1891

than the lithograph and of this a tracing can be made for you.[3] It is a poor map, however; by no means sufficiently accurate to plan upon, even approximately without some study of the ground. There is less surface available for buildings or courts, especially turfy courts, than you are likely to suppose; especially as it is very desirable to avoid occupation of the ground within about a hundred feet of the park face of the wood. Large craggy ledges are the characteristic feature but there is I think good opportunity for (deep rock enclosed) courts for burrowing animals and in which wood-chucks, marmots, badgers prairie dogs and gophers might be exhibited almost in a state of nature. But, of course, the collection must be limited, cruelly, I fear to a naturalist, more so than Mr Ross,[4] at least, has contemplated. What I have hoped is that but little being attempted that little can be a great deal better done than anything within the same limits has been anywhere else. It is my opinion that the result would be more popularly attractive than such a collection as that of New York[5] which would cost fifty times as much to support; even more attractive than such an one as that of Philal[a].[6] Even a child would enjoy more peeping into an old rabbit warren, as described by Jefferies in *Wild Life in a Southern Country*,[7] than in staring into a cage of sulky lions.

Yours Truly,

Fred[k] Law Olmsted.

The text presented here is from a letterpress copy of a handwritten letter signed on the original in Olmsted's hand: A3: 396-98, OAR/LC.

1. Alpheus Hyatt (1838–1902) was a zoologist and paleontologist. He served as curator of the Boston Society of Natural History from 1881 until his death in 1902. He also taught at the Massachusetts Institute of Technology (1870–1888) and Boston University (1877–1902), and helped to found the Woods Hole Institute for the study of marine biology (*DAB*).
2. Hyatt's letter to Olmsted has not been found. In 1887 the Boston Park commissioners had agreed to lease park land to the Boston Society of Natural History for three "Natural History Gardens:" a marine aquarium in Marine Park, a freshwater aquarium near Jamaica Pond, and a New England Zoölogical Garden in Franklin Park (*Thirteenth Annual Report of the Board of Commissioners for the Year 1887* (Boston, 1888), pp. 34–36).
3. In his 1886 report on Franklin Park, Olmsted wrote that the Long Crouch Woods could "be held subject to lease to a suitable organization for a Zoölogical Garden." The topographical plan which he refers to here has not been found, but a later topographical survey of Long Crouch Woods, dated July 1892, shows the rock outcrops and steep topography that would make the construction of a large building, as proposed by the members of the Boston Society of Natural History, expensive and destructive of the surrounding landscape (Frederick Law Olmsted, "Notes on the Plan for Franklin Park and Related Matters," 1886 [*Papers of FLO*, SS1: 488]; plan 918-208, NPS/FLONHS).
4. Matthias Denman Ross, a member of the Boston Natural History Society, had been corresponding with Olmsted about the Society's plans for a zoological garden in Franklin Park (see FLO to Matthias D. Ross, [Dec. 1889], n. 1, below).
5. A reference to the Central Park Menagerie (see Frederick Law Olmsted, *Tenth Annual*

Report, Boston Park Commissioners, Reports on West Roxbury Park and Wood Island Park, [Dec. 1884], n. 2, above; FLO to Calvert Vaux, July 9, 1887, n. 4, above).

6. The Zoological Society of Philadelphia was chartered in 1859 and opened the Philadelphia Zoological Garden in 1874 (Vernon N. Kisling, Jr., "The Origin and Development of American Zoological Parks to 1899," in R. J. Hoage and William A. Deiss, eds., *New Worlds, New Animals: From Menagerie to Zoological Park in the Nineteenth Century* [Baltimore, 1996], pp. 18, 115–16).
7. "By climbing up the mound, and pushing through the brake fern which grows thickly between the bushes, entrance is speedily gained to the wide rolling stretch of open pasture called the Warren. . . . Now, on hands and knees (the turf is dry and soft), creep up one side of the bowl-like hollow, where the thistles make a parapet on the edge and from behind it look out upon the ground all broken up into low humps, some covered with nettles, others plainly heaps of sand. It is the site of an immense rabbit burrow, the relic of an old warren which once occupied half the field. The nettle-covered heaps mark old excavations; where the sand shows, there the miners have recently been at work." (Richard Jefferies, *Wild Life in a Southern County* [London, 1879], p. 218–19.)

To James Hampden Robb[1]

30th March, 1889.

Dear Mr. Robb:

Mr Harrison[2] will in a few days unite with me in making a report of the result of our examination of Central Park, made this week at the request of the West Side Association and the Torrey Club and as I was assured with your cordial sanction. It is delayed by Mr Harrison's occupation at Albany[3] and I do not know precisely what he will be disposed to say. I may privately assure you however, that, provided the probable intention to liberally replant many places where the old plantations had been hopelessly ruined by failure of timely thinning, is to be promptly and largely carried out, we saw no thinning that was not most desirable. The park is in extreme need of a great deal more of the same work and there is no {*possible*} way in which it can now be as much improved as in taking out poor vegetation, replacing it with good and in substituting low bodies of foliage of shrubs and vines for turf where turf, even with very costly maintenance, must be either very shabby or very incongruous with the general character of the associated scenery.

We saw no one and have had no recent communication with any of the park people and shall simply adapt for our report what seems the most natural assumption of your intentions in this respect.

I write this because this is the precise moment of all the year when the greatest liberality and energy is needed in the management of the plantations and if Prof^r^ Sterns's[4] alleged expert advice has had the {*slightest*} weight with you I should like to do all in my power promptly to counteract it. We shall report formally to Mr Van Rensselaer.[5]

Yours Truly

Fred[k] Law Olmsted.

The text presented here is from a letterpress copy of a handwritten letter signed on the original in Olmsted's hand: A3: 426–27, OAR/LC. Two New York organizations, the West End Association and the Torrey Botanical Club, protested what they considered the excessive thinning of trees in Central Park. They asked Olmsted and Jonathan Baxter Harrison, who at the time was the secretary of the American Forestry Congress, to visit the park and report on the situation. Olmsted wrote this letter to James H. Robb, president of the New York City park board, while conducting research for the final report, which was published in April 1889 as *Observations on the Treatment of Public Plantations, More Especially Relating to the Use of the Axe* (Kiliaen Van Rensselaer to FLO, March 5, 1889; FLO to Kiliaen Van Rensselaer, March 9, 1889, A3: 322, OAR/LC; *Observations on the Treatment of Public Plantations, More Especially Relating to the Use of the Axe*, April 30, 1889, below; see also FLO to Joseph S. Fay, April 10, 1889, below).

1. James Hampden Robb (1846–1911) served on the Board of Commissioners of the Department of Public Parks from 1887 to1890. When Robb first learned that Olmsted would be reporting on the department's tree cutting policy, Kiliaen Van Rensselaer (in a letter to Olmsted) quoted Robb as saying, "The subject belongs exclusively to experts in such matters. I trust that Mr. Olmsted's report will be made at an early day." Olmsted and Robb had corresponded regularly in the early 1880s when Robb was serving on the executive committee of the Niagara Falls Association. J. B. Harrison also had worked closely with Robb because he had been the corresponding secretary of the same association. Robb served in the New York State legislature as both an assemblyman in 1882 and a senator from 1884 to 1885. After the legislature created the Niagara Reservation in 1883, Governor Grover Cleveland appointed him to its board of commissioners ("J. Hampden Robb, Ex-Senator, Dead," *New York Times*, Jan. 22, 1911, p. 11; *Year Book of the Pennsylvania Society* [New York, 1912], pp. 80–82; Kiliaen Van Rensselaer to FLO, March 20, 1889; James H. Robb to FLO, Jan. 22, 1883; J. B. Harrison to FLO, Jan. 25, 1883).
2. J. B. Harrison visited Central Park with Olmsted on March 26, 1889 (FLO to Kiliaen Van Rensselaer, March 28, 1889, A3: 418–19, OAR/LC; J. B. Harrison to FLO, March 31, 1889; see also *Observations on the Treatment of Public Plantations, More Especially Relating to the Use of the Axe*, April 30, 1889, n. 1, below).
3. Harrison was in Albany "to promote legislation for the preservation of the Adirondack forests" (FLO to Kiliaen Van Rensselaer, March 28, 1889, A3: 418–19, OAR/LC).
4. Emerson Ellick Sterns (1846–1926) was the member of the Torrey Botanical Club, and on March 13 he presented a report to the park commissioners condemning the cutting of the trees in Central Park. Sterns was also an advocate for the creation of a public botanical garden in Bronx Park (James E. Eckenwalder, *Conifers of the World* [Portland, 2009], p. 639; "Protests Against the Cutting," *New York Times*, March 14, 1889; "The Public Botanic Gardens," ibid., Feb. 16, 1889; FLO to Kiliaen Van Rensselaer, March 14, 1889, A3: 338–40, OAR/LC).
5. Kiliaen Van Rensselaer (1845–1905) owned property on the Upper West Side. He was related through marriage to Mariana Griswold Van Rensselaer and was the chairman of

the Local Improvements Committee of the West End Association. He believed that the parks department was cutting down too many trees in Central Park and invited Olmsted to New York to "help along the cause" ("Kiliaen Van Rensselaer Dies," *New York Times*, Nov. 27, 1905, p. 9; Kiliaen Van Rensselaer to FLO, March 5, 1889; "Protests Against the Cutting," *New York Times*, March 14, 1889).

TO JOSEPH STORY FAY[1]

10th April, 1889.

My Dear Mr. Fay,

In planting the Central Park, especially its bleaker parts, many trees were planted as nurses, and, of species designed to be permanent, two or three were in many parts planted with the intention that gradually the {*poorer*} should be weeded out {*leaving*} the more vigorous and {*promising*}. The business of thinning was in my absence too long neglected and when it began such an outcry was made by {*ignorant*} people that the Commissioners had not the courage to let it go on. At every attempt since it has been the same. This last winter, the present Superintendent[2] began some indispensable thinning—largely the taking out of Norway Spruces planted as nurses 30 years ago, {*mostly*} now, dead or dying trees, and {*again*} the cry of Vandalism was {*raised*} and two associations[3] in which were a number of respectable citizens—respectable but perfectly ignorant in Arboriculture—formally protested against the work and again the Commissioners ordered the work to stop. The protesters showed their good faith by asking that I should be called on in association with Mr Harrison, the Secretary of the American Forestry Association,[4] to review the cutting that had been done and state whether it could be justified. Mr Harrison and I have gone thoroughly through the Park and shall report that we saw nothing wrong except in the evidence of previous neglect of thinning. We saw many dead and dying trees still standing that should have long since either been removed or been {*relieved*} by the removal of others.

We shall {show} that the plantations were made with a view to extensive thinning—regular gradual thinning—and that to plant many more trees than are intended to remain and pursue a course of {*gradual*} removal of nurses and of thinning out the less {*promising*} trees is the usual, and unquestionably the proper, way to obtain fine plantations.

The "superstition" {*that*} prevents the due thinning of plantations is so deep-seated, so general and is everywhere {*working*} such mischief that I {*have*} thought that in publishing an opinion in this case it would be well to give some corroborative evidence. I can, for example, cite the Duke of Atholl's experience in his larch plantations,[5] and the opinion of Loudon and De Candolle,[6] that the best results are obtained when three or four thousand trees are planted to the acre and then thinned gradually and regularly so that at the end of twenty years there shall be standing but four or five hundred. I find brief passages that can be quoted for my purpose from Gilpin, Repton, Cobbett[7] and others. Nothing from Downing[8] or any other American authority, as yet, but I have not given up the search.

Will you give me a brief quotable opinion on this point: — Suppose a *bleak* situation, soil well drained; all deeply and finely tilled ({*trenched*} or subsoiled 20 inches {*deep*}; heavily manured with {*dung*} and treated with composted peat, lime and ashes. Plantations to be narrow and {*so divided*} by open spaces that out of 840 acres 400 shall be planted, so that all will be penetrated by air and sunshine. To consist mainly of maple, bass, ash, elm, oak, catalpa, birch, white pine and hemlock, nursery grown, twice transplanted trees, planted with great care, skillfully staked, watered or mulched while young and no reasonable effort spared {*to guard them*} from vermin or {*other*} injury. The object, to obtain fine masses of foliage, suitable to a public park, to be enjoyed chiefly on the opposite side of lawn-like open spaces by people in movement on roads and paths.

Would you plant the trees much closer than they would finally be allowed to stand?

What proportion of all would good husbandry require to have been removed within thirty years?

Assume that the best possible results are to be aimed at, practically regardless of cost.

I know of no other trees that have grown as large in thirty years as those at the Central Park where they have been kept fairly open. There are hundreds with trunks from two to three feet thick one foot from the {*ground*}. Where crowded many are but half as large.

We are going to plant your Red Pines on the Fens this spring.

Very Truly Yours

Fred[k] Law Olmsted.

Esq. J. S. Fay —

The text presented here is from a letterpress copy of a handwritten letter signed on the original in Olmsted's hand: A3: 462–66, OAR/LC. While writing *Observations on the Treatment of Public Plantations, More Especially Relating to the Use of the Axe* with Jonathan Baxter Harrison, Olmsted contacted several experts for their opinions. Joseph S. Fay responded to Olmsted's request for a "brief quotable opinion" with two long letters (Joseph S. Fay to FLO, April 13, 1889; Joseph S. Fay to FLO, April 14, 1889; see also FLO to James H. Robb, March 30, 1889, above; *Observations on the Treatment of Public Plantations, More Especially Relating to the Use of the Axe*, April 30, 1889, below).

1. Joseph Story Fay (1812–1892) was a nurseryman and member of the Massachusetts Horticultural Society and American Forestry Congress. He experimented with plant-

ing pine trees and exotic species at his estate in Woods Hole, Massachusetts, where he established a nursery in the 1850s. Olmsted bought trees from Fay for planting the Boston Fens and asked for his advice while developing his plan for the Boston Harbor Islands in 1887 (*Transactions of the Massachusetts Horticultural Society* [Boston, 1896], p. 146; *Proceeding of the American Forestry Congress* [Washington, 1886], p. 16; Mary Lou Smith, ed., *Woods Hole Reflections* [Woods Hole, Mass., 1983], pp. 254–55; FLO to Joseph S. Fay, Dec. 3, 1884, A1: 103–4, OAR/LC; FLO to Joseph S. Fay, July 28, 1887, A1: 918, OAR/LC).

2. That is, Samuel Parsons, Jr. (see FLO to Calvert Vaux, July 9, 1887, n. 6, above).
3. Olmsted refers to the West End Association and the Torrey Botanical Club (see *Observations on the Treatment of Public Plantations, More Especially Relating to the Use of the Axe*, April 30, 1889, n. 3, below).
4. The American Forestry Association, organized in 1875, which had merged with the American Forestry Congress in 1882, promoted tree planting and the prevention of wanton forest destruction. Harrison became the corresponding secretary of the Congress around 1887 (Henry Clepper, "The American Forestry Association," *Associates NAL Today*, July–Dec. 1978, pp. 81–84; *Proceedings of the American Forestry Congress At Its Meeting Held at Atlanta, GA., December, 1888* [Washington, 1889]).
5. "Planter John," the fourth Duke of Atholl (1755–1830), was reputed to have planted millions of larch trees around his estates at Dunkeld, Scotland, and at Blair Castle. He recorded his observations about his plantings in his forestry journal (Syd House and Christopher Dingwell, "'A Nation of Planters': Introducing the New Trees, 1650–1900" in T. C. Smout, ed., *People and Woods in Scotland: A History* [Edinburgh, 2003], p. 135; "Forestry for Beauty and Use," *Chambers Journal*, 6:3 [Edinburgh, 1900], p. 680).
6. John Claudius Loudon (1783–1843), the British landscape gardener and author, wrote many books and treatises and edited several magazines and encyclopedias on horticulture and landscape gardening. Augustin-Pyramus de Candolle (1778–1841) was a Swiss botanist noted for reorganizing the botanical gardens at the Societé de Physique et d'Histoire Naturelle in Geneva. He established scientific structural criteria for determining natural relations among plant genera (*DNB*; *EB*).
7. Influential British writers on landscape design and picturesque aesthetics: William Gilpin (1724–1804), Humphry Repton (1752–1818), and William Cobbett (1763–1835).
8. Andrew Jackson Downing (1815–1852), the influential American landscape gardener and author of *A Treatise on the Theory and Practice of Landscape Gardening Adapted to North America* (1841) (see Frederick Law Olmsted, *Annual Report of the Architect of the United States Capitol*, 1882, n. 9, above).

To Thomas Harvey Clark[1]

10th April. 1889.

My Dear Sir;

I have received your note of 6th inst.[2]

I shall enclose herewith a full and detailed memorandum of particulars desirable to be recorded upon a topographical map and also examples of such a map as it would probably be best to provide. Most of the particulars stated can probably be copied from maps in your city surveyor's office. If photographs have been taken of the capitol copies will be an advantage.

Can you give any idea of the scope of expenditure on the ground that may be contemplated? Is good gravel near at hand? Is stone, either {*field*} boulders or quarry?

It is impossible to deal with "precipitate bluffs 20 to 25 feet high" in an inexpensive manner with results that will be long satisfactory. Even here, much more at Montgomery. It is impossible, for example, to keep steep slopes of turf in tolerably neat {. . .} except by inordinate labor. To reduce the ground to moderate slopes will probably require expensive grading. Retaining walls or stone faced terraces, which, with reference to stately architectural effect in the foreground of views toward the capitol may be desired, are still more costly. I mention this as indicating the sort of advice that would be desirably given us as to possible outlay, and the availability of stones of any kind. We are {*just now*} building one such wall of boulders collected on an adjoining field. This is to be completely clothed with foliage.[3] In Alabama it might be covered with evergreen ivy in a manner that would be dignified and pleasing. We are constructing another such wall which will be faced with marble brought from quarries nearly a thousand miles away, at perhaps twenty times the cost of the first.[4]

Respectfully Yours,

Fred[k] Law Olmsted.

Thomas H. Clark Eq[r]
Office of the Governor.
Montgomery, Ala.

The text presented here is from a letterpress copy of a handwritten letter signed on the original in Olmsted's hand: A3: 460–61, OAR/LC. Thomas H. Clark, the recording secretary of Alabama's Governor Thomas Seay, had asked Olmsted in March of 1889 to make recommendations for the improvement of the Alabama Capitol. The Capitol building had been enlarged in 1885 by the addition of an east wing, and at this time plans were being discussed for improvements to the grounds. In June 1889, Olmsted traveled to Montgomery, and he submitted his design for the grounds in July. The governor later determined that the proposed work would be too expensive (Thomas H. Clark to FLO, March 23, 1889; Marie Bankhead Owen, *The Story of Alabama, A History of a State*, vol. 1 [New York, 1949], pp. 210–11; FLO to Thomas H. Clark, April 1, 1889, A3: 436–37, OAR/LC; Thomas H. Clark, "Frederick Law Olmsted on the South, 1889," *South Atlantic Quarterly*, vol. III, Jan., 1904, p. 11; see also FLO to Thomas Seay, July 10, 1889, below; FLO to Thomas H. Clark, Aug. 5, 1889, below).

1. Thomas Harvey Clark (1857–1915), lawyer and journalist, served as Governor Thomas Seay's recording secretary from 1887 to 1890. He was elected to the Alabama Legislature in1892 and served as its speaker from 1895 to 1896. He then moved to Washington,

D.C., where he was a law librarian for the United States Congress from 1899 to 1903, and then the official reporter of the United States Court of Customs Appeals. He also contributed articles during his career to diverse publications, including the Montgomery *Advertiser*, the *Nation*, and the *New York Evening Post* ("Death of Thomas H. Clark," *New York Times*, June 18, 1915, p. 5; Thomas McAdory Owen, *History of Alabama and Dictionary of Alabama Biography* [Spartanburg, S.C., 1978], pp. 335–36).

2. Clark's letter thanked Olmsted for his interest in the project and requested instructions from him for making a topographical map of the grounds. Once the map was completed, Clark wrote that Governor Seay would like to make arrangements for securing the Olmsted firm's services (Thomas H. Clark to FLO, April 6, 1889).
3. A reference to the Overlook (or Playstead Terrace) in Franklin Park. See FLO to JCO, Oct. 5, 1887, above.
4. A reference to the marble terrace being built at this time on the U.S. Capitol building in Washington, D.C. The Vermont Marble Company held the contract for supplying the marble, transporting it from quarries in the northeast (Glenn Brown, *History of the United States Capitol*, vol. II (Washington, D.C., 1900], p. 145).

To Robert Douglas

18th April, 1889.

My Dear Mr. Douglass;

I believe that I told you that I went last year with Mr George Vanderbilt to examine some land which he had bought near Ashville N. C.[1] and to glance at more that he thought of buying if the owners would sell at market rather than Vanderbilt prices. His possessions there now are some 2000 acres in extent and he thinks it probable that his agent[2] will succeed in buying nearly as much more in the course of the next month or two. Nearly all of it has been skinned by poor white farmers; the greater part has a poor second growth of wood upon it now but there are a great many patches of cleared land occupied at present by negroes. Mr V. talked of making a park of it. I advised forest plantations for the greater part and that it should be kept and managed as a commercial forest as a long {*policy*}. Also that he should undertake an Arboretum. In a conversation with him yesterday, I found him {*inclined*} to take this advice but he asked many questions that I could not answer without going over the ground that I had not seen and computing the amount of cleared land on the whole. I need your assistance in devising the scheme, estimating cost of planting, &c. I told Mr V. that probably his best way would be to make contracts with you and he assented to my obtaining offers from you. It was this possible opportunity to which I referred in a letter to you last week. Now, therefore, I write to ask if the intended purchases should have been made, would you, sometime in June, meet me in Ashville and look at the property, with a view to such an arrangement?[3]

Yours Very Truly

Fred[k] Law Olmsted

I presume that you received a note from me asking for a few sentences that I could quote, sustaining the idea that the best results of planting are to {be} obtained by planting at first closely, then gradually and regularly thinning out, year after year, until but a small proportion of the original trees are left, and these the finest.[4] I just have a note from Jno. M. Forbes, saying "My plantation of about 50 years, being exposed to the whole sweep of the Atlantic was under Downing's advice thickly planted but the axe has been vigorously used *every year* and in such use is absolutely essential. Fay's plantations are nearly ruined for want of courage with axe and fast becoming hedges or broomsticks with branches on top."[5]

The text presented here is from a letterpress copy of a handwritten letter signed on the original in Olmsted's hand: A4: 526–27, OAR/LC.

1. Olmsted first visited the proposed Biltmore site at Vanderbilt's request in the summer or early fall of 1888 (FLO to James G. Gall, Oct. 30, 1888, A2: 952–53, OAR/LC; J. M. Bryan, *Biltmore Estate*, p. 31).
2. Charles McNamee was Vanderbilt's agent for land purchases. See FLO to George W. Vanderbilt, July 12, 1889, n. 1, below.
3. Douglas accepted the offer and first visited Biltmore in June 1889 to examine the property and consider the general division of the estate into areas for forestry, a deer park, pasture, and agriculture, as Olmsted had suggested. He sent Olmsted a formal report on his findings, which Olmsted passed on to Vanderbilt in July. Douglas continued to advise and help establish the tree and shrub nursery through the winter of 1889. By 1891 Douglas took a less central role in the project but continued to provide plants when requested (Bill Alexander, *The Biltmore Nursery, A Botanical Legacy* [Charleston, S.C., 2007], pp. 16, 66–67; FLO to Charles McNamee, May 17, 1889, A4:717–20, OAR/LC; FLO to Robert Douglas, June 11, 1889, A4: 852, OAR/LC; FLO to Robert Douglas, July 6, 1889, A4: 924, OAR/LC; Robert Douglas to FLO, [July 1889]; FLO to Charles McNamee, July 6, 1889, A4: 925, OAR/LC).
4. Refers to Olmsted's collecting of quotations from colleagues for the essay he was writing on the necessity of thinning tree plantations. See *Observations on the Treatment of Public Plantations, More Especially Relating to the Use of the Axe*, April 30, 1889, below.
5. John Murray Forbes (1813–1898) was a prominent businessman and landowner. His estate, Milton Hall, in Milton, Massachusetts, contained an extensive plantation of trees. The quote he provided for Olmsted given here appeared in Olmsted's essay. Joseph Story Fay (1812–1897) was a horticulturist and forester. He owned the Woods Hole estate in Massachusetts, where he experimented with tree plantings. See FLO to Joseph S. Fay, April 10, 1889, above (*DAB*; see *Observations on the Treatment of Public Plantations, More Especially Relating to the Use of the Axe*, April 30, 1889, below).

OBSERVATIONS

ON THE

TREATMENT OF PUBLIC PLANTATIONS,

MORE ESPECIALLY RELATING TO

THE USE OF THE AXE.

BY

F. L. OLMSTED,

LANDSCAPE ARCHITECT.

AND

J. B. HARRISON,

CORRESPONDING SECRETARY AMERICAN FORESTRY CONGRESS.[1]

MR. KILLIAN VAN RENSSELAER,[2]

Dear Sir:—We have the honor to present a paper prepared at your suggestion in behalf of the West End Improvement Association, the Torrey Botanical Club,[3] the Park Commissioners of New York and others interested, in relation to the treatment of public plantations.

Your obedient servants,
FREDERICK LAW OLMSTED,
Landscape Architect.
J. B. HARRISON,
Cor. Sec. Amer. Forestry Congress.

30th APRIL, 1889.

It has been said of our old frontier settlers that they seemed to bear a grudge against trees, and to be engaged in a constant indiscriminate warfare with them. If this were so a strong reaction has since set in, of which a notable manifestation appears in the fact that with regard to no other matter pertaining to the public grounds of our cities has public interest taken as earnest, strenuous and effective a form as in respect to the protection of their plantations against the axe.

It has occurred repeatedly of late years that ladies and gentlemen, seeking their pleasure during the winter in public parks, have chanced to see men felling trees, and have been moved by the sight to take duties upon themselves that nothing else short of a startling public outrage would have led them to assume. Sometimes they have hastened to stand before a partly felled tree and have attempted to wrest the axe from the hand of the woodsman. Oftener they have resorted to the press and other means of rousing public feeling, and not unfrequently a considerable popular excitement has resulted. At the time of such excitements a strong tendency has appeared in many minds to assume that the act of tree-cutting marks those who are responsible for it as unsusceptible to the charm of sylvan scenery, and to class them with the old indiscriminately devastating pioneers.

We say that such manifestations of public spirit in respect to the protection of plantations have been frequent. They have occurred, for example, within a few years in Brooklyn, Boston, Washington and San Francisco.[4] They have in some cases affected legislation. They have appeared in the halls of Congress, and statesmen have had part in them.[5] Since the planting of Central Park there have been several in New York. The leaders in them have often been citizens deservedly high in public esteem, more than commonly well equipped with general information, liberally educated, of good social standing and wide influence.

Naturally an effect of such manifestations of public sentiment has been to make those in direct superintendence of public plantations, and the governing boards supervising them, extremely reluctant to use the axe. In some cases, for years not a tree has been cut down; in others only decaying trees which were prominent eye-sores or dangerous to passersby, and even when these were to be dealt with the work has been done in stormy weather, when it was little likely to be observed by visitors, and care has been taken to put the fallen wood out of sight as soon as possible. To guard against the provocation of public feeling even in such extreme cases, a standing order has been made by one Park Commission that not a tree should be cut in its plantations till leave had been granted for it by a majority vote of its Board.[6] One of the best trained and most successful tree growers in the country having been dropped from the service of this Board, a member of it gave as the reason for his dismissal that he had been too anxious to obtain leave to cut out trees.[7] In another case the effect of the agitation was such that a laborer refused to fell a tree when ordered, fearing that he would be punished for it as for a crime.[8]

Early this Spring there was a movement in New York partaking of the character of those which had gone before. In the opinion of some having part in it, trees had been felled in Central Park to an extent, and with a degree of unfeeling indiscrimination and disregard of the landscape effects with a view to which they had been planted and grown, that called for the severest condemnation.

Some difference of opinion having been developed in the course of the proceedings to which this movement gave rise, it was thought desirable that an opinion should be obtained from experts other than those to whose judgment the Commissioners had been leaving the matter. To this end the undersigned were selected,—one the Secretary of the American Forestry Congress, the other one of the designers of the Park, and for forty years a tree grower. The request to them was made in behalf of the West End Improvement Association, the Torrey Botanical Club and the Park Commissioners. The duty which they assumed was to review the plantations of the Park, and report how far the tree-cutting upon them had been in accordance with the requirements of the park design and with approved professional practice.

While no sensible man will deliberately maintain that a tree can never be wisely removed from a public plantation, it will be seen from what has been said, that a public sentiment is liable to be cultivated, the effect of which, in numerous instances, may be to keep trees standing for years that might more wisely be cut, and in a general way to *prevent the free exercise of any specially competent judgment upon the question.*

Hence, instead of simply reporting our own view of the particular case that we have been asked to consider, we have thought it better that we should set forth by quotations what may be regarded as the Common Law view of the duty, in respect to the cutting of trees, of a professional public servant to whom has been given the direction of plantations. We venture to say that no man, however well informed he may be in other respects, can have a respectable understanding of this duty to whom such precepts as are about to be cited are not familiar. It is greatly to be desired that knowledge of them and faith in them should be more generally diffused than it is at present among leaders of public opinion in all our cities. In view of the circumstance that New York has a large scheme of new parks and park improvements before it, a publication of them may be hoped to be useful.*

*Among those to be quoted are the following: *Loudon*, J. C., author of Arboretum Britannicum, the Cyclopedia of Gardening, and many other standard technical works; *De Candolle*, Augustin, an eminent botanist, friend and co-worker with Cuvier and Humboldt; *Lauder*, Sir Thomas Dick, editor and commentator upon the works of Price and Gilpin; *Whateley*, Thomas, a member of the British Parliament, and author of the first standard work on Modern Gardening; *Cobbet*, William, author of "Woodlands" and various famous works on Rural Economy; *Repton*, Humphrey, author of several works in Landscape Gardening and the most distinguished English landscape designer of the present century; *Smith*, C. H. J., author of a treatise on Parks and Pleasure Grounds; *Speechly, Grigor, Main*

1. "It is in the act of removing trees and thinning woods that the landscape gardener must show his intimate knowledge of pleasing combinations, his genius for painting, and his acute perceptions of the principles of an art which transfers the imitative, though permanent beauties of a picture, to the purposes of elegant and comfortable habitation, the ever-varying effects of light and shade and the inimitable circumstances of a natural landscape."—*Repton.*[11]

2. "The old adage, 'PLANT THICK AND THIN QUICK,' holds as good now as centuries ago."—*Douglas.*[12]

3. "Fully half the number of plants inserted per acre should be removed by the time that the most valuable are twenty-five feet high."—*Grigor.*[13]

4. "For the best results, we must plant thickly, keep removing, some here some there, perhaps adding others."—*Beal.*[14]

5. "Thinning is one of the most indispensable operations."—*Brown.*[15]

6. "Of the implements required to produce a fine tree the axe is certainly the first and most important."—*Sargent.*[16]

7. "We now come to the most important consideration connected with forestral questions, that of thinning the trees."—*Hobbs.*[17] (Report to American Forestry Congress, 1886.)

8. "They go on vegetating but hardly growing. The remedy is obvious. *Every year* they need to be thinned." —*Emerson.*[18]

9. "Though they are still far short of their growth, they are [from neglect of thinning] run up into poles, and the groves are already past their prime."—*Whateley.*[19] (Criticism on Clermont Park.)

10. "A natural growth of pine which was thinned when six years old showed an increased rate of accretion three times as great as that of the part not thinned, which was also deficient in height growth."—*Fernow.*[20]

11. "Wherever systematic thinning has been applied the crops are of nearly double the value at a given age." "We divide the several plantations into three portions, and thin one portion regularly and systematically each year successively."—*Brown.*[21]

---

and *Brown*, authors of well-known treatises on Plantations; *Emerson*, G. B., author of a treatise on Trees, prepared at the request of the Legislature of Massachusetts; *Brisbane*, Gen. J. L.,[9] U.S.A.; *Hough, Scott* and *Bryant*, authors of works on Tree Planting and Landscape Gardening, published in the United States; *Fernow*, Editor of U.S. Government Reports of Forestry; *Sargent*, C. S., Professor of Forestry in Harvard University and Superintendent of the Forestry Division of the United States Census, 1880; *Hall*, J. H.,[10] State Engineer of California; *McLaren*, John, Superintendent of Golden Gate Park, San Francisco; *Beal*, Wm. J., Professor of Horticulture, Agricultural College of Michigan; *Fay*, J. S. and *Forbes*, J. M., notable citizens of Eastern Massachusetts who have been in direction of plantations, one above thirty, the other fifty, years; *Douglas*, Robert, the oldest and most successful large planter in North America, his plantings in the arid regions of the far West alone amounting to over three million trees.

12. "It is an undeniable fact that the weakly, unprofitable, and therefore unsatisfactory state of a large extent of plantations is to be attributed to the neglect of systematic thinning." "We frequently see woods growing upon the best land, matured when only some sixty years old: This arises from neglect of systematic thinning." —*Brown*.[22]

13. "At all stages of a plantation, spaces should be gradually allowed, according to the growth of the trees, which, with some sorts, in favorable situations, extends till the plantation is eighty years of age." —*Grigor*.[23]

14. "The thinning may be continued gradually as the trees grow larger." —*Bryant*.[24]

15. *Hough*[25] gives a table showing the number of trees held, as the result of long experiments, by the German Government Department of Forestry, as desirable to be left in thrifty plantations after a growth of from thirty to one hundred years. The number to remain at fifty years is less than half that at thirty, at one hundred years less than half that at fifty.

16. "To form fine ornamental groves or most valuable woods, the trees should be planted thickly, and when they have attained a sufficient length of bole, thinned gradually till each individual tree enjoys a sufficient share of light and air to bring it to its utmost magnitude and perfection." —*Main*.[26]

17. *Loudon*,[27] in Arboretum Britannicum, concludes from an examination of the cultivated larch plantations of the Duke of Athol, that in the most successful practice seven trees out of eight will have to be thinned out in the first twenty years, and quotes *De Candolle*[28] as having reached a similar conclusion from observations in France.

18. *Lauder*, (in a note upon Gilpin's Forest Scenery),[29] says that to make an artificial plantation which shall ultimately resemble a natural plantation, "the best way" is to so manage as that "by a frequent and judicious use of the axe, the best individuals, and those most calculated to associate and harmonize together, are left in permanent possession of the ground." "This mode, be it understood," he adds, "requires constant attention — an attention unremitting from the earliest years of the plantation, till nothing remains but the permanent trees; otherwise, from too long confinement or other causes, stiff and unnatural forms may be produced."

19. "Nurses are surplus trees or shrubs introduced into the plantation for a temporary purpose, for the occupancy of the ground to shelter and protect the permanent plants and to aid in forming them into well shaped trees." "Unless care be taken to subordinate these nurses they will be likely to overwhelm the more valuable plants." —*Brisbane*.[30]

20. "Experience shows us that the oak would make but a slow progress for a number of years were it not for some kind nurses; the birch seems to answer that purpose the best." "After the birches are cut down there is nothing more to be done but thinning the oaks, from time to time, as may be required." —*Speechly*.[31]

21. *Cobbett*[32] records in "Rural Rides" that he saw at New Park two

plantations of oaks, one twelve years old, grown with nurses, the other adjoining, on land thought to be better, twenty years old without nurses. The second "was not nearly so good as the first."

22. "White pine cannot endure our prairie winds if standing exposed, and the same holds good on our Eastern Coast; but intermixed with Scotch pine they have succeeded admirably; the Scotch pine making the most rapid growth during the first five years were overtopped in less than two years [afterwards] and cut out, leaving the White pines to occupy the ground."—*Douglas.*[33]

23. "When the nurses consist of inferior kinds, they should generally be all removed by the time that the plantation arrives at the height of fifteen or twenty feet." —*Loudon.*[34]

24. "From the time that all the nurses are removed, in each of the subsequent thinnings, those trees should first be cut down which appear to press on their stronger and more healthy neighbors, and to deprive them of the room and nourishment needful to their increasing growth."—*Smith.*[35]

25. Addressing the Southampton Chamber of Commerce, Mr. *T. W. Shore,*[36] urging the importance of a School of Forestry, observed that the management of the New Forest was "a national disgrace." "Look," he said, "at the many thousands of young trees choked by their nursing pines." "So many young trees killed before they are grown, and see the pines growing so large and thick as to be at the present time actually killing each other."

26. Consistently with this, Mr. *Gladstone,*[37] speaking on the same topic in the House of Commons, referred to a popular "superstition," which caused the thinning of plantations to be too much neglected, as the most serious difficulty to be overcome in an improvement of British tree-growing.

27. "Now we have trees whose natural habits would produce heads of foliage twenty-five to thirty feet across, at ten to fourteen years of age (and which were planted four to eight feet apart, with the view of gradually cutting out full two-thirds of the number within the years down to this time), still standing in the groups as planted—spindling, bare-stalked saplings within the groups and one-sided shams around the margin thereof; in many cases not a single well-developed specimen in the whole group. In this respect the main large clumps of the older trees are rotten shams, which in a few years, because the individual trees are spindling, weak and light-rooted, and with foliage and branches high up the trunk only, will commence to blow down wholesale." "These trees were never intended to stand permanently in such places. There are thousands which are serving no other purpose than to ruin others."—*Hall.*[38]

28. "I have charge of several hundred acres in forest and ornamental tree growths. My practice has been to plant thick, and thin as soon as the trees showed the slightest indication of interfering with one another. The result has been most satisfactory. Where this work [of thinning] has been neglected, the result has been disastrous."—*McLaren.*[39]

29. "I find the older plantations in very bad condition, which is the result of the neglect of thinning. They are planted thick for various reasons, but have been allowed to stand as planted until the lower branches have died off, and the trees spindled up to their stems." "I have seen whole acres of conifers die off in a single year from these causes" [neglect of thinning].—*McLaren.*[40]

30. Mr. *Forbes* planted extensively fifty years ago, and, on account of the extreme bleakness of the site,[41] under the advice of Mr. Downing,[42] as he writes, "*very thickly;*" but he adds "the axe has been used vigorously *every year*, and a look at the plantations at this time will convince everybody that this was absolutely essential." Of certain other plantations he says: "They were nearly ruined for the want of courage with the axe." "The trees are fast becoming broomsticks with branches on top."[43]

31. "Most trees are gregarious in extreme youth, from habit transmitted through many generations; they love company, and only thrive really when closely surrounded. Close planting is essential, therefore, to insure the best results. As the trees grow, the weaker are pushed aside, and finally destroyed by the more vigorous, and the plantation is gradually thinned. This is the operation which is always going on in the forest when man does not intervene. It is a slow and expensive operation, however, and the result is attained by a vast expenditure of energy and of good material. The strongest trees come out victorious in the end, but they will bear the scars of the contest through life. The long, bare trunk, with a small and misshapen head—the only form of a mature tree found in the virgin forest—tells of years or of centuries of struggle, in which hundreds of weaker individuals may have perished, that one giant might survive. But man can intervene, and by judicious and systematic thinning help the strong to destroy the weak more quickly, and with a less expenditure of vital force. Thick planting is but following the rule of nature, and thinning is only helping nature do what she does herself too slowly, and therefore too expensively. This is why trees in a plantation intended for ornament, like those in a park or pleasure-ground, should be planted thickly at first, and why they should then be systematically thinned from time to time; and it is because this systematic thinning is altogether neglected, or put off until the trees are ruined for any purpose of ornament, that it is so rare to find a really fine tree in any public place or private grounds."—*Sargent.*[44]

It will be observed that all agree that in good practice trees are planted originally much closer than it is desirable that they should be allowed to grow permanently, and that, from every well-planted large body of trees, some are removed every year up to at least eighty years. This for centuries has been the established custom in Great Britain and on the continent of Europe, and it is approved by every American to whom the subject has been one of anything like professional study, whether with reference to the object of sylvan charm of scenery or simply that of growing the largest amount of wood in the shortest time.

Upon this point, we have not, with considerable search, found one man with any claim to be regarded as an authority, differing from those we have quoted. Many writers on Landscape Gardening say nothing about it; but this evidently because they assume that their readers will be of a class not needing to be advised of a principle so well established.

Undoubtedly authorities differ a little in their views as to the extent to which, in the management of plantations for landscape-effect, the thinning process should be pursued. But such differences mainly represent varying degrees of susceptibility to the charm of one or another variety of sylvan scenery, and a consequent disposition to give more prominence in writing to one or another. We may observe that if there can be considered to be two schools in this respect, we should ourselves be classed with that which favors the less uniform use of the axe, and which believes in sometimes sacrificing more of the chances for long and perfect development of trees to the result of a more playful disposition and greater variation of companionship of them. We should, more than some, guard in thinning against making any tree individually conspicuous. We would not have the least confusion between the purpose of a Park and the purpose of an Arboretum.

But no difference in this respect among those who have carefully studied the results of varying practice during many years, subtracts, in the slightest degree, from the unanimity with which they condemn all such management of plantations as it is the tendency of public sentiment to compel public servants to adopt. Instead of saying that if men are seen to be cutting trees out of a plantation there is a presumption of ignorant or unfeeling management, which, practically, is the prevailing disposition with those expressing the most affectionate interest in our parks, they are agreed in teaching that whenever a year passes in which trees are not cut out of any extensive plantation, there is ground for presumption — a very strong presumption — that the management is ignorant or neglectful of its most important duty.

The fact is, nevertheless, that until men, whether non-professional commissioners of public plantations or non-professional planters on their own private account, have learned better by costly lessons of personal experience, they are generally much indisposed to plant as thickly as is necessary and still more indisposed to allow plantations to be thinned as is desirable. Often, therefore, plantations become and remain crowded to a degree which brings many of their trees to death, or to a decrepit and slowly dying condition, and which draws all others into such forms that, even if by a late use of the axe they are at last given ample branch and root room, they are precluded from taking advantage of it. They come to be of senile habit, and it is no longer possible for them to contribute to broad, rich and harmonious compositions of foliage.

The question then will often arise: — What can best be done in places where trees have been more or less seriously injured by crowding; — in what degree is their restoration to be wisely aimed at;—to what extent will it be more judicious to clear the ground and replant? A landscape architect who has had probably as large a private practice as any other in the country, says that no other question oftener comes to him, and no other is a greater tax upon his professional resources. It is easy in any given case, for a shallow, conceited quack to settle it flippantly; it is easy to settle it indolently; it requires experience, close study and sagacious foresight to determine the best practicable settlement of it. Upon this point we present a few additional quotations:—

1. Speaking of a case where due, gradual thinning had been neglected, *Grigor*,[45] in his Treatise on Forestry, (Edinburgh, 1868), says: "Although a thinning is now going on, it is doubtful if the trees left will make much more progress." "The only question is whether it would not be better to clear the trees off at once by rooting them out. Had the ground been in a conspicuous position I should have had no hesitation in recommending that course, for, however common, few scenes more unsightly are to be met with than the display of unshapely trees struggling for existence, and diseased through mismanagement."

2. *Loudon*[46] quotes a passage from *Sang*,[47] urging the importance of timely thinning, observing that if neglected "*the plantation will inevitably be ruined*."

3. "If thinning is delayed too long, the stems will be slender and feeble." "Dead and dying trees should be taken out whenever found."—*Hough*.[48]

4. "Considerable loss is frequently sustained by producing through long confinement tall trunks without a proportionate diameter; and unless the soil is very congenial and the trees of great vigor, they are often slow to become stout or shapely when ample space has at last been afforded to them."—*Grigor*.[49]

5. "The first thing to be decided is the amount of *clean cutting* to be done,—what had better be entirely removed in order that something better may be developed."—*Scott*;[50] Advice as to the Renovation of Old Places.

6. "It is very difficult to determine how to treat plantations that have been neglected in thinning. It is a bad job, and you can only hope to prevent further ruin, but not to entirely remedy that which is now so painfully apparent to any-one who knows about trees and their cultivation. *The trees in some parts are so far gone that they cannot be saved to good purpose. Better cut out spaces* within such groups and around the margins, fertilize the soil, trench it over, plant new trees, and as they grow *cut away the balance of the old ones*."—*McLaren*.[51]

7. "If I were again to set out young trees among the old woods, *I should cut the latter all down clean*."—*J. S. Fay*[52] (Experiments in Tree Planting, U.S. Forestry Report, 1877).

8. "When any plantation has stood long without being thinned, par-

ticularly such as are composed of coniferous trees, it is, we may say, impossible to recover it."—*Brown's Forester*.[53]

9. "This plantation in place of being thinned gradually . . . had been subjected to a severe thinning all at once." "When a pine plantation has been mismanaged in this way, the proprietor should never hesitate but have it cut down at once and the ground replanted."—*J. B. Webster*,[54] in London Garden, April 13, 1889.

We are now prepared to take up the case of the last winter's management of Central Park. What the designers of this Park had in view as to the treatment of its plantations may be inferred from the following passage in a report of theirs. Writing in advance of certain advised plantations, they said:—

> "They are to be thinned out gradually as they come to interlock, until, at length, not more than one-third of the original number will remain; and these, because the less promising will have constantly been selected for removal with little regard to evenness of spacing, will be those of the most vigorous constitution, those with the greatest capabilities of growth, and those with the greatest power of resistance to attacks of storms, ice, disease and vermin. Individual tree beauty is to be but little regarded, but all consideration to be given to beauty and effectiveness of groups, passages, and masses of foliage. The native underwood is to be planted in thickets and allowed to grow in natural forms, enough of it being introduced to prevent, (in connection with the grouping of trees and interspaces of groups, to be formed by the process of thinning the tree plantations), a grove or orchard-like monotony of trunks."*

But in much of the planting of the Park not only were several trees planted of each kind designed to remain permanently, with the object first, of protection, second, of selecting that to remain which should prove most promising of long life and vigor under the circumstances, but nurses were also planted among them. At the time of the earlier planting, the commercial nurseries of the country were overstocked with imported Norway Spruce, and plants of it could be bought by the thousand, of unusual size, at low rates. They were therefore much used as nurses, especially in the bleaker parts on the west side and where the planting was designed to be largely of white pines and hemlocks, which when young grow very slowly and often die if not well nursed.

When the time came for gradually removing these nurses and thinning out the less promising of other trees, the necessary work was restricted within exceedingly inadequate limits, and, as has been stated, at times, was for years wholly suspended. Consequently but a small part of the thinning needed was ever done. Numbers of the spruces intended to serve only as nurses from

*General plan for the improvement of the Niagara Reservation, by Frederick Law Olmsted and Calvert Vaux.[55]

three to six years, remained on the ground after twenty years; some remain yet, after thirty years, and the pines and hemlocks that they were designed to foster have long since disappeared; —either smothered to death or cut out because dwarfed, sickened and mutilated by the oppression of the spruces.

Of the spruces thus brought into undesigned prominence, the late Governor Horatio Seymour[56] stated, from experience on his own farm at Utica:—

> "They grow rapidly when young, but become ragged and thin when they have got to be of any size. Their effect in groups is bad, as their sharp, tapering tops give them a weak, ineffective aspect."

Probably there are localities in which this condemnation would be found too sweeping, but the Central Park is not one of them. Whenever a Norway Spruce has proved worthy to remain, it would appear to be because of an exceptional vigor of constitution, and individual adaptation to the local circumstances.[57] A large majority of all planted in the Park fell into a dwindling condition before they had come to be twenty years old. Four years ago it was observed that much the larger part of those originally planted had disappeared, but many quite dead ones remained; many more were barely alive, and these were disagreeable objects, disgraceful in themselves to the management, but much more disgraceful in the ruin they had made of what would otherwise have been beautiful plantations, contributive to charming passages of sylvan scenery.

Fourteen years ago the professional adviser of the Park Department at the time made a report to the Commissioners, going over much of the ground of the present paper, including in part the citations from eminent tree-growers that have been given above, in support of his statements.[58] He pointed out that the neglect of thinning had already gone far to destroy some of the most important plantations, and that if it continued it was but a question of time when the best thing that could be done, would be to clear considerable areas of ground and replant them.

This report was not published, but as a result of it a special force for thinning was allowed to be employed, and during an inclement season, when few visitors passed through the Park, within less than a month's time, more trees were felled than there had been altogether, probably, in ten years before. The advantage gained where the thinning was most resolute is now conspicuous. It may be seen, for example, on the rising ground, between the two lobes of the North Meadow, the most park-like part of the Park; again on the north side of the eastern half of the road crossing the Park at Mount St. Vincent; on the borders of the drive mounting Bogardus Hill from the south; near the drive opposite Summit Rock; on Cherry Hill and at a few other points. A few complete clearances and replantings were made at this time. A group of hemlocks northwest of the Great Reservoir, for example, occupies ground in which a previous plantation had been ruined by the overgrowth of Norway spruce, the latter having been also ruined a little later, by their crowding of one another. It can be seen that these hemlocks have not been growing thriftily. This is because, in dread of a repetition of the first experience, they were planted too openly.

Within a month, the public indignation was excited and the Commissioners ordered the work to be stopped.*

Not one man with the slightest pretentions to be regarded as an expert in Sylviculture has ever been employed in the service of the Park Department, without making efforts to obtain leave to thin the plantations, or without giving warning that a time was approaching when, if more thorough thinning than the Commissioners were willing to allow, should not soon be made, some of the most important bodies of trees would be ruined, and nothing would remain but to exterminate them and replant the ground.

When we were last passing through the Park before our recent visit, we had observed numbers of dead trees; larger numbers in a dying, and whole groups in a feeble, gaunt and dwindling condition, due to neglect of thinning. It had seemed to us probable that the time was passed when any process of thinning could be successfully used with them. Reading the reports sent this spring, with the request that we would review the plantations, we had been led to suppose that extensive clearings had accordingly been made, and that the principal question that we should have to consider would be whether such clearings had been carried too far, and had been of the insensate character alleged.

On the 20th of March we made an examination of the plantations of the Park, passing nearly from end to end of it four times, walking through all the localities to which our attention had been particularly invited, and bringing under close review all parts of the Ramble and other interior and secluded districts.

It was nowhere apparent to us that trees had been lately removed inconsiderately or without regard for the motives of the original plan. At a number of points what might be regarded as small clearings were found. We saw no reason for doubting that the trees removed in these cases had been ruined for the purpose that had been had in view in the planting of them, by neglect of thinning, and that it had been intended to replant the ground; and at one point we actually found men, so early in the season, beginning the work of replanting.

We saw not a few trees, which in our judgment must die before many

*There is probably no direct connection between the circumstances, but it is worthy of note that immediately following the public protest against the thinning of the Park plantations, of last winter, a bill is introduced to legislate the Commissioners responsible for it out of office. There may be no direct connection, but if public sentiment had been alive to the real character of that work, would those who instigate legislation have been as ready for the move?

years, standing in positions where, if allowed to remain, they will greatly retard the growth of others which if uncrowded would yet become long-lived and umbrageous. It is fair to assume that not a few failing trees thus doing mischief show an incomplete work of improvement.

It was estimated in a report sent us that the quantity of wood cut on the park during the last winter would measure little short of 250 cords. The plantations of the Park are mainly in the form of narrow belts and groups of irregular outline, alternating with spaces of rock, turf, water and roadways; these vacancies being larger on the whole than the planted spaces, so that a large proportion of the trees are open on two sides to light and air. The planted ground was well-drained; the soil taken from the uncovered rocks and the road and water spaces was added to its original soil; many parts had been occupied two years before the planting by small market gardens; the whole was liberally treated with a compost of dung and limed peat, and with phosphates, and finely tilled to a depth of twenty inches. It has since been frequently top-dressed. The trees have been generally growing with extraordinary rapidity. The extent of the planted ground is estimated at 400 acres. The principal tree-planting of the Park was made in 1858, '59 and '60. Having been before thinned much too scantily, would it be thought, by experienced tree-growers, that the taking out of two or three hundred cords of wood from such plantations, at the end of thirty years, was, as has been supposed, an excessive amount?

We cannot think that it would.

Considering how large a proportion of all the felled trees were probably of dead, dying or greatly enfeebled condition, we doubt if they would have borne this year two per cent. of the entire leafage of the Park. We are of the opinion that before midsummer the expanse of leafage that will be gained by new growth will be more than equivalent to all that has been cut off in the winter's thinning. (Let anyone passing through the Park six weeks hence ask if the foliage seems less in amount than it did at the same period last year.)

It is, however, more important to consider the lasting effect. As to this we do not think that a man can be found, of extended experience in plantations of a character corresponding with those of the Park, who, knowing the facts we have recounted, will have the least doubt that the body of foliage on the Park must within two years be considerably larger than it would have been, had the two or three hundred cords of trunks and limbs taken out last winter been left standing.

We have taken for granted that it has been intended to replant various small areas which, because of the destruction by crowding of the originally designed low foliage, were at the time of our visit of dreary aspect. It hardly lies within the duty assigned us, but we may be permitted to add that there are many parts of the Park where ground not now shaded by trees might much more suitably be occupied otherwise than it is. About a hundred paces east of the Springbanks Arch, on the south side of the road, there is a piece of ground of thin soil partly broken by rock, which is charmingly overgrown with low bushes and creepers. It has had much of its present pleasing character for at least twenty-five years, and in that time the annual cost of keeping it has not probably been a fiftieth part as much as the average annual cost of keeping an equal area of the open turf and high shrubbery-studded spaces of the Park. In our judgment a somewhat similar covering would be desirably substituted for turf in many of its smaller openings, which it is never well should be crossed by visitors; in nearly all those, for example, of the Winter Drive and the hill north of it, which are now at large expense kept by lawn-mower and hand-rake, smooth, smug and tame, incongruously with the general character of the designed local scenery. Some slight indications of a desire for improvement in this direction were apparent to us. Should they be liberally followed up, the result, in connection with that of a more courageous management of the old plantations, would, at comparatively small expense, accomplish more for the beautifying of the Park than all that has been done for the purpose in many years. It may be well to say at this point that we have had no recent communication with anyone in the service of the Park, and none for years on the subject of this report. In speaking of the intentions of the management we mean only what is naturally to be surmised in that respect.

At first view it will seem remarkable that complaints so specific and so sweeping as those we have considered should be made by persons of a high degree of general intelligence without any support in the actual facts of the case. It will perhaps be thought hardly credible that the common impression and sentiment of the great body of good citizens as to what is desirable in the management of plantations should be in such direct conflict with what we have shown to be the general conviction of all lovers of natural scenery to whom the question has been one of professional study.

The explanation of the mystery is to be found, we suppose, in the fact that the management of a large park is an art the principles and methods of which are much further from being generally comprehended, even by cultivated men, than is commonly supposed. On this point we offer one more quotation bearing directly upon the particular point of management as to which expert opinion has been asked:

> "To give such general rules for thinning as might be understood by those who never attentively and scientifically considered the subject would be like attempting to direct a man who had never used a pencil to imitate the groups of a Claude or a Poussin."—*Repton.*[59]

And yet it is most undesirable that public-spirited citizens should be led to relinquish any degree of interest that they may now feel in the management of the public grounds of our cities. It is most desirable that they should manifest still greater and more searching interest; that they should influence the management more directly, constantly and effectively. But to do so wisely will require a seriousness of thought upon the subject such as it yet seldom obtains. It will also require a degree of respect for the technical responsibility involved that few have yet begun to realize to be its due.

The text presented here is a privately printed report (Boston, 1889), co-authored by Olmsted and Jonathan Baxter Harrison. Correspondence between the two indicates that Olmsted wrote most of the text and Harrison made editorial comments and suggested changes. On March 5, 1887, Kiliaen Van Rensselaer, chairman of the Local Improvements Committee of the West End Association, had written a letter to Olmsted explaining that his organization was concerned with "how excessively the ax has been used" in Central Park. He asked, at the suggestion of Emerson E. Sterns, a botanist in the Torrey Botanical Club who had written his own report on the subject, if Olmsted and Harrison would "make a brief examination of the park" and present their findings to the park commissioners. Olmsted agreed to consult at no fee but asked for a stipend for Harrison. Tree thinning in the park was being done under the supervision of Calvert Vaux, who since 1887 had served as the department's landscape architect, and the park's superintendent, Samuel Parsons, Jr. Tree thinning was suspended while Olmsted and Harrison prepared this report.

The removal and pruning of trees and shrubs in Central Park had been a contentious issue for many years. When the Tweed Ring took control of the park board in 1870, the new park commissioners ordered the removal of trees and shrubs that they felt obstructed views. Olmsted and Vaux both felt the results were disastrous. In 1873, a new park board passed a resolution declaring that trees could only be removed with their specific approval. In 1882, Olmsted criticized this restriction as being unreasonable. In 1886, Parsons presented a plan for "renewing" Central Park that included tree thinning. Apparently in response to public complaints about the work, William A. Stiles wrote to Olmsted that he had spoken to Vaux and Parsons about tree cutting in Central Park and was reassured that they were acting judiciously. The following year Parsons released a statement claiming that "the trees in the Park have been much injured by being allowed to grow too closely in many places. The cutting for the last month has been perhaps greater than for a long time, but the greatest care has been taken to cut those trees only which it is really necessary to remove" (J. B. Harrison to FLO, March 31, 1889; "Many Trees Cut Down," *New York Times*, March 3, 1889, p. 16; Kiliaen Van Rensselaer to FLO, March 5, 1889; FLO to Kiliaen Van Rensselaer, March 9, 1889, A3: 311, OAR/LC; Kiliaen Van Rensselaer to FLO, March 13, 1889; FLO to Kiliaen Van Rensselaer, March 14, 1889, A3: 338–40, OAR/LC; Kiliaen Van Rensselaer to FLO, March 20, 1889; FLO to Kiliaen Van Rensselaer, March 20, 1889; FLO to Kiliaen Van Rensselaer, March 28, 1889, A3: 418–19, OAR/LC; Roy Rosenzweig and Elizabeth Blackmar, *The Park and the People: A History of Central Park* [Ithaca, 1992], p. 269; FLO to Columbus Ryan, Feb. 27, 1872 [*Papers of FLO*, 6: 523–25]; *The Spoils of the Park* [*Papers of FLO*, 7: 621]; DPP, *Minutes*, Aug. 20, 1873, pp. 217–18; "Renewing Central Park," *New York Times*, Oct. 10, 1886, p. 4; William A. Stiles to FLO, May 20, 1886; "Thinning Out Park Trees," *New York Times*, April 10, 1887, p. 14; see also FLO to James H. Robb, March 30, 1889, above; FLO to Joseph S. Fay, April 10, 1889, above).

1. Jonathan Baxter Harrison (1835–1907) was a journalist and former Unitarian minister who shared many of Olmsted's interests and became a collaborator in several causes. Olmsted met Harrison through their mutual friend, Charles Eliot Norton, after Harrison published accounts of his travels through the South in the *New-York Daily Tribune* and the *Atlantic Monthly* in the early 1880s. Olmsted and Harrison collaborated in 1882 on a series of articles Harrison was writing, at Norton's request, on the subject of landscape preservation and particularly on the need to preserve Niagara Falls. From

1883 to 1885 Harrison served as the corresponding secretary of the Niagara Falls Association. After the creation of the Niagara Reservation in 1885, Charles Sprague Sargent recruited Harrison to write a series of articles arguing for the conservation of the forests of the Adirondack region. In 1887, Norton helped Harrison become an agent for the Indian Rights Association, where he wrote a number of articles on the plight of Native Americans. By 1888 he was serving as corresponding secretary of the American Forestry Congress. Harrison also became a regular contributor to *Garden and Forest* after its creation in 1888. He had great respect for Olmsted, writing in 1885, "I wish you could write a book about Parks, etc. . . . There is more valuable matter in your Reports & Pamphlets than in all the *books* on such subjects" (Albert Fein, *Frederick Law Olmsted and the American Environmental Tradition* [New York, 1972], pp. 44–45; Timothy J. Crimmins, "Frederick Law Olmsted and John Baxter Harrison: Two Generations of Social Critics of the American South," in Dana F. White and Victor A. Kramer, eds., *Olmsted South: Old South Critic, New South Planner* [Westport, Conn., 1979], pp. 137–40; FLO to Charles Eliot Norton, Aug. 14, 1883; FLO to Charles Eliot Norton, May 2, 1885; FLO to Charles Eliot Norton, Aug. 6, 1885; FLO to Joseph S. Fay, April 10, 1889, n. 4, above; Jonathan B. Harrison to FLO, March 22, 1883; see also FLO to James H. Robb, March 30, 1889, above).

2. Kiliaen Van Rensselaer, on behalf of the West End Association, requested that this report be written by Olmsted and Harrison (see FLO to James H. Robb, March 30, 1889, above).
3. The West End Association was organized as the "Citizen's West Side Improvement Association" in 1884 and officially incorporated as the "West End Association" in February of 1889. The association was a group of private citizens, mainly property owners, who oversaw the development of the West Side of New York City between Eighth Avenue and the Hudson River, and 59th Street to 110th Street. Many of the organization's members belonged to the larger West Side Association, organized in 1866. Kiliaen Van Rensselaer was a member of the West End Association and Cyrus Clark was its longtime president.

   The Torrey Botanical Club began meeting under the leadership of John Torrey, Professor of Botany at Columbia College. The early members were amateur botanists, interested in collecting and identifying plants and discussing their findings. The Club had been brought into the Central Park controversy when members of the West End Association invited the club's chairman, Emerson E. Sterns, to present a paper on the subject of tree thinning in Central Park (The West End Association, *The West End Association, organized February 1st 1884* [New York, 1916]; "West Side Property Owners," *New York Times*, Feb. 16, 1884, p. 3; "The Big West Side of Town," ibid., March 31, 1889, p. 6; Edward S. Burgess, "The Work of the Torrey Botanical Club," *Torrey Botanical Club Bulletin*, vol. 27, 1900, pp. 552–58; "Many Trees Cut Down," *New York Times*, March 3, 1889; FLO to Dwight H. Olmstead, July 31, 1887, above; FLO to William R. Martin, June 9, 1888, above; FLO to James H. Robb, March 30, 1889, above).
4. In Brooklyn, several New York newspapers printed editorials and letters in 1887 complaining that the Brooklyn park commissioners were cutting down too many trees in Prospect Park. An editor of the *New York Times* wrote, "There are places where this wretched destruction has ruined the effect carefully developed and guarded by the designers." Complaints against the park commissioners continued into 1888. In Boston, Olmsted responded in 1885 to an anonymous contributor to *American Architect and Building News* who complained that old apple and fruit trees had been cut down as part of the initial site development of West Roxbury Park (Franklin Park). In Washington, D.C., in 1883, Representative Benjamin Wilson of West Virginia called Olmsted a "despoiler" for removing trees from the United States Capitol grounds. In San Francisco,

criticism about tree thinning in Golden Gate Park in 1886 led the park commissioners to ask Olmsted to write a report on the subject with William Hammond Hall (*New York Times*, March 27, 1887, p. 8; "Gibson Victor," *Brooklyn Eagle*, April 23, 1887, p. 4; "Mr. W. Hamilton Gibson Returns to the Charge Against Park Commissioner Somers," ibid., May 29, 1887, p. 4; "Tree Cutting Again," ibid., March 8, 1888, p. 2; "Prospect Park," *Garden and Forest*, July 4, 1888, pp. 217–18; "Vandalism, Excusable or Inexcusable?" *American Architect and Building News*, April 18, 1885, p. 190; "On Points of Views and Methods of Criticism of Public Works of Landscape Architecture," June 20 and June 27, 1885, n. 10, n. 13, above; FLO to Richard P. Hammond, Jr., Oct. 5, 1886, above).

5. In 1874, while Congress was debating an appropriations bill that would employ Olmsted to survey the Capitol grounds, Senator Charles Sumner requested that a beech tree that he deemed "a thing of perfect beauty" not be cut down. Sumner died a few weeks later, and the tree, which Olmsted indeed preserved as part of the new landscape design for the Capitol grounds, was dubbed "the Sumner Beech." A year later, Senator Simon Cameron objected to a walk that Olmsted was planning to build on the Capitol grounds because it would require removal of a large elm tree. In a letter to Justin Morrill, Olmsted asked if he could "induce Senator Cameron to withdraw his objection," but Morrill would not. The tree, dubbed the "Cameron Elm" was saved and the walk was built so that it passed around it (Frederick Law Olmsted, "The National Capitol," *New-York Daily Tribune*, Dec. 5, 1875, n. 7 [*Papers of FLO*, 7: 98]; FLO to Justin Morrill, Sept. 14, 1875; Coy F. Cross, *Justin Smith Morrill: Father of Land Grant Colleges* [East Lansing, Mich., 1999], pp. 134–35).
6. On August 20, 1873, the board of the Department of Public Parks of New York City passed an order banning the cutting of all trees without its approval (DPP, *Minutes*, Aug. 20, 1873, pp. 217–18).
7. Olmsted is likely referring to Oliver Crosby Bullard, whom the New York park board hired with William L. Fischer on March 3, 1875, to supervise the thinning of Central Park's plantations. The board appointed Fischer superintending gardener shortly thereafter (DPP, *Minutes*, March 3, 1875; ibid., March 19, 1875).
8. In *The Spoils of the Park* (1882), Olmsted describes an event during his time at Central Park when there was a standing order "forbidding me to have a single tree felled without a specific order, to be obtained by a majority vote of the Board. Before this order was passed, men seen cutting trees under my directions have been interrupted and indignantly rebuked by individual commissioners, and even by the 'friends' of commissioners, having no more right to do so than they would for like action on a man-of-war. I have had men beg me, from fear of dismissal, to excuse them from cutting trees, and, to relieve them, have taken the axe from them, and felled the trees myself" (*Papers of FLO*, 7: 621).
9. General J. S. Brisbin; see n. 30, below.
10. William Hammond Hall; see n. 38, below.
11. From Humphry Repton, *Observations on the Theory and Practice of Landscape Gardening* (1803) in J. C. Loudon, *The Landscape Gardening and Landscape Architecture of the Late Humphry Repton, Esq.* (London, 1840), p. 195.
12. Appears in Robert Douglas, "The White Pine for Timber," *Garden and Forest*, March 1, 1893, p. 107; but Olmsted likely heard this from Douglas personally some time previous to 1893.
13. From John Grigor, *Arboriculture* (Edinburgh, 1868), p. 91. John Grigor (1806–1881) was a Scottish nurseryman and author of *Arboriculture* (1868) and *Florist and Pomologist* (1881) ("John Grigor," in Ray Desmond and Christine Ellwood, eds., *Dictionary of British and Irish Botanists and Horticulturists* [London, 1994], p. 272).
14. William James Beal (1833–1924) was a leading educator and researcher in applied

plant sciences, and an early advocate of conservation and reforestation. He served as Professor of Horticulture at the Agricultural College of Michigan (1871–1910). He also helped to found several botanical societies, including the Society for the Promotion of Agricultural Science in 1880 (*DAB*).

15. From James Brown, *The Forester*, 4th ed. (Edinburgh, 1871), p. 540. James Brown (1848–1899) was a Scottish forester who was appointed a deputy-surveyor of woods and forests in 1854. His book, *The Forester*, originally published in 1847, was revised and expanded in at least six editions. When the fifth edition was published in 1882, Brown had moved to Ontario, Canada, where he was inspector of woods and forests (House of Commons, *Accounts and Papers*, vol. 29 [1854], p. 19; Peter McDonald and James Lassoie, eds., *The Literature of Forestry and Agroforestry* [Ithaca, N.Y., 1996], p. 40; Richard Refshauge, "Brown, John Ednie (1848–1899)," *Australian Dictionary of National Biography* [Melbourne, 1969], pp. 261–62).
16. From Charles Sprague Sargent, "The Attack on the Niagara Reservation—The Judicious and Systematic Thinning of Trees," *Garden and Forest*, May 22, 1889, p. 242.
17. From John Edward Hobbs, "Lumber Interests—Their Dependence on Systematic Forestry," *American Forestry Congress* (Washington, 1886), p. 46. John Edward Hobbs (b. 1829) was a farmer and forester. He helped to draw up the Maine Forestry Law and was a member of the American Forestry Association (John W. Leonard and Albert Nelson Marquis, "Hobbs, John Edward" in *Who's Who in America* [Chicago, 1889], p. 920).
18. From George Barrell Emerson, *Report on the Trees and Shrubs Growing Naturally in the Forests of Massachusetts* (Boston, 1850), p. 23 (see FLO to Robert Douglas, Dec. 5, 1887, above).
19. From Thomas Whately, *Observations on Modern Gardening* (London, 1770), p. 51 (see "On Gardening," *Art Review*, Fall, 1887, above).
20. Bernhard Eduard Fernow (1851–1923) was a German-born pioneer of American forestry. He was instrumental in organizing the American Forestry Association (1882) and was appointed the head of the U.S. Department of Agriculture's Forestry Division in 1886, a post he held for thirteen years. His views on the benefits of thinning are scattered throughout his annual Reports of the Commissioner of Agriculture (Washington, D.C., 1886+). The quotation given here appears in Fernow's *Report upon the Forestry Investigations of the U.S. Department of Agriculture, 1877–1898* (Washington, D.C., 1899), p. 251. He was also the author of *Economics of Forestry* (1902), *A Brief History of Forestry in Europe, the United States, and Other Countries* (1907), and *The Care of Trees, in Lawn, Street and Park* (1910) (*DAB*).
21. From J. Brown, *The Forester*, p. 552.
22. From J. Brown, *The Forester*, p. 552.
23. From J. Grigor, *Arboriculture*, p. 91.
24. From Arthur Bryant, *Forest Trees, for Shelter, Ornament and Profit* (New York, 1871), p. 35. Peter Rush "Arthur" Bryant (1803–1883) was considered a pioneer of western horticulture. He was the poet William Cullen Bryant's younger brother who, after a short time at West Point, relocated to Illinois (Thomas Meehan, "Arthur Bryant," *Gardeners' Monthly and Horticulturist*, vol. XXV, April 1883, pp. 126–27; William Cullen Bryant II and Thomas G. Voss, *The Letters of William Cullen Bryant*, vol. 1 [New York, 1975], p. 12).
25. From Franklin B. Hough, *The Elements of Forestry* (Cincinnati, 1882), p. 103. Franklin Benjamin Hough (1822–1885) grew up and practiced as a physician in the Adirondack region of New York State. He acted as an inspector for the United States Sanitary Commission during the Civil War, at which time he may have met Olmsted. He also supervised the U.S. Census of 1870, and this work made the rapid rate of depletion of

forests throughout the United States clear to him. Congress appointed him as forestry agent in the Department of Agriculture in 1876. Hough proposed forestry legislation on the state and national level and authored many publications (*DAB*).

26. From J. Main, *The Forest Planter and Pruner's Assistant* (London, 1839), p. 65. James Main (1765–1846) was a British landscape gardener who published several books on vegetable physiology and botany. His works include *Popular Botany* (1835), *The Forest Planner and Pruner's Assistant* (1839) and *The Young Farmer's Manual* (1839). He was an associate of the Linnaean Society from 1829 until his death in 1846 (*The Annals and Magazine of Natural History*, vol. XIX [London, 1847]; William Chambers and Robert Chambers, *Chambers's Edinburgh Journal*, Jan. 31, 1835, p. 199).
27. From John Claudius Loudon, *Arboretum et Fruticetum Britannicum* (London, 1844), p. 2380.
28. Augustin Pyramus de Candolle (1778–1841), Swiss botanist (see FLO to Joseph S. Fay, April 10, 1889, above).
29. From William Gilpin, *Remarks on Forest Scenery, and Other Woodland Views* (1791), edited by Sir Thomas Dick Lauder (Edinburgh, 1834), p. 290. The Reverend William Gilpin (1724–1804) was an English author on picturesque scenery in England and Wales (*DNB*).
30. From General James S. Brisbin, *Trees and Tree-Planting* (New York, 1888), pp. 233, 235. James S. Brisbin (1837–1892), a decorated officer during the Civil War, was an enthusiast of trees and tree-planting and a prolific writer. He was especially concerned about the destruction of American trees, such as the Redwoods in California. His book *Trees and Tree-Planting* (1888) was an encyclopedia of facts he had gathered about American trees ("Gen. James Brisbin," *Chicago Daily Tribune*, Jan. 16, 1892, p. 6; "Current Literature, 'Trees and Tree-Planting,'" *San Francisco Daily Evening Bulletin*, June 2, 1888).
31. From "Letter from William Speechly" in John Evelyn, *Silva: or, A Discourse of Forest-Trees* [1664], edited by Alexander Hunter, 3rd ed. (York, U. K., 1801), pp. 93, 94. William Speechly (1723–1819) was a British agriculturist, and head gardener on several British estates. He wrote several articles about the rural economy that he compiled into *Practical Hints in Domestic Rural Economy* (1820) (*DNB*).
32. From William Cobbett, *Rural Rides*, vol. II, ed. Pitt Cobbett (London, 1885), p. 230. William Cobbett (1763–1835) was a British farmer and political writer. Distressed with the state of agriculture in Britain, throughout 1821 and 1826 he undertook a series of journeys throughout the country to educate himself on the topic, an account of which he later published as *Rural Rides* (1830). He also authored several other works on agriculture, including *Woodlands* (1825) and *The English Gardener* (1829). He also served in the House of Commons in the 1830s (*DNB*).
33. From Robert Douglas to FLO, April 18, 1889, a letter in which he describes his experiences in planting. Douglas's letter reads, ". . . in less than ten years, and cut out, leaving the white pines occupying the ground," although here Olmsted writes "two years" rather than ten.
34. From J. C. Loudon, *An Encyclopedia of Gardening* (London, 1824), p. 962.
35. From Charles H. J. Smith, *Parks and Pleasure Grounds* (New York, 1853), p. 118. Charles H. J. Smith (1810–1895) was a Scottish landscape gardener who emigrated to Australia in 1855 (Richard Aitken, "Charles H. J. Smith: landscape gardener and garden architect," *The Garden History Society Newsletter*, Summer, 2003, pp. 1–2).
36. From T. W. Shore, "Forestry in Hampshire," *Garden*, vol. XXXV (London, 1889), p. 134. Thomas William Shore (1840–1905) was an authority on the geology, forests, and antiquities of Hampshire County, England. He worked for the Hartley Institute in Southampton and was appointed a fellow of the Geological Society in 1878 (*DNB*).

37. William Ewart Gladstone (1809–1898) was a Prime Minster of England and author. The debate that Olmsted is referring to took place on May 15, 1885. See *Hansard's Parliamentary Debates*, vol. CCXCVIII (London, 1885), p. 641 (*DNB*).
38. From "Report of Wm. Ham. Hall, Consulting Engineer," in *The Development of Golden Gate Park* (San Francisco, 1886), p. 13.
39. From "Report of Mr. John McLaren, Landscape Gardener" in *The Development of Golden Gate Park*, p. 29. John McLaren (1846–1943) was a horticulturist appointed superintendent of parks in San Francisco in 1887. He oversaw the development of Golden Gate Park and the grounds of the Panama-Pacific Exposition of 1915 (*DAB*).
40. From William Hammond Hall, Frederick Law Olmsted, and John McLaren, *The Development of Golden Gate Park* (San Francisco, 1886), p. 27.
41. John Murray Forbes's estate, Milton Hall, on Naushon Island in Buzzard's Bay in Massachusetts contained an extensive plantation of trees, including 20,000 white pine and Norway spruce. "The whole place was very bleak and bare when he bought it, and the tree and evergreen shrub planting completely transformed it" (*DAB*; John Murray Forbes and Sarah Forbes Hughes, *Letters and Recollections of John Murray Forbes* [Boston, 1899], pp. 105–6; see FLO to Robert Douglas, April 18, 1889, above).
42. Andrew Jackson Downing (1815–1852) the landscape gardener and author.
43. Olmsted wrote to Joseph S. Fay to solicit a quotation about tree thinning, and Fay responded by encouraging him to visit Milton Hall to discuss with John Murray Forbes his views. Forbes wrote Olmsted in April of 1889 providing the quotation that Olmsted gives here (FLO to Joseph S. Fay, April 10, 1889, above; Joseph S. Fay to FLO, April 14, 1889; FLO to Robert Douglas, April 18, 1889, above).
44. From Charles Sprague Sargent, "The Attack on the Niagara Reservation—The Judicious and Systematic Thinning of Trees," *Garden and Forest*, May 22, 1889, pp. 241–42.
45. From J. Grigor, *Arboriculture*, p. 87.
46. From J. C. Loudon, *An Encyclopedia of Agriculture* (London, 1825), p. 584.
47. The quotation is from Edward Sang's edition of Walter Nicol's *The Planter's Calendar* (1820).
48. From F. B. Hough, *The Elements of Forestry*, p. 50, 103.
49. From J. Grigor, *Arboriculture*, p. 90.
50. From Frank J. Scott, *The Art of Beautifying Suburban Home Grounds of Small Extent* (New York, 1870), p. 239. Frank Jesup Scott (1828–1919) was an architect and landscape gardener who began his career in 1850 working for Andrew Jackson Downing. He established his own practice in Toledo, Ohio, specializing in residential gardening (David Schuyler, "Frank J. Scott," in C. A. Birnbaum and R. Karson, eds., *Pioneers*, pp. 336–38).
51. From W. H. Hall, F. L. Olmsted, and J. McLaren, *The Development of Golden Gate Park*, pp. 27, 28, 29.
52. From Joseph S. Fay, "Experiments in tree-planting" in Franklin B. Hough, *Report upon Forestry* (Washington, D.C., 1878), p. 430 (see FLO to Robert Douglas, Dec. 5, 1887, above; FLO to Joseph S. Fay, April 10, 1889, above).
53. From J. Brown, *The Forester*, p. 550.
54. From J. B. Webster, "Thinning Scotch Fir Forests," *Garden*, vol. XXXV, April 13, 1889, p. 350. John B. Webster (1819–1893) was an Irish forester who published several articles on tree management that he compiled into *Transactions of the Highland and Agricultural Society of Scotland, 1870–71* (Edinburgh, 1871) (R. Desmond and C. Ellwood, eds., *Dictionary of British and Irish Botanists and Horticulturists*, p. 727).
55. From Frederick Law Olmsted and Calvert Vaux, "General Plan for the Improvement of the Niagara Reservation" (1887). Olmsted quotation from the document is not completely accurate. For example, the first sentence in the original reads, "They are to

be thinned out gradually as they come to interlock, until, at length, not more than one-fourth of the original number will remain," not "one-third" (*Papers of FLO*, SS1: 561–62).

56. From Horatio Seymour, "Letter from the Hon. Horatio Seymour," in Franklin B. Hough, *Report upon Forestry* (Washington, 1878), p. 455. Horatio Seymour (1810–1886) was governor of New York from 1852 to 1854 and from 1862 to 1864. He owned a farm in Deerfield, north of Utica, described here (*DAB*).
57. Olmsted observed in 1872 that "Norway spruce and other spirey topped trees are soon likely to be too conspicuous" in Central Park and required thinning (Memorandum [to] Mr Dempker, March 1, 1872, [*Papers of FLO*, 6: 529]).
58. Olmsted served as advisor to the New York City park board in 1875 and 1876, overseeing the Central Park superintending gardener at the time, William L. Fischer. In a letter to the park commissioners, dated March 1, 1875, Olmsted discussed the duties of the office of landscape gardener, including the planting and thinning of trees (*Papers of FLO*, 7: 124–26).
59. From Humphry Repton, *Observations on the Theory and Practice of Landscape Gardening* (1803) in J. C. Loudon, *Humphry Repton*, p. 195. Repton's references are to the landscape painters Nicolas Poussin (1594–1665) and Claude Lorrain (1600–1682) (*EB*).

CHAPTER X

MAY 1889–AUGUST 1889

The documents in this chapter are varied, many of them relating to new or recent commissions. The letter to Alpheus Hyatt is a continuation of Olmsted's discussion with members of the Boston Natural History Society about placing zoological gardens and aquariums in Boston's parks. The two letters to Waldo Hutchins are in response to requests that Olmsted report on work being done on Morningside Park in New York. The report addressed to Thomas Seay contains Olmsted's proposal for the grounds of the Alabama state capitol. The letter to George W. Vanderbilt is Olmsted's first comprehensive description of how the Biltmore property should be laid out. The letter to Calvin C. Laney accompanied five construction plans for the Meadow Park in Rochester, New York. The letter to Leland Stanford is a plea not to modify the plan that Olmsted had developed, since changing one aspect of the plan would require changes throughout. Three letters relate to Boston parks, including a letter to Charles H. Dalton discussing the appropriateness of holding public meetings in Franklin Park, and two letters to William L. Fischer setting forth Olmsted's design intent for planting the Overlook terrace in that park.

Other letters in this chapter relate to diverse topics: the letter to Richard Watson Gilder explains why Olmsted is reluctant to make a public statement concerning the management of the Yosemite grant, and his letter to Thomas H. Clark gives his past views on Reconstruction policies and his present views on race relations in the South.

To Alpheus Hyatt

6th May, 1889.

Dear Profr Hyatt,

Having {*been*} from home your note of 1st did not at once reach me and {*being*} much pressed at this time with {*out-of-door*} occupations I have not been able sooner to reply as I wished.

I thought that in our brief conversation you had taken a very different point of view of the situation from that which appears in your note. I am most sorry to think that you do not and I want very much that there should be no such misunderstanding of my position as would leave you in doubt as to the answer I should make to your suggestion. There could be but one answer.

Some ten years ago it was made my professional duty to think out a scheme for certain purposes. Nothing in the nature of a Zoological Garden was named among them. When the required scheme had been blocked out in its main elements, I asked myself whether without injury to the scheme some parts of the ground to be used might not be made available for what might be designated as "Natural History *Stations*", whereby knowledge of certain forms of brute life might be advanced and distributed. Thinking over this question and taking a little {*counsel*} on it I at length gave it the form in which it is my understanding that it has been presented to your Society.[1] And that is this:—

Here (1) is a place where a large pond could be provided with sea water flowing through it with sites for a range of low constructions such as would be wanted for the ordinary forms of aquaria, {*offices &c.*}. Here, (2) is a place where a small pond or series of pools might be enclosed with a copious supply of fresh water, with sites for a few buildings and the use, if it should be desired, of a pond of fresh water of about 18 acres; ({*this last*} to be open to the public). Here (3) is a place in which there can be no water,* except as it is commonly provided for animals in stables and pastures, as it is in the Central Park Menagerie—no "pond"—but which is good, healthful dry ground, with great rocks and trees and a sheltered southern aspect. Also, with it, could be had the partial use of a range, open to public view, about {*18 acres*} in extent, as a roving ground for a few animals who would be in better health for such a privilege.

Here are three places which I have conjectured might, perhaps, each one of them, be adapted, as one of a series of stations or departments, to some specialty of natural History and which might be used for that specialty in such a manner that the necessary constructions would not be seen from the adjoining ground and so that essentially the free use of the territory as a place of rural refreshment would not be curtailed.

"Is that so or not? Is this conjecture of Mr Olmsted's sound or not? Would you be disposed or not, for example, to take *the third place described, with the*

*"*wholly lacking water*" were the words I used.[2]

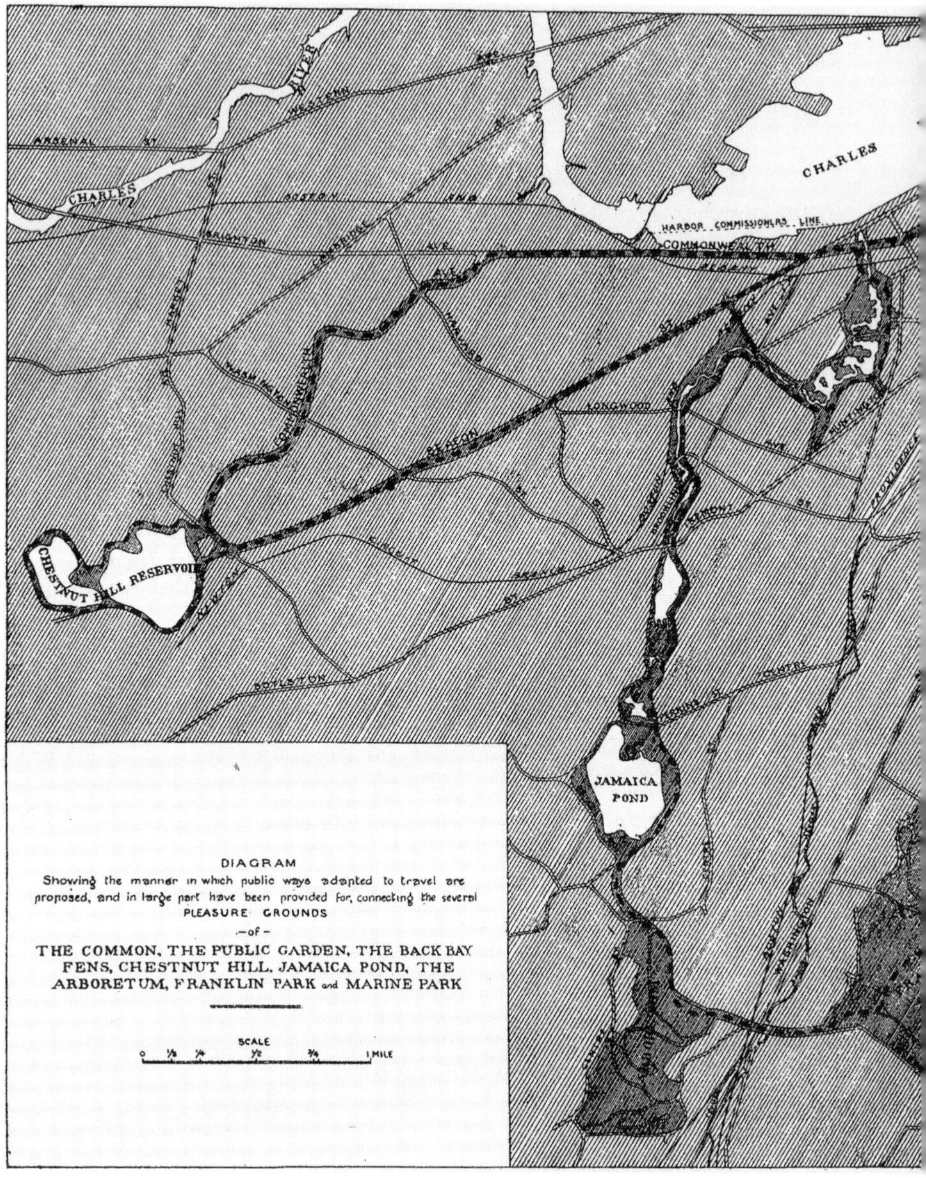

Detail from "Map of the Back

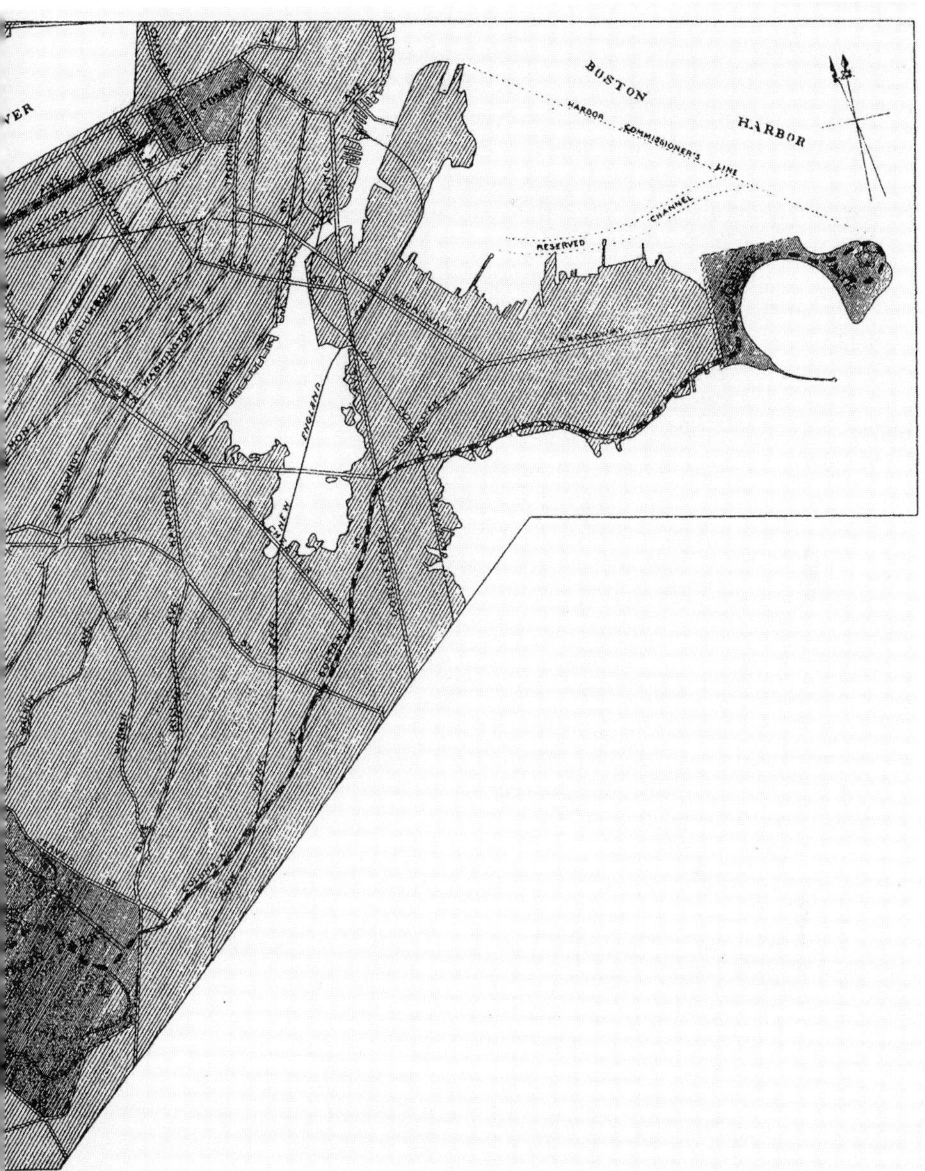

Bay Fens," December 30, 1887.

limitations he suggests, for any particular specialty? If so, what would it be?" These and these only are the questions that have been asked of your Society, as I understand the matter, and which it has had under consideration for a year past. At the root they are one question and a simple one.

Now, because I suggested this question to my employers and shall be professionally responsible for the consequences, you ask certain questions of me. But are your questions branches of that question? Are they not branches of a very different question?

In my conversation and correspondence with you and {*others*} I have taken the greatest pains to point out that I had not thought of placing *the whole* of Long Crouch Woods at your disposal to be used for a special garden or station for some department of natural History but that only so much of it could be used directly for that purpose as would allow a {*margin*} to be maintained in such manner as would exclude the {*remainder*} from view and {*best subserve*} the landscape of the park. I cannot imagine how any other idea can have been had by anyone who was present at the conferences of your Committee with the Commissioners or who has ever conferred with me. It was very distinctly set forth in my letter to Mr Ross of 5th March which you told me had been read to your Committee and with the view of which you heartily concurred. It was as prominently expressed in my note to you of 24th March[3] and in this it was {*stated*} that *the required margin would desirably be 100 feet wide*.

The road[4] to which you refer as being now laid out was laid out three years ago. West of it and passing through what you call the pond is a {. . . } walk that was laid out at the same time and which is expected to be the most frequented walk on the Park. *No part of the pond comes within the ground proposed to be* {*assigned*} *to natural History purposes*; {*none I think within fifty*} feet of it, nor could {*it by*} any process of bending, stretching or {*humoring*} be brought to include any part of the "pond". The road and the walk are a fundamental part of the park.

You speak of an "intended Zoological Garden". I thought it had been long ago fully and cordially agreed that nothing like a Zoological Garden should be aimed at—the term should be dropped as mischievously deceptive. That it was ever used has been a misfortune for which I know that I am responsible. It was used because in a preliminary report upon the park it would strike the only note familiar with the public by which the real intention could be approximately suggested without a long explanation that would not be read.[5] If I was wrong, as I grievously feel that I was in so using it I can only say in extenuation of my folly that from the moment that the subject came under definite verbal discussion I have taken every possible pains, as it seems to me, to present the view which I have again attempted here to set forth. I must say that I cannot think it right that I should be supposed willing to favor any other idea.

I have suggested that without the Long Crouch Wood there might very well be warrens and hutches and paddocks and pits in which there could be exhibited in a semi natural condition a certain class of animals that are often found

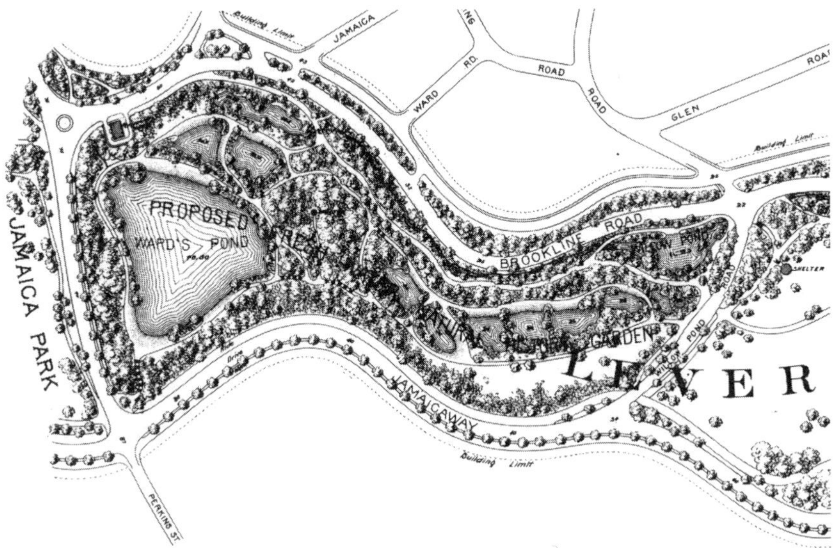

DETAIL FROM "CITY OF BOSTON—PARK DEPARTMENT PLAN OF THE PARKWAY BETWEEN MUDDY RIVER GATE HOUSE AND JAMAICA PARK,'" 1892, SHOWING A SECTION OF LEVERETT PARK WITH THE PROPOSED NATURAL HISTORY STATION

at home in dry regions and for the effective exhibition of which water is wanted in no other way than it is on a sheep range. I have mentioned or others have mentioned in my hearing rabbits, prairie dogs, gophers, squirrels, woodchucks, badgers, coyotes, bears, gophers, field mice, certain deer, certain birds (as the prairie owl) and reptiles, (as horned frogs and tortoises), as illustrations of such a class. I have been told by members of your Society that a very interesting collection of such a class might be perfectly provided for in such a waterless place and assured of their conviction that being provided for in a much better way than the same class ever has been in any Zoological Garden it would prove of great public interest. I am completely mistaken if you yourself did not assure me of your thorough agreement with this conviction. I am sure that two eminent naturalists with whom I have been in conversation since I saw you expressed to me their sense of the importance of limiting the scope of the Franklin Park Station very strictly, in order that what should be attempted might have a unique excellence of performance. Hence in urging this view, which I know is that of the Park Commissioners, I do not feel that I am taking an inexcusable liberty.

If you want for the purposes of the Society a piece of ground in which there is or can be a pool of water, suitably to some other specialty, I do not believe it would be difficult to get it. Within a week a gentleman has expressed to me a disposition to offer a small body of land to the city for a Zoological Garden. It is land wholly unfit for the general purpose—quite as unfit as any that the Park Department has, but it would suit perfectly some other specialty of Natural Science than that to which the Long Crouch site is adapted. A suggestion has been made to me by a prominent city officer that another small body of land should be turned over to the Department. It is exceedingly picturesque and would admirably serve for a special museum and there is no reason it should not be leased to your Society for such a museum, or "station" or special "garden". Why not limit the use of Long Crouch Wood to purposes to which without straining or crowding or reaching out upon the margin, it would be better adapted than any other possible to be had?

Yours Truly

Fred[k] Law Olmsted.

The text presented here is from a letterpress copy of a handwritten letter signed on the original in Olmsted's hand: A4: 649–54, OAR/LC.

1. Olmsted first considered a plan for the Boston park system when the park commissioners invited him to consult in 1875. They officially engaged him to design and oversee the construction of what became the Back Bay Fens at the end of 1878. Over the next several years he developed a comprehensive park plan for what would become known as the "Emerald Necklace," the beginnings of which he first presented in 1881. At that time the park system plan did not include a zoo. He also presented his first design for West Roxbury (Franklin) Park in 1881, which also did not include a zoo. When he presented additional suggestions for Franklin Park in 1884, however, he wrote, "if suitable ground can be found that may be reserved without crippling the park for its main object," an area should be provided for the purpose. In his 1886 plan for Franklin Park, he recommended setting aside the Long Crouch Woods, a relatively secluded area in the north corner of the park, "to be held subject to lease to a suitable organization for a Zoölogical Garden."

   On September 12, 1887, the Boston Society of Natural History asked the park commissioners for space in the city's parks for "a system of zoological gardens, aquaria, etc." The society would oversee these spaces, lay them out, and "stock them with animals." It would charge fees at certain times "to provide for the proper maintenance of the establishment," but allow the public to enter free at other times. The park commissioners referred the society's request "to Mr. Olmsted for suggestion for a reply," and when the commissioners responded to the society on September 30, they suggested the three spaces that Olmsted refers to in this letter: a small zoological garden in Franklin Park, a salt-water aquarium at City Point (Marine Park), and fresh water pools for fish and birds in the "valley below Jamaica Pond" (*Papers of FLO*, 7: 9–13; FLO to Charles H. Dalton, Dec. 29, 1881 [*Papers of FLO*, 7: 567–72]; FLO to Charles H. Dalton, May 17, 1881 [*Papers of FLO*, 7: 528–32]; Frederick Law Olmsted, *Tenth Annual Report, Boston Park Commissioners, Reports on West Roxbury Park and Wood Island Park*, [Dec.] 1884, above; Frederick Law Olmsted, "Notes on the Plan of Franklin Park and Related Matters," 1886 [*Papers of FLO*, SS1: 488]; *Thirteenth Annual Report of the Board of Commissioners for the Department of Parks for the City of Boston, for the Year 1887* [Boston, 1888], pp. 33–44).
2. Written along left margin of letter.
3. FLO to Alpheus Hyatt, March 24, 1889, above.
4. Apparently a reference to Playstead Road, which was laid out in 1887 between the Playstead and Long Crouch Woods. A walk also was built parallel to the Playstead Road. Hyatt's letter has not been found, but he was likely proposing the creation of a pond as part of the Zoological Garden in Franklin Park that would have extended beyond the

Long Crouch Woods into the Playstead (William Jackson, "City Engineer's Report," *Thirteenth Annual Report, Boston Department of Parks, 1887*, p. 78).

5. Olmsted first suggested placing a zoological garden in Franklin Park in his "Notes on West Roxbury Park" in the *Annual Report* in 1884. In the September 30, 1887, correspondence from the park commissioners to the Boston Society of Natural History, Olmsted and the commissioners clarified that they were not proposing an extensive zoological garden, but something closer to what Olmsted refers to in this letter as a "station." They wrote that the twenty acres the commissioners proposed setting aside would be "an ideal site of the more popularly interesting elements of a limited collection such as is suggested in your communication; but for a complete zoölogical garden it is far from being all that is to be desired." The members of the society continued to press for a larger zoological garden in Franklin Park, an effort to which Olmsted responded in his letter to Matthias D. Ross of Dec. 1889, below (Frederick Law Olmsted, *Tenth Annual Report, Boston Park Commissioners, Reports on West Roxbury and Wood Island Parks*, [Dec.] 1884, above; *Thirteenth Annual Report, Boston Department of Parks, 1887*, pp. 33–44).

To Robert Douglas & Sons

Messrs. Robert Douglass & Sons,
Waukegan, Ill.
[Summer 1889]

Dear Sirs;

In the first of three parks which we have to lay out at Rochester, N.Y.,[1] certain land, about 35 acres in extent, as indicated by the tinted portion of the map enclosed, has been prepared with a view to being planted in whole or part this fall.[2] The intention is that it shall be planted so that after thinning and proper treatment it shall have the character of the natural woods of the region, though for reasons of economy and convenience it will not be required that all trees common in such woods shall be represented, nor that there shall be large numbers of any of the trees particularly difficult to be obtained. There should be large proportions of sugar and scarlet maple, elms, ash and bass-wood. Within 100 feet of the railroad, there might be a moderate proportion of alanthus, poplars, canoe birch, locust, honey locust, catalpa, Maclura, and, throughout, Norway and Sycamore maples, white birch etc., may be used for nurses.

The soil is a good wheat-bearing mellow loam. Most of it was, last year, mowing ground. It has this summer been fallowed, (the sod turned under seven inches), subsoiled to a depth of 20 inches, freshly dressed with rotten stable dung 13 cords to the acre, and will have been repeatedly harrowed and rolled, bringing it to a garden condition. It is well drained. All that is to be planted is nearly level.

It is in the Elwanger & Barry quarter of the city[3] and as you know their nursery ground it will give you a fair idea of the eastern part of it. The western part is Genesee bottom land. Young Mr. Barry is one of the Park Commissioners and this is written with his approval.

We are not sure that you would be willing to undertake so small a job but it seems to us that it would be a desirable innovation upon ordinary proceedings in public works if you would, and we venture therefore to suggest it.

Of the trees required we suppose that you have few and that you may not be able to procure them except to some extent of larger size than you commonly provide for forest planting. This we understand would affect the price. Allowing for this we assume that you would be able to procure them and that you might make on the whole a piece of park planting, the result of which would in a few years be regarded as successful and economical as compared with most park planting.

If we are right, will you please make through us a proposition such as you think will best cover the ground and commend itself to the Commissioners.

Yours Respectfully,

F. L. & J. C. Olmsted.

The text presented here is an undated, typed letter signed in Olmsted's hand (see FLO to Edward Mott Moore, Aug. 5, 1888, above; FLO to Edward Mott Moore, Jan. 26, 1889, above; FLO to Calvin C. Laney, Aug. 9, 1889, below).

1. The first three parks laid out at Rochester were Genesee Valley Park (also referred to as South Meadows or Meadow Park), Seneca Park, and Highland Park (also referred to as Reservoir Park).
2. The first Rochester park to be planted was Genesee Valley Park. Grading and other preparations of the site began in the spring of 1889, and planting of trees and ground-cover plants proceeded that fall (*Report of the Board of Park Commissioners of the City of Rochester, N.Y., 1888–1898* [Rochester, 1898], pp. 35–39).
3. George Herman Ellwanger (1816–1906) and Patrick Barry (1816–1890) were horticulturists, authors, and co-founders of the Mt. Hope Nursery (also known as the Ellwanger & Barry nursery) in Rochester. It was the largest nursery establishment in the United States, with many varieties of plants tested there for adaptability to the climate of western New York. Patrick Barry's son William C. Barry served as a park commissioner from 1888–1916. In 1888, Ellwanger and Barry donated twenty acres of land to the city, constituting much of what became Highland Park. See FLO to Edward Mott Moore, Jan. 26, 1889, above (*DAB*; *NCAB*; Alma Burner Creek, "The Family Story: The Ellwangers and the Barrys," *The University of Rochester Library Bulletin*, vol. 35, 1982).

TO WALDO M. HUTCHINS[1]

Brookline, Mass. 8th June, 1889.

The Honorable Waldo Hutchins.
President of the Dpt of Public Parks:

Dear Sir; Appreciating the honor of the request made to me in a communication that I have received from the Secretary of your Department,[2] I wish to state that I have several times during the last ten years been called to New York by like invitations from your predecessors, and with results, on each successive occasion, of such a character that I think it best to advise you as follows:—

I do not wish to be called in occasionally to prepare or aid in preparing details of design for works with regard to which I have no continuous or comprehensive responsibility, such as would be indicated by the title of Advisory or Consulting Landscape Architect and by my being paid in the form of an Annual Salary. I should, however, be pleased to be called in at any time for consultation with Mr Vaux in regard to any matter of the works in the design of which we have been associated. I do not wish to give advice in regard to those works without conference with him. My engagements are such that I do not wish to undertake any duties that would not leave me free to visit works with which I have to do at points distant from New York whenever I may think it desirable.

Judging from the experiences to which I have referred it seems to me probable that what I have thus said will make it unnecessary that you should be put to the expense of my visiting New York at this time. I shall assume this and not come to you unless I hear further.

Yours Respectfully.

Fredk Law Olmsted.

The text presented here is from a letterpress copy of a handwritten letter signed on the original in Olmsted's hand: A4: 838–39, OAR/LC.

1. Waldo M. Hutchins was president of the board of the Department of Public Parks in 1889 (see FLO to Calvert Vaux, June 30, 1887, above; FLO to Waldo M. Hutchins, June 1889, below).
2. Charles De F. Burns was secretary of the Board of Commissioners of the Department of Public Parks from 1885 to 1895 ("Secretary Burns to Go," *New York Times*, Nov. 26, 1895, p. 8).

To Waldo M. Hutchins

Brookline, Mass., June 1889.

The Honorable Waldo Hutchins, President;
Department of Public Parks, New York.
Sir;

I have the honor to report in answer to your inquiries:

First, that in a recent cursory inspection of the Morningside Park work I discovered no variations from the Plan of the Park, as adopted in 1887, except such as are usually and properly made in the elaboration of a plan during the progress of construction.[1] As a rule the variations appear to have been suggested by the disclosure of rock where it had been concealed at the time the plan was studied, and in most cases it was evident to me that they had been adapted to avoid unnecessary outlay without sacrifice of the essential aim of the design. In one place, in the Southwest corner of the ground, the number of stairs has been increased at some cost. The reason appears to have been that the condition of the ledge at this point, when stripped, offered an opportunity for an improvement of grades and for a gain of picturesqueness that has been ingeniously and skilfully taken advantage of. A piece of work has resulted of which the Commissioners may be proud.

Second, the report that at certain points exceedingly steep slopes have been formed and that these slopes have been studded with fragments of rock in a manner that makes them appear unnatural and ugly is true. Such steep slopes would soon crumble, slide and wash out if not partly formed of rock; they are now steeper than the natural rocky slopes near them; to give them a natural appearance when first made, though possible, would be a great deal more costly, than to form them as they have been formed. After weathering for a few years, when seen through a partial screen of foliage such as preparations have been made to provide, there is no reason why the general effect of these artificial rocky slopes should not be consistent with the adjoining natural circumstances, and in all respects pleasing.

Third, as to the progress of the work, the heavier, more difficult and costly part, which, when the park comes into use, is to be out of sight, is nearly everywhere in a great degree complete. I should not think that what remains to be done, that is to say, the superficial covering and dressing of this more substantial structural work, need cost half as much as that which has been done. The most important and tolling part of it will be the planting. The design requires that this should be of an uncommon character, elaborate and skilful. Large and valuable preparations for it have been made. Growth will afterwards be needed under careful horticultural superintendence before the design can be realized, but even within a year the park is likely to be a very interesting and valuable addition to the recreation grounds of the city.

VIEW OF MORNINGSIDE PARK, NEW YORK CITY, N.D

Having thus answered your inquiries I beg leave to add an expression of my judgment upon another point.

I understand that it has been determined by your Board to widen the wheelway of the street on the west of Morningside Park at the expense of the adjoining Promenade.

Considering that there are to be buildings on but one side of the wheelway; that these buildings are likely to be mostly dwellings of greater breadth and with fewer doors upon the street than is usual, it is probable that the Avenue at this point will not be half as much occupied by vehicles standing before doors and by vehicles moving out of direct continuous courses with a view to stoppages, as are most of the avenues of the city. Because of its grades and indirectness of course, it is not likely to be much used as a thoroughfare for freighting vehicles. Taking these circumstances into account it may be questioned whether all purposes of public convenience would not be fairly well provided for by a wheelway of the breadth originally planned. In the determination of the original plan, however, it was considered that this wheelway might very desirably be broader.[2] But it was considered that the Promenade would also desirably be broader than, with the breadth of the wheelway decided upon, it could be. Accordingly the arrangement then adopted was considered a compromise arrangement, the wheelway being

View of Morningside Park, New York City, n.d

made as broad as due consideration of the requirements of the public in the Promenade would allow; the Promenade as broad as due consideration for public requirements in the wheelway would allow. As to the question of convenience it was held that the number of people likely to use the Promenade and to be incommoded by making it narrower would be many times larger than that of the people likely to use the wheelway. As to the question of propriety it was considered that a relation would be felt between the height and massiveness of the retaining wall and its parapet, and the spaciousness of the Promenade directly supported by it.

The retaining wall and its parapets and balconies have since been treated in a much more formal, artificial and showy way than was then intended. The reasons for spaciousness in the Promenade are thus increased, not diminished.

The question has been often under review with me since the original plan was made and with more extended observation of the way such places are used by the public of cities and more mature reflection, I am constrained to say that had I been consulted as to a change I should have been much better prepared to advise gaining more ground for the Promenade at the expense of the wheelway than gaining more ground for the wheelway at the expense of the Promenade. The Promenade on the Heights is in my judgment the dominant and most essential feature of the entire situation. The Park would be a comparatively poor property without it. To reduce the spaciousness of the Promenade will be to lessen the value receivable for every dollar that is spent on the Park, and, in my judgment, establish a standing public grievance.

Your obedient servant,

Fred[k] Law Olmsted.

The text presented here is from a letterpress copy of a typewritten letter signed on the original in Olmsted's hand: A4: 890–94, OAR/LC. As stipulated in a previous letter to Hutchins on June 8, 1889, Olmsted refused to consult with the New York City park board unless he was asked to do so in collaboration with Vaux. Since Vaux had been appointed landscape architect for the park department over a year prior, he contacted Olmsted and they agreed to revisit their 1887 Morningside Park plans together. Olmsted inspected the park on June 17 and wrote this letter soon after (FLO to Waldo M. Hutchins, June 8, 1889, above; FLO to Calvert Vaux, June 7, 1889; FLO to Calvert Vaux, June 9, 1889; FLO to Calvert Vaux, June 12, 1889; FLO to Charles De F. Burns [telegram], June 17, 1889; Calvert Vaux to FLO, [1889]; DPP, *Minutes*, June 26, 1889, p. 79; see also Frederick Law Olmsted and Calvert Vaux, *General Plan For The Improvement Of Morningside Park*, Oct. 1, 1887, above).

1. In 1887 Olmsted and Vaux developed revised plans for Morningside Park, which the park department was using at this point as the basis for construction (Frederick Law Olmsted and Calvert Vaux, *General Plan for the Improvement of Morningside Park*, Oct. 1, 1887, above).
2. In Olmsted and Vaux's original 1873 plan for Morningside Park they specified that the promenade along the western edge of the park, which they called the "mall," should be "nowhere less than twenty feet wide." The accompanying plan showed both the promenade and wheelway to be approximately twenty feet wide. Their revised 1887 plan retained these dimensions (FLO to Salem H. Wales, Oct. 11, 1873 [*Papers of FLO*, 6: 657]; Frederick Law Olmsted and Calvert Vaux, *General Plan For The Improvement Of Morningside Park*, Oct. 1, 1887, above).

To Edward Clark

11th June, 1889.

Mr Ed[d] Clark;
Architect of the Capitol;
My Dear Mr Clark;

I cannot say that I should be satisfied with the Mitchell Vance[1] designs for lamp-posts and vases. They strike me as very inferior. It would be better to have no vases, much as I think them needed, than such as these. Nor do I like the lamp-posts. As to the lamps I do not now see why they should not be identical with those designed by Wisedell,[2] though possibly, with a new design for standards slight modifications might be desirable. If you will send us one of the Wisedell lamps that you like I will have it worked after. And if you can tell me in what way the Mitchell design of standard is less costly than the Walker[3] design I will try to have a new design prepared more refined and not more costly than the Mitchell, for the standards.

Are you not likely soon to be in Boston? I would like to confer with you about the fountain &c.[4] On reflection it appeared to me that in bronze the fountain would soon appear a too disjointed, big black spot. Therefore, I have been

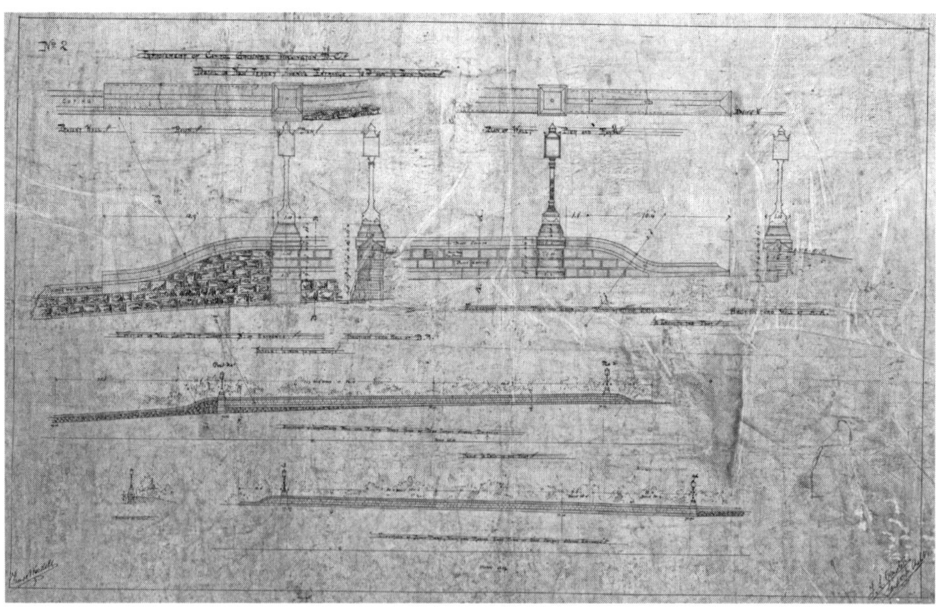

Improvement of Capitol Grounds, Washington, D. C., Detail of New Jersey Avenue Entrance and Lampposts, n.d.

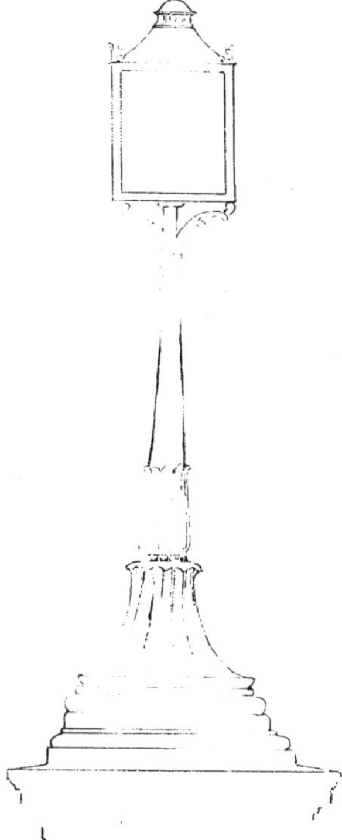

SKETCH OF LAMPPOST FOR U. S. CAPITOL GROUNDS, SEPTEMBER 24, 1889

figuring for it in marble and getting estimates. Returns are not yet complete. If you are coming here please let me know when, as soon as you can that I may not be away. I expect to go Monday next to Pittsfield for a day and to leave on the 22[d] for Asheville, and Montgomery Alabama.

Yours Very Truly

Fred[k] Law Olmsted.

The text presented here is from a letterpress copy of a handwritten letter signed on the original in Olmsted's hand: A4: 857–58, OAR/LC. On March 2, 1889, Congress appropriated $14,000 for the "fountain in front of the terrace" and for "bronze lamp-posts and vases for the north and south terraces" of the U.S. Capitol. On June 7, Edward Clark sent Olmsted drawings of lampposts and vases that would conform "somewhat to the bronze lamps on the Grounds." Clark and Olmsted had been discussing lamps for the terrace since at least 1885, but they had not yet adopted a design and Congress had not yet appropriated funds (Edward Clark to FLO, June 7, 1889, AOC; FLO to Edward Clark, May 15, 1885, AOC; Glenn Brown, *Documentary History of the Construction and Development of the United States Capitol Building and Grounds* [Washington, D.C., 1904], p. 1262).

1. Mitchell Vance and Company of New York was a manufacturer of ornamental electric light fixtures. The drawings to which Olmsted refers have not been found (Richard Edwards, ed., *New York's Great Industries* [New York, 1884], pp. 96–97).
2. Thomas Wisedell (1846–1884) was an English architect who after emigrating became an assistant in the office of Vaux and Withers & Company in New York, and had worked with Olmsted on Prospect Park in Brooklyn. He worked on the Capitol grounds project beginning in 1874 and was responsible for the design of most of the architectural features under Olmsted's jurisdiction, including ornamental bronze lampposts. Wisedell died in September 1884 at the age of thirty-eight (*New York Times*, Aug. 2, 1884, p. 4; plan #2820-46, NPS/FLONHS).
3. Charles Howard Walker (1857–1936) was a Boston architect who, after Wisedell's death in 1884, took over some of his architectural services, collaborating with Olmsted on the west terrace staircases, fountain, and window arches. In the end, Walker designed the simple bronze lampposts that lined the terrace, in deference to Olmsted and Clark's specifications (William C. Allen, *History of the United States Capitol* [Washington D.C., 2001], pp. 348, 356–57; Edward Clark to FLO, Sept. 20, 1889, AOC; FLO to Edward Clark, Sept. 25, 1889, A5: 301, OAR/LC; Edward Clark to FLO, Sept. 28, 1889, AOC; plan #2820-z9, NPS/FLONHS).
4. Morrill requested in 1886 that a fountain be placed between the staircases of the west terrace, and Olmsted, in collaboration with Walker, had been developing designs since then (FLO to Edward Clark, Feb. 15, 1886, above; FLO to Edward Clark, Feb. 11, 1889, above; Edward Clark to FLO, Nov. 18, 1889, AOC; W. C. Allen, *History of the United States Capitol*, pp. 356–57).

To Thomas Seay[1]

[July 1889]

Report of an Examination of the Capitol Ground at Montgomery, Alabama.[2]

To His Excellency,
Thomas Seay, Governor of Alabama;

We have the honor to submit the following observations to which we have been led by a cursory examination, made upon your invitation, of the Capitol Ground at Montgomery.

It is obvious that the position of the Capitol was not determined strictly from considerations of convenience. Had it been its doors would not have been inaccessible to carriages nor would all approaching it on foot have been obliged to mount so many stairs before reaching the lower floor.

The object to which convenience in these and other respects was made to give way was that of giving the Capitol greater dignity as an architectural work, representing and typifying the sovereignty of the State. This advantage of dignity of position was to be attained by elevating it upon a fitting pedestal. For such a pedestal the hill offered good raw material. But to turn it to account something was required to be done with it that has not been done. It was as necessary to the purpose that art should be used in the pedestal as in the dome or the portico. In its present condition the hill is far from adding to the dignity of the Capitol. Within a space of ground of the same extent, of nearly flat surface, with approaches laid out simply as convenience would dictate, and the areas between the approaches occupied by turf kept in neat order as, upon flattish ground, it easily might be, the Capitol would be more commodious than it is at present and much more respectable and pleasing in appearance.

If the Capitol building is thus seen at disadvantage, so also will the Monument adjoining it be.[3] This work promises to be a more than usually successful expression of enduring, reverent regardfulness for that which it commemorates. The ground about it could, by hardly any means, be made to more strikingly express indifference, renunciation and neglect.

Again, the monument has been placed near the building in order that the sympathy of the entire State in the sentiment which the monument betokens may be manifest. This purpose would be much better realized if it were brought into closer association with the building by a unity of design in the treatment of the ground which is the common pedestal of both.

Taking the view thus indicated of the situation as it stands, the question upon which our counsel is desired we consider to be this:— In what way can the ground be now so dealt with that the object of its selection as the site for the Capitol and Monument may be satisfactorily realized?

Excavations for streets have been made through the lower parts of the hill of the Capitol on three sides, leaving high steep banks. The banks are everywhere rude, tattered and infirm, and, at points, are deeply gullied. The surface of the ground above is patchy and squalid. These conditions are as unbecoming as dilapidated walls, hingeless doors and windows stuffed with hats, would be in the building. No superficial repairs or dressings will lastingly remedy what is wrong in these respects. It grows out of the shape of the hill and the character of its soil and subsoil.[4]

As to a radical improvement, if the base of the building were a little less elevated above the streets than it is, or if the space between the building and the streets were a little broader than it is, a satisfactory result might be obtained by so grading and dressing the face of the hill on all sides that it would have the appearance of a natural elevation of turfy slopes with trees and bushes so disposed that they would fall into an agreeable composition with the building and not too much obscure it. Using a common technical term, this would be treating the hill in the natural style of landscape gardening.

Considering what objections there may be to such a treatment it will readily be seen that, unless a space of nearly flat ground is left all about the Capitol building, such sloping of the ground between it and the streets will cause it to appear perched up on a cramped, weak and incommodious base, and that it will, in fact as well as in appearance, be more inconveniently placed than it is at present. It will also be evident that at certain points the slopes must be so steep that it would be impracticable to maintain a good surface of turf upon them. Heavy rains would waste, fret, furrow and gully them as they now do the steeper banks on the edge of the streets. Still more would this be the case if the upper edge of the sloped ground was to be so far out as to leave a fair space of nearly level ground immediately about the building. In neither case could the ground be long kept in seemly order without an outlay for superintendence and labor that to persons unaccustomed to the good management of grounds under similar circumstances, would seem to be extravagant.

The question then is, how can an area of nearly level ground be maintained immediately about the building, and the space between this level area and the streets be so treated as to avoid slopes too steep to be kept in good order at reasonable cost?

In all the older civilized countries having a climate at all similar to that of Alabama, the experience of centuries has made it customary, under similar circumstances, to reduce a hillside to a succession of slopes of such moderate inclination that water passing down them during rains will not acquire a tearing or scouring velocity, the principle being the same with that illustrated in all good management of steep hillside cotton fields. When applied to ground in connection with architectural works, each successive slope ends on the lower side at the top of a wall, by which it is separated from a lower slope and this wall becomes the support and face of what would otherwise be a crumbling bank.

The operation is called hillside terracing. In regions not subject to prolonged heat, where the ground never dries deeply and very heavy rains are unknown, steep turfed banks are sometimes substituted in hillside terracing for walls of masonry. But under the most favorable circumstances these steep turfed banks can be kept in a firm and neat condition such as would befit the Capitol, only by much application of skilled labor. Wherever used in our northern states they are apt, after a few years, to become in some degree dilapidated; often gullies form in them at intervals and where they do not scraps of turf and soil are washed away and they become extremely shabby. Such a result can be prevented only by the constant application of a degree of care and expense that makes the terracing of a hillside with turf banks, if at all extensive, far from economical. Under the circumstances to be dealt with in the case now under consideration it would certainly be a mistake to follow such northern and north of Europe examples.

For reasons thus sufficiently indicated we are reluctantly obliged to express the opinion that it would not be wise for the state to make any notable outlay for the improvement of the Capitol Grounds, except with a view to results that, without excessive care and expense from year to year, would be lastingly

VIEW OF ALABAMA STATE CAPITOL, C. 1889

consistent with the architectural motives of the Capitol building; that such results cannot be secured without a certain degree of terrace wall building and that the cost of carrying out any proper terracing plan would be greater than has probably been contemplated by the legislature in its recent action on the subject.

A plan for such substantial terracing of the Capitol hill as we should advise can be prepared even in outline only upon a detailed survey of the ground giving accurate data for the necessary calculations, but a suggestion may be submitted of what might be the more important features of such a plan, as follows:—

The Capitol building to stand on a nearly level plateau, extending perhaps fifty feet from its west walls; less than that from its south and east walls, and beyond the Monument from its north walls. This plateau to be bordered by a coping, parapet or balustrade, resting on a retaining wall of such height as should be found necessary. From the base of the retaining wall to the street a slope of earth to be formed of varying inclination the upper part having generally a convex, the lower part, a concave curve. It should, if possible, be nowhere so steep as to involve danger of the gullying or washing away of a turfed surface. And, to guard against this it might be found necessary at certain points along the streets to build additional lower retaining walls. If, with such lower walls of moderate height, the slopes at any points should still be thought too steep for a turf surface upon them to be everywhere easily kept in fine order, then at such steeper places, shrubs and vines would be planted which would cover the soil with foliage and by a network of roots prevent it from washing or gullying, temporary provisions for the purpose being used until the rooting shall be adequate.

Except adjoining the entrances where they should be harmonious with the architecture of the building and the stairways leading to it the terrace walls might, if economy required, be of roughly quarried stone, of field stone or of brick, and might be laid with a batter and in the cheapest and rudest way compatible with their permanent firmness, masses of shrubs being planted near their base and vines allowed to grow over their face, so that nothing of beauty would thus be lost. The shrubs to be planted below the wall, in this case would be so selected and adjusted as to position that when grown they would give the building and the monument the effect of rising out of a broad and luxuriant mass of foliage but would not obstruct the view to a distance from the lower windows of the Capitol or from the plateau surrounding it.

The surface of the plateau would be laid out with plots of turf, which, with better soil and the use of water, could be kept as neatly as a parlor carpet, and, with broad walks, form a fine, elevated and breezy promenade. The plateau would be drained and the water carried off so that none would descend upon the slopes, thus lessening the danger of their washing and gullying.

A carriage road should be laid out from the streets on the east and west by which the south entrance to the Capitol could be closely approached. An adjustment of the lines of the plateau would be made to accommodate this feature, and possibly a sheltering roof extended from the south door, so that visitors alighting from carriages could enter the building without exposure to storms.

The text presented here is from a letterpress copy of an unsigned typed letter with edits made in Olmsted's hand: A4: 931–39, OAR/LC. Olmsted had traveled to Montgomery to inspect the grounds of the Alabama State Capitol in late June 1889. In a letter to John C. Olmsted from Montgomery, he expressed his pessimism regarding the possibilities of the site: "The situation here is hopeless—nothing tolerable could be done except by outlay that the state could not contemplate." After the governor decided not to adopt his plan due to lack of appropriation of funds by the legislature, Olmsted replied that he regretted the governor's decision since the more substantial improvements he recommended would be essential in the long run (Thomas H. Clark, "Frederick Law Olmsted on the South, 1889," *South Atlantic Quarterly*, vol. III, Jan. 1904, p. 11; FLO to JCO, June 29, 1889, box H-6, folder 3, OAR/LC; FLO to Thomas H. Clark, July 10, 1889, A4: 949, OAR/LC; Thomas H. Clark to FLO, July 20, 1889; FLO to Thomas H. Clark, Aug. 5, 1889, below; see also FLO to Thomas H. Clark, April 10, 1889, above).

1. Thomas Seay (1846–1896) was a lawyer and plantation owner who, after being a Confederate soldier and a Democratic state senator for ten years, served as governor of Alabama from 1886 to 1890 (*NCAB*).
2. Above title, written in Olmsted's hand is "To be recopied. (Give nearly double as much in margin on the left)."
3. The Confederate Monument on the north front of the Capitol grounds was designed by

Alexander Doyle. The cornerstone was laid in 1886 by Jefferson Davis, and the monument was completed in 1898 (Marie Bankhead Owen, *The Story of Alabama: A History of the State*: vol. I [New York, 1949], p. 213; Peter A. Brannon, "Through the Years: The Confederate Monument on Capitol Hill," *Montgomery Advertiser-Alabama Journal*, Aug. 10, 1947, p. 13B).

4. An earlier version of this paragraph was crossed out by Olmsted:

> With reference to this question, the Capitol building may be considered to have been set upon the highest point of a hill the original shape of which was not very different from that of the half of an egg cut across lengthwise and set with the rounded parts up. The base has been squared in outline by slicing off as it were the outer parts of the egg and upon three sides thus formed there are streets, at the sides of which toward the Capitol rise steep banks. These banks, whatever they may once have been are now in some parts deeply gullied, in all parts are in rough, battered and essentially squalid condition, as unfitting the Capitol, as far as appearance is concerned, as dilapidated brick walls, hingeless doors and broken windows stuffed with hats, would be in the building itself. The surface of the ground is everywhere patched, seedy and forlorn. Its condition is not one that can be made permanently better by any superficial repairs and dressings up. It depends on the shape of the hill and the character of its soil and subsoil.

TO RICHARD WATSON GILDER[1]

10th July, 1889.

Dear Mr Gilder;

Returning from Alabama I have found your note of 4th reinforcing Mr Johnson's of 23d June.[2]

I have a deep and abiding interest in the subject.[3] I shall be glad if Mr Johnson's advice to the Yo Semite Commissioners through Senator Stanford[4] leads them to consult me. I am not sorry that he gave that advice but am obliged to him for having given it. I do not clearly see for what duty it is suggested that the Century would engage me in case the Commissioners decline to do so. But, I am sorry to say that I fear there can be none that would be of much value for the Century's purpose that my engagements will permit me to bind myself to. My views were, I think, fairly well expressed to the "interviewers" of the Examiner,[5] to whose report Mr. Johnson refers but I have not seen that report and it would be singular, according to all my experience, if the interviewer succeeded in not misrepresenting me.

Putting out of view all differences of opinion or purpose directly or indirectly influenced by consideration of politics, jobs and money-making on a large or a small scale, it would probably be found, that, if we could get to the bottom of men's minds, that there are radical differences as to what sh'd be considered to be valuable to the world in the Yo Semite, justifying the Act of Congress in reserving it against a disposition under the influence of ordinary commercial motives.[6] And so intricate and confused are the workings of men's minds in regard to such a question that a statement on the point can hardly be made, assent to which, Theoretically, given the slightest indication of where a man would stand, practically. Before any other discussion, therefore, this is the point upon which a sharply defined proposition is wanted and persuasive, if possible conclusive, at least convincing, argument is wanted. For you will find men, angrily differing as to measures, using the same terms to define their sentiments and intentions, each honestly believing the other to be insincere or quibbling. All argument is thrown away, therefore, upon those with whom you cannot come to an intelligent good understanding on this point at the start. To find a firm {*anchorage*} in this respect is a part of my trade. Unfortunately it is no part of my trade to give good literary form to my convictions, and I am not good at piloting others to sound anchorage. If I could take a Centurion position and say to Galen Clark[7] *do* this and *do* that, I could trust myself with a large responsibility. But for the present business of the Century in the matter I am afraid that if my engagements permitted me to give all the time to the duty that I could ask to do, I could not give it much aid.

I should like to have a talk with Mr Johnson and with Mr Muir[8] on the subject. Are either of them likely to come to you at Marion? If so, might he not find it convenient to let me see him in Boston, or to make me a little visit here.

Yours Truly,

Fred[k] Law Olmsted

The text presented here is a signed letter in Olmsted's hand (see FLO to Robert Underwood Johnson, Oct. 9, 1889, below, and *Governmental Preservation of Natural Scenery*, March 8, 1890, below).

1. Richard Watson Gilder (1843–1909) was an author and editor. He served as assistant editor of *Scribner's Monthly* from 1870 to 1881 and as editor of the *Century Illustrated Monthly Magazine* from 1881 until his death. His summer home in Marion, Massachusetts, was a meeting place for prominent artists and intellectuals of the day (*DAB*; "R. W. Gilder Dies of Heart Disease," *New York Times*, Nov. 19, 1909, p. 1).
2. Robert Underwood Johnson (1853–1937) was an editor, poet, and park advocate whom Olmsted had met earlier in connection with the planning of the East River Park (later Carl Schurz Park) in New York City. Johnson worked as associate editor under Gilder at the *Century Illustrated Monthly Magazine* and succeeded him as editor in 1909. At the time of this letter, Johnson was working with John Muir and others to persuade Congress to establish Yosemite National Park, which was to consist of a large area of the Sierra Nevada Mountains around the then existing state park at Yosemite Valley.

   In the June 23 letter mentioned here, Johnson wrote that on his recent trip to Yosemite Valley he "was shocked in riding over it to see how ignorantly the landscape is being treated. There are numerous fields of stumps in the midst of rank ferns," and "trees are trimmed up out of all natural semblance." Included in this letter was a note from Gilder to Olmsted, saying, "I need hardly tell you that I heartily endorse Mr. Johnson's letter in every detail" (*DAB*; "Robert U. Johnson, Poet, is Dead at 84," *New York Times*, Oct. 15, 1937, p. 23; Robert Underwood Johnson to FLO, June 23, 1889; "Letter 3 — No Title," *Century Illustrated Monthly Magazine*, Jan., 1890, pp. 466–79; "The Treasures of Yosemite," ibid. Aug., 1890, pp. 483–501).

3. In 1864 Congress acted to grant Yosemite Valley and the Mariposa Big Tree Grove to the state of California in perpetuity for public park purposes. The governor of California then appointed Olmsted, who at the time was living in nearby Bear Valley, California, to head the first Yosemite Commission, which was charged with developing a plan for administering the valley as a park. The result was Olmsted's "Preliminary Report upon the Yosemite and Big Tree Grove." Olmsted never returned to Yosemite Valley after leaving for New York later in 1865. His published comments on the situation there in the 1880s were limited to a privately printed report, *Governmental Preservation of Natural Scenery*, March 8, 1890, below (see also, "Preliminary Report upon the Yosemite and Big Tree Grove," Aug. 1865 [*Papers of FLO*, 5: 488–516]).
4. Johnson wanted Olmsted to visit the valley "as the expert appointed by the Yosemite Commission to examine & report ways & means for definite & permanent treatment of the Park." Johnson had raised the idea with Leland Stanford who, he believed, could "control" the Yosemite commission and have Olmsted appointed to the task. If not appointed, Johnson asked Olmsted to write on the subject in any case, with his findings to be published in the *Century* (Robert Underwood Johnson to FLO, June 23, 1889).
5. In December 1888, while in California working on the plan for Stanford University and other business, Olmsted was interviewed by the *San Francisco Examiner* regarding his opinions on the controversy over whether tree cutting and pruning should be allowed in Yosemite Valley. Olmsted partially demurred, stating: "It is many years since I saw the valley, and I cannot speak of its present condition. I would rather not say much on the subject." He was willing to characterize the intentions of the original Yosemite Commission, however, stating: "We stopped tree cutting, and did not intend to permit the felling of any timber for building purposes. The little tree cutting necessary in a national park should be done under the supervision of a landscape gardener, and the ax should be used sparingly. Here and there, the removal of a tree might be an improvement." On the decision of the commissioners to plow and sow with grain "almost every acre" of meadow in the valley, Olmsted was unequivocal: "That is very bad. Nothing can repair that injury. . . . Our idea was that the feed required by the stock of saddle-train and stage companies should be brought in from the outside and not raised in the valley" ("Yosemite Vandalism, A Landscape Gardener Condemns the Commissioners' Work," *San Francisco Examiner*, Dec. 22, 1888; see also Frederick Law Olmsted, *Governmental Preservation of Natural Scenery*, March 8, 1890, below).
6. That is, justifying the Yosemite Grant of 1864, through which Congress ceded the valley to the state of California for public park purposes. The legislation for a larger Yosemite National Park around, but not including, the state park at Yosemite Valley was being advocated at this time and passed in 1890 ("An Act Authorizing a Grant to the State of California of the Yo-Semite Valley, and of the Land Embracing the Mariposa Big Tree Grove,'" U.S. Congress, *Congressional Globe*, 38th Cong., 1st sess., June 30, 1864, Appendix, p. 240; "An act to set apart certain tracts of land in the State of California as forest reservations," *U.S. Statutes at Large* 26 [1890], pp. 650–52).
7. Galen Clark (1814–1910) is considered the first European American to see the "Big Trees" (giant sequoias) of Mariposa County, California, near Yosemite Valley. This grove of giant sequoias was later ceded to the state of California as part of the 1864 Yosemite Grant. Clark served on the first Yosemite Commission with Olmsted and was appointed Guardian of Yosemite Valley and the Big Tree Grove in 1866. He was removed from his

position as Guardian in 1880, reappointed in 1889, and retired in 1897. He wrote *The Yosemite Valley* (1910), *The Big Trees of California* (1907), and *Indians of the Yosemite Valley and Vicinity* (1904) (*Papers of FLO*, 5: 170, n. 9; *Report of the Commissioners to Manage the Yosemite Valley and the Mariposa Big Tree Grove* [Sacramento, 1867], pp. 3–11; Shirley Sargent, *Galen Clark, Yosemite Guardian* [San Francisco, 1964]).

8. John Muir (1838–1914), naturalist, author, and founding member of the Sierra Club, was born in Scotland and emigrated to the United States in 1849. He arrived in California in 1868 and spent the next six years in and around Yosemite Valley, working at a saw mill in the valley and wandering the High Sierra. His published descriptions of his experiences in the wilderness established his career as a writer, and his books include *The Mountains of California* (1897), *Our National Parks* (1901), and *My First Summer in the Sierra* (1911). In 1889 Muir took Robert Underwood Johnson on the camping tour of Yosemite that Johnson described in his June 23 letter to Olmsted. Muir and Johnson worked together in advocating the Yosemite National Park legislation that passed in October 1890 (*DAB*).

To George Washington Vanderbilt

Brookline, Mass., July 12th 1889.

Mr. Geo. W. Vanderbilt:
My Dear Sir; I am advised by Mr. McNamee,[1] that you are expected to arrive in New York next week and will probably be going a few days afterwards to Mt. Desert.[2] If you can offer me a chance to see you as you go through Boston I shall be glad to discuss the matter of your North Carolina Estate with you in a more satisfactory way than I can on paper. Even if this should be practicable, however, you may like to have a report of the movement of my judgment as it has been affected by my recent reconnaissance of the Estate, to be read at your leisure. I will try to give it to you under successive heads.

I

THE RESIDENCE.

The principal points of the residence and its dependencies,[3] as the plan stood when you went away, have been marked on the ground by stout stakes, and two scaffolds have been erected from one of which the view from the Music Room window can be had, from the other the view from the south end of the Terrace. I think that you will be pleased to find how much is to be gained by setting out the building well over the hillside as advised by Mr. Hunt, and also what a considerable variation of view will be had by walking to the end of the Terrace. You will observe that the scope of the scenery to be enjoyed from the house will be much enlarged by cutting down the crest of the hill-top on the East[4] and by breaking into the woods on the North. The woods are poorer near at hand on all sides than they are at a little distance and it will be desirable to thin them boldly.

We shall send you a key-map before you go to the ground, showing the position of the stakes. Letters on the map will correspond with letters on the stakes, and a number on a stake will show, in feet, the cut or fill required to reach the intended level at the point where the stake stands. The building being set so far down the slope, the grading will be a heavy piece of work but the advantage to be gained, is very great.

I have found a better place than that proposed on the preliminary sketch of last spring as a suitable one for the green-house and service garden[5] and have asked Mr. Thompson[6] to extend the survey so as to include this place. When he has done so I shall be prepared to suggest some improvements of the plan south and east from the court.

I doubt whether the court might not with advantage be made a little more spacious.[7] Please consider the question when on the ground and with regard to what I shall later say under the head of The Approach. (vide p. 31.)

II

WATER SUPPLY FOR THE RESIDENCE.

I had thought last year that it was highly important to find, if practicable, means of water supply that, under the most trying conditions of drought, would be abundant without resort to pumping, and had asked Mr. Aston[8] to make certain explorations for this purpose. He apparently was not successful in doing so and proposed instead a source of supply which in my judgment would be inadequate and require engines and pumps. At my request Mr. McNamee had put Mr. Thompson, who succeeds Mr. Aston, upon the line of examination which I originally had in view, and this he had pursued before my visit with results so promising that I instructed him to follow it up thoroughly and prepare a complete project. I expect a report from him and thereupon before long, to advise you fully on the subject.

III

THE FOREST.[9]

Knowing that at no great distance from the Estate and under conditions of climate as far as I could judge, less favorable at least to southern forms of vegetation, there was the finest natural forest and the most varied in its constituents, to be found in the United States, or possibly in the temperate regions of the world, I was last year greatly disappointed to find your property so deficient in respect both to variety of trees and to local beauty of trees in mass. Exploring the narrow valleys I have found this impression a little relived. In the main, however, it remains and it holds with regard to your new as well as to your earlier purchases.

From such study as I could give the circumstances, aided by Mr. Douglass, I was led to think that the defects to which I have referred had been of comparatively recent occurrence and that there had been once and might be again, for any natural obstacles, a much greater variety of trees and shrubs than are found at present on the Estate, and a large majority of them grow to the highest perfection.

As to the way in which the present conditions have been brought about it appears probable that although there have been no permanent residents on the greater part of the Estate it has been occupied for generations past by a succession of campers, squatters and transient settlers in such numbers that the final effect of their operations has been not unlike what would be expected from those of a much denser population. I saw the remains of four saw mills on the Estate, three of which must have been at work a good many years; there have been others, probably, on the Estate, for all that I saw were within much less than half its entire space, and yet others near it, drawing from it. Almost certainly, also, shingles and boards have been worked on it in large quantity without mill saws. For these purposes and those of the mills, every tree desirable for any sort of salable lumber has been felled. What is now seen is the refuse. As is always the case, to get out the best trees, many a little less choice have been felled or broken down and ruined. Of what remained the settlers have taken great numbers for their cabins, fences and fuel. Big fires are the one luxury of the pioneer cabins. Then more have been taken to feed Asheville hearths than you can readily imagine. With many, when anything was wanted from a store, the readiest way to get it was to take a load of fire-wood to town. You may often see distant settlers, even now, drawing jags of hickory cordwood with a runty bull before a creaking cart into Asheville for the same purpose, and, undoubtedly, similar expeditions have been made from the region of the Estate constantly for many years past.

All the large Cherries, Tulips and Black-Walnuts have been taken by speculators to be sold after going through the mills, to cabinets makers; the large Black-Birches if there were any, to bedstead makers; the large locusts have been taken for posts, the large Dogwoods sold for spools and woodcutters blocks. Nearly all of the large trees of any of the species that I have named now standing on the Estate you will find to have long been rotten at the core. These have not been thought worth cutting. But the largest of the standing trees are Chestnuts. These I suppose to have been preserved by the owners of the land as a resource for rails when others should fail. You will observe that there are hardly any medium sized Chestnuts but many stumps, showing where such have formerly stood. The reserved Chestnuts are often hollow-hearted or partly burned or both, so that fewer rails would be obtained from them for the same labor than from those of medium size. Of the trees that remain standing, Oaks greatly preponderate. The reason I suppose to be that Oaks are hard to fell and hard to work, especially with cheap, frontier implements and machinery, while there has been no near demand for oak timber as there has been at all points near the Atlantic coast. For a thousand Oaks with trunks of from two to four feet thick now standing, you may not see more than one Ash, Linden, Sugar-Maple, Liquid-Ambar, Tulip or Locust, of corresponding size. You may pass ten thousand such Oaks without having come upon one Magnolia or Virgilia or White-Fringe or Catalpa, or Honey-Locust, or Persimmon, or Tupelo, or Holly, or White-Pine or Hemlock. Yet of all these species I saw a few small examples on or near the Estate and have no doubt that they were once common. I hoped to find the Silvery Linden which I have seen growing finely on the Blue Ridge but I did not. I hoped to find specimens of a species of Hemlock lately discovered at a point not twenty miles distant from the Estate, but though there are localities exactly suited to it, I found none. Nor did I notice a single native Elm, Coffee-tree, Nettle-tree, Papaw or Silver Bell, all of which are believed to be indigenous to the region. In the narrower glens and swampy places I did find a few splendid Rhododendrons and Kalmias — taller specimens than I remember to have seen in any of the great English collections, but I found none of the Cypresses, Evergreen Magnolias or Andromedas that might naturally have grown in such situations and that undoubtedly would flourish in them if planted. I found no "Jasmines" such as grow elsewhere in the State.

The characteristic and greatly predominating trees of the Estate are Oaks, as I have said. Now Oaks of all the sorts seen, (I found none of the delicate Willow Oak or of the Laurel-leaved Oaks) to exhibit their best character and beauty require, more, perhaps, than any other tree, to be allowed to stretch out their branches horizontally and take spreading and umbrageous forms. I did not see a single large Oak on the Estate that had had this advantage. All the older had evidently been extremely crowded by other trees until they had grown to be too firm in structure to expand when their neighbors were cut out.

I must speak of one other unfortunate circumstance in the present sylvan condition of the Estate. Except near the water courses or in a few rocky or swampy places, there is a remarkable paucity of underwood and of herbaceous plants, so that a great deal of nearly bare ground is seen. Moreover this bare ground has a notably sterile appearance. Often, even in the depths of the woods, not the slightest leaf-mould is to be seen.

With this circumstance another is to be associated:

There are a great many sapling Oaks growing up thickly together and there are as I have said, more scattered Oaks of from two to three feet thickness of trunk than of all other trees. Between Oaks which may have not been growing more than twenty years and these larger ones, that may be a century old, there are few or none. This fact indicates that where other old trees have been cut out and the old Oaks left standing, young Oaks have taken possession of the ground to the exclusion of other young trees. There are two ways of accounting for the circumstance. First, the woods have been a range for stock and the stock has been often hard pressed, forcing the hogs to root searchingly for seeds of trees in the soil and the horned cattle to close browsing. Oak sprouts are comparatively tough and astringent and sprouts of other trees have been selected by the cattle in preference to them.

(I do not mean that Oaks of different upland species have not always predominated in this forest. I am accounting for what I believe to be an extraordinary predominance of young Oaks at this time.)

Second, in addition to the destruction by stock there has been the destruction by fire. I suppose young Oaks to be better able to resist fire than young trees of other of the indigenous species.

Fires have been of two classes; first, comparatively light fires, generally started intentionally in the spring, to clear the surface of dead leaves and stubs so that a better growth of annual grasses and other herbage might spring up for the pasturage of cattle and hogs. This is said to have been a custom of the Indians inhabiting the region and to have been taken up by the earliest white settlers and perpetuated to this time.

Second, fires starting accidentally in the late summer and autumn, which, in times of drought and when forced by strong winds, seizing upon the dead trees and lopped limbs and brushwood of the timber that has been removed, have sometimes been fierce. These fires have, I imagine, destroyed the seed previously in the surface soil, and the younger crop of Oaks has grown from seed subsequently falling from the older Oaks left standing.

To the effect of such fires, I suppose is due, also the absence of undergrowth and of superficial leaf-mould and the sterile aspect of the surface of the ground in many places, where stumps and standing old trees show that it really is not sterile.

I should say that the condition of things that I have described is not at all peculiar to the locality. It is frequently found in all parts of the Cotton States. It is not often found in the better wooded, higher mountain regions of North Carolina because these have had fewer inhabitants; it has been harder to get lumber to market from them and, the summers being shorter and, (because of higher elevation and more frequent showers), less drying, they have been less affected by fires.

Where forests have been systematically cleared for crops, as they have been in many small patches on the Estate, aggregating, I judge near two thousand acres, the ground has been cultivated in a very shallow way, the plow often being a mere prong drawn by one small bullock and its operation a scratch but three or four inches deep. With such tillage, corn and grain and tobacco have been grown year after year until the land was "worn out", which means until the thin upper stratum of cultivated soil had parted with nearly all it had originally possessed of the constituents of these crops. I saw several crops of this year ripening, the value of which would not probably repay the labor, merely of harvesting, at a dollar a day.

When thoroughly exhausted, the land has been "turned out", and then, as a rule, after a few years, a growth of one or two or three species of Pines peculiar to barren lands has sprung up, that most common being known as the Scrub Pine. All the Pine woods of the Estate, several hundred acres in extent, are of this character. The trees never became large; their timber is practically valueless; they sometimes have an agreeable effect in landscape if looked down upon from a distance, but from ground near them or under them they are not pleasing and they are generally recognized as a badge of poverty.

It is a question of great importance relatively to a general plan for dealing with the Estate how far the superficial appearance of the soil that I have described is to be accepted as authentic. I turned this part of my examination largely over to Mr. Douglass who for three days went from end to end of the Estate, sampling soil and subsoil. I shall refer to certain particulars of his report later. The general result of our study is a conviction that, with moderately deep tillage, soil would nearly everywhere be found of a very choice quality for trees, and that if dressed with lime and manure and well tilled, it would probably be productive agriculturally. My belief is that, a clear, fine and lasting grass sod, such as I have never seen in the South, can be formed upon it.

Speaking more particularly of its capabilities for forestry, I should say that I have never examined ground upon which as large variety of trees and shrubs was likely to grow as rapidly.

I will mention one or two circumstances that seem to sustain the view I have taken of the causes of the present apparent barrenness of the soil and of the comparative scarcity of other trees than Oaks.

At a few points on the Estate there are patches of ground that have been parts of clearings and have been fenced in and trees better protected than they otherwise would have been from fires and from the browsing of stock, yet, perhaps because they could not be as conveniently plowed as the rest of the ground enclosed with them, have not been as severely cropped. In some such places I noticed a remarkably thrifty growth of young trees other than Oaks. If, when you are on the ground again, you will follow down the glen that has its head a few hundred yards east from the residence site, until you reach the edge of the old fields that spread south-westerly from Shiloh meeting house, you will find such a place. The present predominating growth is of the Tulip tree. Tulips are outgrowing everything else. They are as fine trees of the species, of their age, as I ever saw and growing with remarkable rapidity. The probability is that Tulip-trees were originally very common; that they grew to majestic size, and that the forest having been cleared of them, had it not been for burning and browsing, seedlings from them would have been now growing everywhere as thriftily as in this accidentally protected locality.

Again, in one valley I found a few Rhododendrons thriving but near by others, larger, that had plainly been ruined by fire not more than two years ago. If sweeping fires, largely due to litter left to become dry by tree cutters, had been avoided, Rhododendrons would probably have been growing abundantly in every valley.

Considering that you were likely to use the Estate as a winter resort I suggested last year that there would be a considerable advantage in having considerable portions of it planted with White Pines, having in view, first a contrast to prevailing Oaks; second, winter verdure; third, the pleasant footing that is always found under a White Pine wood; fourth the agreeable balsamic odor of the tree, and, lastly, its probable future economic value. As to the feasibility of growing it thriftily on the Estate I more particularly sought Mr. Douglas's opinion. This was entirely favorable, and I have asked a proposition from him, looking to the immediate planting on the old fields of several hundred acres of White Pines, by contract. Other suggestions as to general planting and the management of the forest I reserve for the present. I will simply say, at this point, that I am inclined to advise you to have in view the establishment and maintenance of an unbroken forest from the north to the south end of the Estate, to extend from the east border, as a general rule, to the edge of the river bottom on the west, but with a "Park" to be taken out near the residence as to be hereafter proposed. Perhaps with certain fields to be also taken out for agricultural purposes. Your property on the left bank of the river to be also maintained in forest condition and improved.[10]

From these forests you would gradually eliminate the overgrown ill-formed Oaks, replacing them with more valuable and pleasing trees; you would thin out and make thrifty the younger Oaks and other trees, and in desirable localities establish underwood.

The chief peril of forest property is that of fires. And the chief source of forest fires in the future is likely to be railroads. The topography of the Estate is not inviting to new railroads. Your river and tributaries give you advantages for contending against fires spreading from railroads on the West, North and South. It would be desirable to have your forest bounded on the East by a broad road such as is already in considerable part, I believe, provided.

Further, good management will require that the forest be traversed at intervals by common roads and that these be so laid out as to serve as a means of checking the advance of possible fires from one division of it to another. Certain topographical advantages for this purpose, I shall refer to later. Fires are rarely destructive under good forest management.

Looking over what is above written I see that it may not quite clearly indicate the line of policy that I have meant to suggest as applicable to the main body of the ridge land of the Estate. Allow me to make a partial re-statement.

The ridgeland is now occupied chiefly by Oaks of two classes; first, old trees the remnants of a thickly grown forest out of which great numbers of other trees than Oaks have, years ago, been taken. These Oaks have acquired ungainly forms because of the crowding to which they were subject when young. Second, Oaks which have sprung up since the forest was thinned of other trees. These younger Oaks are not now growing very well, partly because many of them are shaded by the older Oaks and partly because the roots of the older Oaks are still taking the lion's share of the moisture and a certain part of the remaining constituents of the soil needed for their nourishment. These younger Oaks are not yet stunted, however, nor are they yet so cramped by crowding that, judiciously thinned, they would not soon acquire fine, characteristic, stalwart and umbrageous forms, such as you have seen Oaks taking in Windsor Forest, for example.[11]

Remove all of the old Oaks that are not of exceptional and admirable character; let the thickets of the younger Oaks be judiciously thinned; give the other trees, (Hickories, Chestnuts, Limes, (Basswood) Tupelos, Beeches, Maples, Tulips, Birches,) that are sparsely growing with them, a fair chance; plant occasional vacant spaces with yet other trees, natural to the circumstances, such as I have named; encourage a growth of underwood, and a forest would result that would easily come in time to be the finest in the country. Finer than any natural forest of the same trees because always in the natural forest, under favorable conditions of soil and climate, the struggle for existence of trees, one with another, prevents the attainment of a high development with any. Finer than any other planted forest because no other yet planted will have equal advantages of soil and climate.

You may ask, if forest undertakings are desirable in this country why are there no notable examples of them other than those recently entered upon by Railway Corporations in the treeless regions of the far West?[12] Simply because no considerable "investment" in forests can be made with the large *early* profits that necessity, and custom growing out of general necessity, lead our people beyond all others to be passionately eager to secure. For the harvest of a forest crop one must look more years ahead than he does months for the harvest of other crops. But, so looking ahead, a well managed forest is likely to be as good a property, all things considered as any other. Mean time, the management of it; the oversight of its development and improvement from year to year, would be a most interesting rural occupation; far more interesting, I am sure, to a man of poetic temperament than any of those commonly considered appropriate to a country-seat life. Certainly there can be no prospect of success, of profit or pleasure from year to year, in any other use to be made of your ridge lands to compare with it. You cannot find an upland farm in all the mountain region that has a thoroughly pleasant aspect; hardly one that does not make a doleful impression. But where the native forest has not been wholly ruined in the manner I have described it to be; wherever it has been but moderately injured, its beauty, its mystery, its solemnity, are really fascinating. Years ago I rode alone for a full month through the North Carolina forests, and it was with great regret that at last I emerged from them. There is no experience of my life to which I could return with more satisfaction.[13]

I have written in a too desultory way but you will see that in what I have said there is the substance of a proposition which is much the most important of all that I have to submit to your consideration. That the subject may be more completely and intelligently brought before you, I advise you to read the pamphlet by my friend Mr. Cleveland that I send herewith.[14] Reading it you will see what I meant when I said last year, that adopting the suggestion, as then less fully presented, you would not only make the best use of the property for the direct satisfaction of yourself and friends but would be doing the country an inestimable service and thus from the start give the Estate a rank like that which Blair Atholl has among the great British estates.[15]

IV

THE QUESTION OF A NAME.

"Blair Atholl" suggests the question of a name. Mr. McNamee has been looking thus far vainly for an Indian name. An Indian name, to be advisable, should have a suitable significance; at least a significance not provocative of punning, sarcasm or ridicule; should be sonorous; should fall trippingly from the tongue, and should not have been appropriated. It is not probable that an Indian name will offer having all these advantages. For a concocted English name there are the following suggestive circumstances: First, the river; second, the forest; third, the ridge or line of hills; fourth the central of both sides of the river. I don't suppose the Indian name of the river is available. If it had been Mr. McNamee would have proposed it. Probably it has been appropriated. French Broad will not do. But possibly something might be done with "Broad", Broadwood, for example, while short, simple, unaffected and appropriate as suggested by the river and the broad wooded hills between which it flows, has to me a quiet respectable air, (perhaps from association with Lord Palmerston's seat, Broadlands.)[16]

V

AGRICULTURE.

You know that what passes with us as "gentleman farming", is generally a very costly, and that after a time, it usually comes to be a very unsatisfactory, amusement. Why should you undertake farming on any large scale? The only reason that I can see is that to a rapid improvement of the Estate as a forestral country seat you need to have at command a great deal more manure than you can economically obtain except by a certain kind of farming. Adopting this as the real motive of what you shall do, incidentally you will have the pleasure of raising and keeping as much fine stock of all kinds as you choose.

Considering fine stock as an incidental feature of your operations, to which you can give as much attention as you please, (making the Estate famous as a head-quarters for particular herds and strains, if your inclination ultimately runs that way), the main agricultural question is how to maintain a large stock most economically.

From the little study that I was able to give this question my impression is that it will be best to confine tillage mainly to the river bottoms and a few fields near them and, as a rule, sell no farm product except live stock and this mostly fat and fine, such as, for example, there will be a growing demand for at special prices, as population and luxury increase in Asheville, Atlanta and other cities not as far away as those on the Atlantic. This policy would lead you to raise as much forage as possible on the ground given to farming. As far as I can judge the bottom lands are all good for forage crops. The poorest are those upon which sand has lodged and the grain crops on them are this year very poor. Mr. Alexander[17] was away during my visit and I could get no information of value from anyone I saw but I am much mistaken if these sandy bottoms would not with fertilizers, bear heavy crops of the coarse forage pea (cowpea, I think it is called) that is elsewhere largely grown at the South, and I have heard that a mixture of this pea with corn-fodder, in silos, makes the best ensilage that is known. Probably you can raise, at first with commercial fertilizers, great crops of fodder corn, alfalfa and clover on the bottoms, while improving their fertility. They have been exhausted by grain growing. Avoid taking grain (including corn) from them until they have recovered fertility. If necessary to fatten off stock for market for the time being, buy corn.

You have unusual advantages (in a number of brooks coming to the bottoms from higher ground and in a more or less sandy soil and good outlets) for an inexpensive trial of water meadows (irrigatable grass lands) hardly ever used in the Eastern States but found highly profitable for forage crops in the south of England.

I think that you will find it best to have two centres of operations, one for the upper, one for the lower bottoms, with silos and feeding stations at each. (The meadows before the residence, I do not think that you will want to cultivate after once putting them in order. They may be made a part of the park, or kept permanently for hay and pasturage.)

As your stock-keeping capacity increases you may bring all the agricultural land of the Estate under a regular system of rotation; manuring for corn, grain, cut fodder and roots, and leaving a due proportion of land, after being thus prepared, to be successively laid down in fields to be kept for a course of years for hay and pasturage; selling off, as a rule, nothing but live stock, and husbanding manure in every reasonable way.

VI

THE PARK.

There is no *park-like* land on the Estate. None in which park-like scenery of a notably pleasing character, could be gained in a life time. Plenty of land in which agreeable, wild, woodland scenery can be had in a few years.

The best place in which to keep deer or other animals where they may be seen to advantage, and which will, as far as practicable, have what is otherwise to be desired in a private park, will be on the westside of the residence where it can be looked into from its windows and terrace. So situated, the inconvenience of having gates wherever transit is to be made in any direction toward or from the residence on the entrance front will be avoided.

The park would differ from the forest in having a much larger proportion of un-wooded ground; in having a larger proportion of its trees standing singly and in groups; in being more free from underwood; and in having a turf surface, forming a fine pasture and giving a pleasant footing for riding or walking freely in all directions. It might be grazed and the turf kept moderately close by herds of the native fallow deer, of the Antelope of the Rocky Mountains and of South Downs or some other herd of small, choice mutton sheep. The latter would probably have to be folded at night on account of dogs.

A park that would answer every desirable purpose would not, I think, exceed two hundred and fifty acres. If much larger it would be a worrisome business to take care of it and the needed fences, gates and other requirements of keeping would be inconvenient. The central parts of it would be nearly midway between the residence and the river. It would include the valley next north of the residence; extend southwardly to the neighborhood of the Alexander place and would take in the lower hill, at present nearly covered with scrub-pine, which is very prominent in the view westward from the scaffolds. Also, probably, the hill on the north of this, beyond the conspicuous road. This road will desirably be abolished and in place of it a road carried on the edge of the bottom land at least as far as the next opening of the hills, where there is now a tolerable farm road. You will observe, when looking from the scaffolds, that by the removal of a few trees a considerably larger space of the river will be brought under view from the windows of the Residence.

VII

THE ARBORETUM.[18]

As to the suggested Arboretum, I have conceived the outline of a plan for it the general nature of which I will try to indicate, but before offering any final recommendation, even as to its general scope, I should want to give the matter more study.

This plan would be to lay out a road starting from the residence in such a manner that, bending to the valley southward, it would follow up Four Mile Creek to the meadow above the second dam, {a}cross from the meadow near, (if I recollect aright) the Hart place, and so to the valley of the next creek south; down this valley to the French Broad bottom-land, then back to the point of departure by the Four Mile valley. A dam could be built on the site of the present lower dam of Four Mile Creek and ten feet higher, which would form a lake, extending up the north valley of the creek to a point a little above where the steam saw mill stood. This lake would probably be visible from the residence garden and perhaps from the terrace. In a branch of the Four Mile valley, where there is now a vacant house a little north east of what would be the head of the lake, is probably the best place for your service gardens, propagating houses, etc.

Such a road as I have thus indicated would make convenient subdivisions of the forest and in connection with the streams which it would follow would be a guard against the spread of fires. It would be a very picturesque road, and on its borders there would be situations of great variety in respect to soil and exposure and generally of the highest fertility to be found on the Estate. Some would be rocky; some marshy; some meadowy; the most, fair upland. My idea, in a word, is to form the Arboretum by cutting back and thinning out the present standing wood on the borders of this road, leaving the best trees and bushes but making place for the planting of the collection, choosing for each representative tree a position adapted to develop its highest character and exhibit it, in several specimens, to the best advantage. Water-side trees by the lake; Ash, on the fertile well-drained meadow; Magnolias in the dingles opening southward; Oaks on the higher upland, and so on.

Without doubt an arboretum could be formed in this way by far finer and more instructive than other in the world, an arboretum to which naturalists would resort from all parts of the world.

It would, of course, be backed at all points by the main forest of the Estate and the trees would group with those of the forest.

VIII

THE APPROACH.

The present roads of the Estate have been laid out as far as practicable on the ridge lands, where they could be made and kept passable at the least cost. Near them the timber has been naturally poorer and has been worse used than elsewhere and the local scenery is monotonous and forlorn. It is in

"Guide Map of Biltmore Estate," 1896, bottom righ

ECTION SHOWS COURSE OF APPROACH ROAD TO THE HOUSE

the valleys or gulches between the ridges that the most interesting foliage is to be seen; where there is the greatest moisture and all conditions are the more picturesque.

I suggest that the most striking and pleasing impression of the Estate will be obtained if an approach can be made that shall have throughout a natural and comparatively wild and secluded character; its borders rich with varied forms of vegetation, with incidents growing out of the vicinity of springs and streams and pools, steep banks and rocks, all consistent with the sensation of passing through the remote depths of a natural forest. Such scenery to be maintained with no distant outlook and no open spaces spreading from the road; with nothing showing obvious art, until the visitor passes with an abrupt transition into the enclosure of the trim, level, open, airy *spacious*, thoroughly artificial Court, and the Residence, with its orderly dependencies, breaks suddenly and fully upon him. Then, after passing through the building, the grandeur of the mountains, the beauty of the valley, the openness and tranquility of the park would be most effectively and even surprisingly presented, from the windows, balconies and terrace.

A sketch map showing a route by which such a result could be obtained will soon be sent you, and when you go to the Estate you will find this route approximately indicated by stakes on the ground.

This plan assumes a crossing of Swananoah creek by a bridge a little below the Haunted House ford, from which point a road would be carried so as to skirt the bottom land to a point where a large beech tree stands on the road you now ordinarily take in visiting the Estate, and where that road is crossed by a brook. Thence it follows near the easternmost and largest branch of this brook, to its source; thence at a slight depression of the ridge, it crosses into a branch of the valley next north of the Residence; runs down this to the brook of the valley; follows up a branch of the brook to its head, where it swings out on the upper part of a hillside, along which it winds to the gate of the Court.[19]

I believe that fairly easy grades, with occasional levels, can be had on all of this line, without heavy construction and without curves that would be inconvenient for four-in-hand driving, but I shall be able to advise you on this point and others much better after Mr. Thompson has made the survey that I have requested of him. As to details, some suggestions will come under the next head.

IX

NURSERY.[20]

Many of the trees, shrubs and vines that you will find it desirable to plant in considerable quantity cannot be obtained at the Commercial nurseries; certainly cannot except in small numbers and at the price of rarities. To

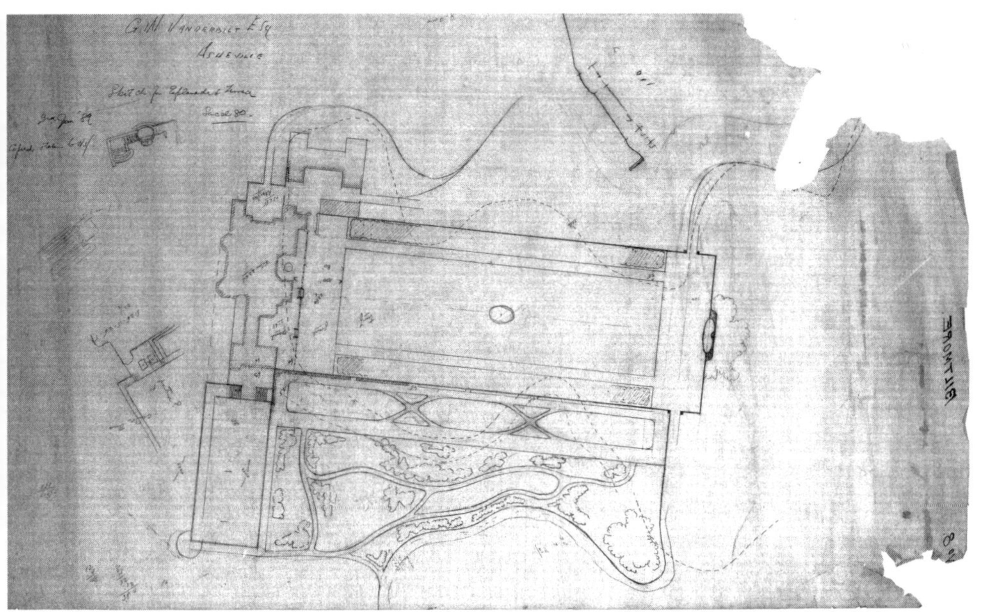

"G. W. VANDERBILT, SKETCH FOR ESPLANADE AND TERRACE," JANUARY 2, 1889, SHOWING THE POSITION OF MANSION AND IMMEDIATE GROUNDS

obtain them in quantity, of a desirable planting size, will take several years. Some can best be propagated on the ground; some obtained as small seedlings in Europe, or from Japan, and advanced in a nursery on the Estate. There are numerous plants that may well be used that are not quite rare but for which there is no demand at the North because of their tenderness and no sufficient demand at the South to have led to their being grown for sale except at the price of rarities and in very small numbers.

I have mentioned several smooth-leaved evergreens of which a few can be found on the Estate, or in the Asheville gardens, showing that they are hardy, such as the evergreen Magnolia, the American Holly and Rhododendron Maximum. There are others which I know from trials at Washington will endure the Asheville climate, and of which for winter enjoyment you should have, near your residence and in sheltered places along your roads, in much larger quantities than they can be obtained at this time from all the nurseries in the country or, as to some of them, in all the nurseries of Europe. Propagating and rearing them on a scale large enough to warrant the employment of a good gardener with a suitable plant for the purpose they would cost you not quarter as much as the commercial price. There are others for which contracts could be made for delivery after two years at half the present market price.

Taking such measures there are shrubs which are yet luxuries, seen only as "specimens", and many of these in New York only under glass, which you could easily have as profusely on the borders of your roads as you see rock ferns and "huckleberries" growing along the roads of Mt. Desert. You can have a stretch of bamboos, at little less cost than one of blackberries, have it quarter of a mile long if you like, provided you make preparations for it three or four years in advance. The nursery price of *Rhododendron Maximum* in New York, three feet high, has been $2.00 a plant. You can have plants gathered for you within twenty miles of your residence, by the thousand, probably at ten cents a plant, and after two years in nursery they will be better plants than I have been able to get from any nurseryman in Europe or America.

Plant 10,000 of them along your road, as a back ground and in front of them 5000 of the most splendid hybrid Rhododendrons (such as they exhibit under tents at the Horticultural Gardens in London) and of the Himalayan and Alpine Rhododendrons; scatter among them clusters of Kalmias, the native and Japanese Andromedas, the Japanese Euonymus of which there are a dozen sorts that will surely be hardy with you, though they cannot live out in Philadelphia; the Japanese Aucubas, the refined little *Abelia rupestris* with a cloud of most delicate bloom (I have had a hundred of them growing fully exposed for several years in Washington though I have never seen a specimen elsewhere except in a hot house); *Mahonia aquifolia* which must be guarded here and is often scorched and sometimes killed, but would be at home with you; the Japanese Mahonia, still less hardy but safe with you; All these are smooth-leaved, (laurel-like) evergreen shrubs, which can be had, under a well organized system, in a few years, by the thousand, costing no more than people generally pay for the commonest deciduous bushes of our northern woods. I suppose that you could naturalize in your woods more than five times as many sorts of fine, smooth-leaved evergreens as can be grown in the open air near New York. Some that I have named rarely grow more than three feet high. Some ten, some twenty feet. *Magnolia Grandiflora*, of which I saw one specimen in Asheville, grows to be a towering, stately tree, sometimes one hundred feet high.

These are hints of the capabilities of the Estate. Making good use of them where would there be anything to compare with it? You would have people crossing the Atlantic to see it.

With these possibilities in view, so unusual with tree buyers that commerce is not in the least adapted to them, the early starting of a propagating house, nursery and trial garden, will recommend itself to your consideration.

Yours Very Truly,

Fred[k] Law Olmsted.
F. L. & J. C. Olmsted;
Landscape Architects.

The text presented here is a typed letter, signed and edited in Olmsted's hand (see FLO to Richard Morris Hunt, March 2, 1889, above).

1. Charles McNamee (1865–1923) was a lawyer from New York whom Vanderbilt invited to Asheville in May 1888 in order to act as his agent in land purchases. McNamee's brother, James, was married to Clara Vanderbilt, George W. Vanderbilt's cousin. McNamee was Vanderbilt's representative and estate manager at Biltmore from 1888 until 1904, when he returned to practice law in New York and then Rome (John M. Bryan, *Biltmore Estate, The Most Distinguished Private Place* [New York, 1994], p. 31; FLO to Charles McNamee, March 13, 1889, A3: 330, OAR/LC; "Biltmore's Manager to Quit," *New York Times*, March 5, 1904, p. 2; "Mr. McNamee in Rome," *New York Times*, May 1, 1910, p. C3; "Death Notice," ibid., April 13, 1923, p. 17).
2. In 1889 Vanderbilt purchased a house on Mt. Desert Island in Maine that had been designed in 1868 by Charles Coolidge Haight. Vanderbilt renovated and enlarged it as a summer residence, which he named Pointe d'Acadie. Olmsted began designing the grounds shortly after Vanderbilt acquired the property (Stephen J. Hornsby, "The Gilded Age and the Making of Bar Harbor," *Geographical Review*, Oct. 1993, pp. 455–69; John M. Bryan, *Maine Cottages* [New York, 2005], p. 74; J. M. Bryan, *Biltmore Estate*, p. 22).
3. At this time the main dependencies planned were the stables, offices, and conservatory. See FLO to Richard Morris Hunt, March 2, 1889, above.
4. That is, the leveling of a hill east of the house, so as to construct the level esplanade. See FLO to Richard Morris Hunt, March 2, 1889, above (J. M. Bryan, *Biltmore Estate*, p. 94).
5. The preliminary plan dated March 1889 shows a proposed conservatory just east of the "winter garden." The walled garden and conservatory were eventually built farther downhill to the south (plan 170-10, NPS/FLONHS; see FLO to Richard Morris Hunt, March 2, 1889, above).
6. William A. Thompson (1845–1933) was an engineer and railroad surveyor in charge of all surveying and engineering operations at Biltmore (FLO to George W. Vanderbilt, Nov. 6, 1889, A5: 465–66, OAR/LC; FLO to William A. Thompson, Nov. 6, 1889, A5: 470–76, OAR/LC; FLO to George W. Vanderbilt, March 26, 1889, A3: 408–9, OAR/LC; "W.A. Thompson Dead; Civil Engineer, 88," *New York Times*, Nov. 10, 1933, p. 21).
7. A sketch for the project dated June 2, 1889, shows the design of the rectilinear esplanade and entry court at the main entrance to the house, essentially as they were built. Olmsted's earlier plan showed a curvilinear approach road and no esplanade or entry court (plans 170-8, 170-10, NPS/FLONHS).
8. J. G. Aston was a local surveyor whom Vanderbilt hired in 1888 to make a topographical map of the central area of the Biltmore estate. William A. Thompson collaborated with Aston and eventually replaced him (FLO to J. G. Aston, Oct. 29, 1888, A2: 950–51, OAR/LC; J. M. Bryan, *Biltmore Estate*, pp. 32, 34).
9. From the beginning of his involvement at Biltmore, Olmsted seized the opportunity to establish the first large-scale demonstration of the principles of scientific forest management in the United States. Vanderbilt eventually acquired over 125,000 acres of mostly forested land, much of which had suffered from over-logging and soil erosion. Acting on Olmsted's advice, in 1892, Vanderbilt hired Gifford Pinchot, then one of the few trained foresters in the country, who developed a forest management plan that called for plantations of new trees, and measures for fire control and selective cutting. In 1895 Pinchot was replaced by Carl Schenck, who in 1898 founded the Biltmore School of Forestry, the first such institution in the country, at Biltmore. In 1915, Vanderbilt's widow, Edith Stuyvesant Vanderbilt (1873–1958), deeded nearly 87,000 acres of the estate to the federal government, creating the core of what is today the Pisgah National Forest (Charles E. Beveridge, "The Olmsteds at Biltmore," *National Association for*

Olmsted Parks Workbook Series, Vol. 5, Biography [Bethesda, Md., 1995], p. 2; Michael Williams, *Americans and Their Forests: A Historical Geography* [New York, 1989], p. 412).

10. Vanderbilt was substantially expanding his land holdings at this time, acquiring property on both the east and west banks of the French Broad River (J. M. Bryan, *Biltmore Estate*, pp. 32, 34).
11. Windsor Forest surrounds Windsor Great Park near Windsor Castle in England. By the eighteenth century Windsor Forest was a tourist destination and the subject of landscape paintings and poetry. The forest was renowned for its ancient oaks (Charles Lyte, *The Royal Gardens in Windsor Great Park* [Whinfield, UK, 1998], pp. 17–21).
12. In the decades following the Civil War, several railroad corporations engaged in forestry experiments west of the Mississippi River. In the 1870s, the Burlington and Missouri Railroad planted willow and cottonwood windbreaks in Nebraska and Kansas, hoping to demonstrate how the Great Plains could be made more amenable to farming and settlement. In 1879, the Kansas City, Fort Scott, and Memphis Railroad hired Robert Douglas, who was working with Olmsted at Biltmore in 1889, to plant a square mile of land in Kansas with catalpa, black walnut, and other species, to see whether such a forest could be established on the prairie (*Transactions of the Massachusetts Horticultural Society, For the Year 1879* [Boston, 1879], p. 133; Sherry H. Olson, "Commerce and Conservation: The Railroad Experience," *Forest History*, Jan. 1966, p. 5; Roy V. Scott, "American Railroads and the Promotion of Forestry," *Journal of Forest History*, vol. 23, April 1979, p. 78).
13. Olmsted made a number of trips through the southern states between December 1852 and August 1854. His journey through the North Carolina forests likely occurred during his trip on horseback from Texas to New York during the summer of 1854. This trip is described in *A Journey in the Back Country*, Chapter VI, "The Highlanders." Olmsted here slightly exaggerates the time he spent in North Carolina, it was closer to ten days than a month. He was in Asheville on July 11, 1854, and climbed Balsam Mountain. He noted in *Back Country* that, "These mountains would therefore be more pleasant to ramble over than the White Mountains, and will probably, when railroads are completed in their neighborhood, be much resorted to for pleasure" (p. 256) (see *Papers of FLO*, 1: 15; *Papers of FLO*, 2: 481–82).
14. Horace William Shaler Cleveland, *The Culture and Management of Our Native Forests for Development of Timber or Ornamental Woods* (Springfield, Ill., 1882).
15. The Dukes of Atholl, inspired by the potential profits from managed forests, planted millions of trees over thousands of acres in Blair and Dunkeld, Scotland, in the eighteenth and early nineteenth centuries (Syd House and Christopher Dingwall, "'A Nation of Planters': Introducing the New Trees, 1650–1900," in T.C. Smout, ed, *People and Woods in Scotland, A History* [Edinburgh, 2003], pp. 135–40).
16. Lord Palmerston was Henry John Temple, the Third Viscount Palmerston (1784–1865). He was Prime Minister of Great Britain from 1855 until his death. His estate at Broadlands in Hampshire was his country home (*DNB*).
17. B. J. and W. J. Alexander owned adjoining farms along the French Broad River. They were prominent farmers and operated grist and saw mills. Their land, more than seven hundred acres combined, was purchased by Vanderbilt in 1889 (Bill Alexander, *Around Biltmore Village*, [Charleston, S.C., 2008], p. 15).
18. The Biltmore Arboretum, the most ambitious arboretum plan of Olmsted's career, was never fully realized. He intended to plant thousands of species of woody plants and a number of trees along the approximately twelve mile long Arboretum Road, outlined here. When completed by 1896, the road started from what was later named the Bass Pond southeast of the house gardens, then followed the Four-Mile Creek southeast through meadows and along other creeks, then traveled southwest along the French

Broad River, cutting inland through the Arrowhead Peninsula and back to the French Broad River. Olmsted hoped that his proposed Arboretum would "advance the science of dendrology; the business of forestry, and the art of landscape improvement." The Arboretum Road, and some site preparation, were the only parts of the plan implemented, although thousands of plants intended for it were propagated and grown at the Biltmore Nursery (C. E. Beveridge, "The Olmsteds at Biltmore," *National Association for Olmsted Parks Workbook Series*, pp. 2–3; FLO to George W. Vanderbilt, Dec. 30, 1893, A31: 814–18, OAR/LC; Paul R. Baker, *Richard Morris Hunt* [Cambridge, Mass., 1980], p. 420; "Guide Map of Biltmore Estate," 1896, plan 170-z5, NPS/FLONHS; Bill Alexander, *The Biltmore Nursery: A Botanical Legacy* [Charleston, S.C, 2007], pp. 49–55).

19. The three mile, winding Approach Road as completed did not follow the route that Olmsted describes here. The proposed location for the road began near where Victoria Road crossed the Swannanoa River, a tributary of the French Broad River on the north side of the estate grounds. It then proceeded southeast past a quarry and along the Ram Branch, a stream running east. The quarry, about one quarter of a mile south of the Swannanoa, was later used for stone for bridges and road construction. From the quarry, the proposed road location proceeded southeast, just over a mile, to an intersection with Shiloh Road. After this intersection, the road turned sharply to the west, and then continued south about one quarter of a mile, finally turning east to arrive at the mansion.

    The Approach Road as completed by 1895 began about one quarter of a mile east of the earlier proposed starting point on the Swannanoa, nearer to what became Biltmore Village. Then, as the first proposed route did, it passed by the quarry. From there it continued much farther east along the valley of the Ram Branch before turning south and arriving at the entrance of the mansion. The 1889 proposed route came to the estate almost entirely on the west side of the grounds, while the completed road approached entirely from the east side (see FLO to William A. Thompson, Nov. 11, 1889, below; C. E. Beveridge, "The Olmsteds at Biltmore," *National Association for Olmsted Parks Workbook Series*, pp. 3–5; J. M. Bryan, *Biltmore Estate*, pp. 94–95; plan 170-20; "Guide Map of Biltmore Estate, 1896," NPS/FLONHS).

20. The Biltmore Nursery, which was established in 1889 to collect and grow plants for the improvement of the estate, eventually covered three hundred acres and became one of the most significant commercial nurseries in the country. It was located between the Swannanoa River and the Southern Railway Company line, near the entrance to the Approach Road and Biltmore Village. James G. Gall began planning the project with Olmsted in 1889 in order to grow and collect the plants required for the Approach Road, Arboretum, gardens, and other estate projects. In the spring of 1890, Chauncey D. Beadle took charge of the nursery, and Olmsted reported in an article for the Asheville *Lyceum* in 1891 that the nursery had about 100,000 trees and shrubs and 500,000 seedlings and cuttings. In addition to providing plants for the Biltmore estate, the nursery became a profitable commercial operation. It eventually provided plants for other Olmsted projects, including the Arnold Arboretum and the Louisville, Kentucky, parks. Vanderbilt's death in 1914 and a flood in 1916 ended the operation (FLO to Frederick J. Kingsbury, Jan. 20, 1891; FLO to James G. Gall, Dec. 11, 1889, A6: 656–59, OAR/LC; B. Alexander, *The Biltmore Nursery*, pp. 11, 18, 67–76).

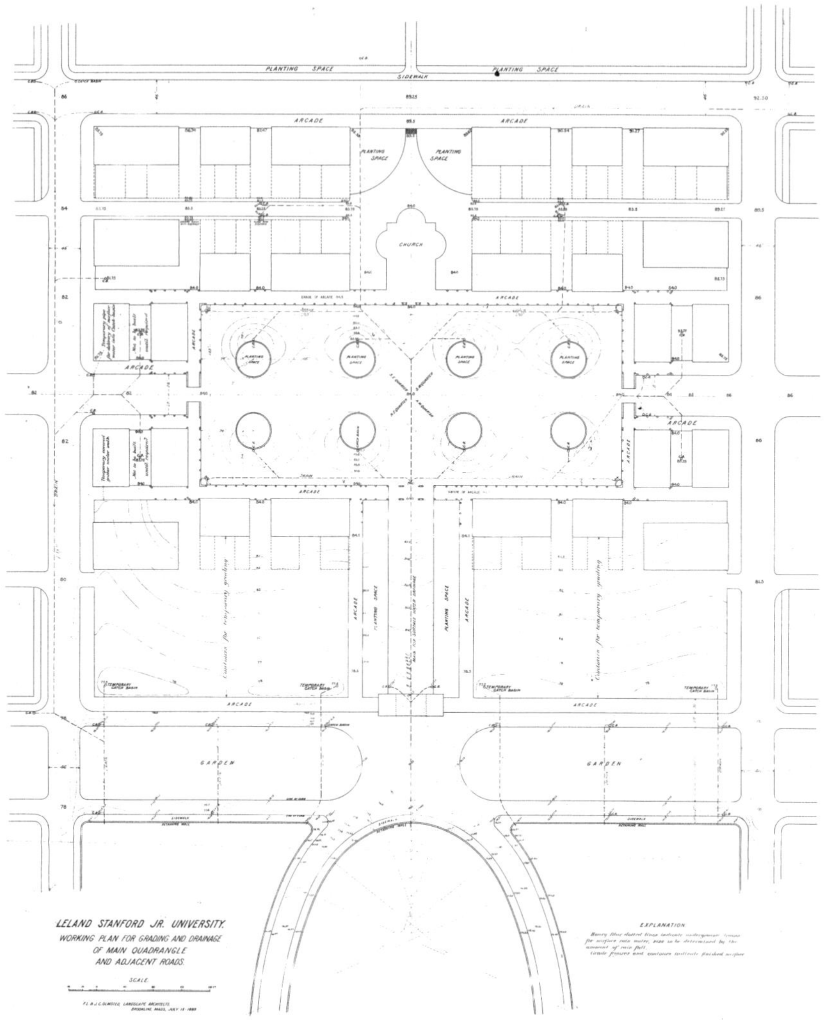

"Leland Stanford Jr. University, Working Plan for Grading and Drainage of Main Quadrangle and Adjacent Roads," July 15, 1889

To Amasa Leland Stanford

Brookline, Mass., 14th July, 1889.

The Hon. Leland Stanford.
Dear Sir; We are completing and expect to send in a day or two the last of the series of working drawings for the grading of the streets and approaches of the University prepared under your instructions of last Fall.[1]

VIEW OF EXTERIOR OF CENTRAL QUAD, STANFORD UNIVERSITY, C. 1900–1906

Among them there will be drawings for the terrace walls north of Garden Avenue designed with a view to the use of a good deal of irregular stone struck off the blocks set in the buildings.

We have today received a note from the Engineer[2] reporting that grading operations are expected to begin tomorrow and to be prosecuted rapidly. But he adds that you have expressed a doubt about adhering to the plan in respect to the panels for shrubbery and an intention to write to us on the subject.[3] We think that we should advise you without delay that a change of the plan in this particular would involve changes in other particulars. We should have given different grades to all of the streets north of Garden Avenue if we had not had that feature in view. If, therefore, you decide to abandon it, the plans should be returned to us at once and a new set prepared. In that case we shall need specific instructions from you what to do with the spaces which we have left with little variation from the natural surface intending that they shall be filled by shrubbery over the surface of which a comprehensive view of the principal buildings of the university would be had by all coming up the main avenue.

The question is as to where the balance of disadvantage lies. Knowing that those of this one plan were very prominent to you, we had been slow to assume it fixed and it had been much on our minds for more than two years without our being able to devise any arrangement to which the objections did not seem to us much more serious and without the suggestion {*of any*

View of Interior of Central Quad, Stanford University, c. 1900–1906, showing early plantings inside Central Quad

View of Interior of Central Quad, Stanford University, c. 1900–1906, showing plantings in Central Quad

VIEW OF EXTERIOR OF CENTRAL QUAD, STANFORD UNIVERSITY, C. 1900–1906, SHOWING SUNKEN PANELS WITH PLANTINGS

other arrangement} coming to us that would meet requirements that you had prescribed.

You will remember that the expedient for keeping the view open was devised after discussion with you in 1887; that with your approval it was incorporated in our plans; was fully set forth, not only graphically, in the large drawings brought to Washington the following spring, but in the explanatory verbal statement printed with them, and that it appeared distinctly in the large perspective drawing of the Architects, afterwards photolithographed. Last fall it was brought again to your attention. We refer to the facts because we should feel not a little mortified to have expended all the labor we have upon these working drawings without having been fully assured that your assent had been well considered, received and made complete and final.

We shall be glad if you can propose a plan less open to objection for accomplishing your object. We have pondered the problem so much that we have no hope of being able to do so. We believe that when the apparent voids are filled up by the growth of the shrub foliage the effect will be satisfactory.

Very Respectfully Yours,

F. L. & J. C. Olmsted.

The text presented here is from a letterpress copy of a handwritten letter signed on the original in Olmsted's hand: A4: 967–70, OAR/LC. By the fall of 1888 the Stanford University plan had gone through significant revisions. Major additions to the plan included the Memorial Arch, over the main entrance to the quadrangle, a proposed arboretum to the south (never fully implemented), several hundred acres of forest plantations on the foothills (not implemented), and an avenue on the north side of the campus leading to a proposed railroad station. On the north side of the quadrangle, where the university library and museum were sited directly opposite the Memorial Church, Olmsted proposed a terrace between the buildings and the head of the approach avenue to the campus. Below the terrace would be "depressed areas, planted with masses of shrubbery over which a broad view of the principal buildings of the University will be had from the head of the Avenue" (Charles A. Coolidge to FLO, May 3, 1887; FLO to Charles A. Coolidge, May 22, 1887, above; FLO to Leland Stanford, April 12, 1888, B74: #1032, OAR/LC; "Notes Explanatory of the Leading Motives of the Plan," May 1888, B74: #1032, OAR/LC, "Plan of the Leland Stanford, Jr., University," *Garden and Forest*, Dec. 19, 1888, pp. 507–9; FLO to John G. McMillan, March 14, 1889, SUA; FLO to Thomas Douglas, Jan. 17, 1890, SUA; see also FLO to JCO, Dec. 1, 1888, Box H6, folder 2, OAR/LC; FLO to JCO, Dec. 5, 1888, Box H6, folder 2, OAR/LC).

1. Leland Stanford's first proposed changes to Olmsted's 1886 design came in May 1887, when he instructed project architect Charles A. Coolidge to rotate the inner quadrangle of buildings ninety degrees so that the Memorial Church would be the central feature of the quadrangle as it was entered. This change blocked the view out to the southern hills, which Olmsted had made the central feature in his 1886 plan. This change also required significant revisions of the proposed grades of the surrounding streets and around the church, and subsequent revisions involved making these adjustments as the work around the main quadrangle was completed (Charles A. Coolidge to FLO, May 3, 1887; FLO to Charles A. Coolidge, May 22, 1887, above; FLO to Leland Stanford, April 12, 1888, B74: #1032, OAR/LC; "Notes Explanatory of the Leading Motives of the Plan," May 1888, B74: #1032, OAR/LC; FLO to John G. McMillan, March 14, 1889, SUA; FLO to Thomas Douglas, Jan. 17, 1890, SUA; see also FLO to JCO, Dec. 1, 1888, Box H6, folder 2, OAR/LC; FLO to JCO, Dec. 5, 1888, Box H6, folder 2, OAR/LC).
2. John Gilmore McMillan (b. 1851), surveyor and civil engineer, had worked for Leland Stanford's Central Pacific Railroad in 1884, then served as chief engineer of construction at the Stanford University site from 1886 to 1890. He was the Santa Clara County surveyor from 1890 to 1914. The note that Olmsted refers to is not extant (Leigh Hadley Irvine, *A History of the New California: its Resources and People* (New York, 1905), p. 402; Stanford University Archives, "Guide to the Correspondence on the Architecture of Stanford University;" FLO to Ariel Lathrop, July 26, 1890, A9: 110, OAR/LC).
3. That is, the sunken earth panels, or "depressed areas," north of the main quadrangle on either side of Palm Drive (then University Avenue) as it approached the University. Olmsted's plan called for these areas to slope down to four feet below adjacent streets, and to be planted with shrubs and other low plants that would thrive in the local climate and soils. This treatment was an alternative to both turf, which would require irrigation, and trees, which would obscure the sight lines he hoped to keep open (FLO and JCO to John G. McMillan, July 16, 1889, SUA; JCO to John G. McMillan, Aug. 2, 1889, SUA; see also FLO to Charles A. Coolidge, May 22, 1887, above; "Study of General Plan," May 1888, B74: #1032, OAR/LC).

To Charles Henry Dalton

29th July, 1889.

My Dear Mr. Dalton;

Mr Lawrence[1] showed me the other day an interesting short letter from you about Richmond Park.[2] I am prompted by it to offer you a suggestion.

You will have seen by the papers that the Boston Park Commissioners, and, with them, the purpose and system they represent, have acquired the fixed virulent enmity of two politically powerful bodies, the Labor Reformers and the Evangelical Alliance, which last, for practical purposes, includes the Young Men's Christian Association and a great number of organizations of good people.[3] The leaders of the attack are pledged to upset the Commission and establish a new order of things, putting the Parks under the control of men holding views the reverse of those adopted under your leadership.

Early in the controversy the Labor reformers asserted that what they asked for was allowed in every other park. I at once addressed notes to a number of Park Commissioners to which the reply, in every case, was that the assertion was unfounded and that the proposition was to be reprobated.

Ground adjoining the Park was offered the Reformers; ground at various other points was offered them. All were disdained and the answer was: "We demand the Park—the right of free speech is denied us if we cannot have our meeting wherever we please in the Park". An absurd proposition, as it seems to me but the Parsons and the Mayor and the Globe newspaper sustain it.[4]

I believe that the cry here is but the taking up by the "Labor Reform" Agitators here, in a senseless, parrot-like way of a party cry originating under a very different state of things, with the old chartist agitators in London.[5]

In London, the claim is made, not entirely without reason, that by ancient prescriptive right, "the people", may meet in Hyde Park. It is not a right to meet anywhere in any of the Parks that is claimed, as I understand, but a right of old usage, in Hyde Park only. The exercise of this alleged right came after a time to be thought inconvenient and dangerous, and attempts, (poor, ill-considered and injudiciously managed, I suppose) to interfere with it were made—once when I was in London. I think in 1856 or 1857, a meeting was held in the Park, perhaps with reference to Sunday mail-carrying, at which there was a fight, and the next day I saw where trees had been broken down and iron fences and a platform, to supply the fighters with clubs. The not fully successful attempts on various subsequent occasions to prevent meetings in Hyde Park and lately at Charing Cross,[6] have made the right to hold meetings at these points, one of the demands of the labor reformers of London. But the original ground of this demand is very different from that upon which the demand of the Evangelicals and the Labor Reformers of Boston is based—being a right of ancient usage, applicable to particular places.

As the ordinance against public meetings in Franklin Park originated with you,[7] it is quite possible that you will be in some way drawn into a discussion of its propriety next winter. And you may find it convenient while in London; you may find it convenient if in Paris, to obtain more definite information on the subject than I have; first, confirmatory or otherwise of what I have above said; second, as to usage in other parks than Hyde; third, as to the results of experience & expert judgment, bearing upon the question of the expediency of allowing preaching and political warfare in grounds devoted to tranquilizing recreation.

Excuse me for suggesting that this would be a pleasant way of passing your vacation!

I hope that you are having a good time and, with kind regards to Mrs. Dalton, remain,

Faithfully Yours

Fred[k] Law Olmsted

The text presented here is from a letterpress copy of a handwritten letter signed on the original in Olmsted's hand: A5: 69–73, OAR/LC.

1. Francis William Lawrence (1839–1903) was a Brookline park commissioner from 1880 to 1890, a selectman from 1876 to 1890, and president of the Brookline National Bank from 1896 until his death ("Prominent in Brookline," *Boston Daily Globe*, March 11, 1903, p. 7).
2. Richmond Park is a large Royal Park in southwest London. Dalton's letter to Lawrence has not been found (Donald Edgar, *The Royal Parks* [London, 1986], pp. 149–60).
3. On July 4, 1889, the Boston park commissioners refused to allow the Central Labor Union to hold a public meeting in Franklin Park, causing members of that organization to protest that their rights had been violated. On July 23, the Evangelical Alliance, an association representing evangelical Christians who were members of unions, joined other trade groups for a formal protest in Faneuil Hall. They argued that public parks had no more important use than that of spaces for public assembly ("Unions Against Mayor," *Boston Daily Globe*, July 3, 1889, p. 5; "Autocrats of the Park: Laboring Men to Make Public Protest," ibid., July 10, 1889, p. 2; "Labor's Voice," ibid., July 24, 1889, p. 1).
4. The "Parsons" presumably were members of the Evangelical Alliance who actively advocated free speech, partly due to their interest in being allowed to preach in public parks. On June 30, 1889, M. R. Deming preached to a large crowd on the Common on the topic of "The Central Labor Union and Franklin Park." Also, A. H. Plumb and A. J. Gordon of the Evangelical Alliance spoke at the Faneuil Hall protest rally on July 23. Although Boston's Mayor Thomas N. Hart did not believe he had the authority to "overrule the park commissioners," a member of the Central Labor Union publicly stated that the mayor told the union that they "were right in asking for Franklin Park." Throughout the month of July the *Boston Daily Globe* covered the protests against the park commissioners and expressed support for the labor unions. On the morning of the Faneuil Hall meeting, the *Globe* editorialized, "The workingmen who were refused the right of assemblage in Franklin Park on the Fourth are to rock the old cradle tonight and give expression to their sense of the injustice done them. Let no guilty man escape!" ("Right of Public Meeting," *Boston Daily Globe*, July 1, 1889, p. 3; "In Faneuil Hall," ibid., July 23, 1889, p. 2; "Unions Against Mayor," ibid., July 3, 1889, p. 5; "Labor's Voice," ibid., July 24, 1889, p. 1; "Editorial Points," ibid., July 23, 1889, p. 4).
5. Chartism was a British political movement in the 1840s that inspired marches and demonstrations in the streets, parks, and commons of London and other cities to demand voting rights for all male citizens, and representative electoral districts (*EB*).
6. Hyde Park is a Royal Park in central London that by the nineteenth century had become the city's principal public park. Individuals and groups also used the park for public speeches and gatherings. Charing Cross, in the southern end of Trafalgar Square, was also a space in London where citizens gathered for meetings and protests. There were

no newsworthy riots in Hyde Park when Olmsted lived in London in the summer and fall of 1856, although the Sunday Trading Bill riots had occurred the previous summer. Despite the riots and related police actions, apparently the precedent of free speech associated with Hyde Park offered some protection for public speaking there. In the 1860s, Parliament began placing more restrictions on assembly in the park and, as debates ensued about the legality of these laws, major meetings continued to occur there. In November 1887, following major riots in Charing Cross, the police commissioner had banned all public meetings in London (Lisa Keller, *Triumph of Order: Democracy and Public Space in New York and London* [New York, 2009], pp. 28, 86–99, 108; *Papers of FLO*, 2: 22–23; Rodney Mace, *Trafalgar Square: Emblem of Empire* [London, 1976], pp. 155–203).

7. The Boston Common Council passed a city ordinance in 1885, during Dalton's tenure as a park commissioner, ordering that "no person shall, except by the permission of the mayor, deliver a sermon, lecture, address, or discourse on the common or other public grounds" (*The Revised Ordinances of 1885, of the City of Boston* [Boston, 1886], p. 135).

To Thomas Harvey Clark

Brookline, Mass., August 5th, 1889.

My Dear Sir:

I duly received your letter of 20th ult°.[1]

I am sorry for the Governor's decision. Perhaps my experience has given me too strong an impression of the disappointment that follows superficial and time-serving operations in matters of my profession and I am too much disposed to guard those who seek counsel of me against it. But I feel sure that if the property-{*holders*} and business men of Montgomery know their own interests they would not let funds be lacking for a more substantial improvement than the Governor thinks practicable. You understand that I have had no interest in the matter but a public and artistic interest.

You kindly say that you would like to know how I look upon the after troubles of slavery. I will tell you.

It was not reasonably to be expected when the war ended that the great body of intelligent whites of the South, should make no great a change in their habits as would be necessary to the placing of the freedmen all at once on a perfect equality with them before the law. It was to be feared that they, or numbers of them, would seek to take courses toward the freedmen that a great many people of the North would regard as outrageous; that they would continuously seek for means to pursue these courses without interference from the general government, and that this would lead to hateful political difficulties. Saying nothing of the better mind of the North, to its mercantile mind the principle gain to those of the winning side for their outlay to the war was escape from the continuous incitements to such difficulties growing out of the attempt of the southern part of the country to perpetuate a peculiar institution utterly inconsistent with the cardinal principle upon which our independence had been declared. There appeared to the mercantile mind danger that this gain would be lost. Then "the better mind" considered, also, that it was a duty to insure the freedmen as far as possible against such impositions upon them as were likely to be attempted under a supposed "social necessity".

And so to the majority of us who were not fanatical or influenced with party spirit, or any venal purpose, it seemed necessary that the freedmen should at once be given the ballot. And it is yet the prevailing judgment of the good people of the North, that only by this means was any permanent assurance to be had that some sort of quasi-slavery, or political subordination, of the freedmen, would not be attempted and thus the old state of sectional division and irritation be drifted into again.

It was not to be denied that the great mass of the freedmen were as yet ludicrously unfit to be trusted with the ballot. That the measures would be likely to lead to great evils, evils under which the whole country would suffer, no sensible man could doubt. A majority of those who favored it did so only as a choice between two dangers.

My choice at the time was the other way and what little influence I could use was directed against the measure. If I could I would have secured to the freedmen the full rights of intending citizens, yet unnaturalized. I would have had placed clearly before them, and at no indefinite or discouraging distance, perfect political equality with white citizens, but this upon conditions of making such political equality a privilege to be earned. I would have taken the chances of the unquestionable danger involved in doing so. I would have preferred this danger to that which was assured in admitting the negroes indiscriminately, at once, to voting citizenship. As far as I could judge those who differed with me did so, for the most part, because they took a more hopeful view than I did of the condition of the mass of the freedmen.

But that is past. I regard it now as one of the fixed conditions of the country, as surely fixed, for all practicable purposes, as its geological conditions, that our people of African blood are to stand on the same political footing as citizens of any other blood. Taking it to be so it remains only for us to make the best of it. Whatever peril it involves should be dealt with squarely, frankly, bravely. I don't believe in school education as a cure-all. But school education will be helpful and the more people do voluntarily to aid the school education of the freedmen the better it is for all of us. I look up gratefully to such men as General Armstrong.[2] I do not favor the "Blair Bill"[3] because I think its effect would be demoralizing. I should like to see laws in the South such as ours in Massachusetts, requiring that a man shall be able to read understandingly before he can qualify as a voter; such a law being applicable, of course, equally to white and black.[4]

The Negroes have been doing a great deal better as freedmen than

I had ever imagined it possible that they would. The whites have accepted the situation about as well as it was in human nature that they should and we have been advancing toward prosperity and in prosperity under the new state of things at the South amazingly more than I thought would be possible in so short a time after so great a catastrophe. And this prosperity is not that of speculation but, for the most part, honorably earned. Hence, I think, firm, lasting and progressive.

Since the war I have had several sons and daughters growing to an age of manhood. It pleases me to see how completely they are clear of the prejudices to political judgment fostered by the war and by what led us into the war. I have just put one of them under examination. The war is a historical circumstance upon which he apparently looks as impartially as upon the French and German war. He feels related to the people of the West no otherwise than to those of the South. More closely to those of the South, he volunteers to say, than to those of the "cattle country". "Canada? But the Canadians are foreigners". "And the Southerners"? Why, they are our people". "And you don't think of the Virginians as a different people from the Pennsylvanians"? "I don't know that I do any more than I think of New Jerseymen as different from Pennsylvanians".

I would not have you think that there is not yet a good deal of jealousy and anxiety and a sense of antagonism among people here growing out of the conviction that the whites of the South are not "playing fair" about the negroes at elections[5] but I am inclined to believe that while most of us deplore the state of things in this respect, we think that it was, for a time, in a large degree, inevitable. We are only anxious to have the more intelligent people of the South show a disposition and purpose to struggle out of it as fast as possible.

I have not meant to write as if I were a man of influence, or as if my views were to be considered those of a man notably thoughtful on the subject, or notably well informed. I have only tried to give you, in an off-hand way, what you have seemed interested to obtain.

Very truly yours,

Fred[k] Law Olmsted.

Hon. Thomas H. Clark;
Montgomery, Ala.

The text presented here is from a letterpress copy of a typed letter signed in Olmsted's hand: Olmsted Family Papers, H2: 13–19, OAR/LC. Thomas H. Clark, recording secretary to Alabama Governor Thomas Seay, published this letter in 1904 on Olmsted's views on the civil rights of African Americans after the Civil War (Thomas H. Clark, "Frederick Law Olmsted on the South, 1889," *South Atlantic Quarterly*, Jan. 1904, pp. 12–15; see also FLO to Thomas H. Clark, April 10, 1889, above; FLO to Thomas Seay, [July 1889], above).

1. Clark's July 20 letter to Olmsted conveyed his regret that he had missed him when Olmsted was in Montgomery. He wanted to meet Olmsted "more particularly because your books on the South made me curious to know something of your opinion on the problems that are before us now, the relics of Slavery" (Thomas H. Clark to FLO, July 20, 1889).
2. General Samuel Chapman Armstrong (1839–1893) was an educator who was best known for founding the Hampton Normal and Industrial Institute in Virginia in 1868, which eventually became Hampton University. An influence on Booker T. Washington, Armstrong's "Normal school" promoted the idea that industrial education would uplift African Americans (*DAB*; Robert Francis Engs, *Educating the Disfranchised and Disinherited* [Knoxville, Tenn., 1999]).
3. The Blair Education Bill was introduced in 1884 by Republican Senator Henry Blair of New Hampshire to provide federal financial aid for public education and, consequently, possibly increase African American and immigrant suffrage, because some states restricted voting rights through literacy tests. The bill passed the Republican controlled Senate, and, although it had bipartisan support, Democratic Speaker John G. Carlisle refused to bring it to a vote on the floor of the House of Representatives. When it was reintroduced in 1889, several Republicans argued that it would create a culture of beggars and, according to the *Chicago Tribune*, destroy the "quality of self-reliance." In 1890, it failed in the Senate and was not reintroduced (Charles W. Calhoun, *Conceiving a New Republic: The Republican Party and the Southern Question, 1869–1900* [Lawrence, Ky., 2006], pp. 198–200, 230–32).
4. Massachusetts adopted a required literacy test for voter registration in 1857. In 1889 the law stated that anyone who had not voted in the previous four years must take a literacy test before they could register to vote (Charles L. Zelden, *Voting Rights on Trial* [Santa Barbara, Cal., 2002], p. 53; Tyler Anbinder, *Nativism and Slavery: The Northern Know Nothings and the Politics of the 1850s* [New York, 1992], p. 138).
5. This concern is an echo of Olmsted's appeal in the concluding letter of his series of articles on the South and slavery in the *New-York Daily Times* in the early 1850s, "Let all who do not think Slavery right, or who do not desire to assist in perpetuating it, whether right or wrong, demand first of their own minds, and then of their neighbors, FAIR PLAY FOR THE NEGRO.'" ("The South," Number 48, *New-York Daily Times*, Feb. 13, 1854).

To William L. Fischer

6th August, 1889.

My Dear Mr Fischer;

I was obliged to leave you this afternoon, in order to meet Colonel Livermore[1] before we had had our talk out.

As I have thought of what you said, since, it has seemed to me to imply quite a decided misunderstanding between us. Let us see what it is. I have supposed that the large number of very conspicuously flowering plants along the base of the overlook wall had been set there as a means to a temporary and provisional effect while the plants necessary to the designed permanent effect *were growing to be large enough to produce that permanent effect*. What you said this afternoon seemed to imply that such a display of flowers as we have had this year was designed to be permanent and that you had not had it in view, and did not suppose that I had, that these plants were to be gradually thinned out as the other plants, (chiefly bushes and vines) grew large enough to be effective.

I have never desired to have any broad or high display of flowers, especially of flowers of herbaceous plants of any kind, either at the Overlook or on the Fens, and if you have at any time thought that I assented to your planting with a view to such displays at either place, it is because I had understood you to wish to use the plants in question as a means of rendering the stones of the Overlook wall, and of its base, less conspicuous, and of covering the nakedness of the ground, *during the period in which the vines and other woody plants would be growing to accomplish these purposes*.

You will remember that in the spring of 1887, I conferred with you very fully on the ground in regard to the permanent planting of the face and the base of the Overlook wall and of the ground below it. I explained to you at length my general views and you fully assented to them. But, to make quite sure that there could be no misunderstanding, before you began planting I sent you a long and careful statement of my views in a plain type-written letter, of which I retained a copy.[2] I have just looked it over, and, as you doubtless have it, I wish that you would oblige me by hunting it up and reading it again. If you had not thought that I was right in what I had in view in that letter, I hope that you would have been careful to tell me so before you began planting. You did not. On the contrary you wrote me that you believed that you fully understood my wishes and that you were well disposed to secure the realization of them.

My intentions on this point had been so carefully considered before the building of the wall was begun, and I had set them before you for discussion so often and so fully, even before I wrote them carefully out for you, that if there has been any misunderstanding between us on this point, I cannot think that it is due to me, or that you can feel aggrieved at my holding more strenuously to my opinions than I am generally apt to do when I find that you do not go with me.

If you have *come later* to think that what I originally proposed is absolutely wrong, that is to say, in *positively bad taste*, then I want you to tell me so and try to make me understand how it is so. You know that I am not disposed to ask you to do anything which *you* think in bad taste. But there is a great difference between asking you to do something which you think in bad taste, and asking to do something which you think is {*only*} not as good as possible.

So, if you do not think such a conspicuous display of flowers as we have hitherto had, both at the Overlook and at the Fens, absolutely necessary to good taste; if you do not think that it would be in positively bad taste to make less display of that kind, you will oblige me by having in view after this a *gradual* reduction of them, and, at the Overlook, a *gradual complete recurrence to the views expressed in my letter to you of the 21st of July, 1887.*

VIEW OF PLAYSTEAD OVERLOOK SHELTER, FRANKLIN PARK, BOSTON, C. 1905

And as to the question of good taste, we often see ladies very splendidly dressed with jewels and bright ribbons and flowers and agree that it is in good taste. We see other ladies dressed quietly without jewelry or any finery of color or material, and we agree that they also are dressed in good taste. If the difference between us is a difference between two ideas, each of which is in good taste, then I think that I have a right to ask you to adopt my more modest rather than your more splendid preference.

Always affectionately Yours,

Fred[k] Law Olmsted

The text presented here is from a letterpress copy of a handwritten letter signed on the original in Olmsted's hand: A5: 106–9, OAR/LC (see "Specifications for Playstead Terrace, Franklin Park," July 30, 1885, above; FLO to William L. Fischer, July 21, 1887, above).

1. Thomas L. Livermore (1855–1918), lawyer and businessman, was best known as a mining financier with the Calumet & Hecla Mining Company. He lived in Boston for much of his life, was a close friend of Francis Amasa Walker's, and served as a Boston park commissioner from 1889 to 1893 (*Fifteenth Annual Report of the Board of Park Commissioner for the Year 1889* [Boston, 1890], p. 30; "Col. Livermore Dies at Age of 74," *Boston Evening Globe*, Jan. 10, 1918; *Nineteenth Annual Report of the Board of Park Commissioner for the Year 1894* [Boston, 1895], p. 82).
2. See FLO to William L. Fischer, July 21, 1887, above.

TO CALVIN COOKE LANEY[1]

Brookline, Mass., Aug. 9th, 1889.

C. C. Laney, Esq.,
Dear Sir;

We send you by express five sheets of plans of the Meadow Park,[2] showing, on a scale of 40 ft. to an inch, the outlines of most of the drives and walks. All of the circuit drive and the approach to it from Elmwood Avenue is shown.

While the immediate purpose of these drawings is to enable you to begin work at once on stripping off the topsoil, it is expected that they will serve also as the working drawings for the construction of the roads and walks except as regards grades. The lines may, however, have to be modified, somewhat, in places, when the grades are more carefully studied out.

We enclose some detailed instructions for the disposition of the topsoil stripped off the road and walk near the river, and the same instructions, in the main, would apply to all the roads and walks on the flat land.

On the hill sides and where a foot or more of cutting or filling will have to be done along the edge of the drives and walks, the stripping will have to be extended beyond the outlines of the drives and walks. As to this you will have to use your judgment.

You may, however, be aided by the general rule that "in forming the side slopes for drives and walks, there should be allowed a level or nearly level border of five feet on steep side hills or in deep cuts or fills and the slopes from this border to the natural surface should be formed to *varying*, *ogee*-curved cross-sections, no part of which should be steeper than one vertical to two horizontal".

"On level or nearly level ground the difference in grade between the natural surface and that of the drives and walks should be overcome by nearly level borders ten feet wide and slopes having long, varying, ogee-curved cross-sections, not steeper than one in ten".

In both cases particular care should always be taken to join the new slope to the natural surface so gradually and gently that no one can tell where the junction has been made. The object of having the border of at least five feet nearly level on top of an embankment next {to} a drive, aside from its greater naturalness, is to lessen the danger of accident, in case of running off the drive, and to lessen the *appearance* of that danger.

The object of having the slope above the drive begin five feet or more from the drive is, aside from its greater naturalness, to allow room for a gentle, hardly perceptible gutter in the turf, which will both withhold the surface water from flowing off the hillside upon the drive and tearing up the gravel, and also take the surface water from the drive itself; thus doing away with the necessity for a paved gutter in the drive.

If you will send us a profile of the natural surface along the {*centre*} line of the road, when staked out, we will indicate a suitable profile for the road.

The elevations of trees coming within ten or twenty feet of the drive should be noted on the profile. After the profile has been established you may send us a few cross-sections of the natural surface and we will draw upon them the proper cross section for the finished surface of the slopes. The profiles should be plotted to 40 ft. horizontal and 4 ft. vertical scales.

Please have copies made of the accompanying "suggestions" and supply your assistants with them and make them thoroughly understand them.

Yours truly,

F. L. Olmsted & Co.

Suggestions for the treatment of the River bank in connection with the construction of the Road and Walk.

Where the west edge of the road is to be within 50 feet of the river bank, a space of about 50 feet should be reserved on the east side of the road {of} which space is not to be prepared for turf until after the road is made.

Upon this space the sod and soil to be excavated for the road and walk beds are to be deposited so that in the end the soil upon this reserved space will be on an average 5 to 8 inches deeper than it is at present, but not uniformly so, there being occasional knolls and hollows, the surface being undulating, with care that the undulations are graceful, nowhere abrupt, and that they play gently into the natural surface still further east, and into the "turf gutters" which will generally be 40 to 60 feet east of the road. The undulations are also to be so managed that there will be occasional depressions of the surface trending transversely to the line of the road, by which water flowing off the road will find its way to the turf gutters. Great care must be taken to avoid uniformity in the size and succession of swells, so that no suspicion will occur that they are artificial or of a different order from those of the natural surface from this {*cant*}.[3]

As a rule the surface on the river side of the walk and immediately bordering it is to correspond with that on the east side of the road but for want of room the undulations can be but slight and but rarely can there be any ground higher than the road. The section between the walk and the water will generally be a perfect "ogee" varying constantly in degree of boldness. At intervals of from 100 to 500 feet there should be spaces in which the inclination is much less steep than elsewhere, the intention being that at these points there shall be gaps in the water side planting and either an unbroken turf slope to the water or to plants on the margin of the water, or a beach. In either case to get the necessary gentleness of inclination it may be necessary to dip the surface of the adjoining walk so that it will be considerably lower than the surface of the drive. In case the character of a beach is to be had in view the walk will be a part of the beach, sloping toward

VIEW OF GENESEE VALLEY PARK, ROCHESTER, N.D.

the water with an inclination not steeper than one in six. The space between the drive and the walk will then desirably be wider than it ordinarily is and will have an ogee section.

The lines of the plan are not to be strictly adhered to, especially in respect to such particulars as are above referred to, but opportunity must be sought in minor inequalities of the natural surface, slight indentations of the shore and natural drainage depressions, for revision and improvement of detail.

Suggestions for Treatment of Slopes of Roads and Walks.

"In forming the side slopes for drives and walks on steep sidehills or in deep cuts or hills, there should be allowed a level or nearly level border of five feet and the slopes from this border to the natural surface should be formed to *varying, ogee* curved cross-sections no part of which should be steeper than one vertical to two horizontal".

"On level or nearly level ground the difference in grade between the natural surface and that of the drives and walks should be overcome by nearly level borders ten feet wide and slopes having long, varying, ogee curved cross-sections, not steeper than one in ten".

In both cases particular care should always be taken to join the new slope to the natural surface so gradually and gently that no one can tell where the junction had been made.[4]

The text presented here is from a letterpress copy of a typewritten letter signed on the original in Olmsted's hand: A5: 130–35, OAR/LC (see FLO to Edward Mott Moore, Aug. 5, 1888, above; FLO to Edward Mott Moore, Jan. 26, 1889, above; FLO to Robert Douglas, [summer 1889], above).

1. Calvin Cooke Laney (1850–1941) worked as a railroad surveyor and opened his own office in Rochester in 1885. In 1888 he became superintendent of the Rochester parks. His first assignment was to survey the lands acquired to create Genesee Valley Park. Over the years, Laney worked closely with the Olmsted firm on construction and maintenance of Highland and Genesee Valley parks as well as other small parks and squares. He also collaborated with horticulturist John Dunbar to create Highland, Maplewood, Cobb's Hill, Seneca, Durand Eastman, and Ontario Beach parks. Laney was made a park commissioner in 1920, a post he held until his retirement in 1928 ("Laney-Hoeing Family" Manuscript Collection, University of Rochester Library, "Collection Overview"; "Calvin Laney Dies; Developed Parks," *New York Times*, Aug. 24, 1941, p. 34; see also FLO to Edward Mott Moore, Jan. 26, 1889, above).
2. That is, Genesee Valley Park.
3. Cant, as in "an inclined or slanting face of a bank, or the like" (*OED*).
4. This is one of the fullest descriptions given by Olmsted of the use of an ogee-curve in grading plans, particularly to blend the surface of a road or walk into the existing topography of a site. An ogee-curve is an S-shaped double curve, which in this case describes a section through the shoulder of the roadway and its adjacent drainage swale.

To William L. Fischer

11th August, 1889.

Dear Mr. Fischer:

You have had so much to do with men who were prejudiced against you and were unjustly disposed to you; who were inclined to disparage your art and your ability, to derogate from your responsibilities and to disregard your feelings, that it would not be surprising if it had affected your habits of mind in a way to make you too ready to look for injustice in those who are not in the least disposed to be unjust. I cannot see otherwise how my note to you of the 6th[1] could have made the impression upon you that from your reply of the 9th it evidently did. On the contrary I do not see how, if I had taken particular pains, to prevent its conveying such an impression, I could have much better guarded against it.

You refer to it as accusing you of having "*planted the Overlook contrary to instructions*". No man reading it fairly can in my opinion find in it the slightest ground for assuming that it was intended to convey such a thought. It certainly was not. I certainly never had such a thought. If I had thought you had in any respect, with deliberate intention, acted in that respect or any other in matters of the Parks contrary to my instructions, do you think I should have written to you about it in such terms as I did write? If I had written to you at all it would have been to ask for your resignation. Then, failing to receive it, I should have asked the Board to drop you, as I asked the New York Board to drop Prof[r] Demcker, for a similar reason.[2]

You assume that having given you a list of plants to be used on the Overlook I have afterwards given you occasion to write to me in this way:—"*I did not know that I was not at liberty to add some herbaceous plants that I thought would improve the effect*". I have never given you reason to say anything like that to me.

My letter to you of 1887,[3] to which you refer as if it might have been intended to give you exact and particular instructions as to all the detail of planting, was not so intended, nor in my note of the 6th did I at all assume that it was. It may have seemed to go further into detail than I often do go in giving instructions to you but that was only because the Overlook wall was a very nice and critical point in the design and it was more difficult to convey to you what I had in mind than it often is. Because of its difficulties and because I could not otherwise be confident that you would understand what effects I was aiming at, I tried to make as clear and plain to you as I could the considerations that had affected my mind and thus convey to you the general principles and motives of the design which I wished you, with your superior botanical and horticultural knowledge, to carry out. It contained no *list* and it referred to no list of the plants that were to be used. It mentioned a considerable number of plants, not for the purpose of prescribing to you what alone should be used, but as illustrations of classes of plants that would have certain characteristics adapting them to be used, and out of which class you would {*select*} at your discretion plants to be used to produce certain effects, some more particularly at the top of the wall, some on its face, some at its base and some in front of its base. These plants that I mentioned were mentioned, I repeat, as an indication of the general character of the plants by which the {*effects desired might be in time be obtained*}. You were not simply at "liberty", as you say, to add other plants if you could find any that you could be sure would add to the designed effects, you were, if I am not mistaken, plainly asked and required to do so. And I suppose that you did carry out these directions faithfully and that you did exercise that discretion, or use that "liberty", {*freely*} and well in your shrubs and vines and the larger part of your perennial planting. I do not think that *some* of the plants that have been {*conspicuous*} since and that I suppose to have been planted mainly after the shrubs had been planted, are adapted to combine with the shrubs and vines so as to blend with them in producing just the effects that in writing you in 1887, I had in view. I had not till now supposed that you had planted them on the supposition that they were. I thought that they were fast and large growing plants that would serve the purpose of quickly furnishing the place and obscuring the heap of stones, while the plants intended for ultimate effect were coming on. If I had supposed that you thought that the plants I refer to were producing the effect that I looked for ultimately, I should sooner have advised you that you were mistaken. What we have to do now is not just what I wanted in all respects; it is not what I now look forward to having in the future, nor is it consistent with what

I want and look forward to. If you have thought it was, as doubtless you have, it is because I have not succeeded in conveying my conception to you. It has simply been a mistake for which I do not hold you responsible, and for which I have not, by a single word, blamed you. If by looking over my note again you can find that I have, then that was an inadvertent word, and I take it back.

But the mistake having occurred it remains now to have it corrected. Therefore and in order that you may correct it I now tell you that the proportion of plants conspicuous for their blooms, in looking toward the face of the Overlook wall from the Playstead is larger than I have designed it to be with reference to permanent effects, and the shrubs and vines and the perennials that are less conspicuous in a general view of the Overlook from the Playstead having this year come to be generally of fairly good size I think it time to *begin* the removal of all plants such as I have considered to have been planted for temporary effect. I do not attempt to instruct you as to the rapidity, or the order, or the amounts of their removal. I say that it should be *gradual* and that it is not to be made certainly on any large scale until you are satisfied that what will be left behind will not be offensive to your own taste, because of its meagerness or otherwise.

I do not understand that you do not like what I like in this matter. I understand that you would prefer to have a good deal more of certain elements *permanently* than I want *permanently*. So the difference between us is simply of degree. A difference as to the degree in which it is desirable that certain forms of bloom should be conspicuously displayed permanently. You mention that *rhododendrons* and *yuccas* and *sedums*, which at certain points I have asked you to plant have as conspicuous blooms as anything you have planted. As this gives an opportunity of *explaining* my views better perhaps, I will take it. There is no place where I have asked you to put any of these plants that I have wished them to be because of their effect during the flowering season. It is because they would, during the summer produce certain *foliage* effects better than anything else that I could think of in those places. I have not asked you to put Rhododendrons on the Overlook because I have not wanted the effect of Rhododendron *foliage* there. I asked you to put sedums on the top of the wall because I know of no other desirable foliage likely to thrive in the crevices of the rocks. I consider the conspicuousness of their *bloom* in that place *an objection* to them. I should prefer them less conspicuous in that respect, and in advising them to be used I had distinctly in view that *Rhus aromatica* would generally be planted outside of them and immediately below and would grow up so that the bloom of the sedums would not be seen from the Playstead or the walk below. I thought too that they would soon be in a great degree obscured by *Genista* and by *Euonymus R.* and *Ampelopsis Veitchii*, growing from the outside over the top of the wall. This was what I was most anxious for and am still anxious for. I am disappointed that the plants I have here named, (as I named them prominently in my letter of 1887), *are not yet grown* so as to *appear in very much larger proportion*.

As to yuccas, my views are the same. When in bloom they are too conspicuous. I would prefer fewer of them in prominent positions along the upper part of the wall. I think that any large bodies of bloom standing out conspicuously so as to attract the eye from general effects of foliage in mass; anything that does not in a general view from a little distance blend with the forms and tints of the foliage, is out of place in this locality. I do not object to a good many small flowers *mixing* with the foliage, and especially if in the shadows of the foliage, so as to be inconspicuous, but I do object to such a display of bloom, that is to say of bright color, in masses and patches and great constellations, as you seem to have supposed that I had had in view in my instructions of 1887.

What I have said on this point applies, as you have inferred, to the Fens as well. At various points in the Fens, as well as at the Overlook, you will please have in view a *more moderate* display of plants conspicuous because of their showy blooms. If you think that I am making a mistake in asking this of you, don't fail to consider that what I ask is greater *moderation* in the carrying out of your ideas where they do not fully accord with mine. No man respects your taste and judgment more than I do, or is more disposed to concede to them where he can.

Yours Truly

Fred[k] Law Olmsted

The text presented here is from a letterpress copy of a handwritten letter signed on the original in Olmsted's hand: A5: 136–43, OAR/LC).

1. See FLO to William L. Fischer, Aug. 6, 1889, above. Fischer's Aug. 9 letter has not been found.
2. Robert Demcker (1821–1925) had joined the New York City Park Department in 1871 as a draftsman in the Bureau of Landscape Gardeners. He was the head of the office of landscape gardeners for Central Park from July 1873 to February 1875. A change in the by-laws of the park department in 1873 made it possible for Demcker to perform supervisory duties that had previously been Olmsted's. During those years, he "had complete control of the exotic and propagation department and was allowed to superintend any landscape plans that the board approved and assigned to him, including his own." Due to the inefficiency of this re-organization and protests by Olmsted, the by-laws of 1873 were repealed and Demcker was fired in 1875. He was replaced, upon Olmsted's suggestion, by Fischer ("To the Board of Commissioners of the Department of Public Parks, New York City, March 1, 1875" [*Papers of FLO*, 7: 124–29]; see also *Papers of FLO*, 7: 81 n. 7, 81–82 n. 14).
3. FLO to William L. Fischer, July 21, 1887, above.

CHAPTER XI

AUGUST 1889–MARCH 1890

In late 1889, Olmsted was planning parks and residential communities in many parts of the United States. Three letters to Charles A. Roberts reflect his frustration with the owners of Perry Park, in Colorado, where Olmsted was designing a residential village, because they wanted to rush construction and were not heeding his advice concerning the creation of a residential community in a semiarid region. Regarding Boston parks, a letter to William L. Fischer provides instructions for planting Ellicott Arch in Franklin Park, and a letter to Matthias D. Ross continues the debate on establishing zoological gardens and aquariums in Boston's parks. The letter to Frederick W. Vanderbilt explores alternative treatments of the grounds of his Rough Point estate. The letters to engineer William A. Thompson and superintendent James G. Gall, Jr., provide instructions for laying out the approach road on the Biltmore estate. A letter to Henry R. Towne is part of a correspondence between Olmsted and several New Yorkers about where in New York to hold the 1893 World's Columbian Exhibition if the city is chosen to host the fair. The August 20, 1889, letter to Sylvester Baxter discusses land the park commissioners of Lynn, Massachusetts, are considering for a forest reserve, and his letter to Philip A. Chase provides an analysis of how Lynn Woods should be managed.

Olmsted continued to be interested in writing and publishing on the theory and definition of the profession of landscape architecture. In a September 2, 1889, letter to Sylvester Baxter, he considers the difference between landscape architecture and gardening, while his letter to the editor of *American Florist* sets forth the difference between ornamental gardening and landscape gardening. Olmsted's letter to Robert Underwood Johnson restates his earlier reluctance to address publicly the present condition of the Yosemite reservation. He reconsiders, however, and five months later writes *Governmental Preservation of Natural Scenery* after the governor of California publishes misleading statements about him and his views on Yosemite. His retrospective letter to Charles Loring Brace of January 18, 1890, is his last surviving letter to one of his oldest friends, who died seven month later.

To Sylvester Baxter[1]

20th Aug. 1889.

My Dear Baxter;

Apropos of Mr Paine's note in Herald today[2] (which follows my note repeated from the Century some time ago)[3] I was asked a few days ago to examine land proposed to be taken by Lynn Park Commissioners—a yet unorganized body—and was delighted with what I saw. The undertaking has been managed quietly to this time, I suppose in order to gain advantage in purchases, but, thinking of you, I asked Mr. Chase, (P. A.)[4] who appears the prime mover, if he wd object to some publication about it now, and he thought not. It is a continuation of the Middlesex Fells,[5] and has all the characteristics of that region. They propose to secure for the public 1000 acres, mainly an amphitheater in any general overlook of which you see nothing but wood, water & rock. The wood is young but promising with some masses of larger fine trees. There will be I should think 200 acres of water in it—basins of Lynn Water Supply, to some extent artificial but to be so crowded about by wood that in broad landscape effect it will tell as if natural. There are several grand rocky eminences, and at one point a view over the town upon the broad ocean.

Its value as a roving ground not for Lynn and the northern suburbs only but for the people of Boston, in the future, cannot well be overestimated. At least I rate it higher than the Commissioners and they are not unappreciative. It shd be to Boston something like Fontainebleau to Paris and Richmond & Windsor to London.[6] The townspeople of Lynn do not appreciate it, I judge. Probably want a park or public garden. It is, what is so much better, a real forest.

I think you could make a good illustrated paper of it, though the character of the scenery is not well adapted to newspaper pictures. The illustrations should be the most sketchy possible, chiefly horizon outlines and merely suggestive indications of continuous bodies of foliage. I should say one from Burrill's Hill looking eastward over the amphitheatre and one from Pine Hill looking seaward. They would be better sketched by an artist with the proper idealization and exaggeration rather than from photographs. Vignette illustrations could be taken from photographs of picturesque bits, near view of craggy rocks &c.[7]

Yours Truly

Fred^{k} Law Olmsted.

The text presented here is a signed letter in Olmsted's hand. Lynn Woods is an area of over two thousand acres of forest, ponds, and granite hills located just inland from the town of Lynn, Massachusetts. Unusable for most agriculture, Lynn Woods remained a forested common until 1706, and afterwards town ordinances restricted the development of the area. In 1870 the city of Lynn acquired Breed's Pond, which served as its water supply. In 1881, a group of citizens established a private trust to accept gifts of land in Lynn Woods and hold the property for the benefit of the public. The trust preserved about one hundred fifty acres in this way as a "Free Public Forest." In 1889, a significant portion of Lynn Woods was flooded to create a larger water source for the town, and new roads were built as part of the project, making the area more accessible, and raising concerns for its future preservation. That year a group of citizens pledged over $20,000 for the acquisition of additional land in Lynn Woods, and in July the city council responded by authorizing the sale of an additional $30,000 in bonds for the same purpose. The first Board of Park Commissioners was formed on November 6, 1888 (Nathan Mortimer Hawkes, *In Lynn Woods With Pen and Camera* [Lynn, Mass., 1893], pp. 1–9; *First Annual Report of the Park Commissioners of the City of Lynn* [Lynn, Mass., 1890]; see FLO to Philip A. Chase, Nov. 29, 1889, below).

1. Sylvester Baxter (1850–1927) was a journalist and a leading advocate for the creation of regional parks around Boston. He became an important ally to Charles Eliot in these efforts. While in the pages of *Garden and Forest* Eliot first suggested the idea for what became The Trustees of Reservations, Baxter wrote in the *Boston Herald* on the need for a metropolitan park commission that would serve the entire region across municipal boundaries. When that regional park commission was established in 1892, Eliot became its landscape architect and Baxter served as its secretary ("Sylvester Baxter, Publicist is Dead," *New York Times*, Jan. 29, 1927, p. 15; Karl Haglund, *Inventing the Charles River* [Cambridge, Mass., 2003], pp. 120–26; FLO to Sylvester Baxter, Nov. 9, 1880 [*Papers of FLO*, 7: 510–12]; Gordon Abbott, Jr., *Saving Special Places: A Centennial History of The Trustees of Reservations* [Ipswich, Mass., 1993], pp. 8–21).
2. Robert Treat Paine (1835–1910) was a lawyer and businessman from Boston who in the 1880s became a leading philanthropist, founding the Wells Memorial Institute for Workingmen and other institutions, including the Associated Charities of Boston. He also served as a director of Charles Loring Brace's Children Aid's Society. In 1884, H. H. Richardson designed Paine's home in Waltham, Massachusetts, Stonehurst, for which Olmsted designed the grounds. The "note in the Herald" that Olmsted mentions here may have been "Buying up the Views," one of the anonymous contributions published in the paper that day. In it, the author lamented the fact that so much of the north and south shores of Massachusetts Bay were in private hands, which prevented the casual summer traveler from enjoying the scenery and benefitting from its spiritual and physical gifts: "It gives the monopoly of nature, at what the world calls its best, to the few, and not to the many. . . . Little has been thought of it while the process was going on, but the fact stares one in the face that at the present time nearly every part of the New England coast which is most attractive to the pleasure-seeking public is in private hands, and cannot be

trodden upon by the stranger, except through the courtesy of the owner" (*DAB*; "Buying up the Views," *Boston Herald*, Aug. 20, 1889).

3. Olmsted may have recently written a "note" to the *Boston Herald* repeating ideas that first appeared in "A Healthy Change in the Tone of the Human Heart," *Century Illustrated Monthly Magazine*, Oct. 1886, above, and Paine's note was a response to it.
4. Philip Augustus Chase (1834–1903), a banker and businessman in Lynn, led the public campaign to raise over $20,000 to acquire the land in Lynn Woods in 1889. He then served in various functions on the Board of Park Commissioners for Lynn from 1889 until 1898. Chase also was first chair of The Trustees of Reservations, a Metropolitan Park Commissioner, a member of the Committee for the Preservation of Beautiful and Historical Places in Massachusetts, and the first president of the Lynn Historical Society (C. J. H. Woodbury, *Philip Augustus Chase: A Memorial Sketch* [Lynn, Mass., 1904], pp. 5–7; *First Annual Report, Lynn Park Commissioners, 1890*, p. 5; *Park Commissioners Report of the City of Lynn, Massachusetts* [Lynn, Mass., 1899], pp. 1, 9; "Lynn Historical Society," *Lynn Item*, Oct. 5, 2002, p. C8; see also FLO to Philip A. Chase, Nov. 29, 1889, below).
5. Middlesex Fells, a wooded area of over two thousand acres, was the site of ponds, wetlands, and rock outcrops northwest of Boston. In 1879, Baxter published an article in the *Boston Herald* in which he suggested the name Middlesex Fells for the area and argued for its preservation. With Elizur Wright and others, Baxter organized the Middlesex Fells Association in 1880 and wrote Olmsted soliciting his advice. Olmsted, who had visited the area in 1879, urged Baxter to "take it as it stands, develop to the utmost its natural characteristics, and make a true retreat not only from town but from suburban conditions" (Sylvester Baxter, *Boston Park Guide, Including the Municipal and Metropolitan Systems of Greater Boston* [Boston, 1898], pp. 50–58; Rosewell B. Lawrence, *Middlesex Fells* [Boston, 1886], pp. 199–205; FLO to Sylvester Baxter, Nov. 9, 1880 [*Papers of FLO*, 7: 510–12]).
6. Olmsted refers to large parks around Paris and London that in the nineteenth century became significant recreational destinations for the growing populations of those cities. The Château of Fontainebleau, to the southeast of Paris, is surrounded by the Fontainebleau Forest, which consists of over six thousand acres. Richmond Park, which is over two thousand acres, is the largest of the Royal Parks in London. Windsor Great Park is a five-thousand acre park adjacent to Windsor Castle in Berkshire and Surrey, England (Patrick Taylor, ed., *The Oxford Companion to the Garden* [Oxford, 2006], pp. 166–67, 287, 516; Kimberly A. Jones, et al., *In the Forest of Fontainebleau* [Washington, D.C., 2008], pp. 4–27; Charles Lyte, *The Royal Gardens in Windsor Great Park* [London, 1998], pp. 17–18).
7. Baxter published an illustrated pamphlet in 1891 titled *The Great Woods Park of Lynn: Lynn's Public Forest: A Hand-Book Guide to the Great Woods Park of the City of Lynn.* It included a transcript of Olmsted's 1889 letter to Chase (FLO to Philip A. Chase, Nov. 29, 1889, below).

To Charles A. Roberts[1]

Brookline, Mass., August 20th. 1889.

Mr. C.A. Roberts;
Denver, Colo.
My Dear Sir; I am sorry that I have not been able sooner to reply to your note of 7th., inst., having been absent on business.

I am too ignorant of the premises to advise you with confidence but I ought to tell you that such apprehension as you found evinced in my last letter to you is rather increased than lessened by your reply to it.[2] I am afraid that you have not taken in the full significance of what I have said or of what was written in the longer of the two communications addressed to General Hughes on the 15th. January.[3]

It is so much my habit to consider turf and foliage, or fresh and lively vegetation in various forms, as a necessity of any pleasant rural abode, that I do not readily conceive of a man's choosing to build a house with a view to enjoyment of the country in a place that has no charms of local domestic vegetation. When I remarked upon the lack, in the place that you first had in view for your summer village, not only of vegetation, but apparently of soil or vegetable mould, and the consequent barren and forlorn aspect of the locality, you said "You have only to put water on it and it will blossom like the rose". I then inquired about the facilities for putting water on it, and from what you and General Hughes said, I supposed that you had the intention of providing liberal water works at once.

The problem that I was studying after that was, how with water and without excessive constant expense and trouble in distributing it, a village could be formed that would be continuously neat and verdant in all its parts. Continuously, I say, because, if, in a village which is generally neat and verdant, there are vacant lots forming neglected squalid places, they are peculiarly offensive and destructive of the attractiveness of the entire village. And this would be the case in a village built on one street around a pond as proposed, more strikingly than in one of cross and parallel streets.

Read now in view of what I have just said, my letter to General Hughes and you will see that it embodies the assumption that to sell lots in sufficient number and at sufficient prices to warrant the operations proposed, the place must have been first made attractive by means that could only be successfully pursued with a liberal use of water.

Building a road around the pond will not increase the attractiveness of the locality as a place for vacation in a cottage, it will greatly lessen it. It will present raw artificial banks to view in place of the present rude wild nature.

And with due deference to your better knowledge of Denver human nature, I greatly doubt if you can find people who will discount in their minds the value to be acquired by carrying out the plan upon which we are engaged. I

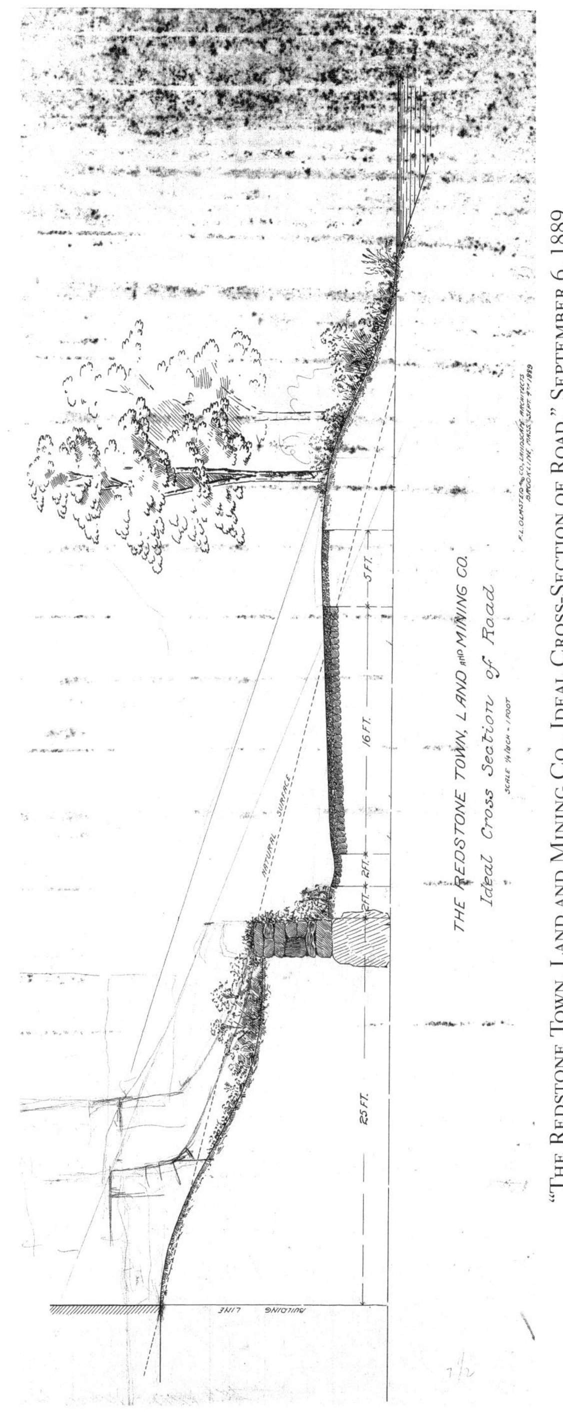

"The Redstone Town, Land and Mining Co., Ideal Cross-Section of Road," September 6, 1889

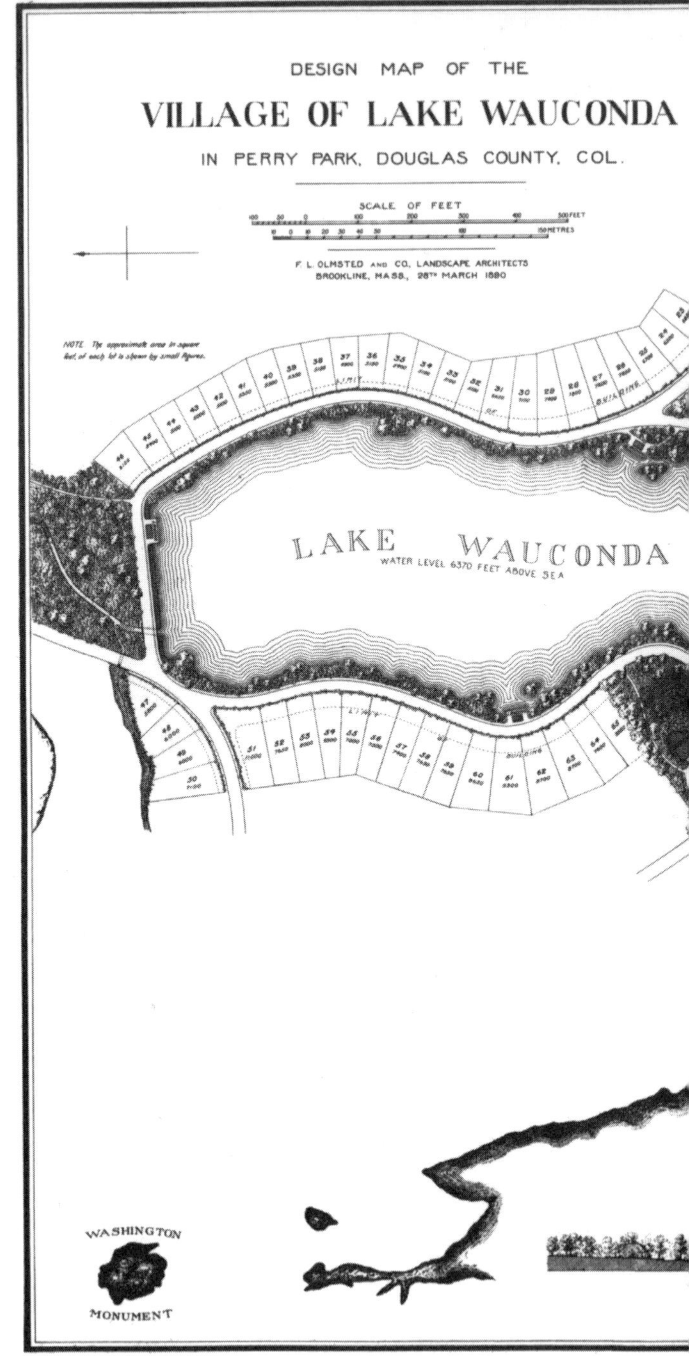

"Design Map of the Village of Lake Wauconda i

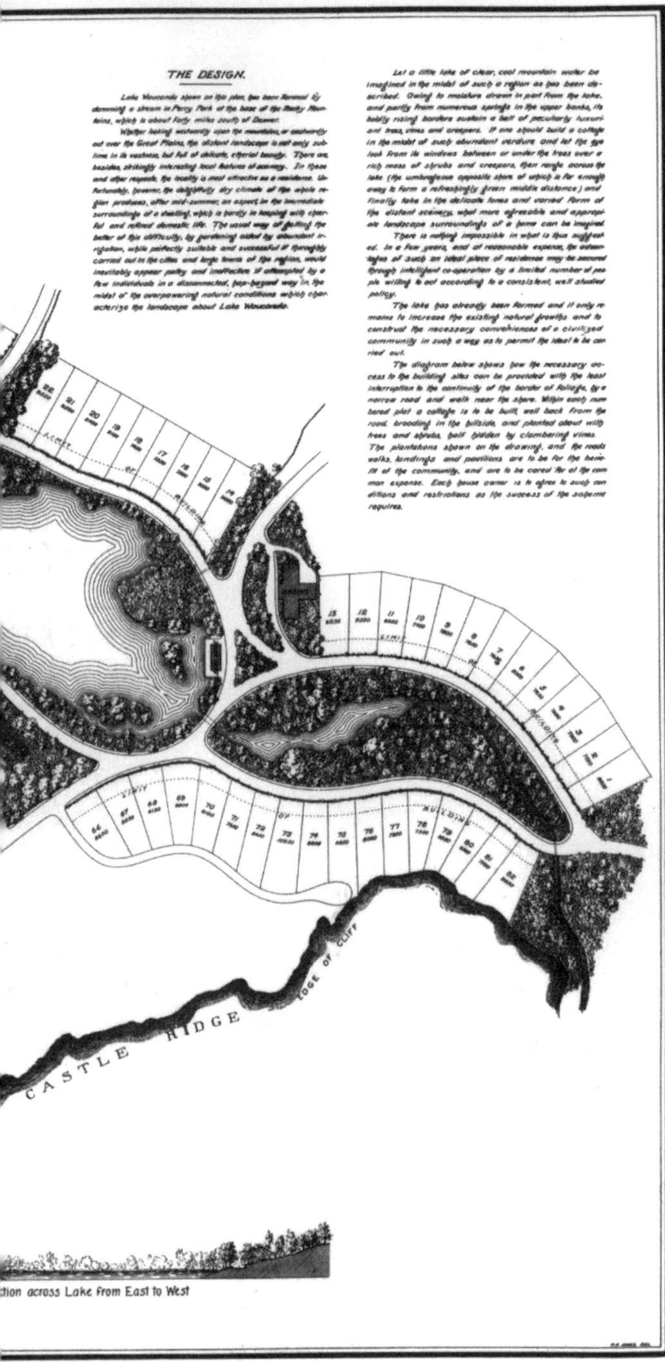

"PERRY PARK, DOUGLAS COUNTY, COLORADO," MARCH 28, 1890

do not believe that you will be able to sell lots in advance of the proposed public improvements in sufficient number and at sufficient price to provide you with means for making these improvements.

To lay out a road and lay off lots upon it is not what you employ us for. What you employ us for is to provide a plan for a pleasing dressing of the village. We can provide no plan for this purpose that does not depend on your water supply. Therefore we must know what your water scheme will be, and what plants can be procured that, with this water, will flourish.

In answer to my inquiry about plants you write that you would use plants readily to be obtained. But we asked the question because we know of no plants to be readily obtained in the requisite numbers. We feel that very few of the plants with which we are familiar can be depended on in your climate.

I do not answer your question about "a pleasure ground in front of the hotel" because I really do not know how to make a pleasure ground under the circumstances. I have never managed an irrigated pleasure ground and I don't imagine that you can do anything without irrigation.

Until you have water laid on, what are your people going to do for water? Until you have sewers what are you going to do with their sewerage? Of course there are temporary expedients which would be *decent* and *tolerable* but that is all you can say for them.

We have hitherto considered that we had to make a plan for a village of summer residents only, to be provided with water liberally by means of a supply that would be cut off in winter. Your instructions about your house showed that this was not your understanding, and really we don't know how to proceed. Without water the plan we have had in view would, it appears to us, be a dead failure. But supposing that you become responsible for that, we must know more accurately what the water works *of the future* are to be. We must see where the pipes and sewers are to be laid, and what the arrangements are to be for drawing and distributing the water from them. We must have a sewer and sewer connections in view. Otherwise we may give you a plan into which the future introduction of a sewer and water system would be extravagantly costly.

We shall be very glad to receive any hints that the lady of whom you speak can give us.[4] Our lack of familiarity with the local conditions is such that we shall be thankful for any light upon them.

If what we have said should satisfy your company that the work could be better planned by someone better acquainted with the conditions to be considered, we shall willingly be relieved of the duty of going further with our study of the plan, and make you no charge for what we have done.[5]

This is written in good faith and not in the least with an idea that you are not disposed to trust us. We only question if you do not trust us more than is justifiable.

Yours Very Truly

Fred^{k} Law Olmsted.

The text presented here is from a letterpress copy of a typewritten letter signed on the original in Olmsted's hand: A5: 159–64, OAR/LC (see FLO to Gen. Bela M. Hughes, [Jan. 15], 1889, above; FLO to Charles A. Roberts, Oct. 5, 1889, below; FLO to Charles A. Roberts, Oct. 14, 1889, below).

1. Charles A. Roberts (d. 1902) was the son-in-law of Gen. Bela M. Hughes and one of the primary stockholders in the Red Stone Town, Land, and Mining Company as well as the company's secretary. Roberts owned a hardware store in Denver and moved to Perry Park in 1891. He devoted considerable effort and money to the venture, but land title disputes, inadequate sources of water, and the lack of a rail connection to Denver contributed to the effective end of the enterprise by 1901 (Ardis Webb, *The Perry Park Story* [Denver, 1974], pp. 24, 36, 38, 42).
2. Roberts's reply has not been found. Olmsted's previous letter to Roberts expressed his apprehensions about the suitability of the site for residential development and doubts about his firm's ability to transform the area into what Roberts envisioned: "We are very apprehensive that your funds and faith and the funds and faith of your costumers will not hold out. And it is perfectly true that we are to proceed upon a very imperfect knowledge and no experience of the requirements of your climate—so greatly differing from that of any region that we are familiar with. We shall do so with reluctance and if there was a man of our profession who had better advantages in this respect, we should strongly urge you to let us shift the responsibility upon him" (FLO to Charles A. Roberts, July 27, 1889, A5: 76–80, OAR/LC).
3. See FLO to Gen. Bela M. Hughes, [Jan. 15], 1889, above.
4. The "lady" may be Miss Sarah Cary Emmons of Detroit, daughter of Mrs. Sarah Emmons, both stockholders in the Red Stone Town Company. Miss Emmons would later correspond with Olmsted in December of 1889, and Roberts later wrote to Olmsted that she was working on a competing plan for Perry Park (A. Webb, *The Perry Park Story*, p. 24; Sarah Cary Emmons to FLO, Dec. 13, 1889, B76: #1091, OAR/LC; Charles A. Roberts to FLO, Dec. 21, 1889, B76: #1091, OAR/LC).
5. In a letter dated August 24, 1889, in response to this letter, Roberts assured Olmsted that he was the most qualified landscape architect for the job. He wrote, "If I knew of anyone who was competent to relieve you, and you *absolutely refused* to give us a plan, why then I should be compelled to give you up, but I should hate awfully to do it and it would be a very great disappointment to me." Olmsted wrote on September 1 that "we stand very far apart; you seeing only beauty in what to me—seeking a summer house—would be repulsive," but told Roberts that his partner Henry Sargent Codman, who was on his way to California to work on Stanford University, would be in Colorado in a few days and that they could then discuss their differences in person (Charles A. Roberts to FLO, Aug. 24, 1889, B76: #1091, OAR/LC; FLO to Charles A. Roberts, Sept. 1, 1889, A5: 215–19, OAR/LC).

To Sylvester Baxter

2[d] Sep[tr] 1889.

Dear Mr Baxter;

A paper read before the late convention of American Florists by McMillan, Supt of the Buffalo Parks,[1] made some stir and I have procured a copy

VIEW OF PUBLIC GARDEN, BOSTON, C. 1890

of it which I think that you will be interested to run through. The view taken is undoubtedly most unpopular just now, and there is here in Boston I apprehend a good deal of feeling against it growing out of Mrs Van Renssalaer's criticism of the Public Garden[2] and Dogue's foolish disposition to attribute that to Profr Sargent's personal hostility to him.[3] I think that Mrs Van R., & McMillan (in this paper), and certainly most others do not sufficiently distinguish between gardening and landscape gardening. It seems to be absurd to criticise the Public Garden from the point of view of landscape gardening. I do not suppose that Dogue really has before him any motive of landscape gardening any more than a sculptor or wood carver has the motives of a painter. I admit that I know of no satisfactory definition of landscape gardening. But suppose that a landscape architect disposes of the materials with which he deals, earth, turf, foliage, water, rocks, with a view to what may be called a general quality in the landscape to result—or, instead of quality say, a sentiment or expression, of landscape. Neither the old fashioned nor the new fashioned flower gardening has anything of that motive. Its motive is much more allied to that of a jeweler or a carpet weaver. And though some things have been done in the original modeling of the Public Garden in the fashion of landscape gardening I do not suppose that now, from year to year, it is ever really thought of. It is considered as a collection of pretty things, and the motive of the disposition of these things is the same with that which directs the disposition of goods in a show window, or of bric a brac on a table. The words "expression", "quality", "sentiment", do not apply to it.

I am writing to no purpose — merely expressing a certain dissatisfaction that I have in all such writings as this of McMillan's because they seem not to do justice to the possible motives of such artists as Dogue. The real thing to be attacked is the going to work with mixed or confused motives; and producing results in which motives of one sort contradict and neutralize motives of another sort. Separate them; work anywhere exclusively for one or the other, and you will get desirable results.

The Gymnasium[4] appears to me a perfect success; just what I hoped for but did not expect. As far as I can estimate 90% of all who use it are young men of the "working class", factory hands &c. Negroes and Jews in their full proportion. The remaining 10 prct chiefly clerks, mostly of low degree, about 1 prct of college men or others coming well dressed and whom you might find at the Athletic Club. It will be used by these, being a better training place than an indoor gym.

Yours Truly

Fred[k] Law Olmsted.

The text presented here is a signed letter in Olmsted's hand.

1. William McMillan, superintendent of Buffalo parks at this time, read a paper titled "Landscape Gardening" during the annual convention of the American Florist Society, held in Buffalo that year. In it he condemned floricultural displays in public parks that featured brightly colored and contrasting flowers and foliage:

   > In the embellishment then of any grounds of sufficient extent to have a distinctive landscape character, the gardener must take into account all the impressive and attractive natural elements of the place. The general aim of his work will be to make a harmonious combination with the dominant characteristics which nature has already stamped upon the site. . . . He will thus avoid all novel conceits, all conspicuous eccentricities, all incongruous intrusions, and be guided by his understanding of the laws of nature, as enacted by the ruling Divinity of the scene, and his sympathy with them.

   Olmsted also discussed McMillan's paper in a letter to the editor of *American Florist*, Jan. 1890, below (*Proceedings of the Fifth Annual Convention of the Society of American Florists held at Buffalo* NY, Aug. 20th, 21st, 22nd, 23rd 1889 [Boston, 1889], pp. 108–18).
2. Mariana Griswold Van Rensselaer, "Correspondence. The Boston Public Garden," *Garden and Forest*, Sept. 12, 1888, pp. 345–46. Her principal criticisms of the Public Garden were that the monuments in various locations, and the bridge over the pond, stood out too strongly. She also commented that the formal flower beds were too abundant, and that the exotic plants were out of place and too numerous.
3. William Doogue (1828–1906) was superintendent of the Boston Common and the Boston Public Garden from 1878 until his death. As part of his duties, he supervised the planting of ornamental beds of flowers, many of them annuals raised in hothouses, in geometric patterns with contrasting colors. While such "gardenesque" planting design enjoyed great popularity in the United States and Europe during the Victorian period,

Olmsted, William Robinson, Van Rensselaer, and Charles Sprague Sargent, among others, condemned what they considered an excessively ornamental and artificial approach to public landscape design. Doogue reprinted Van Rensselaer's critique of the Public Garden in his annual report for 1888, as well as an article published in the *Boston Herald* where he had responded to her criticism and blamed Charles Sprague Sargent for printing her article, "Now let me here say that I do not attribute to this lady critic (?) any of the malice which dictated her article. She simply met the requirements of another party, her employer [Sargent], who has had some of his peculiar schemes, with reference to the Public Garden and some of the other ornamental grounds of Boston, thwarted by me." Doogue then described to the *Herald* reporter several reasons why Sargent, who he said "had been my friend, and done me many acts of kindness" was now his "enemy" (Henry Lee, *The Public Garden: Boston* [Boston, 1988], pp. 10, 28–29; Cynthia Zaitzevsky, *Frederick Law Olmsted and the Boston Park System* [Cambridge, Mass., 1982], pp. 185–86; *Annual Report of the Superintendent of Common and Public Grounds* [Boston, 1889], pp. 6–23).

4. Olmsted included men's gymnastics facilities in his design for the Charlesbank in 1887. In 1891, the gymnasia were expanded to accommodate women and children (C. Zaitzevsky, *The Boston Park System*, pp. 96–99; see also Frederick Law Olmsted, *Twelfth Annual Report, Boston Park Commissioners, Report on Charles River Embankment*, [Dec. 1886], above).

To William L. Fischer

Brookline, Mass., Sept. 30th. 1889.

MR. W. L. FISCHER;
FRANKLIN PARK;

Dear Mr. Fischer;

My notion about the planting of the rocky slope north of Ellicott Arch[1] is that we should avoid obscuring the rocks, using only vines and low-growing shrubs in front of them; and, back of them, and in the broad openings between them, nothing that would much interrupt a view from the drive near the Arch under the wood to the Northward. I would not object to the use of Cotoneaster and of Juniper in small numbers in close connection with some of the rocks but I don't think it desirable that either should be very conspicuous. I would have most of the planting appear as a natural *thicket* spreading out from the edge of the wood. A few foreign plants, not of large, distinctive or very conspicuous foliage, might be introduced among these with possible advantage, but not in such manner that they would, because of their flowers or otherwise, attract special attention or materially affect the native character of the main body of foliage.

From end to end a moderate use of thorny and prickly plants will be desirable as a means of checking the movement of visitors from the top of the hill toward the bridle road.

I should be glad to have whortel-berries moved in considerable numbers from the wood in the rear, if you thought it could be done successfully.

Any or all of the following would be suitable for the low planting, over which the rocks would be seen:—

Rosa lucida and other low wild roses
Rubus canadensis
Myrica cerifera
Vaccinium corymbosum (This is offered by Meehan and other nurserymen, nursery-grown.)
Clethra alnifolia
Spirea tormentosa and *Salicifolia*
Potentilla fruticosa
Symphoricarpus vulgaris
Rhus aromatica
Diervilla trifida
Ceanothus Americanus
Amelanchier Canad. alnifolia (dwarf. offered, nursery-grown, cheap by the hundred.)
Genista tinctoria
Lonicera sempervirens, caerulea and *ciliata*
Vitis indivisa

Any or all of the following to stand on the higher ground and back of, or between, the rocks:—

Privet
Barberry
Sweet briar
Rhus copal.
Rubus Canadensis
Cornus alternifolia and others
Viburnum acerifolia and *cassinoides*
Quercus prinoides.
Prunus pumila
Laurus Bensoin
Azalea nudiflora
Smilax rotundifolia
(Asters, golden rods etc., to mingle in.)

Any of the above that you want I can obtain from American nurseries if ordered soon.

Yours Truly

Fred[k] Law Olmsted.

The text presented here is from a letterpress copy of a typewritten letter signed on the original in Olmsted's hand: A5: 339–42, OAR/LC (see "Specifications for Playstead Terrace, Franklin Park," July 30, 1885, above; FLO to William L. Fischer, July 21, 1887, above; FLO to William L. Fischer, Aug. 6, 1889, above; FLO to William L. Fischer, Aug. 11, 1889, above).

1. Ellicott Arch carries the Franklin Park circuit drive over a pedestrian path near the northwest corner of the park. Built in 1889, the structure consisted of puddingstone boulders, roughly fitted together, with vines and other plants established in the joints. For pedestrians passing under the drive below, the arch formed a gateway between the pastoral Ellicottdale and the picturesque Wilderness sections of the park. The "rocky slope" Olmsted refers to here is north of the arch, in the Wilderness area. The steep pathway up the slope required a large number of stone steps, which became known as the 99 Steps (C. Zaitzevsky, *The Boston Park System*, p. 177; *Thirty-Sixth Annual Report of the City Engineer of Boston for the Year 1902* [Boston, 1903], p. 20).

What is a "Useless Fence."

[October 1889]

The proposition that useless fences should be abolished does not admit of discussion. The question, under what circumstances fences are useless, admits of so much that it cannot be fairly dealt with in the short letter asked of me. I will therefore consider only the case of door-yard fences in village streets.

There is now a reaction from past fashions in respect to those which leads many to take ground with which I am not wholly in sympathy. As there is no danger that all that can be said for their side will not be well presented in your columns I will, if you please, take it upon me to submit a few considerations of an enumerative tendency, which, in the common arguments of the more thorough going abolitionists are, I think, apt to be overlooked.

1st. What is to be seen in looking *from* the dwelling of a family is of more importance than what is to be seen in looking *toward* it.

2nd. It is more important that a garden or lawn should appear to advantage in looking *from* the dwelling to which it is attached than in looking *toward* it.

3rd. It is more important that a home should be loved by those living in it than that it should be admired by the public.

4th. To look point blank into a street is not helpful to the home quality of a house or a garden.

5th. A family dwelling should, wherever practicable, include an out-of-door apartment in which its people, especially its women and girls, may have the benefit of air and sunlight while engaged in occupations to which it is unbecoming that public attention should be invited. ("Apartment: a place separated by enclosure."—*Webster*.)

6th. If such an apartment can best be provided between the house and the street, a desire to please the public eye should not prevent its being provided.

7th. It is better that the combined frontage of a series of homes on a public street should impress those passing with the prevalence of tranquil, refined and modest domestic conditions than that it should be beautiful in any way at all detractive to a general character of that kind. An emphatic line of separation between property in common and the private property of families, such as an unostentatious fence provides, is not necessarily an interference with what is desirable in this respect.

8th. Of lines of small homes in suburban villages those are the pleasanter which make the impression of retreats from the May-fair of the town rather than colonies of it. Whether fences promote or detract from such an impression is a question of the manner of them.

9th. In regard to this question of the manner of a fence, you present the drawing of a lawn, before which, in one case, there is a formal line of thin, slight and weak pickets; in the other, (presumably) a stone side walk. Let us say that, of the two drawings, the one without the fence is the prettier. But if, in the actuality of the case, instead of unsubstantial paling there stood a wall of roughish stone of agreeable texture and tints; if this wall were partly covered with creepers and its crevices filled with small rock plants, and if it were here and there partly over-hung by bushes; if shadows were falling slantingly, and if it were to be overlooked from the usual height of the eye of a man driving through the street, the foreground thus provided would hardly lessen the beauty of the scene.

10th. As to the question of uselessness otherwise than with respect to beauty, there may be communities in which flowers and fruit are yet safe from depredations when not separated by any fence from the public streets, but there are many in which they are not so, and as population increases the moral effect in this respect of even a slight fence becomes increasingly apparent.

FREDERICK LAW OLMSTED.

Brookline, Mass., August 26, 1889.

The text presented here was published in the October 1889 issue of *American Garden*, p. 371, and composed on August 26. The July 1889 issue of the periodical announced a debate on the "useless fence" that would appear in later issues. E. H. Libby, the editor of *American Garden* (1873–1892) asked Olmsted and other leaders in landscape gardening and architecture to contribute letters to these discussions on the "useless fence." Friends and colleagues of Olmsted who also contributed include Charles W. Eliot, Bishop Thomas M.

Clark of Providence, and Edward Atkinson of Boston ("SVR ROSA," *American Garden*, July 1889, p. 241; FLO to E. H. Libby, Aug. 26, 1889, A5: 187, OAR/LC; see also FLO to "Madam," Jan. 16, 1885, above; L. H. Bailey, ed., "North American Horticultural Periodicals," *The Standard Cyclopedia of Horticulture* [New York, 1917], pp. 1559–60).

To Henry Robinson Towne[1]

2d Octr 1889.

Confidential

Mr. H. R. Towne;
New York;
Dear Mr Towne;

I am much gratified by your conclusions as expressed in the Sun and further in your letter of yesterday just received.[2]

I would not like to give an opinion upon the question of occupying the Park, certainly not unless with reference to a definite and somewhat detailed proposition and I have not time to think it well out.[3] Vaux and Parsons are the proper advisers of the Commissioners and of the city on such a point. In strict confidence I may say to you that both are likely to be somewhat predisposed to favor Green's view,[4] and that Green, having once lost his temper and publicly committed himself against your scheme will fight you malignantly and with the most industrious and painstaking, underhanded if not open, labor.[5] I should say that till you get your land outside, the question had better be postponed. Once get your footing and you will shake off a great deal of opposition. What sort of opposition you have to deal with, you may judge from the fact that since I saw you I have received communications from representatives of three rival sites, asking my cooperation;[6] all assuming that you cannot get the land needed outside the park. Be sure they are doing their best to spread this conviction. I decline in each case, and in that to which friendship wd most incline me to give aid have said that I believe that the Fair must go on Bloomingdale Heights or nowhere.[7]

It will be better if possible to get the Commissioners on your side thro' friendly debate. I shd think that the Mayor[8] would deal with them best. Properly managed neither they nor Vaux and Parsons will be likely to refuse all cooperation, and the financial advantage *to the city* of getting a fee from visitors from outside, well presented, will command grave consideration. The freedom of the Park and the absence of fees and drink money—the denial of advantages to the rich man that the poor man cannot command—is, I remember, a point in which Vaux has a certain chivalric interest. Don't be deceived by what you will hear to Vaux's disadvantage. In certain lines—problems of planning for convenience—

he is unsurpassed. He is apt to greatly misrepresent his own mind in talking; a nervous defect.

Hutchings[9] has been engaged in politico-commercial alliances with Green and is probably under his influence more than you could wish. Moreover, he has an indolent sluggish mind and a lawyer-like habit of easily taking sides and shutting off access to his intellect from the opposing side. Yet his indolent habit disposes him not to fight against a plainly strong opposition.

Yours Truly

Fred[k] Law Olmsted

The text presented here is from a letterpress copy of a handwritten letter signed on the original in Olmsted's hand: A5: 357–61, OAR/LC. In 1888 Congress began planning the 1893 World's Columbian Exposition, a fair commemorating the 400th anniversary of Columbus's voyage to the Americas. Washington, D.C., New York City, and Chicago were the final contenders to host the event. Olmsted advised New York on its bid, inspecting possible sites with Henry R. Towne in September 1889. In 1890 Congress chose Chicago as the location for the fair, and Olmsted later designed the grounds (Norman Bolotin and Christine Laing, *The World's Columbian Exposition* [Champaign, Ill., 2002], pp. 1–3; "Arranging the Buildings," *New York Times*, Sept. 29, 1889, p. 11).

1. Henry Robinson Towne (1844–1924) was an engineer, manufacturer, and co-founder and president of the Yale & Towne Lock Manufacturing Company. He was an influential member of the Merchant's Association of New York, and was actively involved in New York's efforts to host the World's Fair. He lobbied Mayor Hugh J. Grant to solicit subscriptions to a provisional fund to pay for the fair, and was chosen by the mayor to represent mechanical engineers on the Committee on Site and Buildings. He prepared three alternative plans for the fair, published by the *Sun* newspaper on September 29, that located the exhibition buildings mainly in the area between Morningside and Riverside parks. Two of the plans also placed some of the buildings immediately north of Central Park, but none suggested buildings in the park (*DAB*; "For the Provision Fund," *New York Times*, Sept. 26, 1889, p. 8; Committees of the Fair," ibid., Aug. 11, 1889, p. 1; "Arranging the Buildings," *New York Sun*, Sept. 29, 1889, p. 11).
2. On October 2, the *Sun* published the Committee on Site and Buildings' recommended site plan. The committee recommended "the adoption of a site comprising Riverside and Morningside Parks, with adjacent lands," that would use "no portion of Central Park for buildings." In Towne's letter to Olmsted, he suggested enclosing the north end of Central Park so that it could serve as "an annex to afford an overflow for the great crowds" going to the adjacent fair grounds. Olmsted had endorsed a similar plan in a published letter to Charles A. Dana, the editor of the *Sun*, a few days before, but rejected the idea of enclosing or placing buildings in any portion of the park ("Defining the Chosen Site," *New York Sun*, Oct. 2, 1889, p. 3; Henry R. Towne to FLO, Oct. 1, 1889; "Mr. Olmsted's View," *New York Sun*, Sept. 26, 1889, p. 1).
3. Olmsted had expressed reservations about any involvement in New York's bid for the World's Fair in his earlier letter to Dana, declaring that "I have no disposition to take part in any controversy on the subject, and I write solely because of inquiries that have been addressed to me and which I feel bound owing to the great importance of a wise decision to answer as well as possible upon brief consideration" ("Mr. Olmsted's View," *New York Sun*, Sept. 26, 1889, p. 1).

4. Calvert Vaux at this time was the supervisory landscape architect for New York City's Department of Public Parks and Samuel B. Parsons, Jr., was the superintendent of parks. Andrew Haswell Green, who was a citizen representative on the Committee on Site and Buildings with Towne, remained antagonistic to Olmsted, but had supported Vaux throughout his career. As a New York park commissioner, Green advocated for Vaux to become the department's landscape architect and helped him secure the commissions for the Metropolitan Museum of Art and the American Museum of Natural History. As a commissioner on the board of the Niagara Reservation, Green demanded that Vaux be hired to develop the design for the reservation. Green also helped Vaux secure architectural commissions for the mansion of William B. Ogden in upstate New York in the mid-1870s, and for the row house of his law partner Samuel Tilden on Gramercy Park in 1881 (DPP, *Minutes*, Dec. 22, 1887, p. 412; ibid., May 25, 1885, p. 75; "Committees of the Fair," *New York Times*, Aug. 11, 1889, p. 1; FLO to William E. Dorsheimer, July 21, 1886; above; Francis R. Kowsky, *Country, Park, & City: The Architecture and Life of Calvert Vaux* [New York, 1998]).
5. Green had publicly opposed Towne's proposals at a meeting of the Committee on Site and Buildings on September 11, 1889 ("Where Will the Site Be," *New York Times*, Sept. 12, 1889).
6. Other people seeking Olmsted's endorsement for their plans included park commissioner John D. Crimmins, whose plan would clear trees from Central Park to accommodate exhibition buildings. Olmsted called Crimmins' scheme "wholly impractical." Albert S. Bickmore, a founder of the Museum of Natural History, asked Olmsted to write a memorandum officially endorsing the idea that platforms be constructed over the reservoirs in Central Park to accommodate exhibition buildings, as Olmsted had suggested in his letter published by the *Sun*. Olmsted wrote Bickmore, however, that he suggested the platforms as a last resort, and that the Water Department would need to determine whether it was feasible. Arthur M. Wellington, the editor of *Engineering News*, asked Olmsted to endorse the idea of using Governors Island, in New York Harbor, for the fair. Olmsted responded that the site would likely be "too difficult," and that he favored Towne's plan (FLO to John D. Crimmins, Sept. 28, 1889, A5: 315–16, OAR/LC; John D. Crimmins to FLO, Sept. 30, 1889; Albert S. Bickmore to FLO, Sept. 27, 1889; "Mr. Olmsted's View," *New York Sun*, Sept. 26, 1889, p. 1; FLO to Albert S. Bickmore, Sept. 30, 1889, A5: 332–33, OAR/LC; Arthur M. Wellington to FLO, Sept. 30, 1889; FLO to Arthur M. Wellington, Oct. 1, 1889, A5: 355–56, OAR/LC).
7. Olmsted had asked J. J. R. Croes not to use a letter he had written on September 28 "defending the Park," because he did not remember what he had written. Regarding Bloomingdale Heights, the area located between Morningside and Riverside parks that Olmsted also called the Bloomingdale plateau, he wrote, "While I have authorized no statement, have made no comparison between the Bloomingdale site and any other, I do think that it would be a very fine site — much finer than any heretofore used for a like purpose and I believe that the Fair must go there or nowhere" (J. J. R. Croes to FLO, Oct. 1, 1889; FLO to J. J. R. Croes, Oct. 1, 1889, A5: 350, OAR/LC; "Defining the Chosen Site," *New York Sun*, Oct. 2, 1889, p. 3).
8. Hugh J. Grant (1857–1910) was mayor of New York City from 1889 to 1892 and a Tammany Democrat. He organized New York City's bid for the World's Fair and agreed with Olmsted's opposition to using Central Park ("Ex-Mayor Grant Dies Suddenly," *New York Times*, Nov. 4, 1910, p. 1; "Don't Spoil Central Park," ibid., July 8, 1889, p. 8).
9. Olmsted is referring to Waldo M. Hutchins, who at this time was president of the New York City park commission. He favored choosing Central Park as the site for the fair ("Don't Spoil Central Park," *New York Times*, July 8, 1889, p. 8; "Opposed to the Site," ibid., Sept. 26, 1889, p. 8; see also FLO to Calvert Vaux, June 30, 1887, n. 4, above).

To CHARLES A. ROBERTS

5th Oct. 1889.

Mr C. A. Roberts
Denver, Col.
Dear Sir; We have just received yours of 1st.

We cannot take your view of the effect of the clause quoted.[1] Is it not the only clause in the report that would interrupt at all the natural impression which an ordinary reader would have in reading the report that it was a common advertizing puff of a land speculation, written to order? As it is, the report has more of that aspect than we should think desirable for your interests. The best way to meet any doubt that this slight reservation may suggest would be to append a few lines from your engineer reporting the amount of water you control.

Mr. Codman's report to us does not remove the impression that you want and intend to do something that we should not advise and will not be responsible for.[2]

For example, if anyone consulting us, proposes to buy a lot with a view of building upon it before a water and sewer system is actually established and in operation we shall advise him not to do so. If any man proposes to buy a back lot such as Mr Codman says you want to sell to poor people and asks our advice we shall tell him that it does not appear to us that you can put the price of such a lot low enough not to make it an extravagance.[3] He had better pay, as an investment, ten times as much — fifty times as much — for a lot on the pond. I would not advise anyone to build even on the pond if a shantee-town was likely to grow up on the hills back of the first tier of lots. I can see nothing attractive in such a place. I think that a sale of lots there will simply insure a neighborhood of people without taste and without thrift or good judgment. I would not live near dwellings of the character which it seems to me would inevitably prevail.

Mr Codman writes that he has sent drawings from California but they have not yet come to us. Yours Very Truly

Fredk Law Olmsted.

The text presented here is from a letterpress copy of a handwritten letter signed on the original in Olmsted's hand: A5: 372–74, OAR/LC (see FLO to Gen. Bela M. Hughes, [Jan. 15,] 1889, above; FLO to Charles A. Roberts, Aug. 20, 1889, above; FLO to Charles A. Roberts, Oct. 14, 1889, below).

1. On January 15, 1889, Olmsted had written a report on the feasibility of a "summer resort" in Perry Park, Colorado, for the Red Stone Town, Land, and Mining Company for them to use for marketing purposes. On October 1, Roberts had asked Olmsted to remove the following passage: "The ground being frozen and lightly powdered with snow and an

unusual drought prevailing, my observations were not such as would be needed for an assured judgment in the questions of water supply and cultural capabilities." The sentence was not removed in the final publication (FLO to Gen. Bela M. Hughes, [Jan. 15,] 1889, above; Charles A. Roberts to FLO and Henry Sargent Codman, Sept. 27, 1889, B76: #1091, OAR/LC; Charles A. Roberts to FLO, Oct. 1, 1889, B76: #1091, OAR/LC; *Perry Park* [promotional pamphlet] [Denver, 1890]).

2. While on his way to California to work on Stanford University, Henry Sargent Codman visited Perry Park to resolve disagreements between Olmsted and Roberts about when and how basic infrastructure (sewerage and water supply) would be built for the Perry Park development. Roberts wrote that Codman claimed that the "cultural capabilities [were] all right" and that Perry Park could get sufficient water in dry times from their reservoir. But Codman's letter to Olmsted was not as reassuring. While in Perry Park, Codman also drew new plans for its development (FLO to Charles A. Roberts, Sept. 1, 1889, A5: 215–19, OAR/LC; Charles A. Roberts to FLO, Oct. 1, 1889, B76: #1091, OAR/LC; Henry Sargent Codman to FLO, Sept. 26, 1889, B76: #1091, OAR/LC; JCO to Charles A. Roberts, Oct. 1, 1889, A5: 346, OAR/LC; FLO to Charles A. Roberts, Oct. 7, 1889, A5: 381, OAR/LC).
3. In his previous letters to Olmsted, Roberts explained that he did not need the plan of the village to be complete before he began selling lots: "You evidently are not used to the Western manner of building towns. If they can find the stakes that mark their boundary lines, they are perfectly satisfied and glad to do the balance of the work themselves." He wanted Olmsted to provide the general layout of roads and a scheme for a landscape design that could be used for publicity. By proceeding quickly to selling lots, investors could begin to realize profits more readily than if they first invested in infrastructure and other improvements. Codman reported to Olmsted that Roberts was also planning to sell "back lots" behind lots along the lake, at a lower price, despite his and Olmsted's protests (Charles A. Roberts to FLO, Aug. 24, 1889, B76: #1091, OAR/LC; FLO to Charles A. Roberts, Aug. 20, 1889, above; Henry Sargent Codman to FLO, Sept. 26, 1889, B76: #1091, OAR/LC).

To Robert Underwood Johnson[1]

Brookline, Mass.
9th Octr 1889.

Mr. R. U. Johnson,
Office of the Century, New York
Dear Mr. Johnson;

I can only ask pardon for my apparent neglect. I have wanted greatly to write something suitable to your purpose,[2] and at last, though exceedingly pressed with engagements, I did steal an entire day for an attempt. I have not been at all satisfied with the result, and have thrown it up.

The truth is I do not like to find fault without better knowledge of the facts; without hearing more of the Commissioners' side of the case; without being more sure where the fault — the organic fault — lies, or *without being able to advise how it is to be avoided.*

The act of Congress prescribes the Commission and the manner it shall be appointed.[3]

Somewhere among its members there is a responsibility for certain operations that, judging from this distance, have been very unfortunate. One of the Commissioners is represented, also, to have expressed an intention which if it were carried out, would eventually result in an irreparable calamity — a calamity to the civilized world.[4]

But there is nothing to show that the Commission as a whole has not proceeded conscientiously and with as good judgment as could be expected of a body similarly elected, similarly organized, and endowed with similar means and powers.

Those who have attentively read the volumes of Whately, Price, Repton and the Gilpins[5] know that a large part of the business of my profession has always been that of contriving expedients for lessening the misfortune into which gentlemen of education and culture, supposing themselves to have a special aptitude to the work, have carried themselves, in undertaking what they have regarded as very simple improvements of their own country places.

To contrive means and methods by which that which is most distinctly valuable to the world in the Yo Semite can be perpetuated, and to provide means by which the world can conveniently and effectively make use of it, which means shall be in the least degree possible conspicuous, incongruous and disturbing to the spirit and character of the scenery, is a problem that no one ought to dabble with. Suppose a tolerably satisfactory plan could be studied out for solving it. How much reason is there to suppose that such a plan would be persistently followed? And how is any man competent for the duty to enter upon it with the fervor and confidence necessary to success with the prospect of such results as are reasonably to be expected?

I am very sorry indeed that I do not {*find myself prepared*} to write anything on the subject at present that I think worthy to be laid before the public. All I could say is that, having at an early day spent several months in the valley under peculiarly favorable circumstances for contemplating it,[6] I know that the question is {*one of far greater*} importance and of far greater difficulty than can be generally realized; that it is most foolish to take it up in an occasional and desultory way as a question of details, or as a question the answer to which will be chiefly important to the people of the present century. It is preeminently a question of our duty to the future.

Very Truly Yours

Fred[k] Law Olmsted.

The text presented here is from a letterpress copy of a typewritten letter signed on the original in Olmsted's hand: A5: 383–85, OAR/LC (see FLO to Richard Watson Gilder, July 10, 1889, above, and *Governmental Preservation of Natural Scenery*, March 8, 1890, below).

1. Robert Underwood Johnson was associate editor of the *Century Illustrated Monthly Magazine* at this time and an advocate for the preservation of Yosemite Valley (See FLO to Richard Watson Gilder, July 10, 1889, n. 2, above).
2. Johnson had written to Olmsted asking him to visit Yosemite Valley and comment on its management by the Yosemite Commission, particularly with respect to the effects of tree cutting and pruning. Johnson sought to have Olmsted appointed to make a report to the commission, and he also offered to publish an article by Olmsted in the *Century* (Robert Underwood Johnson to FLO, June 23, 1889; FLO to Richard Watson Gilder, July 10, 1889, above).
3. The 1864 Act of Congress ceding Yosemite Valley and the Mariposa Big Tree Grove to the state of California stipulated that the governor would appoint eight commissioners to manage the park and that they would receive no compensation for their work (U.S. Congress, "An Act Authorizing a Grant to the State of California of the Yo-Semite Valley, and of the Land Embracing the Mariposa Big Tree Grove,'" June 30, 1864, *Congressional Globe*, 38th Cong., 1st session, Appendix [1863–1864], p. 240).
4. Olmsted later identified the specific "intention" referenced here as "the systematic cutting of all young trees in the Valley." He also made clear, however, that his knowledge of this policy and its effects was limited to what Johnson had described to him (*Governmental Preservation of Natural Scenery*, March 8, 1890, below).
5. Olmsted refers to Thomas Whately (1726–1772), the English landscape gardener and author who wrote *Observations on Modern Gardening* (1770); Uvedale Price (1747–1829), the English landscape theorist and gardener best known for his *Essay on the Picturesque* (1794); Humphry Repton (1752–1818), the English landscape gardener and author of important books on the subject, beginning with *Sketches and Hints on Landscape Gardening* (1795); the "Gilpins" include William Gilpin (1724–1804), the author of many books, including *Remarks on Forest Scenery* (1791); and his nephew, William Sawrey Gilpin (1762–1843), the landscape painter and author (*DNB*).
6. In the summer of 1864 Olmsted and his family, while living in nearby Bear Valley made an extended camping trip to the Mariposa Big Tree Grove, Yosemite Valley, and the High Sierra. Olmsted returned to the valley twice more in 1865 (*FLO, A Biography*, pp. 265–70; *Papers of FLO*, 5: 20–22, 514, n. 13).

To Frederick William Vanderbilt

Brookline, Mass., Oct. 11th. 1889.

Mr. F. W. Vanderbilt,
Rough Point, Newport, R. I.
Dear Mr. Vanderbilt;

Since our conversation of yesterday, I have had the matter under reflection.

What we have all along been driving at is to restore as nearly as practicable, consistently with convenience, what may be supposed to have been the original aspect of the ground on the sea front of your house. Previous occupants had grubbed out the indigenous growth, had filled up natural depressions; reduced elevations, covered rocks, and done much to obtain a smooth garden and lawn-like character. Our grading operations have been wholly directed to an approximate restoration of a natural surface. We suppose that the valleys made are very nearly the original valleys. Such variation from the original conditions of the surface as there may be are favorable to the more rapid flowing off of water in storms; to better outlooks from your windows, and at a few points to prevent people passing on the "Cliff Walk" from being as conspicuous as they otherwise would be.[1]

So much has been done. Unquestionably the aim has been the reverse of that customarily adopted, and which has been sanctioned by fashion, and with results that have become pleasing by association with pleasing social circumstances.

Nevertheless these results would seem incongruous and unbecoming in such close connection as they would need to be in your case, with the ruggedness of the adjoining rocks. They would have the effect of a satin scarf and white kid gloves worn with a shooting jacket. Moreover, we must keep in mind that the sea, the breakers and the rocks make up a landscape, the command of which gives the chief special value to your property. It seems to us that anything like an ordinary, even, lawn-like surface of the narrow space between your house and rocks would be but a feeble and discomposing foreground to such a landscape.

We have thought it would be better to attempt to cover the surface with bodies of low foliage similar, at least in general aspect, to that which occurs naturally along the shore, and which we suppose to have been on your ground before the attempt was made to give it a dressy lawn-like character.

There are objections to making this attempt. (a) There is a question of its complete success. (b) It cannot, at best, be made completely successful in one year or in two. In the mean time, what will be seen, while never as disagreeable as what you have seen this year, may yet seem strange and queer, and to those who cannot regard it as they would regard a structure in the process of building, and as pleasing because of promised results, it will probably continue to give occasion for disparaging comments if not for ridicule. (c) Finally, while we think it certain that if the intended result were once reached, it would be generally thought pleasingly appropriate to the situation, Mrs. Vanderbilt[2] may be right in her conviction that it would not gratify her own, special personal tastes.

From respect to these considerations but more particularly to the last, we cannot longer urge our views.

There are three prominent alternatives.

First; to have nothing but turf between the house and the rocks. This is the easiest, and in respect to early outlay, the cheapest thing to do. A fairly finished result could, with a favorable season, be obtained next year. It would least provoke criticism. It would be more convenient with reference to strolling away from the house toward the sea. It would give the least harbor for mosquitoes.

I need not repeat the objections I have before made to it.[3] If it is to be adopted, we should advise a recurrence to the suggestion that you once made, of carrying on the present rough wall along the north beach so as to connect it with the rocks; completely shutting the "Cliff Walk" and the low ground out of view from the house, and {*making a smooth connection*} between the turf on the North with that to be formed on the sea-front of the house.

Second; modify the last plan slightly by the introduction of low foliage among the rocks and on the steeper places.

Third; aim at something intermediate between what we have hitherto designed and the last, by having considerable breadths of turf in the valleys, but retaining the wall as it now is, and having broadish bodies of low bushes, vines and creepers near the rocks and upon the steeper and rougher places, where it will be difficult to preserve turf in good order.

If on the whole you think it better to adopt the first of the alternatives, above proposed, orders for plants not yet arrived can be countermanded, and such plants as have been obtained can be transferred to your brother for use at Bar Harbor.[4]

It would take longer to secure a finished character to the place under the last method than under either of the others and it would require an unusual exercise of garden handicraft to get the better of hard, unnatural lines along the edges of the mowed ground, but it could be done, and, we think, that, with the necessary exercise of patience, while waiting the growth of the plants under the peculiar difficulties of the locality, the chances are that the results would be gratifying. But there is no doubt that it will require patience in a greater degree than either of the other two and we would not like to have you adopt it unless well assured that you could abide by it.

We sincerely trust that whatever your conclusion as to the planting, you will agree with Mr. Peabody on some form of broad level platform at the foot of the eastern steps.

Please let us hear from you.

Though you decide contrary to our advice we will try to help you to the best results practicable.[5]

Yours Sincerely

Fred[k] Law Olmsted.

The text presented here is from a letterpress copy of a typewritten letter signed on the original in Olmsted's hand: A5: 398–403, OAR/LC (see FLO to Mariana Griswold Van Rensselaer, June 29, 1888, above and FLO to Frederick W. Vanderbilt, Aug. 2, 1888, above).

1. The Cliff Walk was a public path along the rocky eastern shoreline of Newport, Rhode Island. Vanderbilt was concerned about the privacy of the grounds at Rough Point and did not want a connection from the public walk onto his grounds (Frederick W. Vanderbilt to FLO, June 17, 1888, B74: #1036, OAR/LC; John Foreman and Robbe Pierce

Stimson, *The Vanderbilts and the Gilded Age* [New York, 1991], p. 264; see FLO to Mariana Griswold Van Rensselaer, June 29, 1888, n. 2, above).
2. Louise Holmes Anthony Torrance Vanderbilt (1844–1926).
3. See FLO to Frederick W. Vanderbilt, Aug. 2, 1888, above.
4. Olmsted was at this time beginning work on the landscape design of George W. Vanderbilt's Pointe d'Acadie estate near Bar Harbor, Maine (J. Foreman and R. P. Stimson, *The Vanderbilts*, p. 277; *Master List*, p. 207).
5. Olmsted added this handwritten addendum to the typed letter.

To Charles A. Roberts

Brookline, Mass., Oct. 14th. 1889.

Mr. C. A. Roberts,
Denver, Colo.
My Dear Sir;

Reviewing Mr. Codman's report with the drawing sent by him from California,[1] I am sorry to say that the conviction is confirmed that I have before expressed and which has led me to wish that we could, without harm to your Company, be relieved from responsibility in the Lake Wauconda matter.

It is plain that we have been proceeding upon a misunderstanding and that you want a different plan from that which we have undertaken to furnish. You would never have made the engagement you have with us had you realized what we expected to do.

Are we responsible for the fact that you have not realized it? Read attentively our letter of last January to General Hughes; (that in which the report designed, if you should think best, to be published, was enclosed) and you will be satisfied that we are not.[2]

You will see on the first page that we did not presume that the proposed operation on the lake would, in itself, give a sure profit on what it would cost you. We supposed that you would look upon it chiefly as a means for attracting attention to and developing the value of the property as a whole.

You will see, (page third) that a key to our ideas of the plan to be prepared was expressed in the following sentence:—

"THE COMPANY WILL NOT SELL OR LEASE LAND TO PEOPLE WHO ARE UNWILLING TO LIVE IN A MODERATELY COMPACT VILLAGE AND TO TAKE OBLIGATIONS WHICH WILL INSURE BETWEEN EACH HOUSE AND ITS NEIGHBORS A CONSTANT STATE OF TIDY VERDURE."

You will see (page two) that the company was advised to "STRINGENTLY INSIST" that the settlement should not be made in a "straggling, fragmentary or scattered way."

You will see that we looked upon the lake as a means of forming a belt of foliage; that this belt was to be widened by a water supply system, and that every house built was to be within this belt. Every house was to stand (as stated on page two) IN THE MIDST OF A WEALTH OF FOLIAGE.

You will see four passages on the first, second and sixth pages, and from the general tenor of the report, that building of houses was expected to "BE PREVENTED," at points where water for the irrigation of the adjoining ground, could not be had at once, and at all points outside the proposed "COMPACT SETTLEMENT" on the margin of the lake.

You will find nothing to indicate that we considered ourselves instructed to provide lots for you to sell in the rear of those fronting on the lake. Our opinion was, and our opinion remains, that it would be a great injury to your enterprise to provide such lots, and we could not and cannot advise people to buy lots with the intention of building along shore, if the little settlement that would be formed by a continuous line of buildings around the lake is to be surrounded by an outer settlement of houses looking down upon it and shutting it in. Such a settlement would to our mind hardly be a rural retreat.

What you have written us as argument, that a settlement formed as you have it in view that this of Lake Wauconda shall be; what you say of the rushing way in which things are done in Colorado, only tends to strengthen the difference between us.[3] The rush that you anticipate would be a rush toward a state of things which we should think most undesirable for those who are to live on the Lake, and which it would be the leading object of any plan for which we should be willingly responsible to PREVENT.

The case being as I have tried to explain what can now be done justly to the Company and justly to us?

We send you herewith two sketches, one suggesting such a plan as we should recommend to your customers, the other such a plan as we understand that you would prefer.[4]

We can make a drawing for you in general accordance with the last and help you to get a good presentation and advertisement of it. For this we would charge you not over $200.00. But to such a plan we could not give our name. It could be your plan, not ours.

Or, we can give you a plan on the general principle of the sketch No. 1, as a plan that we should advise to be followed. This under our existing agreement.

I am about to go South for perhaps a fortnight. While I am gone, you can look at these sketches, discuss them and return them with a statement of your conclusions.

We do not think that our plan would be immediately popular. We do not advise you to adopt it, as the best for immediate money making. Of course this means that we set our judgment against the judgment of those to whom you wish to sell, and who may be supposed to know the requirements of comfort in your climate better than we can. How can we do so without effrontery? We can because we think that those whom you look to as purchasers are

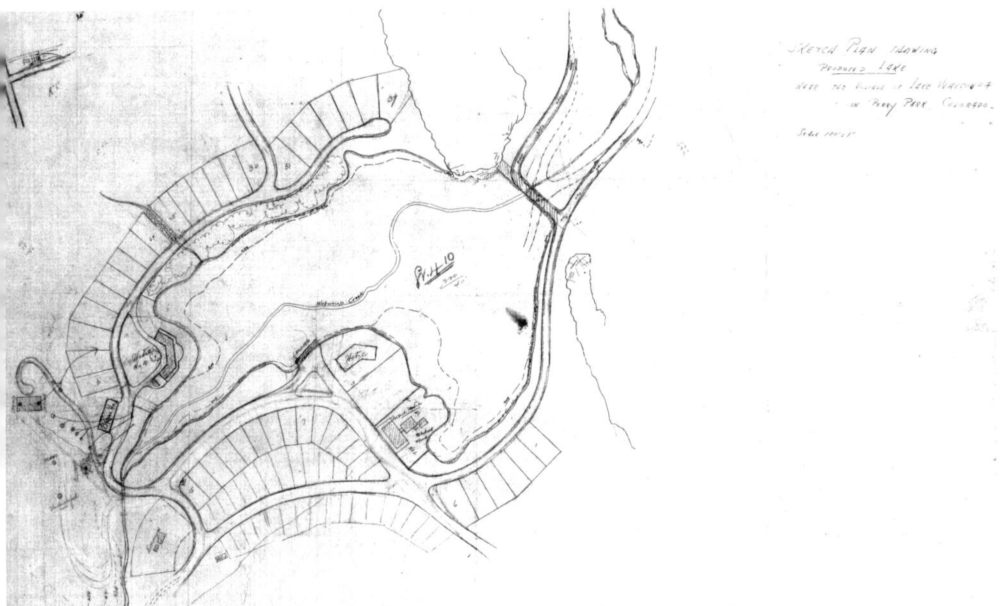

"SKETCH PLAN SHOWING PROPOSED LAKE NEAR THE VILLAGE OF LAKE WAUCONDA, PERRY PARK, COLO.," N.D., ILLUSTRATES FRONT AND BACK LOTS AROUND LAKE

mostly eastern-bred people, with eastern ideas of what is desirable in a country dwelling.

They have not had time nor have their occupations and interests, since they moved from the East, been favorable to anything more than a very imperfect adjustment of their ideas of what is desirable in this respect to the extremely different local conditions of Colorado. The study of special local conditions with a view to the invention of plans of an original character adapted to them has been our life business.

It is because it has, that, in spite of the fact that we have but little personal knowledge of the peculiarities of the climate, or of the requirements of comfort in Colorado, and are liable to error in this respect, you ask us for a plan.[5]

Yours truly

Fred[k] Law Olmsted
F. L. Olmsted & Co

The text presented here is from a letterpress copy of a typewritten letter signed on the original in Olmsted's hand: A5: 411–15, OAR/LC (see FLO to Gen. Bela M. Hughes, [Jan. 15,] 1889, above; FLO to Charles A. Roberts, Aug. 20, 1889, above; FLO to Charles A. Roberts, Oct. 5, 1889, above).

1. Henry Codman sent his report and drawings in a letter to Olmsted, in which he wrote: "I know perfectly well that there are several changes & departures from the theory of

your original scheme but they have been rather forced upon me & I don't see any way out of them." Included in these changes were the "back lots" that he and Olmsted opposed (Henry Sargent Codman to FLO, Sept. 26, 1889, B76: #1091, OAR/LC; FLO to Charles A. Roberts, Oct. 5, 1889, above).

2. See FLO to Gen. Bela M. Hughes, [Jan. 15,] 1889, above.
3. For more on Roberts' preferred design for the development, see FLO to Charles A. Roberts, Oct. 5, 1889, n. 3, above.
4. The recommended plan that Olmsted and Codman sent is plan 1091-7, NPS/FLONHS. An undated plan likely based on Roberts' preference for back-lots is plan 1091-9, NPS/FLONHS.
5. Roberts was able to convince Olmsted to submit a formal plan for the Village of Lake Wauconda at Perry Park, which he did in March of 1890, and it did not include backlots. Olmsted corresponded with Roberts further that year, making suggestions about restrictive covenants, gardeners, and engineers. But by 1891 the company was spending money without being able to sell lots. There was also an inadequate supply of water during dry periods. Olmsted ceased any further consultations in 1891, and his design for Perry Park was never executed. By 1904 all of the original investors had either died or sold their shares (Charles A. Roberts to FLO, Dec. 21, 1889, B76: #1091, OAR/LC; FLO to Charles A. Roberts, Dec. 26, 1889, A6: 731–74, OAR/LC; FLO to Charles A. Roberts, April 25, 1890; FLO to Charles A. Roberts, March 25, 1891, A13: 201–2, OAR/LC; "Design Map of the Village of Lake Wauconda, March 28, 1890," NPS/FLONHS; A. Webb, *The Perry Park Story*, pp. 35–43).

To William A. Thompson[1]

Brookline, Mass., Nov. 11th. 1889.

Mr. W. A. Thompson, C. E.
Asheville, N. C.

Dear Sir; We have received yours of 6th. We were rather expecting to have some map from you which would enable us to review the course of the Approach Road before giving you the memoranda for which you ask, but it is not necessary. Send us as soon as convenient a topographical sketch of the strip of land to be dealt with between Shiloh road and the corn-field, with the plan of the road laid on it and any suggestions for improvement that you can think of.[2]

Without waiting for further discussion or development of the plan you can go ahead with all preliminary operations until you hear from us, (or until my next visit.)

Assume that the wheelway, exclusive of gutters, is to be 18 feet broad; that there is to be no curve in its course of a less radius than 35 feet, and that its grade is to be nowhere steeper than 1 in 20.

In determining the exact lines of the road, particularly where it is to be built as a shelf thrown out from a hillside, allow space for gutters and for graceful borders etc., as follows:—

(1) Wherever the surface of the adjoining ground is to be higher than that of the road there is to be on that side a paved gutter ordinarily from 2 to 3 feet wide outside the 16 ft wheelway, This gutter is never to be so deep that a carriage wheel may not be turned into it without inconvenience or danger: as often as necessary to give it due capacity without making it too deep, provision must be made for the diversion of the gutter stream, and this will ordinarily be by an outlet passing under the bed of the road to the brook. The discharge from the gutter may be from an 18 inch vitrified pipe set on end, with a branch leading into the pipe under the road, and with a cast iron grating at the top.

(2) The surface of the ground outside the gutter is never (under circumstances now anticipated) to rise abruptly or in the form of a {*dead*} inclined plane from the gutter thus:

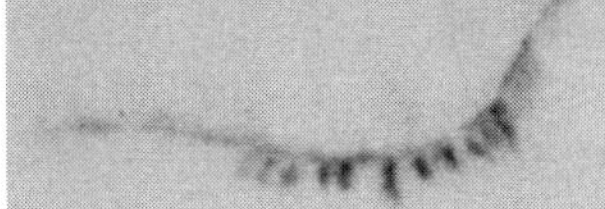

but always with a simple or double ogee curve, thus:

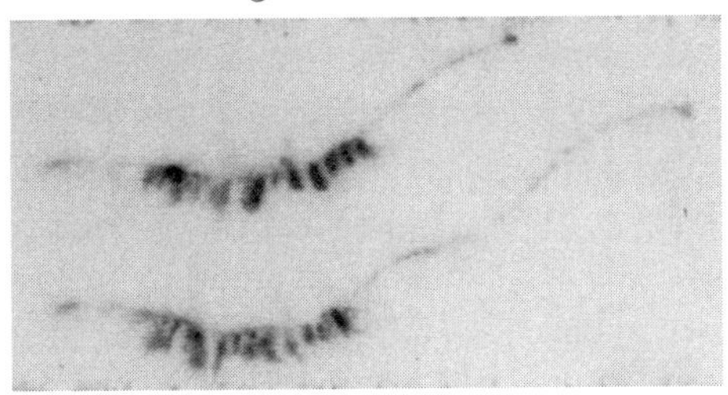

(3) Where the surface rises from the road on both sides, {(*as near the Shiloh road*)}[3] there are to be two gutters.

(4) Where the inclination of the bordering ground toward the road is slight, but the slope extended, provision is to be made for intercepting the flow of water down the slope and carrying it off before it reaches the road gutter. Generally this will be by a broad shallow gutter with a {*curved*} surface.

(5) Where the slope is too steep for the convenient forming of such a gutter and wherever there is reason to apprehend a {*sweeping*} flow of water that in the spring would make the ground soft under the road, a trench at least two feet deep is to be dug along the outside of the gutter and filled to within six inches of the surface with rubble stones, from three to six inches in largest dimension, to act as a blind drain; cross drains under the bed of the road being laid at intervals as outlets.

(6) Where the surface is to rise from both sides of the road and there is no brook into which to carry drainage directly, vitrified pipe is to be laid, ample to take all surface flow, and all gutter water is to be led to it through silt basins.

"General Map of the Estate of George W. Vanderbilt Esq., Asheville N.C.," December 30, 1889

(7) Where the road is crossing from one side to the other, as a causeway, no gutters will be needed but the wheelway is to have a border not less than three feet wide upon which a carriage could be turned out; making, with the wheelway proper, a space {22} feet broad.

(8) As a general rule where there is to be ground lower than the road at the side of the road, there should be a gentle ogee slope between this lower ground and the level of the road; where the difference of the level is considerable, however, a retaining wall with a parapet will be better. A parapet 2 feet high and 2 feet broad may be had in view. In this case, a border of one foot will be enough between the parapet and the wheelway, and this border space may be paved as a gutter and frequent outlets made through the parapet.

(9) Wherever the stream is to be crossed by the road, a {*capacious*} arched bridge is to be had in view, the ends to be of rough, rock-faced blocks with parapets two feet high and two feet thick. As a rule, the channel should be deepened near the bridges and given steep and partially rock-faced banks with a sinuous course. As a rule, also, the road should be graded to rise slightly from both sides toward the bridge.

Topsoil is to be saved wherever ground is broken. Where the road is carried on the hillside, the top-soil can be at once distributed on the upper side of the road.

Within {60} feet each side of the road, all decaying, dilapidated,

VIEW OF CONSTRUCTION OF APPROACH ROAD, BILTMORE ESTATE, C. 1891

spindling-trunked and notably top-heavy or ill-balanced and unhealthy trees are to be removed at once, and conspicuously bad ones within twice that distance. No tree is to be left standing within three feet of the wheelway, but, as pointed out on the ground, the wheelway may, at one or two points be divided and carried on both sides of trees of particular value, there being always a distance of at least three feet between each branch of the wheelway and any tree.

The felling of Beech, Black Gum, Sweet Gum, Sourwood, Chestnut and Hickory trees of more than sapling size is to be avoided as far as practicable; even (where they are of particular value,) by special curves in the course of the roads. All Rhododendrons, Kalmias, Azaleas and other notably fine bushes found in the way of grading work are to be shortened in (Kalmias very closely) and carefully transplanted to points near the edge of the road or of the swampy ground, where they can be left.

Yours Truly

F. L. Olmsted & Co
F. L. O.

The text presented here is from a letterpress copy of a typewritten letter signed and edited on the original in Olmsted's hand: A6: 429–501, OAR/LC (see FLO to Richard M. Hunt, March 2, 1889, above; FLO to George W. Vanderbilt, July 12, 1889, above; FLO to James G. Gall, Jr., Feb. 8, 1890, below.

1. William A. Thompson (1845–1933) was an engineer and railroad surveyor who began his career with the Delaware, Lackawanna & Western Railroad. Vanderbilt hired him as a surveyor, and by November of 1889 he was in charge of all surveying and engineering operations at Biltmore. He spent ten years on the estate and was responsible for building the private railroad that facilitated the transportation of construction materials there (FLO to George W. Vanderbilt, Nov. 6, 1889, A5: 465–66, OAR/LC; FLO to William A. Thompson, Nov. 6, 1889, A5: 470–76, OAR/LC; FLO to George W. Vanderbilt, March 26, 1889, A3: 408–9, OAR/LC; "W. A. Thompson Dead; Civil Engineer, 88," *New York Times*, Nov. 10, 1933, p. 21).
2. Shiloh Road ran perpendicular to the proposed route of the Approach Road, crossing it roughly half a mile northwest of the estate and a little under a mile south of the Swannanoa River, where the road began. It is unknown where the corn-field was. For more on Olmsted's plan for the Approach Road in 1889, see FLO to George W. Vanderbilt, July 12, 1889, n. 19, above (plan 170-20; "Guide Map of Biltmore Estate, 1896," NPS/FLONHS).
3. This phrase was crossed out by Olmsted.

To Philip Augustus Chase[1]

Brookline, Mass., Nov. 29th, 1889.

Mr. Philip A. Chase, Chairman of the Park Commission of Lynn, Mass.:
Sir:—At your request and under your guidance we have made such examination of the property lately coming under the charge of your Board,[2] as we have thought necessary to justify an expression of our professional judgment upon the question of its availability and value as a place of public recreation.

This question at once suggests a consideration of the provisions commonly made elsewhere for the same purpose; more especially in the parks of our larger cities. In a general survey of these, certain common characteristics are so obvious that the term park-like is in general use, as descriptive of a particular character of scenery. The principal elements of park-like scenery are broad, level or gently undulating, areas of smooth, clean turf, bordered by trees with low and spreading branches standing singly and in groups, and interspersed with objects of a decorative character, either natural, as when in the form of flowering shrubs, or artificial, as when in elegant structures, all in a finely dressed condition.

The most striking circumstance of your property is that, although nearby populous and flourishing communities, much of it is in a state of undisturbed nature and, as a whole, it is in a singularly wild, rugged and rude condition. Hardly any of it has been under tillage and were it not for the trees growing spontaneously upon it, it would be a desert. The reason it has been allowed to remain of such a character is found in the outcropping ledges and the bowlders and gravel with which its surface is strewn.

For the same reason you cannot hope to make it ever take on a "park-like" character. If you attempt it the result will be poor and will be obtained at preposterous cost. Nor can you hope ever to introduce decorative features of the sort commonly expected to be seen in parks in such a manner that they will not be discordant with the general character of the scenery and offensive to good taste. Should you be offered a gift of half a million dollars with a condition that it should be applied to such objects it would be a great extravagance to accept it.

Because of the hopelessness of making the property park-like, and, because, being unparklike in other particulars, the decorative features commonly seen in parks would appear fussy and impertinent, everywhere jarring upon the natural scenery, there is danger that the value of the property, as a place of public recreation, will fail to be realized, and that means of profitably adding to its value will be grudged.

To lessen this danger it will be well to consider wherein lies the intrinsic value of public parks. Mainly, a park is valuable to a city, as it offers those resorting to it opportunity to escape with little trouble or cost from their ordinary artificial surroundings. To escape, that is to say, from the neighborhood of objects associated with common conditions of fatigue, wear and tear, and nervous irritation, to others as much as possible foreign to them.

That the scenery offered in parks is not generally, to any great extent, of a rugged and wild forest aspect, is not because such scenery would not be valuable for the purpose of a park, but because, when, in the history of a city, ground comes to be selected for a park, no considerable area can be found within a convenient distance within which a rugged, wild and forest-like character, if it ever existed, has not been destroyed, either for industrial purposes or with the object of adapting portions of the ground to dwelling places, in which these qualities would conflict with domestic convenience. Moreover, it is not often possible to find, near a town, any larger area from within which buildings or artificial constructions, lying outside of it, do not force themselves undesirably upon the attention of visitors. For these and other reasons, in most city parks, an excess of human and artificial elements has been found unavoidable. This being the case, a sense of fitness, congruity and becomingness requires a degree of elegance, finish and neatness, in all that comes under the eye in ordinary city parks, that would otherwise be unnecessary to a satisfactory result.

The advantage of your property, with reference to the same general purpose of supplying a place of refreshing and restful relief from scenery associated with the more wearing part of the life of towns-people, is found in the circumstance that it consists of a series of elevations so disposed about a comparatively depressed area that from most points within its boundaries nothing can be seen of all that lies beyond its boundaries. Though rugged and rocky it is well-watered and densely wooded. The broken topography of the region about it and other circumstances will aid to prevent in the future, as in the past, intrusions from without upon its scenery. The extent of the property is such that with reasonable care and skill all essential accommodations may be provided for the use of it by the public without any marked disturbance of its natural character. As it stands it offers rare opportunities for those forms of recreation which experience shows to be of the most use to the great body of the people of a city. Under good management its value, in this respect, can be greatly increased. Such good management need not be costly. What is mainly required is that a method of improvement shall be pursued steadily, systematically, continuously, for a series of years. It need employ but a small force, provided this force is *constantly* employed and is directed unwaveringly to the accomplishment of certain specific objects.

Of these objects the most important will be the gradual thinning of the native forest, the less promising trees being taken out, leaving those selected to remain to have a larger share of fertility, moisture, air and light, with which advantage they would gradually give the entire forest a character much more impressive and more effective for the purpose of public recreation.

Next in importance would be the introduction, at numerous points, of new vegetation of various kinds, and with a view to different objects of detail. In some cases this would be for the covering of places which, by reason of sterility and hard exposure, are comparatively dreary of aspect, plants being wanted under such circumstances, either that, once started, will flourish under the required conditions, or plants, which growing from occasional small deposits of soil, will spread over and hide large and forlorn intermediate spaces.

In other cases the object in view would be the gradual replacing, in damp places, of the comparatively sickly plants now growing in them by others better adapted to flourish in such localities. In yet others, the aim would be to enlarge, strengthen and emphasize a local character due to an existing growth by adding to that growth and removing growths that are now weakening to the character in question.

A few men kept at work with motives such as these, removing that which, if it remains, will be harmful to a desirable character; replacing it with that which will be helpful, will gradually add greatly to the intrinsic value of the property.

We urge this element of management because the sooner it is entered upon the less will be the cost of results of a given value that can only be obtained by a steady course of operations for a series of years. Roads and walks, bridges, shelters and other constructions, may be obtained within a given short time, when set about. The difficulty of obtaining what is wanted in them is not increased by postponing outlay for it.

Your obedient servants,

F. L. Olmsted & Co.
Landscape Architects.

The text presented here was published in the *First Annual Report of the Park Commissioners of the City of Lynn* (Lynn, Mass., 1890). A draft of the letter is in Papers of FLO/LC. It was printed again in Sylvester Baxter's *The Great Woods Park of Lynn: Lynn's Public Forest: A Hand-Book Guide to the Great Woods Park of the City of Lynn* (Boston, 1891). See FLO to Sylvester Baxter, Aug. 20, 1889, above.

1. Philip Augustus Chase, a banker and businessman in Lynn, Massachusetts, served in various functions on the Board of Park Commissioners for Lynn from 1889 until 1898. See FLO to Sylvester Baxter, Aug. 20, 1889, n. 4, above.
2. Olmsted first visited the Woods in 1879 with the naturalist Thomas Wilson Flagg, who was an early advocate, along with Cyrus M. Tracy, Sylvester Baxter, and others, for the creation of the public trust, established in 1881, to hold gifts of property in Lynn Woods for public park purposes. Olmsted had most recently visited Lynn in July of 1889 (*First Annual Report, Lynn Department of Parks, 1890*, pp. 5–8; FLO to Sylvester Baxter, Nov. 9, 1880 [*Papers of FLO*, 7: 510–12]; FLO and JCO to Edwin W. Rice, July 10, 1889, A4: 966, OAR/LC).

To Matthias Denman Ross[1]

[December 1889]

Mr. M. D. Ross,
Chairman of the Committee of the
Boston Natural History Society.[2]
My dear Sir:—

You asked me last night to candidly review and criticise the paper that you had before left with me.

This paper is a suggestion of a step proposed to be taken by your Society in a negotiation with the Park Commissioners looking to a lease of certain lands, more particularly lands at Franklin Park, desired to be used by the Society.

You know that I think that the adoption of this suggestion would not be favorable to the success of the negotiation and you want to know why I think it would not.

In my judgment it is an essential condition of a satisfactory result of this negotiation that you should fully recognize, appreciate and cheerfully and heartily accept, and inwardly adopt and make genuinely your own, certain considerations that are fundamental with the Commissioners. Any tendency on your part to slur them, obscure them or get round them; any tendency to be dissatisfied and temporize with them, is fatal, in my opinion, to success.

I have often before tried to make these considerations clear to you. This paper shows that I have been unsuccessful. Trying again, I ask you to think of the Park Commissioners as a body of gentlemen serving without pay in the capacity of Trustees of certain lands, of certain funds and of a certain authority to establish ordinances and enforce them, all with reference to the accomplishment of certain ends. It is not necessary to our purpose here to define what these ends are. It is necessary that it should be clearly seen that the purposes for which the Natural History Society exists are not among them. It is no more the business of the Commissioners to use its lands, its funds or its authority, to aid the Society, than to aid the American Board of Foreign Missions or the Boston Theatre. They have no more right to part with the control of any part of the lands entrusted to them in order to promote the success of the Society, than in order to promote the success of a Railroad Corporation or a Whiskey Ring. I beg you to try to fix this thought in your mind and, in reading what is to follow, not lose sight of it.

The case being as thus stated, you may ask how it is then that there has come to be a question of the possible lease of land to your Society at a nominal rent? The answer to this question, as the record stands, is to be found in your communication to the Commissioners of September 1887, this being the initial paper of the negotiation.[3] In this paper it was stated that it had been an important part of the business of your Society for twenty years past to establish a special New England collection and that you now "invoked the aid" of the Commissioners in providing (impliedly as a natural and desirable branch and development of what you had previously been doing in this respect) "a *living* collection of the fauna of New England, under conditions as nearly natural as possible" and adapted to "facilitate public observation of their habits, their native environment, their breeding peculiarities and the rearing of their young."

Observe that these are the very words of your initial communication.

A respectful consideration of this document led the Commissioners at once to this question:—Can what is asked by the Society be granted without a diversion from its designed purpose of the property under the trusteeship of the Commissioners? This question was, as a matter of record, referred to me as their professional adviser and my advice was, in effect, that whether the property would be lessened in value for the purpose for which it had been taken, by allowing the Society such use of it as had been proposed, was a question of the limits within which the proposed collection of New England fauna *could be fixedly and permanently kept*. I pointed out that the value of the land in question as an element of the trust *did not depend on the freedom of the public to pass through it or to occupy it*, but that it resided in that which was to be seen of it, and in its service as a screen or visual border of the park. As the Society proposed to occupy it in such a manner as would exhibit a certain part of a collection of the fauna of New England under conditions as nearly as possible like those of their natural habitat, the gist of the question for the Commission would be simply this: Whether, setting off that part of such a collection as would be more naturally disposed of on the shores of a fresh water stream and pond or on the shores of a salt water tidal basin, the remainder could be satisfactorily so disposed of behind the rocks and among the trees of the Long Crouch Wood as not to lessen its essential value as a screen, a wind-break and an element of the natural rural scenery of the Park?

With my limited knowledge of the Natural History of New England it appeared probable that most of the animals of such a division of a New England collection would be very small and that the spaces required to exhibit them with a reasonable approach to their natural environments would not be larger than would be admissible. But I added that before a final opinion could be given on that point, the plan of the Society needed to be more accurately defined, meaning, for example, that the Commissioners should have before them a list of the animals to be provided for, with some approximate estimate of the space of ground and the extent of sheltering or other structures that would be required for the proper keeping and exhibition of each group of them.

Consistently with this advice the Commissioners prepared their reply to your communication.[4]

Shortly afterwards I personally met your Committee and then informally presented the position of the Park Department as I have presented it above. I said that I knew of no reason why the Commissioners should not grant the request of the Society, provided some way could be found of fixing such a clear and indubitable limit upon what should be granted that the Commissioners might be reasonably sure that under no circumstances would the successors of the present members of the Natural History Society be likely to seek to encroach upon that which it was the first duty of the Park Commissioners to guard from encroachments.

I added that the proposition to restrict the proposed collection to be accommodated in Long Crouch Wood to such part of the fauna of New England as could be better provided for there than between the two other points considered, seemed to me to offer a means of avoiding all difficulty on that score.

The negotiation having reached this point what was the next step to be expected?

Simply, in my judgment, that the Natural History Society should again present the scheme already presented in the terms above quoted, but in a more specific, definite and detailed form, a form, for example, that would supply a lawyer with the necessary data for drawing up a lease. There was no reason obvious to me why that should not be done and within a month or two a provisional lease signed. The Society could than have gone on independently of the Commissioners to deal with the question of ways and means, and, that being settled by its collection of a fund of $200,000, as required, to take possession of its property in Long Crouch Woods.

Many months afterwards it became evident to the Commissioners that the Society was proceeding on a very different course from that thus anticipated, and to me it appeared that it was in a fair way to abandon its purpose of a collection restricted to New England fauna. In conversation with you and others I therefore took occasion to offer a caution that while it was not essential that the proposed collection should be limited to New England fauna it was essential that it should have *some practical, working, fixed and accurately restricted limits; limits about which there could never in the future be any dispute* and limits that would leave no door open to a subsequent exercise of influence that might operate in the least to the detriment of the scenery and the convenience of the public in the intended specifically rural and natural landscape recreative use of the park.

Since then, in writing you and in writing Professor Hyatt,[5] I have aimed to courteously reiterate, explain and emphasize the same caution, and both from you and from him I have had responses indicating that my warning was understood and accepted.

But now this paper says:—

"An exclusively New England collection has been proposed but *this* limit seems undesirable".

Mind you it was your Committee that proposed this limit and made it the foundation of all negotiations with the Department.

But this foundation being at last knocked out, what is proposed to be substituted?

The answer given in your paper reads as follows:—

"The Garden should *start* with the exhibition of such hardy forms and be extended gradually and with great caution *in other* directions." The prescribed limitations should be—"*not inelastic*, otherwise the new enterprise may suffer from not being able to profit by"—"unexpected advantages which are likely to arise."

This appears to me very nearly equivalent to saying that upon further reflection your Committee has come to think that it would be inexpedient for the Society to accept a lease of the ground it first asked for unless the Commissioners are willing to let it do so with a view to its being used simply as a starting point of an enterprise the end of which might be hoped to be a pretty good imitation of a regular and complete Zoological Garden extending over the entire northern border of Franklin Park. And, if I do not misunderstand it, all the rest of the paper bears strongly towards such a conclusion.

There is nothing, for example, in the report of the Superintendent of the Philadelphia Zoological Garden, copied in full in the paper,[6] to indicate that he had been consulted at all in regard to the original proposition of the Society. It all reads as if this gentleman had been asked simply: "How would this place do for a Zoological Garden?": and as if he had answered without the slightest knowledge of any needed restrictions upon the manner or extent of the occupation of the ground; as if in fact the problem for his consideration was much the same with that offered at the outset in Philadelphia in a situation separated by a broad belt of railroads and carriage roads from the scenery of the park and selected with special reference to a fully developed Zoological Garden. It would appear to me that he had not even read the answer of the Commissioners to the request of the Society in which it is distinctly stated, as one of the bases of any negotiation, that Long Crouch Woods are not adapted to a complete Zoological Collection but only to some limited section of such a Collection.

But if the impression which the paper makes upon me in this respect is wrong and your Committee, though discarding the idea of limiting the Long Crouch Collection to New England fauna, still had in view for Long Crouch Wood no more than some section of a collection to which its topography would be particularly suited, has it kept in view with sufficient distinctness the necessity which the nature of the Commissioners' trust compels them to be governed by? The necessity, that is to say, of establishing plain, unquestionable, fixed and permanent limits to the proposed Long Crouch Collection before the Commissioners can intelligently determine whether they have a legal right to lease the land desired for it?

Read the paper over again and I am much mistaken if you can think that it shows that they have.

I have to observe further that the paper seems to have been prepared not only with an overestimate of what the Commissioners could rightly offer on Franklin Park, but with an underestimate of what they might rightly offer below Jamaica Pond and in the proposed land to be made between Dorchester Point and Castle Island. There have been several sketch-plans made for dealing with this latter site, each varying from the other according to a different view of what concessions could be obtained by the Commissioners from the state and the nation.[7] But in every one of them the place upon which your Committee has fixed its eyes has been otherwise appropriated, and the site contemplated for the Natural History enclosure has been either at the extreme north of the proposed bay, or on its east side adjoining the fort where much better advantages would be offered for obtaining cool salt water flowing directly from the ocean. The space had in view has been much larger than that your Committee propose to ask for, amounting in two of the plans to from eight to ten acres.

One other reflection suggested by your paper I may present in the form of a question.

Would such a sum ($200,000) as has been had in view as an assurance that your Society would be able to creditably carry out its suggestion of a New England collection, be equally an assurance of its ability to carry out such a scheme with all its suggested possibilities of expansion, as is now foreshadowed?

Yet one other reflection:—

You have repeatedly observed to me that it would, in your opinion, be well for the Society to begin operations as quickly as possible, even if in a very small and unscientific way. In a way "to please young ladies", you said last night. "With a hen and chickens", you once before said, "if it could start with nothing more". I question whether the Park Commissioners have any more right to lease land in order that the Natural History Society may provide for the amusement of young ladies or may keep a hen and chickens, (or a coon or a bear or a cage of squirrels) than for any other tenant to do so. It is not the business of the Commission, in my judgment, to lease land to be used in any such fashion, even as a means of raising money for something that shall eventually be of substantial scientific value.

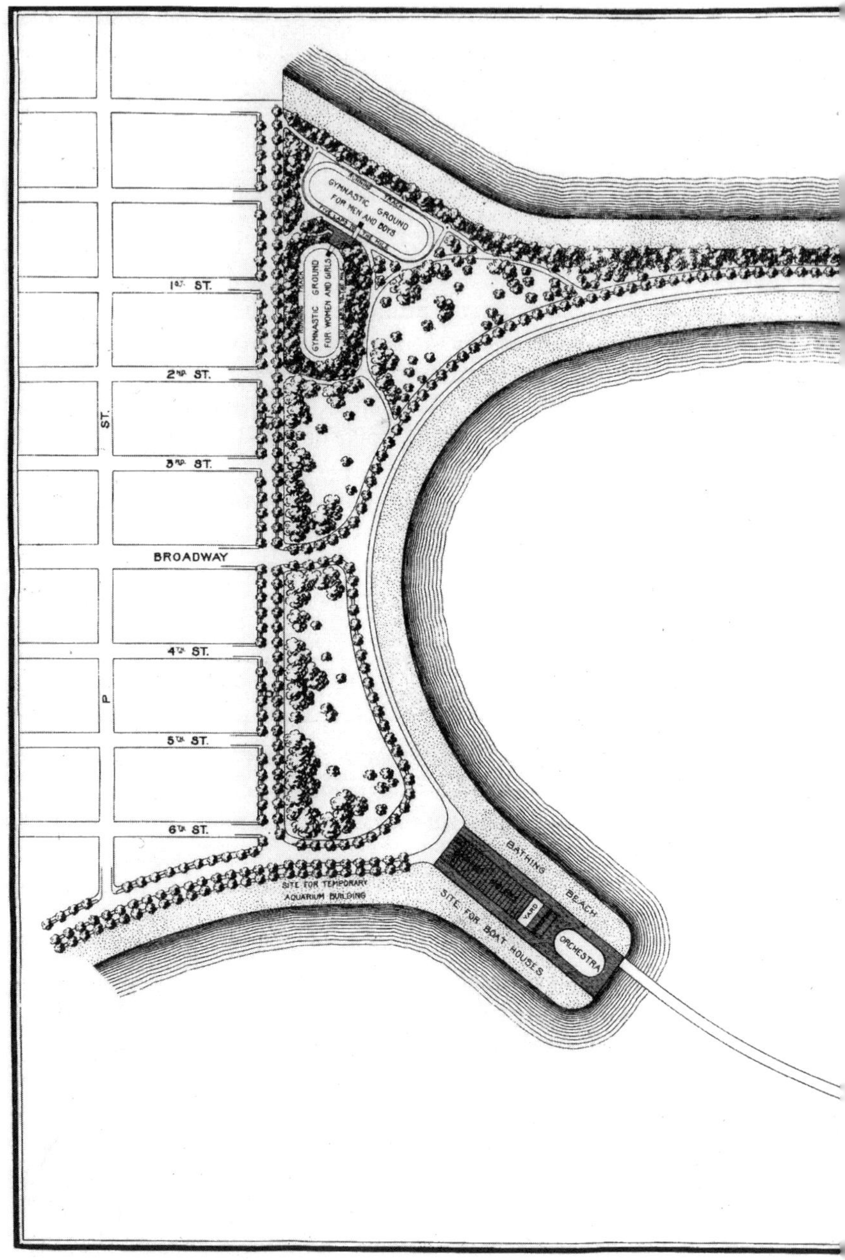

"Revised Study of a Plan for Marine Park wi

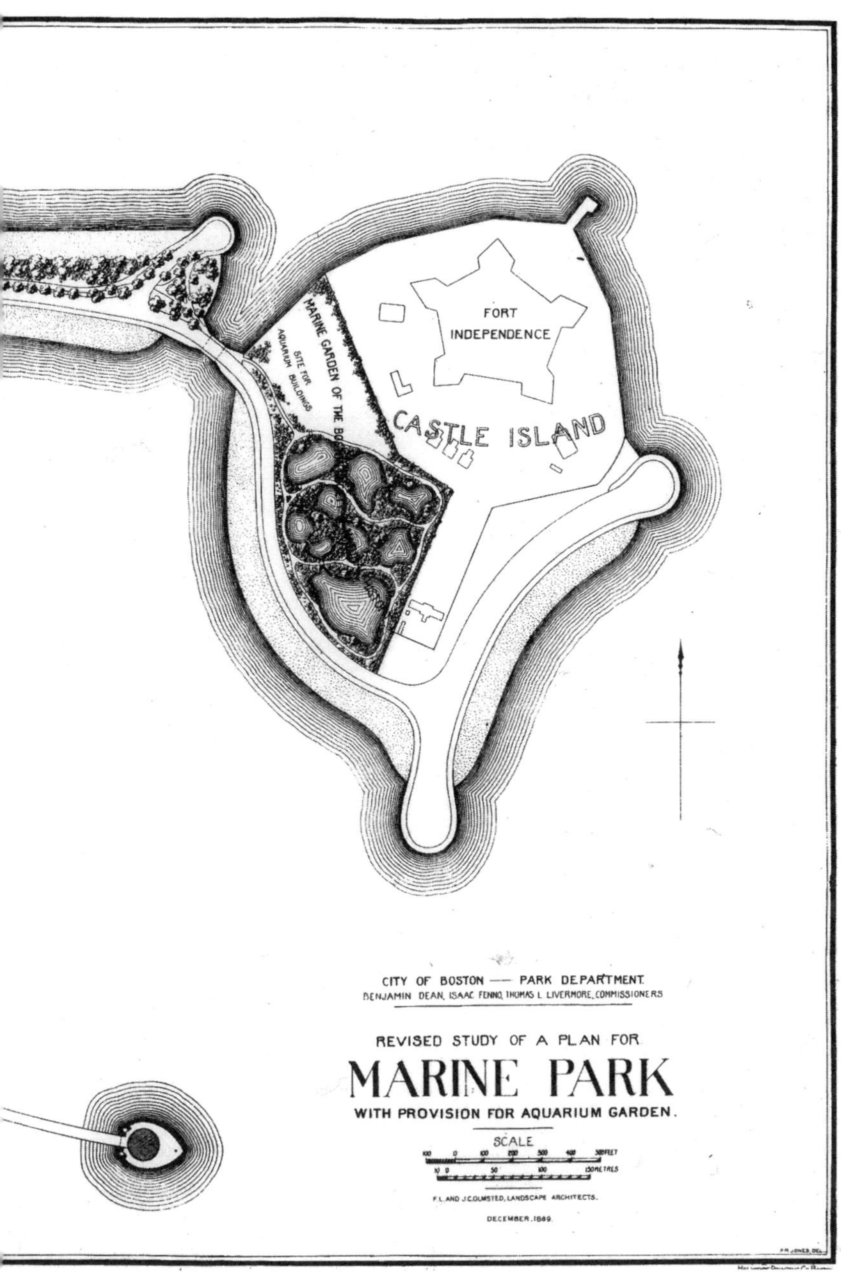

ROVISION FOR AQUARIUM GARDEN," DECEMBER 1889

Your Committee in its letter of December 3d., 1887,[8] in specific terms accepted the requirement of the Commissioners that it should be possessed of a fund of $200,000., pledged to be used in carrying out the plans of the Society, before asking for the proposed lease, and that it should enter upon no undertaking until it was prepared to carry it out with completeness.

To what end did you thus formally record your acceptance of these conditions if not that the Commissioners might be assured that you would not seek to occupy the ground in question in any provisional and temporizing way—any way that might be thought by any of those busy critics who influence public opinion and affect legislation, to be paltry; childish or derogatory to the dignity and reputation of the city as a seat of science? I suppose that to have been a most important, if not the sole, object of the condition, and I had supposed at the time that that was your understanding of it. From the point of view of the Commissioners it is of infinitely greater importance that when any thing is done it should be a complete, comprehensive and thoroughly admirable thing, than that any thing whatever should be done within a year, or two years, or twenty. The land proposed to be leased answers their purpose just as it is. If they wanted what you talk of, they would not ask your Society to supply it. They want of you only that which a body of men devoted to the interests of science—the lasting and large interests of science—can supply with a fund for a beginning of $200,000. They want what Mr. Barnum with ten times that sum could not supply.[9]

I am as far from being disposed to set back or discourage your enterprise as any man in my position well could be. I shall be heartily glad if I have opportunities to aid it. I trust that you will feel that I have proved my good will toward the Society, and toward its primary and essential objects. If so you will not think that I have answered your request in a franker spirit than the circumstances call for.

In closing I must repeat that in my judgment the Society can accomplish nothing with the Park Commissioners without coming nearer than this paper shows that it yet has to the Commissioner's point of view—a point of view from which the objects of the Natural History Society are regarded as coming before the Commissioners but incidentally and in strict subordination to the main object which it is the Commissioners specific, official duty to promote. If the Natural History Society expects more than this of the Commissioners; if it expects to obtain ground out of Franklin Park for a Zoological Garden, even a synoptical Zoological Garden, by any means that will essentially contract Franklin Park as a field of rural recreation independent of Zoological recreation; in my judgment it ought to be and will be disappointed.

I do not write as one representing the Commissioners. I have had no recent consultation with any of them on the subject and for months have not heard it mentioned. I have tried to indicate what it would seem to me reasonable for you to assume as to the point of view from which they will regard your next communication; the point of view which I should expect you to take if you had the responsibilities of a Park Commissioner resting upon you.

The text presented here is a typed, unsigned letter. It was likely written in December 1889 in response to a draft of a paper that Matthias D. Ross of the Boston Society of Natural History was planning to give to the Boston park commissioners. Ross's draft that Olmsted read has not been found, but the final version, dated December 31, 1889, was printed in the board's annual report. It outlined the Society's proposals for three "Natural History Gardens" in Boston's parks: the "Marine Aquarium" at Marine Park, "Fresh Water Aquarium" near Jamaica Pond, and "New England Zoölogical Garden" at Franklin Park. The park commissioners, at Olmsted's suggestion, had agreed in 1887 to lease Long Crouch Woods in Franklin Park to the Society for the purpose of creating a small zoo. But the Society's December 31 letter stated that they wanted to use a larger area of the park:

> The principal difficulty in carrying out even this limited plan is the insufficient surface suitable for such an exhibition. This is nowhere more manifestly true than as regards the ruminants; for within the limits of Long Crouch Woods itself it would be entirely impossible to display in any pleasing or profitable manner those largest forms among our quadrupeds. . . . For this purpose it is absolutely essential that more ground be had, at least so far as a range is concerned. And this it is hoped the commissioners will grant whenever needed, perhaps in the ground which has been set aside as a deer park, [south of Long Crouch Woods].

The Society also asked to use Sargent's Field, which had been planned as a separate area between the two sections of the proposed Deer Park. The Boston park commission voted on February 10, 1890, to cooperate with the Society in carrying out its plans, but reserved "for future consideration the extent to which the ground in the Parks can be devoted to the same." The society, in any case, was unable to raise the sufficient funds to build a zoological garden in Franklin Park at that time.

In the early twentieth century the park commissioners voted to allow the construction of what became the Franklin Park Zoo, covering the entire northeast section of Franklin Park, including the site of the Greeting (the still unbuilt formal promenade and gathering place intended to connect the Playstead and the park entrance at Columbia Road), as well as the Long Crouch Woods, the deer parks, and Sargent's Field. Arthur Shurcliff designed the Franklin Park Zoo, which opened in 1912 (Boston Society of Natural History to the Board of Park Commissioners, Dec. 31, 1889, *Fifteenth Annual Report of the Board of Park Commissioners for the year 1889* [Boston, 1890], pp. 31–40; *Sixteenth Annual Report of the Board of Park Commissioners for the Year 1890* [Boston, 1891], pp. 43–44; "Natural History Garden and Aquaria for Boston," *Science*, April 4, 1890, pp. 213–16; Arthur A. Shurtleff, "Boston Zoological Park," *Landscape Magazine*, Oct. 1912, pp. 1–14).

1. Matthias Denman Ross (1819–1892), a longtime member of the Boston Natural History Society, moved to Massachusetts from Ohio in 1846. He initially oversaw the construction of the Bay State Mill in Lawrence, Massachusetts, and moved to Boston in 1850 to found a firm producing linen thread for fishing lines and nets. He was an early proponent of filling the Back Bay and suggested that land there be set aside for educational and cultural sites, helping to establish the Massachusetts Institute of Technology. Olmsted and Ross corresponded throughout 1889 about the Society's proposals for a zoological garden and aquariums (Julius A. Stratton and Loretta H. Mannix, *Mind and Hand: The Birth of MIT* [Cambridge, Mass., 2005], pp. 162–64; *Memorial Biographies of the New England Historic Genealogical Society* (Boston, 1908); see also FLO to Matthias D. Ross, March 5, 1889, A3: 307–17, OAR/LC).
2. The Boston Society of Natural History was incorporated in 1831 as a body committed to the "encouragement and promotion of the science of Natural History" (*Annual of the Boston Society of Natural History, 1868–69* [Boston, 1868]).
3. "Committee of the Council of the Boston Society of Natural History to the Board of Park

Commissioners, September 12, 1887," *Thirteenth Annual Report of the Board of Commissioners for the Department of Parks for the City of Boston, for the Year 1887* [Boston, 1888], pp. 34–36.

4. The park commissioners specified the conditions for leasing the land to the Society and stressed that the proposed "gardens" not interfere with the original purposes of the parks: "It is the conviction of the Commissioners that the more nearly the Department of Parks is limited to the definite duty of providing the people of the city with opportunities simply of rural recreation, unmixed with other methods of recreation, and of guarding the means under its control for this purpose from being encroached upon in efforts to further other ends, the better will its funds be administered and the public served" ("Board of Park Commissioners to the Committee of the Council of the Boston Society of Natural History, Sept. 30, 1887," *Thirteenth Annual Report, Boston Department of Parks, 1887*, p. 38).
5. See FLO to Alpheus Hyatt, March 24, 1889, above; FLO to Alpheus Hyatt, May 6, 1889, above; and FLO to Matthias D. Ross, March 5, 1889, A3: 307–17, OAR/LC.
6. The paper from Ross that Olmsted read has not been found. The park board did not publish a copy of the Philadelphia Superintendent's report along with the Society's letter in its *Fifteenth Annual Report*. A mention of the superintendent's visit, however, does appear in the *Proceedings of the Boston Society of Natural History*: "The committee has also invited and received the benefit of a visit from an expert of experience, Mr. Arthur Erwin Brown, whose opinion was considered to be of great value on account of his success in conducting the operations of the Zoölogical Gardens at Philadelphia which are under his charge. Mr. Brown was very much pleased with the general aspect and facilities for the exposition of certain classes of animals at Franklin Park and gave the committee the use of his written opinions" (*Proceedings of the Boston Society of Natural History*, vol. XXIV [Boston, 1890], p. 246).
7. In their 1876 park system plan, the Boston park commissioners proposed building a park in part on a landfill between Dorchester Point in South Boston and Castle Island. By 1889, the boundaries of what would become Marine Park had changed several times, and Congress had not granted the park board permission to use Castle Island, which was the site of Fort Independence and federally owned. In 1887 the park commissioners petitioned Congress to use all or part of the island for park purposes, but President Cleveland vetoed the legislation.

   In 1889 the park commissioners again petitioned Congress for the use of Castle Island. Before Congress voted on the resolution, on December 23, Olmsted presented to the park board the two sketches that he mentions in this letter. According to a written statement by Olmsted, each sketch responded to a different scenario. In the first, Congress allowed the park commissioners to extend Marine Park onto Castle Island but insisted it could only be connected to the mainland by a drawbridge. In that sketch Olmsted covered the entire western portion of Castle Island with a "Marine Garden." In the second proposal, Olmsted assumed Congress had not allowed the public to use Castle Island at all, and he placed the "Marine Garden" between "the beach drive and west border of the Park." On May 1, 1890, Congress approved the resolution "authorizing the use and improvement of Castle Island, Boston Harbor," but neither scenario was immediately acted upon. When an aquarium was built in 1912, the park commissioners placed it in the western portion of the park, not on Castle Island (C. Zaitzevsky, *The Boston Park System*, p. 91–94; *Thirteenth Annual Report, Boston Department of Parks, 1887* [Boston, 1888], pp. 30–31; *Fifteenth Annual Report, Boston Department of Parks, 1889*, pp. 23–26; plan 926-30, NPS/FLONHS; *Sixteenth Annual Report of the Board of Park Commissioners for the Year 1890* [Boston, 1891], pp. 37–38; *Seventeenth Annual Report of the Board of Park Commissioners for the Thirteen Months Ending January 31, 1892* [Boston, 1892], pp. 37–38; Anthony Mitchell Sammarco, *South Boston* [Charleston, S.C., 2006], p. 93; see also *Appendix, Report of the Landscape Architect Advisory*, Dec. 30, 1887, above).

8. "Committee of the Council of the Boston Society of Natural History to the Board of Park Commissioners, December 3, 1887," *Thirteenth Annual Report, Boston Department of Parks, 1887*, pp. 41–43.
9. P. T. Barnum (1810–1891) owned a number of successful museums and circuses in the nineteenth century, including the American Museum in New York City and the traveling Barnum & Bailey Circus (*DAB*).

TO THE EDITOR OF *AMERICAN FLORIST*

January 15, 1890

"Landscape."

"Anglo Saxon, landscipe. Scipe is the same as ship in friendship and means the state or condition of being." "A landscape means a piece of the earth's surface, and it is always understood that this piece will have a certain artistic unity, or suggestion of unity, in itself."

PHILIP GILBERT HAMMERTON, Landscape Painter.[1]

"Our art, to appear to advantage, requires some extent of surface, its lines should lose themselves indefinitely, and unite agreeably and gradually with those of the surrounding country."

ANDREW JACKSON DOWNING, Landscape Gardener.[2]

"The masses of light and shade, whether in a natural landscape or a picture, must be broad and unbroken or the eye will be distracted by the flutter of the scene."

THOMAS WHATELEY, (*Observations on Modern Gardening.*)[3]

"The principles of landscape gardening we conclude to be derived from nature or developed by the principles of landscape painting."

JOHN CLAUDIUS LOUDON, (*Encyclopedia of Gardening.*)[4]

ED. AM. FLORIST:—Can debate be profitable between friends who are agreed upon no premises; who take for granted what is not granted, and who use terms vital to the discussion, one in a different sense from the other? If not, a common understanding among all who are called gardeners as to how the following questions should be answered is much to be desired. Whatever will tend to bring us nearer to it is much to be desired.

1. With what significance, under sound usage, is the word landscape to be prefixed to the word gardening? If "landscape gardening" means anything distinctive from "ornamental gardening," for instance, what is the

essence of the distinction? What is the use, what the purpose, of landscape gardening in distinction from other gardening?

2. Can that which is discriminatingly called landscape gardening, and that which is discriminatingly called ornamental gardening be fused together so that a given work may be regarded as a perfect combination of both? Is there, or is there not, a liability in attempting such a combination that the purpose of one will antagonize the purpose of the other and the result be confusion rather than fusion—disunity rather than unity?

3. Have in mind a body of land, like the site of Fairmount Park,[5] which is more than four square miles in area, of beautiful but highly diversified topography, with deep valleys and lofty hills, partly wooded, partly open, here divided by a broad quiet pond-like river, here by a brawling trout stream, its banks some times bold, craggy and sterile, sometimes flat, fertile and grassy. Suppose that from points within such a body of land, views are to be had miles away toward sunset, ending in wooded heights faintly blue in the distance. If landscape gardening, so called, has distinctive purpose, would it be more or would it be less becomingly applied to such a body of land than to a small body of simple topography, the site of the garden before the cathedral in New Orleans, for example, the Bowling Green in New York or the Public Garden in Boston? And how is it with ornamental gardening?

4. Why should some pleasure grounds be described as parks and others as gardens? Does the term "park-like" mean anything that the term "garden-like" does not? If there is any distinction, what are the leading qualities of a garden other than those of a park?

The irreconcilable answers to such questions that must underlie the habits of mind of different men, equally intelligent, well informed and interested in the subject, may be inferred from two or three examples of the manner in which such men manifest their ordinary attitude toward it.

In October you printed a paper that had been read before the convention at Buffalo by Mr. McMillan,[6] the gardener of a large rural park outside of that city. It assumed to present certain views of what was considered by the author to be properly called *landscape* gardening and the key to what he thought the significance of the term was probably expressed when he said that the "lay of the land' is the groundwork of *landscape* gardening, these words meaning, I suppose, much the same as the words of my texts. The gist of the paper seems to be given when it says that in dealing with "any grounds of sufficient extent to have a distinctive *landscape* character, the general aim (of *landscape* gardening) will be to make a harmonious combination with the dominant characteristics which nature has already stamped upon the site. He (the *landscape* gardener) will seek a fuller or a richer development of the essential leading features, simply softening what is hard, clothing what is bare, filling out what is meager and enriching what is beautiful, all in harmony with the original type." These sentences sufficiently suggest how the author would answer the questions that I have submitted.

Afterwards (December 1, page 184 and 186) you printed a review of the McMillan paper from the accomplished pen of "Observer,"[7] who, while expressing warm personal regard and friendship for Mr. McMillan, undertakes to show that his views are "in many respects totally erroneous." In combating them he refers to the slight degree in which he found himself interested in what he properly assumes to be a better exposition of Mr. McMillan's view than could be given in words, namely, his park.

This park has two principle features, one is a slightly undulating plain of turf bordered by masses of wood, mainly natural, but here and there pieced out and connected by new plantings and interspersed with a few scattered trees standing singly and in groups with glades between them. Sheep and cows run at large in it, and looking across it in almost any direction the distance is so great that forms and colors blend together, and all detail on the opposite side is obscure. Its "masses of light and shade are broad and unbroken;" its lines "lose themselves indefinitely and unite themselves agreeably and naturally with those of the adjoining country." No object calls for special admiration by itself. Nothing is obtrusive. There are roads and walks and a single group of low buildings, but they are kept so much behind trees and under their shadow that in a general view they are little seen. There is nothing, indeed, to be seen from many points but a broad, far-reaching stretch of partially wooded, slightly rolling pasture land. The other principle feature is a pond of forty or fifty acres with sylvan shores. This has been made simply by scooping the mire out of a swamp and filling the hole with water, so that the shores, except for a little additional planting, are pretty much what nature made them.

This is what Mr. McMillan may be assumed to mean when he speaks of finding the groundwork of landscape gardening in "the lay of the land." Observer speaks of it as *acres of dreary monotony*. He thinks if what he saw is to be called gardening that it compares with the gardening with which he is familiar as "the rude figures and crude paintings that mark the dawn of art" rank by the side of "the Venus de Medici or the Transfiguration of Raphael." He notices that scarcely any use has been made in Mr. McMillan's park of the immensely varied resources of splendor in color that modern scientific and commercial enterprise has recently provided. He saw no rarities, no *nouveautes*.[8] Even the shrubs and perennials were as old fashioned as a last year's bonnet. His conclusion is that in what Mr. McMillan advocates under the name of landscape he is trying to lead a "retrograde movement," a return to the gardening of a primitive stage of civilization.

What do you suppose Mr. McMillan thinks of these comments? May he not be imagined saying to himself: "My friend does not appear to have understood what I meant by landscape, and he is judging operations for the improvement of the natural scenery of a body of land, within which one can have views more than a mile in length, by standards which might be applied, if not to a conservatory opening out of a drawing room, to an urban garden a stone's throw across, formed on made land and surrounded by tall buildings."

Take another case. In your issue No. 103, page 163, another gentleman, reviewing the same McMillan essay, describes a similar experience.[9] There was nothing in the Buffalo Park, he says, that was worth *to him* the five cents which it cost him to see it, but he recognizes, as "Observer" can not, that it is possible to apply to such a work another standard than that which he is habituated to use. He does not question that *"from a landscaper's point of view"* it may have some interest. What do these words imply? How does a "landscaper's" point of view differ from another man's—say a florist's? There is an article in a recent number of your esteemed contemporary, *Garden and Forest*, that may throw some light on the point—the landscaper's point. The writer of it is describing the recent "improvement" of a park in Paris, which, for one of its limited area, formerly had, he says, a certain degree of landscape beauty. Of late it has been attempted to combine with this beauty a share of ornamental beauty. The manner of the attempt is explained as follows: "Trees are encircled by flower beds, and even isolated exotic plants which are placed near them—as if they were not obtrusive enough in themselves—are surrounded in the same way. A tuft of pampas grass, which would be far better away, is rendered doubly bad by its ring of geraniums, or a wide-leaved palm overshadows a circle of crimson coleus."[10] The result is apparently thought to be that landscape unity is destroyed by the ornaments, while the ornaments are displayed at great disadvantage because of the presence of objects and conditions which, left without ornaments, were adapted to give the place a distinctively landscape charm.

Would the following be a much exaggerated statement of the difference between the point of view thus exemplified, and that apparently occupied by those who are of Observer's way of thinking? Observer regards gardening as an "art," in the sense that painting is an art and sculpture another art, each having distinctive aims, each having distinctive principles. It would be better to say that there are really two arts, each having distinctive aims and principles, to both of which the name gardening is applied and is apt to be confusingly applied. To distinguish one from the other the prefixes *landscape* and *ornamental* or decorative, are sometimes used. How do they differ? If a man blind and deaf from birth were to ask how the art of music and the art of painting differ, a part of the answer would be that they respectively appeal to different emotional sensibilities. So, to explain how the two arts differ that are called by the name of gardening, it may be said that works of landscape art are addressed to one class of human sensibilities, works of ornamental gardening to another. Just this is pre-supposed when one says that a certain passage of landscape may be pleasing to those who are sensitive to landscape, but that he himself is not so, and to him it seems only dull and monotonous.

But one not used to think of landscape gardening and ornamental gardening as different arts, may ask, if they are so, how they happen to have a name in common? A full answer would include the result of some historical inquiry, but, for the occasion, it may be sufficient to say that, regarded from the physical and superficial rather than the metaphysical, spiritual and essential point of view, which latter is the point of view of art, (that is to say of poetic design, motive or purpose to affect the imagination), they are not to be clearly separated, both having largely to do with the same class of materials and both largely employing the same class of mechanical appliances and handicraft processes in dealing with those materials. The common name witnesses this fact, as smith in coppersmith and in silversmith testifies of men of different trades both working in metals, with common appliances and common methods.

There were, a year ago or more, as I remember, two short articles in the AMERICAN FLORIST from which it might be inferred that you, Mr. Editor, were rather inclined to take some such view as has thus been suggested of the difference between landscape gardening and ornamental gardening. One was a discussion of certain observations upon landscape gardening, so called, that had appeared in the *Century* magazine; the other a reply to a correspondent, presumably qualified for ornamental gardening, asking how he could best proceed to make himself a landscape gardener. In both you referred to landscape gardening much as you might, I think, if you regarded it as an essentially different art from that of ornamental gardening.[11]

Before fully adopting such a view, I should be glad, as I am sure that many others would, to see a better presentation than I yet have of the reasons that prevent it from being more generally accepted.

AN ATTENTIVE READER

The text presented here is from *American Florist*, Jan. 15, 1890, pp. 254–56, signed "An Attentive Reader." The Society of American Florists began publication of *American Florist* in Chicago in 1885. The editor was G. L. Grant (Regan Printing House, *Story of Chicago in Connection with the Printing Business* [Chicago, 1912], p. 142; G. L. Grant, "Floriculture for Profit," *Daily Picayune*, Feb. 13, 1888, p. 8; J. C. Vaughan and G. L. Grant, "Protest by the Horticulturists," *Chicago Daily Tribune*, June 18, 1891, p. 7).

1. Quoted from Philip G. Hamerton, *Landscape* (London, 1885), pp. 9–10. The second sentence has been slightly truncated from the original, which reads: "A landscape means a piece of the earth's surface that can be seen at once, and it is always understood that this piece will have a certain artistic unity, or suggestion of unity in itself."
2. Quoted from Andrew Jackson Downing, *A Treatise on the Theory and Practice of Landscape Gardening Adapted to North America* (New York, 1841), p. 19.
3. Olmsted attributes the quotation to Thomas Whately, but it is actually from Humphry Repton, in his *Sketches and Hints on Landscape Gardening* (London, 1794), which Olmsted likely read in J. C. Loudon's edited volume: *The Landscape Gardening and Landscape Architecture of the Late Humphry Repton, Esq.* (London, 1840), pp. 79–80.
4. Quoted from J. C. Loudon, *An Encyclopædia of Gardening* (London, 1835), p. 1168.
5. Fairmount Park is a large park in Philadelphia located on the Schuylkill River.

6. William McMillan, "Landscape Gardening," *American Florist*, Oct. 15, 1889, pp. 107–11. William McMillan, superintendent of Buffalo's parks, whose work Olmsted greatly appreciated, read his paper at the Fifth Annual Convention of the American Florist Society (FLO to William McMillan, March 16, 1885, n. 1, above; *Proceedings of the Fifth Annual Convention of the Society of American Florists, 1889*, pp. 108–18; see FLO to Sylvester Baxter, Sept. 2, 1889, above, for more on McMillan's paper).
7. "Landscape Gardening—A Retrograde Movement," *American Florist*, Dec. 1, 1889, pp. 184–86.
8. *Nouveautés*, meaning novelties.
9. Herbert G. Walker, "Flowers in Parks," *American Florist*, Nov. 15, 1889, p. 163.
10. "Ornamental Planting' in Paris," *Garden and Forest*, Dec. 11, 1889, pp. 590–91.
11. In the fall of 1887, the *American Florist* published articles in reply to an article that appeared in the *Century Illustrated Monthly Magazine* that claimed that there was a scarcity of qualified landscape gardeners in the United States, prompting responses about the differences between gardeners and landscape architects. At least one respondent ("A Gentleman's Gardener") said that this was "the purest nonsense." He asserted that there were plenty of "garden artists" available that were more than capable of completing large commissions, "even though its [the profession's] ranks were swollen by the Olmsteds and Vauxes—marching in the shoes of Downing." He went on to criticize the design of Central Park as "not noble or original," and claimed that a true garden artisan could "easily give points to any landscape architects." There were a number of commentaries in the *American Florist* in 1887 that began to draw divisions among the professions of florists, gardeners, and landscape architects, sometimes with landscape architects identified as being more broadly educated and qualified than the others ("Landscape Gardening and 'Garden Artisans,'" *American Florist*, Oct. 1, 1887, p. 86; "The Florists of the Future," ibid., Aug. 15, 1887, pp. 1–2; "The Education of Gardeners," ibid., Aug, 15, 1887, p. 7; "The Education of Florists," ibid., Sept. 1, 1887, pp. 36–37).

To Charles Loring Brace

18th Jan. 1890.

My Dear Charles;

Returning from Washingtn I find your note of 14th & the book.[1] I cordially congratulate you. It strikes me as your best work from a literary point of view tho' I doubt if as interesting or as helpful as the *Gesta*.[2] It is likely to be more popular, however. I do not see why you should say it is probably your last. Certainly there is a large chance of our dying or being disabled within a week but a sufficient chance of our being in working condition ten years longer to make it wrong not to so order our lives that we can be doing as good work in the future as in the past. If I have lost power in some ways I have gained compensatingly in others, and it must be more so with you & your chances of living vigorously on, with your habits, a great deal better than mine. I never had more before me or less inclination to lay off than now, though my arrangements are such that nobody need be disappointed if I drop out tomorrow, John and Codman being ready to take up all my work and on an average better qualified for it than I am. My office is much better equipped and has more momentum than ever before.

Do you remember a night we passed sleeping upon an earthen floor with our feet toward a peat fire with an old woman who gave us a piteous account of her sufferings in the Famine?[3] It amused me to find that I was entertaining her landlord here in the Earl of Meath.[4] He had a lot of photographs of his seat and taking one up without knowing in what part of Ireland he lived I said:—"Hullo! I seem to remember those hills in the background. Is it Wicklow." "Yes," he answered, "Wicklow; have you been there? Did you go by —, — and — (names I recalled as he mentioned them) and the Seven churches[5] and — and —?" "Yes I think, I did." "Then you passed right through my estate and saw the mountains from very near this point of view."

Yours Very Affcty

Fred[k] Law Olmsted.

The text presented here is a signed letter in Olmsted's hand.

1. Charles Loring Brace, *The Unknown God or, Inspiration Among Pre-Christian Races* (New York, 1890). Brace's letter of the 14th has not been found.
2. Charles Loring Brace, *Gesta Christi or, A History of Human Progress Under Christianity* (New York, 1882).
3. The Great Famine began in Ireland in 1845 with a failure of the potato crop, leading to mass starvation and emigration. In the spring and summer of 1850, Olmsted, his brother, John, and Charles Loring Brace together went on a walking tour of the British Isles, including Ireland, which they visited in late summer. Upon his return, Olmsted published *Walks and Talks of an American Farmer in England* (1852) (*Papers of FLO*, 1: 8–12).
4. Olmsted's guest was Reginald Brabazon (1841–1929), the Twelfth Earl of Meath, who had visited a number of American parks during the summer of 1889, and to whom Olmsted sent statistics on public parks in the United States and Canada in 1890. He was the founder, in 1882, of the Metropolitan Public Gardens Association, a charity devoted to the preservation of public green spaces in London. During Olmsted's walking tour of 1850, however, the Earl of Meath would have been Reginald's grandfather, John Chambre Brabazon (1772–1851), the Tenth Earl (*DNB*, Frederick Law Olmsted, "Contribution to the Public Discussion of the Question of a Park for the People of My Old Home Town," May 19, 1890, A8: 569–81 OAR/LC; FLO to Earl of Meath, Feb. 7, 1890, A6: 843, OAR/LC; FLO to Earl of Meath, May 9, 1890, A8: 483–84; Sylvanus Urban, *Gentleman's Magazine* [London, 1851], pp. 547–48).
5. The Valley of Gledalough is south of Dublin in County Wicklow. The region was known for its medieval monastic ruins, including the Seven Churches (James Fraser, *A Hand Book for Travellers in Ireland* [Dublin, 1844], pp. 102, 388).

To James G. Gall, Jr.[1]

Brookline, Mass., Feby. 8th, 1890.

Mr. James G. Gall, Jr.

Dear Sir: Before the Approach Road through the Valley above the Quarry can be made, or precisely laid out, the water channel of the Valley will have to be considerably modified as to its course and to be much deepened.[2] This must be your work and in this letter we shall give you instructions for it. Please get these well fixed in your mind and use your best judgment in the matter having it in mind from the start that there is nothing in Landscape Gardening that oftener fails of wholly satisfactory results, more especially in respect to naturalness, than an undertaking of this kind. I meant to have had a talk with you upon the matter before I left the Estate last week but did not find you at the office the last day.

You will see that before any other part of the Valley work can be entered upon, the water channel must be made deep enough to allow drain pipes to be discharged into it, which will have been carried under the road, and as those drain pipes must be laid and the road bottom formed and consolidated before stone can be removed to it from the breaker, the sooner this deepening of the channel in preparation for them is done the better. It should not be made necessary to store the broken stone at the breaker or to handle it twice after it falls from the breaker.

You will rough out the revised channel therefore, as fast as you well can, and probably before you come to the stage of detailed slopings and finish. I can go over the ground with you. But you cannot do even the preliminary work well unless you have from the outset a pretty good notion of the character of the result to be obtained at all points, for sameness of character and the repetition of features is to be avoided and, as much as practicable, different qualities should appear in the upper from the lower parts of the Valley. I shall presently lay down a few simple general principles for your guidance and give you certain figures of measurement. Within the limits thus fixed you must exercise your artistic taste and judgment. I don't know whether you have before had occasion to direct such work but you have seen {*three*} rapidly-falling water courses formed under my direction (in the Ramble and in McGowan's Pass, Central Park, and in the Glen, Brooklyn Park)[3] and will have some idea of the manner in which I have proceeded in laying out and directing them. You will have to make such arrangements that the business can be well done without taking much of your time. To this end it will be well to make a careful preliminary study of the ground, digging test-pits if you think best; approximately stake out a course for the stream, and form in your own mind a provisional plan for the work to be modified and elaborated in detail as excavation proceeds and you obtain a better understanding of the subsurface conditions and your imagination is aided by partly done work. The most important matter will be the choice of a foreman. The best man for bossing sewer or railroad work might be the worst for this. If you should find one who can appreciate general principles after a little training; who will take pride in working them out and yet be cautious and unpresuming in the exercise of needed discretion during the intervals of a day or two which there should generally be between your visits to the ground, he will be worth higher wages than most foremen. I have not found gardeners or contractors' foremen suitable for such work. It cannot be done by digging to stakes or set limits. The foreman should have a personal aptitude to take in your ideal and must exercise personal {*ingenuity*} in working it out.

The passage through the wood that has already been cleared may be considered as establishing the course of the road unless, as you examine the ground more closely and get your plan for the channel developed, there should be found occasion to slightly modify it. The grades as arranged by Mr. Thompson will doubtless require some slight adjustments at a few points with a view to convenience and economy in making the channel. You can arrange such adjustments in conference with Mr. Thompson, keeping in mind two points:

First, *it is desirable with regard to landscape effect to have the surface of the road as low as practicable*; it should nearly everywhere be rather below than above the natural surface of the ground immediately on its borders, anything like the effect of a causeway or terrace road being objectionable. That is to say, as a general rule the surface of the road should be flush with the natural surface of the flat valley bottom adjoining it, and the immediate border on the hillside will have to be reformed in adjustment to this lower grade of the road. If the soil of the flat ground to be moved in order to get a solid bottom for the road is more than the intended depth of the road metal (8") the surface of the road will sometimes be *below* the natural surface of the flat ground. Better have it so, commonly, than go to expense in drawing in earth from the hills for a higher bottom. But there will be a question of making the channel sufficiently deep for drainage and other circumstances to be considered, and, as to grade of road, Mr. Thompson, knowing what you want as to channel, must decide.

Second, *the grade of the road will vary from 1 in 100 to 1 in 20 with a very gradual transition between the steeper and the less steep parts*. There should be hardly any absolute plane and nothing approaching an angular change of grade such as is sometimes seen in city streets. In other words you must look out that the profile of the road as well as its course is graceful. I think that a grade of 1 in 30 will have to be exceeded only in the approaches to bridges, and where these occur it will be a question whether you will best accomplish a desirable result by deepening the water course so that the bridge will be low, or, for some distance on the sides of the bridge, elevate the grade of the road above the natural surface. It is a question mainly of economy and to be determined by local conditions. If you find rock near the surface for example you will raise the grade sufficiently to avoid blasting. But other things equal, the low grade is to be preferred.

In order to admit drain tile to pass at sufficient depth under the road and discharge into the water course, the bottom of the water course will need to be generally at least four feet below the level of the finished grade of the road, and in order to avoid crumbling banks, to obtain variety of graceful, dimpled slopes, and to give footing for occasional large shrubs, the middle line of the water course will need to be generally at least 12 feet from the gutter of the road.

At certain points, however, near bridges and where the road passes at the greatest elevation above the water, it will be well to lay out the water course as near as practicable to the road, the middle of it being, say, six feet from the gutter, but, in such cases, the road must be sustained by a strong wall with a parapet at least two feet high, the roadside of which parapet would be one foot from the outer edge of the gutter. It is very desirable to have the top and road side face of parapets and all that shows in the masonry of bridges formed of fitting rock with natural weathered face, carrying moss or lichens or at any rate not of raw color. You can be on the lookout for specially good bits of rock, for prominent places either ledge rock or bowlders, as you move about the neighborhood and if not so found, by and by make search for it, especially on the edges of streams and river banks.

As far as the limits that have been above prescribed will admit, the course of the revised stream will generally follow the course of the present stream but the widening and deepening of it will sometimes be on one side sometimes on the other so that the revised course will be more meandering. It will at some points be best carried as far from the road as practicable in loops, so that it will be momentarily lost sight of from the road but more commonly it will best be at a distance from the road varying from 12 to 20 feet. The water should appear sometimes in still broad pools with low nearly flat immediate banks; sometimes in rapids of varying breadth and more or less obstructed by rocks or pebbly shoals and with bold banks, and sometimes in small cascades with yet bolder banks buttressed with rock.

The localities where the larger loops in the course of the stream can best be made and those in which it will be desirable to introduce a retaining wall, will be obvious in the natural circumstances on the ground; the pools will come in naturally where you find the ground nearest level and the bottom broadest; the rapids where the valley is narrowest and the fall of the present stream most rapid.

There will be places, probably, above the head of cascades or rapids where you cannot well get the bottom of the open channel as much as four feet below the road. Of course you will make provision at these points for a conduit below ground to take the under-drainage of the road to a lower point of discharge.

No more grading work having been done than is necessary to establish the general course and grade of the bottom of the stream, the banks being still generally abrupt and rough, (as they should, in the first instance, be left, systematically) there will remain the detailed modeling of the banks and shores to be taken up as a work by itself. This will mainly follow local suggestions, the surface being "humored" to the best trees and shrubs and to conditions of soil; grace of slope being studied and a pleasing play of one slope into another. Avoid all petty effects; aim to maintain a large scale and broad lights and shadows. Let one character of

Workers and Designers Standing on Approach Road, Biltmore Estate, c. 1891; (*First Row, Second from Right*) G. W. Vanderbilt, (*First Row, Third from Right*) Frederick Law Olmsted

bank contrast with another, high banks with low, concave with convex surfaces, low shelves with high, always of course, keeping in view the methods of nature.

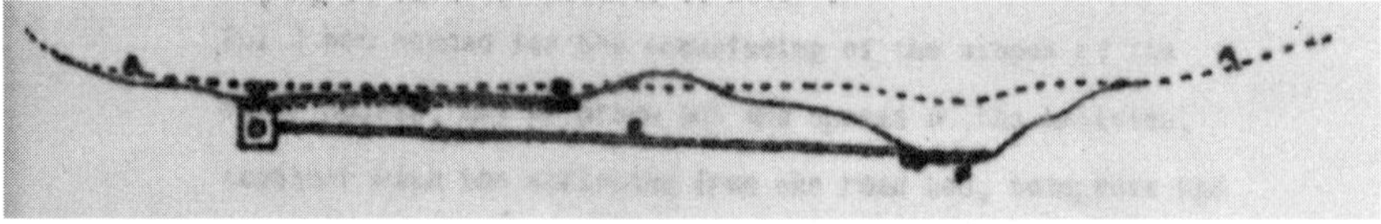

A. A. Natural Surface
B. B. Gutters
C. Road Metal
D. Silt Basin
E. Tile
F. Bottom of stream

Comparative elevations.

Bottom of Stream	0
Tile Outlet	0'. 6"
Bottom of Silt Basin	1.' 0"
Outlet of Silt Basin	2'. 0"
Gutters	3'. 7"
Crown of Road	4'. 0"

The above may be considered as an ideal section applicable under the prevailing circumstances in the narrower parts of the valley.

The road is expected to be made with seven inches evenly broken road metal (on a firmly rolled clean earth bottom) rolled in layers, and one inch screenings; total thickness of stone, eight inches.

We hope that the material excavated for the revised channel will be

View of Approach Road, Biltmore Estate, c. 1891

VIEW OF APPROACH ROAD, BILTMORE ESTATE, C. 1891

nearly all muck (leaf mould) soil or fair loam. All such material, (and all that would not be harmful) not needed for the resurfacing of the slopes of the water course, may be drawn out and spread on the hillside, together with the stripping from the road bed, to improve the soil for Rhododendron and Kalmia plantations.

The text presented here is from a letterpress copy of an unsigned typed letter with edits in Olmsted's hand: A6: 852–61, OAR/LC.

1. James G. Gall, Jr., (d. 1910) was superintendent of landscape construction at Biltmore. Olmsted had worked with him in New York City in the 1850s when Gall was an assistant drainage engineer during construction of Central Park, and Olmsted brought him to Biltmore in 1889. In the interim, Gall had been employed on a number of public works, including railroad construction and the development of the national cemeteries at Vicksburg, Gettysburg, and Arlington. Although Gall and William A. Thompson were both engineers, Gall was in charge of the landscape department under Olmsted, and Thompson was in charge of all engineering projects. Therefore, Thompson and Gall worked together on the Approach Road under Olmsted's supervision ("Obituary Notes," *New York Times*, Feb. 21, 1910, p. 9; *Papers of FLO*, 3: 12; John M. Bryan, *Biltmore Estate, The Most Distinguished Private Place* [New York, 1994], p. 91; FLO to George W. Vanderbilt, March 26, 1889, A3: 408–9, OAR/LC, FLO to George W. Vanderbilt, Nov. 6, 1889; FLO to William A. Thompson, Nov. 6, 1889, A5: 470–76, OAR/LC).
2. That is, the quarry about one quarter mile south of the Swannanoa River near the beginning of the Approach Road. Above the quarry was the valley of Ram Branch, a stream that ran along and at points intersected with the Approach Road. See FLO to William A. Thompson, Nov. 11, 1889, n. 2, above.

3. The Central Park Ramble features a small watercourse, the Gill, that flows down to the Lake, with several small pools and waterfalls formed along the way. McGowan's Pass in Central Park was an existing topographic feature in the north end of the park, near what became the Harlem Meer. A watercourse flowed from the large Pool, located on the west side of the park, through the Ravine, and into the Harlem Meer near McGowan's Pass. The Glen in Prospect Park, also known as the Ravine, featured the Ambergill, a watercourse flowing down through the park's woodlands near the center of the park. All of these streams were engineered in the wooded, picturesque sections of their respective parks (see Charles E. Beveridge and Paul Rocheleau, *Frederick Law Olmsted: Designing the American Landscape* [New York, 1995], pp. 52–83).

GOVERNMENTAL PRESERVATION OF NATURAL SCENERY.

Brookline, Mass.,
8th March, 1890.

In a communication that has been given to the public from the Governor of California to the Senators and Representatives in Congress of that State, I am surprised to find my name introduced in a manner that compels me to make the following statement.[1]

In the year 1864, being then a citizen of California, I had the honor to be made chairman of the first Yosemite Commission, and in that capacity to take possession of the Valley for the State, to organize and direct the survey of it and to be the executive of various measures taken to guard the elements of its scenery from fires, trespassers and abuse. In the performance of these duties, I visited the Valley frequently, established a permanent camp in it and virtually acted as its superintendent. It was then to be reached from the nearest village only by a sixty mile journey in the saddle, and there were many more Indians in it than white men. The office had come to me unexpectedly and in a manner that earned my devotion. So far from a salary coming with it, it was an affair of considerable cost to me, which I have not asked to be reimbursed. Moving out of the State in the autumn of 1867, I presented my resignation of the office, which was accepted by the Governor with expressions of regret and gratitude.[2]

I have not been in the Valley since;[3] but because of some knowledge of this pioneer duty of mine, travelers returning from it have often told me of what they thought missteps in its administration. I have never expressed an opinion on the subject. These travelers have also now and then urged that some proceeding should be taken to expostulate with the State against the manner in which it was believed by them to be abusing its trust. I have always declined to move, or take any part in any movement, for the purpose.

Several years ago, one of the editorial staff of the Century Magazine, Mr. R. U. Johnson, called on me with a letter of introduction. In the conversation that ensued, the subject came up of the danger to treasures of natural scenery that is more and more growing out of modern developments of commerce and modern habits of travel. The thought came to the surface that with reference to this danger, a sentiment needs to be cultivated such as would appear in any crisis threatening a national treasure of art. I do not remember that the Yosemite was referred to, but it followed from the conversation that I wrote a short paper, afterwards published in the Century, upon the duty of towns to guard for their future people eminently valuable passages of scenery near them, and in this paper the Yosemite was mentioned; but not reproachfully to the Commissioners.[4]

Last summer I received a second call from Mr. Johnson.[5] He had just returned from the Yosemite, and his object was to invite me to prepare an article upon it. I declined, giving as one reason for doing so that I could not properly write on the subject without making a prolonged personal examination of the present condition of the Valley and investigating the grounds of the complaints made by travelers as to the management of it. I was then asked if I would undertake to make such an examination and investigation at a suitable professional compensation from the Magazine, taking with me an accomplished artist to prepare illustrations for the desired article. I was loth to decline so liberal a proposition, but concluded that I must in justice to my existing professional engagements.[6]

Mr. Johnson then said that he would be obliged to write it himself, and thereupon mentioned several points upon which he desired my opinion.[7] One was in regard to a proposition which I understood to involve the systematic cutting out of all young trees in the Valley. He asked what I thought of it. A proper system of management for woods valued because of their effect in scenery, must be directed as much to the renewal and perpetuation of the constituent trees as to anything else; a common rule being that for every hundred or thousand trees going off, there shall be a hundred or a thousand more, advancing, to take their place. To provide against accidents, and in order that the replacing trees shall be of choice quality, a much larger number of young trees are kept growing, those not selected to remain because of their choiceness being gradually thinned out. A systematic removal of all the young trees of the Valley would be equivalent to the destruction, in course of time, of just what the State of California stands voluntarily pledged *to "hold, inalienably, for all time."*[8] That is to say, the distinctive charm of the scenery of the Yosemite does not depend, as it is a vulgar blunder to suppose, on the greatness of its walls and the length of its little early summer cascades; the height of certain of its trees, the reflections in its pools, and such other matters as can be entered in statistical tables, pointed out by guides and represented within picture frames. So far, perhaps, as can be told in a few words, it lies in the rare association with the grandeur of its rocky elements, of brooks flowing quietly through the ferny and bosky glades of very beautifully disposed great bodies, groups and clusters of trees. In this respect, its charm is greater than that of any other scenery that, with much searching, I have found. There is nothing in the least like it in the canyon of the Colorado, sometimes foolishly compared with the Yosemite. I felt the charm of the Yosemite much more at the end of a week than at the end of a day, much more after six weeks when the cascades were nearly dry, than after one week, and when, after having been in it, off and on, several months, I was going out, I said, "I have not yet half taken it in." To the perpetuation of this charm nothing is more essential than the constant renewal of its wood. There will always be danger that fire will too much interfere with what is necessary to provide in this respect.

These views having been for years fixed in my mind, to Mr. Johnson's inquiry I replied, that to carry out such a rule as he said had been advocated, would be "a calamity to the civilized world." I remember that I said this because he introduced the phrase in what he afterwards wrote,[9] and this has been my sole contribution, hitherto, to the agitation of the subject. It did not occur to me at the time, nor do I think now, that Mr. Johnson was trying to "make a case" against the State. His questions were such as would be asked by any intelligent man of one known to have given many years of serious and business-like study to a subject about which the inquirer was preparing to address the public. To me he only seemed patient and pains-taking, just and loyal in the performance of a not at all pleasing duty. He was apparently seeking to avoid injustice to the Commissioners whom I judged that he regarded as honest and well meaning men. He distinctly agreed with me in discrediting much that had been charged against them. He spoke disrespectfully of no one of them, but showed, I think, that he had an impression that, as a body, they had taken a narrow, short-sighted and market-place view of the duty of the State in the premises.

I have thus shown all that I have had to do with the matter, and all that I know concerning Mr. Johnson's motives and methods. I believe that the latter were simple, honorable, public spirited and perfectly in character with the distinguished high tone of the Magazine he represents. The Governor has been led to state in an official paper, given to the world, that Mr. Johnson is my nephew, and that all he wanted in this business was to bulldoze the Commissioners into giving me employment, as to the latter of which delusions I may say that I have never been so unfortunate as to need to solicit public employment, or to have any one solicit it for me.

After the above narration, may I not suggest that if the attitude of the State of California toward the trust it accepted in 1864, from the Nation, were what it ought to be, its Governor would hardly have missed the point of the remonstrance of the Century, so completely as his letter indicates that he has.

That remonstrance points to nothing in the methods of the Commissioners that would be objectionable if the concern of the Nation in the matter were of the same kind that it is with the State's dealings with mineral deposits, irrigation, militia, schools, railroads, or even forests. If the Governor and the Commissioners are in error, their error probably lies not in any intentional disregard of the State's obligation, but in overlooking the fact that in natural scenery that which is of essential value lies in conditions of a character not to be exactly described and made the subject of specific injunctions in an Act of Congress, and not to be perfectly discriminated without other wisdom than that which is gained in schools and colleges, counting-rooms and banks. Such qualities as are attributed by the Governor to his Commissioners — integrity, general education, business experience and what is comprehensively called good taste — do not, in themselves, qualify men to guard against the waste of such essential value, much less do they fit them to devise with artistic refinement means for reconciling with its preservation, its development and its exhibition, such requirements of convenience for multitudes of travelers as must be provided in the Yosemite. Whether it is the case with these Commissioners or not, there are thousands of such estimable men who have no more sense in this respect than children, and it must be said that those most wanting in it are those least conscious of the want. Men of the qualifications attributed to the Commissioners are the best sort of men for the proper duties of an auditing and controlling board. There could be no better men for the usual business of a board of hospital trustees, for example. But the best board of hospital trustees would commit what the law regards as a crime, if they assumed the duties of physicians and nurses. Ability in a landscape *designer* is, in some small degree, a native endowment, but much more it is a matter of penetrative study, discipline, training, and the development through practice of a special knack. Even men of unusually happy endowment and education, who have not, also, the results of considerable working experience, can rarely have much forecasting realization of the manner in which charm of scenery is to be affected by such operations as commonly pass under the name of "improvements."

I should say no more had I not observed in a California publication on the subject an assumption that a professional field-student of that which constitutes the charm of natural scenery would be more inclined than other men to crowd the Yosemite with "artificialities." Its error may be shown by quoting the advice, given several years ago, by the Landscape Architects employed by the State of New York to outline a plan for the restoration, preservation, development and exhibition, of the scenery of Niagara Falls. The paragraph which follows was the only italicised passage in their report, this distinction meaning that they regarded the principle stated as the corner stone of their work.

"Having regard to the enjoyment of natural scenery, and considering that the means of making this enjoyment available to large numbers will unavoidably lessen the extent and value of the primary elements of natural scenery, nothing of an artificial character should be allowed a place on the property, no matter how valuable it might be under other circumstances, and no matter at how little cost it may be had, the presence of which can be avoided consistently with the provision of necessary conditions for making the enjoyment of the natural scenery available."[10]

FREDERICK LAW OLMSTED.

The text presented here was published privately (Brookline, Mass., 1890) (see FLO to Richard Watson Gilder, July 10, 1889, above, and FLO to Robert Underwood Johnson, Oct. 9, 1889, above).

1. In early 1890, California Governor Robert W. Waterman (1826–1891) published a statement addressed to the California Legislature defending the Yosemite Commission from criticisms by John Muir, Robert Underwood Johnson, and others. In his statement the governor erroneously asserted that Johnson was Olmsted's nephew and that his motivation for attacking the policies of the commission was to secure an advisory position for Olmsted ("Guide to the Waterman Family Papers, 1839–1906," The Bancroft Library, UC Berkeley; "The Yosemite Controversy," *San Francisco Daily Evening Bulletin*, March 20, 1890, p. 2; "The Yosemite Despoilers," *New York Times*, March 23, 1890; "The Yosemite," *San Francisco Chronicle*, March 21, 1890, p. 6).
2. Olmsted had left California in October 1865 and officially resigned from the Yosemite Commission on October 23, 1866. Governor Frederick F. Low accepted his resignation in January 1867 (*Papers of FLO*, 5: 770–71; F. F. Low to FLO, Jan. 18, 1867, B10: #12301, OAR/LC).
3. Olmsted returned to California three times in the late 1880s to work on plans for Stanford University—September 1886, October through November 1887, and November through December 1888—but he did not visit Yosemite Valley on any of these trips. In 1886, on his first trip back to California since 1865, Olmsted did travel to the Mariposa Big Tree Grove. He was accompanied by Frederick Law Olmsted, Jr., and Henry Sargent Codman, and the group met Galen Clark, who had accommodated Olmsted and his family in the area in the summer of 1864. Clark, a friend who had also been a fellow member of the first Yosemite Commission, may have described the changes that had occurred in the nearby valley since Olmsted had last been there. For whatever reasons, Olmsted's party did not visit the valley then, nor did Olmsted ever return (*FLO, A Biography*, pp. 407–8; FLO to Richard Watson Gilder, July 10, 1889, n. 7, above).
4. Olmsted refers to "A Healthy Change in the Tone of the Human Heart," an essay that describes the importance of preserving natural scenery in and around towns and cities. The essay as published does not, however, mention Yosemite Valley ("A Healthy Change in the Tone of the Human Heart," Oct. 1886, above).
5. For Johnson's letter, see Robert Underwood Johnson to FLO, June 23, 1889.
6. For Olmsted's refusal, see FLO to Richard Watson Gilder, July 10, 1889, above.
7. In a July 19, 1889, letter, Johnson made plans to meet with Olmsted in Boston to discuss Yosemite. During that meeting Johnson likely discussed his intended article (Robert Underwood Johnson to FLO, July 19, 1889).
8. A paraphrase from the 1864 Yosemite Grant legislation, which states that that the grant was made "upon the express conditions that the premises shall be held for public use, resort, and recreation; [and] shall be inalienable for all time" ("An Act Authorizing a Grant to the State of California of the Yo-Semite Valley, and of the Land Embracing the Mariposa Big Tree Grove,'" June 30, 1864, *Congressional Globe*, 38th Cong., 1st session, Appendix [1863–1864], p. 240)
9. Johnson quoted this phrase of Olmsted's in his article "The Care of the Yosemite Valley," *Century Illustrated Monthly Magazine*, Jan. 1890, pp. 474–75 (see FLO to Robert Underwood Johnson, Oct. 9, 1889, above).
10. Frederick Law Olmsted and Calvert Vaux, "General Plan for the Improvement of the Niagara Reservation," 1887 (*Papers of FLO*, SS1: 546).

APPENDIXES
INDEXES

I

CHRONOLOGY OF FREDERICK LAW OLMSTED

1882–1890

1882	
April	Olmsted proposes to Oakes Angier Ames the construction of a memorial cairn adjacent to the Oakes Ames Memorial Town Hall in North Easton, Massachusetts
May 29	Olmsted advises Elizabeth Henderson Guild on treatment of the grounds of her seaside estate in Nahant, Massachusetts
August 22	Olmsted advises Montgomery Schuyler concerning a proposed residential development along the shore of the East River in New York City, between East 81st Street and East 84th Street
Fall	Olmsted submits report to Architect of the Capitol Edward Clark on progress of construction of the U.S. Capitol grounds and his concept for planting them
September	Olmsted's article "Trees in Streets and in Parks" is published in the *Sanitarian*
October 12	Olmsted is made honorary member of the Union League Club of New York
November	Olmsted submits his plan for Belle Isle, *The Park for Detroit*
	Olmsted submits to artist T. Worthington Whittredge a statement on the possible role of a village improvement society in Summit, New Jersey
1883	
January	Calvert Vaux resigns as Superintending Architect of New York Department of Public Parks
January 11	Niagara Falls Association formed

February 23	Olmsted reviews condition of South Park in Chicago for the South Park Commission
Spring	Olmsted acquires and begins renovations of the farmhouse at 99 Warren Street in Brookline that becomes Fairsted
Spring	Charles Eliot joins the Olmsted firm as an apprentice
March	Olmsted elected member of the Saturday Club of Boston
March 13	Olmsted submits his report, *Improvement of Easton's Beach* for the mayor of Newport, Rhode Island
April 30	Governor Grover Cleveland signs law creating New York State Reservation at Niagara Falls
May 10	Olmsted submits his report for the development of Cushing's Island in Casco Bay, Maine
May 21	Olmsted submits preliminary plan to James Cameron Mackenzie for the campus of the Lawrenceville School in New Jersey
July	Olmsted and Eliot travel to Detroit, Buffalo, and Niagara Falls for work on public parks and reservations
July	Olmsted submits report to Edward Clark concerning construction of approach to north terrace of U.S. Capitol and provides an estimated cost of construction of terraces
August 21	Olmsted instructs F. L. Temple concerning the planting of the Beacon Street entrance to the Back Bay Fens
October 7	Olmsted travels to Detroit to present to the Belle Isle commissioners a set of drawings for a steamboat pier and gallery
November 24	Boston park board hires F. L. Temple to plant Beacon Street entrance of the Back Bay Fens
December 22	Olmsted submits report on selection of park lands to park commissioners of Wilmington, Delaware
December 24	Olmsted corresponds with Charles Follen McKim about designing the grounds for Julia and Alice Appleton's country estate in Lenox, Massachusetts
December 24	Olmsted submits *Report of Landscape Architect* to Boston park board concerning the design and construction of the Back Bay Fens
Winter	Olmsted's step-daughter Charlotte is institutionalized due to mental illness

1884

	Olmsted's step-son John C. Olmsted becomes a partner in the Olmsted firm, which is renamed F. L. & J. C. Olmsted, Landscape Architects
February 2	Olmsted advises Charles T. Hubbard concerning the design of his residence Ridgehurst in Weston, Massachusetts
March 7	Olmsted instructs F. L. Temple about planting the Beacon Street entrance to the Back Bay Fens

March 12	Olmsted visits Detroit with John Charles for work on Belle Isle
May 12	Olmsted urges the Detroit park board to build the pier and gallery on Belle Isle
May 30	Olmsted corresponds with John Charles about Belle Isle and other projects
Summer	Henry Sargent Codman joins the Olmsted firm as an apprentice
June	Olmsted publishes "Belle Isle: After One Year"
June	Olmsted firm begins keeping letterpress copies of their outgoing office correspondence, and this practice continues through 1899
August	Olmsted firm prepares plans for Franklin Park
September	Publication of F. L. and J. C. Olmsted, *Beardsley Park. Landscape Architects' Preliminary Report*
September 6	Olmsted reports to Charles H. Dalton concerning Commonwealth Avenue extension near entrance to Back Bay Fens
October	Olmsted advises Charles A. Williams about conversion of a cemetery to a park in New London, Connecticut
December 9	Hugh O'Brien elected mayor of Boston
December 22	Olmsted submits reports to Boston park board on Franklin Park and Wood Island Park, published in *Tenth Annual Report, Boston Park Commissioners*
1885	
January 12	Joint Committee on Buildings and Grounds accepts Olmsted's resignation as advisor on design and construction of terraces of the U.S. Capitol. He continues to serve as advisory landscape architect for the grounds of the Capitol
April 30	Governor David B. Hill signs appropriation bill for creating the Niagara Reservation
May	Mayor O'Brien's Democratic appointees take over the Boston park board, and Olmsted is concerned about his future with the new board
June 20, 27	*American Architect and Building News* publishes Olmsted's essay "On Points of View and Methods of Criticism of Public Works of Landscape Architecture"
July 23	Death of President Ulysses S. Grant
July 30	Olmsted submits specifications for Playstead terrace in Franklin Park
August 6	Olmsted advises John D. Crimmins on placing Grant's Tomb in Riverside Park
September	Charles Eliot leaves Olmsted firm for travel with a group of friends in the southern states to learn about parks and scenery there. Afterwards, he departs for travel and study in Europe
September 12	Boston park commission enters into a new three-year contract with Olmsted for design and supervision of the city's parks

October 23	Preliminary report to Morris K. Jesup concerning his estate Belvoir Terrace in Lenox, Massachusetts
1886	
	The Boston park board publishes Olmsted's "Notes on the Plan of Franklin Park and Related Matters"
February 6	Olmsted advises James Cameron Mackenzie on planting the Lawrenceville School campus and suggests creating an arboretum of trees that would thrive in the region
February 15	Olmsted advises Edward Clark concerning treatment of the area between the staircases of the west terrace of the U.S. Capitol
March	Leland Stanford proposes that Olmsted design the Stanford University campus
March 15	Olmsted corresponds with F. L. Temple concerning the failed planting of the Beacon Street entrance to the Back Bay Fens
April 2	Olmsted reads "Paper on the Back Bay Problem and Its Solution" before the Boston Society of Architects
April 19	Olmsted advises Endicott Peabody on the placement of buildings at the Groton School campus in Massachusetts
April 27	H. H. Richardson dies
June	Olmsted writes Charles Eliot in Europe, asking him to return and assist with the Stanford University design. Eliot declines, preferring to continue his travels in Europe
June 10	Olmsted responds to park commissioner Henry R. Beekman's request for him to review and revise plans for some of the New York parks. Olmsted proposes an arrangement by which he and Calvert Vaux could undertake such a project
July	Crisis concerning proposed installation of windows in west terrace wall of the U.S. Capitol
August 3	Olmsted advises Anne Whitney on the setting for the statue of Leif Ericsson she is creating for a site on Commonwealth Avenue in Boston
August 9	Olmsted corresponds with George W. Vanderbilt about planning the grounds of the Vanderbilt mausoleum on Staten Island
Late August	Olmsted leaves for a trip to the Stanford University campus in Palo Alto, California, accompanied by Frederick Law Olmsted, Jr., and Henry Sargent Codman
October	*Century Illustrated Monthly Magazine* publishes Olmsted's article "A Healthy Change in the Tone of the Human Heart"
October 5	Olmsted writes, from Salt Lake City, a contribution to a report on the development of Golden Gate Park and the thinning of its forest tree plantations
October 18	Olmsted returns home from his California trip
November 3	Niagara Commission engages Olmsted and Vaux to prepare a plan for the Niagara Reservation

December	Charles Eliot establishes his own landscape architecture practice in Boston
December	The Boston park commission publishes Olmsted's report on the Charles River Embankment (Charlesbank) in their *Twelfth Annual Report*
December 4	The *Brookline Chronicle* publishes Olmsted's plan for widening Beacon Street
1887	
January 20	Olmsted leaves for Salt Lake City to meet with members of the Union Pacific Railway Company concerning a commission for planning the grounds of a hotel at Garfield Beach on Great Salt Lake
January 31	Olmsted suffers a leg injury during a train collision while traveling home from Salt Lake City
April 11	Olmsted sends Sherman S. Jewett a report on the proposed extension of the Buffalo park system into the Thirteenth Ward south of the Buffalo River. The Buffalo park commissioners include it in their *Eighteenth Annual Report*
May	The Niagara Reservation commissioners publish Olmsted and Vaux's "General Plan for the Improvement of the Niagara Reservation"
May 5	Olmsted corresponds with Richard Morris Hunt about the Vanderbilt mausoleum design
May 14	The cornerstone of inner quadrangle at Stanford University is laid
June 30, July 9, 13	In their letters, Olmsted and Vaux debate terms under which they will collaborate on work on New York City parks
July 12	Olmsted submits general plan for Shelburne Farms to estate owner William Seward Webb
July 21	Olmsted instructs William L. Fischer on planting the Playstead Overlook in Franklin Park
August 15	Olmsted provides suggestions to Col. C. S. Gzowski concerning the planning of Queen Victoria Park opposite Niagara Falls in Ontario
August 26	New York City park board hires Olmsted and Vaux to develop a revised plan for Morningside Park
Fall	*Art Review* publishes Olmsted's article "On Gardening"
September 9	Olmsted submits a report to Alfred D. Chandler for a hotel and resort on Lake Sunapee in New Hampshire
October 1	Olmsted and Vaux submit *General Plan For The Improvement Of Morningside Park* to the New York City park board
October 5	Olmsted begins a trip to California for work on Stanford University campus
November [21]	Olmsted returns from California

December	Olmsted submits plan and report for Montebello Park in St. Catherine's, Ontario
December 30	Olmsted submits a report for inclusion in the *Thirteenth Annual Report* of the Boston park commissioners, calling for a reforestation program for the Boston Harbor Islands. He also discusses the nomenclature of Boston parks, flooding problems in Back Bay Fens from Stony Brook, and tree-cutting in Franklin Park
1888	
	Publication of F. L. and J. C. Olmsted, Landscape Architects, *Plan of Public Recreation Grounds for the City of Pawtucket*
January	Calvert Vaux reinstated as Landscape Architect of the Department of Public Parks of New York City and retains the post until his death in 1895
February 29	Inaugural issue of *Garden and Forest* published
April 2	Olmsted advises William C. Loring on planning his estate in Beverly, Massachusetts
May	Grading and road construction is underway at the Vanderbilt mausoleum on Staten Island
May 2	*Garden and Forest* publishes Olmsted's article "Plan for a Small Homestead"
June	Mariana Griswold Van Rensselaer publishes the biography *Henry Hobson Richardson and His Works*
June 6	*Garden and Forest* publishes Olmsted's article "Terrace and Veranda–Back and Front"
June 9	Olmsted refuses William R. Martin's request that he accept an engagement to advise the New York City park board on the treatment of Morningside, Riverside, and Central parks
June 26	Olmsted submits his preliminary report on where to site the main residence on Morris K. Jesup's estate in Lenox, Massachusetts
August 2	Olmsted advises Frederick W. Vanderbilt about designing the grounds of his estate Rough Point in Newport, Rhode Island
August 5	Olmsted advises Edward Mott Moore on establishing a park commission in Rochester, New York
August 25	Olmsted corresponds with William D. Sloane about gardening issues at his estate Elm Court in Lenox, Massachusetts
October 1	Olmsted and John Charles submit their *Plan for a Public Park on the Flats South of Buffalo* to the Buffalo park commissioners
October 20	Olmsted corresponds with Morris K. Jesup about his estate Belvoir Terrace in Lenox, Massachusetts
October 24	*Garden and Forest* publishes Olmsted's article "Foreign Plants and American Scenery"
November 16	Olmsted begins a trip to Colorado and California
December 22	*San Francisco Examiner* publishes an interview with Olmsted

	titled "Yosemite Vandalism, A Landscape Gardener Condemns the Commissioners' Work"
1889	
	Henry Sargent Codman is made a partner in F. L. Olmsted & Co.
January 2	Olmsted returns to Brookline from his trip to California
January 15	Olmsted submits a preliminary report to Gen. Bela M. Hughes on the creation of a resort community at Perry Park, Colorado.
January 22, 31, February 11	Olmsted pursues issues with Morris K. Jesup about Belvoir Terrace
January 26	Olmsted presents "Remarks About A Difficulty Peculiar To The Park Department Of City Governments" to the New England Club
January 26	Olmsted recommends to Edward Mott Moore a plan for developing a drive along the banks of the Genesee River south of Rochester and special treatment of the edge of the Genesee gorge north of the city
February 11	Olmsted submits plans to Edward Clark for the space between the western stairways of the U.S. Capitol
February 25	Olmsted reads paper on the history of streets to the Brookline Club
March 2	Olmsted corresponds with Richard Morris Hunt about his recommendations for the treatment of spaces and structures near the mansion at George W. Vanderbilt's Biltmore estate
March 24, May 6	Olmsted discusses with Alpheus Hyatt the placing of zoological gardens in Boston's parks
c. March 25	Olmsted inspects condition of the plantings in Central Park with Jonathan Baxter Harrison, at the request of the West Side Association and Torrey Botanical Club
April 10	Olmsted corresponds with Thomas H. Clark about designing the grounds of the Alabama state capitol
April 30	Olmsted and Jonathan Baxter Harrison submit *Observations on the Treatment of Public Plantations, More Especially Relating to the Use of the Axe* to Kiliaen Van Rensselaer of the West Side Association
June 11	Olmsted corresponds with Edward Clark concerning designs for vases, lamp posts, and a fountain for the west terrace of the U.S. Capitol
July	Olmsted submits his report to Governor Thomas Seay concerning a design for the Alabama state capitol grounds
July 12	Olmsted submits his preliminary report to George W. Vanderbilt for planning of the Biltmore Estate
July 14	Olmsted corresponds with Leland Stanford about the grading of streets and approaches to the campus, as well as the significance of proposed panels of shrubbery on the principal approach route

August–September	Planting operations in Franklin Park continue
August 5	Olmsted describes to Thomas H. Clark his views on race relations in the South after Reconstruction
August 9	Olmsted submits his plans to Calvin C. Laney for Meadow Park (Genesee Valley Park) in Rochester
August 20	Olmsted advises Sylvester Baxter on preserving Lynn Woods in Massachusetts
August 20, October 5, 14	Olmsted corresponds with Charles A. Roberts about the design of Perry Park, Colorado
October	*American Garden* publishes Olmsted's article "What is a Useless Fence"
October 2	Olmsted advises Henry R. Towne concerning a site in New York City for the proposed 1893 World's Exposition
October 11	Olmsted corresponds with Frederick W. Vanderbilt about the treatment of an area on the seaward side of the mansion at Rough Point
November 11	Olmsted instructs engineer William A. Thompson concerning construction of the Biltmore approach road
November 29	Olmsted submits his report to Philip A. Chase about Lynn Woods
December	Olmsted engages in discussions on placing zoological gardens in Boston parks
1890	
January 15	*American Florist* publishes Olmsted's letter to the editor titled "Landscape"
February 24	Congress chooses Chicago as the site for the 1893 World's Exposition
March 8	Olmsted privately prints *Governmental Preservation of Natural Scenery*

II

LIST OF TEXTUAL ALTERATIONS

Each entry in the list gives the page and line number of the altered text, followed by the original form of the text. For documents beginning after the first line of a page, lines are counted from the addressee line or from the first line of the title of the document. Alterations of text in the endnotes of a document are identified by page, note, and line number.

CHAPTER I

To Oakes Angier Ames, April 1882
50: 26 walk forming
52: 12 base are

To Elizabeth Henderson Guild, May 29, 1882
56: 10 less not more costly

To Montgomery Schuyler, August 22, 1882
58: 24 earthen banked sodded

Annual Report of the Architect of the United States Capitol, 1882
119: 41 slope the

To Thomas Worthington Whittredge, 1882
133: 1 insincerity cant or
135: 36 pleasant. Narrow
137: 10 habits in
137: 11 fashions and
141: 29 temporarily annual
144: 27 later. Having
146: 37 Well done the

To the South Park Commission [of Chicago], February 28, 1883
151: 8 upon
151: 13 consequence that
151: 15 Commissioners The
151: 19 scope
151: 25 up
151: 27 out But
151: 31 another
152: 1 elements Could

Report of Fred'k Law Olmsted, to the Trustees of the Cushing's Island Co., May 10, 1883
159: 33 crags shingles

To James Cameron MacKenzie, May 21, 1883
166: 8 none It
166: 17 agrees to

CHAPTER II

To Felker L. Temple, August 21, 1883
171: 22 cultivated plants
171: 38 avoided
171: 42 creeper Jap.

To Charles Henry Dalton, January18, 1884
192: 22 throughout the
192: 33 water Bower

To Charles Townsend Hubbard, February 2, 1884
193: 6 yesterday
194: 1 responsibility The
194: 2 desirable I
194: 18 me

To Felker L. Temple, March 7, 1884
196: 16 Plats A
196: 23 A & C
196: 33 black grass "samphire"
196: 36 Avenue

To John Stirling, May 12, 1884
198: 20 out

To Salem Howe Wales, July 5, 1884
204: 39 actual not the honest cost

CHAPTER III

To Charles Augustus Williams, [October 1884]
215: 25 circumstances the ground lying in the midst of a city it

To Bronson Case Rumsey, November 1884
217: 6 it
217: 18 York less
217: 19 inviting and
217: 21 them The
217: 26 cause Remove
218: 2 London Liverpool
218: 4 market good
218: 5 built their
218: 5 neat drainage
218: 9 New York
218: 13 other Some
218: 16 opportunity
218: 24 life A
218: 27 slatterliness
218: 34 fields raw
218: 34 swamps road
218: 35 gardens shanties
218: 35 shanties dilapidated
218: 39 be And
218: 42 are There
218: 43 New York So
218: 43 Philadelphia
219: 5 Boston
219: 10 upon
219: 15 drainage
219: 20 gardening

To "Madam," January16, 1885
237: 25 stronger firmer

"Specifications for Playstead Terrace, Franklin Park," July 30, 1885
260: 12 (a) At
260: 16 height

To John Daniel Crimmins, August 6, 1885
266: 31 cost be
267: 44 sense
269: 1 ground to

CHAPTER IV

To Charles Eliot, March 4, 1886
290: 9 California Colorado

To Edward Payson Wilbur, April 29, 1886
298: 13 causes as
298: 15 arboretum are

To Mariana Griswold Van Rensselaer, [May] 6, 1886
304: 6 $37. for

To Henry Rutgers Beekman, [June 10, 1886]
304: 3 Henry K. Beekman
308: 8 park no
308: 16 division
308: 20 shady those
310: 7 increased no

To George Washington Vanderbilt, August 9, 1886
326: 9 road much
328: 23 custodian
328: 25 court The
328: 34 custom If
328: 36 injury The
329: 1 drawing, should be retained this
330: 7 deep The
331: 4 roads

To Mariana Griswold Van Rensselaer, August 11, 1886
332: 7 set Putting

CHAPTER V

To Amasa Leland Stanford, November 27, 1886
351: 10 series the
352: 5 to, which

To Mariana Griswold Van Rensselaer, May 17, 1887
388: 12 it but
388: 14 for it that I do
389: 16 exaggeration)
390: 12 away

To Oakes Angier Ames, June 5, 1887
398: 43 planted.

CHAPTER VI

To Calvert Vaux, July 9, 1887
409: 6 11 ock
409: 27 one and

To William Seward Webb, July 12, 1887
415: 40 gate one

To Colonel Casimir Stanislaus Gzowski, August 15, 1887
428: 8 “excursionist, at

To John Charles Olmsted, August 31, 1887
432: 7 knee which
434: 18 interest

To John Charles Olmsted, October 5, 1887
469: 7 papers copy

To Robert Douglas, December 5, 1887
470: 10 *folia*) I

CHAPTER VII

To Mariana Griswold Van Rensselaer, December 21, 1887
474: 17 architects

To William McMillan, January 2, 1888
495: 5 level bolting

To Mariana Griswold Van Rensselaer, June 14, 1888
527: 10 sailed. I

TO FREDERICK WILLIAM VANDERBILT, AUGUST 2, 1888
533: 5 (candle-berry) lambskill

CHAPTER VIII

TO EDWARD MOTT MOORE, AUGUST 5, 1888
538: 32 region. Of

TO EDWIN FLEMING, OCTOBER 20, 1888
548: 11 problem to

TO GENERAL BELA M. HUGHES, [JANUARY 15,] 1889
559: 17 roads you

TO THE BUFFALO PARK COMMISSIONERS, JANUARY 26, 1889
571: 33 Shore which

TO EDWARD MOTT MOORE, JANUARY 26, 1889
575: 8 a parts

TO MORRIS KETCHUM JESUP, JANUARY 31, 1889
579: 43 convenience. Taking

"TALK TO THE BROOKLINE CLUB, HISTORY OF STREETS," [FEBRUARY] 1889
602: 27 is a

CHAPTER IX

TO THOMAS VINCENT WELCH, FEBRUARY 16, 1889
613: 37 Mr Hulberts intimation

TO JOSEPH STORY FAY, APRIL 10, 1889
630: 13 skillfully, staked

CHAPTER X

TO GEORGE WASHINGTON VANDERBILT, JULY 12, 1889
682: 18 Estate three *684: 43* crops I

TO CALVIN COOKE LANEY, AUGUST 9, 1889
715: 14 On level

CHAPTER XI

TO SYLVESTER BAXTER, SEPTEMBER 2, 1889
730: 4 Dogues *730: 4* Sargents

TO CHARLES A. ROBERTS, OCTOBER 14, 1889
746: 18 argument that

TO JAMES G. GALL, JR., FEBRUARY 8, 1890
772: 17 breaker the

INDEX OF PLANT MATERIALS

Entries are presented in alphabetical order in the form that Olmsted wrote them. If Olmsted used a common name or old Latin name, then the current Latin name is given in brackets. Hybrids are denoted with an (×). Cultivars are enclosed in single quotation marks.

GENERAL INDEX